AF669525

힌디어로 발음하는
바라티 실용 한영 사전

Practical Bharati Korean-English Dictionary

with Hindi Pronunciation

by

Prof. Kim Do-Young

FRANK BROS. & CO.

Published by
Frank Bros. & Co. (Publishers) Ltd.
4675-A, 21 Ansari Road, Daryaganj,
New Delhi-110 002
Phones: 23263393, 23279936

Sales and Showroom
IV/85, Chandni Chowk, Delhi-110 006
Phones: 23276791, 23268884

First Edition 2009

ISBN 978-81-8409-640-8

Printed at Ashoka Offset Works, Delhi 110 033

To
The Students

FOREWORD

The present day world of shrinking space and ever-increasing knowledge requires quick and efficient transmission of knowledge and services across nations. The knowledge of a foreign language is a boon for citizens of countries that have close bilateral ties. The *Practical Bharati Korean-English Dictionary* by Prof. Kim Do Young gains in significance in the context of the widely increasing educational, cultural, scientific and technological relationship between India and the Republic of Korea.

In the field of education the relationship between the University of Delhi and some Korean universities commenced in the year 1993, a relationship which is increasing every year. The Korean language was introduced with 3 years part time courses in the Department of East Asian Studies in the year 2003. Prof Kim Do Young has been deeply involved in the teaching of Korean language to Indian students. He had taught Korean language at the Jawaharlal Nehru University, Delhi, for about seven years before joining the University of Delhi as a Visiting Professor in 2003. Prof. Kim had also written a series of books, called *Bharati-Korean, Reading Comprehension* as well as a *Workbook* for the students of Korean language in India. His works have earned a great success and popularity among students and other Korean language teachers in India. He is a scholar with a very good knowledge of Hindi and Indian culture. His rich experience of teaching Korean to Indian students over the years has enabled him to gauge the requirements of Indian students in order to make them well conversant with the language with ease and in the shortest possible time. His present work—*Practical Bharati Korean-English Dictionary*—needs to be viewed in the context of his long-time endeavor, i.e. in the teaching of Korean to Indian students in India.

A dictionary, we all know, consists of an alphabetically ordered list of words. The present *Practical Bharati Korean-English Dictionary* lists over 15,000 Korean words in the Hangul script and according to the alphabetical order of the Korean language. The present dictionary is the first to have attempted transcription of Korean words in Devanagari, and this can be seen both as a major shift and a contribution. It is common knowledge that the sounds represented by Korean letters are not exactly equivalent to the sounds represented by the Devanagari letters for Hindi. The dictionary through its transcriptions will indirectly highlight this problem and make the users aware of the sounds existing in the Korean language, thus enabling them to pick up the Korean pronunciation with ease. Paradoxically the main dictionary is in English language in the roman script. English has been chosen so that it could be used by a wide spectrum of readers in India. This may appear to be contrary to the script of the transcription; however, it is a known fact that the articulation of sounds of the alphabet of English also finds a good amount of variation in India. Hence, for the sake of uniformity of articulation, the use of the Devanagari script may be more apt. Further, the entries do not provide explicitly the grammatical categories of words but the necessary equivalents conform to the grammatical categories of the entries. Word meanings along with synonyms have been provided. In addition, equivalents have also been provided for many useful idiomatic expressions.

The *Practical Bharati Korean-English Dictionary* is meant for use by students of Korean language in India. The volume will also be extremely useful for those who may only be conversant with the Korean script. The present dictionary, in addition to being a basic source material for the learners of Korean in India, also makes a significant contribution towards the teaching of Korean in India.

Ravinder Gargesh
Professor & Head
Department of Linguistics
Arts Faculty Extn.
University of Delhi
Delhi-110007

PREFACE

The rapid expansion of Indo-Korean relationship and mounting interest among Indian students in learning Korean as a foreign language have enthused me to publish a few Korean textbooks in recent years. it is believed that important cornerstones were placed for learning Korean language in India and they contributed to structure Korean language learning field according to Indian ethos and methods. Thus, it became easier for many learners to study it from the initial stage to the advanced practices. However, a hole has been noticed that there was no dictionary obtainable in India, since it hadn't been published ever. Moreover, those dictionaries published in other areas were designed for Korean native speakers for learning English. Due to the enormous difference, serious hurdles were discovered for Indian learners and caused them to be confused in articulation. Indeed, learners of Korean language often have difficulties in grasping the pronunciation and using standard Korean-English dictionaries in reading. It was very necessary that a dictionary which could help them to pick up the pronunciation of Korean words with Indian articulate system should be developed. Their needs were reflected from the perspective of the non-native speakers of Korean in general and for Indian learners in particular. This dictionary for Hindi speakers represents an attempt to overcome these problems related to pronunciation and selection of words through a combination of usable definitions and practical expressions. In the dictionary Korean pronunciation is given in Devnagari script for each Korean word. I hope by using this dictionary the learners are able to enhance their speaking and listening power at large extent in an uncomplicated way. This dictionary is a result of an extensive research during which it has gone through different processes. And for that I owe special thanks to the different organizations and people.

I like to express my sincere gratitude to KBS Korean Language Team and Mr. Lee, Jae-gang, KBS special correspondent, New Delhi. I also thank Mr. Chung Tae-soon, M.D of Sinokor Merchant Marine Co. Ltd. who enable us to publish this dictionary. Prof. Madhu Bhalla, the Head of the department of East Asian Studies, University of Delhi and all the colleagues made academic environment to develop this. Mrs. Kim Young-soon, my wife and colleague for Korean language education in India took care of all the modification. Ms. Jung Son-young, Mr. Shashi Mishra and my students Mr. Gaurav Nigam and few others deserve to be mentioned. They put their hard labor for reviewing each vocabulary of Korean and Hindi and for computerization works. Finally, I thankful to Frank Brothers and Company (Publishers) Ltd. to take hard pain to publish this dictionary.

Kim Do-Young
University of Delhi
New Delhi

한글 HANGUL

It is a well-known fact that earlier Korean language used to be written in Chinese script which was difficult to be learnt and to learn the pictorial character had come a Herculean task for the common people of the country. Therefore, the scholars of the country felt an urgent need to develop their own simple script so that they could make their language readable to their own people. And as result of that they came up with their own set of alphabet called Hangul. The Korean alphabets called Hangul, was invented by a group of scholars under the patronage of King Sejong the great during the 15th century. The king thought of the people's difficulties for not having scripts. At the time of inventing Hangul 14 consonants and 10 vowels were invented. Of its morphology, its consonants were originated from the shape of mouth structure which creates pronunciation whereas its vowels from the shape of sky, earth and man based on Yin-yang theory.

Hangul can give pronunciation with combination of consonants and vowels. There are three ways of combination: first, vowel only, for instance, 아 (a), second, a vowel is added to a consonant, for an example, ㄱ + ㅏ = 가 (ga), and third, combination of a consonant, vowel and consonant, for an example, ㅎ + ㅏ + ㄴ = 한 (han).

Phonologically, Korean vowels consist of monothongs and dipthongs. Mono- thongs and diphthongs. Mono- thongs don't change the position of lips, tongue while being pronounced. Ten vowels, ㅏ, ㅐ, ㅓ, ㅔ, ㅗ, ㅚ, ㅜ, ㅟ, ㅡ, ㅣ belong to this. Dipthongs change the sound of the beginning and endings of the vowels. They are eleven vowels, that is , ㅑ, ㅒ, ㅕ, ㅖ, ㅘ, ㅙ, ㅛ, ㅝ, ㅞ, ㅠ, and ㅢ.

Consonants are classified into two by large, that is, voiced and voiceless. The former is nasal sound ㄴ(n), ㅁ(m), ㅇ(ng) and liquid sound ㄹ(l or r). Among these, ㅁ, ㅂ, ㅃ, ㅍ are labial using both lips. ㄱ, ㄲ, ㅋ, ㅇ are soft palatal touching soft palatal with a tongue, ㅈ, ㅉ, ㅊ are hard palatal touching hard palatal with surface of tongue. ㄷ, ㄸ, ㅌ, ㅅ, ㅆ, ㄴ, ㄹ are called dental touching the tip of tongue to the inner part of upper teeth. Apart from these, ㅎ is from voice chord.

KOREAN ALPHABET AND ITS PRONUNCIATION

1. Vowels

(i) Pure

Korean letter	Hindi equivalent	Hindi sound	English sound
ㅏ 아	आ	आम	as ah
ㅓ 어	औ	औरत	as hut and hot
ㅗ 오	ओ	ओस	as oh
ㅜ 우	उ	उमंग	as do
ㅡ 으	उ	उत्तर	as taken
ㅣ 이	इ	इन्कार	as ink
ㅐ 애	ऐ	ऐनक	as hand
ㅔ 에	ए	एहसास	as met
ㅚ 외	वे	वेद	as wake

(ii) Compound (Diphthong)

Korean letter	Hindi equivalent	Hindi sound	English sound
ㅑ 야	या	गया	as yard
ㅕ 여	यौ	यौवन	as yearn
ㅛ 요	यो	गायो	as yoke

ㅠ 유	यू	यूरोप	as you
ㅒ 얘	यै	नैया	as yam
ㅖ 예	ये	गये	as yes
ㅟ 위	वी	वीरता	as wield
ㅢ 의	उइ	सुई	
ㅘ 와	वा	सेवा	as wine
ㅙ 왜	वै	वैर	as wag
ㅝ 워	वॉ	जवॉ	as won
ㅞ 웨	वे	वेन्डर	as wet

2. Consonants

(i) Simple

Korean letter	Hindi equivalent	Hindi sound	English sound
ㄱ	ग	गाल	as *g*uy
ㄴ	न	नमक	as *n*ame
ㄷ	द	दीमक	as that
ㄹ	र	रात	as rat
ㅁ	म	महल	as *m*other
ㅂ	ब	बेकार	as *b*ook
ㅅ	स	सवाल	as *s*peech
ㅇ	अं	अंगूर	as ki*ng*
ㅈ	ज	जहाज	as *J*ohn

ㅊ	छ	छाता	chance
ㅋ	ख	खरगोश	as *k*ite
ㅌ	थ	थाली	as *tide*
ㅍ	फ	फकीर	as *p*ump
ㅎ	ह	हाथ	as *h*igh

(ii) Tensified

Korean letter	Hindi equivalent	Hindi sound	English sound
ㄲ	क्क	कागज	as s*k*y or Jack
ㄸ	त्त	उत्तर	(no sound)
ㅃ	प	पागल	as s*p*y
ㅆ	स्स	सागर	as e*ss*ential
ㅉ	च	चम्मच	as *ch*air

HOW TO USE THE DICTIONARY

1. Key to Entries

In the dictionary key wards are written in Hangeul Alphabet letters and they are arranged according to the following chart:

ㄱ	ㄲ	ㄴ	ㄷ	ㄸ	ㄹ
ㅁ	ㅂ	ㅃ	ㅅ	ㅆ	ㅇ
ㅈ	ㅉ	ㅊ	ㅋ	ㅌ	ㅍ
ㅎ	ㅏ	ㅐ	ㅑ	ㅒ	ㅓ
ㅔ	ㅕ	ㅖ	ㅗ	ㅘ	ㅙ
ㅚ	ㅛ	ㅜ	ㅟ	ㅝ	ㅞ
ㅠ	ㅡ	ㅢ	ㅣ		

1. The pronunciation of the Korean key words is written in Devnagari script (which is the main purpose of the writer and of this Dictionary as well). Pronunciation of the words written Devnagari script is within [ ] in bold letters. Just after that Chinese equivalent words are written in Hanja again in [ ] in bold letters where it is felt required for Indian students as this dictionary has been prepared keeping the requirement of the Indian learners in to account. Then, meaning of the words have been given in English keeping socio-political, social-psychological and socio-economical requirement in to account. In the middle of the examples given in Korean some-

where written in Hanja have also be given (wherever required).

2. After meaning use of the Korean words has also been given by citing examples in Korean. To show extra explanation (▷….) symbol has been used.
3. To differentiate in British English and American English <英> this symbol has been used before British English and <美> this symbol before American English words and <프> has been used for French words
4. For pronunciation of the Korean words Devnagari script is used. While writing the pronunciation of the Korean words in Devnagari, phonological changes of the Korean sounds have been taken care of.
5. The total number of the words (key words) is approximately 15,000 which are selected according to the requirement of level-1 to level-6 students.
6. To present different meanings of the same word it has been used separately indicated by 1 2 3 …. First meaning is indicated with 1 and so on.
7. There are few words in the dictionary which seem same but of different origins. Each word has been used as a separate key word and indicated with 1 2 3 at the right shoulder of the key word.

8. The dot "ं" in Hindi may be invisible with clarity. When the spelling is combined with the other *Mātras* (phonetic symbols) of Hindi. E.g. "ैं" (with dot), "ै" (without dot). This is caused by Hindi font size unavoidably.

ㄱ

-가 [गा] [**家**] [전문인] a man; a specialist; a professional; a person noted for e.g. 공상가 a day-dreamer

-가[गा] [**價**] [값] price. e.g. 공정가 an official price. 단가 a unit price.

-가 [गा] [**歌**] [노래] a song e.g. 농부가 a farmer's song

가 [गा] [가장자리] an edge; a border; a margin; [절벽 등의] a brink; [경계,주변] a verge e.g. 길가 the road-side / the wayside. 강가 a riverside / a riverbank

가게 [गाग्ये] a store; a shop

가격 [गाग्यौक] [**價格**] [파는 사람이 요구하는] a price; [대가 원가로서의] [a] cost; [가치][a] value. ⇨ 물가

가계 [गाग्ये] [**家**] [집안 경제] household economy; [금전상의] family finance [s]; [생계비] house keeping expenses; [가정의 예산 family budget; [생계] living; livelihood.

가공 [गागोंग] [**加工**] [특히 식품, 농산물등의] process-sing; [기계에 의한 대량의] manufacturing; specific-ation; [보석 등의] cutting. 가공하다 process fruit [cheese]

가관 [गाग्वान] [**可觀**] **1** [볼만 함] e.g. 가관이다 e.g. be well worth seeing / be some-thing to see **2** [꼴사나움] e.g. 가관이다 be a sight / be unbecoming [unsightly].

가구 [गागू] [**家具**] [house-hold] furniture [furni-shings]; household stuff

가급적 [गागुप्चौक] [**可及的**] as ... as possible; as much [far] as possible; as ... as one can[may]; [가능한 한] to the best of one's abi-lity e.g. 가급적 빨리 와라 Come as early as you can.

가깝다 [गाक्काप्ता] **1** [거리가] near; close [▷ close가 near 보다 접근 정도가 강함]; close [near] by; not far away; nearby. e.g. 가까운 집 a nearby house / a house close by **2** [시간이] near; immediate; short. e.g. 가까운 장래에 in the near [immediate] future / at an early date. **3** [사이, 관계가] close <to>; near; intimate <with>; friendly <with> e.g. 가까운 친구 an intimate [a close] friend / a bosom buddy.

가꾸다 [गाक्कुदा] **1** [식물을] culti-vate; raise; grow; rear. **2** [치장하다] [옷으로] dress <one-self>up; [장식물로] deco-rate; adorn; ornament; [얼굴을] make oneself up.

ㄱ

거꾸로 [गौक्कुरो] [아래위를] bottom up; upside down; wrong side up; [안팎을] inside out.

가끔 [गक्कुम] [때때로] sometimes; [every] now and then [again]; occasionally; [이따금] once in a while; [사이를 두고] at intervals.

가난 [गानान] [빈곤] poverty; want; destitution; indigence; penury. 가난하다 poor; needy; poverty-stricken; estitute; impecunious; indigent. e.g. 가난한 집 a poor [needy] family.

가냘프다 [गान्यात्फुदा] 1 [목소리가] [힘이 없다] [feeble; [희미하다] faint. e.g. 가냘픈 목소리로 in a feeble voice. 2 [몸이] [호리호리하다] slim; slender; slight; [약하다] weak; feeble; frail.

가늘다 [गानुल्दा] 1 [둘레가 작다] small; thin; fine; slender; slim e.g. 가는 철사[끈] a small wire [string] 2 [너비가 좁다] narrow e.g. 눈을 가늘게 뜨다 narrow one's eyes

가늠 [गानुम] [판단, 어림] judgement; discernment; estimation; sense of proportion; a guess; a conjecture. 가늠하다 make a guess [conjecture]; use one's sense of proportion <on>; watch; study; weigh <one plan against another>.

가능 [गानुंग] [**可能**] e.g. 가능한 범위내에서 as much [far] as possible / within the limits of the possible [possibility]. 가능하다 possible; [실현이]; feasible.

가능성 [गानुंग्सौंग] [**可能性**] [a] possibility; [잠재적인] [a] potentialities; [능력의] [a] capacity; [기회의] a chance; [객관적으로 본바] likelihood.

가다 [गादा] 1 [목적지를 향해 움직이다] go <to>; [상대방쪽으로 가다] come; [어떤 장소에 가서 잠시 머물다] be <at, in>; [탈것을 타고] take; [출발하다] leave <for>; [방문하다] visit. e.g. 서울 가는 기차 a train[bound] for Seoul. 2 [떠나다] start; leave; go out. e.g. 여행을 가다 start on a journey

가다듬다 [गादादुम्ता] 1 [정신을 차리다] brace. e.g. 마음을 가다듬다 brace oneself [up] / pull oneself together / brace [up] one's spirits / collect one's scattered mind. 2 [조절하다] put <things> in order; set in good order; tidy up; adjust: e.g. 목소리 [목청]를 가다듬다 clear one's throat.

가닥 [गादाक] 1 [줄] a strand; a strip; a ply; [머리의] braid a cut [ting]. 2 [줄기] a streak; a stripe; [빛의] a ray; a beam. e.g. 한 가닥

의 빛 a beam [ray] of light.

가담 [गादाम] [**加擔**] [참여] participation; [공모] conspiracy 가담하다 [편들다] take sides with; side with; stand by [a person's] side; [참여하다] participate [take part] in; be involved in; be a party to; join company with; [공모하다] conspire

가당찮다 [गादांग्छान्था] [**可當-**] [부당하다] unreasonable; unjust; improper; undue; unsuitable; [터무니없다] wild; absurd; preposterous; [지나치다] excessive; outrageous. e.g. 가당찮은 생각 a preposterous idea.

가동 [गादोंग] [**稼動**] operation; work. 가동하다 operate; work; run; put into operation.

가두다 [गादूदा] [사람을] shut in [up]; coop up; lock up [자물쇠를 채워서]; confine; [가축을] impound; shut up in a pen; pen; [맹수를] cage in.

가득하다 [गादुक्ख्वादा] full <of>; chock-full; brimful; filled [to the brim]; packed [crammed / crowded] <with people>. e.g. 방 안에는 술냄새가 가득했다 The room reeked of liquor.

가라앉다 [गाराआन्ता] **1** [내려앉다] sink; go down [to the bottom]; go under; be submerged; [찌꺼기 등이] settle. **2** [진정되다] cool off; cool down; settle down.

가라앉히다 [गाराआन्छिदा] **1** [물 속으로] sink <a vessel>; send <a ship> to the bottoms [전투 등에서] submerge [물 속에 잠기게 하다]; [찌꺼기 등을] settle; lay. **2** [감정을] calm; quiet; compose; [달래다] soothe; appease.

가랑비 [गारांग्बी] [a] drizzle; [a] mizzle; a fine [drizzling] rain.

가량 [गार्यांग] [**假量**] **1** [어림짐작] a guess; a conjecture. 가량하다 guess; conjecture; estimate; make an estimate <of>. **2** [쯤] about; around; some; almost; more or less; approximately. e.g. 1 주일 가량 about a week [or so].

가련하다 [गार्यौंनहादा] [**可憐-**] [불쌍하다] poor; pitiable; pitiful; [애처롭다] pathetic; touching; sad; [비참하다] miserable; wretched.

가렵다 [गार्यौंप्ता] itchy; itching e.g. 등이 가렵다 My back itches. / My back feels itchy.

가령 [**假令**] [गार्योंग] [예를들어] for example; for instance; e.g; let us say; [··· 과 같은] such as; as; say.

가로등 [गारोदुंग] [**-燈**] a streetlight; a streetlamp.

가로 [गारो] **1** [폭] width; breadth; length **2** [옆으로 된 방향] across; crossways; crosswise; horizontally.

가로막다 [गारोमाक्ता] **1** [가로

질러 막다] stop; stem; check e.g. 강물을 가로 막다 stop [stem] a stream / check a current. **2** [앞쪽이 보이지 않게 하다] obstruct; shut out; [빛을] intercept. **3** [방해하다] cut off; block; bar; hinder; [사람의 언행을] head off; interrupt.

가로채다 [गारोछैदा] [낚아채다] snap [away] <from / off>; wrest <from>; take by force; tear [off / away] <a thing> from <a person>. e.g. 오토바이를 탄 젊은 남자가 그녀의 손에서 돈뭉치를 가로채어 도망갔다 A young man on a motorcycle snatched [grabbed] a roll of bills from her hand and ran off with it.

가루 [गारु] [일반적으로] powder; [금,석탄 등의 dust; [주로 체로 친 밀가루] flour; [곡식의 굵은 가루, 맷돌로 탄 것] meal.

가르다 [गारुदा] **1** [쪼개다] cut <into>; divide <into>. e.g. 생선의 배를 가르다 cut [slash] open the abdomen of a fish **2** [분할하다] divide <into>; part <into>; split <into>; [분류하다] separate; sort out; classify. e.g. 편을 가르다 divide [split] <a group> into <two> rival teams **3** [분배하다] share <with>; distribute [divide] <among>; allot. ⇨ 나누다

가르치다 [गारुछिदा] [교육하다] [지식,기술 등을] teach; [음악,미술 등을 개인적으로] give lessons <in>; [지도하다] instruct <in>; train; educate; school

가리다[1] [गारिदा] [덮다] cover; veil; shield; screen. e.g. 베일로 얼굴을 가리다 cover one's face with a veil / veil one's face.

가리다[2] [गारिदा] **1** [고르다] choose; select; pick out; sort out. ⇨ 가려내다 e.g. 그의 작품 에서 최고의 것을 가리다 select [choose] the best of his works. **2** [싫어하다] be shy [bashful]. e.g. 낯을 가리다 be shy of[with] strangers **3** [따져 밝히다] look into; inquire; investigate. e.g. 시비를 가리다 argue about whether it is right or wrong

가리키다 [गारिखिदा] **1** [손가락 등으로] point to[at] e.g. 그는 누이동생을 손가락으로 가리켰다 He pointed his finger at his sister. **2** [지칭하다] mean; refer <to>. e.g. 누구를 가리켜 말하는 것입니까 Who do you mean?

가만히 [गामान्ही] **1** [움직이지 않고] motionlessly; quietly; still. e.g. 가만히 앉아 있다 sit still [motionless]. **2** [조용히] calmly; silently;

quietly; still.

가망 [गामांग] [**可望**] [장래성] hope; promise; [전망] prospect; [가능성] probability; possibility; [a] likelihood; [a] chance.

가면 [**गाम्यौन**] [**假面**][[탈] a mask. **가무**[गामू] [**歌舞**] singing and dancing; all musical and other entertainments.

가문 [**家門**] [गामुन] one's family [clan]. e.g. 가문의 영예 a credit [an honor] to one's family.

가발 [गाबाल] [**假髮**] [전체 가발] a wig; [부분 가발] a hairpiece

가방 [गाबांग] a bag; a portfolio [둘로 접게 된 것] a briefcase [서류용]. ⇨ 손가방

가볍다 [गाब्यौप्ता] **1** [무게가] light; not heavy. e.g. 가벼운 짐 light baggage **2** [가치,정도가] light; slight. e.g. 가벼운 범죄 a minor [petty] offense **3** [경솔하다] rash; thoughtless; careless; frivolous. e.g. 하는 짓이 가볍다 behave frivolously [flippantly]

가불 [गाबुल] [**假拂**] [봉급 등의] an advance; advance payment. 가불하다 advance; pay in advance

가사 [गासा][**歌詞**] [노래의] the words; the text; [오페라의] the libretto.

가사 [गासा][**家事**] [살림을 꾸미는 일] [세탁, 청소 등, 가정의 일상적인 일] housework; [집 안의 잡일] household [domestic] chores

가소롭다 [गासोरोप्ता] [**可笑**–] ridiculous; laughable; absurd. e.g. 네가 나를 가르치겠다니 가소롭다]It is ridiculous to imagine you teaching me anything.

가속 [गासोक] [**加速**] acceleration; speed-up. 가속하다 accelerate; speed up; soup up.

가수 [गासू] [**歌手**] a singer; [여자[유행] 가수] a songstress; [특히 밴드 연주로 노래하는 가수]] a vocalist.

가스 [गासु] [기체] gas; [연료용의] [coal] gas. **2** [뱃속의] gas; wind [방귀]

가슴 [**गासुम**] **1** [가슴팍] the breast; [흉곽] the chest; [여자의] the bust; [품] the bosom. e.g.가슴이 아프다 have a pain in the chest. **2** [심장] the heart. e.g.가슴을 두근거리며 with one's heart throbbing. **3** [마음] one's heart; one's mind; feelings; soul; bosom. e.g. 가슴 깊이 deep in one's heart. 가슴 [이] 아프다 heart-stricken; heart-broken; heartrending; broken-hearted; lamentable; regret-able; <서술적> one's heart aches <at> e.g. 가슴 [이] 아파하다 eat one's heart out <over> be heartsick of

/ grieve <at / over>.

가시 [गाशी] **1** [장미 등의] a thorn; [풀잎 등의] a prickle; [선인장의] a spine; [밤송이, 우엉 등의] a bur; [植] an acantha; an aculeus; an acicula. **2** [생선의] a fishbone; [지느러미의] a spine; [동물의] a [piece of] bone.

가식 [गाशिक] [**假飾**] affectation; dissemblance; dissimulation; ostentation; pretense; hypocrisy. e.g. 가식적인 hypocritical / affected / false. 가식하다 make outward show; put a good face on <a matter>; put a varnish on <a matter>; pretend; dissemble; dissimulate; do hypocrisy; play the hypocrite.

가업 [गाओप] [**家業**] [직업] a family occupation; one's trade [business / calling / profession].

가열 [गायौल] [**加熱**] heating. 가열하다 heat[up]; apply heat <to>.

가엾다 [गायौप्ता] [불쌍하다] poor; pitiable; pitiful; [애틋하다] pathetic; sad; sorry. e.g. 가엾은 고아 a poor orphan.

가옥 [गाओक] [**家屋**] [집]a house; [건물] a building

가요 [गायो] [**歌謠**] [가곡] a song; [전승적인 전설시] a ballad; <집합적> songs and ballads.

가운데 [गाउन्दे] **1** [중앙] the middle; the center. **2** [중에, 속에] in; in the midst of; in the heart [center] of; between; among; through; into; of; out of. e.g. 두 사람 가운데 between the two **3** […하는 중[에] while [in the process of] doing; during [동안에]; amid[st]; in[한창 …하는] with <a person> in attendance; in the presence of <a person>. e.g. 박수 갈채가 울려퍼지는 가운데[amid [st] the applause of the audience.

가위 [गावी] scissors; shears [큰]; clippers [털 등을 깎는]; snips [양철 등을 자르는]; a punch [차표 등을 찍는] e.g. 가위 한 자루 a pair of scissors.

가을 [गाउल] [계절] autumn; fall; falltime.

가이드 [गाइड्] [안내] guiding; [안내자] a <tour> guide; [안내서] a guidebook.

가입 [गाइप] [**加入**] 가입하다 enter <for>; join <an association>; become of member <of>; affiliate oneself with <a society>; send in[up] one's name <to>; subscribe <for>; sign <a treaty>.

가장 [गाजांग [**假裝**] [변장] disguise; guise; masquerade; a fancy dress. 가장하다

disguise oneself <as>; be disguised <as>; wear a disguise; dissemble; dress up. e.g. 가장하여 in disguise; in fancy dress.

가장 [गाजांग] [**家長**] [가구주] the head of a family [household]; a patriarch [남자]; a matriarch [여자]; a paterfamilias <*pl.* patresfamilias>.

가장 [गाजांग] [제일 최고로] most; extremely; exceedingly; to the extreme; supremely. e.g. 가장 안쪽의 innermost.

가장자리 [गाजांग्जारी] the edge; the verge; the brink; the margin; the hem; the border; the fringe; the brim.

가정부 [गाजौंग्बु] [-**婦** a housekeeper; a homemaker; a housemaid [식모].

가정 [गाजौंग] [**假定**] [a] supposition; [an] assumption; [a] postulation; [가설] a hypothesis <*pl.* -ses>. 가정하다 suppose; assume; pre-sume; take it for granted that; take <this fact> for granted; postulate; pre-suppose.

가정 [गाजौंग] [**家庭**] [a] home; a family; a household; the home circle. e.g. 가정의 home / domestic / household / family.

가져가다 [गाज्यौगादा] [몸에 지니고 가다] take <a thing> along [with one]; carry; [가지고 가버리다] take [carry] away; take off; make off [away] <with>. e.g.누가 내 책을 가져갔느냐 Who has taken my book?

가져오다 [गाज्यौओदा] **1** [지참하다] bring [over]; fetch; get; bring [carry / take] <a thing> with <one>; take <a thing> along. e.g. 가져오게 하다 get <someone> to bring send <to a shop> for <something>. **2** [초래하다] bring about [on / forth]; cause; induce; give rise [birth] to <confusion>; result [end] in. e.g. 실패를 가져오다 cause a failure / result in failure

가족 [गाजोक] [**家族**] a family; a household; members of a family; one's people [folks]; [친족]

가죽 [गाजुक] [피부] [the skin; [a] hide [주로 쇠가죽; [무두질한] leather; [모피] [a] fur; [날가죽] a pelt [raw skin / rawhide].

가지 [गाजी][1] [나무의] a branch; [줄기에서 나온 큰 가지] a bough; a limb; [잔가지] a twig

가지 [गाजी][2] [종류] a kind; a sort; a variety. e.g. 여러 가지 물건 things of various kinds / varieties [different kinds] of things.

가지각색 [गाजीगाक्सैक] [-**各色**] every kind and description. e.g. 가지각색의 사람들 all sorts [and conditions] of men / a motley of people.

가지다 [गाजीदा] **1** [손에] have; take; hold; [몸에] carry [with one]; have <a thing> with one [about one]. **2** [소유하다] have; own; possess; be possessed of; be endowed with [타고나다].

가지런하다 [गाजीरौन्हादा] arranged neatly; equal; even; uniform; regular <teeth>; <서술적> be in order. e.g. 신을 가지런 하게 놓다 arrange shoes [in order].

가짜 [गाचा] [**假**–] [모조품] an imitation; a sham; a spurious [false] article; a fake; a make believe; [위조품] a counterfeit; a forgery; < 美 > a duffer; [사람] a charlatan; a pretender; an imposter; a fraud.

가책 [गाछैक] [**呵責**] scolding; chiding; blame; censure; imputation. e.g. 양심의 가책 compunction / the qualms [sting[s]

가축 [गाछुक] [**家畜**] a domestic animal; <집합적> cattle; stock; livestock. e.g. 축을 치다keep[raise / breed] livestock.

가출 [गाछुल] [**家出**] disappearance from home; abscondence [도망] an elopement 여자의] 가출하다 run [go / drith] away from home; leave home one's house]; disappear fly] from home; abscond; elope 특히 여성이 애인과].

가치 [गाछी] [**價値**] value; worth; merit

가치관 [गाछीग्वान] one's sense of values.

가톨릭 [गाथोल्लिक] Catholicism; the Roman] Catholic Church.

가파르다 [गाफारूदा] steep <slope>; sharp <climb>; precipitous <cliff>.

가해 [गाहै] [**加害**] doing harm; inflicting injury; violence; an offense; wrong [doing].

가해자 [गाहैजा] an assaulter; an assailant; a wrongdoer; a murderer [살해자]

가혹 [गाहोक] [**苛酷**] severity; rigor; harshness; [잔혹] cruelty. 가혹하다 severe hard; harsh; rigid; cruel; brutal.

가히 [गाही] [[**可**–] [may] well; fairly well; [might] well; [can] rightly [suitably]. e.g. 가히 당대의 석학이라 할 만한 사람 a man who might well be called the greatest scholar of the age.

각 [गाक] [**各**] each; every; all. e.g. 각 곳 every place / all the places

각 [गाक][**角**] [각도] an angle.

각 각 [गाककाक] [**各各**] ach; all; every; respectively; individually; severally; separately. e.g. 우리는 각각 자기 방이

있다 Each one of us has a room to himself / We each have our own room.

각광 [गाकक्वांग] [**脚光**] [극장의] footlights; floats. 각광[을] 받다[무대에서] appear before the footlights; [세상에서] be highlighted [spotlighted]; be in [move into / step into] the limelight; get into the spotlight.

각국 [गाककुक] [**各國**] [각 나라] every [each] country [nation]; [여러 나라] various countries [states]; [만국] the world; all countries. e.g.세계 각국 world nations.

각별하다 [गाकप्यौर्हादा] [**恪別-**] [유다르다] particular; 특별하다 especial; special; extra-ordinary.

각색 [गाक्सैक] [**脚色**] [각본으로 씀] dramatization; [an] arrangement. e.g. 각색 김종찬 adapted by Kim Chong-ch'an. 각색하다 dramatize <a novel>; adapt [arrange] <a novel> for a movie [play]; [영화로] filmize; cinematize; scen-arize; make a screen version of <a story>.

각선미 [गाक्सौन्मी] [**脚線美**] the beauty of leg lines; a nice leg line; "a well-turned ankle".

각설 [गाक्सौल] [**却說**] 설하다 resume <one's story>; return to the subject; get back from a digression.

각성 [गाक्सौंग] [**覺醒**] awak-ening; disillusion; disenchant-ment. 각성하다 [무지에서] awake <from / to>; wake up <to>; come to one's senses; [잘못에서] be disillusioned

각오 [गागो] [**覺悟**] [마음의 준비[準備] readiness; pre-paredness; [결심] reso-lution; determination. 각오하다 [be ready [pre-pared] for; make up one's mind; form [make] a resolution; be determined

각자 [गाक्चा] [**各自**] each; each [every] one; <부사> each; individually; respect-ively; severally.

-간 [गान] [**間**] **1** [관계] relation; relationship. e.g. 형제간 brotherly [fraternal] relation. **2** [사이] between; among. e.g. 형제간의 싸움 =a quarrel between bro-thers. **3** [간격] an interval; [기간] a period; for; during; in. e.g. 1개월간 for a month.

간 [गान] [**肝**] the liver; <비유> courage. e.g.간이 작은 timid / faint-hearted / chicken-hearted. 간이 콩알만해지다 be fright-ened out one's wits / be scared stiff.

간격 [गान्ग्यौक] [**間隔**] [공간, 거리, 시간] a space;

spacing; an interval; a gap; a distance. e.g. 간격을 좁히다 narrow the distance between / move closer together.

간결 [गान्ग्यौल] [**簡潔**] conciseness; brevity; neatness <of expression>. 간결하다 concise; terse; brief; compact <style>; succinct; pithy.

간과 [गानग्वा] [**看過**] 간과하다 fail to notice; overlook; miss; pass over [by / up]; lose sight of <an important fact>.

간단 [गान्दान] [**簡單**] simplicity 간단하다 simple; brief; short; plain; easy e.g. 간단한 문제 a simple problem [question].

간략 [गाल्ल्याक] [**簡略**] [간단함] [simplicity 간략하다 simple; concise; terse; brief; informal. e.g. 간략하게 하다 make simple / simplify / abbreviate.

간병 [गान्ब्यौंग] [**看病**] nursing; tending <a sick person>. 간병하다 nurse; tend; care for; attend on.

간부 [गान्बु] [**幹部**] the executive members; the management; the leading [principal] members; the managing staff; the leaders; the governing body.

간사 [गान्सा] [**奸詐**] cunningness; slyness; deceitfulness; crath. 간사하 ng; sly; foxy; crath; wily; deceitful; fawning. e.g. 간사 [를] 부리다 play a sly game / be a wily customer.

간섭 [गान्सौप] [**干涉**] [참견함] interference; [타국의 내정 등의] intervention. 간섭하다 interfere <in a matter / a person with>; meddle <in>; intervene <in>; intrude oneself <into an affair>; put [thrust] in one's oar; cut in

간수 [गान्सु] keeping; safekeeping; custody; charge; storage. 간수하다 keep; save; store; take custody [charge] <of>; put aside for future use.

간식 [गान्शिक] [**間食**] a snack.

간신히 [गान्शिन्ही] [**艱辛**–] [겨우] barely; narrowly; hardly; by a [near] shave; [힘겹게] laboriously; with difficulty; [근근히] just; only. e.g. 간신히 도망치다 escape narrowly [by a hairbreadth / by the skin of one's teeth] / have a narrow escape.

간절 [गान्जौल] [**懇切**] arnest [ness]; eagerness 간절하다 earnest; eager; fervent; ardent; sincere. e.g. 간절한 부탁 an earnest request.

간절히 [गान जौही] [**懇切**–] [절실히] eagerly; sincerely.

간접 [गान्जौप] [**間接**] indirectness e.g. 간접의 = 간접적.

간주 [गान्जु] [**看做**] 간주하다

regard <as>; consider; think of <as>; deem; reckon; count <as / for>; look on [upon] <as>; take <for>.

간지럼 [गान्जिरौम] ticklish [tickling] sensation [feeling]; tickling; titillation.

간지럽다 [गान्जिरौप्ता] [몸이] feel ticklish; feel a tickle.

간질이다 [गान्जिरिदा] tickle; titillate e.g. 발바닥을 간질이다 tickle the soles of <a person's> feet.

간첩 [गान्छौप] [**間諜**] spy; an [espionage] agent; a secret agent; an emissary; espionage [행위].

간청 [गान्छौंग] **懇請**] entreaty; solicitation; an earnest request; supplication. 간청하다 entreat <a person to do>; solicit <a person for>; implore; supplicate; request earnestly; beg [earnestly].

간추리다 [गान्छुरीदा] sum up; summarize; digest; epitomize; condense.

간판 [गान्फान] [**看板**] **1** [상점의] a signboard; a sign; [광고판] a billboard [a hoarding]. **2** [학벌] a school career; an academic career [background]. e.g. 간판이 좋다 have a good [brilliant] academic career [background] **3** [인기 인물] a drawing card; an attraction; a draw girl; a beauty lure; [극단 등의] the leading actor; the prima donna [여자]. e.g. 저 예쁜 아이는 그 꽃집의 간판이다 That pretty girl is the florist's drawing card.

간편 [गान्फ्यौन] [**簡便**] convenience; handiness; simplicity. 간편하다 convenient; simple; easy; handy; portable [휴대가 손쉬운]. e.g. 간편한 방법 an easy method / a simple and easy way.

간행 [गानहैंग] [**刊行**] publication. 간행하다 publish; issue; bring out.

간헐 [गान्हौल] [**間歇**] intermittence. e.g. 간헐적인 intermittent.

간호 [गान्हो] [**看護**] nursing; care [of the sick]; tending <a sick person>. e.g. 극진한 간호 careful nursing. 간호하다 [गानहोहादा] nurse; tend <the sick and wounded>; attend on <a sick person>; care for.

간호사 [गान्होसा] [**看護師**] [여자] a [hospital] nurse; a sick nurse; a sister; [남자] a male nurse [attendant].

간혹 [गान्होक] [**間或**] [이따금] occasionally; at times; between times [whiles]; now and then; once in a while [way]; once in a long [great] while; at long [rare] intervals; on rare occasions e.g. 간혹 들르다

drop in once in a while.

갇히다 [गाच्छिदा] be confined [shut up]; be kept in-doors; be locked in; be imprisoned; be behind bars.

갈겨쓰다 [गाल्ग्यौसुदा] write hurriedly [carelessly]; scribble; scrawl; dash off.

갈고리 [गालगौरी] a hook; a crook; a gaff.

갈기갈기 [गालगीगालगी] to pieces; into shreds. e.g. 갈기갈기 찢다 tear [rend] to pieces [ribbons / shreds / threads] / tear into strips / rip <the flag> into tatters.

갈기다 [गाल्गिदा] **1** [때리다] beat; strike; knock; hit; thrash; wallop e.g. 몽둥이로 갈기다 drub / club / cudgel. **2** [글씨를 마구 쓰다] write hastily; scribble; scrawl; dash off.

갈다[1] [गाल्दा] [바꾸다] renew; change <for a new one>; replace <A by [with] B>; substitute <B for A>; attach [fix] anew. e.g. 이름을 갈다 change one's name.

갈다[2] [गाल्दा] **1** [칼 등을] whet; sharpen <a knife / a sword>; grind <an axe>; hone <a razor>; strop <a razor>. **2** [가루가 되 grind [mill] <wheat> into [to] <flour>; grind down; rub fine [into powder]; bray; pulverize; triturate.

갈다[3] [गाल्दा] [땅을 파 뒤집다] till; get <the soil> turned over; plow; plough; cultivate. e.g. 밭을 갈다 till the field.

갈등 [गाल्तुंग] [葛藤] trouble [s]; discord; dissension; a complication; tangle; difficulties; [반목] a feud.

갈라서다 [गाल्लासौदा] **1** [이혼, 절연하다] divorce oneself <from>; be divorced <from>; break <with a person>; break off relations <with a person>; sever [cut] one's connection <with>. **2** [따로 서다] stand apart; line up separately.

갈라지다 [गाल्लाजीदा] **1** [째지다] split; cleave; fissure; [금이 가다 crack [a part]; [땅등이 크게] gape. **2** [분할되다] be divided <into three parts>; [분열되다] break up; split; rend <into two>; part; [분리되다] branch off [out] <from>; diverge <from>; [분기하다] fork [out]. **3** [사이가 틀어지다 be [become] estranged [alienated] <from>; [헤어지다] [हेऔजीदा] part <from / with>; part company with; be parted <from>; be separated.

갈래 [गाल्लै] [분기] a fork <of a road>; [분파] a branch; an offshoot; a sect

[종파의]; [당내의] a faction; a fraction; [구분] a division; a section. e.g. 두 갈래 길 a cross-road [s].

갈리다[1] [गाल्लिदा] [분리되다] be divided <into>;[be] split <into>; be parted; separate; [분기하다] branch off <from>; be forked; fork <into>.

갈리다[2] [गाल्लिदा] **1** [[사람, 물건이] [바뀌다] be changed <for>; be replaced. **2** [[다른 것으로] 갈게 하다] get <a person> to change; have <a person> renew; have [get] <something> replaced.

갈리다[3] [गाल्लिदा] [갈려지다] [칼 등이] be whetted; be ground; be sharpened. e.g. 이 밀은 잘[곱게] 갈린다 This wheat grinds [is ground] well [fine].

갈림길 [गाल्लिमगिल] **1** [갈린 길] a branch road; a side road; a forked road; the fork of a road. e.g. 갈림길에 이르다 come to the fork of a road. **2** [기로] turning point; a crossroad [s]. e.g. 생사의 갈림길에서 헤매다 hover between life and death.

갈비 [गाल्बी] a rib; <집합적> the ribs.

갈비찜 [गाल्बीचिम] beef rib stew; steamed short-ribs.

갈수록 [गाल्सुरोक] [걸어서] as one goes along; [시간이] as time goes on [by]; with the lapse [passage] of time; in the process of time; [할수록] the more [-er] ... the more[-er] ...; the more ... the less. e.g. 갈수록 태산 Things go from bad to worse / Things are worse than ever

갈아입다 [गाराइप्ता] change <one's clothes>. e.g. 갈아입을 옷 a change of clothes / spare clothes.

갈아타다 [गाराथादा] change <cars [trains / planes] at>; transfer <to another car>; [배를] transship; change <for another train / to another line

갈채 [गाल्छै] [**喝采**] [환영의 목소리와 박수] [applause; [환성] cheers; [환영, 칭찬의 환호성] acclamation[s]; [열렬한 찬사] plaudits; [자연적으로 터지는] an ovation.

갈팡질팡하다 [गाल्फांज्जिलफांग्हादा] [당황하다] be flurried; be confused; be bewildered; be at a loss; be in a hurry-scurry.

갈피 [गाल्फी] **1** [책장 등의 사이] a space between layers [folds / leaves]. **2** [일의 어름] [an interval <of / in / between>; an interstice; [요점] the point; the sense; the thread <of meaning>. e.g.

갈피를 못 잡다 cannot make head or tail <of a thing>

갉다 [गाक्ता] **1** [[이, 손톱, 날카로운 도구 등으로] 깔짝깔짝 문지르다 gnaw <at / on / through>; nibble <at>[쥐 등이] scratch. **2** [[갈퀴 등으로] 긁어모으다] [rake up] [together]; scrap together [up]; gather up. e.g.낙엽을 갈퀴로 갉다 rake together fallen leaves

감[1] [गाम] [**感**] [느낌] feeling; sense; sensation [feeling 쪽이 더 주관적]; [인상] [feeling an impression e.g. 만족[적막 / 행복]감 a feeling of satisfaction [loneliness / happiness].

감[2] [गाम] **1** [본바탕이 되는 재료] [a] material; matter; stuff; [천] texture; weave; fabric. e.g. 옷감 dress material / suiting / dress [clothing] fabrics. **2** [적격자] a suitable person; a man fit for the post. e.g. 훌륭한 사윗감 the most suitable man for one's son-in-law

감각 [गाम्गाक] [**感覺**] **1** [감각 기관을 통한 느낌] sense; sensation; feeling; sensibility. **2** [사물을 느끼는 마음의 작용] sense.

감감하다 [गामगामहादा] **1** [거리가] faraway; far off [away]; remote; [시간, 차이 등이] far above [beyond]; long before. e.g. 바다 위에 감감히 흰 돛이 보인다 A white sail is seen far out on the sea. **2** [기억, 지식 등이] entirely forgotten; ignorant <of>. **3** [소식이] hear nothing from <a person>; have no news from <a person>; receive no word from <a person>.

감격 [गाम्ग्यौक] [**感激**] **1** [격동] deep emotion; strong impression [feeling]. e.g. 감격적인 moving / touching / impressive / dramatic. 감격적인 장면 a dramatic [moving / touching / soul-stirring] scene. 감격하다 be deeply moved [touched] <by>; be deeply impressed <with / by>; be inspired <with>; be carried away with emotion. e.g. 감격시키다 impress / move [touch / affect] <another's> heart deeply. **2** [감사] a strong sense of gratitude; deep gratitude; heartfelt thanks. 감격하다 be very grateful; show gratitude.

감금 [गाम्गुम] [**監禁**] confinement; imprisonment; detention in custody. 감금하다 imprison; confine; detain <a person> in custody; place <a person> in confinement; lock up.

감기 [गाम्गी] [**感氣**] a cold; [유행성] influenza; the flu. e.g. 지독한 감기 a bad [severe] cold.

감기다[1] [गाम्गिदा] **1** [눈이] <one's eyes> be shut [closed] of their own accord [of themselves]. **2** [눈을] make <a person's> eyes fall shut; shut [close] <a person's> eyes.

감기다[2] [गाम्गिदा] **1** [감아지다][실, 끈 등이] be wound [rolled] [up]; be coiled <around>; [덩굴 등이] twine together; get twisted [wound] round; twist about. **2** [실, 끈 등을 감게하다 make [let] <a person> wind [roll / coil] <something> around. **3** [옷이 몸에 달라붙다] be [get] caught in <a roller, a wringer, a wipe, etc.>; cling [stick] to; hang on to.

감기다[3] [गाम्गिदा] [머리, 몸을] wash [bath[e]] <a person>; make <a person> wash [bath]. e.g. 어린애의 머리를 감기다 wash a baby's hair.

감다[1] [गाम्ता] [눈을] shut [close] <one's eyes>.

감다[2] [गाम्ता] [씻다] wash; bath [e]. e.g. 머리를 감다 wash one's hair.

감다[3] [गाम्ता] [실, 등을] wind [coil / twine / bind / tie] <something> round <another thing>; reel. e.g. 실을 실패에 감다 wind thread on [to] a reel / wind a reel with thread / roll thread round a reel / reel <thread>.

감당 [गाम्दांग] [**堪當**] 감당하다 be equal to; be capable of carrying out [discharging / performing]; be up to <doing>; be fit for <a job>; be competent <to do>; be able to fulfill the duties <of>.

감독 [गाम्दोक] [**監督**] **1** [단속] superintendence; supervision; direction; con-trol; [감시] surveillance. 감독하다 sup-erintend; supervise; control; manage; exercise super-vision over; oversee; direct; coach [경기를]; look ather; take charge of. e.g. 학생을 감독하다 look ather one's pupils / take charge of one's class [pupils]. **2** [단속자, 감시자] a super-intendent; a supervisor; an overseer; a director; an inspector; [인부, 공원의] a foreman; gaffer; [영화의] director; [교회의] a bishop; [경기 팀의] a manager; [무대의] an impresario <*pl.* ~s, sari>

감돌다 [गाम्दोल्दा] **1** [주위를 돌다] go [turn] round;

circle round; turn about. **2** [길, 물굽이가] wind; meander; curve; follow [a bend]; make a curve <around>. e.g. 굽이굽이 감도는 winding <path> / meandering <stream> **3** [어떤 분위기가 가득하다] linger; hang <in the air>. e.g. 입가에 감도는 미소 a smile on one's lips / a smile playing about one's lips.

감동 [गाम्दोंग] [**感動**] impression; [deep] emotion; excitement; a sensation <among the audience>. 감동하다 be impressed <by / with>; be moved [touched / inspired / affected / electrified] <by>; feel emotion <at>; be struck <by / with>.

감량 [गामन्यांग] [**減量**] a loss in quantity [weight]; [운동 선수의] reduction of one's weight. 감량하다 decrease [reduce] the quantity <of>; [체중을] reduce [one's weight].

감면 [गाम्मयौन] [**減免**] [세금의] reduction <of> and exemption <from taxes>; [형벌의] mitigation and remission; commutation. 감면하다 [세금을] reduce and exempt; [형벌을] mitigate and remit

감명 [गाम्मयौंग] [**感銘**] a [deep] impression. e.g. 감명적인 impressive. 당신의 능란한 교수법에 깊은 감명을 받았다 I am deeply impressed by your skillful teaching / I cannot but admire your teaching skill.

감봉 [गाम्बोंग] [**減俸**] a reduction in salary [pay] 감봉하다 reduce salaries [wages]; cut a person's pay; dock

감사 [गाम्सा] [**監査**] [검사] inspection; superintendence. 감사하다 inspect; superintend; [회계를] audit. e.g. 회계를 감사하다 audit accounts.

감사 [गाम्सा] [**感謝**] thanks; gratitude; appreciation; [신에 대한] thanksgiving. 감사하다 thank <a person for his help>; express [give / tender] one's thanks; express one's gratitude [appreciation]; appreciate; thankful; grateful.

감상 [गाम्सांग] [**感傷**] sentiment; sentimentality. e.g. 감상적인 sentimental / emotional / melodramatic / rosewater

감상 [गाम्सांग] [**感想**] [생각] one's thoughts; [인상] one's impression [s]; sentiments; [느낌] feelings. e.g. 감상을 말하다 give [state] one's impressions <of>.

감상 [गाम्सांग] [**鑑賞**] appreciation. e.g. 취미는 음악 감상입니다 My hobby is listening to music.

감소 [गाम्सो] [減少] [수량의] decrease; [모양이나 정도의] diminution; decline; drop; reduction. 감소하다 diminish; decrease; dwindle; fall off; shrink; lessen; drop; bring down; go down.

감속 [गाम्सोक] [減速] speed reduction; deceleration. 감속하다 reduce the speed; slow down; decelerate.

감수 [गाम्सू] [監修] [editorial] supervision. e.g. 김 박사 감수 edited by [compiled under the supervision of] Dr. Kim. 감수하다 supervise [the compilation of]; be chief editor of the compilation <of>.

감시 [गाम्शी] [監視] [지켜봄] watch; guard; lookout; vigil; observation; [감독] supervision. 감시하다 watch; keep watch on [over]; keep an [one's] eye on; observe; [죄수 등을] guard; [경찰이 장소 등을] stake out.

감싸다 [गाम्सादा] **1** [싸다] wrap <in>; tuck up <in>. e.g. 그녀는 온몸을 담요로 감싸고 있었다 She was covered from head to foot with a blanket. **2** [비호하다] protect <the weak>; cover <a guilty person>; shield [screen / shelter] <a person from>; take <a person> under one's wings; [변호하다] plead [speak up] for <a person>. e.g. 김 씨는 항상 그를 감싸주고 있다 He is always under Mr. Kim's patronage.

감염 [गाम्यौम] [感染] [공기나 물에 의한] infection; [접촉에 의한] contagion; contamination.

감옥 [गामोक] [監獄] a prison; a jail; gaol [▷<美>에서는 보통 [유치장]의 뜻, <英>에서도 prison 쪽을 흔히 씀].

감원 [गाम्वॉन] [減員] reduction of the staff; cutting down of the personnel; a personnel cut [reduction]; [일시적인] a layoff. 감원하다 reduce [cut] the staff personnel]; lay off.

감자 [गाम्जौन] a potato; a white potato; an Irish potato.

감전 [गाम्जौन] [感電] [receiving] an electric shock. 감전하다 receive an electric shock; be struck affected] by electricity.

감점 [गामचौम] [減點] a demerit mark. e.g. 감점을 당하다 receive a cut in marks. 감점하다 give <a person> a demerit mark; make a cut in marks.

감정[1] [गाम्जौग] [憾情] [악감] an unpleasant [ill] feeling; ill [bad] blood; [유감] resentment. e.g. 감정이 있다 be ill [unfavorably] disposed <toward> / have something on one's mind.

감정[2] [गाम्जौग] [**感情**] feeling [s]; [정서] emotion; sentiment; [열정] passion; [충동] impulse. e.g. 그녀는 감정에 치우치기 쉽다 She tends to become emotional.

감지 [गाम्जि] [**感知**] perception 감지하다 perceive; sense; become aware <of>; suspect; scent <a plot>

감지덕지 [गाम्जिदौक्चि] [**感之德之**] very thankfully; with deep gratitude; with many [grateful / hearty / heartfelt] thanks. 감지덕지하다] be [feel] very thankful [grateful] <for>.

감찰 [गाम्छाल] [**監察**] [감사] inspection; [감독] supervision. 감찰하다 inspect; supervise.

감초 [गाम्छो] [**甘草**] a licorice [root]. e.g. 약방에 감초 [필수적인 사물] an indispensable thing <to> / indispensable

감촉 [गाम्छोक] [**感觸**] [the sense of] touch; a feel. e.g. 감촉이 부드러운 smooth to the touch.

감추다 [गाम्छुदा] [몸,물건 등을] hide <one's face>; conceal <one's money>; secrete <stolen goods>; [덮어서] cover <a face>; veil <one's displeasure>; disguise <one's nationality>; conceal <one's identity>; [비밀로 하다] keep <a matter> secret [back] <from>; [숨겨주다] harbor <fugitives>; shelter <a criminal>. e.g. 마음의 동요를 감추다 cover one's confusion.

감탄 [गाम्थान] [**感歎**] admiration <for / of>; wonder; marvel; exclamation. 감탄하다 admire; be struck with wonder [admiration]; marvel <at>; wonder <at>; exclaim <over>.

감퇴 [गामथ्वे] [**減退**] decline; ebb; failing; loss; decrease; recession. e.g. .... 시력 [기억력] 감퇴 failing of eyesight [memory]. 감퇴하다 decline; ebb; recede; fall off. e.g. 식욕이 감퇴하다 lose one's appetite.

감행 [गाम्हैग] [**敢行**] decisive [resolute / daring] action; [수행] carrying out; execution. 감행하다 [गाम्हैगहादा] take decisive [resolute] action; dare to do; venture <an attempt>; carry out resolutely.

감회 [गामह्वे] [**感懷**] [회포] sentiments; feelings; [회상] memories; reminiscences; retrospection. e.g. 감회가 깊다 be deeply moved <by>.

감흥 [गाम्हुंग] [**感興**] interest; fun; inspiration [영감]. e.g. 감흥을 깨뜨리다 spoil fun [interest] / break the spell.

감히 [गाम्ही] [**敢-**] boldly; fearlessly; daringly; without heistation; [주제넘게] affectedly; impudently. e.g. 감히 … 하다 dare [venture / presume] <to do> / make bold <to do> / lend oneself to <a deed>.

갑 [गाप] [**匣**] a case; a casket; a tiny case; a boK a pack [담배 등의]. e.g. 담뱃 갑 a cigarette case / a tobacco box.

갑갑하다 [गाप्काफादा] **1** [답답하다] stifling; suffocating; stuffy; close; [좁다] confined <space>; [uncomfortably] narrow; poky <little room>. **2** [지겹다] boring; tedious; dull; tiresome; feel bored

갑론을박 [गाम्नोनुलबाक] [**甲論乙駁**] arguments pro and con; the pros and cons. 갑론을박하다 [गाबलोनुलबाख्वादा] argue back and forth; argue [discuss] the pros and cons <of a matter>.

갑자기 [गाप्चागी] [별안간] suddenly; on a sudden; all of a sudden; all at once; abruptly; [뜻밖에] unexpectedly; without warning [notice]

갑작스럽다 [गाप्चाकसुरौप्ता] sudden; abrupt; unexpected; unlooked-for; unannounced. e.g. 갑작스러운 초대 a surprise invitation.

갑절 [गाप्चौल] **1** two times; twice; double; twofold; [셀 때] times; as much. **2** <부사> e.g. 갑절비싸다 cost twice as much. 남보다 갑절 일하다 work twice as hard as others.

값 [गाप] **1** [가치] value; worth; merit [장점]. **2** [가격] price; cost; charge [▷ price 는 특히 파는 값. Charge 는 노동 봉사에 대해서 구하는 대가. Cost 는 물건 노동 기타의 획득에 대해 지불하는 값]. e.g. 값이 비싸다[싸다] be expensive [dear costly] / be high in price

값어치 [गाप्सौछी] **1** [값에 알맞는 가치]. value; worth. **2** [사람, 사물의 가치]. e.g. 그런 말을 하면 네 값어치가 떨어진다 It is beneath your dignity to say such a thing.

값지다 [गाप्चिदा] [값나가다] valuable; of value; worthy; [비싸다] expensive; costly. e.g. 값진 물건 a precious object / [진귀한 물건]

갓 [गात] [방금] fresh [green] from; just now; newly; recently. e.g. 갓 구운 빵 bread fresh [hot] from the oven.

갓난아이 [गान्नानाई] a newborn baby; a baby; a babe; an infant.

강 [गांग] [**江**] a river; [강물] a stream; [시내] a brook.

강가 [गांका] [**江-**] a riverside;

ㄱ

a riverbank; an edge of a river.

강간 [गांगान] [**强姦**] rape; violation; outrage; assault. 강간하다 rape; assault; violate; outrage; ravish.

강경 [गांग्यौग] [**强硬**] firmness; toughness; resoluteness; stubbornness. 강경하다 [गांगग्यौगहादा] strong; firm; [단호한] resolute; unbending; unyielding; uncompromising.

강국 [गांगुक] [**强國**] a great power; a strong nation [country]; a powerful state. e.g. 세계의 강국 the powers of the world / world powers.

강단 [गांगदान] [**講壇**] a rostrum <pl. ~ s, -tra>; [학술의] a [lecture] platform; [설교의] a pulpit. e.g. 강단에 서다stand on a platform / take[occupy] the platform [rostrum] / preach a sermon.

강당 [गांग्दांग] [**講堂**] a lecture hall; [계단식] a lecture theater; a hall; [학교의] an auditorium <pl. ~s, -ria>; an assembly hall.

강도 [गांग्दो] [**强盜**] [사람] a robber; a burglar; a housebreaker; [행위] burglary; robbery.

강력 [गांगन्यौक] [**强力**] 강력하다 strong; powerful; mighty.

강렬 [गांगन्यौल] [**强烈**] 강렬하다 [गांगन्यौरहादा] strong; intense; severe.

강론 [गांग्नोन] [**講論**] [토론] exposition; discussion; [설교] preaching; a sermon. 강론하다 expound; discuss; preach; teach.

강박 관념 [गांग्बाक ग्वाँनन्यौम] [**强迫觀念**] an imperative idea [conception]; an obsession. e.g. 강박 관념에 사로잡히다 suffer from an obsession.

강사 [गांग्सा] [**講師**] **1** [연사] a lecturer. **2** [대학의] an instructor; a lecturer.

강산 [गांग्सान] [**江山**] [강과 산] rivers and mountains; [경치] landscape; scenery; [강토] a country; a territory; a realm; a domain. e.g. 십년이면 강산도 변한다 Ten years is an epoch.

강설 [गांग्सौल] [**降雪**] snowing; a snowfall. **강설량** [the amount of] snowfall.

강세 [गांग्से] [**强勢**] **1** [음악, 음성학에서] stress; emphasis; accent. e.g. 강세를 두다 put emphasis <on>. **2** [시장,주식 시세의 오름세] a strong feeling [market]; a firm [high] tone; a bull; a bullish tendency.

강수 [गांग्सु] [**降水**] rainfall; precipitation. **강수량**[the amount of] rainfall [precipitation].

강습 [गांग्सुप] [**講習**] a short

training course [class]; studying; learning. e.g. 강습을 받다 take short-term course <of English> / attend a class / take lessons <in English

강압 [गांगाप] [**强壓**] pressure; oppression; coercion; repre-sssion; compulsion; high-handedness. 강압하다 coerce; oppress; repress; put pressure <upon>.

강약 [गांग्याक] [**强弱**] **1** [힘의 강함과 약함] strength and weakness; [강자와 약자] the strong and the weak. **2** [음의] stress; [a] rhythm; [악센트] accentuation; [음악에서의 강약법] dynamics.

강연 [गांग्यौन] [**講演**] a lecture; an address; a speech; a discourse. 강연하다 [give a] lecture <on>; address <a meeting>; make an address <on>; make a speech

강요 [गांग्यो] [**强要**] a [forcible] demand; compulsion; en-forcement; exaction; ex-tortion. 강요하다 [상대방 의사를 거스르고] force [compel] <a person to do>; [세금, 벌금, 의무, 의견 등을] impose <a thing on a person>; [권위를 갖고] demand forcibly; [지불, 복종 등을] exact; [위협, 압력으로] coerce; high-pressure <a person into doing>. e.g. 복종을 강요하다 exact obedience from <a person>. 노동을 강요하다 force labor <upon a person>

강우량 [गांगउर्यांग] [**降雨量**] [the amount of] rainfall; a rainfall; [the record of] precipitation. e.g. 서울의 연강우량 the annual rainfall in Seoul.

강의 [गांगुइ] [**講義**] a lecture <on>; a discourse; an expo-sition; [설명] an explan-ation. 강의하다 lecture <on a subject>; give a lecture <on>; give a course <in>; teach.

강적 [गांग्जौक] [**强敵**] a power-ful enemy [adversary]; a formidable foe [rival]; [시합의] a powerful rival [opponent].

강점 [गांगजौम] [**强點**] one's strength [power]; a strong point; an element of strength. e.g. … 의 강점이 있다 have the advantage of

강제 [गांग्जे] [**强制**] compul-sion; coercion; constraint; forcing; duress. e.g. 강제적인 compulsory / coer-cive / forced. 강제적으로 forcibly / by force / compulsorily / by com-pulsion / coercively.

강조 [गांग्जो] [**强調**] stress; emphasis; accentuation. 강조하다 emphasize; stress;

accentuate; lay[place / put] stress [emphasis] <on>; highlight; underline.

강좌 [गांगज्वा] [**講座**] [대학의] a chair; a lectureship; professorship; [강습의] a course; a lecture.

강직 [गांग्जिक] [**强直**] [강하고 곧음] integrity; honesty; rigidity; stiffness. 강직 하다 honest; upright; rigid; stiff.

강타 [गांग्था] [**强打**] **1** [강한 타격] a heavy [hard / hethy] blow; a wallop; a slug; [권투에서] a Sunday punch. 강타하다deal <a person> a heavy blow; hit hard; slog; slug; swat [wallop] <a ball>. **2** [야구에서] a terrific [hard / heavy] drive [hit]; [골프, 테니스에서] a powerful drive.

강탈 [गांग्थाल] [**强奪**] extortion; [강도] [a] robbery; [선박, 토지 등의] [a] seizure; plunder; [침입자 등에 의한 약탈] depredation; hijacking; a stickup; [노상 강도 행위] holdup. 강탈하다 extort; rob [despoil / plunder / loot] <a person> of <a thing>; snatch <a thing> from <a person>; seize; hijack; stick up <a person / a bank>.

강하 [गांग्हा] [**降下**] faliing; dropping; a drop; descent; [기압의] depression. e.g. 기온의 강하 a drop in [the] temperature. 강하하다 fall; drop; descend; glide down; [착륙하다] land.

강하다 [गांग्हादा] [**强-**] **1** [강력하다] strong; powerful; mighty. e.g. 강한 나라 a strong nation / a great power **2** [강건하다] robust; stout.

강행 [गांग्हैंग] [**强行**] enforcement; forcing. 강행하다 enforce; force.

강화 [गांगह्वा] [**强化**] strengthening; solidification; consoledating; reinforcement; firming up; fortification. 강화하다 strengthen; intensify; solidify; firm up; reinforce.

갖다 [गात्ता] **1** ⇨ 가지다 e.g. 아이들이 성냥을 갖고 있지 못하게 하시오 Don't let children get hold of matches **2** [가져다가]. e.g. 물을 한 컵 갖다다오 Get me a glass of water. 사장님이 그 서류를 갖다달라고 하십니다 The president is calling for the document. [갖다 놓다] e.g. 사전을 다 썼으면 선반 제자리에 갖다 놓으시오 Put the dictionary back in its place on the shelf when you have finished with it. 갖다 주다 bring [over]. e.g. 맥주 좀 갖다 주시오 Bring us some beer, please.

갖은 [गाजुन] [모든] all; all sorts [manner] of; every; every possible; [빠짐없는] complete; perfect; well-made; [갖가지의] various; a variety of; [골고루 갖춘] assorted; well-assorted. e.g. 갖은 고생 all kinds of hardships [troubles]

갖추다 [गाच्छूदा] **1** [고루 준비하다] be [get] ready; be prepared; have. e.g. 준비는 갖추어졌다 Our preparations are complete. / We are ready. **2** [제대로 완비되다] equip; furnish; complete; assort. e.g. 이것으로 만찬 식기 세트가 갖추어진다 This completes the dinner set.

같다 [गात्था] **1** [동일하다] the same; identical <with>; the self same. **2** [동등하다] equal <to>; uniform; equivalent <to>.

같이 [गाछी] **1** [같게] as; like; in the same way [manner]; similarly; in a similar way; alike; likewise. e.g. 여느 때와 같이 as usual. **2** [동등하게] equally; impartially; alike; indiscriminately. e.g. 같이 분배하다 divide equally **3** [처럼] as if [though]; like; as; as ... as. e.g. 눈같이 흰 as white as snow **4** [함께] together; with; together with; along with; in company with e.g. 다 같이 all together

같잖다 [गाच्चान्था] [눈꼴 사납다] foolish; silly; absurd; nonsensical; unseemly; improper; bothersome; saucy; impertinent; [시시하다] trifle; trivial; small; slight; insignificant; of no account. e.g. 같잖은 물건 a no-good thing / a worthless object / wretched stuff / rubbish / trash / a white elephant.

갚다 [गाप्ता] **1** [돈을] pay back <a loan>; repay <a loan>; clear; return; give back; refund; settle one's account. e.g. 빚을 갚다 pay [repay] one's debts. **2** [보답하다] reward <a person> for; repay <another's kindness>; requite <favors>; [보상하다] recompense <a person> for; compensate for; [보복하다] retaliate <against a person> with; return; requite; [원수를] revenge; avenge.

개 [गै] [**個,箇,介**] a piece; a unit; an item. e.g. 사과 세 개 three apples. 비누 두 개 two cakes [pieces] of soap.

개 [गै] [動] a dog; [암캐] a bitch [a she-dog]; a canine.

개각 [गैगाक] [**改閣**] a cabinet reshuffle; a cabinet shake-up. 개각하다 reshuffle the cabinet.

개간 [गैगान] [開墾] land clearing; reclamation; bringing <wasteland> under cultivation. 개간하다 bring <land> under cultivation; reclaim <wasteland>; clear <land>.

개강 [गैगांग] [開講] 개강하다 give one's first lecture; begin a series of lectures; [대학에서] open a course; begin school.

개개 [個個,箇箇] [गैगै] being individual; each one; an item; [모두] all; every one; everyone. e.g. 개개의 individual / separate / several.

개관 [गैग्वॉन] [開館] the opening <of a hall>. 개관하다 open <a hall>.

개교 [गैग्यो] [開校] the opening of a school. 개교하다 open [inaugurate] a school; found a school.

개구리 [गैगुरी] a frog; [식용의] a bullfrog.

개구쟁이 [गैगूजैंगी] a naughty boy; a mischievous boy; a brat; an urchin; an imp. e.g. 개구쟁이짓 naughtiness / brattiness

개그 [गैगु] a gag.

개그맨 [गैगुमैन] a gagman; gagster.

개근 [गैगुन] [皆勤] perfect attendance; non-absence [throughout a year]; regular attendance [without a day's absence].

개근하다 [गैगुनहादा] attend regularly [without missing a single day]; be not absent a single day.

개념 [गैन्यौम] [概念] a notion; a general idea; [哲] a concept; a conception; an idea.

개다[1] [गैदा] [맑게 되다] [날씨가] clear up; become clear; [눈,비가] hold up; stop <raining / snowing>; cease to <rain / snow>; [안개가] lith; clear away [off]; break away.

개다[2] [गैदा] [섞이게 이기다] sothen with water; knead; mix up; temper; pug; work <clay / mortar>. e.g. 가루반죽을 개다 knead dough.

개다[3] [गैदा] [접어 포개다] fold [up] <bedding>; turn down. e.g. 옷을 개다 fold one's clothes / lay the clothes away.

개론 [गैरोन] [概論] an outline <on>; general remarks [consideration]; [입문] an introduction <to>.

개막 [गैमाक] [開幕] **1** [막을 엶] the raising of the curtain; the commencement of performance. 개막하다 [गैमखादा] raise [draw up] a curtain; begin [commence] the perform-ance. **2** [일의 개시] the opening. 개막하다 [गैमखादा] open;

commence.

개미 [गैमी] [昆] an ant; a pismire.

개발 [गैबाल] [開發] [개척] development; [자원의] exploitation; [식민지의] colonization; [우주 등의] exploration; [계발] enlightenment; development. 개발하다 develop.

개방 [गैबांग] [開放] [열어 놓음] opening; throwing open; [허용] lithing the ban. 개방하다 [गैबांगहादा] open; throw open <a door>; leave <the door> open.

개벽 [गैब्यौक] [開闢] [천지의 창조] the Creation e.g. 개벽 이래 since the beginning of the world

개별 [गैब्यौल] [個別] an individual [a particular] case; individualization. e.g. 개별적으로 individually / [따로따로] separately

개비 [गैबी] a piece of split wood [timber]. e.g. 성냥개비 a matchstick

개선 [गैसौन] [改善] [an] improvement; [a] betterment; amelioration; reform [ation]. 개선하다 improve; better; ameliorate; make <a thing> better. e.g. 생활을 개선하다 better one's standard of living / improve one's way of life

개설 [गैसौल] [開設] establishment; [공식적인] inauguration; opening; installation <of a telephone>. 개설하다 establish; set up; inaugurate; open.

개성 [गैसौंग] [個性] individuality; personality; idiosyncrasy; individual character; characteristic traits.

개시 [गैशी] [開始] start; opening; inauguration; commencement; beginning. begin; commence; open <a game>; enter upon [into] <negotiations>; start <business>; inaugurate <bus service>; launch <an attack>; make a beginning <with>.

개업 [गैऔप] [開業] opening [commencement] of [a] business [a trade]; establishment in business. 개업하다 start [a] business; set oneself up [establish oneself] in business; enter [up] on business; [의사, 변호사가] start practice; practice <medicine / law>.

개요 [गैयो] [概要] an epitome; a summary; an outline; a synopsis; an abstract; a résumé

개운하다 [गैउनहादा] **1** [상쾌하다] <feel> refreshed; feel well [fine / all right]. e.g. 이제 몸이 개운하다 I feel quite well now / Now I feel refreshed. **2** [후련하다] <feel> relieved; free and easy; feel at ease

개울 [गैउल] a brook; a brooklet; a streamlet; a rivulet.

개원 [गैवॉन] [**開院**] [병원 등의] the opening [inauguration] <of a hospital>. 개원하다 open [inaugurate] <a hospital>. **개인** [गैइन] [**個人**] an individual; [사인] a private person [individual / citizen]; a person in his private capacity.

개입 [गैइप] [**介入**] intervention; meddling; interference. 개입하다 intervene [interfere] <in a dispute>; meddle <in a matter>.

개작 [गैजाक] [**改作**] [an] adaptation <from / for>; recasting. 개작하다 adapt <from / for>; recast; rewrite. **개작자** an adapter.

개장 [गैजांग] [**開場**] opening; [증권] the opening session; a session; a call. 개장하다 open; open the door; [증권시장을] hold [open] a session [market].

개점 [गैजौम] [**開店**] 개점하다 open [start] a shop [store]; open shop; establish a shop [store].

개정 [गैजौंग] [**改正**] [수정] [a] revision; [an] amendment; [a] reform; [변경] [an] alteration; [a] change. 개정하다 revise; amend; alter; change; remodel <the rules>.

개조 [गैजो] [**改造**] remodeling; reconstruction; reorganizeation; rebuilding. 개조하다 remodel; reorganize; reconstruct; rebuild.

개종 [गैजोंग] [**改宗**] [a] conversion <to>; proselytism. 개종하다 change one's religion; be converted [proselyted] <to>; proselyte

개죽음 [गैजुगुम] throwing away one's life; an ignominious death; a stupid sacrifice of life; a useless death.

개찰 [गैछाल] [**改札**] 개찰하다 examine tickets; [가위로 찍다] punch [clip] <a ticket>.

개찰구 [गैछाल्गू] a [platform] wicket; a ticket barrier [gate]; a gate.

개척 [गैछौक] [**開拓**] [토지의] clearing; [자원의] exploitation; development; [식민지의] colonization. 개척하다 reclaim [clear] <wasteland>; bring <wasteland> under cultivation; develop [exploit] <resources>; open up <a new field in science>; colonize

개체 [गैछे] [**個體**] **1** [철학에서] an individual; the individual; an independent [individual] existence; a separate entity. **2** [생물학에서] an individual; an individual [independent] organism; an organism existing independently.

개최 [गैछ्वे] [**開催**] 개최하다 hold <a meeting>; open <an exhibition>; have <a

farewell [welcome] meeting>; give <a garden party>.

개탄 [गैथान] [慨嘆] deploring; lamentation; regret. e.g. 개탄을 금할 수 없다 be most deplorable. 개탄하다 deplore; lament; regret; grieve.

개통 [गैथोंग] [開通] opening to traffic. 개통하다 [새로] be opened to [for] traffic; go into operation; open up; [막혔다가] be reopened for service; [교량을] open a bridge formally.

개판 [गैफान] utter confusion or disorder; a mess; a jumble; a topsy-turvy.

개편 [गैफ्यौन] [改編] reorganization; [a] reshuffle; reform; modification. 개편하다 [reorganize; reshuffle; remodel.

개폐 [गैफ्ये] [開閉] opening and [or] shutting; make and break. 개폐하다 open and shut [close]; make and break <circuit>.

개표 [गैफ्यो] [開票] the official counting of votes; ballot counting; official canvass of the votes. 개표하다 count the votes [ballots]; make a canvass <of the votes>; open the ballot boxes.

개학 [गैहाक] [開學] beginning of school 개학하다 open [begin] school; school begins.

개혁 [गैह्यौक] [改革] [혁신] [a] reform; reformation; renovation; innovation; [개선] improvement <of / on>. 개혁하다 reform; make [carry out] reforms; renovate; innovate; improve [개선하다].

개화 [गैह्वा] [開化] 개화하다 be [become] civilized; be enlightened; be illuminated. e.g. 개화한 나라 a civilized country.

개회 [गैह्वे] [開會] [회의의] the opening of a meeting; [의회, 법정의] the opening of a session. 개회하다 [집회를] open; [집회가 열리다] open; meet; [의회, 법정 등이] sit

객관 [गैक्वॉन] [客觀] the object; the material world [물질계]

객사 [गैकसा] [客死] 객사하다 die away from home; die in a strange land; die abroad.

객석 [गैकसौक] [客席] a seat [for a guest]; [관객, 승객용의] the seats [for the audience / for passengers]; [관객, 청중] the audience.

객실 [गैक्शिल] [客室] [여관 등의 방] a guest room; [선실] a passenger cabin; [특등실] a stateroom; [가정의] a drawing room [a parlor].

객지 [गैक्ची] [客地] a strange land [where one is staying on a trip]; one's staying place on a journey; foreign land.

갭 [गैप] a gap.

갱신 [गैङ्शिन] [更新] renewal;

renovation; innovation. 갱신하다 renew <a contract>; renovate; innovate.

갸름하다 [ग्यारूमहादा] somewhat long; slender; oval; pleasantly oval. e.g. 갸름한 얼굴 an oval face.

거구 [गौगु] [巨軀] a huge [massive] figure; a big [gigantic] body [frame / physique].

거금[गौगुम][巨金] a large [big] sum [of money]; a pile of money. ⇨ 거액

거기 [गौगी] **1** [그곳 [에]] that place; there; to that place; thither. e.g. 거기서 기다려라 Wait there. **2** [그것[에]] that; so far; that far; to that extent. e.g. 거기에 비하면 on the other hand

거꾸로 [गौकुरो] [아래위를] bottom up; upside down; wrong side up; [안팎을] inside out. **-거나** [गौना] [열거] and; or; [양보] [even] though [if]; no matter how [what / when / where / who]; whatever, etc; [상반] whether ... or .... e.g. 손벽을 치거나 큰 소리로 웃거나 하지 마시오 Don't slap your hands or laugh loudly.

거느리다 [गौनुरिदा] [이끌다] lead; head <a party>; be at the head <of>; [지휘하다] command <an army>; be in command <of an army>; [부양하다] have; take care of.

거느림채 [गौनुरिम्छै] [建] a detached house [building]; an outbuilding [outhouse]; an annex [e] <to a house>; an extension.

거닐다 [गौनिल्दा] walk [stroll] [aimlessly]; saunter [lei surely]; wander about; loiter; ramble.

거대 [गौदै] [巨大] 거대하다 huge; gigantic; giant; enormous; mammoth; colossal.

거덜나다 [गौदौल्लादा] collapse; crumble; break down; go to pieces; [결딴나다] be ruined; fail; burst; [파산하다] go bankrupt [into bankruptcy]; go broke .

거동 [गौदोंग] [擧動] [처신] conduct; behavior; manner; carriage; demeanor; deportment; [행동] action; movements; doings. e.g. 거동을 주시하다 watch <a person's> movements.

거두다 [गौदुदा] **1** [모아들이다] collect; gather; get[bring] together; take in. **2** [수확하다P얻다] harvest; reap <fields>; gather [in]; take the crop up.

거두 절미 [गौदु जौल्मी] [去頭截尾] 거두 절미하다 cut off the head and tail of <it>; leave out the introduction and the conclusion of; make a short story of <it>.

-거든 [गौदुन] [가정, 조건] provided that; if; when. 바쁘지 않거든 놀러 오시오 Come and see me if you are free [not busy].

거들다 [गौदुल्दा] help; assist; aid; lend [give] a [helping] hand; stand by. e.g. 일을 거들다 help <a person> in [with] his work.

거듭 [गौदुप] [되풀이하여] over and over again; again; once again [more]; repeatedly. 거듭하다 repeat; do again.

거래[गौरै][去來] transaction; dealings; business; trade; a deal; [돈거래] lending and borrowing. 거래하다 deal with <a person in a thing>; transact [do] business <with>; have an account <with>; be connected in business dealings <with>

거룩하다 [गौरूख्दा] divine; sacred; holy; sublime; solemn; venerable; great; grand; glorious.

거르다[1] [गौरुदा] [여과하다] filter; strain [out]; leach [물 등을]

거르다[2] [गौरुदा] [건너뛰다] skip [over]; omit; go without; dispense with e.g. 하루[이틀] 걸러 every other [every third] day.

거름 [गौरुम] [비료] manure; [인분] night soil; [소, 말의 똥] dung; [화학 비료] [a] fertilizer.

거리 [गौरी] [距離] distance; [사정거리] range; [간격] an interval; a gap; a gulf; [차이] a difference.

거리[1] [गौरी] [재료] material; matter; stuff; makings; [근거, 핑계] basis; excuse; pretext. e.g. 걱정 거리 a source [cause] of anxiety [worry].

거리[2] [गौरी] [길거리] a road; a street. e.g. 번화한 [쓸쓸한] 거리 a busy [deserted / lonely] street.

거리끼다 [गौरीकीदा] [꺼림칙하다] be afraid of; be shy of; [주저하다] hesitate <to do>; [가책을 받다] feel uneasy; have scruples about <doing>; [방해가 되다] be restrained [hindered / prevented] <by>. e.g. 그 일이 마음에 거리낀다 That matter weighs heavy on my mind.

거만 [गौमान] [倨慢] arrogance; insolence; haughtiness; self-importance; self-conceit; pomposity; pride; <美> toplothiness. 거만하다 proud; haughty; [건방지다] arrogant

거물 [गौमुल] [巨物] [영향력 있는 사람] a great man; a big [an important] figure; a bigwig; a VIP; [큰 사물] a big thing; a whopper. e.g. 당대의 거물 the lion of the day.

거미 [गौमी] a spider.

거부 [गौबू] [**拒否**] refusal; rejection; disapproval; [부정, 부인] denial; veto disallowance; traverse. 거부하다 refuse; deny; veto; reject; turn down; disapprove of.

거북 [गौबुक] [動] a tortoise; a terrapin; a [sea] turtle

거북하다 [गौबुखादा] **1** [마음이] embarrassing; ill at ease; uncomfortable. **2** [몸이] unwell; out of condition [order].

거세다 [गौसेदा] rough; wild; violent; fierce; strong; furious; tough; coarse; rude; aspirated. e.g. 거센 파도 wild [heavy] sea [waves / waters].

거스르다 [गौसुरूदा] **1** [반대 방향을 취하다] go [act] against; act contrary to; run counter to; oppose; disobey; defy; cross <another's will>; offend <a person>. e.g. 바람을 거슬러서 나아가다 go in the teeth of the wind **2** [거스름돈을 주고 받다] give change; make change. e.g. … 을 받고 10원을 거슬러 주다 give ten won [in return] for .... **거스름돈** [गौसुरूमदोन] change.

거슬러올라가다 [गौसुल्लौओल्लागादा] **1** [흐름을] go [row / sail] upstream. **2** [과거로] go back <to the past>; [소급하다] retroact <to>; retrospect <to>.

거슬리다 [गौसुल्लिदा] [언짢은 느낌이 들다] offend; be offensive; give offense; be against the grain [one's taste]; be unpleasant; rub <a person> the wrong way. e.g. 귀에 거슬리는 소리 a harsh grating noise.

거시적 [गौशीजौक] [**巨視的**] macroscopic; [관점이] all-inclusive; comprehensive.

거실 [गौशिल] [**居室**] [개인의] one's room; one's own [private] room; [가족의] a sitting room; a living room; a parlor.

거액 [गौऐक] [**巨額**] a huge [an enormous] amount of money; a colossal [stupendous] sum; a lot [a great deal] of money.

거역 [गौयौक] [**拒逆**] disobedience; insubordination; opposition; objection. 거역하다 disobey; protest <against>; object <to>; oppose; go [act] against <a person's will>.

거울 [गौउल] **1** a mirror; a looking glass; a speculum. **2** [귀감] a pattern; a model; an example; a paragon; a mirror. e.g. 그의 선행은 세상 사람들의 거울이 되었다 His good conduct set an example for the world.

거의 [गौउइ] [대체로] almost; nearly; practically; all but;

as good as; no more than; next to; well-nigh; [대부분] for the most part; mostly; [약] about; some; <부정적> few; little; hardly; scarcely. e.g. 거의 전부 almost [nearly] all / mostly

거인 [गौइन] [巨人] a giant; a colossus; a Titan; [위인] a great man.

거장 [गौजांग] [巨匠] a [great] master; a great artist. e.g. 악단의 거장 a great [master] musician.

거저 [गौजौ] **1** [일을 안하고] without doing anything [in particular]; idly; lazily; slothfully. e.g. 거저 세월만 보내다 idle away one's time [days] **2** [헐값으로] for a song; dog-cheap; dirt cheap e.g. 거저나 다름없는 값 a nominal price.

거절 [गौजौल] [拒絶] refusal; rejection; rebuff; disapproval; repudiation; < 美 > brush-off. 거절하다 refuse; reject; decline; rebuff; turn down; deny

거주 [गौजू] [居住] residence; dwelling; abode; habitation. e.g. 거주 이전의 자유 the freedom of residence and change of residence. 거주하다 reside; live; dwell; inhabit; make one's home; take [up] residence.

거지 [गौजी] a beggar

거짓 [गौजीत] [속이기 위한 거짓말] a lie; untruth; [진실이 아님] falsehood; hypocrisy; a fabrication; [지어낸 말] misrepresentation; deceit.

거짓말 [गौजीन्माल] [속이기 위한] a lie; [진실이 아님] a falsehood; an untruth; a fabrication; a fake; [사소한] a fib. e.g. 터무니없는 거짓말을 하다 lie like a gas meter. 새빨간 거짓말을 하다 lie in a person's teeth.

거창 [गौछांग] [巨創] 거창하다 huge; enormous; gigantic; immense; monstrous; [말, 글 등이 떠들썩하다] bombastic; [거들먹거리다] pompous; [뽐내다] ostentatious; [표현이 과장되다] exaggerated; [꿈,계획 등이 원대하다] grandiose. e.g. 거창하게 on a large [grand] scale.

거처 [गौछौ] [居處] dwelling <in>; a dwelling place [house]; a residence; an abode. 거처하다 live [dwell / reside] <in / at>; inhabit <a place>.

거추장스럽다 [गौछुजांगसुरौप्ता] burdensome; cumbersome; troublesome; cumbrous; bulky; unwieldy; ponderous.

거침없다 [गौछिमऔप्ता] **1** [막힘이 없다] unhindered; unobstructed; smooth. **2** [거리낌없다] unreserved; unconstrained; unsparing; straightforward; free [from obstruction]; without heistation [reserve / being ashamed].

거품 [गौफुम] a bubble; foam; froth; [발효의] barm; [표면에 뜨는 찌꺼기] scum; suds; [유리 속 등의] an air bell [bubble]; a seed; a blister; [곤충의] spit; spittle.

거행[गौहैंग][擧行] **1**[의식을 치름] celebration; performance; solemnization. 거행하다 perform [conduct / carry out] <a ceremony>; observe [keep] <an anniversary>; [특히 식전을] celebrate; hold [give]. **2** [명령대로 행함] execution of an order. 거행하다 do as one is told; act according to orders [commands].

걱정 [गौक्चौंग] [근심] anxiety; concern; apprehension; worry; care; trouble. 걱정하다 feel anxiety; be anxious <about>; take <a matter> to heart; be concerned <about / for / by>; feel concern <about / for>; take <it> seriously; be apprehensive <of>; feel uneasy <about>; worry [oneself] <about>; feel worried <about>.

건강 [गौन्गांग] [健康] health. e.g. 건강을 해치다 injure [ruin / destroy] one's health / one's health breaks down. 건강하다 healthy; sound; well; wholesome; [노인 등이] hale and hearty; fit; be in good health.

건국 [गौन्गुक] [建國] the founding [establishment] of a country [nation]. 건국하다 found [establish] a country.

건너다 [गौन्नौदा] **1** [넘다, 가로지르다] go [pass] over; go [walk / run] across; cross; ferry [나룻배로]. e.g. 다리를 건너다 cross a bridge. **2** [옮겨지다] be carried; be conveyed.

건너편 [गौन्नौफ्यौन] [-便] the opposite [other] side.

건널목 [गौन्नौल्मोक] **1** [철도의] a [railway] crossing; a grade crossing; a level crossing. **2** [횡단보도] a pedestrian crossing.

건달 [गौन्दाल] [乾達] **1** [빈둥거리는 사람] an idler; a lazybones; a loafer; a good-for-nothing [fellow]; a scamp. **2** [빈털터리] a penniless fellow; a stone- [stony-] broke person.

-건대 [गौन्दै] on the ground of; according to; in accordance with. e.g. 듣건대 I hear [we learn] <that> / according to the rumor / as the rumor goes.

건더기 [गौन्दौगी] 1 [국의] ingredients; a piece of meat and vegetables in soup. **2** [액체에 섞여 있는] solid matter in a mixture of liquid and solids. **3** [내용] substance; [근거] a ground; a foundation. e.g. 변명할 건더기가 없다 have little excuse <for>.

건드리다 [गौन्दुरीदा] **1** [움직이게 하다] touch; jog; give <a thing> a jog; move slightly; stir. **2** [노하게 하다] irritate; fret; provoke; nettle; vex. **3** [여자와 관계하다] make sport [fun] of; play [sport] with.

건들거리다 [गौन्दुल्कौरीदा] **1** [흔들리다] dangle; swing; sway; totter; shake; be shaky; be unstable. **2** [바람이] blow gently [sothly]. **3** [빈둥거리다] idle [loiter / dawdle / fiddle / lounge] one's time away; fiddle about doing nothing.

건립 [गौल्लिप] [**建立**] **1** [탑, 동상 등의] erection; building; construction. 건립하다 erect; build; construct. **2** [기관, 조직체등의] establishment; foundation; organization.

건망증 [गौन्मांग्चुंग] [**健忘症**] amnesia; forgetfulness; failure [slip / loss] of memory.

건물 [गौन्मुल] [**建物**] a building; a structure; an edifice.

건방지다 [गौन्बांगजीदा] [self-] conceited; pretentious; presumptuous; forward; impudent; impertinent; saucy; pert; cocky; cheeky. e.g. 건방진 대답 a pert answer / a saucy reply.

건배 [गौन्बै] [**乾杯**] a toast. e.g. [당신의 건강을 위하여] 건배 To your health! / Here's to you! / Prosit! / Cheers!

건설 [गौन्सौल] [**建設**] construction; erection; building; [설립] establishment. 건설하다 construct; erect; build [up]; [설립하다] establish; found. e.g. 댐[철도 / 교량] 을 건설하다 construct a dam [a railway / a bridge].

건성 [गौन्सौंग] half-heartedness; inattention; lack of attention; abstraction; absent-mindedness. e.g. 건성으로 abstractedly / carelessly 건성으로 듣다 listen to <a person> in an absent sort of way / let <something> go in one ear and out the other.

건성 [गौन्सौंग] [**乾性**] dryness. e.g. 건성의 dry.

건실 [गौन्शिल] [**健實**] steadiness; steadfastness; soundness; reliableness. 건실하다 steady; steadfast; sound; solid; reliable. e.g. 건실한 사람 a steady [trustworthy] person.

건의 [गौनुइ] [**建議**] [제의] a proposal; a recommendation; a suggestion; [진언] a representation; a memorial. 건의하다 [제의하다]

propose; recommend; suggest; [건백하다] make a representation <to>; submit a petition <to>.

건장 [गौन्जांग] [**健壯**] good [robust] health; healthiness; robustness. 건장하다 healthy; robust; strong; sturdy; stout.

건재 [गौन्जै] [**健在**] 건재하다 be well; be in excellent health [condition]; be in good shape; be up and doing; be going strong; be as prosperous as usual [사업 등이].

건전 [गौन्जौन] [**健全**] 건전하다 healthy; sound; wholesome.

건전지 [गौन्जौन्जी] [**乾電池**] a dry cell [battery]; a flashlight battery.

건조 [गौन्जो] [**乾燥**] dryness; aridity; [말림기] drying; seasoning [목재의 건조하다 dry; arid; seasoned [목재가]; become [get] dry [arid]; dry; season [목재를].

건지다 [गौन्जिदा] **1** [물에서] take [bring] out of water; pull [draw] up; refloat [배를]; pick up <a shipwrecked person>. **2** [위험P죽음에서] help <a person> out of; rescue <a person> from; relieve <a person> from; release <a person>from.

건축 [गौन्छुक] [**建築**] [건조] construction; building; erection; [건축물] a building; a structure; <집합적> architecture 건축하다 build; construct; erect; set up; put up.

건축가 [गौन्छुक्का] an architect.

건투 [गौन्थू] [**健闘**] good fight; [노력] strenuous efforts. e.g. 건투를 빕니다 Good luck to you! / I expect you to do your best. 건투하다 fight bravely; put up a good fight; [노력하다] make strenuous [vigorous] efforts.

걷다[1] [गौत्ता] walk; go on foot; tramp; step; hike.

걷다[2] [गौत्ता] **1** [말아 올리다] roll [turn / pull] up <one's sleeves>; tuck up <one's skirt> / bare [strip] <one's arm>; gather up <curtain>; fold up. e.g. 소매를 걷고 with bare arms / with one's sleeves turned over one's elbows. **2** [치우다] remove; take away; take off; [내리다] take down; strike; lower; pull down. e.g. 빨래를 걷다 gather up the laundry / take [bring] in the clothes.

걷잡다 [गौच्चाप्ता] [붙들다] hold; keep; stay; [참다] stop; keep back <one's tears>; [막다] check <the enemy's advance>; keep <a danger> at bay; control. e.g. 걷잡을 수 없는 혼란에 빠지다 get into uncontrollable confusion.

걷히다 [गौच्छिदा] **1** [구름, 안개 등이] be lithed; be dispelled; be cleared away [off]; vanish; be broken up. **2** [곡식, 돈 등이] be gathered; be collected.

걸다 [गौल्दा] **1** [매달다] hang <a thing on a peg>; hook [걸쇠에]; suspend; put up; set up. e.g. 간판을 걸다 hang [put] up a signboard. **2** [잠그다] [자물쇠, 문고리 등을] lock; fasten; turn a key; [빗장을] bar [bolt] <the gate>. e.g. 문의 자물쇠를 걸다 lock a door. **3**[내기로 금품을] bet; stake; wager; [보증금 등을] deposit; pay <earnest money>; [현상을] offer <a prize for>. e.g. 돈을 걸고 마작을 하다 play mah-jongg for money. **4** [목숨 등을] stake; risk. e.g. 목숨 [지위] 을 걸고 at the risk of one's life [position]. **5** [말 등을]. e.g. 남에게 말을 걸다 speak [talk] to a person / address [oneself to] a person.

걸레 [गौल्ले] a floorcloth; a dustcloth; a duster; [자루가 달린] a mop; [갑판용] a swab

걸레질 [गौल्लेजील] wiping with a damp cloth [duster]; mopping; scrubbing; swabbing 걸레질하다 wipe with a [damp] cloth; scrub; mop; swab.

걸리다 [गौल्लिदा] **1** [매달리다] hang <on / from>; be suspended <on / from>. e.g. 못에 걸려 있는 모자 a hat hanging on a peg. **2** [얽히다] catch; be caught <in / by>; hitch <on a nail>. e.g. 바지가 철조망에 걸리다 get one's pants snagged on the barbed wires. **3** [잡히다] be caught [entangled]; be hooked [낚시에] e.g. 거미줄에 걸리다 be entangled [get caught] in a cobweb.

걸맞다 [गौल्मात्ता] [정도가 비슷하다] well-balanced; well-matched; nicely-paired; [어울리다] suitable; be coming; fitting; befitting. e.g. 걸맞지 않은 ill-matched / unsuited / dispro-portionate / improper.

걸음 [गौरुम] walking; stepping; a step; [보조] pace. e.g. 한걸음 한걸음 step by step / by degrees.

걸음걸이 [गौरुमगौरी] one's manner of walking; gait; walk; a step. e.g. 무거운 걸음걸이로 with a heavy [leaden] step.

걸음마 [गौरुम्मा] toddling.

걸작 [गौल्चाक] [**傑作**] [뛰어난 작품] a masterpiece; a great work; a fine piece of work. 이 그림은 르누아르의 걸작이다 This is Renoir at his best.

걸치다[1] [गौल्छिदा] **1** [얹어 걸다, 놓다] put <a thing> on [over]; [건너질러 걸다] lay [place] over [across]. e.g. 도랑에 널빤지를 걸치다 lay a plank across a ditch. **2** [옷을 되는대로 입다] throw [slip] on; huddle on. e.g. 급히 외투를 걸치다 huddle on one's overcoat / slip on one's overcoat hurriedly.

걸치다[2] [गौल्छिदा] [시간, 공간적인 범위에] range <from A to B>; extend; spread <over>; cover; last [계속되다]. e.g. 그의 다방면에 걸친 지식 his multifarious learning. 5년에 걸쳐서 over a period of five years.

걸핏하면 [गौल्फित्थाम्यौन] too othen; readily; easily; at the slightest provocation. e.g. 걸핏하면 …하다 be apt [liable / prone] to <do>.

검 [गौम] [**劍**] [도검] a sword; [군도] a saber; [총검] a bayonet; [단검] a dagger.

검거 [गौम्गौ] [**檢擧**] an arrest; [일제 검거] a roundup. 검거하다 arrest; take up; round up [일제히].

검다 [गौम्ता] [빛깔이] black; dark; swarthy [살결 등이]. e.g. 얼굴이 검다 have a dark complexion / be dark-complexioned.

검문 [गौम्मुन] [**檢問**] [an] inspection; [a] check. 검문하다 [गौम्मुनहादा] inspect; examine; check.

검사 [गौम्सा] [**檢事**] a public prosecutor; a counsel for the Crown; <집합적> the prosecution.

검사 [गौम्सा] [**檢査**] [an] inspection; [an] examination; a test; an overhaul [기계, 선박 등의]; [an] audit [회계의]. 검사하다 inspect; examine; audit <accounts>; overhaul <a machine>.

검색 [गौम्सैक] [**檢索**] [찾아봄] reference; [컴퓨터의] retrieval. 검색하다 refer to <a dictionary>; look up <a word> in <a dictionary>.

검소 [गौम्सो] [**儉素**] [간소] simplicity; plainness; [검약] frugality; economy; thrith. 검소하다 [간소하다] simple; plain; [검약하다] frugal; thrithy; economical.

검열 [गौम्यौल] [**檢閱**] **1** [점검] inspection; examination. e.g. 검열필 <게시> Passed Inspection. 검열하다 inspect; examine. **2** [간행물 등의] censorship

검진 [गौम्जिन] [**檢診**] [a] medical examination [check-up]. 검진하다 examine; give a medical examination; check up <a person's health>.

검토 [गौम्थो] [**檢討**] [an] examination; [an] investigation; scrutiny; study.

검토하다 examine <a theory>; investigate; inquire into; study.

겁 [गौप] [**怯**] [공포] fear; fright; [a] terror; [a] dread; [소심] timidity; cowardice.

겁나다 [गौम्नादा] [**怯**–] be frightened [scared]; be over come with fright; be seized with fear [panic]; get in [to] a funk.

겁내다 [गौम्नैदा] [**怯**–] fear; dread; be afraid <of>; be in fear [terror]; have a horror of; show one's cowardice.

겁먹다 [गौम्मौक्ता] [**怯**–] be frightened <by / at>.

겁탈 [गौप्थाल] [**劫奪**] [약탈] pillage; plunder; [강간] violation; rape. 겁탈하다 [약탈하다] plunder; pillage; [강간하다] violate; rape.

것 [गौत] **1** [유형물] a thing; an object; [물품] an article; <대명사적> a one; the one; [사물] things; a matter. e.g.이 것 this **2** [소유물] a possession. e.g. 내 것 mine. **3** [사람, 동물] a man; a person; <대명사적> a one; the one. e.g. 어린 것 a young one **4** [사실] a fact; [일] a thing; what. **5** [필요] need; necessity. 그가 언제 돌아올 것인지 잘 모르겠다 I don't know exactly when he will be back.

겉 [गौत] **1** [표면] the surface; the face; the right side [옷의]; the obverse [메달 등의]. **2** [외부] the exterior; the outside; [외관] the [outward] appearance. e.g. 겉으로 externally / outwardly / apparently.

겉늙다 [गौन्नुल्ता] look old for one's age; get old before one's time; be prematurely gray. e.g. 머리 모양을 그렇게 하니 겉늙어 보인다 That hair-do makes you look older than your age.

겉돌다 [गौत्तोल्ता] **1** [헛돌다] spin free [바퀴가]; [톱니 바퀴가] do not gear [engage] <with>; be out of gear [mesh]. **2** [사람이 어울리지 못하다] do not get along well; be out of keeping <with>; do not mix [mingle] <with>. **3** [액체 등이 잘 섞이지 않다] do not mix [together].

겉모양 [गौम्मोयांग] [–**貌樣**] outward appearance; outward show; look; front; outlook. e.g. 겉모양으로 사람을 판단하다 judge [of] a person by his appearance.

겉보기 [गौप्पोगी] [outward] appearance; show; look. e.g. 겉보기에는 outwardly / on the surface / in appearance / apparently.

겉잡다 [गौच्चाप्ता] **1** [대강 추산하다] make a rough estimate; estimate roughly. e.g. 손해는 겉잡아서

3천만 원이다 The [amount of] damage is roughly estimated at thirty million won **2** [헤아리다] guess; imagine; get a rough idea <of>. e.g. 겉잡을 수 없는 말을 하다 talk incoherent story.

겉치레 [गौच्छिरे] ostensible decoration [display]; ostentation; outward show; keeping up appearances. 겉치레하다 dress up; keep up appearance; show off; cut a dash; put on a fair show.

겉핥다 [गौत्थालथा] scratch the surface <of a situ-ation>; have a superficial knowledge <of>; have a smattering <of>; smatter in <Latin>; dip into <Philosophy>.

게걸스럽다 [गैगौल्सुरौप्ता] greedy [for food]; voracious; ravenous; gluttonous; have an insatiable appetite; have a wolf in one's stomach. e.g. 게걸스럽게 먹다 eat greedily / gobble / eat like a pig.

게다가 [गेदागा] [거기에 더하여] in addition to <it>; on top of <it>; what is more; [그리고 또한] moreover; besides; [설상가상으로] to make matters worse. e.g. 게다가 요리도 맛있었다 In addition to that, the food was delicious.

게시 [गेशी] [**揭示**] a notice; a notification; a placard; a bulletin. 게시하다 post[put up] a notice; notify; placard <a board with a bill>.

게시판 [गेशीफान] a notice [bulletin] board; a billboard.

게으르다 [गेउरूदा] lazy; idle; indolent; slothful; sluggish.

게으름 [गेउरूम] laziness; idleness; indolence; sluggishness; sloth; [태만] neglect. e.g. 게으름피우다[부리다] be idle [lazy] / loaf / slacken one's efforts / idle one's time away.

게임 [गेइम] a game.

게재 [गेजै] [**揭載**] publication; insertion; printing. 게재하다 [신문, 잡지 등이] carry; run; [광고 등을] insert.

-겠다 [गेत्ता] **1** [결심, 필연성] will do [be]. e.g. 나는 여기 있겠다 I will stay here. **2** [추측, 판단] probably do [be]. e.g. 보기에는 좀 게으르겠다 Judging from his appearance,

겨냥 [ग्यौन्यांग] [겨누기] aim; aiming. 겨냥하다 aim [take aim] <at>; set one's sights <on>.

겨누다 [ग्यौनुदा] [겨냥하다] aim [take aim] <at>; sight <a target>; set one's sights <on>; draw [get / take] a bead <on>; level <a gun at>; point <a gun

at>.

겨드랑이 [ग्यौदुरांगी] [신체의] the armpit; the axilla <*pl.* -lae, ~s>.

겨레 [ग्यौले] [한 자손] offspring of the same forefather; [동포] brothers; brethren; fellow countrymen; one's countrymen; compatriots; [민족] a race; a people; a nation.

겨루다 [ग्यौरूदा] pit <one's skill against>; rival; compete [vie] <with>; struggle <with>. e.g. 힘을 겨루다 measure one's strength <with / against> / measure oneself against another in strength.

겨를 [ग्यौरूल] leisure; leisure time [hours]; free [spare] time; time to spare. e.g. 겨를이 없다 have no leisure / have no time to spare.

겨우 [ग्यौउ] [간신히] barely; hardly; narrowly; [애써서] with much difficulty [effort]; [고작] only; merely; but; no more than. e.g. 겨우 입에 풀칠하다 live barely / keep body and soul together.

겨울 [ग्यौउल] winter; the winter season. e.g. 겨울의 winter / wintry

겨울철 [ग्यौउलछौल] the winter season; the winter [time]

격 [ग्यौक] [格] **1** [지위, 등급] [a] standing; [a] status; [a] rank; [a] class; [a] grade; [an] order. e.g. 우두머리격인 사람 the boss. **2** [자격] capacity; character e.g. 격에 맞지 않는 짓을 하다 go out of one's character / play an unbecoming par. **3** [문법] [a] case. e.g. 주[소유 / 목적]격 the nominative [possessive / objective] case

격돌 [ग्यौक्तोल] [激突] [격렬하게 부딪침] a crash. 격돌하다 crash <into / against>.

격려 [ग्यौगन्यौ] [激勵] encouragement; urging; incitement 격려하다 encourage <a person to do>; cheer [up].

격렬 [ग्यौगन्यौल] [激烈] violence; severity; intensity. 격렬하다 violent; severe; intense.

격리 [ग्यौग्नी] [隔離] [고립] isolation; [전염병 환자의] quarantine; [흑인에 대한] segregation. 격리하다 isolate; quarantine; segregate. e.g. 환자를 격리하다 isolate a patient / keep a patient in isolation.

격식 [ग्यौक्शिक] [格式] [형식의 준수] formality; [사회의 관습] social rules; a [fixed] rule; an established form. e.g. 격식을 리다 be formal / be ceremonious / stand on ceremony / be stiff.

격언 [ग्यौगौन] [格言] [금언] a proverb; [속담] a [common] saying; [처세훈] a maxim.

격조 [ग्यौक्चो] [格調] [문예작품의] tone; style; rhythm; swing; [사람의] character; personality.

격차 [ग्यौक्छा] [格差] [차이] a difference; [간격] a gap.

격찬 [ग्यौक्छान] [激讚] high praise; a high tribute. 격찬하다 praise highly; speak highly of; admire extravagantly.

격퇴 [ग्यौक्थवे] [擊退] a repulse; dislodgement. 격퇴하다 repulse; drive [beat] back [off].

격투 [ग्यौक्थु] [格鬪] a grapple; a fight; a tussle; fisticuffs; a hand-to-hand fight; [난투] a scuffle. 격투하다 fight <with>; grapple <with>; come to fisticuffs [blows]; fight hand to hand <with>.

격파 [ग्यौक्फा] [擊破] defeating; beating out; destruction. 격파하다 [적을] defeat <the enemy>; beat; [put to] rout; crush; [때려부수다] destroy <an enemy warship>; [논파하다] refute <one's opponent>.

격하 [ग्यौक्खा] [格下] demotion; degradation; downgrading. 격하하다 [ग्यौख्खाहादा] demote; lower the status [position] <of>; lower <a person> in rank; demean [oneself]; downgrade.

겪다 [ग्यौक्ता] [경험하다] undergo; suffer; endure; experience; go through.

견고 [ग्यौन्गो] [堅固] solidity; firmness; stability. 견고하다 strong; solid; [확고하다] steady; steadfast; firm. e.g. 견고히 하다 strengthen / make firm [solid] / solidify.

견디다 [ग्यौन्दिदा] **1** [참다] endure; bear; stand; put up with; tolerate; suffer. e.g. 견디기 어려운 unbearable / intolerable. **2** [지탱하다] support; stand; bear; hold [out]; [오래가다] wear; last long. e.g. 열에견디다 stand [bear up against] heat. 그 다리는 홍수에 견디었다 The bridge held out against the flood.

견본 [ग्यौन्बोन] [見本] [상품의] a sample; [표본] a specimen; [무늬 등의] a pattern; [서적의] a sample copy.

견습 [ग्यौन्सुप] [見習] [일] probation; apprenticeship; [사람] a probationer; an apprentice.

견습생 [ग्यौन्सुप्सैग] an apprentice; a student; a trainee; a probationer; a cub.

견인 [ग्यौनिन] [牽引] traction; hauling. 견인하다 pull; draw; haul; tow.

견적 [ग्यौन्जौक] [見積] an estimate; an estimation; assessment; valuation; computation; calculation.

견적서 [ग्यौन्जोक्सौ] an estimate; a written estimate; an estimate [estimation] sheet.

견제 [ग्यौन्जे] [**牽制**] [자유를 방해함] a check; [a] restraint; curbing. 견제하다 check; keep [hold] in check; restrain. e.g. 서로 견제하다 hold each other in check.

견주다 [ग्यौन्जुदा] [비교하다] compare <one thing> with <another>; weigh [measure] <one thing> against <another>; take <something> for comparison; [겨루다] rival; compete <with>.

견지 [ग्यौन्जी] [**見地**] [입장] a standpoint; [관점] a viewpoint; a point of view; an angle. e.g. 내 견지에서 보면 from my point of view [standpoint / viewpoint] / viewed in my [this] light / viewed from my [this] angle.

견학 [ग्यौन्हाक] [**見學**] study by inspection [observation]. 견학하다 inspect; observe; visit <a factory> for study [information]; [체육 시간 등에] look on / sit out <a game> and watch.

견해 [ग्यौन्है] [**見解**] an opinion; a view; an outlook <on>; a slant. e.g. 견해의 차이 a difference of view / conflict of views / divergence of opinion / discrepancy in opinions. **결** [ग्यौल] **1** [나무,돌의] grain; [직물의] texture; [피부의] grain; [skin] texture. e.g. 비단결 a silky [velvety] texture. **2** [물결P숨결의] a wave.

결강 [ग्यौल्गांग] [**缺講**] 결강하다 [교수가] do not give one's lecture; cancel a lecture [class]; [학생이] cut a class [lecture].

결과 [ग्यौल्ग्वा] [**結果**] a result; an effect; an out-come; [자연스런 과정] a consequence; the issue. e.g. 원인과 결과 cause and effect.

결국 [ग्यौलगुक] [**結局**] **1** [끝장] an end; a close; a finish; a termination; [결말] conclusion. **2** [마침내] ather all [긍정, 부정 양쪽에 쓰임]; finally; in the end; in conclusion; in the long run; in the result; in the last resort; in the last [final / ultimate] analysis; ultimately.

결근 [ग्यौल्गुन] [**缺勤**] absence <from>; nonattendance <at>. 결근하다 be absent <from duty [office / one's work]>; be away from work; stay home <from the office>.

결단 [ग्यौल्तान] [**決斷**] [a] definite decision; determination; [a] resolution.

결론 [ग्यौल्लोन] [**結論**] a conclusion; a concluding remark.

결말 [ग्यौल्माल] [**結末**] [끝장] an end; a close; a conclusion; a termination; [결과] a result; an outcome; [낙착]

settlement; fixing up; [대단원] the denouement; the catastrophe [비극의].

결백 [ग्यौल्पैक] [潔白] [깨끗함] purity; [무죄] innocence; [청렴] integrity. 결백하다 [깨끗하다] pure; stainless; immaculate; [죄가 없다] innocent; guiltless; [청렴하다] upright; cleanhanded.

결별 [ग्यौल्बयौल] [訣別] [작별] parting; separation; [고별] leave-taking; farewell; good-bye. 결별하다 part with; take leave of; say [bid] good-by <to>; bid farewell <to>. e.g. 그는 가족과 결별하고 전선으로 떠났다 He parted from his family and leth for the front. **2** [관계,교제를 끊음] a breach <of friendship>; a rupture. 결별하다 break with [off] <a person>; part with[from] <a person>; cut [drop / sever] one's acquaintance [connection] <with>. e.g. 그는 낡은 유파와 결별했다 He broke with the old school.

결산 [ग्यौल्सान] [決算] settlement of accounts; balancing [closing] accounts. 결산하다 settle [balance / square] accounts; balance the books; close the books.

결석 [ग्यौल्सौक] [缺席] absence; nonattendance; a cut; [法] default; nonappearance. be absent <from>; absent oneself <from>; stay away <from>; fail to attended; miss [cut] <one's class>; default; make default.

결성 [ग्यौल्सौंग] [結成] organization; formation. 결성하다organize; form.

결속 [ग्यौल्सोक] [結束] **1** [한 덩이로 묶음] binding together; banding [sticking] together; pulling together. 결속하다 bind together. **2** [단결] union; unity; solidarity. 결속하다 band [stick] together; unite; hang together; get [be] united; pull [hold] together; present a united front <toward>.

결승 [ग्यौल्सुंग] [決勝] **1** the decision <of a contest>. 결승하다 decide victories; fight to the finish [last]; fight it out; play off [무승부 시합에서]. **2** = 결승전.

결실 [ग्यौल्शिल] [結實] **1** [열매 맺기] ripening; fruition; bearing [of fruit]; fructification.결실하다 bear fruit; fructify; fruit; go to seed; develop into fruit. **2** [좋은 결과] realization; a result. e.g. 결실을 보다[거두다] =결실하다 .결실을 보는 연구를 하다 do productive research. 결실을 못보다[결실하지 못하다] come to naught [nothing] / bear no fruit. 결실하다 be successful; achieve [attain] success.

결심 [ग्यौल्शिम] [**決心**] determination; resolution. e.g. 굳은 결심 a firm [a determined / an unshakable / an inflexible] resolution. 결심하다 determine; be determined; make up one's mind; resolve; be resolved; decide.

결여 [ग्यौयौ] [**缺如**] [a] want; [a] lack; absence <of a proof>; deficiency; privation.

결연 [ग्यौयौन] [**結緣**] [인연을 맺음] forming a connection [relationship]. 결연하다 form [establish / enter into] a connection <with>; establish relations <with>.

결원 [ग्यौवन] [**缺員**] a vacancy; a vacant position [post]; an opening. e.g. 결원이 생기다 a vacancy occurs.

결재 [ग्यौल्चै] [**決裁**] sanction; approval; decision. 결재하다 sanction; approve; decide <upon>.

결전 [ग्यौल्चौन] [**決戰**] <fight> a decisive battle <with>; a tug-of-war; a showdown; [경기의] a deciding match [race]; [무승부 후의] a run-off; a play-off. e.g. 결전 단계에 돌입하다 reach [enter into] a decisive stage.

결절 [ग्यौल्चौल] [**結節**] [뼈나 식물의 뿌리의, 또는 결핵의] a tubercle; [피부에 생긴 융기] a node; [마디] a knot. e.g. 결절[모양]의 tubercular / nodular.

결점 [ग्यौल्चौम] [**缺點**] [불완전한 점] a fault; a defect; a demerit; a flaw; a blemish; an imperfection; [약점] a weak point; a weakness; a shortcoming; a failing; one's blind side; [난점] a drawback; a disadvantage.

결정 [ग्यौल्चौंग] [**決定**] [a] decision; [결의] [a] determination; [결론] [a] conclusion; [해결] [a] settlement. 결정하다] decide <on / to do>; determine; set; fix <upon>

결제 [ग्यौल्चे] [**決濟**] settlement; liquidation [빚의].

결코 [ग्यौल्खो] [**決-**] [절대로 … 않다] never; by no means; assuredly [positively] ... not; [어떤 경우에도 … 않다] under no circumstances; [어떤 이유로도] on no account [occasion]; [조금도 …않다] not [bad] at all; not in the least.

결탁 [ग्यौल्थाक] [**結託**] [함께 꾸미기] conspiracy; [사전 비밀 협약] collusion. 결탁하다 conspire <with>; be in collusion[league] <with>.

결투 [ग्यौल्थु] [**決鬪**] a duel; an

affair of honor; [되받아 침] a shootout; a gunfight. e.g. 결투를 신청하다 challenge <a person> to a duel / throw down the gauntlet [glove]. 결투하다 duel <with>; fight a duel <with>.

결판 [ग्यौल्पान] [**決判**] [판가름] [a] judg [e] ment; [결말] settlement; fixing [up]. e.g. 결판 [이] 나다 be settled [fixed] / be finished / come [be brought] to an end [a conclusion].

결핍 [ग्यौल्फिप] [**缺乏**] [없음] [a] want; [a] lack; [a] dearth; [a] famine; poverty; absence; [부족] shortage; deficiency; scarcity; scantiness. 결핍하다 [필요한데 없다] want; lack; be wanting [lacking] <in>; [부족하다] run short <of>; run low [out of].

결함 [ग्यौहम] [**缺陷**] a defect; [완전함에서 약간 모자라는] a flaw; a fault; a shortcoming; < 美 > bugs; a deformity <of one's nature>; [부족] deficiency; shortage; a gap.

결합 [ग्यौहाप] [**結合**] union; combination; cohesion; conjunct-tion <of discoveries and inventions>; coupling; linkage; bond; [원자핵의] fusion; [우주선의] docking.

결항 [ग्यौहांग] [**缺航**] [배P항공기의] a flight cancellation; a canceled flight; suspension of <ferry> service. 결항하다[배가] do not sail[as scheduled]; [비행기가] do not fly [as scheduled].

결혼 [ग्यौहॉन] [**結婚**] [a] marriage; a union; matrimony. 결혼하다 marry; be [get] married <to>; be united; wed; join [hands] [unite] in marriage; enter into matrimony; <美> hitch [up].

결혼식 [ग्यौहॉनशिक] [**結婚式**] a marriage [nuptial] ceremony; a wedding [ceremony].

겸비 [ग्यौम्बी] [**兼備**] 겸비하다 combine <one thing> with <another>; have both; have [possess] <A and B / two things> at the same time; join. e.g. 재색을 겸비한 여성 a woman with beauty and intelligence

겸손 [ग्यौम्सोन] [**謙遜**] modesty; humility; diffidence. 겸손하다 modest; diffident; humble; unassuming; humble [efface] oneself;[아랫사람에게] condescending; [삼가다] reserved.

겸양 [ग्यौम्यांग] [**謙讓**] humbleness; modesty; humility e.g. 겸양의 미덕 the virtue of modesty. 겸양하다 ग्यौम्यांगहादा be modest; humiliate oneself; humble oneself; condescend.

겸업 [ग्यौमौप] [**兼業**] a side job [business / line]; a subsidiary business; a by-business; bywork; a job [business] on the side. 겸업하다 take up a side job; pursue[follow] <another trade> as a side business [in addition to a trade]; have two jobs at the same time.

겸연쩍다 [ग्यौम्यौनचौक्ता] [**慊然-**] abashed; embarrassed; disconcerted.

겸용 [ग्यौम्योंग] [**兼用**] a combined [double / multiple] use; combination. 겸용하다 use in two or more ways; use [both] as <A> and <B>; make <a thing> serve a double purpose.

겸임 [ग्यौमिम] [**兼任**] 겸임하다 [ग्यौमीमहादा] hold an additional [also] post [office] <of>; hold two or more positions concurently; have part-time business in two or more places.

겸하다 [ग्यौम्हादा] [**兼-**] **1** [아울러 가지다] combine [unite] <one thing with another>; possess both <A and B>; [겸용되다] serve both as <A and B>; double as; [A이기도 하고 B이기도 하다] be both <A and B>. e.g. 일과 놀이를 겸하다 combine business with pleasure. **2** [겸직하다] hold <a post> as an additional office [in addition to one's regular office]; combine the office of <A> with that of <B>; hold <two offices> simultaneously [concurrently]; double as <cook>. e.g. 아내가 입원 중이므로 나는 그녀의 일을 겸하여 하지 않으면 안 된다 I have to do my wife's work too, now that she's in the hospital.

겸허 [ग्यौम्ह्यौ] [**謙虛**] 겸허하다 humble; modest; retiring. e.g. 겸허하게 in a humble way / with modesty / modestly / humbly.

겹 [ग्यौप] [포개어 거듭됨] fold; [거듭된 켜] a fold; a layer; [쌓아 올린 켜] a pile; [밧줄 등의 가닥] a ply; [두 배] double; twofold. e.g. 두 겹 twofold. 여러 겹 many folds / over and over again / repeatedly. e.g. 두 겹 twofold

겹다 [ग्यौप्ता] **1** [참기 어렵다] uncontrollable; unrestrainable; irrepressible; irresistible; beyond restraint; be difficult to stand <against>; be unable to bear up. e.g. 흥에 겨워 in the excess of mirth / driven by one's enthusiasm **2** [힘에 부치다] beyond [above] one's capacity; too much for <one>. e.g. 이 일은 내 힘에 겹다 I am not equal to the task.

겹치다 [ग्यौप्छिदा] **1** [포개다] pile up; heap up; put [place] one upon [over] another; lay one on top of another [the other]. **2** [포개어지다] be piled up; overlap each other [one another].

-경 [ग्यौंग] [**頃**] about; around; toward [s]; circa. e.g. 3시경[] about [around] three o'clock.

경각 [ग्यौंगाक] [**警覺**] warning; awakening; remonstration; caution; precaution. 경각하다 warn; awaken; remonstrate; give a warning; caution; admonish.

경각심 [ग्यौंगाविशम] [self-] consciousness; [self-] awakening.

경감 [ग्यौंगाम] [**輕減**] reduction; mitigation; abatement; [고통 등의] alleviation; [형의] commutation. e.g. 고통을 감하다 alleviate [relieve / ease] the pain.

경거 망동 [ग्यौंगौ मांग्तोंग] [**輕擧妄動**] rash [hasty] attempt and blind behavior. 경거 망동하다 do [act] rashly; commit a rash act.

경건 [ग्यौंगौन] [**敬虔**] piety; de-votion; reverence. 경건하다pious; devotional; devout; godly; God-fearing.

경계 [ग्यौंग्ये] [**境界**] a boundary; a border; a frontier; [法] metes and bounds.

경계[ग्यौंगग्ये][**警戒**] **1** [경고] caution; warning; admonition; [주의] precaution. e.g. 경계[를] 시키다 put [set] <a person> on one's guard against / 경계하다 warn; give warning of; exercise [take] precaution; caution <a person> against; admonish. **2** [감시P경비] watch; vigilance; lookout; guard. 경계하다 watch; look out for; keep an eye on; be on the watch; be watchful; [순찰하다] patrol

경고 [ग्यौंगो] [**警告**] warning; admonition; caution; advice; notice. 경고하다 warn; caution <a person> against; give warning; admonish.

경공업 [ग्यौंगोंगौब] [**輕工業**] light industry.

경과 [ग्यौंग्वा] [**經過**] [시간의] passage; lapse; flight; [기한의] expiration; [사건, 상태의 귀추] progress; development; the course <of events>; a trend; a tendency. 경과하다 pass; elapse; go by; expire.

경관 [ग्यौंग्वॉन] [**景觀**] a view; a vista; a scene; a spectacle; a sight; scenery.

경국지색 [ग्यौंगुकिजसैक] [**傾國之色**] a woman beautiful enough to cause the downfall of a country; a Helen of Troy; a siren.

경기 [ग्यौंगी] [競技] [시합] a game; a match; a contest; a competition; a meet; a tournament; [경기의 종목] an event; a sporting event

경기 [ग्यौंगी] [景氣] 1 [형세, 형편] the times; things; condition. 2 [경제 활동의 상황] business conditions; transactions; [the tone of] the market.

경도 [ग्यौंग्दो] [硬度] hardness; solidity. e.g. 다이아몬드의 경도는 10 이다 The hardness of diamond is 10.

경력 [ग्यौंगन्यौक] [經歷] one's [past] career [record]; one's life [personal] history; a career record; personal experiences; antecedents.

경련 [ग्यौंगन्यौन] [痙攣] convulsions; a spasm; a spasmodic; contraction; [근육의] crick; cramp; a jerk; [안면의] a tic; a twitch.

경례 [ग्यौंगन्ये] [敬禮] salutetion; a salute; an obeisance; a courtesy; a bow; [구령] Salute! 경례하다 salute; make a salutation; bow <to>.

경로 [ग्यौंग्नो] [經路] [지나는 길] a course; a channel; a route; [단계] a stage; [과정] a step; a process.

경로 [ग्यौंग्नो] [敬老] respect for the old [aged].

경리 [ग्यौंग्नी] [經理] [처리] management; [회계] accountting; [사무] accountant's business. 경리하다 anage; administer.

경마 [ग्यौंग्मा] [競馬] horse racing; the races; a horse race.

경매 [ग्यौंगमे] [競賣] auction; a public [an open] sale; a sale at [by] auction

경멸 [ग्यौंगम्यौल] [輕蔑] contempt; scorn; disdain 경멸하다 despise; hold <a person> in contempt; look down on [upon]; scorn; slight; think meanly of.

경미 [ग्यौंग्मी] [輕微] slightness; triviality 경미하다 slight; little; not serious; trifling; negligible; insignificant. e.g. 경미한 문제 a trifling [trivial] matter.

경박 [ग्यौंग्बाक] [輕薄] [천박] frivolity; flippancy; levity; fickleness; [불성실] insincerity; untruthfulness. 경박하다 [불성실하다] insincere; [부박하다] light; frivolous; flippant; flighty; [변덕스럽다] fickle; volatile

경범죄 [ग्यौंग्बौम्चवे] [輕犯罪] a minor offense; a misdemeanor.

경보 [ग्यौंग्बो] [警報] an alarm; a warning; a signal

경비 [ग्यौंग्बी] [警備] defense; guard; guarding; policing. 경비하다 defend; guard <against / from>; police; keep watch <on / over / of>. e.g. 해상을 경비하다 patrol [police] the sea.

경비 [ग्यौंग्बी] [經費] [비용]

expense [s]; cost [s]; upkeep; [지출] expenditure; [an] outlay.

경사 [ग्यौग्सा] [**慶事**] a happy event [occasion]; a matter calling for congratulation; an auspicious occasion.

경사 [ग्यौग्सा] [**傾斜**] inclination; a slant <of a roof>; bevel; [언덕의] slope; acclivity [오르막]; declivity [내리막]; [배의] a list; a grade [경사도].

경솔 [ग्यौग्सोल] [**輕率**] [소홀] rashness; hastiness; [부주의] carelessness; imprudence; [무분별] thoughtlessness; indiscretion. 경솔하다 frivolous; flippant; rash; hasty; thoughtless; care-less. e.g. 경솔한 판단 a hasty judgment.

경시 [ग्यौग्शी] [**輕視**] contempt; negligence; slight; disdain. 경시하다 despise; make [think] light of; make little account of; think lightly of; treat lightly; hold <art> in slight [light] esteem; slight; neglect; belittle; minimize. e.g. 문제를 경시하다 treat [take] a matter lightly / underrate the importance of a subject. ...

경악 [ग्यौगाक] [**驚愕**] astonishment; amazement; fright; alarm; consternation; a shock. 경악하다 be greatly surprised <at>; be astonished [frightened / amazed / shocked] <at / by>; be thrown into consternation.

경애 [ग्यौगै] [**敬愛**] respect and affection [love]; love and esteem; reverent affection; veneration. 경애하다 [ग्यौगैहादा] love and respect; hold <a person> in high esteem; have a high regard <for>.

경어 [ग्यौगौ] [**敬語**] an honorific [expression [word]]; a term of respect.

경연 [ग्यौग्यौन] [**競演**] a contest; a match; a competitive performance. e.g. 민요 경연 대회 a folk song concours[recital contest] / <美> a hootenanny.

경영 [ग्यौग्यौग] [**經營**] [관리] management; administration; [운영] operation; running <of a school>; working <of a business>; conduct <of a business>.경영하다 manage <a firm>; conduct <a business>; operate <a hotel>; run[keep] <a store>; administrate; administer; practice <an industry>; work <a mine, a farm, etc.>; carry on <an enterprise>. e.g. 사업을 경영하다 carry on an enterprise / manage [run] a business

경영학 [ग्यौग्यौगहाक] business administration; business economics.

경우 [ग्यौगू] [**境遇**] [때] an occa-sion; a time; a moment; [형편] circumstances; con-ditions; a situation; [사례] a case; an instance. e.g. 지금 같은 경우에[는] at this time [occasion] / as things stand [the case stands] [now].

경위 [ग्यौंग्वी] [涇渭] [옳고 그름] right and [or] wrong; good and [or] bad [evil]; vice and virtue; [판단, 식별력] judgment; discernment; good sense. e.g. 경위야 어떻든 whether it is right or wrong / for good or bad [evil].

경유 [ग्यौंग्यू] [經由] e.g. 대전 경유 대구행 열차 a train for Taegu via [by way of] Taejòn. 경유하다 go via [by way of]; pass [go] through.

경의 [ग्यौंगुइ] [敬意] respect; regard; homage; esteem; deference; honor; reverence. e.g....에 대한 경의의 표시로서 out of respect to / as a mark [token] of respect for / in honor of / in deference to.

경이 [ग्यौंगी] [驚異] [a] wonder; a miracle; a marvel. e.g. 자연계의 경이 prodigies of nature / nature's wonder.

경작 [ग्यौंग्जाक] [耕作] cultivation; farming; tillage. 경작하다 cultivate; farm; till <a field>; plow <land>.

경쟁 [ग्यौंग्जैंग] [競爭] [a] competition; a contest; rivalry; emulation; a race 경쟁하다 compete [contend] <with[against] a person for something>; rival <another in something>; vie [cope] with <another in>; contest <an election>; emulate each other [one another

경쟁률 [ग्यौंग्जैंगन्युल] the competitive rate; the ratio of successful [applicants] to total applicants.

경쟁력 [ग्यौंग्जैंगन्यौक] [競爭力] <develop> competitive power; competitiveness; competitive edge.

경적 [ग्यौंग्जौक] [警笛] an alarm whistle; [경관의] a police whistle; [자동차의] a [warning] horn; a honker; a foghorn [농무 때의]. e.g. 경적을 울리다 whistle a warning / give an alarm whistle / [자동차의] sound [blow] a horn [honker] / honk [a car horn] / hoot.

경전 [ग्यौंग्जौन] [經典] scriptures; sacred books; [불교의] Buddhist scriptures; the Sutras; [크리스트교의] the Scriptures; the [Holy] Bible; [회교의] the Koran; the scripture of Islam.

경제 [ग्यौंग्जे] [經濟] economy; [경제 상태] economics; [재정] finance; [절약] thrith; frugality; saving; economy.

경종 [ग्यौंग्जोंग] [警鐘] an alarm bell; a fire bell [alarm] [화재의]; [경고] warning. e.g. 경종을 울리다 ring [sound] an alarm [bell] / [경고하다] warn / give warning.

경주 [ग्यौङ्जू] [**競走**] a [foot] race; a run; a running match; [단거리의] a dash; a sprint. 경주하다 run [have / do / engage in] a race <with>; race <another

경지 [ग्यौङ्जी] [**耕地**] [경작에 적합한] arable [tillable] land [soil]; [경작한] a cultivated field [area]; plowed [cultivated] land; plowland; a plantation; land under cultivation; farmland.

경지 [ग्यौङ्जी] [**境地**] **1** [상태] a state; a condition; a stage; [심경] a mental state. e.g....의 경지에 도달하다 reach [attain / come to] the stage of .....**2** [분야,영역] a field; a sphere; a ground; a territory; a pro-vince. e.g. 그는 문학에서 마침내 독자적인 경지를 개척했다 He finally broke [struck out / opened up] new ground [a new path] in literature.

경직 [ग्यौङ्जिक] [**硬直**] stiffness; stiffening; rigidity. 경직하다stiffen; get stiff; be-come stiff [rigid].

경찰 [ग्यौङ्छाल] [**警察**] the police; the police force; [경찰서] a police station; [경찰관] a policeman.

경찰관 [ग्यौङ्छालग्वान] [**警察官**] a police officer; a policeman; a constable; <집합적> the police; a cop.

경찰서 [ग्यौङ्छाल्सौ] [**警察署**] a police station; a station house.

경청 [ग्यौङ्छौंग] [**傾聽**] listening closely [intently / attentively]. 경청하다 [ग्यौङ्छौंगहादा] listen [intently / attentively] to <what is said>; have a listen <to>; give ear <to>; be all attention [ears].

경축 [ग्यौङ्छुक] [**慶祝**] congratu-lation; felicitation; celebra-tion. 경축하다 congratu-late; felicitate; celebrate <an event>. e.g....을 경축하여 in celebration [honor] of ... / congratulating

경치 [ग्यौङ्छी] [**景致**] [어느 고장 전체의 경관] scenery; [개개의 경관] a view; [한정된 풍경] a scene; [육지의 경관] a landscape; [바다의 경관] a seascape.

경쾌 [ग्यौङ्ख्वै] [**輕快**] 경쾌하다 [날렵하다] light; nimble <movement>; airy <manner>; [쾌활하다] light hearted; cheerful <tone>; buoyant. e.g. 경쾌한 발걸음으로 with light steps.

경탄 [ग्यौङ्थान] [**驚嘆**] admira-tion; wonder. 경탄하다 admire <the skill>; wonder [marvel] at <the beauty>; be struck with admiration [wonder]; have a great regard [respect] <for>.

경품 [ग्यौङ्फुम] [**景品**] a pre-mium; a free gith; a present; a giveaway.

경향 [ग्यौङ्हांग] [**傾向**] [사물이 쏠리는 방향] a tendency <to / toward / to do>;

[정세] a trende.g. 영문학의 최근의 경향 a recent trend [recent trends] in English literature. 앙등의 경향 a rising [an upward] tendency.

경험 [ग्यौम्हौम] [經驗] [an] experience <of / in

경호[ग्यौम्हो][警護] guard; escort; convoy; patrol.

경황 [ग्यौम्हवांग] [景況] [an interesting] situation; the state of things; conditions. e.g. 경황이 없다 be busy [preoccupied]for / have no time [to spare] / one's mind is too much occupied[to think about other things].

곁 [ग्यौत] [옆] a side; [부근] neighborhood; vicinity. e.g. 곁에 서다 stand by the side of.

곁들이다 [ग्यौतुरिदा] [음식을] garnish <a dish with some vegetable>; add <some vegetable> as a relish; put all on one plate; dress. e.g. 케이크에 버찌를 곁들이다 garnish a cake with cherries.

-계[1] [ग्ये] [系] [계통][गैथोंग] a system. e.g. 태양 계 the solar system

-계[2] [ग्ये] [界] [...사회] a community; a world; a circle; a kingdom; a group. e.g. 동물 [식물 / 광물] 계 the animal [vegetable / mineral] kingdom.

계[1] [ग्ये] [係] [담당] charge; duty; business; [부서] a[sub] section <in charge of>; a <front / an information> desk; [담당자] a person in charge; a clerk [in charge]. e.g. 접수계 a reception clerk / a recaptionist.

계[2] [ग्ये] [契] a fraternity; a fraternal order [society]; a friendly society; a benefit club [society / association]; a mutual aid association; a mutual financing [loan] association; a mutual savings club. e.g. 계를 조직하다 organize a fraternity. 계를 타다get one's share[dividend] from a savings club.

계곡 [ग्येगोक] [溪谷] a valley; a gorge; a glen; a ravine; a dale; a canyon.

계급 [ग्येगुप] [階級] [신분][a] class; estate; caste [봉건적인]. e.g. 지식 계급 the intellectual class [es] / the intelligentsia.

계기 [ग्येगी] [契機] [기회] a chance; an opportunity; an occasion; [시초] a start; a beginning. e.g. 이를 계기로 해서 마음을 고치시오 Take this opportunity to reform.

계단 [ग्येदान] [階段] [층계] stairs; [통로로서의] a stairway; the stairs; [한 계단] a step; [난간 등을 포함한 전체] a staircase.

e.g. 나선 계단 a spiral [corkscrew] staircase / a winding stair.

계란 [ग्येरान] [鷄卵] = 달걀.

계략 [ग्येर्याक] [計略] [책략] a stratagem; an artifice; a design; a trick; a ruse; [함정] a trap; a snare; [계획] a plan; a scheme; [음모] a plot; [공동 모의] a conspiracy. e.g. 깊은 계략 dark designs.

계량 [ग्येर्यांग] [計量] [무게의] weighing; [길이부피의] measuring. 계량하다[길이 양을] measure; gauge; [무게를] weigh.

계몽 [ग्येमोंग] [啓蒙] enlightenment; education; instructtion <of the ignorant>; illumination. 계몽하다 enlighten; illuminate; educate; edify; develop the intellect of <backward people>.

계산 [ग्येसान] [計算] [숫자셈] calculation; reckoning; computation; counting; accounts; figure work; an estimation; balancing 계산하다 calculate; com-pute; figure [out];

계속 [ग्येसोक] [繼續] continuation; continuance; succession. 계속하다 [이어지다] continue; last; run on; follow; [이어서 하다] continue; maintain; keep up <with>; go on <with one's work>; [갱신하다] renew. e.g. 계속되는 불황 a continuous [lasting] recession. 계속되는 가뭄 [한발] a long spell of dry weather / a long drought.

계승 [ग्येसुंग] [繼承] succe-ssion; accession; inheri-tance. 계승하다 succeed <to>; accede <to>; inherit; take over. e.g. [조상으로부터] 계승한 inherited. 왕위를 계승하다 succeed [accede] to the throne..

계시다 [ग्येशीदा] <someone esteemed> be; stay; be located. e.g. 아버지 계시냐 Is your father in [at home]?

계약 [ग्येयाक] [契約] a contract; a compact; a covenant; an agreement [협정]; [매매 계약] a bargain. e.g. 가계약 a provisional contract. 구두계약 a verbal [an oral] contract. 계약하다 contract; make [enter into] a contract [an agreement] <with>; promise; sign a contract [an agreement

계열 [ग्येयौल] [系列] a system; an order of descent; succession; a series

계절 [ग्येजौल] [季節] a season; the time of the year. e.g. 사계절 the four seasons.

계좌 [ग्येज्वा] [計座] an account. e.g. 대체계좌 a postal transfer account.

계획 [ग्येह्वेक] [計劃] a plan <for / of>; a project; a scheme; a design 계획하다 plan <to do>; make a plan; project; scheme; design.

고가 [गोगा] [**高價**] a high [good] price; costliness; expensiveness

고갈 [गोगाल] [**枯渴**] [물의] drying up; [자원 등의] exhaustion; drain. 고갈하다be dried up; run dry; be parched; [자원 등이] become exhausted; be drained.

고개[1] [गोगै] [머리] the head; [목 뒤] the back [scruff] of the neck; [목] the neck. e.g. 고개를 갸우뚱하다 lean one's head to one side / tilt one's head.

고개[2] [गोगै] [산길]. a ridge; a[mountain] pass. e.g. 고개를 넘다 cross [over] a mountain pass [ridge / peak] / pass over the peak [crest].

고객 [गोगैक] [**顧客**] a customer, a patron; <집합적> patronage; custom

고결 [गोग्यौल] [**高潔**] nobility; noble-mindedness; noble character; lothiness; purity. 고결하다 lothy; noble; pure; high-minded [-souled]. e.g. 고결한 사람 a man of noble character / a high-souled [noble-minded] person.

고고학 [गोगोहाक] [**考古學**] arch [a] eology.

고구마 [गोगुमा] a sweet potato <*pl.* –es>.

고국 [गोगुक] [**故國**] one's native [home] country [land]; one's homeland; one's old home.

고군 분투 [गोगुन बुन्थु] [**孤軍奮鬪**] 고군 분투하다 fight alone <with / against>; fight unsupported struggle single-handed.

고궁 [गोगुंग] [**古宮**] an ancient [old] palace; a time-honored palace.

고귀 [गोग्वी] [**高貴**] nobility; valuableness; costliness; expensiveness. 고귀하다 [지위,인품이] noble; exalted; highborn; [값이] expensive; valuable; rare.

고급 [गोगुप] [**高級**] [높은 계급] high rank; seniority; [훌륭한 품질] high class [grade]. e.g. 고급인 [질이 좋은] high-quality [-class / -grade] / [사치스러운] luxury <food>.

고기 [गोगी] [동물의] meat [fish와 poultry를 제외한 식용육]; game [사냥한 들새,짐승의]; flesh <of a beast> [들짐승의 살].

고기압 [गोगीआप] [**高氣壓**] high atmospheric pressure; anticyclone; the barometric maximum.

고난 [गोनान] [**苦難**] distress [es]; suffering [s]; affliction [s]; [박해 등에 의한] tribulation; hardship [s].

고뇌 [गोन्वे] **苦惱**] gnawing; suffering[s]; distress;[an] affliction; anguish; agony; pain. e.g. 고뇌의 생활 a life of suffering / a hell of life.

고단하다 [गोदानहादा] tired; fatigued; exhausted; weary; worn out. e.g. 몹시 고단해 보이는군요 You look done up[all in / run down / beat / fagged].

고달프다 [गोदालफुदा] 1 [심신이] tired [fagged / worn] out; quite [dead / dog] tired; done [used / knocked] up; [totally] exhausted; all [done] in. 2 [일,시간이] tiring; fatiguing; wearing; weary; wearisome; tiresome; hard. e.g. 고달픈 일 tiring [wearing / fatiguing / hard] work.

고대[1] [गोदै] [苦待] 고대하다 [गोदैहादा] wait impatiently [eagerly] <for>; feel [be] impatient <for>; long for; eagerly look forward to <an event>. e.g. 고대하던 소식 the long-awaited news.

고대[2] [गोदै] [古代] ancient [old] times; remote ages; antiquity. e.g. 고대의 [गोदैउइ] ancient / antique / of antiquity.

고도 [गोदो] [高度] [높이][an] altitude; [a] height

고독 [गोदोक] [孤獨] [혼자임] solitude; [혼자 있어 외로움] loneliness [soli-tude는 자기 뜻에 의해 혼자 있는 것이며, 반드시 외로움이 포함되는 것은 아님].

고되다 [गोद्वेदा] tired; fatigued; [일 등이] trying; hard [to bear]; painful; tough; difficult; laborious; arduous. e.g. 고된 일 hard [heavy] work / a toilsome [painful] task / an awful [a horrible] sweat.

고등 [गोदुंग] [高等] e.g. 고등의 high / [상급의] higher / advanced / supreme / [고급의] high-grade / high-class / first-class.

고등학교 [गोदुंगहाकक्यो] [高等學校] [senior] high school; an upper secondary school

고래[गोरे][動] a whale

고려[गोर्यो][顧慮] [잘 생각함] consideration; thinking over; [걱정] concern; solici-tude. 고려하다consider; think over; take <a matter> into consideration; be concerned about.

고령 [गोर्यौंग] [高齡] an advanced [a great / a venerable / a ripe] age. e.g. 80세의 고령으로 죽다 die at the great [advanced / ripe / old] age of eighty.

고르다[1] [गोरुदा] [선택하다] choose; select; make choice of; pick [single / sort] out [선발하다]; fix upon [선정하다]. e.g. 자기가 고른 책 a book of one's own choice..

고르다[2] [गोरुदा] [평평하게 하다] level <the ground>; smooth; make even; roll [롤러로]; bulldoze [불도저로]. e.g. 표면을 고르다

bring a surface to a level.

고르다[3] [गोरूदा] [한결같다] even; uniform; equal; regular. e.g. 이가 고르다 [고르지 않다] have regular [irregular / uneven] teeth.

고리 [गोरी] [끼우는 물건] a ring; a link [사슬의];[실끈 등의] a loop.

고리대금 [गोरीदैगुम] **[高利貸金]** [이자가 비싼 돈] a loan at high interest; [이자가 비싼 돈놀이] usury; loanshar-king.

고리타분하다 [गोरीथाबुन्हादा] **1** [냄새가] ill-[foul-] smelling; stinking; malodorous; rancid; offensive; fetid; rank; rotten [썩어서]. **2** [성질 행동이] low; mean; petty; shallow; narrow-minded; stale; trite; commonplace; banal; meticulous.

고립 [गोरिप] **[孤立]** isolation; helplessness. 고립하다be isolated; stand alone [isolated]; be in isolation; be helpless [friendless]; [정치경제적으로] be qua-rantined. e.g. 고립된 soli-tary / isolated / lone / friendless / helpless. 외계로부터 완전히 고립하다 be entirely cut off from the outside world[from the rest of the world]. 고립시키다 isolate <a person> <from>.

고맙다 [गोमाप्ता] **1** [사물이] grateful; welcome; blessed; appreciated; gracious; bene-volent. e.g. 고마운 주인 a benevolent [kind] master.**2** [감사하다] thankful; app-reciative; gratefully ac-knowledged; obliged; obli-gated; indebted.

고매 [गोमै] **[高邁]** 고매하다 [गोमैहादा] noble; lothy; high-minded. e.g. 고매한 이상 a lothy ideal.

고모 [गोमो] **[姑母]** an aunt; a sister of one's father; a paternal aunt.

고모부 [गोमोबू] **[姑母父]** an uncle; the husband of one's father's sister.

고무 [गोमू] **[鼓舞]** encourage-ment; incitement; inspi-ration; stimulation. e.g. 고무적인 encouraging / ins-piring / stimulative. 고무하다 [गोमूहादा] encourage; inspire <a person with patrio-tism>; inspirit <a person to an action>; incite; stimu-late; stir up <one's mind>; arouse <a person to activity>; cheer up.

고무 [गोमू] [가공품으로서의] rubber; [탄성 고무] India rubber; [재료로서의] gum.

고문 [गोमुन] **[顧問]** [물음에 의견을 제공하는 사람] an advisor [an adviser] <to>; a counselor [a counsellor] [adviser는 지식이나 경험에 입각한 실제적인 조언을 해주는 사람, counselor는 신중히 숙고한 뒤에 조언을 해주는 사람]; a brain truster; [컨설턴트] a con-sultant.

고문[[गोमुन] **拷問]** torture; the

ㄱ

rake; the third degree. 고문하다torture; use torture on <a person>; give <a person> the third degree; put <a person> to torture[the rack]; torture <a person> on the rack.

고물 [गोमुल] [**古物**] [낡은 것] a used item; used things; a worn-out [secondhand] article; used [old] furniture [가구].

고민 [गोमिन] [**苦悶**] agony; anguish [agony는 심신의, anguish는 주로 마음의 괴로움]; worry; trouble; afflicttion. 고민하다 [गोमीनहादा]be in agony [anguish / distress]; suffer mental anguish; agonize <over one's failure>; be worried <about>; be troubled <with>; worry [oneself] <about / over>.

고발 [गोबाल] [**告發**] [法] prosecution; indictment; accusation; charging; a complaint; a formal charge [accusation] <against>.

고배 [गोबै] [**苦杯**] a bitter cup; [승부에서] a sad defeat; hardships. e.g. 고배를 마시다 [들다] drink a bitter cup / drink the cup of agony [humiliation]

고백 [गोबैक] [**告白**] confession; acknowledge-ment [자인]; profession [공표]. 고백하다 confess <of>.

고별 [गोब्यौल] [**告別**] leave-taking; farewell; valediction; parting; good-bye. 고별하다 take leave <of>; bid farewell [adieu] <to>; pay last respects <to>.

고부 [गोबू] [**姑**] mother-in-law and daughter-in-law. e.g. 그의 고부간의 사이가 별로 좋지 않다 His mother and wife don't get along so well.

고분 [गोबुन] [**古墳**] an old burial mound; an ancient [old] tomb; a tumulus <*pl.* ~es, -li>. e.g. 고분을 발굴하다 unearth [dig up] an old tomb.

고비 [गोबी] [절정] the climaK the crest; the height; the peak; the summit; [위기] the crisis <*pl.* crises>; brink; the crucial [trying] moment; the critical situation [stage]; the turning point <of an illness>. e.g. 고비를 넘[기]다 pass the crisis / turn the corner [병세가] / pass the peak [crest] of [물가가].

고사하고 [गोसाहागो] [별도로 하고] setting aside; apart from; [...은 커녕] anything but; far from; not at all; let alone; [말할 것도 없이] not to mention; not to speak of; to say nothing of. e.g. 농담은 고사하고 joking aside.

고상 [गोसांग] [**高尙**] nobleness; refinement; elegance; high-mindedness. 고상하다 noble; lothy; high; [품위가] refined; elegant; high-minded; high-toned; elevated.

고생 [गोसैंग] [**苦生**] **1** [어려운 생활] a hard [tough] life; privation. 고생하다be badly off; be in needy [straitened] circumstances. **2** [고난] trouble [s]; hardship [s]; suffering [s]; difficulty; distress; adversity. 고생하다 be distressed [troubled] <by / with>; have trouble [difficulty]; undergo [suffer / go through] hardships; have a hard [thin] time; be [hard] put to it.

고소 [गोसो] [**告訴**] an accusation; a charge; a [law] suit; a complaint; legal proceedings [steps]; a legal action. 고소하다 complain <to the magistrate of a crime>; make [lay] a complaint <against>; proceed against <a person>; take legal steps <against>; file a bill <in the court>; bring [institute] a suit <against>; charge <a person with a crime>; accuse <a person of theth>; bring a charge against <a person>; sue <a person for damages>; lodge a complaint <against a person

고소득층 [गोसोदुक्चुंग] the high-income bracket.

고소하다 [गोसोहादा] **1** [맛, 냄새가] taste of sesame oil; tasty; sweet; savory; nice; fragrant; <서술적> have a flavor of nut. e.g. 콩을 볶는 고소한 냄새 the aroma of beans being roasted. **2** [남의 일이] <서술적> be pleased to see a disliked person makes a mistake. . e.g. 남의 실패를 보고 고소해 하다 gloat over another's failure.

고속 [**도**] [गोसोक] [दो] [**高速**[**度**]] high [full] speed; [교통] rapid transit. e.g. 고속[으]로 at high speed / at a high rate of speed / at high velocity.

고속도로 [गोसोकदोरो] [**高速道路**] a super-highway; an expressway; an express highway; a speedway; a freeway; a motorway.

고수 [गोसू] [**固守**] 고수하다 [고집하다] adhere [cling] to <the principle>; keep [stick] to <old customs>; hold fast to <one's ideal>; persevere [persist] in <a course>

고스란히 [गोसुरान्ही] [그대로] just as it was; with nothing touched; with no change; [손상없이] without a damage; with nothing damaged; safely; [모두] completely; entirely; wholly; all.

고시[1] [गोशी] [**考試**] an examination; a test; the civil service examination. e.g. 검정 고시 a certificate examination

고시[2] [गोशी] [**告示**] a notifycation; a notice; a bulletin; an [official] announcement; a proclamation. 고시하다 notify <the public of some-

thing>; give notice <of>; issue a notification; proclaim; promulgate; announce.

고심 [गोशिम] [苦心] pains; labor; efforts; trouble; hard work; close application. 고심하다 work hard; take pains; labor; apply oneself to; make every possible effort; [머리를 짜다] rack [cudgel] one's brains.

고아 [गोआ] [孤兒] an orphan [child].

고안 [गोआन]] [考案] a design; a device; a plan; a conception; an idea; a project; a contrivance. 고안하다 devise; contrive; conceive; design; plan; originate.

고액 [गोऐक] [高額] a large amount [sum] [of money].

고약하다 [गोयाखादा] [보기에] ugly; bad-looking; unsightly; [마음이] bad; nasty; ill-natured; evil; wicked; crooked; malicious; foul; troublesome.

고양이 [गोयांगी] a cat; a puss [특히 부르는 말]; a feline [고양잇과의 동물]; a pussy [cat] [애칭,유아어].

고역 [गोयौक] hard work [toil]; a tough job; drudgery; toil; fag.

고온 [गोओन] [高溫] a high temperature.

고요 [गोयो] silence; stillness; calm [ness]; tranquility; quietude; serenity; peace.

고요하다 [गोयोहादा] [조용하다] still; quiet; hushed; silent; [평온하다] calm; serene; tranquil; peaceful; pacific. 고요히 quietly; still; calmly; peacefully; placidly.

고용 [गोयोंग] [雇用] employment; hiring. 고용하다 employ; hire.

고원 [गोवोन] [高原] a plateau <*pl.*, s, -eaux>; a highland; a tableland; [고지] heights.

고유 [गोयू] [固有][특유] characteristics; peculiarity; [천성] inherence; [본질] essence; nativeness. 고유하다 peculiar <to>; proper <to>; characteristic <of>; [of] one's own; essential; inherent <in>; native; inborn; indigenous.

고의 [गोउइ] [故意] [의도적임] intention; deliberation; design; purpose; willful-ness; bad faith. e.g. 고의의 [의도적인] intentional / deliberate / designed / studied / willful / contrived.

-고자 [गोजा] [욕망] wanting to; wishing to; intending to; going to; willing to; [목적] [in order] to; so as to; with the intention of; [so] that ... may; for [the purpose of]. e.g. 그것이 내가 말하고자 했던 거요 That is what I was going to say.

고자질 [गोजाजील] [告者-] tale-telling; talebearing; tattling; squealing; a tale. 고자질하다 tell [squeal / tattle] on <a person>; tell tales <about a person>; inform <a person against another>; let on.

고작 [गोजाक] at [the] most; at

[the] best; at the highest [greatest / largest]; at the outside; as much as one can <do>; no more than; merely; only; but. e.g. 고작 3년 가다 last [wear] for three years at most [at the outside].

고장 [गोजांग] [**故障**] trouble; a breakdown; [결함] defect; something wrong. e.g. 전기의 고장 an electricity failure.

고전 [गोजौन] [**古典**] [옛날의 뛰어난 예술 작품] classics; classical literature; [고서] an old book; [희랍 로마의] the classics.

고전 [गोजौन] [**苦戰**] a hard fighting; a hard [severe] fight; a desperate battle; a bitter battle; [경기 경쟁의] a hard-fought game; a close contest; a tight game [match / race]; hard [tough] going. 고전하다 fight hard; struggle desperately; fight against heavy odds; have a tough [close] game.

고정 [गोजौग] [**固定**] fixation; fixing; [자금의] lockup; tie-up. 고정하다fiK be fixed; fasten; settle; put <a thing> in place [position]; [자본이] be locked [tied] up; [진정하다] calm oneself; calm down <one's excitement [temper]>.

고조 [गोजो] [**高潮**] **1** [절정] the climaK the culmination; the acme; the high point. e.g. 최고조에 이르다 come to [reach] the climax / culminate. **2** [감정의] a rise; a swell; an elevation. e.g. 감정의 고조 an uprush of emotion.

고종 사촌 [गोजोंग साछोन] [**姑從四寸**] a child of [cousin by] one's father's sister.

고주망태 [गोजूमांग्थै] dead drunkenness. e.g. 고주망태가 되다 get [be] dead [beastly] drunk / be under the table / get boozy.

고지식하다 [गोजीशिकखादा] simple and honest; guileless; simple-minded; rigid; naive; formalistic; tactless; too serious [grave]; serious to a fault.

고진감래 [गोजीनगाम्नै] [**苦盡甘來**] 고진 감래하다Sweet ather bitter.; Pleasure follows pain.; Pain is gone, and pleasure is c1me.; No gains without pains.

고집 [गोजीप] [**固執**] [완고] obstinacy; stubbornness; obduracy; [집착] adherence <to>; persistence. e.g. 고집이 센 obstinate / stubborn / obdurate / headstrong.

고찰 [गोछाल] [**考察**] consideration; an examination <of>; [a] study; [an] investigation <of>; [an] inquiry <into>. 고찰하다 consider; examine; study; contemplate; inquire into; investigate.

고체 [गोछै] [**固體**] a solid [body]; solid matter

고충 [गोछुंग] [**苦衷**] distress; a

predication; a dilemma; mental suffering [anxiety / conflicts].

고층 [गोछुंग] [**高層**] [건물의] higher stories; upper floors. e.g. 고층의 multi-story / multi-storied / high-rise / lothy. [대기의] a high layer.

고치다 [गोछिदा] **1** [바로잡다] correct; reform <an evil practice>; redress <abuses>; remedy <an evil>; amend <one's conduct>; mend <one's ways>; rectify <a mistake>; cure; revise; set[put] right. e.g. 잘못을 고치다 correct an error **2** [병을 낫게 하다] heal; cure. e.g. 고칠 수 없는 병 an incurable [uncurable] disease. **3** [수선하다] repair; mend; patch up; set [put] right; put in order; e.g. 기계를 고치다 repair a machine / put a machine in order [to right] **4** [변경하다,새롭게 하다] change; alter; modify; remodel; renew; make renew [again / afresh]; renovate; improve; [번역하다] translate [render / put] <into>. e.g. 고쳐 말하다 express <one's idea> differenttly / restate.

고통 [गोथोंग] [**苦痛**] pain; agony; [심한 괴로움] great pain; anguish; [일시적 격통] pang; suffering; affliction. e.g. 고통을 느끼다 feel a pain / feel painful / suffer pain.

고프다 [गोफुदा] hungry; famished. e.g. 배가 고프다 be hungry / feel [get] hungry.

고함[गोहाम][**高喊**] a shout; a yell; a roar; a howl; a scream; a shriE; an outcry. 고함[을] 지르다[치다] shout; shriek; set up a shout; [떠들썩하게] clamor; bawl [out]; cry [call out] loudly; [응원 등에서] yell; give a yell <to a player>.

고행 [गोहैंग] [**苦行**] [속죄의] penance; [수도자로서의] asceticcism; an ascetic practice [penance]; religi-ous austerities; self-mortification; a religious penance.

고향 [गोह्यांग] [**故鄕**] one's home; one's hometown; one's native place; one's birthplace; one's home country [village]; one's native town [village].

곡 [गोक] [**曲**] [a piece of] music; [곡조] a tune; a melody; an air.

곡물 [गोंग्मुल] [**穀物**] cereals; grain; corn.

곡선[गोकसौन][**曲線**] a curved line; a curve.

곡예 [गोग्ये] [**曲藝**] acrobatics; a trick; an acrobatic feat; a stunt; fancy performances.

곡조 [गोक्चो] [**曲調**] a melody; a tune; strains. e.g. 한 곡조 부르다 sing a tune.

곤경 [गोन्ग्यौंग] [**困境**] distressed [adverse / straitened] circumstances; straits; a fiK a predicament; an awkward [a hard / a difficult] position [situation]. e.g. 곤경에 빠지다 get into trouble / be driven to the wall / be thrown into a fix / be placed in a painful position.

곤란 [गोल्लान] [**困難**] difficulty; a hurdle; a trouble; su-ffering [s]; hardship [s]; distress; embarrassment; perplexity. 곤란하다 difficult; hard; tough; troublesome; embarrassing; perplexing; awkward; <서술적> be in trouble; have a hard time.

곧 [गोत] [금방] immediately; instantly; directly; soon enough; at once; quick [ly]; straight off; [즉석에서] on the spot; [오래잖아] soon; shortly; presently; before long

곧다 [गोत्ता] **1** [물건이] straight; upright; erect; direct. e.g. 곧은 길 a straight road. **2** [마음이] honest; straight-forward; upright; righteous. e.g. 곧은 사람 an honest [righteous] person / a man of integrity.

곤란 [गोल्लान] [**困難**] difficulty; a hurdle; a trouble; su-ffering [s]; hardship [s]; distress; embarrassment; perplexity. e.g. 재정 곤란 financial [pecuniary] em-barrassment [difficulty].

곤충 [गोन्छुंग] [**昆蟲**] an insect; a bug.

곧바로 [गोप्पारो] [똑바로 곧게] straight; direct [ly]; [즉시] at once; immediately; directly.

곧이곧대로 [गोजीगोत्तैरो] [사실 그대로] plainly; straight-forwardly; honestly; frankly; just as it is.

곧이듣다 [गोजीदुत्दा] take <a thing> for truth; accept <a remark> [as true / as truth]; believe <a state-ment> [to be true]; take <it> seriously; believe one's ears.

곧잘 [गोच्चाल] [제법 잘] pretty [fairly] well; well enough; quite well; [쉽사리] [all] readily; quite readily; easily; [자주] othen; fre-quently.

곧장 [गोच्चांग] [똑바로 곧게] straight; direct [ly]; [즉시] right [away]; straight [right] off; without delay.

골 [गोल] a goal. e.g. 골을 넣다 [득점하다] make [score] a goal.

골격 [गोल्ग्यौक] [**骨格**] [고등동물의 뼈의 조직] a frame-work; a skeletal structure; a skeleton; [체격] a frame; build; physique. e.g. 골격이 좋은 말 a horse with plenty of bone.

골골 [गोल्गोल] 골골하다suffer from a chronic disease; suffer constantly from weak health; be sick all the time. e.g. 골골하는 사람 a chronic invalid / a sickly person

골다 [गोल्दा] [코를] snore. e.g. 코를[요란하게] 고는 사람 a [heavy] snorer

골동품 [गोल्दोंग्फुम] [**骨董品**] a curio <*pl.*, s>; objects [articles]

of virtu; brica-brac; an antique [object]. e.g. 가짜 골동품 a faked antique.

골똘하다 [गोल्तोर्हादा] absorbed [engrossed / lost] <in>; intent [keen] <on>; concentrated <on>; given <to>; completely taken up <with>. e.g. 독서에 골똘하다 be intent on reading <a book>.

골목 [गोल्मोक] a side street; an alley; a byway; a bystreet; a narrow street; an alleyway.

골몰 [गोल्मोल] [汩沒] absorption; immersion; engrossment. 골몰하다be immersed [absorbed / engrossed] in; devote oneself to <a task>; give oneself up to; bury oneself in; be hung up e.g. 그는 골프에 골몰하여 왔다 He has thrown himself completely into golf.

골병 [गोलप्यौंग] [-病] a deep-rooted illness [injury]; a disease [an injury] in the inmost part.

골짜기 [गोल्चागी] a valley; a vale; [협곡] a canyon; a ravine; a dale; a gorge.

골프 [गोल्फ़ु] golf.

곪다 [गोम्ता] [상처가] gather; fester; form pus; [일이] <an affair> come to a head; ripen. e.g. 상처가 곪았다 The wound festered. / The wound formed

곯다 [गोल्था] [배를] go hungry; be [always] hungry; be famished; starve. e.g. 곯은 배를 채우다 satisfy [gratify] one's hunger.

곯아떨어지다 [गोल्थादौरौजीदा] [잠에] fall fast asleep; be dead asleep; sleep like a top; [술에] be overcome with liquor; be dead drunk; be helplessly drunk; pass out. e.g. 그는 맥주 한 잔에 곯아떨어졌다 He got quite drunk ather only a glass of beer.

곰 [गोम] [동물] a bear.

곰곰[이] [गोम्गोम][इ] deliberately; thoroughly; deeply; profoundly; seriously; mulling [thinking] over; musing. e.g. 곰곰 생각해 보아라 Put that in your pipe and smoke it. / You should take time to consider it

곰팡이 [गोम्फांगी] mold; <英> mould; mildew; must.

곱다 [गोप्ता] **1** [아름답다] beautyful; lovely; fine; nice; handsome. e.g. 고운 소녀 a nice-looking [pretty / lovely] girl. 고운 얼굴 pretty features / a fair face [countenance]. **2** [마음이] sweet; gentle; pure-minded; noble-minded. e.g. 마음씨 고운 소녀 a kindhearted [a tender-hearted / an affectionate] girl..

곱빼기 [गोप्पेगी] [음식의] double measure; a double-measure of wine; a double [-size] glass; a double-the-ordinary dish.

곱셈 [गोप्सेम] [a] multiplication.

곱셈하다multiply; do multiplication

곱슬곱슬하다 [गोप्सुल्गोप्सुर्हादा] curly; curled; frizzled; frizzly; wavy. e.g. 곱슬곱슬한 머리 curly [frizzled] hair.

곱절 [गोप्चौल] [두배] double; [배] times. 곱절하다 [गोप्जौलहादा] double <it>. e.g. 곱절이 되다 double / be doubled <in value>.

곳 [गोत] [장소] a place; [좁은] a spot; [현장] a scene; [지방] locality. e.g. 사고가 일어난 곳 the spot of the accident.

-공 [गोंग] [工] [일꾼] an artisan; a worker; a mechanic. e.g. 금속공 a metal worker.

공[1] [गोंग] [空] [영] [a] zero; [a] cipher; [무] [a] naught; nothing[허사]. e.g. 나의 모든 노력은 공으로 돌아갔다 All my efforts have come to naught.

공[2] [गोंग] [功] 공로 e.g. 특히 공이 있는 사람 a person of exceptional merit.

공[3] [गोंग] [公] [공무[公 務] public matters; public affairs. e.g. 공과 사를 구별하다 draw the line between public and private matters.

공[4] [गोंग] [볼] a ball; a handball; [원구] a circle; a sphere; a globe.

공간 [गोंगान] [空間] **1** [우주의] space. e.g. 공간의 spacial. **2** [장소] room; [틈] a space; a gap; discontinuity. e.g. 위상 공간 topological space.

공감 [गोंगाम] [共感] sympathy; response.

공감하다sympathize with <a person>; respond to <an appeal>. e.g. 남의 의견에 공감하다 sympathize with a person in his point of view / sympathize with a person's point of view

공개 [गोंगै] [公開] e.g. 공개의 [적인] open[to the public] / public.

공경 [गोंग्यौग] [恭敬] respect; reverence; veneration; deference. 공경하다respect; esteem; honor; revere

공고 [गोंगो] [公告] a public [an official] announcement [notice]; a [public] notifycation 공고하다 notify publicly; announce; give a public notice <of>. e.g. 시험 날짜가 어제 공고되었다 The date of the examination was publicly announced yesterday.

공공 [गोंगोंग] [公共] the public society; the community. e.g. 공공의 public / common / communal.

공공연하다 [गोंगोंग्योन्हादा] [公公然-] open; public; open and public; avowed <enemy>; overt <hostility>. e.g. 공공연한 사실 a fact as clear as day / a fact known to everybody.

공과대학 [गोंग्वादैहाक] [工科大學] a college of engineering; a college specializing in engineering; an institute of technology.

공교롭다[गोंग्योरोप्ता][工巧-] [뜻밖이다] coincidental; wholly unexpected; quite accidental; opportune [inopportune]; timely [untimely]; lucky [unlucky]. e.g. 공교로운 일치 a coincidence.

공구 [गोंगू] [工具] a tool; an implement; an instrument. e.g. 기계 공구 a machine tool.

공군 [गोंगुन] [空軍] an air force; the air service; a flying corps.

공권력 [गोंग्वनन्यौक] [公權力] governmental authority [power].

공급 [गोंगुप] [供給] supply; provision; [전기,수도 등의] service 공급하다 supply [provide] <a person with something / something for a person>; furnish <with>; serve <a town>. e.g. 원료를 공급하다 supply <a factory> with material.

공기 [गोंगी] [空氣] [기체] air.

공덕 [गोंग्दौक] [功德] charity; piety; a pious act; a charitable [virtuous] deed; an act of merit; virtue. e.g. 공덕을 베풀다 [자선하다] perform an act of charity

공동 [गोंग्दोंग] [共同] cooperation; collaboration; union; association; partnership. e.g. 공동의 common / communal / joint / concerted / united / public [공공의].

공들이다 [गोंग्दुरीदा] [功-] make a strenuous effort; labor assiduously; spend [expend] one's labor; put great care <in one's work>; take pains. e.g. 공들인 문장 an elaborate sentence.

공란 [गोंग्नान] [空欄] a blank [an empty / a vacant] column; a blank [space]; empty space; margin. e.g. 공란에 기입하다 fill in the blanks

공략 [गोंगन्याक] [攻略] capture; conquest; reduction; occupation; [침략] [an] invasion; taking by storm. 공략하다 carry; capture; conquer; reduce; take <a fortress> by storm; [침략하다] invade <a country>. e.g. 공략하기 어려운 impregnable <fortress>.

공로 [गोंग्नो] [功勞] meritorious deeds [services]; merits; an exploit. e.g. 공로를 세우다 distinguish oneself in <war> / render distinguished service to <the state> / perform a meritorious deed / do much for <social welfare>.

공룡 [गोंगन्योंग] [恐龍] [古生] a dinosaur; a dinosaurian; a titanosaur

공립 [गोंग्निप] [公立] a public institution. e.g. 공립의 public / communal / [지방 자치제의] provincial / municipal.

공모 [गोंग्मो] [公募] [an appeal

for] public subscription [contribution];[주식 등의] public offering. 공모하다 [invite public participation; [사람을] advertise for <a secretary>;[기부금 등을] solicit <a contribution>. e.g. 현상 소설을 공모하다 open a prize list of novels / invite the public to join in a prize contest for best stories

공무원 [गोंग्मूवॉन] [公務員] <집합적> the civil service; public service personnel; government employees; [개인] a public employee; an official; a civil servant; a servant of the state; a public service worker; a government official; an officeholder.

공문서 [गोंग्मुन्सौ] [公文書] an official document[paper / note]; a state document; archives [보존된]; a communiqué [외교의]. e.g. 지급 공문서 a dispatch.

공백 [गोंग्बैक] [空白] [책 등의 여백] a blank; blank [empty] space; <비유> a vacuum <*pl.* , s, vacua>; a void; a gap. e.g. 공백을 메우다 fill a gap <in> / fill up [in] a blank.

공범 [गोंग्बौम] [共犯] [공모하여 죄를 범함] complicity <with a person in a crime>; conspiracy [공모]. e.g. 공범으로 체포되었다 He was caught as a party to the crime.

공부 [गोंग्बू] [工夫] study; learning; work [on one's studies]; scholarly activity. 공부하다 study; work at [on] <one's studies>. e.g. 법률을 공부하다 study <英> read law..

공사 [गोंग्सा] 工事] construction; construction work; work of construction; engineering work. 공사하다 construct; do[execute] construction work <on>; work <at>; build.

공사 [गोंग्सा] [公社] a public corporation.

공산주의 [गोंग्साजुइ] [共產主義] communism. e.g. 공산주의와 싸우다 battle [struggle] against communism.

공상 [गोंग्सांग] [空想] [an] imagination; a daydream; a fantasy; fancy. 공상하다 imagine; dream; daydream. e.g. 마음껏 공상하다 give full play to one's fancy.

공생 [गोंग्सैंग] [共生] [生] symbiosis; commensalism; [鑛] paragenesis. 공생하다 live together [in symbiosis]; symbiose.

공석 [गोंग्सौक] [公席] [공적인 모임][the presence of] the public; the meeting;. e.g. 공석에서 in public [company] / before[in the presence of] others.

공세 [गोंग्से] [攻勢] an offensive [movement]; the offensive; the aggressive; aggression. e.g. 평화[외교]

공세 a peace [diplomatic] offensive. 노동 공세 a labor offensive.

공손 [गोंग्सोन] [**恭遜**] politeness; courteousness; civility. e.g. 지나친 공손 excessive [over done] politeness.

공식 [गोंग्शिक] [**公式**] **1** a formula <*pl.*, s, -lae>. e.g. 공식으로 나타내다 express in a formula / formulate. **2** [의식,정식] formality; an official ceremony. e.g. 공식의 state / formal / official. 공식으로 formally / officially.

공약 [गोंग्याक] [**公約**]a pledge; a public promise [commitment]; [선거의] an election [a campaign] promise. 공약하다 pledge [commit] oneself <to>. e.g. 정책을 공약하다 commit oneself to a policy.

공업 [गोंगौप] [**工業**] [an] industry; manufacturing industry; <집합적> the Industries

공연 [गोंग्यौन] [**公演**] a public performance. 공연하다 perform; play; stage; present. e.g. 그 연극은 국립 극장에서 공연된다 [공연 중이다] The play will be presented [is on] at the National Theater.

공예 [[गोंग्ये] [**工藝**] industrial arts; technology. e.g. 공예의 industrial / technological..

공용 [गोंग्योंग] [**共用**] common [joint] use. e.g. 공용의 부엌 a kitchen for common use.

공용어 [गोंग्योंगौ] [**公用語**] [관청 용어] official language [terminology]; [국제 회의 등의] an official language <of an international conference>.

공원 [गोंग्वॉन] [**公園**] a park; a public garden; [작은 공원] a square. e.g. 국립 공원 a national park.

공유 [गोंग्यू] [**共有**] joint [common] ownership; co-ownership; community. 공유하다 have [possess] a thing jointly; hold <something> in common. e.g. 재산을 공유하다 communize property.

공익 [गोंगिक] [**公益**] public [common] benefit; common weal. e.g. 공익을 위하여 in the interest [cause] of the public / for public good.

공인 [गोंगिन] [**公認**] official recognition[approval]; authorization 공인하다recognize [approve] officially; give <a person> official recognition; authorize; [법률로] legalize. e.g. 후보자를 공인하다 officially adopt a candidate / nominate a candidate.

공장 [गोंग्जांग] [**工場**] a factory; a plant; a mill; a works; a manufactory

공적 [गोंग्जौक] [**公的**] public; official; formal. e.g. 공적으로 publicly / officially.

공정 [गोंग्जौंग] [**公正**] justice; impartiality; fairness; equity. 공정하다 just; fair; equitable; righteous; impartial. e.g. 공정한 처사 a fair [square] deal.

공제 [गोंग्जे] [**控除**] subtraction; deduction. 공제하다 subtract; deduct; take away [off]; cut off. e.g. 공제할 수 있는 deductible <expenses>.

공존 [गोंग्जोन] [**共存**] coexistence 공존하다 coexist; live together; live and let live. e.g. 두 종파가 공존하기는 어려웠다 It was difficult for the two sects to coexist [live together].

공주 [गोंग्जू] [**公主**] a [royal] princess.

공중 [गोंग्जुंग] [**空中**] the air; the sky; midair; space.

공중도덕 [गोंग्जुंगदोदौक] [**公衆道德**] public morality [morals]. e.g. 공중 도덕을 지키다 take care not to trouble others / act the gentleman in public / be a gentleman in public.

공직 [गोंग्जिक] [**公職**] a public office; an official position. e.g. 공직에 있는 사람 a public official [servant] / a public office holder.

공책 [गोंग्छैक] [**空冊**] a notebook.

공천 [गोंग्छौन] [**公薦**] [합의에 의한 천거] public nomination [recommendation]; [의원 선거 출마자에 대한 정당의 추천] party nomination of parliamentary candidates. 공천하다 recommend publicly; nominate <a candidate>. e.g. 후보자를 공천하다 officially adopt a candidate / nominate a candidate.

공통 [गोंग्थोंग] [**共通**] commonness. e.g. 공통의 이익을 위하여 for the public good.

공통점 [गोंग्थोंग्जौम] [**共通點**] a common point; a point of sameness. e.g. 공통점이 있다[없다] have something [nothing] in common <with>.

공평 [गोंगप्यौंग] [**公平**] impartiality; fairness; fair play; equity; equitability. 공평하다 [정실이 없다] impartial; unbias [s]ed; [공정하다] fair; equitable; [공평무사하다] disinterested; fair and square

공포 [गोंग्फो] [**恐怖**] fear; dread; terror; fright; horror; panic [공황]. e.g. 이유 없는 공포 a groundless [baseless] fear.

공포 [गोंग्फो] [**公布**] promulgation; proclamation; [official] announcement.

공학 [गोंग्हाक] [**共學**] coeducation; mixed education. e.g. 남녀 공학반 a mixed class.

공학 [गोंग्हाक] [**工學**] engineering; technology. e.g. 기계[전기 / 토목] 공학 mechanical [electrical / civil] engineering.

공항 [गोंग्हांग] [**空港**] an airport;

an aerial port; airdrome; an aviation field; an aerodrome

공해 [गोंग्है] [**公害**] [environmental] pollution [환경 오염]; environmental disruption [환경 파괴]; a public nuisance; [a] menace [a threat] to public health; public hazard.

공헌 [गोंग्हौन] [**貢獻**] a contribution; services. e.g. 아시아의 평화적 개발에 대한 미국의 공헌 America's contribution to the peaceful development of Asia..

공화국 [गोंगह्वागुक] [**共和國**] a republic; a commonwealth.

공황 [गोंगह्वांग] [**恐慌**] a panic; a scare; consternation; a financial panic[crisis]. e.g. 주식 공황 a stock market [exchange] panic

공휴일 [गोंगह्युइल] [**公休日**] [법정 휴일] a legal holiday; a bank holiday; [정기적 휴일] a regular holiday; a day-off.

과 [ग्वा] [**科**] [학과] a department; a faculty; [병원의] a department; [병과] an arm [of the military service]. e.g. 수학과의 학생 a student majoring in mathematics.

과감 [ग्वागाम] [**果敢**] [단호함] decisiveness; resolution; determination; [용감함] boldness; daring. 과감하다 [단호하다] resolute; determined; [용감하다] bold; daring; [두려움을 모르다] dauntless

과거 [ग्वागौ] [**過去**] [지나간 때] the past. e.g. 과거를 회상하다 recall [think of] the past.

과격 [ग्वाग्यौक] [**過激**] 과격하다 extreme; excessive; radical; drastic; ultra; violent; rabid <terrorists>. e.g. 그는 곧잘 과격한 말을 쓴다 He othen uses violent language..

과다 [ग्वादा] [**過多**] excess; superabundance; overplus; surplus. e.g. 공급 과다 oversupply / an excessive supply / excess of supply.

과대 [ग्वादै] [**過大**] 과대하다 excessive; exorbitant; unreasonable; undue; extravagant; inordinate; too big[great]. e.g. 과대한 요구 an unreasonable [exorbitant] demand.

과도 [ग्वादो] [**過度**] excess; immoderation; immoderateness. 과도하다excessive; immoderate; too much; inordinate.

과도기 [ग्वादोगी] [**過渡期**] a transition period; a period of transition; an age of transition. e.g. 과도기의 문화 culture in a transition period.

과로 [ग्वारो] [**過勞**] overwork; overexertion; strain. 과로하다work too hard [oneself]; overwork; exert oneself too much. e.g. 자네는 병후 요양 중이니까 과로해

서는 안 되네 You've just gotten better, so you'd better not overdo things.

과목 [ग्वामोक] [科目] [학과] a subject; a course; a [the] curriculum [전과목].

과묵 [ग्वामोक] [寡默] taciturn-nity; reticence. 과묵하다 taciturn; reticent. e.g. 과묵한 사람 a taciturn [reti-cent] person / a man of few words / an oyster of a man.

과반수 [ग्वाबान्सू] [過半數] the majority; the greater part [number] <of>. e.g. 절대 과반수 an absolute majority.

과부 [ग्वाबू] [寡婦] a widow; a woman bereth of her hus-band.

과분 [ग्वाबुन] [過分] 과분하다unmerited; unde-served; unworthy <of>.

과속 [ग्वासोक] [過速] over-speed. e.g. 과속으로 달리다 overspeed.

과수원 [ग्वासूवॉन] an orchard; a fruit garden; a fruit farm.

과시 [ग्वाशी] [誇示] osten-tation; display; showing off; parade. e.g. 힘의 과시 an ostentation[a display] of one's power. 과시하다 show off [proudly]; display ostentatiously; make a display [show / parade] of; parade.

과식 [ग्वाशिक] [過食] over-eating; excessive eating; surfeit. 과식하다eat too much; eat to excess; overeat [one-self]. e.g. 과식하여 탈나다 overeat oneself sick.

과실 [ग्वाशिल] [過失] [잘못] a mistake; an error; [실책] a blunder; a fault. e.g. 과실을 인정하다 admit one's error / admit that one is in error / acknow-ledge one's mistake.

과연 [ग्वायौन] [果然] as ex-pected; sure enough; just as one thought; indeed; really. e.g. 과연 그것은 사실일까 Is it really true?

과오 [ग्वाओ] [過誤] = 과실 e.g. 과오를 범하다 commit a fault / make a mistake[an error].

과욕 [ग्वायोक] [過慾] avarice; greed; greediness; covetous-ness. 과욕하다avaricious; greedy; covetous.

과음 [ग्वाउम] [過淫]l ustful excesses; overindulgence in sexual pleasure; sexual indulgence. 과음하다 in-dulge [oneself] in sE give oneself up [over] to sex life.

과일 [ग्वाइल] <집합적> fruit [age];[낱낱의] a fruit; [딸기류] a berry.

과잉 [ग्वाइंग] [過剩] [잉여] an excess; a surplus; over-abundance; superabun-dance; superfluity. e.g. 공급 과잉 an oversupply.

과자 [ग्वाजा] [菓子] <집합적> confectionery; sweet stuff; [케이크] a cake; [당과] candy; sweets; [파이 등] pastry.

ㄱ

과장 [ग्वाजांग] [課長] t he chief [head] of a section; a section chief.

과장 [ग्वाजांग] [誇張] exaggeration; overstatement; grandiloquence; magniloquence; magnification. e.g. …라고 해도 과장이 아니다 It is not too much to say that ... / It is no exaggeration to say that ..과장하다 exaggerate; overstate; magnify; overdraw; overshoot oneself; stretch; go too far; overpitch; blow up; paint <a thing> in high colors; make a mountain out of a molehill.

과정 [ग्वाजौंग] [課程] 학과 과정, 학과 e.g. 교과 과정 a curriculum / a course of study.

과제 [ग्वाजे] [課題] 1 [문제] a question; a problem. e.g. 해결해야 할 과제 a problem awaiting solution [to be solved]..2 [숙제] homework; a home task; an assignment; exer-cises [연습 문제]. e.g. 여름방학 과제 a summer assignment / summer homework

과중 [ग्वाजुंग] [過重] 과중하다 too heavy; burdensome. e.g. 과중한 노동 excessively heavy work / overwork. 과중한 부담 too great burden / a heavy burden.

과즙 [ग्वाजुप] [果汁] fruit juice.

과찬 [ग्वाछान] [過讚] overpraise; an undeserved praise; excessive compliment. 과찬하다overpraise; praise [compliment] excessively.

과태료 [ग्वाथेर्यो] [過怠料] [法] a fine for default; a negligence fine; penalty; a penalty fee; a civil fine.

과하다 [ग्वाहादा] [過-] too much [good / heavy / severe]; excessive; overly; beyond [all] bounds [limits]; undue; undeserved; unreasonnable. e.g. 술을 과하게 마시다overdrink oneself / drink too much / drink to excess.

과학 [ग्वाहाक] [科學] science.

과학자 [ग्वाहाक्चा] a scientist; a man of science.

-관 [ग्वान] [觀] an outlook; a view. e.g. 인생관 one's view of life / an outlook on life.

관[ग्वान] [棺] a coffin; a casket.

관 [ग्वान] [管] [둥글고 긴 속이 빈 물건] a pipe; a tube; 도관 a duct. e.g. 유리관a glass tube.

관개 [ग्वान्गै] [灌漑] irrigation; watering. 관개하다irrigate; water. e.g. 그들은 황무지를 관개했다 They irrigated the wasteland.

관객 [ग्वान्गैक] [觀客] a spectator; an audience; an attendance. e.g. 많은[적은]관객 a large [small] audience.

관계[ग्वान्ग्ये] [關係] 1 [관련]

relation; relationship; reference; bearing; respect; [이해 관계] an interest; a concern; [연고] connection; [교제] relations. e.g. 거래 관계trade connections. **2** [관여] participation; concern; [연좌] involvement. e.g. 관계를 끊다wash [wipe] one's hands of <an affair>. **3** [영향] influence; an effect; [이유 까닭] reason. e.g. 그것은 나에게는 큰 관계가 없다 It matters little to me.

관공서 [क्वान्गोंग्सो] [**官公署**] a government office; a public office.

관광 [क्वान्ग्वांग] **觀光**] sightseeing; tourism. 관광하다 go sightseeing; go on a [sightseeing] tour; see [do] the sights <of>. e.g. 제주도를 관광하다see[do] the sights of Cheju-do.

관광객 [क्वान्ग्वांगैक [**觀光客**]] a tourist; a sightseer; a visitor; <美> a rubberneck [특히 단체 여행의]; <집합적> tourism.

관념 [क्वानयौम] [**觀念**] [개념 생각] an idea; a concept [ion]; a notion. e.g. 고정 관념 a fixed idea.

관능 [क्वान्नुंग] [**官能**] [육체적 감각] fleshly] sense; [육욕] carnal desires [lust]. e.g. 관능적인여자 a glamour [ous] girl / a sexpot.

관대 [क्वान्दै] [**寬大**] [너그러움] generosity; magnanimity; broad-mindedness; liberality. 관대하다 broad-minded; generous; liberal; magnanimous. e.g. 관대한 태도a generous attitude.

관람 [क्वाल्लाम] [**觀覽**] inspecttion; viewing. e.g. 일반의 관람을 허가하다 [불허하다] be open [closed] to the public. 관람하다 see; view; inspect

관람석 [क्वाल्लाम्सौक] [**觀覽席**] a seat; [극장의] an auditorium; a front; a boK the [spectators'] gallery; [야구장 등의] a stand; a grandstand [정면의] a bleacher [s]

관련 [क्वालल्यौन] [**關 聯**] connection; relation; reference; correlation; association. e.g. 이것은 그것과 아무 관련이 없다] This has no connection with it. / This has nothing to do with it 관련하다be connected <with>; be related <to>; relate <to>; be correlated <to>; bear <on>; have a bearing <on>; refer <to>; connect [up] <with>. e.g.… 과 관련하여 in connection with / in relation to.

관례 [क्वालल्ये] [**慣 例**] [a] custom; a usage; a usual practice; a precedent [전례] a convention [관습].

관료 [ग्वालल्यो] [**官僚**] [관리] a bureaucrat; a government official; <집합적> the bureaucracy; officialdom; government officials.

관리 [ग्वाल्ली] [**管理**] **1** [지배 감독] administration; management; control; supervision; superintendence. 관리하다 administer; manage; control; superintend; supervise. e.g. 학교를 관리하다 manage [administrate] a] school. **2** [돌봄] charge; care. e.g. 재산의 관리를 위임하다entrust one's property to <a person's> care / put one's property in <a person's> charge.

관리 [ग्वाल्ली] [**官吏**] a government official; a public official [servant]; a civil servant; a public functionnary; <집합적> bureaucracy; officialdom. e.g. 고급 관리a high-ranking government official.

관리인[ग्वाल्लीइन] [**管理人**] a manager; an administrator; a supervisor; a superintendent; an executor [유산 유저 등의] a caretaker; a trustee; a custodian; a keeper; [아파트 등의] a concierge; a superintendent; 농장 목장 등의] <美>a majordomo; [사무실 아파트 등의] <美 a janitor; a janitress [여자]

관문 [ग्वान्मुन] [**關門**] **1** [요새,국경의 문] a barrier [station]; a barrier-gate; a gateway <to>; a boundary gate [지계의 [검문소] a checking station; a checkpoint. e.g. 동양에의 관문 a gateway to the Orient. **2** [난관] a difficult situation; [장벽] a barrier; a hurdle; an obstacle. e.g. 고등 고시의 관문을 돌파하다 successfully pass the higher civil service examination.

관세 [ग्वान्से] [**關稅**] customs [duties]; a custom duty; a [custom] tariff.

관습 [ग्वान्सुप] [**慣習**] custom; usage; [a] usual [common] practice; convention; tradition.

관심 [ग्वान्शिम] [**關心**] interest <in>; concern <about / over>. e.g. 관심을 기울이다give thought <to> / take [have] [an] interest <in>.

관여 [ग्वान्यो] [**關與**] participation <in>. 관여하다 participate [take part] in; have [play] a part <in>; be concerned in [with]; have something to do with. e.g. 계획에 관여하고 있는 사람a participant in a plan.

관용 [ग्वान्योंग] [**寬容**] tolerance; magnanimity; generosity; liberality; leniency; forgiveness; forbearance.

관점[ग्वान्जोम] [**觀點**] a point of view; a viewpoint; a

standpoint; an angle [of vision].

관중[ग्वान्जुंग] [觀衆] spectators; viewers; onlookers; <집합적>an audience.

from] government service.

관찰 [ग्वान्छाल] [觀察] observation; view. 관찰하다 observe; make observation <of>; watch. e.g. 내가 관찰한 바로는 according to my observation / as I look at it.

관청 [ग्वान्छौंग] [官廳] a government office; [당국] the authorities.

관측 [ग्वान्छुक] [觀測] [관찰] observation; survey. 관측하다observe; make [take] an observation; survey.

관통 [ग्वान्थोंग] [貫通] piercing; penetration; perforation. 관통하다pierce; bore <through / into>; pass through; penetrate; perforate; [탄환이] shoot [go] through. e.g. 탄환이 그의 다리를 관통했다 The bullet went through his legs.

관하다 [ग्वान्हादा] [關-] [대하다] be connected [concerned] with; be related to; concern; be about; refer to. e.g. 종교[과학]에 관한 책a book on religion [science].

관할 [ग्वानहाल] [管轄] jurisdiction; control; competence. e.g. 이 지역은 서대문 경찰서 관할이다 This district is under the jurisdiction of the Sŏdaemun Police Station. 관할하다] exercise jurisdiction [control] <over a district>; have competence <over a matter>; control.

관행 [ग्वान्हैंग] [慣行] [a] traditional practice; [a] custom; routine. e.g. 관행의 habitual / customary / practical.

관현악 [ग्वान्ह्यौनाक] [管絃樂] orchestral music; an orchestra.

관혼상제 [ग्वान्होनसांग्जे] [冠婚喪祭] the ceremonies of coming of age, marriage, funeral and ancestral worship; ceremonial occasions.

괄목 [ग्वालमोक] [刮目] 괄목하다] watch eagerly [closely]; watch with keen interest. e.g. 괄목할 만한 진보 [eye-opening [startling] progress.

괄시 [ग्वाल्शी] [恝視] negligence; slight; [냉] a cold reception. 시하다neglect; slight; treat <a person> coldly. e.g. 너무 괄시하지 마라Don't hold me so cheap.

괄호 [ग्वाहॉ] [括弧] [소괄호] parentheses <*sing.* -sis> [<英>[round] brackets]; [대괄호] brackets; square brackets; [중괄호] braces [▷모두가 복수형으로 쓰임].

-광 [ग्वांग] [狂] a fan; a

fanatic; a buff. e.g. 경마광 a turfman / a race maniac / a horse racing enthusiast [nut]. **광**[光] **1** [빛][a] light; [광선] rays [of light]; a ray. e.g. 태양광the light [rays] of the sun. **2** [윤기] gloss; luster; glaze; brightness. e.g. 진주의 광 the luster of a pearl

광경 [ग्वांग्यौंग] [光景] [벌어진 일의 상태] a spectacle; a sight; a scene; a view / an aspect. e.g. 즐거운[무서운 / 슬픈] 광경a pleasant [horrid / sad] sight [경치] a scene; <집합적> natural] scenery; a view. e.g. 하늘에서 본 광경an aerial view.

광고 [ग्वांगो] [廣告] an advertisement; ad; <英> an advert; [알림] a notice; an announcement; [선전] advertising; publicity.

광나다 [ग्वांग्नादा] [光-] gloss; glaze; shine; have a gloss [shine / luster / glaze]. e.g. 광나지 않다be dull [dim / lackluster] / <a table> won't polish.

광내다 [ग्वांग्नैदा] [光-] shine <shoes>; polish; make <a thing> shine [bright]. e.g. 광내는 가루약 polishing powder. 구두를 광내다 shine shoes.

광대 [ग्वांग्दै] [가면극의] a masque performer; [인형극의] a puppeteer; [곡예사] an acrobatic performer; a tumbler; [어릿광대] a clown; a buffoon; a jester; [창극의] a feat singer.

광란 [ग्वांग्लान] [狂亂] madness; craziness; fury; frenzy; raving. e.g. 반광란 상태의 half-mad[-crazed].

광명 [ग्वांग्म्यौंग] [光明] [빛light; [희망] hope; a bright future [prospect]. e.g. 한 줄기의 광명a ray [gleam] of hope / a beam of hope <on the horizon>.

광물 [ग्वांग्मुल] [鑛物] a mineral.

광범위 [ग्वांग्बौम्वी] [廣範圍] a wide area [range]; a wide scope. 광범위하다 extensive; wide; widespread; wide-ranging <studies>; comprehensive <plan>; far-reaching <program>.

광복 [ग्वांग्बोक] [光復] glorious restoration; [주권 회복] the restoration of independence <to a country>.

광복절 [ग्वांग्बोक्चौल] [光復節] Independence Day of Korea.

광부 [ग्वांग्बु] [鑛夫] a miner; a mine worker; a pitman; a digger.

광산 [ग्वांग्सान] [鑛山] a mine; a mine field.

광선 [ग्वांग्सौन] [光線] a ray [beam] of light; light.

광야 [ग्वांग्या] [曠野] a wilderness; an extensive [wild] plain; a prairie..

광장 [ग्वांग्जांग] [**廣場**] an open space; [도시의a public square; [대광장] a plaza.

광적 [ग्वांग्जौक] [**狂的**] lunatic; insane; frantic; fanatic [al]; mad. e.g. 광적인 신앙 fanatic belief.

광택 [ग्वांग्थैक] [**光澤**] gloss; sheen; luster; polish; brilliance; a shine. e.g. 광택있는 lustrous / glossy / brilliant.

광활 [ग्वांगह्वाल] spaciousness; extensiveness. 광활하다 spacious; vast; extensive. e.g. 광활한 사막a vast expanse [extent] of desert.

괘도 [ग्वैदो] [**掛圖**] [지도] a wall map; [도표] a wall chart; [그림] a hanging picture.

괘씸하다 [ग्वैशिमहादा] [무례하다] rude; impertinent; insolent; [밉살스럽다] hateful; detestable; dis-gusting; [은혜를 모르다] ungrateful; [발칙하다] outrageous; [믿을 수 없다] unfaithful; untrustworthy.

괜찮다 [क्वैन्छान्था] **1** [쓸만하다] nice; good; not so bad; passable; fair; fine. e.g. 괜찮은 값[수입] a good [fair] price [income]. **2** [무방하다] [사람이] may; can; <서술적> be allowed to <do>; be justified in <doing>; [사물이] justifiable; warrant-able; all right; O.K.; <서술적> will do. e.g. 어느 쪽이든 괜찮다 Either will do. **3** [안심이다] safe; secure; free from danger; all right; O.K. e.g. [위험을 벗어나] 이젠 괜찮다 Now we are out of danger [the woods]. / We are in the clear now.

괜히 [क्वैन्ही] to no purpose; needlessly; uselessly; without reason; fruitlessly; in vain

괴다 [ग्वेदा] [모이다] gather; collect; [정체하다] stagnate; be stagnant. e.g. 괸물 stagnant [standing] water.

괴다 [ग्वेदा] [받치다] prop; support; sustain. e.g. 두 손으로 턱을 괴다cup one's chin in one's hands / support one's chin on one's hands

괴담 [ग्वेदाम] [**怪談**] [무서운 이야기] a ghost story; a spooky story; [이상한 이야기] a strange story.

괴력 [ग्वेर्यौक] [**怪力**] marvelous [physical] strength; Herculean [prodigious / superhuman] strength; Amazonian strength [여자의].

괴로움 [ग्वेरोउम] [곤란 고난] distress; troubles; hardships; sufferings; [근심] worries; [수고] trouble; annoyance; [고뇌] agony; anguish; affliction; [고통 병고] pain; pangs; throes; [시련] trials; ordeals

괴로워하다 [ग्वेरोवॉहादा] **1** [고통을 느끼다] suffer <from>; feel [be in] pain; be afflicted <with>. e.g. 갈증으로 괴로워하다 suffer from thirst. **2** [고민하다]] be distressed; be worried <by>; worry oneself <about / over>; torment with the thought <of>. e.g. 돈 문제로 괴로워하다be pinched [pressed / hard up] for money.

괴롭다 [ग्वेरोप्ता] [고통스럽다] painful; afflicting; distressing; agonizing; [곤란하다] troublesome; hard; difficult; [난처하다] awkward; embarrassing; embarrassed; [곤궁하다] straitened; needy; reduced; <서술적> be indisposed of.

괴롭히다 [ग्वेरोंफिदा] [괴로움을 주다] afflict; torment; harass; agonize; torture; [고통을 주다] cause <a person> pain; distress; excruciate; [난처하게 하다] trouble; worry; annoy; bother; embarrass; [못살게 굴다] persecute; tease; be hard on; [억압하다] oppress. e.g. 강아지를 괴롭히다 torment a small dog / be cruel to a puppy.

괴물 [ग्वेमुल] [**怪物**] [도깨비a monster; [정체를 알 수 없는 인물a mysterious figure; a mystery man. **괴짜** [**怪**]an eccentric [person]; an odd [a peculiar] fellow; a queer fish [fellow]; <美> a screwball; a character; an oddball. e.g. 저 사람은 괴짜야 He is an odd fish. / He is quite a character.

괴팍하다 [ग्वेफारव्वादा] [별나다] eccentric; cranky; [까다롭다] fastidious; finical; fussy; finicky; [완고하다] obstinate; bigoted. e.g. 괴팍한 사람] an eccentric person / a fastidious [finical] person.

굉장하다 [ग्वेंग्जांग्हादा] [**宏壯**-] [크다] grand; magnificent; imposing; [대단하다] spleendid; glorious; grand; excellent; superb; [엄청나다] awful; terrible; tremendous. e.g. 굉장한 부자an awfully rich man.

교가 [ग्योगा] [**校歌**] a school [college] song; an alma mater song.

교감 [ग्योगाम] [**交感**] rapport; mutual response; consensus; [mutual] sympathy. 교감하다sympathize [with each other]; respond[be responsive] to each other; share each other's feeling

교과 [ग्योग्वा] [**教科**] a lesson; a subject; a course of study; the curriculum.

교과서 [ग्योग्वासौ] [**教科書**] a textbook; a schoolbook; a text.

교구 [ग्योगू] [**教區**] a parish; an ecclesiastical district. e.g. 교구의 교회a parish church. 교구의 목사a parish priest.

교권 [ग्योग्वॉन] [教權] [교육상의] educational authority;[종교상의] ecclesiastical authority; ecclesiasticism.

교내 [ग्योनै] [校內] school grounds; a campus [대학의]. e.g. 교내의 intramural <game / team>.

교단 [ग्योदान] [教壇] [학교의] the [teacher's] platform; [교육계]the educational world. e.g. 교단에 서다be a teacher / teach [at a] school / teach a class

교대 [ग्योदै] [交代] [교체] [ग्योछे] [an] alternation; [a] change; [직무의] relief; [근무 시간의] a shith.

교도소 [ग्योदोसो] [矯導所] a prison; a jail jail 은 특히 <美>에서는 미결수, 경범 죄자용을 가리킴. <英> 에서는 공용어로 gaol 이 쓰임] [jail gao < 美 > [주연방의][a penitentiary; a pen. e.g. 교도소에 수감하다put <a person> in prison / send <a person> to prison. 교도소에 수감되다[들어가다] be sent to prison [jail] / be imprisoned.

교류 [ग्योर्यू] [交流] [교환] interchange; exchange. e.g. 한미간의 문화 교류 cultural exchange [interchange] between Korea and America.

교만 [ग्योमान] [驕慢] arrogance; haughtiness; pride; conceit. 교만하다 arrogant; haughty; proud; conceited; puffed-up

교묘 [ग्योम्यो] [巧妙] skill; dexterity; ingenuity; shrewdness; adroitness. 교묘하다 skillful; ingenious; clever; dexterous; shrewd; adroit; deth; adept.

교무 [ग्योमू] [教務] [학교의] school affairs; academic affairs [administration]; [교회 등의] the business affairs of a sect, temple, etc.

교문 [ग्योमुन] [校門] the gate of a school; a school gate.

교복 [ग्योबोक] [校服] a school uniform.

교사 [ग्योसा] [教師] a teacher; an instructor; [주로 초등 학교의] a schoolteacher; a master; <美> a schoolman; [초등 학교의] a schoolmaster; a schoolmistress [여교사a tutor [가정 교사]; a governess [여자 가정 교사

교생 [ग्योसैंग] [教生] a student teacher; a practice teacher. e.g. 교생으로 가다 do practice teaching.

교섭 [ग्योसौप] [交涉] [담판] negotiation; bargaining; a parley; an overture; [논의] discussion; conversation; [관계] connection; relation; dealing 교섭하다

negotiate; bargain; confer; parley; make an overture <to>; approach <a person with a proposal>; communicate <with>. e.g. 직접 교섭하다negotiate directly with <a person> / enter [go] into direct negotiations with <the boss>.

교수 [ग्योसू] [**教授**] [가르침] teaching; instruction; tuition; [대학의 강의자] a professor; <집합적> faculty. e.g. 지도 교수an adviser / a supervisor. 교수하다 teach; instruct <in>; give instruction <in>; give lessons to <a person> in. e.g. 한국어를 교수하다 teach <a person> Korean.

교신[**交信**] [ग्योशिन] communication [s]; contact; correspondence. 교신하다 contact; make [radio] contact <with>; communicate <with>. e.g. 신호로 배와 교신하다 communicate with a ship by signals.

교실 [ग्योशिल] [**教室**] a classroom; a schoolroom; a lecture room; a recitation room; [대학의] a department.

교안 [ग्योआन] [**教案**] a teaching plan; lesson plans. e.g. 교안을 짜다make a teaching plan / form a lesson schedule.

교양 [ग्योयांग] [**教養**] culture; refinement; education; cultivation. e.g. 교양이 있는 cultured / cultivated / educated.

교외 [ग्योवे] [**郊外**] the suburbs; the outskirts; the environs; suburbia.

교원 [ग्योवौन] [**教員**] a teacher; an instructor; [초등학교,중고교의 a schoolteacher; [한 학교 전체의 사] [the [teaching] staff; the faculty [대학의].

교육 [ग्योयुक] [**教育**] education; [학교 교육] schooling; [교수] instruction; teaching; [훈련 training; [훈육] discipline; [교양] culture; [양육] upbringing; breeding.

교장 [ग्योजांग] [**校長**] [국교,중고교의] a principal; a schoolmaster; a headmaster; [여자] a schoolmistress; a headmistress.

교재 [ग्योजै] [**教材**] teaching material [s]; teaching aids.

교정[ग्योजौंग] [**校正**] proofreading; correction of the press; correcting the press. 교정하다 proofread; read proofs; correct the press. e.g. 원고를 교정하다 correct a manuscript

교제 [ग्योजे] [**交際**] association; social intercourse; intercourse; society; company; friendship; acquainttance; fellowship. 교제하다 associate <with>; mix with; have intercourse <with>; keep company <with>; cultivate one's acquaintance

교직 [ग्योजीक] [**教職**] the teaching profession; [대학의][professorship; [종교의] the ministry; [religious orders; the priesthood. e.g. 교직에 있다 follow the teaching profession / be a teacher / teach school.

교직원 [ग्योजीग्वॉन] [**教職員**] the teaching staff; the faculty; [교원과 직원][the [teaching and clerical] staff [of a school].

교차 [ग्योछा] [**交叉**] intersection; crossing; [통신] transposition; crossing over. 교차하다 intersect; cross; [전선을] transpose.

교차로 [ग्योछारो] [**交叉路**] a crossing; an intersection; a crossroads; a cross street; a crossway. e.g. 교차로에서 at the [a] crossroads / at the intersection <of two roads>.

교체 [ग्योछे] [**交替**] replacement; a change; shithing

교칙 [ग्योछिक] [**校則**] school regulations; the statutes.

교탁 [ग्योथाक] [**教卓**] the teacher's desk [in a classroom]; a teaching desk.

교통[**交通** [왕래] traffic; [수송[방 transportation transport]; [연락] communication; [교제] < 英 >] intercourse.

교포 [ग्योफो] [**僑胞**] a Korean resident [national] abroad; a Korean residing abroad; <집합적> overseas Koreans.

교향곡 [**交響曲**] ग्योहयांगोक] a symphony.

교향악단 [ग्येहाकताान] a symphony orchestra.

교화 [ग्योह्वा] [**教化**] enlightenment; culture; edificetion; education; civilization; illumination; [야만인에 대한] reclamation; domestication; taming; [복음에 의한] evangelization. 교화하다 enlighten; civilize; culture; educate; illuminate; [야만인 등을] reclaim; domesticate; tame; [전도하다=] evangelize.

교환 [ग्योह्वान] [**交換**] exchange; interchange; reciprocation; reciprocity; give-and-take;[물물 교환]barter; swap; trade; substitution; [어음 교환][clearing. 교환하다 exchange <one thing for another>; make an exchange; trade; barter; interchange; give and take; counterchange; reciprocate; change <one thing for another>; swap; [어음을] clear <a check

교활 [ग्योह्वाल] [**狡猾**]

cunning; slyness; crathiness; crath; artfulness. 교활하다 cunning; sly; crathy; wily; sneaky; foxy; tricky.

교황 [ग्योह्वांग] [**教 皇**] a pope;[로마의] the Pope; the Sovereign [Supreme] Pontiff; the Vicar; the Holy Father; His Holiness the Pope <경칭> e.g. 교황의 papal.

교회 [ग्योह्वे] [**教會**] **1** [기독교의 단체,종파] [the] Church; an ecclesia. e.g. 가톨릭 교회 the [Roman] Catholic Church. 2 [그 건물] a church; a chapel. e.g. 교회에서 결혼하다be married in church.

교훈 [ग्योहुन] [**教訓**] a lesson; [우화 등의] a moral; instruction; edification; teachings; a precept; an injunction. e.g. 교훈을 주다give a lesson <to a person>.

-구[गु] [**口**] an opening; a mouth; a window; a hole; a wicket. e.g. 개찰 구a [platform] wicket. 출입구an entrance and exit.

구 [गु] [**九**] nine; [로마숫자] IX. e.g. 구배nine times. 구분의 1 a ninth.

구 [गू] [**句**] a phrase; an expression; a passage.

구-[गू] [**舊**] former; one-time; ex-; old; outgoing [퇴임한] e.g. 구세대 the old generation.

구간 [गूगान] [**區 間**] the section <between A and B>; a block [of railroad track]; a service area; an interval.

구강 [गूगांग] [**口腔**] the mouth; the oral cavity. e.g. 구강의 oral / of the mouth.

구걸 [गूगौल] [**求乞**] begging; asking alms; mendicancy. 구걸하다beg <one's bread>; go begging; live by asking alms; ask alms [charity].

구경 [गूग्यौग] **1** [관광] sight-seeing; a visit. 구경하다 see <a play>; visit <a museum>; see [do] the sights of; watch <a game>. e.g. 연극을 구경하다see a play. **2** [방관]. 구경하다 watch [with interest]; look on [at]. e.g. 군중은 그들의 싸움을 구경하고 있었다The crowd looked on at their fight.

구급 [गूगुप] [**救急**] first aid; relief; rescue. e.g. 구급용의 first-aid <medicine>.

구급차 [गूगुप्छा] [**救急車**] an ambulance <car>. e.g. 구급차를 부르다call an ambulance.

구기다 [गूगीदा] [옷 등이[을] 금이 생기[게 하]다] crumple; wrinkle; rumple; crease; crush; muss. e.g. 구겨진[구긴] 종이 조각a crumpled sheet of paper. 구겨지다be crumpled [wrinkled] / be rumpled / get mussed / get rucked up / become crease.

-구나 [गूना] [감탄] how; what; indeed. e.g. 참 불쌍하구나 What a pity! / Poor thing! / Poor fellow!

구내 [गूनै] [構 內] [시설,지의안] premises; precincts; [담벽이 있는] a compound; [학교 등의][ground; an enclosure; [건물에 인접한] a yard; a close [사원,학교의][e.g. 역 구내에[서][in the station yard.

구단 [गूदान] [球團] a corporation which owns a professional baseball [soccer] team.

구덩이 [गूदौंगी] [팬 땅] a [ground] depression; a hollow [place]; a cavity; a pit.

구도 [गूदो] [構 圖] [美] composition <of a painting>; planning. e.g. 구도를 잡다compose <a picture> / draw a rough sketch <of> / design <a picture / a sculpture>.

구독[गूदोक] [購讀] subscription. 구독하다subscribe for [to] <a newspaper / a magazine>; take; take in. e.g. 그는 수종의 잡지를 구독 하고 있다] He subscribes to [has a subscription to / takes] several magazines.

구두[गूदु] [단화] [a pair of] shoes; [장화] high shoes; boots; <집합적> footwear; footgear.

구두[गूदु] [口 頭] word of mouth. e.g. 구두로 전하다 convey [communicate] verbally.

구두쇠 [गूदुस्वे] a miser; a niggard; a stingy [close fisted / tightfisted] fellow; a skinflint; a screw; a penny pincher; a tightwad.

구렁[गूरौंग] **1** [패인 곳] a hollow [place]; a depression; a pit; a cavity. e.g. 구렁에 빠지다] fall into a pit [hole]. **2** [심연][the depths; a gulf; an abyss; an abysmal chasm; nadir. e.g. 가난의 구렁the depths of poverty.

구르다[1][गूरूदा] [데굴데굴] roll [over]. e.g. 굴러 떨어지다[공 등이 roll down <a slope> / [쓰러져 떨어지다] tumble [fell] down <the stairs>.

구르다[2] [गूरूदा] [발을]stamp [one's feet]; tread noisily; beat one's shoes <on the floor>. e.g. 초조하게 발을 구르다tap one's foot impatiently.

구름 [गूरूम] a cloud; <집합적> the clouds

구면 [गूम्यौन] [舊面] an old acquaintance; a familiar face. e.g. 그와 나는 구면이다 I have known him for a long time. / Our acquaintance is of long standing.

구명 [गूम्यौग] [**救命**] life-saving; sparing a person's life; clemency [죄수의]. 구명하다 save a person's life; save a person from death; spare a person's life; [항복자를] give quarter <to a person>. e.g. 그는 구명되었다 His life was saved.

구미 [गूमी] [**口 味**] [입맛] <one's> taste; <one's> palate; appetite. e.g. 구미를 돋우는 tempting / inviting / appetizing.

구박 [गूबाक] [**驅 迫**] ill-treatment; maltreatment; cruel treatment; mistreatment; abuse. e.g. 구박을 참아 내다 endure [bear] the severity of the treatment. 구박하다 persecute; ill-treat; mal-treat; abuse; treat <a person> harshly [roughly / cruelly]; be cruel to <a maid-servant>.

구별 [गूब्यौल] [**區別**] **1** [차이] a difference; [a] distinction; [차별] discrimination 구별하다] tell [know] <A from B>; distinguish <between A and B>; make a distinction <between>; discriminate <between the two things>[▷ difference 는 일반적인 말, distinction 은 미묘한 차이, discrimination 은 가치의 인식이 따름] [difference,distinction discrimination] [차이에 따라 나눔][a] classi-fication. 구별하다classify.

구부러지다 [गूबुरौजीदा] bend; bow; curve; stoop; turn. e.g. 구부러진 곳 a curve / a bend.

구분 [गूबुन] [**區分**] [분할] a division; [구획] a section; [분류] classification; [한계] demarcation. 구분 하다 [나누다] divide; [분류하다] sort [out

구비 [गूबी] [**具備**] 구비하다] possess; have; be possessed of. e.g. 모든 조건을 구비하다 fulfill all the conditions / satisfy all the requisites.

구사 [गूसा] [**驅使**] [자유자재로 씀] free use. 구사하다use freely; command; have a command of. e.g. 영어를 자유로이 구사하다 have a good [perfect / excellent] command of English / be a master of English.

구사일생 [गूसाइल्सैग] [**九死一生**] a narrow [hair-breadth] escape from [the jaw of] death. e.g. 그는 죽음을 모면했으나 그야 말로 구사일생이었다 He fortunately escaped death, but it was a very near thing.

구상 [गूसांग] [**構想**] [계획] a plan; [면밀한 계획][a

design; [착상][a] conception; an idea;[문예 작품의] a plot.

구색 [**गुसैक**] [**具色**] assortment. e.g. 구색을 갖추다 assort a stock of goods / keep [have] a rich [large] assortment of goods [in stock] / have a well-assorted stock.

구석 [**गुसोक**] **1** [모퉁이의 안쪽] a corner; a nook. e.g. 구석 자리a corner seat. **2** [치우친 곳] a recess; a nook; [외딴 곳] a remote [a secluded / a retired / a sequestered / an out-of-the-way] place [corner]. e.g. 시골 구석a remote country place / an out-of-the-way corner in the country / the backcountry. **3** [점,면] a point; a respect; an aspect; a side; an angle; a way; a manner. e.g. 모르는 구석이 없다 know every inch of <the neighborhood> / know <a thing> down to the last detail.

구석기 시대[**गुसौक्की शीदै**] [考] the Old Stone Age; the Pal [a] eolithic period [era].

구석지다 [**गुसौकजीदा**] recessed; retired; sequestered; secluded; covert; out-of-the-way. e.g. 구석진 곳a recess / a [covert] nook / an out-of-the-way place [corner] / the backcountry.

구성 [**गुसौंग**] [**構成**] [각 요소를 하나의 통일체로 만들기] composition; constitution; organization; formation; construction; make-up; configuration [분자의] plot. 구성하다 make; compose; constitute; organize; form; comprise; construct. e.g. 사회를 구성하다form a community / constitute a society.

구세대 [**गुसेदै**] [**舊世代**] the old generation.

구속 [**गुसोक**] [**拘束**] [a] restriction;[a] restraint; constraint; binding; [감금] confinement; detention[in custody]; [체포][an] arrest 구속하다 [제한하] restrict; place restrictions <on>; [규제하다] restrain <a person from doing>; [속박하다] bind; curb; be binding <upon / on>; place <a person> under restraint; detain <a person> in custody; arrest

구수하다 [**गुसूहादा**] **1** [맛이] tasty; pleasant-tasting; savory; [냄새가] nice-[sweet-] smelling; sweet. e.g. 구수한 맛a delicate flavor [savor / taste]. **2** [인품,이야기 등이] engaging; appealing; attractive; entertaining; interesting. e.g. 구수한 사람 an attractive [affable] person / a man of delicate charm.

구술[गुसुल] [口述] an oral statement; dictation. 구술하다 state orally; dictate <a letter to one's typist>. e.g. 그는 연설을 비서에게 구술하였다He dictated his speech to his secretary.

구슬리다[गुसुल्लिदा] [그럴듯한 말로] cajole; coaK wheedle; talk <a person into [out of] doing>; win <a person> over. e.g. 슬슬 구슬려서 만 원을 내도록 하다wheedle [coax] <a person> out of 10,000 won.

구슬프다 [गुसुलफुदा] sad; sorrowful; plaintive; pathetic; touching; doleful; melancholy; mournful. e.g. 구슬픈 이야기a sad [pathetic / sob] story / a sorrowful tale.

구식 [गुशिक] [舊式] an old type[style / fashion / school]. e.g. 그 옷은 구식이다The clothes are out of date.

구실[गुशिल] [직무,역할] [a] duty; an office; a function; a job; a mission; a role; a part; [책무] a] duty;[an] obligation. e.g. 자식 구실 a son's [daughter's] duties / one's filial duties.

구실[गुशिल] [口實] [핑계] an excuse <for>; a pretext; a pretense; a plea; make-believe. e.g. 그럴듯한 구실 a plausible excuse / a specious pretense.

구애[गुऐ] [求愛] courting; courtship. 구애하다court; woo; make advances. e.g. 그는 그녀에게 열렬히 구애하고있다He's doing everything he can to win her love. / He has been making impassioned advances to her.

구애 [गुऐ] [拘碍] adherence <to>; prejudice <against>; scruples. 구애하다adhere <to>; stick <to>; be particular [fussy] <about>. e.g. 비용에 구애받지 않고 without regard to cost / regardless of expense.

구어 [गुऔ] [口語] [the] spoken [colloquial] language; [a] colloquialism; a colloquial word.

구역 [गुयौक] [區域] [지역] an area; a district; a zone; a quarter; [한계] the limits; the boundary.

구역질[गुयौकचिल] [嘔逆-] nauseation; vomiting.

구원[गुवौन] [救援] [구조] relief; rescue; succor; deliverance; [기독교][गीदोक्यो] salvation; redemption. e.g. 구원의 손길을 뻗치다 extend a helping hand <to>.

구이 [गुई] meat [fish] roasted [broiled / grilled] with seasonings; grill [불고기]

구인 광고 [गुईन ग्वांगो] [求人廣告] an advertisement for help; a help-wanted advertisement; a want ad; a situation-vacant advertisement.

구입 [गुइप] [購入] purchase; buying. 구입하다 purchase; buy. e.g. 대량 구입하다make [effect] a heavy purchase <of>.

구전[गुजौन] [口傳] transmitting [conveying] by word of mouth; [oral] tradition. 구전하다 transmit by word of mouth; hand down[by word of mouth]; [소문을] spread; circulate

구절[गुजौल] [句節] [구와 절] phrases and clauses; [글도막] a phrase; a passage; a paragraph.

구정[गुजौग] [舊正] the lunar New Year's Day; the New Year [New Year's Day] by the old [lunar] calendar.

구제 [गुजे] [救濟] relief; help; aid; succor; deliverance; redemption; salvation [영혼의구제하다 relieve; give relief [aid] to; help; succor; save; deliver; redeem. e.g. 구제할 수 가 없는 beyond remedy / past sal-vation [redemption] / <비유> hopeless / irredeemable <criminal>.

구조[1] [गुजो] [救助] rescue; relief; succor; deliverance; aid; help; assistance. 구조하 rescue; relieve; save; aid; help; assist; salvage; succor; pick up [난파선의 사람 들을].

구조[2] [गुजो] [構造] [만듦새] structure; [a] cons-truction; [a] make; makeup; fabric; fabrication; set up; [조직] constitution; organization. e.g. 산업 구조 industrial structure.

구직 [गुजीक] [求職] job hunting; a hunt for a job. 구직하다 seek [for] a job [employment]; look[hunt] for a job.

구질구질 [गुजीलगुजील] 1 [상태가] dirtily; untidily; squalidly; slovenly. 구질구질하다] dirty; untidy; squalid; slovenly; filthy; foul. e.g. 구질구질 한 날씨 nasty [foul] weather. 2 [하는 짓이] meanly; basely; despicably; indecently. 구질구질하다 mean; base; sordid; despicable; indecent. e.g. 구질구질한 수를 쓰다 use a mean [dirty / slimy] trick.

구차하다 [गुछाहादा] [苟且-]1 [변변하지 못하다] clumsy; awkward; strained; ignoble; humiliating; unworthy; insignificant; worthless. e.g. 구차한 목숨 an ignoble existence / a humiliating life. 2 [가난하다] very poor; poverty-stricken; needy; hard-up; badly off; wretched. e.g. 구차한 살림 형편narrow [needy / straitened] circumstances.

구청 [गुछौग] [區廳] a ward

[district] office; a borough office. e.g. 마포 구청the Map'o Ward Office.

구체 [गुछे] [**具體**] e.g. 구체적인concrete / definite. 구체적으로 concretely / in the concrete / in a concrete way[form].

구체화[具體化] [형체 부여] embodiment; concretization; [실현] materiali-zation; actualization. 구체 화하다 embody; concre-tize; give shape[body] to; take [concrete] shape; mate-rialize; actualize.

구축 [गुछुक] [**構 築**] con-struction; building. 구축하다 construct; build. e.g.기반을 구축하다establish[build up] the foundation <of>.

구출 [गुछुल] [**救出**] rescue; deliverance; saving. 구출하다 rescue; save <a person from danger>; relieve; deliver.

구타 [गुथा] [**毆打**] a blow; [a] beating; [法] assault and battery. 구타하다give [deal] <a person> a blow; beat; assault; drub; make an assault on <a person>; assail with blows

구태여 [गुथैयौ] [일부러] inten-tionnally; on purpose; [특별히] especially; particularly. e.g.구태여 반대하지는 않겠다 have no particularly objection to it. / I will not object to it particularly

구토 [गुथो] [**嘔吐**] vomiting; emesis <*pl.* -ses>. 구토하다] vomit; throw up; be sick[at one's stomach].

구하다[1] [गुहादा] [**求-**] **1** [찾다] look for; seek[for / ather]; search for; pursue; want; need. e.g.셋방을 구하다] look for a room to let. **2** [청하다]ask for; call for; solicit[for]; look[turn] to <a person for something>. e.g. 자비를 구하다 ask mercy of <a person>. **3** [얻다] get; have; obtain; [찾아내다] find [out]; [사다] buy; purchase. e.g. 서울에서 구한 물건 a thing bought in Seoul.

구하다[2] [गुहादा] [**救-**] [위험, 죽음에서] rescue <a person> from <danger>; save <a person> from <death>;[고통,가난,나쁜 환경 등에서] relieve <a person> from <suffering>; release <a person> from <pain / distress>; help <a person> out of <a difficulty>; deliver [extricate] <a person> from <a difficulty>;[죄에서] redeem; reclaim.

구현 [गुह्यौन] [**具現**] incar-nation; embodiment; mate-rialization; realization 구현하다] embody; mate-rialize; realize; give con-crete form <to>. e.g. 작가 자신의 철학이 주인공 속에 구현되어 있다], The writer's own philosophy is embodied in the hero.

구형 [गुह्यौंग] [**舊型**] an old model [style / type].

구호[गुहो] [**救護**] **1** [재난,어려움에 처한 사람의] relief; aid. e.g. 따뜻한 구호의 손길을 뻗치다 extend a warm helping hand <to>. 구호하다aid; give aid to; give relief [help] to; relieve; help and protect.**2** [병자,부상자] nursing; tending; [medical] care [treatment]; cure.

구호하다 nurse; tend [attend on]; care for; treat; give <a person> a medical treatment; cure. e.g. 부상자를 구호하다 give aid to the injured [the wounded]

구호[गुहो] [**口號**] [주장을 나타내는 간결한 말 a slogan; a motto <*pl.* ~[e]s>; a catchword; a catchphrase; a rallying word. e.g. … 의 구호를 내걸고[...under the slogan of

구혼 [गुहोन] [**求婚**] a proposal [an offer] of marriage; courtship; wooing. 구혼하다propose [marriage] <to>; court; pay court <to>; seek <a lady's> hand in marriage; woo.

구획 [गुह्वेक] [**區劃**] [구분] division; demarcation; [한 구획] a section; a division; a compartment;[시가 등의] a block;[토지의]a lot [plot] [of land]; [경계] a boundary. 구획하다 draw a line of demarcation; mark off <one lot from another>; divide; partition; demar-cate; compartment; mark out <land>.

-국 [गुक] [**國**] a state; a country; a nation. e.g. 선진국an advanced[a developed] nation.

국[1] [**गुक**] **1** [탕] soup; broth. e.g. 국 건더기 solid stuff [ingredients] in soup. **2** [국물] the liquid part of a dish; <fish / meat> stock.

국[2] [गुक] [**局**] **1** [관청,회사 등의]a bureau; a department. e.g. 사무국a secretariat. **2** [바둑,장기의 승부] a game <of go [chess]>. e.g. 대국 playing] a game of go [chess] <with>.

국가 [गुक्का] [**國歌**] a national anthem.

국가 [गुक्का] [**國家**] a nation; a state; a country[▷ nation은 하나의 독립 정부하에 통일된 것, state는 주권이 있는 국가, country는 사람이 국민으로서 귀속되는 곳] [nation state country] **국경** [गुक्यौंग] [**國境**] a border; a frontier; the [national] boundary [bor-der]; the boundaries of a country.

국경일 [गुक्यौगिल] [國慶日] a national holiday.

국고 [गुक्को] [國庫] the [National] Treasury; the Exchequer; the coffers of the State; the public purse; the fisc.

국교 [गुकक्यो] [國交] diplomatic relations; national friendship; intercourse between nations. e.g. 국교를 맺다 enter into diplomatic relations <with>.

국군 [गूकक्युन] [國軍] [한 나라의 군대] a nation's armed [military] forces; government troops.

국권 [गूकक्वॉन] [國權] [국가 권력] the power of the state; [통치권]national sovereignty.

국기 [गुक्की] [國旗] the national flag [emblem / colors]; [海] an ensign.

국내[गुंग्नै] [國內] the interior. e.g. 국내의 internal / domestic / home [▷<英> 에서는 home을, <美> 에서는 domestic을 쓰는 일이 많음] home. domestic

국력 [गुंग्न्यौक] [國力] the strength [power] of a nation; [자원] the resources of a nation.

국립 [गुंग्निप] [國立] e.g. 국립의national / government-established.

국면 [गुंगम्यौन] [局面] [어떤 일의 형세] the state of affairs; the situation. e.g. 새로운 국면에 접어들다 take a new turn / enter [up] on a new phase / take on a new aspect.

국문 [गुंग्मुन] the national script; [한글] the Korean alphabet; [국어] the Korean language; the national language; [문학] the national literature; Korean literature; [국문으로 쓴 것] writings in Korean.

국문학 [गुंग्मुन्हाक] [國文學] [한국 문학] Korean literature; [학문] the study of Korean literature.

국물[गुंग्मुल] [국 등의] soup; broth; gravy; <fish / meat> stock.

국민[國民] <집합적> a nation; [인민] a people; [개개인] a national; a member of a nation; a citizen; a subject.

국방 [गुक्पांग] [國防] national defense [defence]; the defense of a country.

국보 [गुक्पो] [國寶] a national treasure; a treasure of th untry; an asset to the nation.

국비 [गुक्पी] [國費] national expenditure [expenses / outlay]; [나라의 자금] public funds; public money.

국사 [गुक्सा] [國史] the history of a nation; a national history; [한국사] the history of Korea; Korean history.

국산 [गुक्सान] [國產] home

[domestic] production; [한국산] Korean production.

국산품 [गुक्सान्फुम] [**國產品**] [자기 나라의] a domestic product; domestic goods; home products; home-made articles; home-produced[-manufactured] articles; [한국의] Korean [-made] products; articles made in Korea.

국수 [गुक्सो] noodles; vermicelli; spaghetti

국악 [गुगाक] [**國樂**] Korean classical music; Korean folk music.

국어 [गुगौ] [**國語**] [한 나라의 말] the national language; one's native language; one's mother tongue; the vernacular; [한국말] the Korean language; Korean.

국영 [गुग्यौंग] [**國營**] government [state] management; management by state. e.g. 국영의state-operated [-run] / under government management.

국왕 [गुग्वांग] [**國王**] [왕] a king; [세습 군주a monarch; [주권자] a sovereign; [통치자] a ruler.

국외 [गुग्वे] [**國外**] e.g. 국외로[에] outside the country / abroad / overseas / beyond seas.

국자 [गुक्चा] a dipper; a ladle; a scoop.

국장 [गुक्चांग] [**局長**] [관청의] the director [chief] of a bureau; [우체국 등의] the head of a post [telephone / telegraph] office.

국적 [गुक्चौक] [**國籍**] nationality; citizenship.

국제 [गुक्चे] [**國際**] international intercourse. e.g. 국제적인 international.

국제 연합 [गुक्चे यौन्हाप] [**國際聯合**] the United Nations[略 U.N., UN].

국채 [गुक्छै] [**國債**] [부채] [बुछै] a national debt [loan]; [공채][गोंग्छै] a public loan; [증권] national bonds; < 美 >government bonds; government securities.

국토 [गुक्थो] [**國土**] a country; a territory; a realm; a domain.

국한 [गुख्वान] [**局限**] localization; limitation. 국한하다] localize; confine; limit; set limits to. e.g. 빈곤은 반드시 한 지역에 국한되어 있는 것은 아니다Poverty is not necessarily is confined to only one area.

국호[गुखो] [**國號**] the name of a country.

국화 [गुख्वा] [**國花**] a nation-nal flower

국회[**國會**][गुख्वे] [한국,프랑스의]the National Assembly;[미국의] Congress;[영국의] Parliament; [일본,스웨덴의] the [National] Diet.

국회 의원 [गुख्वे उइवौन] [**國會**

ㄱ

議員] a member of the National Assembly; an[a National] Assemblyman; [미국의] a member of Congress; a Congress-man; a Congresswoman [여자 [영국의] a member of Parliament; an M.P. <pl. M.P.s, M.P's>; [일본의] a member of the Diet; a Dietman.

군[1] [गुन] [君] **1**[경칭] Mister [Mr.][▷ 동료, 친구, 손아랫 남자를 부를 경우, 영어에 서는 이름에 경칭을 붙이지 않음 e.g. 김군 [Mr.] Kim. **2** [자네] you. e.g. 군들 you fellows [people / chaps]. 그것은 군의 잘못 이다 You are to blame for that.

군[2] [गुन] [軍] [군대] an [the] army; a force / [armed] forces; troops; [단위] an army; [군부] military authorities.

군것질 [गुन्गौच्चिल] 군것질하다 eat between meals; <美> piece; spend one's pocket money on candy [sweets].

군계 일학 [गुन्ग्ये इहकि] [群鷄一鶴] the only figure among ciphers; the sun among inferior lights; a Triton among [of] minnows. e.g. 우리 사이에서 그 청년은 군계 일학 같은 존재였다 Among us, the youth looked like a jewel in a heap of trash.

군고구마 [गुन्गोगुमा] a roast [baked] sweet potato.

군대 [गुन्दै] [軍隊] the troops; armed forces; the forces; an army; a corps; the military.

군더더기 [गुन्दौदौगी] [쓸데없이 덧붙은 물건] an excre-scence; a superfluity; [공연히 따라다니는 사람] an unwanted follower; a hanger-on. e.g. 군더더기를 붙이다 add some-thing superfluous.

군데 [गुन्दे] a place; a spot; a point; a part. e.g. 한두 군데의 잘못 one or two mistakes.

군데군데[गुन्देगुन्दे] here and there; sporadically [산재하여Wat[in] places; [in] various places; sparsely. e.g. 군데군데 눈이 쌓이다 be covered with snow here and there. [페인트 등이]

군말 [गुन्माल] an unne-cessary [uncalled-for] re-mark; an expletive; [문장 등의] redundant [super-fluous] words. e.g. 건강의 중요성에 대해서는 군말이 필요 없다We do not need to dwell on [emphasize] the importance of health. 군말하다 say unnecessary things; make an uncalled-for remark.

군복 [गुन्बोक] [軍服] a military uniform; [육군의]

an army uniform; [해군의] a navy [naval] uniform; [공군의] an air-force uniform. **군사**[**軍事**][**गुन्सा**] military

군살 [**गुन्साल**] [군더더기살] flab; superfluous [waste] flesh. e.g. 군살을 빼다get rid of extra flesh / wear [work] off surplus fat.

군소리 [**गुन्सोरी**] [헛소리] talking in one's sleep [delirium]; [쓸데없는 말] an uncalled-for remark. 군소리하다 make an unnecessary remark; talk in one's sleep [delirium]; utter meaningless words.

군인 [**गुनीन**] [**軍人**]a serviceman; a servicewoman [여성]; a soldier [병사]; an officer [장교];[해군의] a sailor; [공군의] an airman; [육군의]a soldier.

군자[**गुन्जा**] [**君子**] a man of virtue [honor / honour]; a [true] gentleman.

군주[**गुन्जु**] [**君主**] [왕국,제국의] a monarch; [최고의 지배자] a sovereign; [통치자] a ruler

군중 [**गुन्जुंग**] [**群衆**] a crowd [of people][▷ 집합체를 가리킬 때는 단수, 군집 속의 하나 하나를 지칭할 때는 복수 취급]a multitude; a throng.

군침 [**गुन्छिम**] excessive saliva; slaver; slobber; drool. e.g. 군침을 흘리다 drivel / slaver / salivate / run [dribble] at the mouth / [부러워하다] be envious <of>. 군침[이] 돌다feel an appetite. e.g. 그는 불고기 냄새를 맡고 군침이 돌았다 His mouth watered when he smelled the roast meat.

굳건하다 [**गुक्कोन्हादा**] strong and steady; solid; reliable; firm; strong-minded; stout-hearted.

굳다 [**गुत्ता**] [굳어지다] become hard [hardened]; harden; become solid; [뻣뻣해지다] become stiffened; stiffen; [응결 하다] set; congeal [엉기다]; clot [피가]; curdle[우유가].

굳다[**गुत्ता**] **1** [딱딱하다] hard; solid; adamant[ine]; unyielding. e.g. 굳은 땅 hard [stiff / tough] soil. **2** [확고,견고하다] strong; firm; fast; tight; secure; steady; steadfast; stable; solid; sound. e.g. 굳은 결심a firm resolve [resolution].

굳세다 [**गुस्सेदा**] [몸이] strong; firm; stout; [마음이] strong-minded; stout-hearted <woman>. e.g. 굳세게 undauntedly / bravely / stout.

굳이 [**गुजी**] strongly; firmly; decisively; strictly; obstinately [고집스럽게][. e.g. 굳이 묻다inquire importunately.

굳히다 [**गुछिदा**] **1** [굳게 하다] harden; make hard; [응결

시키다] congeal; condense; curdle; freeze. e.g. 자갈을 시멘트로 굳히다 bind gravel with cement. **2** [강화하다] strengthen; [견고히 하다 solidify; consolidate; make secure. e.g. 기초를 굳히다 strengthen the basis

굴 [गुल] [**窟**] **1** [터널] a tunnel. e.g. 굴을 파다 dig a tunnel / build [bore / drive / cut / excavate / pierce] a tunnel <through> / tunnel <through> / excavate <the side of a hill>. **2** [동굴] a cave; a cavern; a grotto <*pl.*~[e] s>; an ex-cavation <in a rock>. e.g. 굴의 어귀 [입구] [a cave mouth. **3** [짐승이 사는 구멍] a lair; a den; a holt; an earth [여우등의]; a burrow [barrow] [토끼등의] e.g. 늑대 굴] a wolve's den [lair].

굴곡 [गुल्गोक] [**屈曲**] a bend; a curve; [관절의] flexion; [해안선등의] indentation; [광선의] refraction. e.g. 한국의 남해안은 굴곡이 심하다 The southern coast of Korea frequently runs in and out [is very rugged].

굴다 [गुल्ता] behave <toward>; conduct [bear] oneself; act; treat; demean oneself <like a man>. e.g. 심하게 굴다 act harshly <toward a person>.

굴뚝 [गुल्तुक] [집의] a chimney; [여러개한묶음의] a [chimney] stack; [기관, 기선의] a funnel; [난로의] a stovepipe. 굴뚝 같다 be quite anxious [eager] <to do>; have a strong urge <to do>; feel an irresistible impulse <to do>. e.g. 나도 가고 싶은 마음은 굴뚝같지만 다른 데 방문할 약속이 있다I would very much like [I am dying] to go, but I have another appointment to visit.

굴리다 [गुल्लिदा] **1** [구르게 하다] roll <a barrel / a wheel>; trundle <a cask>; tumble over <a barrel>. e.g. 구슬을 굴리는 듯한 목소리 a sweet silvery voice. **2** [방치하다] neglect; leave <a thing> unattended; lay aside. e.g. 책을 함부로 굴리다 toss a book to one side. **3** [돈놀이하다] lend out. e.g. 돈을 굴리다 lend one's money out at interest / practice usury. 돈을 잘 굴리다 invest one's money profitably. **4** [운행하다] run. e.g. 그는 버스를 5 대 굴린다 He has five buses running for business purposes.

굴복 [गुल्पोक] [**屈服, 屈伏**] sub-mitssion; surrender. 굴복하다 submit [surrender / yield / succumb / give in] <to>; bow one's head <to>; lick [kiss] the dust

굴욕 [गुर्योक] [**屈辱**] humiliation; indignity; disgrace; dishonor; shame; an insult. e.g. 남에게 굴욕을 주다 humiliate a person / subject a person to humiliation

굴절 [गुल्चौल] [**屈折**] **1** [꺾임] bending; a turn. e.g. 굴절이 많은 해안선 an uneven coastline. 굴절하다 bend; turn; make a turn. e.g. 그는 그녀에게 굴 절된 감정이 있다 [His feelings toward her are warped. **2** [理,光] refraction. e.g. 굴절성의 [굴절시키는] refractive [굴절하는] refrangible. 굴절하다 be refracted. **3** [어형 [語形] 등의] inflection; inflexion. 굴절하다 inflect; be inflected.

굴지 [गुल्ची] [**屈 指**] [손가락을꼽음] counting on one's fingers; [뛰어남] eminence; prominence. e.g. 한국굴지의 상업 도시 the leading commercial cities in Korea.

굴하다 [गुर्हादा] [**屈－**] **1** [몸을 굽히다] bend; stoop <to do>; bend over [down]. **2** [굴복하다] [yield [submit / succumb / give in / bow / knuckle under] <to>. e.g. 굴하지 않고 undauntedly / unflinchingly / nothing daunted <by failure> / in defiance of / in spite of.

굵다 [गुक्ता] [몸피가] big; thick; burly; [목소리가] deep; thick; [선이] heavy; [활자 등이] fat; [피륙의 바탕이] coarse; large. e.g. 굵은목소리 a deep voice.

굶기다 [गुम्कीदा] let <aperson> go hungry [foodless]; starve; make <a person> starve. e.g. 굶겨 죽이다] starve <a person> to death.

굶다 [गुम्ता] go foodless [hungry]; skip [miss / lose] a meal; starve; famish; fast. e.g. 굶어 죽다 die of [from] hunger / be starved [famished] to death.

굶주리다 [गुम्जुरीदा] **1** [먹을 것이 없어 주리다 starve; be famished; be hungry [▷ starve 는 식량 부족으로 쇠약 또는 아사하다, be hungry 는 배가 고프다, be famished 는 be hungry 를 과장한 표현] [starve, be hungry, be famished be hungry **2** [욕구가 충족되지 않다] hunger [hanker / thirst] for [ather]. e.g. 그는 지식에 굶주리고 있었다 He was hungry for knowledge. / He hungered ather knowledge **굽 1** [마소의] a hoof <*pl.* ~ s, hooves>. e.g. 갈 라진 굽 cloven hoofs. **2** [신 발의] a heel; [그릇의] a foot; a base; a stem <of a glass>. e.g. 굽이 높은 [낮 은] 구두 high-heeled [low-heeled] shoes.

굽다 [गुप्ता] [만곡하다] bend; curve; be crooked [stooped]; warp. e.g. 굽 은 길 a winding path.

굽다 [गुप्ता] 1 roast [고기를] broil [고기, 생선을]; bake [빵을]; toast [빵 조각이나 김을 e.g. 잘 구워진 well done / well baked. 2 [도자기 등을] [दोजागी दुंगल] bake; fire; make <china>; burn <bricks / lime>; [숯을] produce; burn <charcoal>. e.g. 도자기 [벽돌]를 굽다 bake [fire] pottery [bricks].

굽실 [गुप्शिल] bowing [kowtowing] obsequiously [fawningly]. 굽실거리다 [복종하다] bow [and scrape]; truckle [yield] <to>; [아첨하다] kowtow <to>; cringe <to>; crouch. e.g. 그는 사장 앞에서 늘 굽실거린다 He always kowtows [humbles] himself before the president.

굽히다 [गुफीदा] 1 [구부리다] bend <one's knees>; stoop <oneself>; hook <one's finger>; crook <one's arm>; bow <one's head>. e.g. 허리를 굽히다 bend one's back / bend forward / bend over / bow. 2 [굴하다] yield; submit; give in; bend <to / before>. e.g. 주장을 굽히다 concede a point

굿 [गुत] [무당의] an exorcism; practices of an exorciser

궁궐 [गुंग्वौल] [宮闕] the royal palace. e.g. 궁궐 같은 집 a palatial residence / a palace.

궁극 [गुंगुक] [窮極] finality; extremity; eventuality. e.g. 궁극적으로는 같은 결과가 된다 Ultimately [In the long run / In the end] the result will be the same.

궁금증 [गुंगुक] [-症] x [호기심] curiosity; [염려] anxiety.

궁금하다 [गुंगुम्हादा] anxious [worried / concerned / nervous] <about>; <서술적> feel wonder [curious / curiosity]; wonder <about / if / whether / how / when / who>.

궁둥이 [गुंग्दुंगी] the buttocks; the hips; the backsides; the seat <of one's pants>; the bottom; [마소의] the rump.

궁리 [गुंग्नी] [窮理] [연구] study [research] of the laws of nature; [생각함] deliberation; consideration; thinking [pondering] over 궁리하다 [연구하다] study the laws of nature; [생각하다] ponder [think / mull] over; cast about [in one's mind] <for a good plan>.

궁상 [गुंग्सांग] [窮狀] a sad [sorry] plight; a distressed state [condition]; straitened circumstances. e.g. 궁상스러운 poor-looking.

궁색 [गुंग्सैक] [窮塞] poverty; destitution; want; distress; straitened circumstances. 궁색하다 poor; destitute

<of>; distressed. e.g. 살림이 궁색하다 be in needy [straitened] circumstances / be badly off.

궁여지책 [गुंग्योजीछैक] [窮餘之策] the last resort [expedient]; a desperate measure. e.g. 궁여지책으로서 as the last resort [expedient] / as a desperate measure [shith].

궁전 [गुंग्जौन] [宮殿] a [royal] palace.

궁지 [गुंग्जी] [窮地] **1** [생활의] poverty; destitution. **2** [곤란한 지경] a difficult situation; a predicament; a sad [sorry] plight; a dilemma; extremity; a fix a hot-seat. e.g. 궁지에 몰리다 [몰려 있다] stand [be] at bay / be pushed to the wall / be driven into a corner / be placed in a fix.

궁핍 [गुंग्फिप] [窮乏] destitution; want; distress; indigence; poverty; penury; necessity-ous circumstances. 궁핍하다 destitute; poor; penurious; needy; <서술적> be in poverty [need]; be reduced to poverty; be in needy [straitened] ircumstances

궁하다 [गुंग्हादा] [窮-] **1** [경제적으로] destitute; needy; hard up; indigent; penurious. e.g. 돈이 궁하다 be in need of money. **2** [궁지에 몰리다] cornered; <서술적> be driven to the wall; be in a dilemma [fix]; get into a scrape. e.g. 궁한 새가 품에 날아들면 포수도 쏘지 않는다 Even the hunter will refrain from killing the bird that has flown to him for shelter. / We help those who appeal to us in distress.

궁합 [宮合] [गुंग्हाप] marital harmony as predicted by a fortuneteller. e.g. 궁합을 보다 compare the horoscopes of a young couple.

궂다 [गुत्ता] **1** [언짢다] bad; ill; undesirable; irksome; [불길하다] ominous; [성질이] cross; bad. e.g. 심술궂다 be bad-natured / be cross-minded. **2** [날씨가] bad; foul; nasty; inclement; rainy; snowy; wet; soggy. e.g. 궂은 날씨 nasty weather. **궂은일** [गुजनिल] [언짢은일] an ugly job; an untoward event. e.g. 좋은일이 있으면 궂은일도 있다 Good and evil are interwoven. / Every cloud has a silver lining.

-권 [ग्वॉन] [權] [권력] authority; power; [권리] a right; a claim; [이권] a concession.

-권 [ग्वॉन] [券] a bond; a ticket; a card; a [bank] note. e.g. 백 원권 a 100-won note [bill].

권 [ग्वॉन] [卷] [책의] a volume; a book; a copy

[부수]. e.g: 제 1 권 the first volume / volume one

권고 [ग्वॉन्गो] [**勸告**] <a piece of> advice; counsel; recommendation; expostulation [충고]. 권고하다 advise <a person to do / that>; counsel a person <to do>.

권력 [ग्वॉलल्योक] [**權力**] power <over / with>; authority <over / with>; [세력] influence <over / with>.

권리 [ग्वॉल्ली] [**權利**] [정당한 요구] a right <to / to do / of doing>; a claim <to> [청구권]; a privilege [특권] a title [소유권].

권선 징악 [ग्वॉन्सौन जीगाक] [**勸善懲惡**] promotion of virtue and reproval of vice; encourageing good and punishing evil.

권위 [ग्वॉन्वी] [**權威**] authority; power; [위엄] dignity; majesty; prestige.

권유 [ग्वॉन्यु] [**勸誘**] an inviteation <to>; [운동] canvassing; solicitation; [장려] persuasion; encouragement. 권유하다 ask; invite <to do>; induce; persuade <a person to do / into doing>; canvass <for contributions>.

권익 [ग्वॉनिक] [**權益**] [rights and] interests. e.g. 국가의 권익 national interests.

권장 [ग्वॉन्जांग] [**勸奬**] encouragement; recommendation; promotion. 권장하다 encourage; recommend; promote.

권총 [ग्वॉन्छोंग] [**拳銃**] a pistol; a revolver [연발총] a handgun; a gun; a rod.

권태 [ग्वॉन्थै] [**倦怠**] weariness; fatigue; languor; tedium; ennui. e.g. 권태를 느끼다 feel tired [languid] / become weary [tired / fatigued] / feel languor / be [get] bored / have a tired feeling.

권투 [ग्वॉन्थु] [**拳鬪**] boxing; pugilism; a prize-fight [흥행].

권하다 [ग्वॉन्हादा] [**勸-**] **1** [권고하다] ask; exhort; advise; suggest; encourage; persuade. e.g. 담배를 끊으라고 권하다 advise <a person> to give up [quit] smoking / advise against smoking. **2** [추천하다] recommend. e.g. 책을 권하다 recommend a book <to a person>. 형이 이 사전을 나에게 권했다 My brother recommended this dictionary to me. **3** [음식, 물건을] [offer <a person something>; present <a person with something>. e.g. 담배 [차]를 권하다 offer a cigarette [a cup of tea].

권한 [ग्वॉन्हान] [**權限**] right; authority; power; [관할권] jurisdiction; [관청,법원 등의] competence; competency;

[권능의 한도] the authorized limit of rights [powers].

궐기 [ग्वॉल्गी] [**蹶起**] 궐기하다 rise and go into action; rise; rouse <oneself> to action; spring up; stand up <against>

궤도 [ग्वेदो] [**軌道**] **1** [천체의] an orbit; a circle. e.g. 궤도의 orbital. **2** [어떤 일의 과정, [a] track. e.g. 궤도에 오르다[일이] be started along the right lines / get going.

궤변 [ग्वेब्यौन] [**詭辯**] sophism; [a] sophistry; quibbling; a false [vicious] syllogism; a paradox [역설]. e.g. 그는 궤변을 늘어놓는 버릇이 있다 He has a way of using sophistry.

귀 [**ग्वी**] [듣는 기관] an ear; [청각] hearing. 귀가[번쩍] 뜨이다 (1) [정신이] have one's attention drawn <to>; have <it> brought to one's ears. e.g. 그 일에 귀가 번쩍 뜨이다 have the matter come to one's attention. (2) [이해가] catch on; grasp; begin to understand; get it. e.g. 일에 귀가 번쩍 뜨이다 catch on to the job.

귀- [ग्वी] [**貴**] **1** [당신의] your; your esteemed. e.g. 귀사 your company. **2** [귀한] valuable; noble; precious. e.g. 귀금속 the precious [noble] metals.

귀가 [**歸 家**] return [ing] home; home-coming. 귀가하다 [돌아오다] come home; return home; [돌아가다] go home.

귀감 [ग्वीगाम] [**龜鑑**] a model; a paragon; a pattern; a good [shining] example; a mirror; an exemplar. e.g. 군인의 귀감 a model soldier / a pattern [paragon] of soldiery. 남의 귀감이 되다 exemplify oneself / set an example to the world.

귀걸이 [**ग्वीगौरी**] 귀고리

귀공자 [ग्वीगोंग्जा] [**貴公子**] a young nobleman; a scion of a noble family.

귀국 [ग्वीगुक] [**歸國**] returning home from abroad; home-coming; return to one's country. 귀국하다 go [come / return] home; return [go back] to one's country.

귀금속 [ग्वीगुम्सोक] [**貴金屬**] [쉽게 화학 변화를 일으키지 않는 금속] a noble metal; [값비싼 희귀금속] a precious metal.

귀납 [ग्वीनाप] [**歸納**] induction; generalization. e.g. 귀납적으로 추론하다 reason inductively [a posteriori]. 귀납하다 induce; generalize; make an induction <from>. e.g. 경험에서 일반적 원리를 귀납하다 induce general principles from one's experience.

귀농 [ग्वीनोंग] [**歸農**] returning to the farm [soil]. 귀농하다 return to [go back to] farming; [원래 농민이 아닌 사람이] become a farmer [rancher]; take up farming [ranching].

귀담아듣다 [ग्वीदामादुत्ता] listen willingly [attentively]; listen carefully; stuff one's ears with <a person's words>. e.g. 그는 내 충고를 귀담아듣지 않았다 He turned a deaf ear to my advice.

귀동냥[ग्वीदोंगन्यांग hearsay; second-hand knowledge. e.g. 귀동냥으로 배우다 pick something up from others [others convers-ation] / learn about something by listening to what people say.

귀띔 [ग्वीत्विम] a suggestion; a hint; a tip; an intimation. 귀띔하다 give a hint [tip]; suggest; tip off; intimate; give [make] suggestion. e.g. 남에게 사실을 귀띔해 주다 tip a person off to the fact.

귀머거리 [ग्वीमौगौरी] a deaf person; <집합적> the deaf.

귀빈 [ग्वीबिन] [**貴賓**] an honored [a distinguished] guest; an important guest.

귀성 [ग्वीसौंग] [**歸省**] home-coming; coming home; visiting one's parents at home. e.g. 휴가로 귀성 중이다 He is home for the vacation [holidays].

귀소 본능 [ग्वीसो बोन्नुंग] [**歸巢本能**] the homing instinct.

귀신 [ग्वीशिन] [**鬼神**] **1** [혼령] a departed soul; a spirits; [유령] a ghost; [요괴] apparition. e.g. 귀신이 나오는 집 a haunted house. **2** [뛰어난 사람] a master; an expert; a proficient <in>; a demon <at golf>. e.g. 그는 돈을 버는 데는 귀신이다He is an expert at moneymaking.

귀여워하다 [ग्वीयौवोहादा] love; be affectionate to; treat with affection; pet; make a pet of; be attached to; treat tenderly [kindly]; [애무하다] caress; fondle. e.g. 어머니들은종종 아이들을 너무 귀여워한다 Mothers othen spoil their children.

귀엽다 [ग्वीयौप्ता] lovely; charm-ing; cute; attractive; winn-ing; dear; darling; [예쁘다] sweet; nice; pretty; cute <girl / hat>. e.g. 귀여운 애a lovable [sweet / charming] child.

귀족 [**貴族**] <집합적> the nobility; nobles; the peerage; the aristocracy; blue blood; [훌륭한 가문의 개인] a noble; a nobleman; a noble-woman; a peer; a peeress; an aristocrat.

귀중 [ग्वीजुंग] [**貴重**] precious-ness. 귀중하다 precious; valuable. e.g. 귀중한 보물

precious treasures.

귀찮다 [ग्वीछान्था] troublesome; annoying; bothering; harassing; bothersome; tiresome; pesky; irksome <work>. e.g. 귀찮은 일 troublesome [bothersome] task / a bother.

귀퉁이 [ग्वीथुंगी] [모퉁이] a corner; an edge. e.g. 탁자 귀퉁이 the corner of a table.

귀하 [ग्वीहा] [**貴下**] **1** [당신] you. **2** [께] [남자에게] Mr. <*pl.* Messrs.>; Esq.; [여자에게] Ms[Ms.] <*pl.* Mses, Ms's>; [기혼녀에게] Mrs [Mrs.] <*pl.* Mrs., Mmes.>; [미혼녀에게] [Miss <*pl.* ~ es>. e.g. 아담 스미스 귀하 Mr. Adam Smith / Adam Smith, Esq.

귀하다 [ग्वीहादा] [**貴-**] **1** [고귀하다] noble; august; high; exalted; honorable; venerable. e.g. 귀한 가문 a noble family. **2** [드물다] rare; scarce; few; [진귀하다] uncommon; unusual; curious; precious; valuable; highly prized. e.g. 요즈음은 좋은 쌀이 귀하다 Nowadays good rice is rather rare [hard to get]. 생명보다 귀한 것은 없다 Nothing is so precious as life.

귀화 [ग्वीह्वा] [**歸化**] [국적이전] naturalization.

귓볼 [ग्वीपुल] an earlobe; an earlap; the lobe of the ear.

귓전 [ग्वीचौन] the ear rims. e.g. 귓전에서 about [close to] one's ears. 귓전에 대고 소리치다 yell into <a person's> ear

규격 [ग्युग्यौक [**規格**] a standard; a norm; a gauge.

규명 [ग्युम्यौंग] [**糾明**] a close examination; a searching [grilling / minute] examination. 규명하다 examine <a matter> closely; look [inquire] into <a matter> minutely

규모 [ग्युमो] [**規模**] [규범] a rule; a pattern; [짜임새] a scale; [범위] [a] scope; [설계] [a] plan; [구조] [गुजो] structure. e.g. 규모가 큰large-scale <warfare> / large in scale.

규범 [ग्युबौम] [**規範**] [본보기] a model; an example; a pattern; [법칙,원리] a law; a [fundamental] rule; a regulation; a principle; [표준] a standard; a norm; a criterion <*pl.* -ria, ~s>. e.g. 규범적인 normative.

규율 [ग्युयुल] [**規律**] [질서] order; discipline; observance [수도회의][[조직] system. e.g. 엄격한 규율] rigid discipline.

규정 [ग्युजौंग] [**規定**] [규칙] rules; regulations; [정한 것] stipulations; prescriptions; [조항] provisions.

규제 [ग्युजे] [**規制**] [규칙] regulation; [제한] restricttion; [통제] control. 규제하다 regulate; control; restrict. e.g. 교통을 규제하다 regulate traffic.

규칙 [ग्युछिक] [規則] a rule; regulations. e.g. 규칙을 지키다 observe [stick by] the rules / act upon a rule / keep [conform] to a rule / follow [obey] a rule

규탄 [ग्युथान] [糾彈] impeachment [▷ 특히 <美>에서는 공무원에 대한 탄핵의 뜻이 있음] censure; denunciation; arraignment. 규탄하다 impeach; censure; denounce; arraign <a person for something>; take [call / bring] <a person> to task <for something>.

균 [ग्युन] [菌] **1** ⇨ 균류 **2** ⇨ 세균 e.g. 결핵균 tuberculosis bacilli. **3** ⇨ 병균 e.g. 균이 묻은 옷 infectious clothing.

균등 [ग्युनदुंग] [均等] equality; uniformity; evenness; [a] parity [세력처우 등의] e.g. 기회 균등 equality in opportunity 균등하다 equal; even; uniform.

균열 [ग्युन्यौल] [龜裂] **1** [물체의] a crevice; a chap; a crack; a fissure; a cleth; a crevasse [빙하 등의]. e.g. 지면의 균열] a crack [fissure] in the ground. 균열하다 crack; be cracked; fissure; cleave. **2** [관계의] a break; a rupture; a crack. e.g. 그것 때문에 두 사람의 우정에 균열이 생겼다 That has impaired [caused a crack in] their friendship. 균열하다 break <with>; fall out <with>; split <with>; be at odds <with>.

균일 [ग्युनिल] [均一] uniformity; equality. e.g. 천 원 균일 a uniform rate of 1,000 won.

균형 [ग्युन्ह्यौग] [均衡] balance; [an] equilibrium; equipoise. e.g. 균형이 잡혀 있다 be[well-]balanced / be in balance [equilibrium / equipoise].

귤 [ग्युल] [橘] an orange; [중국 원산의] a mandarin; [북미,남아프리카 원산의] a tangerine. **귤껍질** [ग्युल्कौपचिल] orange peel; the peel of an orange.

그[1] [गु] **1** [그이] that man; that woman; he; she. e.g. 그는[가] he. **2** [그것] it; that. e.g. 그로 인하여 on that account [score] / therefore / consequently.

그[2] [गु] that; those; the; [앞에서 말한] the same; [불확실한] <the man> in question; [강조하여] [the very; [그것의] its. e.g. 그 사람 he / she / that person / that [the] man [woman].

그것 [गुगौत] that one; that; it.

e.g. 그것은 그렇지만 it may be so, but….

그까짓 [गुकाचित] [그 정도의] so trivial; so trifling; [그와 같은] like that. e.g. 그까짓 일로 울다니 You must not weep over a trifle like that.

그나마 [गुनामा] and that; at that; and yet; still; even so; nevertheless. e.g. 그 커피는 2 천 원이나 했는데 그나마 질이 좋은 편이 아니었다 The coffee cost 2,000 won and not a very good one at that.

그날 [गुनाल] <on> that day; [강조하여] <on> the very [same] day. e.g. 그날의 일 the day's work.

그냥 [गुन्यांग] **1** [그대로] as it is; as it stands; intact; in the same way as before; still. e.g. 그냥그대로 있다 remain as it was / remain intact / be leth untouched. **2** [줄곧] all the time [way]; [all] through; throughout; continuously. e.g. 그냥 울고만 있다do nothing but cry.

그네 [गुने] a swing; a trapeze.

그녀 [गुन्यौ] [-女] she.

그놈 [गुनोम] that fellow [chap / rogue]; that guy; that blighter; that bastard.

그늘 [गुनल] **1** [응달] shade. e.g. 큰 나무 그늘에서 in the shade of a big tree. **2** [남의 보호] protection; care. e.g. 부모님 그늘에서 자라다 grow up under the protection [good care] of one's parents / grow up under one's parents wings [one's parental roof]. **3** [드러나지 않는 처지] obscurity. e.g. 그늘에서 사는 사람 a social outcast / a person with a shady past / an ex-convict / a fugitive from justice.

그다지 [गुदाजी] **1** [별로,그리] <not> very[much / greatly]; rarely; seldom; little. e.g. 그다지 춥지 않다 It is not very cold. / I do not feel very cold. **2** [그러한 정도로까지] so; so much; to that extent; that much; to such an extent. e.g. 그다지 먼 길인 줄은 몰랐다 I never thought it would be such a long way.

그대[गुदे] thou; you. e.g. 그대들] ye / you / you people [folks].

그대로 [गुदेरो] as it is [stands]; in the same way as before; like that; that way; intact; untouched. e.g. 있는 그대로의 사실 a plain [an unvarnished / a straight / an undisguised] fact.

그뒤 [गुदवी] since [then]; since that time; ever since; from then on; from that time on. e.g. 그뒤 그에게서 소식이 없다 I have heard nothing from him since

그때 [गुत्तै] then; [at] that time [moment]; [on] that occasion. e.g. 마침 그때 just at that moment / just then

그래 [गुरै] **1** [대답의] yes; so. e.g.너 오겠니? 그래 갈께 Will you come? – Yes, I will. **2** [감탄,놀람] indeed. e.g. 과연 그래 You are quite [too] right. / So it is.

그래도 [गुरैदो] but [still]; and yet; nevertheless; though; still; however; all the same; for all that; at any rate. e.g.이상하게 들릴지 모르지만 그래도 사실이다 It may sound strange, but it is true for all that.

그래서 [गुरैसौ] and; [and] so; [and] then; thereupon; hereupon; accordingly; for that [this] reason; on that account. e.g. 그래서 나는 인천으로 이사가기로 했다 So I decided to move to Inch'ŏn.

그래프 [गुरैफु] a graph.

그램 [गुरैम] a gram [me] [기호]

그러나 [गुरौना] but; however; though; and yet. e.g. 나는 가고 싶었다. 그러나 갈 수 없었다 I wanted to go, but I couldn't.

그러면 [गुरौम्यौन] **1** [그렇게 하면] and. e.g. 구하라. 그러면 너희에게 주실 것이다 Ask and it shall be given you. **2** [그러하다면] [if [it is] so; if that is the case; in that case; then; well; well then. e.g. 그러면 나는 어떻게 해야 하지 In that case, what shall I do?

그러므로 [गुरौमुरो] so; therefore; hence; for that reason; accordingly; on that ground; on that account; consequently. e.g. 그러므로 나는 나의 의도를 단념했다 I accordingly gave up my intention.

그럭저럭 [गुरौक्चौरौक] somehow [or other]; [in] one way or another; by some means [or other]; by hook or by crook; barely. e.g. 그럭저럭 살아간다 manage to get along, one way or another.

그런 [गुरौन] e.g. 그런 경우에는 in that case / in such a case / in case like that.

그런데 [गुरौन्दे] but; however; and yet; by the way; by the bye; now.

그럴듯하다 [गुरौल्दुथादा] **1** [있을 법하다] likely; [수긍할 만하다] plausible. e.g. 그럴듯한 이야기] a likely story. **2** [제법 훌륭하다] fair; passable; considerable; respectable; decent. e.g. 그럴듯한 연설] a speech worth hearing [listening to].

그럼 [गुरौम] [긍정] yes; <美>

yah; yeah; indeed; right; quite so; certainly; of course. e.g. 뜰에 들어가도 됩니까? – 그럼 May I go into the garden? – Yes, certainly.

그렁그렁 [गुरौंग गुरौंग] [액체가] almost full [to the brim]; all watered up;[눈물이] tearfully; suffused with tears. 그렁그렁하다 almost full [to the brim]; brimful; all watered up; tearful; suffused with tears. e.g. 눈물이 그렁그렁한 눈 tearful [watery] eyes / eyes filled [suffused / brimming] with tears.

그렇게 [गुरौख्ये] **1** [그러한 정도까지] [so; so much; like that. e.g. 그렇게까지 to such an extent / so [thus] far / that much. **2** [그러하게][in that manner; [in] that way; like that; so. e.g. 사정이 그렇게 되었다 Such is the case

그렇다 [गुरौथा] [그러하다] so; such; like that; that way; [대답] Yes; No; That's right. e.g. 바로 그렇다 be just [quite / exactly / precisely] so / be just like that.

그렇다면 [गुरौथाम्यौन] e.g. 그렇다면 내가 가겠다 In that case [If that's the case] I will go.

그렇지 않으면 [गुरौछी आनुम्यौन] otherwise; else; or [else]; if not so; were it not so. e.g. 자유를 달라, 그렇지 않으면 죽음을 달라Give me liberty, or give me death!

그렇지만 [गुरौछीमान] but; however; still; nevertheless; though; although; and yet; be that as it may; for all that. e.g. 그렇지만 값이 비쌌어요 It was expensive, though. **그루** [गुरू] **1** [나무의] a stump; a stock;[곡식의] stubbles <of rice plants>. **2** [식물을 세는 단위] a plant; a tree. e.g. 감나무 세 그루 three persimmon trees. 한 그루의 느티나무 a zelkova [tree].

그룹 [गुरूप] a group.

그르다 [गुरूदा] **1** [옳지 아니하다] wrong; erroneous; false; incorrect; mistaken; <서술적> be in error; be in the wrong; be at fault. e.g. 옳고 그름을 가리다 tell [know] right from wrong / discriminate between right and wrong. **2** [잘될 가망이 없다] hopeless; <서술적} be done for; be all over; be all fouled up. e.g. 그 환자는 이제 글렀다 The patient has little chance to pull through. / The patient is hopeless. **3** [상태, 조건 등이 좋지 않다] bad; foul; nasty; ill. e.g. 맛이 글렀다 It tastes bad [flat]. / It is unsavory [unpalatable].

그릇 [गुरूत] [용기] a receptacle; a container; a bowl; [액체를 담는 용기] a vessel. e.g. 밥그릇 a rice bowl. **2** [능력,도량] caliber; [calibre]; capacity; capability; ability. e.g. 그릇이 큰[작은] 사람 a man of high [poor] caliber.

그릇되다 [गुरूत्दवेदा] be mistaken; go amiss [wrong]; go to pot; end in a failure; fail; be spoiled [ruined]; come to naught [nought]. e.g. 그릇된 생각 a mistaken [an erroneous] idea / a wrong opinion.

그리고 [गुरीगो] and; [and] then; and also; as well as. e.g. 방을 먼저 치우고 그리고 공부를 시작했다 First I tidied up my room, and then I began studying.

그리다[1] [गुरीदा] long [sigh / languish / pine] for; yearn ather [for]; be sick for; miss; be attached to. e.g. 고국을 그리다 pine for homeland / be homesick / be filled with a longing to see one's home again.

그리다[2] [गुरीदा] **1** [그림 등을] draw; picture; paint [채색 하여]; sketch [약도로]; [도형을] construct; describe. e.g. 유화를 그리다 paint in oil. **2** [묘사하다] depict; describe; delineate; portray. e.g. 그 작품은 현실 생활을 그린 것이다 The work is a picture of real life.

그리움 [गुरीउम] yearning; longing; attachment; affecttion; nostalgia. e.g. 그리움을 못 이기다 feel an irresistible yearning for [ather].

그리워하다 [गुरीवोहादा] long [yearn / pine] for. e.g. 고향을 그리워하다 have a longing for home / be homesick / pine for home.

그림 [गुरिम] [일반적으로] a picture; [연필, 펜, 크레용화] a drawing [무채색화] [수채화, 유화] a painting; [사생화 a sketch; [삽화] an illustration [▷ 페이지내의 일부에 넣는 삽화는 a cut, 전면적인 삽화는 a plate 라고 함] [a cut, a plate [도형] a figure; [설명도] a diagram.

그림자 [गुरिम्जा] **1** [음영] a shadow; a si'khouette. e.g. 검은 그림자 a dark shadow. **2** [영상] a reflection; an image; a figure; a shadow. e.g. 거울에 비친 그림자 the picture in a mirror. 호수에 비친 산의 그림자 the mountain reflected [mirrored] in the lake. 물속에 비친 자신의 **3** [자취] a shadow; a sign; a trace; a clue. e.g. 그림자도 보이지 않다 be completely [entirely] out of sight / there is no sign of <a person> there.

그립다 [गुरिप्ता] dear; sweet; beloved; longed-for; <서술적> yearn ather [for] <a person>; miss <a friend>. e.g. 그리운 사람 my beloved / my dearest.

그만 [गुमान] **1** [그 정도로] that much and no more; to that extent only; no more than that; [명령형] Stop <doing>. e.g. 그만 울어라 Do not cry any more. **2** [곧] as soon as; no sooner than; immediately; directly. e.g. 그는 화를 버럭 내면서 그만 가버렸다 He went off immediately in a fit of sudden temper [anger]. **3** [부주의로] carelessly; by mistake [accident]; [본의 아니게] involuntarily; unintentionally. e.g. 그만 …하다 do by mistake / be careless enough to do.

그만두다 [गुमान्दुदा] **1** [중지하다] stop <doing / a fight>; discontinue <doing>; cut out; [포기하다] give up; abandon; renounce; [취소하다] call off <a meeting>. e.g. 계획을 그만두다] abandon [give up / lay aside / drop] a plan / give up a project [an idea / a scheme]. **2** [폐지하다] abolish; do away with; discontinue. e.g. 허례를 그만두다] dispense [do away with] formalities. **3** [술P습관 등을] stop <drinking>; give up <smoking>; break oneself of <a habit>; [삼가다] refrain [abstain] from <drinking>. e.g. 술을 그만두다 give up drinking / go on the wagon. 그의 술마시는[담배 피우는] 습관을 내가 그만두게 해주리라 I will cure [break] him of the habit of drinking [smoking]. **4** [사임하다] resign <one's post>; leave [quit / throw up] <one's job>; retire <from office>. e.g. 회사를 그만두다 leave [the service of] the company.

그만큼 [गुमानखुम] [그 분량] as much as that; as [that] much; [그 정도] to that extent; in that degree.

그만하다 [गुमानहादा] **1** [웬만하다] tolerable; so-so. e.g. 그의 학교 성적은 그만하다 His school record it tolerable. **2** [정도가 그것만 하다] much the same; alike; similar; so many [much]; as many [much]; that much; so trifling; so small. e.g. 내 모자의 크기도 그만하다 My hat is of the same size with it.

그맘때 [गुमाम्तै] about that time; that time of day [night / year]. e.g. 사과는

그맘때가 제일 맛난다 That is the time when apples taste most delicious.

그물 **[गुमुल]** [구멍이 나게 얽은 물건] a net; <집합적 netting; network; mesh.

그밖 **[गुबाक]** the rest; the others. e.g. 그밖에 또 필요한 것이 있습니까 Do you want anything else?

그사이 **[गुसाइ]** the while; [in the] meantime; the interval. e.g. 그사이에 우리는 저녁을 먹을 수 있다 [गुसाइए उरीनन जौन्यौगल मैगल सु इत्ता] We can take our supper in that time.

그야말로 **[गुयाम्ल्लो]** [참으로] really; indeed; certainly; [그것이야말로] [that is ... certainly [indeed]; that is the very thing <that>. e.g. 그야말로 아름답다 It is really beautiful.

그윽하다 **[गुउख्वादा]** **1** [장소가] I] secluded; secret; retired; sequestered; hidden; out-of-the-way; solitary lonely; peaceful. e.g. 그윽한 곳 a secluded spot. **2** [생각, 뜻 등이] deep; private; secret; deep-down; profound; recondite; abstruse. e.g. 그윽한 생각] a secret [private] idea **3** [정취가] refined; tasteful; [향기가] sweet. e.g. 그윽한 향기 a sweet scent.

그을다 **[गुउल्दा]** **1** [햇볕에] become suntanned; get sunburnt [browned]; be tanned with the sun; get a tan. e.g. 새까맣게 그을은 deep-[heavily-] tanned. **2** [연기에] smoke; fume; smolder; get sooty; fumigate; get covered [black] with soot. e.g. 연기에 그을은 천장 a smoke-stained ceiling.

그을리다 **[गुउल्लिदा]** [훈제가공을 위해] smoke; [소독,살충을 위해] fumigate; [산화를 위해] oxidize;[연기에] cover [stain] with soot; make [all] sooty; [햇볕에] sunburn. e.g. 그을린] smoked / fumed.

그저 **[गुजौ]** **1** [줄곧] yet; still; without ceasing [stopping]; so far. e.g. 비가 그저 계속해 내리고 있 It keeps on raining. **2** [생각 없이 recklessly; wildly; immoderately; aimlessly; heedlessly; at random; [이유없이] without any reason; [어쨌든] anyhow; anyway; [하는 일없이] without doing anything [in particular]. e.g. 그저 빚을 마구 지다 go into debt recklessly. **3** [신통하지 않다] so-so; all right [but not terribly good]. e.g. 그저 쓸만하다 be just passable. 영화가 재미있었느냐 – 그저 그렇더라 Was the movie interesting? – It was so-so.

그저께 [**गुजौके**] the day before yesterday.

그전 [**गुजौन**] [**-前**] former days [times]; the other day; the past. e.g. 모든 것이 그전과는 다르다 Things are not what they used to be.

그치다 [**गुछीदा**] **1** [멈추다] stop; [끝나다] lith; end; come to stop [an end]; cease; [소리가] die out [fade away]; [바람 등이?] die down; [비,눈이] hold up. e.g. 그칠 새 없이 ceaselessly / continuously / without cease / with no break. **2** [...을 그만두다] [... stop; cease; [끝내다, 제한하다] put an end [a stop] to. e.g. 울음을 그치다stop crying.

그토록 [**गुथोरोक**] so [much]; such an extent. e.g. 자네가 그토록 심하게 말할 것까지는 없다] You don't have to use such harsh words.

그후 [**गुहू**] [-後] [이후] ather that; thereather; subsequently; atherward [s]; [이래] [ever] since; from that time on. e.g. 그후 5 년간 for the five ensuing years

극 [**गुक**] [**劇**] a drama; a play.

극 [**गुक**] [**極**] **1** [지구의] the terrestrial poles; [전기의] [the electric poles; [자석의] the magnetic poles. e.g. 남[북]극 the South [North] Pole. **2** [절정] the height; the zenith; the climax the acme; the extreme; extremity. e.g. 극에 달하다 go to extremes / run to an extreme / reach its climax.

극단 [**गुकतान**] [**極端**] an extreme; extremity; a pole. e.g. 그것은 극단적이다 That's going too far.

극단 [**गुकतान**] [**劇團**] a dramatic [theatrical] company; a theatrical troupe; a theater group; a troupe [company]. e.g. 부길 극단 Pugil and his troupe. 국립 극단 the National Drama Company.

극대 [**गुक्तै**] [**極大**] the greatest; the largest; [數] the maximum. e.g. 극대의 이익[이윤]을 추구하다 seeE the maximum profit.

극도 [**गुक्तो**] [**極度**] the extreme; [최대한] the maximum; [정상] the zenith. e.g. 극도로 흥분하다 be extremely excited / be excited in the extreme / be highly wrought up.

극복 [**गुक्पोक**] [**克服**] conquest; subjugation. 극복하다 overcome; conquer; surmount; subjugate; cope with; deal successfully with.

극비 [**極秘**] strict [absolute]

secrecy; a top secret. e.g. 극비의 closely guarded / in strict secrecy.

극빈 [गुक्पिन] [**極貧**] extreme [dire] poverty; destitution. 극빈하다 extremely poor; destitute; indigent; as poor as a church mouse

극성 [गुक्सौंग] [**極盛**] [세력이] highly flourishing [thriving]; being very prosperous; being rampant; [성질이] extremity. 극성하다 impatient; impetuous; mad; frantic; furious. e.g. 극성스럽다 = 극성하다. 극성맞다 = 극성하다. 극성스러운 사람 [an impatient [impetuous] person.

극심 [गुक्शिम] [**極甚**] intensity; severity; vehemence. 극심하다 extreme; excessive; intense; severe; heavy; enormous; tremendous; terrible; keen. e.g. 극심한 더위 an intense heat.

극장 [गुक्चांग] [**劇場**] a theater; a playhouse.

극적 [गुक्चौक] [**劇的**] dramatic. e.g. 극적으로 dramatically.

극진 [गुक्चिन] [**極盡**] cordiality; heartiness; utter devotion. 극진하다very kind; cordial; hearty; hospitable; devoted.

극찬 [गुक्छान] [**極讚**] high praise. 극찬하다 praise <a person> sky-high; speak very highly of <a person>. e.g. 두 사람의 음악 평론가가 이 젊은 지휘자를 극찬했다 Two music critics spoke very highly of[extolled] this young conductor.

극한 [गुख्खान] [**極限**] the utmost limits; the bounds; an extremity <of pain>; limit. e.g. 극한에 달하다 reach the limit <of patience>. 극한을 넘다[넘지 않다] go beyond [keep within] the bounds [limits] <of>. 인내의 극한에 도달하다 reach the limit of one's endurance.

극히 [गुख्खि] [**極** −] very; exceedingly; excessively; extremely; remarkably; greatly; immensely.

근 [गुन] [**筋**] a muscle; [힘줄] a sinew; a tendon.

근 [गुन] [**近**] about; almost; near [ly]. e.g. 근 한 달 동안 for about a month.

근거 [गुन्गौ] [**根據**] [이유] ground [s]; [기반] a basis <*pl.* −ses>; [전거] authority. e.g. … 에 근거를 두다 [사람이] base <one's argument> on ... / find one's reasons in. / [사물이] afford [provide] a basis for.

근검 [गुन्गौम] [**勤儉**] thrith and diligence [industry]; diligence and economy 근검하다 thrithy [and diligent]; frugal. e.g. 근검한 가정 주부 a frugal hous-Eeeper.

근교 [गुन्ग्यो] [**近郊**] the

suburbs; the outskirts; the neighboring[neighbouring] districts.

근근이 [**गुन्गुनी**] [**僅僅-**] [간신히] barely; narrowly; hardly; with difficulty; [겨우] just; only

근대 [**गुन्दै**] [**近代**] recent [modern] times [ages]. e.g. 근대의 [modern / recent. 근대적인 modernistic / modern. 전근대적인 premodern. 초근대적인 ltramodern.

근래 [**गुल्लै**] [**近來**] recent days; these days e.g. 근래의 사건 recent events. 근래의 late / recent.

근로 [**गुल्लो**] [**勤勞**] work; labor [labour] [▷ work 는 알반적인 말, labor 는 육체 노동 또는 일반적으로 힘이 드는 일 service; industry.

근면 [**勤勉**] [diligence; industry; hard work; [close] application; assiduity. e.g. 근면은 성공의 어머니 Diligence is the mother of success.

근무 [**गुन्मु**] [**勤務**] service; duty; work; business. 근무하다 do duty; be on duty; work; serve.

근방 [**गुबांग**] [**近方**] [근처] the neighborhood; the vicinity; [주변] the surrounding; the environs <of a city>. e.g. 근방에 있는 nearby / close by / in the neighborhood <of>.

근본 [**गुनबोक**] [**根本**] [기초] the foundation, the basis <*pl.* -ses>; [근원] the root; the origin; [본질] the essence. e.g. 근본적인 [기본적인] [fundamental / basic / [철저한] radical, drastic / [각 세부에 걸친] thorough.

근사 [**गुन्सा**] [**近似**] **1** [유사] approximation; [an] approach <to>; resembleance. 근사하다 approximate; close; <서술적> closely resemble; be closely akin to. e.g. 인간에 가장 근사한 동물 animals most nearly allied to man [human beings]. **2** [멋짐] splendidness; wonderfulness.

근사하다 chic; fine; smart; excellent; splendid; wonderful; nice; OK. e.g. 근사한 생각 a happy [good / splendid / capital] idea

근성 [**गुन्सौंग**] [**根性**] **1** [성질] nature; [기질] a disposition; spirit. e.g. 관리 근성 a bureaucratic nature. **2** [견고한 의지] willpower; guts. e.g. 근성이 있는 사람] a man who has guts [plenty of grit].

근세 [**गुन्से**] [**近世**] modern time [ages]; recent times / latter days.

근소 [**गुन्सो**] [**僅少**] 근소하다 few [수]; little [양]; [사소하다] trifling <cost>; small; scanty; insignificant; meager. e.g. 근소한 차로 [win / lose> by a narrow margin.

근시 [गुन्शी] [近視] near [short]-sightedness; near vision; myopia.

근신 [गुन्शिन] [謹愼] 1 [언동을 삼가함] good behavior [conduct]; prudence; discretion; [자제] self-control; self-restraint; [개전][penitence 근신하다 behave oneself; be on one's good behavior; be prudent <in speech and action>; be penitent. 2 [처벌] disciplinary confinement. 근신하다 be confined to one's home..

근심 [गुन्शिम] anxiety; concern; solicitude; uneasiness; apprehension; fear; care; worry; trouble 근심하다 feel anxious <about>; worry <about / over>; be troubled [worried / concerned] <about>; feel concern <for>; be afraid of [for]; be uneasy about; be alarmed; care for.

근엄 [गुन्औम] [謹嚴] seriousness; gravity; austerity. 근엄하다 [진지하다] [serious; [엄숙하다] solemn; grave; austere

근원 [गुन्वॉन] [根源] the root; the origin; the source; the basis <*pl.* bases>; the fountainhead; the beginning; [원인] the cause; [정수] the essence. e.g. 뉴스의 근원 a news source.

근육 [गुन्युक] [筋肉] muscle [▷ 신체 각부의 근육을 구체적으로 가리킬 때는 a muscle]; brawn [팔,다리 등의 불거진 근육].

근접 [गुन्जौब] [近接] approach; nearing; close contact; approximation; appulse; contiguity. 근접하다 draw near; come [go] close <to>; approach. e.g. 근접한 neighboring [neighbouring / nearby] <cities> / [인접한] contiguous [adjacent] <territories>

근처 [गुन्छो] [近處] [이웃] the neighborhood; the vicinity; [주위] the surroundings; the environs.

근하신년 [गुन्हाशीनन्यौन] [謹賀新年] [I wish you] a Happy New Year; Allow me to offer you my hearty congratulations on the arrival of the New Year.; I hope you may have a happy New Year and that all things may prosper with you.

근해 [गुन्है] [近海] the adjoining [near] seas; the neighboring [home] waters.

근황 [गुन्हवांग] [近況] the recent [present] condition [situation].

글 [गुल] 1 [문장] writings; a composition; [문법상의] a sentence; [본문] the text; [문체] style. e.g. 세련된 글 a polished sentence [style]. **2** [글자] a letter; a character; an ideograph [한자등]. e.g. 글을 모르다 be unlettered [illiterate].

글썽글썽 [गुल्सौंगुल्सौंग] with tearful eyes. 글썽글썽하다 <서술적> be filled [brimming / swimming] with tears. e.g. 눈물이 글썽글썽한 눈 eyes suffused [filled] with tears / moist [tear-soaked] eyes.

글쎄 [गुल्से] [주저] [जुजौ] well; say; I think; let me see; [생각할 때] ah; uh; er —. e.g. 글쎄 아무래도 모르겠는데 Well, I am sure I don't know.

글자 [गुल्जा] [-字] a letter; a character; an ideograph [한자등]. e.g. 큰글자[대문자] a capital letter / a cap.

글짓기 [गुल्जीत्गी] composition; writing. 글짓기하다 write [make] a composition; write a theme.

긁다 [गुल्दा] [손톱,연장 등으로] scratch; scrape <off / away / out / down>. e.g. 머리를 긁다 scratch one's head.

긁어먹다 [गुल्गौमौकता] [숟갈 등으로] scrape [scratch] [out] and eat; [이로] gnaw [bite] off and eat. e.g. 참외를 숟가락으로 긁어먹다 scrape out the meat of a melon and eat it. 뼈에 붙은 고기를 긁어먹다 gnaw the meat off a bone.

긁적긁적 [गुक्चोक गुक्चोक scratching and scratching; scraping and scraping. 긁적긁적하다 = 긁적거리다.

금[1] [गुम] [金] **1** [황금] [हांगुम] gold. **2** ⇨금요일 [गुमयोइल]

금[2] [गुम] **1** [균열] a crack; a crevice; a cleth; a chink; a fissure. e.g. 벽의 금 a crack in the wall. **2** [선] a line; [접은 자국] a fold; a crease; [주름] a wrinkle. e.g. 금을 긋다 draw a line.

금- [गुम] [지금] this <time>; the present <term>; the coming <examination>. e.g. 금월 the current [present] month / this month. 금세기 the current century / the present century / this century.

금고 [गुम्गो] [金庫] [화재, 도난 방지용 철제 궤] a safe; a strong boK a moneyboK a cashboK <美> a coffin; a vault [금고실][

금기 [गुम्गी] [禁忌] [a] taboo; tabooing; contraindication. 금기하다] taboo; [음식물을] abstain voluntarily from <certain food>.

금리 [गुम्नी] [金利] interest [on money]; money rates; [이율] a rate of interest. e.g. 대출 금리 loan rate.

금발 [गुम्बाल] [金髮] golden [fair] hair; hair of gold.

금방 [गुम्बान] [今方] [지금

막] just [right] now; just; now; [바로 전에] [just] a moment ago; [곧] at once; in a moment; immediately; [금시라도] every [at any] moment. e.g. 나는 금방 도착했다[돌아왔다] I arrived [came back] just now

금속 [गुम्सुक] [金屬] [a] metal.

금시초문 [गुम्शीछोमुन] [今時初聞] e.g.그것은 금시 초문이다 I have never heard of that. / This is the first time for me to hear about that. I didn't know that.

금액 [गुमैक] [金額] an amount [a sum] of money. e.g. 큰[작은] 금액 a large [small] amount of money.

금연 [गुम्यौन] [禁煙] prohibition of smoking; no smoking.

금욕 [गम्योक] [禁慾] abstinence; ascetic practice; [성욕의] continence / sexual abstinence.

금융 [गुम्यू] [金融] [자금의 대차] finance; financing; monetary circulation.

금의환향 [गुमुइह्वांनह्यांग] [錦衣還鄕] 금의환향하다] go home loaded with honors; return to one's old home in glory.

금일 [गुमिल] [今日] today; this day.

금주 [गुम्जू] [禁酒] abstinence <from alcohol drinks>; temperance [▷ temperance 는 절주를 말하나 완전히 술을 끊는 경우에도 쓰임]. 금주하다 abstain from alcohol [drinking]; give up [stop / quit] drinking; go on the wagon; be temperate; go dry.

금지 [गुम्जी] [禁止] prohibition; inhibition; a ban; an embargo; taboo; interdiction; [발행의] suppression. e.g. 문[도어] 개방 금지 <게시> Don't Leave The Door Open.

금지옥엽 [गुम्जीय्योप] [金枝玉葉] [임금의 집안자손] a person of royal birth; [귀한자손] precious sons and daughters. e.g. 금지옥엽으로 자라다 be brought up like a prince.

금품 [गुम्फुम] [金品] money and goods. e.g. 금품을 요구하다 demand a person of <his> money and valuables.

금하다 [गुम्हादा] [禁-] [금지하다] forbid <a person wine / a song to be sung>; prohibit; proscribe; ban; taboo; bar <the use of poison gas>; interdict <foreign trade>; inhibit <a person from doing>; enjoin <an action / a person from doing>; [금제품으로서] place <something> under a ban; lay an embargo on <something>; place ban <on>.

급 [गुप] [級] [등급] a class; a grade; a rate. e.g.

대사급 회담 a conference on the level of ambassadors [at the ambassadorial level] / an ambassador level conference.

급격 [गुप्क्यौक] [**急激**] 급격하다 [돌연하다] sudden; [빠르다] rapid; [심하다] sharp. e.g. 급격한 정책의 변화 a sudden [rapid] change in policy. 급격히 suddenly; rapidly. e.g. 자동차에 의한 사망자의 수가 급격히 증가했다 The number of deaths from car accidents has increased rapidly. / There has been a sharp increase in the number of deaths from automobile accidents.

급경사 [गुप्क्यौंगसा] [**急傾斜**] a steep slope [incline]; [치받이] steep ascent [acclivity]; [내리받이] steep descent [declivity]; [배의] a heavy list.

급급하다 [गुप्गुफादा] [**汲汲-**] intent [bent] on; engrossed [absorbed] in; busy oneself about; too eager [very anxious] <to do>; think only of. e.g. 명리에 급급하고 있다 be striving hard ather fame and gain / be hungry for fame / be thirsty for reputation.

급기야 [गुप्क्यिा] [**及其也**] at [long] last; finally; in the end; in the long run; in time; ultimately; ather all. e.g. 돈을 물 쓰듯 하더니 급기야 그는 빈털터리가 되었다 He went on squandering his money until [at last] he became penniless.

급락 [गम्नाक] [**急落**] [시세의] a sudden [sharp] drop [decline / fall]; a sharp break; a steep decline; a slump. 급락하다 drop [fall] suddenly; slump; drop sharply; plunge. e.g. 오늘 달러 시세가 700 원으로 급락했다 The dollar plunged [plummeted] to 700 won today.

급료 [गुम्न्यो] [**給料**] a salary; wages; pay [▷ wages 는 일급,주급 등. Salary 는 매달 나누어 지불하는 연봉을 뜻하며, pay 는 일반적으로 보수로 지불되는 것].

급류 [गुमन्यू] [**急流**] a fast flowing [rushing] stream; a rapid [swith / fast] stream; a swith [strong] current; [격류] a torrent; rapids.

급변 [गुप्प्यौन] [**急變**] [갑작스런 변화] a sudden change [turn]. 급변하다 change suddenly; undergo a sudden change; [병이] take a sudden turn for the worse. e.g. 급변하는 주위 환경[세계 정세] the rapidly changing circumstances [world situation].

급선무 [गुप्सौन्मू] [**急先務**] the most urgent business

[necessity]; the most important matter requiring immediate attention; an exigency. e.g. 우리의급선무는 우선 그의 소재를 알아내는 일이다 It is of the most urgent necessity for us to find out where he is.

급수 [गुप्सू] [**級數**] = 등급.

급습 [गुप्सुप] [**急襲**] a surprise [sudden] attack; a raid; [경찰의] a [police] raid <on gamblers>; a round-up [일제 단속]. 급습하다 make a surprise [sudden] attack <on>; suddenly descend <upon>; take <the enemy> by surprise; raid; storm.

급식 [गुप्शिक] [**給食**] [provision of] meals; feeding [동물 등의]. 급식하다 provide [free] lunch for <school-children>; supply [provide] <the poor> with meals; provide meals for <employees>; feed <a bird>.

급여 [गुब्यौ] [**給與**] [an] allowance; a grant; [a] supplies; [봉급] pay; salary; wages. 급여하다 allow; grant; supply [furnish / provide] <a person with something>; pay <a monthly salary of 450,000 won>. den turn.

급정거 [गुप्जौंगो] [**急停車**] a sudden stop. 급정거하다 stop suddenly [short]; come [be brought] to a sudden stop. e.g. 급정거시키다 bring <a car> to a sudden stop / apply [put on] the emergency brake.

급증 [गुप्जुंग] [**急增**] a sudden [rapid] increase <in numbers>; a <populational> jump. 급증하다 increase rapidly [suddenly]; jump <to>.

급진 [गुप्जीन] [**急進**] **1** [빨리 나아감] rapid progress [advance]. 급진하다 advance rapidly; make rapid progress; speed up; push forward; rush. **2** [과격] going to extremes; radicalism. e.g. 급진적인 radical / extreme.

급하다 [गुप्हादा] [다급하다] urgent; pressing; hurried; impending; imminent; [갑작스럽다] sudden; abrupt.

급행 [गुप्हैंग] [**急行**] **1** [급히감]. e.g. 급행의 express / fast / hot-shot <freight train>. 급행하다 hasten [hurry / rush] <to>; go in a hurry; go posthaste <to>. e.g. 현장으로 급행하다 rush [shoot off] to the scene. **2** ⇨ 급행 열차 e.g. 7시 30분 부산행 급행 the 7:30 express for Pusan.

급히 [गुपी] [**急-**] [서둘러] in a hurry; in haste; hastily; hurriedly; [빨리] speedily; quickly; quick; <美> on the double; at a brisk pace [빠른 걸음으로]; [즉시] without delay; promptly;

immediately; at once.

긋다 [गुत्ता] [선 등을 그리다] draw. e.g. 금을 긋다 draw a line.

긍정 [गुँग्जौंग] [**肯定**] affirmation; approbation [시인]. 긍정하다 affirm; answer in the affirmative; answer "yes"; acknowledge. e.g. 긍정적[의] affirmative.

긍지 [गुंग्जि] [**矜持**] pride; dignity. e.g. 긍지를 느끼다 feel proud.

-기 [गी] [**氣**] a feeling <of ...>; a flavor; a touch; a shade; a tinge. e.g. 바람기가 있는 남자 a man with a roving eye.

-기 [गी] [**記**] [기록] a record; [기술] an account; a description; [역사] a chronicle; a history; [연대기] annals. e.g. 체험기 memoirs.

-기 [गी] [**期**] [시대] a period; an age; [기일] a date; a time; [기간] a period; a term; [계절] a season; [지불기의 하나] a quarter; [회기] a session; a sitting; [병의] a stage. e.g. 제 1 기의 폐병 tuberculosis [consumption] in the first stage.

-기 [गी] [**機**] a machine. e.g. 비행 기 an airplane. 세탁기 a washing machine.

기 [गी] [**氣**] **1** [기력, 원기] vigor; energy; vitality; strength; force; spirits; stamina; pep. e.g. 기가 부족하다 be lacking [deficient] in energy / be in low [poor] spirits. **2** [전력] all one's energies [strength / might]; one's utmost [best]; all-out effort. e.g. 기를 쓰다 ⇨ 기쓰다. 기를 쓰고 반대하다 oppose strongly [stoutly] / be [hell-] bent on opposing <a person>. 기[를] 펴다 make oneself comfortable [at home]; put oneself at ease; cheer up; heighten one's spirit; relax

기각 [गीगाक] [**棄却**] [각하] turning down; rejection; dismissal; [포기] abandonment; renunciation. 기각하다 turn down; reject; dismiss; throw <a suit> out of court. e.g. 신청을 기각하다 reject [turn down] an application.

기간 [गीगान] [**期間**] [한정된 시기] a period [of time]; a term.

기겁 [गीगौप] 기겁하다 be astonished [shocked / thunderstruck]; be frightened out of one's wits; [소리지르다] cry out in astonishment [surprise]. e.g. 기겁하여 in a fright / in alarm / with yells of horror.

기계 [गीगे] [**機械**] a machine; a gin; <집합적> machinery; gear; [기계 장치] a mechanism; machinery; setup; works [시계 등의]. **기고**

[गीगो] [寄稿] [a] contribution <to>; a piece written <for>. 기고하다 contribute <to a newspaper>; write <for a magazine>. e.g. 신문에 기고하다 write in [for] the paper [press].

기고 만장 [गीगो म्नजांग] [氣高萬丈] [기세가 대단함] high spirits; elation. 기고 만장하다 elated; <서술적> be in high [roaring / towering] spirits; be puffed up; be big with pride; wear a high hat [술] tracheotomy / bronchotomy.

기관[1] [गीग्वान] [器官] an organ. e.g. 감각 기관 a sense organ. 발성 기관 a vocal organ.

기관[2] [गीग्वान] [機關] [수단] an organ; a means; a vehicle; a medium; an instrument; an agency; a system; [시설] facilities; service; accommo-dations; an institution; [기구] an organization; machinery. e.g. 관리 기관 the governing body. 교육 기관 an educational institution.

기괴 [गीग्वे] [奇怪] 기괴하다 [괴이하다] strange; mysterious; weird; uncouth; uncanny; [망측하다] outrageous; extraordinary;

기교 [गीग्यो] [技巧] art; craths-manship; workmanship; technical skill; technique; technics; mechanism [예술의]; [계책] an artifice; a trick; finesse. e.g. 기교에 치우친 작품 an excessively elaborate work.

기구[1] [गीगू] [崎嶇] [세상살이의 험함] vicissitudes [of life [fortune]]; ups and downs [of life]; adversity. 기구하다 checkered; viciss-itudinous; adverse; hapless; unlucky; strange; unfortun-ate; ill-fated

기구[2] [गीगू] [器具] [도구] a tool; a utensil; [간단한 기계] an appliance; an apparatus; an instrument.

기구[3] [गीगू] [機構] [조직] a system; [an] organization; [a] structure; machinery. e.g. 국제 기구 an international organization.

기권 [गीग्वान] [棄權] abstention <from voting>; renunciation [waiver] <of one's rights>;[경기의] absence; cancellation <of the [one's] entry>. 기권하다 abstain <from voting>; [권리를] renounce [waive] <one's right>; [경기에서] give up <the race halfway>. e.g. 그는 시장 선거 투표를 기권했다 He did not vote in the mayoral election

기근 [गीगुन] [飢饉] [a] famine; failure of crops; [부족] a dearth; [a]

shortage.

기금 [गीगुम] [**基金**] a fund; a foundation; an endowment.

기기 [गीगी] [**機器**] [비품] equipment; [특수한 기능을 가진 기구 일습] [an] apparatus [▷ 복수는 드묾]; [기계] an instrument. e.g. 전자 기기 electronic equipment.

기껏해야 [गीगौत्थैया] at [the] most; at the very most; at the utmost; at [the] best; only; merely; ather all. e.g. 기껏해야 1마일 a mile at the [very] outside.

기념 [गीन्यौम] [**記念,紀念**] commemoration; [추억] a memory; remembrance.

기념하다 commemorate; [축하하다] celebrate.

기념품 [गीन्यौम्फुम] [**記念品**] a remembrance; a memento; a souvenir [▷ rememberance는 상당히 추상적이고, 특정한 것에 대해서는 memento 를 쓰는 일이 많음. Souvenir 는 이를테면 여행지에서 사는 것 등].

기능 [गीनुंग] [**機能**] a function. e.g. 기능적인 functional.

기다 [गीदा] [몸을 엎드리어] crawl; creep [▷ 보통 crawl 은 발이 없거나 있어도 짧은 생물, 엎드려 기는 사람 등에 대하여 씀. Creep 는 네 손발로 기는 사람이나 네발짐승이 천천히 살금살금 나아가는 모양]; grovel [배를 붙이고].

기다리다 [गीदारीदा] [대기하다] wait <for>; await; watch for; be in wait for; be on the lookout <for>.

기대 [गीदै] [**期待,企待**] expectation; expectancy; anticipation; hope. 기대하다 expect; anticipate; hope for; look forward to; look for; count on [upon]; reckon on; look to <a person> for.

기대다 [गीदैदा] [몸을] lean against [on / over]; stand against; recline on [against]; rest on [against]. e.g. 난간에 기대다 lean over the railing.

기도 [गीदो] [**祈禱**] a prayer; [식전,식후의] [a] grace; [one's] devotions [▷ 언제나 복수로].

기독교 [गीदोक्यो] [**基督教**] **1** = 크리스트교. **2** [개신교] Protestantism.

기둥 [गीदुंग] **1** [건축물의] a pillar; a column [두리기둥]; a post; a pole. e.g. 기둥을 세우다 erect [set up] a pillar. **2** [의지가 될 만한 사람] a support; a prop; a stay; a mainstay; a pillar. e.g. 집안의 기둥 the prop [breadwinner] of a family / the support [prop and stay] of a family.

기득권 [गीदुक्वॉन] [**既得權**] vested rights; vested interests [권익]. e.g.

기득권을 침해하다[지키다] infringe upon [protect] <a person's [one's]> vested rights..

기량 [गीर्यांग] [**器量**] ability; talent; capacity; caliber. e.g. 기량이 있는 able / talented.

기력 [गीर्यौक] [**氣力**] [기운] energy; vigor; vigour; force; spirit; vitality; virility; <美> pep; will power. e.g. 기력이 왕성한 energetic / vigorous / full of vitality.

기록 [गीरोक] [**記錄**] **1** [적음] recording; [기록한 것] a record; [문서] a document; documentary literature; [공문서] archives; [의사록] the minutes; proceedings; [연대기] annals; a chronicle. 기록하다 record; register; write [note] down; put on <something> record. **2** [경기 등의 성적] a record. e.g. 100미터 자유형의 기록 the record for the 100-meter freestyle.

기르다 [गीरुदा] [키우다] raise [애완 동물 등에는 쓰지 않음]; keep; breed; rear; feed [먹이다]; grow; cultivate; bring up; foster; nurse. e.g. 새끼 때부터 기른 곰 a bear raised [by a man] since it was a cub / a bear kept from young

기름 [गीरुम] [식물유, 동물유, 광물유] oil; [기계용] grease; [동물의 지방] fat; [정제한 돼지 기름] lard; [소,양의] suet; [고래의] blubber.

기막히다 [गीमाखादा] [놀랍다, 어이없다] amazed; appalled; dum [b] founded; astonished; stunned; taken aback. e.g. 기막히는 일 a horrible thing / an absurdity.

기말 [गीमाल] [**期末**] the end of a term; a term end.

기말 시험 [गीमाल शीहौम] a semester test; a term exam [ination]; [학년 말의] a final [term-end] exam [ination].

기묘 [गम्यो] [**奇妙**] 기묘하다 strange; curious; queer; odd; singular. e.g. 기묘한 운명 a strange fate.

기밀 [गीमिल] [**機密**] secrecy; secret information; a secret. e.g. 국가 기밀 a state secret.

기반 [गीबान] [**基盤**] a foundation; a base; a basis; [지위] footing; foothold; [세력 범위] a sphere of influence; [선거의] a constituency; constituents; [지질의] bedrock. e.g. …을 기반으로 하다 be based [founded] on ....

기발 [गीबाल] [**奇拔**] uncommoness; extraordinariness; originality; novelty. 기발하다 uncommon; extraordinary; peculiar; novel; original; unconventional; fanciful <drawing / pattern>.

기별 [गीब्यौल] [**奇別,寄別**] a

notice; information; news; word; tidings; a letter; report; a message. e.g. 미리 아무 기별도 없이 without previous notice. 기별하다 let <a person> know; tell; inform <a person> of [that]; advise <a person> of; give <a person> notice; report; write to <a person>. e.g. 일주일 전에 기별하다 give <a person> a week's notice.

기본 [गीबोन] [**基本**] [기초] a foundation; a basis; basics; [기준] a standard..

기부금 [गीबुगुम] [**寄附金**] a contribution; a donation; an endowment; a gith of money.

기분 [गीबुन] [**氣分**] feeling; sensation; a frame of mind; mood; atmosphere.

기사 [गीसा] [**技師**] an engineer; [전문 분야의] a technical expert. [▷ 미국에서는 engineer 란 말이 아주 넓은 뜻으로 쓰임. 예를 들면 미화원을 sanitation engineer, 창문 수리공을 casement window engineer 라고 하는 경우가 많음]

기사 [गीसा] [**記事**] [신문의] news; a news item [story]; a report; [논설] an article; an account.

기사회생 [गीसाहवेसैंग] [**起死回生**] resuscitation; revival. 기사 회생하다 restore from death; revive; resuscitate.

기상 [गीसांग] [**奇想**] an original [a fantastic] idea; a fanciful notion; a clever idea; a conceit. e.g. 기상 천외의 most fantastic.

기상 [गीसांग] [**起床**] rising [in the morning]. 기상하다 rise; get up; turn out; <美> roll out.

기상 [गीसांग] [**氣像**] spirit; temperament; nature; temper; disposition; appearance; bearing. e.g. 쾌활한 기상의 사람 a man of cheerful disposition. 씩씩한 기상 a manly [valiant] spirit. 독립[진취]적 기상 an independent [enterprising] spirit.

기색 [गीसैक] [**氣色**] [표정] looks; countenance; appearance; [감정] mood; humor; feeling; [표시] a sign; an indication. e.g. 조금도 두려워하는 기색 없이 without showing the slightest sign of fear.

기성복 [गीसौंग्बोक] [**旣成服**] ready-made[ready-to-wear] clothes; store clothes; hand-me-downs; slops [싸구려].

기세 [गीसे] [**氣勢**] spirit; vigor; ardor; [형세] a position; a situation. e.g.. 기세가 오르다[떨어지다] be in high [in low / out of] spirits.

기숙사 [गीसुकसा] [**寄宿舍**] a

boarding house; a dormitory; a hostel; a dorm; [영국 대학의] a hall of residence; a residence hall [<英>에서 a dormitory 는 침대가 많이 놓인 기숙사의 넓은 한 방].

기술 [गीसुल] [記述] [a] description; an account; writing. 기술하다 describe; give an account of; write up. e.g. 기술하기 어렵다 be beyond description.

기술 [गीसुल] [技術] art; technique; [기량] ability; skill; [과학,공업의] [a] technology; <美> [technical] know-how; [학과목] manual training. e.g. 공업 기술 [engineering] technology.

기슭 [गीसुक] [강의] the bank[s]; [호수, 바다의] the shore; the coast; the border; [산의] the foot. e.g. 강기슭 the edge [brink] of a river.

기습 [गीसुप] [奇襲] a surprise [attack]; a sudden [sneak] attack. e.g. 기습적인 시험 a surprise examination / a pop [snap] quiz [test]. 기습하다 raid; make a surprise attack <on>; attempt a surprise; take unawares; take <a person> off his guard. e.g. 나무

기쓰다 [गीसुदा] [氣-] be hot [bent] <on>; be very eager [going all out] <to>; be mad [frantic] <for>; do with great zeal; vehemently [heatedly / excitedly] do <something>; make desperate [strenuous] efforts; do one's best; exert oneself to the utmost; strain; struggle. e.g. 기써서 일하다 work with all one's might / work to the best of one's ability.

기아 [गीआ] [飢餓,饑餓] hunger; starvation. e.g. 기아로 고통을 받다 suffer from hunger.

기약 [गीयाक] [期約] promise; pledge; engagement; appointment. 기약하다 pledge; promise.

기어이 [गीओइी] [期於-] [꼭] by all [manner of] means; by hook or by crook; without fail; at any cost [price / risk]. e.g. 나는 기어이 이기고야 말겠다 I intend to win no matter what.

기억 [गीओक] [記憶] memory; mind; memorization; remembrance; [추억] recollecttion. 기억하다 [기억하고 있다] remember; remain [live] in one's memory; [잊지 않도록] bear [keep] <something> in mind [remberance / memory]; commit <something> to memory; memorize; [외다] learn [get] <something> by heart. e.g. 단단히 기억하다 fix [bear] <something> firmly [indelibly] in one's memory [mind].

기업 [गीऔप] [**企業**] an enterprise; a business.

기업가 [गीऔप्गा,] an enterpriser; a man of enterprise; an enterprising man; an industrialist; a captain of industry.

기여 [गीयौ] [**與**] contribution; service. 기여하다 contribute <to>; render services <to>; add [much] to; do much toward. e.g. 그는 한국의 경제 발전에 크게 기여했다 He contributed greatly to the economic development of Korea.

기온 [गीओन] [atmospheric] temperature.

기와 [गीवा] a [roofing] tile; <집합적> tiling.

기왕 [गीवांग] [**既住**] [지금보다 이전] the past; bygones; the bygone days; [이미] already; since. e.g. 기왕의 past / bygone. 기왕이면 if it is done / if it has already happened / [선택] if I must take [choose].

기용 [गीयोंग] [**起用**] appointment; employment. 기용하다 [발탁하다] promote; [임명하다] appoint. e.g. 그는 과장으로 기용되었다 He was promoted to chief of his section. 그는 우리 대학팀의 투수로 기용되었다 He was chosen to be the pitcher for our college team.

기우 [गीउ] [**杞憂**] unfounded [groundless / imaginary] fears [apprehensions]; baseless anxiety.

기우뚱거리다 [गीयूदुंगौरीदा] **1** [흔들리다] rock; totter; wobble; sway [move] from side to side. e.g. 기우뚱거리는 의자 a shaky [rocky / rickety] chair. **2** [흔들다] move <a thing> from side to side; rock; sway; tilt [incline] <one's head>. e.g. 몸을 기우뚱거리다 sway one's body.

기운 [गीउन] [힘] [physical] strength; force; power; might. e.g. 기운이 센 strong / powerful / energetic.

기울다 [गीयूल्दा] [한쪽으로 쏠리다] tilt; [특히 서 있는 것이] lean; [배 등이] list. e.g. 태풍으로 배가 좌[우]로 기울었다 The storm caused the ship to list to port [starboard].

기울어지다 [गीउरोजीदा] incline; slant. e.g. 기울어진 널빤지 an inclined [a slanting] board.

기울이다 [गीउरिदा] **1** [한쪽으로 쏠리게 하다] tilt; [서 있는 물건을] lean; incline. e.g. 고개를 기울이다 lean one's head to one side / tilt one's head. **2** [쇠퇴하게 하다] ruin. e.g. 그의 실정이 우리 국운을 기울게 했다 His misrule ruined our country. **3** [집중하다] con-centrate <one's energy,

powers, etc.>; devote oneself <to>; [향하게 하다] direct one's attention <to>; bend <one's mind> to.

기웃거리다 [गीयुक्कौरिदा] [엿보다] peep <through / into>; snoop <around>; get a peep <at>; look in on <a person / a thing>; [고개를] crane <one's neck>; incline [tilt] <one's head>.

기원[1] [गीवॉन] [**起原P起源**] the origin [s]; the beginning [s]; the rise; the genesis.

기원[2] [गीवॉन] [**祈願**] prayer; supplication; petition. e.g. 필승의 기원 a prayer for victory. 기원하다 pray; supplicate; petition; wish. e.g. 영원한 평화를 기원하다 pray for everlasting peace.

기이 [गीई] [**奇異**] 기이하다 strange; queer; odd; singular; curious; eccentric; extraordinary. e.g. 기이한 광경 a curious sight.

기인 [गीइन] [**起因**] the cause; the root. 기인하다 be caused by; originate in; come [arise / spring] from; result from; be due [owing] to. e.g. 이 비극은 질투에 기인하였다 Jealousy was the cause of this tragedy. / This tragedy arose from jealousy.

기일 [गीइल] [**忌日**] the anniversary of <a person's> death; the deathday. e.g. 어머니의 3회 기일 the third anniversary of one's mother's death.

기일 [गीइल] [**期日**] a [fixed] date; an appointed day; [기한] a time limit; a deadline; a due date. e.g.납일 기일 [제품의] the delivery date / [세금 등의] the deadline for payment. 기일 안에 within the time limit / by the appointed day.

기입 [गीइप] [**記入**] entry; filling up [용지에]; recording. 기입하다 make an entry; enter; fill up; register; write in. e.g. 인명록에 이름을 기입하다 enter a name in a directory.

기자 [गीजा] [**記者**] [탐방기자] a reporter; [신문기자] a newswriter; a newspaperman; [통신원] a correspondent; [저널리스트] a journalist. e.g.

기장 [गीजांग] [옷의 길이] the length of a suit; the dress length. e.g. 이 옷의 기장은 너무 짧다 This dress is too short for me.

기재 [गीजे] [**記載**] mention; a statement; description; [장부의] entry; [신문의] publication. e.g. 허위 기재 a false entry. 기재하다 state; mention; record;

[신문,잡지에] print; report; carry; [장부에] enter.

기저귀 [गीजौग्वी] a diaper; a napkin; < 英 > a nappy. e.g. 종이 기저귀 a paper diaper [nappy].

기적 [गीजौक] [**奇蹟**] a miracle; a marvel; a wonder; a mystery. e.g. 기적을 행하다 work [accomplish / perform] miracles / work wonders.

기절 [गीजौल] [**氣絶**] fainting; a swoon; a fainting fit [spell]. 기절하다 faint [away]; lose consciousness [one's senses].

기점 [गीजौम] [**起點**] the starting point; the origin; [도로의] the top; the head; [배의] the home port; [철도의] the terminus <*pl.* –ni, ~es>. e.g. … 을 기점으로 하다 start <from>. 이 건물을 기점으로 하여 거리를 측정하다 measure the distance with this building as its starting point.

기존 [गीजोन] [**旣存**] e.g. 기존의 existing / established.

기종 [गीजोंग] [**機種**] [비행기의] kinds [types] of airplanes [aeroplanes]; [기계의] kinds [types] of machines. e.g. 제조를 중지한 기종 a model which is no longer being made [produced]. 신기종을 발매하다 release a new model of a machine.

기죽다 [गीजुक्ता] become diffident; lose one's nerve. e.g. 그렇게 높은 연단 위에서 연설을 하려니까 기죽어 말도 잘 나오지 않는다 It makes me feel self-conscious to speak from such a high platform.

기준 [गीजुन] [**基準**] [표준] a standard; [판단, 결정 등의] a criterion <*pl.* –ria, ~s>; [기초] a basis.

기증 [गीजुंग] [**寄贈**] presentation; contribution; donation. 기증하다 [गीजुंगहादा] present; contribute; donate.

기지 [गीजी] [**基地**] [軍] a base; [터전] a site; a home [탐험대의].

기진 맥진 [गीजी मैक्चिन] [**氣盡脈盡**] 기진 맥진하다 be worn [tired] out; be wearied [tired] to death; be utterly [totally] exhausted. e.g. 나는 기진 맥진 하였다 I am completely exhausted [beat / drained of energy].

기질 [गीजील] [**氣質**] [a] disposition; [a] temper; [a] temperament [disposition 은 타인과의 관계 등에 있어 나타나는 천성적인 기질, temper 는 자기 억제 등과 관계가 있는 기분, 성향, temperament 는 정서에 관련된 기질]; [a] nature; a cast [frame] of mind; make-up. e.g. 예술가

기질의 사나이 a man with an artistic temperament.

기차 [गीछा] [**汽車**] = 열차. e.g. 서울발 [행] 의 기차 a train from [for] Seoul. 9시 [9시 20분] 기차

기척 [गीछौक] [기색] a sign; [기미] a touch; an indication; traces; a hint. e.g. 인기척이 있다 There is a sign of somebody present.

기체 [गीछे] [**氣體**] [가스] [a] gas; [증기] [a] vapor [<英> [a] vapour]. e.g. 기체의 gaseous / aerial / pneumatic / gasiform. **기체 동력설** [गीछे दोंग्रौकसौल] the kinetic theory of gas.

기초 [गीछो] [**基礎**] **1** [건축물의 토대] the foundation. e.g. 건물의 기초를 쌓다 lay the foundation [groundwork] of a building. **2** [밑바탕이 되는 것] a basis <*pl.* bases>; a foundation; the groundwork. e.g. 문법의 기초 지식 elementary knowledge of grammar.

기침 [गीछीम] a cough; coughing; [醫] a tussis.

기타 [गीथा] [**其他**] the others; the rest; and others; and so forth; and the like; etc. e.g. 피복과 서적 기타 품목 clothes, books, and so forth.

기타 [गीथा] a guitar.

기탁 [गीथाक] [**寄託**] deposition; bailment. 기탁하다 [गीथाकहादा] deposit <a thing with a person>; entrust <a person with a thing>.

기탄 [गीथान] [**忌憚**] scruple; reserve; hesitation. e.g. 기탄없이 말하자면 to be frank <with you> / plainly speaking.

기특하다 [गीथुकखादा] [**奇特-**] commendable; admirable; praiseworthy; laudable. e.g. 기특한 마음씨 a good intention

기틀 [गीथुल] the key [pivotal] point; the crux [of a matter]; [계기] a [most appropriate] moment; a chance; an occasion; [토대, 기반] a base; a basis <*pl.* bases>; a foundation. e.g. 기틀 을 잡다 seize an opportunity <to do / of doing>

기품 [गीफुम] [**氣品**] [위엄] dignity; nobility; grace; [세련] refinement. e.g. 기품이 있는 dignified / refined.

기피 [गीफी] [**忌避**] [꺼리어 피함] evasion; avoidance. 기피하다 avoid <doing>; evade; shirk. e.g. 자기의 책임을 기피하다 shirk [evade] one's responsibility.

기하다 [गीहादा] [**期-**] **1** [날짜, 기한 등을 정하다] fix [decide upon] the date; set [fix] a term [time limit / deadline] <for>; [약속하다] promise; pledge. e.g. 가까운 장래를 기하여 in the near future. **2** [목표로 삼다] aim <at something /

to do>; have <something> in one's mind [in view]; [기대하다] expect; anticipate; hope for; look forward to; look to; [결심하다] determine; resolve; decide. e.g. 만전을 기하다 aim at perfection.

기한 [गीहान] [**期限**] a period; a time limit; a term; a deadline; time; limitation [법률의 효력 등의].

기행 [गीहैंग] [**紀行**] an account of travels; a traveler's journal; a book of travels; a travelog

기형 [गीहैंग] [**畸形**] deformation; [a] malformation; [a] deformity; [a] monstrosity; abnormality [형태상의].

기호 [गीहो] [**記號**] a sign; a symbol; a mark [▷ 보통 문자,숫자 이외의 기호]; emblem; an ideogram [ideograph] [1, 2, +, − 등]; a clef; a signature [조, 박자의].

기회 [गीहै] [**機會**] an opportunity; a chance; an occasion.

기획 [गीहैक] [**企劃**] [계획함] planning; [계획] a plan; a project. 기획하다 plan; make [form / set up] a plan; work out a scheme [program].

기후 [गीहू] [**氣候**] [a] climate; [날씨] the weather [▷ weather 는 나날이 변하는 것, climate 는 어떤 지방의 풍토를 가리키며 오랜 동안에 걸쳐 거의 변화하지 않는 것을 지칭함]; [절후] a season.

긴급 [गिन्गुप] [**緊急**] urgency; [긴급 사태] [an] emergency; [an] exigency; [서류 등에 쓸 때] "Rush"; "Urgent". 긴급하다 urgent <demand>; pressing <problem>; emergent <state>; burning <problem>; exigent <problem>; crying <want>.

긴밀 [गीन्मिल] [**緊密**] [엄밀] strictness; rigidity; [긴하고 가까움] closeness; tightness. 긴밀하다strict; rigid; tight; tightly knit <alliance>.

긴박 [गिन्बाक] [**緊迫**] tension; strain. 긴박하다 tense; acute; strained. e.g. 긴박한 국제 정세 a tense [strained] international situation. 긴박한 용건으로 on urgent business.

긴요 [गिन्यो] [**緊要**] importance; momentousness; [burning] necessity. 긴요하다important; of vital importance; vital; momentous; of moment; weighty; [필요하다] necessary <to>; [없어서는 안 되다] essential; [주요하다] main; indispensable <to>; requisite <to>.

긴장 [गिन्जांग] [**緊張**] strain; tension. e.g.동서의 긴장 완화 easing [relaxation] of East-West tensions. 긴장하다 be strained; become tense; be on the strain [stretch]; be keyed up; gird [string]oneself up <to do>; brace

긴축 [गिन्छुक] **緊縮**] [절약] [strict] economy; retrenchment; curtailment; [통화의] deflation; [생활 태도의] austerity; belt tightening. 긴축하다 [절약하다] economize; tighten; [삭감하다] retrench; curtail; cut down <expenses>; [통화를] deflate.

긷다 [गीत्ता] [물을] draw; ladle [바가지 등으로]; pump [펌프로]. e.g. 우물의 물을 긷다 draw water from a well.

길 [गिल] **1** [도로] a road; a way; [거리] a street; a thoroughfare; [가도] a highway; a highroad; [코스] a route; [작은 길] a path; a lane; a walk [정원 등의]; a pass; a trail [산,숲속의]; a track [밟아 다진]; an alley [골목길]; [통로] a passage; an approach [road] <to> [입구로 가는]. [뉴욕시 등에서 avenue 는 남북으로 통하는 대로, street 는 동서로 통하는 것] **2** [도중] the midst of a way [course]; incidental to a course of action. e.g. 대전으로 가는 길에 on my way to Taejòn. **3** [진로] a course; a way; [경로] a route; a channel; [방법, 수단] a way; a means; [취할 길] a course; a step. e.g. 성공하는 길 the road [way] to success.

길가 [गिल्गा] the roadside; the wayside.

길거리 [गिल्गौरी] a street; a road; an avenue; a thoroughfare.

길눈 [गिल्लुन] [방향 감각] a sense of direction. e.g. 길눈이 밝다 have a good sense of direction. 길눈이 어둡다 have no sense of direction.

길다 [गील्दा] [물체가] long; lengthy. e.g. 긴 소매 a long sleeve.

길동무 [गिल्दौग्मू] a fellow traveler [traveller / passenger]; a traveling companion.

길목 [गिल्मोक] [길모퉁이] a street corner; a turning of a road; <at> a turn in a road; <at> a bend of a road; a road bend. e.g. 길목에 있는 가게 a corner store

길이[1] [गिरी] [긴 정도] length; stature. e.g. 드레스[웃옷]의 길이 the length of a dress [coat].

길이[2] [गिरी] [오래도록] [for] long; for a long time; [영원히] forever; everlastingly; eternally; for many and many years to come. e.g. 길이 길이 for ever [and ever] / eternally / everlastingly / to [through all] eternity / forever.

길일 [गिरिल] [吉日] a lucky day; an auspicious day. e.g. 대 길일 a very lucky day.

길쭉길쭉 [गिल्चुक्किल्चुक] 길쭉길쭉하다 [all] longish; somewhat long. e.g. 길쭉길쭉한 막대기 longish [long] sticks.

길쭉하다 [गिल्चुहादा] longish; moderately [somewhat] long. e.g. 다리가 길쭉한 의자 a chair with spindly legs

길흉 [गिर्ह्युंग] [吉凶] one's fortune; one's [good or bad] luck. e.g. 카드로 길흉을 점치기 fortune-telling with playing cards. 길흉은 꼰 새끼줄과 같다 Good and bad luck are intertwined like the strands of a rope.

김[1] [किम] [해태] laver; sloke; sloak.

김[2] [किम] **1** [수증기] [white] steam; vapor. e.g. 온천에서 솟아오르는 김 steam rising from a hot spring. **2** [입, 코의] breath. e.g. 입김 breath.

김[3] [किम] [기회] an occasion; an opportunity; a chance. e.g. [하는]김에 while / when / as / by the way / by the by [e] / incidentally / on the occasion / at the same time / apropos / while one is at [about] it / in passion. 나가는 김에 just as one is going out.

김장 [किम्जांग] [겨우내 먹을 김치를 담그기] kimchi-making [preparing kimchi / pickling vegetables] for the winter; [담근 김치] kimchi prepared for the winter. 김장하다 [गीम्जांगहादा] prepare [make] kimchi for [use during] the winter; pickle vegetables for winter use.

김치 [किम्छी] kimchi; pickled vegetables. e.g. 김치를 담그다 prepare [make] kimchi / pickle [salt] vegetables.

깁다 [गिप्ता] sew; stitch; mend; patch up [헝겊을 대고]; darn [양말을].

깃들이다 [गित्तुरीदा] [새가] build a nest; nest; put up a nest; roost; <비유> lodge; dwell. e.g. 새는 나무에 깃들인다 Birds roost in[on] trees. 건전한 신체에 건전한 정신이 깃들인다 A sound mind [dwells] in a sound body.

깃발 [गिप्पाल] [旗-] a flag; banner; a standard [군기]; a pennant [pennon][긴 삼각형의]; <집합적> bunting; [기치] one's attitude [stand] [태도]; the platform [plank] [정강]; [구호] a slogan; a motto <*pl.* ~ [e]s>.

깃털 [गित्थौल] a feather;

[장식용] a plume; <집합적> plumage; [엷은 털] down.

깊다 [गिप्ता] **1** [바닥, 속까지의 거리가 멀다] deep; [외지다] secluded; remote. e.g. 깊은 곳 a depth / a deep place / the deeps **2** [짙다, 무성하다] thick; dense; heavy. e.g. 깊은 숲 a dense [deep] forest. **3** [심원하다] deep; profound; in [ner] most; [강렬하다] intense; strong. e.g. 깊은 애정 deep affect-tions **4** [친밀하다] close; fast; intimate; thick. e.g. 깊은 관계 close connec-tions / intimate relations / intimacy.

깊숙이 [गिप्सुगी] deep [down]; deeply; far. e.g. 장롱에 깊숙이 넣다 put deep into a chest.

깊숙하다 [गिप्सुख्वादा] [깊다] deep; [으슥하다] sequest-ered; secluded; retired; covert; inmost. e.g. 깊숙한 골짜기 a deep valley.

깊숙한방a secluded [se-questered] room / an inner room / a back room.

깊이 [गिफी] depth; deepness; profundity. e.g. 깊이를 알 수 없는 bottomless / fathom-less / unfathomable / aby-smal.

까놓다 [कानोथा] **1** (껍질을) [कोप्चीरल] peel [pare] off; take off; (겉이 보이게) (place) (a thing) face up. e.g. 탁자 위에 화투짝을 까놓다 place the cards face up on the table. **2** [털어놓다] open one's heart <to>; speak (out) one's mind; unbosom oneself <to>; confide in <a person>; confide <a secret> to <a person>; lay bare one's mind. e.g. 까놓고 말하면 to be frank with you / frankly speaking / to speak honestly / in plain terms.

까다[1] [कादा] [제하다] take (away / out) <from>; deduct <from>; subtract <from>. e.g. 봉급에서 월부금을 까다 deduct a monthly install-ment one's salary.

까다[2] [कादा] **1** (껍질을) peel; husk; crack; shell. e.g. 귤을 까다 peel a tang-erine. **2** (살갗을) graze; abrade; skin. e.g. 무릎을 까다 have one's knee skinned

까다롭다 [कादारोप्ता] **1** (성미, 취향이) fastidious <about>; overnice; particular <about>; hard to please. e.g. 성미가 까다로운 사람 a fastidious person / a person hard to please. **2** [복잡하다] compli-cated; [어렵다] difficult; hard;
[성가시다] troublesome; vexing; delicate. e.g. 까다로운 문제 a knotty

[com-plicated] problem; a hard nut to crack.

까닭 [कादाक] [이유] a reason; [원인] a cause; [근거] ground; [동기] a motive; account. ⇨ e.g. 무슨 까닭으로 why / for what reason / on what ground

까딱 [कातक] **1** (고개를). 까딱하다 bob; nod. e.g. 알았다고 고개를 까딱하다[] nod in assent. **2** [조금 움직이는 모양]. 까딱하다 move slightly; budge. e.g. 저 게으름쟁이는 손가락 하나 까딱않는다 That lazy fellow would not stir a finger [do a stitch of work]. **3** [자칫]. e.g. 까딱하면 막차를 놓칠 뻔했다 I almost missed [I came very close to missing] the last train.

까르르 [कारूरू] e.g. 아이들의 까르르 웃는 소리가 밖에까지 들려 왔다[] Shrieks [Peals] of children's laughter was heard outside.

까마득하다 [कामदुख्यादा] **1** (거리가) far; faraway; remote; a long way <off>. e.g. 그의 집은 저 언덕 너머 까마아득한 곳에 있다[] His home is far (away) beyond that hill. **2** (시간이) distant; remote. e.g. 내가 런던에 갔던 것은 까마아득한 옛날이다 I was a long time ago that I went to London.

까맣다 [कामात्था] **1** (빛깔이) deep-black; jet-[coal-] black; inky(-black). e.g. 까만 머리 raven(-black) hair / (윤기가 나는) jet-black hair. **2** [아득하다] far; far-off [-away]; in the distance; long way off. **3** [모르고[잊고] 있다]. e.g. 나는 그것을 까맣게 잊고 있었다 I've forgotten all about it. / It has entirely slipped from my mind [slipped my memory]

까먹다 [कमौक्दा] **1** [까서 먹다] [कासौक्दा] peel [rind / shuck / shell / crack] and eat. e.g. 귤을 까먹다 peel [rind] an orange and eat it. **2** [없애다] use up; spend all; squander; run through. e.g. 밑천을 다 까먹다 live on one's capital. **3** [잊다] forget; be forgetful [oblivious] <of>; lose. e.g. 가사[대사]를 까먹다 go blank.

까불다 [काबुल्दा] [우스꽝스러운 짓을 하다] act like a clown; clown; droll; be facetious; be merry; (어린이가) frisk; frolic; make merry. e.g. (어린이에게) 까불지 말고 얌전히 있어라 Where're your manner? / Behave yourself. / Be a good boy.

까지 [काजी] **1** [시간 또는 공간의 종결점] till; until; to; up [down] to(▷ until과 till은 그 뜻의 차이는

ㄲ

없으며 until쪽이 다소 격식 차린 감이 있음); [기한] by; by the time; not later than; before. e.g. 오늘날까지 up to this day / up to date. **2** [장소] to; as far as; [정도,범위] to the extent of; even; [한도] up to; to the limit; so much. e.g. 부산까지의 차표 a ticket to Pusan. **3** [게다가] moreover; besides; what is more; in addition to (that); to make matters worse; what is worse. e.g. 길이 바쁜데 차까지 고장났다 I was in a hurry [pressed for time] and, to make matters worse, even the car broke down.

까탈스럽다 [कथाल्सुरौप्ता] **1** [복잡하다] complicated; complek intricate. e.g. 그렇게 되면 문제가 까탈스럽게 된다 That will complicate the matter. **2** [어렵다] difficult; hard. e.g. 이 문제는 좀 까탈스럽다 The problem is a little too hard to solve. **3** [골치아프다] troublesome. e.g. 일이 생각보다 까탈스럽다 The work is more troublesome than I expected.

깍듯이 [काक्दुशी] politely; courteously; with much courtesy; civilly; in a civil way; respectfully. e.g. 남에게 깍듯이대하다 be polite [civil] to others.

깍듯하다 [काक्तुत्थादा] well-mannered; mannerly; polite; civil; courteous. e.g. 예의범절이 깍듯한 사람 a well-mannered person.

깍쟁이 [काक्जैंगी] **1** [약빠른 사람] a shrewd person; a sharp customer; a cunning fellow; a sly dog. e.g. 그렇게 깍쟁이노릇하지 말아요 Don't be such a stinker. **2** [인색한 사람] a stingy person; a tightwad; a niggard; a miser. e.g. 깍쟁이짓을 하다 be stingy with one's money.

깎다 [काक्ता] **1** (머리를) cut; clip; crop; dress; (단발로) bob; <美> shingle. e.g. 머리를 짧게 깎고 with one's hair cropped short [close]. **2** (잔디, 손톱, 나무 등을) trim; prune; dress; mow. e.g. 잔디 깎는 기계 a lawn mower. **3** (수염, 양털 등을) shave; shear; fleece. e.g. 수염을 갓 깎은 freshly shaven. **4** (값을) cut; reduce; come down; beat [knock / whittle] down the price; lower; take off; abate; make <it> cheaper; slash; bargain down. e.g. 값을 백 원으로 깎다 beat <the dealer> down to 100 won.

깎이다 [काकीदा] **1** [깎게 하다] make [have] <a person>

cut [trim]; get <a person> to cut [mow / peel / pare]. e.g. 머리를 깎이다 have one's hair cut [trimmed. **2** [깎음을 당하다] be shaved [trimmed / sharpen-ed / cut / pared / mowed]. e.g. 저 연필은 잘 깎인다 That pencil sharpens nicely.

깐깐하다 [कानकानहादा] [끈질기다] sticky; [완고 하다] pertinacious; tenacious; [세심하다] meticulous; in-quisitive; careful; [까다롭다] fastidious; particular; hard-grained <character>.

깔깔거리다 [काल्काल्गौरीदा] laugh loudly [aloud]; scream [roar] with laughter; guffaw; burst out laughing; burst into laughter; cachinnate; cackle. e.g. 그는 깔깔거리다거렸다 He gave a loud, cheerful laugh.

깔끔하다 [काल्कुमहादा] (외양이) sleek and clean; smart; neat and tidy [trim]; (성질이) sharp; harsh; fastidious. e.g. 깔끔하지 못한 slovenly / untidy.

깔다 [काल्दा] **1** (깔개 등을] spread; lay [put down] <a carpet on the floor>. e.g. 마루에 돗자리를 깔다 lay mats on the floor. **2** (자갈 등을) pave; pitch. e.g. 도로에 아스팔트를깔다 pave <streets> with asphalt. **3** (방석 등을) sit on [seat oneself] <a cushion>. e.g. 이 방석을 깔고 앉으십시오 Please take your seat on this cushion. / Please take [use] a (floor) cushion.

깔리다 [काल्लीदा] **1** [널리 흩어져 있다] be (over) spread; be covered; be scattered; be dispersed. e.g. 자갈이 깔린 길 a road covered with gravel / a graveled road. **2** [깔림을 당하다] [काल्लीमल दांग्रवादा] be buried [pressed / pinned / held / caught] under; be held down <by>; be sat on <by>. e.g. 자동차에 깔리다 be run over by a car.

깔보다 [काल्बोदा] look down on; think [make] little [nothing] of; despise; disparage; de-preciate; belittle. e.g. 남의 능력을 깔보다 undervalue a person's ability.

깔아뭉개다 [कारामूंग्गैदा] **1** [깔고 뭉개다] press down; compress; squeeze; [앉아서 뭉개다] sit on <a thing> and mash it. **2** (일을) shelve; pigeonhole; put [lay / cast] on the shelf; lay on the table; side track; table; (사실 등을) keep [conceal / hide] <a matter from a person>; repress [cover up / stifle up / smother up] <a fact>. e.g. 제안을 깔아뭉개다 shelve [smother up] a proposal.

깜깜하다 [कामकामहादा] **1** [어둡다] very dark; pitch-dark; <as> dark as pitch; <as> dark [black] as midnight. e.g. 깜깜한 밤 a jet black [pitch-dark] night **2** [모르다] ignorant; blank; unlearned. e.g. 나는 과학에는 깜깜하다 I am unlearned in science.

깜박 [काम्पाक] **1** (등불,별빛 등이) with a flash; with a twinkle.깜박하다flicker; twinkle; blink. e.g. 촛불이 바람에 깜박하다가 꺼졌다 The candle flickered out in the wind.. **2** (눈을) with a blink [blinking]; with a wink. e.g. 눈 깜박할 사이에 in the twinkling of an eye [in a blink / in a wink / quick as a wink / in a flash]. **3** [정신이 순간적으로 흐려지는 모양]. e.g. 깜박 졸다 have a snatch of sleep. 깜박하다 forget for the moment;(일이) escape one's memory; slip from [out of] one's memory. e.g.나는 가끔 깜박한다 My memory othen fails me

깜박거리다 [काम्पाककौरीदा] **1** (별이) twinkle; (불이) flicker; waver; shimmer. e.g. 깜박거리는 등불a blink of light / a flickering light. **2** (눈을) blink (one's eyes); wink; nictitate. e.g. 그녀는 눈물을 감추려고 눈을 깜박거렸다 She blinked to stop the tears. **3** (정신이) be vague [indistinct / hazy / misty / dim]. e.g. 정신이 깜박거린다 My mind keeps giving way [dimming / blacking out].

깜짝[1] [काम्चाक] [눈을 떴다 감는 모양] with a wink; with a blink [blinking]. 깜짝하다wink [blink] (one's eyes); bat one's eyes [eyelids]. e.g.눈 깜짝할 사이에 in the twinkling of an eye / in a twinkling / in an instant / in a flash.

깜짝[2] [काम्चाक] [놀라는 모양] with surprise; with a start. e.g. 세상을 깜짝 놀라게 하다 startle the world / cause the public to gasp with surprise.

깜찍하다 [काम्चिरवादा] [영악하다] too clever for one's age; precocious; too sharp; overly shrewd; cunning; crathy; sly; selfish. e.g. 깜찍한 놈 a foxy fellow.

깡충깡충 [कांग्छुंककांग्छुंग] e.g. 깡충깡충 뛰다 hop / skip / jump up and down / [뛰어다니다] romp / frisk [gambol] about

깡통 [कांग्थोंग] a can; a tin; an empty (tin-) can; [머리가 텅 빈 사람] an empty-headed fellow; a rattlebrain.

깡패 [कांग्फै] hoodlums; a

rough; a good-for-nothing; a gangster; a ruffian; a racketeer; a blackguard; a heavy; a hood; a tough.

깨끗이 [कैक्कुशी] **1** [청결히] clean (ly); cleanlily; [단정히] neatly; tidily. e.g. 깨끗이하다 clean / cleanse / make clean / purify / [치우다] put in order / tidy <up> / make tidy [neat]. **2** [결백하게] clearly; purely; cleanly. e.g. 깨끗이 살다 live cleanly / live an honest [a clean / a pure] life / lead an immaculate life. **3** [완전히] clean; comple-tely; wholly; thoroughly; entirely; once (and) for all. e.g. (병이) 깨끗이 낫다 recover completely <from one's illness> / be quite well again.

깨끗하다 [कैकत्थादा] **1** [청결하다] stainless; unsoiled; clean; [단정하다] neat (and clean); tidy; trim; smart. e.g. 깨끗한 방 a neat [clean] room. **2** [맑다] clear; limpid; clean; [순수하다] pure. e.g. 깨끗한 공기 clean [fresh] air <of the morning> / unpolluted air **3** [완전하다] clean; complete; entire; all; whole. e.g. 깨끗한 청산 clean liquidation. **4** [결백하다] pure; clean; immaculate. e.g. 마음이 깨끗한 사람은 행복하도다 Blessed are the pure in heart.

깨다[1] [कैदा] **1** (잠,꿈에서) wake (up); awake from sleep [a dream]. e.g. 잠이 깨다 awake [be roused] from one's sleep / have one's sleep interrupted. **2** (미혹, 환상에서) awake <from>; be aroused; become sensible; come to one's senses; be disillusioned; have one's eyes opened. e.g. 환상에서 깨다 wake from one's reverie [the illusion]. **3** (술이) become [get] sober; sober off [up]; take off the effects of drink; recover from one's intoxication; [술기운이 가시다] wear off. e.g. 술이 깰 때까지 자라 Sleep yourself sober. / Sleep and get sober.

깨다[2] [कैदा] **1** [부수다] break (into pieces); crack <an egg / a nut>; crush; smash. e.g. 접시를 깨다 break [smash] a dish. **2** [좌절시키다] frustrate <a person's plan>; [파괴하다] break; destroy. e.g. 평화를 깨다 destroy the peace. **3** [취소하다] cancel; dissolve; [어기다] break <off>; violate. e.g. 혼담을 깨다 break up a proposed marriage.

깨닫다 [कैदात्ता] [인식하다, 깨치다] understand; comprehend; realize; [알아채다] see; perceive; discern; be aware of; get wind of; sense. e.g. 위험을 깨닫다 perceive [sense] danger.

깨물다 [कैमुल्दा] bite; gnaw; crunch.

깨우다 [कैउदा] (잠에서) wake up <a person>; awake [arouse / rouse] <a person> from [out of] <his> sleep; call (up) <a person>. e.g. 문을 두드려 깨우다 tap [knock] up <a person>.

깨우치다 [कैउछीदा] [깨닫게 하다] awake [awaken] <a person> to <the realities [facts] of life>; wake <a person> up to; make <a person> realize [understand]; call <a person's> attention to. e.g. 도리를 깨우치다 bring <a person> to reason.

깨지다 [कैजीदा] **1** [조각이 나다] break; be broken [smashed / crushed]; come [go] to pieces (산산조각으로); go smash. e.g. 깨진 접시 a broken dish [plate]. **2** [상처가 나다] get [receive] a wound; get hurt; be broken. e.g. 날아온 돌에 머리가 깨지다 get hurt in the head by a thrown stone. **3** [성사되지 않다] fall through; be broken off; come to [end in] a rupture; be frustrated [ruptured]; fail. e.g. 흥정은 깨졌다 The bargain failed. .**4** [기록 등이 돌파되다] be broken [beaten / smashed]; (흥이) be dampened; be spoiled. e.g. 흥이 깨지다 one's fun is spoiled <by> / one's enthusiasm is dampened <by>.

깽깽 [कैंग्कैंग] yap, yap, yap. e.g. 강아지가 깽깽거렸다 The puppy cried, "Yap, yap, yap.".

꺼내다 [कौनैदा] **1** [밖으로 내다] take [bring] out; draw [pull] out; pick out. e.g. 호주머니에서 지갑을 꺼내다 take one's purse out of one's pocket. .**2** [이야기를 시작하다] bring out <a question>; bring <a matter> up <for discussion>; broach <a matter>; open <the case>; start <one's dis-course>. e.g. 이야기를 꺼내다 broach a matter / introduce a topic [subject].

꺼리다 [कौरीदा] [싫어하다] dislike; have a dislike to [for]; have a distaste for; be reluctant <to do>; [피하다] shun; avoid; alienate. e.g. 세상의 이목을 꺼리다 avert people's eye.

꺼림칙하다 [कौरीम्छीखादा] <서술적> feel uneasy; feel uncomfortable <about>; <something> weigh on one's mind. e.g. 꺼림칙한 예감 [꿈] an ominous premonition [dream].

꺼지다[1] **[कौजीदा]** [불 등이 사라져 없어지다] go [die] out; blow out; be put out; be extinguished. e.g. 꺼진 불[숯] a dead fire [coal].

꺼지다[2] **[कौजीदा]** [움푹 들어 가다] become hollow [depressed]; [땅이 내려앉다] sink <into the ground>; fall [cave] in; subside; [얼음이 깨지다] give; crack; (배가) get hungry. e.g. 지진으로 도로가 꺼졌다 The road sank [caved in] because of the earthquake.

꺾다 [कौक्ता] **1** [부러뜨리다] break (off); snap. e.g. 꽃을 꺾다 break off a spray of flowers / [따다] pluck [pick / pull off] a flower. **2** [방향을 돌리다] turn; make a turn; shith; veer (round); change direction. e.g. 왼쪽으로 꺾다 turn to the leth / turn leth. **3** (기세를) crush; break; squelch; daunt; shake; unnerve; damp (en); dishearten; discourage; (고집을) yield <to>; concede <to>; give in <to>. e.g. 용기를 꺾다 discourage [dispirit / dishearten / unnerve].

꺾이다 [कौकीदा] **1** [부러지다] break; be broken; snap; give way. e.g. 참나무는 휘기는 하지만 잘 꺾이지는 않는다 Oak may bend, but will not break. **2** (방향,길이) turn; make a turn; be bent; be crooked. e.g. 크게 꺾인 커브 a sharply breaking curve / a curve which breaks well. **3** (기세, 용기가) be discouraged; be disheartened; lose heart [courage]; be dispirited; (의지가) bend [bow] <to>; submit [yield] <to>. e.g. 그는 이 실패로 용기가 꺾였다 He was discouraged by this failure. / He lost heart through this failure.

껌 [कौम] chewing gum; a stick of gum (막대기 모양의); a tablet of gum (정제 모양의).

껍데기 [कौप्तेगी] (조개,달걀 등의) a shell; a valve.

껍질 [कौप्चिल] (나무의) bark; (과일 등의) skin (엷은 껍질); rind (단단한 껍질); a peel (주로 벗겨진 껍질).

-껏 [कौत] **1** [있는 대로 모두] as far [much] as possible; to the extent <of>; to the utmost <of>. e.g. 힘껏 일하다 work as hard as one can. **2** [까지] (right) up to <now>. e.g. 여태껏 all this while.

껑충 [कौम्छूंग] with a jump [leap]. e.g. 담을 껑충 뛰어넘다 jump [leap] over a fence.

껑충하다 [कौम्छुंख्वादा] tall and long-legged; lank; lanky; gangling. e.g. 키가 껑충한 사람 a lanky [gangling] man / a man tall as a church steeple.

께 [के] [에게] to [by / for] <a person>. e.g. 하느님께 맹세하다 swear by God.

께서 [केसौ] from <a person>. e.g. 아버지께서 주신 선물 the present that my father gave me.

껴안다 [क्यौआन्दा] embrace; hug; hold <a person> to one's breast [in one's arms]; take into one's arms; [떠맡다] undertake <many responsibilities>.

껴입다 [क्यौइप्ता] wear <a shirt> underneath one's outer clothes; wear extra (layers of) clothing. e.g. 셔츠를 석 장 껴입다 wear three undershirts one over another

꼬끼오 [कोकीओ] cock-a-doodle (-doo). 꼬끼오하다 <roosters> cry cock-a-doodle; crow. e.g. 수탉이 꼬끼오 하고 울고 있다 The cock is crowing [is going cock-a-doodle-doo / is cock-a-doodle-dooing].

꼬다 [कोदा] **1** (새끼 등을) twist; entwist; twine; throw. e.g. 금실 은실을 합쳐 꼬아 만든 끈 a string made of gold and silver threads twisted together. **2** (몸을) twist; writhe. e.g. 다리를 꼬고 앉다 sit with one's legs crossed.

꼬드기다 [कोदुगीदा] [꾀다] tempt; allure; seduce; entice; [선동하다] incite; abet; instigate; egg on; stir up. e.g. 꼬드겨 … 하게 하다 entice [allure / tempt] <a person> to <do> / egg[set] <a person> in a crime / put <a person> up to (commit) a crime.

꼬리 [कोरी] **1** (전반적동물의) a tail. **2** [밑동] a tail; [끝] the end. e.g. 혜성의 꼬리 the tail [train / trail] of a comet. **3** <비유> the rear (뒤쪽); one's true self [colors / character] (정체); a clue (단서). e.g. 말꼬리를 잡다 take up <a person> on a slip of the tongue / catch <a person> in his own words / cavil at <a person's> words. 꼬리(를) 감추다 hide [conceal] oneself; cover one's trace. e.g. 개가 꼬리를 감추고 있다 A dog is hanging its tail between its legs. 꼬리 (를) 물고 one ather another [the other]; in rapid succession. 꼬리 (를) 밟히다 give a clue to <the police>; furnish a clue to the discovery; be traced by. 꼬리 (를) 잡다 find another's faults; catch

<a person> tripping. e.g. 오래지 않아 그도 꼬리를 잡힐 것이다 He will give away one of these days. 꼬리 (를) 치다 [유혹하다] seduce; entice; (al) lure; [아첨하다] flatter; butter <a person> up. e.g. 그는 자기 사장에게 꼬리를 치고 있다 He is fawning on his boss.

꼬박꼬박 [कोबाककोबाक] [머리를 계속 숙였다가 들어] niddle-noddle; bowing repeatedly; [어김없이] humbly obeying; faithfully; obediently; without fail; [고대하여] waiting intently [anxiously]. e.g. 어른의 말을 꼬박꼬박 잘 듣다 readily obey one's elders.

꼬불꼬불 [कोबुल्कोबुल] meanderingly; windingly; zigzag. 꼬불꼬불하다 croo ked; meandering; winding; zigzag; tortuous <curve>; (나무가) snarled. e.g. 꼬불꼬불한 산길 a meandering [a zigzag / winding] mountain path.

꼬이다 [कोइदा] **1** (실 등이) get snarled [twisted]; be entangled; (일 등이) go wrong [amiss]; get fouled up; suffer [meet with] a setback. e.g. 꼬인 것을 풀다 untwist / disentangle / straightenout. **2** (마음이) becomecrooked [distorted / peevish / perverse]; get cross [sour]; get cranky. e.g. 배알이 꼬이다 get cranky / grow peevish.

꼬집다 [कोजीप्ता] **1** (살을) pinch; give a pinch; nip. e.g. 세게 꼬집다 give <someone> a sharp pinch <on the arm>. **2** [비꼬다] make cynical [cutting / sarcastic] remarks about <something>; say spiteful things; criticize. e.g. 아픈 데를 꼬집다 criticize <a person> on a sore spot.

꼬치꼬치 [कोछीकोछी] [따지고 캐묻는 모양] inquisitively. e.g. 꼬치꼬치 따지고 들다 examine <a matter> to a bottom. search into the root of <a matter>

꼬투리 [कोथूरी] **1** [깍지] a <pea> pod; a hull; a peascod (완두의); a shell; a shuck. e.g. 꼬투리를 까다 shell [pod] <peas / beans> .1 [일의 실마리] cause; reason; a lead; a beginning; a start; origin. e.g. 꼬투리를 잡다 invent [make up] a pretext <for a fight [quarrel]> / trail one's coattails.

꼭 [कोक] **1** [단단히] firmly; tightly; fast; close (ly). e.g. 끈을 꼭 묶다 tie [fasten] the strings tight (ly). **2** [빈틈이 없는 모양] exactly; to a tittle; to a nicety; perfectly. e.g. 꼭 알맞은 사람 a suitable person /

the right man.**3** [수량, 시간 등이 맞는 모양] exactly; precisely; punctually; sharp; just; to the minute. e.g. 시간에 꼭 맞게 punctual to the moment. **4** [틀림없이] certainnly; surely; undoubtedly; at any cost; on all accounts; in any case; by all means; by hook or by crook; without fail; always. e.g. 꼭 들러 주십시오 Please drop in by all means. / Do come and see me

꼭대기 [**कोक्तैगी**] [맨 위] the top; the summit (산의); the apek (머리,모자의) the crown; (뾰족한 것의) the spire.

꼭두각시 [**कोक्तुगाक्शी**] (철사나 손으로 놀리는) a puppet; (실을 달아 놀리는) a marionette; <비유> a tool; a cat's paw; a robot. e.g. 그는 정부의 꼭두각시가 되었다 He was made a puppet of the government.

꼴 [**कोल**] [모양] shape; form; [외양] appearance; [복 장] clothes; [상태] a state; plight; [광경] a sight; a spectacle. e.g. 꼴이 말이 아니다 be out of shape / look miserable.

꼴불견 [**कोल्बुल्ग्यौन**] [-不見] unsightliness; unpresentableness; shabbiness; indecency. e.g. 꼴불견이다 be unsightly [ugly / indecent] / cannot bear to see / be unable to stand the sight <of>.

꼴사납다 [**कोल्सानाप्ता**] [보기 흉하 다] ugly; unsightly; shabby; [창피스럽다] indecent; unbecoming; disgraceful. e.g. 꼴사나운 놈 a disgusting [despicable] fellow / "a nasty customer".

꼴찌 [**कोल्ची**] the last; the bottom; the tail (end); the tail ender (최하위자).

꼼꼼하다 [**कोम्कोमहादा**] very careful; meticulous; scrupulous; precise; deliberate; elaborate.

꼼꼼히 [**कोम्कोमही**] carefully; meticulously; scrupulously; in detail; elaborately. e.g. 일을 꼼꼼히 하다 do (one's) work carefully.

꼼짝 [**कोम्चाक**] budging; stirring; moving. 꼼짝 못하다 (1) [움직이지 못하다] cannot move at all / cannot move [budge / stir] an inch. e.g. 그는 그 자리에서 꼼짝도 못했다 He was rooted to the spot. (2) [곤경에 빠지다] be in a fiK be quite helpless; be at a loss; stick in the mud. e.g. 적을 꼼짝 못하게 하다 hold the enemy in check.

꼽다[**कोप्ता**] count <on one's fingers>; number; reckon; take a count <of>. e.g. 손꼽아 세다 count on one's fingers.

꽁꽁 [**कोंग्कोंग**] **1** [언 모양]. e.g. 꽁꽁 얼다 be thickly frozen (over) / be frozen stiff [hard / solid]. **2** [묶는 모양]. e.g. 꽁꽁 묶다 tie up <a parcel>.

꽁초 [**कोंग्छो**] a cigarette-butt [end / stub]; (엽궐련의) a cigar end;

꽂다[**कोत्ता**] **1** [박아 세우다] stick <in / into>; put <into / through>; fix <in / into>; [찌르다] drive <into>; stab; pierce; thrust; [끼워 넣다] insert <in>; inset; (핀으로) pin <up / down>; impale. e.g. 감자에 포크를 꽂다 stick a fork into a potato. **2** [가로지르다] put <a bar> across. e.g. 문에 빗장을 꽂다 bar [bolt] the gate.

꽂히다[**कोछीदा**] [찔리다] be stuck [pinned / impaled]; be stabbed [pierced]; [맞히다] hit; [끼이다] be inserted; [박히다] be embedded; [걸리다] be bolted. e.g. 타이어에 못이 꽂혀 있었다 I found a nail sticking in the tire.

꽃[**कोत**] **1** (초목의) a flower (특히, 관상용의) ; (과 수의) a blossom; [헌화] a floral tribute (▷ flower 는 가장 널리 쓰이는 말, blossom 은 결실을 기대하는 뜻이 포함됨). e.g. 일찍 [늦게] 피는 꽃 an early [late] flower. **2** <비유> [정수] essence; flower; spirit; the pride; pearl; the pick; [청춘] youth; [시절] best days; [미인] a fair woman. e.g. 청춘은 인생의 꽃이다 Youth is the flower of life.

꽃꽂이 [**कोक्कोछी**] flower arrangement [arranging / composition].

꽃답다 [**कोत्ताप्ता**] lovely [pretty / beautiful] (as a flower); flowerlike. e.g. 꽃다운 청춘 the bloom [flower / charm / glow] of youth / the springtime [prime] of life.

꽃봉오리 [**कोफोंगोरी**] a (flower) bud; a button; a budding flower; [청춘] the youth. e.g. 꽃봉오리가 피다 a bud develops into a flower [bursts into blossom].

꽉 [**क्वाक**] **1** [힘을 주는 모양] tight (ly); fast; firmly. e.g. 꽉 쥐다 grasp firmly / grip with force / take a firm grip of / squeeze. **2** [가득 찬 모양] close (ly); tight (ly); fully; compactly; to the full; chockfull. e.g. 트렁크에 꽉 채워 넣다 pack a trunk tight (ly) [close]. 꽉 차 있다[] be packed to the full / be chockfull of / be crammed with.

꽉차다 [**क्वाकछादा**] closely pac-ked; jampacked; full up; crowded (to capacity);

filled solidly. e.g. 이 서랍은 꽉찼다 This drawer is jampacked.

꽝 [क्वांग] **1** with a bang [boom]; with a thump [thud]. 꽝하다 [क्वांग्हादा] bang; boom; thump; thud. e.g. 의자가 꽝하고 넘어졌다 The chair fell over with a crash. **2** [당첨 안 된 제비] a blank. e.g. 꽝 없는 제비뽑기 a lottery without any blanks.

꽤 [क्वै] [제법] quite; pretty; rather; fairly (바람직한 일에 쓰임); considerably; [비교적] comparatively; relatively; [생각보다 더] beyond one's expectation. e.g. 꽤 먼 거리 [] a good distance.

꽥 [क्वैक] with a shout [scream / shriek / yell].

꽥꽥 [क्वैकक्वैक] quacking; shouting and shouting. e.g. 그렇게 꽥꽥 소리를 질러 서는 안 돼 Don't scream [squeal / screech] like that! 꽥꽥하다 = 꽥꽥 거리다].

꾀 [क्वे] **1** [슬기] wise counsel; wit; resources. e.g. 꾀 많은 사람 a man of resources / a resourceful person. **2** [계략,계책] a trick; a ruse; an artifice; a stratagem (군략 등의); a device; a design; a scheme. e.g. 꾀를 써서 이기다 [] outwit <a person>.

꾀다 [क्वैदा] [유혹하다] tempt; lure; entice; seduce; decoy. e.g. 꾀어 내다 [] lure <a person> out

꾀병 [क्वैब्यौंग] [-病] feigned [pretended] illness; counterfeit illness [sickness]; fake sickness; malingering. e.g. 꾀병을 앓다 [] feign illness / pretend to be sick / malinger.

꾀부리다 [क्वेबूरीदा] [게으름피우다] be sluggish; be indolent; be idle; be lazy. e.g. 꾀부리는 사람 [] a sluggard (man) / a lazy fellow / a lazybones.

꾀쓰다 [क्वेसुदा] use a trick; play a trick <on>; resort to wiles [a ruse]. e.g. 목적 달성을 위해 꾀쓰다 use tricks to achieve one's object.

꾀이다 [क्वेइदा] be lured; be enticed [tempted]; be seduced. e.g. 친구에게 꾀이다 be enticed by a friend.

꾀죄(죄)하다 [क्वेज्वेहादा] shabby; dirty; filthy; squa-lid; sordid; seedy; dowdy. e.g. 옷차림이 꾀죄하다 be shabbily dressed [clothed] / be dressed with dirty [soiled] clothes

꾀하다 [क्वेहादा] [계획,획책하다] scheme; plan; devise; contrive; de-sign; project; [서두르다] attempt; (나쁜 짓을) plot;

conspire; hatch <a plot>; machinate; frame up; [추구하다] seE; intend <to do>; aim at; (노력하다) strive [labor] <for>; exert oneself <for>. e.g. 실각을 꾀하다[] plot [design] a person's downfall.

꾸다[1] [कूदा] (꿈을) dream. e.g. 꿈을 꾸다 dream [have] a dream / [꿈에 보다] dream <a thing> / dream of / see in a dream

꾸다[2] [कूदा] [빌려 쓰다] borrow <a thing from a person>; have <money> on loan; have a loan <of>. e.g. 꾼 돈 만 원 the owing 10,000 won.

-꾸러기[कूरौगी] an overindulger; a person who overdoes <something>. e.g. 말썽꾸러기 a burden / a bother / a handful / a nuisance / an imp / a bully.

꾸러미[कूरौमी] [싼 물건] a bundle (in a wrapper); a package; (작은) a packet; a parcel; (큰) a bale (▷ bundle 은 운송이나 저장에 편리하도록 한 묶음으로 만들어 놓은 것. Parcel 은 수송이나 판매의 목적으로 비교적 조그맣게 꾸려 놓은 것이며, package 는 보통 상자나 용기 안에 담은 것을 말함). e.g. 옷꾸러미 a bundle of clothes.

꾸리다 [कूरीदा] **1** (짐을) pack (up); tie up; do up; wrap up; bundle. e.g. 짐을 꾸리다 make a bundle [package]. **2** (일을) manage; deal with; have control of. e.g. 살림을 꾸리다 manage household affairs.

꾸물거리다 [कूमुल्कौरीदा] move slowly; dawdle. e.g. 그는 무슨 일에나 꾸물거린다 He is slow [inefficient] about everything.

꾸미다 [कूमीदा] **1** [장식하다] ornament; decorate <a room with flowers>; adorn; bedeck; dress <a window>; [화장하다] make up <one's face>; put on makeup. e.g. 꽃으로 꾸민 방 a room decorated [blazoned] with flowers. **2** [수식하다] embellish; garnish. e.g. 꾸민 문체 an ornate [a flowery] style.

꾸밈 [कूमीम] [장식] an ornament; a decoration; an adornment; [허식] display; show; ostentation; (의상의) trimmings <for>; trim <on the dress>.

꾸벅거리다 [कूबौक्कौरीदा] nod (in a doze); make repeated bows. e.g. 책을 읽으면서 꾸벅거리다 nod [doze] over a book.

꾸준하다 [कूजुन्हादा] [한결같다] steady; constant; [부지런하다] assiduous; strenuous; [끈기 있다] untiring; unflagging; persistent.

꾸준히 [कूजुन्ही] steadily; constantly; ceaselessly; assiduously; strenuously; untiringly; unflaggingly; persistently; undefatigable

꾸지람 [कूजीराम] a scolding; a rebuke; a reproof; a reproach; a reprimand (공무상의). e.g. 꾸지람을 듣다 be scolded [reproved / rebuked] / catch [have / get] a scolding

꾸짖다 [कूजीत्ता] scold; chide; rebuke; upbraid; reprove; reproach; reprimand; give <a person> a scolding [lecture / lesson]. e.g. 지각했다고 학생을 꾸짖다 scold a student for being late. **-꾼** [कून] a person notorious [noted] for; a man occupied with .... e.g. 씨름꾼 a wrestler.

꿀 [कुल] honey; nectar (꽃의); molasses; honeydew

꿀꺽 [कुल्कौक] [삼킴] at a gulp; holus-bolus. e.g. 꿀꺽 마시다[삼키다] gulp (down) / drink [swallow] at a gulp

꿀꿀 [कुल्कुल] [돼지 소리] grunting (ly); [물소리] bubbling; gurgling.

꿇다 [कुल्था] bend one's knees; kneel (down); fall [drop / go down / throw oneself] on one's knees. e.g. 무릎을 꿇고 on one's knees.

꿇어앉다 [कुरौआन्था] sit on one's knees [legs].

꿈 [कुम] a dream; [환상] a vision; an illusion; [망상] a delusion; a chimera; [백일몽] a daydream.

꿈꾸다 [कुम्कूदा] [바라다] dream <of>; fancy (oneself); desire; wish; have an ambition <to ...>.

꿈틀거리다 [कुम्थुल्कौरीदा] wriggle (about); squirm; wriggle oneself. e.g. 꿈틀거리며 나아가다 wriggle along. **꿉꿉하다** [कूप्कूपादा] dampish; (빨래가) damp-dry.

꿋꿋하다 [कुक्कुत्थादा] [견고하다] strong; firm; solid; tough; hard; (언행이) upright; firm; inflexible; unyielding. e.g. 꿋꿋한 의지 a strong [an iron] will.

꿰다 [क्वेदा] **1** [관통시키다] pass [run] through; thread; string. e.g. 바늘에 실을 꿰다 thread a needle / run [pass] a thread through a needle **2** [찔러 꽂다] pierce; thrust; put through. e.g. 꼬챙이에 꿰다 skewer / transfix.

꿰뚫다 [क्वेतुल्था] **1** [관통하다] pierce; pass [run] through; shoot through (총알이); perforate (구멍을 뚫다). e.g. 정글을 꿰뚫은 도로 a road that pierces the jungle. **2** [통찰하다] discern; penetrate [see] into. e.g. 그의 말은 문제의 실상을 꿰뚫은 것이었다 What he said went [got] to the root of the matter. 꿰뚫어 보다 discern; penetrate [see] into; see through; have an insight into <a person's character>; perceive <another's motive>. e.g. 꿰뚫어 보는 듯한 눈 a penetrating eye.

꿰매다 [क्वेमैदा] [깁다] work in needle and thread; sew; stitch; (조각을 대고) sew (in) a patch; patch (up); put [add] a patch on <a coat>; [수선하다] mend. e.g. 상처를 꿰매다 suture [sew up] a wound [an incision

뀌다 [क्वीदा] break; release <flatulence>. e.g. 방귀를 뀌다 break [make] wind / pass gas / fart.

끄다[कुदा] **1** (타는 불을) put out; extinguish; blow out (입으로 불어서); snuff <a candle>; put <a fire> under; bring [get] <a fire> under control. e.g. 밟아서 끄다 trample [tread out / stamp out] <a fire>. 촛불을 불어 끄다 blow out a candle. 물을 끼얹어 불을 끄다 put out [quench] a fire with water **2** (전기 등을) switch off <an electric light>; turn off [out] <the television / the gas / the radio>; put off [out] <the light>. e.g. 시동을 끄다 stop [kill] an engine.

끄덕이다 [कुदौगीदा] nod. e.g. 재빨리 [가볍게.] 고개를 끄덕이다 nod a quick nod / nod lightly / give a slight nod.

끄떡없다 [कुतौगोप्ता] [탈없이 온전하다] safe (and sound); all right; (물,불 등에) proof <against>; [태연하다] unmoved; unflinching; withstand. e.g. 이 구두는 함부로 신어도 끄떡없다 These shoes will withstand much hard wear.

끄집어내다 [कुजीबौनैदा] **1** (물건을) take [bring / carry] out; draw [pull] out; drag out. e.g. 호주머니에서 편지를 끄집어내다 take a letter out of one's pocket. **2** (말을) bring up <a new subject>; bring <some-thing> into conversation. e.g. 슬슬 금전 문제를 끄집어내다 lead up to the question of money.

끈 [कुन] [줄] a string; a cord (▷ cord 는 string 보다 굵고, rope보다 가늚); a ribbon; a lace; [끈 끈] a braid; a line; a plait; a band.

끈기 [−氣] [कुन्गी] **1** [끈끈한 기운] viscosity; stickiness / glutinousity; adhesiveness. e.g. 끈기 있는 sticky / adhesive / glutinous. **2** [참을성] patience; perseverance; persistence; endurance; energy; stamina; staying power; tenacity; <美> stick-to-itiveness; ability to hang on; grit. e.g. 끈기 있게 기회를 기다리다 patiently await an opportunity.

끈끈하다 [कुन्कुनहादा] **1** [끈적끈적하다] sticky; adhesive; viscous; gluey. e.g. 끈끈한 액체 a sticky liquid. **2** [검질기다] tenacious; persistent; glutinous; sticky. e.g. 성질이 끈끈한 사람 a stickler / a man of great tenacity / a tough guy.

끈적거리다 [कुन्जौक्कौरीदा] **1** [끈끈하여 자꾸 들러붙다] be sticky; be gluey; <美> be gooey; adhere <to>. e.g. 풀이 묻어 내 손이 끈적거린다 My hands are sticky with paste. **2** [검질기다] stick <to>; (be) tenacious; persistent; persist <in>; get on <a person's> nerves; irritate by being persistent. e.g. 끈적거리는 사람 a person of tenacity.

끈질기다 [कुन्जिल्गीदा] strong and sticky; strongly adhesive; [집요하다] steadfast; persistent; tenacious; obstinate; unyielding; <서술적> have tenacity of purpose; stick to <a task>; persist in <doing>. e.g. 끈질긴 노력 a steadfast endeavor / (a) persistent effort

끊다 [कुन्था] **1** [절단하다] sever; cut (off); chop off; break. e.g. 둘로 끊다 cut in two. **2** [단절하다] sever <one's connections with>; break off <relations with a person>; break with; cut <connection>; cut off <communication>; [중단, 차단하다] cut off; stop; shut off; intercept; inte-rrupt; (꼭지, 스위치 등을 조작하여) turn off <the gas / water>. e.g. 끊을래야 끊을 수 없는 인연 an indissoluble tie / a fatal connection.

끊어지다 [कुनौजीदा] **1** [절단되다] be cut; break; snap (실 등이). e.g. 열에 녹아 끊어지다 burn out. **2** [두절,차단,중단되다] break off; be [get / become] broken; be cut off; be interrupted [suspendded / blocked]; cease; discontinue; pause; intermit; be switched off; be disconnected. e.g. 이야기가 끊어졌을 때 in pauses of the conversation / between talks.

끊임없다 [कुनिमऔप्ता] continued; continual; continuous;

ceaseless; unceasing; incessant; uninterrupted; endless; **끊임없이** constantly; continually; continuously; incessantly; ceaselessly; unceasingly; in succession; successively; without cease [ceasing / cessation / interruption / intermission / letup]; without a break; [영원히] perpetually; everlastingly; [항상] always; ever.

끌다 [कुल्दा] **1** [잡아당기다] pull; draw; give a pull; jerk (갑자기); drag [tug / lug / haul] <at> (세게); tow (밧줄로). e.g. 양쪽에서 끌다 tug from both side **2** [질질 끌다] drag; draggle. e.g. 발을 질질 끌다 drag one's feet. **3** [이끌다] lead; guide. e.g. 말을 끌다 lead a horse <by the bridle>.

끌리다 [कुल्लीदा] **1** [당겨지다] be pulled; be drawn <by>; be tugged; be lugged; be hauled; (질질) be dragged; be draggled; be trailed; drag; draggle; trail. e.g. 신발이 끌리다 one's shoes drag <on the ground>. **2** [연행,소환되다] be taken to <a place>; be walked off to <a place>. e.g. 경찰서에 끌려가다 be taken [walked off] to a police station. **3** (마음이) be attracted; be drawn; [매혹되다] be charmed; be fascinated; [감동되다] be moved; be touched <with emotion>; (꾐에) be touted [enticed / solicited]. e.g. 광고에 끌려 attracted [enticed] by the advertisement.

끌어내다 [कुरौनैदा] take [get / pull / draw] out; drag out [forth] (질질); carry <a thing> out of <a house>. e.g. 침대[집]에서 끌어내다 rout <a person> out of bed [the house].

끌어내리다 [कुरौनैरीदा] pull [drag / draw] down; take [bring / carry] down; (기등을) haul [pull] down; (물가를) reduce; cut down

끌어당기다 [कुरौदांगीदा] draw <a thing> near [toward / up to] <one>; pull nearer; drag in; (마음 등을) attract; draw.

끌어올리다 [कुरौओल्लीदा] drag [pull / draw / lug] up; (침몰선을) refloat; (난파선을) salvage; (그물을) land <a net>; (시체를) recover; [승진시키다] promote <a person to a higher position>.

끓다 [कुल्था] **1** [비등하다] boil; seethe; be on the boil. e.g. 끓는 물 boiling [scalding] water. **2** [뜨거

워지다] become very hot; become boiling hot. e.g. 방이 설설 끓는다 A (heated) room is boiling hot. **3** [치밀어 오르다] ferment; stir; burn; glow; be aflame; fret; fume. e.g. 노여움으로 속이 부글부글 끓다 fret and fume / seethe [boil] with anger / be convulsed with anger.

끓이다 [कुरीदा] **1** [끓게 하다] boil; heat; make hot. e.g. 펄펄 끓이다 boil up / bring <water> to the boil. **2** [익히다] cook. e.g. 밥을 끓이다 cook [boil] rice. **3** [속태우다] worry; bother; trouble; vex annoy. e.g. 그 일로 나는 속을 끓였다 This weighed [pressed] heavy on my mind.

끔찍하다 [कुम्चीख्वादा] **1** [참혹하다] cruel; atrocious; horrible; heartless; [으스스하다] ghastly; grim; gruesome; appalling. e.g. 끔찍한 살인 a cruel [cold-blooded] murder. **2** [지독하다] terrible; awful; horrible; tremendous. e.g. 끔찍한 인파 an awful turnout of people / a mammoth crowd. **3**[극진하다] terribly kind; awfully thoughtful [considerate]; very courteous [cordial]; devoted; warmhearted. e.g. 끔찍한 대접 cordial [hearty] hospitality.

끙끙 [कुंगकुंग] (아파서) with groans [moans]; (불평으로) grumbling; (힘이 들어) laboriously. e.g. 그렇게 끙끙 앓지 마라 Don't worry! / No dark brooding! / Cheer up! / Take it easy!

끙끙거리다 [कुंगकुंग्कौरीदा] groan; moan; grumble; labor. e.g. 끙끙거리며 물건을 나르다 drag [carry] a thing with great effort.

끝 [कुत] **1** [최종] an end; a close; a finish; a termination; [종말] the end; the extremity; [결말] (a) conclusion; [기한의 만료] expiration. e.g. 여로의 끝 the journey's end / the end of a journey. **2** [첨단] the point <of a pencil>; the (pointed) head <of a spear>; the tip <of a finger>; the nib <of a pen>; the end [top] <of a pole>; the nozzle <of a hose>; an end; a tip; the tail end; the extremity; [맨 마지막 부분] the edge; the verge; the brink; the border. e.g. 붓끝 the tip of a writing brush. **3** [한도] a limit; limits; bounds; an end. e.g. 끝이 없다 be endless [limitless / boundless] / know no end. **4** [결과] <in the> end; <as the [a]> result; <in> consequence. e.g. 충분히

생각한 끝에 ather due consideration.

끝나다 [कुल्नादा] end; come [be brought] to an end[a close / a conclusion / a termination]; close; be concluded; be over (with); be done; terminate; [완료되다] be finished; be completed; (기한이) expire; [결과를 가져오다] result [end] in; [산회하다] break up; rise; adjourn.

끝내 [कुल्नै] [결국] in the end; finally; ultimately; on top of all this; as the last consequence; as the final outcome; ather all

끝없다 [कुछौप्ता] endless; boundless (넓이가); unfathomable (깊이가); [영원하다] eternal; ever-lasting; [무한하다] unlimited; limitless; interminable; infinite; [다함이 없다] inexhaustible; never-ending; [끊임없다] ceaseless; incessant; [걷잡을 수 없다] uncontrollable.

끝없이 [कुतऔप्शि] boundlessly; endlessly; without end; interminably; eternally; infinitely; to an unlimited extent. e.g. 끝없이 깊은 바다 a bottomless abyss

끼 [की] [끼니, 식사] a meal; a diet. e.g. 한 끼 거르다[] skip a meal.

끼니 [कीनी] a meal; daily meals. e.g. 세 끼니 three meals.

끼다[1] [कीदा] **1** (안개, 연기 등이) gather; hang over; envelop; shroud; screen. e.g. 아침 안개가 끼어 있는 마을들 villages wrapped [veiled / enveloped] in a morning mist. **2** (때,먼지 등이) become dirty; be soiled; be stained <with>; (이끼 등이) be mossed. e.g. 옷에 온통 기름 때가 끼어 있었다 The clothes were smeared all over with greasy dirt.

끼다[2] [कीदा] **1** [끌어안다] embrace; hug; fold <a person> into one's arms; hold <a person> in one's arms; (팔 등을) fold [link] <one's arms>; (몸의 벌어진 사이로) hold <a thing> <under / between / behind>. e.g. 연필을 귀에 끼고 with [holding] a pencil behind one's ear. **2** [착용하다] put on; pull on; wear; slip on. e.g. 장갑을 끼다[] pull [put] on one's gloves.

-끼리 [कीरी] e.g. 가족끼리의 모임 a family party [gathe ring]. 우리끼리의 이야기지만 사태가 아주 좋지 않은 것 같다 Just between you and me, the situation looks very bad

ㄱ

끼어들다 [कीऔदुल्दा] intrude into [upon]; wedge (oneself) in (to); thrust oneself into; (이야기 등에) break [cut / shove] in <on>. e.g. 줄지어 선 틈바구니에 끼어들다 break into the queue / cut in / <英> jump the queue.

끼얹다 [कीऔन्ता] pour [splash] <on>; shower [sprinkle] <on / over>; dash <water> <on a person>. e.g. 몸에 물을 끼얹다 pour [splash] water over [on] oneself / douse oneself with water.

끼우다 [कीउदा] [사이에 넣다] put[get / let] in; insert <in>; hold between; (빠지지 않게) fix [fit] into; set <in>; inlay; [참가시키다] take <a person> into one's circle; let <a person> join <in>. e.g. 유리를 끼운 fitted with glass.

끼이다 [कीइदा] **1** (물건 사이에) get between; be caught in; get jammed [hemmed] in; be sandwiched between; [틈에 박히다] fit (in(to)); be fit for. e.g. 음식물이 이새에 끼었다 A particle of food got caught between my teeth. **2** (양자 사이에) lie [get] between. e.g. 어머니와 아내 사이에 끼어 난처한 처지에 있다 Caught between my mother and my wife, I am in an awkward position off a letter.

끼치다[1] [कीछीदा] (소름이) get (the) gooseflesh; become (all) goose pimples; feel goose-pimply [gooseflesh]; shudder; shiver; thrill <with horror>; feel a thrill; be gooseflesh all over; (사물이) make one's blood run cold; curdle one's blood; send a thrill [chill]; make one's flesh creep. e.g. 무서워서 소름이 끼치다 [कोछीदा] shudder in horror / feel one's hair stand on end with terror.

끼치다[2] [कीछीदा] (폐,영향 등을) cause <harm>; exert [exercise] <influence upon>; give; render. e.g. 걱정을 끼치다 give [cause] <a person> occasion to feel anxiety / cause anxiety to <a person>.

끽소리 [किक्सोरी] a yell of; a squawk of complaint. e.g. 끽소리 못하다 be (utterly) silenced / be in blank dismay [surprise] / be completely nonplused.

낄낄거리다 [किलकिलकोरिदा] giggle; titter; chuckle; snicker; snigger. e.g. 숨어서 낄낄거리다 laugh in one's sleeve.

낌새 [किम्सै] [되어 가는 형편] the course <of events>; the development <of an affair>; the turn <of events>; [기미] niceties; secrets; secret devices; inner workings; delicate signs; the delicate turn (of a situation); [조짐] a sign; an indication. e.g. 옆방에 누가 있는 낌새를 느꼈다 I felt [sensed] someone in the next room.

낑낑거리다 [किंकिंकौरीदा] groan; keep groaning; moan. e.g. 무거운 짐을 지고 낑낑거리다 groan under a heavy load on one's back.

ㄴ

나[1] [ना] [앞 뒤의 상반] but; though. e.g. 가난하나 거짓 말을 할 사람은 아니. Though (he is) poor, he is above telling a lie.2 [동작, 상태를 가림 and; or; whether. or . e.g.크나 작으나 가리지 않고. Regardless of whether it is big or small.

나[2] [ना]; me; myself; self; [자아] ego.

나[3] [ना] 1 [선택] ... or ...; ... and ...; either <A> or <B>; neither <A> nor <B> (부정). e.g. 너나 나나 누구 한 사람이 가야 한다. Either you or I must go.2 [그 어느 것을 막론하고.] and; as well as; (두 가지 물건일때) both ... and. e.g. 그는 밤이나 낮이나 일했다. He worked night and day.

나가다 [नागादा] 1 (밖으로) go [get / head / stir / turn] out; step out (잠깐 나가다) 2 [출근,출석하다] be present at <a ceremony>; attend <a meeting>; [출두하다] appear; report <at>. 3 [근무하다] work <in>; serve <in>; be in the service <of>; be employed <in>; hold an office <in> (관청에).4 [진출하다] go [sally] forth into <the world>; go upon <the world's stage>; launch into; enter upon. 5 [참가, 출전하다] join; participate in; take part in; enter for; go out for; [출마하다] stand <for>; run <for>. 6 [태도를 취하다] assume <an attitude>; take <a move>. [정신이 없어지다] This magazine has the largest circulation in our country. 금년에는 가스 스토브가 잘 나갔다 Gas stoves were in great demand this year.10 [닳다] wear [be worn] out [off]; wear threadbare.. 11

ㄴ

(비용이) be spent; be paid out; (수중의 물건이) be out. **12** (가치가) cost; be worth; (무게가) weigh. **13** [나아가다] advance; go forward; make one's way; [진척하다] make progress; progress; advance; improve. **14** [못쓰게 되다] be broken; go wrong; get out of order; (전기 등이) go out; fail; be cut off.

나그네 [नागुने] [길손] a traveler; a tourist; a wayfarer; [타관 사람] a stranger; [방랑객] a wanderer; a vagabond; [손님] a visitor; a guest.

나긋나긋하다 [नागुन्नागुत्थादा] (태도가) mild; amiable; affable; smooth.

나누기 [नानुगि] divide.

나누다 [नानुदा] **1** [분할하다] divide; part; sever; split (up); whack (up) 2[분배하다] istribute [divide (up)] among>; share; allot; portion out; (트럼프의 카드 등을) deal (out). **3** [구분하다] draw a line between; [분류하다] classify; sort <A> from <B>; assort. **4** [함께 하다] share <something> with <a person>; partake of.

나눗셈 [नानुस्सेम] division. 나눗셈하다 divide.

나다[1] [नादा] **1** [태어나다] be born; come into the world; come into being [existence].]. e.g. 날 때부터 from(the day of) birth. **2** [자라다] grow; [돋아나다] come out; bud(out); spring up; sprout. e.g.비 온 뒤에 난 죽순 bamboo shoots [sprouts] ather a rain. **3** [흘러나오다] flow [run / gush] out; spring (from). e.g.샘이 나다a fountain flows. **4** [발생하다] happen; come to pass [happen]; come about; occur; take place; turn up; break out; rise; arise; spring [come] up. e.g. 연기가 나다have smoke / be smoky / smoke rise [goes up]. **5** [길,구멍이 생기다] be built; be constructed; be made; be open (ed). e.g. 새 길이 났다A new road is built [opened]. **6** [감정, 생각 등이 들다] occur; feel. e.g. 성이 나다get [become / grow] angry.**7** [약효,능률 등이 생기다] get; take; produce. e.g. 약효가 나다 tell [act / work] <on> / talk effect **8** [생산되다] be produced; be yielded; be raised; be grown; be found. [이익이 생기다] issue <from>; accrue <from>; be derived; be obtained. e.g. 이 지방은 쌀이 많이 난다

This part of the country yields much rice. (냄새가) smell; (맛이) taste. e.g. 좋은[나쁜] 냄새가 나다 smell sweet [nasty]. (소리가) sound; come out [forth]; make a sound [noise]. e.g. 높은[날카로운] 소리가 나다sound loud [shrill]. (티가) have an air [a look]; look like; look; show. e.g. 장사꾼 티가 나는 사람 a man looking like a shopkeeper / a man apparently a merchant. **8** (병 등이) get; become; have. e.g. 병이 나다 get sick / fall [be taken] ill

나다[2] [नादा] **1** [계속되어 나아 가다] keep [go on] <doing>. e.g. 차차 자라나면 알게 될 것이다. If you grow older, you'll come to understand it. **2** [완료되다] have (just) finished <doing>. e.g. 한잠 자고 나니 정신이 새롭다. I have had a nap and now I feel much refreshed.

나들이 [नादुरि] going out; an outing; a short visit. 나들이 하다. go out; pay a short visit <to>; go on a(short) visit <to>.

나라 [नारा] **1** [국토] a country; a land; [영토] a territory. **2** [국가] a state; a nation; a country; an empire (제국) a kingdom (왕국) [국적] one's nationality; [고국] one's (native) country; one's home [mother] country; one's homeland [fatherland / motherland].

나란히 [नारान्ही] [줄지어] in a (regular) line [row / file]; side by side; abreast; [가지런히] evenly; uniformly; regularly; in (good / neat / trim) order.

나르다 [नारुदा] [운반하다] carry; convey; [수송하다] transport

나른하다 [नारनहादा] [고단하다] languid; weary; dull; heavy. 나른히 languidly; wearily; languorously; lazily; listlessly.

나름 [नारुम] e.g. 나름이다 depend on / hang [turn] on / be conditional [dependent] on / rest [lie] with. e.g. 자기 [그] 나름대로 in one's [its] own way / ather one's [its] kind. 능력 나름으로 according to one's ability.

-나마 [..नामा] though; however; even if; even. e.g. 맛은 좋지 못하나마 좀 들어보세요 These are not very tasty, but just have some anyway.

나마 [नामा] [···라도] though; however; but anyway; if only; [···마저] even. e.g. 그만한 비나마 와 주니

크게 다행이다 Even that much of rain is of great help

나머지 [**नामौजी**] **1** [잔여] the remainder; the remnant; the rest; the remaining (s); the balance (잔고); [잉여] the surplus; the residue; [남긴 것] leavings; remnants; things leth over; lethovers.**2** 끝(에 (in) the excess (of); (as) a result (of).

나무 [**नामू**] [수목] a tree; a shrub (관목); [초목] a plant; [목재] wood; timber; lumber; [땔나무] firewood; firing; fuel.

나무라다 [**नामूरादा**] [꾸짖다] rebuke <a person for something>; scold; blame; reprove; reproach; [비난하다] censure; accuse; [문책하다] call [bring] <a person> to account; take [call / bring] <a person> to task.

나물 [**नामुल**]**1** (edible) herbs; wild greens [vegetables]**2** (무친 것) cooked potherbs [greens / vegetables]; herb salad.

나불거리다 [**नाबुल्कौरिदा**] **1** [나부끼다] flutter [flap / stream] away. **2** (입을) chatter; prattle; rattle; wag one's tongue; flap about.

나비 [**नाबि**] a butterfly.

나사 [**नासा**] [**螺絲**] e.g. 나사를 박다 [죄다 / 돌리다] drive [put on / turn] a screw / screw

나서다 [**नासौदा**] **1**[나와 서다] come [step] forward; appear; come out [forward / forth / up / along]; turn up; make one's appearance; present oneself. **2** [나타나다] (구하던 것이) turn up; be found; (구하던 사람이) apply <for>; make application <for>; go in for. **4** [가로맡거나 간섭하다] intrude; intermeddle; push [put / thrust] oneself forward **5** [떠나다,출발햐다] leave; set out; start; get out <of>.

나아가다 [**नाआगादा**] [전진하다] advance; go forward; move on [forward]; progress; march; make way.

나아지다 [**नाआजीदा**] become [get] better; improve [be improved]; change for the better; take a favorable turn.

나약 [**नायाक**] feebleness; effeminacy. 나약하다 effeminate; emasculate; feeble-minded; spiritless.

나열 [**नायौल**] [**羅列**] marshaling; an array. 나열하다 arrange (in a row); marshal; enumerate.

나오다 [**नाओदा**] **1** [안에서 밖,앞을 향하여 오다] go [come / get / head] out of; take one's way out; step out **2** (말이) be said [spoken / uttered]; come out. **3** [… 에 모습이 나타나다] appear; show oneself; emerge <from / out of / on>; make one's appearance; come forward; turn [show] up; infest; [드러나다] show itself; assert [reveal / betray] itself; **4** (싹이) shoot; sprout; bud. **5** [참석,출석,출근하다be present at; attend; [출두하다] appear; report <at>.

나이 [**नाइ**] age; years.

나중 [**नाजुंग**] the last; the latter part; the future; the end; the consequences; the next.

나지막하다 [**नाजीमाखादा**] rather low; lowish.

나침반 [**नाछिम्बान**] [**羅針盤**] a compass.

나타내다[**नाथानेदा**] **1** (모습을) appear; show oneself; turn [show] up; make one's appearance. **2** [표시하다] show;speak for; [드러내다] expose; disclose; reveal; betray; bare; lay bare.

나태 [**नाथे**] [**懶怠**] laziness; idleness; indolence; sloth; sluggishness. 나태하다 idle; lazy; indolent; slothful; sluggish.

나흗날 [**नाहन्नाल**] the fourth day of the month.

나흘 [**नाहल**] [4일간] four days.

낙 [**नाक**] [**樂**] [즐거움] pleasure; enjoyment; delight; [기분전환] a diversion; [취미] taste; hobby; [위안] comfort.

낙관 [**नाक्वान**] [**樂觀**] optimism; an optimistic [a rosy / a hopeful] view; sanguine [optimistic / high] hopes.

낙농 [**नांग्नोंग**] [**酪農**] dairy (farming)

낙담 [**नाक्ताम**] [**落膽**] discouragement; disappointment;. 낙담하다 be [get] discouraged; be disheartened [dispirited]; be disappointed; be cast down; lose heart.

낙뢰 [**नांगन्वे**] [**落雷**] the falling of a thunderbolt.

낙마 [**नांग्मा**] [**落馬**] a fall [tumble / spill] from a horse. 낙마하다 all from [be thrown off] one's horse; fall off one's horse.

낙방 [**नाक्पांग**] [**落榜**] failure in an examination; flunk. 낙방하다 fail in an examination; <英> get plucked; flunk <an exam>.

낙서 [**नाक्सो**] [**落書**] [장난으로 씀, 또는 그 글씨나 그림] scribbling (s); a scrawl; (공중 변소의) graffiti

낙선 [**नाक्सौन**] [**落選**] (선거의) defeat [failure] (in an election); (출품의) rejection. 낙선하다 (선거에서)

lose an election; be defeated [unsuccessful] in an election; (출품이) be rejected.

낙심 [नाक्शिम] [**落心**] disappointment; discouragement; disheartenment. 낙심하다 be disheartened.

낙엽 [नाग्योप] [**落葉**] [나뭇잎이 떨어지기] defoliation; [떨어진 잎] fallen [dead] leaves.

낙오 [नागो] [**落伍**] (대열에서의) falling behind; straggling; (시대,사회에서의) being out of step with the times. 낙오하다 drop [fall] out of line [the ranks]; drop out <to the rear>; straggle.

낙원 [नाग्वॉन] [**樂園**] a paradise; Eden

낙인 [नागिन] [**烙印**] [불에 달궈 찍는 도장] a brand; a brand (ing) iron; [그 자국] a brand; a stigma <*pl.* –mata, –s>.e.g. / stigmatize / <비유> brand <a person as a Communist>. 그는 술고래라는 낙인이 찍혀 있다 He has the reputation of being a vicious drinker. 그는 사기꾼으로 낙인이 찍혔다 He was branded a swindler.

낙제 [नाक्चे] [**落第**] failure in an examination; (검사에서) rejection.

낙천주의 [नाक्छोन्जुइ] optimism.

낙천주의자 [नाक्छोन्जुइजा] an optimist.

낙태 a (criminal) abortion; a miscarriage; aborticide. 낙태하다 abort; miscarry; commit feticide.

낙태 수술 [नाक्थै सुसुल] a surgical operation to cause abortion.

낙하 [नाख्वा] [**落下**] falling; dropping; descent. 낙하하다 fall; come down; drop; descend; come to the ground.

낙하산 [नाख्वासान] [**落下傘**] a parachute;

낙후 [नाख्खु] [**落後**] falling behind; straggling. 낙후하다 lag [fall] behind <another in something>; be behind [backward]; be in arrear <the times>; drop [fall] out of line [the ranks]; be out of touch with

낚다 [नाक्ता] **1** (물고기를) angle for; fish (with rod and line); catch <a fish>. **2** [솔깃한 말로 꾀다] allure; decoy; entice; entrap; draw on; attract; take in; cheat; ensnare.

낚시질 [नाक्षिजील] angling; fishing (with rod and line). 낚시질하다 fish (with rod and line); angle <for trout / in a brook>.

난간 [नांगान] [**欄干,欄杆**] a handrail; a railing; (계단등의) a handrail; a guardrail

난감 [नांगाम] [**難堪**] 난감하다 [힘겹다] beyond one's capacity [power]; be too much for <one>; be not equal to <the task>; [견디기 어렵다] unbearable; intolerable

난관 [नांग्वान] [**難關**] [장애] a barrier; an obstacle; [곤란] a difficulty; [난국] a difficult situation; [교착] a deadlock; the crux of the situation.

난다긴다하다 [नान्दागिन्दाहादा] be incomparably deth [adroit]; display versatility [flexibility]; have many strings to one's bow.

난데없다 [नान्देऔप्ता] [뜻밖이다] unexpected; never dreamed of; sudden; abrupt; be out of the blue; unanticipated; [엉뚱하다] wild; fantastic; eccentric; absurd.

난동 [नान्दोंग] [**亂動**] a disturbance; a commotion; a strife; a riot.

난로 [नाल्लो] [**煖爐**] a stove; a heater (▷ stove 는 요리용 렌지도 뜻함); (벽난로) a fireplace.

난류 [नाल्यू] [**暖流**]a warm current.

난리 [नाल्लि] [**亂離**] [전쟁] a war; [반란] a revolt; a riot; [혼란] confusion; commotion.

난민 [नान्मिन] [**難民**] [피난민] refugees; displayced persons (D.P.); [빈민] the destitute; [이재민] sufferers; <flood> victims.

난방 [नान्बांग] [**煖房P暖房**] [데움] heating; [덥게 한 방] a heated [warm] room.

난방 장치 [नान्बांग जांग्छि] [**煖房裝置**] [난방 기구의 설치] heating; axir conditioning; [난방 기구] a heating apparatus [arrangement / system]; a heater; a radiator (복사 난방기).

난색 [नान्सैक] [**難色**] [곤란해하는 기색] disapproval; reluctance; unwillingness.

난잡 [नान्जाप] [**亂雜**] disorder; confusion; a mess; pell-mell; untidiness; disarray. 난잡하다 be in disorder [in a mess]; disorderly; confused; unsystematic; untidy; jumbled up.

난장판 [नान्जांगफान] [**亂場-**] a scene of confusion and disorder; a chaotic scene; a tumult; a turmoil; a mess.

난처하다 [नान्छौहादा] [**難處-**] awkward; annoying; be at a loss; be in a dilemma.

난파 [नान्फा] [**難破**] shipwreck; wreck. 난파하다 be wrecked; be shipwrecked.

난파선 [नान्फासौन] a wrecked ship.

난폭 [नान्फोक] [**亂暴**] violence; outrage 난폭하다 violent; rude; wild; reckless; rough; outrageous.

난해 [नान्हे] [難解] 난해하다 difficult to understand; hard to make out;abstruse.

낟알 [नादाल] a grain; a kernel.

날[1] [नाल] **1** [하루] a day; [시일] time **2** 날이 좋건 나쁘건 in fair weather or foul / rain or shine. **3** [시절,때] on the morrow of; in the event of; a time when; in time [case / the event] of.

날[2] [नाल] (칼 등의) an edge; a blade. 날(을) 세우다 put an edge on; give an edge to; edge; sharpen; whet.

날- [नाल] [익히지 않은] raw; uncookede.g.날고기 [생선] raw meat[fish]. 날계란 a raw egg.

날개 [नाल्कै] the wings

날다 [नाल्ता] (공중을) fly; take wing; take flight; (바람에) blow.

날뛰다 [नालत्विदा] jump (up); leap (up); bound (up); (사납게) rage; rave; raise a row; go [run] wild; get rowd

날려보내다 [नाल्यौबोनैदा] [놓아주다] fly; let fly; (바람이) blow off [away]; (바람에) have <a thing> blown away.

날렵하다 [नाल्यौफादा] smart; sharp; shrewd.

날로[1] [नाल्लो] [날이 갈수록] day by day; every day.

날로[2]. [नाल्लो] [날것으로] raw; uncooked.

날름거리다 [नाल्लमगौरिदा] **1** (혀 등을) let <a tongue / an arm> dart in and out **2** crane one's neck to see.

날리다[1] [नाल्लिदा] **1** (공중으로) fly; let fly; make fly. **2** (이름을) make famous; distinguish; be popular <with / among>; be widely [well] known **3** [일을 대충하다] scamp [skimp] one's work; do slipshod; do hasty job.**4** [없애다] lose <all>; waste; throw away; bring to naught.

날리다[2] [नाल्लिदा] (바람에) wave; flutter; flap.

날마다 [नालमादा] every day; daily; day ather day; day by day.

날숨 [नाल्सुम] an outbreath; exhalation; expiration.

날씨[नाल्षि] the weather; atmospheric conditions; the elements.

날씬하다[नाल्षिनहादा] (몸매가) slender; delicate (-looking); thin; slim; svelte; lithe; (자태가) smart; spruce. 날씬하다 She is trim and slender in figure.

날아가다 [नारागादा]**1** (공중을) fly away; take wings; (바람에) be blown away

[off]. **2** [없어지다] be gone [out]; be used up; go.

날인 [**नारिन**] [**捺印**] sealing; affixing a seal. 날인하다 seal; put [affix / set / stamp] one's seal to.

날짜 [**नाल्चा**] **1** [정해진 날] a date; dating. **2** [일수](the number of) days; time.

날치기 [**नाल्छिगि**] [재빨리 채뜨려 가는 행위] purse-snatching; swiping <things>; [재빨리 채뜨려 가는 사람] a purse-snatcher; a <handbag> snatcher. 날치기하다 snatch (away) <from>.

날카롭다 [**नाल्खारोप्ता**] **1**[예리하다] sharp; [끝이 뾰족하다] pointed.**2** [형세가 매섭다] sharp; poignant.

낡다[**नाल्ता**] [오래되다] old; [시대에 뒤지다] old fashioned; antique; outdated; out of date; outworn.

남[**नाम**][타인] another; other people; others..

남[**男**] [**नाम**]남자[**नम्जा**].

남 [**नाम**] [**南**]⇨ 남쪽[**नाम्चोक**]

남극 [**नाम्गक**] [**南極**] (지구의) the South Pole; the Antarctic; the south pole.

남기다 [**नाम्गिदा**]**1** [(사람,물건을) 뒤에 남게 하다] leave (behind); keep back [in]; [후세에 전하다] leave; hand down..**2** [하지[쓰지] 않고 두다] leave over [undone]; [따로 떼어 두다,돈을 저축하다] save; spare; have in store; set aside.

남남북녀 [**नाम्नाम्बुंगन्यौ**] [**南男北女**] The best men are found in the south and the best women in the north.

남다 [**नाम्ता**]**1** [여분이 있다] remain (over); be leth (over); be in excess [surplus]. **2** [이익을 보다] (사람이) make a profit; make; gain; earn; (사물이) be profitable; yield profits.

남다르다 [**नामदारूदा**] peculiar; <서술적> be different from others

남달리 [**नाम्दाल्लि**] out of the common; extraordinarily

남매 [**नाम्मै**] [**男妹**] brother and sister.

남발 [**नाम्बाल**] [**濫發**] an excessive [a reckless] issue; an overissue.

남부 [**नाम्बु**] [**南部**] the southern part [district / portion].

남부끄럽다 [**नाम्बुकरौप्ता**] ashamed; shameful.

남부럽잖다[**नाम्बुरौप्चान्था**] well-to-do; well-off; wealthy; rich.

남성 [**नाम्सौंग**] [**男性**] [남자] the male (sex); the sterner [stronger] seek a man; [남자 성질] masculinity; manliness.

남용 [**नाम्योंग**] [**濫用**] abuse; misuse; an extravagant [improper] use <of>.

남용하다 misuse; abuse; use improperly [unlawfully]; misappropriate.

남장 [नाम्जांग] [**男裝**] male attire [disguise]. 남장하다 disguise oneself as a man; be dressed like a man; wear [be in] men's clothes.

남짓하다 [नाम्जिथादा]<서술적> be a bit over [above / more than]; be upward of. e.g. 20명 남짓하다 be more than twenty people / be twenty strong.

남편 [नाम्फ्यौन] [**男便**] a husband; one's man; a hub(by); [法] a baron; the worser half (익살로).

남하 [नामहा] [**南下**] 남하하다 go [come] south; advance southwards.

남한 [नामहान] [**南韓**] South Korea

남해 [नामहै] [**南海**] the southern sea.

남향 [नामह्यांग] [**南向**] a southern exposure; facing (the) south. 남향하다 face the south; be exposed to the south.

남향집 [नामह्यांगजीप] a house facing [looking towards] (the) south;

납골 [नाप्कोल] [**納骨**] laying <a person's> ashes to rest. 납골하다 lay a person's ashes in a tomb.

납기 [नाप्कि] [**納期**] (금전의) the time [period] for payment; (물품의) the appointed date [time limit] of delivery.

납득 [नाप्तक] [**納得**] [이해] understanding 납득하다 [이해하다] understand; comprehend; [알아듣다] listen to reason; [깨닫다] be convinced <of / that ...>; satisfy [persuade] oneself <of / that ...>.

납부 [नाप्पु] [**納付**] (금전의) payment; (물품의) delivery <of goods>. 납부하다pay <taxes>; deliver <goods>; supply <goods>

납북 [नाप्पुक] [**拉北**] 납북하다 kidnap [abduct] <a person> to the north; hijack <an airplane> to the north.

납세 [नाप्से] [**納稅**] tax payment. 납세하다 pay one's taxes.

납작 [नाप्चाक] [몸을 바닥에 대고 냉큼 엎드리는 모양] flat; low.

납치 [नाप्छि] [**拉致**] (사람의) kidnaping; abduction; (물건의) seizure by force; hijacking. 납치하다 kidnap; carry away; take <a person> away [captive]; hijack.

납품 [नाप्फुम] [**納品**] [물품을 바침] delivery of goods 납품하다 deliver <goods>; supply <the government with goods>.

낫다[1] [नात्ता] [병이] recover <from illness>; get well; be cured; (상처 등이) heal.

낫다[2] [नात्ता] better <than>; superior <to>; preferable <to>; best <another>; surpass; excel; exceed; outdo; have an advantage <over>.

낭독 [नांगदोक] [**朗讀**] (a) reading (aloud); (a) recitation (암송); (연설투의) (a) declamation. 낭독하다 read aloud <to a person>; recite; declaim; give [deliver] a reading <of>.

낭떠러지 [नांगतौरौजी] a cliff; (바다에 면한) a bluff; (깎아지른) a precipice.

낭랑 [नांगनांग] [**朗朗**] 낭랑하다 (목소리가) clear and ringing; sonorous; silvery <voice>; (달빛 등이) clear and serene.

낭만 [नांगम्न] [**浪漫**] being romantic.

낭비 [नांगबि] [**浪費**] waste; extravagance; squandering 낭비하다 waste; use [spend] wastefully; dissipate; throw away; squander

낭송 [नांगसोंग] [**朗誦**] recitation

낭패 [नांगफै] [**狼狽**] [실패] failure; frustration; a blunder; a fiasco; [곤경] (a) trouble. 낭패하다 fail <in>; fall down <on / at>; make a failure; meet with failure; be frustrated; be in a fix [dilemma].

낮 [नात] [해가 떠 있는 동안] day; the daytime; [대낮] noon; noonday; noontime.

낮다 [नात्ता]**1** (높이,정도가) low; (숫자가) low; small. **2** (신분이) low; humble; mean.

낮잠 [नाच्चाम] a (midday) nap; a noon's nap; a siesta; forty winks

낮추다 [नाच्छुदा] [낮게 하다] lower; bring [let] down; lower; sink; turn down (라디오를).

낮춤말 [नाच्छुम्माल] [言] [하대말] intimate [friendly] speech [terms].

낯 [नात] **1** [얼굴] a face; a visage; features **2** [면목, 체면] face; honor; prestige.

낯가리다 [नाक्कारिदा]**1** (어린 애가) be afraid [shy] of strangers; be bashful.**2** [차별 대우하다] treat with discrimination; discriminate against <a person>.**3** [체면을 세우다] save one's face [honor]; relieve <a person> from disgrace

낯간지럽다 [नाक्कान्जिरौप्ता] ashamed; blushed.

낯두껍다 [नात्तुक्कौप्ता] shameless; unabashed; unblushing; brazen-faced; impudent; audacious

낯부끄럽다 [नाप्पुकरौप्ता] ashamed; shameful; disgraceful.

낯설다 [नात्सौल्ता] [알지 못하다] unknown; [친숙하지 않다] strange; unfamiliar.

낯익다 [नाछ्विक्ता] (사물이) familiar <to>; well known <to>.

낱 [नात]a piece; a unit.

낱낱이 [नान्नाछी]**1** [하나하나] one by one; individually; separately. **2** [모조리] [मोजोरि] in everything; all; entirely**3** [자세히] in detail; in full a grain <of rice>.

낳다 [नाथा]**1** [출산하다] bear; give birth to; be delivered of; bring forth.**2** [생기게 하다,배출하다] bring forth; produce; bear; give rise to.

-내 [.....नै] [내내] [नैनै] through; throughout; all through; in the course of <the day>. e.g. 겨우내 throughout [all through] the winter.

내 [नै] [**內**] within; within the scope of.

내[1] [नै] [연기][यौगि] smoke; fume.

내[2] [नै] 그의 입김에서는 술내가 난다 His breath rees [smells] of liquor.

내[3] [नै] [시내] a stream; a brook.

내[4] [नै] **1** [나] [ना]I; myself. **2**[나의] my.

내- [नै] [**來**] next; coming; forthcoming.

내가다 [नैगादा] take [bring] out; carry out [away]; out with <something>; remove.

내각 [नैगाक] [**內閣**] a cabinet; a ministry; [정부] the government; the administration.

내걸다 [नैगौल्ता] **1** [게양하다] put up; hang out <a sign / a lantern>; display <a flag>. **2** [내세우다] stand for; advocate; maintain; (문제 등을) take up <a problem>.

내공 [नैगोंग] [**耐空**] endurance in flying [flight].

내과 [नैक्वा] [**內科**]

내기 [नैगि] betting; staking; gambling. 내기하다 wager <on>; bet <on>; lay [have] a wager <on>; make a bet <on>; lay down a stake. 내기하다 see who will win <in a contest>.

내내 [नैनै] all the time [way]; (all) through; all during <the vacation>.

내년 [नैन्यौन] [**來年**] next year; the coming year.

내놓다 [नैनोत्था]**1** (밖으로) put out; take out; bring out; pull [draw] out. **2** (가둔 것을) set [make] free; free; liberate; let go [loose]; put [let] out of; release.**3** [드러내다] expose; bare; show. **4** (팔려고) lay <articles> out for sale; put up [offer] <a thing>

for sale; place <a thing> on sale; [진열하다] exhibit <an article> at a show; put <an article> on show. **5** [발간하다] publish; issue; [생산,배출하다] bring [put] out; produce. **6** (돈을) pay; give; contribute (기부); invest (투자). **7** (음식 등을) offer; serve (up); set out <a meal>. [제출하다] present; send in; submit <one's view>; tender; bring forward [up]. **9** [제외하다] exclude; except; leave out; omit. **10** [포기하다] give up; abandon; leave; resign.

내다 [नैदा] **1** (밖으로) put out; [꺼내다] take out; bring out; pull [draw] out. **2**[발휘하다] put [call] forth; muster [pluck / rouse / stir / summon] up <one's courage>; exert; display.

내다보다 [नैदाबोदा] **1** [밖을 보다] look out <of / over / on>; see from within. **2** [예상하다] anticipate; expect; forecast; foresee; look ahead.

내던지다 [नैदौन्जिदा] **1** [냅다 던지다] throw [cast / hurl / fling] out [away]. **2** [포기하다] give [throw] up; abandon; [내버려 두다] neglect; lay aside; leave [let] <a thing> alone.

내란 [नैरान] [**內亂**] [내전] a civil war [strife]; [폭동] an insurrection; [반란] a rebellion; [국내의 소요] internal disturbances [troubles]; a domestic conflict.

내레이션 [नैरिइश्यौन] narration.

내려가다 [नैर्यौगादा] (아래로) go [come] down; get down; move down [to]; descend.

내려놓다 [नैर्यौनोत्था] take down; bring down; put [pull] down

내려다보다 [नैर्यौदापोदा] (아래를) look down <at>; overlook; take a bird's-eye view <of>; see <a place> below one's eyes. **2** [얕보다I] look down upon [on] <a person>; despise; belittle; slight; make light [little] of.

내려앉다 [नैर्यौओन्ता] **1** (아랫자리로) come [get] down <and sit>; take a lower seat. **2** collapse; give way; cave [fall] in; (지붕 등이) subside

내려오다 [नैर्यौओदा] (높은 데서) come [go] down; descend; (명령 등이) be given; be issued.

내려치다 [नैर्यौछ्दिा] strike <a person> a blow <on the head>; bring <a stick> down <on a person's head>; flick [swing] downwards.

내력 [नैर्यौक] [**來歷**] **1** [경력] a career; one's (personal) history **2** 내림

내륙 [नैर्युक] [**內陸**] inland.

내륙 지방 [नैर्युक जीबांग] inland

areas; the interior (provinces) of a country.

내리다[1] [नैरिदा] <자동사>**1** (높은 데서) come [go] down; get [step] down; descend **2** (비,눈,서리 등이) fall; come down; descend. **3**(온도 등이) drop; fall; go down

내리다[2] [नैरिदा] <타동사>**1** (높은 데서) take down; lower; bring down; put [pull] down; lith down; let down [fall]; drop. **2** (탈것에서) set <a passénger> down; drop; get <a person> off. **3** (셔터,커튼 등을) drop; let fall; let down. **4** (값 등을) cut [reduce / lower / drop / br ing down] <the price / wages / fare / freight>.

내리쬐다 [नैरिच्वेदा] beat [strike] down on; shine [glare / blaze] down upon.

내막 [नैमाक] [**內幕**] the inside (facts); concealed [undisclosed] circumstances; inner workings <of a business>.

내맡기다 [नैमाक्किदा] leave <a matter> (entirely) to [with] <a person>; commit <a matter> to a person's care; entrust <a person> with the task <of>.

내면 [नैम्यौन] [**內面**] the inside; the interior.

내몰다 [नैमोल्दा] drive out [away]; turn [force / send] out; bundle off [out]; (직위에서) oust [expel / -dislodge] <a person from a position>; hoof out.

내몰리다 [नैमोल्लिदा]be driven out [away]; be forced out; be expelled.

내밀다 [नैमिल्ता] **1** [한쪽 끝이 나오다] push [thrust] out; stick out <of>; force out. **2** [남에게 미루다] throw <on>; shith <on>; switch <over to>.

내방 [नैबांग] [**來訪**] a visit; a call.내방하다 visit; call on <a person>; call at <a house>; pay <a person> a visit; make a visit to <a person>.

내뱉다 [नैबैत्ता] spit (out); spew; spue; expectorate.

내버려두다 [नैबौयौंदुदा] [등한히 하다] neglect <one's work>; lay aside; [방치하다] leave [let] <a thing / a person> alone [unattended / un-tended]; let <a thing> as it is [stands].

내버리다 [नैबौरिदा] throw [east / fling] away; dump <refuse>.

내보내다 [नैबोनैदा] **1** (안에서 밖으로) let go [get] out; let[send] out; forward; turn <a person> out-of-doors; show <a person>

the door. **2** (직장,거주지에서) give <a person> the sack; fire; evict (셋방 등에서).

내복 [**內服**] [**नैबोक**] **1**내복을 갈아입다 change one's underwear.**2** [약을 먹음] internal use. 내복하다 take [use] <a medicine> internally [orally].

내부 [**नैबू**] [**內部**] the inside; the interior; the inner part.

내분 [**नैबुन**] [**內紛**] an internal trouble [strife]; domestic discord; a storm in a teacup.

내빼다 [**नैप्पैदा**] flee; run away

내색 [**नैसैकं**] [**-色**] one's facial expression [countenance]; expression of one's feeling; betrayal of one's emotion; a revealing look.

내색하다 [**नैसैखादा**] betray one's emotion; show [display] <anxiety> on one's face; let one's face show one's thoughts

내세 [**नैसे**] [**來世**]a better [the next / other] world; the future life [existence] ather death; the world to come; the hereather; Kingdom

내세우다 [**नैसेउदा**] **1** [나와 서게 하다] make <a person> stand; stand; support. e.g. 대열 앞에 내세우다 make <a person> stand before ranks.**2** [나서게 하다] nominate; designate; put up; make [have] <a person> represent [stand for]. **3** [남이 보도록 내놓다] put up [set up / hang out] <a sign>; put <a placard on the sidewalk **4** stand on; insist; bring <a matter> up to one's advantage; speak highly of <one's own achievement>; single

내수 [**नैसू**] [**內需**] domestic [home] demand [requirements]; (소비) domestic consumption.

내숭 [**नैसुंग**] 내숭하다 tricky; crathy; insidious; wily; snaky.

내오다 [**नैओदा**] (안에서 밖으로) take [carry / bring] out; remove.

내왕 [**नैवांग**] [**來往**] [통행] come-and-go; comings and goings; (street) traffic; (편지의) communication; an exchange of letters; [교제] friendly) intercourse 내왕하다 come and go

내외 [**नैवे**] [**內外**] **1** [안팎] the interior and exterior; within and without; the inside and outside. **2** home and abroad; home [domestic / native] and foreign. **3** [부부] man [husband] and wife; a (married) couple. **4** [약간 넘거나 덜함] some; about; around; or so; thereabouts; a matter of

내용 [नैयोंग] [內容]1 [속에 든 알맹이] contents <of a bag>. contents; import.2 (실질) substance.

내우 외환 [नैउ वेहवान] [內憂外患] troubles both at home and abroad [from within and without]; internal and external troubles.

내일 [नैइल] [來日] [명일] tomorrow.

내장 [नैजांग] [內臟] the internal organs; the internals; [창자] the intestines; the bowels; the entrails; the guts; (가축의) innards; viscera; guts; (새의) giblets.

내재 [नैजे] [內在] imamnence; indwelling; inherence. 내재하다 be immanent <in>; indwell <in>; be inherent <in>.

내조 [नैजो] [內助] the wife's help [assistance / aid]. 내조하다 help one's husband.

내주다 [नैजूदा]1 (금품을) take [bring / put] <a thing> out; give; give out [away]; [교부,허가하다] grant; issue; [차려 주다] set <a person> up. 2 transfer; resign; (항복) surrender.

내키다 [नैखिदा] (마음이) have a mind <to>; be [feel] inclined <to do>; feel like <doing>; have an inclination; care to; be disposed <to do>; be willing <to do / for doing>. money in the personal possession of the king; the privy purse.

내후년 [नैहुन्यौन] [來後年] the year ather next; three years hence.

냄새 [नैम्सै] 1 (a) smell; (an) odor; (a) scent; [방향] perfume; aroma; fragrance; a stink; ree. 2 [느낌,티] a smack; a flavor; an odor.

냅다 [नैप्ता] [몹시 빠르고 세차게] with force; hard; actively; with all one's strength; violently.

냉- [नैंग] [冷]iced; cold; chill(ed); cooled.

냉각 [नैंगाक] [冷却] cooling; refrigeration. 냉각하다 [차게 하다] cool (down); refrigerate; [차가워지다] cool (off); get cool.

냉담 [नैंग्दाम] [冷淡] 1 [무관심] coolness; indifference; lukewarmness. 냉담하다 cool; halfhearted; indifferent; apathetic; phlegmmatic. 2 [냉정] cold-heartedness; heartlessness 냉담하다 cold; cold-hearted; indifferent; heartless

냉동 [नैंग्दोंग] [冷凍] freezing; refrigeration 냉동-하다 cool down; refrigerate; deep-freeze.

냉랭하다 [नैंग्लैंगहादा] [冷冷-] 1 [차갑다] cold; chilly;

frigid; icy; freezing. **2** [태도가 쌀쌀하다] cold; cool; indifferent; half-hearted.

냉방 [नैग्बांग] [**冷房**] [찬방] a cold [an unheated] room; [온도를 낮춤] air conditioning; air cooling. 냉방하다 air-condition [-cool] <a room>.

냉소 [नैग्सो] [**冷笑**]a cold [sardonic / derisive / cynical] smile; a jeer; a derision 냉소하다 smile mockingly; sneer <at>; jeer <at>; deride; mock at; laugh in scorn.

냉장고 [नैग्जांगो] [**冷藏庫**]a refrigerator; a freezer

냉정 [नैग्जौग] [**冷靜**] calmness; coolness; composure; presence of mind. 냉정하다 calm; cool; composed; self-possessed; cold-headed; serene; dispassionnate.

냉큼[नैग्खुम] straight [right] away; right now; [재빨리] quickly; promptly; hastily

냉혈 [नैगह्यौल] [**冷血**]**1** [動] cold-bloodedness. e.g. 냉혈의 (a) ematocryal / poikilothermal / cold-blooded. **2** [무정함] cold-heartedness; callousness; heartlessness. e.g. 냉혈의 cold-hearted / heartless.

냉혹 [नैग्होक] [**冷酷**]cold-bloodedness; cruelty; cold-heartedness. 냉혹하다 cruel; heartless; callous; cold-hearted; inhuman

냠냠 [न्यामन्याम] Yum-yum! (=How tasty!) .냠냠하다 [먹고 싶어하다] want [wish / desire] to eat; [갖고 싶어하다] wish for; long [itch] for; be anxious for.

너 [नौ] [2인칭 대명사] you; <古> thou.

너그러이 [नौगुरोई] generously; liberally; with lenience; with a broad mind; indulgently.

너그럽다 [नौगुरौप्ता] broad-minded; generous; liberal; magnanimous; tolerant; lenient; indulgent.

너덜거리다 [नौदौल्कौरिदा] (가닥이) dangle [hang] in tatters; flutter; flap.

너머 [नौमौ] beyond; over; the other [opposite] side <of a mountain>.

너비 [नौबि] width; breadth; range.

너울거리다 [नौउल्कौरिदा] (물결이) wave; surge; roll; swell; undulate; waver; sway (to and fro).

너저분하다 [नौजौबुनहादा] (모양이) shabby; untidy; disorderly; messy; squalid; (행실이) slovenly; untidy; sloppy.

너털웃음 [नौथौरूसुम] a loud [hearty / boisterous] laugh; a guffaw; cachinnation; a roar of laughter.

너희(들) [नौहउइ] [दल] you; ye; you all; you people; you folks.

넉 [न्यौक] four; fourth (순서) 넉달 four months.

넉넉하다 [नौग्नौख्वादा] **1** [충분하다] enough; sufficient; adequate; plenty [plenty-ful]; ample.**2** [풍족하다] rich; well-off; comfortably off.**3** [도량이 넓다] big- [broad-] minded; lenient

넉살 [नौक्साल] shameless-ness; impudence

넋[नौक]a soul; a spirit; a ghost;

넋두리 [नौक्तुरी] 넋두리하다 <a shaman> transmit [con-vey] the words of the departed spirit to the bereaved family. 넋두리하다 [불평하다] grumble <at / about / over>; mutter [murmur] <at / against>; complain <of / about>

넌지시 [नौन्जीशी] indirectly; tacitly; allusively; implicitly; covertly; by hints

널다 [नौल्ता] [펼쳐 놓다] spread out; stretch; [펴서 걸다] hang <something> out <to dry>.

널따랗다 [नौल्तारात्था] wide; broad; roomy; spacious; extensive.

널리 [नौल्लिदा] [너르게] widely; broadly; extensive-ly; far and wide; [보편적으로] universally; genera-lly; [도처에] everywhere; all over

널리다 [न्यौल्लिदा] [흩어져 있다] be spread [scattered] <over / around>

넓다 [नौल्ता] (폭이)] wide; broad <road>; (면적이) large <territory>; extensive

넓이 [नौल्बि] **1** [폭] width; breadth. **2** [면적] (an) area; (an) extent; dimensions.

넓적하다 [नौल्चौख्वादा]

넘겨다보다 [नौम्ग्यौदापोदा] [탐내다] covet; lust <for / ather>; have a desire [lust] for.

넘겨잡다 [नौम्ग्यौजाप्ता] guess; [알아채다] anticipate; fore-cast; foresee; look ahead.

넘겨주다[नौम्ग्यौजूदा]**1** (너머로) pass <a thing> over. **2** [인도하다] hand [turn] over; deliver **3** [양도하다] transfer; assign; convey; part with (내주다). **4** [포기하다] surrender

넘겨짚다 [नौम्ग्यौजीप्ता] guess; make [try] a shot <at>.

넘기다 [नौम्गिदा]**1** [넘어가게 하다] pass <a thing> ov make pass [go] over. **2** [쓰러뜨리다] fell; throw down; trip (다리를 걸어서). **3** [이월하다] carry [bring] over; [다음으로 미루다] carry forward; [연기하다] defer; postpone; put off.

넘다 [नौम्ता] **1** go [get] beyond; [가로지르다] cross; go across <a

mountain>; [통과 하다] pass. exceed; go [pass] beyond <the limit>; be more than **넘보다 [नौम्बोदा]1** [얕잡아 깔보다] look down on; underrate; hold <a person> cheap **2** = 넘겨다보다1.

넘어가다 [नौमैगादा] 1 = 넘다 **2** [쓰러지다] fall over [down]; drop; [망하다] collapse; be overthrown. **3** [해,달이 지다] set; sink; go down.**4** [옮아가다] pass <into / to>; (권리 등이) pass [fall] into another's hand; be transferred. **5** [속다] be deceived [cheated]; be taken in; be played upon.

넘어뜨리다 [नौमौतुरिदा]1 bring [throw] down; (사람을) throw <a person> (to the ground); get <a person> down; knock down**2** [꺾다] defeat; beat.

넘어서다 [नौमौसौदा] pass [get] over.

넘어오다 [नौमौओदा] (넘어서 이쪽으로) come over <a mountain>; come beyond; come across; (역경 등을) overcome [tide over] <difficulties>.

넘어지다 [नौमौजीदा] 1 (서 있는 것이) fall; come [go] down; collapse. **2** [패배하다] be defeated [beaten]; [망하다] be ruined; collapse; be overthrown. ⇨ 넘어가다

넘치다 [नौम्छिदा] 1 [흘러나오다] overflow <the bank>; run [flow] over <the brim>; be overflowing <with>; be superabundant [overabundant]. **2** [지나치다] exceed; be more than

넝쿨 [नौंग्खुल]= 덩굴.**[दौगुल]**

넣다 [नौत्था]1 (속에) put [take / bring] in; let in **2** [끼워 넣다] put <a thing> in (to); set [fit] <a thing> in; insert. **3** [(사람을) 통과시키다] let [allow] in; admit. **4** [수용하다] acco-mmodate; admit (into); take in <a patient>; hold <so many people>; [들어가게 하다] send [put] to..

-네[-ने] [사람,집안의 한 무리. e.g. 우리네 **[उरिने]** we all.

네[1] [ने] 1 [너] [you. **2** [너의] your.

네[2] [ने] [넷] four.

네[3] [ने] = 예.

네모 [नेमो] a square (shape); a quadrilateral.

넥타이 [नेक्थाइ] a necktie; a tie.

넷 [नेत] four.

녀석 [न्यौसौक] [놈] a fellow; a guy; (친근감을 가지고) a chap; a male.

ㄴ

년 [न्यौन] [年]a year.

녘 [न्यौक] [무렵] about; around; toward (s). e.g. 새벽 녘에 around dawn / toward (s) dawn [daybreak].

노고 [नोगो] [勞苦] [애씀] labor; pains; toil; travails.

노곤하다 [नोगोनहादा] [勞困–] languid; heavy; weary; tired; exhausted.

노골적 [नोगोल्चौक] [露骨的] [숨기지 않는] naked; plain; open; undisguised; unreserved; broad; frank; candid; blunt; outspoken; plain-spoken; straightforward.

노긋노긋하다 [नोगन्नोग्थादा] [아주 부드럽다] very soth [limp]; supple; elastic; [유순하다] gentle

노년 [नोन्यौन] [老年] old [advanced] age; declining years

노닥거리다 [नोदाक्कौरिदा] keep talking[chatting / chattering / joking] playfully

노동 [नोदोंग] [勞動] labo (u)r; work; toil. 노동하다 labor; work; toil.

노랑 [नोरांग] [노란 빛] yellow.

노랑 머리 [नोरांग मौरी] a yellow head; yellow hair.

노랗다 [नोराथा] [매우 노르다] yellow.

노래 [नोरै] [가요] a song; a ballad; singing. 노래하다 [नोरैहादा] [노래를 부르다] (가락을 붙여) sing; (작은 목소리로 감상적으로) croon; [새가 지저귀다] sing.

노려보다 [नोर्यौपोदा] glare <at>; scowl <at>; stare fiercely <at>; look angrily [sharply / daggers] <at>.

노력 [नोर्यौक] [努力]effort; endeavour; (an) exertion; labor; strain; industry. 노력하다 endeavor; do one's best; make an endeavor [effort]; strive <for>; exert [bestir] oneself; make [put forth] efforts; work hard

노련 [नोर्यौन] [老鍊] mature experience; expertness; skil (l) fulness. 노련하다 experienced; veteran; old; expert; skilled.

노령 [नोर्यौग] [老齡] old [advanced] age; one's increasing age [advancing years].

노르스름하다 [नोरूसुरूमहादा] yellowish; cream-colored; creamy; cream.

노름 [नोरूम] gambling; gaming 노름하다 gamble; bet; wager; play for money

노름꾼 [नोरूमकुन] a gambler; a gamester

노릇 [नोरूत] [일] a job; work; [기능] function; a role; [직업] an occupation.

노릇노릇 [नोरून्नोरूत] 노릇노릇하다 spotted [dappled] with yellow; yellow here and there; yellowish.

노리다 **[नोरिदा]** **1** [노려보다] glare [scowl] <at>; stare fiercely <at>. **2** [목적하다] aim <at>; have an eye <on>; [기회를 엿보다] watch for; [추구하다] seE; be ather.

노발대발 [नोबाल्तैबाल] [**怒發大發**] 노발대발하다 burn with wrath; be in hot anger [a fume]; get into a rage

노사 [नोसा] [**勞使**] labor and management; capital and labor.

노사 관계[नोसा ग्वांग्ये] the relations between labor and capital

노선 [नोसौन] [**路線**] [일정한 교통선] a route; [기본 방침] a line; a course.

노쇠 [नोस्वे] [**老衰**] infirmity of old age; senility; anility; senile decay [weakness]; decrepitude 노쇠하다 senile; decrepit; old and infirm [feeble].

노숙 [नोसुक] [**老熟**] matured experience; maturity 노숙하다; mellow

노숙 [नोसुक] [**露宿**] camping; camping-out; sleeping outdoors 노숙하다 sleep [pass the night] in the open (air); camp (out)

노심 초사 [नोशिम छोसा] [**勞心焦思**] exertion of the mind; solicitude; anxiety; care; worry. 노심 초사하다 exert oneself mentally; be worried [anxious].

노여움 [नोयौउम] anger; indignation; fury; displeasure 노여움(을) 사다 incur [arouse / provoke] <a person's> wrath [displeasure]

노여워하다 [नोयौवाँहादा] be displeased by [with / at]; take offense at; feel hurt; feel displeasure over; be indignant over [at]; be given offense.

노예 [नोये] [**奴隸**]**1** a bond (s) man; a bondslave. **2** <비유> a slave.

노인 [नोइन] [**老人**]an old [aged] person; an elder; an oldster; <집합적> the aged [old]; old people; old folks

노처녀 [नोछौन्यौ] [**老處女**] an old maid; a spinster

노총각 [नोछोंगाक] [**老總角**]an old bachelor.

노출 [नोछुर्हादा] [**露出**]**1** [드러남,드러냄] exposure; disclosure 노출하다 expose; disclose **2** [寫] exposure.

노크 **[नोख]** [문 등을 두들김] a knock.

노티 [नोथि] [**老-**]signs of (old) age; looking old.

노파 [नोफा] [**老婆**]an old woman; (나쁜 뜻으로) a beldam; a hag.

노파심 [नोफाशिम] [**老婆心**] grandmotherly [old-womanish / excessive] solicitude; solicitude for another's welfare.

노하다 [नोहादा] [怒-] get [become / grow / be] angry <with a person / at something>; be angered [offended / enraged / furious]; get [fly] into a rage; lose one's temper; fume; get mad.

녹 [नोक] [綠] 1⇨ 동록 [दोंनोक] 2 [금속 표면의 산화물] rust; tarnish.

녹다 [नोक्ता] 1 [열에 물러지다] melt (away); thaw; fuse. 2 [용해되다] dissolve; liquefy; melt. 3 [추워서 굳어진 몸이 풀리다] warm up; be warmed; get warm.

녹색 [नोक्सैक] [綠色]a green color; green; verdure. e.g.녹색의 green / verdant / emerald

녹음 [नोगुम] [錄音] (sound) recording; phonographing; (electrical) transcription. 녹음하다 record <a speech / music>;(테이프에) tape; phonograph; transcribe <a program>.

녹이다[नोगिदा]1 (열에) melt (up / down); fuse; smelt; (얼음 등을) thaw. 2 [용해시키다] melt; dissolve; liquefy. 3 (굳은 몸을) warm <oneself> up; take warmth; make oneself warm; thaw. 4 [반하게 하다] enchant; charm; bewitch; fascinate; captivate; steal the heart of; enslave; kill <a man>.

녹차 [नोक्छा] [綠茶]green tea.

녹초 [नोक्छो] [기진 맥진] utter exhaustion; dog-tiredness.

녹화 [नोख्वा] [錄畵] [TV] telerecording.녹화하다 record <a scene on video tape>.

논 [नोन] a rice paddy; a rice field; [무논] a paddy field.

논거 [नोंगो] [論據] the basis [grounds] of an argument; data.

논고 [नोंगो] [論告] the prosecutor's closing argument; prosecution. 논고하다 prosecute; <the prosecutor> address the court.

논란 [नोल्लान] [論難] (adverse) criticism; denunciation; charge; (a) censure; disproof. 논란하다 criticize; denounce

논리 [नोल्लि] [論理] logic.

논문 [नोन्मुन] [論文] (일반적인) a treatise; an essay; (연구상의) a thesis <*pl.* theses>; a dissertation; (학회 등의) a paper; (신문 등의) an article.

논박 [नोन्बाक] [論駁] refutation; confutation. 논박하다 argue against; confute; refute; contradict (반박하다)

논밭 [नोन्बात] rice paddies and dry fields; fields

논설 [नोन्सौल] [論說] [논문] a discourse; [사설] a

leading article; a leader; an editorial.

논설 위원 [**नोन्सौल विवौन**] a leader writer; an editorial writer

논술 [नोन्सुल] [**論述**] statement; enunciation. 논술하다 enunciate; state; set forth.

논의 [नोनउइ] [**論議**] (서로 주장하는) (an) argument; [토의] (a) discussion. 논의하다 discuss <a matter>; argue <about>; debate <on / about>.

논쟁 [नोन्जैग] [**論爭**] a dispute; a controversy; an argument. 논쟁하다 argue; have an argument <with>; dispute; contend; controvert; take issue <with>.

논제 [नोन्जे] [**論題**] the subject [theme / text] of one's argument [article / lecture]; a topic for discussion.

논증 [नोन्जंग] [**論證**] (a) demonstration; proof. 논증하다 prove; demonstrate

논지 [नोन्जि] [**論旨**] the point [gist / drith / tenor] of an argument.

논평 [नोन्फयौग] [**論評**] (a) criticism; a comment; a review. 논평하다 criticize; review; comment <on current topics>.

놀다 [**नोल्ता**] **1** [유희하다] play. **2** [즐기다] amuse [divert] oneself; enjoy oneself.**3** [일하지 않다] be idle; be doing nothing; be loafing and lolling; take one's ease. **4** [사용되지 않고 있다] be not in use; lie [stand] idle.

놀라다 [**नोल्लिदा**] [경악하다] be surprised; be astonished; be astounded; be startled; be taken aback (대경하다).

놀라움 [**नोल्लाउम**] [경악] surprise; astonishment; [경탄] amazement; wonder; horror; terror; scare.

놀랍다 [**नोल्लाप्ता**] wonderful; marvelous; surprising; amazing; alarming.

놀래다 [**नोल्लैदा**] **1** [놀라게 하다] surprise; astonish; startle; give <others> a start **2** scare

놀리다 [**नोल्लिदा**] [조롱하다] banter; chaff; tease; make fun [sport / game] of; kid.

놀림 [**नोल्लिम**] banter; chaff; fun; teasing; a joke

놀아나다 [**नोरानादा**] [방탕해지다] take to fast living; begin to lead a fast life.

놀음 [**नोरुम**] (놀이) [**नोरि**] play; pleasure; fun; (good) sport.

놀이 [**नोरि**] **1** [유희] play. 놀이하다 play. **2** [경기] a game; a sport. **3**[오락] a pastime; pleasure; fun.

놀이터 [**नोरिथौ**] a playground; a pleasure resort **놈** [**नोम**] [남자] a fellow; a chap; a bird; a guy

농 [नोंग] [弄] [장난] sport; fun; play..

농가 [नोंगा] [農家] [농사로 생계를 꾸리는 집] a farmhouse; [농사로 생계를 꾸리는 가정] the household of a farmer

농경 [नोंग्यौंग] [農耕] agriculture; farming; tillage.

농구 [नोंगू] [籠球] basketball.

농기구 [नोंगिगू] [農器具]

농담 [नोंग्दाम] [弄談]a joke; a jest; fun; pleasantry.

농도 [नोंग्दो] [濃度] density; thickness; consistency; intensity; concentration.

농락 [नोंग्नाक] [籠絡] 농락하다 make a person one's puppet; (특히 여자 등을) sport [toy / trifle / fool] <with>

농민 [नोंगमिन] [農民] [소작인] a peasant; [자작농] a farmer; <집합적> the farming population; [소작농민 계급] the peasantry.

농부 [नोंग्बू] [農夫] [농장 노동자] a farm laborer [worker / hand]; [소작인] a peasant; [자작농] a farmer

농사 [नोंग्सा] [農事] agriculture; farming; farm work; agricultural affairs

농산물 [नोंग्सान्मुल] [農産物] agricultural [farm] products; farm produce.

농성 [नोंग्सौंग] [籠城] a stay-in strike. 농성하다 stage a sit-down demonstration.

농수산 [नोंग्सुसान] [農水産] agriculture and fisheries.

농아 [नोंगा] [聾啞] deaf and dumb; a deaf-mute.

농악 [नोंगाक] [農樂] instrumental music of peasants

농약 [नोंग्याक] [農藥] agricultural chemicals [medicines]..

농약 사용 경작 [नोंग्याक सायोंग ग्यौंग्जाक] chemicultivation.

농어촌 [नोंगौछोन] [農漁村] farming and fishing villages [communities].

농업 [नोंगौप] [農業] agriculture; farming; agricultural industry.

농작 [नोंग्जाक] [農作] farming; husbandry; cultivation of land; farming.

농작물 [नोंग्जांग्मुल] [農作物] the crops; a harvest; farm produce [products].

농장 [नोंग्जांग] [農場]

농지 [नोंग्जी] [農地] agricultural land; farmland.

농촌 [नोंग्छोन] [農村]a farm [farming] village; a rural community. e.g. 농촌의 rural / agricultural / agrarian.

농축 [नोंग्छुक] [濃縮] concentration 농축하다 concentrate; enrich.

농후 [नोंग्हू] [濃厚] thickness; density. 농후하다 thick; dense; heavy

높낮이 [नोम्नाजी] [고저] high and low

높다 [नोप्ता] **1** (높이가) high; tall; lothy; elevated **2** (지위,

신분,희망 등이) high; lothy; noble. **3** (정도,비율이) high.

높다랗다 **[नोप्ताराथा]** remarkably high; lothy.

높이[1] **[नोफि]** [높은 정도] height; altitude

높이[2] **[नोफि]** [높게] **[नोफगे]** high; highly; aloth. e.g. 하늘 높이 high up in the air.

높이다 **[नोफिदा]** **1** [높게 하다] raise; lith; [증진하다] promote; heighten <an effect>; elevate <one's ideal>; enhance <value>**2** [받들다] respect; honor; reverence

높임말 **[नोफिम्माल]** an honorific (expression / word)

놓다 **[नोत्था]** **1** [두다] [put; lay; set (세워서); place. e.g. 손을 테이블 위에 놓다 rest one's hands on a table. **2** [해방하다] set free; release; unloose; turn [let] loose;(손을) let go [off]; take off one's hand; let go one's hold <of>; quit one's grasp e.g. 그는 그녀의 손을 쥐고 있다가 놓았다 He held her hand and then let it go.

놓아두다 **[नोआदूदा]** [내버려두다] leave; allow; let

놓아주다 **[नोआजूदा]** turn [let / cast] loose; let go [off]; release; unloose; free; set free.

놓이다 **[नोइदा]** **1** (물건이) be put [laid / placed / set]. e.g.책상 위에 놓인 꽃병a flower vase set on the table. **2** (마음이) feel [be] relieved; feel at ease; be relaxed. e.g. 마음이 놓일 때가 없다 [have no moment of ease.

놓치다 **[नोछिदा]1** (잡고 있던 것을) miss one's hold **2** (기회 등을]) let <an opportunity> slip **4**(차를) miss; lose; fail to catch.

뇌 [न्वे] [**腦**]a brain; a cerebrum; an encephalon; [두뇌] brains.

뇌리 [न्वेरि] [**腦裡**] the brain; one's mind; one's memory. e.g. 뇌리에서 떠나지 않다 haunt one [one's memory] / be ever present in one's mind.

뇌물 [न्वेमुल] [**賂物**] a bribe

누 [नू] [**累**] implication; involvement; trouble; an evil influence [effect]. e.g. 남에게 누를 끼치다 give [cause] a person trouble [annoyance] / worry / inconvenience / implicate [involve] others in trouble.

누구 **[नूगू]** **1** [특정인인 경우] <주격> who; <소유격> whose; <목적격> whom. **2** [일정치 않은 사람] <긍정문> somebody; someone (좀 형식적); some (누군가); (누구나 다) everybody; everyone; <의문문,조건문> anybody; anyone; any; <부정문> anybody;

L

anyone; none. **3** <양보절에서> whoever

누그러뜨리다 [नुग्रौतरिदा] so then <one's attitude>

누그러지다 [नुग्रौजीदा] **1** (날씨가) get milder [warmer / better] e.g. 추위가 누그러졌다 The cold has abated [moderated]. / The cold has decreased [relaxed] in severity.**2** (감정P태도 등이) sothen e.g. 그녀의 친절한 말에 그는 마음이 누그러졌다 He melted at her kindly words.

누나 [नूना] <a boy's> elder [older] sister.

누누이 [नूनूइ] [**屢屢**−]many times (over); time and (time) again; over and again; repeatedly

누더기 [नूदौगि] tattered clothes; tatters; rags; duds.

누락 [नूराक] [**漏落**]an omission; a lacuna <*pl.* –nae, ~s>. 누락하다 omit; leave out; fail to enter.

누렇다 [नूरौथा] quite [deep] yellow; golden yellow.

누르다 [नुरूदा] **1** [어느 부분에 힘을 가하다] press; push; hold [press / keep / pin] down e.g.벨을 누르다 push [press] the bell.**2** [억압하다,진압하다] suppress; put down; repress; subdue; control; oppress; [저지하다] check; [위압하다] overpower; overwhelm. e.g. 반란을 누르다 suppress a rising / put down a rebellion.

누르스름하다 [नुरूसुरूमहादा] yellowish; somewhat yellow.

누리다 [नूरिदा] enjoy; have; be blessed with.

누명 [नुम्यौंग] [**陋名**]a false [an unjust] charge [accusation / imputation]; groundless [unfounded] suspicion.

누비다 [नूबिदा] quilt.

누설 [नूसौल] [**漏泄,漏洩**]**1** (액체 등의) a leak; leakage. e.g. 가스 누설 a gas leak. 누설을 막다 stop [plug] a leak.누설하다 leak; let leak. **2** (비밀의) leakage; disclosure; divulgence. e.g. 군기누설a leakage of military secret. 누설하다 tell others; let <a secret> out; divulge <one's secret>; reveal; disclose; betray; break; give away; leak (out).

누이 [नूइ] a boy's sister.

누이다[1] [नूइदा] [눕히다] lay down; lay on the side

누이다[2] [नूइदा] (대소변을) make [let / have] <a child> urinate [defecate].

누적 [नूजौक] [**累積**] accumulation; cumulation. 누적하다 accumulate; cumulate; increase cumulatively.

누전 [नूजौन] [**漏電**] an

electric leakage; a short circuit; a leak; a fault. 누전하다 short (-circuit); leak.

누추 [नूछु] [陋醜] 누추하다 filthy; squalid; sordid; shabby; untidy.

누출 [नूछुल] [漏出] leakage; leak 누출하다 leak <out>; ooze out; escape (가스가)

눅눅하다 [नुंग्नुख्वादा] damp; (공기 등이) humid; moist; dampish. 눅눅한 옷 wet [damp] clothes.

눈[1] [नुन] **1** [물체를 보는 기관] an eye **2** [시력, 시각] sight; eyesight; vision; eyes. e.g. 눈이 어둡다[나쁘다 have bad eyes [defective vision] / have a poor [bad] sight [vision]. **3** [주목,주시] (public) notice; attention; watch. e.g. 세상 사람들의 눈이 두렵다I am afraid of the eye of the people [the public eye].**4**[안목,안식] an eye; judgment; insight; discernment. . e.g. 사물을 보는 눈이 있다[없다] have [haven't] the seeing eye / have an eye [no eye] <for> / be a good [poor] judge <of> / be [be not] sharp-eyed.

눈[2] [नुन] [설] snow; a snowfall (강설); snows (적설).

눈가림 [नुंगारिम] (a) sham; (a) pretense; camouflage. 눈가림하다 pull the wool over <a person's> eyes; hoodwink; camouflage; blind the eyes <of>; blindfold; cover up; gloss over; make <A> look like <B>; give <a thing> an air [appearance] of.

눈감다 [नुन्गाम्ता] **1** [눈시울을 마주 붙이다] shut [close] one's eyes.**2** [죽다] die; breathe one's last.**3** [못 본 체하다] shut [close] one's eyes <to>; blink [wink] at; connive at; turn a blind eye <on / to>; overlook.눈감아 주다 overlook; look over; pass over

눈금[नुन्गुम]graduations <on a thermometer>; scale

눈대중 [नुन्दैजुंग] eye measurement [estimation]; measuring with one's eye. e.g. 눈대중으로 by the [one's] eye / by eye measure.

눈동자 [नुन्तोंजा] [-瞳子] the pupil (of the eye); the apple of the eye

눈뜨다 [नुन्तुदा] (감았던 눈을) open one's eyes; [잠을 깨다] wake (up); awake; [깨닫다P본능 등이 발동하다] awake [awaken / wake up]

눈맞다 [नुन्मात्ता] (남녀가) fall in love with each other.

눈물 [नुन्मुल] a tear; [동정심의 비유] sympathy.

눈물짓다 [नुन्मुल्चित्ता] shed

tears; (눈이) be filled with tears; one's eyes moisten [glisten] with tears; moisten at one's eyes. e.g. 그녀는 눈물지으며 고개를 떨구었다 She hung her head with tears in her eyes.

눈발 **[नुन्बाल]** snow flakes.

눈보라 **[नुन्बोरा]** a snowstorm; a shower of snow; a snowdrith.

눈부시다 **[नुन्बूशिदा]** **1**(빛이) dazzling; glaring; blinding <flash>. [현란하다] gorgeous; showy; gaudy; dazzling; brilliant; radiant. e.g.매우 눈부신 태양 the hot glaring sun**3** <비유> striking <achievement>; remarkable <development>; splendid <exploit>; brilliant <success>e.g. 눈부신 발전 remarkable [striking] development.

눈빛 **[नुन्पित]** [눈의 빛깔] the color of one's eyes; [표정] the expression of one's eyes.

눈사람 **[नुनसाराम]** a snowman

눈사태 **[नुनसाथै]** **[-沙汰]**a snowslide; an avalanche (of snow) (큰).

눈살 **[नुन्साल]** 눈살(을) 찌푸리다 frown <at / on> e.g. 눈살을 찌푸리고 with a frown

눈속임 **[नुन्सोगिम]** cheating; deceiving; hoodwinking; camouflage. 눈속임하다 눈속이다

눈시울 **[नुन्षिउल]** the edge of an eyelid; the eye rims. e.g. 눈시울이 뜨거워지다 be (almost) moved to tears / melt into tears / one's eyes moisten (with tears) / be touched <by>.

눈싸움 **[नुन्साउम]** [설전(雪戰)] a snowball fight [battle]; snowballing. 눈싸움하다 have a snowball fight [battle]; snowball.

눈썰미 **[नुनसौलमि]** a quick eye for learning things.

눈썹 **[नुन्सौप]** an eyebrow.

눈앞 **[नुनाफ]1** [면전] 눈앞에서 before <a person's> eyes; under <a person's> (very) eyes [nose] / in <a person's> presence [sight] / (just) before one.**2** [직전]. e.g. 눈앞에 close [near] at hand / just ahead. **3** [현재] e.g. 눈앞의 immediate

눈여겨보다 **[नुन्यौग्यौबोदा]** observe carefully; watch intently; take a good [close] look <at>.

눈요기 **[नुन्योगि]** **[-療飢]**a feast [joy] to the eye; visual pleasure. 눈요기하다 feast one's eyes on <something>.

눈웃음 **[नुनुसुम]** a smile with [about / in] one's eyes.

눈웃음(을) 치다 smile with one's eyes; wear a smile about [in] one's eyes

ㄴ

눈치 [नुन्छि] **1** 센스] tact; sense; quick [ready] wit. **2** [마음의 기미] one's frame of mind; one's mental attitude toward <a person>; one's intention [design / wish]; [기색] looks; (facial) expression; a sign; a hint; an indication.

눈흘기다 [नुनहल्किदा] look askance [sideways] <at a person> with hate [reproach] in one's eyes

눌리다 [नुल्लिदा] **1** [누름을 당하다] be pressed down; be kept [held] down.**2** [압도당하다] be suppersed; be put down; be repressed

눌어붙다 [नुरौबुत्ता] [한 곳에 오래 머물며 떠나지 않다] remain in the same place [position]; settle down; stay on.

눕다 [नुप्ता] lie down; lay oneself down; stretch oneself; prostrate oneself.

뉘앙스 [न्विआंस] a nuance

뉘엿거리다 [न्वियौक्कौरिदा] (해가) be going [ready] to set; be about to set [sink].

뉘엿뉘엿 [न्वियौन्वियौत] (해가) e.g. 해가 뉘엿뉘엿 지다 the sun is sinking in the west.

뉘우치다 [न्विउछिदा] Regret; repent; be sorry <for>; be penitent [repentant] <for>; feel regret [remorse] <for>.

뉴스 [न्यूस] news

느긋하다 [नुगुत्थादा] [만족하다] quite satisfied [contented / gratified] <with>; well pleased; [마음 편하다] comfortable; relaxed

느끼다 [नक्किदा] **1** [감각,지각하다] feel; be conscious of; experience <inconvenience>; be sensible of [to]; have a feeling <that ...>.**2** [감동하다] be impressed <by / with>; be struck <by / with>; be affected [moved / touched] <by>. ⇨ 감동**3** [흐느끼다] sob; be choked with [drowned in] tears.

느끼하다 [नक्किहादा] (맛이) greasy; fatty; oily; thick; heavy.

느낌 [नक्किम]**1** [감각] feeling; sense; sensation; [감촉] touch; feel. **2** [인상] an impression; [기분] sentiment; feeling

느낌표 [नक्किम्फ्यो] [一標] [문법] an exclamation mark [point].

느닷없다 [नदासौप्ता] abrupt; unexpected.

느닷없이 [नदासौप्षि] [돌연히] abruptly; suddenly; (all) of a sudden; out of the blue

느리다 [नरिदा]**1** [더디다] slow; tardy; slow-going; sluggish. **2** [짜임새가 성글다] loose <in weave>

느림 [नरिम] [장식으로 늘어뜨린 것] a tassel.

느릿느릿 [नरिन्नरित] **1** (동작이) slowly; sluggishly; tardily; idly. **2**[성기게] loose (ly); slack.

느슨하다 [नुसुनहादा] **1** [헐겁다] loose; slack; lax. **2** (마음이 relaxed; slack.

느지막하다 [नुजीमाख्वादा] rather [quite] late.

늑대 [नुक्तै]a wolf <*pl.* wolves>.

늑장부리다 [नुक्चांगबूरिदा] dawdle <over>; linger; loaf <on the job>; dally away

-는[-नन]-ing. e.g. 흐르는 물 running [flowing] water / a running stream.

는[नन] e.g. 그는 의사다He is a doctor.

-는지 [-नन्जि] [막연한 의문,감탄] if; or; either ... or; I wonder .... e.g.그가 집에 있는지 사무실에 있는지 모른다I don't know whether he is at home or in [at] the office

늘 [नल] [어느 때나,항상] always; all the time; usually; habitually; ceaselessly; continuously.

늘다[नुल्दा]**1** (수,양이) increase <in number, in quantity, etc>; multiply (배로); gain(힘,무게 등이); swell (팽창하다); augment; rise (강물이); accrue (증식되다). **2** [향상되다] improve; advance; make (good) progress.

늘리다 [नुल्लिदा]**1** (수량을) increase; add <to>; raise; multiply; augment.**2** [확대하다] extend; expand; enlarge.

늘씬하다[नुल्शिनहादा]⇨날씬하다 늘씬히⇨ 날씬히(⇨날씬하다)

늘어가다[नुरौगादा] (수량이) go on increasing [growing / swelling]; be (steadily) increasing; be on the increase (실력 등이) make (good) progress; advance [progress] <in>

늘어나다 [नरौनादा] extend; lengthen; stretch; grow longer; expand.

늘어놓다 [नुरौनोत्था] **1** [벌여놓다] arrange <goods>; range; [정돈하다] put [place] <things> in order; [진열하다] display <goods>; show <samples>; exhibit <paintings>; (요리를) spread <dishes>. e.g. 한 줄로 늘어놓다 place <things> in a row. **2** [흩어 놓다] scatter (about); put in disorder; leave <one's clothes> lying about <in the room>. e.g. 옷을 방안에 늘어놓다 leave one's clothes lying about in the room.

늘어뜨리다 [नुरौतुरिदा] hang down; suspend; slouch (축); droop <the tail>; drop; lower <one's head>.

늘어서다 [नुरौसौदा] be in a row; stand in a row [line]; be drawn up; [열을

만들다] line up; rank; (차례를 기다리며) queue [line] up; line up in a queue.

늘어지다 [नुरौजीदा]**1** [아래로 처지다] hang down; dangle; droop; be pen-dent.**2** [길어지다] extend; lengthen; stretch; spread. **3** (몸이) droop; languish; get exhausted; grow languid.

늘이다 [नुरिदा]**1** [길게 하다] lengthen; make <something> longer; stretch; extend; draw out. **2** (아래로) [आरेरो] hang down; droop

늙다 [नुल्ता] grow [get] old; age

늙은이 [नुल्गुनि] an old person; an aged person; an elder; <집합적>the aged [old]

늠름하다 [नुम्नुमहादा] [凜凜-] imposing; manly; commanding.

능 [नुंगा] [陵]a royal mausoleum <*pl.* -lea>; a royal tomb.

능가 [नंगा] [凌駕] 능가하다 surpass; exceed; excel; be superior to; outdistance; outdo; outrival; stand above; outstrip.

능글맞다 [नुंगुलमात्ता] tricky; sly; snaky; cunning; insidious; wily; crathy; foxy; slick. e.g. 능글맞은 웃음 <make> an insidious smile.

능동 [नुंग्दोंग] [能動] activity; activeness.

능동태 [नुंग्दोंग्थे] [문법] the active voice.

능력 [नुंगन्यौक] [能力] [일을 할 수 있는 힘] (an) ability; [특수한 지력] a faculty; [적성] competence; [그 자체에 갖추어진 잠재적인 힘] capacity.

능률 [नुंगन्यूल] [能率] **1**일의 진척] efficiency. **2** (기계의) moment.

능선 [नुंगसौन] [稜線] a ridge-line

능숙 [नुंगसुक] [能熟] skill; expertness; proficiency 능숙하다 skilled; skillful; expert <in / at>; proficient <in>; good <at>.

능청 [नुंछौंग] dissemblance; feigning; false pretense; hypocrisy.

능청스럽다 [नुंछौंगसुरौप्ता] deceitful; cunning; tricky; wily; hypocritical.

능통 [नुंग्थोंग] [能通] proficiency; mastery; cleverness; skill. 능통하다 skillful; proficient; expert; versed.

능하다 [नुंग्हादा] [能-]skillful; dexterous; adept; expert; proficient

능히 [नुंग्ही] [能-] capably; competently; ably; [손쉽게] easily; without difficulty [trouble].

늦다 [नत्ता] (시간적으로) late.

늦더위[नत्तौवि] the lingering summer heat; the heat of

late summer.

늦잠 [नच्चाम] oversleeping; late rising

늦추다 [नाच्छुदा]**1** (띠,고삐를) loosen; slacken; (마음을) relaK ease. e.g. 조금 늦추다make <one's belt> a little looser.**2** (속도를) slow down; reduce one's speed; ease (up) <the speed>; slack; slacken. e.g. 걸음 [속도] 을 늦추다 slack (en) [relax / reduce / slow down] one's pace [speed].**3** (시간,날짜를) delay; defer; put off; postpone; extend e.g. 시계를 1시간 늦추다 put [set / turn] back a clock [watch] one hour.

늪[नुप]a marsh; a swamp; a bog.

-님 [-निम] [경칭] (남자의) Mr. (Mister 의 약어); Esq. (Esquire의 약어); (여자의) Mrs. (Mistress 의 약어); Mme. (Madame 의 약어); Miss (미혼 여성)

다[दा] **1** [모두] all; wholly; altogether; all through; in all [full]; everything; everybody; everyone; both. e.g. 둘 다 both of them / both together. **2** [완전히] completely; quite; all; utterly; perfectly; thoroughly! e.g. 다 죽어 가는 목소리 a faint voice.

다가서다 [दागासौदा] get near (er); come [walk / step] up to; approach closer; come [go] nearer. e.g. 다가서서 보다 take a near [get a closer] view of / see <a picture> close at hand.

다가앉다 [दागाआन्ता] sit close [closely]; sit up; move forward (on one's knees); slide oneself forward; e.g. 얘기 좀 하게 다가앉아라 Sit a little closer, so we can have a talk.

다가오다 [दागाओदा] **1** [접근하다] approach; near; step [come / go / walk] up to; get near <a place>; move on toward. e.g. (배가) 육지에 다가오다 approach land / close with the land / draw toward the shore. **2** [임박하다] e.g. 다가오는 coming / to come / next.

다각 [दागाक] [多角] e.g. 다각의 many-sided / multilateral / diversified / multiple.

다각적 [दागाक्चौक] [**多角的**] many-sided; versatile; diversified; multilateral. e.g. 다각적인 취미 many-sided interests [tastes

다감 [दागाम] [多感] sensibility; susceptibility; sentimentality. 다감하다 [느끼기 쉽다 susceptible; [감동하기 쉽다] emotionnal; impressionable; sensitive

다과회 [दाग्वाह्वे] [茶菓會] a tea party; a tea.

다국적 [दागुक्चौक] [多國籍] multinationality.

다급하다 [दागफादा] pressing; urgent; imminent; exigent; impending

다녀가다 [दान्यौगादा] drop in for a short visit; call at <a house>; drop in <on a person> [come round to see <a person>] and then go on; look <a person> up; stop [come] by.

다녀오다 [दान्यौओदा] drop in <on a person> and then come back; go round to see <a person> and then return; get [come] back <from visiting>; return; be (back) home.

-다니[-दानि] [의외] how [why] should ...; I am sorry that ...; I regret ...; It is a pity that .... e.g. 여기서 너를 만나다니 (생각도 못했다)] This is the last place where I expected to meet you.

다니다 [दानिदा] **1** [왕래하다] go to and from <a place>; go to <a place> and back; make a trip to and from <a place e.g. 부산과 제주를 다니는 배 a ship plying between Pusan and Cheju. **2** [통근,통학하다] commute; attend <school>; go to. **3** [자주 가다] go frequently <to>; frequent; hang around; hang out at. e.g. 버스로 학교에 다니고 있다 I go [commute] to school by bus. 그들은 매일 아침 걸어서 공장에 다닌다

다다르다 [दादारुदा] [장소에 닿다] come to; arrive <at>; reach; get to <a place>; gain; attain.

다다익선 [दादाइक्सौन] [多多益善] The more, the better.

다달이 [दादारि] every [each] month; from month to month; monthly; a [per] month.

다듬다 [दादुम्दा] **1** 매만지다] trim [spruce] up; adorn; embellish; refine; polish; elaborate; file; e.g.. 문장을 다듬다 polish one's writing. **2** (나무,잔디 등을) prune; trim e.g.. 잔디를 다듬다 mow a lawn / cut the grass.

다량 [दार्याङ] [多量] a large quantity <of>; a great deal <of>; plenty <of>; a lot <of>.

다루다 [दारुदा] 1 [처리,취급하다] handle; manage; deal with; treat of <a subject>; transact [carry on / handle / conduct]

<business>; deal in <goods>. e.g. 다루기 쉬운 manageable / easy to handle [to deal with.2 [(사람을) 대하다] treat; deal with. e.g. 다루기 쉬운 사람 an easy person to handle.

다르다 [दारुदा] [상이하다] different <from>; unlike; dissimilar <to>; diverse; divergent; variant; [별개이다] distinct; [유별나다] extraordinary; uncommon; peculiar; unusual. e.g. 다른 것 something else / the other thing.

다름없다 [दारुमऔप्ता [같다] the same; not different <from>; similar <to>; alike; [변함없다] constant; never-changing; steady; unwavering.

다름없이 [दारुमऔप्शि] [똑같이] similarly; equally; alike; in like manner; [변함없이] unvaryingly; unchangingly; without a change;

다리 [1] [दारी] **1** (사람, 동물의) a leg; pins; a limb; an arm.. e.g. 비쩍 마른 다리 a lean [thin] leg **2** (책상 등의) a leg; a leg piece. e.g. 안경 다리 the bows of a pair of glasses [spectacles].

다리 [2] [दारी] [교량] a bridge; [구름다리] a viaduct; [현수교] a suspension bridge. e.g. 돌 다리 a stone bridge

다리다 [दारिदा] iron (out) <a shirt>; press <the trousers>; do the ironing. e.g. 바지를 다리다 iron out trousers [pants] / crease one's trousers

다리미 [दारिमी] an iron; a flatiron; a goose.

다만 [दामान] [오직 그뿐] only; merely; simply; just; but; alone. e.g. 다만 …하기만 하면 되다 have only to <do> / an one has to do is to <do>.

다목적 [दामोक्चौक] [多目的] multipurpose. e.g. 다목적의 multiple-purpose

다물다 [दामुल्दा] shut [close] <one's mouth>. e.g. 굳게 다문 입 a compressed [a firm] mouth / tense lips.

다발 [दाबाल] bundle; a bunch; a sheaf <*pl.* sheaves> (벼 등의); a faggot (장작 등의); a stack; a coil (새끼 등의). e.g. 꽃 [열쇠] 다발 abunch of flowers [keys

다방 [दाबांग] [茶房]a teahouse; a tearoom; a teashop; a coffee shop [a coffee house];

다방면 [दाबांग्म्यौन] [多方面] [여러 방면] many quarters; [여러 방향] many directions; [여러 취미] many-sideness; [여러 재능] versatility. e.g.

다방면으로 in many directions [fields

다섯 [दासेत] five. e.g. 다섯배 (의) fivefold / quintuple

다소 [दासो] [多少] 어느 정도 a little; some; <의문,조건> any; somewhat; to some extent [degree]; in some [a] measure; e.g. 다소 이름이 알려진 사람 a man of some note.

다소곳이 [दासोगोशी] [온순하게] obediently; quietly; submissively; gently; e.g. 다소곳이 남의 말을 듣다 listen to another's advice obediently [with one's head dropped].

다소곳하다 [दासोगोथादा] [고개를 숙이다] modest and quiet with one's head lowered; [온순하다] modest; quiet; gentle; obedient. e.g. 다소곳한 태도 an obedient (and courteous) attitude.

-다손 치더라도 [-दासोन छिदोरादो] even) though; (even) if; granted [granting] that; no matter how [who / what / when / which]. e.g. 그렇다손 치더라도 even if it were so / granting that it is so.

다수 [दासू] [多數] **1** [많은 수] a large number; a multitude <of readers>; numbers; a heap; a multiplicity <of errors>; a plurality <of causes>; a host; an army.**2** (과반수) (a) majority <of>; a predominance <of>; a greater part <of>

다수결 [दासूग्योल] [多數決] decision by majority. e.g. 다수결 원칙 majority rule / majoritarian principle..

다스리다 [दासुरिदा] [통치하다] rule [reign] over; govern; administer; [관리하다] conduct; manage; direct; preside over. e.g. 나라를 다스리다 rule over [govern] a country / manage a state.

다시 [दाशि] [되풀이하여 또] again; once more [again]; another time; a second time; repeatedly; twice..-

다시피 마찬가지로] as; like; similar to; sort of; in the same way <that>; [같은 정도로] almost; nearly; practically; all but; as good as. e.g.보다시피 as you (can) see.

다양[दायांग] [多様] variety; diversity. 다양하다 various; diverse

다용도 [दायोंग्दो] [多用途] many purposes.

다운[दाउन] **1** [쓰러짐] a knock-down.. e.g. 다운시키다 [권투] knock down / < 美 > floor.**2** [지쳐서 떨어짐]. e.g. 지난 주에는 독감으로 다운되고 말았다 I was down with (the) flu last week.

ㄷ

다음[दाउम] the next; the second; the sequel <of a story>; <형용사적>[바로 뒤의] (the) next; following; ensuing; [오는] coming; [둘째] second; the rest; [인접한] adjacent; adjoining.

다작 दाजाक] [多作] abundant production; prolificacy in writing. 다작하다 produce [write] abundantly; be prolific (in writing).

다정 [दाजौ] [多情] [감정이 풍부함] tenderness; humaneness; kind-[warm- / tender-] hearted-ness. affectionate; tender; kind [warm- / tender-] hearted; emotional; passio-nate.

다정 다감 [दाजौ दागाम] [多情多感] sentimentality. 다정다감하다 sentimental; passionate; emotional; ardent.

다지다 [दाजीदा] 1 [단단하게 하다] harden; make hard. e.g. 땅을 다지다 harden the ground / tamp (down) / ram.2 [다잡다] emphasize; underscore; make sure of [that ...]; press <a person> for a definite answer [promise]; keep ather <a person>. e.g. 마음을 다지고 그 난 문제에 착수했다 I tackled the difficult problem with determination.

다짐 [दाजीम] [확약] a definite promise; a promise; a pledge; an oath; an assurance; vouching. 다짐하다 assure; pledge; make sure; pledge oneself <to>; give one's word.

다짜고짜(로) [दाच्चागोच्चा][रो] [예고 없이] without notice [warning]; [느닷없이] suddenly; abruptly; unexpectedly; without preamble; [이유 없이] with neither rhyme nor reason; peremptorily; arbitrarily. e.g. 다짜고짜 따귀를 때리다 slap <a person> on the chee all of a sudden.

다채롭다 [दाछेरोप्ता] [多彩-] colo (u) rful; multicolor (u) red; varicolo (u) red; variegated. e.g. 다채로운 행사 variegated functions.

다치다 [दाछिदा] 1[부상하다] be [get] hurt [wounded / injured]; hurt oneself; come to grief. e.g. 다친 개 an injured dog. 2 [손상하다] be damaged / sustain an injury. e.g. 어두운 곳에서 책을 읽으면 시력을 다치게 된다 You will ruin your sight if you read books in a dark place.

다투다 [दाथुदा] [말다툼하다] quarrel [have a quarrel] <with a person over a matter>; have a cross word <with>; squabble; wrangle; brawl. e.g. 사소한 일로 다투다 quarrel about [over] trifles.

다툼 [दाथुम] [말다툼] a quarrel <with / between>; a [verbal] dispute; a wrangle; a brawl; a squabble; [불화] discord <with> (▷ fall out 은 의견 대립의 원인으로 다툼)..

다하다[1] [दाहादा] **1** [다 없어 지다] be exhausted; run out; be used up [consumed / spent / gone.] .] e.g. 기름[식량] 이 다하다 food] / The oil [food] is all gone. **2** [죽다] die; pass away; meet one's end [fate]. e.g. 목숨이 다할 때까지 as long as one lives.

다하다[2] [दाहादा] **1** [있는대 로다 들이다] exhaust; use up; run out of; do everything possible. e.g. 최선을 다하여 to the best of one's ability.**2** [끝내다] finish; go through; be through <with>. e.g.일을 다하다 finish one's work / get [be] through with one's work / get one's work done.

다행 [दाहे] [多幸] (good) luck; good fortune; happiness..

닦다 [दाक्ता] **1** 윤내다 polish; give <a thing> polish; burnish <metal>; brighten; shine (▷ 이 뜻으로는 규칙 동사) grind <a lens>; cleanse <a watch>. e.g. 반들반들하게 닦은 작은 시렁 a well-polished display shelf. **2** [물로 씻다] clean; wash; brush; [훔치다] wipe (off[from]); mop (up); dry (물기를) wipe clean.. e.g. 창문을 닦다 clean a window.**3** [길,터를 다지다] level; improve; make even; smooth. e.g. 길을 닦다 improve a road.

닦이다 [दाक्किदा] **1** [닦음을 당하다] be polished [shined / burnished / brightened]; be wiped [mopped]; be cleaned [brushed / scrubbed / washed]. e.g. 이 마루는 잘 닦였다 This floor is well polished.**2** [혼닦이다] be rebuked; be scolded; be given a talking-to. e.g. 호되게 닦이다 have [be given] a good scolding.

단[1] [दान] [單] [하나, 홀] only (one); no more than; single; [겨우] mere (ly); sole. e.g. 단 한 사람 only one man.

단[2] [दान] [團] [모임] a group; a body; a corps; a team (경기의) a gang (악한의); [일행] a party; [극단] a company; a troupe. e.g. 관광 단 a tourist party. 외교 단 a diplomatic corps.

단[3] [दान] [묶음] a bundle; a bunch; a sheaf <*pl.* sheves> (짚 등의) a load; a faggot (장작 등의). e.g. 시금치 세 단 three bunches of spinach.

단[4] [दान] ⇨ 옷단 e.g. 단을 올리다 take the hem up.

단가 [दांगा] [**單價**] a unit cost [price]. e.g.생산 단가 unit cost of production.

단거리 [दांगौरी] [**短距離**] a short distance; (사격의) a short [close] range.

단결 [दानग्यौल] [**團結**]unity; union; (공통의 목적,이해에서 생기는) solidarity; combination.
단결하다 unite; stand [hand / hold] together; combine.

단계 [दांग्ये] [**段階**] **1** [등급] a level; a rank; a grade. e.g. 4 단계로 나누다 divide into four levels [ranks]. **2** [순차적인 과정] a step; a stage; [국면] a phase.. e.g. 4 단계로 나누다 divide into four levels [ranks].

단골[दांगोल] [늘 거래하는 손님] a (regular) custommer; a patron; a client; a frequenter; [늘 거래하는 집] a customary [regular / familiar] establishment; <집합적> custom; connection; patronage.

단기 [दांगी [**短期**]= 단기간. e.g. 단기의 short / short–period / of short duration.

단념 [दान्यौम] [**斷 念**] abandonment; despair; resignation; relinquish-ment. 단념하다 give up <an idea>; abandon; fore-go; relinquish; despair <of>; get resigned to (one's loss); [손떼다] wash one's hands <of>.

단단하다 [दानदानहादा] [굳다] hard; solid; adamantine; [견고하다] firm; [오래 견디다] durable.. e.g. 단단한 돌 a hard stone.

단단히 [दानदानही] [튼튼하게, 견고히] hard; solidly; firmly. e.g. 기초를 단단히 닦다 make a solid foundation / establish a firm ground

단락 [दाल्लाक] [**段落**] **1**[일의 결말] settlement; conclusion; an end; a stop. e.g. 일에 단락을 짓다 put an end to a job.**2** (문장의) the end of a paragraph; a full stop. e.g. 이 작문은 세 단락으로 되어 있다 This composition is made up of three paragraphs.

단란 [दाल्लान] [**團欒**] a happy (home / family) circle; a fire–side circle; [화합] harmony. 단란하다 harmonious; happy; <서술적> sit in a happy circle; make a happy group.

단련 [दालल्यौन] [**鍛 鍊**]

(심신의) training; discipline; drilling.. 단련하다 train; drill; discipline.

단맛 [दान्मात] sweetness; a sweet flavor [flavour]; a sweet taste; a sugary taste.

단면 [दानम्यौन] [斷面] **1** [잘라 낸 면] the cut end; a section; (지층의) a profile. **2** e.g. 사회 생활의 한 단면 a slice [phase] of social life.

단모음 [दान्मोउम] [單母音] a single [simple] vowel; a monophthong.

단발 [दान्बाल] [短髮] short hair; crop.

단발 [दान्बाल] [斷髮] bobbed hair; a bob. 단발하다 cut [bob] one's hair; have one's hair bobbed; wear bobbed hair..

단번에 [दान्बौने] [單番-] at a stroke; at one coup; at one try; in a single effort; at once. e.g. 붓을 떼지 않고 단번에 그린 그림 a picture drawn without lithing the pen from the paper.

단서 [दान्सौ] [但書] a proviso <pl. ~(e)s>; a provision; a provisory [conditional / saving] clause. e.g. 단서가 붙은 conditional. …이라는 단서를 붙여서 with [add] the proviso that

단서 [दान्सौ] [端緖] [발단] the beginning; the start; [시초] the first step; [실마리] a clue <to>; a key; a trace.. e.g. 문제 해결의 단서 the first step toward the solution of the question / a clue for solving a problem.

단속 [दान्सोख्वादा] [團束] [규제] control; regulation; a crackdown; [감독] supervision. 단속하다 control; regulate; manage; supervise; keep control over; keep (anything) in order. .

단수 [दान्सू] [斷水] (a) suspension of water supply. 단수하다 cut [shut] off the water supply; stop [suspend] the supply of water.

단순 [दान्सुन] [單純] simplicity. 단순하다 sim-ple; uncomplicated; plain; simple-minded [-hear-ted];

단순화 [दान्सुनहादा] [單純化] simplification. 단순화하다 simplify.

단숨에 [दान्सुमे] [單-] [한 번에] at [in] a breath; in one breath; [계속하여] at [on] a stretch; in a single spell; at a heat; without a break e.g. 책을 단숨에 읽다 read a book at a [one] stretch [sitting].

단식 [दान्शिख्वादा] [斷食] a fast; fasting; abstinence <from food>. 단식하다 fast; observe a fast; abstain from food.

단어 [दानौ] [單語] a word; a vocabulary

단언[दानौन] [斷言] affirmation; (positive) assertion; asseveration; a positive [definite] statement; declaration. 단언하다 affirm; assert; asseverate; declare; say [state] positively;

단역 [दान्योक] [端役] [대단치 않은 역할] a minor role [part]; a small part; a bit; a walk-on (part

단오[दानो] [端午] the *Tano* festival (on the fithh of the fithh month of the year according to the lunar calendar).

단원 [दान्वॉन] [團員] a member <of an association [a party]>;

단원 [दान्वॉन] [單元] [학습 단위] a unit.

단위 [दान्वी] [單位] [기준 수치] a unit; (화폐의) a denomination; (유수(流水) 측정의) module.

단일 [दानिल] [單一] singleness; unity; simplicity. 단일하다 single; singular; sole; simple.

단잠 [दान्जाम] a sweet [good / sound] sleep.

단장 [दान्जांग] [丹粧] [화장] a make-up; (a) toilet; [옷치장] dressing.

단장하다 [화장하다] make up <one's> face; put on <one's> make up; make one's toilet

단절 [दान्जौल] [斷折] cutting; severance; section; amputation. 단절하다 cut; cut off; chop; sever; amputate.

단점 [दान्चौम] [短點] [결점] shortcoming; a fault; a defect; [약점] a weak point.

단정 [दान्चौंग] [端正] correctness; rightness; justness; uprightness; decency; propriety; (복장의) neatness. 단정하다 correct; right; just; upright; decent; proper. e.g. 용모가 **단정하다** have classical [neat] features.

단정 [दान्चौंग] [斷定] [결론] conclusion; [결정] decision; [판단] judgment. 단정하다 conclude; decide; judge; come to a conclusion; make up one's mind e.g. 성급하게 단정해서는 안 된다 We must not jump at conclusions.

단조롭다 [दान्चोरोप्ता] [單調-] monotonous; dull; flat; humdrum; drab; (음악이) monotonic; (억양이) singsong; (일하는 방법이) simple; tactless.

단지 [दान्जी] [團地] a (public) housing development; an apartment development [area]; a development; a housing [an apartment-house] complex e.g. 공업

단지 an industrial complex

단짝 [दान्चाक] a bosom[an intimate] friend; a great [close] friend; a chum; one's pal [partner / mate / fellow]; a crony;

단체 [दान्छे] [團體] **1** [일단] a party; a company; a group; a body; a corps >. e.g. 단체를 구성하다[만들다] make up a party [body]. **2** [조직체] an organization; a corporation; a society; an association; a unit. e.g. 교섭[연구] 단체 a negotiation [research] body.

단추 [दान्छु] a button; a stud (장식의)

단축 [दान्छुक] [短縮] shortening; reduction; contraction; curtailment; condensation; abridge (e) ment; abbreviation. 단축 하다 shorten; reduce; contract; curtail; cut (down); condense; abridge; abbreviate.

단편 [दान्फ्यौन] [斷片] a fragment; a piece; a shred; a scrap; a snippet; odds (and ends). e.g. 단편적인 지식 fragmentary knowledge.

단풍 [दान्फुंग] [丹楓] (나무) a maple (tree); (잎) red [scarlet-tinged] leaves; yellow [golden] leaves; tinted autumnal leaves; crimson foliage; (색) autumn [autumnal] tints [colors]. e.g. 단풍잎 (scarlet) maple leaves

단행본 [दान्हैंगबोन] [單行本] a book; a separate volume; an independent volume.

단호히 [दान्होही] [斷乎] 단호하다 [굳다] firm; [결연하다] determined; resolute; decisive; [과감 하다] drastic 단호히 firmly; resolutely; positively; squarely; conclusively; in a determined manner; with a set purpose

닫다 [दात्ता] (문을) shut; close. e.g. 문을 닫다 shut [close] a door. 문을 꼭 닫다 keep a door tightly shut

닫히다 [दाछिदा] [닫아지다] be shut; be closed; shut; close. e.g. 저절로 닫히다 shut of itself. 대문이 닫혀 있다 The gate is shut [closed]. 문이 잘 닫히지 않는다 The door won't shut.

달 [दाल] [지구의 위성] the moon. e.g. 달의 이지러짐 wane.

달갑다 [दाल्काप्ता] satisfactory; desirable. e.g. 달갑지 않은 undesirable / unacceptable / objectionable. 달갑지 않은 손님 an unwelcome visitor [guest].

달걀 [दाल्ग्याल] an egg.

달다[1] [दात्ता] **1** [졸아들다]

be boiled down [dry]; boil down. e.g. 탕약이 다 달았다 The decoction is parched up. **2** [물건이 뜨거워지다] become (red-) hot; glow (벌겋게). e.g. 벌겋게 단 red-hot <iron>. **3** [몸이 뜨거워 지다] feel hot [warm]; flush; burn. e.g. 흥분해서 얼굴이 달다 lush with excitement. **4** [마음이 초조해 지다] be [feel] irritated <at / by / with>; be fretful; fret [be in a fret] <about / at / over>; [안달하다] be [feel] impatient <at / by / for / with>. e.g. 애인이 보고 싶어 애가 달다 be dying to see one's sweetheart.

달다 2 [दाल्ता] [걸다] hang (up); suspend; put up; dangle. e.g. 기를 달다 hoist [raise] a flag.

달다 3 [दाल्ता] (무게를) weigh (a thing). e.g. 저울로 달다 weigh <a thing> in the balance

달다 4 [दाल्ता] [달콤하다] sweet; sugary; sweet-flavored. e.g. 설탕으로 달게 하다 sweeten (coffee) with sugar.

달라붙다 [दाल्लाबुत्ता] [밀착하다] stick <to>; [서로 들러붙다] be[stick] close together; be sticky <to>; be adhesive <to>; be glutinous <to>; [e.g. 구두창에 추잉검이 달라붙어 있었다 Chewing gum got stuck to the sole of my shoe.

달라지다 [दाल्लाजीदा] [변화하다] change; undergo a change; alter; be altered; shith; turn e.g. 마음이 달라지다 change one's mind. 주소가 달라지다 have one's address changed.

달래다 [दाल्लैदा] (좋은 말로) soothe; pacify; calm (down); mollify; [가라앉히다] appease; placate; comfort. e.g. 우는 아이를 달래다 soothe [still] a crying child.

달려가다 [दालल्यौगादा] run [rush / dash / hasten / hurry] <to the spot>; run [rush] up to <a person>. e.g. 의사에게 달려가다 hasten [run] to the doctor's.

달려오다 [दालल्यौओदा] come running; hasten [hurry / rush] to <a place>.

달력 [दालल्यौक] [-曆] a calendar; an almanac.

달리 [दाल्ली] [다르게] differently; dissimilarly; [갖가지로] variously; [특수하게] distinctively; in a different way; in some other way; [따로] apart; separately; e.g.생각했던 것과는 달리 contrary to one's expectations

달리기 [दाल्लिगी] a run;

(경주) a race; a footrace; (말의) a gallop.

달리다 [दाल्लिदा] **1** [열매 등이 붙어 있다] hang <on / from>; hang down <from>; dangle; be suspended <from>. e.g. 먹음직한 사과가 나무에 달려 있었다 Juicy apples hung on the tree **2** […에 의존하다] depend <on / upon>; hang <on>; turn <on / upon>; rest <with>; hinge <on>. e.g. 성패는 너의 노력에 달려 있다 Your success depends on how much effort you make. dissimilar <in>

달빛 [दाल्पित] moonlight; moonshine; a moonbeam. e.g. 달빛 비치는 밤 **दाल्पित बीछीनन बाम** a moonlit night.

달성 [दाल्सौंग] [**達成**] achievement; attainment; accomplishment. 달성하다 achieve; attain; accomplish. e.g. 이리하여 그 위업은 달성되었다 That was how this great work was achieved [accomplished].

달아나다 [दारानादा] **1** [빨리 내닫다] speed; scurry <away / off>; run off [away]; fly off [away] (새가); run fast. e.g. 차는 쏜살같이 달아났다. The car sped away. **2** [도망가다] run away [off]; fly; escape (위험, 체포 등에서); flee; take flight (추적 등에서)

달아보다 [दारापोदा] 무게를) weigh <a thing>; check the weight of. e.g. 짐을 달아보다 weigh a bundle / check the weight of bundle.

달아오르다 [दाराओरुदा] **1** [물건이 뜨거워지다] become red-hot; glow; get very hot. e.g. 달아오른 쇠 red-hot iron. **2** [얼굴이 화끈해지다] feel hot [warm]; burn; flush. e.g. 빨갛게 달아오른 그녀의 얼굴 her face glowing [aglow] with red.

달이다 [दारीदा] 간장 등을) boil down; reduce by boiling; (약제를) decoct; infuse; brew. e.g. 차를 달이다 brew tea.

달인 [दारिन] [**達人**] [기예에 숙달한 사람] an expert; a (past) master; a master-hand; [인생을 달관한 사람] a master mind; a philosopher; a farsighted person; a man of wisdom.

달짝지근하다 [दाल्चाक्चिगुनहादा] rather sweet; sweetish; pleasantly sweet.

달콤하다 [दाल्खोमहादा] **1** [맛이 달다] sweetish; sweet (flavo(u)red); nicely sweet. e.g. 달콤한 멜론 a sweet melon. 달콤한 사랑 sweet love. 맛이 달콤하다 taste sweet / have a sweet flavor. **2** (말이) honeyed; sugary; sweet; flattering;

smooth; oily; well-oiled e.g. 달콤한 말에 넘어가다 be caught by <a person's> sweet talk / be soth-soaped.

달팽이 [दाल्पैंगी] a snail.

달하다 [दाहादा] [達 -] (수량,정도에) reach; extend <to>; cover; range <over> amount to; come (up) to; mount [run] up to. e.g. 지원자가 천명에 달하다 the number of appli-cants mounts up to one thousand .

닭 [दाक] (암탉) a hen; (수탉) a cock; a rooster; (병아리) a chicken

닭고기 [दाक्कोगी] chicken; fowl.

닭싸움 [दाक्साउम] cock-fighting; a cock-fight. e.g. 닭싸움을 시키다 fight cocks.

닮다 [दाम्ता] [look] like <an-other>; be alike; resemble; take ather <one's father>; have a likeness <to>; be similar <to>.

닳다 [दाल्था] [해지다] wear [be worn] out [off]; be rubbed off [down]; (옷이) wear threadbare. e.g. 닳은 구두 worn-out shoes

담 [दाम] (벽돌 등의) a wall; [울타리] a fence. e.g. 돌[벽돌] 담 a stone[brick] wall.

담그다 [दाम्गुदा] **1** (액체 속에) soak [dip / immerse / steep] <in>. e.g. 옷을 물에 오래 담가 두다 give the clothes a long soak. **2** (김치 등을) prepare [make (kimchi); ickle (vegetables) ;(소금에 절이다) salt; preserve with salt[in brine]; (술P장 등을) prepare; brew; ferment. e.g. 김치를 많이 담그다 get a large quantity of vegetables pickled into kimchi.

담기다 [दाम्गिदा] (그릇에) be filled; be put in; hold; (음식이) be served [helped]; be dished up [out]; (병에) be bottled; (

담다 [दाम्ता] **1** [그릇 안에 넣다] put in; fill; (음식을) serve; help; dish up [out]; (병에) bottle. e.g. 바구니에 과일을 담다 put fruit in a basket **2** [포함시키다] put into; incorporate <in>; include; comprise; comprehend. e.g. 정성을 담은 선물 a gith from <a person> with his best wishes.

담담하다 [दामदामहादा] [淡淡-] (마음이) unconcerned; indifferent; disinterested; cool. e.g. 지금의 심경은 담담합니다 Now I am in a serene state of mind.

담당 [दाम्दांग] [擔當] charge; undertaking; one's post. 담당하다 take charge <of>; be in charge <of>. e.g.

저는 이 지역의 판매를 담당하고 있습니다 I'm in charge of sales in this district.

담당자 [दाम्दांग्सा] the person in charge <of>.

담대 [दाम्दांग] [膽大] 담대하다 daring; bold; plucky; audacious. e.g. 그는 담대한 사람이다 He is a man of great courage.

담력 [दामन्यौक] [膽力] courage; pluck; heart; nerve; mettle; grit; guts. e.g. 담력이 없다 [약하다] be timid [cowardly] / be wanting in pluck..

담론 [दाम्नोन] [談論] (a) discussion; argument; discourse. 담론하다 discuss; argue; discourse.

담배 [दाम्बै] tobacco; a tobacco; a cigarette (te) (궐련) ; a cigar (엽궐련); leaf tobacco (잎담배) cut [pipe] tobacco (살담배); chewing tobacco (씹는 담배)

담배 꽁초 [दाम्बै कोंग्चो] a cigarette [cigar] butt [stub / end]; a half-smoked [-consumed] cigarette [cigar];

담벼락 [दामप्यौराक] [담의 표면] the surface of a wall.

담보 [दाम्बो] [擔保] (a) security; (a) mortgage (빚의 보증으로 넣는 것) collateral (융자의 담보 물건) e.g. 대물 담보 impersonal security.

담소 [दाम्सो] [談笑] a chat; chatting; a familiar [friendly] talk; a confabulation.

담쌓다 [दाम्साथा] **1** [담을 두르다] build [set up]a wall; surround <a place> with a wall. **2** [관계를 다] break with <a person>; break off relations with <a person>; e.g. 그와는 담쌓은지 이미 오래다 I broke with him long since.

담요 [दाम्यो] a blanket; a rug.

담판 [दाम्फान] [談判] (a) negotiation; bargaining; a conference; a parley; talks. e.g. 강경하게 담판하다 press hard / make strong [peremptory] demands.

담화 [दाम्ह्वा] [談話] [이야기] (a) talk <with>;(a) conversation <with>; a colloquy 담화하다 talk [converse] <with>; have a talk [chat] <with>.

답 [दाप] [畓] answer

-답다 [दाप्ता] like; worthy <of>; becoming <to>; -ly; -like. e.g. 남자다운 거동 manly behavior.

답답하다 [दाप्दाफादा] [沓沓-] (갑갑한) stuffy; close; stifling; suffocating; choking; (옷등이) tight <coat>; (가슴이) <feel> oppressed; heavy. e.g. 답답한분위기 an oppressive atmosphere.

답례 [दामन्ये] [答禮] [호의에

대한 인사] a return favor [favour]; a gith in return; a return courtesy; a return call [salute].

답변 [दापप्यौन] [答辯] an answer; a reply; [변명] an explanation; (피고측의) a defense; a plea.

답사 [踏査] a survey; (an) exploration; an investingation; reconnaissance. e.g. 현지 답사 <make> an on-the-spot survey / <make> a field investigation.

답안 [दाबान] [答案] [해답] an answer; (용지) an examination paper; an answer sheet

답장 [दाप्चांग] [答狀] an answer; a (written) reply; a reply letter.

-당 [दांग] [當] per ...; (for) each; apiece. e.g.1 인당 per capita <라> य [head] / for each person.

당 [दांग] [黨] [정당] a party; [무리] a group. e.g. 공화 [민주]당 the Republican [Democratic] party.

당구 [दांगू] [撞球] billiards; <英> pills; pool.

당국 [दांगुक] [當局] the (relevant) authorities; the competent authorities.

당근 [दांगुन] [植] a carrot. **당근즙** carrot juice.

당기다 [दांगिदा] **1** [끌다] draw; pull; haul; tug; jerk. e.g. 밧줄을 당기다 pull (on) a rope. **2** [팽팽하게 하다] stretch <a rope> tight; strain; tighten <a rope>. e.g. 밧줄을 팽팽히 당기다 tighten [strain] a rope / stretch a rope tight. **3** [기일을 줄이다] advance; move [carry] <a day> up [forward]; make earlier. e.g. 결혼 날짜를 사흘 당기다 shith the wedding date three days ahead.

당당하다 [दांगदांगहादा] [堂堂-] [번듯하다] stately; [위압하는 듯하다] imposing; [위엄 있다] dignified. e.g. 당당한 저택 a stately mansion

당대 [दांग्दै] [當代] [이 시대] <in> the present age; [당시] those days. e.g. 당대의 present / contemporary / of the day / of our time / of the age.

당돌하다 [दांग्दोर्हादा] [唐突-] **1** [다부지다] staunch; bold; daring; plucky; spunky. e.g. 키는 작지만 그는 매우 당돌하다 Though small in stature, he is quite a daring fellow. **2** [무례하다] rude; abrupt; blunt; forward; presumptuous e.g. 그는 당돌하게 입을 열었다 He abruptly spoke up

당번 [दांग्बौन] [當番] [차례] being on duty; being on guard [watch]; [번드는 사람] a person on duty. e.g. 청소 당번 one's turn for sweeping.

당부 [दाग्बू] [**當付**] a request; an entreaty. 당부하다 ask [request / solicit / tell / beg / bid] <a person> to do <something>; make a request

당분간 [दाग्बुन्गान] [**當分間**] for the present [time being]; for some time (to come); for a while [time]; temporarily.

당사자 [दाग्साजा] [**當事者**] the parties [person] concerned. e.g. 결혼 당사자 the contracting parties in a marriage.

당시 [दाग्शी] [**當時**] at that time; in those days; then. e.g.당시의 then / of those days [times] / at that time.

당신 [दाग्शिन] [**當身**] **1** [2 인칭의 높임말] you. e.g. 당신의 책 your book. **2** [웃어른] he; she; himself; herself. e.g. 이 음식은 당신께서 손수 장만하신 것이다 This food was cooked by my mother herself.

당연 [दाग्योन] [**當然**] 당연하다 rightful; proper; fair; reasonable; natural; justifiable; just;

당일 [दागिल] [**當日**] the day; that day; the appointed day; the day in question; on that day; at the date named.

당일치기 [दागिलछिगी] [**當日-**] 당일치기 여행을 하다 make a day trip.

당장 [दाग्जाग] [**當場**] <부사> [그 자리에서 즉시] on the spot [instant]; in no time; now and here; at once, right away; immediately; promptly; directly. e.g. 당장해야 할 일 business [work] in hand.

당직 [दाग्जीक] [**當直**] duty; (감시,야경 등의) watch.

당직하다 be on duty [watch] (duty 는 근무에 임하고 있음, watch 는 선원 등이 감시를 하는 것) [duty

당첨 [दाग्छौम] [**當籤**] rize winning; drawing a prize; a prize lot. e.g. 그는 당첨 운이 있는[없는] 사람이다 He is always lucky [unlucky] in lotteries.

당하다 [दाग्हादा] [**當-**] **1** [겪다, 만나다] have; encounter; experience; come; arrive; happen; confront; come upon [across]. e.g. 상을 당하다 have a death in the family / have a sad bereavement in one's family. **2** [맞서다] match [equal / rival] <a person>; be a match for; compare with; stand <against / up to>; cope with; keep up with <a person>. e.g. 당할 수 없다 be no match for. [속다] be deceived [cheated / taken in]; be outwitted; [얻어맞다] be struck; receive a blow. e.g. 깜쪽같이 당했다 I was fairly caught. / I was fooled. / I was taken in.

당혹 [दाङ्होक] [當惑] [곤혹] perplexity; puzzlement; embarrassment; [진퇴 양난] dilemma; [혼란] confusion.

ㄷ

당황하다 [दाङ्ह्वाङ्हादा] e perplexed; be puzzled; be bewildered; be nonplussed

닻 [दात] an anchor.

닿다 [दात्था] 1 [접하다] touch; come in [into]; contact [touch] with; be close to; get to [at]; attain to. e.g. 무엇인가가 발에 닿았다 Something touched my foot. / I felt something touch my foot. 2 [도착하다] reach; arrive at[in / on]; get to. e.g. 무사히 닿다 arrive in safety / (물건이) arrive in good condition [order].

-대 [दै] [代] 1 [대금] [दैगुम] a price; [요금] a charge; a rate. e.g. 도서대 a book fee. 2 [연령의 대강의 범위]. e.g. 10 대의 어린이 a teen-ager. 3 [연대의 대강의 범위]. e.g. 1960 년 대에 in the 1960's [1960s].

대 1 [दै] [代] [계승의 순위, 그 기간] a generation; [치세] a reign; [시대] [शीदै] an age; an era. e.g. 5 대째의 대통령 the fithh President. 대를 잇다 succeed <a person>.

대 2 [दै] [大] [큼] largeness; bigness; greatness; [대형] [दैह्यौंग] large size; [크기] size. e.g. 대중소 세 가지 형이 있다 There are [It comes in] three sizes, large, medium and small.

대 3 [दै] [臺] 1 [받침] a stand; a rest; a rack (걸쳐놓는); a table (탁자); a support (버팀); (비석 등의) a pedestal; [지주] a support; a stool. e.g. 텔레비전 (받침)대 a television stand. 2 [차, 기계 등을 세는 단위] a car; a cart; a plane. e.g. 자동차가 한 대 지나갔다 A car passed by. 3 [수량의 범위] a level; a mark. e.g. 수억 대의 자본가 a capitalist with billions

대 4 [दै] 1 [줄기] a stalk; a stem; a pipe; (대나무, 벼 등의) a culm; (완두 등의) ha (u) lm; (사탕수수 등의) a cane; [막대] a pole; a staff; a rod; [붓,펜대] a holder; [담뱃대] a pipe. 2 ⇨ 줏대 (主-) e.g. 대가 약하다 be weak kneed / be timid / be fainthearted. 3 [곧고 긴 물건을 세는 단위] a smoke; a puff; a whiff; a cigarette (te); a fill (양). e.g. 담배 한 대 a pipeful of tobacco / a cigarette 4 [때리는 횟수를

세는 단위] a blow; a stroke; a punch; a hit; (주사의) a shot; an injection. e.g. 한 대에 at a [one] blow [stroke] / by a (single) blow.

대- **[दै]** [**大**] **1** [큰] large; great; vast; [거대한] grand; large-scale; wholesale. **2** [중대한] grave; serious. **3** [뛰어난] great; prominent. e.g. 대 예술가 a great artist. 대 작곡가 a prominent composer.

대기업 **[दैगीऔब]** big traders [enterprises].

대가 **[दैगा]** [**大家**] [거장] a (great) master; a past [passed] master <in / at>; a maestro <*pl.* ~s, -tri>; [권위자] an authority; leading figure; (학문의) a great [an eminent / a distinguished] scholar

대가 **[दैगा]** [**代價**] [대금] [दैगुम] (a) price; [비용] (a) cost. **2** [희생] a cost. e.g. 어떤 대가를 치르더라도 단념하지 않는다 I will not give it up no matter what the cost.

대가족 **[दैगाजोक]** [**大家族**] [많은 수의 가족] a large family. e.g. 대가족을 거느리고 있다 have a large family to support.

대강 **[दैगांग]** [**大綱**] 대충] roughly; about; approximately; [거의] nearly; [간략하게] briefly; cursorily; [가볍게] lightly; almost; [대체로] generally; in general. e.g. 대강 끝나다 be almost [practically] finished.

대개 **[दैगै]** [**大概**] [대부분] most <of>; the (a) great part <of>; a great [large] portion <of>; the majority <of>.

대거 **[दैगौ]** [**大擧**] [한꺼번에] in a body; in (great) force; in large [great] numbers; <프> en masse; [대규모로] on a grand scale. e.g. 대거 적을 공격하다 attack an enemy in full force.

대견하다 **[दैग्यौन्हादा]** [흡족하다] <be> satisfied; contented; content; [훌륭 하다] fine; admirable; praiseworthy; great; [소중하다] valuable; dear; precious. e.g. 대견하게 여기다 take <a person / a thing> admirable [laudable] / put much importance on / make much [highly] of / be proud of.

대결 **[दैग्यौल]** [**對決**] 맞섬] confrontation; a face-to-face meeting; a showdown; [승부] a contest; a match; a game; a bout

대교 **[दैग्यूमो]** [**大橋**] a large [big] bridge. e.g. 한강의 대교들 large bridges over the Han River.

대규모 **[दैग्युम]** [**大規模**] large [big / grand] scale.

대금 **[दैगुम]** [**代金**] [산 물건에

치루는 돈] (a) price; (a) cost; (a) charge; the money; a bill; a fee. e.g. 대금을 치르다 pay for <an article> / pay the price <for>.

대기 [दैगी] [待機] watching and waiting for a chance; standing by. e.g. 경찰에 대기 명령을 내리다 alert the police.

대낮 [दैनात] [백주] broad daylight; [정오] high noon; midday. e.g. 대낮처럼 밝다 be as bright as day [noontime].

대다[1] [दैदा] **1** [접촉시키다] put; apply; hold; place; lay; press. e.g. 수화기를 귀에 대다 hold a receiver to one's ear **2** [닿게 하다] touch; lay [put] one's hand <on / against>. e.g. 이마에 손을 대다 put one's hand to one's forehead / place one's hand against <another's> forehead.

대다[2] [दैदा] **1** (물을) draw <water> into; water; irrigate <rice fields>. e.g. 사막에 물을 대다 irrigate the desert / drew water into the desert. **2** [공급, 후원하다] supply [provide / furnish / serve] <a person> with. e.g. 돈을 대어 주다 furnish [provide] <a person> with money.

대다[3] [दैदा] [동작의 정도가 심함] e.g. 웃어 대다 laugh a heavy laugh / laugh oneself to death.

대다수 [दैदासू] [大多數] a large [great / heavy / crushing / thumping] majority; an enormous majority; the greater part <of>; the mass [bulk] <of>. e.g. 압도적 대다수 an overwhelming majority.

대단원 [दैदावोन] [大團圓] (연극,소설의) a denouement; the (grand) finale; the end; a catastrophe (주로비 극적인) e.g. 대단원의 막이 내리다 come to an end.

대단하다 [दैदानहादा] **1** [수가 많다] many; a great [large / good] number of; [양이 많다] much; a great [good] deal of; [엄청나다] count-less; innumerable; enormous; immense. e.g. 대단한 금액 a colossal [huge / vast] sum. **2** [중대하다] important; serious; grave. e.g. 그것은 대단한 일이 아니다 That does not make much difference. **3** [놀랍다, 비상하다] horrible; terrible; awful; awesome; dreadful; tremendous; [놀랄 만하다] wonderful; amazing; <반어적> nice; fine; precious. e.g. 대단한 부자 a very wealthy man / a man of great wealth.

대담 [दैदाम] [對談] [마주 보고 이야기함] a talk; a face-to-face talk; a convers-ation; a tête-à-tête <pl. tête(s)-à-têtes>; a colloquy; a dialogue; [회견] an interview.

대답 [दैदाप] [對答] a reply; an answer; a response.

대답하다 [दैदाफादा] reply; answer; make [give] an answer [a reply]; respond <to>.

대대 [दैदै] [代代] successive generation. e.g. 대대로 전해 내려오는 물건 a hereditary article.

대두 [दैदू] [擡頭] rise <of nationalism>.
대두하다 raise [show] one's [its] head; come to the fore [front]; become influential [powerful]; be on the rise.

대들다 [दैदुल्दा] defy; stand against; turn <against / upon>; go at; challenge; oppose; rose against; lith a finger against; lash (out) <at>; put a chip on one's shoulder.

대등 [दैदुंग] [對等] equality; an equal [a level] footing; equal [even] terms; parity; par. 대등하다 equal; on an equal status [footing]; even; level.

대뜸 [दैदुम] at once; outright; forthwith; on the spot; instantly; promptly; immedi-ately; in no time; offhand; extempore. e.g. 대뜸 대답하다 answer immediately / give a ready answer.

대략 [दैर्याक] [大略] [개략] an outline; a summary; an epitome; the gist. e.g. 대략을 말하자면 to sum up / to give a general account of.

대량 [दैर्यांग] [大量] a large [great] quantity <of>; enormous volume; a lot <of>; a pile <of>.

대량 생산 [दैर्यांग सैंगसान] [大量生産] mass [quantity] production; production on a large scale. 대량 생산하다 mass-produce; produce <a thing> in commercial quantity

대로 [दैरो] **1** [··· 처럼] as; like; [그 모양과 같이] as it is; as it stands; intact; [본떠서] ather. e.g. 느낀 대로 이야기하다 speak just as one feels. **2** [···에 따라] as; according to [as]; in accordance with; true to; in pursuance of. e.g. 약속 대로 as promised **3** [즉시] as soon as; directly. e.g. 도착하는 대로 as soon as one arrives / on one's arrival.

대륙 [दैर्युक] [大陸] a continent.

대리 [दैरी] [代理] [일을 대신하는 행위] represent-ation; agency; proxy; [法]

procuration; attorneyship; subrogation; [일을 대신하는 사람] a proxy; a deputy; an agent.

대리하다 [दैरीहादा] act (as substitute) for; act in place [behalf] of; act in another's name; stand [be] proxy for; represent <another person>; stand in the place of; deputize for. e.g. 대리시키다 substitute <a person> for <another> / make <another> one's proxy / subrogate.

대리인 [दैरीइन] [代理人] a representative; a proxy; an agent; a procurator; (소송의) an attorney. e.g. 법정 대리인 a legal representative.

대리점 [दैरीजौम] [代理店] an agency; an agent.

대립 [दैरीप] [對立] confronting; opposition; antagonism. e.g. 민족간의 대립 the antagonism of one race against another.

대머리 [दैमौरी] baldead; a baldheaded person; a baldpate.

대면 [दैम्यौन] [對面] an interview; a meeting; [마주봄] facing; confrontation.

대명사 [दैम्यौन्सा] [代名詞] [문법] a pronoun

대목 [दैमोक] (시기) the most important occasion; the height of a certain period; the vital moment; (상인의) a rush period. e.g. 대목을 노리고 물건을 쌓아 두다 stock goods to provide for the rush period. **2** (글의) a passage; a paragraph. e.g. 재미있는 대목 an interesting passage

대문 [दैमुन] [大門] a gate; the front [main] gate [entrance].

대문자 [दैमुन्जा] [大文字] (로마자의) a capital letter.

대번에 [दैबौने] [단숨에] at a breath; at a stroke [blow]; at one coup [try]; by a single effort; at once; immediately; directly; promptly; instantly; [쉽사리] very easily; without difficulty [effort]; readily; [서슴지 않고] without hesitation.

대범하다 [दैबौमहादा] [大泛-, 大汎-] large-hearted; broad-minded; liberal; generous; magnanimous; open-handed; catholic. e.g. 대범한 태도 an air of magnanimity / loth manners / free and open manners.

대법원 [दैबौब्ऑन] [大法院] the Supreme Court; (영국의) the Supreme Court of Judicature; (프랑스의) the Court of Cassation.

대변 [दैब्यौन] [大便] [인분] f (a) eces; excrements; stools; dung; evacuation; excreta; motions; movements. .e.g. 대변이 마렵다 want to go to the toilet / have a call of nature

대변 [**दैब्यौन**] [**代辯**] speaking by proxy. 대변하다 speak for; be a mouthpiece for; act as a spokesman <of>.

대보다 [**दैबोदा**] [비교하다] compare <A with B>; measure; balance; make a comparison <between A and B>; [대조하다] contrast. e.g. 번역을 원문과 대보다 compare a translation with the original.

대본 [**दैबोन**] [**臺本**] (연극의) a playbook; a(play) script; (영화의) a (film) script; a scenario <*pl.*~s>; (오페라의) a libretto <*pl.* ~s, -ti>..

대부 [**दैबू**] [**貸付**] oaning.

대부분 [**दैबूबुन**] [**大部分**] [거의 모두] for the most part; most (ly); nearly; practically; on the whole; [전체량에 거의 가까운 수효,분량] the bulk <of>; a major [great / large] portion <of>.

대비 [**दैबी**] [**對備**] [준비] provision <for / against>; preparations <for>; preparedness <for / against>; [방비] defenses. **대비하다** prepare <for>; make preparations <for>; provide <for / against>.

대비 [**दैबी**] [**對比**] [대조] contrast; contradiction. e.g. 색의 대비 color contrast / contrast of colors. 대비하다 contrast <A> with [and] <B>; set <A> against <B>. **2** [비교] comparison; a side-by-side comparison <of A and B>. 대비하다 compare; draw <A> into comparison with <B>.

대사 [1] [**दैसा**] [**臺詞, 臺辭**] (배우의) speech; words; one's line. e.g. 독백 대사 a monolog (ue) / a soliloquy. 대사가 없는 역 a walk-on [nonspeaking] role.

대사 [2] [**दैसा**] [**大使**] an ambassador; an ambassadress (여성).

대사관 [**दैसाग्वान**] [**大使館**] an embassy.

대상 [**दैसांग**] [**對象**] [정신 활동의 목적물] the object; the subject; [목표] a target.

대서양 [**दैसौयांग**] [**大西洋**] the Atlantic (Ocean).

대서 특필 [**दैसौ तुक्पिल**] [**大書特筆**] a feature (story); a cover story; a wide news coverage; featuring; special mention. 대서특필하다 publish <the news> with heavy headlines; crack the headlines; play up <the event> with abanner; splash the news; headline; banner; feature. e.g. 그 지방 신문들은 대통령의 방문을 대서 특필했다 The localnews-papers featured the President's visit.

대설 [दैसौल] [大雪] [많이 오는 눈] a heavy (fall of) snow; a heavy snowfall.

대성공 [दैसौगोंग] [大成功] a great [big / huge / brilliant] success; a successful [big] hit; a splendid result; (공연 등의) a brilliant performance; a box-office performance.

대세 [दैसे] [大勢] [형세, 추세] the general trend [drith / situation] <of the times [affairs]>; the general tendency <of the world>; the general current <of thought>.

대소 [दैसो] [大小] [대와 소] great and small sizes; [크기] (relative) size; dimensions; magnitude. e.g. 대소에 관계없이 regardless of size / whether large or small.

대소변 [दैसोब्यौन] [大小便] [변] urine and feces; [용변] urination and defecation. e.g. 대소변을 보다 relieve oneself [nature] / ease nature.

대수롭다 [दैसूरोप्ता] important; significant; valuable; useful. e.g. 대수롭지 않은 일 a matter of no importance [weight / consequence / account] / a trivial [trifling] affair [matter] / a trifle.

대승 [दैसं] [大勝] [크게 이김] a great [a signal / a decisive / an easy] victory; (선거의) a landslide [sweeping] victory; a sweep.

대식가 [दैसिक्का] [大食家] a great [large / big / hearty] eater; a glutton; a go (u) rmand; a large [huge / gross / heavy] feeder; a good trencherman.

대신 [दैषिन] [代身] [대리, 대용] substitution; vicariousness; [대용품,대리인] a substitute; a sub; [대리인] a deputy; a proxy; an alternate; [교대자] a relief. 대신하다 take the place of; act as a substitute; take <a person's> place; be substituted <for a person>; [교대하다] relieve <a person>. e.g. 내 아들이 나를 대신할 것이다 My son shall be my proxy.

대안 [दैआन] [代案] an alternative plan [proposal]; a substitute <measure / bill>.

대야 [दैया] a basin; a washbasin; a washbowl.

대양 [दैयां] [大洋] an ocean; the main.

대여 [दैयौ] [貸與] lending; a loan 대여하다 lend; give the loan of <a thing>; lease; loan; grant the use of.

대역 [दैयौक] [代役] [어떤 역을 대신 맡는 행위] substitution; [역을 대신 맡아 하는 사람] a substitute actor [actress]; a substitute; an understudy; (급할 경우의) a pinch hitter; a stand-in; a double. 대역하다 play as a substitute for; play the part of <another actor>; act in <another's> place; double [stand in] for.

대용 [दैयोंग] [代用] substitution. e.g. 이 상자는 의자 대용이 된다 This box will serve as a chair. / We can use this box as a chair.

대우 [दैउ] [待遇] [취급] treatment; [접대] [जौप्तै] reception; entertainment. e.g. 차별 대우 discriminative treatment. 파격적인 대우를 하다 make an exception of one's case [in one's favor].

대원 [दैवौन] [隊員] a member <of a fire brigade [an ~xpedition team]>.

대응 [दैउं] [對應] [마주대함] correspondence. 대응하다 e.g. 그 한국말에 정확하게 대응하는 말이 영어에는 없다 In English there is no precise equivalent for that Korean wor 대응하다 e.g. 젊은 여성에게는 쉽사리 대응하지 못한다 I cannot deal with young women easily.

대인 관계 [दैइन ग्वांग्ये] personal relations [relationship]. e.g. 그는 대인 관계가 원만 하지 않다 His personal relationships are not going well.

대인 [दैइन] [大人] [어른] an adult; a grown-up person. e.g. 입장료 대인 3 백 원 Admission: 300 won per adult.

대작 [दैजाक] [大作] [걸작] a masterpiece; a monumental [great] work; [문학 등에서 대규모의 작품] a voluminous work; [대규모의 미술 작품] a large-scale work <of art>.

대장 [दैजांग] [隊長] 지도자] a leader; a captain; [지휘하는 사람] a commander; (군대의) a commanding officer.

대장 [दैजांग] [臺帳] [회계장부] an account book; [원장] a ledger. e.g. 토지 대장 a land register. 그는 금액을 대장에 기입했다 He entered the sum in the ledger [the account book].

대장부 [दैजांबु] [大丈夫] a man; a manly [worthy] man; [용사] a heroic [brave] man; [큰 인물] a great man. e.g. 대장부 답게 굴어라 Be a man. / Play the man. / Behave [Act] like a man.

대접 [दैजौब] [待接] [대우] treatment; reception; service; [환대] welcome; entertainment; hospitality. 대접하다 [대우하다] treat; receive; [환대하다] entertain; show [give] <a

person> hospitality

대조 [दैजो] [**對照**] 대비 (a) contrast; antithesis; [비교] (a) comparison; [맞추어 보기] (a) collation; check (up). 대조하다 contrast; compare <A with [and] B>; set <A> against <B>; check <A> up with <B>. e.g. 나는 그것을 그의 자료와 대조했다 I checked it against his data.

대주다 [दैजुदा] supply [provide / furnish] <a person with something>; find <a person with something>; give <rations to>. e.g. 의식을 대주다 provide <a person> with food and clothing / issue food and clothing <to a person> / feed and clothe <a person> financial aid [pecuniary help] / finance <a person

대중 [दैजुंग] [**大衆**] the masses (▷ 약간 경멸적); the mass of people; the multitude; the populace; the general public; the public at large; grassroots.

대책 [दैछैक] [**對策**] 방책] measures; a step; [대항책] a counter measure; a counterplan; a countermove.

대체[1] [दैछे] [**大體**] [개요] an outline; a summary; an epitome; an adumbration; the gist; the substance; the drith; the tenor; [취지] the purport; [요점] the principal parts; the main [chief] point(s). e.g. 대체적인 general <idea> / main <points> / rough / loose

대체[2] [दैछे] [**代替**] substitution; [교체] alternation; replacement <of worn-out parts>. 대체하다 substitute <one thing for another>; replace <with>; alternate <with>; substitute <one thing for another>; replace <with>; alternate <with>.

대체로 [दैछेरो] [**大 體** –] generally; in general; generally speaking; as a rule. e.g. 이탈리아인은 대체로 쾌활하다 Generally (speaking), Italians are cheerful.

대출 [दैछुल] [**貸出**] (금전의) a loan; lending; (가불) an advance; (물건,책 등의) lending; a loan. 대출하다 lend; loan; advance; let out on hire.

대충 [दैछुंग] 대강

대치[दैछी] off (against). e.g. 대치 하고 있는 두 거봉 two lothy peaks facing each other.

대통령 [**大統領**] [दैथोंगन्योंग] [공화국의 원수] a president; the President

대포 [**大砲**] [दैफो] [포탄을 쏘는 병기] a gun; (구형의) a cannon <*pl.* ~s, ~>;(a piece of) ordnance; <집합적> artillery.

대폭 [大幅] [दैफोग] [썩 많이] sharply; steeply; by a large margin. e.g. 가격의 대폭 인상 a steep raise in prices / a sharp increase / a heavy boost.

대표 [代表] [दैफ्यो] [여러 사람을 대신함] representation; [대표 하는 사람] a representative; a delegate. 대표하다 represent; stand [act] for. e.g. 그는 학급을 대표하여 학생회에 참석했다 He represented his class at the student council meeting.

대피 [दैफी] [待避] 대피하다 take shelter <in / under>; [철도] shunt. e.g. 사람들은 그 위험 지구로부터 대피했다 The people were evacuated from the danger zone.

대하다 [दैहादा] [對-] **1** [마주 하다] face; confront; be opposite to; be over against. e.g. 적을 대하다 confront an enemy / engage [deal with] an enemy **2** [상대하다, 대접하다] see; face; address; receive ; treat. e.g. 사람을 대하기 싫어하다 don't like to see people.

대학 [दैहाक] [大學] (종합 대학) a university; (단과 대학) a college.

대학생 [दैहाक्सैंग] [大學生] a university [college] student; a college man [woman]; an undergraduate; a collegian.

대학원 [दैहाक्वॉन] [大學院] a graduate [postgraduate] school

대한 민국 [दैहान मीन्गुक] the Republic of Korea (R.O.K.).

대합실 [दैहाप्शिल] [待合室] room; (은행 등의) a lobby.

대항 [दैहांग] [對抗] [맞겨룸, 대립] opposition; antagonism; [대결] confrontation; emulation; rivalry 대항하다 oppose; confront; face; meet; counter; set up against; [경쟁하다] emulate; rival; cope [vie] with; compete with.

대행 [दैहैंग] [代行] vicarious execution. e.g. 수출 [수입] 대행업자 an export [import] agent. 대행하다 execute <business> for <another>; act for <another>; execute as proxy <for>; act for <a person>.

대형 [दैहयौंग] [大形, 大型] a large [full] size; oversize.

대화 [दैहवा] [對話] [의견 등의 교환] a dialogue; a dialog; [담화] a conversation.

대회 [दैहवे] [大會] [큰 회합] a mass meeting; (특정 목적을 위한) a rally; [총회] a general meeting [assembly]; [회의] a conference; a convention; (경기의) a meet; a tournament; a tourney.

-댁 [दैक] [宅] […의 아내] Mrs. ...; the wife of <a

person>. e.g. 김씨 댁 the wife of Mr. Kim / Mrs. Kim.

댁 [डैक] [宅] **1** [가정] a home; [주택] a house; a residence; [상대의 집] your home; [남의 집] a person's home; [가족] your [his] family. e.g. 댁은 어딥니까 Where is your home? / Where do you live? **2** [당신] you. 댁의 부인은 친절한 분이시군요 Your wife is really kind hearted.

댐 [डैम] a dam.

더 [दौ] (수량,정도) more; some more; (시간) longer; (거리) farther; [더욱] still more; further; <부정과 함께> less; still [much] less. e.g. 나는 딸기를 더 먹고 싶다 I want more strawberries e.g.

-더니 [दौनी] **1** [원인,이유] as; so; since; because (of); owing to; but now [then]; and now [then]. e.g. 그는 열심히 공부하더니 시험에 일등으로 합격했다 He studied so hard that he topped the list of successful examinees. **2** [회고] used to be ...(but now). e.g. 그때는 낚시꾼도 드물더니 Then there used to be very few anglers (but now ...).

더듬거리다 [दौदुम्कौरीदा] **1** (손으로) grope; fumble for; feel about [around] for. e.g. 어둠 속에서 더듬거리다 grope about in the dark for <a doorknob>. **2** (말을) stammer; falter; stutter; stumble; [우물우물 말하다] mumble; speak indistinctly; mouth one's words. e.g. 어린애의 더듬거리는 설명으로는 according to the child's faltering explanation.

더듬다 [दौदुम्ता] **1** (손으로) grope <for>; fumble <in the darkness> for <a thing>; feel [grope] about for <a thing>; feel ather <the handle>. e.g. 회중전등을 찾으려고 더듬다 grope for a flashlight [torch]. **2** (말을) stammer; falter; stutter; stumble; be stuck for a word; have an impediment in one's speech. e.g. 말을 더듬으며 stammering (ly) / stuttering (ly). 그는 몹시 말을 더듬는다 He stammers badly. 그는 말을 더듬는 버릇이 있다 He is apt to stutter [falter in speaking]. **3** (근원, 기억 등을) trace; retrace; tread; follow (up); pursue; explore.

더디다 [दौदीदा] **1** [늦다] late; tardy; dilatory; behind time [schedule]. e.g. 그는 돌아오는 것이 더디다 He is long in returning. / He's been gone long [a long time]. **2** [느리다] slow; tardy; retarded. e.g. 걸음이

더디다 be slow [laggardly] of foot.

-더라 [**दौरा**] [회상, 감탄] found [discovered] that; I noticed that; it has been observed that; it is known that; as we all [I] know; I hear [have been told] that; [···이라고 한다] they say; it is said that. e.g. 그는 앓고 있다 더라 (I am not sure but) I hear he is sick.

더러워지다 [**दौरौवॉजीदा**] **1** (사물이) become dirty [filthy]; be stained; be soiled; be polluted; be defiled; be blemished [smudged]; be contaminated. e.g. 더러워진 dirty / unclean / filthy / stained / tainted / defiled. **2** (마음 등이) become mean [base / low / sordid / despicable / dirty]. e.g. 마음이 더러워지다 become mean-spirited [base-minded].

더럽다 [**दौरौप्ता**] **1** [불결하다] dirty; filthy; foul; unclean; soiled; squalid; nasty; stained; grimy; shabby. e.g. 더러운 물dirty [impure] water **2** [비열하다] mean; base; low; dirty; [추잡하다] indecent; obscene; filthy; nasty. e.g. 더러운 놈 a mean [low] fellow / a dirty guy [dog].

더럽히다 [**दौरौफीदा**] **1** [불결하게 하다] make <a thing> dirty [unclean]; stain; soil; foul; defile; blemish; slur; taint; contaminate; pollute <air>. **2** (명예 등을) disgrace; dishonor; bring disgrace <upon>; sully; defile; tarnish; [모독하다] desecrate <a shrine>; profane <a temple>.

더미 [**दौमी**] a heap; a pile; an accumulation; (건초 등의) a stack; a rick.

더부룩하다 [**दौबुरुक्खादा**] **1** (머리, 수염 등이) tuthy; fringy; bushy; thick; unkempt; shaggy; (풀 등이) thick; rank; rampant; luxurious. e.g. 더부룩한 머리 unkempt hair. **2** [뱃속이 시원하지 않다] <서술적> feel stodgy; feel [sit] heavy on the stomach; be heavy; be not easily digested; feel bloated.

더불어 [**दौबुरौ**] **1** [함께] together; [···과 함께] with; together [along] with; in company with; [··· 에 따라서] as; with. **2** [한가지로] alike; equally. e.g. 남녀[노소]가 더불어 men and women [young and old] alike.

더없이 [**दौओप्शी**] 더할 나위 없이] most of all; best (of all); supremely; superatively; in the last degree.

더욱 [**दौउक**] [한층 더] more; more and more; still [much] more; all the more; <부정> less and less; still [much] less. e.g. 더욱 중요한 것은 what is more important.

더위 [दौवी] [더운 기운] heat; warmth; hot weather.

더하다[1] [दौहादा] **1** [심해지다] get [become] worse; worsen; grow harder; increase in violence; get serious; gather strength; go from bad to worse; be aggravated; grow in intensity; become intensified. e.g. 그의 병세는 차차 더해갔다 His illness is steadily worsening. **2** [보태어 늘리다] add <up>; sum up; add <one number to another>; [부족분을 보태어 메우다] make up <for>. e.g. 8 에 5 를 더하면 13 이 된다 Five added to eight makes [is / equals] thirteen. **3** [늘리다] increase; augment; gain; grow; add to; enlarge. e.g. 낮은 목소리가 그의 위엄을 더하고 있다 His low voice adds to his dignity.

더하다[2] [दौहादा] [(비교하여) 더 많거나 심하다] more; much; all the more [better / worse]. e.g. 그도 술꾼이지만 그의 아버지는 더한 술고래다 He is (quite) a drinker, but his father is an even heavier drinker.

덕 [दौक] [德] [미덕] (a) virtue; morality; goodness; moral excellence; a merit. e.g. 덕이 있는 virtuous / respectable.

덕망 [दौग्मांग] [德望] (a) moral influence; a reputation for virtue; high moral repute. e.g. 덕망이 있다 have a moral influence <over>

덕택 [दौकथैक] [德澤] indebtedness; [은혜] favor; grace; patronage; boon; [조력] help; aid; assistance; [후원] support; backing.

던지다 [दौन्जीदा] **1** (물건을) throw; hurl; fling; cast; pitch; (창 등을) dart; toss (가볍게). e.g. 공을 던지다 throw [pitch] a ball. **2** [투표하다] cast a ballot; ballot <for>; cast a [one's] vote <for>; poll. e.g. 깨끗한 한 표를 던지다 cast a clean vote.

덜 [दौल] less; incompletely; little; insufficiently. e.g. 덜 취한 half-tipsy / half-drunk.

덜다 [दौलदा] **1** [빼다] subtract; deduct <from>; take off; [적게 하다] decrease; lessen; abate; reduce. e.g. 3 분의 1 을 덜다 reduce one-third **2** (고통, 슬픔 등을) lessen; ease; relieve; allay; alleviate; lighten; mitigate; (돈 등을) save; spare; curtail; cut (down). e.g. 수고를 덜다 save <a person> trouble / save labor.

덜덜 [दौलदौल] [떠는 모양]

trembling(ly); shivering(ly); shaking(ly); quivering(ly). e.g. 손을 덜덜 떨면서 with trembling hands.

덜되다 [दौल, ढेदा] **1** [미완성 되다] incomplete; unfinished. e.g. 덜된 작품 an unfinished work <of art>. **2** (사람됨이) <서술적> be no good; be wretched [poor / sorry / sad] stuff; be a failure; leave much to be desired; be not up to the mark; be a complete botch.. e.g.덜된 놈 a good-for-nothing fellow / a greenhorn / a wretched fellow / a silly ass. **3** [덜익다] unripe; immature; green. e.g. 덜된 과일 green [unripe] fruits.

덜렁거리다 [दौल्लौंग्गौरीदा] (행동이) be restless; conduct [behave] oneself flippantly; act hastily [rashly / carelessly / frivolously]; be always on the go. e.g. 덜렁거리는 사람 a flighty [hasty] person / a bustling fellow.

덜커덩거리다 [दौल्खौदौंग्गौरीदा] keep banging [crashing / rattling / clattering]. e.g. 미닫이를 덜커덩거리며 닫다 shut the sliding door noisily

덜컥 [दौलखौक] **1** [갑자기] suddenly; unexpectedly; with a pop. e.g. 덜컥 죽다 die suddenly / pop off / drop dead. 덜컥 겁이 나다 be struck with awe [get into a funk] all of a sudden.**2** (가슴이). e.g. 그의 말에 가슴이 덜컥 내려앉았다 His words shocked me. 전보라면 언제나 가슴이 덜컥 내려앉는다 A telegram always gives me a turn.

덜하다 [दौलहादा] **1** [정도가 낮아지다] decrease; diminish; lessen; abate. **2** [줄이다] decrease; diminish; lessen; abate; (수를) subtract <from>. **3** [견주어 한쪽이 적다] less.

덤[दौम] an addition; a premium; something extra; something thrown in; a throw-in; [경품] a free gith; a giveaway.

덤덤하다 [दौमदौमहादा] **1** [말이 없다] silent; speechless; closemouthed; mum; <서술적> keep [remain] silent; holone's tongue; keep one's mouth shut; keep dumb. e.g. 덤덤하게 앉아 있다 sit in silence. **2** [차분하다] calm; serene; placid; peaceful; [탐탁하지 않다] ordinary; common; <서술적> keep calm [cool]; keep a cool head; do not get excited.

덤벙거리다 [दौलबौंग्गौरीदा] act frivolously [rashly / flippantly / lightly]; frivol. e.g. 덤벙 거리는 사람 a careless [hasty] person / a scatter-brain.

덤비다 [दौमबीदा] **1** [대들다] go at; turn [fall] upon; defy; challenge; strike (out) at <a person>; attack; assault; spring [jump / leap / pounce / fly] upon [at]; fling [throw] oneself upon; set upon; rush [fly] at. e.g. 두 사람이 악당에게 덤볐다 Two of them attacked [made an attack on] the ruffian. **2** [서두르다] hurry; hasten; be in a hurry; make (undue) haste; be in hot haste; fluster; busy oneself <with>; bustle [act helter-skelter] (당황). e.g. 덤비지 말고 calmly / with calmness [composure].

덥다 [दौप्ता] hot; warm (hot 는 미국에서, warm 은 영국에서 흔히 씀); sultry; <서술적> feel hot [warm].

덥석 [दौप्सौक] [급히] quickly; suddenly; with a quick movement; all of a sudden; all at once; hastily; [단단히] firmly; tightly. e.g. 덥석 물다 snap at <food>.

덧나다 [दौन्नादा] (병이) worsen; become [grow] worse; go from bad to worse; take a bad turn; change [take a turn] for the worse; be aggravated; (종 기가) be [get] inflamed; [곪다] form [generate] pus; fester; suppurate. e.g. 엉터리 약을 먹고 감기가 덧나 폐렴이 되었다 The cold developed into pneumonia due to a quack medicine.

덧붙이다 [दौप्पुछीदा] **1** [더 붙이다] add [attach / stick] <one thing to another>; append; affiK annE join [fix] <on top of another>. e.g. 물건에 편지를 덧붙여 보내다 send <a person> a thing with a letter. **2** (말을) add; say further [in addition]; make an additional remark; (인용구 등을) tag <one's speech> with; tack on [onto]. e.g. 편지에 추신(追 伸)을 덧붙이다 add a postscript to a letter.

덧셈 [दौस्सैम] addition.

덧없다 [दौतऔप्ता] [공허하다] vain; hopeless; empty. e.g. 덧없는 노력 vain efforts

덧입다 [दौतइप्ता] put on [wear] <a coat> over a garment.

덩굴 [दौंगुल] a bine; a vine (포도 등의); a runner [creeper] (땅을 기는); [植] a voluble stem.

덩달다 [दौंग्दालदा] do the same as <a person> does; follow suit; chime in with; echo; tag along; follow <another> blindly. e.g. 덩달아 웃다 smile in sympathy / laugh following suit.

덩어리 [दौंगौरी] [뭉쳐진 덩이] a lump; a mass; a clod; a gobbet <of meat>; a dollop

<of butter>. e.g. 얼음덩어리 a lump of ice pack (큰 것).

덩치 [दौन्ची] physique; frame; build; physical constitution; bulk; mass; size; volume.

덫 [दौत] a trap; [올가미] a snare; a hook; a gin.

덮개 [दौप्कै] a cover; a covering; a casing; [침구] bedding; bedclothes.

덮다 [दौप्ता] **1** [씌우다] cover <with>; put <a thing> on; veil; overspread; overlay. e.g. 산꼭대기를 덮은 구름 clouds hanging over the top of the mountain. **2** [은폐하다] hide; conceal; cover up; keep <a matter> secret. e.g. 죄를 덮어 주다 cover up <a person's> crime / keep <a person's> crime secret.

덮어두다 [दौफौदुदा] ignore; disregard; let go; lay aside <a question>; wink at; connive at; overlook; leave <a matter> unnoticed [out of consideration]; shut one's eyes to; take no notice of; pass over; tolerate <a misstep> without question; (비밀로) keep <a matter> secret [dark]. e.g. 남의 잘못을 덮어두다 shut one's eyes to a person's faults / overlook a person's mistakes.

덮어쓰다 [दौफौसुदा] **1** [누명을 쓰다] take <another's fault> upon oneself. **2** [가리다]. e.g. 그는 비옷을 머리에 덮어쓰고 들어왔다 He came in with his raincoat over his head.

덮어씌우다 [दौफौस्वीउदा] **1** [가리다, 덮다] cover <with>; cover over; put <a thing> on; plate <a thing> with. **2** [책임,죄 등을 지우다] put[lay / pin] <the blame> on <a person>; charge <the guilt> on <a person>; blame <an error> on <a person>; ttribute [ascribe] <the failure> to <a person>.

덮치다 [दौप्छिदा] **1** [겹쳐 누르다] press down; press upon <a thing>; throw [cast / pop] <a thing> over; hold [get] <a person> down; keep [hold / pin] down; lie one upon [on top of] another; overlap each other [one another]; [습격하다] attack; assail; raid; assault; invade; make an attack [onset / onslaught] on; come upon; set upon; deliver an assault on; strike [go] at; make a raid on; force down; descend on; fall [swoop / pounce] upon. e.g. 놀음판을 덮치다 raid [make a raid upon / move in on] a gambling den. **2** [동시에 닥치다] come [happen] all at the same time; be pressed with [by] business; suffer from pressure of business. e.g.

여러 가지 일이 덮치다 have many things to do all at the same time / things come all bunched up at once

데 **[दे]** [곳] a place; a spot; [점] a point; [특징] a feature; a distinction; [대목] a passage (문장등의); a part (부분); [경우] a case; an occasion. e.g. 요리를 하는 데에는 물이 필요하다 Water is needed for cooking.

데다 **[देदा]** **1** [뜨거운 것에 닿아 살이 상하다] get [be] burnt; have [suffer] a burn; burn oneself; get [be] scalded (뜨거운 물에); get [be] scorched (부젓가락 등에). e.g. the scar of a burn [scald]. **2** [혼나다] have a bitter experience; have [experience] difficulty; find <something> troublesome [difficult] to deal with; have had enough <of>; find [know] <a thing> to one's cost. e.g. 못된 고리 대금업자 를 만나 몹시 데었다 I had a hell of a time dealing with a bad usurer.

데려오다 **[दैर्यौओदा]** bring <a person> with one; come bringing along; make <a person> come back; come in company with; fetch; [불러오다] send for; summon; call in. e.g. 딸을 집으로 데려오다 bring one's daughter home. 의사를 데려오다 bring a doctor <along with one>.

데리다 **[दैरीदा]** [가까이에 있게 하다] take [bring] <with>; be accompanied by; be attended by. e.g. 데리고 with / accompanied by. 집에 데려다 주다 see <a person> to a house / escort <a person> home. 데리러 가다 go for <a person> / go to fetch <a person> / call for <a person>.

데모 **[देमो]** a demonstration; a rally; a demo.

데우다 **[दैउदा]** warm; make warm; heat; heat [warm] up.

데이트 **[देइथु]** [날짜,남녀간의 만남] a date.

데치다 **[दैछीदा]** [살짝 익히다] scald; parboil; boil slightly.

-도 **[दो]** [비록 …이라도] even if; although; in spite of; notwithstanding; despite; no matter <what, how, who, etc.>. e.g. 적어도 세 번은 내가 그에게 전화를 했다 I phoned him at least three times

도[度] **[दो]** [온도, 각도, 경도의 단위] a degree. e.g. 영상 [영하] 7 도 seven degrees above [below] zero

도[1] **[道]** **[दो]** [행정 구역의 하나] a province; a district; a *do*.

도[2] **[दो] 1** [및] and; as well as; both ... and; [또한, 역시] too; also; [···도 ···이 아니다] not ... either; neither ... nor .... e.g. 나도 그를 알고 있다 I know him, too. / I also know him.

도구 [दोगु] [道具] 1 [연장] a tool; (비교적 정밀한 것) an instrument; (가사에 쓰는 것) a utensil; (어떤 목적을 위한) an implement (흔히 복수형으로); [설비] equipment; tackle; (작고 편리한) a gadget. **2** [수단,방편] a means; a tool; a stepping-stone; an instrument; a vehicle; [앞 잡이] a cat's-paw. e.g. 결혼을 출세의 도구로 삼다 use marriage as a tool for one's advancement.

도굴 [दोगुल] [盜掘] (무덤의) grave robbery. 도굴하다 rob a grave.

도금 [दोगुम] [鍍金] (금속의) plating; gilt.

도기 [दोगी] [陶器] <집합적> earthenware; pottery; ceramic ware; [사기 그릇] crockery; [도자기] china ware..

도끼 [दोक्की] (자루가 긴) an ax (e); a hatchet (손도끼).

도난 [दोनान] [盜難] theth; [강탈] (a) robbery; [밤도둑, 빈집털이] (a) burglar

도달 [दोदाल] [到達] [목적지에 다다름] arrival; reaching; [달성] attainment. 도달하다 arrive in [at / on]; get to [at]; attain; touch; come to; make it <to>

도대체 [दोदैछे] [都大體] [도무지] (not) in the least; (not) the slightest; (not) at all. e.g. 도대체 알 수 없다 cannot understand (it) at all / be all Greek to (me) / be utterly at sea.

도덕 [दोदोक] [道德] [행동의 바름] morality; [사회에서 받아들여지고 있는 기준에 맞춘 행위] morals.

도도하다 [दोदोहादा] arrogant; haughty; proud; overbearing; lordly; toplothy; uppish; puffed-up; stuck-up

도둑 [दोदुक] a thief <*pl.* thieves>; [강도] a robber; [밤도둑] a burglar; [좀도둑] a pilferer; a filcher; a shoplither; [도둑질] (a) theth; (a) robbery; (a) burglary.

도둑질 [दोदुक्चिल] [절도] theth; thievery; stealing; [강도질] robbery; burglary; [좀도둑질] pilfering; filching.

도래 [दोरै] [渡來] (사람의) a visit; (사물의) introduction; importation; influx. e.g. 불교의 도래 the introduction of Buddhism.

도련님 [दोर्यौन्नीम] [시동생] an unmarried younger brother of one's husband.

도로 [दोरो] [道路] [길] a road; [거리] a street; [대로, 공로] a thoroughfare; a highway; [코스] the route.

도로 [दोरो] [되짚어서] back; (over) again. e.g. 오던 길을 도로 가다 go back over one's way / go back where one came

도로아미타불 [दोरोआमीथाबुल] [-阿彌陀佛] [애쓴 일이 허사가 됨] a relapse; a setback. e.g. 도로아미타불이다 be no better than what one used to be / wind up just where one started / have lost all one gained.

-도록 [दोरोक] **1** [목적] (so as) to <do>; in order to <do>; so [in order] that one may <do>; that one may <do>. e.g. 나는 급행열차를 탈수 있도록 일찍 일어났다 I got up early so as to be in time for the express. **2** […때까지] till; until; to; up [down] to. e.g. 밤늦도록 till late at night

도리 [दोरी] [道理] **1** [이치] reason; [정당] right; [정의] justice; [진리] truth; [본분] (a) duty. **2** [방도] a way; a method; a process; the ways and means; an alternative. e.g. 사태가 이 지경이니 딴도리가 없다 Now that things have come to this, there is no more that can be done

도리어 [दोरीओ] [반대로] on the contrary; instead; [오히려] rather; all the more. e.g. 익을 올리기는커녕 도리어 큰 손해를 봤다 It brought us no profit, on the contrary [instead], we incurred a heavy loss.

도망 [दोमांग] [逃亡] (an) escape; (a) flight; desertion; decampment; abscondence; elopement.

도맡다 [दोमाथा] [혼자서 책임지다] undertake alone; take all upon oneself; shoulder <something> alone; take [bear] responsibilities by oneself <for something>; run the whole thing. e.g. 모든 책임을 혼자서 도맡다 take the whole responsibilities alone.

도매 [दोमे] [都賣] wholesale trade. **도매하다** sell (by / at) wholesale; wholesale.

도면 [दोम्योन] [圖面] [스케치, 도화, 선화, 그림] a drawing; a sketch; [설계도, 겨냥도 평면도] a plan; [청사진] a blueprint.

도모 [दोमो] [圖謀] planning; devising; contriving; designing; scheming.

도모하다 plan; devise; contrive; scheme; plot; [애쓰다] labor [work / strive] <for>.

도무지 [दोमुजी] [전혀] utterly; entirely; quite; altogether; never; <not> at all; <not> in the least. e.g. 그는 도무지 아무것도 모른다

He knows nothing at all. / He is utterly ignorant.

도박 [दोबाक] [賭博] [노름] gambling; a game of chance; gaming; a gambling game. e.g. 사기 도박 fraudulent [crooked] gambling.

도발 [दोबाल] [挑發] provocation; excitement; incitement; stimulation.

도발하다 [दोबाल्हादा] provoke; arouse; stir up; excite; incite; stimulate; be provocative of. e.g. 호기심을 도발하다 excite <a person's> curiosity.

도배 [दोबै] [塗褙] papering <of the walls and ceiling of a room>; paperhanging.

도배하다 paper [hang paper on] <the walls [ceiling] of a room>.

도보 [दोबो] [徒步] walking; going on foot; pedestrianism. e.g. 도보로 on [by] foot / afoot.

도사 [दोसा] [道士] **1** [도를 닦은 사람] [a man of high moral sense. **2** [불교의 교리를 깨달은 사람,스님] a (Buddhist) priest; [도교 수행자] a Taoist.

도사리다 [दोसारीदा] **1** [웅크리다] sit [squat (down)] cross-legged [tailor-fashion]; sit with one's legs crossed. **2** (뱀 등이) coil itself (up). e.g. 도사리고 있는 뱀 a snake lying in a coil. (뱀이) 도사리고 있다 be coiled.

도산 [दोसान] [倒産] [재산을 잃고 망함] (a) bankruptcy; insolvency; failure. 도산하다 go bankrupt; go under; be bankrupt (ed); become bankrupt [insolvent].

도살 [दोसाल] [屠殺] slaughter; butchery.

도서 [दोसौ] [圖書] books; [간행물] publications; [문헌] literature.

도수[दोसू] [度數] [횟수] (the number of) times; frequency; incidence. **2** (온도,각도 등의) the degree; (렌즈의) a degree; a diopter. e.g. 안경의 도수 the power of glasses **3** (알코올분의) proof. e.g. 도수가 높은 위스키 high-proof whisky.

도시 [दोशी] [都市] a city; a town; an urban community; towns and cities; an asphalt jungle.

도시락 [दोशीराक] lunch; luncheon; a packed [box] lunch; (상자) a lunch [chip] boK(옛날의) a small willow basket (for carrying food); a lunch basket.

도심 [दोशिम] [都心] the heart [center] of the Metropolis [the city]; the downtown

도심지 [दोशिमजी] the central area of a town; the downtown [mid-town] area.

도안 [दोआन] [圖案] a design; an ornamental design; a

device; a sketch; a plan. **도안하다** design; draw a design <of>; make a design <of>.

도약 **[दोयाक]** [**跳躍**] a jump; a leap; a spring; a skip; a take-off; jumping (경기). **도약하다** jump; leap; spring; skip; prance; <a horse> make [cut] a curvet.

도예 **[दोऐ]** [**陶藝**] ceramic art; ceramics (단수 취급); pottery.

도와주다 **[दोवाजुदा]** [조력하다] help <a person (to) do>; help <with>; give help [aid] <to>; help out; assist; give [lend / reach out] a helping hand <to>.

도용 **[दोयोंग]** [**盜用**] (기타의) surreptitious use; using by stealth; plagiarism. 도용하다 use by stealth; make a fraudulent use of <another's registered design>; [표절하다] plagiarize. e.g. 사인을 도용하다 use another's private seal by stealth.

도움 **[दोउम]** [조력] help; aid; assistance; [후원] support. e.g. 남의 도움을 청하다 seE the support of a person.

도자기 **[दोजागी]** [**陶磁器**] ceramic ware; ceramics; china and porcelain; pottery; earthenware.

도장 **[दोजांग]** [**圖章**] [인장] a seal; [소인,압인] a stamp; a handstamp..

도저히 **[दोजौही]** [**到底** –] <cannot> possibly; <cannot> by any possibility; <none> at all; not nearly <so>; [전혀] utterly; absolutely. e.g. 해결은 도저히 불가능하다 No settlement is remotely possible.

도전 **[दोजौन]** [**挑戰**] a challenge; [권위 등에 대한 반항] defiance. **도전하다** challenge <a person to a fight>; make [give] a challenge; defy; bid defiance <to>; call <a person> to combat; fling [throw] down the gauntlet [glove] <to>; provoke a battle.

도주 **[दोजू]** [**逃走**] = 도망.

도중 **[दोजुंग]** [**途中**] e.g. 도중에(서) on the way <to / from> / on one's way <to> / on the road / en route <to / for> / on route <to / from> / in the middle of / in the midst of / in the course of / in transit (운송중) / (중도에서) halfway; midway. e.g. 학교로 가는 도중에 on one's way to school.

도중 하차 **[दोजुंगहाछा]** [**途中下車**] a stopover; a layover **도중 하차하다** stop over [make a stopover] <at a way station>; stop off; break one's journey; lay over.

도지다 [दोजीदा] [병이 재발하다] a relapse occurs; (사람이) relapse <into illness>; have [suffer] a relapse [return] <of a disease>; become serious again; suffer a setback; take a critical [serious] turn.

도착 [到着] [दोछाक] arrival. 도착하다 arrive at [in / on]; [도달하다] reach; get to; (편지,화물이) come to hand.

도처 [दोछो] [到處] everywhere. e.g. 도처에 wherever one goes / all over <the world> / throughout <the country> / far and wide [near / nigh] / in every quarter / in all directions / on all sides / on every hand / here, there, and everywhere.

도청 [दोछोंग] [道廳] a provincial office [government]; the administeration hall [office] of a province.

도취 [दोछ्वी] [陶醉] **1** [거나하게 취함] intoxication. 도취하다 be intoxicated. **2** [감격에 젖음] fascination; rapture. e.g. 자기도취 narcissism. 자기 도취자 a narcissist. 도취하다 be fascinated [charmed / carried away] <by>; be enraptured <with>; be in rapture [ecstasies] <over>. e.g. 자연의 아름다 움에 도취하다 be intoxicated with [fascinated by] the beauty of nature. 승리의 환희에 도취하다 be intoxicat-ed with [lost in the rapture of] the joy of victory. 그는 그 그림의 아름다움에 도취했다 He was intoxicated with [fascinated by] the beauty of the picture.

도치 [दोछी] [倒置] turning upside-down; [문법] inversion. **도치하다** invert; reverse; put upside-down.

도톰하다 [दोथोम्हादा] ⇨ 두툼하다

도통 [दोथोंग] [都統] [전혀] (not) at all; absolutely. e.g. 그 사람 일은 도통모른다 I know absolutely nothing about him. / I don't know him from Adam.

도표 [दोफ्यो] [圖表] a chart; [도식] a diagram; [그래프] a graph.

도피 [दोफी] [逃避] (an) escape; evasion; (a) flight <from the world>.

도피하다 escape; fly. e.g. 사회로부터 도피하다 seclude oneself from society.

도형 [दोहयोंग] [圖形] a figure; a device; a diagram.

독 [दोक] [毒] [유독 물질] (a) poison; poisonous substance.

독감 [दोकगाम] [毒感] (malignant) influenza; (Spanish) grippe; flu(e); a bad [nasty] cold.

독과점 [दोकगवाजौम] [**獨寡占**] monopoly and oligopoly.

독단 [दोकदान] [**獨斷**] [전단] arbitrary decision. e.g. 독단의 arbitrary / peremptory.

독립 [दोंग्निप] [**獨 立**] **1** [자립] independence; self-help; self-reliance. e.g. 경제상의 독립 economic independ-ence. 독립하다 become independent <of one's parents>; stand on one's own legs [feet]; stand alone; end one's dependence <on>; set up for oneself. **2** [자주] independence; freedom. e.g. 독립을 선언하다 declare independence / declare <itself> independent.

독무대 [दोंगमूदै] [**獨舞臺**] **1** [혼자서 연기하기] playing alone [by oneself]. **2** [한 사람의 연기가 특히 뛰어난 판국] the sole master of the stage [field]. e.g. 독무대다 be the sole figure in the scene / outshine all other actors.

독백[दोक्बैक] [**獨 白**] a monologue; monolog; a soliloquy. 독백하다 soliloquize; utter a soliloquy; speak aside.

독보 [दोक्बो] [**獨 步**] e.g. 독보적인 unique / matchless / peerless / unparalleled / unequaled / unrivaled / unchallenged. 당대의 독보적인 시인 the greatest poet of the age [day].

독살 [दोकसाल] poisoning; killing by poison.

독서 [दोकसौ] [**讀書**] reading.

독설 [दोकसौल] [**毒 舌**] a spiteful tongue; a venomous remark; malicious language; vituperation.

독성 [दोकसौंग] [**毒 性**] virulence; toxicity. e.g. 독성이 강한 화학 약품 a highly toxic chemical. 독성이 있는 virulent / poisonous / toxic / toxicant.

독수 공방 [दोक्सू गोंग्बांग] [**獨守空房**] (남편이 출타 중의) solitude [a lonely life] in one's husband's absence; (별거,사별) a lonely life in separation; a widowed life. **독수 공방하다** live in solitude with one's husband away from home; live separate; live as a widow.

독신 [दोविशन] [**獨身**] celibacy; a single life; bachelorhood (남자); spinsterhood (여자).

독실 [दोविशल] [**篤 實**] sincerity; faithfulness. 독실하다 sincere; faithful; true.

독약 [दोक्याक] [**毒藥**] poison; a poisonous drug [medicine

독자 [दोकजा] [**讀 者**]

독자[दोकजा] [**獨 自**] a reader; [구독자] a subscriber <to a magazine / to a newspaper>; (사회 전반의) the reading public.

[저 혼자]. e.g.독자적인 individual / personal. 독자적 견해 one's personal views.

독재[दोक्जै] [**獨 裁**] dictatorship; despotism; autocracy; absolute rule; absolutism. 독재하다 have <a country> under one's despotic rule; hold an absolute authority <over a project>; manage [run / operate] <a company> on one's sole authority.

독점 [दोक्जौम] [**獨占**] [독차지] exclusive possession. e.g. 독점적인 monopolistic / exclusive. ··· 의 독점물이 되다 become the exclusive property of .... 독점하다 have [keep] <a thing> to oneself; obtain the exclusive possession of; monopolize.

독주 [दोक्जु] [**獨走**] **1** [혼자 뜀]. 독주하다 run alone. **2** [남을 떼어놓고 선두를 달림]. 독주하다 have a large [sizable] lead <on [over] the others>; be far ahead of <a person>; leave <other> far behind.

독주 [दोक्जू] [**獨奏**] a recital; a solo (performance). e.g. 피아노 독주 a piano solo [recital]. 독주하다 play a solo; play alone.

독지가 [दोक्जीगा] [**篤志家**] [자선가] a benevolent [charitable] person; [솔선자] a volunteer; a person interested; a supporter (후원자).

독차지 [दोक्छाजी] [**獨** –] exclusive possession; having [keeping] all to oneself; monopolizing. 독차지하다 have [keep] all to oneself; possess exclusively; monopolize; engross; get the exclusive possession of.

독창 [दोक्छांग] [**獨唱**] a (vocal) solo.

독창적 [दोक्छांग्जौक] [**獨創的**] e.g. 독창적인 original / creative. 독창적인 복장 original clothes.

독특 [दोक्थक] [**獨 特**] 독특하다 [고유하다] peculiar <to>; [특징이 있다] characteristic; [독자적이다] ow ; [유일 무이하다] unique.

독파 [दोक्पा] [**讀 破**] 독파하다 read (through) <a book>; read <a book> to the last page; finish reading <a book>.

독하다 [दोखादा] [**毒** –] **1** [독기가 있다] poisonous; venomous; mephitic; deleterious; toxic; noxious. e.g. 독한 가스 poisonous air**2** [진하다] strong; severe; intense; sharp. e.g. 독한 냄새 a strong [heavy] smell

독학 [दोखाक] [**獨 學**] self-education; self-instruction; solitary studies. **독학하다**

study by oneself; teach [educate] oneself; learn without a teacher.

독후감 [**दोखुगाम**] [**讀後感**] <one's> impressions of a book [an article].

ㄷ

돈[**दोन**] [금전] money; juice; <美> dough; [현찰] cash; [경화] coin; [자금] funds.

돈독 [**दोन्दोक**] [**敦篤**] 돈독하다 gentle (and sincere); humane; courteous; affable; friendly; amicable.

돈푼 [**दोन्फुन**] a small sum of money; a small fortune; a snug hoard of money. e.g. 돈푼깨나 모으다 save a pretty penny / acquire [amass] a competency / make a small fortune.

돋구다 [**दोक्कुदा**] [높이다] raise; make higher. e.g. 안경의 도수를 돋구다 make one's glasses stronger.

돋다 [**दोत्ता**] **1** (해P달이) come up; rise. e.g.해는 동쪽에서 돋아 서쪽으로 진다 The sun comes up [rises] in the east and goes down [sets] in the West. **2** (싹 등이) sprout; bud; come up; shoot. **3** (피부에) break out; come out; erupt; form. e.g.그는 온몸에 두드러기가 돋았다 He has a rash all over the body / The eruption broke out all over him.

돋보기 [**दोप्पोगि**] **1** [노안경] convex glasses [spectacles] for the aged; reading glasses (for the aged). e.g. 그는 돋보기를 끼고 책을 보고 있다 He is reading with his reading glasses on. **2** [확대경] a magnifying glass; a magnifier.

돋보이다 [**दोप्पोइदा**] look better (than actually is); set off; make a fine show; look [show] to advantage. e.g. 붉은 옷이 그녀를 더욱 돋보이게 했다 The red dress showed her off to advantage.

돋우다 [**दोदुदा**] **1** [끌어올리다] raise; turn <a thing> up. e.g.그는 스토브 심지를 돋우어 불이 타오르게 했다 He poked up a blaze in the stove. **2** [높이다] make higher; raise; bank. e.g. 땅을 돋우다 raise the ground. 길을 돋우다 bank the road. 베개를 돋우다 make one's pillow higher / raise one's pillow.

돌[1] [**दोल**] (천연의) (a) stone; [조약돌] a pebble; a rock.

돌[2] [**दोल**] **1** [주년] an anniversary (기념일); one full year; a full day. **2** [첫돌] a baby's first birthday.

돌격 [**दोलग्यौक**] [**突擊**] a charge; a rush; a dash;

(백병(白兵)의) an assault. **돌격하다** charge <at / on>; rush [dash] <at>; make a dash at; raid; make an assault upon.

돌다 [दोल्ता] **1** [회전하다] turn (round); (축을 중심으로 하여) rotate; (축을 중심으로 빨리) spin; (원궤도를) revolve; gyrate; (원을 그리며) circle. e.g. 왼쪽으로 빙빙 돌다 turn round and round to the leth. **2** [순회하다] go (one's) round; make a round; [주유하다] make a tour <of>; travel about [around]. e.g. 선거 유세를 돌다 make an electioneering tour / take the stump / stump (it). **3** [미치다] go off one's head [chump]; go balmy [barmy]; be off one's nut[rocker]; be batty. e.g.그는 머리가 좀 돌았다 He is touched in the head. / He's gone off his head.

돌려놓다 [दोल्यौनोथा] change the position <of>; change direction; put the other way round; turn(about); shith; veer (round).

돌려보내다 [दोल्यौबोनैदा] = [도로 보내다] return; give back; send back; [돌아가게 하다] let <a person> go back; release; remand <a case>.

돌려보다 [दोल्यौबोदा] have a look <at a thing> by turns; read and pass on; send round <a notice>; passing <a thing> around; circulate. e.g.책을 돌려보다 pass a book around reading it in turns.

돌려쓰다 [दोल्यौसुदा] borrow <a thing from person>.

돌려주다 [दोल्लयौजुदा] [반환하다] return; give back; hand back; pay back. e.g. 돈을 돌려주다 pay the money back / pay one's debt / return the borrowed money.

돌리다 [दोल्लिदा] **1** [회전시키다] turn; spin; trundle; revolve; roll; rotate; wheel; whirl; screw. e.g. 병마개를 돌려 열다 [닫다] screw the top off [onto] a bottle. 꼭지를 돌려 물을 틀다 [잠그다] turn the tap on [off]. **2** [몸의 방향을 바꾸다] turn <to>; (얼굴을) look <to / toward (s)>; turn one's head [face] <toward(s)>; veer <around>; direct <to / towards>; shith; sheer; wheel.

돌림병 [दोल्लिमप्यौंग] [-病] = 유행병 (⇨ 유행).

돌멩이 [दोल्मैंगी] a stone; <美> a rock; [자갈] a pebble; a piece of stone.

돌발 [दोल्पाल] [突發] an [a sudden] outbreak; (out-) burst. e.g. 돌발적 (으로) sudden (ly) / unforeseen (ly) / unexpected (ly) / unpredictable (예상할 수 없는).

돌변 [दोलप्यौन] [突變] a sudden change [turn]; an accident. 돌변하다 change suddenly; take a sudden turn; (병세가) take a sudden turn for the worse; take a serious turn.

돌보다 [दोल्पोदा] [보살피다] care for; take (gsood) care of; look [see] ather; attend to; tend.

돌아가다 [दोरागादा] 1 [집,고향 등으로 다시 가다] go [come] back <to>; return; [물러가다] leave. e.g. 집으로 돌아가다 go (back) home. 돌아갈 채비를 하다 prepare <oneself> for going home [back]. 우리는 왔던 길을(되)돌아가야 했다 We had to go back the way we had come. 2(원상태로) return <to>; be restored to; turn back; revert <to>. e.g.(죽어서) 흙으로 돌아가다 fall back to dust. 스프링은 본래 대로 돌아갔다 The spring has unwound itself.

돌아다니다 [दोरादानिदा] [쏘다니다] go [walk] about; wander [roam] about; walk to and fro; get [go / pace] around; (놀러) gad about; (맹수, 도둑 등이) prowl <about>; be on the prowl; [여행하다]. (make a) tour; travel about.

돌아보다 [दोराबोदा] 1 (뒤를) look back <at>; turn around; turn one's face [head]; (어깨 너머) look over one's shoulder. 2 [과거를 다시 생각해 보다] reflect [look back] <upon>; recall; recollect; review; retrospect; reflect on [upon] oneself (반성하다)

돌아서다 [दोरासौदा] 1 [뒤로 바꾸어 서다] turn away [the other way]; turn one's back on <a person>; turn on one's heels; [방향을 바꾸다] turn around <toward>; turn about.2 [등지다] turn one's back on; turn against; fall out [quarrel / disagree] with; break up with; become estranged [alienated] <from>; dissent.

돌아오다 [दोराओदा] 1 [제자리로 도로 오다] come [get / be / turn] back; return. e.g. 돌아올 때에 on one's return / as one returns. 2 [차례,때가 닥치다] return; come round; come again. e.g. 차례가 돌아오다 one's turn comes (round).

돌연 [दोरयौन] [突然] 돌연히 suddenly; abruptly; unexpectedly; on [all of] a sudden; all at once; without notice [warning].

돌연 변이 [दोरयौन ब्यौनि] [突

然變異] (a) mutation.

돌이키다 [**दोरिखिदा**] **1** [고개, 몸을 돌리다] turn [look] round; turn one's face [head]; face about. **2** (원상으로 돌아가다) get back; regain; recover; restore; retrieve; undo. **3** [회상하다] look back upon; retrospect; review; [반성하다] reflect on oneself. e.g. 돌이켜 생각하니 (up) on second thought(s) / on(further) reflection / to look at the matter from a different angle. **4** (마음을) change <one's mind>; reverse <a decision>; make <a person> change <his mind>; [재고하다] think better of; reconsider; reflect on.

돌입 [**दोरिप**] [**突入**] nrush; a thrust <into>. 돌입하다 rush [dash / run] in; charge [plunge] in.

돌잔치 [**दोल्चान्छि**] a baby's first-birthday party [feast]; the birthday party for one-year-old baby.

돌진 [**दोल्चिन**] [**突進**] a rush; a dash; an onrush; a charge. 돌진하다 rush <at / for / to>;(make a) dash <at>; make a dart <at>; charge <at>; storm.

돌출 [**दोल्छुल**] [**突出**] [쑥 내밂] projection; protrusion; [두드러짐] prominence; jutting [popping] out. 돌출하다 project; protrude; jut [pop] out. e.g. 돌출한 projected / projecting / prominent.

돌파 [**दोल्फा**] [**突破**] **1** [뚫고 나감] breaking through; a breakthrough. e.g. 중앙 돌파 a frontal breakthrough. **2** (곤란 등의) surmounting. 돌파하다 surmount <a difficulty>; overcome; get over. e.g. 입시의 난관을 돌파하다 (successfully) pass a difficult entrance examination <to a college>.

돌풍 [**दोल्फूंग**] [**突風**] a gust (of wind); a blast.

돕다 [**दोप्ता**] **1** [조력하다] help <a person with>; help <a person (to) do> (▷ 지금은 뿐만 아니라 <美> 에서도 특히 구어체에서 는를 생략함); assist; aid **2** [구제하다] relieve; give relief to; give <a person> a helping. e.g. 가난한 사람을 돕다 relieve the poor / help the needy. 곤경에 처한 사람을 돕다 help a person out of difficulties.

돗자리 [**दोच्चारि**] a (rush) mat; <집합적> (rush) matting. e.g. 돗자리를 깔다 spread a mat <on a floor>.

동 [**दों**] [**東**] east (E). e.g. 동아시아 East Asia. **동** [**洞**] [마을] a village; [행 정

구역] a *dong.*

동 [दोंग] [棟] [집채의 수를 세는 말] e.g. 3 동 three buildings [houses]. 1 (호)동의 2 층 the second [first] floor of building No. 1. 서울 아파트 7 동 120 호 Rm. 120, Seoul Apt. No. 7.

동 [दोंग] [同] [위와 같은] the same; the said; [똑같은] equal; [마찬가지 의] similar. e.g. 동 대학에서는 in [at] the (above-mentioned) college [college mentioned above].

동감 [दोंगाम] [同感] [같은 의견] agreement (in opinion); concurrence; [같은 느낌] the same sentiment; sympathy. 동감하다 [같은 느낌이다] sympathize [think] with; feel the same way <as>; share <a person's> feeling; [같은 의견이다] agree [concur] with; be of the same opinion; see eye to eye <with a person over a issue>.

동갑 [दोंगाप] [同甲] [같은 나이], the same age; [나이가 같은 사람]a person of the same age; <one's> contemporary.

동갑내기 [दोंगाप्नैगि] one's age-fellow.

동강 [दोंगांग] a piece; a part. 동강(이)나다 break into pieces [parts]. e.g. 칼이 두 동강났다 A sword was broken into two pieces.

동거 [दोंगौ] [同居] [함께 삶].동거하다 live together [with]; live in the same house [room] <with>. e.g. 나는 숙부댁에서 동거하고 있다 I live with my uncle [uncle's family].

동격 [दोंग्यौक] [同格] [같은 지위] the same rank [status / standing]; an equal footing; equality. e.g. 그와 동격인 사람 his equal.

동결 [दोंग्यौल] [凍結] freezing; a freeze <of / on>. e.g. 물가 [임금]의 동결 a price [wage] freeze / a freeze on prices [wages].

동경 [दोंग्यौंग] [東經] the east longitude.

동경 [दोंग्यौंग] [憧憬] yearning; longing; aspiration; a yen; [숭배] adoration; admiration. 동경하다 yearn [hanker] ather [for]; long [sigh] for winter season [time]; winter.

동계 [दोंग्ये] [同系] e.g. 동계의 akin / of the same stock / cognate. 이들 부족은 모두 동계이다 All these tribes are of the same descent [stock]. / All these tribes are related to one another. **동굴** [दोंगूल] [洞窟] [산허리 등의 굴] a cave; (지하의 커다란) a cavern; a grotto <*pl.* ~s, ~es>.

동그라미 [दोंगरामि] [원] a

circle; a circlet (작은).

동그랗다 [दोंगराथा] (원형의) round; rotund; (고리 모양의) circular; (공 모양의) globular; spherical. e.g. 동그랗게 round / in a circle.

동급 [दोंगप] [同級] [같은 등급] the same rank [level]; equality; [같은 학급] the same class [grade].

동급생 [दोंगप्सै] [同級生] a classmate; a classfellow.

동기 [दोंगि] [動機] a motive; an inducement; an incentive (motive 는 심리적, 감정적인 자극, incentive 는 외부적인 자극을 말하며 특히 보수(報酬)를 의미함).

동남 [दोंनाम] [東南] the southeast. e.g. 동남의 southeast / southeastern. 동남으로 southeastward(s).

동냥 [दोंन्यांग] [구걸] begging; mendicancy (탁발승의); [구걸한 돈, 물건] an alms; a handout. 동냥하다 beg <food, money, etc.>; beg one's bread.

동네 [दोंने] [洞 –] [사는 근처] the neighborhood; the (whole) town; the (whole) street; [마을] a [one's] village. e.g.동네 사람(단수) a villager / (복수) village folk [people]; <집합적> the whole village.

동년배 [दोन्यौन्बे] [同年輩] (about) the same age bracket. e.g. 동년배의 사람 one's contemporary.

동동거리다 [दोंदोंगोरिदा] jump up and down; stamp [stomp] one's feet <on the ground>; beat [thump] one's shoes <on the floor>. e.g. 분해서 발을 동동거리다 stamp with vexation [chagrin] / be hopping mad.

동등 [दोंगदुंग] [同等] [같음] equality; the same rank (지위가); equivalence; par; parity. **동등하다** equal; coordinate e.g.동등한 권리 equal rights.

동떨어지다 [दोंगतौरोजीदा] 1 [멀리 떨어지다] be far apart <from>; be remote <from>; be far [distant] <from>; be divorced <from>. e.g. 동떨어진 곳[a remote [an out-of-the-way] place. 2 [심히 다르다] be quite different <from>. e.g. 나는 내 취미와 아주 동떨어진 일을 하고 있다 I am engaged in a work quite alien to my taste.

동료 [दोंग्न्यो] [同僚] a colleague; an associate (일과 연관이 있는); a coworker (함께 일하는); a fellow worker (직장의).

동맹 [दोंग्मैग] [同盟] an alliance; a union; a league.

동면 [दोंगम्योंग] [冬眠] winter sleep; hibernation.

동명 [दोंबगम्यौग] [**同名**] the same name.

동명 이인 [**दोंगम्यौग ईइन**] [-**異人**] a person of the same name; a namesake; a homonym.

동무 [**दोंग्मू**] [친구] a friend; a pal; a chum; a mate; a companion.

동문 [दोंग्मुन] [**同門**] [동창] a fellow pupil [student / disciple]; a classmate; [졸업생] an alumnus <*pl.* -ni>; an alumna <*pl.* -nae> (여자).

동문서답 [दोंग्मुन्सौदाप] [**東問西答**] an irrelevant answer; an incoherent reply. e.g. 자네 말은 아주 동문서답이군 What you say is irrelevant.

동물 [दोंग्मुल] [**動物**] an animal; [생물] a (living) creature; [짐승] a beast; <집합적> animal life.

동물원 [दोंग्मुलवन] [**動物園**] zoological gardens;.

동반 [दोंग्बान] [**同伴**] company. e.g. 그는 부인 동반으로 회합에 참석했다 He attended the meeting, accompanied by his wife. 동반하다 accompany; go (in company) with; go in <a person's> company. winter dress (부인의); a winter jacket (학생의)

동봉 [दोंगबोंग] [**同封**] 동봉하다 enclose. e.g. 동봉한 편지 the enclosed letter.

동북 [दोंग्बुक] [**東北**] the northeast (略 NE, N.E.).

동분서주 [दोंग्बुनसौजू] [**東奔西走**] 동분서주하다 be greatly pressed; busy oneself about [(in) doing] ; run [bustle] about.

동사 [दोंग्सा] [**凍死**] death from cold [exposure] 동사하다 die of [from] cold [exposure]; be frozen to death; freeze to death.

동사 [दोंग्सा] [**動詞**] [문법] a verb.

동사무소 [दोंग्सामूसो] [**洞事務所**] a down-block office; a *dong* office.

동산 [**दोंग्सान**] a hill [hillock] (near a village);(정원의) an artificial [a miniature] hill; a mound.

동상[1] [दोंग्सांग] [**銅賞**] (the) third prize; the bronze prize. e.g. 그는 동상을 받았다 He won third prize.

동상[2] [दोंग्सांग] [**凍傷**] frost-bite; chilblains. (▷ frost-bite 가 정도가 심함) e.g. 동상에 걸리다 be [get] frostbitten / get [have] chilblains <on one's hands>.

동상[3] [दोंसांग] [**銅像**] a bronze statue; a statue in bronze.

동서[1] [दोंग्सौ] [**同壻**] [자매의 남편] the husband of one's wife's sister; [형제의 아내] the wife of one's husband's brother; a sister

-in-law.

동서 [2] [दोंग्सौ] [**東西**] [동쪽과 서쪽] the east and the west.

동서남북 [दोंसौनामबुक] [**東西南北**] the (four) cardinal points; north, south, east and west (영어에서는 흔히 이 순서로 말함).

동석 [दोंग्सौक] [**同席**] 동석하다 sit together; sit in company with.

동성 [दोंग्सौंग] [**同性**] [성별이 같음] the same sex [동일한 성질] homogeneity; homogeneousness; congeniality.

동시 [1] [दोंग्शि] [**童詩**] children's verse; (a) nursery rime [rhyme].

동시 [2] [दोंग्शि] [**同時**] the same time [period]. e.g. 동시에 at the same time / simultaneously <with> / (일시에) at a time / at once.

동시대 [दोंग्शिदै] [**同時代**] [같은 시대] the same age [period]; [시대를 같이함] contemporaneousness. e.g. 우리와 동시대의 사람들 our contemporaries.

동식물 [दोंग्शिग्मुल] [**動植物**] animals and plants; (어느 지역,시대의) fauna and flora.

동심 [दोंग्शिम] [**童心**] the child's mind [heart]; the juvenile mind.

동아리 [दोंगारी] [무리] a group; faction; companions composed of the people with the same purpose.

동안 [दोगान] [**童顔**] a boyish face. e.g. 그는 여전히 동안이다 He still has a boyish look.

동안 [दोंगान] (a space of) time; a period; a span; a while; [간격] an interval; a space; <부사적> in; for <a weE / three days>; during <the vacation>; between; [사이] in the course of <the dinner>; as[so] long as.

동양 [दोंग्यांग] [**東洋**] the Orient; the East.

동업 [दोंगौप] [**同業**] the same trade [profession]; the same line of business. 동업하다 business inpartnership <with>; run business together. e.g. 동업하는 정의로 이 일은 비밀로 해 주시오 Please keep to yourself out of professional courtesy.

동요 [दोंग्यो] [**動搖**] [흔들림] shake; quake; tremble; (배의) rolling (좌우로); pitching (상하로). 동요하다 tremble; shake; stir; quake; (차가) jolt;(배가) pitch and roll; rock. e.g. 지동차가 몹시 동요한다 The car jolts badly. **2** [불안] restlessness; unrest; disquietude; [흥분] excite-

ㄷ

ment; agitation; [소요] disturbance; commotion; (a) tumult; [움직임] oscillation; fluctuation. e.g. 물가의 동요 a fluctuation in prices.

동요 [दोंग्यो] [童謠] child verse; a children's song; a nursery rhyme.

동원 [दोंग्वन] [動員] mobilization. 동원하다 mobilize; set [drew] in motion; (군대 등의 출동) call out. e.g. 그 쇼는 많은 관객을 동원했다 The show attracted [drew] a large audience.

동의 [दोंगुइ] [同意] [같은 의견] the same opinion; [승낙, 찬성] consent; assent; agreement; approval.

동일 [दोंगिल] [同一] [꼭 같음] identity; sameness; oneness; [무차별] equality; indiscrimination.

동일하다 identical; equal; nondiscriminatory; (one and) the same.

동일시 [दोंगिल्शी] [同一視] 동일시하다 identify <a thing> with <another>; treat <matters> without discrimination; regard <A> in the same light with <B>; put on a par <with>; put <a thing> in the same category [class].

동작 [दोंग्जाक] [動作] action; movements; motions; [거동] carriage; bearing; behavior; deportment; demeanor; manners; [몸짓] gestures; an act.

동절 [दोंग्जौल] [冬節] winter; the winter season; winter time.

동점 [दोंग्जौम] [同點] a tie score; a draw; the same grade [mark / score]. e.g.동점이 되다 tie with / draw (level) with.

동정 [दोंग्जौंग] [同情] sympathy; compassion; fellow feeling; pity; commiseration **동정하다** sympathize with <a person>; feel sympathy for <something>; have compassion on; be compassionate toward; take pity upon; pity for <a person>. e.g. 남의 불행을 동정하다 commiserate <a person> on his misfortune

동조 [दोंग्जो] [同調] alignment; tuning; syntony; synchronism; the same key [pitch / tune]. 동조하다 align oneself <with>; side [ally oneself] <with>; fall in <with>; follow suit; act in concert <with>.

동족 [दोंग्जोक] [同族] [같은 종족] the same race [tribe]; one's kind; [동포] brethren; fellow countryman; [혈족] the same blood; consanguinity; [일족] the same family.

동지 [दोंग्जी] [冬至] the winter solstice; the shortest day

of the year. e.g. 오늘이 동지다 Today is the winter solstice.

동지 [दोंग्जी] [**同志**] [뜻이 같음] the same mind; the congenial spirit; a kindred mind; [뜻이 같은 사람] a like-minded person; a friend; a comrade; fellow thinkers.

동질 [दोंग्जिल] [**同質**] [같은 성질,품질] the same quality [nature]; [같은 종류임] homogeneity. e.g. 동질의 of the same quality / homogeneous / cognate / coessential.

동쪽 [दोंग्चोक] [**東**−] the east.

동참 [दोंग्छाम] [**同參**] participation. 동참하다 participate <in>; take part <in>.

동창 [दोंग्छांग] [**同窓**] a fellow student; a schoolmate; a schoolfellow; an alumnus.

동창회 [**दोंग्छांगह्वे**] [동창 모임] a graduates' association; an alumni association; an old boys' [pupils'] association; [동창 모임] an alumni meeting [reunion]; a meeting of old boys.

동침 [दोंग्छिम] [**同寢**] **동침하다** sleep together; sleep with <a person>; share a bed with <a person>.

동파 [दोंग्फा] [**凍破**] 동파하다 be frozen to burst [rupture].

동포 [दोंग्फो] [**同胞**] [형제] brothers; [같은 겨레] brethren; fellow countrymen; one's countrymen; compatriots; [인류] fellowmen; fellow creature.

동하다 [दोंग्हादा] [**動**−] [마음이 흔들리다] be shaken [perturbed]; be upset; (감동, 욕망 등이) be move [touched]; be [feel] inclined to <do> e.g. (마음이) 동하기 쉽다 be (easily) excitable / be easily affected [moved / influenced] <by> / be susceptible <to> / be sensitive <to>.

동해 [दोंग्है] [**東海**] the East Sea.

동행 [दोंग्हैंग] [**同行**] going together; traveling together. 동행하다 go (along) with; accompany <a person>; go in company with; go in <a person's> company; traveling together; [호송] escort.

동향 [दोंगह्यांग] [**動向**] a tendency; a trend; a movement; an attitude. e.g. 여론[시세]의 동향 the trend of public opinion [the times].

동화 **1** [दोंगह्वा] [**同化**] assimilation; [순응] adaptation; anabolism.

동화 **2** [दोंगह्वा] [**童話**] [어린이를위한 이야기] a children's story; a juvenile story; [옛날 이야기] a fairy [nursery] tale.

돛 [दोत] a sail; a canvas; muslin.

돼지 [दवेजी] [가축] a pig; a hog

되- [द्वे] [다시,도로] re-; again; back; [도리어] reversely; conversely; on the contrary; in return; instead; contrary to what you might expect. e.g. 되묻다 ask in return. 되돌려보내다 send <a person> back.

되뇌다 [द्वेन्वेदा] retort [talk back] again and again; say over again.

되는대로 [[द्वेननदैरो] **1** [함부로] at random; at hap-hazard;irresponsibly; [무성의하게] lukewarmly; half-heartedly. e.g. 되는대로 지껄이다 talk irresponsibly [at random] / say whatever comes into one's head. **2** [되어 가는 대로] e.g. 그날그날 되는 대로 on a day-to-day.

-되다 [-द्वेदा] **1** <동사적 명사에 붙어> be; become; get to be. e.g. 악화되다 take a serious turn / change [take a turn] for the worse. **2** <형용사적 명사나 부사적 어근에 붙어> be. e.g.막되다 be ill-mannered [-bred] / be wild.

되다 [द्वेदा] **1** [다 이루어지다] be done; be completed; be finished; (준비가) be ready. e.g.일이 다 되었다 The work is finished. **2** […하게 되다] begin to <do>; come [get] to <do>; learn to <do>; set in; […으로 발전하다] develop into; grow into. e.g. 감정적이 되다 become emotional.

되도록 [दवेदोरोक] **1** [될 수 있는 한] as ... as possible [practicable]; as ... as one can; [될 수 있으면] if possible [practic-able]; if it can be so arranged; if circumstances allow; <부정(否定)> no more than one can help. **2** [될 수 있도록] (so as) to <become>;(so [in order]) that one may <become>.

되돌다 [दवेदोल्ता] turn back around. e.g.그는 되돌아서 달려갔다 turned around and ran off.

되돌리다 [दवेदोल्लिदा] **1** [반환하다] return; give back. e.g. 돈을 되돌려 주다 give back the money <one borrowed>. **2** [원상태로 놓다] restore. e.g. 책을 다 읽으면 제자리에 되돌려 놓으시오 When you are through with the books, put them back where they were.

되돌아보다 [दवेदोराबोदा] look over one's shoulder; turn one's head; turn round; look back [round]. e.g. 과거를 되돌아보다 think back to the past days / think backward / look back upon the past.

되돌아오다 [दवेदोराओदा] **1** [원래의 상태로 돌아오다] return <to>. e.g.마치 제 2 차 세계 대전 당시로 되돌아 온 것 같다 It looks as if time had been turned back [backward] to world War II **2** [원래의 장소,주인에게 돌아오다] be returned. e.g. 폭풍우 때문에 나는 도중에서 되돌아왔다 I turned back halfway because of the storm.

되묻다 [दवेमुत्ता] [다시 묻다] ask again; repeat one's question.

되새기다 [दवेसैगिदा] (음식을) chew over and over again (because of poor appetite); (소 등이) ruminate; chew the cud; (마음 속으로) meditate <on / upon>; ruminate <about / of / upon / over>; relive.

되어가다 [दवेओगादा] **1** (일이) go (on); work; progress; advance. e.g. 잘되어가다 go well [right] / work well / go on smoo-thly [without a hitch]. **2** (물건이) be getting finished [completed / attained / accomplished]. e.g. 동상이 거의 되어가고 있다 The bronze statue is nearly completed. 연이 다 되어간다 The kite is being finished.

되풀이 [दवेफुरि] [반복] (a) repetition; a repeat; reiteration. 되풀이하다 repeat; reiterate; do <something> over again.

된소리 [दवेन्सोरि] a fortis <*pl.* fortes>.

된장 [दवेन्जा] [一醬] *toenjang*; fermented soybean paste.

됨됨이 [दवेम्दवेमि] (사람의) the man; one's nature [disposition / character / personality]. e.g. 됨됨이가 귀골스럽다 look noble / have the appearance of a high personage.

두 [दू] two; a couple <of>. e.g. 두 가지 two kinds <of> (종류) / two ways (방법).

두각 [दूगाक] [頭角] [뛰어남]. e.g. 두각을 나타내다 cut [make] a conspicuous [brilliant] figure <in> / distinguish oneself / stand head and shoulders <above others> / rise into prominence

두고두고 [दूगोदूगो] [여러 차례] many times; repeatedly; over and over (again); [오래도록] (for) long; for a long time; for a good while; [영원히] forever; eternally; for good (and all); through all eternity [ages].

두고보다 [दूगोबोदा] [지켜보다]

watch (intently); keep (a good) watch <over>. e.g. 두고보자일의 결과를) See how things will shape up. / Watch and wait. / (위협적으로) You will have to pay dearly for it.

두근두근 [दुगनदुगन] pit-a-pat; palpitating; throbbing. 두근하다=두근거리다.

두껍다 [दुक्कौप्ता] thick; heavy; massive.

두께 [दुक्के] thickness.

두뇌 [दुल्वे] [頭腦] a head; a brain; brains.

두다[1] [दुदा] **1** [놓다] put; place; set; emplace; position; park; deposit (일정한 장소에). e.g. 제 자리에 갖다 두다 put it back in its place. **2** [남겨 두다] leave (behind). e.g. 두고 온 물건 a thing [an article] leth behind.

두다[2] [दुदा] [동작의 결과를 지니어 감] do something to get <it> out of the way; get <it> done; do <it> once and for good; get <it> over with; finish (up); do <it> thoroughly now(so it will not have to be done again). e.g. 미리 조사해 두다 examine beforehand / have <it> examined before ....

두둑하다 [दुदुख्खादा] **1** [매우 두껍다] thick; heavy. e.g. 밖이 꽤 추우니 두둑하게 입고 가거라 It's pretty cold outside, so you'd better bundle up. **2** [풍부하다] plenty; quite a lot; ample; satisfactory. e.g. 두둑한 사례를 받다 be given a liberal [handsome] reward / be rewarded generously.

두둔 [दुदुन] 두둔하다 back <the weak>; shield [screen / shelter] <a person from>; support; give support to; stand by; side with; [변호하다] plead[speak up] foe <a person>. e.g. (싸움에서) 자기 자식을 두둔하다 back one's own child (in a quarrel).

두드러기 [दुदुरोगि] hives; nettle rash; urticaria.

두드러지다 [दुदरोजीदा] [뚜렷하다] conspicuous; prominent <figure>; marked <event>; remarkable <fellow>; notable <person>; striking; exceptional; distinct; clear-cut <skyline>. e.g. (신문에서) 두드러진 사건 a highlighted news event

두드리다 [दुदरिदा] [치다] strike; beat; hit; knock; thrash; slap (손바닥으로); rap (똑똑); tap [pat] (가볍게); pound [slog / bang] (세게); clap <hands> (마주치다); maul (두드려 상처를 내다)

두려움 [दुर्यौउम] [공포] fear; (a) terror; dread; horror;

[염려] apprehension(s); anxiety; concern; [외경] reverence; veneration; awe.

두려워하다 [**द्रयौवॉहादा**] **1** [무서워하다] fear; dread; be afraid [fearful] of; stand in fear of; be frightened [scared / terrified] at; have a horror [dread] of; be overawed. e.g. …을 늘 두려워하다 be [live] in constant fear of. **2** [걱정하다] fear; be afraid of; apprehend; be apprehensive of. e.g. 최악의 사태를 두려워하다 fear the worst.

두렵다 [**द्र्यौप्ता**] **1** [무섭다] fearful; scared; frightened; terrified; <서술적> be afraid of. **2** [염려스럽다] feared; fearful; apprehended; <서술적> be afraid of; be in danger of.

두루 [**द्रू**] [빠짐없이] without exception; thoroughly; [전면적으로] all over; all around; [일반적으로] generally; universally; [널리] widely; extensively; far and wide

두르다 [**द्ररुदा**] **1** [둘러싸다] put around; surround <with / by>; enclose <with / in>; encircle; hem [shut] in. e.g. 식탁보에 레이스로 테를 두르다 border [edge] a tablecloth with lace **2** [입다,차다] wear [wrap] about one; engird (le). e.g. 허리에 띠를 두르다 bind a belt about [round] one's waist.

두리번거리다 [**द्रुरिबौंगौरिदा**] stare about; look around (restlessly); glance round. e.g. 눈을 두리번거리며 with unsteady eyes

두말 [**दुमाल**] a double tongue; equivocation. e.g. 두말할 것 없이 of course / without saying this or that [anything further].

두목 [**दुमोक**] [**頭目**] a chief; a head; a boss; a captain

두발 [**द्रबाल**] [**頭髮**] 머리털 [**मैरिथौल**].

두절 [**द्रजौल**] [**杜絶**] stoppage; cessation; interruption; suspension (중절). 두절하다 be stopped; be cut off; be interrupted; be blocked; cease; be paralyzed. e.g. 차량 소통이 두절되었다 The flow of traffic stopped.

두텁다 [**दुथौप्ता**] warm; affectionate; kind; cordial; hearty; deep <friendship>. e.g. 두터운 우의 a warm [deep] friendship

두통 [**दुथोंग**] [**頭痛**] (a) headache.

두툼하다 [**द्रथुमहादा**] (very) thick; heavy. e.g. 두툼한 외투 a thick [heavy] overcoat

둑 [**दुक**] [제방] a bank; a dike; [호안(護岸)을 위한 제방] an embankment; a levee.

둔감 [**दुंगाम**] [**鈍感**] insensibility; stolidity; obtuseness of feeling. 둔감하다 insensible; [감각,감정의 반응이 둔하다] insensitive <to>; dull; stolid; obtuse; [무신경하다] thick-skinned; thickheaded.

둔갑 [दुंगाप] [**遁甲**] 둔갑하다 take the form [shape] <of>; turn [change / transform] <oneself into something>. e.g. 사람으로 둔갑한 여우 a fox in the shape of man / a fox in [assuming] human shape [form].

둔하다 [दुनहादा] [**鈍-**]**1** (성질, 머리 등이) dull; slow; stupid; blunt; thickheaded; slow-witted; dull-witted. e.g. 감각이 둔하다 be dull-headed / be thick-skinned. **2** (동작, 상태 등이) slow; sluggish; inactive; inert. e.g. 둔하게 살찐 사내아이 a chubby boy.

둘 [दुल] two.

둘러대다 [दुल्लौदैदा] [꾸며대다] give an evasive answer; cook up [concoct] an excuse; explain away; sophisticate. e.g. 이리 저리 둘러대어 그 자리를 모면했다 I managed to get [talk myself] out of trouble for the time being with some excuse or other.

둘러보다 [दुल्लौबोदा] look around [about]; take a glance around; make a survey <of>; survey

둘러싸다 [दुल्लौसादा] **1** (주위를) enclose; environ; encircle; surround; (벽, 담으로) wall in; (울타 리로)] fence. e.g. 그녀를 둘러싼 5 인의 남성 the five men around her. **2** (관계, 문제를) surround. …을 둘러싸고 centering [pivoting] around ... / in connection with / concerning. e.g. 그의 실종을 둘러싼 비밀 a secret surrounding his disappearance.

둘러싸이다 [दुल्लौसाइदा] be besieged [invested / surround / enclosed / girded].

둘러앉다 [दुल्लौआन्ता] sit round [around]; sit in a circle [ring]; gather around in a circle.

둘레 [दुल्ले] [바깥 언저리] (a) circumference; girth; surroundings

둘째 [दुल्चै] the second; number two.

둥 [दुंग] […하는 듯도 하고 아니하는 듯도 함]. e.g. 남의 말을 듣는 둥 마는 둥 하다 listen to a person in an absent sort of way / pay little attention to a person's talk.

둥글다 [दुंगल्ता] (원형의) round; rotund; (고리 모양의) circular; (구형의) globular; spherical.

둥글둥글 [दुंगल्दुंगल] **1** [몹시 동그란 모양]. 둥글둥글

하다 round; rotund; circular; globular **2** [원만하게] peacefully; amicably; smoothly; harmoniously. e.g. 그는 사람이 둥글둥글하다 He has well-rounded corners. 그녀는 성품이 둥글둥글하다 She is easy to get along with.

둥지 [दुंग्जी] = 보금자리.

뒤 [द्वी] **1** [뒤쪽] the back; the rear. e.g. 뒤의 back / rear **2** [다음,나중] atherward(s); later. e.g. 지금부터 5년 뒤에 five years from now.

뒤늦다 [दविनत्ता] late; tardy; belated; delayed. e.g. 뒤늦은 경고 a belated warning.

뒤덮다 [दविदौप्ता] cover <over / up>; overspread; overlay; hang over. e.g. 산꼭대기를 뒤덮은 구름 clouds hanging over the top of the mountain.

뒤덮이다 [दविदौफिदा] be covered (all over) <with>; be veiled; be overspread [overlaid]; be hung over

뒤돌아보다 [दविदोराबोदा] **1** [회고하다] look back on. e.g. 과거를 뒤돌아보다 think back to the past days / think backward / look back upon the past. **2** [반성하다] reflect upon. e.g. 나의 일상 생활을 뒤돌아보면 when I consider [think of] everyday life. **3** 뒤쪽을 돌아보다] look back <at>; turn about to see; take a backward glance <at>.

뒤떨어지다 [दवितौरौजीदा] **1** [뒤에 처지다] be <a long way> behind; [뒤에 남다] leave (behind); remain [stay] behind. e.g. 혼자 뒤떨어지다 be leth (all) alone **2** (시대,유행에) get [fall / lag / drop] behind; be in arrear of (the times). e.g. 시대[유행]에 뒤떨어지다 be behind the times [fashion]. 시대에 뒤떨어지지 않도록 하다 keep abreast of the times / keep up with tShe times. (학력,지능이) be inferior; be worse than; be below; fall behind; be behindhand; drop out. e.g. 수학이 특히 남보다 뒤떨어지다 be behind the others in mathematics above all.

뒤뚱거리다 [दविदुंगौरिदा] totter; stagger; falter; waver; be unsteady.

뒤바꾸다 [दविबाक्कुदा] reverse; turn around <in position / order>; invert; switch; get (it) backwards. e.g. 순서[자리]를 뒤바꾸다 reverse the order [their positions].

뒤범벅 [दविबौम्बौक] a jumble; a hotchpotch; a mess; a medley; a muddle; a pell-mell.

뒤섞다 [दविसौक्ता] [혼합하다]

mix <up / together>; jumble together; [휘젓다] stir.

뒤섞이다 [दविसौविक्दा] be mixed [jumble] (up / together); be intermixed [mingled / blended]; mix in a confused way; commingle

뒤숭숭하다 [द्वीसुंगसुंगहाहा] [정신이 어수선하다] nervous; distracted; uneasy; awkward; fidgety; jumpy; restless. e.g. 마음이 뒤숭숭하다 feel [be] nervous [uneasy] / be in a fidget / be ill at ease.

뒤엉키다 [दविऔखिदा] **1** (밧줄, 실 등이) get [become] entangled; get [become] entangled; get [become] raveled. e.g. 뒤엉킨 실을 풀다 untie entangled knots / unravel a thread **2** (이야기 등이) get onfused [mixed];(사건 등이)] get complicated; become involved.

뒤엎다 [द्वीऔप्ता] **1** [전복시키다] upset; overturn; (배를) capsize. e.g. 찻잔을 뒤엎어 버렸다 I upset [kicked over] the tea cup. **2** [타도하다] overthrow; undermine; subvert; (결정을) overrule; reverse. e.g. 판결을 뒤엎다 overrule a decision / reverse a sentence.

뒤적거리다 [दविजौक्कौरिदा] ransack; rummage; (책 등을) browse; (더듬어서) fumble [feel / fish] <in>. e.g. 서류를 뒤적거리다 rummage among papers.

뒤적이다 [दविजौगिदा] 뒤적거리다

뒤져보다 [दविज्यौबोदा] search [look / hunt] <for>; make [prosecute] a search<for>; rummage [fumble] <for>. e.g. 돈이 있는지 호주머니 속을 뒤져보다 fumble [fish] in one's pocket to see if there is any money.

뒤좇아가다 [दविजोछागादा] [따르다] follow; go ather; [추적하다] pursue (ather); chase; give chase to; run ather; hunt up; course.

뒤죽박죽 [दविजुक्पाक्चुक] in disorder; pell-mell; in confusion; topsy-turvy; all mixed up; all jumbled up; in a mess. e.g. 뒤죽박죽을 만들다 mix [jumble] up [together] / turn (things) topsy-turvy.

뒤지다[1] [दविजीदा] [뒤떨어지다] fall [drop] behind; fall back; be backward; be behind; be inferior to; (경주에) lose the lead to <one's opponent>. e.g. 지능이 뒤지는 아이 a backward [retarded] child.

뒤지다[2] [दविजीदा] [휘젓다] rummage <for>; [찾다] ransack; fumble <in>; search. e.g. 책상 서랍을 샅샅이 뒤지다 ransack

[rummage in] the desk drawers

뒤집다 [दविजीप्ता] **1** [안팎을 뒤바꾸다] turn <a sleeve> inside out; turn the other side; turn wrong side out; turn upside down; reverse; (카드의 겉면을 위로) turn up; (호주머니 등을) turn out. e.g. 뒤집어 말하면 to put (it) the other way / stated reversely. **2** [위, 아래를 바꾸다] overturn; turn up; capsize; turn over. e.g. 책을 뒤집다 turn a book over / lay a book facedown. **3** [일을 틀어지게 하다] reverse; change; overrule e.g. 계획을 뒤집다 upset a plan / balk (a person) in his plan / change one's plan.

뒤집어쓰다 [दविजीबौसदा] **1** (머리에) put on; wear; cover. e.g. 모자를 뒤집어쓰다 wear a hat. **2** (온몸에) cover with; put on; draw [pull] over. e.g. 담요를 뒤집어쓰다 be wrapped [wrap oneself] up in a blanket / wrap a blanket about oneself / pull a blanket (up) over one's head.

뒤집히다 [दविजीफिदा] **1** (안팎이) be turned [turn] inside out; be turned over. e.g. (우산이) 바람에 뒤집히다 be blown inside out. **2** [뒤집혀 엎어지다] overturn; capsize. e.g. 보트가 뒤집혔다 The boat capsized [tipped over / overturned]. 차는 군중에 의해 뒤집혔다 The car was overturned by the mob. 쟁반이 뒤집혔다 The tray tipped over. **3** [순서가 바뀌다] be reversed; be changed [switched]. e.g. 순서가 뒤집히다 The order is reversed [changed]. **4** (속이) feel sick [nausea]; (정신이) go [run] mad. e.g. 속이 뒤집히다 have a sick stomach.

뒤척거리다 [दविछौक्कौरिदा] [누운 몸을 뒤척뒤척하다] toss [roll] about (in bed); toss and turn. e.g. 그는 잠을 못 이루어 밤새껏 몸을 뒤척거렸다 He could not sleep a wink and tossed and turned all night long.

뒤통수 [द्वीथोंग्सू] the back (part) of the head; the occiput <*pl.* ~s, -pita>.

뒤틀리다 [दविथल्लिदा] **1** [비틀리다] be twisted; be distorted [wrenched]; grow [become] warped. **2** (마음이) become perverse; get distorted; become crooked; get warped. **3** (일이) miscarry; fail; be frustrated; be baffled; be upset; be foiled; go wrong [amiss].

뒤흔들다 [दविहन्दल्ता] [마구흔들다] shake [swing /

sway] violently [hard]; jolt; convulse. e.g. 천지를 뒤흔드는 큰 음향 [a sound loud enough to shake heaven and earth.

뒷간 [दविक्कान] [-間] a toilet; a water closet (W.C.); a rest room.

뒷거래 [दविक्कौरै] [-去來] backdoor [illegal] dealing [business].

뒷걸음 [द्वीक्कोरुम] a backward step. e.g. 뒷걸음(을) 치다[(1) [뒤로 물러서다] step [move / walk] backward; step [draw] back; back down. 몇 발짝 뒷걸음 치다 fall [draw] back a few steps. (2) [꽁무니를 빼다] shrink [hang / hold] back; back out; flinch [recoil] <from>.

뒷골목 [दविक्कोलमोक] an alley; a backlane; a back street; an alleyway (좁은); a by-street.

뒷모양 [द्वीम्मोयांग] [-貌樣] 뒷모습

뒷바라지 [दविप्पाराजी] looking ather; giving aids; a help; taking care of; care. e.g. 그 여자는 애들의 뒷바라지에 바쁘다 She is busy with the care of her children.

뒷받침 [दविप्पाछिम] [지지] backing; backup; support; [증명] proof <of / that>; evidence <of / that / to do>; substanti-ation; [보증] guarantee; ndorsement; [기반] foundation.

뒷받침하다 back (up); upport; endorse; substantiate; prove; give substance to <words>; add support to <the rumor>.

뒷북치다 [दविप्पुकिछ्दा] fuss about belatedly; pother ather the event. e.g. 미련한 놈 뒷북친다 Fools are wise ather the event.

뒷수습 [द्वीस्सुसप] [-收拾] settlement <of an affair>. e.g. 사건의 뒷수습을 하다 settle an affair.

뒷이야기 [द्वीतियागी] a sequel to the story. 사건의 뒷이야[a sequel to the event.

뒷일 [द्वीतिल] **1** [뒤의 일] the athermath of an event [affair]; the rest; the sequence; later happening. e.g. 소송의 뒷일을 처리하다 dispose of the athermath of a lawsuit. **2** [장래에 생길 일] uture affairs; (사후의) affairs ather one's death. e.g.먼 뒷일을 생각하다 have future in view of posterity at heart.

뒷조사 [दवित्चोसा] [-調査] a detailed [secret] investigation [inquiry]. **뒷조 사하다** investigate secretly [in secret]; make secret [confidential] inquiries into <a matter>.

뒷짐 [द्वीच्चिम] **뒷짐을 지다** clasp

one's hands behind one's back.

뒹굴다 [**ढीगुल्दा**] **1** [누워서 구르다] roll [tumble] about [over]; throw oneself down; (고통으로) writhe. e.g. 잠자리에서 뒹굴다 toss [tumble] about in one's bed **2** [빈둥빈둥 놀다] idle [loaf] one's time away; be on the loaf; loaf around; live at ease; eat the bread of idleness. e.g. 평생을 뒹굴며 지내다 drith aimlessly through life.

드나들다 [**दनादल्ता**] [출입하다] come in and go out; go [come] in and out; (자주 가다) go othen; frequent <a house>; m ke frequent visits <to>.

드넓다 [**दनौप्ता**] spacious; wide; large; open; extensive; vast.

드디어 [**ददिऔ**] at last; finally; eventually; at length; ather all; in the end; in the long run; ultimately. e.g. 그는 드디어 성공했다 At last he got a success.

드라마 [**दरामा**] a drama; a play.

드라이브[**दराइब**] a drive; motoring; a motor ride; a joyride.

드러나다 [**दरौनादा**] [표면에 나타나다] come into view; come out; appear; crop out (광맥이); emerge <from>; be exposed; be bared. e.g. 어깨가 드러나다 one's shoulders are exposed [bare].

드러내다 [**दरौनैदा**]**1** [노출하다] expose;lay bare [open]; bare; uncover; disclose. 드러낸 naked / bare / uncovered. e.g. 가슴을 드러내다 expose [bare] one's breast.**2** [보이다] show; indicate; display; exhibit; manifest; [입증하다] prove; speak for; bespeak. e.g. 정직함을 드러내다 speak for one's honesty.

드러눕다 [**दरौनुप्ता**] lie down; lay oneself down; throw oneself down; lie on one's back; stretch oneself.

드럼[**दरौम**] [북] a drum.

드레스 [**दरेस**] a dress.

드르렁거리다 [**दरौरौंगौरिदा**] keep snoring (loudly); snore. e.g.코를 드르렁거리다 be snoring away.

드리다 [**दरिदा**] **1** [주다] give; offer (up); present <one's compliments>; make a present <of>; dedicate; serve. e.g. 기도를 드리다 offer [put up] prayers <to God **2** [팔다] sell; let <a person> have; offer. e.g. 무엇을 릴까요(가게에서) What can I do for you? / May I help you?

드릴 [**दरिल**] [천공기,송곳] a drill.

드문드문 [**दमुनदमुन**] **1** (시간적으로) once in a (long)

while; at (rare / long) intervals; from time to time; occasionally;now and then. e.g. 드문드문 찾아 오다 come once in a while / show up from time to time. **2** (공간적으로) at intervals; here and there; sporadic-cally; sparsely; thinly; scatteredly. e.g. 나무를 드문드문 심다 plant trees at intervals [here and there].

드물다 [दमुल्ता] [진귀하다] rare; uncommon; unusual; [수효가 적다] scarce; few; (few and) far between; [특이하다] unique. e.g. 드물게 rarely / seldom / uncommonly / on rare occa-sions / at rare intervals.

드세다 [दसेदा] (사람이) wild <nature>; savage <dispo-sition>; violent <temper>; (일이) rough; tough; difficult.

득 [दक] [**得**] [이득](a) profit; (a) gain; interest (s); [유리] advantage; benefit. e.g. 득이 되는 profitable / advantageous / gainful / paying / economical. 득이 되다 turn [prove] to one's profit <to> / do <a person> good.

득남 [दंग्नाम] [**得男**] 득남하다 have a baby boy; beget a baby boy (남성에 대하여 말함).

득녀 [**得女**] [दंगन्यौ] 득녀하다 have a baby girl; beget a baby girl (남성에 대하여 말함).

득실 [दक्षिल] [**得失**] [얻음과 잃음] gains and losses; [이익과 손해] profits and losses; [성패] success and failure; [장단점] merits and demerits; advan-tages and disadvantages [short-comings].

득점 [दक्चौम] [**得點**] the marks obtained; (경기의) the points made; the runs scored; a score; scoring; [야구] runs [R].

든든하다 [दनदनहादा] **1** [굳세다] robust; healthy; stout; strong; hardy; sturdy. **2** [단단하다] firm; solid; secure; steady. e.g.든든한 기초 a solid foundation. **3** [미덥다] secure; con-fident; reassuring; encoura-ging; reliable; safe. e.g. 든든한 사람 a reliable person. **4** [배가 부르다] full; replete. 배가 든든하다] have a full stomach [belly] / have the stomach full. e.g. 배가 든든하지 않으면 일을 할 수가 없다 One cannot work on an empty stomach. / A full belly counsels well.

-든지 [.....दन्जि] **1**[더라도] even if; although; though; no matter <who / what / when / where / how>. e.g. 무엇을 하든지 whatever (it be found that) one does. **2** [무엇이나 가리지 않고] or; either or; whether or. e.g. 비가 오든지 안 오든지 간에 whether it may rain or not / rain [wet] or shine.

든지 [दन्जि] **1**[무엇이나 가리지 아니함][either or; whether or. e.g. 사과든지 배 든지 either apples or pears. **2** [까지도] even; even if [though]; -ever. e.g. 내가 할 수 있는 일이라면 무엇이든지 하겠다 I am willing to do everything in my power to help you.

듣다[1] **[दत्ता]** **1**[효험이 있다] be effective;be efficacious <against fever>; have an effect <on>; be good <for a cold>; act [work / tell] <on>. e.g. 잘 듣는 약 a very efficacious medicine / a medicine of marvelous efficacy / a drug of great virtue [정상적으로 움직이다] work; act. e.g. 오른손이 말을 안 듣다 lose the use of one's right arm / one's right hand is out

듣다[2] **[दत्ता]** **1** (소리를)] hear <music>; listen to; give ear to; lend an ear to; heed. e.g. 남이 듣는 데서 in the audience of a person / in a person's audience. **2**(소식, 소문 등을) hear of; be informed [told] of [about]; learn <something from [of] a person>; understand; (사물이) come to one's ears [knowledge]. e.g. 많이 들어본 이름 a familiar name. **3** (칭찬,꾸지람을). e.g. 칭찬을 듣다 be praised [admired / extolled / applauded] <by> / catch [get] it <from dad> / catch [have / get] a scolding.

-들 [-दल] 우리 들 we / us. 사람들] people / other people / others.

들 1 [दल] a field; [전답] the fields; [평야] a plain

들 2 [दल] [등등] and so on [forth]; and others [other things] (of the same kind); and [or] the like; and what not; et cetera (略 &c., etc.). e.g.책상 위에 노리개며 책 들이 많이 놓여 있었다 The table was loaded with toys, books, and what not

들것 [दलकोत] a stretcher; a litter.

들끓다 [दलकल्था] **1** [많이 모이다] swarm <about / in / with>; gather <round>; crowd; [특히 해충,도둑 따위가 설치다] infest. e.g. 쥐가 들끓는 집 a house infestedwith rats. **2** [흥분하다,술렁거리다] be excited; seethe; ferment; be in an uproar. e.g. 들끓는 군중 a boiling [an excited] crowd. 들끓는 소동 an uproar / a ferment.

들녘 [दल्यौख an open field; a plain; a flat; a flat country (지방)

들다[1] [दल्ता] (날 등이) cut(well); be keen; be sharp. e.g. 잘 드는[잘 안 드는] 칼 a sharp [dull] knife.

들다[2] [दल्ता] (나이가) grow older [in years]; get on [up] in years; take [put] on years; advance in age [years]. e.g. 나이가 듦에 따라 as one grows old (er) / with advancing years. 나이 든 사람 an old [aged] person / <집합적> the aged [old] / old people.

들다[3] [दल्ता] **1** [들어가다] go in [into]; get in [into]; come in [into]. e.g. 범주 안에 들다 fall under [come within] the category <of>. 잠자리에 들다] go to bed. **2** [시작하다] begin. 8 월 들어](곧)] (early) in August. e.g. 이 달 들어 몹시 추워졌다[The weather has been extremely cold since the beginning of this month. **3**[포함하다] hold; contain; be contained; be included; [부류에 들다] come [fall] unde <the category of>; [수용하다] accomodate; admit. 병에 든 물] water in a bottle. e.g. 3 천 원이 든 지갑 a purse with 3,000 won in it. **4** [가입,가담하다] join; enter; go into; associate oneself <with>; [합격하다]] enter <a school>; pass into. e.g.보험에 들다 insure oneself / take out (a policy of) insurance <on> / carry <10,000,000 won> insurance <on one's life **5** [물들다] dye; be dyed; take(up) color; [감염하다] be stained [tainted / infected]. e.g. 검게 물이 들다 be dyed black. 물이 잘 들다[들지 않다] dye well[badly]. **6** [소요되다] take; want; need; require; cost;[(사물이)필요하다]]be necessary [needed]; be required. e.g. 돈이 얼마가 들더라도 at any cost / regardless of expense. **7** (햇볕 등이) come [shine] in [into]; pour in [into]. e.g. 저녁 햇살이 드는 방 a room open to sunshine from the west. **8** [상태, 때가 되다] become; get; grow; come round; set [close] in. 멍이 들다] get bruised. e.g. 버릇이 들다 I get [fall] into a habit <of> / get in the way <of doing> / acquire [pick up] a habit <of>. **9** (생각 등이). 생각이 들다 come across [into] one's mind / come into one's head / occur to one / hit [strike] one. e.g.

잡념이 들다 be lost in idle thoughts.

들다[4] [दल्ता] **1** [위로 올리다] raise; lith (up); put [set] up; hold up; heave; hoist. e.g. 돌을 들다 lith (up) a stone **2** [손에 쥐다] hold <a book in one's hand>; take hold of; have <a thing> in one's hand; [휴대하다] take[have / carry] <a thing> with [about] one. e.g. 칼을 빼 들고 with a naked sword [blade] in one's hand **3** [예증하다] give <an example>; mention <a fact>; produce <evidence>; [인용하다] quote <a passage from a book>; cite <an instance>. e.g. 예를 들면 for instance[example].

들뜨다 [दलतुदा] **1** [붙은 것이 틈이 생겨 일어나다] come off [undone]; get loose [free]; become unfastenned. e.g. 장판이 들떴다 The layer of oil paper came off the floor. **2** (살이) sallow and swell. e.g. 누렇게 들뜬 얼굴[피부] a sallow and swollen [bloated] face [skin]. **3** [마음이 들썽거리다] grow restless [giddy / unstable / unsteady / fickle]; be in high spirits; treat [walk] on air. e.g. 그는 마음이 들떠 있었다 He was quite distracted

들락날락 [दल्लांग्नाल्लाक] 들락날락하다 go in and out frequently; make frequent entrance and exit [egress and ingress]; frequent. e.g. 아이들은 노상 들락날락한다 Children are always popping in and out

들러붙다 [दल्लौबुत्ता] **1** [부착하다] stick to; cling to; adhere to; cleave to. e.g. 찰싹 들러붙다 stick fast <to>. **2** (사람이) stick [cling / adhere / cleave] <to>. e.g. 귀찮게 들러붙다 hang about <a person> / pester <a person> to death.

들려주다 [दल्यौज़ूदा] [알리다] tell; inform <a person of [about] a matter>; let <a person> hear [know] <of>; (읽어서) read <a thing> (out) to <a person>; (연주하여)[play for <a person>; give <a person>a tune. e.g. 노래[음악]를 려주다 sing [play] for a person.

들르다 [दुल्लदा] [방문하다] call at <a house>; step at <a place>; drop [stop] in for a short visit; [지나가다] drop in <on a person / at a place>; drop into <an office>; look <a person> up; stop [come] by; go by <a house>; (배가) call [touch / stop] at. e.g. 책방에 들르다 drop into a bookstore [bookshop].

들리다[1] [दल्लिदा] **1** [자연히 귀에 들어오다] (사람이) (can) hear; catch;(소리가) be heard; be audible; reach [fall on] one's ear; meet [greet] the ear. e.g.잘 들리지 않는 difficult [hard] to hear. **2** [울리다,의미가 이해되다] sound; ring; seem. e.g. 역설적으로 들리다 sound paradoxical.

들리다[2] [दल्लिदा] [귀신 등이 들러붙다] be possessed <by / with>; be obsessed <by>; be bewitched. e.g. 그는 신들린 것처럼 공부했다 He studied like one [as if] possessed. / He studied like mad.

들리다[3] [दल्लिदा] (병이) catch; contract; be taken [fall] ill; be attacked [affected] by <a disease>; be seized [afflict-ted] with <a disease>;

들리다[4] [दल्लिदा] [올려지다] be lithed(up); be raised; [올리게 하다] let <a person> raise [lith(up)] <something>; let <a person> heave [ele-vate]. e.g. 책상 다리가 들렸다 The legs of the desk were lithed.

들먹거리다 [दुल्मौक्कौरिदा] **1** (몸이) <one's shoulders [buttocks]> move up and down; (가슴, 심장이) go pit-a-pat; throb; thump; flutter; pound; (마음이) become restless; be excited [tempted] <to do>; be inclined <to do>; be eager <to>. e.g. 궁둥이가 들먹거리다 one's buttocks move up and down / become restless. 그 소식에 가슴이 들먹거렸다[The news made my heart fall into a flutter. **2** [언급하다] men-tion; speak of; refer to; specify by name. e.g. 그녀까지 들먹거릴 필요야 없지 않느냐 You don't have to mention her name.

들볶다 [दल्पोक्ता] annoy; tease; harass; torment; pester; nag at; make it tough [rough / hot] for <a person>; be hard [rough / severe / tough] on <a person>; be cruel [hard] to <a person>; urge <a person to do>; press <a person for a thing>. e.g. 못 견디게 들볶다 make it too hot [warm] for <a person> / huff <a person> to pieces.

들숨 [दल्सुम] inspiration; inhalation; air breathed in; air that is being inhaled.

들썩거리다 [दल्सौक्कौरिदा] = 들먹거리다

들어가다 [दरौगादा] **1** [안으로 가다] enter <a room>; go [get / come] in; go [get / come] into <a house>; walk[step] in; walk [step] into <a room>; turn in; make one's entry into <a

place>; find one's way into; set foot inside <a house>; let oneself in. e.g. 창으로 들어가다 enter by [through] a window. **2**[움푹 패다] sink; sag; be hollow; cave [fall] in; be sunk(en). e.g. 깊숙이 들어간 만 a landlocked bay. **3** [모임,단체 등의 구성원이 되다] join; enter; go into; associate oneself with <a society>;(회사 등에) join; go to work for <a firm>; find [take] service in [with]; be employed <by>; (학교에) enter <a school>; pass into <Harrow>. **4** [수용 능력이 있다] hold; accommodate; house. e.g.이 회관은 1,500 명 들어간다 This hall seats [can accommodate / hold] 1,500 people. **5**[소유가 되다] fall into <a person's> hands [power]. e.g.…의 손에 들어가 있다 be in the hands of **6** (비용이) cost; be spent; be consumed; be put in; be sunk. e.g .집을 짓는 데 많은 돈이 들어갔다 Much money has gone into building the house.

들어내다 [दरोनेदा] [밖으로 내놓다] remove; lith out; take[bring / carry / get] out; whip out; (재난을 피하려고) save; re cue. e.g. 몰래 들어 내다 smuggle <something> out of <the house>.

들어맞다[दरोमात्ता] **1** [적합하다] fit; fit in <with>; be fit <for>; suit; be suited <to>; go on(신발 등이). e.g. 꼭 들어맞는 옷 a perfect fit. **2**[일치하다]fit together; agree <with>; be in accord <with>; coincide <with>; tally <with>; square [conform] <with>; answer to; meet. e.g. 그들의 이야기가 들어맞는다 Their accounts tally [square] with each other.

들어붓다 [दरोबुत्ता] **1** (비가) fall [rain] heavily; pour down; rain cats and dogs; rain in torrents; rain(in) buckets. e.g. 들어붓는 비 a pouring [heavy / driving] rain / a pelting rain [shower] / a downpour(of rain) / a cloudburst. **2** (물 등을) pour <water> into [on / out of] <something>. e.g. 솥에 물을 들어붓다 pour water into an oven.

들어서다 [दरोसोदा] **1** (안으로) enter; step [tread] in; set foot inside; come [go / get] into. e.g. 마당[집안]]에 들어서다 step [walk] a garden [a home]. 구내에 들어서다 enter the premises. **2** [접어들다] begin; set in. e.g. 노년기에 들어서다 arrive at sen- escence / become

ㄷ

senescent / reach old age.

들어오다 [दरौओदा] **1** (안으로) enter; co me [get] in; come [get] into; walk [step] in [into]; turn in; let oneself in; set foot inside; (도둑 등이) burgle; burglarize; break in [into]; enter <a house> by force. e.g. 항구에 들어오다 enter [make] port / come into port. **2** [입회하다,참가하다] join; come into; enter; participate [take part] in; take a hand in. e.g.우리 클럽에 들어오다 join our club / be enrolled in our club. **3** (수입 등이) have; get; receive; make. e.g. 월 30 만 원 들어온다 I get [have an income of] 300,000 won a month.

들어주다 [दरौजुदा] (요구,부탁을) comply with <a person's request>; grant <a request / a favor>; entertain <a person's request>; concede [listen to] <a request>; accede [assent] to <a proposal>; hear [answer] <a person's prayer>;(충고 등을) take [follow] <a person's advice>.

들여놓다 [दर्यौनोथा] **1** (물건을) take [bring / get / carry] in (and put down). e.g. 방에 책상을 들여놓다 bring a desk in a room. **2** (발을) set foot <in / on>; put one's foot <in / on>; step into <a bog>; tread <on>. e.g. 위험한 곳에 발을 들여놓다 tread on dangerous ground. **3** (사람을) let [allow] in; admit; show [usher] in. e.g. 남을 그곳에 들여놓지 않다 keep a person from the place. **4** [사들이다] purchase; buy (in) <books>; take in <a fresh supply of fuel>; lay in <a stock>. e.g. 월동용으로 식량과 연탄을 들여놓다 lay in provisions and briquets for the winter.

들여다보다 [दर्यौयोदा] **1** (안을)] look in [into]; peep [peek] into <a room>; peep through <a hole>; snoop into <a home>. e.g. 현미경으로 들여다보다 **2** (자세하게) look [go] over; look [inquire] into; examine closely [carefully]. e.g. 서류를 들여다보다 look over [dig into] the documents.

들여보내다 [दर्यौयोनैदा] send <a person / a thing> into; let <a person> in [into]; allow to enter; allow in; admit. e.g. 남을 집으로 들여보내다 send a person in (to) the house.

들여오다 [दर्यौओदा] **1** (밖에서 안으로) bring in; carry in;takein. e.g. 음식물을 호텔에 들여오다 [bring [take] food and drink into a hotel. **2** [사들이다] buy;

get(in); [주문하다] order; (우편,주문판매로) send (away) for; [수입하다] import. 오스트레일리아에서 양모를 들여오다 import wool from Australia.

들이다 [दरिदा] **1** (안으로) let [allow] in; admit; show [usher] in. e.g. 신선한 공기를 들이다 let fresh air in. **2** [입회시키다] let join [participate]; enlist; receive; admit; let in. e.g. 새 회원을 들이다 admit a new member. **3** [자본,시간,비용,노력 등을 어떤 필요에 쓰다] invest <capital>; lay out [sink] <capital in some venture>; spend <money on clothes / time in toilet>; expend <time on>; consume; make efforts. e.g. 많은 시간을 들여서] with a great sacrifice of time. **4** [고용하다][employ; engage; take <a person> into one's service; (양자를) adopt; take into the family. e.g. 요리사를 새로 들이다 engage [hire] a new cook. **5** [들여놓다] take [bring] in; carry in [into]. e.g. 볏섬을 뜰에 들이다 bring rice bags into the yard **6** [맛을 붙이다] get [acquire] a taste <for>; take to. e.g. 돈에 맛을 들이다 get a taste for money. **7** [염색하다] dye. e.g. 검정 물을 들이다 dye <a thing>(in) black. 무슨 물을 들일까요 What color shall I dye it? 머리를 갈색으로 물들였다 I have my hair dyed brown.

들이닥치다 [दरिदाक्छिदा] draw [come] near; be close [near] at hand; descend upon; raid; rush in; make a rapid approach to; storm <a place>; fall on. e.g. 눈앞에 들이닥친 위험 an imminent [a pressing] danger.

들이대다 [दरिदैदा] **1** [바싹 가져다 대다] thrust <a thing> before <a person>; put [place] under <a person's> nose; point <a gun> at [to / toward]. e.g. 권총을 들이대다 point [aim] a revolver at <a person>. **2** [대들다] resist openly; defy; protest; go at; challenge. e.g. 윗 사람에게 들이대다 set oneself against one's superior.

들이마시다 [दुरिमासिदा] (기체를) breathe in; inhale; draw [take] in; (액체를) suck in; drink in; gulp down. e.g. 담배를 깊이 들이마시다 take a deep pull [drag] at a cigarette.

들이받다 [दरिबात्ता] run [bump / strike / knock / hit] against; run into; butt; bunt hard. e.g. 자동차로 담벼락[전주]을 들이받다 run [crash] a car into a wall [an electric pole].

들이쉬다 [दरिस्विदा] breathe in; inhale; inspire; draw <a breath>. e.g. 급히 숨을 한번 들이쉬고 [with a rapid intake of breath.

들이치다 [दरिछ्दिा] (바람 등이) blow in [into];(비 등이) drive into [through]. e.g. 바람이 불면 비가 들이친다 When it's windy it rains in

들짐승 [दल्यिमसुंग] wild animals.

들쭉날쭉 [दल्चुंग्नाल्चुक] jaggedly; ruggedly; unevenly. 들쭉날쭉하다 jagged; indented; notched.

들추다 [दल्छुदा] **1** [폭로하다] disclose [let out] <a secret>; uncover; reveal; expose; dig up [into]; bring to light. e.g. 남의 잘못을 들추다 expose a person's fault. **2** [뒤지다] search; ransack; rummage <in>. e.g. 호주머니 속을 들추다 fumble in one's pocket <for>.

들추어내다 [दल्छुऔनैदा] **1** [찾아내다]] find out; hunt out; rummage out. **2** [드러내다] expose; disclose; lay bare; un-mask.

들키다 [दल्खिदा][발견되다] be found (out)[discovered / detected / caught] <doing / in the act of doing>; come out. e.g. 장난하다 선생님에게 들키다 be caught up to some mischief by the teacher.

들통나다 [दल्थोंग्नादा] be detected [revealed / disclosed]; be brought [come] to light; get found out. e.g. 그의 거짓말이 들통나고 말았다 His lie was discovered [exposed]

들판 [दल्फान] [들을 이룬 벌판] a plain; a field.

듬뿍 [दम्पुक] plenty; much; quite a lot; to the brim; to the full. e.g. 빵에 잼을 듬뿍 바르다 spread a lot of jam on the bread.

듬성듬성 [दम्सौदम्सौ] sparsely; thinly; scatteredly; sporadiccally; here and there.

듯 [दत] e.g. 듯 마는 듯하다 it hardly seems one way or the other / it hardly feels as if / one hardly knows whether. 비가 올 듯말 듯했다 I was not sure if it would rain or not.

듯싶다 [दत्षिफदा] [인 듯 생각되다] seem; it seems (to me) that; [일 것 같다] be likely <to>; probably.

듯이 [दषि] as if; as though; like; giving the appearance of. e.g. 그는 네가 생각하듯이 그렇게 대학자는 아니다 He is not such a great scholar as you think.

등 [दुंग] the back. e.g. 등을 돌리다 turn one's back <on>.

등 [दुंग्बुल] [燈] a light; a lamp; a lantern. e.g. 등을

켜다 light a lamp / light up <a room> / (전등을) turn [put] on the light.

등 [दुंग] [**等**] **1** [등급] a class; a grade; a degree; a rank. e.g. 1 등 the first class [grade]. **2** [… 따위] and the like; and so forth [on]; et cetera (etc.); and such like <things>; and what not. e.g. 한국, 중국, 일본 등의 나라에서 in these three countries of Korea, China, and Japan.

등고선 [दंगोसौन] [**等高線**] a contour line.

등골 [दंगोल] **1** [등줄기] the line of the backbone; the hollow along the spine. e.g. 등골이 오싹해지는 광경 a spine-chilling sight. **2**= 척수(脊 髓). e.g. 등골(이) 빠지다 suffer extremely; have a very hard time of it.

등교 [दंग्यो] [**登校**] attending school; school attendance.

등급 [दंगप] [**等級**] a class; a grade; a rank; a degree; (별의) magnitude.

등기 [दंगि] [**登記**] Registration; registry.

등단 [दंगदान] [**登壇**] [단위에 오름]. 등단하다 take [go on / proceed to / ascend] the platform; take [mount] the rostrum.

등대 [दुंगदै] [**燈臺**] a lighthouse; a light tower; a beacon; <詩> a pharos.

등등 [दुंगदुंग] [**等等**] and so Son; and so forth; and all that sort of thing; and what not; et cetera (略 etc.). e.g. 우리는 물통, 냄비, 접시 등등을 샀다 We bought buckets, pots, plates, etc [and so forth / and so on].

등록 [दंग्नोक] [**登錄**] Registration; (경기,단체 등에의) entry; enrollment. **등록하다** register oneself with [at] the unemploy-ment office.

등록금 [दुंग्नोक्कम] a Registration fee; (학교의) university expenses; school fees.

등반 [दुंगवान] [**登攀**] climbing.

등분 [दुंग्बन] [**等分**] [an equal division; division into equal parts **등분하다** divide equally [in equal parts]; share equally. e.g. 사[삼] 등분하다 divide into quarters [three equal parts] / quadrisect [trisect].

등불[दुंग्बुल] [**燈**–][a light; a lamplight; an electric light (전등).

등산 [दुंग्सान] [**登山**] mountain climbing; mountaineerring (은 본격적인 등산)

등수 [दुग्योंग] [**等數**] [등급에 따라 정한 차례] a grade; a rank; a rate.

등용 [दंग्योंग] [**登用**] [임용] appointment; assignment; [승진] elevation; promotion; advancement. 등용하다 appoint [assign] <a person to a position>; [승진시키다] promote [advance] <a person to a higher position>; elevate. e.g. 그는 법관으로 등용되었다 He was appointed (as a) judge. / He was raised to the bench.

등용문 [दुग्योंग्मुन] [**登龍門**] an opening to honors; the gateway to success (in life).

등잔 [दुग्जान] [**燈盞**] an oil cup for a lamp; a lamp-oil container. e.g. 등잔 밑이 어둡다<속담> The beacon does not shine on its own base. / At the foot of the candle it is dark. / One has to go abroad to get news of home.

등장 [दुंग्जांग] [**登場**] [무대에 나타남] (an) appearance <on the stage>.

등재 [दुग्जै] [**登載**] Registration; record. e.g. 등재하다 register; record.

등정 [दुंग्जौंग] [**登頂**] [정상에 오름]. e.g. 일행은 등정에 성공했다 The party succeeded in reaching the summit.

등지다 [दुंगजिदा] **1** [틀어지다] fall out <with a person about trifles>; become estranged [alienated] <from>; break [split] <with>. e.g. … 과 등지고 있다 […be on bad terms with <a person> / be at odds with <a person>. **2** [배반하다] rise [turn] against [on / upon]; betray; [돌아서다] turn one's back on; [떠나다] leave. e.g. 나라를 등지다 turn against one's country / leave one's native country. **3** [등 뒤에 두다] <one's back> lean against. e.g. 관중을 등지고 [with one's back to the audience.

등치다 [दुंग्छिदा] [빼앗다] extort <money from a person> (by intimidation [threats]); blackmail; pinch; squeeze; wring [screw / bully / scare] <money out of a person>; <美> racketeer. e.g. 등쳐 먹는 사람 a blackmailer / <美> a racketeer.

디디다 [दिदिदा] [밟다] step on; tread (up) on. e.g. 외국땅을 디디다 step [set foot] on foreign soil.

디딤돌 [दिदिम्दोल] 고 오르내리는 돌] a stepstone; [수단] a stepping stone; a springboard. e.g. 남을 디딤돌 삼아 출세하다 improve one's position at the expense of another.

디스크 [दिसख्] a disc; a disk.

디자이너 [दिजाइनौ] a designer.

디자인 [दिजाइन] a design; designning.

디저트 [दिजौथ] a) dessert.

디지털 [दिजीथौल] digital. **딜레마** a dilemma. e.g. 딜레마에 빠지다 be in a fix / be on the horns of a dilemma / be caught between the devil and the deep blue sea [between Scylla and Charybdis] / come up against a dilemma.

ㄹ

ㄹ [र/ल] **1** [일반적 사실].)할 일 things to do. **2** [미래 의일] .e.g.c 그것을 할 작정이다 I expect to do it.

-ㄹ것이다 [-र गौसीदा] **1** [추측 예상] I think [suppose] (that) ...; I hope (that) ... (▷ 좋은 일을 예상하여) **2** [당연]. e.g. 달이 떴으니 밖은 아주 밝을 것이다] Since the moon is out, it must be quite light outside. **3** [예정] e.g. 그는 곧 집에 돌아올 것이다 He is expected to come home soon.

-ㄹ 바에 [-र बाए] [어차피 그러할 것이면]. e.g. 그를 믿을 바에, 그에게 모두 맡겨 두어라 If you trust him at all, leave all to him.

-ㄹ 터이다 [-र थौइदा] [의지, 예정] intend to <do>; will; mean to <do>; be going to <do>; [추측] should; ought to <do>; must.

-ㄹ걸 [- र गौल] **1** [후회]. e.g. 네가 그것을 보았으면 좋았을걸 You should have seen it. / If only you could If you could only] have seen it. **2** [추측] I dare say; I should say; perhaps; probably; maybe; possibly; I suppose; I think; I presume; I guess. e.g.아마 그럴걸 It may be so. / I should think so.

-ㄹ게 [-रगे] [행동의 약속]. e.g. 잠깐 다녀올게` I will be [come] back soon.

-ㄹ까 [-रक्का] **1** [의문,추측] I wonder; I am afraid; I fear. e.g. 저 사람은 누구일까 I wonder who that man is. **2** [제의]. e.g. 산책할까 How about taking a walk? / Let's go out for a walk, shan't we? **3** [부탁]. e.g. 전화 번호를 가르쳐 주실 수 있을까요 Will you kindly give me your phone number?

-ㄹ까 말까 [-रक्का म्लक्का] **1** [망설임] hesitatingly; with hesitation. e.g. 이라고 말할까 말까 망설이다 have [feel] hesitation in saying that .... **2** [미달] less than; not more than; scarcely; barely. e.g. 일년이 될까 말까 해서 in less than a year. 생후

-ㄹ라 [-र रा] [염려]. e.g. 서둘러라, 학교에 늦을라 Hurry up, or you will be late for school.

-ㄹ망정 [-रमंगजौग] [비록 그러하지만 그러나] (even) though; although; (even) if;(and) yet; nevertheless; however; but. e.g. 가난할 망정 poor as he is / though (he is) poor.

-ㄹ밖에 [पाक्के] cannot (choose) but <do>; cannot help <doing>; cannot do otherwise than; have no choice but <to do>. 그의 충고에 따를밖에 I have no choice but to[cannot choose but] follow his advice.

-ㄹ뿐더러 [-रपूनदौरौ] [뿐만 아니라 다른 일이 더 있음] not only [merely] ... but (also); as well as. e.g. 그것은 품질이 좋을뿐더러 가격도 싸다 It is both good and cheap.

-ㄹ수록 [-र सूरोक] [어떤 일이 더하여 감] the more [less]…, the more [less]. e.g. 싸면 쌀수록 좋다 The cheaper, the better.

-ㄹ지 [-रजी] [추측으로 의심을 나타냄] whether (...or); if. e.g. 내가 가야할지 모르겠다 I wonder whether I should go(or not). 그가 올지 어떨지 I wonder whether he will come.

-ㄹ지라도 [-र जीरादो] [비록 …하더라도] though; even if[though]; no matter <who / what / when / where / how>. e.g.무슨 일이 생길지라도[मुसन इरी सैंगीलचीरादो] whatever may happen / come what may.

ㄹ지언정 [-रजीऔनजौग] evenif [though]; rather [sooner] than. e.g. 죽을지언정 노예로 살진 않겠다 I would sooner [rather] die than live in slavery.

-라고 [-रागो] **1** [명령] e.g. 그에게 들어오라고 할까요 Shall I ask him in? **2** [인용] e.g. 네 실언은 취중이었기 때문이라고 하여 빠져나갈 수는 You can't get away with your slip of the tongue by saying you'd been drinking.

-라는 [रानन] […라고 하는]. e.g. 그린 씨라는 분 a certain Mr. Green

-라니 [रानी] **1** [… 라 고 하니]. e.g. 이 집을 나가라니 나가겠소 I will get out of this house as you told me to. **2** [의문,의외]. e.g.그 사람이 스파이라니 To hear that he is a spy! / That he should be a spy!

라도 [रादो] if; even if [though]; though; although; however; any. e.g. 언제라도 오십시오 You may come any time [day].

라디오 [रादीओ] radio (▷ 종종 the radio); wireless; [수신기] a radio; a radio [wireless] set.

-라면 [राम्यौन] [가정,조건] if; in case; suppose; suppose-

ing; provided; as for; for. e.g. 하라면 해라 Do as you are told.
라면 [राम्यौन] [중국국수] Chinese noodles [vermicelli].
라이벌 [लाइबौल] a rival.
라이터 [लाइथौ] a (cigarette) lighter.
란제리 [रानजेरी] <프> lingerie.
랑 [रांग] and; or; and so on [forth]; etc.; [함께] (together) with. e.g. 너랑 나랑 you and me.
랑데부 [लांगदेबू] a rendezvous <*pl.* –vous (▷ 복수에서는 s 를 [z]로 발음함)> a date.
-래서 [रैसौ] [···라고 하여서]. e.g. 그 소년은 어머니에게 오천 원을 달래서 책을 샀다 The boy asked his mother for 5,000 won and bought a book. 그가 그 책을 달래서 주었다 I gave him the book because he asked it.
랜턴 [लैनथौन] a lantern.
램프 [लैम्फ] a lamp. e.g. 석유 램프 an oil [a petroleum / a kerosene] lamp.
랭킹 [रैङ्खिंग] ranking. e.g. 국내[국제] 랭킹 national [international] ranking.
-랴 [ल्या] **1** 반어] e.g. 어찌 내가 그런 일을 할 수 있으랴 How on earth [ever] can I do such a thing?**2** [문의]. e.g. 돈을 주랴 I Shall I give you some money?
러브 [लौब] [사랑] love; [정구] [무득점] love.₩
레몬 [लेमोन] a lemon.
레벨 [लेबेल] [표준,수준] a level. e.g. 레벨이 높다 [낮다] be on a high [low] level.
레스토랑 [रेसथोरांग] a restaurant.
레슨 [लेसन] a lesson. e.g. 피아노 레슨 a piano lesson / a lesson in piano.
레슬링 [लेसुल्लीग] wrestling
레이스 [रेइस.] [수예 편물] lace; lacework. e.g. 레이스를 달다 trim with lace.
레저 [रेजौ] leisure; leisure time amusement.
레코드 [रेखोदु] **1** [기록] a record; a mark. **2** [녹음된 음반] a (phonograph / gramophone) record; a disk; a disc.
레크리에이션 [रेखुरीएइसियौन] (a) recreation.
레퍼토리 [रेफौथोरी] a repertory; a repertoire.
렌즈 [लेन्जु] a lens <*pl.* ~es>.
-려고 [रियौगो] [의도] with the intention of <doing>; with a view to <doing>; [목적] in order to <do>; in order that ...; for the purpose of ... e.g. 시험에 합격하려고 in order to pass the examination
-려는 [रियौनुन] [···려고 하는] e.g.만나려는 분이 누구요 Who(m) do you want? / Who(m) are you going to

ㄹ

see?

-려는데 [रियौननदे] [···려고 하는데]. e.g. 내가 자리를 뜨려는데 그녀가 왔다 She came as I was leaving.

-려다가 रयौ दागा [··· 려고 하다가]. e.g. 고향에 내려 가려다가 말다 give up [abandon / relinquish] the idea of going home.

-려면 [रियौम्यौन] [··· 려고 하면] e.g. 내가 하려면 할 수는 있는데 I could do so, if I would.

-로 [रो] [**路**] a route; a street; a road; an avenue. e.g.교통로 a traffic route. 십자로 a cross-roads.

로 [रो] **1** [수단,기구] by; by means of; with; in; on. e.g.기계로 짠 양탄자 a rug woven by machine **2** [방향,목적지] for; to; toward; into; in. e.g. 해변가로 가다 go to the seaside. **3** [재료] of; [원료] from. e.g.나무로 만든 상자 a box made of wood. **4** [원인,동기] because of; owing to; of; at; with; from; through. e.g.그는 티프스로 죽었다 He died of typhoid fever.

-로구나 [-रोगुना] [감탄]. e.g. 그 여자 정말 미녀로구나 She is a beauty indeed! 벌써 12 시로구나 It is already 12 o'clock! 정말 구경거리로구나 What a sight it is!.

로맨스 [रोमैनसु] a romance; a love affair; [연애 사건] affairs of the heart; a love story.

로봇 [रोबोत] [인조 인간] a robot; [허수아비] a figure-head.

로비 [लोबी] a lobby.

로서 [रोसौ] **1** [지위, 신분,입장,자격을 가지고] as; for; in the capacity of; in [under] the character of. e.g.학자로서 as a scholar. 부모로서의 의무 one's duty as a parent. 부부로서 어울리지 않는 쌍 an ill-mated pair. **2** = 로부터.

로켓 [रोख्वेत] [비행체] a rocket.

로테이션 [रोथेइस्यौन] rotation. e.g. 로테이션으로 <do something> by [in] rotation.

록 [रोक] rock

-론 [रोन] [**論**] **1** [논의] (an) argument; (a) discussion; a discourse; a dispute; (a) controversy; (a) debate (토론) **2** [이론] a theory; a doctrine. e.g. 유심론 spiritualism.

-롭다 [रोप्ता] be; be characterized by. e.g. 새롭다 new / fresh

-류 [र्यू] [**類**] **1** [종류] a sort; a kind; a variety; a class; a genus <*pl.* genera>; a description; a type; a species. e.g. 거미류 a genus of spider. **2** [강] a class; [목] an order. e.g. 갑각류 Crustacea.

를 [रुल] e.g. 동아일보를 보니 according to the Dong-A Ilbo. 자전거를 타다 ride a bicycle. 시계를 주다 give <a person> a watch.

-리 [री] [裡] in; amid (st). e.g. 극비리에 with absolute secrecy. 암암리에 secretly / covertly.

리 [री] [理] reason; possibility. e.g. 일 리가 없다 cannot be / must not be / It is hardly possible <that>. 그것이 사실일 리가 없다 It cannot be true

리듬 [रीदम] (a) rhythm.

-리라 [-रीरा] **1** [추측] may[might] <be / do>; must; would; I think [suppose]. e.g. 그녀는 틀림없이 성공하리라 She will certainly succeed. / She is sure to succeed. **2**[의지] I will [shall]; I would; I am going to. e.g. 실패하더라도 한번 더 해보리라 If I should fail, I would try again.

리셉션 [रीसेपश्यौन] a reception. e.g. 리셉션을 열다 hold [give] a rece-ption.

리스트 [लीस्थु] a list. e.g. 리스트에 기재된 이름 listed names.

리포트 [रीफोथ्] [보고] a report; (학교의) a term [research] paper.

리허설 [रीहौसौल] a rehearsal.

릴레이 [रिल्लेई] a relay (race). e.g. 400 미터 릴레이 [साबैकमीथौ रील्लेई] 400-meter relay

립스틱 [लिपसफथीक] a lipstick; a lip pencil.

링크 [लिंख़ु] a link.

-마 [मा] [魔] devilish; diabolic; fiendish. e.g. 살인마 a devilish murderer. 색마 a male flirt / a wolf.

마감 [मागाम] conclusion; a close; an end; a finish;(기한 등의) closing; closure. 마감하다 end; close; finish; drop <a matter>; bring <a matter> to an end[a close]; put an end to. e.g.계산을 마감하다close the account.

마개 [मागै] (병 등의) a stopper; a stop; a stopple; a cork (코르크로 된); (금속제의) a crown cap.

마구 [माग़ु]. recklessly; blindly; carelessly; haphazard-dly; at random; roughly; in a disorderly way; without discretion [discrimination]; lapdash; hit-or-miss; happy-go-lucky; wantonly. e.g. 돈을 마구 쓰다spend money freely [extravagantly] / lavish money / spend money fast [recklessly

마구(간) [मागू गान])[馬廐(間)] a stable; a(horse) barn. e.g. 마구에서 일하는 사람a stableman / a stabler. 마구에 넣다stable <a horse> / put [lodge] in a stable.

마귀 [माग्वी] [魔鬼] [잡귀]an evil spirit; a devil; a demon; evil influence.

마냥 [मान्यांग] [그저] solely; only; but; intently; [끝없이] endlessly; ceaselessly. e.g. 마냥 어리석기만 하다be in a bottomless ignorance [stupidity].

마늘 [मानुल] [植] a garlic; [향료] garlic. e.g. 마늘 한 조각a clove of garlic. 마늘 냄새가 나는garlicky / smelling of garlic.

마다 [मादा] [낱낱이] each; every; all. e.g. 밤마다 every evening / every night.

마다하다 [मादाहादा] [싫어하다] dislike; hate; loathe; detest. e.g. 나는 어떤 일도 마다하지 않겠다I don't mind doing any job.

마당 [मादांग] **1** [뜰] a yard; a court; a garden. e.g. 안마당a courtyard / a [an inner] court. **2** [경우] an instance; a case; [때] the moment. e.g. 이 마당에on this occasion / at this time [juncture].

마디 [मादी] **1** [관절] a joint; [손가락 관절] a knuckle. **2** [결절](대나무 등의) a joint; (나무의 옹이) a knot; a knob; a lump; a nod; [실 등의 매듭] a knot. e.g. 나무의 마디a knar / a gnarl**3** (말의) a word; a phrase; (노래의) a snatch; a tune; a melody; [소절] a bar; a measure. e.g. (노래의) 첫째 마디 the first measure / measure 1.

마땅하다 [मातांगहादा] [적합하다] becoming; befitting; right; proper; appropriate; suitable; apposite; [상당하다] fair; reasonable. e.g. 마땅한 값에 사다 buy at a reasonable price

마땅히 [मातांगही] [의당 당연히] properly; naturally; exactly; justly; necessarily; of necessity; deservedly; of course; as a matter of course. e.g. 마땅히 … 해야 하다ought to <do> / it is (just and) proper that <one> should <do

마라톤 [माराथोन] a marathon (race); (운동을 위한) long-distance running.

마련 [मार्योन] **1** [준비] preparation; provision; arrangement; [계획](a) plan; [설비] furnishing. e.g. 혼자 살아갈 만한 마련은 되어 있는 몸이오 I've got what it takes to be able to go it alone. 마련하다 prepare <seats>; provide; arrange; furnish; get ready <for>;

make ready for; plan. e.g. 술자리를 마련하다 hold a banquet **2** [당연]. e.g. 겨울 등산은 위험하기 마련이다 Mountain climbing in winter is always risky.

마렵다 [मार्यौप्ता] feel an urge to urinate [defecate]; have a call of nature; want to relieve oneself. e.g. 똥이 마렵다 have to defecate / feel like going to stool. 오줌이 마렵다 have a desire to urinate [pass water]. 마렵지 않다feel no urge to ease nature. 엄마, 오줌[똥] 마려워 Mammy, I want to do my needs.

마루[मारू] (집의) a (wooden) floor; a flooring.

마르다[मारूदा] 1 [건조하다] dry (up); get [become] dry;(목재가) be seasoned; (초목이) wither; be withered. e.g. 마른 수건 a dry towel. **2** [여위다] become lean [thin]; grow gaunt [slim]; lose (one's) weight; (병으로) lose flesh; (사랑,근심으로) pine away. e.g. 마른 사람a thin [lean / skinny / scrawny / scraggy] person

마름질 [मारूमजील] cutting (out). e.g. 마름질을 시작하다 begin to cut <cloth>. 마름질하다 cut out <a garment>. e.g. 마름질이 바느질보다 어렵다고 한다 Cutting is said to require more skill than tailoring.

마리 [मारी] a head <단수 복수동형>; the number <of animals>. e.g. 두 마리의 개[곤충 / 뱀] two dogs [insects / snakes]. 다섯 마리의 새끼 고양이five kittens. 물고기 세 마리 three fishes.

마모 [मामो] [**磨耗**] wear (and tear); abrasion. e.g. 이 재질은 마모에 견딘다 This material resists abrasion. 마모하다 be worn away. e.g. 이 기계는 상당히 마모되어 있다 This machine is badly worn.

마무리 [मामूरी] [완성] finishing; completion; conclusion; [마지막 손질] the finish; the finishing touches [strokes];(벽 시멘트칠의) a setting [finishing] coat 마무리하다 settle; arrange; finish; complete; conclude; get through with. e.g. 정교하게 마무리한 조각 a sculpture with a fine finish.

마법 [माबौब] [**魔法**] magic; sorcery; black art; witchcrath (여자의); wizardry (남자의

마비 [माबी] [**痲痺**] paralysis; palsy; numbness; monoplegia; stupor (정신의); an (a) esthesia (약에 의한).

마사지 [मासाजी] <give> a massage; a rubdown.

마술 [मासुल] [**魔術**] [마력을

부리는 술법] magic; [사악한 마법] witch-crath; the black arts; [악령의 도움을 빌려 행하는 술법] sorcery.

마스크 [मास्ख] **1** [얼굴을 가리는 것] a (face) mask; a face guard. **2** [용모] looks; features.

마시다 [माशीदा] 1 (액체를)] drink; have; take; [삼키다] swallow [약을 먹다] 의 경우는 일반적 으로) take. e.g. 차를 마시다 drink tea. **2** (기체를) breathe in; inhale; inspire; draw <air> into <the lungs>. e.g. 신선한 공기를 마시기 위해 창문을 열다 open the window to let in fresh air.

마약 [मायाक] [痲藥] a narcotic; a drug; a dope

마을 [माउल] [동네] a hamlet; a rural community.

마음 [माउम] **1** [정신] mind; spirit; [생각] an idea; (a) thought; [심성] mentality. e.g. 마음과 몸the mind and the body. **2** [심정] (the) heart; [감정] sense; feeling; [기분] mood; frame of mind; humor. e.g. 마음이 편치 않다feel ill at ease / feel constrained [awkward. **3** [의지] will; [의향] mind; design; inclination; intention. e.g. 정말로 갚을 마음만 있으면 갚을 수 있는 금액이다 The debt is small enough that he could pay it back if he really intended [wanted] to.

마음가짐 [माउम्गाजीम] **1** [마음의 자세] a mental attitude; the attitude [a frame] of mind. **2** [각오] determination; resolve; resolution. **3** [의도] intention; [주의] care; [신중함] prudence. e.g. 마음가짐이 좋으니까 내가 외출할 때는 언제나 갠단 말야 (농담 조로) My heart is in the right place so it never rains when I go out.

마음껏 [माउम्कौत] [실컷] to one's heart's content; to the utmost [hilt]; as much as one likes [pleases]; all on wants. e.g. 마음껏 … 하다 give free play to / give rein to.

마음대로[माउम्तैरो] [하고 싶은 대로] as one pleases [likes / wishes]; at one's pleasure; [독단으로] at one's (own) discretion; on one's own authority; [자유의사로] at (one's own sweet) will; freely; [무단으로] without leave [permission]. e.g. 마음대로 하다have one's (own) way <in everything>.

마음속 [माउम्सोक] one's inmost feelings; (deep within) one's heart; the bottom of one's heart; one's innermost thoughts; one's bosom. e.g. 마음속으 로는

in one's heart / inwardly.

마음씨 [माउम्शी] (a) nature; (a) temper;(a) disposition; a turn [cast] of mind. e.g. 마음씨가 고운tender in sentiment / sweet-tempered / well-disposed.

마저 [माजौ] [남김없이] without leaving any; with everything else; with all the rest. e.g. 마저 듣다hear the last of it.

마저 [माजौ] [까지도] besides; what is more; even; also; on top of; to the length [extreme / extent] of; so far as; into the bargain; in addition to. e.g. 도둑질마저하다go to the length [extent] of committing theth / go so far as to commit theth.

마주보다 [माजुबोदा] [마주 대하다] be opposite <to>; face each other; confront; (눈으로) exchange looks [glances]; look at each other. e.g. 놀라서 서로 마주보다exchange looks of astonishment.

마주잡다 [माजुजाप्ता] 1 [서로 잡다] take each other; take [hold] together. e.g. 손에 손을 마주잡고hand in hand <with 2 [제휴하다] go hand in hand with; join [shake] hands with; join together; [협동하다] co-operate <with>. e.g. 손을 마주잡고 사업을 하다 do a business in cooperation with each other.

마주치다 [माजुछीदा] 1 [충돌하다] crash together [against / into]; collide <with>; knock [bump / dash] against; run against [into]. 2 [우연히 만나다] happen to meet; chance [hit] upon; come [fall / run] across; fall [drop] in with; meet with. e.g. 딱 마주치다 come [be brought] face to face with <a person>.

마중 [माजुंग] meeting; going [coming] out to meet <a person>; reception (영접). e.g. 마중을 나가다go to meet a person.

마지막 [माजीमाक] 1 [맨 끝] the last; [결말] the conclusion; the end. e.g. 마지막날the last [closing / concluding / final] day <of a show>. 2 [죽음P임종] one's last moment; one's death [end]; one's fate. e.g. 마지막을 지켜보다 be present at <a person's> deathbed / watch <a person> die.

마지못하다 [माजीमोत्हादा] <서술적> be obliged [forced / compelled] to; cannot help [but]; be under the ecessity [compulsion] of; be driven by dire necessity to. e.g. 그는 마지못해 승낙했다He consented unwillingly [reluctantly / with bad grace]. / He gave unwilling [reluctant] consent.

마진 [माजीन] a margin <of profit>.

마차 [माछा] [馬車] a (horse-drawn) carriage; a coach; a (horse) cab;(짐 실는) [जीम शित्ता] a cart; a wagon.

마찬가지 [माछानगाजी] the (very) same; sameness; the selfsame; one and the same; [유사] likeness; similarity. e.g. 둘 다 마찬가지다The two are much the same. / There is nothing to choose between the two.

마찰 [माछाल] [摩擦] [접촉면의 저항] friction. e.g. 마찰의 frictional. [불화, 알력] (a) discord; (a) trouble; friction. e.g. 좌파와 우파 사이의 마찰 conflict [friction] between the leth and right wings.

마취 [माछ्वी] [痲醉] an (a) esthesia; narcotism. e.g. 국부 [전신 / 척수] 마취 local [general / spinal] anesthesia. 에테르 마취 etherization. 마취 에서 깨어나다 come out from under the anesthetic.

마치 [माछी] [꼭] just; just [exactly] like; [흡사(…과 같이)] like; as; just as; as if[though]; as it were. e.g. 마치 나가라는 듯이as if to say "get out".

마치다 [माछीदा] [끝내다] end; finish; get [be] through <with>; make an end of; complete; conclude; [수행하다] accomplish; [졸업하다] graduate <from>.

마침 [माछिम] [운좋게] luckily; fortunately; as good luck would have it; [시기에 맞게] in the very nick of time; in good time; just in time [season]; opportunely; seasonably; [그때에] just at the time; just then. e.g. 마침 오다[지나가다] happen to come [pass] by

마침내 [माछिमनै] [드디어] at (long) last; finally; at length; [결국] ather all; in the end; ultimately; in the long run; [오랜 시간이 지나] at length

마침표 [माछिमप्यो] [-標] a period; a full stop. e.g. 마침표를 찍다put a period <to>.

마크 [माख्र] [표] a mark; [레테르] a label; [상표] a trademark; [휘장] a badge

마흔[माहुन] [幕] forty.**막** [माक] **1** [임시로 지은 집] a temporary shed [shelter]; a booth; a shack; a hut; a shed. e.g. 원두막a look-out shed. 막을 짓다put up a booth [shed]. **2** [장막] a curtain; a hanging screen; hanging; [천막] <set up / fold up> a tent.

e.g. 막을 치다stretch a curtain. **3** [연극의 단락] an act. e.g. 단막극a one-act play / a play in one act. **4** [끝장] an end; a close; a conclusion. e.g. 전쟁의 막을 내리다 put an end to the war

막 [माक] [방금] just; just [right] at the moment; just now. e.g.막 …하려 하다be about to <do> / be ready to <do> / be on the point [edge / verge] of <doing>.

막간 [माक्कान] [**幕間**] <during> an intermission; an interval (between the acts [scenes]). e.g. 15분간의 막간 a fitheen minutes' interval.

막강 [माक्कांग] [**莫强**] 막강하다mighty; having [of] the greatest power; enormously powerful. e.g. 막강한 군사력 great military strength.

막내 [मांगनै] the lastborn; the youngest of the family.

막다 [माक्ता] **1** [닫다] close; shut; [채우다] stop up <a hole>; fill (up) <a hole>; fill (up) <a crevice>; clog <a pipe>; block(up). e.g. 구멍을 종이로 막다 close up an opening with paper. **2** [둘러막다] wall (up); fence (round); enclose. e.g. 집을 돌담으로 막다 enclose a house with a stone wall. **3** [가로막다] block up (장애물로); [방해하다] obstruct; hinder; [저지하다] stop; check; interrupt <the progress>; hold in check. e.g. (자신의) 입을 막다)] hold a hand over one's mouth / (남의) cover <a person's> mouth / gag <a person> / (비밀이 새지 않게) silence <a person> / buy <a person's> silence. **4** (칸을) screen off; partition; compart. e.g. 방의 칸을 막다 partition a room. **5**[방어하다] defend <oneself against the enemy>; protect <from / against>; [저항하다] resist; [접근을 시키지 않다] keep [hold] off; keep [hold] <the enemy> at bay; [방지하다] keep away [out / off / back]; hold in check; ward off <danger>; [예방하다] prevent; guard against. e.g. 적의 공격을 막다stop the enemy's attack.

막대 [माक्तै] [**莫大**] 막대하다 vast; huge; immense; colossal; enormous; tremendous; fabulous. e.g. 막대한 빚 [माक्तैहानबीत] a vast debt.

막대기 [माक्तैगी] a stick; a rod; a bar; a staff; a club (곤봉); a baton(지휘봉) .

막되다 [माक्द्वेदा] ill-bred; ill-mannered; rude; boorish; wild; outrageous; lawless. e.g. 막된 놈 an ill-bred fellow / an ill-mannered person / a wild guy; a boor.

막둥이 [मावतुंगी] = 막내아들 (⇨ 막내)

막론 [मावनोन] [莫論] 막론하다 go without question; be a matter of course; be needless to say; there is no need to speak <of>. 남녀를 막론하고 regardless of sex / (no matter) whether it be man or woman.

막막 [मांग्माक] [漠漠] 막막하다vast; boundless; extensive. e.g. 막막한 벌판 a vast plain.

막무가내 [मांग्मुगानै] [莫無可柰] e.g. 막무가내로 stubbornly / doggedly / obstinately / resolutely / firmly.

막바지 [मावपाजी] [끝] the end [bottom] <of a street>; the very [dead] end. e.g. 언덕 막바지 the top of a hill.

막상[मावसांग] [급기야] ultimately; really; actually; in reality; ather all. e.g. 막상 일을 해보면 꽤 어려운 법이다 When one comes to doing it, one finds it rather difficult

막상막하 [मावसांगमाख्वा] [莫上莫下] nothing better and nothing worse. e.g. 막상막하의 열전a nip and tuck race / an evenly-matched contest.

막심 [मावशिम [莫甚] 막심하다 extreme; immense; enormous; tremen-dous; serious; heavy. e.g. 후회가 막심하다I regret it very much

막아내다 [मागानैदा] keep away [out / off / back]; hold in check; hold off; ward off <danger>; [방어하다] defend <against>; protect <from / against>. e.g. 적을 막아내다 hold the enemy in check / check the enemy's onslaught.

막역 [माग्यौक] [莫逆] intimacy; closeness; familia-rity. 막역하다 intimate; familiar; close. e.g. 막역한 사이 intimate relations.

막연 [माग्यौन] [漠然, 邈然] 막연하다 vague <idea>; obscure <meaning>; ambiguous <attitude>; hazy <notion>; misty <conception / recollection>; dim <memory>; indefinable <word>; nebulous <idea>. e.g. 그의 생각은 막연하고 요령부득이다 His ideas are vague and pointless.

막일 [मागिल] rough work; physical labor; toil; heavy [rough] work; < 美 > a roughnecking job. 막일하다 be engaged in rough work.

막판 [मावफान] [마지막판] the last round; the final scene [stage]; [위기] the last [critical] moment; the eleventh hour. e.g. 막판에 가서 at the last moment / at the eleventh hour.

막히다 [मार्कीदा] **1** (구멍 등이) be stopped [plugged] up; be [get] clogged; be obstructed; be choked. e.g. 숨이 막히다 be choked / be suffocated / be stifled. **2** (길 등이) be blocked (up); be barred; be obstructed; be interrupted; be suspended; stop. e.g.앞이 막힌 골목a blind[dead] alley[lane]. **3** (말,생각 등이) stick <in one's speech>; get tongue-tied; be at a loss for <an answer>; be driven to one's wit's end; come to the end of one's tether. e.g.막힌 사람a blockhead / a thickhead / a halfwit.

만[1] [मान] [灣] a bay (작은); a gulf (큰)

만[2] [मान] [萬] ten thousand; [다수] a myriad; many; all.

만[3] [मान] **1** [단지,다만,뿐] only; alone; merely; just; [한 도,범위] as many [much] as; as [so] far as. e.g. 사람은 빵만으로 살아갈 수 있는가Can man live by bread alone? **2** [적어도] at least. e.g. 나는 한 달에 만 원만은 저금하고 싶다I want to save at least ten thousand won every month.**3** […쯤] by. e.g. 반만 줄이다 reduce by half.

만감 [मानगाम] [萬感] a flood [crowd] of emotions. e.g. 만감이 북받쳐 가슴을 메웠다 A thousand emotions crowded in on my mind.

만기 [मान्गी] [滿期] expiration <of a term>; expiry <of a contract>;(어음의) maturity (略 mat.). e.g. 계약이 만기가 되었다The contract has expired.

만끽 [मानक्कि] [滿喫] 만끽하다 [마음껏 마시고 먹다] have [eat / drink] one's fill <of>; eat [drink] to one's heart's content; do ample justice to <the dinner>; [마음껏 즐기다] enjoy fully [to the full

만나다 [मान्नादा] **1** [얼굴을 대하게 되다] see; meet; [맞닥뜨리다] come across; run into; [면회하다] see; interview; have an interview <with>. e.g. 우연히 만나다come across / [재회하다] meet again by chance. **2** [일,때를 당하다] meet with <an accident>; encounter <the enemy>; come upon [across]; suffer <a calamity>; experience <hardship>; be confronted by <a crisis>. e.g. 재난을 만나다suffer [be visited by] a calamity / meet with a misfortune

만년필 [मान्यौनफिल] [萬年筆] a fountain pen; a self-feeding pen

만능 [मान्नुंग] [萬能] omnipotence; being almighty; having an all-round capability.

만두 [मान्दू] [饅頭] a steamed (bean-jam) bun; a bun; a dumpling.

만들다 [मान्दुल्दा] **1** [창조하다] make; create. e.g. 태초에 하느님이 천지를 만드시니라In the beginning God created (the) heaven and (the) earth. **2** [제작,제조하다] make; (기계 등을 사용하여 대규모로) manufacture; [급히 만들다] knock up. e.g. 잘[서투르게] 만든 물품a well-made [poorly-made] article / an article of fine [poor] make.

만들다 [मान्दुल्दा] […하게 하다] make [have / let] <a person do>; get [induce / cause / force] <a person to do>. e.g. 가게[믿게] 만들다 make <a person> go [believe <in

만료 [मान्र्यो] [滿了] expiration [expiry] <of a term>; termination <of office>. e.g. 계약 만료 the termination of an agreement.

만류 [मान्र्यु] [挽留] [붙들고 말림] .만류하다 [मान्र्युहादा] detain; keep [hold] back <a person from fighting>.

만만 [मानमान] [滿滿] 만만하다 be full of ambition / be highly ambitious. 자신 만만하다 be full of self-confidence.

만만하다 [मानमानहादा] **1** [다루기 쉽다] easily ; easy to deal with; tractable; docile. e.g. 만만한 사람 <美> an easy mark / <美> a pushover. **2** [대수롭지 않다] negligible; slight; insignificant; trivial; of little importance; of no account. e.g. 우리는 적이 만만찮다는 것을 알았다 We found in them no despicable foes.

만물 [मान्मुल] [萬物] all things (under the sun); [하느님의 창조물] all creation

만발 [मान्बाल] [滿發] full bloom.만발하다 be in full bloom [blossom / flower]; bloom all over [in pro-fusion].

만병 [मानब्योंग] [萬病] all (kinds of) diseases [maladies]. e.g. 감기는 만병의 원인A cold may lead to all kinds of diseases. / A cold may develop into all kinds of illness.

만사 [मान्सा] [萬事] everything (in the world / under the sun); all things [affairs

/ matters]; all(sorts of things). e.g. 만사 오케이 All's well. / Everything's O.K.

만성 [मान्सौंग] [慢性] [醫] chronicity; (being) chronic. e.g. 만성적 실업 chronic unemployment

만세 [मान्से] [萬歲] [외치는 소리] a hurrah; hurray; rah; cheers; cheering. e.g. 그들은 만세를 불렀다 [외쳤다] They hurrahed.

만수 무강 [मान्सु मुगांग] [萬壽無疆] a long life; longevity. e.g. 만수 무강을 빕니다 Long life to you!

만신 창이 [मान्शिन छांगी] [-瘡痍] being covered all over with wounds.

만약 [मान्याक] [萬若] = 만일

만연 [मान्यौन] [蔓延,蔓衍] spread; diffusion. e.g. 발진티푸스의 만연을 막다 prevent [check] the spread of typhus. 만연하다 [널리 퍼지다] grow thick (ly); spread; prevail; diffuse; be prevalent; be widespread

만우절 [मानुजौल] [萬愚節] All Fools' Day; April Fools' Day. e.g. 나는 만우절 놀림을 당했다 I was made an April fool. / I fell for an April Fools' Day joke.

만원 [मान्वॉन] [滿員] no vacancy; a full [capacity] house(극장의); congestion (교도소 등의) e.g. 열차는 초만원이었다 The train was crowded beyond capacity [jammed full].

만일 [मानिल] [萬一] [만약] if; in case <of> (… 의 경우에는); provided [supposing] (that)(조건) by any chance (만에 하나라도). e.g. 만일 비가 오면if [in case] it rains / in case of rain.

만장 일치 [मान्जांग इल्छी] [滿場一致] unanimity (of the whole assembly). e.g. 의안은 만장 일치로 통과되었다 The bill was passed unanimously [without dissent].

만점 [मान्जौम] [滿點] 1 [최고점,무감점] full marks; a perfect score. e.g. 역사에서 만점을 받다get a perfect score in history / gain [win] full marks in history. 2 [만족할 만한 정도]. e.g. 그녀의 요리는 만점에서 아주 거리가 멀다 Her cooking is far from satisfactory [ideal].

만조 [मानजो] [滿潮] a high [full] tide; high water.

만족 [मानजोक] [滿足] [흡족함] satisfaction; contentment; gratification (욕망의) complacency; complacence. 만족하다 satisfactory; gratifying; <서술적> be satisfied <with>; be gratified <with / by>; be contented [content] <with>; content oneself

<with>; find satisfaction [contentment] <in>.

만지다 [मान्जीदा] touch; feel; feel of; handle; (흐트러진 머리를) comb [smooth] down; dress; [가지고 놀다] play with; (손가락으로) finger.

만천하 [मान्छौनहा] [**滿天下**] the whole world.

만취 [मान्छ्वी] [**滿醉**] dead drunkenness. 만취하다 get dead [beastly / blind] drunk; be fuddled [muddled] with drink; get tanked up.

만큼 [मान्ख्वम] [정도를 나타내는 의존명사] an extent; a degree; a measure. e.g. 어느 만큼 to what extent [degree] / how far (거리) / how long (시간)

-만하다 [मान्हादा] **1** [같은 정도이다] be to the extent of; be as much [little / many / big / small / high / tall / large / deep / thick] as; be the size of. e.g. 그만한 것은 나도 알고 있다I know as much. **2** […보다 더하지 않다] be not more (than). e.g. 그의 병세는 그저 그만하다His condition is getting neither better nor worse.

만하다 [मान्हादा] **1** [가치가 있다] be worth; be worthy of; deserve (of); merit; claim; be entitled to. e.g. 볼 만한 것 a sight / a spectacle / an attraction / highlight. **2** [가능하다] be likely <to do>; be probable; be in all likelyhood [probability]; [적절하다] be fit <for service>; be fitted <to>; be suited <to>; be suitable <for one's purpose>; [족하다] be sufficient <to do>; be enough <to>. e.g. 쓸 만하다 be fit for use / can be used.

만행 [मान्हैंग] [**蠻行**] barbarity; savagery; brutality; cruelty; an atrocity; a savage deed; an outrage. e.g. 만행을 저지르다 commit an act of brutality.

만화 [मान्ह्वा] [**漫畵**] comics; [풍자,시사 만화 등] a cartoon; [풍자적인 희화] a caricature; [이야기를 그림과 문장으로 엮은 극화] story comics.

만회 [मान्ह्वे] [**挽回**] retrieval; recovery; restoration; revival. 만회하다 retrieve <one's fortune / credit>; restore [redeem] <one's honor>; recover <one's good reputation>; revive <activity in the market>; regain. e.g. 세력을 만회하다 regain one's strength.

많다 [मान्था] (수가) many <things / persons>; many a <thing / person> (▷ 단수 취급); a good [great] many; a large number of

<things / persons> (▷ 복수 취급); lots of <things / persons>; (양이) much; plenty of; a good [great] deal of; a large quantity of; lots of

많이 **[मानी]** [다수] in large [great] numbers; aplenty; plentifully; in plenty; amply; abundantly; in abundance; in profusion; in large quantities; in a large amount; in full measure.

맏 **[मात]** = 맏이

맏이 **[माजी]** the firstborn <son>; the eldest <child>. e.g. 맏이로 태어나다 be born first / be the eldest.

말 **[माल]** [末] **1** [끝,마지막] the end [close] <of>. e.g. 9월말에 at the end of September. 8 월말경에 귀성 합니다I'll go home in late August. **2** [야구] the second [lower / last] half; the bottom. e.g. 양키즈는 3회 말에 2점을 얻었다 The Yankees scored two runs in the bottom half of the third inning.

말 **[माल]** a horse

말 **[माल]** [언어] language; speech; [단어] a word; a term; <집합적> wordage; (두 단어 이상의) an expression; a phrase; (글로 쓴) a written word; parlance (어법); [표현] phraseology; diction; wording; an expression; [언어] a language; a tongue; [방언] a dialect; [진술] a statement; a remark; [언사] what one says; a remark; a statement; an observation; [담화] a talk; (a) conversation; a chat; [연설] a speech; an address.

말갛다 **[माल्गाथा]** clear; clean; limpid; pure. e.g. 말간 물 clear [crystal] water. 말갛게 하다 clear / make clear / clarify.

말거리 **[माल्गौरी]** **1** ⇨ 말썽거리 e.g. 말거리를 일으키다 raise [make] trouble / cause trouble / lead to a dispute / raise [kick up] a dust / have a [get into] trouble <with>. **2** [화제] a subject <of talk>; a topic <of conversation>. e.g. 말거리가 동이 났다We have no more topics to talk about. / We have emptied the bag.

말고 **[माल्गो]** not ... but ...; instead of ...; except; but. e.g. 그 사람말고 그의 부인이 왔었다 It was his wife, not he, that came. 너말고 누가 그런 짓을 하겠느냐 Who would do such a thing but you? 그말고는 믿을 사람이 아무도 There is no one

말괄량이 **[माल्ग्वाल्लयांगी]** a hussy; a minx; a flapper; a hoyden; a tomboy; a tomboyish girl; a kitten; a romp; a romping [bouncing] girl; a giglet; a giglot; a filly; a shrew.

말굽 [माल्गुप] a horse's hoof; a horseshoe (편자)

말귀 [माल्ग्वी] [말뜻] the import [meaning] of the words; [알아듣는 총명] hearing; understanding; catching on; an ear <for words>. e.g. 말귀를 못 알아듣다can't make out what <a person> says.

말기 [माल्गी] [末期] the end; the close; the last period [years / days / stage]; the late stage (s). e.g. 말기 증상의 환자a terminal patient / a patient in the terminal stage.

말끔하다 [माल्कुमहादा] clean (ly); clear; neat and tidy; pretty; comely; fair; fine; graceful. e.g. 말끔한 집[방] a neat house [room].

말끝 [माल्कुथ] the end of words [speech]; concluding remarks; the ending [termination] of a word. e.g. 말끝을 흐리다 slur the end of one's words [sentence] / leave one's statement vague / give a vague answer.

말다 [माल्दा] [돌돌 감다] roll <paper>; roll <a thing> up <in paper>. e.g. 돛을 말다 furl [hoist] a sail.

말다 [माल्दा] (물이나 국에) put <boiled rice> into soup [water]; mix <food> with <soup / water>. e.g. 국에 밥을 말다 put rice into soup.

말다 [माल्दा] [그만두다] stop; cease; discontinue; break [leave / lay / call] off; give [throw] up; quit; abandon; cut off; desist from <doing>. e.g. 먹다 만 바나나 a half-eaten banana.

말다 [माल्दा] [금지] don't; keep [refrain] from <doing>. e.g. 잊지 마라 Don't forget. [필경] end up <doing>; finally do; get around to <doing>. e.g. 그는 술 때문에 죽고 말았다 Drink ended him

말다툼 [माल्दाथुम] [말싸움] a (verbal) quarrel; [논쟁] an argument; a dispute; a wordy conflict [battle]; a row; a wrangle; an altercation; bickering (s); (exchange of) high words; a brawl; a rhubarb; a fracas; a jangle.

말대꾸 [माल्दैकु] a retort; a back talk; <give> a back answer; answering [talking] back; contradiction; <美> a crack. 말대꾸하다 answer <a person> back; talk [speak] back <to a person>; contradict <a person>; retort; give <a person> a retort [back talk]; sass

말똥말똥 [माल्तोंगमाल्तोंग] e.g.

말똥말똥 얼굴을 쳐다보다 stare a person in the face / look [stare] hard at a person / gaze steadily at a person. 말똥말똥하다(잠이 안 와서) wakeful; wide-awake. e.g. 시계가 두 시를 쳤는데 눈은 더욱 말똥말똥했다 he clock struck two, and my wakefulness increased.

말뚝 **[माल्तुक]** a stake; a post; a pile; a picket (울타리 등의)

말라깽이 **[माल्लाकैंगी]** a skinny [very lean / scrawny] person; a (living) skeleton; a bag of bones.

말랑말랑하다 **[माल्लांगमल्लांगहादा]** soth; spongy; tender plastic; squashy (과일 등이 너무 익어서); e.g. 말랑말랑한 군고구마nice and soth sweet potatoes <hot from the oven>.

말려들다 **[माल्यौदुल्दा]** [연루되다] be implicated in; be involved [entangled] in; get mixed up in; be concerned with. e.g. 싸움에 말려들다 get entangled in [be dragged into] a quarrel.

말리다 **[माल्लिदा]** [만류하다] <try to> stop [keep / prevent / dissuade] <a person from doing something>; <try to> persuade <a person not to do from> cutting the forest trees.

말리다 **[माल्लिदा]** [마르게 하다] dry; make [let] dry; weather; (식물을) let die; (목재를) season; (우물, 재원 등을) exhaust; draw off <water>; drain off [away]; air(빨래를)

말막음 **[माल्मागुम]** [입막음] hushing [shutting] up; avoiding [forestalling] <another's> words. e.g. 나는 그에게 말막음으로 만 원을 줬다I paid [gave] him 10,000 won hush money. / I bought his silence for 10,000 won.

말머리 **[माल्मौरी]** **1** [말의 첫머리] the beginning of one's speech [talk]; introductory remarks; opening words; one's first few words. **2** [말의 방향] the subject of one's speech. e.g. 말머리를 돌리다 change the [one's] subject / change the topic [subject] of conversation / shith the conversation.

말문[－ 門] **[माल्मुन]** one's mouth when speaking. e.g. 말문이 막히다 be at a loss for words / not know what to say [answer] / be dumbfounded / be struck dumb <with surprise> / be speechless / be agape <with wonder>..

말미 **[माल्मी]** [末尾] the end; the close; the tip. e.g. 말미의 last / final.

말미암다 **[माल्मीहाम्दा]** come

from; arise from; be derived from; be owing to; be due to; be caused by; be in consequence of. e.g. 말미암아 owing to / because of / in consequence of / due to / in accordance with.

말버릇 [माल्बौरूत] one's manner of speaking; one's way of talking. e.g. 야비한 말버릇 a mean [low] expression. 말버릇이 나쁜 다 have a foul tongue / be rude in speech [address]. 말버릇 좀 고쳐 봐라 Mind your speech! 무슨 말버릇이 그러냐 How dare you talk to me like that? / <반어적> That's nice way to speak

말벗 [माल्बौत] a conversational partner; a friend to talk with; a companion to chat with

말살 [माल्साल] [抹殺] 있는 것을 아주 없앰 liquidation; annihilation. 말살하다 kill; get rid of; liquidate; annihilate.

말상대 [मालसांग्दै] [-相對] a companion; a conversational partner; someone to talk to; [상담 상대] an adviser; a consultant. e.g. 나는 말상대 가 없다 [있으면 한다] I have no one [want someone] to talk to.

말세 [माल्से] [末世] the end of the world; [타락한 세상] a degenerate [corrupt] age; these latter days; the hopeless world; [최후의 심판일] the doomsday; the judgment day.

말소 [माल्सो] [抹消] erasure; effacement; cancel; obliteration; blot; writing-off. 말소하다 erase; efface; cancel; obliterate; blot out; strike [cross] out [off]; write off. e.g. 소송을 말소하다 withdraw a suit.

말소리 [माल्सोरी] a voice; (속삭임) a whisper; a murmur. e.g. 옆방에서 사람들의 말소리가 들렸다I heard several voices talking in the next room.

말솜씨 [माल्सोम्शी] one's way of speaking; eloquence

말수 [माल्सू] [-數] the number of words one speaks; words; speech. e.g. 말수가 적은 사람 a taciturn [reticent] person / a man of few words.

말실수 [माल्शिल्सू] [-失手] a tongueslip; a slip of the tongue; a slip [mistake] in speaking; a verbal lapse; an impropriety in speech. 말실수하다 make slip [lapse] of the tongue; make a slip [mistake] in speaking; use improper language [words]; commit an impropriety in speech; one's tongue slips.

말썽 [माल्सौंग] trouble; difficulties; complaint; criticism; a dispute (분쟁) complication

(분규).

말썽꾸러기 [माल्सौंकुरौगी] = 말썽꾼

말쑥하다 [माल्सुकहादा] clean; neat; smart; tidy; neat and clean; trim. e.g. 옷차림이 말쑥한 사람 a neatly-dressed person.

말씀 [माल्सुम] words; speech; talk; saying; language. 말씀하다 e.g. 도와 드릴 수 있는 일이 있으면 말씀해 주십시오 If there is anything I can do (for you), just let me know.

말씨 [माल्सी] **1** [말하는 버릇,태도] one's way [manner] of speaking; use of words; (표현) wording; expression; diction; grammar (문법) **2** [말에 나타나는 어조] a dialect; a brogue; an accent. e.g. 약간 서울 말씨로 말하다 speak with a trace of the Seoul accent.

말없이 [मारौप्शी] [조용히] in silence; silently; dumbly; without saying anything; without a word [comment]; [이의 없이] without objection; without question; [말썽 없이] without causing any trouble; without ado; [무단으로] without leave [permission]; without notice

말엽 [मार्यौप] [末葉] the end; the close; the last [closing] days <of the Chosòn>. e.g. 19세기 말엽 toward (s) the end [close] of the 19th century.

말일 [मारिल] [末日] the last day; the end. e.g. 4월 말일 the end [last day] of April.

말재주 [माल्जैजू] [-才-] a talent for words [language]; eloquence; the gith of (the) gab. e.g. 그는 말재주는 있지만 듣는 재주는 없다 He is a good talker, but a poor hearer.

말조심 [माल्जोशिम] [-操心] care in speaking. 말조심하다 be careful in one's speech [of one's language].

말주변 [माल्जूब्यौन] talking ability; tact in speech; oratorical skill [talent]; the gith of gab. e.g. 말주변이 좋은 (능변의) eloquent / (유창한) fluent / (수다스러운) talkative / (입심 좋은) glib / (말이 많은) voluble.

말짱하다 [माल्चांगहादा] **1** [흠 없다] flawless; faultless; spotless; sound; free from blemish [damage]; perfect; [온전하다] whole; complete; intact; [깨끗하다] clean; tidy; neat. e.g. 말짱한 옷 spotless [clean] clothes. **2** [(정신이) 또렷하다] <서술 적> be in one's senses; be in one's right mind; (술취 하지 않고) be dead [cold] sober; be not drunk. e.g. 말짱한 때에 in one's sober times / when (one is) not drunk

말참견 [माल्छामैन] [-參見] [남의 말에 끼어 드는 일] interference; meddling; officiousness; meddlesomeness; [끼어 들어 하는 말] an impertinent remark [comment]; gratuitous advice 말참견하다 interfere; intervene in; meddle in [with]; put in a word; make an uncalled-for remark; break [cut / butt] in; make comment <on>; put [shove] in one's oar; poke [thrust] one's nose.

말치레 [माल्छीरे] a compliment; flattery; using fair [fine / pretty / honeyed] words; making a specious remark. 말치레하다 pay compliment; flatter; use fair [fine / pretty / honeyed] words; say nice [pretty] things; make a specious remark.

말캉말캉 [माल्खांगमाल्खांग] ⇨ 물컹물컹

말투 [माल्थू] [-套] one's way [manner] of talking [speaking]; delivery; turn of words.

말하다 [माल्हादा] [말을 꺼내다] say; speak; talk [이야기 하다] tell

말하자면 [माल्हाजाम्यौन] [… 으로[하게] 말하면] if we are to speak <about>; if we must say; speaking [talking] of ...; it reminds me ...; [이를테면] so to speak [say]; so to call it; as it were; in a manner (of speaking); in a way [sense / kind / sort]; as one might put it; in a word (한마디로 말해) say.

맑다 [माक्ता] **1** (물,소리 등이) clear; clean; limpid; pure; transparent; fresh; crystal; lucid. e.g. 맑은 공기fresh [limpid] air. **2** (날씨가) fine; clear; fair. e.g. 맑은 날씨 fine [fair] weather. **3** (마음,기분 등이) clear; fresh; pure; refreshing. e.g. 머리가 맑아지다 have a clear head. [맑게 하다] make clear [clean]; purify; clean; clarify; settle; cause to be-come clear; cleanse. e.g. 물을 맑히다[] clear the water. 정신을 맑히다 refresh one's mind / make one's mind fresh.

맘 [माम] ⇨ 마음

맘껏 [माम्कौत] ⇨ 마음껏

맙소사 [माप्सोसा] Oh, no!; Good God [Lord / me]!; Good gracious [heavens]!; Gracious Heaven [goodness]!; Gracious!; Goodness!; Save us!; My eye(s)!

맛 [मात] **1** (음식의) taste; flavor; savor. e.g. 매운 맛 a hot [biting / spicy] taste. **2** [묘미] relish; taste; zest; gusto; aroma; charm. e.g. 그녀는 글 맛을 알고 있다 She has a relish for [appreciate] literature. **3** [경험] experience; (a practical) knowledge; a taste. e.g. 나는 빚진 고통의 맛을 알고 있다I know what it is (like) to be in debt. **4** [혼나기] e.g. 어디 맛좀 봐라 Wait and see. / See what I will do. / You shall have your due in time. / You will haveE to pay for this. (어디 두고 보자).

맛깔스럽다 [मात्कालसुरौप्ता] [입에 맞다] agreeable [pleasing] to the taste; pleasant-tasting; palatable; toothsome; suit [be to] one's taste [palate]; be nice to the palate. e.g. 맛깔스러운 음식 [맛] an agreeable food [taste].

맛나다 [मान्नादा] [맛있다] tasty; delicious; sweet; savory; palatable; [맛이 돌다] taste good [nice]; have a good flavor <of>.

맛들이다 [मात्तरीदा] 1 [맛이 들게 하다] season [flavor] with; give [impart] a flavor; add seasoning to; make <something> ripe [mature] enough to. e.g. 소금으로 맛들이다 season with salt / give a salty taste / **2** [재미를 붙이다] get [acquire] a taste <for>; take a liking for [to] ...; be interested <in>; find pleasure <in>. e.g. 돈에 맛들이다 get a taste for money.

맛보다 [मात्पोदा] 1 [시식하다] taste; get [have] a taste of; sample; try (the flavor of); foretaste; degust. e.g. 간을 맛보다 taste <a dish> to see how it is seasoned with salt. **2** [경험하다] taste; know; experience; go through; undergo; learn. e.g. 슬픔의 쓴 잔을 맛보다drain [drink] the cup of sorrow to the bottom

맛없다 [मात औप्ता] (음식이) tasteless; unsavory; unpalatable; untasty; ill-tasting; flavorless; insipid; flat; <서술적> taste bad.

맛있다 [मातइत्ता] (음식이) tasty; delicious; palatable; dainty; savory; sweet; nice; flavorous.

-망 [मांग] [**網**] [조직] a network. e.g. 법망 the net [grip / clutches / toils / meshes] of the law / justice.

망 [मांग] [**網**] [그물] a net; <집합적> netting.

망 [望] [मांग] [동정을 살핌] watch; lookout; observation; vigilance; guard; surveillance; vigil. e.g. 망을 세우다 set [post] a lookout <for> / place a guard <at the door> / keep guard <over the house>.

망가뜨리다 [मांगातुरीदा] [부수다] break (down); destroy; demolish; [손상하다] injure; damage; ruin; spoil; wreck; [고장 내다] put [get]

<a watch> out of order; [망치다] upset; frustrate <one's designs [scheme]>; [찌그러뜨리다] crush; smash. e.g. 모자를 망가뜨리다 smash [squash] a hat.

망가지다 [मांगाजीदा] [부서지다] break; be broken; be wrecked; be demolished; be ruined; fall to ruin; [파손되다] be damaged / be destroyed / break [come] down; [고장나다] get out of order; [찌그러지다] be crushed; be smashed. e.g. 망가진 우산 a broken umbrella.

망각 [मांगाक] [忘却] lapse of memory; oblivion; forgetfulness; obliteration. 망각하다 forget; be forgetful [oblivious] of; consign <something> to oblivion [limbo].

망나니 [मांग्नानी] [못된 사람] [मोतदवैन सारम]a rough-and-tumble man; a hard-boiled egg; a rascal; a rough; a rowdy. e.g. 망나니 짓을 하다 play the gangster.

망년회 [मांग्न्यौन्ह्वे] [忘年會] a year-end (dinner) party [social gathering]. e.g. 망년회를열다 give a year-end party / celebrate the outgoing year.

망라 [मांग्ना] [網羅] 망라하다 [모든 것을 포함하다 include [comprehend / contain] all ...; [남김없이 모으다] collect all .... e.g. 모든 것을 망라한comprehensive / all-inclusive / exhaustive

망명 [मांग्म्यौग] [亡命] flight from one's own country; exile. 망명하다 flee from one's own country <for political reasons>; exile oneself; seek [take] refuge <in a foreign country>.

망보다 [मांग्बोदा] [望-] keep watch <for / against / on>; be on the watch [lookout] <for>; watch; keep an eye on; picket.

망상 [मांग्सांग] [妄想] a fancy; a wild [vagrant] fancy; a fantasy; a fantastic idea; an impossible idea; a delusion

망설이다 [मांग्सौरीदा] hesitate; waver; hang [hold] back; vacillate; shilly-shally; think twice <about>; jib[balk] at; be irresolute.

망신 [मांगशिन] [亡身] shame; disgrace; dishonor; infamy; ignominy; humiliation; loss of reputation. e.g. 그는 우리 집안의 망신감이다 He is a disgrace [dishonor] to our family. / He is a blot on our family name.

망아지 [मांगाजी] [작은 말] a pony; [말새끼] a colt (수컷) a filly (암컷); a foal (통성).

망언 [मांगौन] [妄言] a reckless remark; thoughtless words; a slip of tongue; a blunder; [못된 말] abusive language.

망언하다 make reckless [thoughtless] remarks; use abusive language.

망연 자실 [मांग्यौन जाशिल] [茫然自失] abstraction; stupefaction; entrancement.

망연 자실하다 <서술적> be stupefied [abstracted] <with grief>; be dazed [stunned] <by the news>; be distrait; be at one's wit's end; feel all at sea. e.g. 아버지가 돌아가셨다는 소식을 듣고 그녀는 망연 자실했다 She was stunned by the news of her father's death.

망원경 [मांगवौन्ग्यौग] [望遠鏡] a telescope; a spyglass (소형의); [쌍안경] a binocular; field glasses.

망측 [मान्छुक] [罔測] 망측하다 [불쾌하다] offensive; disgusting; [상스럽다] low; abominable; mean; lascivious; indecent <talk>; [추잡하다] nasty; vicious; [꼴사납다] ugly; bad-looking; unsightly; shabby

망치 [मान्छी] a hammer (쇠망치) a mallet (나무 망치) 큰 망치) a maul; a sledge (hammer) (대장간의); (의장이나 경매인의) a gavel.

망치다 [मान्छीदा] [亡-] spoil; mar; ruin; destroy; damage; work [play] havoc with; make a mess [muddle] <of>. e.g. 계획을 망치다[frustrate [upset] a plan / throw a wet blanket over a project.

망하다 [मांगहादा] [亡-] [멸망하다] perish; cease to exist; die out; meet with destruction; [영락하다] be ruined; go [come] to ruin; go to the bad [the dogs / the devil]; [파산하다] go [become] bankrupt.

맞고소 [माक्कोसो] [-告訴] a cross action; a counteraction; a counterclaim; a counter-suit. 맞고소하다 counterclaim <against a person for a matter>; plead a counter-claim; bring a cross action <against a person for a matter>.

맞다[1] [मात्ता] **1** [영접하다] meet; go (out) to meet; receive; greet. e.g. 반가이 맞다 welcome / make <a person> welcome / receive <a person> with delight. **2** [받아들이다] invite; engage. e.g. 아내를 맞다 take a wife / get married. **3** (어떤 때를). e.g. 새해를 맞다greet [hail] the New Year. **4** (비, 바람 등을) be exposed to; expose oneself to. e.g. 비를 맞다 be exposed to rain / be caught in a rain. **5** [어떤 일을 당하다] meet with; encounter <a difficulty>; come upon [across]; suffer. e.g. 도둑을 맞다 (사람이) have <a thing> stolen / be relieved [robbed] of <one's

purse> / (물건이) be stolen. **6** (매, 총 등을) get a blow; be struck; be beaten; be knocked; be lashed; be whipped;(총에) be shot. e.g. 뺨을 맞다be boxed on the ears / be slapped across the face. **7** (주사를) get [have] <an injection>; take <a needle>; (도장, 검인을) receive <a seal [a stamp] of approval>. e.g. 팔에 모르핀 주사를 맞다 get [have] a morphine shot in [on] the arm. **8** (점수를) get; receive; gain; take. e.g. 90점을 맞다 get a 90 percent rating.

맞다[2] **[मात्ता]** **1** [옳다] be right; be correct; (시계가) keep good time; (계산, 장부가) balance. e.g. 맞는 답a correct [right] answer. **2** [적합하다] suit <one's taste>; answer [serve] <the purpose>; meet <one's wishes>; come <measure> up to <one's expectations>; befit. e.g. 입에 맞는[맞지 않는] 음식 an agreeable[a disagreeable] food **3** [일치하다] agree <with>; accord <with>; be in accord <with>; be consistent <with>; conform <to>; [부합하다] coincide <with>; correspond <with>; tally <with>; square <with>; be in concordance <with>. e.g. 사실과 맞지 않다 conflict with the facts. **4** (몸 등에) fit; suit; be suited <to>; (뚜껑 등이) fit on. e.g. 몸에 잘 맞는 양복 a well-fitting suit.

맞닥뜨리다 [मात्ताक्तुरीदा] meet (with); meet up with; encounter <the enemy>; come across; face; be confronted by [with]. e.g. 딱 맞닥뜨리다 come face to face with.

맞닥치다 [मात्ताक्छीदा] face (up to); confront; be confronted with [by]; be faced with; come face to face with. e.g. 위험에 맞닥쳐서 in (the) face of danger.

맞닿다 [मात्ताथा] come in touch [contact] <with>; touch each other. e.g. 땅과 하늘이 맞닿은 지평선 the horizon where the earth and(the) sky seem to meet

맞대다 [मात्तेदा] **1** [마주 대다] bring [put] <them> into contact (with each other); [마주 대하다] face <with>. e.g. 과 얼굴을 맞대다 come [be] face to face with **2** [대면시키다] bring <one person> face to face with <another>; bring <two persons> together; confront <a person> with <another>. e.g. 살 사람과 팔 사람을 맞대다 bring parties to a sale together.

맞들다 [मात्तुल्दा] **1** [마주 들다] lith (up) together; hold up together. e.g. 책상을 맞들다 lith a desk together. 백지장도 맞들면 낫다 Two heads are better than one. **2** [힘을 합하다] cooperate; unite [join] efforts; join forces <with>. e.g. 일을 서로 맞들어 하다 cooperate [help one another] in doing a job.

맞먹다 [**माम्मोक्ता**] **1** [상당하다] be equal [equivalent] to; be worth; be worthy of. e.g. 석달치의 봉급에 맞먹는 보너스a bonus equivalent to three month's pay. **2** [필적하다] be a match for; match; be as good as; be equal to; rival; stand comparison with. e.g. 맞먹을 자가 없다 have no equal [match / parallel] / be without a match [peer] / be unrivaled / be peerless.

맞물리다 [**माम्मुलिदा**] go [be] in gear <with>. e.g. 맞물려 있다[있지 않다] be in [out of] gear.

맞바꾸다 [**माप्पाकुदा**] barter <A for B>; exchange <one thing for another>; trade; truck. e.g. 시계와 카메라를 맞바꾸다 exchange a watch for a camera.

맞바람 [**माप्पाराम**] a head wind; a contrary [an adverse / a foul] wind. e.g. 배가 맞바람을 받아 잘 가지 못한다 The ship is held back by a head wind.

맞받다 [**माप्पात्ता**] **1** (정면으로) receive [face] head-on [directly]. e.g. 햇빛을 맞받다 receive the sunlight directly. **2** [들이받다] crash head-on <into>; collide head-on <with>. e.g. 이마를 맞받다 bump [knock] heads together / bang heads with each other / bump against [into] each other. **3** [응수하다] give [pay] <a person> tit for tat; make a retort. e.g. 상대방의 악담에 그도 지지 않고 맞받아 주었다Undaunted by his opponent's abuse, he retorted as sharply.

맞벌이 [**माप्पौरी**] working together (for a living); working in double harness; the joint bread-winning <of husband and wife>. 맞벌이하다 work together for a living; earn a livelihood together; work [run] in double harness.

맞부딪치다 [**माप्पुछिदा**] run [bump / hit / dash] against; run [crash] into; collide with. e.g. 머리를 맞부딪치다 bump each other's head.

맞붙다 [**माप्पुत्ता**] **1** (한데) stick [cling] together. e.g. 그 두 점포는 서로 맞붙어 있다 The two shops stand close to each other. **2** [격투하다] wrestle [grapple / close] with; be matched against. e.g. 그는 도둑과 맞붙었다 He grappled with the burglar.

맞붙이다 [मापुछ्दिा] **1** (물건을) stick [plaster / glue / fix] <things> together. e.g. 고무 풀로 종이 두 장을 맞붙이다 stick [put] two sheets of paper together with gum. **2** (사람을) bring <them> together [into contact]; (경기 등에서) match one competitor with [against] another; pit one against another. e.g. 저 두 사람을 맞붙이면 누가 이길까 If those two were set against each other, which (do you think) would win?

맞상대 [मात्सांग्दै] [-相對] a man-to-man fight; a single (-handed) combat [fight]; a straight fight.

맞서다 [मात्सौदा] **1** [마주 서다] stand face to face <with>; face each other; be opposite <to>; confront. **2** [대항하다] stand against [up to]; rise against <one's lord>; oppose; turn against [upon]; defy; [필적하다] be a match for; stand comparison with. e.g. 어른에게 맞서다 defy one's elders [superiors] / turn upon one's elders.

맞선 [मात्सौन] a (formal) meeting with a view to marriage; a marriage meeting.

맞아들이다 [माजादुरीदा] receive; invite [ask] <a person> in; show [usher] <a person> into <a house>. e.g. 아내를 맞아들이다 take a wife.

맞아떨어지다 [माजातौरौजीदा] tally; be correct. e.g. 계산이 맞아떨어지다 a calculation is correct / the figures tally. 내 계산은 네 계산과 맞아떨어진 My figures tally [check] with yours.

맞은편 [माजनफ्यौन] [-便] [상대편] the opposite [other] party; one' opponent jopposite [over the way / across the street].

맞이 [माजी] meeting; greeting; welcoming; reception. 맞이하다 [영접하다] meet; go(out) to meet; [접대하다] receive; play host to; [환영하다] welcome; make <a person> welcome; greet; hail; [맞아들이다] invite; engage; (때를) meet; face; be confronted <by>; [즈음하다] be on the eve of <a general election>.

맞장구 [माच्वांगू] [남의 말에 동조함] e.g. 맞장구(를) 치다 give responses that make a conversation go smoothly / echo <another's words> / make agreeable responses / chime in <with others>; flatter [ingratiate oneself with] a person.

맞추다 [मात्छूदा] **1** [대조하다] compare <with>; check <with>; collate <with>; verify; tally <with>. e.g. 원장과 맞추다 compare with [refer to] the ledger. **2** [조립하다] assemble; fix up; put [fit / piece] together. e.g. 시계를 분해했다가 다시 맞추다 reassemble [overhaul] a watch. **3** [맞게 하다] set [fit / adjust / adapt / conform / square / gear] <one thing to another>; tune <someth-ing to the purpose>; bring <a thing> into line <with another>. e.g. 피아노[테이프에 녹음된] 반주에 맞추어 노래하다 sing to piano [taped] accompany-ment.

맞춤 [**मात्छूम**] [주문] an order; [주문품] an article ordered; a thing made to order; an order.

맞춤법 [**मात्छूमबौम**] orthography; the rules of spelling; ortho-graphical rules.

맞히다 [**माच्छिदा**] **1** (목표에) hit <the mark>. e.g. 잘 맞히다 make a good hit. **2** [물음에 옳은 답을 하다] guess right; make a good guess [hit]; hit the truth; hit the nail on the head. e.g. 답을 맞히다 answer right / give a right [correct] answer **3** (비, 바람 등을) expose <to>; subject <to>. e.g. 비[바람]를 맞히다 expose to [leave out in] the rain [air]. 비를 맞히지 않도록 하다 protect [keep] <a thing> from the rain.

맡기다 [**माक्कीदा**] **1** [보관시키다] entrust [trust] <a person with a thing / a thing to a person>; deposit [leave] <a thing with a person [in a bank]>; place [leave] <a thing> in <a person's> charge [hands]; put <a thing> in charge of <a person>; leave [check] <a thing> with <a person>; give <a thing> into <a person's> keeping [custody]. e.g. 돈을 맡기다 entrust a person with one's money / trust one's money to a person. **2** [위임하다] assign; entrust <a matter> to <a person>; entrust <a person> with <a task>; leave <a matter> (up) to <a person>; leave <a person> with <a matter>; trust <a person> with <something>; commit [leave] <something> to <a person's> care; delegate <a task> to <a person>. e.g. 임무를 맡기다 [ईम्मूरल म्खीदा] charge <a person> with a duty / assign <a person> to a task [job] / place a duty upon <a person **3** (사람을) put <a child> with <a person>; leave <a child> in the care of <a person>; place <a child> under <a person's> care; give <a person> charge of <a child>. e.g. 환자를

의사에게 맡기다 leave a patient to the doctor's care.

맡다[1] **[मात्था]** **1** [보관하다] keep; receive <a thing> in trust [custody]; take charge of <a thing>; take <a thing> in charge; take <a thing> under one's charge; have the custody of <a thing>; be entrusted with <a thing>; take over. e.g. 출발 2시간 전까지 이 항공표를 맡아 두겠습니다 We will hold the ticket until two hours before flight time. **2** [책임지다, 담당[감독] 하다] undertake; take on; take [have] charge of; be in charge of <a class>; take in hand; take <it> upon oneself <to do>; charge oneself <with the work>; have <a boy> under one's charge [care]; assume the care of <children>; take <a person> in charge. e.g. 그 사무를 맡은 사람 a man in charge of the business. **3** [허가 등을 받다] get; obtain; receive; be given; have; take out <a license>. e.g. 허가를 맡다 obtain [be granted] permission / get a permit.

맡다[2] **[मात्ता]** **1** [냄새를 느끼다] smell; scent; (개 등이) sniff. e.g. 냄새 잘 맡는 사람a person sensitive to odor / a person of sensitive nostril. **2** [낌새를 알다] scent; get wind of; smell a rat; smell out <a secret>; detect a secret; get wise; smoke out. e.g. 계략의 낌새를 맡다

매[1] **[मै]** (막대 끝에 가죽끈, 노끈을 매단) a whip; (가죽으로 된) a lash; (막대 모양의) a rod; (교사용의) a pointer. 매를 때리다 lash / flog / whip / swish / cane / switch <a boy with a cane> / tan / give <a person> the rod [a caning / a thrashing]. 매를 맞다 be whipped / be lashed / be caned / get the cane / be flogged.

매[2] **[मै]** [鳥] a hawk;a falcon.

매[3] **[मै]-** [**每**] every; each; apiece. e.g. 매분 per minute.

매각 **[मैगाक]** [**賣**] sale; disposal (by sale). 매각하다 sell (off); dispose of (by sale). e.g. 그는 집을 매각했다 He sold his house.

매개 **[मैगै]** [**媒介**] intermediation; intervention; mediation; agency; mediacy. 하다 (inter) mediate [intervene] <between two parties>; act as (an) intermediary; serve as a medium; [전파하다] carry <germs>. e.g.

모기는 종종 전염병을 매개한다 The mosquito is othen a carrier [vehicle] of infectious disease.

매관 매직 [मैग्वान मैजिक] [賣官賣職] corruption in the government personnel administration; trafficking of official posts; [엽관 제도] spoils system. 매관 매직하다 traffic in government positions; practice payoff deals for appointive offices.

매국 [मैगुक] [賣國] selling one's country; betrayal of [treachery to] one's country. 매국하다 sell [betray] one's country; be treacherous to one's country

매기다 [मैगिदा] [정하다] decide; set; put; fix. e.g. 값을 매기다 price / mark the price on <an article> / set [put] a price on <an article>.

매끄럽다 [मैक्रोप्ता] [반드럽다] smooth; sleE; velvety; glassy; [미끄럽다] slippery; greasy; lenis; 매끄럽게[smoothly / [막힘없이] without a hitch.

매너 [मैनौ] manners

매너리즘 [मैनौरीजुम] a mannerism. e.g. 매너리즘에 빠지다become stereotyped / fall into mannerism.

매년 [मैन्यौन] [每年] every year; yearly; annually; per year.

매니저 [मैनिजौ] a manager; (프로 복싱 등의) a handler; (흥행의) an impresario; a proprietor.

매니큐어 (a) [मैनिक्युऔ] manicure

매다[1] [मैदा] [동여 묶다] tie (up); fasten (together); bind; lash; lace; [매듭을 짓다] make [tie] a knot; (높은 곳에) hang oneself <on a tree / down from a tree branch>. e.g. 단단히 매다tie securely [hard] / tie [bind / make] fast.

매다[2] [मैदा] [풀을 뽑다] weed (out). e.g. 김을 매다 sweep off weeds / weed out.

매달 [मैदाल] [每-] every [each] month; monthly.

매달다 [मैदाल्दा] [달아매다] hang (up); suspend; swing; sling; dangle

매달리다 [मैदाल्लिदा] **1** [늘어지다] hang down <from>; be hung (down); be suspended <from>; dangle; swing. e.g. 공중에 매달리다 hang in the air [midair]. **2** [달라붙다] hold on to; stick(fast) to; adhere to; cling to. e.g. TV. 밤새도록 나는 그 보고서에 매달려 있었다I devoted myself to the report throughout the night. **3** [의지하다] depend [rely / lean] on [upon]; place [put] dependence on; place [put] reliance on

[in]. e.g. 아들에게 매달리다 depend upon one's son for support / lean on one's son. **4** [애원하다] appeal to; entreat [implore] <a person to do>. e.g. 남의 자비심에 매달리다 throw oneself on a person's charity / appeal to a person for mercy.

매도 [मैदो] [**罵倒**] denunciation; condemnation; scathing [severe] criticism; abuse; raillery. 매도하다 denounce; condemn; abuse; decry; criticize severely; hurl abuse <at>; rail <at>; cry down; call <a person> hard names.

매듭 [मैदुप] **1** (끈의) a knot <in a rope>; a tie; a bend. **2** [일의 해결] a settlement; [결말] a conclusion; an end; [합의] an agreement.

매듭짓다 [मैदुप्चीदा] **1** (끈 등을) knot; make [tie] a knot. **2** [결말짓다] settle; fix (up); finish; conclude; bring <a matter> to an end [a conclusion]; put an end to; be through with; close up <one's affairs>. e.g. 매듭지어지다[결말이나다 be settled [fixed] / be concluded / be finished / be completed / be brought to completion / [타협되다] reach [arrive at / come to] an agreement / be brought to an agreement / be arranged.

매력 [मैर्यौक] [**魅力**] (a) charm; a bewitching [spellbinding] power; (a) fascination; glamo(u)r; attractiveness; (an) appeal; an allure; a lure. e.g. 매력이 있는 [매력적인] charming / fascinat-ing / attractive / appealing.

매료 [मैर्यो] [**魅了**] 매료하다 charm; fascinate; captivate; cast a spell <on>; hold <the audience> spellbound. e.g. 그는 경치의 아름다움에 매료되었다He was fascinated [captivated] by the scenic beauty of the spot

매립 [मैरिप] [**埋立**] (land) reclamation; filling-up. 매립하다 fill in <a moat>; fill up <a pond with earth>; reclaim [gain] <land from the sea>; recover. e.g. 그들은 바다를 매립하여 공업 지대로 만들었다hey reclaimed land from the sea and made it into an industrial area.

매만지다 [मैमान्जिदा] adjust <one's dress>; tidy [do] up; tend; trim; groom; care for. e.g. 머리를 매만지다 fix [arrange] one's hair / smooth one's hair down / give a smooth to the hair.

매매 [मैमै] [**賣買**] buying and [or] selling; purchase and [or] sale; [거래] trade; dealing; transaction; a bargain; traffic <in furs, in

narcotics, etc.>; a deal cancel a contract [deal]. 증권거래소에서는 약 20만주의 매매가 있었다 About 200,000 shares changed hands on the Ex

매매 계약 [मैमै गैयाक] [賣買契約] a sales contract; a bargain. e.g. 매매 계약을 한 주권 engagements / stocks bought [sold]. 매매 계약을 맺다 make a contract <with> / conclude a sale.

매몰 [मैमूल] [埋沒] burying. 매몰하다 bury <in / under>. e.g. 산사태로 집이 매몰되었다 The house was buried under the landslide.

매몰차다 [मैमूलछौदा] very cold; very unkind; hard; harsh; heartless; merciless. e.g. 그런 짓을 하다니 그도 매몰차구나 It is cruel of him to do such a thing.

매물 [मैमूल] [賣物] an article for [on] sale; offerings.

매번 [मैबौन] [每番] every time; very othen e.g. 그는 매번 똑같은 말을 한다 He says the same thing every time.

매사 [मैसा] [每事] [일] each [every] affair [matter]; [사업] every business [undertaking]; [계획, 시도] each step [attempt / plan]; [상황] every circumstance.

매상 [मैसांग] [賣上] **1** [물건을 팖] sale; selling. **2** 수입품의 매상이 오르고 있다The sales of imported goods are on the increase [going up]. 어제는 20 만 원의 매상을 올렸다 The sales of yesterday amounted to [totaled] 200,000 won.

매섭다 [मैसौप्ता] strict; fierce; violent; severe; sharp; acute; stern. e.g. 매서운 공격 a severe attack / [비난] a bitter criticism.

매수 [मैसू] [買收] [사들임] purchase; buying up [off]. 매수하다] purchase; buy up; take over. e.g. 회사를 매수하다 buy up a company.

매스 미디어 [मैसमीदीओ] the mass (communication) media (원래는 복수형이지만, 오늘날에는 단수형으로 취급되는 일도 많음)

매연 [मैयौन] [煤煙] [연기] sooty smoke; smoke; [검댕] soot; [자동차의 배기 가스] automobile exhaust fumes; exhaust gas.

매우 [मैउ] very; greatly; excessively; very much; awfully; terribly; remarkably; extraordinarily

매이다 [मैइदा] **1** (끈 등으로) be tied; be fastened; be bound. e.g. 구두끈이 매이다 shoelaces are fastened / one's shoes are tied. **2** [구속되다] be bound [fettered / tied / restricted]. e.g. 시간에 매이다 be restricted by time.

매일 [मैईल] [每日] e.g. 매일 day ather day / day by day

매입 [मैईब] [買入] [사들임] buying; purchase; stocking; laying in; (공사채 등의) a subscription. 매입하다 buy; purchase; make purchases; lay in. e.g. 대량으로 매입하다 make a large purchase of <rice> / lay in a large stock of <coal>.

매장[1] [मैजांग] [埋葬] 1 (시체의) burial; <文> (an) interment. e.g. 가 매장 provisional burial [interment]. 2 (사회적인) social ostracism e.g.. 그는 사회에서 매장되어야 한다 He ought to be ostracized from society.

매장[2] [मैजांग] [賣場] [파는 장소] a counter; a sale(s) room; [점포] a shop; a store.

매장[3] [मैजांग] [埋藏] 1 [묻어서 감춤] burying underground. 매장하다 [मैजांगहादा] hide underground; bury in the ground. e.g. 매장해 두었던 보석 jewels buried in the ground. 2 (지하 자원의) deposits <of minerals>. 매장하다 have <oil> deposits underground

매점 [मैजौम] [賣店] a stand; a stall; a booth; [공원,역 등의 간이 매점] a kiosk; [공원, 극장, 백화점, 슈퍼마켓 등에 서의 대여 판매 코너] a concession stand.

매정하다 [मैजौंगहादा] [무정하다] heartless; hard-hearted; [냉혹하다] cruel; merciless; [인정이 없다] unfeeling; pitiless.

매진[1] [मैजीन] [賣盡] a sell-out; being sold out. e.g. 매진되다 [मैजीनदवैदा] be sold out / be out of stock.

매진[2] [मैजीन] [邁進] pushing on; dash. 매진하다 push on [forward]; dash on [forward]; struggle on; [노력하다] strive <for>. e.g. 일에 매진하다get on with one's work

매체 [मैछे] [媒體] a medium <*pl.* ~s, -dia>.

매출 [मैछुल] [賣出] (a) sale; selling.

매치 [मैछी] 1 [시합] a match. e.g. 타이틀[리턴 / 태그] 매치] a title[return / tag] match. 2 [조화]. 매치하다 match (with); go well <with>. e.g. 그녀의 모자가 옷에 잘 매치한다Her hat matches [goes with] her dress well.

매캐하다 [मैखैहादा] [연기 냄새가 나다] smoky. e.g. 매캐한 냄새 a smoky smell.

매트리스 [मैथरीस] a mattress.

매표 [賣票] [मैफ्यो] selling of tickets. 매표하다 [मैफ्योहादा] sell tickets.

매표소 [मैफ्योसो] a ticket office;

a booking office.

매혹 [**मैहोक**] [**魅惑**] (a) charm; (a) bewitchment; captivation; fascination.

맥 [**मैक**] [**脈**] 1 평맥[부정맥] a regular [an irregular] pulse. e.g. 맥이 없는 pulseless. 맥이 뛴다 The pulsebeats. **2** 기운,힘] spirit; vigor. 남자는 여자의 눈물을 보면 맥을 못 쓴다 Men are a pushover for women's tears. 맥 (도) 못 추다 e.g. 여자 앞에서는 맥도 못 추다 get weak-kneed in the presence of a woman. 맥(을) 보다[맥을 짚다] feel [take / exa-mine] <a person's> pulse; have one's fingers on <a person's> pulse; [살피다] sound out <a person>; feel out <a situa-tion>. 맥(이) 빠지다 (1) be discour-aged; be dis-appointed; be dejected; be damped; be dispirited; be disheart-ened. e.g. 맥 빠진 문체 style.

맥락 [**मैग्नाक**] [**脈絡**] [연결] (a line of) connection; cohe-rence; logical connection. e.g. 맥락이 있는 [없는] 이야기 a coherent [an incoherent] account.

맥박 [**मैकबाक**] [**脈搏**] pulsation; the pulse; the stroke of the pulse.

맥없다 [**मैगौप्ता**] [**脈**–] [기운이 없다] weak; feeble; feel tired [exhausted / enervated / worn out / done in]; [풀이 죽다] dispirited; dejected; be in low spirits; be in the dumps; feel blue.

맥없이 [**脈**–] [**मैगौप्शि**] [기운 없이] weakly; spiritlessly; in low spirits. e.g. 맥없이 앉아 있다 sit exhausted / sit dejected [disappointed]. 맥없이 지다 be beaten too easily.

맥주 [**मैक्यू**] [**麥酒**] beer; ale; lager (저장 맥주)

맨 [**मैन**] [가장] most; extreme; the very. e.g. 맨 끝[말단] a (tail) end / the tip / [뒤끝] the rear. 맨 왼쪽의 lethmost. 맨 꼭대기에on (the) top <of>. 맨 꼴찌다 be at the end [bottom] <of a class>.

맨 [**मैन**] bare; naked; nothing but; just; unadulterated. e.g. 맨발 bare feet. 맨손bare [empty] hands. 맨밥just rice (without any side dishes).

맨몸 [**मैनमोम**] **1** [벌거벗은 몸] a naked body; nakedness; nudity; a nude. e.g. 맨몸으로 in the nude / with nothing on / in one's birthday clothes. **2** [무일푼] penn-ilessness. e.g. 맨몸의 penniless. 맨몸이 되다 be-come penniless. go (clean) broke.

맨션 [**मैनसयौन**] [고급 아파트의 한 세대의 구획] an apart-ment (of a better class); a flat

(of a better class); (건물) an [a ferroconcrete] apartment house; a block of flats; (분양식의) a condominium
1 [손에 아무것도 갖지 않음] an empty [a bare] hand. e.g. 맨손으로 [아무것도 갖지 않고] with one's bare hands / with empty hands / [무기 없이] unarmed.
2 [수단, 기술, 자본을 갖지 않음]맨손으로 [मैनसोनउरो] without art or crath / without capital / empty-handed. e.g. 맨손으로 장사를 시작하다 start a business with practically no capital.

맨송맨송하다 [मैनसोंगमैनसोंगहादा]
1 [털이 없이 반반하다] hairless; bald; bare. e.g. 턱이 맨송맨송하다 be / have no beard / have a bald chin. 2 [나무나 풀이 없다] treeless; bald; bare. e.g. 맨송맨송한산a treeless mountain. 3 [술마셔도 정신이 말짱하다] sober; not drunk; unintoxicated. e.g. 맨송맨송함 soberness / sobriety.

맨주먹 [मैनजूमैक] a naked fist; an empty fist; a bare [an empty] hand. e.g. 맨주먹의 barefisted / empty-handed / with one's bare [naked] hands [fists] / barehanded.

맵다 [मैप्ता] 1 [혀를 쏘는 듯하다] hot; [자극성이 있다] pungent; [후추같다] peppery; sharp; spicy. e.g. 매운 맛a harp[pungent] taste. 2 [혹독하다] severe; intense; inclement. e.g. 참 추위가 맵군요 How intense the cold is!

맵시 [मैप्सी] shapeliness; smartness; figure; form; appearance; a style. e.g. 몸맵시one's figure [carriage].

맹 [मैंग] -[猛] e.g. 맹연습 strenuous [hard] training. 맹반격a terrific counter-attack.

맹독 [मैंगदोक] [猛毒] (a) deadly [virulent] poison; (동물의) deadly venom. 맹독성의 fatally poisonous. 맹독의 뱀a very poisonous [highly venomous] snake.

맹랑하다 [मैंगरांगहादा] [孟浪-] [허망하다] false; untrue; [믿을 수 없다] incredible; unbelievable; [근거 없다] groundless; unfounded; unreliable; [터무니없다] absurd; fabulous; nonsensical; unreasonable e.g. 맹랑한 사람 an unreliable [a disappointing] erson

맹렬하다 [मैंगरयौलहादा] [猛烈-] violent <storm>; vehement <wind>; furious <anger>; fierce <hatred>; keen <competition>. e.g. 맹렬한 더위 intense heat.

맹목적 [मैंगमोकजौक] [盲目的] blind; reckless. e.g. 맹목

적 사랑 blind love. 맹목적 모방 blind [servile] imitation.

맹물 [**मैंगमुल**] **1** [물] plain [tasteless] water; insipid [flat] stuff; dishwater (싱거운 음료) e.g. 이것은 맥주가 아니고 맹물이다 This isn't beer — it's dishwater! **2** [야무지지 못한 사람] a dull [an uninteresting] person; a dull drink of water; a drip. e.g. 그 사람은 맹물이다 He is a dull drink of water.

맹세 [**मैंगसे**] an oath (▷ 성경에 손을 얹고 하는 것과 같은) a vow; a pledge; a promise (약속)맹세코 upon my oath [word / honor / life] / by God [Jove / Jupiter]. 맹세를 지키다[어기다] keep [break] one's vow [oath].

맹수 [**मैंगसू**] [**猛獸**] a fierce [ferocious] animal; a savage beast; a predatory animal; a beast of prey.

맹신 [**मैंगशिन**] [**盲信**] a blind belief; overcredulity. 맹신하다 believe unquestioningly; be over-credulous.

맹아 [**मैंगा**] [**盲啞**] a blind and dumb person; the blind and dumb; the blind and the dumb.

맹연습 [**मैंग्यौनसब**] [**猛練習**] hard [intensive] training; heavy [vigorous] practice. 맹연습하다 do hard training; carry out vigorous practice [exercises].

맹점 [**मैंगजौम**] [**盲點**] a blind spot[point]; a scotoma <*pl.* ~s, -mata>.

맹탕 [**मैंगथांग**] **1** [싱거운 국] insipid [watery] soup; flavorless soup; unseasoned soup. e.g. 이국은 맹탕이다 This soup is mere wash. **2** [싱거운 사람] a dull [an uninteresting] person; an empty person; an insipid person.

맹훈련 [**मैंगहुल्यौक**] [**猛訓練**] hard [intense] training. 맹훈련하다 carry out intense training; train hard.

머리 [**मौरी**] 1 [두부] the head. e.g. 머리를 들다 raise [lith] one's head. 2 [머리털] hair;a hair. e.g. 희끗희끗한 머리gray hair. 머리가 돌다 go off one's head; become [go] mad [insane]; lose one's mind [wit / reason]. e.g. 그는 머리가 돌았다 He is crazy [mad]. / He is off his head [out of his mind]. 그러지다 e.g. 그의 노력에 는 머리가 수그러진다 I take off my hat to him for his effort. / I admire him for his effort. 머리 (를) 굽히다 =굴복하다. e.g. 저 녀석에게만은 절대로 머리를 굽히고 싶지 않다 He is the one person I couldn't bear to give in to. 머리(를) 깎다

(1) [중이 되다] become a bonze; shave one's head in order to enter the priesthood. (2) [교도소에 복역하다] be sent to jail; serve a prison term. 머리(를) 들다 e.g. 회원들 사이에 불만이 머리를 들기 시작했다 Discontent began to show itself among the members. 머리(를) 숙이다 = 머리(를) 굽히다. 머리(를) 식히다 머리를 식히고 시작하라 You must calm down [cool off] before you start. 머리(를) 썩이다 e.g. 교사들은 학생들의 폭력에 머리를 썩이고 있었다 The teachers were worried [concerned] about student violence.머리(를) 쓰다 think; view <a matter> from every angle. 머리(를) 짜다 cudgel [rack] one's brains; puzzle; think hard <of / about>. e.g. 그들은 사고 방지를 위해 머리를 쥐어짜고 있다 They are racking [cudgeling] their brains for ways of preventing accidents 머리 (를) 흔들다 (1) =거절하다 (2) =부인하다

머리말 [मौरीमाल] a preface; an introduction; a foreword (▷ preface 는 저자가 쓰는 머리말, 본문의 목차나 내용을 언급하는 foreword 는 보통 저자 이외의 사람이 쓰는 간단한 머리말, introduction 은 본론의 예비적 해설)

머리말 [मौरीमात] one's bedside [pillow-side]. a long tress of hair.

머리카락 [मौरीखाराक] a hair (of one's head).

머리 핀 [मौरीफीन] a hair pin.

머릿수 [मौरीतसू] [-數] the number of persons; a head count; numerical strength; (의회의) quorum.

머무르다 [मौमूरदा] **1** [정지하다] stop; halt; come to a halt [standstill]. **2** [그대로 있다,유숙하다] stay <at / with>; remain. e.g. 돌아가려는 그를 우리는 말려 머무르게 했다 As he was leaving, we stopped [detained] him.

머뭇거리다 [मौमूतगौरीदा] hesitate

머슴 [मौसम] [농가,농장의 일꾼] a farmhand; a farm servant; a farmer's man.

머지않아 [मौजीआन्आ] [이윽고] soon; presently; before long; in a short time; by and by; [때가 되면] in due course of time; in due course [time]; [불원간] some [one] day; at no distant date.

멎다 [मौत्ता] 멈추다] stop; [그치다] cease; come to a stop [an end]; (바람 등이) die down; (소리 등이) die away. e.g. 바람이 멎었다 The wind has died down.

메뉴 [मैन्यू] a menu; a bill of fare; a (menu) card.

메다 [मैदा] (어깨에) shoulder <a gun>; carry [bear / take] <a load> on one's shoulder. e.g. 총을 메고 행진하다 march with guns on one's shoulder.

메다 [मैदा] [막히다] be [get] choked [filled / stopped / plugged] (up); be [get] blocked; get clogged; be glutted; be obstructed. e.g. 목이 멘다 My throat is choked.

메달 [मैदाल] a medal; a medallion (대형의

메마르다 [मैमारूदा] 1 [땅이 건조하다] very dry; dried-up; arid; parched; [땅이 기름지지 못하다] sterile; barren; meager; infertile. e.g. 메마른 땅 [मैमरून ताग] barren [poor / sterile / unproductive] soil [land] / wasteland. 2 (피부 등이) dried-up; withered; shriveled; rough. e.g. 메마른 살갗 a dry [parched] skin. 메마른 손 a dry, rough hand. 3 (마음이) hard (-hearted); cold (-hearted); harsh; severe. e.g. 메마른 마음 cold [a hard / an unfeeling] heart / a heart of stone.

메모 [मैमो] a memorandum <*pl.* ~ s, -da>; a memo <*pl.* ~ s>; a note.

메스껍다 [मैसकौप्त्ता] 1 [토할 것같다] sickening; nauseous; nauseating; <英> sick. e.g. 메스꺼워지다 feel sick [nausea / queasy] / feel like vomiting. 2 [아주 불쾌하다] disgusting; abominable; loathsome; offensive; revolt-ing; sickening. e.g. 메스꺼운 아첨 nauseating [sickening] flattery.

메시지 [मैसीजी] a message.

메아리 [मैआरी] an echo; echoes. e.g. 메아리치다 echo / resound / be echoed / reverberate

메우다 [मैउदा] 1 (틈, 구멍 등을) fill up [in]; plug (up); fill [cover] in; stop up; choke up; (바다, 호수 등을) reclaim; (군중 등이) jam. e.g. 구멍을 메우다 [गूमैंल मैउदा] fill [block / stop] up a hole / stop a gap. 2 (모자라는 것을) supply; make up for; (결함을) stop [fill up] <a gap>; offset <a fault>. e.g. 결원을 메우다 fill up a vacancy / fill a vacant place.

메이커 [मैइखौ] a maker; a manufacturer. e.g. 메이커 제품 [मैइखौ जेपूम] name-brand goods

메이크업 [मैइखओप] [얼굴 화장] makeup. 메이크업하다 make (oneself) up; put on makeup; use makeup.

메카 [मैख्वा] [동경의 땅, 중심지] a mecca

멜로드라마 [मैल्लोदराम] a melodrama.

멜로디 [मैल्लोदी] a melody; a tune.

멤버 [मैमबौ] a member.

멤버십[मैमबौसीब] membership.

며 [मयौ] [둘 이상의 사물 열거] and. e.g. 사과며 복숭아며 기타 여러 과일 apples, peaches and many other fruits.

며느리 [मयौनरी] a daughter-in-law .

며칠 [मयौछील] [일수] how many days; how long; [수일] several days; a few days. e.g. 며칠 동안[मयौजील नोंगान] for (a few) days.

멱살 [मयौकसाल] the flesh of the throat; the throat; [멱 부분의 옷깃] a collar; a lapel. e.g. 멱살을 잡다 seize [grab / take] <a person> by the collar [lapels].

-면 [मयौन] if; unless; when. [가정적 조건] e.g. 가능하다면 if possible.

면[1] [मयौन] [綿] cotton.

면[2] [मयौन] [面] **1** [얼굴] a face; one's features; dignity; prestige; face; honor. **2** the surface; the face. **3** an aspect; a side; a field. e.g. 인생의 어두운 면 the dark side of life. **4** [지면] a page. e.g.제 1 면the front [first] page. 사회면 the local [city] news page. **5** [측면] a side; (다면체의) a facet; a face; [평면] a plane; (활자의) the face. e.g. 수평면 a level surface

면담 [मयौनदाम] [面談] an interview.

면도 [मयौनदो] [面刀] [수염을 미는 일] shaving.

면도칼 [मयोनदोख्वाल] [面刀-] a razor.

면목 [मयौनमैक] [面目] [명예] honor; honour; [체면] face; countenance. e.g. 면목을 세우다 [मयौनमैकल सैउदा] [손상시키다] raise [harm] one's reputation / rise [fall] in public estimation / earn a high reputation [lose one's dignity]. 면목(이) 없다 be ashamed of oneself; be put out of countenance; have no face to show. e.g. 면목 없는 짓을 하다 do a shameful [disgraceful] thing.

면밀하다 [मयौनमीलहादा] [綿密] [세밀하다] minute; detailed; close; nice; [정확 하다] exact; [빈틈없다] careful; [세심하다] scrupulous; meticulous; elaborate.

면상 [मयौनसांग] [面上] the face. e.g. 면상을 치다 strike <a person> in the face.

-면서 [मयौनसौ] **1**

[동작,상태의 진행] ...ing; [··· 하면서 (동시에)] while; as; between; during; over; with; at the same time (that). e.g. 가난하게 살면서 while living in poverty. **2** [··· 이지만] though; [··· 에도 불구하고] but; yet; still; in spite of; for [with] all. e.g. 싫어하 면서(도) against one's will / reluctantly.

면세 [मयौसे] [**免稅**] exemption from taxation; tax [duty] exemption; immunity from taxes; re-mission of taxes.

면역 [मयौनयौक] [**免疫**] (병원균 등에 대한) immunity (from a disease). e.g. 면역이 되다 [मयौनयौकी दवैदा] become [be rendered] immune <to / against / from>.

면역성 [मयौनयौकसौंग] [**免疫性**] immunity.

면적 [मयौनजौक] [**面積**] (an) area; square measure; size <of land>; superficial content (s); floor space

면접 [मयौनजौप] [**面接**] an interview. 면접하다 interview; see; receive; have an interview. e.g.한 사람 한 사람 면접하여 앙케트 조사를 했다I interviewed each person to collect information for a questionnaire.

면제 [मयौजे] [**免除**] (an) exemption; immunity; impunity; discharge; excuse; remission; release (▷ exemption 은 의무나 이행 등으로부터 해방되는 것. Immunity 는 의무, 속박, 벌,고통 등으로부터 해방 보호되는 것. Impunity 는 벌을 면제받는 것

면하다 [मयौनहादा] [**免**–] **1** [모면하다] escape <danger, arrest, conscription, etc.>; be saved [rescued] from <drowning>. e.g. 죽음을 면하다 escape death / be saved from death **2** [회피하다] escape <responsibility>; evade <one's duty>; elude <taxation>; get round <the law>; excuse oneself from <responsibility>. e.g. 책임을 면하려고 하다 shirk [shith off] one's responsibility.

면허 [मयौनहौ] [**免許**] permission; license.

면허증 [मयौनहौजग] [**免許證**] a license; a licence; a certificate (증명서) a permit (허가증) a charter (특허장)

면회 [मयौनहवै] [**面會**] [만나봄] a meeting; [회견] an interview.

멸망 [मयौलम्ग] [**滅亡**] [절멸] extinction; [몰락] a fall; a downfall; ruin; collapse; destruction.

멸시 [मयौलसी] [**蔑視**]

contempt; disdain; disregard. 멸시하다 [मयौलसीहादा] regard <a person> with contempt; despise; disrespect; disregard; disdain; hold <a person> cheap; make light [little] of; slight; neglect.

멸종 [मयौलजोंग] [滅種] extermination of a stock [race].

멸하다 [मयौलहादा] [滅-] [멸망하다] go to ruin; perish; [멸망시키다] ruin; destroy; exterminate.

명 [命] [मयौग] **1** [목숨] life e.g. 명이 길다 [मयौगी गील्दा] live long / last on / have a long life **2** [명령] **an order; a command** e.g. (당국의) 명에 의하여 by order (of the authorities) / under government orders.

명 [मयौग] [名] [사람수] a man; a person; persons. e.g. 20 명 twenty persons [people.].

명곡 [मयौगोक] [名曲] a famous tune [piece of music]; a musical masterpiece.

명단 [मयौगदान] [名單] a register [list] of names.

명당 [मयौगदांग] [明堂] [좋은 묏자리] a propitious site for a grave; [좋은 터] a very good place

명랑 [म्यौगनांग] [明朗] brightness; cheerfulness; livelyness; gaiety. 명랑하다 clear; bright; cheerful; gay; sunny; sunshiny.

명료 [म्यौगल्यो] [明瞭] clearness; plainness; lucidity; perspicuity; distinctness. 명료하다 clear <meaning>; plain <language>; obvious <reason>; evident <fact>; distinct [articulate] <pronunciation>; lucid <style>; perspicuous <expression>.

명망 [म्यौग्माग] [名望] reputation; renown; popularity. e.g. 명망있는 reputed / renowned / popular.

명맥 [मयौगमैक] [命脈] life; the thread of life. e.g. 간신히 명맥을 이어가다 barely keep <itself> in existence / maintain <its> slender existence.

명명 [मयौगमयौग] [命名] christening; naming.

명명하다 [मयौगमयौगहादा] name; christen; give a name <to>; call; designate; denominate. e.g. 본회를 상우회라 명명한다 This society shall be called [designated as] "Sanguhoe".

명명백백 [मयौगमयौगबैकबैक] [明明白白] obviousness; patency; distinctness. 명명백백하다 as clear as day [daylight]; as plain as a pikestaff.

명목 [मयौगमोक] [名目] a name; a title; an appellation; a pretext. e.g. 그는

명목상의 사장이다 He is a president in name only

명문 [मयौगमून] [名門] a noble [distinguished] family.

명문화 [मयौगमूनहवा] [明文化] stipulation.
명문화하다 [मयौगमूनहवाहादा] stipulate; put in a statutory form

명물 [मयौगमूल] [名物] [어떤 특색으로 이름난 것] a feature; an attraction. e.g. 이 식당은 냉면이 명물이다 This restaurant features iced vermicelli [noodles].

명백 [मयौगबैक] [明白] 명백하다 [분명하다] obvious; [애매하지 않다] clear; [확실히 알 수 있다] plain; [틀림없다] unmistakable [positive / undeniable]; [상황으로 보아 확실하다 evident; apparent; manifest; explicit; distinct; patent; open-and-shut; indisputable [indubitable].

명복 [मयौगबोक] [冥福] heavenly bliss; happiness in the other world. e.g. 명복을 빌다 pray for the repose of <a person's> soul / pray for the souls of the departed / bless <a person's> memory.

명부 [मयौगबू] [名簿] a register [list] of names; a nominal; a register; a nominal list [register / roll].

명분 [मयौगबून] [名分] [본분] [बोनबून] one's moral duty [obligations]; [정당성] (moral) justification; justice; a just cause. e.g. 명분이 서는.

명사 [मयौगसा] [名士] a celebrity; a man of note; a notable; a man of distinction; a distinguished [celebrated / prominent] person; a prominent figure; a big name; a swell

명사 [मयौगसा] [名詞] a noun; a (noun) substantive.

명상 [मयौगसांग] [瞑想] meditation; contemplation. 명상하다 imeditate <on>; contemplate.

명색 [मयौगसैक] [名色] a name; a title; an appellation. e.g. 명색뿐인 학자 a scholar in name only.

명석 [मयौगसौक] [明晳] clearness. 명석하다 clear; bright; lucid; distinct.

명성 [मयौगसौंग] [名聲] fame; (a) reputation; renown; a kudos. e.g. 그는 명성을 전세계에 떨쳤다He has become world-famous. / His fame has spread throughout the world.

명세서 [मयौगसैसौ] [明細書] a detailed [full] statement; details; specifications; a minute description; a list of particulars; a detailed account.

명소 [मयौगसो] [名所] [유서 깊은 곳] [यूसौ गीफन गोत] a

noted place; a place of interest [note]; a celebrated locality; sights(to see); a place rich in [with many] historical associations; a beauty [scenic] spot; a picturesque site; a place of scenic interest

명시 [मयौगशी] [明示] clear statement; elucidation. 명시하다 express [describe] clearly; specify; state plainly [clearly / expressly]; clarify. e.g. 자기 의사를 명시하다 express one's wishes clearly.

명실 [मयौगसील] [名實] name and reality. e.g. 명실상부한 대정치가 a great statesman worthy of his reputation [the name].

명심 [मयौगसीम] [銘心] 명심하다 [मयौगसीमहादा] bear [keep] <something> in mind; take <the advice> to heart; have <something> stamped [engraved] on one's mind; impress <a fact> on one's mind. e.g. 명심해야 할 일 things that should be remembered [borne in mind].

명암 [मयौगाम] [明暗] light and darkness [shade]. e.g. 명암이 뚜렷하지 않은 사진 a flat picture.

명언 [मयौगऔन] [名言] [사리에 맞는 훌륭한 말] a wise [witty] remark; [유명한 말] a famous [wellknown] saying; a wise [golden] saying.

명예 [मयौगये] [名譽] [영예] [यौग्ये] honor; honour; glory; [명성] [मयौगसौग] fame; reputation; distinction; renown; [신망] credit.

명의 [मयौगउइ] [名義] [이름] a person's name. e.g. 남의 명의를 사칭하다 assume a false [another's] name.

명작 [मयौगजाक] [名作] a masterpiece; a fine piece <of literature>; a fine work <of art>; a masterwork.

명절 [मयौगजौल] [名節] a festive day; a national holiday; a gala [fête] day.

명제 [मयौगजे] [命題] [論] a proposition; a position; a thesis.

명중 [मयौगजूंग] [命中] hit. 명중하다 hit <the mark>; tell. e.g. 과녁에 명중하다 hit the target

명찰 [मयौगछाल] [名札] a name card; (an identification tag; a nameplate [tag]; a place card

명칭 [मयौगछीग] [名稱] [이름] [इस्म] a name; a title; a term; a designation; an appellation; (종파, 화폐 단위 등의) a denomination

명쾌 [मयौगख्वै] [明快] clearness; lucidity; explicitness. 명쾌하다 clear; lucid; explicit. e.g. 명쾌한 발언 a clear statement.

명품 [मयौंगफूम] [**名品**] [훌륭한 물건] a fine article; a gem; [뛰어난 작품] a masterpiece.

명함 [मयौंगहाम] [**名銜**] a calling card; a visiting card; a business card.

명화 [मयौंगह्वा] [**名畵**] [탁월한 그림] a masterpiece (of painting); a beautiful [masterful] drawing [painting]; [유명한 그림] a famous [celebrated / great] picture; [훌륭한 영화] an excellent film; a noted film

명확 [मयौंगह्वाक] [**明 確**] clearness; definiteness. 명확하다 clear; [확실하다] definite; [정확하다] precise.

몇 [मयौत] 1 [부정의 수] [ब्रूजौंगउइ सू] some; a few; several. e.g. 일 년 몇 개월 one year and some month 2 [의문] how many <days / weeks / months> (수); how much (양,금액); how far (거리); how long (시일); how old(연령); what time (시간). e.g. 가족은 몇 명입니까 How many people [members] are there in your family?

몇몇 [मयौत मयौत] e.g. 몇몇의 a few / some / several.

모[1] [मो] [**某**] **1** [어떤 사람] a certain person; Mr. K (이름을 모를 경우) Mr. So-and-so; somebody; Mr. –. e.g. 김 모(씨) a certain (Mr.) Kim / a man called Kim / a [one] Mr. Kim. **2** [어떤 사물] one; a; certain. e.g. 모 일 a certain day / one day.

모[2] [मो] [벼의 싹] rice sprouts; sprouts of rice; a rice seedl-ing. e.g. 모를 내다[심다] transplant rice seedlings / set [bed] out rice plants.

모[3] [मो] **1** [각] an angle. e.g. 모가 난 angular / angled. 세모꼴 a triangle. **2** [성깔이나 가탈] angularity; stiffness; harshness. e.g. 모나지 않은 사람 an affable [a sociable] person.

모계 [मोग्ये] [**母系**] the maternal line; one's mother's side; the uterine descent; the matrilineal descent. e.g. 모계의 maternal / on the maternal [mother's] side / umbilical / matronymic.

모교 [मोग्यो] [**母 校**] one's alma mater (▷ 주로 고교,대학을 말함); one's (old) school.

모국어 [मोगुकौ] [**母國語**] one's mother tongue

모금[1] [मोगुम] (액체의) a drath [drought]; a gulp; (뜨거운 차 등의) a sip; (담배의) a puff; a whiff. e.g. 물 한 모금 a drath [drought] of water.

모금² [मोगुम] [募金] fund-raising; collection [invitation] of subscriptions; collection of contributions [donations].

모기 [मोगी] a mosquito <*pl.* ~s, ~es>.

모나다 [मोनादा] **1** (물건이) angle; be angular; be angulated; be angled; (뾰족하게) be pointed; be sharp. e.g. 모난 얼굴[턱] an angular [a squarish] face. **2** (성격,행동이) be angular [stiff / harsh / severe]; be unsociable [unaffable / uncompromising]. e.g. 모난 성격[사람] an unaffable character [person].

모내기 [मोनाःगी] rice-planting; rice transplantation. e.g. 모내기로 바쁘다 be busy planting the rice.

모녀 [मोन्यौ] [母女] mother and daughter. e.g. 모녀간 between [the relation of] mother and daughter.

모니터 [मोनीथौ] a monitor.

모닥불 [मोदाकबुल] a bonfire; a fire in the open air; (야영의) a campfire.

모던 [मोदौन] 모던하다 modern.

모델 [मोदेल] **1** [모형, 본보기, 본] a model <of honesty>. **2** (그림, 소설 등의) a model; a sitter.

모독 [मोदोक] [冒瀆] [신, 신성한 것을 더럽히기] profanity; [독신적인 욕] blasphemy; [신성한 것, 장소를 더럽히기] sacrilege; [신성한 것의 악용, 남용] desecration; [존경하지 않음] disrespect.

모두 [मोदु] all (▷ 사람은 복수 취급, 사물은 원칙적으로 단수 취급); [모든 사람] everyone; everybody (▷ 단수 취급); [모든 사물] everything (▷ 단수 취급); in all; in a body; all together; one and all; altogether; without an exception; in the gross.

모든 [मोदुन] all; every (▷ every 뒤에는 가산 명사의 단수형. all은 가산, 불가산 명사의 어느 것이나 쓰임); each; each and every.

모래 [मोरे] sand; grit (굵은).

모략 [मोर्याक] [謀略] strategy; a stratagem; an artifice; a trick; a scheme; a plot. e.g. 모략을 꾸미다 devise a stratagem / concoct [work out] a plot.

모레 [मोरे] the day ather tomorrow.

모르다 [मोरूदा] **1** [알지 못하다] do not know; be ignorant of; be innocent of. e.g. 아무 것도 모르고 unknowingly. **2** [이해하지 못하다] do not understand; have no idea of; (사물이) be above [beyond / past] one's comprehension.

e.g. 의 뜻을 모르다 do not understand the meaning of a sentence. **3** [안면이 없다] be not acquainted with; be unfamiliar; be a stranger. e.g. 모르는 얼굴 a strange [an unfamiliar] face / a stranger

모름지기 [मोरूमजीगी] = 마땅히 e.g. 아이들은 모름지기 부모를 따라야 한다 Children should obey their parents.

모면 [मोमयौन] [謀免] escape; evasion; avoidance; shirking; elusion. 모면하다 escape; avoid; evade; shirk; elude; excuse oneself from <responsibility>. e.g. 모면할 수 없는 unavoidable / inescapable / inevitable / ineluctable.

모멸 [मोरूमयौल] [侮蔑] contempt; disdain; scorn. e.g. 모멸적인 언사 a word of contempt. 모멸하다 despise; disdain; scorn; abase; contemn; look down on [upon] <a person>. traitor.

모발 [मोबाल] [毛髮] <집합적> hair (of the head); [털 하나] a hair.

모방 [मोबांग] [模倣] imitation; copying; mimicry.

모병하다 [मोब्यौगहादा] recruit <troops>; drath.

모사 [मोसा] [模寫] copying; a copy (모사물); a reproduction (미술 작품); a facsimile; a replica (▷ facsimile는 [치수는 다를지 모르나 정확한 모사 복사], copy는 가장 일반적인 말로 [원물의 복사]이며 흔히 [근사한 모방]의 뜻으로도 쓰임 모사하다 copy (out); trace; reproduce; facsimile; hit off. e.g. 피카소의 그림을 모사하다 copy from [make a copy of] a painting by Picasso.

모색 [मोसैक] [摸索] [더듬어 찾음] groping. e.g. 암중모색 groping in the dark. 모색하다 grope <for>; fumble <for>. e.g. 모색하여 in search of <a better solution>.

모서리 [मोसौरी] [물건의 쑥 나온 부분] a corner; [가장자리] an edge; an angle. e.g. 책상 모서리 the corners of a desk. 뾰족한 바윗돌 모서리 the sharp edges of a rock. 모서리를 죽이다 round off the angles.

모성 [मोसौग] [母性] motherhood; maternity. e.g. 그녀에게는 모성의 자각이 없다 She has no sense of responsibility as a mother.

모순 [मोसुन] [矛盾] (a) contradiction; contradictoriness; (an) inconsistency; an antinomy; (a) discrepancy; a conflict <of evidence>. e.g. 무모순성

consistency. 모순되다 [반대이다] be contradictory <to> / [일관성이 없다] be inconsistent <with> / [양립하지 않다] be incompatible <with> / [대립하다] conflict <with>.

모습 [मोसुप] **1** [몸의 모양] a figure; a form; [얼굴 모양] features; (outward) looks. e.g. 죽은 누님의 모습을 생각하다 remember one's (dead) sister's look [face]. **2** [외관] appearance; [옷차림] guise; dress. e.g. 이상한 모습을 한 사나이 a funny-looking man / a man with a strange appearance. **3** [상태] a state; a condition; [양상] an aspect; a phase; a picture. e.g. 인생의 여러 가지 다른 모습 diverse aspects of human life

모시다 [मोश्दा] **1** [섬기다] attend [wait] (upon) <a person>; be in attendance on <a person>; minister to <a person>; serve; take service under <a person>. e.g. 부모를 모시다 have one's parents with him / serve [support] one's parents / wait upon one's parents. **2** [인도하다] show [usher / conduct] <a person> in [into]. e.g. 선생님을 상좌에 모시다 seat the teacher at the head / give the teacher the place [seat] of honor. **3** [초청하다] invite; ask. e.g. 의사를 모시러 보내다 send for a doctor.

모양 [मोयांग] [模樣, 貌樣] **1** [형상] (a) shape; (a) form; make; [외관] appearance. e.g. 도끼 모양의 흉기 an ax-shaped weapon. **2** [차림새, 맵시] appearance; a look; an air. e.g. 그녀는 그 옷을 입으니까 모양이 우습다 She looks funny in that dress. **3** [상태] the state [aspect / phase / situation / position] of affairs [things]; circumstances. e.g. 살아가는 모양 (living) circums-tances.

모양새 [मोयांगसै] [模 樣 −] [모양의 됨됨이] (a) shape; (a) form;(a) figure; an appearance.

모어 [मोओ] [母語] [자기 나라 말] one's mother tongue; [言] [모체가 되는 언어] a parent language.

모여들다 [मोयौदुलदा] gather [flock] (together); assemble; come [get] together; meet [throng / draw] together.

모욕 [मोयोक] [侮辱] insult; affront (▷insult는 상대에게 창피를 주려 하는 언동, affront 는 맞대고 하는 무례한 언동); contempt; indignity; slight; outrage. 모욕하다 insult; affront;

throw contempt on; put a slight on; subject <a person> to insult.

모유 [मोयु] [母乳] mother's milk; breast milk.

모으다 [मोउदा] **1** (사물,인원을) gather; get [bring / put] together; collect; make a collection of; round up <scattered cattle>. e.g. 여러 가지 과일을 한데 모은 것 an assortment of fruit. **2** [집중시키다] focus <on>; concentrate <one's energy on something, rays of light into a focus, etc.>. e.g. 정신[힘]을 모으다 concentrate one's attention [strength] on <one's work>. **3** [저축하다] save; lay [put / set] by; store; lay up; accumulate; amass. e.g. 어렵게 모은 돈 one's hard-saved money.

모음 [मोउम] [母音] [聲] a vowel (sound).

모이 [मोइ] feed. e.g. 닭모이 chicken feed

모이다 [मोइदा] **1** [몰려들다] gather [flock] (together); come [get] together; crowd; swarm; cluster. e.g. … 의 둘레에 모이다 gather [crowd / flock / swarm / cluster] about [around] .... **2** [회동하다] meet; assemble; congregate. e.g. 회의하려고 모이다 meet [assemble] for a meeting. 모인 사람이 많다 have a large attendance. 어디로 모일까 Where shall we meet? **3** [걷히다] be collected [gathered]. e.g. 모인 돈 the collected money / the money collected. 모금으로 모인 돈이 20이었다 The money collected [Contributions] amounted to 200,000 won. / Two hundred thousand won was collected through the campaign.

모임 [मोइम] [회합] a meeting; [회동] a gathering; [집단] a group; [동호인] a set; [파티] a party; [비공식적인 회합] a get-together (스포츠 등의); a meet; a meeting; an assembly; a congregation; a party

모자[1] [मोजा] [母子] mother and child.

모자[2] [मोजा] [帽子] a hat (테있는); a cap (챙달린); a bonnet (여자용); a hunting [sporting] cap (사냥모); a derby (hat) (중산모); a soth [felt] hat; a bowler; <집합적> headgear.

모자라다 [मोजारादा] **1** [부족하다] be not enough; be insufficient [deficient]; lack; want; be lacking [wanting / short of]; [만족스럽지 못하다] (사물이) be unsatisfactory; be not gratifying; be not (good)

enough; (사람이) be dissatisfied <with>; be discontented <with>. e.g. 역량이 모자라다 be wanting in ability / be incapable **2** [지능이 낮다] dull-[half-] witted; stupid; dull (brained) (▷ dull 은 이해력, 사고력이 부족하며, stupid 는 지능이 떨어짐을 의미). e.g. 좀 모자란 사람 a dull [slow-witted] person.

모자이크 **[मोजाइख्]** a mosaic. e.g. 모자이크식의 건물 바닥 a mosaic floor.

모정 **[मोजौंग]** [**母情**] maternal love [affection]; a mother's love.

모조 **[मोजो]** [**模造**] [모방하여 만듦] imitation. e.g. 모조의[मोजोउइ] imitation / counterfeit / faked (-up) / sham / artificial (인조의). 모조하다 imitate; copy <from>; reproduce <from>; counterfeit; fake.

모종 **[मोजोंग]** [**某種**] a certain kind. e.g. 모종의 [मोजोंगउइ] a certain / some / unnamed. 모종의 이유로 for a certain reason.

모지다 **[मोजीदा]** **1** = 모나다. **2** ⇨ 모질다

모직 (**물**) **[मोजीक मुल]** [**毛織(物)**] woolen stuff [goods]; (천) woolen fabric [cloth]. e.g. 모직을 입고 있다 be dressed in woolen. 모직은 명주보다 질기다 Woolen outwears silk.모직물 공업 the woolen manu-facturing industry.

모직물 공장 **[मोजीक मुल गोंगजांग]** a woolen mill.

모질다 **[मोजीलदा]** **1** [잔인하다] ruthless; cruel; atrocious; harsh; hardhearted; merciless; wicked; pitiless; brutal. e.g. 모진 사람 a brute / a wicked man / a hard-hearted [coldblooded] person. **2** [배겨내다] patient; persevering; tenacious; unremitting; long-suffering. e.g. 모진 목숨 one's contemptible life / one's wretched [miserable] life / one's hard [heavy] lot.

모집 **[मोजीब]** [**募集**] **1** (지원자 등의) invitation; collection; registration (학생의). 모집하다 invite; collect; raise; advertise for (광고를 내어). e.g. 사무원을 모집하다 invite applications for the position of clerk. **2** (기부금 등의) raising; collection; subscription; solicitation; an appeal. e.g. 기금 모집 운동을 벌이다 carry on [run] a drive to raise funds.

모처럼 **[मोछौरौम]** [오래간만에] ather a long time [interval / silence / absence / separation]; (고대했던) long-awaited; much-awaited. e.g. 모처럼 맞은 좋은 날씨

the first fine day in a long time / fine weather ather a long spell of rain.

모친 [**मोछीन**] [**母親**] a mother; a female parent.

모터 [**मोथौ**] a motor; [발동기] an engine

모텔 [**मोथैल**] [자동차 여행자용 숙박소] a motel; an auto court.

모퉁이 [**मोथुंगी**] a corner; a turn; a turning.

모피 [**मोफ़ी**] [**毛皮**] a fur (부드러운); a fell; a skin (거친); a pelt (생가죽).

모함 [**मोहाम**] [**謀陷**] false incrimination; a plot to entrap <a person>. 모함하다 intrigue against <a person>; falsely incrimi-nate; frame (up); entrap; ensnare.

모험 [**冒險**] [**मोहेम**] an adventure; a venture; a risky [hazardous] attempt; a hazard; a risk. 모험하다 venture; risk; run a risk [hazard]; make a venture; take chances [a chance]. e.g. 목숨을 걸고 모험하다 stake [venture] one's life / risk one's neck.

모형 [**मोह्यौग**] [**模型**] a model; (기계 등) a pattern; (주조의) a mold.

모호하다 [**मोहोहादा**] [**模糊-**] dim; vague; faint; obscure; ambiguous; equivocal. e.g. 모호한 태도를 취하다 take an equivocal [dubious] attitude.

목 [**मोक**] **1** [모가지] a neck. **2** [머리] a head. e.g. 죄인의 목을 치다 behead [decapitate] a criminal. 그는 갑자기 창밖으로 목을 내밀었다 He popped his head out of the window. 그녀는 목을 움츠렸다 She shrugged her shoulders. **3** [직책, 목숨]. e.g. 목이 떨어지다 be dismissed / be fired / < 英 > get [receive] the sack. 그 녀석은 아직 목이 붙 있다 He has not been dismissed [fired] yet.

목각 [**मोक्काक**] [**木刻**] [나무에 새김] wood carving; wood-crath; [그 작품] a wood carving. 목각하다 carve [engrave] wood; make a woodcarving [woodcut]

목걸이 [**मोक्कौरी**] a necklace; a necklet; a rivière (보석); a choker (목에 꼭끼는 짧은 것);(개의) collar.

목격 [**मोकक्यौक**] [**目擊**] observation; witnessing; sighting. 목격하다 witness; see with one's own eyes; observe. e.g.목격되다 come under one's yes [notice / observation

목덜미 [**मोक्तौल्मी**] the nape [back / scruff] of the neck. e.g. 목덜미를 붙잡다 seize [grab] <a person> by the collar

목도리 [**मोक्तोरी**] a (neck)

scarf; a muffler; (긴 털실로 만든) a comforter; a (neck) wrap;

목돈 [मोक्तोन] [모갯돈] a (good) round sum; a sizable [tidy] sum [amount] (of money). e.g. 목돈을 좀 만들다 scrape together some money.

목례 [目禮] [मोक्ल] a nod; nodding. e.g. 목례를 주고받다 exchange nods.

목록 [目錄] [मोंग्नोक] 1 (상품,장서의) a catalog; a catalogue; (재산, 상품의) an inventory. 2 = 목차.

목마 [木馬] [मोंग्मा] [목제의 말] a wooden horse; [흔들목마] a rocking horse; a hobbyhorse. e.g. 회전 목마 a merry-go-round / a roundabout / a carousel. 회전 목마를 타다 ride a carousel pony.

목마르다 [मोकमारूदा] 1 [갈증나다] thirsty; <서술적> be [feel / get] thirsty; have a dry throat. e.g. 나는 목이 마르다 I am [feel] thirsty. 2 [갈망하다] be thirsty ather [for / of] <know-ledge>; have a thirst for <money, knowledge, etc.>; thirst [crave / yearn] for <money>; hunger for <knowledge, affection, etc.>. e.g. 목마르게 기다린 비 long-awaited rain / the long-looked-for rain.

목매 (달)다 [मोंग्मै (दाल) दा] (남을) hang <a person>; (스스로) hang oneself. e.g. 나무에 목매다 hang oneself on a tree[down from a tree branch].

목메다 [मोंग्मैदा] be choked [stifled / suffocated] <with / by>. e.g. 목메어 우는 소녀 a sobbing girl / a girl choked with tears.

목사 [牧師] [मोकसा] a clergy-man; <집합적> the clergy

목석 [木石] [मोक्सौक] [나무와 돌] trees and stones; [생명이 없는 물건] inanimate objects; stocks and stones. e.g. 목석 같은 사람 an unfeeling [a callous] person / stocks and stones.

목소리 [मोकसोरी] a voice; a tone (of voice).

목수 [मोकसू] [木手] a car-penter.

목숨 [मोकसूम] life. e.g. 귀한 목숨 one's most precious life / one's dear (est) life 목숨 (을) 걸다 risk [haz-ard] one's life; risk one's neck. e.g. 목숨을 걸고 맹세하다 swear on [upon] one's life. 목숨(을) 끊다 (남의) take <a person's> life; kill; (스스로) take one's own life; kill oneself. 목숨(을) 바치다 offer [lay down / sacrifice] one's life. e.g. 나라를 위해

목숨을 바치다 offer [lay down / sacrifice] one's life for one's country / die for one's country.

목쉬다 [मोकश्वीदा] become [get / grow] hoarse [husky / harsh].

목요일 [मोग्योइल] [木曜日] Thursday (Thur(s).).

목욕 [मोक्यौक] [沐浴] a bath; bathing; ablution. 목욕하다 have [take] a bath; bathe; bath; wash oneself; wash up; clean up; have a tub

목욕탕 [मोग्योकथांग] [沐浴湯] a bath; a bathhouse; a bathroom. e.g. 대중 목욕탕 a public bath [bath-house].

목장 [मोक्यांग] [牧場] a stock farm; [방목장] a pasture (ground); a pasturage; [목초지] a meadow; a ranch.

목재 [मोकजै] [木材] wood; (건축용) (house) timber; lumber; <집합적> timbering.

목적 [मोक्चौक] [目的] a purpose; an object; an end (in view); [의도] a design; an intention; [목표] a goal.

목전 [मोक्चौन] [目前] e.g. 목전의 before [under] one's eyes / immediate / immi-nent / impending. 목전의 위험 an imminent danger 목전에서 일어난 사건 an event which happened under one's eyes.

목젖 [म्कजोछ] the uvula <*pl.* -lae, ~s>.

목제 [म्कजे] [木製] wooden construction [structure].

목조 [म्कजे] [木造] 목조 [म्कजे] = 목제. e.g. 그 집은 목조이다 The house is built of wood.

목차 [म्कछा] [目次] (a table of) contents.

목청 [मोक्छौंग] 1 [후두 중앙부의 발성 기관] the vocal c(h)ords [bands]. e.g. 목청을 울리다 vibrate the vocal chords. 2 [목소리] one's voice; one's tune (of voice). e.g. 목청껏 at the top of one's voice [lungs] / at the pitch of one's voice.

목초 [मोकछो] [牧草] grass; pasture; pasturage.

목축 [मोकछुक] [牧畜] (live) stock-farming; cattle breeding [raising]; pasturage (방목).

목축업 [मोकछुगौप] [牧畜業] stock-farming; cattle-breeding [-raising].

목표 [मोकफ्यो] [目標] 1 [표지] a mark; a landmark; a sign. e.g. …을 목표로 하여 나아가다 advance with ... for a guide. 2 [목적] a goal; a target; an object; an objective; an aim; [표준] (a) standard.

e.g. 학습의 목표 the aim of a lesson.

몫 [मोक] a share; a portion; an allotment; a quota; a whack; a cut; <美> a rake-off; a split; a divvy; the quotient(q.). e.g.자기 몫 one's share / one's winnings

몰골 [मोलगोल] <unshapely> figure[features]. e.g. 몰골 사나운 unshapely / shapeless / misshapen / unsightly / indecent.

몰다 [मोलदा] **1** [마소,차 등을 운전하다] drive. e.g.차를 몰다 drive a car. **2** [쫓다] pursue [chase] (ather); give chase to; go [run / take] ather; hunt up; course. e.g. 토끼를 몰다 chase [hunt up] a hare. **3** (궁지에) drive [chase] <into>; corner. e.g. 궁지에 몰다 corner / drive into a (tight) corner / drive [push] to the wall.

몰두[मोलदु][沒頭] devotion <to>; absorption <in>; immersion <in study>. 몰두하다 be immersed in; be absorbed [lost / engrossed] in; immerse oneself in; be devoted to; devote oneself to; give oneself up entirely to; bury oneself in; be up to the eyes [neck / elbows] in <one's work>.

몰라보다[मोल्लाबोदा] fail to recognize; cannot [do not] recognize; [무시하다] ignore; fail to appreciate; show no appreciation of <the kindness>. e.g. 친구를 몰라보다 fail to recognize one's friend / neglect [disregard] one's friend

몰락 [मोल्लाक] [沒落] 몰락 [파멸] ruin; fall; collapse; downfall; wreck; [파산] bankruptcy. 몰락하다 fall; go to ruin; be ruined; be wrecked; go to the dogs; [파산(하다] become [go] bankrupt

몰래[मोल्लै] stealthily; by stealth; quietly; secretly; in secret; privately; surreptitiously; imperceptibly; furtively; in a stealthy way; on the quiet; clandestinely.

몰려가다 [मोल्लयौगादा] **1** [쫓기어 가다] be driven [chased / pursued]. e.g. 구석지로 몰려가다 be driven into a corner. **2** [떼지어 가다] crowd [flock] <to>; throng (to) <a place>; storm <a theater>; go in groups; besiege. e.g. 응원하러 몰려가다 turn out (in droves) to cheer [support] <a team>.

몰려나다 [मोल्लयौनादा] **1** [쫓기어 나가다] be expelled [turned / put / sent / driven] out; be booted out; (직장에서) be ousted [dislodged] <from a position>; (셋집 등에서) be evicted [ejected] <from a rented house>. e.g. 회사에서 몰려나다 be kicked out of a company. **2** [떼지어 나가다] go out in groups [crowds / swarms / flocks]; turn out en masse; sally forth. e.g. 야구장에서 많은 군중이 한꺼번에 몰려났다 A big crowd surged out of the baseball stadium.

몰려다니다 [मोल्लयौदानीदा] **1** [쫓기어 다니다] be driven round [about]; be chased about. e.g. 구름이 바람에 몰려다니다 Clouds are driven about by the wind. **2** [떼지어 다니다] walk in groups [crowds / swarms / flocks]; throng about [round]. e.g. 아이들이 몰려다니며 놀고 있었다 Children were playing about [around] in groups [clusters / bunches].

몰려들다 [मोल्लयौदुलदा] **1** [쫓기어 들어오다] be driven [chased / pursued] into. e.g. 도둑이 골목으로 몰려들었다 The thief was driven [chased] into an alley. / The hunted robber rushed into an alley. **2** [떼지어 들어오다] come in groups [crowds]; crowd [flock / swarm] in. e.g. 해안으로 몰려들다 flock to the seaside.

몰려오다 [मोल्लयौओदा] **1** [쫓기어서 오다] come driven [chased / pursued] (back). **2** [떼지어 오다] come in crowds [flocks / groups]; flock; throng; storm <a place>.

몰리다[1] [मोल्लीदा] **1** [밀리다] be driven; be pressed; be pushed. e.g. 일이 몰리다 be pressed with work / be driven by business. **2** (궁지에) be driven to a corner; be cornered; [궁해지다] be hard up; be pressed for <money>; [난처해지다] be at a loss for <an answer>; be driven to one's wit's end. e.g. 궁지에 몰리다 be placed in fix / be in a tight corner / stand[be] at bay / be pushed to the wall / be driven into a corner **3** [한쪽으로 여럿이 밀리다] gather[flock](together); come [get] together; crowd; swarm; cluster; throng. e.g. 돈이 한곳으로 몰리다 money flows into one place / money is poorly distributed.

몰리다[2] [मोल्लीदा] **1** [쫓기다] be pursued [chased] (ather); be trailed [hunted up]. e.g. 도둑이 몰려서 골목으로 뛰어들었다 The hunted robber rushed in an alley. **2** [···으로 다루어지다] be accused of; be charged with; be blamed for. e.g. 살인죄로 몰리어 on a charge of murder.

몰살 [मोल्साल] [沒殺] extermination; annihilation; (무차별의) (a) total slaughter; (무저항자에 대한) a massacre; (국민, 민족 등에 대한) genocide. 몰살하다 kill (the enemy) to a man; massacre; annihilate; exterminate; wipe out. e.g. 온 가족을 몰살하다 murder the whole family.

몰상식 [मोल्सांगसीक] [沒常識] lack of (common) sense; senselessness; thoughtlessness; absurdity; irrationality. 몰상식하다 absurd; preposterous; thoughtless; <서술적> have no common sense

몰아가다 [मोरा गादा] **1** [몰아서 데리고 가다] drive (away). ⇨ 몰다 1 e.g. 소를 풀밭으로 몰아가다 drive cattle (out) to pasture. **2** [휩쓸어 가다] take away in a lump [in bulk / by the gross / in one lot / en masse]; sweep away; [몰아서 사다] buy <things> in a mass [lot]; buy up. e.g. 시장의 밀을 몰아가다 corner the stock of wheat on the market.

몰아내다 [मोरा नैदा] [내쫓다] turn [get / put / send / drive] out; kick [run] <a person> out <of the house [company / army]>; (지위에서) oust [expel] <a person from a position>; (셋집에서) evict [eject] <a tenant from the house>. e.g. 적을 도시에서 몰아내다 drive the enemy from the town.

몰아넣다 [मोरानोत्था] **1** [들어가게 하다] drive [chase / push] in [into]. e.g. 돼지를 우리 안에 몰아넣다 drive a pig into the pigpen. **2** (궁지에) corner <a person>; get [drive] <a person> into a (tight) corner; drive [push / thrust] to the wall; put <a person> in a fix [hole]. e.g. 궁지에 몰아넣다 corner <a person> up / drive <a person> into a corner. **3** (휩쓸어) put [push / press] all into <a place>. e.g. 옷을 트렁크에 몰아넣다 ram [squeeze] all the clothes into a trunk.

몰아주다 [मोराजुदा] (한꺼번에) give [pay] in a lump [in one lot / by the gross]; give [pay] all at once [at a time]. e.g. 1 년 생활비를 몰아주다 give <a person> the living expenses for one year in a lump sum.

몰아치다 [मोराछीदा] **1** [몰아 닥치다] make [rush] for; (비바람이) storm; (파도가) surge [rush] upon. e.g. 눈이 몰아쳤다 It was snowing thick and fast. **2** [한 곳으로 몰다] drive [chase] to <a place>; drive [push / thrust] to the wall; press <a fugitive> close [hard]. **3** [급히 서두르다] do [work] all at once; speed up <one's business>; make short work (of it); bundle off in quick [short] order. e.g. 시험 공부를 몰아쳐서 하다 cram [get crammed] for an examination.

몰염치 [मोर्यौम्छी] [**沒廉恥**] impudence; shamelessness. 염치하다 impudent; shameless; <서술적> be without shame; have no shame.

몰입 [मोरिप] [**沒入**] [몰두] immersion; devotion; absorption. 몰입하다 be immersed [absorbed] in <one's work>; get oneself absorbed in <one's study>.

몸 [मोम] **1** [신체] the body; [체격] physique; build; constitution (체질); frame (뼈대); [신장] stature; [크기] size; [모습] figure. e.g. 사람의 몸 the human body. **2** [몸통] the body; the trunk (of the body); the torso. e.g. 여자 머리에 사자 몸을 가진 스핑크스 the sphinx with a women's head and lion's body. **3** [건강] health. e.g. 몸이 튼튼한[약한] 아이 a healthy [delicate] child. 몸(을) 던지다 throw oneself <into a river>. 몸(을) 망치다 shatter one's constitution; (건강이) fall into ill health; injure [lose] health. 몸(을) 아끼다 spare oneself <the trouble>. e.g. 몸을 아끼면 살이 찔 것이다 You will put on weight if you don't work [don't do any manual work].

몸가짐 [मोम गाजीम] [태도] demeanor, demeanour; [거동, 행동 거지] manners; (a) carriage; movements.

몸값 [मोम गाप] [화대] money paid for prostitution; (포로 등의) ransom; price of redemption; the money [price] for flesh traffic (for a slave).

몸매 [मोम्मै] one's figure; one's shape; one's form. e.g. 날씬한 몸매 a slender figure

몸부림 [मोमबुरीम] **1** [버둥거림] writhing; squirming; a (violent) struggle. 몸부림하다 =몸부림치다 **2** [잠자리에서의 몸을 뒤치는 짓] turning over in bed; tossing about in sleep.

몸부림하다 = 몸부림치다.

몸부림치다 [मोमबुरीम छीदा] **1** [버둥거리다] struggle; writhe; flounce; wriggle; flounder; squirm. e.g. 괴로워서 몸부림치다 writhe in agony. **2** (잠자리에서) turn [heave] (over / round) in sleep; toss [roll] about in bed.

몸살[मोमसाल] illness from fatigue; general [great] fatigue.

몸서리 [मोमसौरी] **1** [무서워서 다시는 하고 싶지 않은 마음] a shudder; a quiver; a thrill; a quake; a tremble; a shiver; quivering; shuddering; trembling; shivering. e.g. 그것은 듣기만 [생각만] 해도 몸서리난다 I shudder at the mere mention [thought] of it. **2** [지겨움] weariness; tiresomeness. e.g. 가난한 생활에는 몸서리난다 I am tired of my humble life.

몸소 [मोमसो] personally; in person; <do it> oneself. e.g. 몸소 방문하다 make a personal call <on / at>.

몸져눕다 [मोमजयौनुप्ता] take to one's bed; be ill in bed; lie in one's sickbed; be laid up <with a cold>; keep one's bed. e.g. 그는 폐병으로 몸져누워 있다 He is laid up with consumption.

몸조리 [मोमजोरी] [－調 理] taking care of one's health; (병후의) recuperation. 몸조리하다 take care of one's health; (병후에) recuperate (oneself); recruit t(oneself).

몸조심 [मोमजोसीम] [－操心] **1** [건강을 위함] care of one's health. 몸조심하다 take (good) care of one's health; be careful of one's health. e.g.병에 걸리지 않도록 몸조심하라 Take care not to make yourself ill. **2** [언행을 삼감] prudence; discretion; behaving oneself. 몸조심하다 behave oneself prudently; be prudent [use prudence] in action. e.g. 그 사건 이후 나는 매우 몸조심하고 있다 The accident has rendered me very cautious.

몸집 [मोमजीब] the stature; one's build; the frame. e.g. 몸집이 작은 small-sized.

몸짓 [मोमजीत] a gesture; (a) gesticulation; (an) action; (a) motion.

몸치장 [मोमछीजांग] [－治 粧] adornment (of one's person); dressing (oneself) up; decking oneself out; trimming oneself up. 몸치장하다 (옷으로) dress (oneself) up; be gaily [gaudily] dressed; be dressed up; (장식물로) ornament [adorn / deck] oneself <with>

몸통 [मोमथोंग] the trunk; the body; the bulk of one's body; girth.

몸풀다 [मोमफुलदा] **1** [해산하다] give birth to <a baby>; be delivered of <a baby>. **2** [피로를 덜다] relieve [banish] one's fatigue; take a rest.

몹시 [मोप्सी] **1** [대단히] very (much); exceedingly; excessively; extremely; greatly; immensely; terribly; highly. e.g. 몹시 기뻐하다 be highly [much] pleased. **2** [심하게] severely; violently; intensely; heavily; badly. e.g. 몹시 아프다 feel [suffer] a severe pain.

몹쓸 [मोप्सुल] [나쁜] bad; evil; ill; immoral; sinful; [사악한] wicked; ill-natured; malicious; villainous; roguis

못[1] [मोत] (금속으로 만든) a nail; [대못] a spike; [나무못] a peg.

못[2] [मोत] [불가] (definitely) not; won't; [불능] cannot <do>; unable <to do>; incapable <of doing>. e.g. 어두워서 못 읽겠다 It is too dark to read.

못 본 체하다 [मोतबुन छेहादा] (보고도) pretend not to see [to have seen] <something>; (관대하게) overlook; look over; pass over <a matter> in silence; let <it> pass [go]; connive <at>.

못나다 [मोन्नादा] **1** [못생기다] plain; ugly; bad-[ugly- / plain-] looking; ill-favored; homely (-looking); uncomely. **2** [어리석다] foolish; stupid; silly; dull; witless; fatuous; asinine; daffy; zany.

못내 [मोन्नै] [그지없이] immeasurably; incalculably; [잊지 않고] unforgettably; [늘] always; ever. e.g. 이별을 못내 아쉬워하다 be deeply sorry to part from <a person

못되다 [मोल्देदा] [나쁘다] bad; evil; wrong; [사악하다] wicked; ill-natured; malicious; criminal. e.g. 못된 생각 an evil intention / a mistaken idea.

못마땅하다 [मोम्मात्तांगहादा] [(사물이) 마음에 안 들다] disagreeable [offensive / distasteful / unacceptable] <to>; not to <a person's> liking; unsatisfactory; undesirable; [불만스럽다] displeased [dissatisfied] <with something>.

못살게 굴다 [मोस्साल्गे गुल्दा] [학대하다] persecute; oppress; torment; be hard (up) on <a person>; be cruel to <a dog>; ride <a person> (hard); (장난삼아) tease; annoy; (신입생 등을) haze; rag.

못생기다 [मोस्सैंगीदा] **1** [잘나지 못하다] ugly; (용모가) bad-looking; (특히 여자가) plain; homely (▷ homely, plain 은 완곡한 표현임 **2** [어리석다] foolish; stupid; dull; thickheaded; soth-[dull-] witted.

못쓰다 [मोस्सुदा] [쓸모 없다] useless; worthless; unfit for use; bad; (금지) must not <do>; shall not <do> (2, 3인칭에); ought not to <do>; should not <do>.

못지않다 [मोच्चीआन्था] no less (than); just as good (as); not inferior <to>; by no means inferior <to>; equal <to>. e.g. 남자 못지않은 여자아이 a strong-minded girl.

못질 [मोच्चिल] 못질하다 nail (up) <a box>; nail down <a lid>; fasten with nails.

못하다[1] [मोत्थादा] **1** [할 수 없다] cannot <do>; be unable <to do>; be incapable <of doing>; [··· 할 여유가 없다] cannot afford <to do>. e.g. 그것은 어려워서 나는 못하겠다 It is too difficult for me to do. / It's too much for me. **2** [하지 못하다] fail to <do>; miss <doing>. e.g. 승진하지 못하다 fail to be promoted.

못하다[2] [मोत्थादा] [뒤떨어지다] inferior [second] to <another>; worse than; below; unequal to; not as good as; not on a level [par] with. e.g. 약간 못하다 fall (a little) behind <another> / be a cut below <a person>.

몽둥이 [मोंगदोंगी] a stick; a club; a cudgel.

몽땅 [मोंगतांग] (one and) all; everything; entirely; wholly; completely; in its entirety; in a body.

몽롱 [मोंगनोंग] [朦朧] dimness; obscurity; indistinctiveness; vagueness. 몽롱하다 dim; indistinct; vague; faint; fuzzy; obscure; opaque; hazy; cloudy; misty; foggy

몽상 [मोंगसांग] [夢想] a dream; a vision; a fancy; a daydream; a fantasy. e.g. 몽상에 잠기다 fall into [be lost in] (a) reverie / be given to daydreaming.

몽실몽실 [मोंगसील मोंगसील] plumply; fleshly. e.g. 몽실몽실 살찐 아기 a chubby baby.

몽유병 [मोंग्युबयौग] [夢遊病] [醫] sleepwalking; somnambulism. e.g. 몽유병의 somnambulant. **몽유병자** a sleepwalker; a somnambulist.

몽환 [मोंगहवान] [夢幻] dreams and phantasma; (a) fantasy; visions. e.g. 몽환적 dreamlike / dreamy / phantasmal.

묘 [मयो] [墓] = 무덤.

묘기 [मयोगी] [妙技] [기술] wonderful skill; [곡예] a miraculous [wonderful] feat; (연예 등에서의) a wonderful performance; (야구 등에서의) a fine play.

묘목 [मयोमोक] [苗木] a (young) plant; a nursery tree; a sapling; a seedling.

묘미 [मयोमी] [妙味] exquisiteness; charm; beauty; a nicety; a nice point.

묘비 [मयोबी] [墓碑] a tombstone; a gravestone; a funerary slab; a mortuary monument

묘사 [मयोसा] [描寫] (a) description; (인물,풍물의) a portrait; <文>(a) depiction; delineation; representation

묘안 [मयोआन] [妙案] a happy [bright] idea; an excellent [ingenious] plan [scheme]. e.g. 묘안을 생각해내다 hit on [be struck with] a capital idea / a bright idea strikes one.

묘연 [मयोयौन] [杳然] 묘연하다(거리가) far away; remote; [기억이 흐릿하다] dim; vague; indistinct; (소식이) unknown; missing. e.g. 그의 행방이 묘연하다 No one knows his whereabouts.

묘지 [मयोजी] [墓地] a graveyard; a burial ground [place];(공동묘지) a (public) cemetery; (교회 부속의) a churchyard; God's acre.

묘하다 [मयोहादा] [妙-] [기묘하다] strange; curious; odd (▷ strange는 낯설고 불가사의한, curious 는 호기심을 돋우는, odd 는 보통과 다른 기묘함); queer; funny; singular; rum.

무 [मू] [無] [없음] nothing; naught; nil; nihility; nullity; zero. e.g. 무에서 유는 생기지 않는다 Nothing comes of [from] nothing.

무감각 [मुगामगाक] [無感覺] **무감각 1** [감각이 없음] insensibility; senselessness; [마비되어 있음] numbness; [무감동] apathy; impassiveness; callousness; callosity. 무감각하다 insensible <to pain>; anesthetic; numb; apathetic; callous; thick-skinned; dead <to pity>; <서술적> have no feeling. e.g. 남의 고생에 대하여 무감각하다 be callous [apathetic] to the sufferings of others **2** [감수성이 둔함] insensitivity; [무신경] callousness. e.g. 미에 대한 무감각 a lack of sensitivity to beauty. 무감각하다 insensitive <to>; insensible <of>; callous. e.g. 그는 치욕[모욕]에 대해서 무감각하다 He doesn't seem to feel shame [insults] at all.

무겁다 [मुगौप्ता]**1** [무게가 많다] heavy; weighty. e.g. 무거운 발소리 a clamp / a heavy tramp. **2** (입이) taciturn; ncommunicative; reticent; quiet; reserved <in speech>; (행동이) pru-dent; serious; grave; ponderous. e.g. 입이 무거운 사람 a taciturn [reticent / discreet / tight-lipped] person.**3** [기분이 침울하다] heavy; depressed; dull; languid. e.g. 무거운 분위기 an oppressive atmosphere.

무게 [मूगे] **1** [중량] weight; heth. **2** [침착하고 의젓한 정도] weight; importance; dignity; authority; prestige. e.g. 무게 있는 말 a remark carrying weight [authority / conviction].

무경험 [मूग्यौगहौम] [**無經驗**] inexperience; lack [want] of experience; greenness

무계획 [मूग्येहवीक] [**無計劃**] 무계획하다 unplanned; haphazard; [무모하다] reckless

무고 [मूगो] [**無辜**] innocence. 무고하다 [사실과 다르다] false; [결백하다] innocent; guiltless. e.g. 무고한 죄 a false charge.

무관(계) [मूगवान ग्ये] [**無關(係)**] no connection; no relation; irrelevance; impertinence. 무관하다 unconnected; unconcerned; unrelated; indifferent; <서술적> have no connection <with>; have no relation <to / with>; have nothing to do <with>; be not connected <with>; be not concerned <in / with>; be independent <of>; be irrelevant <to>. e.g. 문제에 무관한 사항 a matter foreign [extraneous] to the question.

무관심 [मूगवान सीम] [**無關心**] indifference; unconcern; nonchalance; apathy; callousness; lacking interest <in>. 무관심하다 indifferent <to>; unconcerned <about / with>; apathetic; nonchalant; callous <to>; uninterested <in>; careless <about / of>.

무궁 무진 [मूगुंग मुजीन] [**無窮無盡**] infinitude; endlessness. 무궁 무진하다 infinite; endless; bound-less; inexhaustible. e.g. 그 지방에는 철광이 무궁 무진하게 있다 The region has inexhaustible deposits of iron ore.

무근 [मूगुन] [**無根**] groundlessness; baselessness. e.g. 그것은 사실 무근이다 There's not a grain [an ounce] of truth in it. 무근하다 groundless; baseless; unfounded; false. e.g. 전혀 사실 무근한 이야기 a pure fabrication. 그 보도는 사실 무근하다 The report is unfounded [a pure fabrication]. / There is no foundation for the report.

무급 [मुगुप] [無給] e.g. 무급의 unpaid / unsalaried / gratuitous / honorary. 무급으로 without pay [salary] / for nothing / gratuitously.

무기 [मुगी] [武器][전투에 쓰이는 기구] a weapon; <집합적> arms; weaponry; ordnance; armament.

무기력 [मुगीरयौक] [無氣力] enervation; lethargy; languor; languishment; leadenness; tameness. 무기력하다 [생기없다] spiritless; enervate; nerveless; [불활발하다] lethargic; languid; leaden; flabby.

무기명 [मुगीमयौग] [無記名] e.g. 무기명의 unregistered / (무서명의) unsigned / (주식,채권 등이) blank / uninscribed. 무기명식의 (배서 등이) blank / general / (지참인 지불의) <a check> payable to bearer / bearer <check>.

무기한 [मुगीहान] [無期限] an indefinite period; no time limit. e.g. 무기한의 limitless / indefinite / without a time limit.

무난 [मुनान] [無難] **1** [쉬움] being easy; being without difficulty [trouble]. **2** [무던함] faultlessness; passableness. 무난하다 fairly good; moderate; passable; acceptable; flawless; free from fault. e.g. 무난한 작품이 적었다 There were few passable [tolerable] works.

무남 독녀 [मुनाम दोकन्यौ] [無男獨女] an[the] only daughter; a daughter and only child <of>.

무너뜨리다 मुनौतुरीदा] break down; pull down; tear down; destroy; demolish.

무너지다 [मुनौजीदा] **1** [붕괴하다] crumble; go [fall] to pieces; collapse; break; give way; be destroyed; come down; [함몰하다] cave in. e.g. 눈의 무게로 지붕이 무너졌다 The roof collapsed [caved in] under the weight of the snow **2** [질서 등이 파괴되다] break; give way; be thrown into disorder [confusion]; be routed. e.g. 군대가 무너졌다 The army gave away [was routed].

무능 [मुनुंग] [無能] incompetency; inefficiency; lack of ability; inability; incapacity; inadequacy; inequality <to a task 무능하다 incompetent; inefficient; incapable; ineffective; talentless; lacking in ability [efficiency]; good-for-nothing.

무능력 [मुनुंगरयौक] [無能力] inability <at / in / to do>; lack of ability; [法] incomepetence; incapacity <for / to do>; disability.

무늬 [मूनउइ] a pattern; a figure

무단 [मूदान] [**無斷**] [허가 없음]. e.g. 무단 출입 금지 <게시> No trespassing.

무담보 [मूदामबो] [**無擔保**] e.g. 무담보의 unsecured / naked / without collateral [security]. 무담보로 대부하다 grant <a person> a loan without security.

무당 [मूदांग] [**巫 堂**] an exorcist; a (female) shaman; a sorceress; a witch; [영매] a (psychic) medium <*pl.* ~s>.

무대 [मूदै] [**舞臺**] **1** (연극의) the stage; the boards. e.g. 원형 무대 a theater-in-the-round. **2** (활동의) the sphere [field] <of activity>; the arena; the stage; theater. e.g. 경쟁 무대 the arena of competition

무더기 [मूदौगी] a pile; a heap; a deposit; a lot; a mound

무더위 [मूदौवी] sultriness; hot and humid weather; (high) humidity; sultry weather; sweltering heat.

무던하다 [मूदौकहादा] (성질이) generous; broad-minded; liberal; quite good [nice]. e.g. 무던한 사람 a good-natured man.

무던히 [मूदौनही] **1** 어지간히] quite; pretty; fairly; considerably; [매우,몹시] extremely; exceedingly. e.g. 무던히 애쓰다 make considerable efforts.**2** [너그럽게] generously; kindly; nicely; satisfactorily; courteously; warmly. e.g. 무던히 굴다 behave nicely.

무덤 [मूदौम] **무덤** a grave; a tomb; a resting place; a sepulcher.

무덥다 [मुदौपता] sultry; sweltering; muggy; close and hot; hot and damp; steaming; humid. e.g. 무더운 날씨 muggy [sultry] weather.

무도회 [मूदोह्वे] [**舞蹈會**] a ball; a dancing party; a dance.

무드 [मुद] [기분] a mood.

무득점 [मूदुकजौम] [**無得點**] e.g. 무득점의 scoreless / [야구] runless.

무디다 [मूदीदा] **1** [날이 예리하지 못하다] dull; blunt; obtuse; pointless; edgeless. e.g. 무딘 면도날 a dull razor blade. **2** [둔하다] dull; slow; thick-headed; slow-witted; dense. e.g. 감각이 무디어지다 get dull of one's sense.

무뚝뚝하다 [मूतुक्तुकहादा] [퉁명스럽다] blunt; brusque; abrupt; short; [붙임성없다] unsociable; [멋없다] curt; [쌀쌀맞다] cold

무럭무럭 [मूरौक मुरौक] [자라는 모양] rapidly; well; perceptibly; quickly. e.g. 무럭무럭 자라다 grow up quickly [rapidly] / (키가) become taller with rapidity [day by day].

무려 [मुर्यौ] [無慮] [자그마치] to the prodigious [vast] number of; as many as; no less than. e.g. 무려 5 천명 as many as five thousand.

무력 [मुर्यौक] [武力] military force [power]; armed might [force]; force of arms; the sword [saber]; the mailed fist. e.g. 무력으로 by (force of) arms / at the point of the bayonet [sword].

무렵 [मुर्यौप] [때] time; [즈음] about; around; toward(s); […할 즈음] about the time when ... e.g. 무렵에 at the time / on the occasion / when / as.

무례 [मुरये] [無禮] [실례] impoliteness; rudeness; discourtesy; disrespect; [불손] insolence; impertinence. 무례하다 impolite; rude; dis-courteous; disrespectful; indecent; uncivil; insolent; impertinent. e.g. 그런 말을 묻는 것은 무례한 일이다 It is impolite [bad manners] to ask such a question.

무료 [मुर्यो] [無料] no charge; free of charge. e.g. 무료로 제공되다 be offered free [without cost].

무료 [मुर्यौ] [無聊] [심심함] tedium; ennui; wearisomeness; dullness; [열없음] awkwardness. e.g. 무료를 달래다 beguile the tedium / while away [kill] the time.

무르다[1] [मुरुदा] (산 것을) take back [redeem] money cancelling a purchase; get a refund; (판 것을) give back [return] money cancelling a sale; give a refund. e.g. 대금을 무르다 refund the price paid.

무르다[2] [मुरदा] [연하다] soth; tender; flabby; flaccid; mushy; pulpy; limp; weak <foundation>; frail <structure>. e.g. 무른 고기 tender meat.

무르익다 [मुरुइकत्ता] **1**(과일 등이) ripen; mellow; mature; become [get] ripe; come to maturity. e.g. 무르익은 술 mellow [well-mellowed] wine / rich wine.**2** (시기나 일이) be ripe for; (음모 등이) come to a head. e.g. 기회가 무르익기를 기다리다 wait for a ripe opportunity [moment] / wait till the time is ripe <for

무릅쓰다 [मुरबसुदा] risk; brave [defy / face] <a danger>; venture; dare; run <a risk, a hazard, etc.>(▷ brave는 [각오하고 견디어]라고 하는 느낌에 대해 defy는 [건방지게 무시한다]는 느낌). e.g. 죽음을 무릅

쓰고 항거하다 face death to resist.

무릉 도원 [मुरूंगदोवॉन] [**武陵桃源**] an Arcadia; a Utopia; the Happy Valley. e.g. 무릉 도원의 꿈 a Utopian dream.

무릎 [मुरूफ] a knee; a lap; a genu <*pl.* -nua>.

무리[1] [मूरी] [**無理**] **1** [도리에 어긋남] unreasonableness. e.g. 네가 웃은 것도 무리는 아니다 Now I see why you laughed / No wonder you laughed. **2** [불가능] impossibility.e.g. 무리한 일을 하려고 하다 attempt the impossible / try to do something beyond one's power. 너는 무리한 짓을 하고 있다 You are trying to do the impossible.

무리[2] [मुरी] a band; a party; a gang; a group e.g. 무리를 짓다 band together.

무마 [मूम] [**撫摩**] [달램] (a) consolation; (a) solace; soothing; pacification. 무마하다(노여움을) appease; pacify; (싸움 등을) suppress; quell; put down. e.g. 소동을 겨우 무마시켰다 We had much difficulty in putting down the sedition.

무명 [मुम्यौग] [**無名**] **1** [이름이 없음] being nameless. e.g. 무명의 [nameless / unnamed.**2** [유명하지 않음] obscurity. e.g. 그녀는 무명의 사나이와 결혼했다She has married a nobody.

무모 [मूमो] [**無謀**] recklessness; rashness; temerity; imprudence; thoughtlessness. e.g. 무모하게 recklessy

무미 건조 [मूमी गोनजु] [**無味乾燥**] 무미 건조하다 dry(as a chip); dry-as-dust; dusty; (flat and) insipid; uninteresting; dull; vapid; jejune; tasteless; prosaic. e.g. 무미 건조한 농담a dry [flat] joke.

무방하다 [मूबांगहादा] [**無妨-**] <서술적> [해가 되지 않다] do <one> no harm; be harmless; [지장 없다] be no obstacle [hindrance / impediment]; [이의가 없다] have no objection; [상관없다] do not matter; make no difference; [해도 좋다] may; can; be allowed to <do>; be all right; [없어도 좋다] can do without. e.g. 자네가 없어도 무방하다I can do without you.

무법 [मूबौब] [**無法**] [불법] injustice; unlawfulness; outlawry; wrongfulness; outrage; violence; [이치에 어긋남] lawlessness; unreasonableness; absurdity. e.g. 무법한 요구 an unreasonable [unlawful] demand.

무법 천지 [मूबौब छौनजी] a lawless world; a state of extreme disorder.

무보수 [मुबोसु] [無報酬] non-payment; no compensation; no pay

무분별 [मुबुनबयौल] [無分別] [사려 없음] indiscretion; thoughtlessness; imprudence; [경솔] rashness; reck-lessness. 무분별하다 indiscreet; thoughtless; imprudent; rash; reckless; injudicious; ill-considered[-judged]. e.g.무분별하게] indiscreetly / imprudently / thoughtlessly / recklessly / rashly.

무비판 [मुबीफान] [無批判] e.g. 무비판적(으로) uncritical (ly) / indiscriminate(ly).

무사 [मुसा] [無事] [안전] safety; security; [평온] peace; quietness; tranquility; [탈없음,건강] good health. 무사하다 [안전하다] safe; secure; [평온하다] peaceful; quiet; calm; uneventful; [탈없다] (quite) well; doing well [nicely]. e.g. 무사하기를 빌다pray for <a person's> safety.

무상 [मुसांग] [無常] [변하기 쉬움] mutability; [덧없음] uncertainty; vanity; transiency; impermanency. e.g. 인생의 무상을 절실히 느끼다 feel keenly the precariousness [capriciousness] of life / feel deeply the pathos of life.

무상 [मुसांग] [無償] no compensation. e.g.초등 학교 교과서는 무상으로 배포된다 Elementary school textbooks are distributed (to children) free of charge.

무색 [無色] [मुसैक] **1** [빛깔이 없음] colorlessness; lack of color. e.g. 무색의[मुसैकउइ] colorless / achromatic. **2** [부끄러워 볼 낯이 없음] shame; disgrace. 무색하다 <서술적> feel shame; be ashamed <of>. e.g. 전문가를 무색케 하는 연기 acting which outshines that of a professional.

무생물 [मुसैगमुल] [無生物] a lifeless thing; an inanimate object.

무서움 [मुसौउम] fear; fearfulness; dreadfulness; formidableness; ferocity; terror; horror; frightfulness; terribleness. e.g. 그는 무서움을 모른다 He does not know what fear is.

무서워하다 [मुसौवॉहादा] fear; be afraid <of>; be frightened <at / by>; be scared <at>; be in fear <of>; be in a fright; be timid <of>; be nervous <about>

무선 [मुसौन] [無線] radio; wireless.

무섭다 [मुसौबदा] [끔찍하다] fearful; frightful; terrible; dreadful; dread; fright-

ㄷ

tening; horrible; horrific; awful; scary; [으스스하다] grim; uncanny; weird; [사납다] fierce; ferocious; truculent; savage; villainous; [상대하기에 겁나다] formidable; [두렵다] be afraid <of / that>; be apprehensive; be scared [frightened

무성 [मूसांग] [茂盛] 무성하다 thick; dense; luxuriant; exuberant; profuse; rank; rampant; close-grown (▷ rank 는 바람직하지 않은 식물에 사용). e.g.무성한 잡초 rank weeds / a tangled growth of wild grass.

무성음 [मूसौगम] [無聲音] a voiceless [an unvoiced] sound.

무성의 [मूसौगउइ] [無誠意] insincerity; bad faith. 무성의하다 insincere; unfaithful; false; fickle. e.g. 무성의하게 [मूसौगउइहागे] insincerely / unfaithfully.

무소속 [मूसोसोग] [無所屬] e.g. 무소속의 independent / unattached / affiliated with no party / neutral.

무소식 [मूसोशिक] [無消息] no news <from a person>. e.g. 무소식이 희소식 <속담> No news is good news.

무수 [मूस्] [無數] an infinite [untold] number; immensities. e.g. 무수의 innumerable / countless / numberless. 무수하다 numberless; innumer-able; incalculable; count-less. e.g. 무수한 예를 들다 give no end of exam-ples.

무술 [मूसुल] [武術] the military [martial] arts.

무슨 [मुसन] [의문] what; what kind [sort] of; [어떤] some; some kind of. e.g. 무슨 일이나 in everything / in all matters [things].

무승부 [मूसंगबु] [無勝負] a drawn game; a tie; a draw <in a game>; an undecided match. e.g. 무승부로 끝나다end in a tie [draw] / be drawn / tie [draw] <with>.

무시 [मूसी] [無視] disregard <for rules>; neglect <of consequence>. 무시하다 disregard; ignore; defy; discount; neglect; take [make] no account <of>; set <the rules, etc.> at naught [nothing]. e.g. 규칙을 무시하다 disregard the rules.

무시무시하다 [मूशीमूशीहादा] frightful; [송장 같다] ghastly; [초자연적이다] weird; [불가사의해서 기 분 나쁘다] uncanny; [귀신같다] spooky; [소름끼치다] creepy; horrible; cruel; brutal; dismal; terrible; dreadful; fearsome. e.g. 무시무시한 사건 a ghastly [horrible] incident.

무식 [मूशीक] [無識] ignoreance; illiteracy. 무식하다 ignorant; [읽고 쓰지 못하다] illiterate; unlettered; [교육받지 못하다] uneducated. e.g. 무식한 탓으로 due to ignorance.

무신경 [मुशीनग्यौग] [無神經] insensibility; apathy; indifference; callousness; stolidity. 신경하다 pathetic; indifferent; stolid; dull; [둔감하다] insensitive; [냉담하다] callous; [뻔뻔스럽다] thick-skinned. e.g. 그는 이웃 사람의 고통[비탄]에 대하여 무신경하다 He is callous [unfee-ling] about the distress of his neighbors. 심 [मुशीम] [無心] [생각 없음] detachment; innocence; heedlessness; inadvertence; absent-mindedness.

무심하다 [मुशीमहादा] innocent; casual; [관심 없다] unconcerned; [인정 없다] heartless; hard; inconsiderate.

무심코 [मुशीम्ख्वो] [無心 -] [아무 생각 없이] unintentionally; involuntarily; [문득] casually; by chance; accidentally; [부주의하게] carelessly; [저도 모르게] unconsciously; in spite of oneself. e.g. 나는 무심코 있다가 정류장을 세 곳이나 지나쳐 갔다I was daydreaming and [My thoughts were elsewhere and I] was carried three stops beyond my destination.

무아 [मुआ][無我] self-effacement; self-renunciation; annihilation of self; selflessness. e.g. 무아의 경지에 이르다 attain a spiritual state of perfect selflessness / rise above self / go into an impersonal state.

무안 [मुआन] [無顔] shame; disgrace; dishonor. e.g. 무안을 주다 put <a person> to shame [the blush] / put <a person> out of countenance. 무안을 당하다 be put to shame / disgrace oneself / bring disgrace upon oneself. 무안하다 ashamed; feel shamed at; lose face; humiliate oneself by; blush with shame. e.g.무안해서 고개를 떨구다hang one's head with shame.

무언 [मुऔन] [無言] silence; muteness; reticence; taciturnity. e.g. 두 사람 사이에는 무언의 이해가 있었다 There was a tacit understanding between the two.

무엇 [मुऔत] what; which; something; anything. e.g. 이것은 무엇입니까What's this?

무역 [मुयौक] [貿易] trade; commerce.

무예 [मुये] [武藝] military [martial] arts; feats of arms.

무용 [मुयोंग] [舞踊] [춤을 춤]

dancing; [한 차례의 춤] a dance. e.g. 민속 무용a folk dance.

무용지물 [मुयोंगजीमुल] [無用之物] a useless thing [person]; a good-for-nothing.

무의미[मूउइमी][無意味] meaninglessness; insignificancy; purpose-lessness <of an act>. 무의미하다 [뜻이 없다] meaningless; insignificant; pointless; [무익하다] purposeless; [어리석다] absurd; senseless; nonsensical. e.g. 무의미한 토론a meaningless argument.

무의식 [मूउइसीक] [無意識] unconsciousness; involuntariness; [정신 분석] the unconscious. e.g. 무의식 중에 한숨이 나오다 sigh unconsciously.

무이자 [मूइजा] [無利子] no interest; without interest; interest-free.

무익 [मूइक] [無益] uselessness; unprofitableness; futility. 무익하다 useless; futile; unavailing; unprofitable; no good; fruitless.

무인 [मूइन][無人] e.g. 무인의 manless / unmanned / uninhabited / desert.

무인도 [मूइनदो] [無人島] a desert island; an uninhabited island. e.g. 그 섬은 무인도이다 The island is uninhabited.

무일푼 [मूइलफुन] [無一] penniless ness. e.g. 그는 무일푼으로 사업을 시작했다 He started his business with practically nothing.

무임 승차 [मूइम सुंगछी] [無賃乘車] a free ride; deadheading. 무임 승차하다 ride free; (부정으로) cheat (the railway); steal a ride; pinch a free ride.

무자격 [मूजाग्यौक] [無資格] disqualification; [法] incapacity; incompetence. e.g. 무자격의 disqualified / incompetent / [무면허의] unlicensed / uncertificated / [허가가 없는] unqualified.

무자비 [मूजाबी] [無慈悲] mercilessness; cruelty; harshness; brutality; ruthlessness. 무자비하다 merciless; ruthless; cruel; pitiless; heartless; hard-hearted. e.g. 무자비하게 mercilessly / without pity.

무작위 [मूजाकवी] [無作爲] e.g. 무작위의 unintentional / unintended. 무작위로 [아무 생각 없이] unintentionally / [임의로] at random.

무작정 [मूजाकजौंग] [無酌定] lack of any definite plan; lack of definite view in mind; recklessness; rashness; <부사> with no particular plan [view] in mind; without any goal in mind; recklessly; blindly. e.g. 무작정 남이 하는 대로하다 imitate [follow] <a

person> blindly.

무장 [मुजांग] [武裝] arms; (국가의) armament; (병사의) equipment. e.g. 비무장 지대 a demilitarized zone (略 DMZ). 완전 무장 <in> full kit. 무장하다 arm <a person, a ship, etc.>; equip <an army>; (스스로) equip [arm] oneself <with rifle>; bear [take up] arms. e.g. 국가를 무장시키다 militarize a nation.

무저항 [मुजौहांग] [無抵抗] 무저항 nonresistance.

무적 [मुजौक] [無敵] invincibility. e.g. 그 팀은 천하 무적이다 The team is unrivaled throughout the nation.

무전 여행 [मुजौन यौहैंग] [無錢旅行] a penniless trip; a vagabond journey. 무전 여행하다 go on a penniless journey; (남의 차로) hitchhike.

무절제 [मुजौलजे] [無節制] lack of control; immoderation; intemperance; excesses; incontinence; incontinency 무절제하다 immoderate; intemperate; incontinent; <서술적> commit excesses

무정 [मुजौग] [無情] heartlessness; hardness of heart; cruelty. 무정하다 [인정 없다] heartless; hard-hearted; cold-hearted; inhuman; cruel; [무자비하다] merciless; pitiless

무정부 [मुजौगबु] [無政府] anarchy. e.g. 무정부의 anarchic (al). 무정부 상태에 있다 be in a state of anarchy / be in an anarchical state.

무제 [मुजे] [無題] no title. e.g. 무제의 without a title / untitled. 무제(그림 등의 제목) No title.

무제한 [मुजेहान] [無制限] e.g. 무제한으로 입장을 허락하다 admit people without any restriction.

무조건 [मुजोगौन] [無條件] e.g. 무조건으로 조약에 조인하다 sign a treaty without any conditions.

무죄 [मुजवी] [無罪] innocence; guiltlessness

무중력 [मुजुंगरयौक] [無重力] zero gravity; weightlessness; zero G; nongravitation.

무지 [मुजी] [無知] [모름] ignorance; [문맹] illiteracy; [어리석음] stupidity. e.g. 자신의 무지를 드러내다 betray one's ignorance / display one's lack of knowledge.

무지개 [मुजीगे] a rainbow.

무지막지 [मुजीमकजी] [無知莫知] 무지막지하다 ignorant and uncouth. e.g. 무지막지한 행동을 하다 act rudely / be wild / commit an outrage.

무지하다 [मुजीहादा] [無知-] 1 [놀라울 만큼 대단하다] horrible; awful; awesome;

dreadful. e.g.무지한 부자 a very wealthy man / a man of great wealth. **2** [우악스럽다] rough; rude; wild; violent. e.g. 무지하게 굴다 behave rudely / play it through.

무직(업) [मुजीक] [औब] [**無職(業)**] inoccupation. e.g. 그는 지금 무직이다 He is unemployed [out of work] at the moment.

무진장 [मुजीनजांग] [**無盡藏**] 무진장하다 inexhaustible; unlimited; limitless; infinite; unfailing. e.g. 무진장한 천연자원 inexhaustible natural resources.

무질서 [मुजीलसौ] [**無秩序**] disorder; confusion; absence of order; disorderliness; chaos. 무질서하다 disordered; lawless; confused; chaotic. e.g. 무질서하게 without any order [system] / randomly.

무찌르다 [मुचीरुदा] **1** [마구 죽이다] kill off; wipe out; mow [cut] down. e.g. 수천의 적군을 무찌르다 mow down thousands of the enemy.**2** [공격하다] attack; assault; launch an attack <on>; fall upon; set upon; [유린하다] devastate; overrun; conquer. e.g. 적의 성을 무찌르다 assault [devastate] an enemy castle.

무차별 [मुछबयौल] [**無差別**] indiscrimination; nondiscrimination.

무참 [मुछाम] [**無慘**] 무참하다 cruel; atrocious; pitiless; ruthless; merciless. e.g. 사고 현장은 실로 무참한 광경이었다 The scene of the accident presented a horrible [dreadful] spectacle. 무참히 cruelly; pitilessly; mercilessly; without pity [mercy]. e.g. 우리 희망은 무참히도 깨어졌다 Our hopes were sadly crushed.

무책임 [मुछैकइम] [**無責任**] [책임(감)이 없음] irresponsibility; lack of a sense of responsibility. 무책임하다 irresponsible.

무척 [मुछौक] very; extremely; greatly; highly; exceedingly. ⇨ 대단히 e.g. 무척 오랫동안 나는 집을 비워 두고 있었습니다 I have been away from home for a very long time.

무치다 [मुछीदा] season; dress <vegetables> with <some condiment>. e.g. 나물을 무치다 season vegetable.

무턱대고 [मुथौक्तैगो] **무턱대고** [무분별하게] recklessly; needlessly; indiscreetly; [준비[까닭]없이] without any preparation [reason]; [닥치는 대로] haphazardly; at random; [무차별하게] indiscriminately; blindly. e.g. 무턱대고 돌진

하다 rush forward blindly [recklessly].

무표정 [मूफ्यूजौग] [**無表情**] absence [lack] of expression. 무표정하다 expressionless; blank; wooden

무한 [मूहान] [**無限**] infinity; [영구] eternity. 무한하다 limitless; infinite; boundless; [무진장하다] inexhaustible; [영원하다] eternal. e.g. 무한한 공간 infinite space.

무해 [मूहै] [**無害**] harmlessness; innocence; innocuousness; innoxiousness. 무해하다 harmless; innocent; inoffensive; innocuous; innoxious; <서술적> do <a person> no harm; produce no ill effects. e.g. 이 약은 인체나 가축에 무해하다 This drug is harmless to men and farm animals.

무허가 [मूहौगा] [**無許可**] no permit. e.g. 무허가의 [무인가P무면허의] unlicensed <doctors> / [무등록의] unregistered <brokers> / [무자격의] unqualified.

무협 [मूह्यौब] [**武俠**] chivalry; heroism.

무형 [मूह्यौग] [**無形**] e.g. 무형 의 [형체가 없는] formless / shapeless / [비물질적인] immaterial / [만질 수 없는] intangible / [정신적인] spiritual / moral.

무효 [मूह्यो] [**無效**] [실효] invalidity; nullity; [통용-되지 않음] unavailability; [보람이 없음] ineffectiveness; futility; no effects

무휴 [मूह्यू] [**無休**] e.g. 연중무휴 <게시> Open throughout the year. / Open through Dec. 31. / Open all year.

묵과 [मूकगवा] [**默過**] connivance. 묵과하다 overlook; look over; pass over <a matter> in silence; let <it> pass; let <a person> go unchallenged [unpunished]; connive [wink] <at>

묵념 [मूकनयौम] [**默念**] = 묵상.

묵다[1] [मूकदा] [오래되다] become [get / grow] old; become antiquated [outdated / outmoded / out of date / old-fashioned]. e.g. 묵은 관습 an old custom / a worm-eaten custom.

묵다[2] [मूकदा] [숙박하다] stay <at / in / with>; lodge <in / with>; put up [stop] <at a hotel>; register <at a hotel>. e.g. 호텔에 묵다 put up [stay] at a hotel.

묵독 [मूकतोक] [**默讀**] silent reading. 묵독하다 read <a book> silently.

묵묵 [मूकमुक] [**默默**] 묵묵하다 silent; mute; dumb. 묵묵히 silently; in (stony) silence; mutely. e.g. 그들은 묵묵히 행진했다 They marched in silence.

묵살 [मुकसाल] [**默殺**] 묵살하다 take no notice of; pass (over) <a matter> in silence; treat <it> with silent contempt; ignore(by keeping silence).

묵상 [मुकसांग][**默 想**] (a) meditation; contemplation. e.g.묵상에 잠기다 be lost in contemplation[reflection / (a) reverie] / be absorbed [buried] in meditation.

묵인 [मुगीन][**默 認**] tacit [silent] approval [consent]; tacit admission; (나쁜 짓의) connivance <at / with>; toleration. 묵인하다 permit tacitly; tolerate; connive [wink] at. e.g. 이런 부패가 묵인되다니 참 한탄할 노릇이다 It is matter for sincere regret that such corruption should be overlooked.

묵직하다 [मुगजीक हादा] 묵직하다 **1** (무게가) rather heavy [massive / weighty]. e.g.묵직한 스웨터 a heavy [bulky] sweater. **2** (기분이) heavy; depressed. e.g. 머리가 묵직하다 feel heavy in the head.

묵히다 [मुगहादा] leave unused [wasted]; let <a thing> lie idle; keep <money> idle. e.g. 팔다 남은 스키복을 다음해까지 묵히다 keep [hold over] unsold ski wear till the following year.

묶다 [मुकता] **1** [매다] tie up; bind (▷ 묶어서 움직이지 못하게 하는 데는 tie 도 bind 도 쓸 수 있으나 개를 기둥에 묶어 매다는 경우에는 tie 를 씀); fasten; bundle; tie up in a bundle; cord (끈으로). e.g. 볏단을 짚으로 묶다 tie up [bind] sheaves of rice with straw **2** [속박하다] bind; fetter; tie; restrict; restrain; chain. e.g. 낮은 수준으로 묶어 놓은 임금 wages pegged at a low level.

묶음[मुकुम] a bundle;(같은 종류의 것의) a bunch; (볏단 등의) a sheaf <*pl.* sheaves>; (장작 등의) a faggot; (건초 등의) a truss

묶이다 [मुकीदा] **1** (사람,물건이) be bound [tied / fastened / trussed / sheaved]; be chained [fettered / tied up / bound together / restricted / screwed down]. e.g. 두 손을 뒤로 묶여 with one's hands tied behind. **2** [속박되다] be tied [fettered / restricted] by; be bound by <a rule>. e.g. 시간에 묶이다 be restricted by time / be not the master of one's time.

문[1] [मुन] [**文**] **1** [문장] writings; a composition; (문법상의) a sentence; [본문] the text; [문체]

style. e.g. 단[복/중]문 a simple [complex / compound] sentence. **2** [문학] literature; letters. e.g. 문은 무(武)보다 강하다 The pen is mightier than the sword.

문[2] **[मुन]** [門] (방문) a door;(장지) a sliding door; (창문) a window;(대문) a gate (way); (회전문) a revolving door.

문과 [मुनक्वा] [文科] the liberal arts; (대학의) the school [college] of liberal arts. e.g. 문과의 학생 a student in the school of liberal arts / a liberal arts major.

문구[1] **[मुनगु]** [文具] ⇨ 문방구

문구[2] **[मुनगु]** [文句] a passage; a paragraph; a sentence; words; a phrase; a clause; [표현] an expression. e.g. 편지의 문구 the wording of a letter.

문단[1] **[मुनदान]** [門段] [문장을 크게 나눈 단락] a para graph.

문단[2] **[मुनदान]** [文壇] [문학계] the literary world; literary circles; the world of letters. e.g. 문단에 명성을 떨치다 win literary fame / become a famous writer.

문단속 [मुनदानसोक] [門團束] fastening [locking] the doors. e.g. 밤에 문단속을 하다 lock up for the night.

문드러지다 [मुनदुरौजीदा] (썩어서) rot; decay; disintegrate; decompose; (익어서) be overripe; (상처,피부가) be sore; be inflamed; [곪다] fester; ulcerate.

문득 [मुनदुक] [갑자기] suddenly; [우연히] by chance [accident]; casually; accidenttally; unexpectedly (생각지 않게). e.g. 문득 생각나다 occur to <one> / flash across one's mind.

문란 [मुल्लान] [紊亂] disorder; confusion; disorganization; derangement. 문란하다 disordered; disorderly; confused; corrupt; loose; lax. e.g. 풍기가 몹시 문란하다 Public morals are very lax [sadly decayed].

문맥 [मुनमैक] [文脈] the context <of a passage>; the line of thought.

문맹 [मुनमैग] [文盲] [글을 모름] illiteracy; [문맹자] an illiterate [uneducated] person

문명 [मुनमयौग] [文名] literary fame[reputation]. e.g. 문명을 떨치는 작가 a famous [an eminent] writer. 문명을 떨치다 win literary fame / make a name for oneself as an author. 그는 이 작품으로 문명을 떨쳤다 With this work, he made his name[a name for himself] as a writer. / This work made him a famous writer.

문명 [मुनमयौग] [**文明**] civilization; [문화] culture.

문물 [मुनमुल] [**文物**] the products of civilization.

문밖 [मुनबाक] [**門**−] [문의 바깥] the outside of a house. e.g. 문밖에(서) out of doors / outdoors. 문밖 출입을 하지 않다 keep [remain] indoors.

문방구 [मुनबांगगु] [**文房具**] stationery; writing materials.

문법 [मुनपौप] [**文法**] grammar; rules of composition

문서 [मुनसौ] [**文書**] [서류] a document; [기록] a record; archives; [통신] letters; notes.

문신 [मुनसीन] [**文身**] [먹물로 살갗에 그림 등을 새김] tattooing;(무늬) a tattoo <*pl.* ~s>; tattoo marks.

문안 [मुनआन] [**問安**] an inquiry [asking] ather <a person's> health; sending kind regards. e.g. 환자에게 문안을 드리다 express one's concern for a sick person.

문어 [मुनौ] [**文語**] [문장어] written [literary / classical] language; [문어의 한 단어] a literary word.

문예 [मुनये] [**文藝**] [문학과 예술] the arts; literature [learning] and the arts; [문학] literature; [학예] liberal arts.

문의 [मुनि] [**問議**] an inquiry; a reference; a re-quest for information. 문의하다 make inquiries <about>; inquire; check; ask. e.g. 우리는 마감 일자를 문의했다 We inquired [made an inquiry] about the deadline.

문자 [मुनजा] [**文字**] [글자] a letter; a character (한자 등).

문장 [मुनजांग] [**文章**] **1** [글월] writing; [작문] a composition; [문체] (a) style; [논문] an article [essay]; [산문] prose. **2** [문(文)] a sentence.

문제 [मुन्जे][**問題**] **1** [답을 구하는 질문] a question; (해답에 계산,작도 등을 필요로 하는) a problem. e.g. 시험 문제 an examination question [paper (전체)]. **2** [해결해야 할 일] a question; a problem; [쟁점] an issue; [과제] a subject. e.g. 문제가 되지 않다 be out of the question / [대수롭지 않다] do not matter [figure] / matter little / [하찮다] be insignificant / be negligible / count for nothing

문지르다 [मुन्जीरुदा] [무엇에 대고 비비다] rub <in / into>; scour; scrub

문책 [मुनछैक][**問責**] (a) censure; (a) reproof; reprehension. 문책하다 censure; reprimand; reprehend; reprove; rebuke. e.g. 남의 실수를 문책하다 censure a person for his blunder.

문체 [मुनछ्ये] [文體] a (literary) style; a style; a style of writing; language. e.g. 자기류의 문체를 만들어 내다 make [cultivate] a style of one's own.

문턱 [मुनथौक] [門 -] a threshold; a doorsill.

문틈 [मुनथुम] [門-] a crack [chink] in door.

문학 [मुनहाक] [文學] literature; letters.

문헌 [मुनहौन] [文獻] (어떤 주제에 관한) literature; [기록 자료] documents.

문화 [मुनह्वा] [文化] culture; [문명] civilization.

문화재 [मुनह्वाजै] [文化財] cultural assets [properties].

묻다[1] [मुत्ता] [질문하다] ask; [조사하다] inquire <of a person about a thing>(▷ ask보다 격식차린 말). e.g. 남의 안부를 묻다 ask [inquire] ather a person's safety.

묻다[2] [मुत्ता] [들러붙다] stick <to>; adhere <to>; be stuck; be covered; (더럼,때 등이) be stained [smeared] <with>. e.g. 옷에 잉크가 묻었다 My dress was stained with ink.

묻다[3] [मुत्ता] **1** [파묻다] bury <in / under>; inter; inhume; cover (up). e.g. 시체를 묻다 bury a corpse [body]. **2** [숨기다] hide [conceal / keep] <a matter from a person>; keep <a matter> secret <from>. e.g. 살인 사건을 비밀로 묻어 두다 keep a case of murder (a) secret.

묻히다[1] [मुछीदा] [매장되다] be buried <in>; [숨겨지다] be hidden [concealed] <from a person>; be kept secret <from>. e.g. 무덤 속에 묻혀 있다 be buried in the ground / lie beneath a grave.

묻히다[2] [मुछ्दिा] [묻게 하다] stain; smear; cover. e.g. 신발에 흙을 묻히다 get mud on one's shoes / have one's shoes muddy.

물 [मुल] (일반적인) water.

물가[1] [मुलगा] [物價] price (s). e.g. 물가가 오르다 prices rise [go up].

물가[2] [मुलगा] [강변] a riverside; a riverbank; [바다,호수의 가장자리] a shore; [연안] the coast; the beach; the waterside; the water's edge. e.g.호수 물가에 있는 통나무집 an arbor on the shore of the lake

물감 [मुलगाम] [빛깔을 들이는 색소] dyestuffs; dyes; colors;

stain.

물거품 [मुलगौफुम] **1** [물의 거품] bubbles(▷ 보통 복수형); a foam; froth. e.g. 물거품 같은 foamy / frothy / bubble. **2** 없는 것] transience. e.g. 물거품 같은 사랑 a short-lived love.

물건 [मुलगौन] [物件] [물체] a thing; an object; [물품] an article; goods; [재료] material; stuff; [재고품] stock; [소유물] a possession

물결 [मुलग्यौल] a wave

물결치다 [मुलग्यौल छीदा] move in waves; undulate; surge; swell; roll; billow(크게).

물고기 [मुलगोगी] a fish <*pl.* ~, ~es>(▷ 종류를 말할 때는 fishes); [어육] fish.

물고늘어지다 [मुलगोनुलौजीदा] **물고늘어지다** **1** (이빨로) bite at something and hang on. e.g. 목을 물고 늘어지다 sink one's teeth in the throat and hangs on. **2** (약점 등을) hang [hold] on to; stick to; cling to; get a firm grip on <one's rival>; <美> latch on to. e.g. 끝까지 물고늘어지다 stick to one's last.

물구나무서다 [मुलगुनामुसौदा] stand on one's hands [head]; do a handstand [headstand]. e.g. 물구나무서서 걷다 walk on one's hands.

물기 [मुलकि] [-氣] [수분] water; [습기] moisture; dampness; wetness; [액즙] juice.

물끄러미 [मुलकुरौमी] with a blank [vacant] look; staring (with fixed eyes). e.g. 그는 그 그림을 물끄러미 쳐다보았다 He gazed [looked intently] at the painting.

물놀이 [मुलनोली] [물가에서의 휴양] a waterside vacation. e.g. 물놀이가다 go to a summer resort / go swimming <to the seaside>.

물다[1] [मुलदा] (개 등이) have a bite <at>; bite[snap] <at>. e.g. 다리를 물다 bite <a person> in the leg

물다[2] [मुलदा] [돈을 치르다] pay; repay. e.g. 벌금을 물다 pay a fine / pay one's penalty [forfeit].

물들다 [मुलदुलदा] **1** 빛깔이 들다] dye; get dyed; take (up) color. e.g. 파랗게 물들다 be dyed blue. **2** [감염되다] be imbued [infected / contaminated / stained / tainted] <with>; be influenced <by>; be steeped <in>; catch. e.g. 서양[미국] 풍습에 물든 사람 a Europeanized[an Americanized] person who affects a European [an American] manner.

물들이다 [मुलदुरीदा] [채색하다] color; tint; paint; tinge. e.g. 손톱을 빨갛게

물들이다 tint [paint] one's nails with carmine[red] polish.

물량 [मुल्लयांग][物量] the amount [quantity] of materials [resources].

물러가다 [मुल्लौगादा] **1** [뒷걸음쳐 가다] move backward; draw [fall / pull] back; back; retrogress; recede; retreat. e.g. 한 발짝 물러가서 생각해 보면 전체 상황이 더 잘 보이게 된다 You can see the whole situation better if you step back a little. **2** [사임,은퇴하다] retire <from>; resign(from) <a post>. e.g. 공직에서 물러가다 resign[withdraw] from public life. 무대에서 물러가다 leave [quit] the stage.

물러나다 [मुल्लौनादा]**1** [후퇴하다] retreat; withdraw <from>; leave; recede; move [go] backward; back. e.g. 옆으로 물러나다 step [move] aside. **2** [사임하다] retire <from service>; withdraw. e.g. 직위에서 물러나다 leave office / resign one's post in an office.

물러서다 [मुल्लौसोदा] **1** [뒤로 나서다] step [stand] back; back; [후퇴하다] retreat; recede; [길을 내어 주다] make way <for a person>; get out of the way <of>. e.g. 거리에서 멀찌감치 물러서 있는 집 a house (standing) for[well] back from the street **2** [사임하다] retire; resign; withdraw. e.g. 정계에서 물러서다 retire from the political world.

물러앉다 [मुल्लौआन्ता] **1** (자리를) draw [move] one's seat back; sit back. e.g. 그는 아버지 앞에서 물러앉았다 He gave the seat of honor to his father. **2**(관직 등에서) retire; resign; leave. e.g. 세속에서 물러앉다 live a retired life. 직위에서 물러앉게 하다 dismiss <a person> from office / relieve <a person> of his post [office / duty].

물렁하다 [मुल्लौगहदा] **1** (물건이) soth; tender; squashy; juicy; overripe. **2** (성질이) yielding; soth; weak-kneed; compliant; flabby; flaccid.

물려받다 [मुल्लयोपात्ता] [넘겨받다] take over; (양도증서에 의해) obtain by transfer; succeed to <the throne>; [상속하다] inherit. e.g. 부모에게서 물려받은 재산 property inherited from one's parents.

물려주다 [मुल्लयोजुदा] turn [hand / make] over; transfer; [남겨 주다] leave; (왕위를) abdicate; (동산을) bequeath; (부동산을) devise. e.g. 정권을 물려주다 hand over the reins of government [power].

물론 [मुल्लोन] [勿 論] of course; to be sure; undoubtedly; naturally; needless to say. e.g. 그녀는 영어는 물론이고 프랑스어도 말할 줄 안다 She speaks French, not to mention English. / She speaks French as well as English. / She speaks not only English but also French.

물리다[1] [मुल्लीदा] [싫증나다, 따분하다] be bored <by / with>; [진저리 나다] be fed up <with>; get [grow] tired <of>; get sick <of>; lose interest <in>; want nothing more to do <with>; (음식에) be sick [tired] of eating; be satiated [sated] <with>; have enough <of>. e.g. 나는 잔소리에 물렸다 I have heard enough of scolding

물리다[2] [मुल्लीदा] **1** [연기하다] put off; postpone; defer. e.g. 기한을 물리다 extend the term <from ... to ...>. **2** [뒤로 옮기다] change direction; turn; shith; switch over; remove; get around. e.g. 의자를 물리다 push back a chair.**3** [물려주다] hand over; leave; bequeath; transfer; yield; convey; (지위,권리) abdicate. e.g. 소유권을 아우에게 물리다 yield one's right of possession to one's little brother.

물리다[3] [मुल्लीदा] **1** (곤충, 동물 등에) be [get] bitten. e.g. 물린 상처투성이의 얼굴 a face covered with stings. **2** [물게 하다]. e.g. 톱니바퀴를 마주 물리다 engage a gear / put <a machine> in gear.

물리치다 [मुल्ली छीदा] **1** [거절하다] refuse; turn down; reject. e.g. 뇌물을 물리치다 spun a bribe.**2** [격퇴하다] drive[turn / send] away; beat off; repel; expel; [멀리하다] keep away. e.g. 그들은 적의 공격을 물리쳤다 They beat off[repelled / repulsed] the enemy's attack.

물리학 [मुल्लीहाक] [**物 理 學**] physics; physical science. e.g. 물리학적 physical. 물리학적으로 physically.

물망 [मुलमांग] [**物望**] popular expectations[prospects]. e.g. 물망에 오르다 be popularly [widely] expected.

물물교환 [मुल्मुलग्योहवान] [**物物交換**] barter; bartering truck; dicker; dickering 물물교환하다 barter <A for B>; trade; truck; swap. e.g. 그들은 원주민들과 무기와 식량을 물물 교환했다 They bartered weapons for food with the natives.

물방울 [मुल्पांगुल] a drop of water; (a) spray;(튀긴) a splash; [이슬] a dewdrop.

물벼락 [मुल्बयौराक] splashing [dashing] water <on a person> all of a sudden; dousing <a person> with water. e.g. 지나가던 버스가 우리에게 물벼락을 안겼다 The bus spattered us with muddy water [spattered muddy water on us] as it passed.

물색 [मुल्सैक] [**物色**] [찾음] looking for; [고름] selecting. 물색하다 [찾다] look for; search for; cast about for; hunt up; [고르다] select; pick [single] out.

물쓰듯 [मुल्सुदत] 물쓰듯하다 spend money like water; be a free spender; spend money unsparingly. e.g. 여자에게 미쳐서 돈을 물쓰듯하다 spend money freely on a woman.

물씬 [मुल्सीन] [냄새가 심하게 코를 찌르는 모양]. e.g. 냄새가 물씬 풍기다 (일반적으로) smell strongly <of> / (지독한 악취가) stink <of>.

물어내다 [मुलौनैदा] [변상 하다] pay for; compen-sate; indemnify; make good.

물어뜯다 [मुलौतुत्ता] gnaw on; bite (hard); bite [snap]off; bite <at>; tear off with one's teeth.

물어보다 [मुलौबोदा] [묻다] ask; inquire; question; query; [조회하다] make inquiries <about>; refer to; apply to; [확인하다] ascertain (by inquiry).

물어주다 [मुलौजुदा] pay <for>; compensate; reimburse; make good; make up for. e.g. 비용을 물어주다 compensate <a person> for (the) cost.

물음 [मुलउम] a question; a query; an inquiry; an interrogation. ⇨ 질문

물의 [मुऊम] [**物議**] public criticism [censure]; public discussion[comment]; trouble. e.g. 자주 물의를 일으키는 사람 a stormy petrel

물자 [मूल्जा] [**物資**] [공급물] supplies; [물품] goods; [상품] commodities; [자원] materials; resources. e.g. 물자를 확보하다 secure the supply of goods.

물장구 [मूल्जांग्गु] (헤엄칠 때) the beating; the flutter kick; the thrash. e.g. 물장구 치다 make flutters[flutter kicks] / swim with the thrash.

물정 [मूल्जौंग] [**物情**] [세상의 형편](the condition of) the world; worldly matters; [세상 인심] public feeling. e.g. 세상 물정을 모르는 젊은이 an ingenuous youth

물질 [मूल्जील] [**物質**] (정신에 대하여) matter; [물체를

이루는 본바탕] substance; [재료] material.

물체 [मुल्छ्ये] [**物體**] [물건의 형체] an object;(물리에서) a body; [고체] a solid (body); a material object.

물컹거리다 [मुल्खौंगगौरीदा] be very soth[pulpy / squashy / mushy]. e.g. 나는 어둠 속에서 무엇인가 물컹거리는 것을 밟았다 I stepped on something soth [mushy] in the dark.

물통 [मुल्थोंग] [-**桶**] a (water) pail [bucket]; a water tank; a cistern. e.g. 물통에 가득찬 물 a bucketful of water.

물품 [मुल्फुम] [**物品**] [물건] an article; [상품] a commodity; goods (▷ 복수 취급; 수사를 붙이지 않음).

묽다 [मुकता] (농도가) watery; washy <milk>; thin <coffee, porridge, paste, etc.>; sloppy <food>.

뭉개다 [मुंग्गेदा] [짓이기다] crush; smash; squash; mash (감자를); (일을) make a mess of. e.g .뭉갠 감자 mashed potatoes.

뭉그러뜨리다 [मुंग्गुरौतुरीदा] demolish; pull down; destroy; level (down). e.g. 돌담을 뭉그러뜨리다 demolish a stonewall.

뭉그러지다 [मुंग्गुरौजादा] crumble; go [fall] to pieces; collapse; break; give away; be destroyed; come down. e.g. 비바람을 맞아서 뭉그러지다 fall to pieces as the result of exposure to wind and rain. 돌담이 뭉그러졌다 The stone wall fell down.

뭉뚱그리다 [मुंग्तुंगगुरीदा] **1** [대강 싸다] wrap [pack / do] up <a parcel> in a slipshod way; throw together hastily; bundle up crudely. e.g. 짐을 뭉뚱그리다 bundle up a package crudely. **2** [총괄하다] lump [put] together; sum up. e.g. 전부 뭉뚱그려서 all put together / in total / (all) in all / in the lump.

뭉치 [मुंग्छी] [덩이] a bundle; a roll; a lump; a clod.

뭉치다 [मुंग्छीदा] **1**[단결하다] unite; stand[hold / hang / band] together; be banded [leagued] together; combine. e.g. 투철한 애국심과 확고한 역사 의식으로 굳게 뭉치다 be firmly united with patriotic spirit and perspectives regarding history.**2** [덩이지다] lump; mass; cake; conglomerate. e.g. 풀이 뭉친다 Paste lumps. / Paste forms a hard mass.

뭉클하다 [मुंग्खुलहादा] (가슴이) be choked <with grief>; be filled <with emotion>; feel a lump in one's throat. e.g. 슬퍼서 가슴이 뭉클했다 My heart was choked with sorrow.

뭍 [मुत] ⇨ 육지 e.g. 뭍쪽으로 landward.

뭐 [मवॉ] ⇨ 무엇 e.g. 너 뭐 좀 먹어야지 Surely you have to eat something, don't you?

뮤지컬 [मयूजीख्वौल] a musical.

-므로 [मुरो] [까닭으로] on account of; owing to; as; because(of); since. e.g. 그는 몸이 허약하므로 심한 육체 노동은 할 수가 없다 He cannot do hard muscular labor because of his delicate health [because he is weak in health].

미[1] [मी] [美] [아름다움] beauty; the beautiful; grace; charm. e.g. 남성미 masculine [manly] beauty.

미[2] [मी]-[未] un-; in-; not yet. e.g. 미발표 작품 an unpublished work / a work not yet published.

미각 [मीगाक][味覺] the (sense of) taste; the palate; the gustation.

미간 [मीगान] [眉間] the middle of the forehead; the brow; [解] the glabella <*pl.* -lae>; the glabellum <*pl.* -la>.

미개 [मीगै] [未開] [발전이 없이 문화 수준이 낮음]. e.g. 미개 상태에 있다 be in a state of nature. 미개하다 uncivilized; benighted; savage; barbarous; wild.

미결 [मीग्यौल][未決] pendency. e.g. 그 문제는 아직 미결이다 The question is still open [unsettled].

미결제 [मीग्यौलजे] [未決濟] e.g. 미결제의 [미결산의] unsettled / outstanding / [미불의] unpaid.

미관 [मीग्वान] [美觀] a fine [pretty / lovely] view; a fine [beautiful] sight; a charming [beautiful] spectacle; beauties (보통 복수형). e.g. 여기저기 붙은 포스터가 거리의 미관을 해치고 있다 The posters put up here and there spoil the appearance of the streets [make the streets look bad].

미국 [मीगुक] [美國] he United States (of America) (略 U.S., U.S.A.); America; the Union; the States.

미궁 [मीगुंग] [迷宮] a labyrinth; a maze.

미끄러지다 [मीकुरौजीदा] 1 [활주하다] slide; glide; slip; skid. e.g. 계단에서 미끄러져 떨어지다 slip [slither] down the stairs. 2 [낙방하다] fail(in) an examination; get plucked in an examination. e.g. 나는 대학 입시에서 미끄러졌다 I failed my university entrance examinations.

미끄럽다 [मीकुरौपदा] slippery; slithery; greasy; [반드럽다] smooth; sleek.

미끈하다 [मीकुहादा] 1 (사물이)

sleek; slick; smooth; streamlined. e.g. 미끈한 자동차 a streamlined motorcar. **2** (사람이) slender; slim; (옷맵시가) neat; gay; flashy. e.g. 미끈한 얼굴 a sleek face / a good-looking face.

미끼 [मीकी] 1 [낚시용 먹이] a bait. e.g. 낚시 미끼 a fish bait / a bait for fish. **2** [유혹물] a bait; a decoy; a lure; an allurement. e.g. 미끼에 걸려들다 be lured / get decoye

미남(자) [मीनाम जा] [美男(子)] a handsome[good-looking] man; an Adonis; an Apollo.

미납 [मीनाप] [未納] <make> default in payment; nonpayment. e.g. 그의 수업료는 아직 미납이다 His tuition has not yet been paid.

미녀 [मीन्यौ] [美女] a beauty; a belle; a good-looking girl; a beautiful woman; <美> a knockout.

미니 [मीनी] a mini.**미니 스커트** a miniskirt.

미닫이 [मीदादी] a sliding door

미달 [मीदाल] [未達] shortage; lack; deficiency; insufficiency. e.g.체중 미달 underweight.

미담 [मीदाम] [美談] a praiseworthy[fine / laudable / commendable] anecdote [episode]; a moving story; an impressive tale

미덕[मीदौक][美德] a virtue; a noble attribute; a grace(of character); a good trait; a good deed(선행). e.g. 인내는 미덕이다 <속담> Patience is a virtue.

미덥다 [मीदौपता] reliable; trustworthy; sure-footed; (장래가) hopeful; promising. e.g. 미더운 사람 a reliable [trustworthy] person.

미래 [मीरे] [未來] 미래 [다가올 앞날](the) future; time[days] to come. e.g. 그는 미래의 내 남편이다 He is my future[intended] husband

미련[1] [मीर्यौन] [未練] [애착] lingering attachment [affection]; [섭섭함] regret; reluctance to give <it, a person, etc.> up. e.g. 그는 아직도 그 여자에게 미련이 남아 있다 Still he cannot give her up

미련[2] [मीर्यौन] stupidity; dullness; silliness; asininity. 미련하다 stupid(as an owl); dull; thickheaded; weak-headed; soth-[dull-] witted; imbecile. e.g. 미련스럽다 =미련 하다. 그렇게 행동하다니 내가 미련했어 It was stupid of me to behave like that.

미로 [मीरो] [迷路] a maze; a labyrinth

미루다 [मीरूदा] 1 [연기하다] put off; postpone; defer; [기한을 연장하다] prolong; extend; protract; [지연

시키다] delay; hold off. e.g. 회의를 내주의 수요일로 미루자 Let's postpone[put off] the meeting until next Wednesday. 2 [전가하다] lay [throw] <the blame on a person>; shith [shuffle off] <a responsebility on another's shoulders>; pass the buck <to>. e.g. 책임을 서로 미루다 shith the responsibility back and forth / keep passing the buck.

미리 [मीरी] beforehand; in advance; previously; in anticipation; ahead of time. e.g. 남에게 미리 알려주다 let a person know beforehand [ahead of time].

미만 [मीमान] [未滿] e.g. 미만의 under / below / less than.. 18세 미만 입장할 수 없음 <게시> No admittance to those under eighteen years of age.

미망인 [मीमांगिन] [未亡人] a widow.

미모 [मीमो] [美貌] good [attarctive] looks; pretty features; a beautiful [handsome] face; a fair face; personal beauty; beauty of person; charming personal attraction.

미묘 [मीम्यो] [微妙] delicacy; subtlety; nicety. 미묘하다 subtle; delicate; fine; nice e.g. 미묘한 뜻의 차이 delicate [fine] shades of meaning.

미비 [मीबी] [未備] [불완전, 불충분] imperfection; insufficiency; defectiveness; inadequacy; [부족] lack; deficiency; [미비점] a defect; an imperfection; a loophole (법률 등의). e.g. 제도상의 미비 institutional inertia.

미사 [मीसा] [彌撒] [가톨릭] <라> Missa;(a) mass; Mass.

미사일 [मीसाइल] a missile.

미상 [मीसांग] [未詳] e.g. 미상의 [불명의] unknown / [미확인의] unidentified / not exactly known. 사고로 인한 부상자의 성명, 연령 등은 미상이다 The man injured in the accident is still unidentified. / Nothing is yet known about the identity of those injured in the accident.

미생물 [मीसैंगमुल] [微生物] a microbe; a microorganism; a microscopic organism; a germ; minute forms of life. e.g. 미생물의 microbial / microbic.

미성년 [मीसौंगनयौन] [未成年] minority; nonage; (legal) infancy. e.g. 미성년의 minor / infant / under age. 미성년이다 be under age / be not yet of age.

미세 [मीसे] [微細] [극소] minuteness; fineness; [상세] details; particulars. 미세하다 [아주 작다]

minute; fine; nice; infinitesimal; microscopic; [세밀하다] minute; detailed; full; particular

미소 [मीसो][微笑] a smile. e.g. 미소짓는 얼굴로 with a smile.

미수 [मीसु] [未遂] e.g. 방화 미수 attempted arson. 살인 미수 an attempted murder / a murder attempt.

미숙 [मीसुक][未熟] immaturity; [미경험] inexperience. 미숙하다(과실이) unripe; [원숙하지 않다] immature; [경험이 없다] inexperienced; [숫되다] naive; green.

미술 [मीसुल] [美術] art; (the) fine arts (▷ 회화,건축, 조각, 공예를 가리킴. 영어에서는 그 밖에 음악, 시 등을 포함하는 경우도 있음).

미스 [मीसु] [미혼 여성의 성 앞에 붙이는 호칭] Miss; [미혼의 여성] an unmarried girl[woman]. e.g. 그녀는 아직 미스다 She is still unmarried. / She still remains single.

미스터리 [मीसुथोरी] [이상한 일] (a) mystery.

미식가 [मीसीकगा] an epicure; a gourmet; a gourmand; a gastronome (r); a good [high] liver; <프> a bon vivant <*pl.* bons vivants>.

미신 [मीसीन][迷信] (a) superstition; a superstitious belief

미아 [मीआ][迷兒] a stray [lost / missing] child

미안 [मीआन] [未安] 미안하다 regrettable; sorry. e.g.I am sorry to have put you to so much trouble. 그 초대를 수락하지 못해 미안한 생각이 든다

미어지다 [मीऔजीदा] be [get] torn; tear; rip (open); be rent; rend; wear [be worn] out. e.g. 가슴이 미어질 듯한 heart-rending <sorrow> / heart-breaking <sorrow>.

미연 [मीयौन][未然] e.g. 미연에 before <it> happens / beforehand / previously. 사고를 미연에 방지하다 prevent an accident from happening / take precautions against possible accidents.

미온적 [मीओन जौक] [微溫的] (철저하지 않은) lukewarm; tepid; (좋지도 나쁘지도 않은) indifferent; half-hearted. e.g. 지금까지 너무 미온적인 정책을 펴 왔다 Up to this point, the measures we have taken have been too lukewarm.

미완성 [मीवानसौंग] [未完成] incompletion. e.g. 저 건물은 미완성이다 The building is not yet finished.

미용 [मीयोंग] [美容] beauty culture. e.g. 미용과 건강을 위해 조깅을 한다 I jog for the sake of my health and figure.

미용사 [मीयोंगसा] [美容師] a beauty artist [expert]; a beauty-culturist; a beauty doctor [specialist]; a cosmetologist; <美> a beautycian; (머리 만지는) a hairdresser.

미움 [मीउम] hatred; hate; enmity; animosity; rancor; bad [ill] blood; [밉살스러움] hatefulness; [불쾌] displeasure; disfavor; disgrace. e.g. 미움을 받다 be hated [detested / disliked] <by>. 미움을 사다 incur <a person's> enmity / become an object of loathing. 그녀는 어디를 가나 미움을 받는다 She is an unwelcome guest everywhere. 저 사람한테서 미움을 살 만한 짓을 한 적이 없다 I don't remember having done anything to incur his hatred.

미워하다 [मीवोहादा] hate; detest; abhor; abominate; have a hatred <for>; have a spite <at / against>. e.g. 서로 미워하다 hate each other / be hateful to one another

미인 [मीइन] [美人] [용모가 아름다운 여자] a beauty; a belle; a beautiful [lovely] woman [lady]; a pretty girl; a lovely; <美> a good-looker; a peach; <美> a pin-up(girl); a bombshell.

미인계 [मीइनग्ये] [美人計] a badger game. e.g. 미인계를 쓰다 pull a badger game (▷ 영국에는 이에 해당하는 말이 없음).

미적 [मीजौक] [美的] 미적 aesthetic (al). e.g. 미적으로 aesthetically.

미적지근하다 [मीजौक जीकुनहादा] **1**미지근하다] tepid; lukewarm. e.g. 미적지근한 물 tepid [lukewarm] water.**2** 비유> indecisive; vague; dubious; lukewarm; irresolute; undetermined; shilly-shally. e.g. 미적지근한 대답 a dubious [vague] reply / a noncommittal reply.

미주알고주알 [मीजु आलगो जुआल] [속속들이 캐묻는 모양] inquisitively; overcuriously. e.g. 그렇게 미주알고주알 캐묻지 마라 Don't be so inquisitive.

미지 [मीजी] [未知] e.g. 미지의 unknown / strange / unacquainted <with>.

미지근하다 [मीजुकुनहादा] **1** [온도가 낮다] tepid; lukewarm; not warm enough. e.g. 이 차는 미지근해서 못 마시겠다 The tea is too tepid to drink. **2** [엄하지 않다] slack; laK mild; lenient; not strict [severe] enough. e.g. 미지근한 조치 a halfway measure.

미처 [मीछो] 미처 yet; before; as yet; up to now; so far; hitherto; to this day. e.g.

나는 그걸 미처 몰랐다 I didn't know that before.

미천 [मीछौन] [**微賤**] 미천하다 lowly; humble; ignoble; obscure; of humble origin. e.g.미천하게 태어나다 be base born / be of humble origin.

미취학 [मीछ्वीहाक] [**未就學**] **미취학** e.g. 미취학의 not (yet) attending school / preschool.

미치다[1] [मीछीदा] **1** [정신이 상이 되다] go mad [out of one's mind]; become [go] insane [crazy]; lose one's head [wits / mind]; go crackers [nuts]. e.g. 미친 mad / crazy / insane / crackbrained / cracked. 미친 듯이 frantically / frenziedly / like mad [crazy] / madly. 미친 사람 = 미치광이. 자기 자식을 잃은 그 어머니는 미쳐 죽었다 The mother who had lost her child died mad [crazed] with grief. **2** [열중하다] be absorbed [engrossed] <in>; be devoted <to>; be given up <to>; [열광하다] be crazy <for>; be a fanatic. e.g. 그는 여자에게 미쳐 있다 He is infatuated with [He has lost his head over] a woman.

미치다[2] [मीछीदा] **1** [이르다] reach; attain to; amount to; come to; come up to <the standard>; [걸치다] extend <to / over>; stretch; range over <the whole country, wide subjects, etc.>. e.g. 손이 미치는 곳에 within one's reach **2** [닥치다] visit; befall <a person>; happen to <a person>. e.g.그에게 재난이 미쳤다 A misfortune befell him. / An accident happened to him.**3** [필적하다] match; equal; be a match for; rival <another> in; come up with; (힘이) lie in one's power [ability]. e.g. 힘이 미치는 한 as much as lies in one's power / to the best of one's power

미터 [मीथौ] [길이의 단위] a meter [a metre]. e.g. 100미터 경주 the hundred-meter dash.

미팅 [मीथीग] [집회,모임] a meeting. **미풍 양속** [-**良俗**] established social morals and good manners [customs]. e.g. 한국에서는 윗사람의 의견을 따르는 것이 미풍 양속으로 되어 있다 In Korea it is considered proper to go along with the ideas of one's superiors.

미해결 [मीहैग्यौल] [**未解決**] e.g. 미해결의 unsolved / unresolved / unsettled / pending / outstanding.

미행 [मीहैग] [**尾行**] 미행하다 follow (up); shadow; trail;

(ather) <a person>; dog <a person's step>.

미혼 [मीहोन] [未婚] e.g. 미혼의 single / unmarried

미화 [मीहवा] [美化] beautyfication; idealization (이상화). 미화하다 beautify <a city>; make <the look of the town> beautiful; landscape (조경으로); idealize <death> (이상화하다). e.g. 젊은 이는 죽음을 미화하는 경향이 있다 Young people are apt to romanticize death.

미흡 [मीहब] [未洽] insufficiency; inadequacy; unsatisfactoriness. 미흡하다 (사람이) unsatisfied <with>; dissatisfied <with>; (사물이) insufficient; unsatisfactory; unsatisfying; inadequate.

민간 [मीनगान] [民間] e.g. 민간의(공(公)에 대하여) private / nonofficial / nongovernmental / (군에 대하여) civilian / civil / nonmilitary. 민간에서 among the people / in nongovernmental circles. 그것은 오랫 동안 민간에 전해 내려오는 치료법이다 That is a care which has long been handed down among the common people.

민간인 [मीनगानइन] [民間人] a non-official civilian; a nongovernment person.

민감 [मीनगाम] [敏感] sensitiveness; sensitivity; susceptibility; susceptivity. 민감하다 sensitive; susceptible; susceptive. e.g. 지나치게 민감한 oversensitive / oversubtle.

민란 [मीनरान] [民亂] a riot[revolt] of the people; an uprising [insurrection] of the people. e.g. 민란을 일으키다 raise [start / get up] a riot [an insurrection] / rise in revolt [rebellion].

민망하다[मीनमंग हादा] **1** [측은하다] pitiable; pitiful; piteous; miserable; sad; sorry. e.g. 민망한 생각이 들다 feel pity [compassion] <for / toward>. 민망히 pitiably; pitifully; piteously; miserably; sorrily. **2** [열없다] awkward. e.g. 나는 가진 돈이 적어 민망했다 I felt awkward to find myself short of cash.

민박 [मीनबाक] [民泊] a private residence temporarily taking lodgers; a home-stay. 민박하다 [मीनबाक हादा] take lodgings at a private house.

민생 [मीनसैंग] [民生] the livelihood of the people [nation]; public welfare. e.g. 민생의 안정 the stabilization of the people's livelyhood.

민속 [मीनसोक] [民俗] folk [ethnic] customs; folkways.

민심 [मीनशिम] [民心] popular feeling; public [popular]

sentiment; the mind of the people. e.g. 민심의 안정을 꾀하다 work to prevent popular unrest.

민영 [मीनयौंग] [民營] private management [operation]. e.g. 민영의 privately-managed[-operated] / private / nongovernment (al).

민요- [मीनयो] [民謠] a folk song; a popular ballad.

민원 [मीनवॉन] [民怨] public resentment[grievance]; popular discontent. e.g. 민원의 대상이 되다 become a target of public grievance. 민원을 사다 incur the enmity of the people.

민족 [मीनजोंक] [民族] a race; a nation; a people; a nationality; an ethnic group.

민주 [मीनजु] [民主] democracy. e.g. 이 회사는 민주적인 운영이 이루어지고 있다 This company is run democratically.

민주주의 [मीनजुजुउइ] democracy; democratism; democratic principles.

민중 [मीनजुंग] [民衆] the people; the mass of people; the masses; the public; the populace; people in general; the multitude.

민첩 [मीनछौब] [敏捷] agility; nimbleness; alacrity; quickness; promptitude; smartness; shrewdness. 민첩하다 quick; prompt; nimble; agile; smart; shrewd.

민폐 [मीनफ्ये] [民弊] public harm[damage]; an abuse suffered by the public; a public nuisance (대중 상대의); a private nuisance (특정인 상대의); [금전의 갈취] extortionate practices by public officials; [공직자의 비행] a malpractice. e.g. 민폐를 끼치다 cause a nuisance to the people / cause inconvenience to the general public / make trouble for the people.

믿다 [मीत्ता] [의심치 않다] believe; put belief in; credit; give credit [credence] to; put credit in; accept <a thing> as true; be convinced of <a fact>; be persuaded <of / that>. e.g. 믿을 수 있는 credible / believable. 나는 그가 말하는 것을 믿는다 I believe him [what he says].

믿음 [मीदुम] **1** [믿는 마음] trust; confidence; credit; reliance; credence. e.g. 믿음을 얻다 be trusted by <a person> / get <a person's> credit[trust] / be in <a person's> confidence[trust]. **2** = 신앙. e.g.믿음이 없는 사람 an impious person / an infidel.

믿음직하다 [मीदुमजिख्वादा] reliable; dependable; trustworthy; authentic; authoritative; [유망하다] hopeful;

promising. e.g. 그는 믿음직한 사람이다 He is to be depended upon[a reliable / a trustworthy] man.

밀고 [मीलगो] [密告] secret information <against>; an anonymous report [notice]; betrayal; a tip-off; a tip. e.g. 익명의 사람으로부터 그가 여기에 있다는 밀고를 받았다 We received information [a tip] from an anonymous person that he was here. / We were informed [tipped off] by an anonymous person that he was here. 밀고하다 inform against [on]; lay [lodge] information <against>; turn informer <on a person>; peach [squeal] <on a person>; tip off <about / that>; blow the gaff <to the police>; snitch <on>. e.g. 자기 친구를 밀고하다 inform

밀다 [मीलदा] **1** [힘을 주어 앞으로 나아가게 하다] push; shove; thrust; jostle; give a push; elbow (팔꿈치로); bunt (머리나 발로); bob (약간). e.g. 승객을 만원인 전차에 밀어 넣다 squeeze passengers into a (crowded) train. **2** [깎다] shave; plane; [문지르다] rub; scrub; [눌러 펴다] press; roll. e.g. 턱수염을 밀다 shave off one's beard. **3** [추천하다] recommend; propose; nominate (지명하여); [지지하다] support; back (up); boost. e.g. 한 배우를 아낌없이 밀다 patronize an actor munificently.

밀담 [मीलदाम] [密談] a private [secret] conversation; a confidential talk.

밀도 [मीलदो] [密度] [조밀의 정도] density.

밀려나다 [मीलल्यौनादा] be pushed [thrust / forced] out; be elbowed [hustled] out; (씨름에서) be pushed out(of the ring);(지위 등에서) be ousted [expelled / dislodged] <from>; be squeezed [shoved] out of; (하위로) be relegated <to>. e.g.사장 자리에서 밀려나다 be squeezed out of the president's seat.

밀려오다 [मीलल्यौओदा] [밀어닥치다] advance [come / press] on <a castle>; make [rush] for <the door>; rush [surge / crowd] into; besiege <one's house>; (파도가) surge[beat / rush] upon <the shore>. e.g. 주문이 밀려오다 have a rush [flood] of orders

밀렵 [मीलल्यौब] [密獵] poaching. 밀렵하다 poach (for) <pheasants>; steal game; trespass on game [fish]; take game [fish] by illegal method.

밀리다 [मीललीदा] **밀리다 1** [일이 쌓이다] be leth undone; be delayed [retarded]; be piled up; be accumulated; be in arrears <with>. e.g. 주문이 밀리다 orders pile up. **2** [미지불이 늘다] fall into arrears; be in arrears <with>; be leth unpaid; be overdue; be outstanding. e.g. 밀린 봉급 back pay [salary]. **3** [떠밀리다] be pushed; be shoved; be thrust. e.g. 인파에 밀리다 be jostled in the crowd / be swept along in the crowd.

밀매 [मील्मै] [密賣] an illicit sale <of>; illicit traffic <in>; smuggling; (주류의) bootlegging. 밀매하다 sell secretly; deal secretly <in>; smuggle; practice smuggling; bootleg (주류를). e.g. 그는 밀수품을 밀매하고 있다 He illegally sells smuggled articles.

밀물 [मील्मुल] the inflow [rising] of the tide; (조수) the flowing [rising / swelling] tide.

밀봉 [मील्बोंग] [密封] sealing up; sealing tightly. 밀봉하다 seal hermetically; seal up. e.g. 밀봉한 편지 a sealed letter.

밀수 [मील्सू] [密輸] smuggling; contraband (trade). 밀수하다 [밀수입하다] smuggle <goods> in (to) <the country>; import through illegal channels; [밀수출하다] smuggles <goods> abroad [out of the country]; export <an article> unlawfully; run.

밀실 [मील्सील] [密室] 밀실 a secret room [chamber]; a closet.

밀어넣다 [मीलौनौथा] push [force / squeeze / thrust] in. e.g. 작은 방에 많은 사람을 밀어넣다 crowd a lot of people into a mall room.

밀어붙이다 [मीलौबुथीदा] push [drive] <a person> to; push [thrust] against; pin against (움직이지 않도록); hold against; (힘있게) press hard. e.g. 벽 쪽으로 밀어붙이다 drive <a person> to the wall.

밀어젖히다 [मीलौजौतहादा] push away [aside / by]; thrust aside [away]; force[push] aside [out of the way]; crowd [squeeze] out; shove [brush] aside; elbow <a person> out [aside / to one side] (팔꿈치로). e.g. 사람을 밀어젖히다 push people aside.

밀입국 [मीलइपकूक] [密入國] illegal entry into a country; smuggling oneself into <a country>; stowing away. 밀입국하다 smuggle oneself into <a country>; enter [slip into] a country secretly [illegally]; stow away.

밀접 [मील्जौब] [密接] 밀접하다 close <to>; intimate <with>; near. e.g. 그것과 이것은 밀접한 관계가 있다 It is closely related to this.

/ The two are closely related.

밀집 [मील्जीब] [密集] 밀집 massing; concentration. 밀집하다 crowd; swarm; close up [together]; aggregate densely; cluster together; from in close order. e.g. 광장에는 사람들이 밀집해 있었다 The square was crowded with people.

밀착 [मील्छाक] [密着] [꼭 붙음] close adhesion. 밀착하다 stick (fast) to; adhere closely to; be glued <together / to>. e.g. 붕대가 상처에 밀착되어 떨어지지 않는다 The bandage is stuck to the wound and will not come loose.

밀치다 [मील्छीदा] push; shove; thrust; give a push [thrust]; push [thrust] away [aside]. e.g. 서로 밀치다 jostle [push / hustle / crowd / elbow] one another.

밀폐 [मील्फ्ये] [密閉] 밀폐하다 shut tight (ly); cover [close] up tight; seal hermetically; make [keep] airtight; seal [glue] up. e.g. 밀폐한 상자 an airtight box / a hermetically sealed box

밀항 [मील्हांग] [密航] a secret passage; stowing away; smuggling oneself. e.g. 화물선으로 밀항을 기도하다 attempt to [try to] stow away on a cargo boat.

밉다 [मीबता] [싫다] hateful; disgusting; detestable; odious; [가증스럽다] abominable; cursed; [심술궂다] spiteful; [얄밉다] provoking.

밉살스럽다 [मीब सालसुरौबता] [싫다] hateful; detestable; disgusting; [지긋지긋하다] abominable; cursed; odious; horrible; [심술궂다] spiteful; [얄밉다] provoking; offensive

밋밋하다 [मीत्मीतहादा] [굴곡이 없다] flat; even; plane; plain; smooth; smooth and flat; [곧고 길다] slender and tall; straight and long. e.g. 얼굴이 밋밋하다 have a smooth expressionless [blank] face.

밍밍하다 [मीगमीगहादा] tasteless; flat; insipid; weak [watery] <tea>; thin <porridge>; washy <milk>; mild <tobacco>; light <liquor>. e.g. 밍밍한 국 thin soup.

및 [मीत] and; also; as well as; in addition to; besides; both ... and. e.g. 이 법령은 부산 및 인천에서 실시되고 있다 This ordinance is in effect in Pusan and Inch'ŏn.

밑 [मीथ] **1** [아래쪽] the lower part; the foot; the base; the bottom. e.g. 나무 밑에서 하늘을 올려다 보다 look up at the sky from under a tree. **2** [하위]. e.g. 그는 나보다 세 살 밑이다 He is three years my junior [younger than I].

3 [조건,환경]. e.g. 선생 밑에서 바이올린을 배우다 study violin under a teacher.

밑돌다 [मित्तोल्दा] do not amount <to>; fall short <of>; be less [lower] than; be [fall] below <the average>; be a fraction <of>. e.g.(결과가) 예상을 밑돌다 fall short of one's expectation(s).

밑바닥 [मिप्पादाक] **1** [물건의 바닥] the bottom; the base; the bed <of a river>. e.g. 구두의밑바닥 the sole of a shoe.**2** 최하층] the bottom; the depths; the abyss; the nadir <of one's fortune>. e.g. 사회의 밑바닥에 있는 사람들 people at the very bottom of society [lowest level of society].

밑바탕 [मिप्पाथांग] **1** [본질] essence; [기초] the foundation; the basis; the groundwork; the ground. e.g. 서구 민주주의의 밑바탕 the basic ideas of western democracy. **2** [본성] the original nature; the inherent character; one's true colors. e.g. 밑바탕이 좋다[나쁘다] be good [bad] by nature.

밑줄 [मिच्चुल] an underline.

밑지다 [मिच्चिदा] lose on the cost [price]; do not cover the first cost; [손해보다] lose <over>; suffer [incur] a loss; do not pay. e.g. 밑지는 장사

밑천 [मिच्छौन] [자본] capital; funds; stock; [원금] the principal; [원가] the cost [prime] price; (도박의) a stake. e.g. 적은 밑천으로 사업을 시작하다 start business on a small capital.

바가지 [बागाजी] a gourd (dipper); a calabash. 바가지(를) 긁다 nag[snap / yap] <at>; speak crossly <to>; grumble <at>.바가지(를) 쓰다 be overcharged be charged high(be made to) pay through the nose pay exorbitantly.

바구니 [बागुनी] a basket <집합적> basketry a crate (큰 것).

바깥 [बाकाथ] [바깥쪽] the outside [옥외] the outdoors out-of-doors the open(air); [겉면] the exterior.

바깥일 [बाक्काथइल] 1 [주로 남자들이 하는 일] the job [work] of one's husband a man's work[job]. 2 [집 밖의 일] outdoor work. e.g. 바깥일을 하다 work in the yard[garden / field]. 3 [세상일] the affairs [occurrences / happenings] in the world. e.g.집 안에만 있어서 바깥일은 모른다 I always stay at home, so I don't know what happens in the streets.

바꾸다 [बाक्कुदा] 1 [교환하다] exchange[change / barter] <one thing for another>; [전환하다] convert [change / turn] <one thing for another>. e.g. 수표를 현금으로 바꾸다 cash a check.2 [변경하다] change alter e.g.주소를 바꾸다 change address

바뀌다 [बाक्कवीदा] [변하다] change be [get] changed undergo a change alter be altered shith turn (풍향이) shith (round) <to>; turn veer come around [about]; [개선되다] be impro-ved be bettered [교정되다] be corrected be reformed [대체되다] be replaced

바나나 [बानाना] a banana.

바느질 [बान्जील] needlework sewing. 바느질하다 do needlework sew

바늘 [बानल] 1 (바느질의) a (sewing) needle.2 (낚시의) a hook (시계의) a hand <on the clock

바늘방석 [बानलबांगसौक] [-方席]<비유> a bed of thorns. e.g. 난 바늘방석에 앉아 있는 기분이었다 I felt as if I were sitting on thorns.

바다 [बादा] the sea [대양] the ocean

바닥 [बादाक] 1 [평면을 이룬 부분] the broad the flat. e.g. 방바닥 a floor (of the room).2 [물체의 밑부분] the bottom the sole the bed. e.g. 강바닥 a river-bed 바닥(이) 나다 be exhausted be used up be consumed run out be gone come to an end give out.

바닷가 [बादात्का] the beach the seaside the seashore.

바라다 [बारादा] [원하다] wish <for / to do / that>; desire <to do / that>; want <to do / that>; long [crave / yearn] for seek care for; [기대하다] hope <for / to do / that>; expect <to do / that>; look for look for-ward to.

바라보다 [बाराबोदा] 1 [건너다보다] look at watch see [응시하다] gaze at[on]; stare at [관망하다] take [get] a view <of>; view look over. **2** [방관하다] look on sit back [tight] and watch remain a spectator.

바람[1] [बाराम] **1** [공기의 움직임] a wind (미풍) a breeze (외풍) a drath a draught (돌풍) a blast [gust] (of wind); (폭풍) a storm (외기) air a current (선풍기 등의). **2** [공 R 타이어 등의 공기] air. e.g. 바람을 넣다 fill <a football> with air / pump up <a tire>. 3 [들뜬 마음] inconstancy fickle-ness [들뜬 행동] an amour. 바람(이) 나다 ⑴ [이성

관계로 마음이 들뜨다] become fickle [flippant / dissipated]; take to fast living take to amours have a secret love affair. 바람(을) 맞다 (1) [속다] be fooled[cheated / deceived / swindled]; be taken in. (2) [퇴짜맞다] be rejected [refused / rebuffed]; get [be given] the cold shoulder <from>; get the mitten be stood up. 바람(을) 맞히다 [퇴짜를 놓다] reject refuse snub give the cold shoulder <to>; give the gate <to>; [헛기다리게 하다 keep a <person> waiting in vain break[fail to keep] an appointment stand up.

바람 2 [बाराम] 1 [어떤 일에 따른 기세] conjunction; process; result; conesquence; outcome; influence; effect; impetus; motive. e.g. 경기는 비가 오는 바람에 연기되었다 The game was put off on account of rainy weather. 2 [차림새]. e.g. 파자마 바람으로 in pajamas only / without one's trousers on.

바람둥이 [बारामदुंगी] [바람 피우는 사람](남자) a playboy a licentious man a Don Juan an inconsistent lover philanderer (여자)a flirt a fickle[wanton] woman a woman of easy virtue a light-o'-love.

바람직하다 [बारामजीख्वादा] desirable advisable [환영할 만하다] welcome

바래다 1 [बारेदा] [빛이 변하다] (물건이) lose [cast] color [colour]; discolor [discolour]; be discolored [discoloured]; get washed out (물건 또는 빛깔이) fade (away); (빛깔이) go [come] off.

바래다 2 [बारेदा] = 배웅하다 (⊠ 배웅). 바래 (다) 주다 바래주다 see [take] <a person to a place>; escort see <a person> off [leave].

바로 [बारो] 1 [굽지 아니하고 바르게] right straight upright erect [정당하게] justly rightly properly duly [정확하게 correctly accurately [진실되게] truly honestly truthfully straightforwardly. e.g. 바로 앉다 sit properly / sit up straight 2 [지체 않고 곧] at once directly immediately right now [off]; promptly without (a moment's) delay [hesitation]; right [straight] away. e.g. 저녁 식사 후 바로 right ather dinner.

바로잡다 [बारोजाब्दा] 1 [굽은 것을 곧게 하다] straighten make straight [right]; (나뭇가지 등을) set up again train. 2 [잘못된 것을 고치다] correct redress reform <evil practices>;

remedy rectify <an error>; cure set right set [put / bring] to rights straighten.

바르다[1] [बारुदा] 1 [붙이다] (종이 등을) stick paste plaster affix put post (장지문 등을) paper <a sliding door>. 2 [묻히다] apply <one thing to another>; paint (칠을); spread <on>; plaster (회반죽 등을); daub bedaub coat (그림 물감 옻 등을); varnish (바니시를); lacquer (옻칠을); rub (in) (문질러서); use put on make

바르다[2] [बारुदा] [발라내 다] open [split] (and take out the inside of); split [scrape / strip] off cleave shell husk. e.g. (생선) 가시를 바르다 bone [fillet] fish.

바르다[3] [बारुदा] 1 [곧다] straight erect upright. e.g. 바른 자세 good posture 2 [참되다] honest upright true straight [솔직하다] straightforward frank [옳다] right true just [정확하다] correct accurate exact. e.g. 마음이 바른 righteous / right-hearted / right-minded / upright / honest.

바보 [बाबो] a fool a simpleton an ass a donkey a goose

바비큐 [बाबीख्यु] [통구이] a barbecue.

바쁘다 [बापुदा] 1 [틈없다] busy <서술적> be occupied be engaged be all tied up be not free. 2 [급하다] pressing urgent immediate hurried hasty.

바삐 [बाप्पी] 1 [분주하게] busily like a busy bee. 2 [급히] in a hurry in a hurried manner hurriedly in haste hastily in a rush [즉시] at once without delay [loss of time]; immediately.

바삭 [बासाक] (잎 등의) with a rustle [a rustling sound]; rustlingly (깨물 때의) with a crunch.

바삭거리다 [बासाकौरीदा] rustle crinkle crunch (again and again).

바스락거리다 [बासराकौरीदा] rustle; make a rustling sound. e.g. 바람에 낙엽이 바스락거렸다 The fallen leaves were rustling in the wind. / The wind rustled the fallen leaves.

바싹 [बास्साक] 1 [물기가 없게] <dried up> completely; in a parched manner; bone-dry; scorched; [타버리게] burnt up [off]. e.g. 목이 바싹 마르다 I am parched. / My throat is as dry as dust. 2 [밀착하여] closely; close to; side by side; hard (by). e.g. 바싹 붙어 앉다 sit closely together / sit close to each other

바야흐로 [बायाहुरो] 1 [한창] at the height <of>; in full swing [operation]; [바로]

just really truly. e.g. 바야흐로 봄이다 Spring is really here. / We are now in the midst of spring. 2 [이제 곧] <be> about to <do>; on the point [brink / verge] of <doing>; almost nearly. e.g. 해가 바야흐로 지려고 하고 있다 The sun is about to sink [set].

바위 [बावी] a rock a crag (울퉁불퉁한); a reef (암초).

바이러스 [बाइरौस] a virus.

바이올린 [बाइओलीन] a violin a fiddle.

바지 [बाजी] 1 (a pair of) trousers pants

바치다 [बाछीदा] 1 [드리다] give <to a superior>; present make a present <of>; dedicate (저서 음악 등을); offer <to a god>; make an offering <to>; consecrate <to>. e.g.남에게 저서를 바치다 dedicate a book to a person. 2 [진력하다] devote [희생하다] sacrifice. e.g. 일신을 바치다 devote [dedicate / give] oneself to <a cause>.

바퀴 [बाख्वी] 1 [수레바퀴] a wheel a rundle (무거운 가구 등에 다는) a caster. 2 [도는 횟수] a round a turn [회전] a turn a revolution a rotation. e.g. 연못을 한 바퀴 돌다 walk around [round] a pond.

바탕 [बाथांग]1 [성질] nature (a) disposition temperament temper character [재질] endowments giths ability talent [소지소질] an inclination the making [체질] (physical) constitution. e.g. 바탕이 좋은 사람 a man of good disposition. 2 [물건의 바닥] (the) ground field (직물의) texture weave. e.g. 검은바탕에 흰 무늬 a white pattern [design] on a black ground. 3 [기초] foundation groundwork basis <pl. bases>. e.g. 에 바탕을 두다 be based [founded] on ....

박다 [बाकता] 1 (말뚝 등을) drive [strike / knock]; ram down <a stake>; wedge in (쐐기 등을). e.g. 기둥에 못을 박다 drive a nail into a pillar. 2 [재봉하다] sew (by backstitch). e.g. 재봉틀로 커튼의 가장자리를 박다 stitch the edge of a curtain on one's sewing machine.

박람회 [博覽會] [बांगनामह्वे] an exhibition an exposition a fair.

박력 [बांगन्यौक] [迫力]force power drive wallop. e.g. 박력 있는 strong / powerful / able / convincing / forcible.

박멸 [बाकम्यौल] [撲滅] eradication extirpation extermination destruction suppersssion annihilation (질병이나 악습의) stamping out. 박멸하다 eradicate extirpate ex-terminate destroy suppress annihilate wipe out (of existence); make an end of put down stamp [wipe] out.

박물관 [बाकमुलग्वान] [博物館] a museum.

박사 [बाकसा] [博士] [대학의 가장 높은 학위(를 지닌 사람)]] a doctor [정통한 사람] an expert [학자식 자] a learned man

박살 [बाकसाल] [撲殺] [때려죽임] clubbing [beating] <a person> to death. 박살하다 club [beat / knock / strike] <a person> dead [to death]. e.g. 박살당하다 be beaten to death.

박수 [बाक्सु] [拍手] hand clapping (a) clapping of hands a handclap 박수하다 clap (one's hands in applause).

박수 갈채 cheers cheering and clapping applause plaudits.

박식 [बाकिशक] wide [extensive] knowledge encyclop (a) edic knowledge erudition. 박식하다 erudite learned well-informed knowledgeable.

박애 [बाकै] [博愛] love of mankind philanthropy [자선] charity benevolence humanity. 박애하다 love (mankind); engage in philanthropy. 박애주의자 a philanthropist.

박자 [बाकचा] [拍子] time rhythm measure beat timing a musical time pattern.

박차 [बाकछा] [拍車]a spur a rowed spur (톱니가 달린); [촉진] speeding up acceleration. 박차를 가하다(말에) set [put] spurs to one's horse spur (on) one's horse <비유> spur [put] <a person> <to do / into action>; accelerate give impetus to.

박치기 [बाकछीगी] butting (서로의) bumping of heads. 박치기하다 give <a person> a butt of head (서로가) bump into [against] each other bump heads together.

박탈 [बाकथाल] [剝奪] 박탈하다 deprive [strip] <a person> of <his office>; divest <a person> of <his rank>.

박하다 [बाखादा] [薄 –] [인색하다] illiberal stingy niggardly tight hard (점수가) severe [strict] in marking (인정이) inhuman unfeeling tough. e.g. 인심이 박한 세상 a hard [tough] world to live in.

박학 [बाख्वा] [博學] erudition extensive learning wide [encyclop (a) edic] knowledge. 박학하다 erudite learned well-read well.

박해 [बाखै] [迫害] persecution oppression torment. 박해하다 persecute oppress torment.

박히다 [बाख्वीदा] 1 [들어가 꽂히다] stick be stuck run into get stuck [imbedded / driven in]. e.g. 별이 정점이 박힌 하늘 a sky studded with stars / a star-studded sky. 2 e.g. 그녀는 온종일 방안에 박혀 있다 She keeps her room all day long.

밖 [बाक] 1 [바깥쪽] the outside [외부] the exterior [옥외] the outdoors the open(air). e.g. 창문 밖을 내다보다 look out of the window. 2 [이외] another the other the rest outside of (a limit); with the exception <of>; [다른] else [다만 … 뿐] only but no more than merely barely. e.g. 이 밖의 장미는 모두 붉다 All the rest of the [All the other] roses are red.

ㅂ

반 [1] [बान] [班] [집단] a party a company a group a set a team a unit [학급] a class a section a squad. e.g. 상급 [하급] 반 the senior [junior] class.

반 [2] [半] [बान] 1 [절반] (a) half. e.g. 수박을 반으로 자르다 cut a watermelon in half. 2 중앙] the middle the center [중도] halfway. e.g. 인생의 반을 지나다 pass the middle milepost of life.

반- [1] [बान] [半] half semi-; demi-; hemi-. e.g. 반숙의 half-cooked. 반영구적인 semipermanent.

반- [2] [बान] [反] anti-. e.g. 반주류파 an antimainstream association.

반감 [बान्गाम] [反感] (an) antipathy animosity ill feeling an antagonistic feeling a feeling of revolt (a) revulsion of feeling. e.g. 반감을 사다 rouse <a person's> antipathy / antagonize <a person>. a half-life half (-life) period.

반갑다 [बान्गाप्ता] glad joyful joyous happy welcome delightful pleasant <to see>.

반격 [बान्ग्योक] [反擊] a counterattack a responsive attack a counteraction a counteroffensive a counter-drive a counterblow a counterbuff. 반격하다 make a counterattack counterbuff strike [fight / beat / hit] back.

반기 [1] [बान्गी] [半期] a half term [year]; a semester. e.g. 상 [하] 반기 the first [latter] half of the year.

반기 [2] [बान्गी] [反旗 R 叛旗] a standard [banner] of revolt [rebellion]. 반기(를) 들다 raise the standard of revolt rise in revolt [rebellion] <against>; take up arms <against>; be up in arms <against>.

반기다 [बान्गीदा] be [look] glad <about>; be pleased [delighted] <at / with>; rejoice [be rejoiced] <in / at / over / to do>; [환영하다] greet welcome.

반나절 [बानाजौल] [半-] a quarter of a day half the morning several hours of the day.

반납 [बान्नाम] [返納] return restoration. 반납하다 return give [send] back restore.

반년 [बान्नयौन] [半年] half a year a half year. e.g. 반년마다 half-yearly / semi-annually.

반대 [बान्दै] [反對] 1 [두 사물의 위치, 내용이 서로 등진 상태] the reverse the inverse the opposite the contrary. 2 [남의 의견, 행동에 맞서서 거스름] opposition resistance antagonism hostility kick [이론] objection dissension. 반대하다 oppose be opposed <to>; offer opposition <to>; object <to>; take exception <to>; raise [make / have] an objection <to>; take a stand <against>; stand <against>; antagonize.

반도 [बान्दो] [半島] peninsula.

반도체 [बान्दोछे] [半導體] a semiconductor.

반동 [बान्दोंग] [反動 reaction counteraction (총 등의) kick recoil (탄력체의) resilience. 반동하다 react (총 등이) kick recoil rebound (탄력체가) resile spring back.

반드시 [बान्दुशी] [꼭] certainly surely infallibly positively upon one's life by God [틀림없이] without fail [기필코] by all (manner of) means / at any cost at all costs.

반들거리다 [बान्दलकौरीदा] [윤이 나다]shine have a gloss get glossy [lustrous].

반듯하다 [बान्दत्हादा] 1 [곧다] straight upright erect [고르다] even square and level. e.g. 반듯한 길 a straight road. 2 [흠없다] flawless decent [단정하다] neat tidy [정연하다] orderly regular in good order [shape]. e.g. 반듯한 집안 a decent [respectable] family. 3 [반반하다] comely well-shaped clear-cut nice-looking. e.g. 반듯한 용모 finely-chiseled features.

반란 [बान्लान] [反亂, 叛亂] a rebellion a revolt (an) insurgency [폭동] an insurrection [봉기] a rising an uprising 반란군 a rebel army insurgent [mutinous] troops.

반론 [बान्रोन] [反論] a refutation a counter-argument an opposing argument a polemic <against>.

반말 [बान्माल] [半-] [거친 말] crude language rough talk words lacking in respect impolite speech slipshod [insolent] speech [얕잡은 말] a neutral style of speech (ignoring social differences). 반말하다 talk roughly [slovenly]; speak impolitely use the low forms of speech <to>.

반면 [बानम्यौन] [反面] the other side the reverse the

opposite.

반문 [**बान्मुन**] [**反問**] 반문하다 [되받아묻다] ask a question in return [반대 신문하다] cross-question cross-examine.

반바지 [**बान्बाजी**] [**半-**] knee trousers [pants]; knee [short] breeches knickers knickerbockers.

반박 [**बान्बाक**] [**反駁**] (a) refutation confutation disputation contradiction disproof retort rebuttal (원고의 반증에 의함); rebutter (피고의 반증에 의함). 반박하다 refute confute contradict dispute disprove rebut answer [shoot / talk / argue] back take issue <with>.

반반 [**बान्बान**] [**半半**] [반과 반 절반] half-and-half fithy-fithy. e.g. 반반으로 half-and-half / in half [halves]. **반반하다** 1 [판판 하다] smooth even level flat. e.g. 반반한 길 a level road. 2 [예쁘장하다] comely pretty handsome attractive charming nice-looking.

반발 [**बान्बाल**] [**反撥**] 1 [되받아 퉁기기 repulsion [되퉁겨짐] rebounding a backlash a rally recovery.반발하다 repel repulse bound [spring] back rebound rally recover. 2 [반항] opposition resistance rebellion. 반발하다 oppose resist defy rebel <against>.반발력 repulsive [repelling] power repulsive [repellent] force.

반복 [**बान्बोक**] [**反復**] (a) repetition a repeat iteration reiteration epistrophe aphora (악절의); (시 노래의) a refrain a burden. 반복하다 repeat iterate reiterate do over again.

반비례 [**बान्बीरये**] [**反比例**] an inverse proportion a reciprocal proportion. 반비례하다 be in inverse pro-portion <to>; be inversely proportional <to>.

반사 [**बान्सा**] [**反射**] reflection reflexion reverberation.

반상회 [**बान्सांगह्वे**] [**班常會**]a neighborhood meeting a monthly neighbor's meeting.

반색하다 [**बान्सैख्वादा**] show great joy rejoice <in / at / over / to do>; be delighted <in>; light [brighten] up with joy be all smiles smile a welcome <to>. e.g. 반색하며 승낙하다 give one's hearty approval / consent with pleasure.

반석 [**बान्सौक**] [**盤石磐**] [큰 바위] a huge rock a crag [견고함] firmness. e.g. 반석 같은 as firm as a rock / adamantine.

반성 [**बान्सौंग**] [**反省**] self-examination reflection introspection reconsideration (재고). 반성하다 examine oneself reflect(on) / search one's heart [soul]

<on a matter>; introspect reconsider.

반소매 [**बान्सोमै**] [**半-**] a half (-length) sleeve. e.g. 반소매 셔츠 a shirt with half-length sleeves.

반송 [**बान्सोंग**] [**返送**] 반송하다 return send back

반숙 [**बान्सुक**] [**半熟**] [반쯤 익힘]. e.g. 반숙 half-[soth-] boiled / half-cooked / half-done.

반숙하다 boil <an egg> soth [lightly]; be half-boiled [half-done].

반신 반의 [**बान्सीन बानउइ**] [**半信 半疑**] 반신 반의하다 be half in doubt throw some doubt on do not quite believe have [entertain] a doubt about be doubtful [suspicious / distrustful] of.

반역 [**बान्यौक**] [**反逆 叛逆**] (high) treason breach of faith [allegiance]; treachery (an) insurrection (a) rebellion (a) revolt insurgency mutiny insubordination 반역하다 turn traitor (권위에 대해) revolt [rebel] <against>; rise in revolt [mutin>.

반영 [**बान्यौंग**] [**反映**] reflection [영향] influence. 반영하다 reflect influence be reflected be reflective of.

반응 [**बानंग**] [**反應**] [반작용감응] counteraction [반향] a response [효과] an effect (a) reaction

반장 [**बान्जांग**] [**班長**] a squad [section / party / group] leader (학급의) a monitor a class president (직공의) a foreman (동네의) the head of a neighborhood association.

반전 [**बान्जौन**] [**反轉**] [뒤바뀜] [turning over reversal inversion. 반전하다 [거꾸로 돌다] turn reversely [the other way round]; [거꾸로 되다] be reversed [거꾸로 되게 하다] reverse invert [거꾸로 돌아오다] reverse its [one's] course **반점** [**बान्जौम**] [**斑點**] a spot a speck a speckle a dot a fleck. e.g. 둥근 반점 무늬 <a towel with> a spotted pattern.

반주 [**बान्जु**] [**伴奏**] an accompaniment. 반주하다 accompany <a person>; play <a person's> accompaniment play music [장단을 맞추다], keep [beat] time.

반죽 [**बान्जुक**] dough paste <of bread>. 반죽하다 knead dough mo(u)ld <clay>.

반지 [**बान्जी**] [**半指 斑指**] a (finger) ring.

반지르르 [**बान्जीरुरु**] [미끄럽고 윤이 나는 모양] glossily sleekly lustrously lubricously. 반지르르하다 greasy and smooth slippery lubricous glossy sleek lustrous.

반지름 [**बान्जीरुम**] [**半-**] a radius a semidiameter.

반질거리다 [बान्जील्कौरीदा] 1 [매끈거리다] be slippery be smooth be glossy be sleeky be oily. e.g. 사나이들의 얼굴은 비지땀으로 반질거리고 있었다 The men's faces were shiny [gleaming] with grease. 2 [교활하다] be sly be cunning be crathy.

반짝이다 [बान्चागीदा] glitter; glisten; sparkle; gleam; glimmer; glint; twinkle; (순간적으로) flash; glance; glimpse; wink (▷ shine 은 빛나다, 빛을 내다, twinkle 은 별이나 먼 불빛이 반짝이다 glitter 는 눈부시게 반짝거리다, sparkle 은 반짝 반짝 빛나거나 눈 등이 생기가 넘치도록 반짝거릴 때도 씀 e.g. 반짝이는 별처럼 like the twinkling stars.

반찬 [बान्छान] [飯饌] a (side) dish dishes served to go with rice subsidiary articles of diet.

반창고 [बान्छोंगो] [絆創膏] a sticking plaster an adhesive plaster (테이프 모양의) an adhesive tape (상표명) a Band Aid an Elastoplast.

반칙 [बान्छीक] [反則] (a) breach of regulations (an) infringement [violation] of rules an irregularity (a) foul play a foul. 반칙하다 violate [act against] the rules (play) foul commit a foul.

반포 [बान्फो] [頒布] [공포] proclamation promulgation (a) public announcement [발표] publication. 반포하다 proclaim promulgate announce publicly make public [known]; publish.

반하다 [बानहादा] [反 –] 1 [반대되다] oppose be opposed to. 2 [어긋나다] be contrary <to>; go against run counter <to>; be contradictory <to>; (규칙 등에) violate <a law>; infringe <a rule>; break <the regulations>. e.g.그들의 행위는 이 운동의 취지에 반한다 Their action goes against [is out of step with] the aim(s) of this movement.

반하다 [बान्हादा]1 1 [연모하다] fall in love <with>; be enamored <of>; be attached <to>; take a fancy <to>; lose one's heart <to>; be taken <with her / by her beauty>; be keen <on>; fall for be mashed on. e.g. 첫눈에 반하다 fall in love <with a girl> at first sight / take a fancy <to a person> at first meeting. 2 [감탄하다] admire be charmed [넋을 잃다] forget oneself be entranced [enraptured] <by / with>. e.g. 아름다운 목소리에 반하다 be entranced with <a person's> sweet voice.

반항 [बान्हांग] [反抗] [저항]

resistance insubordination recalcitration recalcitrance [권위 등의 무시] defiance [대항] opposition [적대] hostility antagonism [반역] rebellion revolt mutiny (병사의). 반항하다 [저항하다] oppose resist offer resistance <to>; [복종 하지 않다] disobey be insubordinate <to>; [권위를 무시하다] defy bid defiance <to>; [적대 하다] antagonize be antagonistic <to>; rebel <against>; turn upon <a person>; lith [raise] one's hand to [against] <a person>.

반향 [बान्हयांग] [反響] 1 an echo <pl. ~es>; reverberation. 2 [영향] repercussions influence [반응] reflection an echo <pl. ~ es>; a response(a) reaction.

반환 [बान्हवान] [返還] return restoration repayment (돈의); retrocession (영토의); rendition (토지 사람의); restitution (정당한소유주로의

-받다 [बात्ता] [입다, 당하다] receive <an action>; suffer. e.g. 주목받다 receive attention. 그녀는 한 어린애를 점지 받았다 She was blessed with a child.

받다[1] [बात्ता] **1** [수령하다] get have receive take obtain be given be presented <with>; [받아들이다] accept [수여되다] be awarded. e.g. 물건을 고맙게 받다 accept a thing gratefully. 2 [당하다] receive <an insult>; suffer incur <a loss>; be subjected [exposed] to <an insult>. e.g. 그는 절도 혐의를 받았다 He was suspected of theth.

받다[2] [बात्ता] 2 [음식이 잘 먹히다] agree with <a person>; suit one's taste [palate]; be to one's taste. e.g. 몸에 받는[받지 않는] 음식 an agreeable [a disagreeable] food.

받들다 [बातलदा] 1 [공경하다] respect revere esteem venerate hold <one's teacher> in esteem [reverence]; pay respect to <a person>; [모시다] serve work under [for]. 2 [지지하다] hold up uphold support [보좌하다] assist aid help [추대하다] have <a person> over [따르다] obey follow [신봉하다] believe in [embrace] <Christianity>.

받아들이다 [बादादरीदा] [영수하 다] accept receive [동의하다] assent [agree / consent] to [들어주다] grant <a person a request>; listen to comply with [승인하다] accept <a newly independent nation into the UN>; [따르다] follow

[take] <a person's advice>; [포용하다] tolerate comprehend [도입하다] introduce [채택하다] adopt. 받아쓰기 a dictation writing to dictation.

받아치다 [बादाछीदा] receive and give back [권투] counter.

받치다 [बाच्छीदा] 1 [우산 등을 받다] hold up <an umbrella>; hold <an umbrella> over one's head put up [raise] <an umbrella>. 2 [괴다] prop [bolster / shore] (up); support (with a prop); underpin hold up. e.g. 기둥으로 받치다 support <a wall> with a post.

받침 [बात्छीम] 1 [지주] a prop a stay a support a strut a shore a fulcrum <pl. ~s, -cra>; underpinnings (앉히는₩) a stand a pedestal (앉는) a mat a pad. e.g. 책받침 a celluloid board [cardboard] (laid under writing paper). 2 a consonant placed under a vowel.

받히다 [बाथीदा] [부딪히다] be butted butted be gored be struck be hit be bumped. e.g. 트럭에 받히다 be run [struck] against by a truck.

-발 [बाल] [發] 1 [출발] departure. e.g. 서울역 6 시 20 분발 기차 the train leaving Seoul at 6:20 / the 6:20 train from Seoul. 2 [발신] sending. e.g. 3 월 9 일발 전보 the cable dated March 9.

발 [बाल] 1 a foot <pl. feet>; a paw (고양이 등의 발톱이 있는); (오징어 R 낙지 등의) a tentacle an arm (발굽이 있는 동물의) a hoof <pl. ~s, hooves>. 2 [걸음] walking walk [보조] a step [걷는 속도] pace speed. e.g. 발이 빠른 [느린] 사람 a quick [slow] walker. 3 (기물의) a foot a leg. e.g. 발이 셋인 의자 (세발 의자) a three-legged stool.

발가락 [बालकाराक] a toe a digit a dactylus. e.g. 새끼발가락 the little toe.

발가벗다 [बालकाबौत्ता] strip oneself of all one's clothes strip oneself bare [stark-naked]; take off one's clothes undress. e.g. 발가벗은 산 a bare [bald] mountain [hill].

발각 [बालकाक] [發 覺] detection revelation discovery disclosure exposure. 발각하다 find out discover detect.

발간 [बालकान] [發刊] publication issue. 발간하다 publish bring out issue start <a magazine>; launch <a newspaper>.

발걸음 [बालकौरम] a step a pace a tread.

발견 [बालक्यौन] [發 見] discovery revelation [발각]

detection. 발견하다] discover make a discovery find (out); detect spot (우연히) chance (up)on <a thing>; light upon <a fact>; strike out <a theory>.

발굴 [बाल्कुल] [發掘] (an) excavation (시체의) exhumation. 발굴하다 dig(out / up); excavate unearth turn up (시체를) exhume disentomb untomb disinter.

발권 [बाल्क्वॉन] [發券] the issue of banknotes note issuing.

발그레하다 [बाल्कुरेहादा] reddish tinged with red (안색이) ruddy rubicund aglow reddened flushed <서술적>be aglow. e.g. 발그레한 뺨 ruddy cheeks.

발그스름하다 [बाल्कुसरमहादा] reddish somewhat red light red.

발급 [बाल्कप] 발급하다 issue.

발길 [बाल्कील] 1 [차는힘] (the force of) a kick. e.g. 발길로 차다 give <a person> a kick / kick <a person>. 2 [걸음] a step [왕래] coming and going. e.g. 발길이 닿는 대로 가다 go where one's feet lead one.

발길질 [बाल्कील्चील] kicking. 발길질하다 give <a person> a kick; kick out at <a person>; kick.

발깍 [बाल्काक] 1 [갑자기 성내거나 힘쓰는 모양] all of a sudden in a sudden outburst with a burst. 2 [소동이 나는 모양] topsy-turvy in a great bustle in a turmoil [hubbub / mess]; in utter confusion pell-mell every which way. e.g. 온 집안이 발깍 뒤집혔다 All is confusion in the house. / The house is all torn up. / The whole house was in a terrible confusion.

발단 [बाल्तान] [發端] [일이 벌어짐일의 첫머리] the origin the opening the start the beginning the commencement the outset the inception. 발단하다 originate <from / in / with>; be originated start <from>; begin commence.

발달 [बाल्ताल] [發達] [성장] development growth [진보] progress advance advancement.발달하다 develop grow (up); progress make progress advance. e.g. 저 아이는 정신도 육체도 아직 발달하지 않았다 The child is underdeveloped both in mind and body [has not fully developed in mind or in body

발돋움 [बाल्तोदुम] [발끝으로 서기]. 발돋움하다 stand on(one's) tiptoe(s). e.g. 발돋움하여 책을 선반에서 내리다 take [reach] down a book from a shelf on tiptoe.

발등 [बाल्दुंग] the top side of the foot. e.g. 발등을

ㅂ

밟다 step [tread] on <another's> foot.

발라내다 [बाल्लानैदा] shuck <corn>; hull <peas>; crack <a chestnut>; remove. e.g. 생선의 가시를 발라내다 clean [bone] a fish.

발라드 [बाल्लाद] a ballad.

발맞추다 [बाल्माचुदा] keep pace <with>; fall [get] into step <with>; (행동상) act in concert <with>.

발매 [बाल्मै] [發賣] sale. 발매하다 sell put <books> on the market [on sale]; release <a new record>.

발명 [बाल्म्यौंग] [發明] [신고안] invention contrivance. 발명하다 invent devise contrive. e.g. 그가 발명한 새 장치 the new device of his invention. 이 장치는 그가 발명한 것이다 This device is his invention.

발명품 [बाल्म्यौंगफुम] [發明品] an invention [신고안품] [सीन्गोआन्फुम] a contrivance a device

발목 [बाल्मोक] the ankle. e.g. 발목을 삐다 sprain one's ankle.

발바닥 [बाल्पादाक] the sole [bottom] of the [one's] foot. e.g. 발바닥에 티눈이 생기다 get a corn on the sole of one's foot.

발버둥이치다 [बाल्पोदुंगीछीदा] (아이가) flutter one's feet (kick and) struggle do not sit still be restless [몸부림치다] squirm wriggle struggle [헛애를 쓰다] make vain effort make a useless struggle. e.g. 붙잡힌 범인은 도망가려고 발버둥이쳤다 The captured criminal struggled to escape.

발벗다 [बाल्पौत्ता] 1 [맨발이다] be barefoot (ed); have bare [naked] feet. 2 [전력을 다하다] do one's best[utmost]. e.g. 발벗고 나서다 throw oneself into <a matter> with eagerness [enthusiasm].

발사 [बाल्सा] [發射] [총포 등을쏨] discharge firing shooting (로켓의) launching blast-off lith-off. 발사하다 discharge [fire / let off] <a gun>; shoot <a rifle / a bullet from a rifle>; launch[blast off / put up] <a guided missile>; emit emanate radiate send forth. e.g. 권총을 발사하다 discharge [fire] one's revolver.

발산 [बाल्सान] [發散] [밖으로 퍼지어 흩어짐] exhalation (증기 냄새 등의); emanation (빛 등의); diffusion (확산). 발산하다 give forth [out / off]; send forth emit exhale <from>. e.g. 불이 발산하는 열과 연기 heat and smoke emitted by fire.

발생 [बाल्सैंग] [發生] [발현생김] occurrence (an) outbreak [창생] origination genesis birth creation [출현] appearance (생물, 열 전기 등의) generation production [생육] growth development.

발설 [बाल्सौल] [發說] disclosing divulging revealing announcement publication. 발설하다 disclose tell mention reveal divulge announce publish make known give out.

발성 [बाल्सौंग] [發聲] utterance speaking vocalization phonation exclamation ejaculation. e.g. 발성을 공부하다 study voice. 너의 발성이 좋지 않다 You vocalize poorly [have poor vocaliz-ation]. 발성하다 make voice utter speak exclaim ejaculate.

발송 [बाल्सोंग] [發送] sending forwarding dispatch shipping. 발송하다 send out [forth]; forward dispatch ship (우편물을) mail out post.

발신 [बाल्शीन] [發信] [편지를 내기] dispatch [despatch] of a message [letter]; [전신을 보내기] sending [dispatch of] a telegram. 발신하다 send <a letter / a telegram>; dispatch <a message>; telegraph cable (해외로). 발신국 the sending office [station].

발아 [बारा] [發芽] germination sprouting budding gemmation. 발아하다 germinate be germinant sprout (out); bud(out); pullulate put forth buds..

발악 [बाराक] [發惡] [욕] abusive language revilement [모진 짓] infernality atrocity. 발악하다 use abusive language abuse revile rail <at>; rave inveigh <against>; do infernal things kick and struggle.

발육 [बारयुक] [發育] growth development progress. e.g. 발육이 늦은 아이 a retarded child.

발음 [बारम] [發音] [言] pronunciation enunciation articulation (음절로 나누어서의).

발자국 [बसल्चागुक] a footprint a footmarka spoor <美> a track [행방] a trace.

발자취 [बाल्चाब्वी] 1 [발자국] a footprint a footmark <美> a track [종적] a trace. e.g. 발전의 발자취 signs [traces] of progress. 2 [더듬어 온 길] a course. e.g. 지난 20 년간의 발자취를 회고하다 think of [recollect] the course one has followed for twenty years.

발작 [बाल्चाक] [發作] a fit a spasma paroxysm an access an ictus <pl. ~(es)>. e.g. 발작을 일으키다 have a fit [spasm / paroxysm].

발전 [बाल्चौन] [發展] [뻗어나감] expansion ex-

ㅂ

tension-enlargement development growth. 발전하다 develop growexpand extend. e.g. 발전하는 도시 a developing city [town].

발전소 [बाल्चौनसो] [發電所] a power plant [station]; a powerhouse a generating plant[station].

발췌 [बाल्छ्वे] [拔萃] [뽑아 냄] extraction excerption-selection [뽑아 낸 것] an extract an excerpt [적요] an abstract a summary [선집] a selection. e.g. 신문의 발췌 newspaper cuttings [<美> clippings].

발칙하다 [बाल्छीख्वादा] [무법하다] lawless [무례하다] insolent rude [포학하다] outrageous [용서할 수 없다] inexcusable unpardonable. e.g. 발칙한 놈 an insolent [a rude] fellow.

발코니 [बाल्ख्वोनी] a balcony.

발탁 [बाल्थाक] [拔擢] selection choice. 발탁하다 select pick [single / sith] outchoose <out of / from among many>; draw <from>.

발톱 [बाल्थोप] (사람의) a toenail (짐승의) (जीम्संगउइ) a claw (독수리 매 등의) a talon.

발판 [बाल्फान] [-板] [발돋음 받침] a stepa stool a footstool [발판 사닥다리] a stepladder.

발표 [बाल्फ्यो] [發表] [공표] (an) announcement–publication [성명] a statementa communiqu_; (정견등의) (a) manifestation [표현] expression. 발표하다 announcemake public publish make <something> known give outlay <a matter> before the public-issue <a statement>; expressrelease present <the results of study>.

발행 [बारहैंग] [發行] (도서잡지의) publicationissue. 발행하다 publish issue bring output into circulation. e.g. 잡지를 발행하다 publish [start] a magazine.

발효 [बारह्यो] [醱酵] fermentation zymosis. 발효하다 ferment undergo fermentation. e.g. 발효시키다 ferment / leaven / sweat.

발휘 [बारह्वी] [發揮] demonstration display manifestationexhibition. 발휘하다 display exhibit show-demonstrate make mani-fest. e.g. 재능을 발휘하다 display [exhibit / show / demonstrate] one's ability.

밝기 [बाल्की] [밝은 정도] luminosity.

밝다[1] [बाल्ता] [날이 새다] dawnbreak. e.g. 날이 밝기 시작한 하늘 the dawn sky / the sky at dawn.

밝다[2] [बाल्ता] 1 [광선이 충분하다] light [조명 이 충분하다] (well-) lighted [빛나고 있다] bright [빛을

발 하다] luminous. e.g. 밝은 곳에서 in the light. 2 [빛깔 이 산뜻하다] light. e.g. 밝은 녹색 bright green. 3 [눈귀가 좋다 sharp acutekeen quick. 4 [정통 하다] well acquainted <with>; well informed [versed] <in>; expert <in / at>; familiar <with>. 5 [표정분위기가 유쾌하다] cheerful spirited. e.g. 밝은 얼굴 a cheerful face [look]. 6 [장래 등에 기대를 걸 수 있다] bright promising-rosy. e.g. 밝은 장래 a bright future.

밝히다 [बाल्खीदा] [밝게 하다] light up brightenlighten. e.g. 불빛[등불]을 밝히다 turn up the light / make the lamp brighter.

밟다 [बाल्दा] 1 [디디다] step on tread upon [on] (with the feet); [짓밟다] trample <on>; stamp. e.g. 밟아 다져진 길 a beaten path. 2 [수속 등을 거치다] go through <formalities>; undergo [마치다] finish complete. e.g. 절차를 밟다 go through formalities / take proceedings.

밤 [बाम] 1 night [저녁] [evening (▷ evening 은 일몰이나 저녁 식사때부터 취침시까지, night 는 일몰에서 태 양이 비추지 않는 시간을 가리킴

밤거리 [बाम्कोरी] night streets the town at night.

밤길 [बाम्गील] a night journey [walk / trip].

밤낮 [बामनात] [밤과 낮] day and nightnight and day [언제나] night and day constantlyalways all the time day in, day out <文> day in and day out. 밤사이 the nighttime <부사> during[in] the night. e.g. 밤사이 맹위를 떨친 폭풍우로 on account of the storm that has been raging overnight.

밤새우다 [बामसैउदा] pass a night without sleep sit [stay] up all through the night keep [stay] awake all night. e.g. 독서로 밤새우다 sit up all night reading [over] a book.

밤일 [बामील] [밤에 하는 일] night work a night shith (교대 작업의 야근

밤잠 [बामजाम] night sleep sleeping at night.

밤중 [बामजुंग] [－中] [밤의 한가운데] <in> the middle of the night <in> the dead of night [자정] <at> midnight.

밥 [बाप] 1 [쌀밥] boiled [cooked] rice [잡곡밥] any boiled cereal. 2 [식사] a meal food. e.g. 밥을 먹다 take[have / eat] a meal.

밥값 [बाप्काप] [밥벌이 정도 의 구실] the price for a meal [식비] food expenses (하숙의 (the charge for)

ㅂ

board. e.g. 그는 밥값도 못한다 He is a good-for-nothing.

밥맛 [बाम्मात] 1 [밥의 맛] the taste of boiled rice. 2 = 식욕.

밥벌이 [बाप्पौरी] (a means of) living breadwinning live-lihoodone's bread and butter. 밥벌이하다 earn one's bread make a livelihood [living]. e.g. 밥벌이를 못하다 be unable to earn one's bread / cannot make a living.

밥상 [बाप्सांग] [–床] a (dining) table. e.g. 밥상 앞에 앉다 sit down at the table (to eat).

밥솥 [बाप्सोथ] a rice cooker an iron pot.

밥줄 [बाप्चुल] ⇨ 직업 e.g. 밥줄이 끊어지다 lose one's means of livelihood [job].

밥짓다 [बाप्चीत्ता] [밥을 하다] boil [cook] rice prepare food.

밥투정 [बाप्थुजौग] 밥투정하다 grumble at [about / over] one's food complain about the inadequacy of one's food.

밧줄 [बीत्चुल] a rope; a line; a stay.

–방 [बांग] [房] a store <英> a shop. e.g. 금은방 a gold and silversmith's shop. 복덕방 a real estate agent.

방 [बांग] [房] a rooma chamber.

방과 [बांग्वा] [放課] dis-missal of a class. e.g. 방과 후 ather school / ather-school hours.

방관 [बांग्वान] [傍觀] on-looking looking on as a spectator standing idle by [aside]. 방관하다 look on remain a spectator [an idle on-looker]; sit [stand] by and watch be on the hedge.

방귀 [बांग्वी] wind a fart. e.g. 방귀를 뀌다 fart / break wind / pass gas.

방그레 [बांगुरे] smilinglybea-mingly with a sweet [gentle] smile. e.g. 방그레 웃다 smile sweetly <at a person> / smile a sweet smile / beam <upon a person>.

방금 [बांगम] [方今] a moment ago just now right now. e.g. 방금 말씀드린 대로 as I have just said.

방긋 [बांगत] 1 [웃는 모양] smilinglybeamingly with a (bland) smile. e.g. 방긋 웃다 smile sweetly <at a person> / beam <upon a person> / break into a smile. 방긋하다 =방긋거리다 2 [열린 모양]. e.g. (꽃이) 방긋 피어 있다 be half out [open] / be in half bloom.

방대 [बांग्दै] 방대하 bulky massive vastvoluminous copious extensiveenor-mous stupendous coloss-alfabulous mammoth hugegigantic enormous. e.g. 방대한 계획 a grand plan.

방도 [बांगदो] [方道方途] a way a method a meansa measure. e.g. 돈 버는 방도 how to make money / the art of making money.

방랑 [बांगनांग] [放浪] wandering roaming rovinga Bohemian life. 방랑하다 wander about roam rovet-ramp lead a Bohemian life.

방망이 [बांगमांगी] a club a billy (club) (경찰관의); a cudgel (무기로 쓰는).

방면 [बांगम्यौन] [方面] 1 [방향] a direction a sidea way [지역] a quarter a district. e.g. 서울 방면 Seoul districts. 2 [분야] a field a spherea line [각도] an angle [국면] an aspecta phase. e.g. 각 방면에서 (견지, 각도) from every point of view / from all angles.

방목 [बांगमोक] [放牧] grazing pasturing.방목하다 graze <cattle>; put [turn out] <cattle>to grass pasture. e.g. 소를 방목하다 put the cattle out to pasture.

방문 [1] [बांगमुन] [房門] a door (of a room).

방문 [2] [बांगमुन] [訪問] a call a visit an interview. 방문하다 visitcall on <a person>; call at <a place>; pay <a person>a visit. e.g. 친구의 집을 방문하다 call at a friend's home.

방문객 [बांगमुनगैक] [訪問 客] a caller a visitora guest. e.g. 방문객을 만나다 receive a caller [visitor].

방바닥 [बांगबाताक] [房-] the floor of a room the room floor. e.g. 방바닥이 눅눅하다 The floor is wet [damp].

방방곡곡 [बांगबांग्गोक्कोक] [坊坊曲曲] everywhere throughout the country all over the country every nook and corner [cranny] of the land.

방범 [बांगबौम] [防犯] prevention of crimes crime prevention. e.g. 그곳 주민의 긴밀한 유대가 방범에 기여하고 있다 The close bonds between the residents help to prevent crime in the neighborhood. 방범하다 prevent crimes take preventive measures against crimes.

방법 [बांगबौप] [方法] [목적을 이루기 위해 취하는 방식] a way [체계적인 방법] a method [방책] a plana system [...식, 양식] a manner [수단] a means [책략] a schemea device a program [조치]] a stepa measure [과정] a process [절차] a procedure [처방] a recipe a formula <pl. ~s, -lae>.

방사능 [बांगसानंग] [放射能]

radioactivity.

방석 [बांगसौक] [方席] a (Korean) cushion.

방세 [बांगसे] [房貰] a room rent.

방송 [बांगसोंग] [放送] (텔레비전, 라디오의) (TV / radio) broadcasting (1 회의 라디오 방송) a radio broadcast (1 회의 텔레비전 방송) a television broadcast a telecast.

방식 [बांगसीक] [方式] [공식] a formula <pl. ~s, -lae>; [형] a form [양식] a mannera mode [방법] a method a waya system (계통적); [절차] formalities [관례] usage. e.g. 사고 방식 one's way of thinking.

방심 [बांगसीम] [放心] [부주의] carelessness inattention [대비없음] unpreparedness. 방심하다 [부주의하다] be careless about [경계 를 게을리 하다] be off one's guard <toward>; be un-watchfulrelax one's attention.

방아쇠 [बांगास्वे] the trigger <of a gun>. e.g. 방아쇠를 당기다 pull [press] the trigger / trigger <a rifle>.

방안 [बांगान] [方案] a plan a program a schemea device. e.g. 방안을 세우다 draw up [formulate] a plan / lay out[frame] a scheme.

방앗간 [बांगात्कान] [–間] a mill

방어 [बांगो] [防禦] defense [<英> defence]; pro-tection safeguard. 방어하다 defend protect safeguard-bulwark shield.

방언 [बांगौन] [方言] (표준어에 대하여) a dialect [그 지방 특유의 말, 표현 a provincialism.

방역 [बांग्यौक] [防疫] the prevention of epidemics [infectious diseases]; communicable diseases controldisinfection quarantine. 방역하다 prevent an epidemic of take preventive measures against (epidemics).

방영 [बांग्यौंग] [放映] televising <a movie>; television broadcasting. 방영하다 <a movie>; broadcast on television telecast.

방울 [बांगुल] 1 [종] a small bell. e.g. 방울을 달다 bell <a cat> / tie [attach] a bell. 2 [둥근 액체 덩이] a drop. e.g. 눈물 방울 drops of tears.

방위 [बांगवी] [防衛] defense [< 英 > defence] <against>; protection safeguard. 방위하다 defend <against / from>; protectsafeguard shield. e.g. 국토를 방위하다 defend one's land [country].

방음 [बांगम] [防音] soundproofing sound insulation [absorption / arresting / isolation]. 방음하다 (make it) soundproof absorb [arrest] sound. 방음 구조 sound-proof construction.

방임 [बांगीम] [放任] noninterference noninterven-tion do-as-you-please <프> laissez-faire. 방임주 의 a hands-off [let-alone / noninterference / permissive] policy (경제적) a laissez-faire policy [principle]; liberalism.

방정맞다 [बांगजौंगमात्ता] [경망스럽다] light-headed flightyfrivolous rash giddyunreliable.

방조제 [बांगजोजे] [防潮堤] a tide embankment a seawall a sea dike.

방책 [बांगछैक] [方策] [꾀하기계략] a plana device [계획음모 a scheme [정책] [a policy [방법수단] a measure a step.

방청 [बांगछौंग] [傍聽] hearingattendance. 방청하다 hear listen to attend <a lecture>. e.g. 국회를 방청하다 visit the National Assembly in session / attend a sitting of the National Assembly.

방출 [बांगछुल] [放出] (저장 물자 등의) release 방충제 an insecticidemothballs (좀약).

방치 [बांगछी] [放置] leaving [letting] <a thing> alone letting <a thing> as it is[stands]; [등한시] negligence. 방치하다 [상관않다] leave [let] <a thing, a person, etc.> alone leave <a matter> as it is [stands]; leave <a matter> to chanceleave <a thing> to take its own course [등한히 하다] neglect <one's work>; lay aside.

방침 [बांगछीम] [方針] [일을 처리해 나갈 방향] a coursea line a tack [정책] a (line of) policy [계획] a plan [주의] a principle [목적] an aim an object (in view); a purpose.

방탕 [बांगथांग] [放蕩] dissipation profligacy prodigalitydebauchery dissoluteness vicious coursesloose habits riotous [dissolute] living. 방탕하다 dissipateddissolute prodigal profligate. e.g. 방탕한 생활을 하다 live [lead]a fast [dissipated / wild] life / take [be given] to dissipation.

방파제 [बांगफाजे] [防波堤] a breakwater a bulwark a mole

방패 [बांगफै] [防牌] [창화살을 막는 데 쓰던 무기] a shielda buckler (둥근 방패); a screen (작은) an escutcheon (문장이 있는) a targe (작고 둥근).

방편 [बांगफ्यौन] [方便] [수단] an expedient a shitha means <단수, 복수 동형>; an instrumentality [도구] an instrument.

ㅂ

방한 [बांगहान] [訪韓] a visit to Korea.

방해 [बांगहे] [妨害] [훼방] disturbance (잠 행동 등의); obstruction (진행통행 등의); block [간섭] interruption-interference check prevention-trouble (전파의) jamming [장애 지장] a hindrance an obstaclean impedement a barrier an inconveniencean encum-brance.

방향 [बांगहयांग] [方向] 1 [향하는쪽] a direction <one's> bearingsa quarter a situation a waya point of the compass (진행의) a course a line. 2 [뜻이 향하는 곳] one's course [aim / object]. e.g. 방향을 바꾸다 change one's object [course].

방화 [बांगहवा] [放火] [불을 지름] incendiarismarson. e.g. 그 화재는 방화였다 The fire was caused by arson. 방화하다 set fire to <a house>; set <a house> on fire raise a firecommit incendiarism [arson].

방황 [बांगहवांग] [彷徨] 방황하다 (길을 잃고) lose one's way <in darkness, in a wood, etc.>; [정도(正道) 에서 벗어나다] go astray swerve [stray] from the right path wander [roam / stray / knock / hang] aboutrove hover <about / in>.

밭 [बात] a (dry) fielda farm a patch a gardenan orchard.

밭농사 [बागनोंगसा] [-農事] dry-field farming.

배 [1] [बै] [倍] 1 [갑절] two times twicedouble twofold. e.g. 배의 double / twice / twofold. 2 [곱] times -fold. e.g.1 배 once / <美> one time.

배 [2] [बै] 1 [복부] [बोक्पु] the abdomen the belly one's side [위] the stomach [장] [tkax] the bowels [生] the ventral side.

배 [3] [बै] 2a boat (작은 배 기선); a vessel (대형의) a ship (노를 쓰지 않는 대형의); a steamer (기선) a liner (정기 항로의); a barge (바닥이 평평한 짐배); <집합적> shipping (water) crath.

배고프다 [बैगोफदा] hungry sharp-set <서술적> feel [be / get] hungry.

배구 [बेगु] [排球] volleyball.

배급 [बैगप] [配給] distribution supply rationing (식량의).

배급하다 [बैगुपफादा] distributesupply deal out (식량을) ration. e.g. 식사를 배급하다 distribute [provide] boiled rice.

배낭 [बैनांग] [背囊] a knapsack a rucksack (등산용); a packsack (여행용). e.g. 배낭을 꾸리다 pack <things> in a knapsack / pack a knapsack with <things>.

배다[1] [बैदा] 1 (물기 등이) soak <through / into>; permeateinfiltrate sink <into>; penetrate. e.g. 연기 냄새가 집안에 배었다 The odor of smoke permeated [pen-etrated] the house. 2 (버릇 일이) be [get] accustomed to be [get] used to be [become] habituated to get in the way <of doing>; be experienced <in>. e.g. 몸에 밴 일 a familiar work / a job one is experienced in / one's accustomed work.

배다[2] [बैदा] [아이, 알 등을 뱃속에 가지다] conceive become pregnant bear in the womb. e.g. 그 여자는 아이를 뱄다 The woman is pregnant. / The woman is in the family way.

배달 [बैदाल] [配達] delivery (service); distribution.

배드민턴 [बैदमींथौन] badminton.

배반자 [बैबानजा] [背反者] a traitor a betrayer [밀고자] an informer [파업 방해자] a strikebreaker a scab [변절자] a turncoat a quisling a rat.

배변 [बैब्यौन] [排便] the action [movement] of the bowelsa bowel movement (의학에서) an evacuation defecation. 배변하다 open [move / empty / evacuate] the bowel complaint.

배부 [बैबु] [配付] distribution. 배부하다 distribute <blankets to the poor>; pass out <papers to them>;deal out.

배부르다 [बैबुरुदा] [양이 차다] full [cloyed / satiated] (with food); <서술적> have a full stomach have the stomach full. e.g. 배부르게 먹다 eat one's fill / eat heartily / have enough [plenty] / eat to one's heart's content 2 [넉넉하다] rich affluent well-off well-fixed. e.g. 신세지는 처지에 배부른 소리야 할 수 있나 A beggar must not be a chooser.

배분 [बैबुन] [配分] distribution division apportionmentallotment. 배분하다 distribute <to / among>; divide <among>; shareportion out apportion <to>; allot <to>.

배상 [बैसांग] [賠償] reparation indemnity compensationrecompense remedy redressindemnification restitution satisfaction. 배상하다 indemnify [변상하다] compensate recompense <for>; make reparation <for>; give compensation <for>; make [give] satisfaction <for>; make restitutionmake good <a loss>; make up for <a loss>.

배설 [बैसौल] [排泄] excretion evacuation dischargedejection. 배설하다 excreteevacuate purge dischargeeject egest.

배신 [बैसीन] [背信] betrayal infidelity (a) breach of trust [confidence / faith]. 배신하다 betray <a person's> confidence break faith with <one's friend>. e.g. 당신은 나를 배신하였다 You have betrayed my trust.

배심 [बैसीम] [陪審] (a) jury. e.g. 배심 구성의 절차 the proceedings of composing a jury. 배심은 유죄 평결을 내렸다 The jury brought in a verdict of guilty.배심하다 hold (a) juryparticipate in a trial as juryman serve [sit / be] on a jurydo jury duty.

배심원 [बैसीमवौन] [陪審員] <집합적> [जीफाप्वौक] a jury (개인) a juryman a jury-womana juror (남녀).

배양 [बैयांग] [培養] cultivation nurture culture 배양하다 cultivateculture nurture breedraise grow. e.g. 세균을 배양하다 culture [cultivate] bacteria. 배양가 a grower a cultivatora culturist. 배역 [配役] the cast <of a play>.

배열 [बैयौल] [排列配列] arrangement disposition disposal.배열하다 arrangedispose put[place / set] in orderarray set in array.

배우다 [cSmnk] learn be taught take lessons <in>; study [연습하다] practice [교훈을 얻다] draw a lesson [<much> instruc-tion] <from>. e.g. 선생에게 배우다 study under [with] a teacher.

배우자 [बैउजा] [配偶者] a spouse a consort a life partnera companion for life a partner in life a wife (아내); a husband (남편)

배움 [बैउम] learning study. e.g. 배움에 뜻을 두다 aspire to learning.

배웅[बैउंग] seeing <a person> offa send-off. 배웅하다 see <a person> offsend <a person> offgive <a person> a send-off.

배정 [बैजौंग] [配定] assignment allotment allocation-apportionment quota. 배정하다 assign allot allocate-apportion parcel [map] out.

배제 [बैजे] [排除] exclusionremoval elimination [法] abatement 배제하다 make [do] away with exclude remove eliminate. e.g. ...을 배제하고 to the exclusion of ....

배척 [बैछौक] [排斥] rejection expulsion exclusionostr-acism boycott. 배척하다 drive out reject excludeexpel proscribe ostracizeboycott pip. e.g. 모두에게 배척 당하다 be scorned [shunned / left] by all.

배출[1] [बैछुल] [輩出] 배출하다 come forward in successionappear one ather another produce a large [great] number of

<scholars>. e.g. 그 고장은 인재를 많이 배출했다 The place has produced many men of distinguished talent [has turned out a great many talented men].

배출 [2] [बैछुल] [排出] discharge exhaust excretion (배설) 배출하다 draw off discharge transpire exhaust-tissue egest eliminate. e.g. 노폐물을 체외로 배출하다 eliminate waste matter from the system.

배치 [बैछी] [排置] arrangement. 배치하다 arrangeset in place lay out.

배치 [बैछी] [配置] arrangement disposition stationing-posting placement deployment. e.g. 공격 [방어] 배치 offensive [defensive] disposition. 배치하다 arrange distribute make distributions for dispose deploy (부서에) post stationdetail. e.g. 나는 돌을 정원에 배치했다 I arranged the stones in the garden.

배타 [बैथा] [排他] exclusion <of others>. e.g. 배타적(인) exclusive clannish cliquish. 배타하다 exclude expel debar.

배탈 [बैथाल] a stomach disorder [trouble / upset]. e.g. 배탈나다 have a stomach ache / have a pain in the stomach / suffer from indigestion.

배터리 [बैथोरी] [축전지] a battery. e.g. 자동차의 배터리 a car battery.

배포 [बैफो] [配布] (wide) distribution division apportionment. 배포하다 distribute <among / to>; deal out divide <among>; apportion <to>.

배필 [बैफील] [配匹] a spouse a consort a life partnera life's companion a companion for life a matea wife [husband]; one's better half.

배합 [बैहाप] [配合] 1 [조화] match harmony. e.g. 색의 배합 the combination [arrangement] of colors / a color scheme [harmony]. 2 [혼합] mixture blending. 배합하다 mix compound blend. e.g. 배합되다 get mixed [compounded].

배회 [बैह्वे] [徘徊] loitering (about); saunteringhovering (about); knocking aboutrambling about wandering [roaming] about < 美 > hanging around. 배회하다 loiter (about); saunterhover (about); hang around [about]; wander [roam / ramble / knock] about (도적이) prowl (about).

배후 [बैहु] [背後] the rear the back. e.g. 배후 관계를 조사하다 inquire into the hidden circumstances that led up to the case / (흑막을) (gaxekxy) investigate who is pulling the wires.

백 [बैक] [百] a [one] hundred. e.g. 3 백 three hundred.

백- [बैक] [白] white. e.g. 백설탕 white sugar.

백 미러 [बैकमीरे] a rearview [rear-vision] mirror.

백- [बैक] [白] white.

백과 사전 [बैक्वा साजौन] 百科辭典] encyclopedia [an encyclopaedia].

백년가약 [बैगन्यौनगायाक] conjugal [matrimonial] tie; a marriage bond. e.g. 백년 가약을 맺다 tie the nuptial knot / become man and wife for weal and woe / cast in one's lot with a partner for life.

백문 [बैगमुन] [百聞] e.g. 백문이 불여일견 (不如一見) <속담> Seeing is believing. / A picture is worth a thousand words. / The proof of the pudding is in the eating. / To see for oneself is worth all the books of travel. / There's nothing like seeing for oneself.

백발[बैगबाल] [白髮] white [gray] hair; snowy [snow-white / hoar(y)] hair.

백발백중 [बैकपालबैकचुंग] [百發百中 1 (탄환이) hitting [making] the bull's-eye one [a] hundred percent. e.g. 그는 백발백중의 명사수이다 He [His shot] never misses the mark. / He is an ace marksman. / He is a dead [crack] shot. 백발백중하다 never miss the target [mark]. **2** [틀리지 않음]. e.g. 백발백중이다 be infallible. 금주의 일기 예보는 백발백중이었다 The weather fore-casts for this week were all correct [right on target].

백방 [बैकपांग] [百方] **1** [온갖 방법] various ways; every way. e.g. 백방으로 위로하다 console <a person> in every way. 백방으로 힘쓰다 make every effort / exert oneself to the utmost. **2** [여러 방향] every direction; all sides. e.g. 백방으로 사람을 구하다 look all round [all over] for a person.

백분 [बैकबुन] [百分] e.g. 백분의 percent / centesimal. **백분율** [비 (a) percentage.

백사장 [बैकसाजाग] a white sandy plain; a white (sandy) beach.

백색 [बैक्सैक] [白色] [흰 빛] white (color). e.g. 백색의 white / of white color / white-colored.

백수 건달 [बैसुगोनदाल] [白手乾達] bum [tramp]; a good-for-nothing; an out-and-out libertine; a debauchee; a ne'er-do-

백인 [**बैगइन**] [白人] a white man; a Caucasian; a white.

백전 백승 [**बैकयौनबैकसुंग**] [百戰百勝] an -victorious record; invincibility.

백지 [**बैकची**] [白紙] **1** [흰 종이] white paper; Korean paper made from mulberry fiber. e.g. 얼굴이 백지장 같다 look as white as a sheet / look pale. **2** [공지(空紙)] a blank sheet of paper. e.g. 백지 답안을 내다 give [hand] in blank paper. **3** ⇨ 백지 상태 e.g. 백지로 돌리다 call off / nullify / cancel / start afresh / start with a clean state / make a fresh start / go (all) over it again.

백치 [**बैगछी**] [白痴, 白癡] (상태) idiocy; imbecility; (사람) an idiot; an imbecile; a moron. e.g. 백치미인 a beautiful fool. 백치의[와 같은] idiotic.

백화점 [**बैगहवाजोम**] [百貨店]

뱀 a snake; a serpent (구렁이).

뱃살 [**बैस्साल**] the skin [flesh] of the belly [abdomen]; abdominal muscle.

뱉다 [**बैत्ता**] (입 밖으로) spew; spit out; expectorate; salivate. e.g. 침을 뱉다 spit <on> / eject saliva / expectorate.

버럭 [**बौरोक**] [갑자기] <shout> suddenly; abruptly; (all) of a sudden; outright; on a sudden. e.g. 버럭 화를 내다 be roused to anger / fly into a passion / burst into a passion / explode with rage / burn up / see red.

버릇 [**बोरुत**] **1** [습관] a (personal) habit [way]; a customary practice; a habitual practice; an acquired tendency; [성벽] a propensity; an idiosyncrasy (체질적인); a characteristic; a peculiarity; a peculiar way. e.g. 말 버릇 one's peculiar way of speaking. **2** [예의] (good) manners; etiquette; breeding; courtesy; propriety; decorum; politeness; civility; behavior; respectful deportment. e.g. 버릇 들이기 teaching manners / (home) discipline.

버리다[1] [**बौरीदा**] **1** [내던지다] throw [fling / chuck / cast] away; (쓰레기 등을) dump. e.g. 쓰레기를 버리다 dump refuse. 필요없는 것을 버리다 drop [throw] a useless thing into the discard. 한 번 쓰고 버리다 use <something> only once and then throw <it> away. **2** [망치다] spoil; mar; ruin; (해치다) harm; injure; impair; (더럽히다) soil; stain. e.g. 건강을 버리다 injure [ruin / destroy] one's health.

버리다[2] [**बौरीदा**] [끝내다]

finish; get through; do completely; get <it> done; dispose of <a job>. e.g. 다 써 버리다 be used up / be exhausted / spend out.

버선 [बौसौन] Korean socks; sweat socks.

버섯 [बौसौत] a mushroom; a fungus <*pl.* –gi>; a toadstool (유독한).

버스 [बोस] a (motor) bus <*pl.* bus (s) es>; an autobus; a motor coach.

버젓하다 [बौजोत्थादा] respectable; decent; stately; fair and square; good. e.g. 버젓한 직업a respectable occupation.

버티다 [बौथादा] [겨루다] resist; oppose; do not give in; stand up to; hold one's ground; hold out [firm]; stand out [fast / firm]; be unyielding; (주장을) insist <on / upon>; persist <in>. e.g. 끝까지 버티다 persist to the last / hold out to the end / stand it out / stick to one's own opinion (의견을) / carry one's point **2** [견뎌내다] endure; bear up <under>; stand up <to>; hold <out / on / up>; maintain; keep. e.g. 버티어 나가다 endure through / persevere.

버팀목 [बोथीम्मोक] [－木] a prop; a stay; a strut; a support. e.g. 버팀목으로 받치다 prop(up) <a pillar> / support <a wall> / stick (식물에).

벅차다 [बौकछीदा] **1** [힘에 겹다] beyond one's power [capacity]; above one's ability; too much for <one>. e.g. 벅찬 일 work beyond [that surpasses] one's power / a stiff [formidable] task. **2** [넘칠 듯이 가득하다] full; overflowing. e.g. 나는 가슴이 벅차서 말도 나오지 않았다 My heart was too full for words.

번 [बौन] [番] [횟수] **1** a time. e.g. 두번 twice / two times. **2** [번호] a number (No.). e.g. 일번 타자 [야구] the leadoff batter [man]. **3** [때경우] time; occasion. e.g. 지난 번 last time / the other day.

번갈아 [बोन्गारा] [番－] alternately; by turns; in turn; by spells; in rotation <with>. e.g. 번갈아하다 take by spell / take spell and spell.

번개 [बौन्गै] (a flash of) lightning.

번거롭다 [बोन्गौरोप्ता] **1** [복잡하다] complicate; complex intricate; [어수선하다] entangled; confused; [귀찮다] troublesome; [성가시다] annoying; cumbersome. e.g. 번거로운 규칙 vexatious rules. **2** [수선스럽다] noisy; boisterous; turbulent; clamorous; tumultuous.

번뜩 [बौन्तुक] with a flash. e.g. 그들이 자객이 아닌가 하는 의심이 그의 머리에 번득 들었다 The suspicion flashed across him [his mind] that they might be assassins.

번복 [बोन्बोक] [飜覆, 飜覆] 번복하다 change; turn; reverse; upset. e.g. 그는 앞서 한 발언을 번복했다 He changed his former opinion.

번성 [बौन्सौंग] [繁盛] = 번창 (繁昌).

번성 [बौन्सौंग] [蕃盛] (자손의) prosperity; thrith; abun-dance; (수목 등의) luxuri-ance of growth; exuberancy.번성하다 flourish; prosper; (초목이) grow wild [vigorously / rank]; thrive; luxuriate; gad.

번식 [बौन्शिक] [繁殖, 蕃殖] propagation; breeding; re-production; multiplication; increase (증식); [배양] culture.

번역 [बौनयौक] [飜譯, 飜譯] (a) translation; rendering; a version.

번영 [बौनयोंग] [繁榮] pro-sperity; flourish.

번잡 [बौनजाप] [煩雜] [번거로움] troublesomeness; [복잡함] complexity; com-plicatedness; intricacy; [혼잡] confusion. 번잡하다 troublesome; complicated; compleK intricate; crowd-ed; confused.

번지다 [बौनजीदा] 1 (잉크 등이) spread; run; blot. e.g. 빨아도 번지지 않는 물감 dyes that do not run in washing. 이 블라우스는 빨면 처음에는 두세 번 물감이 번집니다 This blouse is not colorfast for the first two or three washings. 2 (질병 등이) spread; prevail; diffuse; be prevalent. e.g. 독이 온 몸에 번졌다 The poison has passed into his system.

번창 [बौनछांग] [繁昌] pro-sperity; flourish; success. 번창하다 prosper; flourish; thrive; succeed <in / as>; be successful; do well. e.g. 번창하게 하다 make pro-sperous.

번호 [बौनहो] [番號] a number.

벌 [बौल] [罰] (a) punish-ment; penalty; chastise-ment; [천벌] divine punish-ment.

벌[1] [बौल] [짝] a set <of cups>; a pair <of>; a suit <of clothes>. e.g. 옷 2 벌 two suits / (여성의) two dresses. 찻잔[식기] 한 벌 a tea [dinner] set.

벌[2] [बौल] [꿀벌] a (honey) bee; [참벌] a wasp; [말벌] a hornet; [땅벌] a ground wasp; a bumblebee.

벌거벗다 [बौल्गौपौत्ता] ⇨ 발가벗다

벌거숭이 [बौल्गौसुंगी] **1** [알몸뚱이] a naked body; a nude. **2** [흙이 드러나 보일 만큼 나무가 없는 산]. e.g. 그 산은 벌거숭이다 The hill is bald [is stripped of all vegetation].

벌금 [बौलगुम] [罰金] a fine; a (monetary) penalty; [위약금] a forfeit; a penalty.

벌다 [बौलता] **1** [돈을 얻다] make [earn / gain / clean up] <money>; find one's account <in>; cash in <on>; come off a gainer; [이익을 얻다] profit <by>; make [get / obtain / realize / derive] a profit <from>. e.g. 애써 번 돈 hard-earned money. **2** [자초하다] bring [draw] upon <one-self>; incur; court; invite. e.g. 매를 벌다 incur [invite] whipping.

벌떡 [बौल्तौक] [급히 일어서는 모양] suddenly; with a jerk[start]; quickly; rashly; abruptly; [자빠지는 모양] on one's back; with the face upward; flat; supinely.

벌떡거리다 [बौलतौककौरीदा] **1** (심장 등이) go pit-a-pat; palpitate; throb; thump; pound; beat. e.g. 벌떡거리는 가슴 a beating [palpitating] heart. **2** [들이마시다] gulp down; quaff; guzzle; swig; swill. e.g. 물을 벌떡거리며 마시다 gulp down a glass of water.

벌레 [बौल्ले] [곤충] an insect; a bug; a grub [ground beetle] (땅벌레); a beetle (딱정벌레 등); a cricke t(여치 등); a moth (나방 등); (송충이 등) a caterpillar; (구더기 등) a worm; [해충] vermin <집합적>; [유충] a larva <*pl.* -vae>.

벌름거리다 [बौल्लुमकौरीदा] swell and subside alter-nately; quiver.

벌리다 [बौल्लीदा] [열다] open (up); unfold. e.g. 입을 벌리고 with an open mouth / with one's mouth open / open-mouthed / agape

벌목 [बौलमोक] [伐木] felling; cutting; logging; lumber-ing; timbering.

벌벌 [बौलबौल] tremblingly; shiveringly; shakingly. e.g. 벌벌 떨다 tremble / shiver / shake.

벌써 [बौलसौ] [오래 전에] long ago [since]; [이미] already; yet (의문문에서); [어느새] so soon. e.g. 벌써 정오다 It is already noon.

벌어지다 [बौरोजीदा] **1** [틈이

생기다] crack (apart); become open; [넓어지다] widen; become wider; (밤송이 등이) split [burst] open; crack. **2** [소원해지다] be estranged [alienated] <from>; fall away <from>. e.g. (두 사람) 사이가 벌어지다 be alienated [estrang-ed] from each other. **3** [일이 발생하다] arise; happen; take place; come up [about]; turn up.

벌이 [बोरी] moneymaking; income; earnings; gainings; pay. e.g. 벌이가 되다[안 되다] pay [do not pay] / be profitable [unprofitable].

벌이다 [बोरीदा] 1 [시작하다] begin; open; start; [착수하다] set about; enter into [upon]; take to. e.g. 사업을 벌이다 start [get launch-ed on] an enterprise. **2** [베풀어 놓다] hold; give; <美> throw <a banquet>. e.g. 술잔치를 벌이다 hold [give] a banquet / give a feast. **3** [늘어놓다] arrange <goods>; display <goods>; show <samples>; exhibit; (음식을) spread <dishes>. e.g. 가게에 물건을 벌여 놓다 arrange [put] goods in a show window.

벌집 [बौलजीप] [벌이 생활하는 집] a beehive; a hive; a honeycomb; a comb.

벌채 [बौलछै] [伐採] felling; lumbering; deforestation. 벌채하다 cut down; cut over; fell <trees>; lumber; log. 벌초하다 mow; cut the weeds [mow the grass] around a grave.

벌칙 [बौलछीक] [罰則] penal regulations [clauses]; punitive provisions.

벌컥 [बौलखोक] ⇨ 발깍

벌판[평야] **[बौलपफान]** a field; a plain; [초원] a green; [대초원] a prairie; [황야] a wildness; a moor.

범국민 [बौमगुकमिन] [汎國民] e.g. 범국민의 [범국민적(인)] pan-national / nation-wide (전국적인).

범람 [बौम्नाम] [氾濫, 汎濫] [넘쳐흐름] inundation; flooding; overflow; a deluge; [홍수] a flood; spate; [마구 쏟아져 나와 나돎] a flood; oversupply. 범람하다 overflow; flow [run] over <the banks>; flood; be inundated.

범벅 [बौमबोक] [여러 사물이 뒤섞인 상태] (utter) confusion; a muddle; a jumble; a mess; a pell-mell. 범벅(이) 되다 get [be] mixed up; be jumbled together; be muddled up [together].

범위 [बौमवीद] [範圍] extent; a scope; a sphere; an ambit;

(the) limits [bounds / confines] <of>; the province <of>; the purview <of>; a range.

범인 [बौमईनं] [犯人] criminal; a culprit; an offender; a convict (기결수); a suspect (피의자).

범재 [बौमजै] [凡才] [평범한 재주] common [ordinary] ability; mediocrity; [평범한 인재] a person of common [average] ability; a (man of) mediocrity; a mediocre person.

범죄 [बौमज्वैदं] [犯罪] offense; a crime; (a) delict; guilt.

범주 [बौमजुं] [範疇] category; a class.

범하다 [बौमहादा] [犯 –] **1** [잘못 등을 저지르다] commit; perpetrate; sin against <morality>. e.g. 과오를 범하다 commit [make] a fault [an error] / err. **2** [규칙,법률 등을 어기다] violate; infringe; break; offend against; transgress; trespass against.

법 [बौप] [法] **1** [법칙] a law; a rule; [법률] the law; <집합적> the legislation; an act; a regulation (조례); a rule (법규); [법전] a code (of laws); [사법] justice. **2** [방법] a method; a way; a manner; [과정] a process; [기술] an art; technique (예술상의).

법관 [बौपक्वानं] [法官] judicial officer; a judge; <집합적> the judiciary; the bench.

법규 [बौपग्यू] [法規] law and regulations; legislation.

법률 [बौमन्युल] [法律] law; <집합적> (the) law; legislation.

법석 [बौपत्सोकं] noise; a hubbub; a clamor; an uproar; fuss; ado; bustle. e.g. 사람들은 클린턴 대통령이 내한한다고 야단 법석이다 People are agog with excitement over the expected visit of President Clinton.

법안 [बौपआनं] [法案] bill; a measure. e.g. 법안을 제출하다 introduce [bring in / submit] a bill.

법원 [बौपवान] [法院] [소송 사건을 심판하는 국가 기관] a court of justice [law]; a lawcourt; a courthouse.

법적 [बौपचौक] [法的] legalistic.

법전 [बौपचौन] [法典] code (of laws); a body of law.

법정 [बौपचौग] [法廷] (law) court; a court of justice [law]; a courtroom; a tribunal; a judgment hall; the bar.

법칙 [बौपछीक] [法則] law; a rule. e.g. 자연 법칙 a law of nature / a natural law.

법하다 [बौफादा] **1** [당위] <서술적> have (a) good reason to be [do]; be reasonable; it is natural [proper] that <a person>

is .... e.g.그가 성날 법하다 He has (a) good reason [every right] to be angry. / He should be angry. **2** [타당한 상정, 기대] <서술적> it seems reasonable <that>; there is reason to expect <that>; it can be ex-pected <that>; ought [be supposed] to be. e.g. 그녀가 왔을 법하다 She must have arrived

법학 [बौपपाफाकसूंय] [法學] jurisprudence

벗 [बौत] friend; a companion; a comrade; a pal; a chum; company.

벗겨지다 [बौक्यौजिदा] **1** (옷,신 등이) come off; be taken [stripped] off; get undressed; slip off [down / out]; (단추 등이) be unbuttoned [unzipped]. e.g. 장화가 벗겨지지 않는다 My boots will not come off **2** (칠,비늘 등이) fall [come] off; (거죽,껍질 등이) get stripped off; peel off[away]. e.g. 래커칠이 군데군데 벗겨져 있다 The lacquer is (worn) off in places **3** (덮개 등이) get removed; be taken off. e.g. 걸쇠가 벗겨졌다 The hook came undone.

벗기다 [बौक्कीदा] **1** (옷 등을) unclothe; undress; strip <a person> of <his clothes>; take off <a person's clothes>. e.g. 옷을 벗기다 unclothe [undress / disrobe] (a person) / strip [divest] <a person> of his clothes. **2** (껍질 등을) chip [slice / flake] off; peel <an orange> (손가락으로); pare <an apple>(칼로); shuck <corn>; hull <peas>; (가죽을) skin (off) <an animal>; strip off; flay <a rabbit>; (곡식을) husk. e.g. 때를 벗기다 wash off the dirt.

벗다 [बौत्ता] **1** (옷 등을) take [peel / leave / shuck] off <one's coat>; strip [divest] oneself of <one's shirt>; remove <one's hat>; (스르르) slip off <one's clothes>; (홀렁) fling [throw] off <one's boost>; (잡아당겨서) pull off <one's gloves>. e.g. 황급히 벗다 rush out of <one's nightgown>. **2** (책임,의무를) be freed from one's duty; get rid of one's responsibility; shith off one's duty; (짐, 부담을) unload; unburden oneself of. e.g. 나는 그것으로써 나의 책임을 벗게 된다 I will be relieved of my responsibility with it. **3** (누명을) clear [divest] oneself of <a false charge>. e.g. 오해를 벗다 remove the misunderstanding.

벗어나다 [बौसौनादा] **1** [에서

헤어나다] get out of <difficulties>; get rid of; be relieved of <trouble>; escape from <danger>; free oneself of [from] <a bondage>; break away from [rid oneself of] <a bad habit>. e.g. 가난에서 벗어나다 overcome poverty. **2** [눈에 들지 못하다] be out of <a person's> favor; incur [fall under] <a person's> displeasure; lose <a person's> favor. e.g. 그녀는 하는 짓이 남의 눈에서 벗어난다 Her ways fail to find favor in the eyes of another. **3**[어긋나다] be contrary to; be against; (정도에) depart from; deviate [swerve] from. e.g. 도리에 벗어나다 be contrary to reason.

벗어지다 [बौसौजीदा] **1** (몸에 걸친 것이) come off; slip off [down]. e.g. 내 장갑[구두]이 좀처럼 벗어지지 않는다 My gloves [boots / shoes] won't come off. **2** (머리가) become [go / grow] bald; be [get] bold (in front); lose one's hair. e.g. 이마가 벗어진 bald at the forehead.

벙어리 [बौंगओरी] (말 못하는) a mute; a dumb person; a dummy; [농아] a deaf-mute.

베개 [बेगै] pillow; [긴 베개] a bolster.

베끼다 [बैकीदा] **1** [옮겨쓰다] copy; take a copy <of>; transcribe. e.g. 원고를 베끼다 make a copy of a manuscript. **2** [모사하다] imitate; copy; trace. e.g. … 을 실물대로 베끼다 make an exact copy of ....

베다[1] [बेदा] (베개 등을) rest [lay] one's head on <a pillow / a thing>. e.g. 베개를 베고 자다 sleep with one's head on the pillow.

베다[2] [बेदा] **1** [자르다] cut; chop; hash (잘게); slice (얇게); slash; hack <to pieces> (토막내다); saw (톱으로); shear; clip (가위로); fell; hew; cut down (나무를); mow (풀을); reap; gather in; harvest (곡식을). S **2** [상처를 내다] cut; wound; inflict a wound <on>; injure; scratch. e.g. 손가락을 베다 cut one's finger <on a knife>.

베어내다 [बेओनैदा] [오려내다] cut [clip] (out) <from>; [떼어내다] cut off [down]; cleave; cut out [away]; [쳐내다] lop off [away] <branches>; prune (off) <twigs>; (나무를) clear (away); get <timber> out <of>; (풀 등을) mow; cut down.

베어먹다 [बेओमौक्ता] cut off and eat; take a slice and

eat it; take a bite out of. e.g. 사과를 한 입 베어먹다 take a bite out of an apple.

베풀다 [बैपुल्दा] **1** (잔치 등을) give [have] <a party>; hold <a banquet [meeting]>; throw <a party, a banquet, etc.>. e.g. 당신을 위하여 연회를 베풀고자 합니다 I'd like to give a party in your honor. **2** (자비심, 동정, 사랑등을) have mercy <on>; [은혜를 누리게 하다] do a person a kindness; [자선 금품을 주다] give alms <to the por>; bestow <a favor on a person>. e.g. 자선을 베풀다 give alms / render aid <to a person>.

벼 [ब्यौ] [포아풀과의 한해살이풀] a rice plant; (열매) unhulled rice; a grain of (unhusked) rice (낟알).

벼농사 [ब्योनौसा] [-農事] (재배) rice growing [farming]; (수확) a rice crop.

벼락 [ब्यौराक] thunderbolt; a thunderstroke; a stroke of lightning.

벼랑 [ब्यौरांग] cliff; a precipice; a bluff (바닷가의); palisades (강가의).

벼룩 [ब्यौरोक] flea.

벼르다 [ब्यौरुक] [미리 마음먹다] plan; design; aim <at>; intend <to do>; contemplate <doing>; be intent [bent] <on>; have <something> in mind; keep both [one's] eyes wide open <for>; look forward <to>; be determined <to do>; be eager <for / to do> .e.g. 기회를 벼르다 watch for a chance / be on the lookout for an opportunity.

벼슬 [ब्योसुल] government [an official] post [position]; official rank.

벽 [ब्यौक] [癖] [치우치게 즐기는 성벽] a craze <for>; a mania <for>. e.g. 수집벽 a mania for <stamp> collecting / a collecting mania.

벽 [ब्यौकं] [壁] wall; [칸막이] a partition (wall).

벽걸이 [ब्यौककौरि] [壁-] wall decorations; a wall tapestry. e.g. 벽걸이 전화기 a wall telephone set.

변 [ब्यौन] [變] [돌발사] a sudden happening; an unexpected occurrence [event]; [사고] an accident; a mishap; [재앙] a calamity; a disaster; a misfortune; [비상사] an emergency; a contingency; [난리] a disturbance; an uprising; an agitation. e.g. 변이 나다 an accident [incident] happens [occurs].

변 [ब्यौन] [便] [대소변] excreta; excrement; [대변] f(a)eces; stool(s); motions; movements.

변경 [ब्यौन्दौक] [變更] (전체 또는 부분적인) (a) change;

(부분적인) (an) alteration; [수정] (a) modification; (an) amendment.

변덕 [ब्यौनदोक] [變德] (a) caprice; capriciousness; a (passing) whim; fickleness; a change of mind. e.g. 변덕스러운 (가을) 날씨 changeable [unstable / fickle] (autumn) weather

변동 [ब्यौनदोंग] [變動] (a) change; (an) alteration; (시세 등의) (a) fluctuation

변두리 [ब्यौनदुरी] **1** [교외] the o utskirts [environs] <of a town>; a suburb. **2** [가장자리] the outer edge; the brim; the rim; the margin; [주위] the circumference.

변론 [ब्यौल्लोन] [辯論] **1** [논쟁] discussion; argument; controversy; disputation; [토론] debate. **2** (법정의) pleading; oral proceedings [pleadings]; debate; argument; a forensic speech. 변론하다 proceed orally; argue; plead (at the bar / before the court).

변명 [ब्यौम्यौ] [辨明] an explanation; an excuse; [정당화] (a) justification; [항변] a defense [defence].

변모 [ब्यौमो] [變貌] (a) transfiguration; (a) transformation; a change in one's looks [of appearance]; a metamorphosis <*pl.* –phoses>. 변모하다 change; undergo a complete change; be transformed [transfigured]; assume a different aspect.

변방 [ब्यौनबां] [邊防] the frontier defenses.

변변하다 [ब्यौनब्यौन] (사람, 사물의 질,내용 등이) fairly good; tolerable; passable; fair; decent; respectable; proper. e.g. 그는 영어로 변변한 편지 한 장 못쓴다 He can't write a letter in English properly.

변상 [ब्यौनसांग] [辨償] compensation; indemnification; reparation; reimbursement. 변상하다 compensate; indemnify; reimburse; repair; make up for; make good; pay for <damage>.

변소 [ब्यौनसौ] [便所] a lavatory; a water closet (略 W.C.); a privy; a convenince; a latrine (공장,학교 등의); a toilet (room); a washroom; (욕조 등이 있는) a bathroom; <英> a loo; (회사,은행,역 등의) a ladies' [men's] room; a rest room; (배,군함의) the head; the john; <美> the can.

변신 [ब्यौन्शिन] [變身] **1** = 변장. **2** transformation; metamorphosis. 변신하다 change <into>; turn <into>; be transformed [metamorphosed] <into>; transform oneself <into>.

변심 [ब्यौनछौन] [**變 心**] [마음이 변하기] a change of heart [mind]; [배반] betrayal; treachery; [변덕] fickleness. 변심하다 [마음을 달리 먹다] change one's mind; have a change of heart; [배반하다] turn traitor; betray <a person>. e.g. 너 언제 변심했니 When did you change your mind?

변이 [ब्यौनई] [**變 移**] (a) change; (a) shith; (an) alteration; (a) mutation; (a) transmutation; [化] a conversion. 변이하다 change; mutate.

변장 [ब्यौनजांग] [**變 裝**] (a) disguise. 변장하다 put on a makeup; disguise oneself <as>; be disguised <as>; wear a disguise; make up <as>; [가장하다] mas querade <as>.

변조 [ब्यौनजो] [**變造**] [개조] (an) alteration; [위조] (a) forgery; falsification. 변조하다 alter; forge; falsify; raise <a check>.

변질 [ब्यौनजील] [**變 質**] [성질이 변하기] change in quality; [품질 등의 악화] deterioration; degeneration; (연금술의) transmutation. 변질하다 change in quality; deteriorate; degenerate; transmute; (음식물이) go bad.

변천 [ब्यौनछीन] [**變 遷**] a change; [추이] (a) transition; (인생,처지 등의) vicissitudes; ups and downs. 변천하다 change; undergo a change. e.g. 시대는 변천했다 Times have changed.

변하다 [ब्यौनहादा] [**變**–] [사물이 달라지다] change; undergo a change; make a change; become different; alter; be altered; shith; vary; (풍향이) come round [about]; work round; shith; […으로 변형하다] change [turn] <into>; be turned <into>; be transformed <into>; be metamorphosed <into>.

변형 [ब्यौनहयौग] [**變形**] [모양, 형태를 바꿈] transformation; variation; modification; metamorphosis; deformation; [바꾼 모양] a variety; a modification; a deformity (기형). 변형하다 [바꾸다] change; transform; metamorphose; [바뀌다] transform <into>; change <into>; turn <into>; be transformed [metamorphosed] into.

변호 [ब्यौनहो] [**辯 護**] **1** [변명] defense; defence; exculpation; vindication; justification; explanation. e.g. 자기 변호 self–justification. **2** 법정에서의)

defense (피고의); pleading (원고 및 피고의). e.g. 변호를 의뢰하다 employ [approach] a lawyer / take one's case to an advocate / brief

변호사 [ब्यौनहोसा] [辯護士] a lawyer

변화 [ब्यौनहवा[變 化] [바꿈,바뀜] (a) change;(a) vari-ation; [변경] (an) alter-ation; [변전](a) mutation; (변천) a transition.

변환 [ब्यौनहवान] [變 換] change; [전환] conver-sion. 변환하다 change; convert

별 [ब्यौल] [別] e.g. 학생들은 남녀[연령]별 그룹으로 나뉘었다 The pupils were divided into groups according to their sex [age]..

별 [ब्यौल] **1** a star; <집합적> the stars; (이칭(異稱)) the eyes of heaven [night] **2** [군인의 계급장] a star; (표지) a mark. e.g. 별이 셋인 장군 a three-star general / a lieutenant general.

별개 [ब्यौलकै] [別個] [구별이 되는 딴 것] a different thing; another thing; a separate [distinct] one; exception; a special case. e.g. 이것은 별개의 문제다 This is another [a separate] problem [question].

별관 [ब्यौलग्वान] [別館] an anneK an annexe; a dependency; an extension; an outhouse; an outbuilding. e.g. 박물관의 별관 an annex to the museum / the museum annex.

별나다 [ब्यौलनादा] [別 -] eccentric; quaint; queer; peculiar; out of the usual [ordinary]; unusual; odd; singular; uncommon; bizarre; novel; viewy; wacky; extra-ordinary. e.g. 별난 취미 bizarre taste / a liking for things that normally put people off / a taste for odd things.

별다르다 [ब्यौलदारुदा] [別 -] particular; special; extra-ordinary; exceptional. e.g. 별다른 명시[지정]가 없는 한 unless otherwise specified.

별도 [ब्यौलदो] [別途] [딴 방면] a separate way; another way; [추가] addition; extra. e.g. 이 일에는 별도의 수당이 붙는다 I am paid extra for this work.

별로 [ब्यौलो] [別 -] in particular; particularly; speci-ally; especially; <not> very; <not> much. e.g. 오늘은 별로 바쁘지 않다 I am not particularly busy today.

별명 [ब्यौलम्यौंग] [別 名] [남들이 지어 부르는 이름] a nickname; a byname.

별미 [ब्यौलमी] [別味] [특별히 좋은 맛] delicate

[exquisite] flavor [taste]; [특별히 좋은 음식] a (choice) delicacy; a tidbit; a dainty.

별별 [ब्यौल ब्यौल] [別別] of various [different] and unusual sorts. e.g. 별별 음식 all sorts of rare dishes.

별사람 [ब्यौलसाराम] [別 -a queer (kind of) person; an oddity; an eccentric (person); a queer fish [bird / card / customer]; an odd fish; <美> an oddball. e.g. 별사람도 다 있군 I have never seen such a case [crank] as him.

별세 [ब्यौलसे] [別 世] decease; demise; passing (away). 별세하다 die; decease; pass away; depart this world.

별세계 [ब्यौलसैगे] [別世界] 1 [이 세상 밖의 다른 세상] another world [planet / sphere]; a different [new] world. e.g. 그는 별세계에서 온 사람 같다 He looks as if he came from another [a different] world. 2 [경치 등이 아주 좋은 곳] a fairyland.

별수 [ब्यौलसु] [別-] 1 [달리 어떻게 할 방법] a special [an effective] means [way]; a secret key [method]; the secret; the mystery; a magical formula; a capital [brilliant / particular] idea. e.g. 별수가 없으면 내가 돈을 내겠다 I will pay for it, if nothing else can be done about it [if there's no other way]. 2 [여러 방법] every means; all resources. e.g. 별수를 다 쓰다 try every means available / try every possible [imaginable] method.

별스럽다 [ब्यौलसुरोप्ता] [別-] 별나다.

별안간 [ब्यौलआनगान] [瞥眼間] [눈 깜빡할 동안] in the twinkling [blink] of an eye; before one can bat an eyelash; quick as a wink; in a flash; in an instant; [갑자기] suddenly; on [all of] a sudden; abruptly; [느닷없이] unexpectedly; without the slightest notice [warning]. e.g. 별안간에 일어난 일이라서 나는 놀랐다 It surprised me, as I had not expected it

별일 [ब्यौरील] [別-] [특별한 일] a particular thing [event]; an unusual event; [별별일] all sorts [kinds / manner / shades] of unusual matters [affairs]; [이상한 일] an odd thing; a strange thing.

별장 [ब्यौलजांग] [別 莊] (대규모의) a villa; a country house; (소규모의) a cottage; (산중의) a cabin; (여름의) a summer house.

병[1] [ब्यौंग] [甁] a bottle; (아가리가 큰) a jar

병² [ब्यौंग] [病] **1** (일반적으로) sickness; illness; (특정한 병) a disease; a malady; an affection; (가벼운) an indisposition; an ailment; (국부적인) a trouble; a complaint; a disorder. e.g. 눈병 eye trouble. **2** [결점, 나쁜 버릇]. e.g. 거짓말을 하는 것이 그의 병이다 His failing [weakness] is that he tells lies.

병나다 [ब्यौंगनादा] [病 –] [병이 생기다] fall [get / be taken] ill [sick]; suffer from a disease; take a disease; be affected by a disease. e.g. 과식하여 병나다 make oneself ill by overeating.

병들다 [病–] [ब्यौंगदुल्दा] 병나다

병력 [兵力] [ब्यौंगन्यौक] military power [force]; force of arms; [군사수] the strength <of an army>.

병력 [ब्यौंगन्यौक] [病歷]a case [clinical] history; the history of a case.

병렬[ब्यौंन्यौर] [竝列] arranging in a row[line]. e.g. 병렬의 parallel.

병명 [ब्यौंगम्यौंग] [病名] the name of a disease.

병역 [ब्यौंग्यौक] [兵役] military service.

병원 [ब्यौंगवन] [病院] a hospital; [진료소] a clinic; a doctor's office; [학교, 공장 등의 부속 진료소] an infirmary.

병폐 [ब्यौंग्यौक] [病弊] evils; ills; evil practices. e.g. 사회적[도시의] 병폐 social [urban] ills.

병행 [ब्यौंगहैंग] [竝行] **1** [나란히 감]. 병행하다 go side by side; go abreast <of>; keep pace <with>; run parallel <to / with>. e.g. 전동 열차와 급행 열차가 병행하여 달려갔다 An electric train and an express train sped away side by side. **2** [동시에 행함]. 병행하다 do [perform / practice] <two things> simultaneously [at the same time].

볕 [बौत] 햇볕

볕들다 [बौतदुल्दा] shine <into / in / upon>. e.g. 쥐구멍에도 볕들 날이 있다 <속담> Every dog has his day.

보강 [बोगांग] [補講] a supplementary lecture; a makeup lesson. e.g. 보강을 받다 take supplementary [makeup] classes [lectures]. 보강하다 give supplementary [makeup] classes [lectures].

보강 [बोगांग] [補强] reinforcement. 보강하다 reinforce <a bridge>; strengthen. e.g. 졸업생이 몇 명 가담해 준 덕택에 육상부가 현저

하게 보강되었다 The track and field club was strengthened remarkably by a number of graduates joining it.

보건 [बोगौन] [保健] preservation of health. e.g. 세계 보건 기구 the World Health Organization (WHO).

보건소 [बोगोनसो] a (public) health center.

보고 [बोगो] [報告] [말,글 등으로 알리는 것] a report; an account; <美> (a) briefing; information

보관 [बोग्वान] [保管] custody; charge; keeping; safekeeping; (a) deposit; storage. 보관하다 keep; take custody [charge] <of>; take <a thing> into one's custody; keep <a thing>(in custody); hold <money> on deposit.

보금자리 [बोगुमजारी] a nest; a roost; a home.

보급 [बोगप] [普及] diffusion; spread; propagation; extension (확장); [대중화] popularization 보급하다 (지식, 병 등을) spread; (학문, 문화 등을) diffuse; (사상, 소식 등을) propagate; extend; make popular; [대중화시키다] popularize.

보급 [बोगप] [補給] supply; replenishment. 보급하다 supply; replenish. e.g. 비행기에 연료를 보급하다 refuel an airplane.

보기 [बोगी] [예] an example; an instance; a case; an illustration. e.g. 보기를 들면 for example [instance].

보내다 [बोनेदा] **1** [물건, 사람 등을 다른 곳으로 가게 하다] send; dispatch; forward; transmit; (상품을) consign; (배,차로) ship; [송금하다] remit. e.g. 답장을 보내다 send a reply. **2** [시간이나 세월을 지나가게 하다] pass (time); pass away <one's time>; kill time; spend <one's time>; live [lead] <a life>; while-dawdle] away. e.g. 그 젊은 미망인은 매일 눈물로 보냈다 The young widow did nothing but weep night and day. **3** [신호P뜻을 전달하다]. e.g. 그 감독은 투수에게 사인[신호]을 보냈다 The manager gave the pitcher a signal.

보너스 [बोनस] [상여금] a bonus.

보다[1] [बोदा] **1** (일반적으로) see; look <at>(see는 눈에 들어옴, 보임. look at 은 보기 위해 눈을 돌림); get(a) sight <of>; set[lay] eyes <on>; [목격하다] witness. e.g. 며칠 전에 나는 도서관에서 그녀를 보았다 I happened to see her in [at] the library a few

days ago. **2** [관찰하다] observe; look <at>; view; see; [시찰하다] inspect; visit. e.g. 미국 체류 중에 본 것 what one observed during one's stay [while] in America.

보다[2] **[बोदा]** [시험 삼아 하다] try; have a try <at>; test. e.g. 코트를 입어 보다 try on a coat / try a coat on.

보다[3] **[बोदा]** **1** [한층 더] more; still [much] more. e.g. 보다 힘드는 일 (much) harder work.. **2** [비교] than; to. e.g. … 보다 못하다[낫다] be inferior [superior] to / be worse [better] than.

보다못해 [बोदामोतहे] unable to stand by (any longer). e.g. 보다못해 나는 그들의 싸움을 말렸다 Unable to stand by, I drew the combatants apart.

보답 [बोदाप] [報答] (a) repayment; (a) return; reward; (a) recompense; (a) requital.

보도 [बोदो] [報道] news; a report; information. 보도하다 report; inform [notify] <a person> of; let <a person> know.

보람 [बोराम] [효과] (an) effect; fruit; worth; benefit. e.g. 보람있는 일 [의욕을 돋우는 일] a challenging job / [애쓸 만한 일] a worthwhile job / work worth doing. 보람없는 일 a thankless task.

보류 [बोर्‍यु] [保留] reservation; [중지] suspension; (법안 등의) pigeonholing; shelving. 보류하다 reserve; defer; withhold

보름 [बोरुम] [열닷새 동안] fitheen days; a half month.

보릿고개 [बोरीतकोगे] the farm hardship period; spring cessation to the peasant; the spring austerity; the barley hump. e.g. 보릿고개를 넘기다 get over the barley hump.

보모 [बोमो] [保姆] a (dry) nurse; a nursery governess. e.g. 유치원의 보모 a kindergarten teacher / a kindergart (e) ner.

보물 [बोमुल] [寶物] a treasure; a highly prized article; valuables.

보복 [बोबोक] [報復] revenge; retaliation; (a) reprisal (국가 간의); retortion; requital. 보복하다 revenge <oneself on>; retaliate; take [exact] revenge; get even with; make [carry out] a reprisal <on>.

보살 [बोसाल] [菩薩] [보리살타] a Bodhisattva; a Buddhist saint. e.g. 외면은 보살 내심은 야차 An angel without, a devil within.

보살피다 [बोसालपफीदा] [뒤를

돌보아 주다] take care of; look [see] ather <a person>; have <a person> under one's charge; have [take] charge of; see to.

보상 [बोसांग] [報償] compensation; consideration; remuneration. 보상하다 indemnify losses [damages] / make compensation [reparation] for a loss.

보석 [बोसोक] [寶石] a jewel; a precious stone; (연마한) a gem; (시계의) a ruby; <집합적> jewelry [jewellery].

보송보송하다 बोसोंगबोसांगहादा [살결 등이 곱고 보드랍다]. e.g. 보송보송한 살결 soth and moistureless skin.

보안[बोआन] [保安] the preservation [maintenance] of public peace [security].

보약[बोयाक] [補藥]a restorative; a tonic (medicine); an invigorant.

보어 [बोओ] [補語] [문법] a complement. e.g. 주격 [목적] 보어 a subjective [an objective] complement.

보유 [बोयु] [保有] possession; retention; maintenance 보 유하다 possess; hold; keep; retain; maintain

보육 [बोयु] [保育] childcare; nurture; upbringing.

보육원 [बोयुकवान] [고아원] an orphanage; an orphan asylum; a day nursery; a nursery school.

보이다[1] [बोईदा] **1** (눈에) see; catch sight of; (사물이) be seen; be visible; show; be in sight; be open to the view. e.g. 보이지 않는 눈 a sightless eye. **2** […인 것 같다] look(like); seem; appear. e.g. 젊어 보이는 사람 a youthful appearing man.

보이다[2] [बोईदा] [보게 하다] show; let <a person> see [look at]; [전시하다] display; exhibit; evince; (감춰진 것을) disclose (to view); reveal. e.g. 실력을 보이다 show [display] one's ability.

보일러 [बोईललो] a boiler

보자기[बोजागी] [褓 -] a wrapping cloth; a kerchief.

보잘것없다worthless; valueless; trifling; beneath notice; trivial; useless. e.g. 보잘것없는 녀석 a nobody / a man of straw.

보장 [बोजांग] [保障] [보증] guarantee; [확보] security 보장하다guarantee; secure; assure

보조 [बोजो] [補助] **1** [원조] assistance; help; aid. 보조하다 assist; help; aid; subsidize. e.g. 재정적으로 보조하다 give financial aid [assistance] <to>. **2** [보충] supplement. 보조하다

ㅂ

supplement. e.g. 수동 브레이크는 제동 장치의 기능을

보조개 [**बोजोगे**] a dimple on one cheek.

보좌[**बोज्वा**] [**補佐**] assistance; aid.

보증 [**बोजुंग**] [**保證**] (품질, 내용 등의) a guarantee; a warranty; [法] (a) security. e.g. 보증을 서다 go [give / stand] security <for>; stand [go] surety <for>.

보채다 [**बोछैदा**] fret; be fretful [peevish]; beg [whine / tease] for <things>; importune; grizzle. e.g. 보채는 아기 a fretful baby.

보초 [**बोछो**] [**步哨**] a sentry; a sentinel; a guard. e.g. 보초를 서다 stand [keep] sentinel / stand sentry / be on sentry duty

보충 [**बोछुंग**] [**補充**] [보태어 채우기] replenishment; [추가] supplementation; [보태어 넉넉하게 함] (a) supplement; (교체에 의한) replacement; recruiting (병력의).보충하다 supplement; replenish; replace; fill up; supply; recruit (병력을).

보태다 [**बोथैदा**] **1** [더하다] add <A to [and] B>. e.g. 보태어 말하다 exaggerate a story / make one's story tall [high] **2** [보충하다] make up (for); make good; supply; supplement. e.g. 모자라는 것을 보태다 make [fill] up the deficiency.

보통 [**बोथोंग**] [**普通**] [예사로움] commonness; normality; the common run. e.g. 보통의 [평소의] ordinary / commonplace / [흔한] common / [평균의] average / [중간치의] medium / [범상의] mediocre

보편[**बोप्योन**] [**普遍**] universality; generality; ubiquity (편재). e.g. 그것은 보편적으로 인정된 진실이다 That is a universally acknowledged truth.

보폭 [**बोफोक**] [**步幅**]a step; a pace; (길게 잡은) a stride

보행 [**बोहैंग**] [**步行**] [걸어감] (a) walk; walking; ambulation. e.g. 보행의 자유를 잃다 be crippled.

보행자 [**बोहैंजा**] [**步行者**] a walker; a pedestrian; a foot passenger.

보험 [**बोहोम**] [**保險**] insurance; assurance (보통 생명보험).

보호 [**बोहो**] [**保護**] [지키기] protection; (경찰에 의한) protective custody; shelter; safeguard; harborage; guardianship; [돌봄] care; [보존,유지] preservation; conservation (▷ 국가 등에 의한 자연 보호에 쓰이는 일이 많음).

복 [**बोक**] [**福**] fortune; good luck; blessing; bliss; happiness

복고 [बोक्को] [復古] [옛 것대로 돌아감] (a) restoration; revival (of the ancient regime); [손실의 회복] recovery.

복고하다 restore; recover

복구[बोक्कु] [復舊] rehabilitation; recovery; restoration; restitution.

복권 [बोकक्वन] [福券] a (public) lottery; a raffle.

복귀[बोकक्वी] [復歸] a return; a comeback; reinstatement.

복귀하다 return <to>; come back <to politics>; be restored <to>; rebert <to

복도 [बोकतो] [複道] a passage (way); a corridor; a gallery; a hallway; a lobby (극장 등의)

복무 [बोकमु] [服務] (public) service. 복무하다 serve; [복무중이다] be in (public) service. e.g. 군대에 오래 복무하다 see much (military) service.

복받치다 [बोकपातछीदा] [솟아 나오다] well up; gush out [forth]; [감정이 치밀어 오르다] be filled [seized] <with>; have a fit <of>; (사물이) fill one's heart. e.g. (감동하여) 뜨거운 것이 가슴에 복받치다 feel a lump rise in one's [the] throat.

복사 [बोकसा] [複寫] [원본을 베끼는 것] copying; duplication; [복제] re-production. 복사하다 copy; [복제,모조하다] reproduce; duplicate; manifold; take [produce] a copy of; make a duplicate [copy] of; transfer <a picture>; facsimile; reprint.

복수 [बोकसु] [復讐] revenge; [격렬한 복수] vengeance; vendetta; [보복] retaliation; requital.

복스럽다 [बोकसुरोप्ता] [福-] happy-looking; fat and well-looking <face>. e.g. 그녀는 살이 쪄서 복스러워 보이는 노파였다 She was a plump and happy-looking old woman.

복습 [बोकसब] [復習] (a) review; <英> (a) revision. 복습하다 review; go over [through] <one's lesson>; revise.

복싱 [बोकसींग] boxing.

복원 [बोक्वान] [復元,復原] [원래대로 회복함] restoration; restitution; rehabilitation; [재건] reconstruction. 복원하다 restore; reconstruct.

복잡 [बोकचाप] [複雜] complexity; complication; intricacy; involvedness. 복잡하다 complicated; complex intricate

복장 [बोकचाग] [服裝]dress; clothes; <집합적> clothing; (풍속으로서의) costume. e.g. 복장을 단정히 하다 tidy oneself up.

ㅂ

복제 [बोकचे] [複製] (facsimile) reproduction; duplication; reprinting; [복제물] a reproduction; a replica (▷ 종종 원작자의 손에 의함); a facsimile (▷ 크기가 다를 경우도 있음); [똑같은 것] a duplicate.

복종[बोकचोंग] [服從] obedience; submission; subordination; [묵종] acquiescence. 복종하다 [명령에 따르다] obey; be obedient <to>; [항복하다] submit oneself <to>; [묵종하다] acquiesce <in>; [굴복하다] yield <to>.

복통 [बोकथोंग] [腹痛] a stomachache

복판 [बोकपफान] [한가운데] the (very) middle; the center; the heart. e.g. 복판의 middle / central.

복합[बोकहाप] [複合] composition; compositeness; complex 복합하다 compound; pound together; unite; be united; miK be mixed.

볶다 [बोकता] **1** (커피콩,땅콩 등을) roast; (콩,곡식 등을) parch; scorch; singe; pan-broil. e.g. 땅콩을 볶다 roast peanuts. **2** [성가시게 굴다] tease; pester; annoy; plague; harass; torment. e.g. 과자를 사 달라고 어머니를 볶다 tease [pester] one's mother for candy.

볶음[बोकुम] pan-broiled [roasted] food; a roast; a broil

본[1] [बोन] **1** ≤本≥ ⇨ 본보기 e.g. 본을 보이다 set an example <for the children>. **2** 형지(型紙). e.g. 드레스의 본을 뜨다 cut out a pattern for a dress.

본[2] [बोन] [本] [이] this <year>; [우리] our; [당면한] the present. e.g. 본건 the case in question / the problem at issue.

본[3] [बोन] [本] **1** [중심의] main; chief; principal; head. e.g. 본점 a head office. 본루 home plate [base]. **2** [진짜의] real; [정식의] regular. e.g. 본명 a person's real name. 본무대 the center stage / the main stage.

본건 [बोनगोन] [本件] this case [affair / matter]; the matter in question [at issue]; the matter under consideration; the case (lying) before us.

본격 [बोनग्योक] [本格] fundamental rules; a regular style. e.g. 본격화하다 become serious / get into <its> stride.

본관 [बोनग्वान] [本館] (별관,분관에 대하여) the main building.

본능 [बोननुंग] [本能] (an) instinct.

본당 [बोनदांग] [本堂] [불교] the main [inner] temple; the main building [hall / sanctuary] (of a temple); [가톨릭] a parish church.

본디 [बोनदी] [本−] [본래, 원래] originally; primarily; [처음부터] from the outset [beginning / first]; [나면서부터] by nature; naturally; [본질적으로] essentially; intrinsically.

본뜨다 [बोनतुदा] [本−] [원형, 모형을 만들다] cut out a pattern <for one's socks>; model [pattern] <on / ather>; [모방하다] imitate; copy <from>; [본보기로 삼다] follow the example [model] of <a person>; take example [pattern] by <a person>.

본뜻 [बोन्तुत] [本−] **1** [의도, 목적] one's original purpose; one's (real) intention [will / motive]. 2 [본래의 의미] the original [primary] meaning; the original import; the true [basic / literal] meaning [sense / conception].

본래 [बोल्लै] [本來] 본디.

본론 [बोल्लोन] [本論] he main discourse [issue / subject].

본명 [बोनम्यौंग] [本名] **1** one's real name; (필명, 예명에 대하여) one's autonym.

본문 [बोनमुन] [本文] [주문(主文)] the text <of a book / of a contract>; the body <of a letter>; (삽화에 대하여) the letterpress.

본바탕 [बोनबाथांग] [本−] [본질] essence; (real) substance; intrinsic [true] nature; essential quality; one's disposition; one's true colors [quality]; [밑바탕] the ground; (도자기의) the body.

본받다 [बोनबात्ता] [本−] imitate; follow; model oneself <on / ather>; make <a person> one's model; take pattern by <another>; follow the example [model] of <a person>. e.g. …을 본받아 ather / ather the example [model / fashion / style] of / in [ather] the manner of / on [along] the lines of / in imitation of.

본보기 [बोनबोगी] [本−] [교훈] a lesson; [모범] an example; [경고] a warning; a model; a pattern. e.g. 본보기로 as an example.

본부 [बोनबू] [本部] the head [main / front] office; the headquarters; the seat (연맹의); the ministry proper (정부 부처의)

본분 [बोनबून] [本分] one's duty; one's part. e.g. 자기의 본분을 다하다 do [discharge / fulfill] one's duty.

본사 [बोनसा] [本社] (지사에

대하여) the head [main] office

본색 [बोनसैक] [本色] [본디의 특색,정체] one's real character; one's characteristic; one's true colors; one's true quality. e.g. 본색이 드러나다 show one's true colors / come out in one's true colors.

본선 [बोनसौन] [本選] [최종 선발] the final selection.

본성 [बोनसोंग] [本性] [본래의 성질] one's true character [colors]; one's real nature.

ㅂ

본심 [बोनसीम] [本心] [진심] one's real intention (s); [속마음] one's heart. e.g. 본심을 드러내다 bare one's heart.

본업 [बोनओप] [本業] one's regular [principal / main] occupation [profession].

본연 [बोनयौन] [本然] 본연의 [자연적인] natural / [나면서부터의] inborn / innate / inherent / proper.

본인 [बोनईन] [本人] [사람 자신] the person himself [herself]; the subject; [(문제의) 당사자] the said person; the person in question; the principal (대리인에 대하여). e.g. 본인 자신이 in person / personally.

본전 [बोनजौन] [本錢] 1원금.2 [밑천으로 들인 돈] capital; fund; a stake (노름의); [원가] the (prime [original]) cost; the cost price (원가). e.g. 이 장사는 본전도 못 뽑는다 This business doesn't pay.

본점 [बोनजौम] [本店] (지점에 대하여) the head [main] office [shop / store]. e.g. 백화점의 본점 the main branch of a department store.

본토 [बोनथो] [本土] the mainland; the country proper. e.g. 본토에서 멀리 떨어져 있는 섬 an island far from the mainland / a remote island. 볼1 [बोल] 1 [뺨의 한복판] a cheek. 2 [물건의 너비] the width of a long and narrow object. e.g.볼이 넓은 발 a broad foot.

볼 [बोल] 공1.

볼록거리다 [बोललोककौरीदा] 불룩거리다

볼록하다 [बोललोकहादा] 불룩하다

볼륨 [बोलल्युम] 1[양감 (量感)] volume. e.g. 그녀는 볼륨이 대단하다 [뚱뚱 하다] She's really fat. / [글래머이다] She has some [quite a] build.2 [음량] volume. e.g. 볼륨 있는 목소리 a very power-ful [loud] voice.

볼일 [बोरील] business; affairs; [할 일] things to do; an engagement; work; (심부름의) an errand. e.g.

볼일이 남아 있다 have something more to do.

봄 [बोम] spring; [봄철] springtime.

봉급 [बोंगुप] [**俸給**] (a) salary; pay; wages.

봉기 [बोंगी] [**蜂起**] an uprising; a revolt; (an) insurrection.

봉변 [बोंगब्यौन] [**逢變**] [변을 당함] meeting with a mishap; a mishap; an insult; humiliation. 봉변하다 [변을 당하다] meet with a mishap; [망신을 당하다] be insulted [humi-liated]; have bitter experi-ences; have a hell of a time; have a hard time of it.

봉사[1] [बोंगसा] [**奉仕**] (고객에 대한) service; (국가에 대한) (a) public duty [service]; [시중 들기] attendance; [근무하기] (a) service. e.g. 그는 봉사 정신이 희박하다 He lacks [is wanting in] public spirit. 봉사하다 serve; attend; render service(s) <to>.

봉사[2] [बोंगसा] [**奉事**] [소경] a blind person.

봉쇄 [बोंगश्वै] [**封鎖**] [출입을 막음] a blockade; blocking; bottling up

봉오리 [बोंगोरी] 꽃봉오리 e.g. 피어나는 (꽃)봉오리 bursting buds.

봉우리 [बोंगुरी] 산봉우리 e.g. 소백 산맥의 봉우리를 타다 walk along the ridges of the Sobaek mountain chain.

봉제 [बोंगजे] [**縫製**] needle-work; sewing (by machine); dressmaking. 봉제하다 make [sew] <a dress> with a sewing machine.

봉지 [बोंगजी] [**封紙**] **1** [종이 주머니] a paper bag [sack]. e.g. 봉지에 가득한 과자 a paperful of biscuits. **2** (셀 때) a pack (age) <of>. e.g. 약 한 봉지 a packet of medicinal herbs / a (pa-ckaged) dose of medicine.

봉착 [बोंगछाक] [**逢着**] 봉착하다 encounter; confront; face <with>; meet <with>; come upon [across].

봉투 [बोंगथु] [**封套**] an envelope.

봉하다 [बोंगहादा] [**封** –] **1** (봉투,문을) seal <a letter>; seal up <a window>; glue up; fasten. e.g. 봉한 [봉하지 않은] 편지 a sealed [an unsealed] letter. **2** (구멍을) close [stop] up <a hole>. e.g. 창구멍을 봉하다 cover a hole in a paper window. **3** (입을) shut <one's mouth>; seal. e.g. 입을 봉하고 말이 없다 keep one's lips tight / keep one's mouth shut / keep silent.

뵙다 [बेप्ता] humbly see [meet]; have an audience [interview] with. e.g. 처음

ㅂ

뵙겠습니다 How do you do?

부[1] [बू] [**附**] **1** [작성,발송한 시일] dated; under the date of. e.g. 8월 15일부의 편지에 대해 감사드립니다 Thank you for your letter of [dated] August 15. **2** [소속,부속] attached <to>; belonging <to>; in attendance <upon>; bea-ring. e.g. 그는 주영 대사관부로 발령되었다 He was attached to the Korean Embassy in London.

부[2] [बू] [**父**] 아버지.

부[3] [बू] [**部**] **1** [부분] a part; a portion; a section. e.g. 회원의 일부 (a) part of member. 제1부 section I. [헨리 4세] 제1부 the first part of King Henry the fourth. 2부로 된 소설 a novel in two parts. **2** [부서] a ministry; a department (▷ 우리 나라 회사의 [부]에 해당. [과]는 a section); a bureau; a division; [클럽] a club. e.g. 경리부 the accountants' department. 국방부 the Ministry [Department] of National Defense. **3** (책을 셀 때) a copy <of a book, magazine, etc.>; [권] a volume. e.g. 3 [4] 부작 a trilogy [tetralogy] / a three-[four-] volume work. 1부에 3천 원 three thousand won a [per] copy.

부[4] [बू] [**富**] riches; wealth; a fortune; [풍부] opulence. e.g. 부의 분배 distribution of wealth [riches].

부[5] [बू] [**副**] assistant; vice-; deputy; sub-; under-; adjutant; substitute; accessory; alternate. e.g. 부통령 a vice president. **부가** [बूगा] [**附加**] addition; supplement; annexation. 부가하다 [덧붙이다] add <to>; make additions to; [보충하다] supplement <with / by>; [첨부하다] append; annex [추가하다] subjoin.

부각 [बूगाक] [**浮刻**] relief; relievo; embossed carving. 부각하다 emboss; raise; [새기다] carve in relief. e.g. 부각되다 be embossed / stand out in bold relief / <비유> be brought to the fore / be highlighted.

부계 [बूग] [**父系**] "the paternal side [line]; the male line; the patrilineage.

부고 [बूगो] [**訃告**] an announcement of <a person's> death; an obituary (notice); an obit.

부과 [बूग्वा] [**賦課,附課**] (세금 등의) (a) levy; (의무, 책임 등의) imposition; assessment; incidence.

부귀 [बूग्वी] [**富貴**] wealth and rank; riches and hono

(u) rs. 부귀하다 wealthy [rich] and noble. e.g. 부귀한 사람 a noble and wealth man.

부근 [बुगन] [附近] [근처] the neighborhood; the vicinity; environs; a part (지역).

부글거리다 बुगोलकोरिदा **1** (물이) boil (over); seethe; come to a boil; simmer. e.g. 내 뱃속이 부글거렸다 My belly growled. / The bowels rumbled.**2** (거품이) bubble; foam; froth; rise in bubble.

부녀 (자) [婦女(子)] बुन्यौ a woman; <집합적> women-folk (s); the fair [weaker / gentle / sother / tender] sex.

부녀 [बुन्यौ] [父女] father and daughter.

부닥치다 [बुढ़ाकछीदा] **1** [만나다] face; encounter; confront; meet with; be faced [confronted] with; come upon [across]; come face to face with. e.g. 난관에 부닥치다 encounter [be faced with] difficulties **2** [충돌하다] run [knock / hit / bump / collide / dash] against; run [crash] into; strike.

부단 [बुदान] [不斷] cons-tancy; ceaselessness; con-tinuity. 부단하다 cons-tant; ceaseless; incessant; continual; persistent; per-petual; steady. e.g. 부단한 발전 continuous develop-ment.

부담 [बुदाम] [負擔] a bur-den; a charge; a load; res-ponsibility (책임); obli-gation (의무); liability (채무); defrayment (지출); inci-dence (조세의).

부당 [बुदांग] [不當]injustice; wrongfulness; impropriety; unreasonableness. 부당하다 unjust; unfair; un-reason-nable; wrongful; improper; unwarrantable; [지나치다] excessive; un-merited; undue; unde-served; exorbitant

부대 [बुदै] [部隊] a (military) unit; a corps <단수, 복수 동형>; an outfit; a party; a detachment (파견대); a squad (분대); troops.

부대끼다 [बुदैकीदा] **1** [시달리다] be pestered <by>; be harassed <by / with>; be annoyed <by>. e.g. 빚쟁이에게 부대끼다 be worried by creditors. **2** [괴로움을 당하다] suffer <from>; be troubled <with>; be afflicted <with>. e.g. 속이 부대 끼다 feel un-comfortable with one's stomach loaded with heavy food.

부도 [बुदो] [不渡] dishonor; nonpayment. e.g. 부도를 내다 dishonor [fail to pay] a bill [check].

ㅂ

부도덕 [बुदोदौक] [**不道德**] (an) immorality; lack of morality; bad morals; vice. 부도덕하다 immoral; unvirtuous; wicked; vicious; dissolute; licentious; depraved; profligate

부동 [बुदोंग] [**不動**] immovability; firmness; stability; immobility. e.g. 부동의 신념 firm belief.

부동산 [बुदोंसान] [**不動産**] real [fixed / immovable] property [estate]; immovables; realty; a landed estate.

부두 [बुदु] [**埠頭**] a wharf <*pl.* wharves, ~s>; a quay; a pier; a jetty.

부둥키다 [बुदुंख्वीदा] hold [take] <a person> in one's arms; clasp; grasp; clutch. e.g. 부둥켜안다 embrace / hug / give <a person> a hug.

부드럽다 [बुदुरोप्ता] **1** (촉감이) soth; tender; (빛 등이) mellow; subdued; gentle. e.g. 부드럽게 so-thly / tenderly. **2** (성질, 태도가) gentle; tender; soth; mild (mannered); suave; smooth; meek. e.g. 부드러운 미소 a ge-ntle [soth] smile. **부득부득** [बुदुक] बुदुक persistently; obstinately; stubbornly; doggedly; importunately; tenaciously.

부득이 [बुदुगी] [**不得已**] unavoidably; inevitably; of [from / out of] necessity; unwillingly. e.g. 만 부득이 out of sheer necessity.

부들부들 [बुदुल बुदुल] [몸을 떠는 모양] tremblingly; quiveringly; shiveringly. e.g. 부들부들 떨다 tremble all over [like an aspen leaf] / shiver like a jelly / flutter.

부디 [बुदी] [꼭] by all means; without fail; at any cost; at all costs; in any case; [바라건대] (if you) please; pray; kindly; I beg. e.g.부디 … 해 주십시오 have the goodness to <do>.

부딪치다 [बुदीछीदा] **1**[맞다] strike; hit; [충돌하다] run against [into]; collide with; run foul of (배가); crash into [against / together]; knock [bump / dash / strike / butt] against. e.g. 남과 부딪치다 bump into a person.**2**[직면하다] face; face up to; be confronted by. e.g. 난관에 부딪치다 face [run up against] a difficulty / be confronted by a difficulty. **3**[해보다] try; risk; chance; [담판하다] negotiate directly with. e.g. 운을 하늘에 맡기고 부딪쳐 보다 run [take] a risk [chance] / chance [risk] it.

부딪히다 [बुदीछीदा] be

bumped [crashed] into; be bumped [run] against; be collided with. e.g. 자동차에 부딪히다 be run over [knocked down] by a car / be hit by a car.

부랑자 [बुरांग्जा] a vagabond; a loafer; a tramp; <美> a hobo; a bum; a vag; <美> a gold brick.

부랴부랴 [बुर्या बुर्या] in haste; in a hurry; hurriedly; hastily. e.g. 부랴부랴 떠나다 make a hurried departure.

부러뜨리다 [बुरौतुरीदा] break (off); snap (딱소리 내며); fracture (뼈를). e.g. 이를 하나 부러뜨리다 have a tooth knocked out.

부러워하다 [बुरौवॉहादा] envy; be envious [jealous] of; feel envy of.

부러지다 [बुरोजीदा] break; be [get] broken; give way; snap (딱하고); fracture (뼈가). e.g. 그는 말에서 떨어져 팔이 부러졌다 A fall from the horse resulted in a broken arm. /

부려먹다 [बुर्यौमोक्ता] work <a person> hard [like a horse]; drive <a person> hard; keep <a person> trotting [on the trot]; keep [hold / put] another's nose [face] to the grindstone; have <a person> at one's beck (and call). e.g. 싼 임금으로 부려먹다 underpay and sweat one's workers

부록 [बुरोक] [附錄] a supplement; an appendix <*pl.* –dixes, –dices>; extra; an addendum <*pl.* –da>; a postscript (발문).

부루퉁하다 [बुरुथुगंहादा] **1** (부어서) swollen; bloated; bulging; dropsical. e.g. 얼굴이 부루퉁하다 have a swollen [bloated] face. **2** (불만스러워서) sullen; sulky; cross; mumpish; peevish; sour; pouty. e.g. 부루퉁한 얼굴 a sulky look [face] / a sullen look.

부류 [बुरय] [部類] a class; a head (ing); a group; a category; an order; a division.

부르다[1] [बुरुदा] **1** [소리내다] call; call out <to>; hail; call ather (뒤에서); invoke (신을). e.g. 부르면 들리는 곳에 within call [hail / earshot]. **2** [오게 하다] call <a person> to one; summon; (사람을 보내어) send for [ather]; call in; (연예인 등을) engage; hire. e.g. 전화로 부르다 telephone for <a person>. **3** [청하다] invite; ask; [끌어들이다] attract; draw over. e.g. 잔치에 손님을 부르다 invite guests to a feast. **4** [일컫다] call; name; christen; style;

ㅂ

term; designate. e.g. … 이라고 부르다 call <it> ... / give <it> the name of.

부르다² [बूरुदा] **1**(배가) full; satisfied. e.g. 배부르게 먹다 eat heartily / eat one's fill / eat to one's heart's contents / have a hearty meal. **2** (임신하여) pregnant; big with <child>. e.g. 배가 잔뜩 부른 암소 a cow big with calf.

부르주아 [बुरूजुआ] [중산 시민] a bourgeois <*pl.* ~>; a man of means; <집합적> the bourgeoisie; [유산 계급] the moneyed [propertied] class (es).

부르짖다 [बुरूजीत्ता] **1** [소리 치다] cry; shout; shriek; let out a yell; exclaim; ejaculate; scre-am; utter [give] a cry. e.g. 큰 소리로 부르짖다 cry [call] out. **2** (사회에 대해서) cry <for>; clamor <for>; advo-cate; set forth. e.g. 개혁을 부르짖다 cry (loudly) for reform.

부르트다 [बूरुथुदा] blister; rise in blisters; form vesicles [blebs] <on>; get [have] a blister <on>. e.g. 발바닥이 부르트다 get [have] a blister [blisters] <on> / blister / vesicate.

부릅뜨다 [बूरुपतुदा] (눈을) make <one's eyes> glare; glare fiercely; goggle. e.g. 눈을 부릅뜨고 with one's eyes wide open.

부리 [बूरी] **1** [새의 주둥이] a bill; (특히 갈고랑이 모양의) a beak.**2** [물건의 뾰족한 끝] the tip; the end; the nozzle <of a hose>. e.g. 발부리 the tips of the toes. 총부리 the muzzle (of a gun).

부리나케 [बूरीनाखै] hurri-edly; in a (great) hurry; in (great) haste; hastily; speedily; at great speed; with flying feet. e.g. 부리나케 가다 hurry <to> / rush <to> / hotfoot(it).

부리다 [बूरीदा] **1** (사람, 동물을) manage; handle; use; keep; employ. e.g. 하인을 부리다 keep a servant / work a servant. **2** [조종하다] manage; work; operate; handle; control. e.g. 기계를부리다 handle [operate] a machine. **3** (꾀,재주, 말썽을) play; practice; do. e.g. 마술을 부리다 juggle / do conju-ring tricks.

부리부리하다 [बूरीबूरीहादा] big and bright; flaring. e.g. 부리부리한 눈 big bright eyes / big eyes full of fire.

부모 [बूमो] [**父母**] [양친] pa-rents.

부부 [बूबू] [**夫婦**] a young [an old] couple.

부분 [बूबुन] [**部分**]a part; a portion; a section

부사 [बूसा] [**副詞**] [문법] an adverb.

부산하다 [बूसानहादा] [바쁘다] (noisily) busy; restless; bustling. e.g. 부산한 거리 a bustling [busy] street.

부상 [बूसांग] [**負傷**]an injury; a wound

부서지다 [बूसोजिदा] break; be broken; crack; be cracked; smash; be smashed; pulverize; [파손되다] be destroyed; break [come] down; go out of repair(집 등이).

부설 [बूसौल] [**附設**] attachment; annexation; adjunct. 부설하다 attach [annex(e)] <a thing to another>.

부성애 [बूसोंगऐ] [**父性愛**] father's [paternal] love..

부속 [बूसोक] [**附屬**] [딸려서 붙음] attachment; affiliation; addendum.

부수 [बूसु] [**部數**] [책 등의 수효] the number of copies; [발행 부수] a circulation.

부수입 [बूसुईप] [**副收入**] (가외의) (a) side income; extra benefit; [음성 수입] a perquisite; a perk.

부스러기 [बूसुरोगी] broken pieces; fragments; scraps; ends; crumbs; chips; odds and ends.

부스럭거리다 [बूसुरोक्गोरिदा] 바스락거리다

부스스 [बूसूसू] **1** [느리게 슬그머니] gently; slowly; quietly. e.g. 잠자리에서 부스스 일어나다 sit up slowly in one's bed.**2** [머리털 등이 헝클어진 모양].부스스하다 disheveled; unkempt; shaggy; untidy.

부시다 [बूशीदा] (눈이) dazzling; glaring; blinding <flash> (전등 등이).

부식 [बूशीक] [**腐蝕**] corrosion; (주로 물이나 바람에 의한) erosion; [썩음] rot; decay; [녹] rust.

부식하다 corrode; erode; eat <into>; [녹슬다] rust[eat] away.

부실 [बूशील] [**不實**] **1** [허약하다] weak; delicate; infirm; sickly; feeble; <서술적> be not strong. e.g. 몸이 부실하다 be poor [delicate] in health / be in poor health / be weak.**2** [부족하다] insu-fficient; wanting; lacking; deficient; short. e.g. 양식이 부실하다 be scant [short] of food.

부양 [बूयांग] [**扶養**]support; maintenance. 부양하다 keep up; support; maintain.

부업 [बूओप] [**副業**] a side job; a by-job; a sideline; a side business; subsidiary work; an auxiliary [a minor / a sideline] occupation.

부엌 [बूऔख] a kitchen.

부여 [बूयौ] [**附與**] [가지거나 지니게 하여 줌] grant; bestowal; allow-

ㅂ

ance. 부여하다 give; (요청에 의해) grant; (권리 등을) invest

부연 [बुयौन] [敷衍] expatiation; amplification; enlargement; dilatation. 부연하다 expatiate [dilate / enlarge / dwell / elaborate] on; amplify; extend; expand; develop

부옇다 [बुयौथा] 보얗다 e.g. 달빛이 부옇게 비추고 있었다 The moon was giving off pale light.

부유 [बुयू] [富裕] wealth; richness; opulence; affluence; a heavy [long / well-filled / well-lined] purse. 부유하다 rich; wealthy; opulent; affluent; well-heeled; well-fixed

부응 [बुउंग] [副應] 부응하다 meet; satisfy; gratify; fulfill (기대 등에); answer (희망 등에). e.g. 현실에 부응하는 교육 education based on reality / education adopted to meet the demands of reality

부인[1] [बुईन] [夫人] [남의 아내] a wife <*pl.* wives>; [기혼자] a married lady; a dame; a matron.

부인[2] [बुईन] [否認] denial; negation; nonrecognition; disaffirmance; disaffirmation; repudiation.

부인[3] [बुईन] [婦人] a (married) woman; a lady (신분, 교양이 있는).

부임 [बुईम] [赴任] 부임하다 start [leave / go] for one's new post; proceed to one's post. e.g. 새로 부임해 온 교사 a new teacher.

부자[1] [बुजा] [父子] father and son.

부자[2] [बुजा] [富者] a rich [wealthy] person; a man of wealth [means / property]; rich folk (s); <집합적> the rich; the moneyed class

부자연 [बुजायौन] [不自然] unnaturalness; [인위적] artificiality. 부자연하다 unnatural; against nature; artificial; factitious; (… 인 체하는) a forced smile [style].

부작용 [बुजाग्योंग] [副作用] a <usually adverse> side [secondary] effect <on>.

부잣집 [बुजातचीब] [富者-] [부유한 가정] a rich [wealthy] family; [부호] a rich man's house.

부장 [बुजांग] [部長] the head [chief / director] of a department [division]; a department manager [head / chief].

부재 [बुजै] [不在] absence. e.g. 나의 부재중에 during [in] my absence / while I was away.

부적격 [बुजौक्यौक] [不適格]

disqualification; inappropriateness; inaptitude; inadequateness; inadequacy; impropriety. 부적당하다 unsuitable; unfit <for>; inappropriate <to / for>; inadequate; impertinent; out of place; improper; ineligible; inapplicable

부정 [बुजोंग] [否定] (a) denial; (a) disavowal; (a) disclaimer; (a) contradiction; negation. 부정하다 deny <a fact>; negative <a statement>; negate; gainsay; say no <to>; disown; disavow; contradict.

부정확 [बुजोंकह्वाक] [不正確] inaccuracy; incorrect-ness; inexactness; uncer-tainty; imprecision. 부정확 하다 inaccurate; incorrect; uncertain; inexact; imprecise.

부조 [बुजो] [扶助] (결혼 때의) making [sending] a wedding [congratulatory] gith; contribution to the expenses of a wedding; (상가에 대한) offering condolence money [goods]; making [giving] a donation to help out a bereaved family; [조력] aid; help; assistance.

부조리 [बुजोरी] [不條理] absurdity; irrationality; unreasonableness; improperness; <프> absurde.

부조화 [बुजोह्वा] [不調和] inharmoniousness; inharmony; disharmony; discord; discordance; incongruity; disparity; disagreement; dissonance; dissonancy. 부조화하다 inharmonious [disharmonious / dis-cordant / incongruous / ill-sorted / inharmonic]; do not harmonize [match] <with>.

부족 [बुजोक] [不足] [불충분] insufficiency; [모자람] shortage; deficiency; deficit (특히 금전의); [결핍, 고갈] want; lack; scantiness; scarcity; dearth; famine <of coal [water]>. 부족하다 There are very few jobs available. / Jobs are scarce [few and far between].

부주의 [बुजुवी] [不注意] carelessness; heedlessness; incautiousness; inadvertence; want of care [attention]; inattention; negligence.

부진 [बुजीन] [不振] dullness; depression; inactivity; stagnation; a slump.

부질없다 [बुजिरैप्ता] idle; vain; useless; unprofitable; futile; trivial. e.g. 부질없는 이야기 a useless [silly] talk / idle gossip.

부착 [बुछक] [附着, 付着] sticking; adhesion (점착); bond (ing); cohesion (고착);

ㅂ

agglutination; conglutination (딱 달라 붙음).부착하다 adhere [stick / attach / cling] to; agglutinate; conglutinate.

부채[1] [बुछै] [**負債**] a debt; liabilities; dues.

부채[2] [बुछै] a fan; [쥘부채] a folding fan

부처 [बुछो] [불타] Buddha; Gautama [Gotama] Buddha; [성인] a Bu-ddhist saint;

부추기다 [बुछुगीदा] stir up; instigate; incite; urge [egg] on; abet; (개 등을) set <a dog> on [at] <a person>; set on <a dog>. e.g. 부추겨서 … 시키다 incite [instigate] <a person to an action [to do]> / cajole [wheedle] <a person into doing> / egg <a person on to an act [on to do]>.

부치다[1] [बुछीदा] [힘이 모자라다] be beyond [out of] one's capacity [power / strength]; be too much for <one>. e.g. 힘에 부치는 일 work beyond one's power [capacity / ability / skill].

부치다[2] [बुछीदा] [부채,풍 구로 바람을 일으키다] fan; use a fan. e.g. 불을 부치다 fan a fire.

부치다[3] [बुछीदा] [물품 등을 보내다] send; forward; transmit; consign (상품을); ship (배,차로); [발송하다] dispatch; [송금하다] remit; [우송하다] mail; post; send [forward] <something> by post [mail]. e.g. 남에게 소포를 부치다 send a person a parcel / send a parcel to a person.

부치다[4] [बुछीदा] [음식을 지지다] griddle; fry; cook [bake] in a greased pan [on a griddle]. e.g.. 빈대 떡을 부치다 cook lentil [green gram] pancake.

부탁 [बुथाक] [**付託**] [당부] a request; a favor; [간청] a solicitation. e.g. 친구의 간곡한 부탁 <at> the pressing request of a friend

부터 [बुथो1] [사람] from; of; through; with. e.g. 멀리 있는 친구로부터 온 편지 a letter from a friend far away. **2**[장소] from; out of; off; through; by; with; at; in; on; down. e.g. 부산까지 from Seoul to Pusan. **3**[시간] from; at; on; in; since (이래); on and ather (어느 날 이후). e.g. 3월 1일부터 on and ather March 1

부패 [बुफै] [**腐敗**] **1**[썩음] decomposition; rot (tenness); putrefaction; decay; sepsis 부패하다 rot; become rotten; putrefy; be decomposed; be vitiated; decay; go bad; be spoilt. e.g. 부패한 rotten / decomposed / putrid / decayed / bad / addled <egg> / tainted <meat> / turned <milk>. **2** [타락] corruption; degeneration; depravity; deterioration; taint.

부풀다 [बुपफुल्दा **1**] (살가죽 등이) swell; become swollen. e.g. 살가죽이 부푼다 The skin swells (up). **2** (물건이) swell out; get big; [팽창하다] expand; be inflated; rise (만두 등이). e.g. 빵이 잘 부풀었다 The bread rose well.**3** (희망 등으로) be buoyant; be lighthearted; be cheered up. e.g. 희망에 가슴이 부풀어 있다 I am full of hope. / My breast swelled with hope.

부품 [**部品**] [बुपफुम] (machine) parts; spare parts; components. e.g. 라디오와 부품 a radio set and parts. 텔레비전의 부품 parts for a TV set.

부하 [बुहा] [**部下**] a subordinate; a follower; (폭력단 등의) a hench-man; <경멸> an underling; <집합적> one's men; a person's following.

부합 [बुहाप] [**符合**] [일치] coincidence; [상응함] correspondence. 부합하다 coincide with; agree with; accord with; correspond with; conform with; tally with; check up with.

부호[1] [बुहो] [**符號**]**1**[기호] a mark; a symbol. e.g. X표[별표]의 부호를 붙여 주십시오 Mark with an "X" [an asterisk]. **2**[數] a sign. e.g. 양[음]의 부호 a plus [minus] sign.**3** [코드] a code. e.g. 부호화하다 code. **부호표** a table of signs; a list of symbols.

부호[2] [बुहो] [**富豪**] a rich [wealthy] man; a man of wealthy; [백만 장자] a millionaire; a billionaire. e.g. 대부호 a multimillionaire. 그는 굉장한 부호다 He is as rich as Croesus [a Jew]. / He is rolling in gold.

부화 बुह्वा [**孵化**] hatching; incubation. e.g. 인공 부화 artificial incubation. 부화하다 be hatched; hatch; incubate.

부흥 बुहुंग[**復興**] [재흥](a) revival; restoration; rehabilitation; [재건] reconstruction.

북 [बुक] a drum.

북극 [**北極**] [बुककुक] the North Pole.

북녘 [बुकन्यौख] [**北**-] the north (ward); the northern part [district].

북돋우다 [बुकतोउदा] [원기, 힘을] enliven; raise; stimulate; encourage; cheer up; strengthen; invigorate. e.g. 허영심 [흥미]을 북돋우다 excite [stir up] a person's vanity [interest].

북받치다 [बुकपातछीदा] 복받치다

북방 [बुकपांग] [**北方**] 북쪽. **2** 북녘.

북북 [बुकपुक] [긁는 소리] with a scraping sound; [찢는 소리] <rip> to pieces. e.g. 다리를 북북 긁다 scratch one's leg roughly. **북상** [बुकसांग] [**北上**] going north; northing. 북상하다 go(up) north. e.g. 태풍이 북상중이다 The typhoon is moving northward.

북쪽 [बुकचौक] [**北-**] the north (ward).

북한 [बुकहान] [**北韓**] North Korea; (공식명) the Democratic People's Republic of Korea.

분납 [बुननाप] [**分納**] (금전의) payment in [by] installments; installment payment; (상품의) installment delivery. 분납하다 (금전을) pay in [by] installments; (물품을) deliver in parts [installments].

분노 [बुननो] [**忿怒, 憤怒**] anger; (a) rage; (a) fury; wrath; resentment; indignation. e.g. 분노에 찬 목소리 an angry voice.

분단 [बुनदान] [**分斷**] dividing into sections; division; partition.

분담 [बुनदाम] [**分擔**] assignment; allotment; share; division of works (분업).

분담하다 [일 등을 나누다] divide; [공유하다] share; [할당하다] assign.

분량 [बुनरांग] [**分量**] [계량할 수 있는 것의 양] a quantity; [총량] an amount; (약의) a dose. e.g. (수)화 물의 분량 the quantity [amount] of baggage [luggage].

분류 [बुल्लयु] [**分類**] assortment; (조직적인) classification; grouping; [生] diagnosis.

분립 [बुल्लीप] [**分立**] [분리] separation; [독립] independence.

분만 [बुनमान] [**分娩**] 해산(解産).

분말 [बुनमाल] [**粉末**] 가루.

분명 [बुनमौग] [**分明**] clearness; obviousness. 분명하다 clear; obvious; evident; plain; unquestionable; distinct. e.g. 분명한 사실 an obvious fact.

분발 [बुनबाल] [**奮發**] strenuous exertions [efforts]; a spurt. 분발하다 strain [exert] oneself; make strenuous efforts; put forth one's efforts; spurt; stir up oneself. 남을 분발시키다 inspire a person with courage / rouse a person <into

activity>.

분배 [बुनबै] [分配]
[배급] distribution; [나누어 줌] division; [할당] allotment; allocation. 분배하다 distribute <among / to>; divide <among / between>; share (out) apportion; portion (out); allocate; allot.

분별 [बुनब्यौल] [分別] [구분] division; [분리] separation; [차별] distinction; discrimination; [분류] classification; assortment. 분별하다 [구분 하다] classify; assort; [化] fractionate.

분분하다 [बुनबुनहादा] [紛紛-] [소란하다 하다 judge; discern; discri-minate; use [exercise] discretion.] tumultuous; [어수선하다] complicated; scattered; pell–mell; [다르다] diverse; divergent; various; conflictting. e.g. 이 문제에 대해서 의견이 분분하다 There are various opinions about [Opinion is divided on] this question.

분사 [बुनसा] jet; spray; injection. 분사하다 jet <water>; shoot <water> at [into]; shoot out <water>; eject.

분석 [बुनसोक] [分析] analysis <*pl.* –ses>; (금속의) assay (ing).
분석하다 analyze; resolve; assay <a drug / an alloy>; make an analysis; reduce <a thing> to its element; take apart.

분식 [बुनसीका] [粉食]our; powdered [pulverized] food; flour–based meals

분신 [बुनसीन] [焚身] 분신하다 set fire to oneself; burn oneself (to death).

분실 [बुनसील] [紛失] loss; losing. 분실하다 [잃어버리다] lose; miss; [없어지다] be lost; be missing. e.g.시계가 분실되었는데 찾을 수가 **분야** [बुनयांग] [分野] a field; a sphere; a division; a realm; a branch; one's speciality [line].

분양 [बुनयांग] [分讓] sale (of land) in lots [parcels]. 분양하다 sell <land> in lots [parcels]; divide <one's estate> into lots [parcels] and sell; lot out; parcel out.

분업 [बुनओप] [分業] division of labor [labour]; specialization.

분열 [बुनयौल] [分裂] division; dissolution; dismemberment; disintegration; disunion; (사람이나 당파 간의) split; (종파 등의) schism; (세포의) segmen-tation; disorganization. 분 열하다 split; segment; disunite; break up; be split [disunited]; be disrupted; be divided; be fragmented; be torn.

분위기 [बुनवीगी] [雰圍氣]

[대기] the atmosphere; the air; [환경] an environment; [느낌] an atmosphere.

분장 (배우의) बुनजांग [**扮裝**] makeup; getup; impersonation (배역의); [변장] disguise.

분쟁 [बुनजैंग] [**紛爭**] a dispute; (a) complication; trouble; [다툼] a quarrel.

분주 [बुनजु] [**奔走**]분주하다 busy. e.g.분주한 사람 a busy person.

분출 [बुनछुल] [**噴出**] gushing; spouting; gust; spurt; jet; ejection; effusion; effusiveness; (화산의) eruption; belch; (용암의) extrusion; ebulli-tion; extravasation. 분출 하다 spout; gush (out); well out; jet; spurt; effuse; (온천 등이) boil out; (불길, 연기 등이) spout; belch out; [뿜어내다] vomit; emit; eject.

분투 [बुनथु] [**奮鬪**]a (hard) struggle; hard fighting; a plucky [desperate] fight; a tight [close] fight; strenuous effort (s). 분투하다 fight; struggle; strive <for>; exert oneself; make a strenuous efforts. e.g. 끝까지 분투하다 fight to the finish [to the bitter end] / fight it out.

분포 [बुनपफो] [**分布**] (a) Distribution

분필 [बुनफील] [**粉筆**] chalk.

분하다 [बुनहादा] [**憤**-] [원통하다] vexatious; mortifying; vexing; [화가 나다] be mad at oneself.

분할 [बुनहाल] [**分割**] [나누어 쪼갬] division; partition; dismemberment. e.g. 토지 [국토]의 분할 the partition of land [a country]. 황금 분할 the golden section [mean]. 분할하다 divide (up); cut [carve] up; split; partition; lot out; parcel off [into lots]; dismember; separate.

분해 [बुनहै] [**分解**] [해체] disjointing; disintegration; disassembly; dismantling; partition. 분해하다 disjoint; dismantle; disassemble; disintergrate; break down; take <a machine> apart [down]; parse (문장을).

분홍색 [बुनहोंगसैक] [**粉紅色**] pink.

붇다 [बुत्ता] **1** [물에 젖어 커지다] swell up; grow [become] sodden; sodden; macerate. e.g. 더운 물에 불어 버린 손 a hand sodden [swollen] with hot water. **2** [늘다] increase; multiply; grow bulky (부피가); mount [run / go] up <to a large sum> (비용,지출이); accumulate (쌓이다); (물이) rise (high); swell; go up. e.g. 물이 불은 강 swollen river / a river in flood

불 [बुल] **1** (a) fire; [화염] flame; blaze **2**화재 e.g. 큰 불 a big [large] fire / a conflagration. **3** [어둠을 밝히는 것] a light; a lamp. e.g. 전깃불 electric light. **4** [격렬한 정열,감정] burning passion; flame; fire. e.g. 애국심에 불타다 be burnt up with patriotism.

불- [बुल] [不]not; non-; un-; im-; ir-; il-; dis-. e.g. 불합리 irrationality / illogicality / unreasonableness.

불가능 [बुलगानुंग] [不可能] impossibility. 불가능하다 impossible; unattainable; impracticable; unfeasible; inexecutable; beyond the range of possibilities.

불가분 [बुलगाबुन] [不可分] indivisibility; impartibility. e.g. 불가분의 [나눌 수 없는] indivisible / [뗄 수 없는] undetachable / inseparable.

불가사의 [बुलगासाउ] [不可思議] a mystery; a wonder; a miracle; a riddle. 불가사의하다 [이상하다] wonderful; [불가해하다] incomprehensible; [기묘하다] strange; [신비하다] mysterious; [기적적이다] miraculous; [기이하다] odd.

불가피 [बुलगाफी] [不可避] inevitableness; unavoidableness. 불가피하다 unescapable; inevitable; unavoidable; ineluctable. e.g. 불가피하게 un-avoidably / inevitably / out of (sheer) necessity

불결 [बुलग्यौल] [不潔] uncleanliness; dirtiness; filthiness. 불결하다 unclean; dirty; filthy

불경기 [बुलग्यौंगी] [不景氣] bad [hard] times; [불황] a depression; [경기 후퇴] a recession; [침체] dullness; a slump.

불고기 [बुलगोगी] grilled [broiled] (slices of) meat.

불공평 [बुलगोंगफ्यौंग] [不公平] [공정하지 않음] unfairness; [편파적임] partiality; injustice; inequity.
불공평하다 unfair; partial; unjust; inequitable; biased; discriminating.

불과 [बुलग्वा] [不過] only; merely; no more than; nothing but. e.g. 불과 일주일 전에 but [only] a week ago

불교 [बुलग्यौ] [佛敎] Buddhism

불구 [बुलगु] [不具] [신체 일부의 기능 마비나 기형 상태] deformity; malformation; abnormity; disablement. e.g. 불구의 deformed / malformed / maimed / crippled / lame / [자유롭지 못한] disabled / (얼굴이) disfigured.

불균형 [बुलग्युनहौंग] [不均衡]

imbalance; unbalance; disproportion; inequality; disparity.

불길 [बुलगील] [不吉] an ill omen; inauspiciousness. 불길하다 unlucky; ominous; sinister; inauspicious; unpropitious; malign; malignant

불길 [बुलगील] the flames; the fire; blazes.

불나다 [बुलनादा] a fire breaks out [starts / occurs].

불다[1] [बुलदा] (바람이) blow.

불다[2] [बुलदा] **1**(입으로) blow on <a fire, one's hands, etc.>; breathe out (입김을). e.g. 뜨거운 차를 훌훌 불어 식히다 blow on hot tea to cool it. **2** (관악기를) blow [play] <a trumpet>; play(on) <a flute>.

불량 [बुलयांग] [不良] **1** [질의 열등] badness; inferiority. e.g. 영양 불량 malnutrition **2** [품성이 나쁨] delinquency. 불량 하다 wicked; delinquent; depraved.

불량배 [बुलयांगबै] a gang of hoodlums [hooligans]; the depraved.

불러내다 [बल्लौनैदा] [불러서 나오게 하다] call <a person>(out); call <a person> to <the office>; (전화통에) call [ring] <a person> to (on the phone); call <a person> to the telephone; [꾀어내다] decoy; lure; (마술로) invoke [conjure up] <evil spirits>.

불러오다 [बुल्लौओदा] [불러서 오게 하다] call <a person> to come; [소환 하다] summon; (사람을 시켜) send for. e.g. 사람을 보내 불러오다 send for <a person>.

불러일으키다 [बुल्लौइरुखीदा] rouse [gather] up; arouse; stir up; excite; call forth. e.g. 센세이션을 불러일으키다 create a sensation. 기억을 불러일으키다 recall something to one's mind.

불룩하다 [बुल्लुकखादा] swollen; baggy; bulging; fat; inflated; protuberant; bulky. e.g. 불룩한 가방 a bulky [bulging] bag.

불륜 [बुललयून] [不倫] [인륜에서 벗어남] immorality; obliquity; [비인 륜적 행위] immoral conduct; a liaison (이성간의).

불리 [बुलली] [不利] disadvantage; a drawback; a handicap. 불리하다 disadvantageous; unfavorable; bad; adverse; impolitic.

불리다[1] [बुललीदा] [(배를) 부르게 하다] fill. e.g. 배를 불리다 fill one's stomach / stuff out the belly / <비유> enrich oneself / feather one's (own) nest.

불리다[2] बुललीदा1 [부름을 받다] be called; [소환되다] be summoned <to>; [초대받다] be invited <to>. e.g. 그는 선생님에게 불려 갔다 He was called before a teacher. **2** (…이라고) be called; be named. e.g. 그는 어렸을 때 신동이라고 불렸다 As a child he was called an infant prodigy.

불리다[3] [बुललीदा] **1**(액체에) steep; soak; sodden; macerate. e.g. 쌀을 물에 불리다 soak rice in water. 물에 불려 두다 keep <a thing> steeped [soaked] in water.**2** [재물을 붇게 하다] add to; increase <one's fortune>. e.g. 재산을 불리다 increase [add to] one's fortune.**3** [과장하다] exaggerate; magnify; stretch <the fact>; [분량을 늘리다] pad; (자본 등을 과대평가하여) water.

불만 [बुलमान] [不滿] dissatisfaction; discontent; [불평] a complaint; (특히 부당한 취급에 대한) a grievance

불면증 [बुलम्यौनजुंग] [不眠症] insomnia; sleeplessness; vigilance.

불멸 [बुलम्यौल] [不滅] (정신적) immortality; (물질적) athanasia; indestructibility; imperishability.

불명예 [बुलम्यौम्ग्ये] [不名譽] dishonor; disgrace; discredit; ignominy; infamy; shame

불문 [बुलमुन] [不問] 불문하다 take no notice of; do not ask [question]; do not care whether ... or ...; ignore; disregard. e.g. 다소를 불문하고 regardless of quantity.

불법 [बुलबौप] [不法] [위법] unlawfulness; illegality; illegitimacy; [무법,무리함] lawlessness; outrage; [도리에 어긋남] wrong(fulness); injustice; iniquity.

불변 [बुनब्यौन] [不變] unchangeability; immutability; constancy; permanence. 불변하다 do not change; be unchangeable [invariable / inalterable / immutable / constant].

불복 [बुलबोक] [不服] **1**불복종.**2** [복죄 아니함] a disapproval; a denial <of one's guilt>; a protest; an objection; a dissatisfaction. 불복하다 deny one's guilt; plead not guilty; be dissatisfied; protest against; object to.

불분명 [बुलबुनम्यौग] [不分明] indistinctness; obscurity; ambiguity; unclearness; vagueness. 불분명하다 indistinct; obscure; be not clear; ambiguous.

불붙다 [बुलबुत्ता] catch(on) [take] fire; light up; kindle; ignite. e.g. 불붙는 데 키질[부채질]하기 casting oil in the fire; making matters worse. 불붙기 쉽다 kindle [catch fire] easily / be easy [quick] to catch fire / be combustible / be inflammable.

불붙이다 [बुलबुचीदा] set <a piece of paper> alight; set <kindling> on fire; light (up); kindle; ignite; apply <a fire / a flame> to (도화선 등에); <비유> touch off <a quarrel>.

불상사 [बुलसांगसा] [不祥事] a disgraceful [deplorable] affair; a scandal; an unhappy [ill] event. e.g. 시험 문제가 누설되는 불상사 the scandal of the examination questions being leaked.

불손 [बुलसोन] [不遜] haughtiness; arrogance; insolence. 불손하다 haughty; arrogant; insolent; presumptuous; assuming; overbearing.

불신 [बुलसीन] [不信] mistrust; distrust; disbelief; discredit; lack [want] of confidence <in>. 불신하다 distrust; discredit; disbelieve.

불쌍하다 [बुलसांगहादा] [가엾다] poor; pitiful; [애처롭다] sad; pitiable; piteous; [비참하다] miserable; wretched; [불행하다] unfortunate; [동정이 가다] pathetic; touching; [가슴아프다] regrettable. e.g. 어미없는 불쌍한 망아지 a poor [pitiful] motherless colt.

불쑥 [बुलसुक] [갑자기 쑥 내미는 모양] suddenly; unexpectedly; abruptly; unusually; (별안간, 뜻밖에) all of a sudden; unexpectedly; (예고없이) without (previous) notice [warning]; unawares. e.g. 창밖으로 머리를 불쑥 내밀다 pop one's head out of the window.

불안 [बुरान] [不安] **1** [걱정] uneasiness; anxiety; worry; apprehension; misgivings; suspense; fear. 불안하다 uneasy; ill at ease; restless; anxious. e.g. 불안해지다 feel uneasy **2** [불안정] insecurity; [사회적 동요] unrest. 불안하다 insecure; precarious; uncertain. e.g. 불안한 정계 the unsettled political world.

불어나다 [बुरौनादा] increase; grow; accumulate; run [go / mount] up; pile [roll] up; rise. e.g. 강물이 불어나다 the river rises.

불완전 [बुरवानजौन] [不完全] incompleteness; imperfection; defectiveness; faultiness. 불완전하다

[부족한 부분이 있다] incomplete; [완벽하지 않다] imperfect; [결함이 있다] defective; faulty.

불우 [बुरू] [不遇] [불행] misfortune; ill fortune [luck / fate]; [역경] adversity; [세상에 알려지지 못함] obscurity. 불우하다 ill-fated; ill-starred; unfortunate; unfavored; adverse; hapless; obscure.

불운 [बुरून] [不運] (a) misfortune; bad luck 불운하다 unfortunate; unlucky; luckless; (숙명 처럼) ill-fated; hapless; evil-[ill-] starred; infelicitous.

불응 [बुरुंग] [不應] non-acceptance; noncompliance; declination; disobedience; [거부] refusal; rejection. 불응하다 do not accept [grant / meet / comply with / consent to]; decline; do not answer [respond to]; disobey; refuse; reject; turn down; turn a deaf ear to.

불의 [बुरुइ] [不意] suddenness; unexpectedness. e.g. 불의의 [돌연한] sudden / abrupt / [우연의] incidental / casual / [예상밖의] unexpected / unlooked-for / unforeseen / [긴급의] emergent / contingent.

불의 [बुरुी] [不義] **1** [부도덕] immorality; impropriety; [부정] injustice; iniquity; unrighteousness.**2** [도의에 벗어난 남녀 관계] illicit intercourse; criminal [improper] connection; misconduct; liaison; intrigue; adultery.

불이익 [बुरीइक] [不利益] disadvantage; a handicap; a loss; a drawback; inadvisability; inexpediency.

불일치 [बुरीलछी] [不一致] disagreement; [불화] discord; discordance; [일관성이 없음] inconsistency; [통일성이 없음] lack of unity; dissonance; incongruity; inconformity; dissidence.

불임 [बुरईम] [不姙] Sterility

불장난 [बुलजांगनान] **1** [아이들이 불을 가지고 노는 장난].불장난하다 play with fire [matches].**2** [위험한 행위의 비유]. e.g. 대통령은 상대국을 도발하는 언사로 위험한 불장난을 하고 있다 The President is playing with fire by using provocative language to the other nation.

불장난하다 play with fire.

불조심 [बुलजोसीम] [-操心] precautions against fire.

불찰 [बुलछाल] [不察] [부주의] carelessness; negligence; lack of attention; thoughtlessness; imprudence; [실수] a fault; a mistake; a blunder; [미숙]

inexperience; [무능] incompetence. e.g. 손님의 출발 시간을 적어 두지 않았던 것은 나의 불찰이었다 It was very careless of me not to write down the time [hour] of the guest's departure.

불참 [बुलछाम] [不參] absence; nonattendance; a failure in attendance; default; nonappearance. 불참하다 be absent <from>; absent oneself <from>; fail to attend [appear <in>]; stay away <from>; do not participate <in>.

불청객 [बुलछोंगकैक] [不請客] a self-invited [an unin-vited / an unbidden] guest; a gate-crasher; a crasher.

불충분 [बुलछुंगबुन] [不充分] insufficiency; imperfection; inadequacy. 불충분하다 insufficient; not enough; deficient; scanty; imperfect; incomplete.

불친절 [बुलछीनजौल] [不親切] unkindness; unfriendlyness; inhospitality. 불친절하다 unkind; unfriendly; disobliging; inhospitable.

불쾌 [बुलख्वै] [不快] **1** [기분이 좋지 않음] displeasure; discomfort; unpleasantness. 불쾌하다 [싫다] unpleasant; displeasing; [마음에 들지 않다] disagreeable; offensive [거북하다] uncomfortable; [기분이 좋지 않다] displeased; ill humored; [부아가 나다] provoking; [짜증이 나다] irritating; [분하다] exasperating. **2** [몸이 찌부드드함] indisposition; an ailment; malaise. 불쾌하다 <서술적> be not well; be [feel] unwell; be indisposed; be out of condition [form / sorts].

불타다 [बुलथादा] **1** [불이 붙어 타다] burn; blaze; be in flames. e.g. 빨갛게 불타고 있는 난로 a red-glowing stove. **2** [정열 P의욕 등이 끓어오 르다] burn; glow; be aflame. e.g.불타는 사랑 a burning [passionate] love / an ardent love / flaming love.

불통 [बुलथोंग] [不通] (교통, 통신의) impassability; suspension; interruption (of telephone service); stoppage; tie-up. e.g. 열차 [전신]의 불통 the interruption of train service [telegraphic communication].

불투명 [बुलथुम्योंग] [不透明] opacity. 불투명하다 opaque; turbid; thick; milky. e.g. 불투명한 태도 a vague [an ambigu-ous] attitude / an uncertain [a noncommittal] attitude.

불편 [बुल मण्हण्यौन] [**不便**] **1**[편리하지 못함] (an) inconvenience; inexpediency; incommodiousness; unhandiness. 불편하다 inconvenient; incommodious; unhandy; unwieldy. **2** [몸,마음 등이 편하지 못함] (an) indispo-sition; (a) discomfort; a disorder; a bad condition; an ailment; malaise. 불편하다 <서술적> be not well; be [feel] unwell [ill]; be indisposed; be [feel] out of sorts [form / condition].

불평 [बुलपफ्यौग] [**不 平**] [불만] discontent; dissatisfaction; displeasure; (정치상의) disaffection; [불평의 말] a grievance; a murmur; an idle complaint; a grouse; <美> a beef.

불평등l [बुलपफ्यौगतग] [**不平等**] nequality. 불평등 하다 unequal; [불공평 하다] unfair

불피우다 [बुलपफीउ्दा] make [build] a fire <in a stove>; get a fire going.

불필요 [बुलफीरयो] [**不必要**] 불필요하다 [필요하지 않다] unnecessary; needless; [쓸모없다] useless; [남아돌다] superfluous; [청하지도 않다] uncalled-for; [사용하지 않다] disused.

불합격 [बुलहापक्यौक] [**不合格**] [낙제] failure; [실격] disqualification; rejection.

불합리 [बुलहाम्नी] [**不合理**] irrationality; absurdity; illogicality; unreasonableness; unreason; inconsistency. 불합리하다 [이성을 결하다] irrational; [논리에 맞지 않다] illogical; [도리에 맞지 않다] unreasonable; [터무니없다] preposterous; [모순되다] inconsistent.

불행 [बुहैंग] [**不 幸**] [행복하지 않음] unhappyness; infelicity; misery; [불운] misfortune; ill fortune [luck]; adversity; [재난] a disaster; a calamity; an accident; a mishap; woe.

불허 [बुहौं] [**不許**] disapproval; nonpermission; disapprobation; disallowance. 불허하다 disapprove; do not permit [allow / grant / admit]; disallow; reject; turn down

불현듯 (बुरहौन्तुत sudde-nly; on [all of] a sudden; unexpectedly. e.g. 하려는 생각이 불현듯 일어나다 have a sudden desire to (do) / be seized with a desire to (do) / suddenly feel like (doing).

불협화음 [बुलह्यौपहवाउम] [**不協和音**] **1** 안어울림음.**2** [일치하지 않는 관계]. e.g. 최근 양국간에 불협화음이 생기고 있다 There has

been discord between the two nations recently.

불호령 [बुलहोरौंग] [-**號 令**] [급하고 무서운 명령] an impetuous order; a fiery command; [비난] thunder; a roaring scolding. 불호령 하다 issue an impetuous [a fiery] order; give a strict command; storm <at a person>.

불화 [बुलह्वा] [**不和**] [사이가 좋지 않음] discord; [분쟁] trouble; [의견의 차이] differences.

불확실 [बुलह्वाक्शिल] [**不確實**] uncertainty; unrelia-bility; unauthenticity. 불확실 하다 [확실하지 않다] uncertain; [불안정하다] insecure; unsteady; [위태 롭다] precarious; [미덥지 않다] unreliable; [의심스 럽다] doubtful.

불황 [बुलह्वांग] [**不**] (일시적인) (a) recession; bad business; a weak market; (심각한) a depression.

불효 [बुलह्यौ] [**不孝**] [부모를 공경하지 않음] want of filial piety; unfilial behavior [behaviour]; [부모에게 순종하지 않음] disobedience to one's parents. 불효하다 un-duti-ful; unfilial; impious; disobedient; <자동사> treat one's parents disrespect-fully.

붉다 [बुकता] red; ruddy; (심홍색의) crimson; (진홍색의) scarlet; rubicund <face>; (병적으로) hectic; (사상이) communistic. e.g. 붉은 빵 red [rosy] cheeks.

붉히다 (बुलख्वीदा) blush; color up; change color. e.g. (부끄러워) 얼굴을 붉히다 blush (for [with] shame) / turn red with embarrass-ment.

붐비다 [बुमबीदा] <서술적> be crowded [thronged] <with people>; be bus-tling; bustle; be packed [congested / jammed / jam-packed]; [만원이다] be full up.

붓다[1] [बुत्ता] **1** [살가죽이 부풀어오르다] swell (up / out); bloat (out) become swollen [dropsical] (▷ dropsical 은 수종으로 부었을 때를 말함). e.g. 부은 swollen / bloated / tumid. **2** [성이 나다] get angry <at>; become sullen; get sulky [cross / peevish]; sulk; fret; get sore <at / on / over>. e.g. 부은 angry / cross / sulky / sullen / sour.

붓다[2] [बुत्ता1] (액체를) pour <in / into>; fill <a cup> with <coffee>; put <water in a bowl>; feed <a lamp with oil>. e.g. 콘크리트를 틀에 붓다 pour concrete into a form. **2** [뿌리다] sow <seed>. e.g. 모판에

씨앗을 붓다 sow seeds in a seedbed.**3** [불입금,곗돈 등을 치르다] pay in[by] install (l) ments. e.g. 월 5만 원씩 붓다 pay a monthly install (l) ment of 50,000 won.

붕 [बुंग1] [방귀소리]. e.g. 방귀를 붕 뀌다 break wind / let a fart / fart / poop.**2** (벌 등의) humming; buzzing; droning; (비행기 등의) whirring; buzzing.**3** (엔진 등의) whirring; humming.

붕괴 [बुंग्वे] [**崩壞**] [허물어짐] a fall; a breakdown; (a) collapse; (건물,광산 등의) a cave-in.

붕대 [बुंगदे] [**繃帶**] a bandage.

붙다 [बुत्था] **1** [부착하다] stick <to>; cling <to>; cleave <to>. e.g. 전단이 벽에 붙어 있었다 A bill was pasted up [stuck] on the wall. **2** [의지하다] live with (a person at his expense); be a parasite <to>; be a dependent <on>. e.g. 친척집에 붙어 살다 live [sponge / hang] on one's relations.**3** [좇아서 따르다] belong to; be attached to; join; (편들다) take sides [a side] with; take the side of; side with. e.g. 반대당에 붙다 join the opposite party. **4**[바싹 가까이하다] keep [stand] close <to>. e.g. 벽에 꼭 붙어서다 stand close to the wall / < 美 >hug the wall. 그렇게 꼭 붙어서 걷지 마라 Don't walk so close to me

붙들다 [बुत्तुल्दा1] [꽉 쥐다] catch; (갑자기, 힘껏) seize; take [get / catch / lay] hold of; [움켜잡다] grasp [grip / grab]. e.g. 팔을 붙들다 seize <a person> by the arm**2** [붙잡다] catch; arrest; capture; apprehend; nab. e.g. 도둑을 붙들다 arrest [catch / capture / nab] a thief. 경찰은 유괴범을 붙들었다 The police arrested [caught / captured] the kidnapper.

붙들리다 [बुत्तुल्लिदा] be caught; be detained; be arrested [apprehended]; be made to stay. e.g. 붙들리지 않고 있다 remain at liberty [large].

붙박이 [बुप्पागी] a fixture; a fixed [built-in] article; a fitting.

붙어다니다 [बुथौदानिदा] follow <a person> about [around]; shadow; tag along.

붙이다 [बुछीदा] **1**stick; (풀로) paste. e.g. 천조각을 이어 붙이다 patch pieces of cloth. **2** [서로 닿게 하다]. e.g. 양무릎을 바짝 붙이고

서다 stand with one's knees close together. **3** [말을 걸다] speak [talk] to[address (oneself to)] <a person>.**4** [의견P설명 등을 첨가하다] add <to>; attach <to>; affix <to>; annex <to>; append <to>.

붙임성 [बुच्चिमसौंग] [- 性] sociability; affability; amiability; companionableness; friendliness. e.g. 붙임성 있는 태도 an affable [a sociable] manner.

붙잡다 [बुच्चाप्ता1] [잡다] catch; seize; take [get / catch] hold of <a thing>; hold; clasp; clutch; [쥐다] grab; grasp. e.g. 소매를 붙잡다 catch [seize] <a person> by the sleeve **2** [체포하다] arrest; capture; collar; nab. e.g. 도둑을 붙잡다arrest [seize / catch / capture] a thief. **3**[못 가게 말리다] detain; hold <a person>. e.g. 사람을 붙잡고 긴 이야기를 늘어놓다 buttonhole <a person>.

붙잡히다 [बुच्चाफिदा] [잡히다] be taken hold of; be grasped; [체포되다] be caught; be arrested; [남의 수중에 빠지다] fall into <a person's> hands [clutches]; [만류당하다] be detained. e.g. 붙잡히지 않도록 하다 keep out of <a person's> clutches.

브레이크 [बुरेइख्] a brake.

브로치 [बुरोछी] a brooch; a breastpin.

브로커 [बुरोखो] a broker; a middleman.

블라우스 [बुल्लाउस] a blo-use; a shirtwaist.

비[1] [बी] [費]비용. e.g. 여행비 traveling expenses

비[2] [बी] [碑] [묘비] a tombstone; a gravestone; [기념비] a monument.

비[3] बी [非] [그름,잘못] (an) injustice; (a) wrong; a mistake; an error

비[4] [बी] [比]a) ratio <*pl.* ~ s>. e.g. 8대 3의 비 a ratio of 8 to 3 / an eight-to-three ratio / the ratio 8:3. 남녀의 비는 3대 2였다 The ratio of men to women [the male-female ratio] was three to two.

비[5] [बी] (내리는) rain; (한 번의 강우) a rain; a rainfall; a shower (소나기).

비[6] [बी] [非] non-; un-; anti-. e.g. 비과학적 unscientific.

비겁 [बीगोप] [卑怯] [야비함] meanness. 비겁 하다 mean; [남자답지 못하다] unmanly; [부정(不正) 하다] foul; unfair

비결 [बीग्यौल] [秘訣] a secret <of>; the mysteries <of>;

a key <to>. e.g. 건강[성공]의 비결 the secret of [the key to] good health [success].

비공개 [बीगोंगे] [**非公開**] e.g. 비공개의 private / secret / not open to the public / closed-door <session>.

비공식 [बीगोंसीक] [**非公式**] informality; unofficialness.

비관 [बीग्वान] [**悲觀**] pessimism; [낙심] disappointment. 비관하다 be pessimistic <about / of>; take a pessimistic [dark] view <of>; look on the gloomy side <of>; despond <of the future>; [낙심하다] be disappointted; lose heart.

비교 [बीग्यो] [**比較**] (a) comparison; a parallel.

비극 [बीगक] [**悲劇**] (a) tragedy; a tragic drama.

비기다 बीगीदा [승부를 가리지 못하다] tie [draw] <with>; end in a tie [draw]; be drawn; come out even. e.g. 그 경기는 비겼다 The game [match] was drawn [a tie]. / The game [match] ended in a tie[draw].

비난 [बीनान] [**非難**] (an adverse) criticism; blame; (a) reproach; reprobation; (a) censure; denunciation (공공연한); [공격] (an) attack 비난하다 criticize unfavorably [adversely]; censure; blame; reproach; denounce; condemn; attack; blast; cry out on [upon]; make a charge against; charge [accuse] <a person> with <a fault>.

비누 [बीनू] soap.

비늘[बीनल] a scale; a shard; a squama <*pl.* -mae>.

비능률적 [बीनंगरयुलचौक] [**非能率的**] inefficient

비닐 [बीनल] vinyl.

비다 [बीदा] (속이) empty <cupboard>; vacant <space>; hollow <tree trunk>; unoccupied <room>; free <of engagements>. e.g. 빈병 [깡통] an empty bottle [can].

비단[1] [बीदान] [**非但**] merely; simply; only. e.g.비단 …뿐 아니라 … not only [merely] ... but also .... 그것은 비단 건강에 해로울 뿐만 아니라 비경제적이다 It is not only unhealthy but also wasteful.

비단[2] [बीदान] [**緋緞**]silk fabrics; silk goods [stuff]; silk(s); satin (공단).

비단결 [बीदानग्यौल] [**緋緞-**]the texture of silk; a velvety texture. e.g. 그녀의 피부는 비단결 같다 Her skin is a velvety texture

비례 [बीरे] [**比例**] [**緋緞-**] [비교] (a) proportion; (a)

ratio (비율). 비례하다 be proportioned [proportionate / proportional] <to>; be in proportion <to>. e.g. …에 비례하여 in proportion to. A는 B에 비례한다 A is proportional to B.

비로소 [बीरोसो] for the first time; not ... until [till] .... e.g. 나는 그 때 비로소 부모님의 은혜를 알았다 I realized then for the first time how much I owe my parents.

비록 [बीरोक] if; even if; (even) though; although; admitting [granting / supposing] that. e.g. 비록 농담으로라도 even in joke.

비롯하다 [बीरोतथादा] [처음 시작하다] begin; start; commence; [기원하다] originate <in>; have <its> origin [rise] <in>; arise <from>. e.g. …을 비롯하여 including ... / ... and / as well as ... / beginning with ... / headed by ....

비료 [बीर्यो] [肥料] (자연의) manure; (인조의) (a) fertilizer.

비리다 [बीरीदा] (생선이) fishy; smelling of fish; (피가) bloody; smelling of blood.

비만 [बीमान] [肥滿] corpulence; fatness; obesity; portliness. 비만 하다 [보기 흉하게 살찌다] obese; corpulent; [비계살이 찌다] fat; [체격이 크다] stout (▷완곡한 말씨); [통통하게 살찌다] plump; (아이가) chubby.

비매품 [बीमैपफुम] [非買品] an article not for sale; <게시> "Not For Sale"; "Not to be sold"; "Privately Printed [Distributed]."

비명 [बीम्यौंग] [悲鳴] [놀라서 지르는 소리] a scream; a shrill [piercing] cry; [새된 소리] a shriek. e.g.비명을 지르다 scream / give [let out] a scream / shriek / give a shriek.

비무장 [बीमुजांग] [非武裝] demilitarization. e.g. 비무장의 unarmed / demilitarized.

비밀 [बीमील] [秘密] secrecy; confidentiality; [비밀인 일] a secret; a confidence; a mystery.

비방 [बीबांग] [誹謗] slander; slanderous statements; calumny; vilification; abuse; reprobation. 비방하 다 slander; abuse (▷slander는 명예를 손상케 하는 일, abuse 는 비난, 욕설을 하는 뜻); calumniate; malign; reprobate; defame; speak ill of.

비번 [बीबौन] [非番] off duty; (경계의) off guard.

비범하다 [बीबौमहादा] [非凡-] extraordinary; uncommon; unique; unusual; remarkable; prodigious. e.g.

비범한 사람 a man of unusual ability / (천재) a genius.

비법 [बीबौल] [秘法]a secret method [process]; a mystique; a mystery; (약의) a secret recipe [for-mula]. e.g. 비법을 전수 하다 initiate <a person> into the mysteries [secrets]

비보 [बीबो] [悲報] [슬픈 소식] sad news; [사망 소식] a death notice. e.g.

비비다 [बीबीदा1] [문지르다] rub; scrub (박박); grate; [비벼서 떼내다] scrape. e.g. 양손을 비비다 rub one's hands together. **2** [버무리다] mix <food>. e.g. 밥을 비비다 mix boiled rice with subsidiary articles of diet / make(a) hash (with rice).

비빔밥[बीबिम्पाप] boiled rice with assorted mixtures.

비상 [बीसांग] [非常] **1** [보통이 아님] being extraor-dinary; unusualness; exce-ssiveness; uncommonness. 비상하다 extraordinary; out of the ordinary; unusual; uncommon; remarkable; exceptional; excessive; ex-treme; immense. e.g. 비상한 솜씨 remarkable [exce-ptional] ability / unusual [uncommon / great] skill. **2** [이변, 긴급] a con-tingency; an emer-gency; an unlooked-for event. e.g. 비상에 대비 하다 prepare for the worst.

비상시 [बीसांगसी] [非常時] an emergency; a crisis. e.g. 비상시에 in case of emergency / in an emer-gency.

비서 [बीसो] [秘書] [요직자 밑에서 기밀문서 등의 용무를 맡은 사람] a (private) secretary.

비석 [बीसोक] [碑石] [묘비] a tombstone; a graves-tone; a stone; [기념비] a (stone) monument; [考] a stele.

비스듬하다 बीसुदुमहादा slant (ing); sloping; skew; obli-que; diagonal.

비슷하다 [बीसुतहादा] [거의 같다] similar; (a) like; resembling. e.g. … 과 비슷한 데가 있다 there is something that resembles

비싸다 [बीसादा] [상품의 값이 너무 많다] dear; expen-sive; costly; high in price; high-priced. e.g. 비싼 값 a high price.

비아냥거리다 [बीआन्यांगगोरिदा] make cynical remarks; be sarcastic <about>. e.g. 그는 내게 비아냥거렸다 He made insinuations against [insinuating re-marks about] me.

비애 [बीऐ] [悲哀] [슬픔] sorrow; grief; sadness; misery; pathos.

비약 [बीयाक] [飛躍] **1** [뛰어

오름] a jump; a leap. 비약하다 jump; leap. **2** [활약] activity. 비약하다 be active; play an active part. **3** [빠른 진보P향상] rapid progress. e.g. 비약적으로 진보하다 make rapid progress. 이제 우리는 일대 비약을 할 때이다 Now is the time for us to take a great leap forward. **4** (논리 등의) a jump. e.g. 당신의 말에는 논리의 비약이 있다 There's a gap in your reasoning. / There's an illogical jump in what you say. 비약하다 fly; jump. e.g. 화제는 개에서 골프로 비약했다 The conversation jumped from dogs to golf.

비옥 [बीओक] [肥沃] fertility; richness <of the soil>. 비옥하다 fertile; rich; productive; fruitful

비옷 [बीउत] a raincoat; a mac (k) intosh (고무를 입힌).

비용 [बीयोंग] [費用] [지출] an expense; [특정한 사물에 출비하는 금액] expenses; [특정한 값에 대하여 지불된 돈] a cost; [경비] costs.

비우다 [बीउदा] **1** [비게 하다] empty <a box, a glass, etc.>; exhaust <the water in a vessel>; clear out the contents of. e.g. 상자를 비우다 **2** (점유지, 건물을) vacate; evacuate; (외출하여) leave <one's house> empty; [쓰지 않고 빈 채로 두다] leave <a house> vacant; leave <a place> clear; hold <a position> open <for a person>.

비운 [बीउन] [非運] misfortune; ill [hard] lu.

비웃다 [बीउतता] sneer <at>; be cynical <about>; [조롱하다] jeer <at>; [짓궂게 놀리다] ridicule; [흉내내며 조소하다] mock; [빈정거리다] be sarcastic <about>. e.g. 세상을 비웃다 mock [satirize] the world.

비웃음 [बीउस्‌अम] a sardonic [cynical / scornful] smile [laugh]; a mocking laughter; a sneer; ridicule. e.g. 비웃음을 사다 incur [excite] ridicule / bring [draw] ridicule upon oneself.

비위 [बीवी] [脾胃] **1** [기호] taste; liking; palate; choice. e.g. 비위에 맞는 음식 a favorable food. **2**[기분] humor; temper; mood. e.g. 비위를 맞추기 힘든 사람 a person hard to please.

비유 [बीयू] [比喩, 譬喩] a figure of speech; a simile (직유); a metaphor (은유); [우화] an allegory; a parable.

비율 [बीयूल] [比率] (a) ratio; (a) percentage; rate; proportion.

비일비재 [बीईलबीजै] [非一非再] 비일비재하다 frequent; repeated; <서술적> occur othen. e.g. 그런 일은 비일비재하다 It is just one of those common things. / It is of frequent occurrence.

비자 [बीजा] a visa; vis

비장, [बीजांग] 悲壯 비장 하다 pathetic; touching; tragic. e.g. 비장한 각오 a tragic but brave resolution / a tragic decision in one's mind / a heroic resolve.

비전 [बीजोन] (a) vision; foresight. e.g. 비전이 있는 사람 a foresighted person.

비정, [बीजोंग] [非情 [인정이 없음]. 비정하다 unfeeling; heartless; cold-hearted. e.g. 비정한 사람 a cold-hearted person.

비정규 [बीजोंग] [非正規] 비정규의 irregular.

비좁다 [बीजोपदा] narrow; confined; cramped; incomemodious. e.g. 비좁은 집 a narrow [cramped] house

비중 [बीजुंग] [比重] [중요성의 정도] relative importance. e.g. 시험 결과보다 출석에 비중을 두다 place more weight on students' attendance than no examination results.

비즈니스 [बीजनेस] [사업, 영업] business.

비지땀 [बीजीताम] beads of sweat; heavy sweat. e.g. 비지땀을 흘리다 sweat heavily / perspire profusely / get into a profuse [heavy] perspiration / sweat one's guts out.

비집다 [बीजीपदा] [틈내다] split open; [벌리다] pull [force] open; spread apart. e.g. 비집어 열다 wrench [pry / prize] open / break [force] open. 비집고 들어가 wedge (oneself) in [into] / thrust [squeeze] oneself in [into].

비참 [बीछम] [悲慘] misery; wretchedness. 비참하다 [몹시도 불행하다] miserable <surroundings>; wretched; [가엾게 보이다] pitiable; [가련하다] pathetic <stories>; [비극적 이다] tragic <events / death>. e.g. 비참한 광경 a pathetic [horrible] sight.

비추다 [बीछुदा] **1** [빛을 보내다, 빛을 받게 하다] shine on; shed [throw] (a) light on; flash <on>; light (up). e.g. 불빛을 비추다 flash a beam <on a thing> / light up <the dark corner>. **2** [빛이 통하게 하다] old (up) <a thing> to [before / against] the light. e.g. 나는 지폐를 불빛에 비추어 보았다 I looked at the bill [note] through the light.

비축 [बीछुग] [備蓄] saving for [against] emergency; storing; a stock <of

ㅂ

goods>. 비축하다 store; stockpile; save for emergency.

비치 [बीछी] [**備置**] equipment; provision; fitting. e.g. 교무실의 비치 도서 books kept in the teacher's room. 비치하다 [설비하다] furnish; provide <with>; equip <a factory with machinery>; fit; install <a telephone>; [준비해 놓다] keep [have] <a thing> ready.

비치다 [बीछीदा] **1** (빛이) shine <in / into / upon>. e.g. 쨍쨍 비치다 blaze away. **2**[투영하다] be reflected; be imaged; be mirrored; be projected; fall [be thrown] upon. e.g. 텔레비전에 비친 그의 얼굴 his face (projected) on the television. **3** [인상을 주다] impress; [···으로 보이다] appear <to>. e.g. 좋게 비치다 impress <another> favorably [in one's favor] / leave a favorable impression on <a person's mind> / give <another> a favorable impression. **4** [투시되다] show through; be seen through; be transparent. e.g. 훤히 비치는 transparent / clear / limpid. 살이

비켜나다 [बीख्यौनादा] step [move] aside <from>; sidestep; step back; get out of the way <of>; (자리를) retire; withdraw.

비켜서다 [बीख्यौसोदा] stand [move] aside; step back [aside]. e.g. 뛰어서 비켜서다 spring [jump] aside

비키다 [बीख्रीदा] **1** (길을) move (out of the way); make room [way] <for>; get out of the way <of>; stand clear of <the door>; (옆으로) step [move] aside <from>; sidestep; move off; (뒤로) step back; [피하다] dodge; make a dodge; turn aside. **2**[옮기다] move <a thing> aside. e.g. 의자를 조금만 비켜 주시겠습니까 Will you please move your chair a little aside? **3** (자리를) retire; withdraw. e.g. 자리를 좀 비켜 주시겠습니까 Would you kindly leave me [us] alone?

비타민 [बीथामीन] vitamins

비탄 [बीथान] [**悲嘆**] grief <over / about / for>; deep sorrow <for / over>; anguish; lamentation. e.g. 그녀는 비탄으로 거의 미칠 지경이었다 She was driven almost insane by grief. / She went nearly mad with grief. 비탄하다 grieve; mourn; sorrow <over / on>; lament; deplore.

비탈 [बीथाल] (오르막, 내리막의) a slope; an incline; a hill; (오르막) an upward slope; an ascent; an acclivity; (내리막) a downward slope; a descent; a declivity. e.g. 완만한 [가파른] 비탈 a gentle [steep] slope [incline

비통 [बीथोंग] [**悲痛**] intense grief; bitterness; pathos. 비통하다 sad; grievous; sorrowful; bitter; touching; affecting; pathetic. e.g. 비통한 마음을 안고 with bitter grief in one's heart.

비틀거리다 [बीथुल्कौरीदा] [이리저리 쓰러질 듯이 걷다] totter; (균형을 잃고) stagger; (현기증 등으로) reel; (발이 물건에 걸려) stumble; trip <against / over / on>. e.g. 돌부리에 걸려 비틀거리며 넘어지다 stumble [trip] over a stone and fall.

비틀다 [बीथुल्दा] **1** (손으로) twist; give <a rope> a twist; wrench; screw; wring; wrest; distort; warp. e.g. 사과 꼭지를 가지에서 비틀어 따다 wrench an apple off a branch. **2** [몸을 틀다] twist; bend. e.g. 허리를 비틀다 twist one's body at the waist. 그 선수는 몸을 1회전 반 비튼 다음에 착지했다 The athlete landed ather doing one and a half twists.

비틀어지다 बीथुरौजिदा1 [꼬이다] get twisted [distorted]; grow warped. e.g. 날씨가 가물어서 비틀어진 판자 a board warped by dry weather. **2** (마음이) become perverse; get crooked.**3** (일이) go wrong [amiss]; be spoilt; be ruined.

비판 [बीफान] [**批判**] (a) criticism; (a) comment; (a) critique; (a) forum <*pl.* ~ s, fora>. 비판하다 [비평하다] criticize <for>; [논평하다] comment <on> (▷ criticism, criticize 는 종종 [혹평]의 뜻으로 씀); pass judgment <upon>.

비평 [बीफ्यौग] [**批評**] [비판] (a) criticism; (a) critique; [논평] (a) comment; [신문, 잡지 등에 실리는 단평] a notice (▷ mixed notices, rave notices 처럼 복수형으로 쓰는 일이 많음). 비평하다 [비판하 다] criticize [criticise] <for>(▷ that 절은 쓰지 않음); [논평하다] comment <on>; [서평을 쓰다] review; [감상을 말하다] remark <that / on>.

비품 [बीफुम] [**備品**] <집합적> equipment; [부착된 것] fixtures; [비치 하는 가구] furnishings. e.g. 부엌의 비품 kitchen fixtures. 사무용 비품 office equipment [appointments]. 실험실의 비품 laboratory [lab] equipment.

비하 [बीहा] [**卑下**] [자신을

낮춤] abasement; self-humbling; [땅이 낮음] low level of ground; [지위가 낮음] low standing [position]; humbleness. 비하하다 disparage oneself.

비하다 [बीहादा] [**比-**] compare <one thing> with [to] <another>. e.g. 비할 수 없을 만큼 beyond (all) comparison.

비합리 [बीहापनी] [**非合理**] irrationality. e.g. 비합리 적인 irrational / unreaso-nable.

비합법 [बीहापपोब] [**非合法**] illegality. e.g. 비합법적(인) illegal / unlawful / out of order.

비행 [बीहैंग] [못된 행위] misconduct; misdeed; misdemeanor; an evil deed; an irregularity; a malpractice; wrongdoing. e.g. 청소년의 비행 juvenile delinquency

비행 [बीहैंग] [**飛行**] a flight; flying; [항공] a plane flight; aviation; aerial navigation; air voyage 비행하다 fly (in the air); make a flight; take the air; travel by air; aviate.

비행기 [बीहैंगी] [**飛行機**] [항공기] an airplane; a plane; an aeroplane; <집합적> aircrath.

빈곤 [बीनगोन] [**貧困**] [가난] indigence; poverty; pauperism; [궁핍] need; want; destitution; [결여] lack; dearth; shortage. e.g. 사상의 빈곤 poverty of ideas.

빈궁 [बीनगुंग] [**貧窮**] 빈곤

빈도 [बीनदो] [**頻度**] frequency. e.g. 높은 사용 빈도 hight frequency of use.

빈둥거리다 [बीनदुंगगोरिदा] loaf [idle / laze / dawdle / snooze] one's time away; loaf; idle; loiter; lounge; be on the loaf; lead an idle life. e.g. 빈둥거리고 있을 때가 아니다 This is no time for idling.

빈말 [बीनमाल] [실속이 없는 말] (an) idle [empty] talk; an empty promise; empty prattle; empty [hollow / vain] words; lip service. e.g. 빈말로 하는 칭찬 empty words of praise / empty [hollow / idle / mere] compliments / flummery

빈민 [बीनमीन] [**貧民**] poor people; the poor; paupers; the needy; the indigent; poverty-stricken people.

빈방 [बीनबांग] [**-房**] (비어 있는) a vacancy; a vacant room; (사람이 없는) an empty room; [셋방] a room for rent [to let]. e.g. 빈방 없음 (호텔 입구에 붙는 게시) No vacancies.

빈번하다 [बीनबौनहादा] **繁-, 頻煩-**] frequent; incessant. e.g. 교통이 빈번한 거리 a busy [bustling] street / a street with heavy traffic.

빈부 [बीनबू] [**貧富**] [가난과 부유] wealth and poverty.

e.g. 빈부의 차가 심하다 There is a tremendous gap between the rich and the poor.

빈속 [बीनसोक] an empty stomach. e.g. 빈속에 술을 마시다 have a drink on an empty stomach.

빈손 [बीनसोन] empty hands. e.g. 그는 빈손으로 나갔다 He went out empty-handed. / He wasn't carrying anything when he went out.

빈약 [बीनयाक] [貧弱] poorness; scantiness; meagerness. 빈약하다 poor; scanty; meager; limited

빈자리 [बीनजारी] **1** [빈 좌석] a vacant [an unoccupied] seat; [여지] room. e.g. 빈자리가 눈에 띄었다 There were a conspicuous number of vacant seats. **2** [결원] a vacancy; an opening; a vacant post. **3** [여백] a space; a blank. e.g. 빈자리가 많은 페이지 a short page.

빈정거리다 [बीनजौंगौरीदा] [놀리다] poke fun at; make fun [sport] of; tease; banter; ridicule; gibe; [비 꼬다] speak ironically; make cynical [caustic / sarcastic] remarks; be cynical [sarcastic] <about>; insinuate; take a dig <at>.

빈집 [बीनजीप] [비어 있는 집] a vacant [an empty] house; [사람이 살지 않는 집] an unoccupied [an uninhabited / untenanted] house.

빈칸 [बीनख्वान] a blank column; a blank (space).

빈터 [बीन्थौ] [공지] vacant land; an open space; [건물이없는땅] unoccupied ground; a vacant lot.

빈털터리 [बीनथौल्थौरी] a penniless person; a fellow without a penny; a person destitute of money.

빈틈 [बीनथुम] **1** [벌어진 틈] a gap; an opening; a crack; a chink; an aperture; [여백] a space; a blank; [여지] room; space. e.g. 빈틈없이 closely / compactly / leaving no space (between them). **2** [허술하거나 부족한 점] unpreparedness; a blind side; an unguarded moment [point]; an opening (for attack); [부주의] inattention; carelessness; imprudence; unwatchfulness; incautiousness; [방심] a slip; an oversight; inadvertence.

빌다[1] [बीलदा] 빌리다

빌다[2] [बीलदा] **1** [구걸하다] beg; ask; [간청하다] solicit; plead <for>; appeal <for>. e.g. 밥을 빌다 beg one's bread / beg food. **2** [기원하다] pray <to

God>; invoke; supplicate; wish; entreat. e.g. 두 손 모아 빌다 pray with folded [joined] hands **3**[사과하다] ask [beg] <a person's> pardon; apologize <a person> for; make [beg] an apology <to a person>. e.g. 용서를 빌다 beg [implore] forgiveness / ask [seek] <for> forgiveness.

빌딩 **[बीलदीग]** a building; an office building.

빌리다 **[बीललीदा]** **1** [차용하다] borrow; have [get] the loan <of>; [대여하다] lend; loan; advance <money>; accomodate <a person with money>; spare. e.g. 빌려 주는 사람 a lender. **2** [임대하다] hire [let] out <carriages and horses by the day>; (토지를) lease; let out <land> on lease; (가옥,토지 등을) let <one's house for the winter>; rent <a house to a person>; rent out <a mansion>. e.g. 토지를 빌려 주다 lease [rent] land. **3**[남의 도움을 받다] have [get] <a person's> help [aid]; enlist the help of; employ <a person's> assistance. e.g. 다수의 힘을 빌려서 on the strength of majority.

빗 **[बीत]** a comb

빗금 **[बीक्कुम]** an oblique (line); a slant (line); (and / or 경우의) a slanting stroke; a slash (mark); a virgule.

빗기다 **[बीक्कीदा]1**[빗어주다] comb <a person's hair>. e.g. 동생의 머리를 빗기다 comb one's (younger) sister's hair. **2**[빗게 하다] get someone to comb <a person's hair>. e.g. 하녀에게 개털을 빗기다 have the maid comb the dog.

빗나가다 **[बीन्नागादा]** (총알 등이) miss; go wide [astray]; miss the mark; dart aside; (계획 등이) go wrong [amiss]; miscarry; fail; (이야기 등이) deviate [diverge] <from>; wander <from>.

빗다 **[बीत्ता]** comb <a person's hair>; pull [run] a comb through <a person's hair>; (양털, 삼 등을) card. e.g. 잘 빗은 머리 well-combed hair.

빗대다 **[बीत्तैदा]** [빙 둘러서 말하다] have a sly dig <at>; make an insinuating remark <at>; hint (obliquely) at; give an indirect cut; insinuate; satirize; satirise. e.g. 그의 말은 실은 나를 빗대어 하는 말이다 He is really talking at me. / His remark is intended for me [a cut at me / directed at me].

빗맞다 **[बीम्मात्ता]** **1** [목표와 다른 곳에 맞다] miss the

mark; go wide of the mark; glance off. e.g. 어뢰가 빗맞았다 The torpedo missed its mark [went wild]. **2** [뜻한 일이 잘못 되다] go wrong [awry / amiss]; miscarry; backfire; misfire; be baffled.

빗발 [बीप्पाल] streaks of rain; lines traced by rain as it falls. e.g. 빗발이 날리기 시작했다 It began to rain. / It started raining.

빗방울 बीप्पांगुल a raindrop

빗자루 [बीच्चारू] (쓰는) a broom; a besom.

빗줄기 [बीच्चुल्गी] great streaks [sheets] of rain. e.g. 빗줄기가 세차다 It pours down. / It rains cats and dogs.

빗질 [बीच्चील] combing <one's hair>. 빗질하다 comb <one's hair>. e.g. 엉킨 머리카락을 빗질하여 풀다 comb [brush] the knots [tangles] out of one's hair.

빙 [बीग] **1** [한 바퀴 도는 모양] round; around. e.g. 섬을 한 바퀴 빙 돌다 go round the island / make a tour of the island. **2**[둘러싼 모양] (all) round; in a circle. e.g. 빙 둘러싸다 surround <a person / a thing> / encircle / shut in on all sides. **3**[아찔해지는 모양]. e.g. 머리가 빙 돌다 get dizzy [giddy] / one's head swims [spins] / be stunned (얻어맞고).

빙그레 [बीगुरीदा] with a smile; smilingly; beamingly; with a beaming face. e.g. 빙그레 웃다 smile / beam <upon a person> / beam with [break into] a smile.

빙그르르 [बीगुरूरू] <turn / skate / glide> around smoothly. e.g. 빙판을 한 바퀴 빙그르르 돌다 take a smooth turn around the ice.

빙글빙글 [बीगगूलबीगगूल] [도는 모양] round and round smoothly. e.g. 빙글빙글 돌다 [돌리다] turn round and round / spin / twirl.

빙빙 [बीगबीग] round and round; repeatedly. e.g. 자리에서 일어서자 나는 머리가 빙빙 돌았다 My head swam [I felt dizzy] when I stood up.

빙수 [बीगसू] [氷水] [잘게 부순 얼음에 설탕과 감미료를 섞은 음료] shaved ice with syrup. e.g. 빙수 한 그릇 a bowl of shaved ice with sugar syrup.

빙하 [बीगहा] [氷河] a glacier

빚 [बीत] **1**[남에게 갚아야 할 돈] a debt; a loan; liabilities; what one owes. e.g. 엄청난 빚 a heap of debts / a mammoth debt. **2** [남에게 입은 은혜]. e.g. 당신에게는 많은빚을 지고 있습니다 I am much indebted to you.

ㅂ

빚내다 [बीन्नैदा] borrow money <from>; get [float] a loan; obtain a loan <from>.

빚다 [बीत्ता] **1** (술을) brew; ferment; distil. e.g. 술을 빚다 brew rice wine. **2** (송편 등을) shape dough for <rice cakes>; roll into balls <as dumplings>. **3**(어떤 부정적인 사태를) bring about [on]; give rise to; cause; breed; engender.

빚지다 [बीच्चीदा] Fall [run / get] into debt; contract [incur] a debt [loan]; owe. e.g. 많이 빚지다 make a lot of debts.

빛 [बीत] **1** [광명] (a) light; [광선] a ray; a beam; [섬광] a flash; a gleam (어둠 속의); [광휘] a luster; radiance; twinkle (별의); a sparkle (보석 등의); a glitter; (희미한) a glimmer. **2** [표정이나 몸가짐에 나타나는 안색, 태도] complexion; color; a look; an expression; an air; a sign; a mark; an indication. **3**[희망] hope; a bright future [prospect]. e.g. 희망의 빛 a ray [gleam] of hope.

빛깔 [बीक्काल] a color; a hue; a shade; a tint; a tinge (색조).

빛나다 [बीन्नादा] **1** [비치다, 번쩍이다] shine; be bright [brilliant]; be radiant; be luminous; glitter (금은 등이); glimmer (희미하게); gleam (어둠속에서); glisten (반사하여); glint; beam; twinkle (별이); sparkle (보석 등이) [번득 이다]; flash; [윤이 나다] be lustrous [glossy]. e.g. 하늘에 빛나는 별 twinkling stars in the sky / stars sparkling in the heavens. **2**[영광이 드러나 다] be glorious [splendid]; shine brilliantly. e.g. 빛나는 장래 promising future / bright prospects.

빛내다 [बीन्नैदा] [빛나게 하다] light up; make <a thing> shine; brighten; [광을 내다] luster; give luster <to>; gloss; glaze; polish up; burnish; [영광 스럽게 하다] bring glory [fame / distinction] to; glorify. e.g. 국위를 빛내다 enhance (the) national prestige / bring glory to one's country.

사[1] [सा] [四] four. e.g. 사차원 the fourth dimension.

사[2] [सा) [社] [회사, 신문사 등을 줄이어 칭하는 말] a company; a corporation; a firm; [사무

소] an office. e.g. 신문사 a newspaper publishing company / a newspaper office.

사각거리다 [साग्गाक्कौरिदा] crunch; crisp; be crisp; eat crisp [brittle / short]. e.g. 사과 씹는 소리처럼 사각거리다 be as crisp as the munch of an apple.

사각형 [सागाख्यौंग] [四角形] a quadrangle; [사변형 a quadrilateral; a tetragon.

사건 [सागौन] [事件] [주목을 끌 만한 일큰] an event; (우발적인) a happening; (작은) an incident; (문제가 되는) a matter; an affair; (살인 도난 등의) a case; [사고] an accident; [음모] a plot; [말썽] complications; a trouble; a difficulty; [추문] a scandal.

사격 [साग्यौक] [射擊] [표적을 향해 총을 쏨] target [rifle] practice; shooting; firing; fire; gunshot.

사고 [सागो] [事故] [나쁜 사건] an accident; [비교적 작은 불행한 사건] mishap; [진행 등의 뜻하지 않은 지장] a hitch; an incident; an untoward event; a crack-up; trouble.

사고뭉치 [सागो मुंछी] [事故-] a trouble maker.

사공 [सागोंग] [沙工] [뱃사공] a boatman; a skipper; a waterman; the master of a junk; a ferryman (나룻배의)

사과 1 [साग्वा] [沙果] [사과나무의 열매] an apple.

사과 2 [साग्वा] [謝過] an apology <for>. 사과 하다 lapologize; make an apology [excuse] <for>; beg [ask] pardon <of a person>; offer <a person> an apology; beg <a person's> forgiveness <for>; express regret <for>

사교 [साग्यो] [社交] social contact; society; social intercourse; social life; the social round.

사교성 [साग्योसौंग] [社交性] sociability; sociality; a social nature.

사귀다 [सागुइदा] [친하게 되다 make friends <with>; become [get] acquainted <with>; strike up a friendship [an acquaintance] <with>; [교제하다] keep company with; associate with; hold intercourse with. e.g. 남자[여자]를 사귀다 become involved with a man [woman] / have [take] a lover [mistress].

사그라지다 [सागुराजीदा] go down; subside; recede;

wither; (썩어서) rot away; decompose; (녹슬어서) rust away; (녹아서) melt away; (종기 등이) resolve; be resolved.

사극 [साग्युग] [史劇] [역사극] a historical play [drama].

사근사근하다 [साग्युनसाग्युनहादा] (성품이) affable; amiable; agreeable; pleasant; pleasing; engaging; companionable; compliant; sweet and gentle. e.g. 사근사근한 사람 an affable person

사기 [साग्गी] [士氣] morale; fighting spirit. e.g. 사기가 왕성하다 have high morale / be full of fighting spirit.

사기 [साग्गी] [詐欺] trickery; a swindle; a trick; [신용거래에서의 협잡] a confidence trick [game]; (a) fraud; swindling; a swindle; a hoaK <文> (an) imposture; (승부에서의) foul play. e.g. 사기를 치다 play a trick <on a person> / swindle / practice deception <on a person> / [부정을 하다] do something crooked / (승부에서) play foul [dirty] / cheat. 나는 사기를 당해 돈을 빼앗겼다 I was swindled out of my money.

사나이 [सानाइ] [남자] a male; a man; the male [sterner] sex.

사납다 [सानाप्ता] fierce <animal>; rough [heavy] <sea>; rude; wild <waves>; harsh; violent; outrageous; ferocious; savage; truculent; (운수가) unlucky. e.g. 사나운 짐 승 a wild animal / a fierce beast.

사내 [सानै] 사내대장부 a man / a great man.

사냥 [सान्यांग] [수렵] hunting; a hunt; [총사냥] shooting. 냥하다 hunt; have a hunt; shoot.

사냥꾼 [सान्यांगकुन] [사냥하는 사람] a hunter; a huntsman (영국에서 hunter 는 사냥에 쓰는 말); a huntress (여자); a sportsman.

사다 [सादा] **1** [구입하다] buy; purchase (▷ 격식차린 말). e.g. 귤을 1 개 100 원에사다 buy oranges at one hundred won a piece. **2** [초 래하다] incur; invite; evoke; bring [draw] upon oneself. e.g. 그는 상사의 노여움을 샀다 He incurred his superior's displeasure.

사다리 [सादारी] 사대주의 worship of the powerful; flunkeyism; toadyism; a trimming policy. **사돈** a member of the family of one's daughter-[son-]

in-law; a relative [relation] by marriage; in-laws.

사라지다 [साराजीदा] disappear; go away; vanish; fade (away); die away [out / off]; go out of sight; go (물건, 아픔, 희망, 구름 등이); fall (빛, 소리, 냄새 등이); be gone.

사람 1 [इल्ल्यू] [인류] man; mankind. **2** [개 개의 사람] a person; (남자) a man; (여자) a woman. **3** [세상 사람] people; men; [남들] another; others; other people.

사랑 [सारांग] love; (지속적이고 잔잔한) affection; [애착] attachment; tender passion [sentiment]. 사랑하다 love; [친애하는 감정을 가지다] have an affection for; be fond of; [애착을 느끼다] be attached to; set one's affection on; have a tender feeling <toward>.

사려 [सार्यौं] [주의깊은 생각] thought; [고려] consideration; prudence; discretion; (good) sense. 사려 깊은 [주의를 기울이는, 남의 사정을 헤아리는] thoughtful / considerate / [신중한] prudent / discreet / [분별있는] sensible / judicious / well-advised.

사례 1 [शाल्लये] [事例] [실례] an example; an instance; a case; [전례] a precedent.

사례 2 [शाल्लये] [謝禮] [감사] thanks; gratitude; acknowledgment; appreciation; [보수] a reward; (a) remuneration; (의사, 변호사 등의) a fee; (강연 등 지적 봉사에 대한) an honorarium <*pl.* ~s, -ria>; a recompense; a consideration; a recognition. 사례하다 reward; remunerate; recompense; give a reward; pay a fee to; fee.

사로잡다 1 [सारोजाप्ता] [생포하다] catch [take / capture] <animal> alive; capture <a person>; take <a person> prisoner [captive]. e.g. 토끼를 사로잡다 catch [capture] a hare alive. **2** [생각, 마음을 한쪽으로 쏠리게 하다] captivate; enslave; seize; win; enthrall; hold in thrall. e.g. 여자의 마음을 사로잡다 win a woman's heart [hand].

사로잡히다 1 [붙잡히다] be caught [seized / taken] alive; be captured; be taken [led] prisoner [captive]. **2** [생

각, 마음이 매혹되다] be fascinated [captivated] by; be a captive to; be enslaved by; be a slave to; [얽매이다] be a slave to; stick [adhere] to; be shackled by; be prepossessed by [with]; (격한 감정 등에) be seized [stricken] with

사료 [सार्यो] (일반적인) feed; provender; [마소 의 여물] fodder; [목장 의 목초] forage.

사리 [सारी] reason; facts; propriety. e.g. 사리를 (분별할 줄) 아는 사람 a man of (good) sense / a sensible man / an enlightened person / a fair-minded

사립 [सारी] [私立] e.g. 사립의 private / non-governmental.

사막 [सामाक] [沙莫,砂莫] a desert.

사망 [सामांग] [死亡] death; decease; demise; passing (away). 사망하다 die; pass away.

사망자 [सामांग्जा] [死亡者] a dead person; <집합 적> the dead; [특정 고인] the deceased (▷ 단수, 복수 취급); (사고 등에 의한) persons killed; deaths.

사면 초가 [साम्यौन छोगा] [四面楚歌] e.g. 그들은 사면 초가였다 They had the whole world against them. / They were surrounded by enemies [foes] on all sides. / They were forsaken by everybody.

사명 [साम्यौंग] [使命] [맡겨진 임무] an appointed task; [천직] a calling; a vocation; [사자 (使者) 로서 받은 명령] a mission. e.g. 사명을 다하다 accomplish [execute / perform / fulfill / discharge] one's mission.

사모 [सामो] [思慕] [그리워함] longing <for>; yearning <for>; deep attachment. 사모하다 long [pine] for; love; yearn ather; have a deep attachment <to>. e.g. 그는 내 누이를 사모하고 있다 He is very much attached to my sister.

사모님 [सामोनिम] [師母-] **1** [스승의 부인] one's teacher's wife. **2** [남의 부인에 대한 경칭] madam; your (good) lady; Mrs.; your ladyship; milady.

사무 [सामू] [事務] 주로 책상에서 처리하는 일] clerical work; desk work [job]; office work [jobs / labor]; [실무] business; [업무] affairs.

사무치다 [सामूछिदा] pierce;

penetrate; come [go] home to <one>; be brought home to <one>; strike <one> home. e.g. 가슴에 사무치다 pierce [come home to] one's heart / go to one's heart / cut one to the heart / sting one to the quick / sink deep in one's mind.

사물 [सामुल] [**私物**] one's (private) property; one's personal effects.

사물 [सामुल] [**事物**] things; affairs; a matter.

사뭇 [सामुत] **1** [거리낌없이 마구] as one pleases [likes / wishes]; willfully; foolhardily. e.g. 술을 마시면 사뭇 시부렁거리게 된다 Wine loosens people's tongues. **2** [줄곧] without break; all through. e.g. 한 달 내내 사뭇 바빴다 I was busy all through the month. **3** [매우] wholly; utterly; very (much); quite. e.g. 생각했던 것과는 사뭇 다르다 It is quite different from what I thought

사발 [साबाल] [**沙鉢**] a (china) bowl.

사방 [साबांग] [**四方**] the four quarters; four sides; all directions.

사법 [साप्पोप] [**司法**] [재판, 법무의 운용] the administration of justice; judicature.

사별 [साब्यौल] separation by death; bereavement. 사별하다 be bereaved <of one's husband>; be separated from <one's parents> by death.

사복 [साबोक] [**私服**] [관복, 제복이 아닌 보통 옷] plain [ordinary] clothes; private [civilian] clothes; civvies; muthi (군인 등의).

사본 [साबोन] [**寫本**] a copy; a transcript (등사물); a duplicate (부본); [필사본] a (book in) manuscript (略 MS); a written copy.

사부 [साबू] [**師父**] = 스승.

사비 [साबि] [**私費**] one's own expense; private expense.

사뿐 [सापुन] sothly; lightly; with a soth step.

사사롭다 [सासारोप्ता] personal; private; informal. e.g. 사사로운 감정[일] personal feeling [affairs].

사살 [सासाल] [**射殺**] 사살하다 kill by shooting; shoot <a person> dead [to death].

사상 [सासांग] [**想**] [सासांग] thought; an idea; [이데올로기] an ideology.

사상자 [सासांगजा] [**死傷者**] casualties; the killed and the injured [wounded]; losses.

사색 [सासैक] [**思索**] speculation; thinking; cogitation; contemplation; meditation. 하다 think; muse [speculate / meditate] on; contemplate (on); cogitate; ponder.

사생활 [सासैंगहवाल] [**私生活**] one's private life.

사서 [सासौ] [**司書**] a librarian.

사석 [सासौक] [**私席**] an informal [an unofficial / a private] occasion.

사선 [सासौन] [**斜線**] = 빗금 사선을 그은 부분 the shaded portion.

사설 [सासौल] [**私設**] e.g. 사설의 private.

사설 [सासौल] [**辭說**] **1** [언사] words; speech; [기술한 글] (a) des-cryption; an account; (노래, 연극 사이의) narration; description. **2** [잔소리] tattering; babbling; prattling; [불평] grumbling; nagging.

사슬 [**सासल**] **사슬** a chain; (개를 매는) a tether. **사슬고리** [**सासल गोरि**] a link.

사슴 [**सासम**] a deer

사실 [साशिल] [**事實**] **1** [실제의 일] a fact; an actual fact; a reality; actuality (현실); [法] a factum <*pl.* –ta>; [진실] the truth; the case. e.g. 그 소문은 사실과 다르다 The rumor is contrary to the fact. **2** [실제로] actually; really; [사실인즉] in fact; [실은] as a matter of fact. e.g. 그는 괴짜라는 평이 있는데 사실 그렇다 He is said to be eccentric and he really is.

사실주의 [साशिलजूउइ] [**寫實主義**] realism; literalism.

사심 [साशिम] [**私心**] selfishness; a selfish motive; self–interest.

사십 [साशिप] [**四十**] forty; [제 40] the fortieth. 사십대의 사람 a person in his forties.

사악 [साआक] [**邪惡**] wickedness; [악덕] vice. 사악하다 [도덕에 어긋나다] wicked; evil; [악의가 있다] malicious; vicious.

사양 [सायांग] [**辭讓**] [양보] declining in favor of another; concession; [사절] courteous refusal [declination / denial]; refusal with appreciation; [삼감] reserve; restraint; deference; modesty; holding back. 사양하다 [양보하다] decline <something> in favor of another; give way to <another>; make room for <another>; concede; make a concession;

사업 [साऔप] [**事業**] **1** [기업] an enterprise; [실업] an industry; a business. **2** [일] work; [인계받은 또는 꾸민 일] an undertaking; [계획적인 일] a project. e.g. 사회 [교육 / 자선] 사업 social [educational / charitable] work. **3** [업적] an achievement; a deed. e.g. 큰 사업을 이룩하다 do [achieve] a great thing.

사연 [सायौन] [**事緣**] [사정] circumstances; considerations; the state of things [matters / affairs]; [연유] the matter; the case; the story. e.g. 말 못할 사연이 있어서 for some secret [inexpressible] reasons.

사연 [सायौन] [**辭緣**] [내용] content(s); [취지] the import; the gist; the point. e.g. 편지 사연은 무엇이냐 What is the letter about?

사용 [सायोंग] [**使用**] use; employment; application (응용); consumption (소비) appropriation (충당) 사용하다 use; make use of; put <a thing> to use; (도구, 수단 등을) employ; apply; consume; appropriate; devote.

사용료 [सायोंगन्यो] [**使用料**] a rental fee; the rental; the rent; the hire.

사용법 [सायोंगबौप] [**使用法**] how to use [handle / treat]; usage; directions (for use) (약 등의)

사우나 [साउना] [증기 목욕] a sauna.

사운드 [साउन्द] [음향] a sound.

사원 [सावन] [**社員**] an employee; a member of the staff <of a company>; a partner (조합원); <집합적> the staff.

사원 [सावन] [**寺院**] a (Buddhist) temple; (기독교의) a temple; a church; a monastery (수도원); (회교의) a mosque.

사월 [सावौल] [**四月**] April (略 Apr.).

사위 [सावि] a son-in-law <*pl.* sons-in-law>.

사유 [सायु] [**私有**] [개인의 소유 또는 소유 물] private possession. e.g. 사유의 privately owned / private.

사유 [सायु] [**事由**] a reason; a cause; a ground; conditions. ⇨ 이유[इयु]

사유 재산 [सायु जैसान] [**私有財産**] private property.

사육 [सायुक] [**飼育**] breeding [raising] <of cattle>; earing. 사육하

다 breed; raise.

사의 [साउइ] [**辭意**] [사임 할 의사] one's resolution [intention] to resign. e.g. 사의를 비추다 [표명하다] intimate [announce] one's intention of resigning <from one's office>.

사이 [साइ] **1** [공간] an interval; (a) distance; a space; [틈] a gap; an opening; [둘 사이] between; [여럿 사이] among(st); [한가운데] amid(st); [중도] halfway; midway; [도중] on the way. e.g. 사이에 든 사람[중개자] a go-between / a middleman / [조정자] a mediator. **2** [시간적인 겨를] an interval; time; while; a space; a period; a span; a spell; a pause; a break; a gap; [여가] leisure; spare time; time to spare; odd moments; (a) rest. e.g. 잠깐 사이에 in a minute [moment] / in no time / in an instant **3** [서로 맺은 관계] a relationship; a relation (relationship 이 보다 현대적임); [사귀는 정분] terms. e.g. 부모 자식 사이 the relation [ties] between parent and child / the parent-child relationship.

사이렌 [साइरेन] a siren; a whistle.

사이비 [साइबि] [**似而非**] <형용사적> false; would-be; sham; pretended; mock; spurious; pseudo(o)-; quasi-; <프> soi-disant.

사이사이 [साइसाइ] **1** [사이와 사이] intervals; spaces; gaps. e.g. 줄 사이사이를 메모로 채우다 fill (in) interlinear spaces with Memos. **2** [틈틈이] intervals <of / in / between>. e.g. 그녀는 출연 시간 사이사이에 자주 뜨개질을 했다 Between her appearances on stage, she othen did some knitting.

사이즈 [साइज] size; (여성 신체의) vital statistics; [옷 등의 치수] a size.

사인 [साइन] **1** [서명] a signature (▷서명의 뜻의 명사로 sign 을 쓰는 것은 잘못임); [유명인의 자필 서명] anautograph. **2** [부호, 암호] a sign

사임 [साइम] [**辭任**] resignation; retirement from office; stepping out [down]; going out of office. 사임하다 resign (from) <one's place>; step out; go out of office. e.g. 관직을 사임

하다 resign a government office.

사자 [साजा] [**獅子**] a lion; (암컷) a lioness; (별명) the king of beasts

사장 [साजांग] [**社長**] the president of a company; the head <of a firm

사적 [साचौक] [**私的**] private; personal; individual; unofficial.

사적 [साजौक] [**史蹟**] a place [spot] of historical interest; a historical site; historical relics [remains / landmarks].

사전 [साजौन] [**事前**] e.g. 사전의 beforehand / before the fact / advance.

사전 [साजौन] [**辭典**] a dictionary; a wordbook; a lexicon; (용어 해설) a glossary; (전문어, 학술 어의) a nomenclature; (보전) a thesaurus.

사절 [साजौल] [**謝絶**] (a) refusal; (a) rejection; [거절] declining. 사절하다 refuse (단호하게); decline (정중하게); deny.

사정 [साजौग] [**私情**] [사사로운 정] personal feelings [regard / consideration / sentiment]; bias. e.g. 사정에 좌우되다 be swayed by one's personal feelings.

사정사정 [साजौगसाजौग] [**事情事情**] pleadingly; imploringly. 사정사정하다 beg <a person's> consideration(s) [leniency / indulgence]; plead <for>; earnestly request [ask for]; implore; solicit; entreat.

사정없다 [साजौगौप्ता] [**事情－**] merciless; heartless; relentless; ruthless; unsparing; severe; inexorable.

사제 [साजे] [**司祭**] a Catholic priest; (미사 등의) a celebrant.

사제 [साजे] [**師弟**] master and pupil; teacher and student.

사죄 [साज्वे] [**謝罪**] an apology <*pl*, −gies>. 사죄하다 apologize; beg a person's pardon [forgiveness]; make an apology. e.g. 그는 무릎을 꿇고 아버지에게 자신의 비행 을 사죄했다 He got down on his knees and apologized to his father for his misbehavior.

사주 [साजू] [**四柱**] the horoscopic data <of a bride [bridegroom]>; the "four pillars" e.g. 사주보다 have one's fortune told / consult a fortuneteller.

사주 팔자 [साजू फाल्चा] [**四柱八字**] the Four Pillars and the Eight Characters

(for the year, month, day and hour of one's birth); [운수] fate; destiny; fortune; one's lot.

사직 [साजीक] [**辭職**] (a) resignation. 사직하다 resign <one's office [post]>; check out (of office); give [throw] up one's office; quit [go out of] office; step out [down].

사진 [साजीन] [**寫眞**] a photograph; a photo <*pl.* ~s>; a picture; [스냅 사진] a snap (shot).

사진기 [साजीनगि] a camera.

사찰 [साछाल] [**寺刹**] = 절[1]

사채 [साछै] [**私債**] a private loan [debt]; a personal liability.

사체 [साछे] [**死體**] = 시체

사촌 [साछोन] [**四寸**] a cousin; a first [full] cousin.

사춘기 [साछोनगि] [**思春期**] [청년기] adolescence; [성적으로 성숙한 시기] puberty.

사치 [साछि] [**奢侈**] [필요 이상으로 돈이 듦] (a) luxury; [분에 넘침] (an) extravagance; extravagancy. 사치하다 be extravagant; indulge in luxury; live [roll] in luxury

사치스럽다 [साछिसरौप्ता] [**奢侈**–] (사물이) luxurious; extravagant; expensive; sumptuous; fine; (사람이) extravagant; indulge in luxury.

사칭 [साछिंग] [**詐稱**] misrepresentation; a false statement. e.g. 신분 사칭 misrepresentation of one's identity [position].

사탕 [साथांग] [**砂糖**] [과자] candy [candies]; <英> sweets; sweetmeats; confection

사탕발림 [साथांगबाल्लिम] [**砂糖**–] 림 sugar-coated [honeyed / sweet] words; cajolery; flattery; blarney; soth soap; a mere show; deceptive appearance; oil. e.g. 사탕발림에 녹다 be coaxed by honeyed wor

사태 [साथै] [**事態**] the situation; the state [position] of affairs [things]; the aspect [look] of affairs. e.g. 심상치 않은 사태 a serious situation / the gravity of the situation.

사퇴 [साथ्वे] [**辭退**] [그만두고 물러남]. e.g. 자진 사퇴 voluntary resignation. 사퇴하다 [퇴거하다] take one's leave of an elder; excuse oneself from a senior's presence; [사직하다] resign <one's post [office]>. e.g. 공직에서 사퇴하다 resign [abdicate] one's office / resign from public life / leave [retire from] one's office.

사투 [साथ्रू] [**死鬪**] a desperate struggle; a mortal combat. 사투 하다 fight desperately; engage in a life-and-death [life-or-death] struggle <with>; (뒤얽 혀서) grapple [scuffle / close] <with a person> in mortal combat.

사투리 [साथूरि] an [a provincial] accent; a dialect; a patois; a provincialism. e.g. 시골 사투리로 말하다 speak in a country [local] dialect.

사표 [साफ्यो] [**辭表**] a (written) resignation; a letter of resignation. e.g. 사표를 내다 send [hand] in one's resignation (▷ hand in 은 직접 건네주다

사필귀정 [साफिलक्विजौंगे] [**事必歸正**] [당연한 결과] a corollary; a natural result.

사학 1 [साहाक] [**私學**] [개인이 세운 학교] a private school [college / university].

사학 2 [**史學**] [साहाक] [역사학] history; historical studies [science]; study of history.

사항 [साहांग] [**事項**] [일] matters; [사실] facts; data; [항목] articles; particulars; items. e.g. 조사 사항 matters for investigation.

사형 [साह्यौंग] [**死刑**] capital punishment; death on the scaffold; (a) death penalty; the punishment of death. 사형하다 condemn <a person> to death; put <a person> to death.

사활 [साह्वाल] [**死活**] life and [or] death. e.g. 그것은 내게 있어 사활의 문제다 It is a matter of life and death to me.

사회 [साह्वे] [**社會**] [공동 생활의 집단]₩ (a) society; [지역 사회] (a) community; [세상] the world; (군대, 감옥 등에서 본) the outer world; the public.

사회 [साह्वे] [**司會**] [회의 등을 진행함] direction of [directing] a meeting [ceremony]; chairmanship; chairing <a meeting>. 사회하다 preside at [over] <a meeting>; take the chair; conduct; (목사 등이) officiate <at a ceremony>; (방송 등의) act as master [mistress] of ceremonies <for>; emcee <a show>.

사회적 [साह्वेजौक] [**社會的**] social; societary; societal. e.g. 사회적으로 보아 from a social point of view / socially speaking.

사회화 [साहवेहवा] [**社會化**] socialization. 사회화하다 socialize <industry>.

사후[1] [साहू] [**死後**] e.g. 사후에 ather one's death / posthumously.

사후[2] [साहू] [**事後**] e.g. 사후의 [에] [ए] ather the fact / <라> [रा] expost facto. 그들은 사후처리를 잘못했다 They made a mistake in dealing with what had happened

사흗날 [साहन्नाल] [셋째 날] the third day.

사흘 [साहल] [3 일] three days. e.g. 사흘마다 every three days.

삭감 [साक्काम] [**削減**] a cut; (a) curtailment; (a) reduction; a cutback. 대삭감 a drastic reduction [cut]. 삭감하다 (비용 등을) cut (down); curtail; reduce; slash; [남아도는 것을 깎다] trim;

삭다 [साक्ता] **1** (옷 등이) wear thin [threadbare]; get rotten; decay; crumble into decay. e.g. (옷이) 삭아서 너덜 너덜해지다 be worn to rags. **2** (죽 등이) become sloppy [watery]; turn bad; (종기가) resolve; be resolved. e.g. 종기는 곧 삭을 게다 The tumor will soon be resolved.

삭막 [सांगमाक] [**索莫,索漠**] 삭막하다 [생각이 잘 나지 않다] dim [vague] (in one's memory); [황량하다] bleak; desolate. e.g. 삭막한 풍경 [bleak] scene.

삭발 [साक्पाल] [**削髮**] hair-cutting; (a) tonsure; (짧은) close cutting; short cropping. 삭발하다 tonsure; shave the head of; have one's hair cut.

삭월세 [साग्वौलसे] [**朔月貰**]

삭이다 [सागिदा] **1** [소화시키다] digest <food>. **2** [가라앉히다] mitigate; alleviate; appease; calm down. e.g. 노여움을 삭이다 mitigate [swallow / appease] one's anger.

삭제 [साक्चे] [**削除**] [깎아 [지워] 없앰] deletion; elimination; erasure; cancellation; striking out. 삭제하다 delete; remove; cancel; strike out [off]; cross out; erase; [인쇄] kill.

삭히다 [साखिदा] [발효시키다] ferment <a thing>; [익히다] make (a thing) ripe.

삯 [साक] **1** [품삯] wages; pay; hire; [보수] remuneration; a reward.. e.g. 삯을 내리다 lower [cut down] wages **2** [물건 등을 이용한 대가] (a) rent (집 [땅] 세); a fare

(찻삯); freight (짐삯); carriage (운반비); a charge (사용료); a fee (수수료).

-산 [सान] [産] [산물] a product; manufacture <of>. e.g. 외국산 [국산] 담배 foreign [home-grown] tobacco

산 [सान] [山] [산악] a mountain; a mount; (봉우리) a peak; a hill (구릉) a knoll (둥근 언덕); a height (고지);

산고 [सान्गो] [産苦] [출산의 고통] birth [parturient] pangs; travail.

산골 [सान्गोल] [山-] a mountain [mountainous] district; a secluded place.

산골짜기 [सान्गोल्चागि] [山-] hills and valleys; a ravine; a gorge; a glen.

산기슭 [सान्गिसक] [山-] <at> the foot [base] of a mountain.

산꼭대기 [सान्कोक्तैगि] [山-] the summit [top] of a mountain [hill]; the mountaintop; a peak; a crest.

산나물 [सान्नामुल] [山-] wild edible greens.

산더미 [सान्दौमि] [山-] a heap; a pile; a great mass; a huge amount; a mountain <of>; an accumulation. e.g. 산더미 같은 숙제 a ton [pile] of homework.

산들바람 [सान्दलपाराम] [시원하고 가볍게 부는 바람] a soth wind; a gentle [light] breeze.

산등성이 [सान्दंगसौंगि] [山-] a (mountain) ridge; the ridge [back / spine] of a mountain.

산뜻하다 [सान्तथादा] 1 [깨끗하다] clean; neat and tidy; [빛깔, 모양 등이 선명하다] vivid; bright [fresh] <color>; [보기좋다] splendid; beautiful; smart; clear-cut. 2 (성격이) frank; open-hearted; (음식 맛이) plain; simple; light <meal>; racy. 3 [상쾌하다] cool; fresh; crisp <weather>.

산란 [सान्लान] [産卵] laying eggs; egg-laying; (어패류의) spawning; (곤충의) oviposition. 산란하다 (새 등이) lay eggs; (어패류 등이) spawn; (곤충이 과일 등에) blow.

산림 [सान्लिम] [山林] 1 [산중의 숲] a forest in the mountains. 2 [산과 숲] mountains and forests.

산만 [सान्मान] [散漫] distraction; diffuseness; vagueness; desultoriness; looseness. 산만하다 vague <notion>; loose <thinking / style>; vagrant <thought>; distracted <attention>; discursive <mind>; desultory <reading>.

산맥 [सान्मैक] [**山脈**] a mountain range [chain].

산모 [सानमो] [**産母**] a woman delivered of a child; a woman in childbed [in her confinement / in the state of maternity].

산문 [साम्मुन] [**散文**] prose.

산물 [साम्मुल] [**産物**] **1** [산출물] a product; a production; <집합적> produce. 주요 산물 staple products [produce]. **2** [어떤 결과로 얻어지는 것] a result; a fruit; an outgrowth; a product; an outcome. e.g. 노력의 산물 the fruit [harvest / product] of sheer labor [hard work]

산봉우리 [सान्बोंगूरि] [**山**-] a (mountain) peak; the summit [top] of a mountain.

산부인과 [सान्बूइनक्वा] [**産婦人科**] obstetrics and gynecology.

산불 [सान्बुल] [**山**-] a forest fire on a mountain; a wood fire. 산불 조심 <게시> Prevent forest fires.

산사태 [सान्साथै] [**山沙汰**] a landslide; [규모가 작은 것] a landslip; a landfall.

산산이 [सानसानि] [**散散**-] [조각조각으로] to [in] pieces [fragments]; to atoms [smithereens]; [흩어져서] scatteringly; scatteredly; sporadically; [따로따로] separately; severally. e.g. 산산이 부서지다 break [be broken] to fragments [splinters]

산산조각 [सानसानजोगाक] [**散散**-] broken pieces; bits and pieces; atoms; fragments; smithereens. e.g. 산산조각이 나다 come to pieces / (무너져서) crumble into dust

산성 [सान्सौं] [**酸性**] [化] acidity. 산성의 acid / [산이 많은] acidic / (맛이) sour.

산소[1] [सान्सो] [**酸素**] [化] oxygen (기호 O).

산소[2] [सान्सो] [**山所**] a grave; a tomb.

산수 [सान्सू] [**算數**] **1** [산술을 가르치는 학과목] arithmetic. **2** [계산] calculation; reckoning.

산수화 [सान्सूहवा] [**山水畵**] (화법) landscape painting; (그림) a landscape.

산아 제한 [साना जेहान] [**産兒制限**] birth control; birth [family] limitation.

산악 [सानाक] [**山岳, 山嶽**]

mountains.

산업 [सानौप] [**産業**] industry.

산전 수전 [सान्जौन सूजौन] [**山戰水戰**] [세상 일에 대한 어려운 고비를 다 겪어 본 것] fighting all sorts of hardships; being buffeted by the waves of adversity.

산지 [सान्जि] [**産地**] (물건의) a production center; a producing area; (동식물 등의) the home; the habitat; a breeding center (말 등의) a growing district (식물의); a locality; (사람의) a birthplace; a home. e.g. 이 동물의 산지는 남미이다 This animal comes from South America.

산책 [सान्छैक] [**散策**] a walk; a stroll; a lounge; an airing; a promenade; a constitutional (건강을 위한) 아침 산책 a morning walk. 산책하다 stroll; promenade; saunter; ramble [lounge] about; take the air; take a walk [stroll].

산촌 [सान्छोन] [**山村**] a mountain village.

산출 [सान्छुल] [**産出**] production; output; yield; [제조] manufacturing. 산출하다 produce; yield; bring forth; manufacture; turn out.

산타클로스 [सान्थाख्लल्लोस] Santa Claus; Father Christmas.

산하 [सान्हा] [**傘下**] e.g. 산하의 subsidiary / affiliated / under the influence [protection] <of>. 미국의 산하에 있다 be under the umbrella of the United States

산호 [सान्हो] [**珊瑚**] **1** coral. **2** [산호충] a coral insect; a polyp.

산화 [सान्हवा] [**酸化**] [化] oxidation; oxidization; oxygenation; combustion.

산후 [सान्हू] [**産後**] e.g. 산후의 [에] postpartum / ather childbirth [parturition] / ather one's confinement.

살 [1] [साल] (뼈를 둘러 싼) flesh. e.g. 살의 fleshy / sarcous. 살이 찐 [많은] fleshy / fat / meaty.

살 [2] [साल] [나이] [नाइ] age; years (of age). e.g. 다섯 살 난 사내아이 a five-year-old boy / a boy of five (years) / a boy five years old.

살갑다 [साल्काप्ता] [마음이 너르다] broad-minded; liberal; generous; open-handed; [다정하다] kind; warm (-hearted); genial.

살균 [साल्क्युन] [**殺菌**] sterilization; pasteurization; disinfection. 살균하 다

sterilize; pasteurize; disinfect.

살그머니 [साल्कमौनि] stealthily; secretly; furtively; by stealth; in secret; on the sly; quietly. e.g. 살그 머니 들어오다 [나가다] sneak in [out].

살금살금 [साल्कमसाल्कम] stealthily; secretly; furtively; sneakingly; by stealth; in secret; quietly; on the sly [quiet]. e.g. 살금살금 걷다 pussyfoot / walk noiselessly [stealthily] / walk on tiptoe

살기 [सालगी] [**殺氣**] [독살스러운 기운] a thirst for blood; blood thirstiness; [긴장된 분위기] a stormy atmosphere. e.g. 살기가 등등해 있었다 There was a wide-spread thirst for blood

살길 [साल्किल] a means to live; a livelihood. e.g. 살길을 찾다 seek a way to make a living.

살다 [साल] **1** [생존하다] live; subsist; exist; [소생하다] revive. e.g. 산 물고기 a live fish. **2** [생계를 잇다] live; make a [one's] living; support oneself; earn one's livelyhood [bread]. e.g. 이런 박봉으로는 살 수 없다 I cannot live on such a wretched salary **3** [생활을 영위하다] live; get on [along / by]; lead [live] a life.]. e.g.혼자 사는 노인 an old man living alone. **4** [거주하다] live <in / on / at>; reside <in> (▷ 격식차린 말); [서식하 다] inhabit (▷ 진행형 으로 쓸 수 없음). e.g. 살기에 적합한 inhabitable / good [fit] to live in.

살랑거리다 [साल्लांगौरिदा] (바람이) blow gently [sothly]; [소리나다] rustle; whisper; e.g. 나뭇잎이 산들바람에 살랑거렸다 The leaves were rustling in the breeze.

살리다 [साल्लिदा] **1** [소생시키다] revive; resuscitate; bring <a person> back to life; bring round [to]. e.g. 잃어버린 풍습을 살리다 revive lost customs. **2** [산 채로 두다] spare a person's life; let <a person> live; keep <an animal / a fish> alive. e.g. 낚은 물고기를 활어조에 살려 두다 keep one's catch alive by putting it in a fish crawl.

살림 [साल्लिम] [생계] (a) living; (a) livelihood; [생활] life; subsistence; existence; [살림 형편] circumstances; [살림살

이] a household (establishment); housekeeping. 살림하다 keep house; manage a household; housekeep.

살며시 [साल्म्यौशि] **1** [살그머니] stealthily; furtively; secretly; in private. **2** [가만히] quietly; gently; lightly; sothly; cautiously.

살벌 [साल्पौल] [**殺伐**] 살벌하다 bloody; [살기를 띠다] bloodthirsty; [잔인하다] savage; [사납다] fierce; sanguinary; brutal; violent; warlike <people>.

살살[1] [सालसाल] sothly; quietly; gently; stealthily

살살[2] [सालसाल] [배가 약간 아픈 모양]. e.g. 배가 살살 아프다] have a slight pain in the stomach.

살생 [सालसैंग] [**殺生**] destruction of life; butchery; shooting and fishing (새, 물고기의).

살신성인 [साल्सिनसौङ्न] [**殺身成仁**] 살신성인하다 sacrifice oneself to preserve one's integrity; become a martyr to humanity.

살아가다 सारागादा **1** [생명을 이어가다] lead a life; live; get along; sustain [maintain] life; keep on living. e.g. 간신히 살아가다 keep body and soul together. **2** [살림을 영위하다] live; make a [one's] living; earn one's livelihood [bread]. e.g. 분수에 맞게 살아가다 live within one's means.

살아나다 [सारानादा] **1** [소생하다] revive; recover consciousness; come to oneself [to one's senses]; be brought round; return to life. e.g. 인공호흡으로 살아나다 be resuscitated by artificial respiration **2** [구조되다] be saved [rescued / relieved]; be spared; survive <a disaster>; [모면하다] escape <death>; live. e.g. 간신히 살아나다 have a narrow [bare] escape / escape by a hair's breath **3** (불 등이) burn [flame up] again. e.g. 숯불이 다시 살아난다 The charcoal fire grows again.

살아남다 [सारानाम्ता] survive; live through; outlive. e.g. 살아남은 surviving <people>.

살의 [साऊइ] [**殺意**] murderous intent; intent to murder [kill]; [法] malice aforethought [prepense]. e.g. 살의를 품고 with murderous intent / with intent to kill

<a person>.

살인 [सालिन] [**殺人**] murder; manslaughter; homicide (▷ 법률 용어에서 murder 는 모살, manslaughter 는 살해 의도 없는 살인 우발적 살인, homicide 는 위 둘을 포함한 일반적인 말). 인하다 commit murder [homicide]; kill [murder] <a person>; do murder.

살짝 [साल्चाक] **1** [남이 모르게] furtively; by stealth; stealthily; quietly; secretly; on the quiet [sly]. e.g. 살짝 만나다 have a clandestine meeting. **2** [손쉽게] effortlessly; adroitly; easily; skillfully; dethly; [간단히] lightly; simply. e.g. 살짝 해치우다 do it cheap

살찌다 [सालचिदा] [살이 많아지다] grow stout [fat] (▷ fat 은 일반적으로 쓰이는 말, stout 는 주로 단단하게 살찐 것을 말함. 또 살찐 여자에 대해서는 fat 을 피하고 [stout 를 씀); (주로 사람이) gain weight; fatten; fat (up); put [take] on flesh; gather [gain / get] flesh. e.g. 나는 요즘 살이 꽤 쪘다 Recently I have gained [put on] a lot of weight

살충 [साल्छुंग] [**殺蟲**] 살충하다 kill [destroy] insects; destroy worms; vermifuge.

살충제 [साल्छुंजे] [**殺蟲劑**] an insecticide; a vermicide; a pesticide; an insect powder (가루); a larvicide (유충의); an adulticide (성충의).

살코기 [साल्खोगि] lean [red] meat.

살판나다 [सालफान्नादा] become rich; be lucky; have a stroke of luck; strike it rich; come into a fortune; one's ship comes in.

살펴보다 [सालप्यौबोदा] [잘 보다] observe [watch] carefully; [확인하다] make sure <of>; look around [about]; watch for; look into; examine.

살포 [सालफो] [**撒布**] 살포하다 [분말,액체 등을 뿌리다] sprinkle; (분무기 등으로) spray; (가루를) dust.

살포시 [सालफोशि] sothly; gently; quietly; lightly; [살며시] stealthily; by stealth; on the sly. e.g. 나뭇잎이 살포시 땅바닥에 떨어졌다 A leaf dropped sothly [fell gently] to the ground.

살피다 [सालपिदा] **1** [관찰하다] observe; make observation <of>; [조사하다] examine; take a good look at; inspect; study; [고찰하다] consider; inquire into; [판단하다] judge; read. e.g. 기색을 [눈치를] 살피다 study the pleasure of <a person>. **2** [주의하다] pay [give] attention <to>; keep close watch <on>; [경계하다] look out <for>; beware of. e.g. 교통 신호를 살피다 look [pay attention] to traffic signals

살해 [सारहै] [**殺害**] killing; [살인 a murder (case); homicide. 살해하다 [생명을 빼앗다 kill; (불법으로) murder; slay; [대량으로 죽이다, 도살하다] slaughter.

삶 [साल्म] living; subsistence; existence; [생활] life.

삶다 [साल्मता] [끓이다] boil; seethe; cook; (뭉 근한 불로) simmer.

삼[1] [साम] [**三,参**] **three.**

삼[2] [साम] [**蔘**] [산삼과 인삼] the wild ginseng and the ginseng.

삼가다 [साम्गादा] **1** [억제하] restrain oneself; abstain [refrain / keep] from; be restrained [moderate / temperate] <in>. e.g. 나는 술[담배]을 삼가고 있다 I'm refraining [abstaining] from drinking [smoking] **2** [조심하다] be prudent [careful]; be cautious; caution oneself <against>; be discreet; be circumspect; reserve e.g. 삼가는 [조심스럽고 마음을 터놓지 않는] reserved / [절도 있는] restrained.

삼각 [साम्गाक] [**三 角**] triangularity

삼각 관계 [साम्गाक ग्वानग्ये] [**三角關係**] the eternal triangle; a triangular [triple] love affair; a three-cornered romance; a love triangle.

삼각형 [साम्गाख्यौं] [**三角形**] a triangle; a trilateral.

삼강 오륜 [साम्गांग ऒयुन] [**-五倫**] the three bonds and the five moral disciplines in human relations.

삼거리 [साम्गौरि] [**三-**] a crossing with three corners; a concourse of three streets; a forked road.

삼겹실 [सामग्यौप्शल] [**三-**] three-ply thread.

삼권 분립 [साम्ग्वौन बुल्लिप] [**三權分立**] the separation of the three branches [of the administrative, legislative, and judicial branches] of government.

삼다 [साम्ता] […으로 정하다] make; make <a thing>

of; have [use / regard] <a thing / a person> as. e.g. 소일삼아 just to kill time. 장난 삼아 half in fun.

삼라 만상 [साम्ला मान्सांग] [**森羅萬象**] all [the whole of] creation; all nature; the universe; Nature.

삼림 [साम्लिम] [**森林**] a wood; woods; a forest (▷ a forest 가 woods 보다 큼)

삼삼오오 [सामसामओओ] [**三三五五**] by twos and threes; in groups (of twos and threes).

삼삼하다 [सामसामहादा] **1** [기억에 생생하다] fresh; vivid.. e.g. 그것은 지금도 내 기억에 삼삼하다 It is still vivid [fresh] in my memory **2** [싱거우면서 맛있다] rather unsaline [unsalty] but dainty [nice]. e.g. 이 콩나물 무침은 너무 삼삼하다 This cooked bean sprouts is seasoned too light.

삼엄 [सामौम] [**森嚴**] solemnity. 삼엄하다 solemn; grave; awe-inspiring. e.g. 그는 경찰의 삼엄한 경계망을 뚫고 도망쳤다 He ran away [disappeared himself] through tightly-guarded police

삼일절 [सामिल्चौल] [**三一節**] Anniversary of the *Samil* Independence Movement.

삼일 천하 [सामिल छौन्हा] [**三一天下**] a very brief reign; a short-lived rule [reign].

삼자 [साम्जा] [**三者**] **1** [세 사람] three persons; the three parties. e.g. 삼자 간의 tripartite <discussion> / triple <alliance>. **2** (당사자 이외의) the third party; [국외자] an outsider

삼촌 [साम्छोन] [**三寸**] [숙부] an uncle (on the father's side).

삼총사 [साम्छोंगसा] [**三銃士**] a triumvirate; a trio.

삼키다 [साम्खिदा] **1** [목구멍으로 넘기다] swallow; gulp down; choke down; take [get] down; down; drink in. e.g. 단숨에 [꿀꺽] 삼키다 gulp down <water> / swallow <the pills> at one gulp **2** [억지로 참다] bear; suppress. e.g. 눈물을 삼키다 keep back one's tears / gulp [choke] down one's sobs **3** [횡령하다] misappropriate; appropriate (for [to] oneself); pocket; embezzle; peculate; take to [for] oneself. e.g. 공금을 삼 키다 divert public money into one's own pocket.

삼한 사온 [सामहान साओन] [**三寒四溫**] a cycle of three

cold days and four warm days.

삽 [साप] a shovel; a spade; (소형의) a scoop.

삽시간 [साप्शिगान] a moment; an instant; a second; a flash. e.g. 그녀의 기쁨은 삽시간에 사라졌다 er joy was but short-lived.

삽입 [साबिप] [挿入] 삽입 insertion; inter-position; Interpolation. 삽입하다 insert; put in [between]; interpose; interpolate.

삽화 [साफहवा] [挿畵] an illustration [a cut-in]; a cut.

-상 [1] [सांग] [相] a minister. e.g. 외상 the Foreign Minister / the Minister of [for] Foreign Affairs. 재무상 the Finance Minister

-상 [2] [सांग] [商] [장수] a merchant; a dealer; a tradesman; [장사] business; commerce; trade. e.g. 도매상 (상인) a wholesale merchant [dealer] / (장사) wholesale business [trade].

-상 [सांग] [上] […이라는 점에서 보아] from the viewpoint [standpoint] of <morality>; viewed in the lightflk <discipline>; as a matter of <fact>. e.g. 교육상 from the educational point of view [stand point / viewpoint]. 역사상 historically / from the historical point of view.

상 [1] [सांग] [床] a (dining) table; a small table (for one person); a desk. e.g. 상을차리다 set [lay] a meal before <a person> / lay the table <for dinner> / set a dinner table.

상 [2] [सांग] [上] **1** [위, 상부 upper. 상반신 the upper half [part] of the body. e.g. 상반신 the upper half [part] of the body **2** [윗길이 되는 등급] the first (class / grade); the best; the superior; the top (class). e.g. 그의 학교 성적은 상에 속한다 His schoolwork [school record] is rather good. **3** [책의 상권] the first book [volume]; Book [Volume] One. e.g. 상중하 3 권 a set of three volumes.

상 [3] [सांग] [相] **1** [인상(人相)] physiognomy; lineaments; [용모] countenance; features; [표정] a look; a face. e.g. 울상 a face ready to cry / a sad face. **2** [상태] an aspect; a phase; a facet. e.g. 사회 상 an aspect of society / a phase of social life.

상 4 [सांग] [喪] mourning. e.g. 상을 입다 go into [take to] mourning for <one's father> / observe mourning.

상 5 [सांग] [像] [사람, 사물의 형체를 본떠 만든 것] an image; figure; a statue; [그림] a picture; a portrait. e.g. 성모 마리아의 대리석 상 a marble image of the Virgin Mary.

상 6 [सांग] [賞] a prize; an award; a reward (보수).

상가 [सांग] [商街] a business section [quarter / center]; a commercial quarter; a shopping district [center]; a downtown.

상거래 [सांगोरै] [商去來] a commercial transaction; a business transaction [deal]; commercial dealings. e.g. 상거래가 활발하다 Business transactions are briskly carried on there.

상경 [सांगौग्यौग] [上京] e.g. 상경 중이다 be in the capital [in Seoul]. 상경하다 come [go] up to the capital; leave for Seoul.

상공 [सांगोग] [上空] [하늘] the sky; the skies; [하늘의 높은 곳] the upper air [regions].

상권 [सांग्वौन] [商權] [法] commercial rights; [상업상의 권력] commercial power [supremacy]. e.g. 상권을 장악하다] acquire commercial supremacy / dominate the market.

상금 [सांगग्म] [賞金] [현상금] prize money; a prize; an award; [보상금] a reward; a premium. e.g. 상금을 타다 win [get] a prize / (경기 등에서) win a purse.

상급 [सांगप] [上級] [위의 등급] an upper [a higher] grade; (학교의) an upper [a higher] class; (과목) an advanced course.

상기 [सांगि] [想起] recollection; remembrance. 상기하다 recollect; remember; recall; call [bring] to mind.

상납 [सांग्नाप] [上納] tax payment to the government [authorities]; (뇌물의) offering a bribe <to one's superior>. 상납하다 pay to the government [authorities

상냥하다 [सांगन्यांग] [부드럽다] gentle; tender; soth; suave; [다정하다] sweet; affectionate; kind (hearted); [붙임성이 있다] amiable; affable. e.g. 그는 누구에게나 상냥하다 He is nice to everyone. / He makes himself agreeable to everybody.

상념 [सांगन्यौम] [**想念**] a thought; a notion; a conception; an idea.

상담 [सांगदाम] [**相談**] (a) consultation; counsel; (a) conference; advice; a talk; a confab. 상담하다 consult <a person / with a person about a matter>; confer <with a person about a thing>; have a talk <with>; talk over <a matter with a person>; seek [ask] <a person's>; advice; take counsel <with [of] a person>. e.g. 상담하러 가다[오다] go [come] to <a person> for advice.

상담소 [सांग्दांगसो] [**相談所**] an information bureau; a consultation office.

상당하다 [सांग्दांगहादा] [**相當**-1] [적당,합당하다] suitable; proper; fit; due; appropriate; adequate; [어울리다] becoming; befitting; [걸맞다] <서술적> be proportionate to. e.g. 능력에 상당하는 급료 a salary proportionate to one's ability. **2** [어지간하다] considerable; pretty; fair; good; tolerable; passable; [부끄럽지 않다] decent; respectable. e.g. 상당한 교육 a good education.

상대 [सांगदै] [**相對**] **1** [대면] facing [confronting] each other; being opposite to each other; [만나 봄] an interview. 상대하다 face [confront / see] each other; be [stand] over against each other; be opposite to each other. **2** [친구] a companion; a mate; a fellow; a date (남녀 교제의); [짝] a partner; a pal (단짝) [대상] an object. e.g. 놀이 상대 a playmate. **3** [적수] an opponent; a rival; a competitor; an antagonist; an adversary; [호적수] a match; an equal; [상대방] the other man [person]; the other [opposite] party.. e.g. 나는 상대를 쉽게 이겼다 I beat my opponent hands down. 상대하다 deal with; contend <with>; play (against) <a person>; take <a person> up on a challenge. e.g. 아무나 나와, 내가 상대해주 겠다 Let any one come, I am his man

상류 [सांगन्यू] [**上流**] **1** (강의)

the upper stream; the upper reaches [waters] of a river. e.g. 저 멀리 상류에 far up the stream. **2** [지위, 생활 정도 등이 높음] the upper [higher] classes; polite [fashionable] society; high society. e.g. 그는 상류 가정 출신이다 He comes of an upper-class family

상륙[सांऽग्न्युक] [**上陸**] landing; disembarkation; [going ashore.] 상륙하다 land <in a country / at a port>; make a landing; get to land; (군대가) disembark; (선원이) go [come] on shore; (태풍이) [थेफुंड] strike.

상반 [सांऽबान] [**相反**] being contrary to each other; conflicting with each other; mutual contradiction; reciprocity. 상반하다 be contrary to <each other>; run counter to <each other>; disagree with <each other>; conflict with <each other>; be mutually contradictory.

상반 곡선 [**सांऽबान गोक्सौन**] a reciprocal curve.

상반기 [सांऽबानगी] [**上半期**] the first half (of the year); the first half year.

상봉 [सांऽबोंग] [**相逢**] 상봉하다 meet [see] (each other). e.g. 부자 (父子) 는 2 년만에 상봉했다 Father and son met ather twenty years' separation.

상부 상조 [सांऽबु सांऽजो] [**相扶相助**] interdependence; mutual dependence; mutual help [aid].

상비 [सांऽबी] [**常備**] e.g. 상비의 standing / permanent / regular / [예비의] reserve. 상비하다 [예비하다] reserve <something> for <a sudden need>; [준비해 두다] have <something> always ready [on hand].

상사 [सांऽसा] [**上司**] one's superior; one's boss; <집합적> the company higher-ups; one's chief.

상사병 [सांऽसाब्यौंग] [**相思病**] lovesickness.

상상 [सांऽसांग] [**想像**] imagination; (a) fancy; [가정] (a) supposition; [추측] (a) guess; (a) conjecture. 상상의 imaginary / fanciful / fancy / fancied / [가정적인] supposed. 상상하다 imagine; fancy; conceive (in imagination); picture [figure] to oneself; [가정하다] suppose; [추측하다] conjecture.

상상력 [सांगसांगन्यौक] [**想像力**] imaginative power [faculty]; (power of) imagination.

상세 [सांऽसे] [**詳細**] details; particulars. 상세하다 minute; detailed; full; circumstantial.

상속 [सांग्सोक] [**相續**] succession; inheritance. 상속하다 succeed [fall heir] to <the estate of a person>; inherit

상술 [सांग्सुल] [**商術**] [장사 요령] a trick [knack] of the trade; [상재] business ability [talent / acumen]; [상혼] commercialism.

상술 [सांग्सुल] [**詳述**] expatiation; a detailed explanation; a full account. 상술하다 explain in full [detail]; make a detailed explanation <of>; give a full account <of>; enlarge [expatiate] <of>; detail <a matter>.

상스럽다 [सांग्सरौप्ता] [**常-**] vulgar; low; indecent; gross; mean; sordid; contemptible; boorish. e.g. 상스러운 사람 a vulgar [mean] person.

상습 [सांग्सुप] [**常習**] (세상의) a convention; a usage; a regular [an established] custom; a common practice; (개인의) a habit; an inveterate habit. e.g. 상습적(인) habitual / confirmed / regular. 상습적으로 habitually.

상승 [सांग्सुंग] [**上昇**] a rise <in temperature>; the ascent <of a balloon>; ascension; [상승 경향] upward tendency; a rising trend; an upturn.

상시 [सांग्शि] [**常時**] ordinary [normal] times; <at> all times.

상식 [सांग्शि] [**常識**] common sense; practical sense [wisdom]; mother wit; [양식] good sense. e.g. 상식적인 common-sense / sensible / wise / matter-of-fact / practical / (보통의) [ordinary / normal.

상실 [सांगशिल] [**喪失**] loss; forfeiture. e.g. 권리의 상실 the forfeiture [loss / lapse (소멸에 의한)] of one's right. 상실하다 lose; be deprived <of sight>; forfeit; divest oneself <of>

상심 [सागंशिम] [**傷心**] a broken heart; heartbreak; grief; distress; sorrow. 상심하다 grieve; be grieved (at heart); be heartbroken; sorrow; be sorrow-stricken; be distressed. e.g. 남편을 잃고 상심하다 be grieved over the loss of one's husband

상아탑 [सांगआथाप] [**象牙塔**] a tower of ivory; an ivory tower. e.g. 상아탑주의 ivory-towerism. 상아탑에 틀어박히다 live in [keep to] an ivory tower / remain behind cloistered walls / lead a scholastic life detached from the world.

상업 [सांगऔप] [**商業**] [산업] commerce; trade; [장사, 거래] [जांसा गौरे] business. e.g. 상업의 commercial / business / mercantile.

상업화 [सांगओप्हवा] [**商業化**] commercialization. 상업화하다 commercialize; put on a commercial basis.

상여 [सांगयौ] [**喪輿**] a "death carriage"; a hearse; a bier; a catafalque. e.g. 상여를 메다 bear [take / carry] a bier on the shoulders / shoulder a bier.l a bier-carrier.

상여금 [सांगयौगम] [**賞與金**] [보너스] [बोनौस] a bonus; [상금] prize money; a prize; a reward. e.g. 연말 상여금 a year-end bonus.

상연 [सांगयौन] [**上演**] dramatic presentation; presentation [staging] <of a play>; performance. 상연하다 perform; present (▷ perform 은 주로 배우의 입장에서, present 는 흥행주의 입장에서 말할 때 씀); put <a drama> on the stage; stage.

상영 [**上映**] [सांगयौ रंग] **상** screening; showing. 상영하다 screen; put on the screen; show; exhibit; run off; play. e.g. 영화를 상영하다 show a movie.

상온 [सांगोन] [**常溫**] [보통온도] normal temperature.

상용 [सांगयोंग] [**常用**] **1** [일상적 으로 사용함] common [constant / ordinary] use; daily [everyday] use. 상용하다 use commonly. **2** [상습적 으로 사용함] habitual [regular] use. 상용하다 use habitually [regularly]; make regular use of <a medicine>.

상위 [सांगवी] [**上位**] a higher [an upper] rank; a high position; precedence. e.g. 지금은 여성 상위 시대다 Women are placed above men today.

상응 [सांगुंग] [**相應**] **1** [대응] [दैउं] correspondence. 상응하다 correspond <to>; answer <to>. **2** [적합] fitness; suitability. 상응하다 be suitable <for / to>; suit; be suited;

상의[1] [सांगुइ] [**上衣**] a coat; a jacket; an upper garment; a blouse; a shirtwaist; a tunic (군복의) e.g. 상의를 입다 [벗다] put on [take off] one's coat.

상의[2] [सांगुइ] [**相議**] **1** 의논] (a) consultation (▷ 복수로 쓸 경우가 많음); (a) conference; a talk; a confab. e.g. 상의 중이다 be in consultation [negotiation] 상의하다 consult <a person / with a person about a matter>; have a talk <with>; talk <with a person over a matter>; discuss <a matter with a

person>. **2** [조언을 구함] 상의하다 consult <a lawyer>; take counsel <with [of] a person>; ask [seek] <a person's> advice. e.g. 신상 문제를 상의하다 consult <a person> [seek <a person's> advice] about one's personal affairs.

상인 [सांगिन] [**商人**] a merchant; a tradesman; a dealer <in rice>; [소매 상인] a storekeeper; a shopkeeper; <집합적> tradespeople.

상자 [सांगजांग] [**箱子**] a case; a packing case; a bin (큰) a casket (작은)

상장 [सांगजांगजां] [**上場**] 상장하다 list <stocks>. e.g. 증권 거래소 2 부에 우리 회사 주식이 상장되었다 Our company is listed on the Second Market.

상장 [सांगजांगजां] [**賞狀**] a certificate of merit; <honor with> a testimonial.

상점 [सांगजांगजौम] [**商店**] a store; a shop.

상정 [सांञ्जौंग] [**上程**] lay-ing before the House; presentation <of a bill>. 상정하다 (일정에) introduce [present] <a bill> on the agenda; (의회에) lay <a bill> before the House; (토의에) bring up <a bill> for discussion. e.g. 의안을 국회에 상정하다 introduce a bill in the National Assembly / present [place] a bill before the National Assembly

상조 [सांगजांगजो] [**相助**] mutual aid [help / assistance]; interdependence. 상조하다 aid [help / assist] each other; cooperate.

상종 [सांञ्जोंग] [**相從**] association; intercourse; company; society; friendship; acquaintanceship. 상종하다 associate <with>; hold intercourse <with>; keep company with; mix <with>. e.g. 상종 하지 못할 놈 a despicable [contemptible] fellow.

상주 [सांगजांगजू] [**常住**] 상주하다 reside (habitually) <in / at>. e.g. 한국에 상주하는 외국인 the foreign residents in Korea.

상중하 [सांगजुंगहा] [**上中下**] [3 단계] the first, the second, and the third grades [classes]; (품질, 능력 등의) good, better, and the best; the three grades of quality [ability] — good, fair, and poor. 상중하 3 권 a set of three volumes / (소설) a three-decker.

상징 [सांञ्जींग] [**象徵**] a symbol <of>; an emblem; [모양 으로 나타내기] symbolic representation. 상징적(인) symbolic(al). 백합은 순결의 상징이다 A lily is symbolic of purity. 상징하다 symbolize; emblematize; be symbolic <of>; stand as a symbol

<for>

상책 [सांगछैक] [**上策**] the best plan; a good [capital] plan [idea]; the best policy; the wisest thing <to do>. e.g. 도망치는 것이 상책이다 It is best to run away.

상처 [सांगछौ] [**傷處**] **1** [부상] an injury (사고 등에 의한 상처); a wound (전,총,칼 등에 고의로 입혀진 상처); a hurt; a cut (벤 상처) a bruise; a scratch (타박상) **2** <비유> [피해를 입은 자취]. 상처 받은 마음 a wounded heart.

상체 [सांगछे] [**上體**] the upper (part of the) body

상충 [सांगछुंग] [**相衝**] contra-dicttion; conflict. 상충하다 contradict; conflict <with>.

상쾌하다 [सारव्वैहादा छुंग] [**爽快 –**] refreshing; exhilar-ating <drink>; bracing; invigo-rating; crisp <breeze>..

상큼하다 [सारव्वमहादा] slender-legged; long-legged; lanky.

상태 [सांगथै] [**狀態**] a state (▷ 보통 단수형) a condi-tion; [상황] conditions (▷ 보통 복수형); [국면] a situation; [광경] a sight; [양상] an aspect. e.g. 건강 상태 one's state of health. 지금 상태로는 그는 좀처럼 일자리를 구할 수 없을 것이다 As things are with him now, he will never be able to find a job. 그는 태풍의 피해 상태를 얘기했다 He described the havoc wreaked by the typhoon. / He gave an account of the damage done by the typhoon.

상통 [सांगथोंग] [마음과 뜻이 통하는 것] mutual under-standing; coincidence; accordance. 상통하다 under-stand each other; coincide <with>; be in accord <with>; together. e.g. 너는 그녀와 마음이 **2** [공통] common-ness; community. 상통하다 [सांथोंहादा] have something in common <with>.

상투 [सांगथ्रू] [**常套**] conven-tionality; commonplaceness; platitude; triteness; stale-ness... e.g. 상투적 (인) [틀에 박힌] conventional / [흔해빠진] commonplace / hackneyed.

상패 [सांगफै] [**賞牌**] a medal; a medallion.

상표 [सांगफ्यो] [**商標**] a trade-mark; a brand; a label.

상품 [सांगफुम] [**商品**] a com-modity; an article of com-merce [trade]. <집합적> merchandise; goods; wares; commodities. e.g. 가정용 상품 코너 the household goods corner.

상품권 [सांगफुमग्वौन] a gith certificate; a merchandise bond [coupon]; a credit slip; an exchange ticket [check].

상품 [सांगफुम] [**賞品**] a prize;

a trophy; a pot.

상하 [सांग्हा] [上下] **1** [위와 아래] top and bottom; the upper and lower sides [parts]. e.g. 상하의 up-and-down / vertical. **2** (신분, 지위 등의) the upper and lower classes; high and low; superiors and inferiors. e.g. 상하 구별 없이 irrespective of social standing / without distinction of social standing / both high and low.

상하다 [सांग्हादा] [傷 -] **1** (물건 등을[이]) damage; be damaged; hurt; be hurt; injure; be injured; e.g. 상한 토마토 a rotten tomato **2** (몸을 [이]) grow haggard; become thin; be emaciated; (건강이) be broken <in health>; injure <one's health>. e.g. 얼굴이 상하다 have a face all pinched and drawn.**3** (마음, 기분 등을[이]) hurt; get [be] hurt; injure; be injured; impair; harm; worry; be worried about; grieve; be grieved <at>; be distressed [troubled] <with>. e.g. 기분이 상하다 take offense <at> / get out of humor.

상해 [सांग्है] [傷害] (an) injury; bodily harm. e.g.… 에게 상해를 가하다 inflict bodily injury on a person

상행 [सांग्है ग] [上行] 상행의 up. e.g. 다음 상행 열차는 몇 시입니까 What time is the next up train?.

상행위 [सांग्है गवि] [商行爲] a commercial [business] transaction.

상향 [सांगह्यांग] [上向] **1** [위쪽을 향함]. e.g. 상향의 upward. 상향환기 upward ventilation. **2** [(시세의) 오르는 기세] an upward tendency; an upturn; an upswing.

상호 [सांग्हो] [相互] reciprocity; mutuality. e.g. 상호간의 mutual / reciprocal

상환 [सांगह्वान] [償還] (a) repayment; (a) refund;(a) reimbursement; (공사채의) redemption; (연부의) amortization. e.g. 국채 상환액 the amount of the national loan redeemed.

상황 [सांगह्वांग] [狀況] the state of affairs [things]; conditions; a situation; circumstances (▷ circumstances 는 자기의 주위 상황을 말함). e.g. 부대 상황 attendant condition.

샅샅이 [सात्साछि] all over; in every nook and corner; throughout; all through; thoroughly; everywhere e.g. 집안을 샅샅이 뒤지다 ransack the house <for> / search the whole house.

새 1 [सै] [조류] a bird; a feathered creature; a fowl; (참새) a sparrow.

새 2 [सै] [새로운] new; [신기한] novel; [신선한] fresh; [최근의] recent; latest; hot; [현대적 up-to-date; modern. e.g. 새 사상 an up-to-date idea. 새 살림 a new home

새- [सै] [빛깔이 짙고 산뜻함] deep; dark; intense. e.g. 새빨간 거짓말 a downright lie / a pure fabrication.

e.g. 새빨간 거짓말 a downright lie / a pure fabrication.

새겨듣다 [सैग्योदत्ता] (주의해서) listen attentively[intently / carefully] to <a person>; [알아듣다] [catch[get] the meaning of what <a person> says. e.g. 내 말을 새겨들어라 Note what I say. / Now understand me!

새근거리다 [सैगनगोरिदा] breathe quick and hard; breathe roughly

새근새근 [सैगनसैगन] [자는모양] camly; quietly; peacefully e.g. 아기는 새근새근 자고 있었다. The baby was sleeping calmly.

새기다 [सैगिदा] **1** [조각하다] carve <in / on / out of>; [표면에 파다] engrave; sculpt; sculpture; cut; (끌로) chisel; inscribe; [칼자국을 내다] nick; notch. e.g. 석불을 새기다 carve a Buddhist figure out of [from / in] stone. **2** [명심하다] impress (deeply); stamp; engrave; inscribe. 가슴 [마음 속] 깊이 새기다] (사람이) be deeply impressed <with / by> / grave <the words> in the heart / (사물이) be brought home to <one> / be deeply impressed on [engraved in] one's mind.

새까맣다 [सैक्कामथा] deep [coal] black; jet (-black).

새끼 [सैक्कि] 1 [동물의 어린 것] [<집합적>] the young; (가금류의 a chick; a newly-hatched bird; (갓 날기 시작한) [a fledg (e) ling; (한 마리) [] a young; a youngling; (여우, 곰, 사자의 a cub; (개, 여우, 이리 등의) a puppy; a pup; (고양이의) [a kitten; a kitty; (소의) a calf <*pl.* calves, calfs>; (말, 사슴의) [a colt; (양의) [a lamb; (치어, 개구리의) [a fry; (염소의) a kid (조류의) [a young bird; a baby bird. e.g. 코끼리 새끼 a baby elephant / an elephant calf. **2** [자식] one's son [daughter]; [욕하는 말 a fellow; a guy; a chap. e.g. 그 새끼 that fellow [swine / brute]. 그 운전사 새끼 that wretch of a cabby.

새끼손가락 [सैक्किसोन्गाराक] a little [small] finger.

새다 1 [सैदा] [날이 밝다] dawn; break. e.g. 날이

새기 전에 before dawn [daybreak] / before daylight.

새다[2] **[सैदा]**1 (액체, 기체 등이) [leak; escape;] get[find] vent; run out. e.g. 물이 새지 않는 천 waterproof cloth **2** (불빛 등이) come [shine / break] through; e.g. 나무 사이로 새어 들어오는 햇빛 sunlight shining through the trees. **3** (말,감정 등이) get [find] vent; find expression. e.g. (그의 입에서자기도 모르게) 욕이 새어 나왔다] A curse escaped his lips. **4** (비밀이) [get [slip] out; leak (out); transpire; be disclosed. e.g. 비밀이 샜다 The secret was out [has leaked out].

새댁 [**सैदैक**] [**-宅**] a bride; a newly married woman

새로 (이) [**सैरोइ**] new (ly); anew; afresh. e.g. 새로 지은 집 a newly-built house.

새롭다 **[सैरोप्ता]** [지금까지 있은 적이 없다] new; [생생하다] fresh; [최신이다] latest; [현대적,진보적이다]] up-to-date; modern; [신기하다] novel; [독창적이다] original. e.g. 그 사건은 아직도 기억에 새롭다 The event is still fresh in my memory.

새벽 **[सैब्योक]** [날이 밝을 무, 먼동이 트기 전, 여명] dawn; daybreak; the break of day; the peep of day; the crack of dawn.

새빨갛다 **[सैपाल्काथा]** [짙게 빨갛고 새뜻하다] deep red; crimson (짙은 다홍빛) [scarlet (주홍 빛)].

새살 **[सैसाल]** granulation tissue; proud flesh. e.g. 새살이 돋다 granulate.

새삼스럽다 **[सैसामसरोप्ता]** e.g. 새삼스럽게 anew / afresh / again / specially (특히) / formally (형식적으로) / now (이제 와서)]. 나는 새삼스럽게 그의 친절에 감동되었다 I was all the more deeply moved by his kindness. / I realized his kindness afresh [anew].

새색시 **[सैसैक्शि]** a bride; a newly married [wedded] woman.

새싹 **[सैसाक]** [새로 돋는 싹] [a sprout; a shoot; [어린 잎, 꽃눈] a bud.

새옹지마 **[सैओंजीमा]** **[塞翁之馬]** blessing in disguise. e.g. 인간 만사 새옹지마다 Inscrutable are the ways of heaven [providence]. / It is impossible to know [tell] man's destiny beforehand.

새우다 **[सैउदा]** [철야하다] sit [stay] up all night; sit the night out. e.g. 이야기로 밤을 새우다] talk the night away / talk all (through) the night

새출발 **[सैछुल्पाल]** [**-出發**] a fresh start [departure]. 새출

발하다 make a fresh start [a new beginning]; set out anew.

새치기하다 [सैछिगिहादा] break into the queue; cut in; <英> jump the queue; snatch <another's portion>. e.g. 새치기하지 마시오 In order, please.

새침하다 [सैछिमहादा] e.g. 새침한 소녀 a prim girl. 남자 아이가 다가오면 그녀는 새침했다 When the boys came by, she assumed a prim air.

새콤하다 [सैखोमहादा] sourish; tartish; vinegarish.

새파랗다 [सैफाराथा] **1** [짙푸르다] deep blue <sky>; indigo (-blue). e.g. 새파란 바다 the deep blue sea. **2** [몹시 질려 있다] deadly [ghastly] pale; as white as a sheet. e.g. 그녀는 무서워서 [화가 나서] 새파래졌다 She turned white with fear [rage]. **3** [썩 젊다] young; green. e.g. 새파란 젊은이] a green youth.

새하얗다 [सैहयाथा] pure-white; snow(y)-white; (as) white as snow; immaculately white.

새해 [सैहे] the New Year; a new year.

색 [色] [색조] [सैक]**1** [색채] a color; a hue; a tint; a tinge; a tincture; [농담] a shade; (그림 물감의) a color. **2** the same sort. e.g. 색다른 것 something that is out of ordinary.

색다르다 [सैक्तारुदा] [色 -] extraordinary; unusual; uncommon; out of the way [ordinary]; offbeat; unconventional; (신기한) novel; (기묘한) strange; curious; peculiar; singular <personality>; odd; queer. e.g. 색다른 풍채 an extraordinary [odd] appearance.

색맹 [सैक्मै] [色盲] color [colour] blindness.

색상 [सैक्सांग] [色相] [색의 3 요소의 하나] the hue; the tone of color; a color tone.

색색거리다 [सैकसैक्कौरिदा] breathe lightly [sothly].

색안경 [सैगानग्यौग] [色眼鏡] **1** <a pair of> colored [coloured] glasses; dark glasses [sunglasses]. e.g. 색안경을 낀 여자 a woman in dark glasses. **2** [편협한 관찰] e.g. 사물을 색안경을 쓰고 보다 look at things from a biased viewpoint.

색연필 [सैग्यौनफिल] [色鉛筆] a colored [coloured] pencil.

색인 [सैगीन] [索引] an index <*pl.* ~es, -dices> <to a book>.

색종이 [सैक्चोंगी] [色-] colored [coloured] paper; a square sheet of thick paper (for writing poems, or painting pictures on).

색채 [सैक्छै] [色彩] **1** [빛깔] a color; a colour; coloring; coloration. e.g. 강렬한 색채

loud colors **2** [기미] a color; a colour; coloring; a tinge. e.g. 지방적 색채 local color.

색출 [**सैक्छुल**] [**索出**] e.g. 부정 공무원의 색출 exposure of corrupt officials. 색출하다 [뒤져서 찾아내다] find (out).

색칠 [**सैक्छिल**] [**色漆**] 1 [칠] colored lacquer. **2** [칠하기] coloring; painting. 색칠하다 paint; color; apply colored lacquer.

샌드위치 [**सैन्दविछि**] a sandwich

샌들 [**सैन्दल**] <a pair of> sandals.

샐러드 [**सैल्लौद**] salad.

샐러리 맨 [**सैल्लौरि मैन**] an office worker; a white-worker; a salaried worker.

샘 [1] [**सैम**] a spring; a fountain.. e.g. 물이 콸콸 솟는 샘 a gushing [live] spring.

샘 [2] [**सैम**] jealousy; (green) envy; the green-eyed monster. e.g. 샘이 나다 feel jealous <of> / feel envy <of / at>. 그가 성공했다는 소식을 듣고 나는 샘이 났다 The news of his success aroused [excited] my envy.

샘플 [**सैम्फुल**] a sample.

샛길 [**सैत्किल**] [큰 길에서 갈린 작은 길] a branch road; a byroad; a bystreet; a byway; a side road; a by-passage. e.g. 우리는 샛길로 빠져서 숲속으로 들어갔다 We took a branch road and entered a forest.

샛별 [**सैप्यौल**] **1** [금성] the morning star; venus. e.g. 초저녁의 샛별 **2** [인기있는 사람] a star. e.g. 오페라의 샛별 a star of the operatic world / an opera (tic) star.

-생 [**सैंग**] [**生**] **1** (생년의) born in <a year> [on <a date>]. e.g. 저는 5 월생입니다 I was born in May **2** [학생] a student of .... e.g. 법학 [의학]생 a law [medical] student.

생- [**सैं**] [**生**] **1** [조리하지 않은] raw <fish>; uncooked; [덜 조리된] underdone; half-boiled; rare; [날것의] unripe; green; e.g. 생야채 fresh vegetables. **2** [방송 등이 녹화[녹음]가 아님] live. e.g. 생방송 [연주] a live broadcast [performance]. **3** [살아있는] live; living; e.g. 생백신 live vaccine / live-virus vaccine. **4** [엉뚱한, 공연한] unreasonable; irrational; arbitrary; forced. e.g. 생트집 a false change [accusation]. 생사람 잡다 inflict injury upon an innocent person.

생가 [**सैंगा**] [**生家**] the house where one was born; the house of one's birth; one's parent's [paternal] home.

생각 [सैंगाक] **1** [사고 (思考)] thinking; [사상] a) thought; ideas e.g. 진보적인 생각을 가진 사람 a man with progressive ideas / a progresssive thinker. **2** [관념,착상] an idea; a notion; a conception; a thought. e.g. 좋은 [멋진] 생각] a capital [bright / happy / good] idea. **3** [의견] an opinion; a view; [신념] a belief; one's persuasion; [인상] an impression; [제안] a suggestion. e.g. 이 점에서 너와 나는 생각이 다르다 I don't agree with you on this point.

생각나다 [सैंगांग्नादा] (사물이) come to mind [one's recollection]; occur to one [one's mind]; flash on one [one's mind]; strike one; (사람이) think of; remember; recall; call [bring] to mind; recollect; hit upon.

생각되다 [सैंगाकत्वेदा] **1** [… 으로 보이다] seem; appear; look; [… 으 로 들리다] sound; [인상을 주다] strike <a person> as; impress <a person> as. e.g. 그가 큰 인물로 생각되었다 He has impressed me as a great man. **2** [여겨지다] be thought of <as>; be supposed; be considered; [간주되다] be regarded <as>. e.g. 그는 당의 장래의 지도자로 생각되고 있다 He is regarded [looked upon] as a future leader of the party. **생각하다** **1** [사고 하다] think <of / on / about / that ...>; have a think <about>; consider; give (a) thought to. e.g. 생각해야 할 일 something to think about. **2** [의견, 견해를 갖다] view <a thing>; take a view <of a thing>; be of (the) opinion <that>. e.g. 사물을 피상적 으로 [깊이] 생각하다 have a superficial [deep] view of things. **3** [의도 하다] intend to <do>; mean to <do>; think of <doing>; plan to <do>; contemplate <doing>. e.g. 그는 노부인을 속여 돈을 빼앗으려고 생각했다 He thought of cheating the old woman out of her money.

생계 [सैंग्ये] [**生計**] a living (▷ 단수형으로만 쓰임) (a) livelihood.

생계비 [सैंग्येबी] [**生計費**] living expenses; the cost of living

생기[सैंगि] [**生氣**] life; vitality; vigor [vigour]; animation; spirit. e.g. 생기 있는 lively. 생기 없는 lifeles

생기다 [सैंगिदा] **1** [없던 것이 새로 있게 되다] come into being [existence]; form. e.g. 새 정당이 생겼다 A new political party was formed [organized / born]. **2** [얻다] obtain; get; come by. e.g. 돈이 좀 생기다 get some money / come into some money.**3** (아기가) be born; have <a baby>; (친구가) make <a friend>; (애인이) have <a girl friend>. e.g. 그들에게 딸이 생겼다 A girl baby was born to them.

생김새 **[सैंगिमसै]** [형상] (a) form; (a) shape; [외관] (an) appearance.

생년 [सैन्यौन] [**生年**] the year of one's birth. **생년월일** **[सैन्यौनवौरिल]** the date of one's birth.

생동 [सैन्दोंग] [**生動**] a lively motion; vividness. 생동하다] move lively; be full of life; be vibrant with life; be vivid [lifelike / graphic / true to life].

생득 [सैदक] [**生得**] e.g. 생득의 innate / inborn.

생략 [सैन्याक] [**省略**] [뺌] (an) omission; [문법] (an) ellipsis <*pl.* ellipses>; 생략하다 [빼다] omit; leave out;. e.g. 제 5 장은 생략하기로 한다 We shall omit Chapter Five.

생리 [सैनि] [**生理**] [생물이 생활하는 원리] physiology. e.g. 생리적인 physiological.

생리대 **[सैनिदै]** a hygienic band; a sanitary napkin [towel / belt].

생맥주 [सैंग्मैक्यू] [**生麥酒**] drath [draught] beer; beer on drath [draught]; beer on tap.

생명 [सैम्यौ] [**生 命**]**생명 1** [목숨] life. e.g. 생명이 없는 것 lifeless things. **2** [가장 중요한 점] the life; the soul. e.g. 그의 소설의 생명은 그 해학성에 있다 The soul of his novel lies in its humor.

생모 [सैंग्मो] [**生母**] one's own [real / natural] mother.

생물 [सैंगमुल] [**生物**] a living [an animate] thing; a [living] creature; an organism; <집합적> life.

생물학 [सैंमुरहाक] [**生物學**] biology

생방송 [सैंगबांगओंग] [**生放送**] live broadcasting; live <TV> coverage; a live broadcast; a live telecast; a live program 생방송하다 cover [carry] <an event> live <by radio / television>; broadcast [televise / channel] <an event> live.

생사 [सैंग्सा] [**生死**] life and [or] death; (안부) safety; (운명) face. e.g. 생사가 걸린 문제 a matter of life and [or] death / a vital question.

생사람 **[सैंग्साराम]** [**生 –**] **1** [아무 잘못없는 사람] an innocent person [party]. **2** [관계없는 사람] an unrealted [unconnected] person; an outsider; the third party; a disinterested person.

생산 [सै`सान] [**生産**] production. e.g. 국내 생산 domestic production. 국민 총생산 the gross national product (GNP). 생산하다 produce; make; turn out; (기계를 사용하여 대규모로 제조하다] manufacture.

생산성 [सै`सानसौ] [**生産性**] productivity.

생산자 [सैसानजा] [**生産者**] a producer; a maker.

생산지 [सै`सान्जि] [**生産地**] a producing center [district].

생색 [सैसैक] [**生色**] a demonstration of benevolence; patronage; a credit. 생색(을) 내다 take credit to oneself <for>; do oneself proud [credit]; emphasize the favor done to <a person>; demonstrate benevolence. e.g. 이 정도 선물 가지고 생색을 내는구먼 You are doing yourself proud by giving this small present, aren't you?

생생하다 [सैसैहादा] [**生生-**] fresh; lively; vivid; green; lifelike; vivacious; graphic; full of life. e.g. 생생한 뉴스 hot news.

생선 [सैसौन] [**生鮮**] fresh [raw] fish; fish <*pl.* ~(es)>.

생성 [सै`गसौ`ग] [**生成**] creation; formation; generation; [哲] becoming. 생성하다 [생겨나다] be created; be formed; come into being [existence]; become; [생기게 하다 create; form; generate; make.

생소 [सैगसो] [**生疏**] **1** [낯섦] unfamiliarity; ignorance. 생소 하다 unfamiliar <with>; be a stranger <to>; new <to / at>; unaccustomed <to>; unacquainted [unconversant] <with>; uninformed [ignorant] <of>. e.g. 생소한 사람 a stranger / an unacquainted person. **2** [서투름] inexperience; lack of experience; want of practice. 생소하다 inexperienced; inexpert; unskillful; unpracticed; unaccustomed.

생식 [सै`गशिक] [**生殖**] reproduction; procreation; generation. 생식하다 reproduce; procreate; generate.

생식기 [सै`गशिक्कि] [**-期**] a period of reproduction; a reproductive period.

생신 [सै`गशिन] [**生辰**] [어른의] birthday.

생애 [सैगै] [**生涯**] a life; one's lifetime; a career. e.g. 화려한 생애 a glorious [brilliant] career.

생업 [सैगौप] [**生業**] an occupation; a profession; a calling; a business; a trade; a vocation. e.g. 농사를 생업으로 삼다 make a living by farming

생으로 [सै`गुरो] [**生-**] [날로]

raw; fresh; uncooked. e.g. 생선을 생으로 먹다 eat fish raw [fresh].

생이별 [सैंगिब्यौल] [**生離別**] a lifelong separation [parting]. 생이별하다 part <from a person> never to meet again; part <from a person> for life [for ever].

생일 [सैंगिल] [**生日**] one's birthday; one's natal day. **생일 잔치** [**सै गिल जान्छि**] <give> a birthday party [feast].

생전 [सैंगजौन] [**生前**] **1** [살아 있는 동안] one's lifetime. e.g. 그가 생전에 이룩한 업적 his achievements reached before his death [while alive / in life / during [in] his lifetime]. **2** [전혀] entirely; wholly; quite; completely; totally; altogether; never. e.g. 생전 모르는 사람 a total [complete] stranger

생존 [सैंगजोन] [**生存**] existence; being; life; subsistence; [살아 남음] survival. 생존하다 exist; live; [살아 남다] survive

생쥐 [सैंगजीव] [**動**] a (house) mouse <*pl.* mice>; [사향뒤쥐] muskrat.

생태 [सैंगथै] [**生態**] **1** [살아 가는 모양] a mode of life. e.g. 현대 중학생의 생태 the (mode of) life of [the facts about] today's junior high school students. **2** 生] [생물의 생활 상태] the habits of living things; ecology. e.g. 곰팡이의 생태 the ecology of molds

생트집 [सैंगथजीप] [**生−**] fault-finding; a false accusation [charge]. 생트집(을) 잡다. e.g. 그는 걸핏하면 생트집을 잡는다 He is ready to find fault with others.

생판 [सैंगफान] [**生−**] **1** [전혀 모름] utter [complete] ignoreance. e.g. 그녀는 집안 살림에 대해서는 생판이다 She is completely ignorant of housekeeping. **2** [아주 (생소 하게)] wholly [totally / utterly / entirely / quite-completely] <ignorant of>; [터무니없이 (무리하게)] groundlessly; unreasonably; unfoundedly; unjustly; forcibly. e.g. 생판 모르는 사람 a perfect [a total / an utter] stranger <to>.

생포 [सैंगफो] [**生捕**] capturing [catching] alive. 생포하다 catch [take / capture] <an animal> alive; take <a person> captive [prisoner].

생화 [सैंगह्वा] [**生花**] a natural flower.

생활 [सैंगहवाल] [**生活**] [살아 나감] life; existence; [생] livelihood; living; subsistence. 생활하다 live; exist; [생계를 세우다] make a living; subsist.

생활비 [सैंगहवाल्पि] [**生活費**]

living expenses; cost of living.

생활 수준 [सैंगहवाल सूजुन] [生活水準] a standard of living; a level of life; a living standard.

생후 [सैंगहू] [生後] ather [since] one's birth.

샤워 [स्यावॉ] a shower (bath). e.g. 샤워를 하다 have [take] a shower (bath) / shower

샤프하다 [स्याफहादां] [날카롭다] sharp; shrewd.

샴푸 [स्यामफू] (a) shampoo.

서 [सौ] [署] an office; a station. [경찰서] a police station.

서[सौ] [西] (the) west

서가 [सौगा] [書架] a bookshelf <*pl.* –shelves>; (도서관의) a bookstack; the stacks.

서구 [सौगू] [西歐] [서양] Europe; the West; the Occident;

서구화 [सौगूहवा] [西歐化] Europeanization; Westernization; Occidentalization

서글서글하다 [सौगलसौगरहादा] [너그럽다] generous; liberal; magnanimous; open-minded; broad- [large-] minded; [부드럽다] soth; tender; gentle; suave; [상냥하다] amiable; affable; sociable. e.g. 서글서글한 눈 gentle eyes / bright [clear] eyes.

서글프다 [सौगलफ्दा] sad; sorrowful; plaintive; melancholy; lonesome; lonely; forlorn; [언짢다] cheerless; dreary; inconsolable. e.g. 서글픈 노래 a touching [plaintive] song.

서기 [सौगि] [西紀] the year of grace [Christ / our Lord]; the dominical year; the Christian 'e'ra;

서너 [सौनौ] three or four; a few; several.

서늘하다 [सौनरहादा] **1** [선선하다] cool; refreshing. e.g. 서늘한 날 [바람 a cool day [breeze]. **2** (마음이) <서술적> be [feel] chilled; feel a chill; [오싹해지다] shudder <at>; be horrified; be frightened; have a thrill of horror. e.g. 놀라서 가슴이 서늘했다 [I was chilled with fright.

서다 [सौदा] **1** (사람이) stand; take a stand <at>. e.g. 똑바로 서다 stand erect. **2** (물건이) stand erect; (높은 것이 rise; tower; soar. e.g. 게시판이 서 있다 There is a bulletin board put up there. **3** [(사람이) 일어서다 stand up; rise; get on [rise to] one's feet; draw oneself up. e.g. 자리에서 (일어) 서다 rise from one's seat. **4** [정지하다] stop; halt; come to a stop [stand / halt]; make a stop [halt]; roll to a stop (차가)]; draw [pull] up (말, 차 등이배가) fetch up; heave to; (동력이 run down. e.g. 시계가 서다 a watch stops [runs down]. **5** (건물이) stand; [건립되다] be built; be erected; be set up; rise; go up; [설립되다] be established; be founded. e.g. 우리 집 주변에 주택들이 자꾸 (들어) 선다 Houses are springing up all over my neighborhood.**6** […의 위치에 서다 stand. e.g. 증인으로 서다 stand [be] witness / be on [take] the witness stand

서당 [सौदां] [**書堂**] a village school [schoolhouse]; a private school for the study of Chinese classics.

서두[1] [सौदू] [**書頭**] [서론] an introduction <to a book>; an introductory part <of a book>.

서두[2] [सौदू] [**序頭**] the beginning; the inception; the opening (sentence); (연극 등의) a prolog (ue); a prolusion; (말 등의) a preliminary statement.

서두르다 [**सौदूरदा**] [빨리 하다] hasten; hurry (up); nip; make haste; make time; step on it; <美> get a move on; [빨리 걷다] walk fast [quickly]. e.g. 몹시 서두르고 있다 be in a great [big / deadly] hurry / be in a big rush

서랍 [**सौराप**] a drawer.

서러워하다 [**सौरौवौहादा**] grieve <at the news / over a friend's death>; be grieved <at / over>; be sad <at>; feel sad <about>; be sorrowful; feel sorrow <for>; have a heavy [broken] heart; [통탄하다] deplore; lament; mourn <for / over>; regret.

서럽다 [**सौरौप्ता**] sad; sorrowful; mournful; doleful; plaintive; lamentable; deplorable; grievous. e.g. 서러운 표정 a sad look [countenance / face].

서로 [**सौरो**] mutually; reciprocally; with each other (주로 두 사람]; with one another (주로 세 사람 이상) e.g. 서로의 이익을 도모하다 consult mutual interests

서론 [सौरोन] [**序論, 緖論**] an introduction; introductory [prefatory] remarks; a proem.

서류 [सौर्यू] [**書 類**] [(공) 문서] a document; [일반 서류] a paper.

서류 전형 [**सौर्यू जौनहयौं**] [**書類銓衡**] selection [screening] of candidates by examining their report cards [personal histories] (for further examination).

서른 [**सौरन**] thirty.

서리 [सौरि] [가루 얼음] frost; hoar [hoary / white / rime] frost. e.g. 된서리 a heavy [hard / severe / strong / sharp] frost. 무[illegible][첫] 서리 the first frost of the year [season]. 서리가 내린 아침

a frosty morning.

서먹 (서먹) 하다 [सौमैक सौमैक हादा] [낯이 설다] unfamiliar; estranged; alienated; [무간하지 않다 reserved; formal; [어색하다] awkward; <서술적>feel awkward [nervous / out of place]; feel small [cheap / embarrassed] <in company>; feel ill at ease; be not at home.

서명 [सौम्यौ] [署名] a signature; an autograph (자기의 사진,저서 등에 하는; [서명하기] signing; autographing. 서명하다 [sign [write (down)] one's name; sign <a treaty>; autograph; affix [attach / put] one's signature <to a document>; subscribe one's name <to a document

서민 [सौमिन] [庶民] the (common / ordinary) people; the populace; the commonality; the masses; (한 사람) a commoner.

서방 [सौबां] [書房] [남편] one's husband [man]; a hubby.

서법 [सौबौप] [書法] penmanship; calligraphy.

서부 [सौबू] [西部] the western part (s); the west.

서비스 [सौबिस] [봉사] [बोंसा] service. e.g. 서비스가 좋다 [나쁘다] They give good [poor] service <in that hotel>. 그 식당은 서비스가 좋다 [나쁘다] The service at that restaurant is good [bad].

서사 [सौसा] [敍事] [修] narration; description. 서사하다 narrate; describe.

서서히 [सौसौहि] [徐徐-] slow (ly); gradually; little by little; by (slow) degree.

서성거리다 [सौसौगौरिदा] walk up and down restlessly; hover <about>; hang about [around] <a house>. e.g. 그는 어찌할 바를 몰라서 집 주위를 서성거렸다 He hovered around the house, uncertain what to do.

서수 [सौसू] [序數] an ordinal (number).].

서술 [सौसुल] [敍述] descryption; depiction; delineation; narration; [predication. 서술하다 describe; depict; delineate; narrate.

서슴다 [सौसमदा] hesitate; scruple; waver; hang [hold] back; be shy <of doing>; vacillate; falter; shilly–shally; be irresolute [heistant]. e.g. 그는 살인도 서슴지 않을 사람이다 He will not stick at murder.

서슴없다 [सौसमऔप्ता] unhesitating; <서술적> be not hesitant; have no scruples about; make no scruple of; do not stick at. e.g. 좋고 싫은 것을 서슴없이 말하다 [express one's likes and dislikes in no measured terms.

서식 [सौशिक] [書式] a (due [prescribed]) form. e.g. 제 5 호 서식 form No. 5. 서식대로 in due [proper] form / in accordance with [according to] the form prescribed.

서식 [सौशिक] [棲息] inhabitation. e.g. 서식에 적합한 in habitable. 서식하다 inhabit <the earth> (▷ inhabit는 장소를 목적어로 하여 타동사로만 씀) live <in the river>.

서식지 [सौशिक्चि] a habitat; a haunt; a home.

서신 [सौशिन] [書信] [편지 왕래] [correspondence; communication; [편지] a letter; an epistle; a note; a missive.

서약 [सौयाक] [誓約] an oath (▷ 성서 등에 걸고 하는 선서; a vow; a pledge (▷ 굳게 약속함; a recognizeance. 서약하다 swear; vow; pledge; make [take / swear] an oath <that>; give one's pledge [word] <that>; make a vow <to do / that>; pledge [bind / commit] oneself <to do>; make a covenant <to do / that>.

서양 [सौयांग] [西洋] the West; the Occident; Europe; Europe and America; [서양 여러 나라] Western countries.

서열 [सौयौल] [序列] rank; ranking; grade; order. e.g. 서열에 따라 in order of importance

서운하다 [सौउनहादा] (마음이) sorry; regrettable; unsatisfied; (하는 짓이) unsatisfactory; heartless; indifferent; unkind; unfair; displeasing. e.g. 이별이 서운하다 be sorry [sad] to part from <a person>.

서울 [सौउल] **1** [수도] a capital; a metropolis. e.g. 영국의 서울 런던 London, the capital of England. **2** [한국의 수도] Seoul.

서재 [सौजे] [書齋] a study; a library.

서적 [सौजौक] [書籍] books; publications

서점 [सौजौम] [書店] a bookseller's; a bookstore; a bookshop.

서정 [सौजौं] [抒情,敍情] delineation [description] of feeling [passions]; lyricism. e.g. 서정적인 lyric (al). 서정적으로 lyrically

서쪽 [सौचोक] [西-] the west (W).

서체 [सौछे] [書體] [글씨체] a style of handwriting; (활자의) a style of type.

서커스 [सौखौस] a circus.

서투르다 [सौथूरदा] unskillful; inexpert; poor; awkward; clumsy; unhandy; bungling; [익숙하지 않다] unfamiliar <with>; unaccustomed [unused] <to>; ignorant <of>; strange; new <to / at> e.g. 서투른 목수 an incompetent [unskilled] carpenter.

서평 [**सौफ्यौ**] [**書評**] a book review.

서포터 [**सौफोथौ**] (사람) a supporter

서해 [सौहै] [**西海**] the western sea; [황해] the Yellow Sea.

서행 [सौहै] [**徐行**] 서행 <게시> Go Slow / Drive Slowly. / Slow Down. 최고 서행 <게시 >Slow Down To Limit. / Dead Slow. 서행하다 [천천히 나아가다] o slow (ly); go at a slow speed; [속력을 떨어뜨리다] slow down.

석 [**सौक**] three. e.g. 석 달 three months.

석가모니 [**सौक्कामोनि**] S(h) akyamuni; Buddha

석간 [**सौक्कान**] [**夕刊**] [석간지] an evening paper; (조간에 대하여) an evening edition

석굴 [**सौक्कुल**] [**石窟**] a stone cave [cavern]

석권 [**सौक्वौन**] [**席卷**] 석권하다 [휩쓸다] carry everything before one; sweep <over / across>; pour over <a land>; [정복하다] conquer; make a conquest of. e.g. 외국 자본이 국내 시장을 석권했다 Foreign capital overwhelmed our market (s). **석기시대** [**सौक्कि शिदै**] [**石器時代**] [考] the stone Age.

석방 [**सौक्पांग**] [**釋放**] (a) release; discharge; liberation; (an) acquittal. 석방하다 release <a person>; set <a person> free; let off; turn loose; liberate; acquit.

석사 [**सौक्सा**] [**碩士**] [학위] Master. e.g. 문학 [이학 / 공학] 석사 a master of arts [science / engineering] (M.A.; M.Sc.; M.Eng.).

석상 [**सौक्सांग**] [**席上**] e.g. 석상 에서 [회합에서] at the meeting [assembly] / [사람들 속에서] [in company [public] / [그때] on the occasion. 공개 석상에서 [on a public occasion.

석양 [**सौग्यांग**] [**夕陽**] the setting sun; the evening sun; the declining [westering] sun. e.g. 석양은 산너머로 졌다 The sun set behind the mountain.

석연하다 [**सौग्यौनहादा**] [**釋然–**] (사람이) satisfied <with the explanation>; relieved from doubt; feeling free from doubt; (사물이) satisfactory; comprehendsible; understandable. e.g. 무언가 석연하지 않은 데가 있다 There is something inexplicable in the matter. / There is something to be clarified.

석유 [**सौग्यू**] [**石油**] oil; petroleum; (등유) kerosene.

석조 [सौक्चो] [**石造**] stone construction. e.g. 석조의 stone / made of stone.

석차 [सौक्छा] [**席次**] [성적의 순위] (academic) standing <in one's class>; ranking. e.g. 그의 석차가 10 등올랐다 [떨어졌다] His standing [rank] in the class has risen [fallen] ten places

석탄 [सौक्थान] [**石炭**] coal; [무연탄] [hard coal.]

석탑 [सौक्थाप] [**石塔**] a stone pagoda [tower].

석학 [सौख्याक] [**碩學**] [학문이 깊은 사람 an erudite scholar; a man of great [profound] learning.

섞다 [सौक्ता] [한데 합치다] mix <A and B / A with B>; (분리할 수 없을 정도로 blend <A and B / A with B>; admik compound; mingle.

섞이다 [सौक्किद्दा] be mixed; be blended (▷ be mixed 는 섞은 것이 식별 되는 경우나 식별되지 않는 경우에도 쓰지만 be blended 는 잘 섞여서 식별할 수 없을 때 씀

-선 [सौन] [**船**] a ship; a vessel. e.g. 외국선 a foreign ship / a foreigner.

-선 [सौन] [**線**] [노선,전선] a line; a wire. e.g. 상행[하행]선](고속 도로 등의) the inbound [outbound] lane (of traffic).

선[1] [सौन] an interview [a meeting] with a view to marriage; a marriage meeting.

선[2] [सौन] [**善**] the good; goodness; virtue; [선행] a good deed. e.g. 선과 악을 확실히 구별하다 make a clear distinction between right and wrong [good and evil].

선각자 [सौगाक्चा] [**先覺者**] a pioneer (leader); a leading spirit; a forerunner; a far-sighted leader; a path-finder; a prophet.

선거 [सौनगौ] [**選擧**] (an) election.

선견지명 [सौग्गयौनजीम्यौग] [**先見之明**] foresight; far-seeing intelligence [wisdom]. e.g. 선견지명이는 farseeing / foresighted / farsighted / longsighted / prescient.

선고 [सौगो] [**宣告**] [결정 사항 등의 통고] (a) pronouncement; announcement; (특히 판결의] a sentence; a verdict; adjudication. e.g. 피고의 유죄를 선고하다 adjudge a defendant (to be) guilty of the crime.

선교 [सौनग्यो] [**宣教**] propagation; (특히 기독교의) missionary work. 선교하다 propagate; preach the gospel; evangelize.

선교사 [सौनग्योजा] [**宣教師**] a

propagator; a missionary (worker).

선구자 [सौंगूजा] [**先驅者**] a pioneer; a herald; a forerunner; an outrunner; a precursor; a pathfinder; a man of light and leading.

선글라스 [सौंगल्लास] (a pair of) sunglasses; <wear> dark glasses.

선남 선녀 [सौंन्नाम सौंन्यौ] [**善男善女**] good [virtuous] men and women; [불교][pious people [men and women]; the faithful; Buddhists.

선녀 [सौंन्यौ] [**仙女**] a fairy; a celestial maiden; a dryad; a nymph (▷강이나 산 등에 사는 요정)

선도 [सौंन्दो] [**先導**] guidance; leadership. 선도하다 lead (the way); guide; go ahead of; conduct; precede.

선동 [सौंन्दोंग] [**煽動**] instigation; abetment; (an) incitement; demagogy; demagogism; demagoguery; (an) agitation (▷ 정치적, 사회적인 일 등으로. 선동하다 agitate; instigate; abet; [부추기다 incite; stir up; set [egg] (a person) on <to (do) something>; fan.

선두 [सौंन्दू] [**先頭**] [행렬 등 이어진 것의 맨 앞] the head; the front; the top; the lead; the van; the first. e.g. 선두가 되다 get ahead of (others in a race); get [have] the lead (in a race).

선득 [सौंन्दक] 선득하다 (추워서) chilled; <서술적> feel chilly; feel a chill [cold]; (놀라서) shudder <at>; have a thrill of horror.

선뜻 [सौंन्तत] [빨리 quickly; nimbly [쾌히] readily; willingly; [서슴없이] without hesitation; [즉석에서] instantly; at once; offhand; right away; [가볍게] lightly; lightheartedly. e.g. 선뜻 승낙하다응하다] readily [willingly] consent <to it> / comply willingly [with a good grace] / give a ready consent.

선량 [सौंलल्यांग] [**善良**] goodness. 선량하다 good; virtuous; right; good-natured.

선례 [सौंल्ये] [**先例**] prejudication.

선로 [सौंल्लो] [**線路**] a (railroad / railway) track [line].

선망 [सौंन्मांग] [**羨望**] envy. e.g. 선망의 눈초리로 보다 gaze enviously <at>. 선망하다 envy; be envious <of>; feel envy <at>; regard <a person> with envy; look enviously <at>.

선명 [सौंम्योंग] [**鮮明**] clearness; distinctness; lucidity; vividness. 선명 하다] clear; clear-[sharp-] cut; distinct; sharp; plain; [생생 하다] vivid.

선물 [सौंन्मुल] [**膳物**] [선사품 a present; a gith; [바치

는것] a tribute; [기념품] a souvenir. 선물 하다 give <a person> a present.

선박 [सौन्बाक] [**船舶**] a vessel; a ship; a bottom; <집합적> shipping; seacrath.

선반 [सौन्बान] [**-盤**] a shelf <*pl.* shelves>; (그물, 격자 모양의) a rack.

선발 [सौन्बाल] [**選拔**] selection; choice; picking out. 선발 하다 select; pick out; choose; mark out <for>; single out; drath.

선배 [सौन्बै] [**先輩**] a senior; a superior; an elder; a predecessor; an old timer

선별 [सौनब्यौल] [**選 別**] sorting; selection; (광석의) concentration; dressing. 선별 하다 sort; [좋은것을 가리다] select; concentrate; dress. e.g. 흠 있는 물건을 선별 하다 sort out defective articles

선불 [सौन्बुल] [**先拂**] advance payment; payment in advance; prepayment; cash before delivery (C.B.D). 선불하다 pay [disburse] in advance; advance (money); make an advance; prepay (of wages).

선비 [सौन्वी] [학자] a (classical) scholar; a learned man;

선사 시대 [**सौन्सा शिदै**] the prehistoric age.

선사 [**सौन्सा**] [위로, 존경, 친근, 애정 등의 뜻으로 선물 을줌] presentation. 선사 하다 give [make / send] <a person> a present; make a gith <to a person>; present <a person with a thing>.

선산 [सौन्सान] [**先山**] [조상의 무덤] one's family graveyard; one's ancestral burial ground.

선생 [सौन्सैंग] [**先生**] (일반적으로) a teacher; a master; an instructor.

선서 [सौन्सा] [**宣誓**] an oath; parole. 선서 하다 swear; take [make / swear] an oath; pledge one's word of honor; lith (up) the hand

선선하다 [सौनसौनहादा] [시원하다] cool; refreshing. e.g. 선선한바람 cool [refreshing] breeze

선수 [1] [सौन्सू] [**選手**] a player; a representative player; an athlete (▷player 는 야구, 축구 등 게임의 선수)

선수 [2] [सौन्सू] [**先手**] [기선을 제압하기] forestalling; the initiative; anticipation. e.g. 선수를 빼앗기다 [앞질리다 be forestalled / [주도권을 빼앗기다 lose the initiative / [후진에서 활약하다] act as rearguard

선술집 [**सौन्सुल्चिप**] a tavern; a (stand-up) bar; a saloon; a groggery; a public house; <英> a pub.

선심 [सौन्शिम] [**善心**] **1** [선량한 마음] virtuous mind; virtue; conscience; moral sense. **2** [자비로운 마음] a merciful heart; mercy; benevolence; kindness; [너그러운 마음] generosity; liberality 선심(을) 쓰다 have mercy on <a person>. e.g. 그들이 선심을 써 주는 바람에 사장을 만날 수가 있었다 They were kind [good] enough to let me see the president.

선악 [सौनआक] [**善惡**] good and evil [bad] [정사(正邪)] right and wrong; virtue and vice.

선약 [सौन्याक] [**先約**] a previous engagement. 선약이 없다 have no previous engagement / be disengaged / be free.

선언 [**宣言**] [규약, 규정에 따른 통고 a) declaration; (a) proclamation; [정식 발표 an) announcement. 선언 하다 declare; make a declaration <of>; proclaim; announce.

선원 [सौन्वौन] [**船員**] a sailor; a seaman; <집합적 the crew; a ship's company; officers and crew; (한사람) one [a member] of the crew [the ships company]; a crew member; a crewman; a seaman; a mariner.

선의 [सौन्ुइ] [**善意**] [좋은 뜻] a favorable sense; [좋은 의도] good will; good intentions; [法] good faith. e.g. 선의로 in good faith / with good intent [intentions]

선임 [सौनिम] [**選任**] [선출] (an) election; [임명] (an) appointment; (an) assignment. 선임 하다 elect; appoint; assign. e.g. 그는 사회당 위원장으로 선임되었다 He was elected chairman of the Socialist Party.

선입관 [सौनिपक्वान] [**先入觀**] a preconception; a preoccupation; a prepossession; a prejudice; a bias; a preconceived idea [notion]. e.g. 선입관을 가지다 [have a preconceived idea [opinion].

선잠 [सौन्जाम] a nap; a doze; a snooze; a dogsleep; a light [short] sleep; slumber (s). e.g. 선잠을 자다 take a nap / doze / snooze / slumber / have a light [short] sleep

선장 [सौन्जांग] [**船長**] the captain of a ship; a (ship's / sea) captain; the master (of a ship); a master mariner; a commander; a skipper (소형 상선,어선의) [; a ferry master (연락선의).

선전 [सौन्जौन] [**宣傳**] propaganda (정부 등이 유리한 정보를 흘림 publicity (이름을 일반에게 알림; propagation; propagandism; [광고] advertisement; an advertising campaign; buildup. 선전 하다 propagate; publicize; propagandize; give publicity <to>; conduct [make] propaganda; disseminate; spread abroad; [광고 하다 advertise; give a buildup <to>. e.g. 대대적으로 선전 하다 carry on propaganda on a large scale / give a big buildup <to>.

선전 [सौन्जौन] [**善戰**] 선전 하다 fight well [magnificently / admirably]; fight a good fight [battle]; make [put up] a good fight. e.g. 그들은 선전했 음에도 불구하고 패했다 [Although they fought very well [hard], they were defeated.

선조 [सौन्जो] [**先祖**] an ancestor; a forefather; a progenitor; a predecessor; [法] a stirps <*pl.* stirpes>.

선진 [सौन्जिन] [**先進**] [앞섬] being advanced; [선배] a senior; a superior; an elder; a predecessor; a progenitor; [선구자] a pioneer; a precursor; a farsighted leader. 선진의 advanced / developed.

선착 [सौन्छाक] [**先着**] [먼저 도착함 the first arrival. e.g. 선착순으로 줄을 서 주세요 Please line up in the order of arrival.

선착장 [सौन्छाक्चांग] [**船着場**] [부두] a wharf; [상륙지][a landing place.

선처 [सौन्छो] [**善處**] amicable [adequate] management; proper dealing. 선처하다 make the best of <a bad bargain>; tide over <difficultties>; act with prudence; use discretion <in>; deal adequately [wisely] with <a difficult situation>; deal with <something> as one thinks fit; adjust oneself <to>.

선천(성) [सौन्छौनसौ] [**先天(性)**] apriority; innateness; inbornness; inherence. e.g. [선천적 인성의] native / inborn / innate / congenital / [유전적인] inherited / hereditary.

선출 [सौन्छुल] [**選出**] election; choice. 선출하다 elect; return. e.g. 그녀는 학급 대표로 선출되었다 She was elected class representative.

선택 [सौन्थैक] [**選擇**] (a) choice; (a) selection; option; selectivity. 선택 하다 select; choose; pick up; make a [one's] choice. e.g. 선택하는 데 갈피를 못 잡다 be at a loss which to choose. 잘 선택하다 make a good choice.

선포 [सौन्फो] [**宣布**] proclamation; promulgation; announcement. 선포 하다 proclaim; make public; promulgate; announce; publicize; make promulgation of; issue a proclamation. e.g. 전쟁을 선포하다 declare war.

[계엄령을 선포하다] proclaim martial law.

선풍기 [सौन्फुंगि] [**扇風機**] an electric fan; a motor fan

선하다 [सौनहादा] vivid [fresh] <before one's eyes>; graphic; feel as if one actually saw. e.g. 눈에 선하다 be fresh in one's memory / live vividly in one's memory.

선행 [सौनहै] [**先行**] precedence; antecedence; preceding; going first; walking ahead <of>. 선행 하다 precede; be [go / walk] ahead <of>.

선행 [सौनहै] [**善行**] good conduct; a good deed. e.g. 선행을 쌓다 accumulate [keep on doing] good deeds.

섣불리 [सौत्पुल्लि] [어설프게 awkwardly; clumsily; tactlesssly; [부주의하게] [carelessly; thoughtlessly; heedlessly; inadvertently. e.g. 남의 말을 섣불리 믿다 believe too easily what o ne hears [what they say].

설 [सौल] [새해의 첫날] [New Year's Day; the first [opening] day of the year; [새해의 첫머리 the New Year (season).

설 [सौल] [**說**] **1** [의견, 주장] an opinion; a view; (종교상의 a doxy. e.g.그 기원에 대해서는 여러 설이 있다 [There are a variety of views about its origin. **2** [학설, 신조] a theory; a doctrine. e.g. (새로운) 설을 주창하다 advance [propose / put forward] a (new) the

설거지 [सौल्कौजी] [그릇을 씻어치움] dish-washing; washing-up. 설거지하다] do the dishes [washing-up]; wash the dishes; wash up

설계 [सौलक्ये] [**設計**] (건물 등의)a plan; (형체, 구조, 외관 등의)a design. 설계하다 plan; design; project; make a plan; work out a design <for>; [도면을 그리다] lay out; draw up a plan.

설교 [सौलक्यो] [**說教**] **1** [교리를 가르침] a sermon; preaching; a preachment; a religious discourse. 설교하다 preach <a sermon>; deliver [give] <a person> a sermon; occupy the pulpit. e.g. 열변을 토하며 설교하는 사람 a pulpit orator. **2** [훈계] a moralizing discourse [lecture]; [잔소리] scolding; remonstrance; admonition; preaching; a lecture; a lesson

설날 [सौल्लाल] New Year's Day; the first of the year.

설다[1] [सौल्ता] **1** [덜 익다] be half-boiled [half-cooked

/ half-done]; be undercooked [underdone]; (과일 등이) be unripe. e.g. 선밥 half-boiled [undercooked] rice. **2** (술 등이] be not thoroughly fermented; (김치 등이) be not fully pickled.

설다[2] [सौल्ता] [생소하다] unfamiliar; strange; [서투르다] inexperienced; green. e.g. 선 무당 a green [novice] shaman. 이 곳은 낯이 설다 I am a stranger here.

설득 [सौल्तक] [**說得**] persuasion. 설득 하다 persuade; prevail on; solicit <assistance>; talk <a person> into compliance; talk <a person> over [round]; urge [induce] <a person to do>; reason with <a person> (▷ persuade 는 설득하여 그것이 성공하였 음을 뜻함)

설렁하다 [सौल्लौंहादा] chilly; rather cold; somewhat [slightly] cold.

설레다 [सौल्लेदा] [마음이 들떠서 두근거리다] throb (audibly / violently); beat high <with the hope of>; palpitate; flutter. e.g. 설레는 가슴 a loudly throbbing heart.

설레설레 [सौल्लेसौल्ले] (머리를) waving; shaking; (꼬리를) swishing (소가) wagging (개가) e.g. 고개를 설레설레 젓다 [shake [wag] one's head.

설령 [सौल्यौं] [**設令**] even if [though]; though; although; granting [supposing] that .... e.g. 설령 그렇다 치더라도 granting [admitting] that it is so / even if it were so.

설립 [सौल्लिप] [**設立**] establishment; foundation; setting up; institution; (회사 등의) promotion; incorporateion; flotation; organization. 설립하다 establish; found; set up; institute; promote; incorporate; organize.

설마 [सौल्म] surely <not>; <not> possibly [by any possibility]; it is not [least] likely <that ...>; by no means; on no account; never. e.g. 설마 [सौल्मा] Indeed! / Impossible! / The idea! / You don't say so! / You're telling me! / What do you know? / Well, I never! / Well, I declare! 설마 자네는 아니겠지 – 물론 아니지 [Surely it wasn't you? – Never!

설명 [सौल्म्योंग] [**說明**] explanation; account; exposition; interpretation; elucidation; illustration (도해) presentation; enucleation; description; a legend (도표 등의) [a caption (사진 등의) 설명 하다 explain; give an explanation <of>;

account <for>; give an account <of>; interpret; make clear; elucidate; describe; expound; illustrate. e.g. 설명할 수 있는 explainable / explicable.

설문 [सौल्मुन] [**設問**] a question.

설비 [सौल्बि] [**設備**] equipment; provision; installation; arrangements; appointments; conveniences; faci-lities <for> (시설) accommodations (숙박, 수용 설비) e.g. 가정용 난방 설비 home heating equipment. 과잉 설비 excessive facilities 설비하다 equip [fit / provide / furnish] <with>; install <electriclights>; accommodate; arrange; appoint; organize. e.g. 호화 롭게 설비된 방 a gorgeously furnished room

설빔 [सौल्पिम] the New Year's garb; a fine dress worn on the New Year's Day.

설사 [सौल्सा] [**泄瀉**] [**醫**] diarrh(o)ea; laxity [looseness] <of the bowels>; loose bowels 설사하다 have diarrhea; have loose bowels (▷ 전자가 많이 쓰임.)

설산 [सौल्सान] [**雪山**] snow-covered mountains; snowy mountains; a mountain covered with snow.

설상가상 [सौल्सांगासांग] [**雪上加霜**] misfortune on top of misfortune. e.g. 설상가상으로 to make matters worse / to add to one's misery / on top of all other misfortunes / as if to rub salt in [into] the wound.

설왕설래 [सौल्वांसौल्लै] [**說往說來**] 설왕설 래하다 argue back and forth; bandy [cross] words <with>; wrangle.

설익다 [सौरिक्ता] **1** [음식이 덜 익다. e.g. 설익은 half-done [-boiled / -cooked]. **2** (과일이 be unripe [un-derripe / partly ripe].

설전 [सौल्चौन] [**舌戰**] e.g. 설전을 벌이다 [wage wordy warfare <with> / exchange verbal attacks with each other.

설정 [सौल्चौं] [**設定**] establishment; creation; fixing; setting up; institution. 설정하다 establish; set up; create; institute. e.g. 규칙을 설정하다 fix a rule

설치 [सौल्छि] [**設置**] [설비 equipment; (기구 등의) [installation; (가구 등의 furnishing; institution; (기관 등의) establishment; (학교 등의) foundation. 설치하다 [equip <with>; fit up <with>; install; found; institute; establish; found. e.g. 모금 위원회를 설치하다 set up [organize] a fund-raising committee.

설치다 [सौल्छिदा] **1** [중도에서 그치다] [leave <a thing>

half-done; stop <work> halfway; (잠을 fail to get to sleep (enough); sleep badly; be sleepless. e.g. 그는 잠을 설친 모양이다 Sleep seemed to have deserted his pillow.2 [몹시 날뛰다] run wild [amuck / riot]; rave [ramp / rage] about; be rampant; overrun; infest; be unruly. e.g. 데모 대가 거리를 설치고 다녔다 The demonstrators stormed through the street.

설탕 [सौल्थांग] [**雪糖**] sugar.

설화 [सौरह्वा] [**說話**] [옛이야기] a tale; a story; [우화] [a fable. e.g. 설화 적인 [narrative.

섬 [सौम] [도서] an island; [작은 섬] an islet; (시어 [शिऔ]) an isle.

섬광 [सौमग्वां] [**閃光**] a flash (of light); a glint [sudden gleam] of light; [天] scintillation.

섬기다 [सौम्गिदा] serve <one's master>; be in <a person's> service; render service to <one's country>; work under <another>; [모시다] attend on; wait on. e.g. 부모를 섬기다 take care of one's parents / be devoted to [dutiful toward] one's parents.

섬뜩하다 [सौम्तख्वादा] frightened; horrified; <서술적>. have a fright [scare]; be taken aback. e.g. 섬뜩 하여 in a fright.

섬세 [सौम्से] [**纖細**] [가냘프고 가늚 slenderness; [찬찬하고 세밀함] delicacy; fineness. 섬세 하다 delicate; fine; nice; exquisite; subtle. e.g. 섬세한 감수성 a) delicate [fine] sensibility.

섬유 [सौम्यू] [**纖維**] (a) fiber [<英> (a) fibre]; a strand; textiles.

섭렵 [सौल्यौप] [**涉獵**] extensive reading. 섭렵하 다책을) read extensively; range over; scour. e.g. 널리 문헌을 섭렵하다 range extensively [dig deeply into] the literature <connecting something>.

섭리 [सौ] [**攝理**] [하느 님의 뜻] providence; dispensation; economy. e.g. 신의 섭리 divine providence [disposal] / the Providence of God.

섭섭하다 [सौपसौफदा]1 [헤어지기가 어렵다] [sad; sorry; regretful; <서술적>. be reluctant <to do>. e.g. 헤어지기가 섭섭한 듯이 reluctantly; lingeringly / wistfully / with a regretful glance. 2 [유감스럽다] sorry; regrettable; regretful; [서운하다] miss. e.g. 참으로 섭섭하다 it is really [highly] regrettable that ..3 [원망스럽다] reproachful; rueful; [불만스럽다] [disappointed. e.g. 섭섭한 듯한 모습으로 with a reproachful look / with a wistful regret.

섭씨 [सॉप्शि] [**攝氏**] [온도계의 눈금 명칭] centigrade (C., C, Cent.); Celsius (C., C, Cels). e.g. 섭씨 10 도 2 분 ten point two degrees centigrade / 10.2℃.

섭외 [सॉब्वे] [**涉外**] [대외관계] public relations (P.R.); [조직간의 연락] liaison (work).

섭취 [सॉप्छ्वि] [**攝取**] (음식, 영양분의) intake; ingestion; intussusception. e.g. 단백질의 섭취 the intake of protein. 섭취하다 [take; ingest; incept; take in; swallow. e.g. 영양을 섭취하다 take nutrition.

성 1 [सॉग] [**姓**] a surname; a family name; a last name. e.g. 성과 이름을 대다 give one's full name.

성 2 [**सॉग**] [노여운 감정] anger; rage; indignation; wrath; displeasure; offense. e.g. 성이 나게 하다 make <a person> angry

성 3 [सॉग] [**性**] **1** (남녀의) a) sex. e.g. 성관계 sexual relations. **2** [본성] nature. e.g. 인간의 본성은 선하다 All men are born good. / Man is naturally good. **3** [문법] gender. e.g. 남[여 / 중] 성 the masculine [feminine / neuter] gender.

성 4 [सॉग] [**城**] a castle; a fortress; a citadel; [성벽] a wall; (castle) walls.

성가시다 [**सॉगाशिदा**] [귀찮다 bothersome; troublesome; harassing; annoying; burdensome; vexatious; irksome; [주체스럽다] cumbrous; [끈덕지다] [pertinacious; (자꾸 캐물어서) inquisitive; (졸라대어서) importunate. e.g. 성가신 아이 a troublesome child. 성가신 사람 a nuisance.

성격 [सॉग्योक] [**性格**] character; personality. e.g. 성격의 차이 disparity [dissimilarity] in character.

성경 [सॉग्यौंग] [**聖經**] the (Holy) Bible; a holy book; the Scriptures; the Holy Writ.

성공 [सॉगोंग] [**成功**] **1** [뜻을 이룸] [तसल इरूम](a) success; [히트] [शिथ] a hit; a coup; [일의 성취] achievement. e.g. 성공을 거두다 [achieve [gain / win] success / make [pull off] a coup. 성공하다 (사람이 succeed <in>; be successful <in>; win [achieve] success; (사물 이) succeed; be [prove] successful. **2** [출세를 함] success in life [the world]; [번영] prosperity. e.g. 그는 학자로서 성공했다 He was a success [succeeded] as a scholar.

성과 [सौग्वा] [**成果**] a result; a fruit; a product; an outcome. e.g.노력의 성과 the result of one's efforts / the fruit [product] of one's labor.

성교육 [सौग्योयुक [**性教育**] sex education; sex information.

성금 [सौगम] [**誠金**] a gith of money; a donation; a contribution; a subscription.

성급하다 [सौगुफादा] [**性急-**] hasty; impatient; impetuous; rash; quick-[short- / hot-] tempered. e.g. 성급한 기질 a hasty temper / impetuous disposition.

성기 [सौगि] [**性器**] sexual [genititial, generative] [organsholy] vessel.

성기다 [सौगिदा] [거리, 간격이 뜨다] loose; sparse; coarse; rough; thin; open. e.g. 성긴 수염 a thin moustache.

성나다 [सौनादा] [화나다] get [become / grow] angry <with a person / at something>; feel angry <with [at] a person>; be furious; be angered [offended / enraged] <by>; get mad; fly into a fury [passion]; be in a fume [huff]

성냥 [सौन्यांग] a match.

성년 [सौन्यौन] [**成年**] adult [full / lawful] age; man's [woman's] estate; majority. e.g. 성년에 달하다 come of age / reach [attain] one's majority / reach full age / arrive at manhood [womanhood].

성능 [सौनुंग] [**性能**] efficiency; capacity; power; (기계의) performance; property (특질). e.g. 고성능 엔진 a high-performance engine.

성당 [सौदांग] [**聖堂**] (천주교의) a (Catholic) church.

성대 1 [सौन्दै] [**盛大**] grandeur; magnificence. 성대하다 grand; magnificent; splendid; pompous; flourishing; prosperous. e.g. 성대한 결혼식 a grand [magnificent] wedding ceremony.

성대 2 [सौन्दै] [**聲帶**] the vocal cords[bands]. e.g. 가성대 a false vocal cords.

성량 [सौंन्यांग] [**聲量**] the volume of (one's) voice. e.g. 성량이 풍부한 목소리 a voice of great volume / a powerful voice.

성립 [सौनिप] [**成立**] **1** [생겨남] coming into existence [being]; [실현] realization; materialization. 성립하다 come [be brought] into existence [being]; be materialized [realized]; materialize e.g. 그런 이론은 성립되지 않는다 [Such a theory is not valid [does not hold water]. **2** [조직됨] formation; organization. e.g. 새 위원회의 성립은 그의 열의에 힘입은 바가 크다

[The formation of the new committee owes a great deal to his zeal. **3** (조약, 협정 등의) conclusion. 성립하다 be concluded. e.g. 두 사람의 혼인이 성립되었다 They became man and wife. / They were [got] married.

성명 [सौंग्म्यौग] [**聲明**] a declaration; a proclamation; a statement; an announcement; a manifesto. e.g. 공동 성명 a joint statement. 공식 성명을 내다 [issue [deliver] an official statement.

성명 [सौंग्म्यौग] (a) (full) name; one's family name and given name. e.g. 성명 부지의 사람 an unidentified person / a man whose name is unknown.

성묘 [सौम्यो] [**省墓**] a visit to one's ancestral grave. 성묘하다 pay a visit [one's homage] to one's ancestor's grave; visit one's ancestor's grave; worship at one's ancestor's grave.

성미 [सौंगमि] [**性味**] [성질] nature; disposition; [기질] temperament; temper; spirit; 성격 character; [성정과 취미] bent. e.g. 성미가 고약한 ill-natured / ill-disposed / evil-minded / wicked / vicious / malicious.

성범죄 [सौबौमज्वे] [**性犯罪**] a sex [sexual] offense [crime].

성별 [सौब्यौल] [**性別**] the distinction of sex.

성사 [सौसा] [**成事**] accomplishment; achievement; attainment; fulfil (l) ment; realization; success. 성사하다 accomplish; achieve; attain; fulfil (l); realize; be settled; be arranged; succeed.

성서 [सौसौ] [**聖書**] the (Holy) Bible; the Scriptures; the Holy Writ.

성수기 [सौसुगि] [**盛需期**] a high-demand season.

성숙 [सौसुक] [**成熟**] [충분히 발육됨] full [complete] growth; maturity. 성숙하다 reach [come to] maturity; attain [reach] full growth; mature; ripen; grow into adulthood. e.g. 성숙하여 여자답게 되다 [ripen into womanhood. 요즘 아이들은 빨리 성숙한다 Recently children have begun to mature earlier

성스럽다 [सौंग्सुरौप्ता] [**聖**-] [신성하다] holy; sacred; divine; heavenly; [장엄하다] solemn; sublime.

성실 [सौंगशिल] [**誠實**] sincerity; honesty; integrity; faithfulness; fidelity; devotion; earnestness; seriousness. 성실하다 sincere; honest; faithful; truthful; devoted; earnest; serious.

성악 [सौंगाक] [**聲樂**] vocal music. 성악가 a vocalist; a singer.

성업 [सौंगौब] [**盛業**] a thriving business. e.g. 성업 중이다 [장사가 drive a thriving [prosperous / roaring / booming] trade / (병원 등이) [ब्यौवौन दंड] have [enjoy] a large practice.

성우 [सौङु] [聲優] (TV 영화의) an actor [actress] specializing in dubbing films; (라디오 방송의) [a radio actor [actress].

성원 [सौन्वान] [聲援] **1** [격려] (a shout of) encouragement; (경기의) cheering; <美> rooting. e.g.열렬한 성원을 보내다 give enthusiastic encouragement <to> / (경기에서)] <美> root wildly <for a team> / give <a person> a big yell. 성원하다 encourage; shout encouragement <for / to>; cheer <a team on to victory>; <美> root <for a team>. **2** [도와줌] support; patronage. 성원하다 support; give one's support <to>; patronize. e.g. 앞으로도 계속해서 저희를 성원해 주시기 바랍니다 [We hope you will favor us with your continued patronage.

성의 [सौउइ] [誠意] sincerity; good faith; a true heart; devotion. e.g. 성의가 없는 insincere / false / fickle / faithless / hollow-hearted / heartless / empty.

성인 [1] [सौगिन] [成人] an adult; a grown-up (person). e.g. 성인의 날 Coming-of-Age Day.

성인 [2] [सौइन] [聖人] a sage; a saint; a holy man.

성장 [सौगजांग] [成長] growth. e.g. 경제 성장 economic growth / growth in economy. 성장하다 grow (up); be brought up.

성적 [सौच्चौक [性的] sexual.

성적 [सौजौक] [成績] **1** 일 등의 성과] performance; a result; a showing; a record; (개인의) merit. e.g. 영업 성적 a firm's) business performance / business showing. **2** [敎] [학업의 기록] a (school) record; [시험 등의 결과] results; [성적의 평가]a grade; a mark. e.g.시험 성적 the result of an examination.

성적표 [सौजौक्फ्यो] (학교의) [a list of students records; a report card [a term report] (통지표경기의 a scorecard.

성전환 [सौजौन्हवान] [性轉換] the change of sex a sex change. 성전환하다 change one's sex.

성전환 수술 [सौजौनहवान सुसुल] a sex change operation.

성지 [सौग्जी] [聖地] a sacred place; holy ground; (팔레스타인의) the Holy Land. e.g. 성지 순례를 하다 make [go on] a pilgrimage

to the Holy Land / visit the Holy Land.

성직 [सौन्जीक] [**聖職**] [가톨릭, 기독교] the clergy; the ministry (▷영국에서는 주로 성공회 이외의 a religious vocation; (holy) orders.

성직자 [सौजीक्चा] a churchman; a clergyman.

성질 [सौन्जील] [**性質**] **1** [마음의 바탕] one's nature; one's disposition; one's temperament; one's temper. e.g. 성질이 좋다 나쁘다] good-natured [ill-natured]. **2** [사물, 현상의 고유의특성] a property; a nature; a quality; character. e.g. 어떤 종류의 풀에는 병을 낫게 하는 성질이 있다

성찰 [सौन्छाल] [**省察**] reflection; introspection; self-examination. 성찰하다 reflect; introspect; examine oneself.

성취 [सौन्छ्वी] [**成就**] accomplishment; fulfil(l)ment; achievement; attainment; completion; consummation; realization. 성취하 다 accomplish; fulfill; achieve; attain; complete; consummate; realize; effect. e.g. 내 소원이 성취되었다 My prayers were answered. / I have my desire fulfilled. / I have my wish realized.

성탄절 [सौथान्जौल] [**聖誕節**] [기독교, 가톨릭] Christmas (Day).

성패 [सौन्फे] [**成敗**] success or failure; [결과] the result. e.g. 성패에 관계 없이 whether successful or not / whatever the result may be.

성품 [सौन्फुम] [**性品**] [성질] nature; disposition; [기질] temper; temperament. e.g. 성품이 좋은 사람 a good-natured man / a man of good character / a man of the right kidney.

성하다 [सौहादा] **1** [온전하다] intact; undamaged; whole; sound; flawless; faultless; spotless. e.g. 깨지지 않고 성한 접시라고는 하나도 없다 Not a plate is left whole. / There isn't a whole plate left. **2** [병이나 탈이 없다] healthy; (safe and) sound; (alive and) well; fit; robust. e.g. 성한 몸 a healthy [sound] body

성함 [सौन्हाम] [**姓銜**] ⇨ 성명 (姓名) e.g. 성함이 어떻게 되십니까 May I have your name, please?

성행 [सौन्हे] [**盛行**] prevalence; vogue; a fad; a rage. 성행하다 prevail; be prevalent; have a great vogue; be much in fashion [vogue]; be in the height of fashion; be very popular; rage; be rife; be rampant e.g. 투기가 성행하고 있다 Speculation is widely prevalent.

성향 [सौन्हयांग] [**性向**] an inclination; a disposition; a propensity; a tendency. e.g. 소비 성향 the propensity to consume..

성형 [सौन्हयौग] [**成形**] **1** [외과] correction of deformities; (얼굴의) face-lithing. **2** [工] forming; shaping; molding. 성형하다 mold; cast. e.g. 찰[금속]을 성형하여 소상을 만들다 cast a statue in clay [metal] / cast clay [metal] into a clay.

성형 수술 a plastic operation.

성황 [सौन्हवांग] [**盛況**] prosperity; a boom; a success. e.g. 성황을 이루다 be prosperous / be thriving / be flourishing / enjoy prosperity / (상점 등이 be doing a flourishing business / do thriving business / (모임 등이) be a success / be well attended.

세[1] [से] [**歲**] age; years. e.g. 80 세 노인 an old man of eighty.

세[2] [से] [**稅**] [조세] a tax a duty; an imposition; dues; rates (지방세 등) [과세] taxation. e.g. 상속세 a death [a succession / an inheritance] tax.

세[3] [से] [**貰**] [임대, 임차] lease; tenancy; location (부동산의) hire; hiring (물건의) charter (배의) [임대료] (a) rent; hire; charterage (선박의) e.g. 세를 든 [낸] 사람 a hirer / a lessee / a tenant / a leaseholder (부동산의)

세[4] [से] [셋] [सेत] three. e.g. 세 three times / thrice.

세게 [सेगे] [강하, strongly; stoutly; powerfully; firmly; intensely; [세차게] hard; severely; violently; [통렬하게] keenly; [인상적으로] impressively; [강조하여] with emphasis; forte (f). e.g. 세게 때리다 hit [strike] hard [vigorously].

세계 [सेग्ये] [**世界**] [온세상] the world; [지구] the earth; the globe.

세공 [सेगों] [**細工**] [잔손질이 많이 가는 수공] work; workmanship; crathsmanship. 세공하다 work <in / on>; crath.

세균 [सेग्यून] [**細菌**] a bacillus <*pl.* bacilli>; a bacterium <*pl.* bacteria>; a germ; a microbe. e.g. 세균의 bacterial / bacillar / bacillary. 세균이 없는 우유 bacteria-free milk.

세금 [सेगम] [**稅金**] a tax dues; the rates (지방세) a duty <on> (물품세 a toll (통행세) e.g. 부당한 세금 an irrational [unreasonable] tax. 미납 세금

unpaid taxes.

세기 [सेगि] [世紀] a century. e.g. 금세기 this [the present] century.

세내다 [सेनैदा] [貰-] hire <a boat, a horse, etc.>; engage <a carriage>; rent <a house, land, etc.>; take <a house, a room, etc.>; lease <land>; (배를) charter <a vessel>.

세놓다 [सेनोथा] [貰-] hire [let] out <a boat>; (집을) let [rent] <a house to a person>; rent out <a mansion>; locate; (토지를)] lease.

세뇌 [सेन्वे] [洗腦] brainwashing; indoctrination. 세뇌하다 brainwash <a person>; indoctrinate. e.g. 그는 세뇌당하여 비밀을 털어놓고 말았다 He was brainwashed into revealing the secret.

세다[1] [सेदा] [머리털이 희어지다] turn white [gray]; become grizzled [grizzly]; [얼굴이 혈색이 없어지다] turn pale[white] <with fear>. e.g. 센 머리 gray [white / hoary] hair.

세다[2] [सेदा] (수를) count; reckon; calculate; number; numerate; enumerate; take count of <votes>. e.g. 다시 세다 recount / count (all over) again / count over. 잘못 세다 [count wrong / miscalculate / miscount.

세다[3] [सेदा] **1** (힘이) [많다] strong; powerful; mighty; vigorous; muscular; robust (강건하다) e.g. 힘이 센 사람 a strong [powerful] man / a brawny man. **2** (마음이 [강하다 tough; firm; stubborn. e.g. 고집이 세다 be stubborn [obstinate]. **3** [강렬하다] violent; strong; hard; severe; fierce; intense; heavy; rough; forcible; keen e.g. 센 바람 a strong [heavy / violent] wind. **4** [능력, 수준이 정도 이상이다 good <at>; strong <in>. e.g. 그는 바둑이 세다 He is a good *paduk* player.

세대 [सेदै] [世代] a generation.

세력 [सेर्योक] [勢力] **1** [지배력] influence; power; strength; might; sway. e.g. 안정 세력 a stabilizing force [factor]. **2** [물리적 힘] force; energy. e.g. 태풍의 세력이 약해졌다 The typhoon weakened [lost strength].

세련 [सेर्योन] [洗練, 洗鍊] polishing; refinement.

세련되다 [सेर्योनदवेदा] [洗練-] polished; refined; finished; elegant. e.g. 세련된 신사 a polished [refined] gentleman.

세례 [सेर्ये] [洗禮] baptism;

palingenesis; christening (유아의) e.g. 유아 세례 pedobaptism.

세로 [सेरो] [가로에 대하여 length; [높이 height; 수직으로 perpendicularly; vertically; lengthwise; longitudinally; endwise

세면 [सेम्यौन] [洗面] washing up (one's face). 세면하다 wash one's face; have a wash.

세면대 [सेम्यौन्दै] a washstand; a washing stand; a washhand stand.

세모 [सेमो] triangularity. e.g. 세모난 모자 a three-cornered [tricornered] hat.

세무 [सेमु] [税務] taxation business; tax affairs.

세미나 [सेमिना] a seminar <on public finance>.

세밀 [सेमिल] [細密] minuteness; elaborateness. 세밀하다 minute; detailed; fine; close; elaborate. e.g. 세밀한 관찰 close observation.

세배 [सेबै] [歲拜] [정초에 하는 인사, 절] the New Year's greetings [call / visit]; a formal bow of respect to one's elders on New Year's Day. 세배하다 perform [make] a New Year's bow; exchange the New Year's greetings

세뱃돈 [सेबैत्तोन] the New Year's gith of money given to one's juniors; a handsel.

세부 [सेबु] [細部] details; particulars; the fine parts; the minutiae. e.g. 세부를 조사하다 go into details [particulars].

세상 [सेसांग] [世上] **1** [세계] the world; (a) society (사회 the public (사람들) [인생, 생애] life; existence; one's life time. e.g. 이 세상 this world [life]. **2** [시대] [शिदै] the age; the era; the period; the times. e.g. 세상의 변천 the change of the times / the march of times.

세상 물정 [सेसांग] [世上物情] (the condition of) the world; the ways of the world; worldly matters; [인간의 속성] human nature; humanity. e.g. 세상 물정에 밝은 사람 a man of the world / a sensible man.

세상에 [सेसांगे] [世上-] <how / what / why> on earth [in the world / in the name of God]. e.g. 세상에 이게 무슨 일이냐 What in the world is it? 세상에 별일 다 보겠다 Of all things! / Well, now I've seen everything!

세세하다 [सेसेहादा] [細細-] **1** [미세하다] small; fine; minute. e.g. 세세한 물건 small things. **2** [상세하다] detailed; minute; circumstantial; [정밀하다] close. e.g. 극히 세세한 점에 이르기까지 to the remotest

particulars [minutest details].

세속 [सेसोक] [**世俗**] [풍습] common [popular / vulgar] customs; [세상] the (mundane / secular) world; the common people. e.g. 세속의 common / worldly / mundane / vulgar / secular / temporal / lowbrow.

세수 [सेसू] [**洗手**] face [hand] washing. 세수하다 wash one's face and hands; have a wash; wash oneself. e.g. 식사 전에 세수하다 wash up before a meal.

세습 [सेसुप] [**世襲**] transmission by heredity; descent. e.g. 세습의 hereditary / patrimonial. 세습의 칭호 a hereditary title. 세습하다 transmit from generation to generation.

세심 [सेशिम] [**細心**] carefulness; circumspection; scrupulosity; prudence. 세심하다 very careful; prudent; scrupulous; circumspect; elaborate; deliberate; attentive. e.g. 세심한 주의 scrupulous care / careful attention.

세안 [सेआन] [**洗眼**] eyewashing. 세안하다 wash one's eyes; have one's eyes washed. e.g. 나는 세안을 했다 I had my eyes washed [bathed].

세우다 [सेउदा] **1** [서게 하다] stand <a candle>; make <a thing> stand; erect; raise; set up; put up <a notice board>; set <a book> on edge [end]; stand <a long thing> on end; hoist <a flag>; plant <a car>. e.g. 간판을 세우다 put up a sign (board). **2** [멈추게 하다] stop; put a stop to; bring to a stop [halt / standstill]; hold up [on]. e.g. 차를 세우다 bring a car to a halt [to rest] / (불러서) call a halt / [주차시키다] park a car. **3** [날카롭게 하다] sharpen; put [forge] an edge <on>; give an edge <to>; edge; hone; set <a razor>. e.g. 칼날을 날카롭게 세우다 put a sharp edge on a knife. **4** (뜻을) have <an object> in view; establish in one's mind; set <an object before one>; be determined to <do>; be inspired by ambition; have <a fixed purpose> (in life). e.g. 정치가가 되고자 뜻을 세우다 [aspire to be a politician. **5** [건조하다] build; construct; erect <a statue / monument>; set [put] up; raise (an edifice); rear. e.g. 동상을 세우다 erect [put up] a bronze statue. **6** [설립, 조직하다] establish <a school / firm>; found; set up; organize <a

union>; institute. e.g. 학교 [회사] 를 세우다 start [establish / found] a school [company]. **7** (제 도, 조직 등을) institute <a system>; lay down <rules>; establish <regulations>; enact <a law>. e.g. 규칙 을 세우다 lay down rules / establish regulations. **8** (계획을) form [make / lay] <a plan>; shape; lay (down) <one's course>; map out <a program>. e.g. 예산 [예정] 을 세우 다 make [draw up] a budget [a plan].

세월 [**सेवौल**] [**歲月**] **1** [시간] time (and tide). e.g. 긴짧 은]세월 a long [short] period [space] of time. **2** [시세, 경기 the) times; things; business; conditions. e.g. 세월이 좋다 [없다] The times are good [bad / hard]. / Business [The market] is brisk [dull / quiet].

세율 [**सेयूल**] [**稅率**] the tax [taxation] rate; the rate of taxation; (관세의)] a tariff.

세일 [**सेइल**] a sale. e.g. 바겐크리스마스] 세일 [**सेइल**] a bargain [Christmas] sale.

세일즈맨 [**सेइल्जमैन**] a salesman; (지방으로 도는) a traveling salesman; a commercial traveler

세제 [**सेजे**] [**洗劑**] a detergent; (a) cleanser; a cleansing agent; a detersive.

세주다 [**सेजूदा**] [**貰 -**] hire [let] out <carriages and horses by the day>; (가옥, 토지 등을 let <one's house for the winter>; rent <a house to a person>; rent out <a mansion>; locate; (토지를] lease; let out <land> on lease; grant a lease.

세차 [**सेछा**] [**洗車**] car washing; car wash. 세차하다 wash a car [an automobile]. **세차장** [**सेछजां**] a car wash.

세차다 [**सेछदा**] violent; strong; vehement; fierce; furious. e.g. 세찬 바람 a strong [severe / violent / sharp] wind.

세척 [**सैछैक**] [**洗滌**] washing; cleansing; cleaning; rinsing; lavation; irrigation; lavage (물을 내쏘아서 하는) toilet (수술 후의 세척하다] [씻다] wash; [깨 끗이 하다]] clean; (상처 등을 irrigate. e.g. 위를 세척하다 carry out a gastric lavage.

세탁 [**सेथाक**] [**洗濯**] e.g. 애벌 세탁] preliminary washing.

세탁소 [**सेथाक्सो**] a laundry; the cleaner's.

세탁기 [**सेथाक्कि**] [**洗濯機**] a washing machine; a washer.

세태 [**सेथै**] [**世態**] [세상의 형편] the prevailing state of society; the order [condition

/ current] of the world; [사회 정세] social conditions; [생활의 양상 a phase [an aspect] of life.

세트 **[सेथ]** **1** [기구 등의 한 벌]] a set <of>; (가구의) a suite <of>. e.g. 홍차 세트 a tea set **2** [극, 영화의 장치] a set. e.g. 세트에 들어가다들어가 있 다] go [be] on the set. **3** [수신기] e.g. 라디오 [텔 레비전]세트 a radio [television] set. **4** (경기 의) a set. e.g. 5 세트의 시합 a five-set match. 테니스를 3 세트하다 play three sets of tennis.

세포 [सेफो] [**細胞**] [生] a cell. e.g. 세포의 cellular

섹스 **[सेक्स]** sex. e.g. 섹스의] sexual.

섹시하다 **[सेक्शिहादा]** sexy; sexually attractive [appealing]; having sex appeal; glamorous.

센세이션 **[सेन्सेइस्यौन]** a sensation. e.g. 그의 최근의 소설은 센세이션을 불러 일으켰다 [His latest novel caused [created] a sensation.

센터 **[सेन्थौ]** [종합적 시설]. e.g. 서비스 센터 a service center. 의료 센터 [उइरयो सेन्थौ] a medical center.

센티미터 **[सेन्थिमिथौ]** a centimeter [a centimetre] (cm).

셀프서비스 **[सेल्फसौबिस]** self-service. e.g. 셀프서비스식의 레스토랑 [a self-service restaurant / a cafeteria.

셈[सेम] [계산] count; counting; reckoning; calculation; computation. e.g. 셈이 빠르다[느리다] be quick [slow] at figures [accounts]. 셈하다 count; reckon; calculate; compute.

셈나다 **[सेम्नादा]** know better; grow sensible; acquire good sense; attain one's years of discretion; cut one's wisdom teeth; begin to understand what is going on around one; become possessed of discretion.

셋 **[सेत]** three; III (로마 숫자)

셋방 [सेत्पां] [**貰房**] a room for rent; a room [an apartment] to let; (관광객을 위한 a tourist apartment; [세든 방] a rented room. e.g. 셋방에 살다 live in a rented room.

셋집 [सेत्चिप] [**貰**-] a house for rent; a house to let; a rental [rented] house; (빈민들의)] a tenement (house). e.g. 가구 딸린 셋집 a furnished house for rent [to let]. 셋집 주인 an owner of rental houses.

셋째 **[सेत्च्वै]** the third.

셔츠 **[स्यौछ]** [와이셔츠, 스포츠 셔츠 a shirt; [내복]] an undershirt; a vest. e.g. 티셔츠 a T-shirt.

소 [1] [सो] [少] [적은] little; few; scarce; [젊은] young.

소 [2] [सो] [小] smallness. e.g. 소를 죽이고 대를 살리다] sacrifice small things to save great ones.

소 [3] [सो] [암소] a cow; [수소] a bull; [노역용의 거세한 수소 an ox <*pl.* oxen>; [새끼 낳기 전의 젊은 암소 a heifer; [송아지] a calf <*pl.* calves>; <집합 적> cattle.

소- [सो] [小] small; little; minor; lesser; miniature. e.g. 소아시아 Asia Minor. 소위원회 a subcommittee. 소극장 a small theater

소각 [सोगाक] [燒却] destruction by fire; incineration; cremation. 소각하다 destroy <a thing> by fire; incinerate (먼지, 쓰레기 등을) cremate; burn up; commit <a thing> to the flames; throw into fire; reduce to ashes.

소감 [सोगाम] [所感] one's impressions [thoughts]. e.g. 소감을 말하다 [묻다] give one's [ask for a person's] impressions <of>.

소개 [सोगै] [紹介] **1** [인사시킴] an) introduction; presentation. e.g. 자기소개 (a) self-introduction. 소개하다 introduce; (정식으로) present. e.g. 나는 친구를 아저씨에게 소개했다 I introduced my friend to my uncle. **2** [추천, 알선] good [kind] offices; a service; recommendation. e.g. …의 소개로 through the good offices of. / at the recommendation of.

소거 [सोगौ] [消去] [말소] erasure; [제거] elimination. 소거하다 erase; eliminate.

소견 [सोग्यौन] [所見] one's view(s); one's opinion; one's impression. e.g. 어떤 건에 대해서 소견을 말하다 give one's view(s) on a matter.

소곤거리다 [सोगोंगौरिदा] talk in a whisper [subdued tone]; whisper; murmur; speak under one's breath. e.g. 소곤거리는 소리 a whispering [suppressed] voice / a whisper.

소굴 [सोगुल] [巢窟] a den; a haunt; a nest; a lair; (범죄의) a breeding place; a hotbed; <美> a hangout. e.g. 도둑의 소굴 a den of robbers [thieves] / a robber's hideout.

소규모 [सोग्यूमो] [小規模] a small scale. e.g. 소규모 가족 a peanut-size family.

소극 [सोगक] [消極] the negative pole; the negative; the cathode; (작용) depolarization.

소극적 [सोगक्चौक] [消極的] negative; passive; half-hearted (▷ negative 는 부정적 passive 는 수동적 half-hearted 는 마음이 내키지 않음을 뜻함 conservative. e.g. 성질이 소극적인 사람삼가는) a man of retiring disposition.

소금 [सोगम] salt. e.g. 식탁용 소금 table salt.

소나기 [सोनागि] a (sudden) shower; a passing rain

소나무 [सोनामू] a pine(tree).

소녀 [सोन्यौ] [少女] a young [little] girl; a maiden.

소년 [सोन्यौन] [少年] a boy; a lad; a youth.

소독 [सोदोक] [消毒] disinfection; (끓이기 등에 의한) sterilization; (우유 등의) pasteurization; [훈증] fumigation; [정화] decontamination. 소독하다 kill (the) germs; disinfect; sterilize; pasteurize; fumigate; decontaminate. e.g. 소독한 disinfected / sterilized.

소동 [सोदोंग] [騷動] [법석] a) disturbance; (an) uproar; an upheaval; [옥신각신 a strife; a dispute; a trouble; [싸움] a quarrel; a brawl; [혼란] confusion; disorder; a row; a tumult; [동란] a commotion; [폭동] a riot; an uprising; [사건 an affair. e.g. 이혼 소동 the fuss about a divorce.

소득 [सोदक] [所得] [수입] [सुइप] income; [수익] [सुइक] earnings; profits. e.g. 개인 [법인]] 소득 individual [corporate] income. 국민 소득 [national income.

소란 [सोरान] [騷亂] [소동] [सोदों] a disturbance; a commotion; a riot; fuss; ado; bustle; stir; [시끄럼] [शिकरौम] (a) noise; (an) uproar; a hubbub; a clamor; a din; a tumult; a row. 소란하다 disturbing; noisy; boisterous; uproarious; clamorous; vociferous; tumultuous <crowd>.

소량 [सोर्यांग] [少量] a small quantity [amount / portion / dose]; a little; a modicum; a touch; a dash; a hint; a suspicion; <프> a soup?n; a morsel <of>. e.g. 소량의 위스키 a little whisky.

소름 [सोरम] gooseflesh; goose pimples [bumps]; horripilation. 소름(이) 끼치다 get (the) gooseflesh; be gooseflesh [goose pimples] all over; feel a chill creep over one; feel a shudder.

소리 [सोरि] **1** [음향] (a) sound; [소음] a noise; a report (총포 등의) a din (왁자지껄하는]; a roar (굉음) e.g. 방울 소리 the sound of a bell. 큰작은 소리 a loud [low] sound. **2** [목소리] a voice; a tone (of voice); [외침 소리] a cry; an outcry; (새, 벌레

의) notes; call; chirp; a song. e.g. 벌레가 우는 소리 the chirping of insects. **3** [판소리 등 노래 a folk song; a ballad. e.g. 소리를 잘하다 sing (a tune) well. **4**[말] a talk; a word; a statement; a remark. **5** [항간의 소문] a rumor; a report; news; an account.

소리지르다 **[सोरिजीरदा]** **1** [소리를 크게 내다] yell; shout; cry (in a loud voice); speak loudly; raise [lith(up) / put forth] one's voice. **2** [큰 소리로 부르다]] call out; hail; sing out.

소망 [सोमांग] [**所望**] (a) desire; a wish; a hope; a request; an expectation. 소망하다 desire; wish for; hope (for).

소매[1] **[सोमै]** a sleeve; (양복의)] an arm.

소매[2] [सोमै] [**小賣**] retail (ing); retail sale. 소매하다 retail; sell (at) retail; sell by retail.

소매치기 **[सोमैछिगि]** (사람) a pickpocket; a cutpurse; <美> a dip (per); (행위) pocketpicking; <美> dipping. 소매치기하다 pick <a person's> pocket <of a purse>; <美> dip <a watch from another's pocket>; commit pocket-picking.

소멸 [सोम्यौल] [**消滅**] [전멸] extinction; extinguishment; [소실] disappearance; [실효] nullification; termination. 소멸하다 [전멸하다] become extinct; cease to exist; disappear; vanish; lapse; become null [void]; be nullified; be extinguished; terminate; be expiated (죄가).

소모 [सोमो] [**消耗**] consumption; [완전히 써 버림] exhaustion; dissipation; waste; wear and tear; (체력의) emaciation. 소모하다 consume; exhaust; dissipate; waste; use up. e.g. 정력을 소모하다 dissipate [waste] one's energy.

소문 [सोमुन] [**所聞**] a rumor; a report; hearsay; gossip; common talk; <美> scuttlebutt.

소박하다 [सोबाख्वादा] [**素朴-**] simple (and honest); unsophisticated; ingenuous; artless; naive. e.g. 소박한 생각 an unsophisticated [a naive] idea.

소방 [सोबांग] [**消防**] fire fighting; fire service; the prevention and extinction of fires.

소방관 **[सोबांग्वान]** a fire fighter; a fire officer; a fireman.

소방서 **[सोबांसौ]** a fire (-brigade) station; a fire department; a firehouse.

소변 [सोब्यौन] [**小便**] e.g. 소변의 uric / urinary. 소변을 누다][보다] urinate / pass [discharge / void] urine /

make [pass] water / answer a call of nature / micturate / pass / pee.

소비 [सोबि] [**消費**] [소모] consumption; [지출] [जीछुल] expenditure; spending. 소비하다 consume; use (up); (시간, 정력 등을 expend.

소비자 [सोबिजा] [**消費者**] a consumer.

소비재 [सोबिजै] [**消費財**] consumption goods; consumer [consumers'] goods [items].

소설 [सोसौल] [**小說**] a novel; a (fictional) story; a romance; a tale; <집합적>[e.g. 교양 소설 an educational novel. **소소하다** [**小小**] trivial; trifling; insignificant; small.

소속 [सोसोक] [**所屬**] one's position [post / place]. 소속하다 belong <to>; be attached <to>; affiliate oneself <with>; be under the command [control] <of>. e.g. 소속시키다 attach / assign / put under the command [control] of.

소송 [सोसोंग] [**訴訟**] a lawsuit; a suit; an action (at law); litigation; legal proceedings [steps]; [고 소] a complaint. 소송하다 sue <a person for dam-ages>; bring an action [a suit] <against a person for a matter>; go to suit; go to law <with [against] a person over a matter>; take [institute] legal proceedings <against>. e.g. 그 사건을 소송하지 않고 해결하는 길은 없을까 Is there no way to settle the matter out of court?

소수 [सोसू] [**小數**] a decimal (fraction).

소수 [सोसू] [**少數**] a small number; a minority.

소스라치다 [सोसराछिदा] take fright [alarm]; be taken aback; be frightened; be startled; be stunned.

소식 [सोशिक] [**消息**] [전갈] word; [뉴스] news; tidings; [보고] a report; [통지] a notice. [편지] a letter. e.g. 오늘의 소식 today's news.

소신 [सोशिन] [**所信**] [신념] one's belief [conviction]; [의견] one's opinion [view]. e.g. 소신을 굽히지 않다 be firm [unshaken] in one's convictions / stick [hold fast] to one's view [belief

소심 [सोशिम] [**小心**] [겁이 많음] timidity; cowardice; [도량이 좁음] narrow- [small-] mindedness. 소심하다 [겁많다] timid; cowardly

소아 [सोआ] [**小兒**] an infant; a small child; a young [little] child. e.g. 소아 시절에 as a small child in one's infancy [early childhood]. **소아과** [सोआग्वा] [**小**

兒科] pediatrics; pediatry.

소액 [सोऐक] [**少額**] a small [petty / limited] sum [amount] <of money>.

소양 [सोयांग] [**素養**] a grounding <in>; knowledge <of>; [조예] acquirements; attainments; accomplishments. e.g. 소양이 있다 have a grounding <in> / have some knowledge <of>.

소외 [सोवे] [**疎外**] (an) estrangement; alienation; neglect. 소외하다 estrange; alienate; neglect; slight; avoid [shun] <a person's> company; keep <a person> at a distance. e.g. 친구들 에게 소외당하다 be treated distantly by one's friends.

소요 [सोयो] [**所要**] what is needed [required]; the need; requirement. e.g. 소요의 [필요한 necessary / [요구되는] required. **소요 시간** the time required.

소용 [सोयों] [**所用**] [쓸데] a use; service; [유용성] usefulness; [쓰임] what is used; the use; necessaries; expenses. 소용(이) 없다 useless; of no use. e.g. 소용 없는 노력 wasted labor.

소원 [सोवौन] [**所願**] [소망] a desire; a wish;(a) hope; one's prayer (신에 대한) e.g. 이루지 못한 소원 an unfulfilled desire.

소원 [सोवौन] [**疏遠, 疎遠**] estrangement; alienation. 소원하다 estranged; alienated; distant. e.g. 소원해지다 be [become] estranged [alienated] <from>.

소위 [सोवि] [**所謂**] what is called; what you [we / they] call; <경멸> so-called. e.g. 그는 소위 음악의 천재이다 He is what we call a musical genius.

소유 [सोयू] [**所有**] possession; ownership. 소유하다 have; own; possess; hold; be in possession of; hold possession of; be possessed of; have <a thing> in possession. e.g. 그는 호텔 세 개를 소유하고 있다 He owns [has] three hotels.

소유권 [सोयूग्वौन] [**所有權**] [法] (the right of) ownership [proprietorship]; proprietary [proprietorial] rights; a right [title] <to a thing>; proprietary; property; possessive rights; (토지) 의 dominium; dominion.

소음 [सोउम] [**騷音**] noise; a racket; (지속적인) a) din (▷ racket 이나 din 이나 혼란스런 소음이 뜻으로는 복수형이 되지 않음) [; (특히 외침소리의) an) uproar.

소인 [सोइन] [**小人**] [어린이] a child; a minor

소임 [सोइम] [**所任**] [임무] duties; a task; [공직 an

office; [지위 a post; [사명] a mission.

소작 [सोजाक] [小作] tenancy; tenant farming; sharecropping. 소작하다 tenant <a farm>; engage in tenant farming; [수확 물의 일부를 소작료로 내 다] sharecrop.

소장 [1] [सोजांग] [所長] a head [chief / manager] <of an office / a factory>. e.g. 영어 교육 연구소 소장 the director of the English Language Education Institute.

소장 [2] [सोजांग] [所藏] one's possession.소장하다 possess; own; have. e.g. 이 도서관은 약 100 만권의 도서를 소장하고 있다 This library owns [houses] about a million volumes.

소재 [सोजे] [素材] a material; [제재] subject matter; (신문 기사 등의 copy.

소재 [सोजे] [所在] (사람의) one's whereabouts; (the place) where a person is; (물건의) the place) where a thing is (kept); (건물 등의) the location; the site; [위치] the position; the situation. e.g. 소재를 알 수 없다 one's whereabouts is unknown / be missing.

소중 [सोजुंग] [所重] 소중하다 [중요하다 important; weighty; momentous; significant; [귀중하다] valuable; valued; dear; precious. e.g. 소중한 물건 a valuable [treasured] article / a treasure / <집합적 valuables.

소지 [सोजी] [所持] possession. 소지하다 [소유하다] possess; own; [휴대하다] have <money> about [with / on] one; have <a revolver> on one's person; bear; carry <with one>. e.g. 그렇게 많은 현금을 소지하고 있으면 위험하다 It's not safe to carry so much cash around (with you).

소지품 [सोजीफुम] [所持品] one's things [belongings]; one's (personal) effects.

소질 [सोजील] [素質] [자질] makings; temperament; character; nature; fiber; [재능] talent; [체질] constitution; make-up; [경향] a tendency. e.g. 문학적 소질이 있는 사람 a person of a literary turn (of mind).

소집 [सोजीप] [召集] call; (명령에 의한) a summons <*pl.* ~ es>; (회의 등의) convocation; (군대의) a call-up; conscription; a muster; a levy; a drath. e.g. 국회의 소집 the convocation of the National Assembly.

소탈 [सोथाल] [疎脫, 疏脫] informality; unceremoniousness; lack of ceremony. 소탈하다 informal; free and easy; unceremonious; unconstrained; bohemian; freely-thinking and freely-acting.

소탐대실 [सोथाम्दैशिल] [**小貪大失**] incurring a great loss by pursuing a small profit. 소탐대실하다 suffer a big loss in going ather a small gain.

소탕 [सोथांग] [**掃蕩**] sweeping; clearing; a sweep. 소탕하다 sweep; clear; scour; stamp [wipe] out; get rid of; (잔적 등을) mop up; clean up; clear out. e.g. 적을 소탕하다 clear [sweep / rid] <the sea> of the enemy.

소통 [सोथोंग] [**疏通**] (의사의) mutual understanding; communication; (물 등의) drainage. e.g. 두 사람은 의사 소통이 부족했다 There was a lack of understanding [communication] between the two of them.

소파 [सोफा] a sofa.

소포 [**小包**] [सोफो] a package; a parcel. e.g. 국내 국제]소포 domestic [international] parcels. 보험 소포 insured parcels.

소품 [सोफुम] [**小品**] **1** (문학의) a short piece [work]; a (literary) sketch; (음악의) a short (musical) composition; (회화의) a small work of art; a small painting; (조각의) a small sculpture. **2** [자그마한 도구] small tools; (무대의 stage) properties; props.

소풍 [सोफुंग] [**逍風**] [바람 쐬기] taking the air; airing one-self; [산책,피크닉] an excursion; a holiday expedition; a walking tour; an outing; a hike; a tramp; [들놀이] a picnic.

소형 [सोह्यौंग] [**小型**] a small size; a pocket size. e.g. 소형의 [सोह्यौउड] small / small-sized <cups>.

소홀 [सोहोल] [**疏忽**] negligence; carelessness; indifference. 소홀하다 negligent; neglectful; remiss; careless; [경솔하다] rash; slipshod; sloppy.

소화 [सोह्वा] [**消化**] **1** (음식의) digestion. 소화하다 digest. e.g. 반숙한 달걀은 잘 소화된다 A soth-boiled egg is easy to digest [easily digested]. 위는 음식물을 소화한다 The stomach digests what has been eaten. **2** (지식,기술 등의) digestion; [흡수] assimilation. 소화하다 digest; assimilate; understand; take in. e.g. 나는 이 책을 소화할 수 없다 This book is too difficult [tough] for me

소화제 [सोह्वाजे] a digestive; a digester; a peptic.

소화 [सोह्वा] [**消火**] fire

extinguishing; fire fighting. 소화용의 [으로] for fire-extinguishing [fire-fighting] purposes. 소화에 힘쓰다 fight a fire. 마을 사람들 모두가 소화에 나섰다 All the villagers fought the fire. 소화하다 put out [extinguish] a fire. **소화기** a fire extinguisher.

소환 [सोहवान] [**召喚**] a summons <*pl.* ~es>; a call; (a) monition; (a) citation; a subp(o)ena. 소환하다 summon; call; cite; subp(o)ena. e.g. 관계자를 소환하다 summon the parties concerned / serve summonses on the parties concerned.

속 [**सोक**] **1** [안] the inside; the interior; the inner part; the innermost [inmost] recess; the heart e.g. 동굴 속 깊숙한 곳에 in the inner part of [at the back of] a cave. **2** [마음, 이면] the depth; the bottom; the heart. e.g. 속이 깊지 않은 사람 a shallow personality. 속(을) 끓이다=속(을) 태우다(1). e.g. 사소한 일에 속을 끓이는 사람 a worry-wart / a worry-guts. 속(이) 보이다 be transparent; be easily seen through. e.g. 속 보이는 짓을 하다 resort to a shallow trick. 속(이) 상하다 [마음이 좋지 않다] feel sore <about>; feel depressed [distressed]; be troubled [unhappy]; [짜증스럽다] be irritated [fretful]; [분하다] be feel] vexed <at one's failure>; be annoyed; be exasperated <at>; [걱정스럽다] be worried; feel anxious; be troublesome; be distressing; be worrisome. e.g. 속상하는 일투성이다 be full of cares and vexations. 속(이) 시원하다 e.g. 속 시원한 대답 [a smart answer. 속(이) 타다 be distressed <about / by>; be vexed [irritated] <at>; be worried <about / that>; be nervous; be harassed [annoyed]; be fretful. e.g. 속타는 마음 an aching [a troubled] heart. 속(을) 태우다 (1) (스스로) worry (oneself) <about>; bother (oneself) <about>; trouble oneself <with>; be anxious [nervous] about>; be troubled [distressed / worried]; be annoyed [bothered / vexed]. e.g. 하찮은 일에 속을 태우다 worry over trifles. (2) (남을) vex annoy; worry; cause worry [anxiety]; bother; distress; trouble; make nervous. e.g. 친구를 속태우다 cause anxiety to friends.

속눈썹 [**सोंग्नुन्सौप**] eyelashes; lashes; winkers. e.g. 긴 속눈썹 long eyelashes. 인조 속눈썹 false eyelashes.

속다 [सोक्ता] be [get] deceived [cheated / deluded / hoaxed / defrauded / fooled]; be imposed (up)on; be taken in; be caught in a trap. e.g. 잘 속는 사람 a dupe / a sucker / a credulous person.

속단 [सोक्तान] [**速斷**] [너무 이른 단정 a hasty conclusion. 속단하다 conclude hastily; form [come to / leap to] a hasty conclusion; make [draw] a hasty conclusion; jump to [at] a conclusion; decide hastily. e.g. 이것으로 성공은 틀림없다고 속단해서는 안 된다 You must not jump to the conclusion that this will ensure your success.

속담 [सोक्ताम] [**俗談**] a proverb; a (common) saying; an adage.

속도 [सोक्तो] [**速度**] **1** (a) speed; (a) velocity (▷ speed 와 velocity 는 거의 같은 뜻으로 쓰이나[과학 용어로서는 후자를 쓰는 것이 보통임; a pace; (a) rate. e.g. 초 [종]속도 initial [final] velocity. **2** [樂] (a) tempo.

속독 [सोक्तोक] [**速讀**] rapid [speed] reading (▷ speed reading 은 특수한 기술로 초속도로 읽는 일속독하다 read <a book> fast [rapidly].

속되다 [सोकत्वेदा] [**俗-**] [세속적이다] secular; earthly; worldly; mundane; [통속적이다] common; popular; [천한] vulgar; low; coarse. e.g. 속된 말로 하면 in common parlance. 속된 사람 a worldly (-minded) person.

속뜻 [सोक्तुत] **1** [참뜻] the inner [true] meaning [sense / significance]. **2** [본심] one's real intention; one's true motive. e.g. 그의 속뜻을 알 수 없다 I can't see what he really means. / I can't make out what he is driving at.

속력 [सोंगन्यौक] [**速力**] (a) speed; (a) velocity; (a) rate.

속마음 [सोकूमाउम] one's inmost heart [thought(s)]; one's real intention; the bottom of one's heart. e.g. 속마음으로는 at bottom / at heart.

속물 [सोंग्मुल] [**俗物**] **1** [속사에만 마음이 이끌리는 사람] a worldly-minded person; a completely materialistic person; a person who values money, position, and fame. **2** [속된 물건] mean [vulgar] stuff.

속박 [सोक्पाक] [**束縛**] binding; [억제] restraint; [제한] restriction; [구속물] fetters; shackles; trammels; a yoke. 속박하다 restrain; restrict; trammel; shackle; enchain; fetter; bind; lay [place] under restraint. e.g. 사람을 속박하다 restrain a person

속보 [सोक्पो] [**速報**] a prompt [quick] report [announcement]; a (news) flash. 속보하다 report promptly; announce quickly; make a quick report <on>. e.g. 사고의 뉴스는 텔레비전으로 속보되었다 The news of the accident was flashed onto the television screen immediately.

속삭이다 [सोक्सागिदा] whisper; murmur; talk in whispers; speak under one's breath. e.g. 사랑의 속삭임 sweet whispers of love / soth nothings.

속살 [सोक्साल] (옷속의) the part of the body usually covered by clothing. e.g. 속살이 내비치는 블라우스 a see-through blouse.

속세 [सोक्से] [**俗世**] the [this] world; (secular) society; mundane life; earthly existence.

속셈 [सोक्सेम] [마음 속으로 하는 셈] inner calculation [thought (s)]; an ulterior motive [purpose]; one's secret [real] intention; a deep design. e.g. 그의 속셈을 모르겠다 I don't understand what he has in mind. / I cannot quite see his motive [idea / design].

속수 무책 [सोक्सू मुछैक] [**束手無策**] helplessness; resourcelessness. e.g. 나는 속수 무책이었다 I was at a loss what to do.

속옷 [सोगोत] underwear; an undergarment; an undershirt; underlinen; underclothes; underclothing; (여성의) lingerie; undies.

속이다 [सोगिदा] **1** [기만하다] deceive; cheat; swindle; trick; hoaK gull; dupe; fool; take in; impose [play] upon; hoodwink; play <a person> a trick (▷보통 heat 는 부정한 수단사기 등으로 trick 은 교묘한 책략으로, deceive 는 거짓말 등으로 남을 속임 e.g. 속이기 쉬운 gullible / credulous. 속이기 쉬운 사람 [a dupe / a gull / a sucker. **2** [거짓말을 하다]lie; tell a lie; fake; falsify; misrepresent.

속임수 [सोगिम्सू] [**-數**] trickery; swindle; imposture; humbug; juggling; a fake; a trick; fraud; deception; a hoax. e.g. 속임수를 쓰다 cheat / deceive / swindle / take [let] <a person> in / play <a person> a (deceitful) trick / play a trick <upon> / practice an imposture <on>.

속전 속결 [सोक्चौन सोक्यौल] [**速戰速決**] blitz warfare; an intensive [all-out] surprise offensive [attack]; <독> a blitzkrieg.

속죄 [सोक्च्वे] [**贖罪**] atonement for [expiation of]

one's sin(s). 속죄하다 atone [make amends] for one's sin / expiate one's sin / make amends for one's offenses [crime]. e.g. 과거를 속죄하다 make amends for the past.

속출 [सोक्छुल] [**續出**] successive [frequent] occurrence. 속출하다 appear [occur] in succession [one ather another]; crop up. e.g. 말썽거리가 속출했다 We had a crop of troubles.

속하다 [सोख्वादा] [**屬-**] [관계되어 딸리다]] belong <to / in / among / with>; appertain [pertain] <to>; be among [one of] <the great cities in Korea>; (분류) come [fall] under [within] <a head>; (나라가 be subject to <another nation>; be under the rule [sway] of <a greater nation>. e.g. 호랑이는 고양잇과에 속한다 The tiger belongs [Tigers belong] to the cat family.

손 [सोन] **1** the hand. e.g. 오른왼]손 the right [left] hand. 손으로 만든 물건] a handmade article. 바로 손이 닿는 곳에 within ready reach <of a person> / where one can reach <it> handily. **2** [도움이 되는 힘 e.g.손을 빌려주다 give [lend] a hand / give [lend] <a person> a helping hand. **3** [일손,도움] a hand; a help. e.g. 여러 사람의 손으로 된 번역[य a translation by various hands. **4** [소유,권력의 범위 possession; hands. e.g. 손에 들어오다 come into one's possession / come to [fall into] one's hands. **5** [수고] trouble; [돌봄] care; charge. e.g. 손을 덜 수 있다 (일이 save trouble. 그것으로 크게 손을 덜 수 있다 That saves much trouble.

손가락 [सोन्काराक] a finger.

손가락질 [सोन्काराकचील] **1** [가리킴].손가락질하다 point <to / at>; point(with) the finger <to / at>; indicate <the door>. e.g. 손가락질하는 것은 실례이다 It is impolite to point. **2** [흉봄] 손가락질하다 point at <a person>; talk about <a person> with scorn [in contempt e.g. 손가락질 받다 be pointed at [talked about] with scorn / be talked of in contempt / be an object of social contempt.

손금 [सोंगम] the lines of the palm. e.g. 손금을 보다 [read (in) <a person's> palm [s hand] / tell hands / tell fortune by the lines of the hand

손길 [सोंगिल] **1** [손가락을 펴고 늘어뜨린 손 hands

(let down). e.g. 손길(을) 잡다 hold [take] <a person's> hands. [내밀어 뻗는 손] one's reach; arm('s) reach e.g. 손길이 닿는 곳에 within one's reach [hands]. **3** [보살펴 매만지는 손] a <helping> hand. e.g. 따뜻한 구호의 손길을 뻗다 extend a warm helping hand <to a person>.

손꼽다 **[सोंकोप्ता]** [손가락을 꼽아 수를 세다] count <the days> on one's fingers; [두드러지게 뛰어나다 stand [tower] high above the others; distinguish oneself; come out on top <of>. e.g. 손꼽는 leading / principal / prominent / outstanding.

손녀 (딸) **[सोन्नयौ]** [**孫女**-] a grand-daughter.

손님 **[सोन्निम]** **1** [방문객] a caller; a visitor; company <단수, 복수 동형> e.g. [손님을 맞다만나다] receive [see] a visitor [caller] / receive company. **2** [초대되어 온 사람] a guest; [체류객] a sojourner; (호텔 의) [a guest; (하숙의) a boarder; (아파트의) a lodger. 손님을 초대하다 invite a guest. **3** [고객]] a customer; a patron; <집합 적 custom; <집합적> trade. e.g. 극장의 손님집합적> an audience

손대다 **[सोन्दैदा]** **1** [건드리다]] touch; lay[put] one's hands on. e.g. 절대로 손대지 못하게 하다] keep a thing absolutely intact. **2** [착수하다] turn[put / set] one's hand to <a task>; set about <work>; set to <work>; get started <on a literary work>; [···에 관계하다 concern oneself with; have a finger[a hand / an oar] in **3** [때리다] beat; strike; knock; hit; give [deal / deliver] <a person> a blow. e.g. 어떤 일이 있어도 아이들에게 손대서는 안 된다 [You must not strike [raise your hand against] your children in any circumstances.

손들다 **[सोन्दल्ता]** **1** [손을 들다]] raise [lith] a [one's] hand; hold up one's hands; (때리려고) lith one's hand against <a person>; (찬성하여) show one's hand. e.g. 손들어 Hands up! / (강도가) Hold'em up! **2** [지다] be defeated; throw up one's hands (in despair). e.g. 완전히 손들다 be beaten hollow. **3** [애먹다] be annoyed <at / by / with>; be [get] floored; be worried <by>; [어찌할 바를 모르다 be dum (b) founded; be stumped <by>; be at one's wit's [wits'] end.

손떼다 **[सोन्तेदा]** [관계를 끊다] get <something> off one's hands; wash one's hands of; sever connection with; withdraw oneself <from ...>; break with <a person>; break away from; back out; [끝내다] finish; bring to a close [an end]; get [be] through <with>; put an end <to>. e.g. 이제 와서 손뗄 수는 없다 [It is too late now to get out of it.

손목 [सोन्मोक] a wrist; [解] a carpus <*pl.* −pi>.

손바닥 [सोन्बादाक] the palm [flat] of the hand; the palm; the hollow of the hand. e.g. 손바닥만한 땅 a tiny plot / a tiny of land.

손발 [सोन्बाल], [손과 발] hands and feet; hand and foot; limbs. e.g. 그는 손발이 부자유스럽다 He has trouble using his limbs [hands and feet]. / [전혀 못 쓴다] He has lost the use of his limbs. 손발 (이) 맞다 e.g. 파업자들은 손발이 맞지 않았다 There was lack of unity among the strikers. 손발이 되다 e.g. 그는 내 손발이 되어 돌봐 주었다 He took care of my every need. / He waited on me hand and foot.

손버릇 [सोन्बौरत] any habitual action of the hands; 도벽 a habit of stealing. e.g. 그는 손버릇이 나쁘다 He is light-fingered. / He is a compulsive thief.

손보다 [सोन्बोदा] [돌보다] care for; take care of; [수리하다] repair <a house>; service <a car>; mend; (원고 등을) correct; touch up. e.g. 집을 좀 손봐야 겠다 My house wants [needs] repairing.

손봐 주다 [सोनब्वा जूदा] [도와주다] help; give [lend] a (helping) hand to; [고쳐 주다] repair [fix] <a car> for <a person>. e.g. 일을 손봐 주다 lend a hand with <a person's> work.

손뼉 [सोनप्यौक] the flat of the hand. e.g. 손뼉을 쳐서 하녀를 부르다 clap hands for a maid.

손상 [सोन्सांग] [損傷] damage; (an) injury. e.g. 신체 내부의 손상 an internal injury. 손상하다 damage; injure; impair; hurt; damnify. e.g. 나라의 명예 를 손상시키다 [stain [besmirch] national honor.

손색 [सोन्सैक] [遜色] inferiority. e.g. 이것은 전문가의 작품으로서 손색이 없다 This work would do credit to a professional.

손수 [सोन्सू] with [by] one's (own) hand(s); [몸소] in person; personally; <do it> oneself. e.g. 손수 만든 of one's own making / homemade

손수건 [सोन्सूगौन] [−手巾] a handkerchief <*pl.* ~s>.

손쉽다 [सोनस्विप्ता] easy;

simple; light. e.g. 손쉬운 방법 the easy way.

손실 [सोन्शिल] [損失] a loss. e.g. 인명 손실 casualties.

손쓰다 [सोनस्दा] take measures; adopt [resort to] a measure; take a course; take action. e.g. 미리 손쓰다 take preventive measures <against>.

손아래 [सोनारै] juniority. e.g. 손아래의 younger / junior / subordinate. 다섯 살 손아래인 동생 a brother five years one's junior.

손위 [सोन्वि] seniority. e.g. 손위의 older / elder(ly) / senior / superior.

손익 [सोनिक] [損益] profit and loss; loss and gain; [이익과 불이익] advantages and disadvantages; pluses and minuses.

손자 [सोन्जा] [孫子] a grandson.

손잡다 [सोनजाप्ता] **1** [손을 붙잡다] [take <a person> by the hand; grasp another's hand; [악수하다] shake hands; clasp hands <with>. e.g. 손잡고 걸어가다 walk hand in hand. **2** [화해하다] make peace <with>; [제휴, 합작하다 join[clasp] hands <with>; cooperate <with>; join together; tie up <with>; go hand in hand <with>; [동맹하다] combine <with>; join forces <with>. e.g. 그들은 선거 운동에서 손잡았다 They joined forces in the election campaign.

손잡이 [सोनजाबि] a handle; a grip; (문 등의) a doorknob. e.g. 손잡이가 한쪽에만 있는 냄비 a pan with a handle / (깊은 것) a saucepan / a pot with a handle.

손재주 [सोनजैजू] [-才-] [손으로 뭘 잘 만드는 재주] hand skill; dexterity [dethness] of hand; manual dexterity [adroitness]. e.g. 그녀는 손재주가 있다 She is a dexterous person. / She is quick and clever [skillful] with her fingers.

손질 [सोन्जिल] **1** 수리, 수선] repair(s); mending; remodeling. 손질하다 repair <a house>; make repairs; mend <shoes>; remodel. e.g. 손질하고 있다 be under repairs. **2** 매만짐, 보살핌 care; pruning; trimming (나무, 뜰, 머리 등의) e.g. 손질이 잘된 정원구석 구석까지 손질이 미친) a well-kept garden / a garden that is well cared for.

손짓 [सोन्जित] a gesture; (a) gesticulation; signs; a hand signal; dumb show. 손짓하다 gesture; gesticulate; make gestures; motion <for a person to do>; give a hand signal

손찌검 [सोन्चिगौम] a blow; beating; striking; hitting.

손찌검하다 beat; strike; knock; hit; slap; give [deal / deliver] <a person> a blow.

손톱 [सोन्थोप] a nail; a fingernail

손톱깎이 [सोन्थोप्काक्कि] nail clippers; <a pair of> nail scissors.

손해 [सोनहै] [損害] [손상] damage; (an) injury; harm; [손실] a loss.

손해 배상 [सोनहै बैसांग] [損害賠償] (a) compensation for damages [a loss]; reparation for injury; indemnity (for damage done). e.g. 자동차 손해 배상 보장법 [법] [बौप] the Automobile Accident Compensation Security Act.

솔 [सोल] [브러시] a brush. e.g. 옷[구두]솔 [सोल] a clothes [shoe] brush.

솔깃하다 [सोल्किथादा] welcome; encouraging; inviting; <서술적 be interested <in>; be enthusiastic <about>. e.g. 귀가 솔깃해지는 조건 a tempting offer / inviting terms.

솔로 [सोल्लो] a solo <*pl.* ~s, -li>. e.g. 바이올린 솔로 a violin solo.

솔선 [率先] 솔선하다 take the lead[initiative]; take up the running. e.g. 솔선해서 on one's own initiative.

솔직 [सोल्चिक] [率直] straightforwardness; frankness; candidness; openheartedness. 솔직하다 straightforward; frank; candid; plain; honest; straight; open; outspoken (▷ frank 는 기탄없는 candid 는 정직하게 있는 그대로의, open 은 숨김이 없는, straightforward 는 에두르거나 모호함이 없음을 뜻함

솜 [सोम] cotton (wool). e.g. [이불옷]에 넣는 솜 cotton wool / batting / wadding / padding.

솜씨 [सोम्शि] a way of moving [using] one's hands; [교묘함] skill; dexterity; dethness; knack; [만듦새] performance; make; hand; workmanship; [수완] ability; capacity; (교제의 tact. e.g. 훌륭한 솜씨기술면에서) excellent skill/ (만듦새면에서] fine workmanship / (경기에서) a) fine [good / nice] play.

솟구치다 [सोत्कुछ्दा] rise quickly; (불길이) blaze up; burn [go] up (in a flame).

솟다 [सोत्ता] **1** (샘 등이) gush out [forth]; spring. e.g. 상처에서 피가 솟았다 Blood gushed out of the wound. **2** [우뚝 서다] rise; tower; soar. e.g. 하늘 높이 솟아 있는산 [a mountain soaring high into the sky. **3** (불길이) flame [blaze] up; burst into flame. e.g. 불길이 창문에서 솟았다 Flames leaped [poured]

from the window.

솟아나다 [सोसानादा] (물이) gush [spring] out [forth]; spout; spurt; [흘러나오다 flow[stream] out [forth]; (우물물처럼) well up [out / forth]; (거품이 일며 bubble up.

송곳 [सोंगोत] a gimlet; [구멍 뚫는 기계 a drill (▷주로 금속, 돌 등에 씀) (구둣방에서 쓰는 an awl; (나사송곳) an auger; 종이용의 an eyeleteer; 얼음 깨는 an ice pick.

송구 [सोंगू] [**悚懼**] 송구하다 [감사하다] <서술적> be much obliged to a person for a thing; be thankful [grateful] to a person for a thing; [죄송하다] be sorry; [창피하다] be ashamed; feel small. e.g. 송구스럽다 =송구하다. 송구할 따름입니다 I am deeply ashamed.

송구 영신 [सोंगू यौंशिन] [**送舊迎新**] 송구 영신하다 see the old year out and the new year in; ring out the old and ring in the new; speed the old and welcome the new.

송금 [सोंगुम] [**送金**] (a) remittance; (생활비 등의) (an) allowance. 송금하다 remit [send] money <to>; make(a) remittance <to>. e.g. 우편환으로 송금하다] remit [send] by postal money order.

송년 [सोंगन्यौन] [**送年**] bidding the old year out (and the new year in).

송두리째 [सोंग्दुरिचै] root and branch; all; completely; thoroughly; whole. e.g. 송두리째 가져가다 take away everything (one can lay hands on).

송별 [सोंगब्यौल] [**送別**] a farewell; a send-off. 송별하다 bid <a person> farewell; give <a person> a send-off.

송송 [सोंगसोंग] **1** [물건을 잘게 빨리 써는 모양] chop) into small pieces; finely. e.g. 파를 송송 썰다 chop scallion into small pieces. **2** [구멍이 많이 뚫린 모양] full of small holes; perforated. e.g. 종이에 송송 구멍을 뚫다 perforate paper. **3** [땀방울이 많이 난 모양] e.g. 그의 이마에는 땀방울이 송송 맺혀 있었다 [beads of sweat stood on his forehead. / Perspiration stood in beads on his forehead.

송신 [सोंग्शिन] [**送信**] transmission (of a message). 송신하다 transmit [dispatch] a message <to>.

송아지 [सोंगाजी] a calf <*pl.* calves>.

송이 [सोंगी] **1** (꽃의 a flower; a blossom; (과일의) a bunch; a clusters. e.g. 포도 한 송이 [a bunch [cluster] of grapes. **2** (눈의) a flake <of snow>.

송환 [**सोंगहवान**] [**送還**] [불법 입국자 등의 국외 추방] [deportation; [국외 도망 범인 등의 인도 extradition; (포로, 망명자 등의 repatriation. 송환하다 send back; (본국으로 send home; repatriate; deport. e.g. 그는 밀항자로서 송환되 었다 He was sent back home as a stowaway.

솥 [**सोत**] an (iron) pot; a kettle; a ca(u) ldron (큰 솥)

쇄도 [**स्वेदो**] [**殺到**] a rush; a flood; a stampede. 쇄도하다 [rush <in / to>; come with a rush; rush [pour] in; [밀어닥치다] rush [throng] to (a place); storm (a place); swoop down on (the enemy). e.g. 그 책의 주문이 쇄도했다 There was a rush of orders for the book.

쇄신 [**स्वेशिन**] [**刷新**] (a) complete reform; (a) renovation; (an) innovation; a cleanup. 쇄신하다 reform completely; introduce [make] a reform; renovate; innovate; clean up. e.g. 공직 사회의 기강을 쇄신하다 renovate the discipline in bureaucracy.

쇠 [**स्वे**] iron

쇠고기 [**स्वेगोगि**] beef.

쇠다 [**स्वेदा**] (명절을) observe; keep (one's birthday); celebrate. e.g. 명절을 쇠다 [observe [celebrate] a festival day.

쇠사슬 [**स्वेसासल**] a chain; an iron chain. e.g. 쇠사슬에 묶인 죄수 a criminal in chains. 쇠사슬에 줄줄이 묶인 죄수들 a chain gang.

쇠약 [**स्वेयाक**] [**衰弱**] weakness; infirmity; debility; prostration; (a) break-down; enervation; collapse; asthenia; emaciation. 쇠약하다 weak; enfeebled; (노령으로) infirm; emaciated (야윈) e.g. 쇠약해지다 become [grow] weak / weaken / decline / sink / be debilitated / be enervated / be worn out / be emaciated.

쇠퇴 [**स्वेथ्वे**] [**衰退**] a decline; decay. e.g. [체력 건강] 의 쇠퇴 the decline of one's strength [health]. 기억력의 쇠퇴 the failing of one's memory. 쇠퇴기에 있다 be on the decline / be at a low ebb. 쇠퇴하다 decline; decay; fall off; be deserted; become desolate

쇠하다 [**स्वेहादा**] [**衰-**] [쇠약해지다] become weaker; decline; lose vigor; be enfeebled; be weakened; be enervated; waste away; be languish; be run down; flag; atrophy; [쇠퇴하다] fall off [away]; fail; dwindle; go downhill; ebb (away); decline; decay; go [fall]

into decay; (기운 등이) sink; wane; collapse; slacken.

쇼 [स्यो] a show. e.g. 패션 쇼 a fashion show.

쇼크 [स्योख] a shock. e.g. 쇼크를 주다 give <a person> a shock.

쇼킹 [स्योखिं] 쇼킹하다 shocking.

쇼핑 [सयोफिं] [사기] shopping. 쇼핑하다 shop; do one's [the] shopping [marketing]; make a purchase

수[1] [सू] [**數**] e.g. 많은 [적은] 수 a large [small] number. 상당한 수의 군대 a good-sized army.

수[2] [सू] [수컷의 동식물 a male; (조류와 새우, 게, 연어 등의 a cock; (오리, 집오리의 a drake; (어린 가금의 a cockerel; (사슴 염소, 토끼, 쥐 등의 a buck; (거세하지 않은 돼지의) a boar; (코끼리, 고래, 거세하지 않은 소 등의 a bull; (거세한 소의) an oK (고양이의) a tom [cat]. e.g. 수꽃] a male flower. 수소 a bull / [거세한 소] an ox. 숫양 a ram.

수[3] [도리, 수단] **1** a means <단수, 복수 동형> a way; a resource; help. e.g. 나는 웃지 않을 수 없다 I can't help laughing **2** [가능성, 능력], ossibility; likelyhood; ability; capability. e.g. 영어를 말할 수 있는 사람 a person who speaks [can speak] English.

수감 [सूगाम] [**收監**] confinement; imprisonment; commitment. 수감하다 imprison <a person>; put <a person> in prison. e.g. 수감되다 be put away / be thrown in jail / be locked up / <美> be sent up / <英> go down.

수갑 [सूगाप] [**手匣**] handcuffs; manacles (▷ 족쇄도 뜻함) cuffs. e.g. 수갑을 찬 범인 a criminal in handcuffs.

수강 [सूगां] [**受講**] taking lectures. 수강하다 take lectures; attend a lecture class; become a trainee; join a seminar.

수강생 [सूगासैंग] a trainee; a student attending a lecture [class]; a person present at a lecture class; a participant (참가자)

수건 [सूगौन] [**手巾**] a (hand) towel; [세수 수건] a facecloth; a washcloth; a [face] flannel. e.g. 세수 수건 a face towel.

수고 [सुगो] trouble; labor; toil; pains (▷ 이 의미로는 복수형) efforts. e.g. 헛수 고 wasted effort / a complete [sheer] waste of effort. 수고하다 take pains [trouble] <about>; take the trouble <to do>; make efforts; labor (hard).

수공 [सुगोंग] [手工] manual arts [work]; handicrath; handwork; handiwork. e.g. 수공이 들다 take much trouble / involve much labor / be laborious.

수공업 [सुगोंऔप] [手工業] manual industry; handicrath manufacturing; handicrath industry

수그러지다 [सुगरौजीदा] **1** [머리가 숙어지다] hang down; become low; lower; sink; droop; drop. e.g. 그의 고개가 푹 수그러지고 눈이 감겼다 His chin sank on his chest and his eyes shut. **2** [태도, 기세가 누그러지다] sothen; become calm; calm down; be pacified; flag; (병세가) be relieved; be suppressed; be subdued; (바람 등이) go [die / calm] down; subside; sink; abate.

수금 [सुगम] [收金] collection (of money); bill collection [collecting]. 수금하다 collect money [bills]. e.g. 지대 [जीदै] (地代) 를 수금하다 collect <rent> from a tenant.

수긍 [सुगंग] [首肯] assent; consent; a nod. 수긍하다 nod; assent <to>; consent <to>; nod one's assent <to>; agree <to something / with a person>; [납득하다] be convinced <of / that>; be persuaded <of / that>. e.g. 수긍할 수 있는 없는] convincing [unconvincing].

수기 [सूगि] [手記] a note; [각서] a memorandum <*pl.* -da, ~ s>; [회상록] memoirs. e.g. 수기를 쓰다 note [take / put] down / take notes <of> / make memoranda <of>.

수난 [सूनान] [受難] sufferings; [혹독한 시련] ordeals; severe trial. e.g. 그리스도의 수난 the Passion / the Crucifixion. 수난하다 suffer; undergo hardships [trials].

수납 [सुनाप] [收納] **1** (금전 등의) receipt. **2** [안에 넣음] e.g. 양곡 수납 collection [purchase] of food grains. 수납하다 put <a thing> away [up]; put <a thing> away <in a box>.

수녀 [सुन्यौ] [修女] a nun; [가톨릭] a sister.

수년 [सुन्यौन] [數年] several [some / a few] years; a number of years. e.g. 나는 수년 전에 외국 여행을 했었다 I traveled abroad several years ago.

수다 [सूदा] [말이 많음] talkativeness; [재잘거리기] prattle; loquacity; chattering. 수다하다 talkative; garrulous; loquacious. e.g. 수다스럽다=수다하다. 술

을 마시면 그는 수다스러워 진다 Alcohol makes him talkative.

수단 [सुदान] [**手段**] a means <단수, 복수 동형> a measure; a way; a step; [고안] a device; [편법] an expedient; a shith; a resource; [도구] an instrument. e.g. 부정 수단 a foul means / an unjust step.

수당 [सुदांग] [**手當**] [봉급 외에 지급되는 돈] extra benefits; an allowance. e.g. 가족 [주택]수당 a family [housing] allowance.

수더분하다 [सुदौबुनहादा] good-natured [-tempered]; tenderhearted; kindhearted; <서술적> have a sweet temper; be of gentle [good] disposition.

수도 [सुदो] [**水道**] **1** [상수도 시설] a water supply; [수돗물] tap water. e.g. 수도를 끌다[놓다] have water pipes laid / have water supplied / lay on water. **2** [수로] a channel. e.g. 한려 수도 the Hally Channel.

수도꼭지 [सुदोकोक्चि] a tap; a hydrant. **수돗물** [सुदोत्मुल] tap [city / running / piped] water.

수도 [सुदो] [**首都**] a capital; a metropolis. e.g. 수도의 metropolitan.

수도권 [सुदोग्वौन] [**首都圈**] the National Capital region; the Metropolitan [Capital] area. e.g. 수도권 방위 the defense of the Metropolitan area.

수동 [सुदोंग] [**手動**] e.g. 수동의 hand-operated [worked] / manual. 이 펌프는 수동이다 This pump is worked by hand.

수동 [सुदोंग] [**受動**] passivity; passiveness. e.g. 수동적 성의 passive. 수동적으로 passively.

수두룩하다 [सुदुरूख्वादा] (다량) much; a good [great] deal of; a lot [wealth] of; plenty [lots] of; plentiful; <서술적 abound in [with]; (다수) many; a good [great] many; a large number of; numerous; [흔하다] common; stock <examples>. e.g. 할 일이 수두룩하다 [have much [a lot / many things] to do.

수락 [सुराक] [**受諾**] acceptance. 수락하다 accept <an offer>; agree to <the conditions>. e.g. 선뜻 수락하다 [give ready consent <to>.

수량 [सुर्यांग] [**數量**] (an) amount; (a) quantity. e.g. 수량적으로 quantitatively. 수량이 늘다 [줄다] increase [decrease] in quantity.

수렁 [सुरौगं] a quagmire; a mire; a morass; a bog; a slough. e.g. 수렁에 빠지다 fall in the mire / sink in a bog / <비유>be bogged [mired] down / get stuck in a bog / mire oneself <in>.

수레 [सुरे] a wagon; a cart; a handcart (손수레)]; a carriage (마차) an oxcart (소가 끄는) e.g. 수레 목수 a wheelwright / a cartwright.

수력 [सुर्योक] [**水力**] water-power; hydraulic power. e.g. 수력으로 움직이는 water-powered / hydraulic.

수력 발전 [सुर्योक बाल्चोन] [**水力發電**] water-power [hydro-electric power] generation.

수련 [सुर्योन] [**修練, 修鍊**] training; practice; culture; discipline; drill. e.g. 주야로 수련을 쌓다 practice [rehearse] day and night. 수련하다 train; practice [practise]; cultivate; discipline.

수렴 [सुर्योम] [**收斂**] **1** [거두어들임] extortion [exaction] of taxes; laying [imposing] crushing taxes <on>. 수렴하다 extort [exact] heavy taxes <from>; tax heavily; impose heavy unjust taxes <on>. **2** [오그라들게함] astriction; convergence. 수렴하다 be astringent; be astrictive; converge. **3** [여론 등을 한데 모으는 것] collecting; (a) reflection. 수렴하다 collect.

수령 [सुर्योंग] [**受領**] receipt; acceptance. e.g. 이 장부는 수령 전용이다 This ledger is used solely for receipts. 수령하다 receive; accept. e.g. 연금을 수령하다 receive a pension.

수로 [सुरो] [**水路**] a water-course; (항행할 수 있는) a waterway; [강,바다,호수 등의 뱃길] a channel; [운하] a canal. e.g. 관개수로 an irrigation canal.

수록 [सुरोक] [**收錄**] 수록하다 [모으다] gather; collect; [기재하다] record; write down; mention; [자기 테이프에 녹음하다] tape. e.g. 이 책에 수록되어 있는 논문은 20 편이다 Twenty theses are printed in this book.

수리 [सुरि] [**修理**] repair(s); mending 수리하다 repair; mend; fix (▷ repair 는 비교적 복잡한 물건의 수리, mend 는 간단한 수리에 각각 쓰임 fix 는 어느 쪽으로도 쓸 수 있음 e.g. 나는 시계를 수리 했다 I had my watch repaired.

수립 [सुरिप] [**樹立**] establish-ment; founding; setting-up. 수립하다 establish; found; set up. e.g. 외교 관계를 수립하다 set up diplomatic relations [ties] <with>.

수만 [सुमान] [**數萬**] tens [scores] of thousands. e.g. 1 년 동안에 수만명의 인구가 증가했다 The population increased by tens of thousands in a (single) year.

수면 [सुम्यौन] [水面] the surface of the water. e.g. 수면에서 2 미터 위아래] two meters above [below] the surface (of the water).

수면 [सुम्यौन] [睡眠] sleep; slumber. e.g. 수면을 제대로 취하다 sleep regular hours. 수면을 방해하다 disturb [interrupt] one's sleep [slumber]. 수면하다 sleep; slumber; have a sleep [slumber].

수명 [सुम्यौंग] [壽命] **1** [목숨]] life; man's [the human] life span; the span of life; one's lifetime; the length of one's days. e.g. 인간의 평균 수명 the average span [longevity] of human life [human beings] / the (average) life expectancy. **2** (물건의) wear; durability; life. e.g. 기계의 수명 a machine's life.

수모 [सुमो] [受侮] contempt; scorn; disdain; insult; affront; indignity. 수모하다 be held in contempt; suffer an insult [indignity / affront]; be insulted [slighted / despised]; be subjected to indignity. e.g. 수모받다 [당하다] = 수모하다.

수박 [सुबाक] a watermelon. **수박 겉 핥기** superficiality; shallowness. e.g. 수박 겉 핥기의 superficial / shallow / half-read. the head. e.g. 내각 수반 the head of a cabinet / the prime minister / the premier.

수반 [सुबान] [隨伴] **1** [수행] accompaniment; attendance (on a journey). 수반하 다 accompany; attend <a person on a journey>; be attendant on [upon]; follow. **2** [어떤 일과 함께 생김] accompaniment; concomitance 수반하다 accompany; be attendant on [upon]; follow; attend; carry. e.g. 행정 개혁에 수반하는 여러 문제 the problems accompanying [concomitant with] administrative reforms.

수배 [सुबै] [手配] [범인 체포를 위한 조치] (a) search. e.g. 수배 중인 강도범 a man wanted [sought] for robbery.

수백 [सुबैक] [數百] hundreds. e.g. 수백명의 사람] hundreds of people.

수범 [सुबौम] [垂範] 수범하다 set [give / afford] an example; set a good example; set the pattern; exemplify oneself. e.g. 네가 솔선 수범해야 한다 You should first [take the initiative and] set an example for [to] the others.

수법 [सुबौप] [手法] [작품 등의 일정한 방법 a technique; technical skill. e.g. 그는 유화의 수법을 체득

했다 He learned the techniques of oil painting.

수북하다 [सुबुख्हादा] **1** [쌓이어 있다] heaped up; heaping. e.g. 수북한 오렌지 a heap of oranges. **2** [살이 부어 있다] swollen. e.g. 수북한 눈 a swollen eye.

수분 [सुबुन] [**水分**] water; [습기] moisture; humidity; [액즙] juice; [수액] sap. e.g. 수분을 제거하다 dehydrate / remove water [moisture] <from> / dehumidify / anhydrate

수비 [सुबि] [**守備**] defense; defence; garrisoning. 수비하다 defend; guard; garrison. e.g. 요새를 수비하다 defend a fort.

수사 [सुसा] [**搜査**] (a) criminal investigation; [수색] a search; a manhunt (범인의) 수사하다 investigate; make [conduct] an investigation <into / of>; [수색하다] search <for>; make a search <for>.

수상 [1] [सुसांग] [**水上**] e.g. 수상의 aquatic / water-surface. 잠수함이 수상에 모습을 드러냈다 The submarine surfaced.

수상 [2] **가옥** a house built on stilts over the water.

수상 [3] [सुसांग] [**受賞**] 수상하다 win [receive] a prize; be awarded a prize.

수상 [4] [सुसांग] [**殊常**] 수상하다 strange; mysterious; questionable; dubious; doubtful; unreliable; suspicious; suspicious-looking; shady; fishy; queer. e.g. 수상스럽다 = 수상하다. 수상한 사람 a suspicious (-looking) person / a dubious [suspicious] character / a questionable [shady] character.

수상 [सुसांग] [**首相**] the prime minister; the premier; the chancellor (독일의) e.g. 전 수상 an ex-premier / a former prime minister.

수색 [सुसैक] [**搜索**] (a) quest; a search; a manhunt (범인의); [수사] (an) investigation. 수색하다 search [look / hunt] <for>; make [prosecute] a search <for>; rummage; drag. e.g. 샅샅이 [철저히] 수색하다 search thoroughly <for> / comb. 몸을 수색하다 frisk <a person> / conduct a body search / rub down <a person>.

수석 [सुसौक] [**首席**] [맨 윗자리] the top seat [place]; [우두머리가 되는 사람 the head; the chief. e.g. 외교단의 수석 the doyen of the diplomatic corps. 수석으로 졸업하다 graduate first (on the list).

수선 [1] [सुसौन] noise; fuss;

ado; bustle. 수선하다 noisy; clamorous; vociferous; bustling. e.g. 수선스럽다 = 수선하다. 수선스러운 분위기 a rowdy [rough] atmosphere / a noisy atmosphere.

수선 2 [सुसौन] [修繕] repair(s); mending. e.g. 수선 중이다 be undergoing repairs / be under repair. 수선하다 repair; make repairs <on>; mend; fix (up); do up; recondition. e.g. 수선해야 하다 need repairing [mending] / be in want of repairs.

수소문 [सुसोमुन] [搜所聞] 수소문하다 ask around; inquire here and there.

수속 [सुसोक] [手續] (a) procedure; formalities;(a) process; proceedings; steps. e.g. 입국 수속 formalities for entry.

수송 [सुसोंग] [輸送] transport; transportation; transit; conveyance; traffic; carriage; deportation. 수송하다 transport; convey; deport; carry. e.g. 항공기는 승객뿐만 아니라 우편과 화물도 수송한다 Planes transport [carry] not only passengers but also mail and freight.

수수 방관 [सूसू बांग्वान] [袖手傍觀] 수수 방관하다 merely watch; stand by idly and watch; look on <a scene> with folded arms; sit back and watch; be [remain] an idle onlooker.

수수께끼 [सूसूकेक्कि] a riddle; a conundrum; a puzzle; an enigma; a mystery.

수수료 [सुसुर्यो] [手數料] [구전] a commission; brokerage (거간의 [요금] a fee; a charge. e.g. 등록 수수료 the registration fee.

수수하다 [सुसुहादा] (맵시가) ordinary-looking; plain; simple; quiet; (질이) moderate; average; 빛깔이 sober; [점잖다] unpretentious; restrained; undemonstrative; uninteresting. e.g. 수수하게 unaffectedly / plainly / simply / quietly / soberly. 수수한 빛깔의 블라우스 a blouse of a quiet [subdued] color.

수술 [सुसुल] [手術] a surgical operation; an operation. 수술하다 operate; perform [conduct] an operation. e.g. 맹장을 수술하다 perform an appendectomy.

수습 [सुसप] [收拾] control; settlement. 수습하다 control; get under control; save. e.g. 수습하기 어려운] difficult [hard] to deal with / hard to manage [control / settle]. 민심을 수습하다 gain public opinion / win the hearts of the people.

수습 [सुसप] [修習] apprenticeship; probation. e.g.

수습 중이다 be on probation / be in training. 수습하다 practice oneself <in a trade>; receive training <in>; learn <by observation>. e.g. 사무를 수습 하다 learn the business routine of an office. 수습 간호사 a student nurse

수식 [सुशिक] [**修飾**] [장식] (a) decoration; ornamentation; embroidery; (an) adornment;(an) embellishment; (a) figuration;(문장 등의 a rhetorical flourish. e.g. 그는 수식이 많은 문장을 쓴다 He writes in ornate[florid] style.

수신 [सुशिन] [**受信**] reception; the receipt of a message. e.g. 라디오 수신 radio reception. 단파 수신 short-wave reception. 수신하다 receive; receive a message [letter]. e.g. 라디 오로 수신한 음악 a music received by radio.

수심 [1] [सुशिम] [**愁心**] anxiety; worry; sorrow; grief; apprehension(s); gloominess; melancholy. e.g. 수심의 빛 a worried [an anxious] look / a melancholy [gloomy] air.

수심 [2] [सुशिम] [**水深**] the depth of water. e.g. 수심이 깊은 항구 a deep-water harbor.

수십 [सुशिप] [**數十**] scores; dozens; several tens. e.g. 수십 만 원 hundreds of thousands of won.

수압 [सुआप] [**水壓**] water pressure; hydraulic pressure. e.g. 수압이 높다 [낮다] The water pressure is high [low].

수양 [सुयांग] [**修養**] cultivation (of the mind); moral [mental] culture; (mental) training; character-building. e.g. 정신 수양 spiritual [moral] culture. 수양하다 improve oneself; cultivate one's mind; train. 젊었을 때 수양해야 한다 You should train [improve] yourself while young pursue knowledge; study; get one's education [training] <from>. e.g. 의학을 수업하다 study medical science.

수업 [सुओप] [**授業**] teaching; instruction; (학교 전체의] school; (학급의 a class; [과업] (school) lessons.

수없다 [सुओप्ता] [**數-**] [셀 수 없이 많다] numberless; countless; innumerable; incalculable; uncounted. e.g. 수없이 countlessly / innumerably / without [out of] number / in large numbers / beyond [out of] count.

수여 [सुयौ] [**授與**] (증서 등의) conferment; presentation; (상품의) awarding. e.g. 졸업 증서 수여 the presentation of diplomas.

수여하다 give; grant; confer <a degree on a person>; award <a medal to a winner>; present <a thing to a person / a person with a thing>; decorate <a person with an order>.

수염 [सुयौम] [**鬚髥**] 수염 [콧수염] a mustache; a moustache; [구레나룻] whiskers; [턱수염] a beard; [염소 수염] a goatee. e.g. 가짜 수염 a false mustache [beard].

수영 [सुयौंग] [**水泳**] swimming; bathing; a swim; a bathe. 수영하다 swim; bathe <in the sea>; have a swim; have a bathe. e.g. 수영하러 가다 go swimming [for a swim] / go bathing [for a bathe].

수영복 [सुयौंग्बोक] a swimming [bathing] suit; a swimsuit; [남자용 팬츠] <a pair of> swimming trunks.

수영장 [सुयौंग्जांग] a swimming [bathing] place; a swimming pool [tank].

수온 [सुओन] [**水溫**] the temperature of the water; water temperature.

수완 [सुवान] [**手腕**] ability; capability; capacity; skill; faculty. e.g. 수완이 있는 able / capable / competent / talented.

수요 [सुयो] [**需要**] demand; request. e.g. 꾸준한 수요 steady demand.

수요일 [सुयोइल] [**水曜日**] Wednesday (略 Wed.).

수용 [सुयौंग] [**收容**] accommodation; reception; admission; seating; housing; (난파선원 등의 picking up; a picking. 수용하다 accommodate; admit; seat; receive; intern; house; pick up. e.g. 그 호텔은 1,000 명까지 수용할 수 있다 The hotel can accommodate up to a thousand people. / The hotel has accommodations [accommodation] for a thousand people.

수월하다 [सुवौरहादा] easy; simple.

수위 [सुवि] [**水位**] water level.

수위 [सुवि] [**守衛**] [지키는 일] guard; [경비원] a guard; a security guard; [문지기] a doorman; a doorkeeper; a gatekeeper; a janitor; a porter.

수유 [सुयू] [**授乳** nursing; breast-feeding; lactation. 수유하다 nurse; feed; suckle; give suck [the breast] to; lactate

수의 [सुउइ] [**獸醫**] [**醫**] a veterinary surgeon; a veterinarian; a vet.

수익 [सुइक] [**收益**] profit; earnings; gainings (이익) income (소득,수입) a return <on the investment> (▷노동, 투자, 장사 등의 이익으로, 흔히 복수형

proceeds (판매 등의 이익).

수익금 [सुइक्कम] earnings; gains; [매상금] proceeds; profits.

수입 [1] [सुइप] [**收入**] [소득] an income; earnings; [세입] a revenue; [매상금] receipts; [수익] proceeds; takings. e.g.고정 수입 a fixed [regular / periodical] income. 국가 수입 national revenues.

수입 [2] [सुइप] [**輸入**] (산물의) import; importation; (제도, 사상등의 introduction. e.g. 무환(無換) 수입] no-drath import. 밀수입 smuggling ⇨자유 수입 free import. 수입하다 import; introduce. e.g. 우리 나라는 브라질에서 커피를 수입하고 있다 Our country imports coffee from Brazil.

수자원 [सुजावौन] [**水資源**] water resources. e.g. 수자원의 적극적인 개발 positive exploitation of water resources.

수재민 [सुजैमिन] flood sufferers [victims]; sufferers from a flood.

수재 [सुजै] [**秀才**] [뛰어난 재주] great ability [talent]; genius; [그런 재주를 지닌 사람] a brilliant person; a genius; a prodigy; a talented person. e.g. 학급 제 1 의 수재 the brightest student in a class.

수저 [सुजौ] [숟가락과 젓가락] spoon and chopsticks. e.g. 은수저 한 벌 a set of silver spoon and chopsticks.

수절 [सुजौल] [**守節**] 수절하다 (절개를) keep one's integrity unsullied; keep [remain faithful to] one's principles; hold [stick / live up] to one's principles; (정조를 defend one's chastity; retain one's virtue; (과부가) do not remarry. .

수정 [सुजौंग] [**修正**] an amendment (▷ 법안이나 헌법에 쓰이는 경우가 많음 a revision; (a) modification; (an) alteration; (잘못의 a) correction; (a) rectification. 수정하다 amend; revise; modify; correct; rectify. e.g. 의안을 수정하다 amend a bill.

수정 [सुजौंग] [**受精**] fertilization; fecundation; [植] pollination. e.g. 인공 수정 artificial insemination.

수제 [सुजे] [**手製**] e.g. 수제의 [손으로 만든] handmade / handwrought / made by hand / [자가 제작의 homemade (식품이) / made by oneself.

수제자 [सुजेजा] [**首弟子**] one's best pupil [disciple] <of>.

수조 [सुजो] [**水槽**] a water tank; a cistern.

수족관 [सुजोक्वान] an aquarium <*pl.* ~s, aquaria>.

수준 [सुजुन] [**水準**] **1** [수평면] water level. **2** [표준] a standard; [정도] a level. e.g. 최고 수준 the highest level / the peak / the high-water mark <of English poetry>.

수줍다 [सुजुप्ता] shy; bashful; diffident; timid; (소녀가) coy e.g. 아이는 수줍게 웃었다 The child smiled shyly.

수줍음 [सुजुबउम] shyness; coyness; self-consciousness; timidity.

수중 [सुजु] [**手中**] e.g. 수중의 <a thing> in one's hands. 수중에 넣다 secure / capture / take [gain] possession of / get <something> in one's pocket.

수중 [सुजुंग] [**水中**] e.g. 수중의 underwater / subaqueous / aquatic. 수구는 수중에서 하는 경기이다 Water polo is an aquatic sport.

수증기 [सुजंगि] [**水蒸氣**] (aqueous / water) vapor [vapour]; steam.

수지 [सुजी] [**收支**] income and expenditure; earnings and expenses; incomings and outgoings. e.g. 국제수지 the balance of international payments / the international balance of payments.

수직 [सुजीक] [**垂直**] perpendicularity; verticality. e.g. 수직의 perpendicular / vertical (▷ perpendicular 는 어떤 것에 대해서 직각 vertical 은 수평선에 대해서 직각 / plumb. 수직으로 perpendicularly / vertically / plumb / sheer / at right angles <to>.

수질 [सुजील] [**水質**] the quality [(degree of) purity] of water; the water quality.

수집 [सुजीप] [**收集**] collection; gathering; ingathering. 수집하다 gather; collect. e.g. 정보를 수집하다 collect information / get information.

수척 [सुछोक] [**瘦瘠**] emaciation; gauntness; leanness; haggardness. 수척하다 emaciated; gaunt; haggard; worn; wasted. e.g. 수척한 얼굴 a haggard face. 수척해지다 lose a lot of weight / become emaciated / grow very thin / waste away.

수천 [सुछोन] [**數千**] (several) thousands. e.g. 수천 명의 군중 a crowd of several thousand people.

수첩 [सुछोप] [**手帖**] a (pocket) notebook; a reminder [memorandum] book; a pocket book; a (pocket) diary.

수축 [सुछुक] [**收縮**] contraction (근육 등의) shrinking; shrinkage (열 등으로 오그라듦) constriction. 수축하다 shrink; contract; be constricted; deflate (배기

하여) e.g. 뜨거운 물은 모직물을 수축시킨다 Hot water shrinks woolen cloth.

수출 [सुछुल] [**輸出**] export; exportation. 출하다 export; ship abroad. e.g. 우리 나라는 아시아의 여러 나라에 카메라를 수출하고 있다 Our country exports cameras to Asian countries.

수취 [सुछ्वि] [**受取**] receiving; receipt; (어음 등의) an acknowledgment. 취하다 receive; bear; accept.

수치[1] [सुछि] [**數値**] [계산측정하여 얻은 값] the result. e.g. 현재의 대기 오염 정도를 수치로 나타내다 explain the present state of air pollution numerically[in numbers]

수치[2] [सुछि] [**羞恥**] shyness; shame; dishonor; reproach; ignominy; [명예를 더럽히는 일] (a) disgrace. e.g. 수치를 참다 bear a shame / suppress the feeling of shame.

수치스럽다 [सुछिसरौप्ता] [**羞恥-**] shameful; disgraceful; dishonorable; infamous; ignoble. e.g. 수치스러운 일 a shameful thing / a shame.

수컷 [सुख्वौत] a male (animal); a cock (새의) a bull (코끼리, 고래, 물소 등의 a he.

수평 [सुफ्यौग] [**水平**] horizontality. e.g. 수평의 level / horizontal (▷ level은 보통 면에 대해서 horizontal 은 수직에 대응하는 말로서 흔히 선에 대해서 말함수평으로 horizontally / at a level <with>.

수평선 [सुफ्यौसौन] [**水平線**] the horizon; [수평한 선] a horizontal line.

수포 [सुफो] [**水泡**] e.g. 그의 모든 노력은 수포로 돌아갔다 All his efforts have come to nothing. / All his efforts ended in vain. / All his efforts went down the drain[went up the spout]. / All his hard work went for nothing.

수표 [सुफ्यो] [**手票**] a check; a cheque.

수필 [सुफिल] [**隨筆**] an essay; stray [random] notes; an occasional essay; miscellaneous [occasional] writings; a miscellany.

수학[1] [सुहाक] [**修學**] pursuit of knowledge; study; learning; education. 수학하다 pursue knowledge; study; learn; get an education.

수학[2] [सुहाक] [**數學**] mathematics; math; <英> maths.

수학 여행 [सुहाक यौहै] [**修學旅行**] <go on> an observation tour [trip]; a tour [trip] for study [information]; a school excursion [trip].

수해 [सुहै] [**水害**] [홍수 피해]

flood damage; [참화] flood disaster; [홍수] a flood; an inundation. e.g. 수해를 입다 (사람이) suffer from a flood / (물건이) be damaged by a flood.

수행 [सुहैं] [**遂行**] accomplishment; execution; performance; achievement; prosecution <of a war>. 수행하다 [이룩하다 accomplish; perform; [실행하다 execute; carryout (▷ execute 는좀딱딱한말) e.g. 임무를 수행하다 perform [execute / carry out] one's duties.

수험 [सुहौम] [**受驗**] undergoing [going through] an examination. 수험하다 take a test; take [undergo / go through] an examination; sit [go in] for an examination. **수험료** [सुहौमन्यो] the examination fee; the expense for the examination.

수혈 [सुह्यौल] [**輸血**] (a) blood transfusion. e.g. 나는 수혈을 받았다 I had [was given] a blood transfusion.

수혈하다 [सुह्यौरहादा] give a blood transfusion <to a person>; transfuse <a person's> blood <into another>; transfuse <a patient>.

수호 [सुहो] [**守護**] protection; guard; safeguard; defense. e.g. 신의 수호에 의해 through [by / as the result of] divine protection. 수호하다 protect; guard; keep guard <over / around>; keep <a place> safe <from>; defend. e.g. 나라를 수호하다 guard [protect] the nation.

수화 [सुह्वा] [**手話**] [손짓으로 말함] talking with the hands [fingers]; [그 말W] sign [finger] language.

수화기 [सुह्वागि] [**受話器**] a (telephone) receiver; an earpiece; a headpiece; (무전의) radio earphones; a receiving set. e.g. 수화기를 들다 pick up [lith] the receiver.

수화물 [सुह्वामुल] [**手貨物**] [휴대하는 짐] personal) luggage; < 美 > (hand) baggage

수확 [सुह्वाक] [**收穫**] [곡식을 거두어들임 harvesting; [수확물] a harvest; a crop; a yield. e.g. 수확 중인 밭 a harvest field. 수확하다 gather (in) a harvest; harvest; [베어 들이다] reap; gather [take] in. e.g. 사람들은 벼를 수확하기에 바쁘다 People are busy harvesting [gathering in] the rice.

수효 [सुह्यो] [**數爻**] a number; a figure; an amount. e.g. 수효가 많다 [적다] be many [few] / be large [small] in number.

숙고 [सुक्को] [**熟考**] (mature / due) consideration; deliberation; meditation; mature reflection. 숙고하다 think over <a matter>; ponder on [over] <a problem>; consider (carefully); deliberate <over / on / about>; meditate; reflect upon <a problem>; chew the cud. e.g. 숙고한 끝에 ather due [careful / mature] consideration / ather mature reflection / on second thought(s).

숙녀 [सुंगन्यौ] [**淑女**] a lady; a gentlewoman <*pl.* –women>. e.g. 숙녀다운 ladylike / becoming (to) a lady.

숙달 [सुक्ताल] [**熟達**] proficiency; mastery; skill. e.g. 영어 숙달법 how to master English. 숙달하다 attain proficiency <in English>; become proficient [skillful / skilled / adept] <in teaching>; gain in [acquire] skill; master <English>.

숙련 [सुंगन्यौन] [**熟練**] (veteran) skill; dexterity; adroitness; expertness; facility; mastery; 연습 practice. 숙련하다 become skillful [dexterous] <in [at] the trade>; get skilled <in riding>.

숙면 [सुंगम्यौन] [**熟眠**] a sound [profound / heavy] sleep. 숙면하다 sleep well [soundly / heavily]; have a good sleep; fall [sink] into a deep sleep; sleep like a top [log].

숙명 [सुंगम्यौ] [**宿命**] fate; destiny; fatality; karma. e.g. 숙명적 (인) fateful.

숙모 [सुंग्मो] [**叔母**] an aunt; the wife of one's father's younger brother.

숙박 [सुक्पाक] [**宿泊**] (a) lodging; (군대의) billeting; quartering. 숙박하다 lodge <in / at>; stay <at / with>; stop <in / at>; put up <at>; take up one's lodging; be registered <at a hotel>; check in <at a hotel>; (군대가) be billeted; be quartered. e.g. 여관에 숙박하다 stay [put up] at an inn.

숙박료 [सुक्पांगन्यो] [**宿泊料**] hotel charges [expenses]; a hotel bill; accommodation [lodging] charges.

숙소 [सुक्सो] [**宿所**] one's address; one's place of abode; one's lodgings [quarters]; [여관] an inn; a hotel. e.g. 숙소를 정하다 [잡다] take up one's lodgings [quarters] <in a house> / .

숙식 [सुक्शिक] [**宿食**] board and lodging; bed and board. 숙식하다 board and lodge. **숙식비** [सुक्शिक्पि] the charge for board and lodging.

숙연하다 [सुग्यौनहादा] [**肅然–**]

[조용하다] silent; quiet; hushed; [엄숙하다] solemn; austere; [경건하다] reverential. 숙연히 silently; quietly; solemnly.

숙이다 [**सुगिदा**] (몸을) bend oneself (forward); stoop; (머리를) hang down <one's head>; bow [droop / bend / drop / incline / sink] <one's head>. e.g. 고개를 숙이다 bow one's head / (풀이 죽어 창피해서) hang one's head.

숙제 [**सुक्चे**] [**宿題**] **1** (학교의) homework; a home task; an assignment; home lessons. e.g. 방학 숙제 a holiday task. **2** [검토 중인 문제] a pending question; [미결 문제 an open question. e.g. 숙제를 해결하다 settle a pending question.

숙지 [**सुक्चि**] [**熟 知**] full knowledge; familiarity. 숙지하다 know well[fully / thoroughly]; be well aware [informed] of <a fact>; be [become] familiar [well acquainted] with <a matter>; have thorough [full / an intimate] knowledge of <a matter>. e.g. 그것을 숙지하고 있다 I am fully aware of it.

숙직 [**सुक्चिक**] [**宿 直**] night duty; night watch. e.g. 어젯밤 숙직은 누구였나요 Who was on duty last night? 숙직하다 be on night duty; keep night watch.

-순 [**-सुन**] [**順**] [순서] order; [차례] turn. e.g. 성적순 <in> the order of merits [the scholastic rank of a student. 날짜순으로 in sequence of date.

순 [**सुन**] [**旬**] [10 년] a decade e.g. 칠순 노인 a person of seventy years old.

순간 [**सुंगान**] [**旬刊**] 순간의 <a magazine> published [issued] every ten days.

순간 [**सुंगान**] [**瞬間**] a moment; a second; an instant. e.g. 순간의적인 momentary / instantaneous.

순결 [**सुंग्यौल**] [**純潔**] [결백] purity; integrity; [티없음] innocence; immaculacy; [동정 chastity; virginal purity; maid (en) hood. e.g. 순결을 더럽히다 sully [stain] the purity <of a woman> / deflower <a maiden>.

순경 [**सुनग्यौग**] [**巡警**] [순찰] patrol (ling); [경관] a policeman; an officer (▷ 부를 때는 officer! 라고 함) a police officer; a (police) constable; a patrolman; <美> a cop(per); <집합적> the police. e.g. 교통 순경 a traffic policeman.

순교 [**सुनग्यो**] [**殉教**] religious martyrdom; baptism of blood. 순교하다 become a martyr; die a martyr for one's faith; martyrize oneself; be martyred; die for one's belief [faith]; suffer martyrdom. e.g. 그는 기독교 박해의 희생이 되어 순교했다 He died a martyr to the persecution of Christians.

순국 [सुंगुक] [**殉國**] dying for one's country. 순국하다 die for one's country. e.g. 그는 순국할 각오가 되어 있다 [He is ready to die for his country.

순국 선열 [**सुंगुक सौन्यौल**] a (patriotic) martyr.

순례 [सुल्ये] [**巡禮**] a pilgrimage. 순례하다 make [go on] a pilgrimage. **순례자** [**सुल्येजा**] a pilgrim; a palmer.

순리 [सुल्लि] [**順理**] submission to reason; reasonableness; rationality. e.g. 순리적 reasonable / rational / right / proper.

순면 [सुनम्यौन] [**純綿**] 순면의 all-cotton. 순면의 셔츠 an all-cotton shirt

순박 [सुन्बाक] [**淳朴, 醇朴**] (rustic) simplicity; homeliness; lack of sophistication [guile]. 순박하다 (성질이) simple; naive; simple and honest; unsophisticated; simple-hearted; simple-minded; (풍속이) homely; simple-mannered <people>. e.g. 순박한 시골 노인 an old country man, simple and honest by nature.

순방 [सुन्बांग] [**巡訪**] a round of calls [visits]. 순방 하다 make a round of calls; visit one ather another. e.g. 각국을 순방 하다 make a tour of various countries.

순백 [सुन्बैक] [**純白**] a pure [snowy] white; sheer [virginal] white. e.g. 순백의 식탁보 a snow-white [pure-white] tablecloth.

순번 [सुन्बौन] [**順番**] [순서] order; [차례] turn. e.g. 순번을 틀리게 하다 mix up [confuse] the order. 순번을 기다리다 wait for one's turn.

순서 [सुन्सौ] [**順序**] [차례] (sequent) order; sequence; [방법] a system; a method; [절차] procedure; course; formalities.

순수 [सुन्सु] [**純粹**] purity; pureness; genuineness. e.g. 영어의 순수성을 깨끗이 보존하다 preserve the pure well of English undefiled. 순수하다 pure; genuine <Celtic people>; real; incorrupt; (잡것이 섞이지 않은 unalloyed; unmixed <blessing>; unadulterated <friendship>; undiluted

순순하다 [सुनसुनहादा] [**順順-**] obedient; gentle; meek; docile; unresisting; submissive. 순순히 meekly; gently; tamely; obediently; submis-

sively; without resistance; quietly e.g. 순순히 자백 하다 own up / confess without concealment [with a good grace].

순식간 [सुन्शिक्कान] [瞬息間] a brief instant; a moment; a second. e.g. 순식간에 in a moment / in an instant / in [like] a flash / in a twinkling / in the twinkling of an eye / in a wink / instantly / in almost no time / (as) quick as a flash [wink].

순위 [सुन्वि] [順位] order; ranking; standing; placing; precedence. e.g. 순위를 다투다 contend for precedence. 순위를 결정하다 [decide ranking.

순응 [सुनुंग] [順應] adaptation; accommodation; adjustment; sympathy. 순응하다 adapt[adjust / accommodate / acclimate] oneself <to new circumstances>. e.g.…에 순응하여 in sympathy with <the national policy>.

순이익 [सुनिइक] [純利益] a net[neat / clean / pure] profit [gain]; net proceeds e.g. 3 만 원의 순이익이 있다 have a net gain of 30,000 won

[सुन्जौन] [純全] 순전하다 [순수하다] pure (and simple); sheer; genuine; [진정하다] true; real; [완전하다] absolute; utter; perfect; downright; entire; total; complete; 100-proof; out-and-out; thorough. e.g. 순전한 사기 [거짓말] a downright swindle [lie]. 순전한 사삿일 a purely personal matter.

순정 [सुन्जौ] [純情] a pure (and simple) heart[mind]; pure-minded feeling <for a person> e.g. 순정적인 naive / pure in heart / unsophisticated.

순조롭다 [सुन्जोरोप्ता] [順調-] favorable; fair; satisfactory; smooth; normal; (날씨가) seasonable. e.g. 순조로운 날씨 seasonable [favorable] weather.

순종 [सुन्जोंग] [順從] (meek) obedience; (tame) submission. 순종하다 follow <a person> obediently; obey <a person> meekly; submit to <a person> tamely

순직 [सुन्जिक] [殉職] death at one's post (of duty); death in the line of duty; death in harness. 순직하다 die at one's post (of duty); die in the line of duty; be killed at work[in the pursuit of one's duties]; die in harness.

순진 [सुन्जिन] [純眞] naivety; purity; innocence. 순진하다 naive; pure; genuine; sincere; ingenuous; innocent;

unsophisticated. e.g. 순진한 웃음 an innocent smile.

순차 [सुन्छा] [**順次**] order; turn. e.g. 순차로[적으로] in (serial / consecutive) order / successively / in regular succession [sequence / series].

순찰 [सुन्छाल] [**巡察**] a round of inspection; a patrol. 순찰하다 make [do] one's rounds; make [go] a round of inspection; patrol. e.g. 경찰관은 순찰하러 나갔다 The policeman went out on patrol.

순탄 [सुन्थान] [**順坦**] 순탄하다길이) even; level; smooth; (일 등이) favorable; fair; smooth. e.g. 순탄한 길 a (broad-) level road / a royal road.

순하다 [सुनहादा] [**順-**] **1** [온순하다] gentle; mild; meek; [고분고분하다] obedient; submissive; tame; docile. e.g. 순한 성질 a gentle nature / a meek disposition. **2** [맛이 독하지 않다] mild <tobacco>; light <wine>; bland. e.g. 순한 맛의 맥주**순화** refinement; sublimation. e.g. 국어 순화 운동 <launch> a campaign to refine [purify] the Korean language.

순환 [सुनहवान] [**循環**] **1** circulation; rotation; cycle. 순환하다 circulate <through>; rotate; cycle; recur; repeat; move in a cycle; go in cycles [circles]. e.g. 주기적으로 순환하다 move in a cycle.**2** (혈액의) circulation of blood.

순회 [सुनहवे] [**巡廻**] (의사 등의) a round; (경찰, 정찰대 등의) a patrol; a tour. 순회하다 go round; go [make] one's [the] rounds; walk one's round(s); go the circuit; make[go / walk] the round <of a district>; patrol; make [go on] a tour <of inspection>; circulate.

숟가락 [सुत्काराक] a spoon.

술 [सुल] [취하는 음료] liquor; alcoholic drink; an intoxicant; wine; spirits. e.g. 독한[약한] 술 a strong [weak] wine / a hard [light] liquor.

술김 [सुल्किम] the influence of liquor. e.g. 술김에 under the influence of liquor [alcohol] / emboldened by liquor

술래잡기 [सुल्लैजाप्कि] tag; tig; touch; touch-last; (a game of) hide-and-(go-) seek; hy spy; I spy. 술래잡기하다 play tag [tig] / play hide-and-seek.

술렁거리다 [सुल्यौंगौरिदा] be disturbed [perturbed]; be stirred [agitated]; be unsettled; be restless [uneasy]; be in (a) commotion. e.g. 온 나라가 승리로 술렁거리고 있었다 The whole nation was astir [alive] with the excitement of victory.

술술 [सुल्सुल] [거침없이] soth-flowing (물 등이) smoothly; swimmingly; without a hitch; without let or hindrance; [막힘없이] fluently; facilely; [쉽게] easily; with ease; readily. e.g. 어려운 문제를 술술 풀다 solve a hard question easily [without (any) effort].

술자리 [सुल्चारि] a drinking party; a banquet; a feast. e.g. 술자리를 마련하다 hold a party.

술집 [सुल्चिप] [주류 판매점] a wine seller's; a liquor store.

숨 [सुम] [호흡] a breath; breathing; respiration e.g. 숨을 내쉬다 breathe out [forth] / give out breath / exhale. 숨 (을) 거두다 breathe one's last (breath); gasp one's life away; expire; die; give up one's breath. e.g. 할아 버지는 오늘 아침에 숨을 거두셨다 My grandfather died [breathed his last] this morning. 숨 (이) 넘어가다 breathe one's last; gasp one's life away [out]; expire; die. e.g. 숨넘어 가는 소리로 말하다 gasp [pant] out. 숨(을) 돌리다 take [gather] breath; recover one's breath; pause for breath; [쉬다] take a pause. e.g. 숨돌릴 겨를도 주지 않고 giving <a person> not a moment's respite.

숨기다 [सुम्गिदा] **1** (모습, 물건 등을) hide <oneself>; conceal <one's money>; ensconce <oneself>; secrete <stolen goods>; bury <one's mistakes>; [덮어 가리다] cover <a fact>; veil <one's displeasure>; draw [throw] a veil over <a fact>; cloak <one's ignorance>; dissemble <a fact>; [막아 가리다] screen; obstruct.**2** [비밀로 하다] keep <a matter> secret [back] <from>; keep <a matter> dark; [숨겨 주다] harbor; shelter <a criminal>; give refuge [shelter / harbor] to <a runaway>.

숨다 [सुम्दा] **1** [몸을 감추다] hide <behind the door / among the trees>; hide [conceal] oneself; take cover; be[lie] in hiding; lie hidden; [피난하다] take [seek] refuge[shelter] <in / under / behind / with>; [보이지 않게 되다]] disappear (from sight);**2** [은둔하다] live in seclusion; retire from the world. 그는 숨어살고 있다 He is living an obscure life. / He remains [has remained] quiet.

숨막히다 [सुम्मखिदा] be choked; be suffocated; be stifled. e.g. 숨막히는 침묵 an oppressive [a breathless] silence. 숨막히는 방 a stuffy[close] room.

숨바꼭질 [सुम्बाकोक्चिल] (a game of) hide-and-(go-) seek; I spy; hy spy. 숨바꼭질하다 play hide-and-seek.

숨쉬다 [सुमस्विदा] breathe; respire; draw(one's) breath; take breath. e.g. 코로 숨쉬다 breathe through the [one's] nose.

숨죽이다 [सुम्जुगिदा] 1 [(일순간) 숨을 멈추다] hold [catch / keep / bate] one's breath; stop [shut out] one's breath. e.g. 숨죽이고 지켜보다 watch with breathless attention.2 [조용히 하다] keep quiet [still]; be silent. e.g. 숨죽이고 이야기하다 speak in a calm tone.

숨지다 [सुम्जिदा] breathe one's last; gasp one's life away [out]; expire; die. e.g. 교통사고로 숨지다 die[be killed] in a traffic accident.

숨차다 [सुम्छादा] be out of breath; be short of breath [wind]; be breathless; be short-winded[-breathed]. e.g. 숨찬 목소리로 말하다 gasp [puff / pant] out [forth / away].

숫- [सुत] pure; virgin; spotless; immaculate; undefiled; innocent. e.g. 숫처녀 a virgin / an innocent girl / an immaculate virgin.

숫기 [सुक्कि] [-氣] manly openness; boldness. 숫기가 없다 be shy [bashful / diffident]; be coy 숫기(가) 좋다 be unabashed[bold / confident / outgoing].

숫자 [सुच्चा] [數字] a figure; a number (▷ 일반적인 말) a numeral (▷ number 보다 딱딱한 말)

숫처녀 [सुत्छौन्यौ] [-處女] a pure [an undefiled] virgin; an innocent[immaculate] virgin.

숫총각 [सुत्छोंगाक] [-總角] a (male) virgin; an innocent bachelor.

숭고 [सुंगो] [崇高] sublimity; lothiness; the sublime. 숭고하다 lothy; sublime; grand; noble.

숭배 [सुंबे] [崇拜] worship; adoration; admiration; cult. e.g. 개인 숭배 the cult of personality 숭배하다 worship; venerate; adore; admire; idolize; make an idol of.

숭상 [सुंसां] [崇尙] respect; veneration. 숭상하다 respect; venerate; esteem; revere

숱 [सुत] (머리털 등의) thickness; density; richness; (분량) quantity. e.g. 숱이 많은 검은 머리 thick [abundant] black hair.

숱하다 [सुथादा] [많다] plentiful; abundant; copious; rich; [흔하다] very many; numerous. e.g. 숱한 불평 잘못] numerous complaints [errors.

숲 [सुफ] (마을 부근에 있고 forest 보다 작은) a wood; woods (▷ < 美 >에서는 단수 취급하는 수도 있음) 나무 그늘의 잡초를 베어 낸, 작은 a grove

쉬 [स्वि] [조용히] hush!; sh!; mum!; [쫓는 소리] scat!; shoo! 쉬 조용히 해 Hush! / Be quiet! / Silence!

쉬다[1] [श्विदा] (음식이) go bad; turn sour; spoil. e.g. 쉰 내 a sourish [stale] smell. 쉰 밥 spoiled rice.

쉬다[2] [श्विदा] (목소리가 get [become / grow] hoarse [husky / harsh]; hoarsen. e.g. 쉰 목소리로 말하다 speak in a husky [hoarse] voice.

쉬다[3] [श्विदा] 1 [휴식하다] rest (up); take [have] a rest <from>; repose [rest] (oneself); stop <from work>. e.g. 5 분간 쉬고 나서] ather five minutes rest. 2 (일,활동을) knock off[drop] <work>; take a rest from <one's work>; give oneself rest. e.g. 휴일에 일한 대신 쉬다 take a day off to make up for having worked on a holiday.3 [중단하다] suspend; pause; discontinue.

쉬다[4] [श्विदा] (숨을) breathe; respire; draw (one's) breath; (한숨 을) sigh; heave [draw / fetch] a sigh. 깊이 숨을 쉬다 draw [take] a deep [full] breath.

쉬쉬하다 [स्विस्विहादा] hush [cover / smother] up <a scandal>; hush-hush. e.g. 쉬쉬하며 말하다 talk hush-hush.

쉬엄쉬엄 [स्विओमस्विओम] with frequent rests; by easy [short] stages; off and on; on and off; in an off-and-on way; intermittently. e.g. 쉬엄쉬엄 가다 go resting at frequent intervals / travel by easy stages.

쉰 [स्विन] fithy. 쉰살] fithy years of age.

쉼표 [स्विमफ्यो] [-標] [樂] a rest; a pause. e.g. 온 2 분 / 4 분 / 8 분쉼표 a whole [a half / a quarter / an eighth] rest / a semibreve [minim / crotchet / quarter] rest.

쉽다 [स्प्ता] 1 [용이하다] easy; [간단하다] simple; [평이하다] plain. 쉽게 easily; with ease [facility]; without difficulty [great effort]; plainly; simply; [바로] readily. e.g. 쉬운 질문 an easy question. 2 [경향이 있다] be susceptible to; be liable to; be apt to; be prone to. e.g. 깨지기 쉬운 자기 fragile china.

쉽사리 [स्विप्सारि] (very) easily; readily; with ease [facility]; without trouble [difficulty]; without effort; with no effort; hands down. e.g. 그는 쉽사리 속는다 He is easily deceived.

슈퍼마켓 [स्यूफौम्खेत] a supermarket.

슛 [स्यूत] (축구P농구 등에서) a shot.

스낵 [सनैक] [간단한 식사] a snack.

스님 [सनिम] [사승] one's teacher [master] in Buddhist faith; (호칭) (the) Rev. (=Reverend) .

-스럽다 [.....सरौप्ता] <서술적> be(like); look (like); seem. e.g. 영광스럽다 be glorious.

-스름하다 [..सरमहादा] **1** (빛깔이) tinged with ...; somewhat; -ish. e.g. 불그 스름하다 be tinged with red / be reddish [some-what red]. **2** (형상이) somewhat; -ish. 동그스름하다 be roundish.

스무 [समु] twenty. e.g. 스무날 the 20th day / twenty days.

스물 [समुल] twenty; a score; [스무 살] twenty years of age; one's twentieth year

스미다 [समिदा] **1** (액체, 기체 등이) soak in [into / through]; sink in [into]; infiltrate <into / through>; filter into; permeate <the soil>; penetrate; pierce. e.g. 스며 나오다 ooze out / exude / percolate / filter through / seep / transude / soak out. **2** (감정, 사상 등이) sink into; be impresssed <on one's mind>; filter into [through]; be imbued. e.g. (교훈 등이) 가슴에 스미다 sink into one's mind / come home to one's heart.

스스럼없다 [सुसुरोमओप्ता] unreserved; unconstrained; free (from constraint); unshy. e.g. 스스럼없는 친구 a friend you can feel free with.

스스로 [सुसुरो] [혼자 힘으로] for oneself; by oneself; unaided. e.g. 스스로 결정하다 decide <a matter> for oneself.

스승 [सुसंग] a teacher; a master (▷ master 는 예술의 거장 등에 씀) a mentor; a preceptor; an instructor. e.g. 옛 스승 one's former teacher.

스웨터 [सुविएथौ] a sweater; a jersey; [풀오버] a pull-over (sweater); (앞이 트인 것) a cardigan.

스위치 [सुविछि] a switch.

스치다 [सुछीदा] graze; barely touch; go past by <a person>; brush past <a person>; rub [scrape] <against / past>; (수면

등을) skim along; scud; (생각 등이) flit. e.g. 두 열차는 전속력으로 스쳐 지나갔다 The two trains passed each other at full speed.

스카우트 [सुख्वाउथ] a scout. e.g. 딴 팀에서 인기 선수를 스카우트하다 entice popular players away from other teams.

스캔들 [सुख्वैन्दल] a scandal.

스커트 [सुख्वौथ] a skirt.

스케이트 [सुख्वेइथ] [운동 기구의 하나] <a pair of> skates.

스케일 [सुख्वेइल] [규모] a scale.

스케줄 [सुख्वेजुल] a schedule <for>; a program. e.g. 꽉 짜인 스케줄 a crammed [crowded / heavy / tight] schedule.

스케치 [सुख्वेछि] [사생(화)] sketching; a sketch. 스케치하다] sketch; make [do] a sketch <of>.

스크랩 [सुख्खुरैप] scraps; a clipping; a cutting (from a magazine). 스크랩하다 make a clipping [cutting] of an article; cut out an article.

스크린 [सुख्खुरिन] [영사막] a screen.

스키 [सुख्वि] (기구) <a pair of> skis; (운동) skiing.

스타일 [सुथाइल] [독특한 방식, 문체, 양식, 화풍] style.

스타킹 [सुथाखिं] <a pair of> stockings [nylons].

스탠드 [सुथेन्दु] 1 [관중석] the stands; (지붕이 없는) the bleachers. e.g. 스탠드에서 우레 같은 박수가 터졌다 A storm of applause rose from the stands. 2 [전기 스탠드] 탁상용) a desk lamp; (바닥에 놓는)] a floor lamp; a standard lamp

스탬프 [सुथैम्फ] [도장] a stamp; [소인] a postmark.

스테이크 [सुथेइख्व] a steak.

스텝 [सुथेप] (춤 등의) a step. e.g. 왈츠의 스텝을 밟다 practice a waltz step.

스토리 [सुथोरि] [이야기 줄거리] a story.

스톱 [सुथोप] [정지] stop. 스톱하다 stop.

스튜디오 [सुथ्यूदिओ] a studio <*pl.* ~s>.

스튜어디스 [सुथ्यूऔदिस] [항공기의 여자 서비스원] a stewardess; an air hostess.

스트레스 [सुग्बू] [생체가 나타내는 방어 반응] stress. e.g. 나는 도시 생활의 스트레스를 느끼기 시작했다 I'm beginning to feel the stress [pressures] of urban life.

스티커 [सुथिख्वौ] a sticker; an adhesive label

스팀 [सुथिम] [증기] steam. e.g. 스팀 난방 steam heat / central heating. 스팀으로 방을 덮게 하다 heat a room by steam.

스파이 [सुफाइ] [간첩] a spy; a secret agent; (행위)

espionage.

스페어 [सुफेओ] [여분] a spare; spare parts.

스펠링 [सुफेल्लिंग] spelling.

스포츠 [सुफोछ] sports; (개개의) a sport. 스포츠의 sport / sports. 스포츠를 즐기다 enjoy sports / take part in sports.

스폰서 [सुफोन्सौ] **1** [광고주] a sponsor. **2** [기부금, 자금을 내는 사람] a sponsor; a patron; a financial supporter.

스프레이 [सुफुरेइ] [분무][a spray; [분무기] an atomizer; a sprayer.

스프링 [सफरि] [용수철] a spring **스프링클러** [सुफुरिंग] [빌딩 천장 등의 자동 살수 장치 또는 관개용 살수 기구] a sprinkler.

스피드 [सुफिद] [속력, 속도] speed.

스피치 [सुफिछि] [연설] a speech.

스피커 [सुफिखौ] [라디오, 텔레비전 등의 확성기] a (loud) speaker

슬그머니 [सल्कमोजी] 남몰래 secretly; in secret; by stealth

슬기롭다 [सल्किरोप्ता] Intelligent; sagacious; wise; bright; prudent; sensible; witty. e.g. 슬기로운 사람 a man of wisdom / a wise man

슬다 [सल्ता] [녹이 생기다]] gather [form] rust; get [become] rusty; (곰팡이가) gather mold; become [get] musty [moldy]; mildew. e.g. 녹슨 칼 a rusty sword [knife].

슬럼프 [सल्लौम्फ] a slump. e.g. 슬럼프에 빠지다 hit [be in] a slump.

슬로건 [सल्लोगौन] a slogan; a motto <*pl.* ~es, ~s>. …

슬리퍼 [सल्लिफौ] (a pair of) slippers; (뒤축이 없는)] backless slippers; scuffs

슬슬 [सलसल] **1** [천천히] slowly. e.g. 슬슬 걷다 walk slowly. 슬슬 떠나기로 가보기로] 하지 Let's be going. / Shall we be going? **2** [가만히 문지르는 모양, 부드럽게 부는 모양] [sothly; gently; lightly. e.g. 슬슬 문지르다 rub lightly / give (something) a light rub. **3** [녹는 모양] melt) well; imperceptibly. e.g. 이 과자는 입안에서 슬슬 녹는다 This cake melts in the mouth.

슬쩍 [सल्चौक] 남몰래 furtively; stealthily; by stealth; quietly

슬퍼하다 [सल्फौहादा] feel sad [be sorrowful] <at>; grieve <at / over>; have a heavy [broken] heart; [통탄하다] deplore; lament; mourn <over / for>; be distressed <over>; regret. e.g. 남의 불행을 슬퍼하다 feel sorry for another's misfortune. 남의 죽음을

슬퍼하다 mourn [lament] another's death / grieve [wail] over another's death.

슬프다 [सल्फुदा] **1** (마음이) sad; sorrowful; unhappy; doleful; mournful; miserable. e.g. 슬픈 목소리 a plaintive [sorrowful] voice. **2** (일이) sad; sorrowful; pathetic; touching; doleful; plaintive; [통탄스럽다] lamentable; deplorable; grievous. e.g. 자식을 잃은 어머니의 슬픈 노래 a lament of a mother who lost her child.

슬픔 [सल्फम] (a) sorrow; sadness; [비통] (a) grief; [비탄] lamentation; [애도] mourning; [괴로움] distress.

슬하 [सरहा] [**膝下**] (under) one's paternal roof [care]; the care of one's parents. e.g. 부모 슬하를 떠나다 leave one's paternal roof [home].

습격 [सपक्यौक] [**襲擊**] a surprise attack; a sudden assault (▷ attack 보다 격렬함) a raid (습격하다 raid; attack; assault.

습관 [सपक्वान] [**習慣**] [버릇, 습성] a habit; [관례] a custom; a practice (▷ a custom 은 그 사회의 구성원의 공통적인 a habit 은 개인적인 장기간의 습관 a practice 는 양쪽 모두에 쓰임)

습기 [सप्कि] [**濕氣**] moisture; humidity; damp (ness); wet (ness). e.g. 습기가 차다] get damp / (쿠키 등이) get soggy / go soth.

습도 [सप्तो] [**濕度**] humidity.

습득 [सप्तक] [**拾得**] 습득하다 [발견하다] find; [줍다] [जुप्ता] pick up. e.g. 보도에 떨어져 있는 지갑을 습득했다 I found [picked up] a coin purse lying on the sidewalk.

습득 [सप्तक] [**習得**] learning; acquirement. e.g. 기술의 습득 acquirement of technics. 습득하다 [배우다] learn; [배워서 몸에 익히다] acquire (a skill); [숙달하다] master.

습성 [सुप्सौंग] [**習性**] a habit; behavior [behaviour]; a peculiarity; a habitude. e.g. 그는 고릴라의 습성을 연구하고 있다 He is studying the behavior [habits] of gorillas.

습하다 [सफादा] [**濕-**] damp; moist; wet; dampish; humid; [축축하다] soppy; soggy.

승 [सुंग] [**勝**] a victory; a win. e.g. 3 승 1 패 with) three victories [wins] and [against] one defeat.

승강 [सुंगांग] [**昇降**] [오르내림] going up and down; ascent and descent; [상하] rise and fall. 승강하다 go [come] up and down; ascend and descend; rise and fall. **승강기** [**संगांगि**] an elevator; a lith.

승객 [**सुंगैक**] [**乘客**] a passenger; a fare (택시 등의)

승낙 [**सुंग्नाक**] [**承諾**] consent; (an) agreement; acceptance; assent. 승낙하다 consent; agree <to>; give one's consent [assent] <to>; assent

승리 [**सुंग्नी**] [**勝利**] a victory; a triumph (▷승리감이 따르는)

승마 [**सुंग्मा**] [**乘馬**] horseback riding; riding; horsemanship; a riding horse (말). 승마하다 ride a horse; get on [mount] a horse. e.g. 승마하러 가다 go for a ride.

승무원 [**समूवौन**] [**乘務員**] <집합적> the crew; (한 사람) a crew member; a member of the crew; (열차의) a train man; <집합적> a train crew; (전차 등의) a carman; (비행기의) a crewman; <집합적> a flight crew (여자 승무원여객기의) a stewardess / an air hostess.

승부 [**सुंग्बू**] [**勝負**] [승패] victory or defeat; the outcome; the issue; [시합] a contest; a game; a match; a bout. 무승부 a drawn game / a draw / (경주에서) a dead heat.

승산 [**संसान**] **勝算**] prospects of success [victory]; one's chances (of winning). e.g. 승산 없는 싸움 a hopeless battle [struggle].

승선 [**संसौन**] [**乘船**] (an) embarkation. 승선하다 get on; board; go on board; embark

승소 [**सुंग्सो**] [**勝訴**] 승소하다 (사람이) win [gain] the case [one's suit]; (사건이) in favor of one.

승승장구 [**संसंजागू**] [**乘勝長驅**] 승승장구하다 make a long march flushed with victories; follow up a [one's] victory; win victory ather victory.

승용차 [**संग्योंगछा**] a (passenger) car; a (motor) car; an automobile.

승인 [**सुंग्नि**] [**承認**] [공인] recognition; acknowledgement; admission; [동의] consent; agreement; [인가] approval; approbation. 승인하다 recognize; acknowledge; approve; admit; consent <to>; hold with.

승자 [**संग्जा**] [**勝者**] a victor; (게임 등의) a winner.

승진 [**संग्जीन**] [**昇進**] promotion; advancement; preferment; a rise in rank. 승진하다 obtain [win / get] promotion; be promoted [advanced] <to>; rise (in rank); move up

승차권 [**सुंग्छाग्वौन**] [**乘車券**] a (railway / streetcar) ticket; a passenger ticket.

승패 [संफै] [**勝敗**] victory or defeat; the issue [outcome] <of a battle>.

시 [1] [शि] [**時**] [시간]] an hour; [시각] o'clock; time.

시 [2] [शि] [**市**] [도시 a city; a town; [행정 구역] a municipality

시 [3] [शि] [**詩**] <집합적> poetry; (한 편) a poem; lines; [운문] verse.

시- [शि...] [**媤**] of the husband; <an aunt> on the husband's side; <a woman's father>-in-law. e.g. 시누이 a sister of one's husband.

시가 [शिगा] [**時價**] the current price <of strawberries>.

시각 [1] [शिगाक] [**視角**] **1** [理] the optic angle; one's angle of vision. e.g. 시각을 바꾸어 보다 look at a thing from a different angle. **2** [사물을 생각하는 입장]] one's viewpoint; a point of view; a way of looking <at>. e.g. 시각의 차이 a difference of viewpoint.

시각 [2] [शिगाक] [**視覺**] (the sense of) sight [vision]; visual sensation; eyesight; seeing. e.g. 시각적(으로) visual (ly).

시각 [3] [शिगाक] [**時刻**] time; the hour. e.g. 약속의 시각 the appointed time.

시간 [शिगान] [**時間**] **1** [시간을 세는 단위 an hour. e.g. 한 시간 이내에 within an hour. **2** [때] [तै] time. e.g. 소요 시간 the time required.**3** (수업, 근무, 휴식 등의) hours; [수업 시간] school hours. e.g. 영업 시간 business [office] hours.

시간표 [शिगान्फ्यो] [**時間表**] a timetable; a (class) schedule.

시계 [शिग्ये] [**時計**] (탁상 시계) a (table) clock; (벽 시계) a (wall) clock; (회중, 손목 시계) a watch; a wrist watch (손목 시계)자명종) an alarm clock; <집합적> a timepiece; a timekeeper.

시골 [शिगोल] (도시에 대하여] the country; the countryside; [전원] rural districts; [지방] local areas; the sticks (▷경멸적으로 씀 [고향] one's home; one's native place; one's birthplace. e.g. 시골의 rural / country / [소박한] rustic / [지방 특유의 또는 편협한] provincial.

시국 [शिगुक] [**時局**] the situation; the (current) state of affairs [things]. e.g. 중대 시국 a critical juncture.

시공 [शिगों] [**施工**] construction; execution; operation. 시공하다 construct; carry out (a construction project); undertake construction

시급 [शिगप] [時急] urgency; emergency; exigency. 시급하다 urgent; pressing; emergent; immediate; imminent. e.g. 시급한 필요 an urgent [a pressing] need

시기 [1] [शिगी] [時期] [정한 때] time; the times. e.g. 중대 [적당] 한 시기 a crucial [an appropriate] time.

시기 [2] [शिगी] [猜忌] jealousy; green envy. 시기하다 be jealous <toward>. e.g. 그는 너의 명성을 시기하고 있다 He is jealous of your good name.

시기 [3] [शिगी] [時機] [기회] an opportunity; a chance; the time; season; [알맞은 때] the (proper) moment. e.g. 시기에 알맞은적절한] opportune / timely / appropriate / well-timed / seasonable.

시꺼멓다 [शिक्कौम्था] **1** (색깔이) deep-black; jet- [coal-] black; inky (-black); sooty. e.g. 시꺼멓게 타다 be scorched black. **2** (마음이) blackhearted; evilhearted; malicious; wicked. e.g. 그는 뱃속이 시꺼멓다 He is wicked at heart [black-hearted].

시끄럽다 [शिक्करौप्ता] **1** [소란하다] noisy; loud; boisterous; uproarious; clamorous; tumultuous; <美> rip-roaring. e.g. 시끄럽게 하다 make noise.**2** (의론, 여론이) much-talked-of; much-discussed; vexed. e.g. 시끄러운 문제 a controversial [much-discussed / burning] question.

시나리오 [शिनारिओ] a scenario <*pl.* ~s>; a screenplay.

시내 [1] [शिने] the city; the area within the city limits. e.g. 시내에 있는 학교 the schools in the city.

시내 [2] [शिने] a stream; a brook (개울) a creek; a brooklet; a rivulet; a streamlet.

시네마 [शिनेमा] cinema.

시누(이) [媤-] one's husband's sister; a sister-in-law.

시늉 [शिन्युंग] [흉내] mimicry; imitation; apery; aping; a take-off; 체하기] false) show; (a) pretense; make-believe; sham; simulation. e.g. 우는 시늉을 하다 pretend to cry.

시니컬하다 [शिनिख़ौरहादा] [냉소적이다] cynical.

시다 [शिदा] (맛이) sour; acid; tart; vinegary. e.g. 신 포도 sour grapes.

시달리다 [शिदाल्लिदा] be troubled <with>; be worried <with>; be annoyed <by / with / at>; be harassed [molested / vexed]; suffer <from> (병에) be jostled <in a crowd>; (세파 등에)

be tried; see [experience] hardships. e.g. 가난에 시달리는 가족 a poverty-stricken family.

시대 [शिदै] [**時代**] **1**[때의 형세] the times. e.g. 시대의 흐름 the current of the times.**2** [역사상의 연대] an era; an age. e.g. 조선 시대 the *Chos?* Period.**3** [시절, 인생의 한 시기] days. e.g. 청년 시대에 in one's youth..

시댁 [शिदैक] [**媤宅**] one's husbnd's family [home]

시도 [शिदो] [**試圖**] a trial; a try; a tryout; an attempt; a venture (모험적인) an experiment. 시도하다 make plans [take steps] to carry out; implement; try to realize [to put into effect]; try out; test; (make an) attempt <at / to do>.

시동 [शिदोंग] [**始動**] starting. e.g. 시동을 걸다 switch on the ignition / start <a machine>.

시동생 [शिदोंसै] [**媤同生**] one's husband's younger brother; a brother-in-law.

시들다 [शिदल्ता] **1**(초목이) wither (away / up); wilt (▷ wither 는 한창때를 지나, 또는 수분 부족이나 기후 때문에 생기를 잃음. wilt 는 주로 수분 부족으로); shrivel (쭈그러들다) droop; fade (away); languish.**2** (기운이) [गिउनि] weaken; lose strength; wane; (매력, 청춘이) wither; go [run] to seed. e.g. 인기가 시들다 lose [fall in] popularity.

시들하다 [शिदरहादा] [마음에 차지 않다] unsatisfactory; dissatisfied; [내키지 않다] halfhearted; lukewarm; reluctant; unwilling; uninterested; [흥미가 없다] unattractive; uninteresting; [대수롭지 않다] trivial; of no account [value].

시럽 [शिरौप] sirup; syrup. e.g. 과즙 시럽 fruit syrup.

시력 [शिर्यौक] [**視力**] sight; eyesight; vision; visual power.

시련 [शिर्यौन] [**試鍊, 試練**] a trial (고난) an ordeal (특히, 가혹한 시련) a test; [神] a probation.

시류 [शिर्यू] [**時流**] [그 시대의 흐름, 풍조] the current of the times; the trend of the world; the general drith of affairs; [유행] the fashion of the day. e.g. 시류를 따르다 follow the fashions of the day. 시류에 영합하다 curry favor with the public.

시름 [शिरम] anxiety; apprehension (s); worry; care; trouble; grief; sorrow; heaviness of mind. e.g. 시름을 놓다 [덜다] be relieved of one's anxiety / feel relieved / set [have] one's mind [heart] at rest [ease] / unload one's mind.

시름시름 [शिरमशिरम] lingeringly. e.g. 그는 시름시름 앓았다 He was long in recovering from his illness.

시리다 [शिरिदा] (achingly / painfully) cold; chilled. e.g. 귀가 시려서 떨어져 나갈 것 같다 My ears tingle with the cold.

시리즈 [शिरिज] [문고, 총서, 연속 영화나 경기] a series.

시립 [शिरीप] [市立] e.g. 시립의 municipal / city. 그 유치원은 시립이다 That nursery school is run by the city.

시무룩하다 [शिमुरुखादा] sullen; grim (기분이 언짢다) taciturn (말이 없다) peevish; sour; glum; grumpy; ill-humored. 시무룩한 얼굴 a sulky look [face].

시민 [शिमिन] [市民] [개인] a citizen; <집합적> the citizens; the townsmen; the townspeople; the townsfolk; the citizenry. e.g. 서울 시민 a citizen [the citizens] of Seoul.

시범 [शिबौम] [示範] showing [setting] an example; a model for others. e.g. 시범적으로 by way of showing an example / as a model. 시범하다 show [set / give / offer] an example <to others>.

시부모 [शिबुमो] [媤父母] one's parents-in-law; the parents of one's husband.

시비 [शिबि] [是非] **1** [잘잘못] right and[or] wrong; [적부] the propriety <of>. e.g. 시비의 판단 discrimination of right and wrong. 시비하다 comment <on>; criticize. **2** [말다툼] a dispute; a quarrel; a wrangle; an altercation; an argument. e.g. 시비가 벌어지다 get into an altercation <over> [arguments <with>

시사 [शिसा] [時事] current [present] events [affairs / questions]; the events [news] of the day. e.g. 시사에 밝다 be well-informed of current events [affairs] / be in touch with the times.

시상 [शिसाग] [施賞] 시상하다 award <a person> a prize; bestow a prize <on>.

시상식 [शिसांशिक] a ceremony of awarding a prize.

시선 [शिसौन] [視線] one's eyes; one's gaze. e.g. (…로) 시선을 돌리다 turn one's gaze [eyes] on / look at.

시설 [शिसौल] [施設] [건물] an institution; an establishment; [설비] facilities; equipment; [수용소] a home <for the aged>. e.g. 공공 시설] a public institution / a public service. e.g. 교육 시설 educational facilities

[institution].

시속 [शिसोक] [**時速**] speed per hour.

시술 [शिसुल] [**施術**] the administration of medicine. 시술하다 administer medicine <to a person>; give medical treatment; perform an operation <on a person>.

시스템 [शिसथेम]a system.

시승 [शिसुंग] [**試乘**] a test [trial] ride [trip]. 시승하다 take a test ride; test <a car>; have a trial ride; try out; make a trial trip

시시각각 [शिशि गाकगाक] [**時時刻刻**] every moment [hour / minute]; <부사> momently; hourly; momentarily; from hour to hour; from moment to moment; moment by moment. e.g. 시시각각 변하는 날씨 ever-changing weather.

시시비비 [शिशिबिबि] [**是是非非**] [잘잘못] right and [or] wrong. e.g. 시시비비를 가리 distinguish between right and wrong / tell right from wrong.

시시콜콜(히) [शिशिखोलखोल] [हि] inquisitively. e.g. 시시콜콜 따져 묻다 inquire of <a person> about every detail of <a matter> / catechize <a person> to the last details about <a matter

시시하다 [शिशिहादा] [사소하다] trifling; trivial; petty; inconsiderable; insignificant; of little importance; of no consequence [account]; [쓸데없다] useless; of no use; [가치없다] worthless; valueless; unworthy; [평범 하다] common; monotonous; flat; prosaic; [어리석다] stupid; foolish; silly; despicable. e.g. 그들은 시시한 일로 다투고 있다 They are quarreling over a trifling matter.

시식 [शिशिक] [**試食**] 시식하다 sample; try; taste; have a foretaste <of>. e.g. 인도네시아 요리를 시식하다 try [sample / have a taste of] Indonesian dish.

시야 [शिया] [**視野**] **1** [시력의 범위] a field [range] of vision; a visual field; one's view; (a field of) view; sight. e.g. 시야를 가리다 obstruct <a person's> field of vision. **2** [식견, 사려의 범위] one's mental [intellectual] horizon; outlook. e.g. 시야가 좁은 [넓은] having a narrow [wide] mental horizon.

시어머니 [शिओमोनि] [**媤**-]a mother-in-law; one's husband's mother.

시연 [शियोन] [**試演**] a demonstration; a trial performance; a preview. e.g. 공개 시연 a public demonstration / a public rehearsal. (시연하다시험 적으로) give a trial performance <of a play>; [연습하다] rehearse <a play>.

시외[शिवे] [**市外**] the outskirts of a city; outside the city limits; the suburbs. e.g. 우리 학교는 서울 시외에 위치하고 있다시의 바깥에) Our school is situated on the outskirts of(the city of) Seoul. / (교외에) Our school is in the suburbs of Seoul.

시원섭섭하다 [शिवौनसौपसौफादा] <서술적>feel relief and sorrow at the same time; feel mixed emotions of joy and sorrow. e.g. 막내 딸을 시집보내고 나니 시원섭섭하다 I feel relieved but sad at having married off my youngest daughter.

시원스럽다 [शिवौन्सरौप्ता] e.g. 성격이 시원스러운 사람 a person of frank disposition.

시원시원하다 [शिवौनशिवौनहादा] (성격이) frank; unreserved; open-hearted; (말이) clear; outspoken; straight-forward; (행동이) bright; brisk; active; lively; prompt; quick; snappy; crisp. e.g. 말씨가 시원시원한 사람 a man with a crisp manner of speaking. 시원시원 frankly; unreservedly; briskly; clearly; actively; fluently; without reserve; promptly. e.g. 그는 시원시원히 대답했다 He answered frankly [candidly]. / He gave a frank [an unreserved] answer.

시원찮다 [शिवौनाशिवौनही] [좋지 않다] not good; poor; humble; [만족스럽지 않다] unsatisfactory; unsatisfying; [보잘것없다] worthless; of little value [importance]; little; small. e.g. 시원찮은 음식 poor food.

시위 [शिवि] [**示威**] show of force; demonstration; display. e.g. 불만을 품은 노동자들이 시위를 벌였다 A demonstration was staged [carried out / held] by dissatisfied [disaffected] workers. 시위하다 show force; demonstrate; display.

시음 [शिउम] [**試飲**] 시음하다 sample; taste; try.

시인 1 [शिइन] [**詩人**] a poet (남자) a poetress (여자) [यौजा].

시인 2 [शिइन] [**是認**] admission; acknowledgement; approval; approbation. 시인하다 admit; acknowledge; approve of; approbate; endorse. e.g. 그는 어머니의 꽃병을 깨뜨렸음을 시인했다 He admitted breaking his mother's vase.

시일 [शिइल] [**時日**] **1** [때와 날] the date; the day. e.g. 회합의 시일을 정하다 set

a date for the meeting. **2** [기일, 기한] time; days. e.g. 시일의 경과 the passage [laps / progress] of time.

시작 [शिजाक] [**始作**] **1** [개시, 착수] the beginning; the start; the opening; the commencement; the outset. 시작하다 [begin; start; open; commence; make a start [beginning]; initiate; set about; take to; enter into [upon]; take up; fall to <doing>; embark in [(up) on]. e.g. 웃기 시작하다 begin to laugh / burst out laughing. **2** [처음] origin; beginning.
시작하다 originate <in>; have <its> origin [rise] <in>; arise <from>; begin. e.g. 이 의식은 고려 시대에 시작되었다 This ceremony originated [was begun] in the Kory Period.

시장 [शिजांग] hunger. e.g. 시장이 반찬 Hunger is the best sauce. / A good appetite is a good sauce. 시장하다 hungry; starving; famishing. e.g. 몹시 시장하다 I'm hungry. / I am good and hungry. / I am (as) hungry as a hunter.

시장 [शिजांग] [**市長**] a mayor

시장 [शिजांग] [**市場**] a market; a fair; a mart; a market place; [거래소] an exchange.

시절 [शिजौल] [**時節**] [일정한 시기] the time; an occasion; days. e.g. 저 거지도 한때는 좋은 시절이 있었다 The beggar has seen better days.

시점 [1] [शिचौम] [**視點**] [관점] a point of view; a viewpoint. e.g. 시점을 바꾸어서 생각해 보시오 Try to think about it from a different point of view.

시점 [2] [शिजौम] [**時點**] a point in[of] time. e.g. 현시점에 at present / at this time [stage]. 이 시점에서는 그것이 최선의 길일지도 모른다 That may be the best we can do at this stage [point / juncture].

시정 [शिजौंग] [**是正**] correction. 시정하다 correct; put right; rectify; set <something> to rights. e.g. 사회의 폐습을 시정하다 put right [redress] social abuses.

시제 [शिजे] [**時制**] [문법] a tense. e.g. 현재미래 / 완료시제 the present [future / perfect] tense.

시조 [शिजो] [**始祖**] the founder; the originator; the father; the progenitor.

시종 [शिजोंग] [**始終**] [처음부터끝까지] from start [beginning] to finish [end]; from first to last; all the time [while]; all [right] along; all the way; all through; throughout. e.g. 시종 일관 consistently. 그들은 인질을 시종 감시하고 있었다 They kept the hostage under constant guard.

시중 [शिजुंग] attendance; attending; waiting on; serving; (식탁에서의) service (at table). 시중하다 attend (on); wait on[upon]; serve <a person>; do <a person> a service; [돌보다 take care of. e.g. 환자를 시중하다 attend [care for] an invalid.

시즌 [शिजन] a season. e.g. 야구수영시즌 the baseball [bathing] season.

시집 1 [शिजीप] [媤-] one's husband's home [family]; the family a woman marries into; a woman's in-laws. e.g. 시집 식구들 a woman's in-laws.

시집 2 [शिजीप] [詩集] a collection of poems; collected poems; an anthology (명시선).

시집가다 [शिजीप्कादा] [媤-] marry <a man / into a family>; be[get] married to <a doctor / lawyer>; take a husband. e.g. 좋은 데로 시집가다 marry [be married] well / get well married / make a good marriage.

시집살이 [शिजीप्सारि] [媤-] a woman's married life [housekeeping] (in the home of her husband's parents). e.g. 시집살이를 잘하다] keep house well (inone's parents-in-law's home).

시차 [शिछा] [時差] [지방 시의 차] a [the] difference in time; a time difference.

시청 1 [शिछों] [市廳] a municipal [city] office; (청사) a city [municipal] hall; the City Administration Building.

시청 2 [शिछों] [視聽] looking and listening; [주의] attention. e.g. 텔레비전 시청료 a TV subscription fee. 시청하다 look and listen; see and hear. e.g. T 를 시청하다 teleview / watch television.

시청각 [शिछोंगाक] [視聽覺] (the senses of) sight and hearing; the visual and auditory senses.

시청률 [शिछोंन्यूल] [視聽率] [TV] a program [an audience] rating; a (popularity) rating.

시청자 [शिछोंजा] [視聽者] [TV] a (TV) viewer; a televiewer; <집합적> the TV audience.

시체 [शिछे] [屍體] a (dead) body; a corpse; one's remains.

시초 [शिछो] [始初] the beginning; the inception; the

start; the outset; [기원] the origin; the source; the genesis; [원인] the cause.

시치미 **1** [शिछिमि] feigned [assumed] innocence [ignorance]; false pretense; dissimulation. 시치미(를) 따다=시치미 (를) 떼다시치미 (를) 떼다 feign [affect] ignorance [innocence]; play [do] (the) innocent; pretend to be ignorant <of>; pretend not to know; assume an air of innocence; keep a straight face; wear [put on] an innocent look; keep a straight face; put on a blank [poker] face.

시큰둥하다 [शिख्वन्दुंहादा] [건방지다] impertinent; saucy; pert; forward; cheeky; impudent; smart aleck; fresh. e.g. 시큰둥한 대 a pert answer / a saucy reply.

시키다 [शिखिदा] (강제) make <a person do>; cause <a person to do>; force [compel] <a person to do>; induce <a person to do>; (허락, 방임) let <a person do>; allow <a person to do>; (부탁, 의뢰) get <a person to do>; have <a person do>; (일러서) tell <a person to do>; bid <a person do>; (주문) order <something from a person / a person to do>; call for <an ice cream> .e.g. 일을 시키 make <a person> work / put <a person> to work. 그 일은 제게 시켜 주십시오 Let me do it, please.

시트 [शिथु] **1** [자리] a seat. e.g. 그 자동차의 뒤쪽 시트는 세 사람이 앉을 만큼 충분히 넓다 The back seat of the car is wide enough for three people. **2** (침대의)] a (bed) sheet; sheeting. e.g. (침대의) 시트를 갈다깔다 change [spread] a sheet.

시판 [शिफान] [**市販**] marketing; sale at a market. 공동 시판 joint marketing. 시판하다 market; put [place] <goods> on the market; place on sale; sell at a market. e.g. 시판되고 있는 공책 a notebook sold [obtainable] at a store.

시퍼렇다 [शिफौरौथा] **1** deep blue; (안색이) deadly [ghastly] pale; pallid. e.g. 시퍼런 바다 the deep blue sea. 시퍼렇게 멍들도록 때리다 [꼬집다] beat [pinch] <a person> black and blue. **2** [당당하다 powerful; influential; stately. e.g. 권세가 시퍼렇다 be very powerful [influential]. 시퍼렇게 살아 있다 be in the land of the living / remain on two legs.

시합 [शिहाप] [**試合**] (주로 오락으로서) a game; (테니

스, 크리켓 등의) a match; a contest; an event; a bout; a meet; a tilt; (권투의 a fight; <美> an encounter; (일련의) a tournament; (연속적인 a series; [시합하기] play; playing.

시행 [शिहै] [**施行**] enforcement; operation. 시행하다 (법률을) enforce; put in force; put into operation; give effect <to>; carry into effect; execute; [실제로 행하다] carry out; conduct. e.g. 그 법률은 아직 시행되지 않고 있다 The law is not yet in force [being forced] (▷ be in force 는 법률이 유효하다 be enforced 는 정해진 법률을 지키게 하고 있음을 뜻함) **시행 착오** [**शिहै छागो**] trial and error. e.g. 그는 많은 시행 착오 끝에 그 발명에 성공했다 He succeeded in the invention ather many trials and errors.

시험 [शिहौम] [**試驗**] **1**(사람의 능력, 지식 등을 시험하기 위한) [an examination; an exam; a teat; (교실에서 간단히 행하는 a quiz <*pl.* quizzes>; an interview (면접) e.g. 시험에 합격하다 pass an examination [a test] / succeed [be successful] in an examination. 시험에 떨어지다 낙제하다 fail in an examination [a test] / fail an examination / flunk a quiz. 시험 잘 쳤나 How have you fared in your exam? **2** [실험] an experiment; a test; a trial; a try. e.g. 강도 [내구성] 시험 a strength [durability] test. 시험하다 experiment <a substance>; make an experiment <on / with / in>; test; put <a thing> to trial [the test]; give <a thing> a trial; try (out); have a try at; make a trial <with / of>. e.g. 기계를 시험하다 test a machine.

시험대 [शिहौम्दै] [**試驗臺**] a test board [desk]; a testing stand; a wire chief desk. e.g. 그 나라는 민주주의의 시험대다 The country is a 'guinea pig' for democracy.

시현 [शिहयौन] [**示現**] revealation; manifestation. 시현하다 [reveal; manifest.

식 [शिक] [**式**] **1** [의식] a ceremony; rituals; rites (종교상의) <집합적> rituals; a (ceremonial) functions; a celebration; an observance; <inauguration> exercises. e.g. 개회폐회] 식 opening [closing] exercises.**2** [방식] a method; a system; [양식] a style; a form; a type; a fashion; a mode; a way; a manner; [기둥 양식] an order. e.g. 미국식 교육 the American method of education.**3** (수리의) an expression; [공식] a formula <*pl.* ~s, -lae>; [방정식] an equation. e.g.구조식 a structural [constitutional] formula.

식견 [शिक्यौन] [**識見**] knowledge; judgment; insight; discernment; vision; intelligence; [견해] one's view; opinions; ideas. e.g. 식견이 높은 사람 a man of exalted ideas / a man of great insight.

식구 [शिक्कु] [**食口**] mouths to feed; one's dependents; members of a family; one's family. e.g. 식구가 많은 집 a large [big] family. 그는 나를 한 식구처럼 대해 준다 He treats me like [as] one of the family.

식다 [शिक्ता] **1** [차게 되다] cool(down[off]); get cold. e.g. 다 식은 커피 stone-cold coffee. **2** [줄거나 가라앉다] abate; subside; lapse back [away]; (열성 등이)[flag; be dampened; cool down [off]. e.g. 열의가 식다 lose interest <in> / grow less enthuse-astic.

식단 [शिक्तान] [**食單**] a menu; a (menu) card; a bill of fare. e.g. 식단을 짜다 make out a menu.

식당 [शिक्तांग] [**食堂**] a dining room [hall]; (군대, 공장 등의) a mess hall; (역, 열차 내의) a buffet; a refreshment room; (대학, 수도원 등의) a refectory; [음식점] a restaurant; (삼류 식당)an eating house.

식대 [शिक्तै] [**食代**] (식당의) [the charge for food; (하숙의) (the charge for) board; (가정의) table expenses.

식량 [शिंगन्यांग] [**食糧**] Food; Foodstuffs; e.g. 비상 식량 emergency rations 우리는 여행갈 때 일주일분의 식량을 갖고 갔다 We took a we'ek's provisions on our journey.

식료품 [शिंगन्योफुम] [**食料品**] [음식의 재료가 되는 채소 등의 물품] an article of food; foodstuffs; <집합적> foodstuffs; provisions; groceries; eatables; victuals.

식모 [शिंग्मो] [**食母**] a kitchen maid; a maidservant; a maid; a housemaid; a (home) help; a domestic; a domestic help.

식목일 [शिंग्मोगिल] a tree-planting day; Arbor Day.

식물 [शिंग्मुल] [**植物**] a plant; <집합적> vegetation; plant life; [한 지역, 한 시대의 식물의 총칭] a flora <*pl.* ~s, -rae>; the botany <of Korea>. e.g. 고산 [열대] 식물 an alpine [a tropical] plant.

식민 [शिंग्मिन] [**植民**] colonization; settlement; (사람) a colonist; a settler; a colonial. 식민하다 colonize (in) <a land>; settle (in) <a region>; plant <a country> with colonists.

식민지 [शिग्मिन्जि] [**植民地**] a colony; a settlement; [史] a plantation.

식별 [शिकप्यौल] [**識別**] discrimination; identification; discernment. 식별하다 discriminate [distinguish] <A from B / between A and B>; discern; tell[separate] <A> from <B>.

식비 [शिक्पी] [**食費**] food expenses; (the charge for) board (하숙의) table expenses (가정의) **식사**[**食事**] [शिक्सा] a meal; dinner; fare; a diet (특히 규정된); board (기숙의) 식사하다 have [take] a meal; dine; eat.

식상 [शिक्सां] [**食傷**] [배탈] a stomach trouble; indigestion; [물림] surfeit; glut. 식상하다 have a stomach trouble; suffer from indigestion; [물리다] be surfeited [cloyed / sated / satiated] <with>; be fed up <with>; glut oneself <with>. e.g.나는 인도에서 카레에 식상했다] I had so much curry in India that I got sick and tired of it

식생활 [शिक्सैहवाल] [**食生活**] (식사 전반에 관한) eating habits; (식사의 질,양) diet. e.g. 식생활의 변화 a change of diet / a change in one's eating [dietary] habits.

식성 [शिकसग] [**食性**] taste; preference; palate. e.g. 식성에 맞는 음식 agreeable [favorite] food.

식욕 [शिकयौक] [**食慾**] appetite; desire to eat. e.g. 식욕을 돋우는 냄새 an appetizing smell.

식은땀 [शिगउन्ताम] (a) cold sweat (▷cold perspiration 이라고는 하지 않음) e.g. 식은땀을 흘리다흘리고 있다] break into[be in] a cold sweat.

식은죽 [शिगउन्जुक] [- **粥**] cold gruel [porridge]. e.g. 식은죽 먹기<비유> an easy task [job] / a piece of cake. 그런 것은 식은죽 먹기다 That's nothing. / Nothing is easier. / That's (as) easy as pie. / <美> That's a cinch.

식음 [शिगउम] [**食飮**] eating and drinking. e.g. 식음을 전폐하다 give up eating and drinking / fast.

식이 요법 [शिगि योबौप] [**食餌療法**] alimentotherapy; a diet [dietary] cure; a dietetic treatment.

식장 [शिक्चांग] [**式場**] the hall [place] of ceremony; the place where a ceremony is held; a ceremonial hall.

식전 [शिक्चौन] [**食前**] 식전에 [밥 먹기 전에] before a meal / [아침밥 먹기 전에] before breakfast / [아침 일찍이] early in the morning.

식중독 [शिक्चुंदोक] [**食中毒**] [음식 중독] food poisoning. e.g. 식중독에 걸리다 get [suffer from] food poisoning / (음식이) disagree with one.

식탁 [शिक्थाक] [**食卓**] a (dining) table; the board; a mess table (함선의)

식품 [शिक्फुम] [**食品**] an article of food; foodstuffs; groceries. e.g. 저칼로리 식품] low-calorie food.

식후 [शिख्रु] [**食後**] 식후에 ather dinner [a meal].

식히다 [शिखिदा]**1**[차게 하다] cool; let <a thing> cool; (얼음으로)] ice. e.g. 수프를 식히다 cool soup.**2** (열의를) dampen <one's eagerness>; cast a damper on <one's enthuseasm>; pall; spoil.

신 **1** [शिन] [**神**] (일신교의) God; the Almighty; Providence; the Supreme Being; the Lord; the Creator; the Divinity; (회교의) Allah; (다신교의) a god; a goddess (여신) a deity; a divinity; a spirit (신령) a demo (악신)

신 **2** [शिन] footgear; footwear; shoes. 갖신 Korean leather shoes. 고무신 rubber shoes. 나막신 wooden clogs. 에나멜신 patent-leather shoes.

신경질 [शिग्योंजील] [**神經質**] a nervous temperament [constitution]; nervousness; nervosity.

신고 [शिंगो] [**申告**] a report (보고) a return; a declaration (세관에서) report, return 은 주로 수입 (收入) 에 대해 쓰는데 declareation 은 관세품과 수입에도 쓸 수 있음) a notice; a statement; a notification; filing. 신고하다 report; make [send in] a report; declare; state; give [submit] notice; notify <the authorities>; file <a return>; register. e.g. 습득물을 경찰에 신고하다 hand over [turn in] a find to the police.

신규 [शिन्ग्यु] [**新規**] a new regulation; a new project. e.g. 신규의 new / fresh. 신규로 anew / afresh / newly.

신기 [शिंगि] [**神奇**] marveloussness; wonderfulness. 신기하다 marvelous; wonderful; mysterious; miraculous; magic (al); supernatural.

신기다 [शिंकिदा] put <shoes> on <a person>; get <a person> to put on <shoes>. e.g. 아이에게

양말 [신] 을 신기다 put socks [shoes] on a child / have a child put on his [her] socks [shoes] / make a child have his [her] socks [shoes] on.

신나다 [शिन्नादा] be very glad[pleased / happy / rejoiced]; be elated; be on the top of the world; (사물이 be very interesting [entertaining]; be highly amusing [exciting]. e.g. 신나는 이야기] a highly amusing story / a very interesting [entertaining] talk.

신년 [शिन्यौन] [**新年**] the New Year

신념 [शिन्यौम] [**信念**] (a) belief; (a) faith (굳은 신념. 반드시 이성에 결부되는 것은 아님. 이런 뜻으로 복수형을 취하는 경우는 없음) a conviction (확신) e.g. 신념에 따라 in accordance with one's beliefs.

신다 [शिन्ता] (동작) put on; get on; (상태) wear <shoes>; have <shoes> on. e.g. 구두를 갈아 신다 change one's shoes

신도 [शिन्दो] [**信徒**] a believer; a devotee; [지지자] an adherent <of scientism>; a follower; <집합적> the faithful; (기독교의 the flock.

신동 [शिन्दों] [**神童**] a (child) [an infant] prodigy; a wonder boy [child]; a boy wonder. e.g. 그 아이는 신동이다 The child is a marvel.

신랄 [शिल्लाल] [**辛辣**] 신랄하다 [날카롭다] sharp; [통렬하다] bitter; [엄하다] severe; [귀에 따갑다] harsh; [찌르는 듯하다] biting.

신랑 [शिल्लां] [**新郞**] a bridegroom; a groom; a newlywed husband.

신록 [शिल्लोक] [**新綠**] fresh verdure; tender [spring] green; new

신뢰 [शिल्वे] [**信賴**] confidence <in>; trust <in>; reliance <on>; dependence <on>.신뢰하다 [신용하다] trust; put confidence <in>; [의지하다 rely <on>; depend <on>. e.g. 신뢰할 수 있는 trustworthy / reliable / dependable / worthy of one's trust.

신망 [शिन्मांग] [**信望**] confidence and popularity; prestige. e.g. 신망을 떨어뜨리다] lose one's good reputation.

신명 [शिन्म्योंग] 신명(이) 나다 get [become] lighthearted [cheerful / gay (-spirited) / enthusiastic]; be exhilarated; get excited. e.g. 신명나서 in the excess of mirth / in a merry mood / enthusiastically.

신문 [शिम्मुन] [**新聞**] a (news)

paper; a paper; a journal; <집합적> the press.

신문 [शिम्मुन] [訊問] questioning; (cross-) examination <of a witness>; a query; an inquest; an inquiry; an interrogation.

신문사 [शिम्मुन्सा] [新聞社] a newspaper publishing company; a newspaper office.

신발 [शिन्बाल] footwear

신변 [शिनब्यौन] [身邊] one's person; oneself. e.g. 신변의 위험을 무릅쓰고 at the risk of one's personal safety.

신봉 [शिन्बों] [信奉] belief; faith. 신봉하다 [믿다]] believe <in>; [굳게 믿다] have faith <in>; [따르다]] follow <the teachings of Christ>.

신부 [शिन्बु] [新婦] a bride.

신부 [शिन्बु] [神父] [가톨릭] a father; the Reverend (略 the Rev.).

신분 [शिन्बुन] [身分] **1** [지위] (a) social standing [status]; (one's) rank. **2** [재력] e.g. 신분에 맞게맞지 않게 생활하다 live with in [beyond] one's means.**3** [처지] e.g. 학생 신분에 벤츠 자동차는 너무 사치스럽다 A Bentz is too luxurious for a student like you.**4** [태생]. e.g. 신분이 높은 [낮은] 사람 a person of high [low] birth.

신비 [शिन्बि] [神秘] (a) mystery. 신비하다 mysterious; mystic (al); miraculous; occult.

신빙성 [शिन्बिंसौंग] [信憑性] [신용도] reliability; [확실성] authenticity.

신사 [शिन्सा] [紳士] a gentleman <*pl.* -men>; <집합적> gentry. e.g. 신사적인 gentlemanly / gentlemanlike.

신생아 [शिन्सैंगा] [新生兒] a new(ly) born infant.

신선 [शिन्सौन] [新鮮] freshness. 신선하다 fresh <vegetables, fish, etc.>; new. e.g. 신선한 달걀 fresh eggs.

신설 [शिन्सौल] [新設] establishment; organization; founding. 신설하다 establish; organize; found.

신성 [शिन्सौंग] [神聖] holiness; sacredness; sanctity. 신성하다 holy; sacred; divine (▷ sacred 는 [신에 관한 것, 숭배할 가치가 있는]을 말하며, 또한 [세속적인] secular) 과 대조적으로 쓰임 divine 은 sacred 에 가까운데 [신의, 신에 의한] 의 뜻이 더욱 강함 holy 는 대개 올바른 것, 신적인 것을 말함)

신세 [शिन्से] [身世] **1** [일신상의 처지와 형편] one's lot [condition / circumstances]; one's personal affairs. e.g. 거지 신세가 되다 be reduced to beggary**2** [은혜] a favor; an obligation; (a) moral obligation; a debt of gratitude; [도움,돌봄] help; care; support; [친절] kindness; goodness; [의지] dependence; [폐](a) trouble; a burden. e.g. 신세는 언제까지나 잊지 않겠습니다] I will[shall] never forget your kindness [what you have done for me]

신세대 [शिन्सेदै] [**新世代**] the new generation.

신속 [शिन्सोक] [**迅速**] promptness; quickness. 신속하다 [민첩한] quick; [날쌘] swith; [급속한] rapid; [고속도의] speedy; [즉석의] prompt. e.g. 그들은 행동이 신속하다 They are swith in action.

신식 [शिन्शिक] [**新式**] [새 유행, 신형 the present fashion; (모양) a new style [type]; (방법) a new method.

신신 부탁 [शिनशिन बुथाक] [**申申付託**] (an) entreaty; solicitation; supplication; imploration; an earnest [a repeated] appeal [request]. 신신 부탁하다 [ask [appeal / request] repeatedly [earnestly / over and over again]; entreat; solicit; supplicate; implore.

신실하다 [शिन्शिरहादा] [**信實–**] steady and honest; sincere; faithful; truthful.

신심 [शिन्शिम] [**信心**] faith; belief; piety; devotion; reverence for God.

신앙 [शिनांग] [**信仰**] [종교적 믿음] faith; [일반적으로 신념, 믿음 belief.

신용 [शिन्योंग] [**信用**] [신뢰] confidence; trust; faith; reliance 신용하다 believe; trust; have [put] trust <in>; place confidence <in>. e.g. 신용할 수 있는 reliable / trusty / trust-worthy. **2** [평판] reputation; [거래 상대의 신용도] credit.

신용 거래 [शिन्योंग गौरै] [**信用去來**] (증권에서) a margin transaction; margin trading; (상업에서) credit transactions; sale on credit.

신원 [शिन्वौन] [**身元**] [일신에 관계되는 자료] one's birth and parentage; (정체) one's identity. e.g. 신원을 조사하다] (가문을) inquire into a person's birth and parentage / (출생과 전력을 inquire into a person's birth and antecedents / look into [check up on] a person's background.

신음[शिनुम] [**呻吟**] a groan; a moan (▷groan 이 소리가 더 낮음) 신음하다 [앓는 소리를 내다]] moan; groan; [괴로움,고 통으로 고생하다] suffer severely. 그들은 상처의 아픔 때문에 신음하고 있다 The pain of their wounds is making them groan [moan].

신의 [शिनउइ] [**信義**] faith; fidelity; truthfulness; loyalty. e.g. 신의를 중히 여기는 사람 a man of honor. 신의를 지키다저버리다] keep [break] faith <with a person> / be faithful [unfaithful]

신인 [शिनिन] [**新人**] [새로 나타난 사람] a new figure; (예능계 등의) a new face [star]; (스포츠의) a rookie.

신임[शिनिम] [**信任**] confidence; trust. e.g. 신임을 얻다 win [gain] the confidence <of>. 신임을 잃다 lose the confidence <of>.

신입 [शिनिप] [**新入**] 신입의 new / incoming / entering. **신입생** [शिनिप्सै] a new pupil; a new student; (대학, 고교의) a freshman; <英> a fresher.

신장 [1] [शिन्जांग] [**伸張**] extension; expansion. 신장하다 extend; expand; elongate. e.g. 세력을 신장하다 extend one's influence.

신장 [2] [शिन्जांग] [**身長**] height; stature.

신정 [शिन्जौं] [**新正**] [양력설] the New Year ('s Day) according to the new calendar.

신조 [शिन्जो] [**信條**] **1** [신앙의 조목] a creed; an article of faith.**2** [신념]a belief; [주의] a principle. e.g. 나의 신조 my belief / what I believe.

신중 [शिन्जुंग] [**愼重**] prudence; discretion; circumspection; caution; care. 신중하다[사려 깊은] prudent; [조심성 있는] cautious; [행동,말 등에 신중한 discreet; [주의 깊은] careful.

신진 대사 [शिन्जिन दैसा] [**新陳代謝**] metabolism

신참 [शिन्छाम] [**新參**] (고참에 대하여) a newcomer; a freshman; [미숙한 사람] a new [green] hand.

신청 [शिन्छौंग] [**申請**] [제의, 제안] a proposal; an offer <of marriage>; an overture <of peace>; [도전] a challenge <to a duel>; [요청, 의뢰] a request <for an interview>; (재심 등의) [法] (a) motion. 신청하다 propose; offer <mediation>; make an overture <of peace>; lodge [file] <a protest with a person against a matter>; enter (oneself) for <a contest>; challenge <a person>; request <a loan>; ask for <an interview>; [法] move <for a rehearing>.

신청서 [शिन्छौसौ] [**申請書**] a written application; an application (in writing); (용지) an application (form); an application blank.

신체 [शिन्चे] [**身體**] the body.

신체 검사 [शिन्चे गौम्सा] [**身體 檢査**] [건강 진단] a physical [medical] examination; a medical checkup; a physical checkup; a physical.

신축 [शिन्छुक] [**伸縮**] expansion and contraction; elasticity. 신축하다 expand and contract; be elastic; be stretchy

신축성 [शिन्छुक्सौं] elasticity.

신통 [शिन्थों] [**神通**] supernaturallness; wonder; miraculousness. 신통하다 [신기하게 통달하다] wonderful; miraculous; marvelous; divine; admirable; extraordinary; [만족할 만하다] satisfactory; desirable; good; favorable.

신형 [शिनह्यौं] [**新型**] a new [the latest] style [model / fashion / design].

신호 [शिनहो] [**信號**] a signal; (몸짓 등의 a sign; (무대 등에서의) a cue. e.g. 경계 신호 a warning [cautionary / caution] signal. 신호하다 signal; give [make] a signal; (손짓 등으로) make a sign; (몸짓으로) motion <a person to do>. e.g. 순찰중이던 경찰관이 나에게 자전거를 세우라고 신호했다 A patrolling policeman signaled (to) me to stop my bicycle

신호등 [शिनहोदुंग] a signal lamp [light]; a blinker (명멸 방향 지시등 등의)

신혼 [शिनहोन] [**新婚**] a new marriage. 신혼하 be newly married; become a newlywed

신혼 여행 [शिनहोन यौहैंग] [**新婚旅行**] a honeymoon; a wedding trip [tour / journey]; a bridal journey.

신화 [शिनह्वा] [**神話**] a myth; <집합적> mythology.

신흥 [शिनहुंग] [**新興**] 신흥의 rising / burgeoning / new / newly-rising [-risen / -arisen]. 신흥하다 newly rise.

신흥 계급 [शिनहुंग्यैगुप] a newly-rise [-rising] class; a newly-awakened class. e.g. 신흥 부유 계급 the new-rich(class).

싣다 [शित्ता] **1** (운반할 목적으로) load (up) <a truck> with <goods>; carry; freight; put on board; have [take] on board; take in [on]; (배에) ship <a cargo>; (말에) pack. e.g. 짐 실은 배 a laden vessel.**2** [기사 등을 게재하다] publish <an article> in <a newspaper>; carry; record; put <an event> on record; put [place]; enter; print; insert; mention. e.g. 일주일간 광고를 싣다 run an advertisement for a we eK.

실 [शिल] (재봉용) thread; (직물, 편물용의) yarn.

실감 [शिल्काम] [實感] actual feeling [sensation]; solid sense; realization. e.g. 실감나는 realistic / true to nature / lifelike / graphic.

실격 [शिलक्यौक] [失格] disqualification; elimination. 실격하다 [자격을 잃다] be disqualified <from / for>; [제외되다] be eliminated <from>; (경주에서) be put out of the race. e.g.그는 준결승전에서실격되었다 He stayed from the course and was put out of the race.

실권 [शिलक्वौन] [實權] real power [control].

실기 [शिल्कि] [實技] actual technique [technics]; practical [actual] skill [talent]; (체육의) practical [physical] training. e.g. 체육 [음악] 실기 시험 a test of one's practical skills [ability] in sports [music].

실내 [शिल्लै] [室內] indoors; the interior of a room. 실랑이 (질) 실랑이하다 [을 못살게 굴다] bother [pester] <a person>; nag; [승강이하다] quarrel; wrangle; have an altercation.

실력 [शिल्यौक] [實力] [실제의 역량] one's (real) ability [power]; efficiency; merit; capacity; competence; competency; [학력] attainments; acquirements; [지식] knowledge. e.g. 어학 실력 one's linguistic ability. 실력으로 through ability / by (sheer) talent.

실례 [शिल्ये] [實例] an example; an instance; a concrete case; a case in point; an illustration. e.g. 실례를 들다 cite [give] an instance / set [give] a concrete example [illustration].

실룩거리다 [शिल्लुक्कौरिदा] twitch (and twitch); wink (repeatedly); quiver.

실리 [शिल्लि] [實利] utility; (an actual) benefit [profit]; material interests [gain]. e.g. 실리적 (인) utilitarian / practical.

실리다 [शिल्लिदा] **1** [기재, 기록되다] be reported; be recorded; be mentioned; be printed; be given; be put on <a book>. e.g. 신문에 실리다 appear [be printed / be reported] in a newspaper / be carried [published] in a daily **2** [실음을 당하다] [<a car / goods> be loaded (up); be put on board; <a ship> be freighted. e.g. 실려 가다 be carried [taken] away / be carted away.**3** [싣게 하다] get <goods> loaded; have <a person> load (up) <a car / goods>; let <a cargo> be put on board [be stowed aboard].

실리 [शिल्लि] [實利] utility; (an actual) benefit [profit];

material interests [gain]. e.g. 실리적 (인) utilitarian / practical.

실마리 [शिल्मारि] **1** [일의 단서] a clue; a key; a lead. e.g. 이것을 실마리로 하여 with this clue to go upon **2** [발단] a start; a beginning. e.g. 실마리를 찾으면 이 계산은 간단하다 This calculation is easy if you know where to start.

실망 [शिल्मांग] [失望] disappointment; despair 실망하다 be discouraged; be dejected; be let down; be disappointed <at / in / of / with>; despair <of>; lose one's hope [heart]; be thrown into despair. e.g. 실망시키다 let down / disappoint / dash [crush] a person's hope.

실명 [शिलम्यौंग] [失明] loss of one's eyesight; blindness. 실명하다 lose one's eyesight [sight]; become sightless; become [go] blind.

실무 [शिल्मू] [實務] practical business affairs. e.g. 실무에 밝다 be familiar with office routine / be versed [experienced] in business.

실물 [शिल्मुल] [實物] [실제의 물건] the real thing; the actual object; [진짜] a genuine article; (그림에 대하여) real life; (사진에 대하여) he original. e.g. 실물과 똑 같은 초상화 a lifelike [true-to-life] portrait. 그녀의 사진은 실물과 다르다 (실물이 나은 경우 The photo does not do her justice. / [사진이 나은 경우] She looks better in the photo.

실상 [शिल्सांग] [實相] real facts[aspects]; the real [true] state of affairs; reality. e.g. 북한의 실상 [the real state of affairs in North Korea. 그 조직의 실상은 외부 사람으로서는 알 수가 없었다 was impenetrable to outsiders.

실생활 [शिल्सै ह्वाल] [實生活] real [actual / practical] life; (the realities of) life. e.g. 실생활에서 취재한 이야기 a tale taken from real life.

실성 [शिल्सौंग] [失性] mentalderangement; distraction; insanity; madness; (a) frenzy. 실성하다 becomementally deranged [unbalanced]; go mad; become insane; lose one's head; go out of one's mind. e.g. 절망한 나머지 실성하여 in a frenzy of despair.

실소 [शिल्सो] [失笑] sudden uncontrollable [irrepressible] laughter. 실소하다 laugh in spite of oneself. e.g. 그녀의 엉뚱한 대답에 모두들 실소했다 Everybody burst out laughing at her funny answer.

실속 [शिल्सोक] [實-] substance; matter; substantiality; real worth; solidity. e.g. 실속있는 substantial / solid / meaty / voluminous / instructive.

실수 [शिल्सू] [失手] [실책] a blunder; a mistake; a bungle; a mess; a mess-up; [실패] a failure; [부주의] carelessness; [못 보고 빠뜨림] an oversight; [잘못] an error; a fault; a slip; [무례] impoliteness. e.g. 실수를 저지르다 do a careless thing / make a blunder [stupid mistake] / blunder / make a mess. 실수하다 make a mistake [slip]; commit an error [a fault]; err; blunder; bungle; make [commit] a blunder; botch; goof. e.g. 경찰이 실수하여 범인을 놓쳤다 The police made a bad job of it and let the culprit get away.

실습 [शिल्सुप] [實習] practice; (practical) exercise; [연습] drill; training; probation. 실습하다 practice; have (practical) training.

실시 [शिल्शि] [實施] enforcement; operation; execution; implementation; practical application; [法] effectuation. 실시하다 put into effect; put <a law> into force; enforce [give effect to] <a law>; carry <a program> into effect; execute; implement; effect-uate. .

실신 [शिल्शिन] [失神] a swoon; a faint; a coma; a fainting fit; a blackout. 실신하다 swoon; faint (away); fall into a swoon; fall unconscious; lose consciousness [one's senses]; black out.

실언 [शिरौन] [失言] a slip of the tongue; a verbal lapse; an impropriety in speech. 실언하다 make a slip of the tongue; use improper language [words]; commit an impropriety in speech; one's tongue slips <in one's statement>; put [stick] one's foot in the [one's] mouth.

실업 [शिरौप] [失業] unemployment; loss of employment; joblessness. 실업하다 lose one's employment [work / job]; fall[be thrown] out of employment [work].

실업자 [शिरौप्जा] [失業者] a person who is out of work; an unemployed person; a jobless person;

실없다 [शिरौप्ता] [성실하지 못하다] insincere; faithless; untrustworthy; unreliable; hollowhearted; [무의미하다] nonsensical; silly; foolish; absurd; idle. e.g. 실없는 소리 absurd remarks / silly talk / non-sense.

실연 [शिरयौन] [失戀] disappointed [unrequited / unreturned] love; a disappointment in love; a broken heart. 실연하다 be disappointed [crossed] in <a person's> love. e.g. 실연한 사람 a brokenhearted person..

실온 [शिऑन] [室溫] the temperature of a room; room temperature

실외 [शिरवे] [室外] e.g. 실외의 outdoor.

실용 [शिरयोंग] practical use; utility. e.g. 실용 본위의 가구 [의복] utility furniture [clothes].

실의 [शिरूइ] [失意] disappointment; despair; dejection. e.g. 실의에 빠진 사람 a disappointed [broken] man / [실연한 사람] a man with a broken heart.

실재 [शिल्चे] [實在] real [actual] existence; actual being; actuality; reality; [哲] essence; entity. 실재하다 exist (really); be in existence; have a real existence. e.g. 실재하지 않는 도시 an imaginary[a fictitious] town.

실적 [शिल्चौक] [實績] (actual) results; one's record of performance; solid results; positive achievements. e.g. 수출 실적 actual exports / the actual export record.

실전 [शिल्चौन] [實戰] actual fighting [fight / warfare]; a battle; an action; active service; (스포츠에서) a real game [match / fight]. e.g. 실전 경험이 많은 노병] a veteran of considerable combat experience.

실점 [शिल्चौम] [失點] (경기 등에서) points given up; runs given up (야구) points lost (정구 points [runs] one allows one's opponent in a game. e.g. 나는 요즈음 실점을 거듭하고 있다 I am in the middle of a losing streak. / I have lost many matches in a row. /

실정 [शिल्चौं] [實情] the actual condition [circumstances]; the real state of affairs [things]; the real condition; the facts <of a case>; the real situation; the lowdown. e.g. 실정을 알다 know the actual circumstances / know how the matter (really) stands.

실제 [शिल्चे] [實際] [사실] the (exact) truth; a fact; [실정] an actual state; the actual condition of things; [실지] practice; [현실 reality; actuality. e.g. 실제의 practical / actual / real / [사실상의] virtual / [구체적] concrete / <美> down-to-earth.

실존 [शिल्चोन] [實存] existence. 실존하다 exist.용은 실존하는 동물이 아니다 Dragons never really existed.

실종 [शिल्चों] [**失踪**] disappearance; missing; abscond-dence 실종하다 disappear; abscond; drop from sight; [행방 불명되다] be missing.

실직 [शिल्चिक] [**失職**] unemployment; loss of employment. 실직하다 lose one's employment [work / job]; fall[be thrown] out of employment [work].

실질 [शिल्चिल] [**實質**] [실체] substance; [본질] essence; [소질] quality; [재료] matter; material; [내용] contents.

실책 [शिल्छैक] [**失策**] a blunder; a slip; a bungle; an error; a mistake; a misstep. e.g. 실책을 저지 르다 do <a matter> amiss / commit an error [a blunder] / bungle / fall into an error

실천 [शिल्छौन] [**實踐**] practice. 실천하다 practice; put <a theory> in practice; execute. e.g. 자기의 신념을 실천하다 live up to one's beliefs [principles]..

실체 [शिल्छे] [**實體**] substance; subject; (phenomenon 에 대한) noumenon; entity; [본성] the true nature <of>. e.g. 실체가 있는 substantial / solid. 실체가 없는 unsubstantial / incor-poreal / insubstantial / impalpable <forms and figures>..

실추 [शिल्छु] [**失墜**] loss; fall. e.g. 권력의 실추 one's fall from power. 실추하다 [잃다] lose; forfeit; [떨어지다] fall; sink. e.g. 위신이 실추되다 lose (one's) prestige. 권력이 실추하다 fall from power.

실측 [शिल्छक] [**實測**] (actual) measurement; (a) survey. 실측하다 measure; survey; make a survey of <a forest>.

실컷 [शिल्खौत] to one's heart's content; to one's satisfaction; heartily; as much as one likes [wishes]; to the full; to the fullest measure; to the utmost; to the hilt; without reserve; unreservedly (거리낌없이) e.g. 그 식당에서는 3,000 원이면 실컷 먹을 수 있다 At that restaurant you can eat as much as you like [all you want] for 3,000 won..

실탄 [शिल्थान] [**實彈**] (소총의) a live cartridge; a solid (bullet); (대포의) [a loaded [live] shell; a solid [round] shot; <집합적 >live ammunition

실태 [शिल्थै] [**實態**] the actual condition [state]; the realities. e.g. 실업자의 실태를 조사하다 investigate the actual conditions of [among] the unemployed

실토 [शिल्थो] [**實吐**] a true confession; telling the whole truth; speaking with sincerity. 실토하다 confess (to); disclose one's real intention; spit out the truth; tell the whole truth; reveal one's real motive.

실패 [शिल्फै] [**失敗**] (a) failure; ill success; blunder; a flop; a washout; a goof. 실패하다 (사람이) fail; be unsuccessful <in>; be frustrated [foiled / balked] <in an attempt>; draw a blank; [영락하다] sink [come down] in the world; (일이) fail; miscarry; prove [turn out] a failure; end [result] in (a) failure; meet with failure; go wrong [amiss]; come to naught. e.g. 그는 입학 시험에 실패 했다 He failed [was unsuc-cessful] in the entrance examination.

실하다 [शिरहादा] [**實**−] **1** [튼튼하다] strong; solid; firm; substantial; sturdy; strongly built. **2** [재산이 넉넉하다] well-to-do; wealthy; solid; sound. e.g. 장사 밑천이 실하다 have enough [sufficient] business funds.

실행 [शिरहैंग] [**實行**] [실천] practice; action; deed; [수행] execution; performance; prosecution; [이행] fulfilment; [실시] enforcement; implementation; [실현] realization. 실행하다 practice; put <something> in [into] practice; execute; implement; carry out <a plan>; carry <a plan> into execution [effect]; enforce.

실험 [शिरहौम] [**實驗**] (과학의) experimentation; (실험실에서의) laboratory work; (한 번의) an) experiment; [시험] a test. 실험하다 experiment <on / in>; make [conduct] an experiment [a test] <on / in / with>; put <a thing> to the test[proof]; experimentalize.

실현 [शिरह्यौन] [**實現**] realization <of one's hopes>; materialization; attainment; actualization; fruition. 실현하다 realize; actualize; materialize; fulfill; effectuate; bring to fruition [realization]; (꿈, 희망이) come true. e.g. 실현할 수 있는 realizable / possible of realization.

실형 [शिरह्यौ] [**實刑**] a prison sentence; imprisonment; (기간) the real term of imprisonment.

실화 [शिरहवा] [**實話**] a true story; a story (taken) from real life; an authentic account.

실황 [शिरहवांग] [**實 況**] [실정] the real [actual] condition; the actual state of things; [광경] the actual scene; [실시 상황] actual oper-ation. e.g. 실황을 조사하다 inspect actual conditions / make an on-the-spot inspection.

실효 [शिरह्यो] [**實效**] [효과] a practical effect; efficacy;

practical results; [능률] efficiency. e.g. 실효 있는 effective [ineffective].

싫다 [शिल्था] [불쾌하다] disagreeable; unpleasant; distasteful; disgusting; odious; offensive; nasty; nauseous; [달갑지 않다] undesirable; unwelcome; [지긋지긋하다] hateful; loathsome; abominable; <서술적> dislike; hate; detest (▷ 이 순서로 뜻이 강해짐) be willing [reluctant] <to do>.

싫어하다 [शिरोहादा] dislike; have a dislike to[for]; grudge <doing>; be unwilling [reluctant] <to do>. e.g. 몹시 싫어하다 hate / loathe / detest / have a distaste for / have an aversion [antipathy] to / have a hatred for / be prejudiced against / feel repugnance for / abhor / be averse to.

싫증 [शिल्चुंग] [-症] an aversion; dislike; disgust; a repugnance <to / for>; weariness. 싫증 (이) 나다 feel a repugnance to[for]; be [get / grow] tired of; get sick of; be [become] disgusted with; become weary of; be bored <with>; lose interest in.

-심 [शिम] [心] a heart; a mind; a spirit; a sense. e.g. 욕심 a mercenary spirit.

심각 [शिम्गाक] [深刻] 심각하다 serious; grave; keen; acute; poignant. e.g. 심각한 인구 문제 a serious population problem. 심각한 표정으로 with a serious [grave] look. 심각한 얼굴을 하다 look serious [grave] / assume [put on] a serious [grave / sober] look.

심경 [शिमग्योंग] [心境] a frame [state] of mind; a mental attitude [state].

심금 [शिमगम] [心琴] heartstrings. e.g. 심금을 울리다 touch [pull at] <a person's> heartstrings / touch a cord [string] in <a person's> heart / touch the lutestrings of <a person's> heart.

심기 [शिम्गि] [心氣] (a) humor; a temper; a mood; feelings. e.g. 심기가 불편하다 be in an ill [bad] humor [mood] / be out of humor [temper] / be in a bad temper / be displeased.

심다 [शिम्ता] **1** (식물을) plant; set (out); transplant (옮겨 심다) e.g. 정원에 나무를 심다 plant trees in a garden / plant a garden with trees. **2** 사상 등을) implant; plant; fiK inculcate; inoculate; impregnate; imbue. e.g. 국민에게 자신감과 희망을 심어 주다 implant self-confidence and hope in the people.

심드렁하다 [शिमद्रंहादा] [탐탁지

않다] rather unwilling <to>; uninterested <in>; indisposed <to do>.

[心亂] perturbation [disturbance] of mind. 심란하다 <서술적> be disturbed [confused] in mind; be upset [agitated].

심려 [शिमन्यौ] [心慮] uneasiness of heart; anxiety; worry; concern; apprehensions. e.g. 심려를 끼치다 give [cause] <a person> occasion to feel anxiety / cause anxiety to <a person> / give <a person> trouble.

심령 [शिमन्यौ] [心靈] spirit.

심리 [शिम्नि] [心理] a state of mind; a mental state; mentality; psychology. e.g. 군중 심리 mass [mob] psychology. 미묘한 심리 delicate shades of psychology.

심리학 [शिम्निहाक] [心理學] psychology; the science of mind; mental psychology.

심문 [शिम्मुन] [審問] a trial; an inquiring; a hearing; an inquest; an examination; a formal interrogation. 심문하다 try; inquire; hear <a case>; give a hearing <to a case>; put <a person> to trial; examine [into] <a case>; interrogate <a witness>; question closely <a witness>

심보 [शिम्बो] [心-] nature; disposition; spirit; mind; temper. e.g. 심보가 나쁜 evil-minded / perverse / crooked. 심보가 고약한 사람 an ill-natured man.

심부름 [शिम्बूरम] an errand; a message; a mission; running errands. 심부름하다 do [run] an errand; run errands.

심사 [शिम्सा] [審査] [검사] an) examination; (an) inspection; [조사] [जोसा] (an) investigation; [감정] judgment; [선별] screening. 심사하다 examine; inspect; investigate (into); judge; screen.

심사 숙고 [शिम्सा सुक्को] [深思熟考] meditation; mature [due] consideration; deliberation; rumination; deep thought. 심사 숙고하다 meditate <on>; contemplate; ruminate <on / over>; muse <on / upon>; consider <a matter> carefully; give deep thought; be deep in meditation

심상[1] [शिम्सांग] [尋常] being ordinary [common / normal]; the commonplace; usualness. 심상하다 [ordinary; common; usual; average; [평범하다] commonplace; [범용하다] mediocre; [이상 없다] normal. e.g. 심상치 않은 unusual / extraordinary / uncommon / serious / alarming / important.

심상 [2] [शिम्सांग] [**心像, 心象**] [心] an image; a mental picture [image].

심성 [शिम्सौ ग] [**心性**] [마음씨] mind; mentality; [타고난 성질] nature; disposition; temperament.

심술 [शिम्सुल] [**心術**] a cross temper; ill nature; perverseness; perversity; cantankerousness; crabbedness. e.g. 심술궂다 perverse / cross (-minded) / cross-grained [-tempered] / ill-natured

심신 [शिम्शिन] [**心身**] mind and body; body and mind [soul]. e.g. 심신의 피로 mental and physical exhaustion.

심심풀이 [शिमशिमफुरि] killing time; beguiling tedious hours; a pastime; (a) diversion. e.g. 심심풀이로 by way of killing time / to kill (one's) time / to beguile an idle hour / to pass the tedious hours / as a pastime.

심심하다 [शिमशिमहादा] [무료하다] be bored; feel ennui; find <the evening> very dull; feel weary. e.g. 심심해서 because one has nothing to do / to relieve the ennui.

심야 [शिम्या] [**深夜**] the dead of night; the middle of the night; midnight. e.g. 심야에 at [in the] dead of night / at midnight.

심오하다 [शिमओहादा] [**深奧-**] deep; profound; abstruse; esoteric.

심의 [शिमउइ] [**審議**] [심사하고 토의함] deliberation; consideration; careful discussion; review; (철저한) [a going-over].

심장 [शिम्जांग] [**心臟**] [解] the heart.

심정 [शिम्जौ] [**心情**] one's heart; one's feelings. e.g. 심정을 알아주다 enter into <a person's> feelings [sentiment] / (동정하다 feel for <a person> / sympathize with another.

심지 [1] [शिम्जि] [**心-**] a (lamp) wick. e.g. 심지를 자르다양초의) snuff a candle / (램프의) crick [trim] a wick [lamp]

심지 [2] [शिम्जि] [**心地**] nature; temper; disposition; character. e.g. 심지가 고운 사람 a tender-hearted person.

심지어 [शिम्जिऔ] [**甚至於**] what is worse; worst of all; the extreme case is ...; not so much as; on top of all this. e.g. 그는 심지어 자기 이름조차 쓸 줄 모른다 He cannot even his own name.

심취 [शिमछ्वि] [**心醉**] [어떤 일에 깊이 빠져 도취함]

admiration; adoration; idolization; [몰두] devotion. 심취하다 be fascinated <with>; be devoted <to>; adore; idolize

심통 [शिम्थोंग] [心-] ill nature; a cross temper. e.g. 심통이 나다 get cranky / become perverse.

심판 [शिम्फान] [審判] (재판 등) judgment; adjudgment; decision; verdict (배심원의)경기의) refereeing; umpireship; umpirage; (신의) judgment; trial. 심판하다 referee <a game>; umpire; act as (an) umpire; judge; adjudge

심하다 [शिमहादा] [甚-] **1** [지나치다] extreme; excessive; heavy <damage>; [격렬하다] severe; violent; intense; hard. e.g. 심한 감기 a bad [nasty] cold. **2** [잔인하다] cruel; harsh; rough; merciless; heartless; [난폭하다] outrageous; atrocious; [부당하다] [unjust; unfair. e.g. 심한 처사 (a) cruel treatment / (a) cruelty / harsh usage.

심혈 [शिमह्यौल] [心血] the heart's blood; <비유> heart and soul; one's whole energy. e.g. 심혈을 기울여 heart and soul / with one's heart's blood.

심호흡 [शिमहोह्प] [深呼吸] deep breathing [respiration]; a deep breath. 심호흡하다 breathe deeply; do deep breathing; take a deep breath; draw a deep [full] breath; take deep breathing exercises.

심화 [शिमह्वा] [深化] deepening. 심화하다 [शिमह्वाहादा] deepen.

십 [शिप] [十] ten; [로마 숫자] X. e.g. 제 십 the tenth.

십대 [十代] [शिप्दै] (연령의 one's teens. 십대의 teen-age(d) / of teen age / in one's teens. 십대의 사람] a teen-ager / a teener / a teen-age boy [girl].

십상 [शिप्सांग] **1** the right thing <for>; the very thing wanted; just the thing <for>. e.g. 십상인 ideal / suitable <for> / fit <for> / the very / right / just.**2** <부사>just <well>; right; exactly; fairly; perfectly. e.g. 낚시하기에 십상 좋은 날씨다 It is an ideal weather for angling.

십자가 [शिप्चागा] [十字架] a cross; [기독교] the Holy Rood. e.g. 성십자가 the holy [real / true] cross.

십중팔구 [शिप्चुंफाल्गु] [十中八九] <부사> in nine cases out of ten; ten to one; most likely; in all probability; in all (human) likelihood; <美> nine-tenths; [거의] almost; nearly. e.g. 그는 십중팔구 성공할 것이다 Ten to one he'll succeed.

싱겁다 [शिंगौप्ता] **1** [짜지 않다] insufficiently [slightly] salted; not salty enough; not well salted; [별 맛이 없다] flat; tasteless; insipid; (술, 담배 등이) weak [mild] <cigarette>; watery [light / thin] <liquor>. **2** [언행이 멋적다 dull; pointless; tedious; boring; irksome; wearisome; flat. e.g. 싱거운 사람 a boring person / a wishy-washy person.

싱글벙글 [शिंगल्पौंगल] with a broad smile; with a smiling face; smilingly; beamingly. 싱글벙글하다=싱글거리다

싱숭생숭하다 [शिंसुंसैसुंहादा] <서술적> feel restless [fidgety / nervous / uneasy]; be in a fidget; be ill at ease. e.g. 봄이면 그녀는 마음이 싱숭생숭해지곤 했다 Her mind used to wander during the springtime.

싱싱하다 [शिंशिंहादा] young and fresh; fresh as paint; fresh (and juicy); fresh-looking; juicy; green. e.g. 싱싱한 생선 a fresh fish / a fish fresh from the water / freshly caught fish. 싱싱한 야채 fresh vegetables.

싶다 [शिप्ता] **1** […할 의향이 있다] <서술적> want <to do>; wish <to do>; should [would] like to see [hear]. e.g. 꼭몹시] …하고 싶다 be anxious [eager / impatient / dying] to <do>. **2** […일 것같다] <서술적> look; seem; appear; be likely <to do>. e.g. 비가 올 듯싶다 It looks like rain.

싶어하다 [शिफौहादा] want to; desire to; be desirous of; be eager to; be anxious to. e.g. 몹시 … 하고 싶어하다 be eager [anxious / impatient] to <do>.

싸구려 [सागूर्यौ] a cheap [low-priced] article.

싸늘하다 [सानरहादा] **1** [한랭-하다] cold; chilly; cool; frigid; icy; [황폐하여 쓸쓸하다] wintry; dreary. e.g. 싸늘한 바람 a cold wind. **2** [냉담하다] cold; icy; frigid; distant; indifferent; cold-hearted; cold-blooded. e.g. 싸늘한 태도 a cool [cold] attitude / a distant air.

싸다 [1] [सादा] (대, 소변을) excrete <urine or feces>; void; discharge. e.g. 오줌을 싸다 pee / wet one's pants / (잠자리에서) wet the bed / make [pass] water.

싸다 [2] [सात्ता] [물건을 포장하다] wrap (in); do up <a parcel>; pack (up) <goods>; bundle <clothes>. e.g. 보자기에 싸다 tie [do / wrap] up <things> in a cloth wrapper. **2** (도시락을) fix a lunch; prepare a luncheon; put up a lunch; pack a lunch basket [box].

싸다[3] [सादा] [(입이) 가볍다 glib (-tongued); talebearing; tattling; talkative; loquacious; prattling; gabby. e.g. 입이 싼 사람 a talkative person / a blabber / a tattler / a chatterbox (여자,아이 등).

싸다[4] [सादा] **1** (물건 값이) cheap; inexpensive; low (-priced); of low price; moderate; moderately-priced (▷cheap 은 [싸구려]의 느낌을 나타낼 때가 있음). e.g. 싼 집세 a low rent. **2** [(죄에 대한 벌이) 마땅하다] <서술적 be well deserved; be none too little. e.g. 욕먹어도 싸다 deserve censure / need to be scolded.

싸우다 [साउदा] **1** fight; [논쟁하다] dispute; argue; have a dispute [an argument]; [말다툼하다] quarrel; wrangle; exchange [have] words; [사이가 틀어지다] disagree <with one's wife>; fall out <with>. e.g. 옆방에서 싸우는 소리가 들렸다 I heard the voices of people quarreling in the next room. / I heard raised voices coming from the next room. **2** [전쟁을 하다] make war <on / against>; [전투를 하다 fight; do battle <with / against>. e.g. 우세한 대군[적군] 과 싸우다 fight against overwhelming odds [with an enemy]. **3** [경쟁하다] contend <with>. e.g. 김군과 박군은 우승을 놓고 싸웠다 Kim and Park fought for the championship. / Kim fought [contended / strove] with Park for the championship. 정정당당히 싸우자 Let's play fair.

싸움 [साउम] **1** [말다툼] a quarrel; a fight; [시끄러운 말다툼] a row; (사소한 일로 인한) a squabble; [논쟁] [नोन्जै] a dispute; (시끄러운) a brawl; [격투] a scuffle; [가족, 씨족 등의 반목] a feud; [불화] a) discord; strife. 싸움하다=싸우다 1. **2** [전쟁] (a) war; warfare; [전투] a fight; a battle; an encounter; an engagement; an action; a campaign; (1 대 1 의) a combat; (소규모의) a scuffle; a skirmish. 싸움하다 = 싸우다 2. **3** [시합,경쟁] a contest; a contention; a competition; (a) rivalry. 싸움하다 = 싸우다 3.

싸이다 [साइदा] get [be] wrapped [covered]. e.g. 어둠에 싸이다 be wrapped in darkness

싹[1] [साक] **1** a bud; (나무의) a leaf bud; (햇가지의) a sprout; a shoot; (씨에서 돋아난) a seedling. 싹(이) 트다(1) [움트다] sprout;

bud; put forth buds [shoots]; shoot out buds; (나무가) burgeon; come [burst] into leaf.

싹[2] [साक] **1** [완전히] quite; entirely; completely; thoroughly. e.g. 다음 날 아침 나는 그 일을 싹 잊고 있었다 중요한 일을 By the next morning it had completely slipped my mind. / (싫은 일을) By the next morning I had forgotten all about it. **2** 베는 소리,모양] with a (single) snip [swish]; with a swishing sound [motion]. e.g. 종이를 싹 베다 cut paper with a snip.

싹둑싹둑 [सावतुकसावतुक] snip-snap. e.g. 종이를 싹둑싹둑 자르다 cut paper up snip-snap.

싹수 [सावसु] a good omen; hope(s); promise; possibility; probability; (a) chance; likelihood. e.g. 싹수가 없다 노랗다 / 틀렸다 be hopeless / show no promise of success / have no prospect <of> / There is not a dog's[cat's] chance. / <美> There's a fat chance.

싹싹 [साकसाक] **1** [완전히] completely; clean(ly); [힘들여] roughly. e.g. 싹싹 쓸어내다 sweep <the dirt> out [away] thoroughly. **2** [베는 모양, 소리] with a snip [swish]; with a swishing motion [sound]. **3** [비는 모양] imploringly; entreatingly; humbly. e.g. 눈물을 흘리며 싹싹 빌다 beg for forgiveness with tears in one's eyes.

싹싹하다 [साकसाख्वादा] affable; amiable; suave; open-hearted; good-humored; sociable; jolly. e.g. 싹싹한 사람 a soth-soaper.

쌀 [साल] [벼껍질을 벗긴 알맹이] raw / uncooked) rice

쌀쌀하다 [सालसारहादा] **1** (날씨가) [차다] chilly; rather cold; cool; [음산하다] dreary; dismal; melancholy; gloomy. e.g. 쌀쌀한 날씨 gloomy [chilly] weather. **2** (사람이) distant; cold-hearted; chilly; indifferent; cool; unkind; frigid. e.g. 쌀쌀한 인사 a curt [brusque] greeting.

쌈 [साम] [상추 등에 밥과 반찬을 싼 음식] cooked rice wrapped in lettuce [laver]. e.g. 상추 [김] 쌈 lettuce-[seaweed-] wrapped rice.

쌍 [सांग] [雙] [짝] a pair; twins; [암수] a couple; a brace <단수, 복수 동형>. e.g. 꿩 한 쌍 a brace of pheasants

쌍둥이 [सांगदुंगी] [雙-] twins; twin children; twin sons [daughters]; twin brothers [sisters]; (그 중의 한 사람)

a twin.

쌍방 [सांगबांग] [雙方] e.g. 쌍방의 both / mutual. 노사 쌍방의 양보에 의해 through concessions by both management and labor.

쌍벽 [सांब्यौक] [雙璧] [우열을 가릴 수 없이 뛰어난 둘] the two greatest authorities; the matchless twin stars. e.g. 현대 한국 화단의 쌍벽 the twin master painters of contemporary Korea.

쌓다 [साथा] **1** [포개어 올리다] pile(up); (난잡하게) heap (up); (건초,짚 등을 정연하게) stack (up); lay; make a pile; pile one above [on] another. e.g. 흙[모래]을 쌓아 올리다 heap up earth [sand]. **2** [구축하다] build; erect; raise; construct. e.g. 성을 쌓다 build a castle. 돌담 둑][을 쌓다 construct a stone wall[an embankment]. 탑을 쌓다 erect a tower. **3** [축적하다] accumulate; acquire; store up; amass. e.g. 부(富)와 명성을 쌓다 build up a reputation and a fortune / amass a fortune and make a name for oneself.

쌓이다 [साहिदा] **1** [퇴적되다] be piled up; lie <on>. e.g. 책이 높이 쌓였다 The books were piled up high. **2** [일이 밀리다] stagnate; be stagnant; be left undone. e.g. 일이 잔뜩 쌓여 있다 There is a good deal of work undone **3** (원한 등이) be pent up; be congested; (빚 등이) accumulate; get accumulated. e.g. 쌓이고 쌓인 원한 suppressed [pent-up] hatred

써넣다 [सौनौथा] write in; fill in; enter <in a register>; make an entry <in>; inscribe <in>; make [write] notes; interline (행간에) e.g.. 카드에 이름을 써넣다 fill in one's name in a card.

써먹다 [सौमोक्ता] use; make use of; utilize. e.g. 써먹을 만하다 be useful [usable] / be of use.

썩다 [सौक्ता] **1** [부패하다] rot; go bad [rotten]; decompose; spoil; decay; corrupt; (달걀 등이) addle; (우유 등이) turn sour; (고기 등이) putrefy; (생선이) become stale; (물이) become foul; (금속이) corrode. e.g. 썩은 생선 rotten fish. **2** [재능, 사물이 활용 되지 않다] gather dust; become [get] rusty; be left to rust; rust away. e.g. 도서관에서 책이 썩고 있다 The books are gathering dust on the library shelves. **3** [타락하다] be corrupted; become depraved; be morally tainted. e.g. 그의 정신이 완전히 썩어 있었다 He was utterly corrupt. **4** [걱정 등으로

마음이 상하다] feel depressed [gloomy]; become heavy; be disheartened. e.g. 방탕한 아들 때문에 그녀의 속이 썩었다 She was sick at heart because of her prodigal son.

썩이다 [सॉक्सिदा] **1** [부패시키다] rot; putrefy; corrupt; let <a thing> rot [spoil]. e.g. 낙엽을 썩여서 거름을 만들다 let dead leaves decay to make compost. **2** [안 쓰다] keep <something> idle; let <something> go to waste. e.g. 이렇게 훌륭한 물건을 썩인다는 것은 부끄러운 일이다 It is a shame to leave such a fine article to rust. **3** (마음을) worry (oneself) [be worried] <about / over>; be anxious <about>; bother (oneself) <about>; make one's heart break. e.g. 방탕한 아들의 일로 속을 썩이다 eat one's heart out with the matter of one's prodigal son.

썰다 [सॉल्ता] cut; chop (up); hack (to pieces); hash <meat>; slice; shave (얇게); mince (가늘게); dice; cube; cut in dice[cubes / chunks](▷chunks는 꽤 큰 것을 두껍게 토막친 것, cubes는 가지런한 것, dice는 작고 가지런한 것을 말함 cubes와 [वा] dice는 야채에, chunks는 살코기나 큰 생선, 일부의 야채에 씀]. e.g. 깍두기 꼴로 썬 야채 diced [cubed] vegetables

썰매 [सॉल्मै] a sled; a sledge; (주로 말이 끄는) a sleigh; (미국, 캐나다의) a toboggan.

쏘다 [सोदा] **1** [화살, 총 등을 나가게 하다] shoot <an arrow / a birds>; fire <a gun>; discharge. e.g. 총을 쏘다 fire [shoot] a gun. **2** [벌 등이 침으로 찌르다] sting. e.g. 톡 쏘는 맛이 나는 biting to the taste **3** [날카롭게 말하다] make cutting remarks; make a sharp [cutting] retort; say spiteful things; deliver <a person> pinpricks.

쏘다니다 [सोदानिदा] gad [wander] about; run [bustle] about; loiter; <美> bum around

쏘이다 [सोइदा] (벌레에) be stung. e.g. 벌에 쏘이다 get stung by a bee

쏜살 [सोन्साल] a shot arrow. e.g. 그는 골을 향해 쏜살같이 달렸다 He dashed full tilt for the goal.

쏟아지다 [सोदाजीदा] pour on [out / down]; (물 등이) gush out [forth]; spout; spurt; get [be] spilt. e.g. 쏟아지는 비 (a) pouring rain.

쏠리다 [सोल्लिदा] **1** [기울다] lean <to / toward>; incline

<to>. **2** [경향을 띠다] incline <to>; tend <to>; lean [trend] <toward>. e.g. 자연주의로 쏠리다 lean to naturalism. **3** [시선, 마음 등이 집중되다] focus <on / at>; center <on / in / at>; converge <on>. e.g. 예쁜 처녀에게 시선이 쏠리다 have one's eye on a pretty girl.

쐐기 [स्वेगि] 자형의) a wedge; (바퀴나 통의) a chock; (차바퀴의) linchpin. 쐐기를 박다 wedge; drive in a wedge. e.g. 그가 약속을 지키도록 쐐기를 박아 둘 필요가 있다 We must take steps to make sure that he will keep his promise.

쐬다 [स्वेदा] expose (to the wind); air; bare. e.g. 바람을 쐬다 (물건을) expose (thing) to the air / (사람이) expose oneself to the wind / air oneself (바깥 공기를).

쑤다 [सुदा] boil; make; prepare. e.g. 죽을 쑤다 boil rice into gruel / cook gruel / simmer porridge.

쑤셔넣다 [सुस्यौनोथा] thrust [shove / tuck] in[into]; stuff [cram / pack] into; poke [strike] into; ram [bump] into.

쑤시다[1] [सुशिदा] (구멍 등을) pick; poke. e.g. 이를 쑤시다 pick one's teeth

쑤시다[2] [सुशिदा] [아프다] ache; smart (손가락 등이); tingle; throb with pain (종기 등이); jump; fester; rankle (염증을 일으켜); be sore; twine; prick; prickle. e.g. 머리] [골치] 가 쑤시다 have a splitting headache.]

쑥 [सुक] **1** [내밀거나 들어간 모양] (protruded) way out; (sunken) way in. e.g. 쑥 나온 턱 a prominent jaw. **2** [밀어 넣거나 뽑는 모양] with a jerk; with a vigorous pull. e.g. 이불 속으로 쑥 들어가다 slide [slip] between sheets [불쑥] suddenly; abruptly; all at once; unexpectedly. e.g. 쑥 나타나다 make an abrupt appearance / appear unexpectedly / pop in [up] / bob up.

쑥스럽다 [सुक्सुरौप्ता] **1** [걸맞지 않다] unbecoming; improper; unseemly; indecent. e.g. 쑥스럽게 굴다 behave unseemly / cut a ridiculous figure. **2** [겸연쩍다] awkward. e.g. 쑥스러워하다 feel awkward [nervous] <before an audience> / feel small [cheap / embarrassed] <in company> / be [feel] abashed / be self-conscious.

쓰다[1] [सुदा] (글씨를) write <a letter>; (글을) compose

<an essay / a poem>; write <a story>; make <a composition>; [적다] put (down) <one's opinion> in writing; put [lay / jot / set] down; [기술하다] describe. e.g. 새로 쓴 소설[희곡] a newly written novel [play].

쓰다[2] [सुदा] s **1** [착용하다] put on; wear (▷put on 은 동작, wear 는 상태를 나타냄); cover. e.g. 안경을 쓴 남자 a man wearing glasses / a man with glasses on. **2** (우산을) hold [put] up <an umbrella> over one's head. e.g. 우산을 쓰고 under an umbrella. **3** [뒤집어쓰다] pour <water> on <oneself>; be covered with <dust>; pull [draw] <the bedspread> over <one's head>. e.g. 담요를 쓰고 자다 sleep with the blanket pulled over one's head. **4** (죄를) be falsely [wrongly] charged <with murder>; be falsely [unjustly] accused <of stealing>.

쓰다[3] [सुदा] **1** (물건을) use; make use of; put to use; employ; [취급하다] work [operate] <a machine>; handle a tool; manipulate <an instrument>. e.g. 아직 쓸 수 있는 중고차 a serviceable secondhand car. **2** (사람을) employ; hire; take <a person> into one's service; [고용하고 있다] keep [have] <a person> in one's employ [service / pay]; keep <a servant>; [잘 다루다] handle; manage. e.g. 시험 삼아 써 보다 take <a person> on trial / give <a person> a trial. **3** [채택하다] adopt; follow; take; apply (적용하다). e.g. 별별 수단을 다 쓰다 use [try] every conceivable means. **4** [소비하다] spend (돈을); consume; use (소모품을). e.g. 시간을 유효적절하게 쓰다 make good use of one's time. **5** [말하다] speak. e.g. 독일어를 쓰다 speak German.

쓰다[4] [सुदा] (맛이) bitter; [쓰라리다] hard; trying.

쓰다듬다 [सुदादम्दा] [손으로 쓸어 어루만지다] stroke; pass one's hand over [across] <one's face>; smooth; caress; (가볍게 두드리듯) pat.

쓰라리다 [सरारिदा] **1** 상처가) smart; sore; tingling; burning. e.g. 상처가 아직도 쓰라리다 The wound still smarts **2** [괴롭다] painful; sore; bitter; trying; hard (to bear). e.g. 쓰라린 생활 [세상] a hard life [world].

쓰러뜨리다 [सुरौतरिदा] **1** (서

있는 것을) bring down; throw down; level <a house to the ground>; blow down (바람이 집을); lodge; lay (벼 등을); fell (베어 넘어뜨리다); (사람을) throw <a person> to the ground; floor <a person>; knock down; trip up (발을 걸어) topple [bring down] <a person>. e.g. 집을 쓰러뜨리다 (지진 등이) demolish [destroy] a house / [헐다] pull down a house. **2** [지우다] defeat; beat; [멸망시키다] overthrow; ruin; [죽이다] kill. e.g. 그는 강적을 쓰러뜨렸다 He defeated a powerful opponent.

쓰러지다 [सुरोजीदा] 1 (서 있는 물건이) fall; come [go] down; (흔들려서) topple (over); collapse; (사람, 동물이) fall; fall over [down]; drop; go [roll] over; be off one's feet; sink to the ground. e.g. 금방 쓰러질 것 같은 집 a tumbledown house. **2** (과로 등으로) break down; have a breakdown; crack up; succumb [give way] to <a disease>; [졸도하다] fall senseless; fall in a faint. e.g. 일사병으로 쓰러지다 be laid low by sunstroke.

쓰레기 [सुरेगि] (일반적 또는 주방의) garbage; [폐물] trash; rubbish; junk; [먼지] dust; refuse; sweepings; waste.

쓰리다 [सुरिदा] 1 [아프다] smart; sore; tingling; burning. e.g. 속이 쓰리다 have a burning feeling in one's stomach / have a sour stomach. **2** (마음이) sore; bitter; heartrending; heart-aching.

쓰이다[1] [सुइदा] 1 [써지다] be written <with>; write. e.g. 글씨가 잘 쓰이는 종이 a paper on which a pen writes well. **2** [쓰게 하다] get <a person> to write <a letter>; have <a letter> written.

쓰이다[2] [सुइदा] 1 [사용되다] be used; be made use of; be utilized; be employed; serve. e.g. 일상 생활에 쓰이는 물건 articles in daily use. **2**[소용되다] be spent; be consumed; be used; require; need. e.g. 겨울철에는 등유가 많이 쓰인다 A great deal of kerosene is consumed during the winter.

쓱 [सक] [슬쩍] <slip away> quickly and quietly; [척] <bolt> abruptly; [빨리] <pass by> rapidly; [슬슬] <rub> dethly [lightly]. e.g. 방문을 쓱 열다 open the door quietly.

쓴맛 [सुन्मात] a sharp [bitter] taste. e.g. 쓴맛이 나다

taste bitter / be bitter. 인생의 쓴맛 단맛을 다 보다 taste the bitters and sweets [joys and sorrows] of life.

쓴웃음 [सुनुसम] <smile> a bitter [wry] smile (▷bitter smile 은 속이 상했을 때의 몹시 언짢은 기분, wry smile 은 종종 자기를 비웃는 기분을 나타냄).

쓸다 [सल्ता] **1** (비로) sweep (with a broom). e.g. 마루를 쓸다 sweep the floor. **2** [유행병이 널리 퍼지다] spread; sweep; prevail; be prevalent [widespread]; (홍수 등이) sweep; (황폐시키다) devastate. e.g. 전염병이 전국을 쓸었다 An infectious disease was prevalent throughout the country. / An epidemic swept all over the country. **3** [일소하다] sweep away [off]; clear off [away]; clean out; wipe; banish; make a clean sweep <of>; [근절하다] make an end of; stamp [root] out.

쓸데없다 [सल्तेऔप्ता] [쓸모없다] useless; unserviceable; of no use [avail / good]; [필요없다] needless; unnecessary; [군더더기이다] superfluous; redundant; [청한 바 없다] unwanted; uninvited; uncalled-for. e.g. 쓸데없는 것 a useless object

쓸모 [सल्मो] use; usefulness; utility; help; convenience; worth; (a) merit; value. e.g. 쓸모가 없는 사람 a good-for-nothing(person).

쓸쓸하다 [सलसरहादा] [적적하다] lonely; lonesome; cheerless; [황량하다] desolate; deserted; [외롭다] solitary. e.g. 쓸쓸한 고독 a bleak loneliness.

씀씀이 [समसमि] expenditure; expense. e.g. 씀씀이가 헤픈 사람 a spendthrith / an extravagant person

씌우다 [सउइउदा] **1** [덮다] cover <a thing> with; put <a thing> on; [도금하다] plate <a thing> with. e.g. 아이에게 모자를 씌우다 put a cap on a child. **2** (죄 등을) charge [fix] <a guilt on a person>; fasten [pin] <a crime on a person>; put <the murder upon others>; impute <a crime to a person>; lay <the guilt upon / a blame at another's door>; (오명을) fasten <a stigma upon a person>. e.g. 남에게 죄를 덮어 씌우다 charge a person with a crime / lay the blame for a crime on a person / fasten a crime on[upon] a person.

씨 [1] [शि] [氏] **1** [씨족] a family; a clan. e.g. 김씨(네) the Kim family[clan]

/ the Kims. **2** (남자에게 붙여서) Mr. <*pl.* Messrs.>; (여자에게 붙여서) Mrs. <*pl.* Mmes.>; Miss; Ms.(▷ Ms.는 Mrs.나 Miss 의 구별을 싫어하는 여자에게 붙임. <英>에서는 마침표를 생략하는 경향이 있음). e.g. 박 김 양씨 Messrs. Park and Kim. **3** (특정인을 가리켜) the gentleman; he. e.g. 씨에 의하면 according to him / in his opinion / he says that .... 씨는 공주 출신입니다 He comes[is] from Kongju.

씨 [2] [शि] **1** [종자] a seed <*pl.* ~ (s)>; [과실의 핵] a stone; (사과 등의) a pip **2** [가축의 품종] a breed; a strain; a stock. **3** [사물이 발생한 근원] a cause; a source. e.g. 자기가 뿌린 씨는 자기가 거두어야 한다 You must reap what you have sown.

씨름 [शिरम] (운동) wrestling; a wrestling match.

씨앗 [शिआत] seeds (of grain / vegetables).

-씩 [..शिक] [같은 수효로 나눔]. e.g. 하나에 백 원씩 a hundred won apiece.

씩 [शिक] [싱겁게 웃는 모양] with a quick smile. e.g. 씩 웃다 grin.

씩씩거리다 [शिकशिक्कौरिदा] gasp (for breath); pant; breathe hard [heavily]; (천식 등으로) wheeze. e.g. 화가 나서 씩씩거리다 huff and puff / fume (with rage). 씩씩거리며 말하다 gasp [pant / puff] out.

씩씩하다 [शिकशिक्यादा] manly; virile; valiant; vigorous; brave; strong; energetic. e.g. 씩씩하게 걷다 step lively / walk briskly.

씹다 [शिप्ता] chew; masticate. e.g. 씹는 담배 chewing tobacco.

씹히다 [शिपिदा] [씹어지다] be chewed; be masticated; [씹게 하다] let <a person> chew [masticate] <on>.

씻기다 [शिविकदा] **1** [씻음을 당하다] be washed [wiped]. e.g. 잘 씻기다 be washed easily [well].**2** [씻게 하다] let [have] <a person> wash <a thing>. e.g. 딸에게 그릇을 씻기다 have one's daughter wash dishes.

씻다 [शित्ता] **1** (물 등으로) wash <one's face>; cleanse <a wound>; rinse <a bottle>; bathe <one's eyes in warm water>. e.g. 물로 씻다 wash in water. **2** [닦아 내다] wipe (away); mop(up); swab (걸레 등으로). e.g. 이마의 땀을 씻다 wipe the sweat off one's brow. **3** (오명, 치욕 등을) clean [clear] oneself of the stain; wipe; mop (up). e.g. 씻을 수 없는 치욕 an indelible disgrace

/ an ineffaceable humiliation.

ㅇ

아 [अ] **1** [감동,놀람 등을 나타내는 소리] Ah!; Oh! (▷ ah **2** [슬픔,실망 등을 나타내는 소리] Ah!; Alas! e.g.아 슬프다 Alas! / Woe is me! 아 이제는 늦었구나 Alas! It's too late. 아 슬프다, 그는 이제 가고 없구나 Alas, he is dead and gone! **3** [깨우침, 응답, 동조 등을 나타내는 소리] Oh; O; O yes; Ah; Well. e.g. 아 이제 알겠다 Aha! Now I get it! 아 그렇군요 Oh, I see. **4** [말을 걸 때의 소리] Oh; O; Well; I say; Listen. e.g. 아 여보세요 Hello! / I say! / Hey! 아이 사람아 Say [I say], you! / Hey, you!

아가미 [आगामी] the gill(s) <of a fish>; the branchiae <*sing.* branchia>. e.g. 아가미가 있는 gilled / branchiat

아가씨 [आगाश्शी] a young lady; (부르는 말) Miss; young lady a country [town] girl. 어여쁜 아가씨 a lovely [charming] little girl., young lady.

아군 [आगुन] [**我軍**] our forces [troops / army]; friendly troops [army].

아궁이 [आगुंगी] a fuel [fire] hole; the opening of a firebox.

아기자기하다 [आगीजागीहादा] **1** [잘 어울려 보여서 예쁘다] harmonious in appearance; visually charming; picturesque. e.g. 아기자기한 방 a(n) harmonious room **2** [잔재미가 있다] (이야기 등이) juicy; colorful; interesting; amusing; jolly; (분위기 등이) harmonious; on intimate [friendly] terms. e.g. 아기자기하게 harmoniously / happily / affectionately.

아까 [आका] a short while ago; a short time ago. e.g. 아까부터 for some time / since a while ago.

아깝다 [आकाप्ता] **1** [소중하다] precious; dear; valuable; worthy; ill-spared. e.g. 아까워하다 value / set [put] much [a high] value on[upon] / make much of. [아쉽다] wasteful; too good <for>; worthy of a better cause. e.g. 아까운 듯이 grudgingly / with an air of reluctance / reluctantly. 그는 비서로 있기에는 아까운 사람이다 It's a waste for him to remain a secretary. **3** [유감이다] regrettable; pitiful; disappointing. e.g. 그가 이 경험에서 배운 바가 없었다니 참 아까운 일이다 It is a pity that he should not have learned from this experience.

아끼다 [आकीदा] **1** [소중히 여기다] prize; value; set great value on; esteem (highly); think [make] much of; hold <a thing> dear. e.g. 소중히 아끼다 take great care of a thing.

아낌없이 [आकीमौप्सी] [미련없이] without regret; ungrudgingly; [후하게] freely; generously.

아나운서 [आनाउन्सौ] an announcer; [뉴스 보도자] a newscaster, announcer.

아낙네 [आनांग्ने] a woman. e.g. 아낙네들 the womenfolk.

아날로그 [आनाल्लोग] [電] analogu(e)

아내 [आनै] a wife <*pl.* wives>; [배우자] a spouse.

아늑하다 [आनुख्वादा] snug; cozy; neat; compact; trim. e.g. 아늑한 방 a cozy room / a snug room.

아니 [आनी] (대답이 부정일 때) no; nay; (대답이 긍정일 때) yes;

아니꼽다 [आनीकोप्ता] **1** [속이 메스껍다] sick; nauseated; <서술적> be sick at the stomach; feel sick [nausea / queasy]. e.g. 보기만 해도 속이 아니꼽다 The mere sight of it makes me sick [turns my stomach]. / My stomach turns [rises] at the mere sight of it. **2** 쾌하다] saucy; sickening; revolting; offensive; repulsive. e.g. 아니꼬운 사람 an affected person

아니다 [आनीदा] not; no. e.g. 도 아니고 … 도 아니다 neither ... nor ....

아니라고 [आनीरागो] <say> that it is not ...; saying that it is not. e.g. 그는 그것이 자기 것이 아니라고 주지 않았다 He wouldn't give it to me saying that it was not his (own).

아니라도 [आनीरादो] even if [though] (it is) not .... e.g. 그는 그 돈을 전부는 아니라도 절반 이상이나 써 버렸다 He has spent more than half the money, if not all.

아니면 [आनीम्यौन] either ... or; [그렇지 않으면] or; (or) else. e.g. 맥주로 할까 아니면 위스키로 할까 Which will you have, beer or whisky?

아담 [आदाम] [雅淡] 아담하다 [단아하다] elegant; refined; graceful; [조촐하다] nice; neat; trim; tidy;

아동 [आदोंग] [兒童] a child; a juvenile; [학동] a pupil; <집합적> children; boys and girls

아드님 [आदुनीम] your [his] esteemed son

아득하다 [आदुख्वादा] **1** (거리가)

far; faraway; far-off; distant; remote; <서술적> be a long way off. e.g.갈길이 아득하다 have a long way to go. **2** (시간이) remote; far-off. e.g. 아득한 옛날을 생각하다 think of the days long past / think of far-off times. **3** (정신이) vague; dim; hazy; obscure; indistinct; fuzzy. e.g. 정신이 아득하다 have a dim consciousness.

아둘 [आदल] a son; a boy

아뜩하다 [आचीलहादा] suddenly dizzy; giddy; dazed; stunned; vertiginous. e.g. 눈앞이 아뜩한 높이에서 at a giddy [dizzy] height.

아랍 [आराब] Arab. e.g. 범아랍주의 Pan-Arabism. 통일 아랍 공화국 the United Arab Republic.

아랑곳 [आरांक्कोत] [관여] concern; interest; [유의] heed; attention; notice; regard; [간섭] meddling; interference.아랑곳하다 be concerned about; concern oneself about; take(an) interest in; take notice of;

아랑곳없다 [आरांक्कोसौप्ता] <서술적> have no concern with; have nothing to do with; have no interest in. e.g. 그것은 나에게는 아랑곳없는 일이다 I have nothing to do with the matter. / It's no concern of mine.

아래 [आरै] **1** [하부, 아래쪽] the lower part; the bottom; the foot; the base. e.g. 아래의 under / lower / downstair(s). [하위]. e.g. 맨 아래 아이 the youngest child. 3 [영향 등이 미치는 범위]. e.g. 아래에서 [을 받아] under / [… 에 의거하여] on / under / [(선생) 밑에서] under. …의 지휘[지도 / 감독] 아래 under the command [direction / supervision] of ... / under ....

아래위 [आरैवी] top and bottom; the upper and lower sides [parts]. e.g. 남의 아래위를 훑어보다 look a person up and down / survey a person from head to foot.

아래쪽 [आरैचोक] [아래 방향] a downward direction. e.g. 아래쪽 방향으로 downward / in a downward direction.

아래층 [आरैछुंग] [-層] the lower floor [story]; the downstairs

아랫도리 [आरैत्तोरी] [하체] the lower part of the body; [하의] lower garment. e.g. 아랫도리를 더 낮추어 밀어라 Use the lower half of your body more when you push.

아랫목 [आरैन्मोक] the warmer [lower] part of an *ondol* floor.

아랫배 [आरैत्पै] the lower

abdomen; the belly (▷ 위 등을 포함하는 일도 있음); the stomach; [장] the intestines; the bowels. e.g. 갑자기 아랫배가 몹시 아팠다 I felt a sudden sharp pain in my stomach. / I suddenly got a bad bellyache.

아랫사람 [आरैत्साराम] [손아랫 사람] one's junior; [부하] a subordinate; an underling; a minion; <집합적> a following; one's men; men under one's orders; a staff

아량 [आरयांग] [**雅量**] tolerance; magnanimity; generosity. e.g. 아량이 있는 tolerant / magnanimous / broad-minded. **아련하다** dim ; faint; vague; indistinct; obscure; hazy; misty. e.g. 아련한 달빛 a dim moonlight.

아령 [आरयौंग] [**啞鈴**] a dumb-bell

아로새기다 [आरोसैगीदा] engrave [carve] delicately; make an elaborate bas-relief. e.g. 그는 반지에 꽃무늬 장식을 아로새겼다 He engraved the ring in a floral pattern.

아뢰다 [आरवैदा] tell; inform; say; mention; state. e.g. 전날에 아뢴 바와 같이 as I told you the other day.

아류 [आरयू] [**亞流**] **1** [같은 유파의 사람] a follower. e.g. 아류의 사람들 those in the same school.**2** [모방하는 사람] an imitator; [모방한 물건] a poor imitation. e.g. 아류의 imitative. 그는 피카소의 아류이다 He is just an imitator of Picasso.

아르 [आरु] [면적의 단위] an are (기호 a).

아르바이트 [आरबाइथ] <독> Arbeit; a part-time job.

아르헨티나 [आरहैन्थीना] (남아메리카) Argentina [공식 국명: 아르헨티나 공화국] the Argentine Republic

아른거리다 [आरुनकौरीदा] Haunt; flicker; glimmer; shimmer; quiver; blink

아름 [आरुम] an armful. e.g. 한 아름의 마른 풀 an armful of hay.

아름답다 [आरुम्दाप्ता] beautiful; pretty; lovely; fine; eye-filling; handsome; good-looking; fair; charming.

아리다 [आरीदा] **1** (맛이) hot; pungent; acrid; biting; burning; <서술적> taste hot; have a biting [burning] taste. **2** (상처, 살갗 등이) smart; tingling; burning; biting; prickling. e.g. 연기 때문에 눈이 아리다 The smoke make my eyes sting. / My eyes smart from the smoke

아리송하다 [आरीसोंख्वादा] ⇨ 어리숭하다 1 e.g. 아리송한 답변[설명] an equivocal [evasive] answer [explanation]. 아리송하게 대답하다 give

ㅇ

an equivocal [a vague] answer / give a noncommittal answer.

아리아 [आरीआ] an aria <*pl.* ~s, arie>. e.g. 오페라의 아리아 an operatic aria.

아마 [आमा] probably; perhaps; possibly;

아마추어 [आमाछूऔ] an amateur.

아메리카 [आमेरीख्वा] America. ⇨ 미국

아멘 [आमेन] Amen! e.g. 아멘이라고 하다 say amen.

아무¹ [आमू] (사람) anyone; anybody; any person; (부정) no one; nobody; none. e.g. 아무나 붙들고 의논하다 consult anyone one can find. 그 집안 사람들은 아무도 모릅니다 I don't know anyone in that family.

아무² [आमू] [어떠한,아무런] any; (부정) no; not at all. e.g. 그는 아무 이유도 없이 사직했다 He resigned from his post without any reason.

아무개 [आमूगै] a certain person; Mr. K Mr. [Mrs. / Miss] so-and-so; (Mr.) what's-his-name; (Mrs. [Miss]) what's-her-name; Mr. –. e.g. 김 아무개 a man called Kim or something / a(certain) Kim. 그 아무개 말이야, 그 사람은 어떻게 됐지 What has become of him – that Mr. what's-his-name?

아무래도 [आमूरैदो] [어떻든] in any way; anyhow; [반드시] surely; inevitably; must; [싫건 좋건] whether willing or not; willingly or unwillingly; will-nilly; [결국] in the end; ather all; [어느 면으로 보나] in all respects; in every respect; all things considered; to all appearances; to all appearance. **2** [아무리 하여도] by any means; on any account; possibly; by any possibility; at all; for anything; for all the world; <英> for nuts. e.g. 아무래도 그 사람의 이름이 생각나지 않는다 I just can't remember his name.

아무러면 [आमूरोम्यौन] whatever it is; no matter what [how] it is; whatever anybody may do; whoever does [says] it. e.g. 그거야 아무러면 어떤가 What does it matter? / Let that go. / What of that?

아무런 [आमूरौन] [아무러한] any; (부정) no; not at all. e.g. 아무런 생각 없이 unconsciously / unintentionally / unwittingly.

아무렇거나 [आमूरौख्वौना] anyway; anyhow; whatever [however] it may be; at any rate.

아무렇게나 [आमूरोख्वेना] [되는대로] at random; at [by] haphazard; haphazardly;

by guesswork; [건성으로] carelessly; half-heartedly; indifferently;.

아무렇든지 [आमूरौथुनजी] at any rate; in any case [event]; anyway; anyhow; at all events; whatever; however. e.g. 아무렇든지 출발 전에 알려주겠다 In any event, I will let you know before I start.

아무렴 [आमूरयौम] Of course!; Certainly!; Naturally!; Sure

아무리 [आमूरी] <부사> however; whatever

아무쪼록 [आमूचोरोक] [될 수 있는 대로] as much [far] as one can; as much [far] as possible [practicable]; [꼭] by all means; [부디] kindly; (if you) please; [힘껏] to the best of one's ability.

아무튼 [आमूथुन] anyway; anyhow; at any rate; in any case [event]; at all events; somehow or other.

아물다 [आमुल्दा] heal [close] (up); be healed. e.g. 상처가 아물었다 The wound has closed.

아버지 [आबौजी] **1** a [one's] father **2** 일을 처음 완성한 사람] the father. e.g. 영소설의 아버지 the father of the English novel. **3** [가톨릭, 기독교] Father.

아부 [आबु] [**阿附**] flattery; sycophancy; adulation; toadyism.

아비 규환 [आबी ग्यूह्वान] [**阿鼻叫喚**] **1** [불교] Avici and Raurava, two of the eight burning hells in Buddhism. **2** <비유> shrieking in agony; agonizing cries; appalling confusion; pandemonium. e.g. 사고 현장은 그야말로 아비 규환이었다 The scene of the accident was simply hell.

아사 [आसा] [**餓死**] 어 죽는 것] death from hunger; (death by) starvation. e.g. 아사시키다 starve <a person> to death / starve out <a person>. 아사 지경에서 헤매다 be on the verge of starvation.

아삭거리다 [आसाक्कौरीदा] be crunchy [crisp]; crunch. e.g. 아삭거리며 당근을 먹다 eat a carrot with a crunching sound / crunch a carrot.

아삭아삭 [आसाग्आसाक] crunching; crisping. 아삭아삭하다 = 아삭거리다.

아쉬워하다 [आश्वीवॅाहादा] (없어서) miss; feel the loss [want / miss] of; feel regret at [feel keenly] the absence of; [서운해하다] be unwilling; be reluctant. e.g. 이별을 아쉬워하다 be reluctant [sorry / unwilling / loath] to leave [part from] a person.

아쉽다 [आश्वीप्ता] want for; miss; feel inconvenienced

by the lack of; be unsatisfied [discontented] with the lack [miss] of; be [stand] in need[want] of. e.g. 아쉬운 소리를 하다 make a request <of a person> / ask a favor of <a person>. 아쉬운 것 없이 지내다 live in comfort / be comfortably off / be above want / be well off

아스팔트 [आस्फाल्थ] asphalt. e.g. 아스팔트로 포장하다 pave [lay] <a road> with asphalt / asphalt <a road>.

아스피린 [आस्पीरीन] [藥] aspirin. e.g. 아스피린을 세 알 먹다 take three aspirin tablets / take three aspirins.

아슬아슬하다 [आसुरआसुरहादा] [위태롭다] risky; dangerous; perilous; thrilling; critical; [차이가 근소하다] close / narrow; near; hairbreadth; touch-and-go.

아시아 [आशीआ].g. 아시아의 Asian / Asiatic.

아야 [आया] Ouch!; How it hurts!; That hurts!

아양 [आयांग] coquetry; flirtation 아양(을) 떨다[부리다/피우다] play the coquette; behave in a coquettish manner; act coquettishly [seductively]; speak in coquettish tone

아역 [आयौक] [兒役] [어린이 역] a child's part[role] <in a play>.

아연 [आयौन] [啞然] [놀라거나 기가 막힌 모양]. e.g. 아연 실색하다 turn pale with surprise [fright].

아열대 [आयौल्तै] [亞熱帶] the subtropical zones [regions]; the subtropics. e.g. 아열대의 subtropic (al) / near-tropical.

아예 [आये] **1** [애초부터] from the outset [beginning / start] **2** [절대로] <not> at all; altogether; entirely; never. e.g. 거짓말은 아예 하지 마라 Never tell a lie. 어제는 아예 외출하지도 않았다 I didn't go out at all yesterday.

아옹다옹하다 [आओंग्ताओंग्हादा] [하찮은 일에 서로 자꾸 다투다] quarrel <with>; dispute; argue; altercate; bicker; wrangle; squabble; engage in wordy warfare; bandy words <with>.

아우 [आऊ] [동생] a man's younger [little / kid] brother; a woman's younger [little / small] sister.

아우성 [आऊसौंग] a shout; an outcry; a clamor; a hubbub; a bawl; a howl; a squawk. e.g. 아우성치다 clamor / bawl (out) / bawl and squall / set up a clamor [shout] / (응원 등에서) yell / give a yell <to> / (불만으로) let out a squawk.

아울러 [आऊल्लौ] [동시에 함께] (joining) together. e.g. 그는 장점과 단점을 아울러 갖고 있다 He has [is endowed with] both strengths and weaknesses

아이 [आइ] [자식, 후사] a child <*pl.* children>; one's issue; one's offspring; a kid; [아들] a son; [딸] a daughter; <집합적> offspring (▷ 단수, 복수 동형으로 동사는 어린이가 둘 이상이면 복수형).

아웃 [आउत] [야구] an out; a put-out (PO); (판정) Out!

아이고 (머니) [आइगो] [반갑거나 좋을 때 내는 소리] Ah!; Oh! e.g. 아이고 고맙기도 해라 Thank you very much. 아이고 좋아라 What a delight! / Hallelujah!

아이디어 [आइदीऔ] an idea.

아이러니 [आइरौनी] (an) irony.

아이보리 [आइबोरी] [상아, 상아색] ivory.

아이스 [आइस] ice.

아이템 [आइथेम] an item.

아장거리다 [आजांग्कौरीदा] (아기가) toddle; totter; shamble. e.g. 아장거리는 아기 a toddler.

아저씨 [आजौस्सी] **1** [삼촌] an uncle. **2** [부모 또래] a man; [호칭] Mister; Sir; Pop; Uncle. e.g. 낯선 아저씨 a strange gentleman.

아전 인수 [आजौन इन्सू] [**我田引水**] drawing water to one's own mill; turning everything to one's own advantage; seeking [promoting] one's own interests; arguing from a self-centered angle; interested consideration. e.g. 아전 인수의 selfish / self-seeking / self-centered [<英> -centred]. 아전 인수격인 견해 a selfish view.

아주 [आजू] [대단히] very (much); exceedingly; excessively; extremely; remarkably; greatly.

아주머니 [आजूमौनी] 1 [숙모] an aunt; an older[a younger] sister of one's father [mother **2** 항렬의 남의 아내] an auntie[aunty]. **3**[부인] a lady.

아줌마 [आजूम्मा] ⇨ 아주머니

아지랑이 [आजीरांगी] heat haze; waves of heat; heat waves; (a veil of) heat shimmer; shimmering of heated air

아지트 [आजीथ] 은신처] a hiding place; a safe house <for underground activists>;

아직 [आजीक] [어떤 일이 이루어질 때가 채 못 되어] (not) yet; still; as yet; with no change; even now; so far; [계속해서] still more; [겨우] only.

아집 [आजीब] [**我執**] [자기만을 내세움] egocentricity; self-centeredness [self-centredness]; egoistic attachment; egotism; tenacity; obstinacy.

아찔하다 [आस्सीरहादा dizzy; giddy; faint. e.g. 나는 정신이 아찔해졌다 I began to feel faint [woozy].

아차 [आछा] [잘못된 것을 갑자기 깨닫고 내는 소리] Heavens!; Hang it!; Damn it!; Oh my

아첨 [आछौम] [阿諂] flattery; adulation; sycophancy; toadyism; a compliment; sugary [sweet] words

아치 [आछी] an arch. e.g. 아치 모양의 arch-shaped / bow-shaped

아침 [आछीम] **1** (때) morning; morn. **2** ⇨ 아침밥

아침밥 [आछीम्बाप] breakfast; the morning meal.

아카데미 [आखादेमी] an academy

아킬레스건 [आखील्लेसगौन] [-腱] the Achilles' tendon; <비유> one's Achilles' heel; a vulnerable point.

아파트 [आफाथ] [한 가구 분의 방] an apartment.

아편 आफ्यौन] [阿片] pium. e.g. 아편을 함유한 opiumized.

아프다 [आफुदा] (육체적으로) painful; sore (염증 등으로); hurt; [욱신거리다] prickle; feel prickly; smart; ache. e.g. 아픈 상처 a painful wound. 가슴이 아프다 I have a pain in my chest.

아프리카 [आफरीखा] Africa e.g. 아프리카의 African.).

아픔 [आफुम] [통증] a pain; an ache; a sore; (마음의) (mental) pain; [슬픔] grief; sorrow; (쑤시는) a smart.

아하 Dear me!; My goodness!; Well!; What-do-you-know!

아홉 [आहोप] nine

아흔 [आहुन] ninety. e.g. 아흔째(의 것) ninetieth. 아흔째의 the ninetieth.

악[1] [आक] badness; (an) evil; wickedness; crimes; [악덕] (a) vice. e.g.

악[2] [आक] [남을 놀라게 할 때 지르는 소리] Bo!; Boh!; Boo!; [놀랐을 때 지르는 소리] Ugh!; Oh!; Wow!; Ooh!

악[3] [आक] [모질게 쓰는 기운] desperate effort; franticness; desperation; [노한 감정] desperation; anger; exploding [pent-up] feelings.

악감 (정 [आकाम]) [惡感(情)] [나쁜 감정] ill feeling; an ill will; animosity; an unfavorable impression; [반감] antipathy.

악공 [आकोंग] [樂工] a court musician.

악귀 [आक्वी] [惡鬼] an evil spirit; a demon; a devil; the Evil One

악극 [आक्कुक] [樂劇] a musical (drama / play); an operetta.

악기 [आक्की] [樂器] a musical instrument. e.g. 현[관 / 타]악기 a stringed [wind /

percussion] instrument. 건반 악기 a keyboard instrument.

악단 [आक्ताल] [**樂團**] [음악 연주를 위해 조직된 단체] a (musical) band; (관현 악단) an orchestra.

악담 [आक्ताम] [**惡談**] [저주 하는 말] a curse; a malediction; [욕] abusive [bad] language; abuse.

악당 [आक्तांग] [**惡黨**] a rascal; a villain; [깡패] a hooligan; a hoodlum. e.g. (이) 악당 같으니 (You) Devil! / (You) Bastard! / (You) Son of a bitch!(▷ 이 같은 표현은 쓰지 않는 것이 바람직함).

악대 [आक्तै] [**樂隊**] a (musical) band; (취주악의) a brass band

악덕 [आक्तौक] [**惡德**] (a) vice; corruption; immorality; evil conduct. e.g. 악덕을 쌓다 commit a series of vicious acts / commit one vice ather another.

악독] [आक्तोक] [**惡毒**] infernality; atrocity; perversity; harshness; villainy. 악독하다 most wicked; infernal; atrocious; brutal; devilish; villainous. e.g. 악독스럽다 = 악독하다. 악독한 짓 an atrocious [infernal] act / an atrocity.

악랄 [आंग्नाल] [**惡辣**] 악랄하다 vicious; wicked; [파렴치하다] unscrupulous; [비열하다] mean; dirty; [교활하다] crathy; wily. e.g. 악랄한 상술 crooked dealing. 악랄한 방법 a vicious way to do things. 악랄한 짓을 하다 play a mean[dirty] trick / play foul. 그는 악랄한 방법으로 큰 돈을 벌었다 He made a big profit by unscrupulous means.

악마 [आंग्मा] [**惡魔**] the Devil; Satan; a fiend; a demon; Old Serpent; [악령] an evil spiritevil spirits <from a person>.

악명 [आंग्म्यौंग] [**惡名**] [나쁜 평판] a bad reputation; ill repute [fame]; a bad name; notoriety; infamy.

악몽 [आंग्मोंग] [**惡夢**] [나쁜 꿈] a bad dream; [무서운 꿈] a nightmare; [불길한 꿈] an ominous dream.

악물다 [आंग्मूल्दा] clench [clamp / set] <one's teeth>.

악바리 [आक्बारी] [영악한 사람] a hard shrewd person.

악보 [आक्बो] [**樂譜**] <집합적> music; (한 장의) a sheet of music; a score (총보); a music book (악보집).

악사 [आक्सा] [**樂士**] a band(s) man; a musician.

악상 [आक्सांग] [**樂想**] a musical motif; a theme; a melodic subject. e.g. 악상을 다듬다 work on a motif.

악센트 [आक्सेन्थु] **1** [고저, 강약의 변화] an accent; [강세] a stress. **2** [강조점].

e.g. 이 블라우스는 칼라의 자수가 악센트다 The embroidery on the collar accents [sets off] the blouse.

악수 [आक्सू] [**握手**] **1** [손을 맞잡고 하는 인사] a handshake; handshaking. **2** 사이좋게 지냄].악수하다 [협력하다] join hands [forces] <with>; [화해 하다] make up <with>.

악순환 [आक्सून्ह्वान] [**惡循環**] a vicious circle; a vicious spiral.

악쓰다 [आक्सुदा] **1** [소리치다] shout [bawl] out; bawl and squall; yell <in anger [protest]>. e.g. 부하 직원 [남편] 에게 악쓰다 bawl at one's subordinate [husband]. 악쓰면서 울다 shout [yell] in tears. 악써서 목이 쉬다 roar oneself hoarse. **2** [기를 쓰다] try hard

악어 [आगौ] [**鰐魚**] [動] a crocodile (아프리카산); a gavial (인도산); an alligator (북미산); a cayman (남미산).

악역 [आझौक] [**惡役**] the role of a villain; a villain's role [part]

악연 [आक्यौग] [**惡緣**] [좋지 못한 인연] a bad [an undesirable] relationship; [불행한 결혼] a bad [poor] match; an unsuccessful [unhappy] marriage.

악영향 [आझौग्हयांग] [**惡影響**] a bad [harmful] influence; infection; an adverse [a baleful] effect.

악용 [आझोंग] [**惡用**] abuse; misuse; an improper use.

악운 [आगून] [**惡運**] [운이 나쁨] bad [ill] luck.

악의 [आगूउइ] [**惡意**] [나쁜 마음] ill will; [적의] malice.

악인 [आगीन] [**惡人**] a bad [wicked] man; a villain; an evildoer; a scoundrel; a hoodlum (불량배)

악장 [आकजांग] [**樂章**] a movement (of music); a chapter.

악전고투 [आकजौनगोथू] [**樂章**] a desperate struggle; a tough fight; a hard battle; a close game (경기); a tight match; a close contest (경쟁). e.g. 우리는 악전 고투 끝에 겨우 이겼다 We finally won the game ather a tough fight.

악조건 [आकजोगौन] [**惡條件**] adverse [unfavorable] conditions [factors / circumstances]; bad conditions; a handicap.

악질 [आकजील] [**惡質**] bad [inferior] quality; evil nature; malignancy; wickedness.

악착 [आकछाक] [**齷齪**] e.g. 악착같이 [끈질기게] perseveringly / persistently / [악을 쓰고] desperately

악천후 [आकछौन्हू] [**惡天候**] [몹시 나쁜 날씨] foul [bad / poor / unfavorable] weather; [사나운 날씨] rough [stormy / inclement] weather.

악취 [आकछ्वी] [**惡臭**] a bad

[foul / nasty] smell; an offensive odor [odour]; a stench; a stink; a malodor.

악평 [आकफ्यौंग] [**惡評**] 나쁜 평판] a bad reputation; ill fame; [헐뜯는 비평] unfavorable [unfavourable] criticism.

악필 [आकफील] [**惡筆**] bad [poor] handwriting; <write> a bad [poor] hand; (알아볼 수 없는) illegible handwriting. e.g. 그는 악필이다 His handwriting is very poor. / He writes a bad [poor] hand.

악행 [आखैंग] [**惡行**] evildoing; (개개의) an evil deed; a wicked act; a misdeed; a sinful deed. e.g. 악행에 빠지다 be given to evil ways.

악화 [आख्वा] [**惡化**] (형세, 상태의) a change [turn] for the worse; aggravation; getting worse [more serious]; (품질 등의) deterioration; debasement; ingravescence; (풍속 등의) degeneration; corruption. ed.

안[1] [आन] [**案**] **1** 제안] a proposal; a proposition; a suggestion. **2** [고안] an idea; a device; a design. [계획] a plan; a program; a project; a scheme. **4** 초안] a drath. e.g. 안을 짜다 prepare [frame] a drath. **5** [의안] a bill.

안[2] [आन] [내부] the interior; the inside. e.g. 안에 in / into / within / inside / inward. 기차 안의 사람들 the passengers in [on] the train.

안간힘 [आन्गान्हीम] e.g. 안간힘을 쓰다 hold back an urge / restrain <one's indignation> / strain / struggle / make great [strenuous] efforts.

안감 [आन्गाम] lining (material); a cloth for lining.

안개 [आन्कै] (a) mist; (짙은) (a) fog; (a) haze.

안건 [आन्कौन] [**案件**] a matter; a case; an item; [의안] a bill.

안경 [आन्ग्यौंग] [**眼鏡**] glasses; <a pair of> spectacles; specs (▷ gla-sses 쪽이 흔히 쓰임); [강풍, 먼지, 광선을 막는 보호 안경] goggles.

안과 [आन्ग्वा] [**眼科**] ophthalmology; (병원의) the department of ophthalmology.

안구 [आन्गू] [**鞍具**] saddlery; saddle gear; horse gear; harness.

안기다 [आन्गीदा] [안음을 당하다] go [move] into <a person's> arms; throw oneself in <a person's> arms; be embraced; be in <a person's> arms.

안기다 [आन्गीदा] **1** [안게 하다] make <a person> hold [take / carry] <someone> in his arms; make <a person> embrace [hug].

ㅇ

e.g. 어머니에게 아기를 안기다 put the baby in its mother's breast[bosom]. **2** (책임 등을) charge <a person with responsebility>; lay <a duty on a person>; put <the responsebility for something> on <a person>; entrust <a person with a task>. e.g. 친구에게 책임을 안기다 give a friend the responsebility. **3** [상품을 떠맡기다] force [press] <a person> to buy <the wares>; force(a sale) on; intrude on; tout; (가짜를) pass [palm] off <a thing upon a person>; foist [impose] <a thing upon a person>. e.g. 나쁜 물건을 안기다 palm [impose] a bad article upon <a person>.**4** (알을) make <a hen> sit on <eggs>; set <a hen> on <eggs>. e.g. 닭에게 알을 안기다 set the hen(on the eggs). **5**[치다] lodge a blow; give[deal / deliver] <a person> a blow. e.g. 주먹을 한대 안기다 give <a person> a punch [clout] (on the head).**6** (기타). e.g. 선물을 안기다 press giths on <a person>.

안내 [आन्नै] [**案內**] [인도] guidance; conduct; lead; [청해 들임] showing in; [통지] information; (a) notice; [초대] invitation.

안녕 [आन्नयौंग] [**安寧**] **1** 안전하고 태평함] (public) peace; tranquility; [복지] welfare; well-being. e.g. 사회의 안녕을 지키다 maintain peace and order (in a society) / maintain social stability **2** [평안] peace; calm (ness); quiet (ness); [건강] good health. 안녕하다 [평안 하다] peaceful; calm; uneventful; [건강하다] healthy; in good health; hale and hearty (노인 등이); <서술적> be(quite) well; be doing well. e.g. 어머님께서는 안녕하시냐 **3** [인사]. e.g. 안녕하십 니까 How are you? / (오전 중에) Good morning! / (오후에) Good atheroon! / (친한 사이에, 오전,오후 관계없이) Hello! 안녕하셨 습니까 How have you been? **4** [작별 인사] good-by (e); (I'll) see you again [later]; by(e)(now); so long; (특히 어린애가) bye-bye; farewell. e.g. [안녕!] 이라고 인사하다 say good-bye <to> / bid a person good-bye

안다 [आन्ता] **1** [껴안다] hold [take / carry] <a person> in one's arms; [포옹하다] embrace; hug; give <a person> a hug; cuddle. e.g. 아기를 품에 안다 embrace a baby / hug a child. **2** [맞받다] meet; confront. e.g. 돛이 바람을 안았다 The sail was filled with wind **3** [입다] suffer; sustain; incur; receive. e.g. 손해를 안다 suffer [receive] damage / suffer [sustain] a loss. **4** [떠맡다] undertake <another's responsibility>; bear [assume / shoulder] <the responsibility for [of]>; hold oneself responsible for; answer for. e.g. 빚을 안다 hold oneself liable for a debt / shoulder another's debt (남의 빚을). **5** [알을 품다] sit [brood] <on eggs>; set. e.g. 암탉이 알을 안았다 A hen set on her eggs

안달 [आन्दाल] fret; fuss; impatience; stew. e.g. 안달이 나다 grow impatient

안대 [आन्दै] [**眼帶**] an eye bandage; a patch over the eye.

안도 [आन्दो] [**安堵**] relief; reassurance. e.g. 안도의 한숨을 쉬다 heave a sigh of relief / feel greatly relieved / breathe again freely.

안되다 [आन्देदा] **1** [유감이다] regrettable; sympathize <with>; be [feel] sorry <for / to hear that ...>; be a pity; have [take] pity <on>; feel pity <for>. e.g. 안 된 이야기지만 to my regret / I regret to say that ... **2** 금지하다] must [should] not <do>; ought not to <do>; be not allowed. e.g. [텔레비전을 보면 안 됩니까] [안 돼] "Can't I watch TV?" "No, you can't.". **3** (필요) must <do>; have (got) to <do>; need to <do>; it is necessary <to do>. e.g.그 집은 수리하지 않으면 안 된다 The house must be repaired. / The house needs [wants] repairing. (의무,도리) should <do>; ought to <do>; be bound to <do>; shall <do>. e.g. 부모에게 복종하지 않으면 안 된다 One should be obedient to one's parents. [쓸모 없다] <서술적> be useless; be of no use; won't do [work]; do not serve the purpose. e.g. 그 돈으론 안 된다 That amount of money will not do\ **6** [실패, 미달이다] <서술적> be a failure; be unsuccessful; fail. e.g. 일이 안되다 one's work is not done / fail in one's attempt. [조심하다]. e.g. ... 하면 안 되니까 for fear ... may [should] / so as not to / so that one may not <be / do> / lest ... should. 비가 오면 안 되니까 우산을 갖고 가거라 Take your umbrella with you in case it rains.

안락 [आल्लाक] [**安樂**] comfort; ease.

안락사 [आल्लाकसा] [**安樂死**] (artificial) euthanasia; mercy-killing; an easy death. e.g. 그는 고양이를 안락사 시키려고 독약을 한 컵 먹였다 He gave the cat a cup of poison to put him out of his pain.

안료 [आल्लयो] [**顔料**] **1** cosmetics; a face paint. **2** a color; a paint; [색소] a pigment.

안마 [आन्मा] [**按摩**] massage; shampoo (ing).

안면 [आन्म्यौन] [**顔面**] **1** = 얼굴 **2** [친분] acquainttance. e.g. 안면이 있는 사람 an acquaintance / a person one knows by sight.

안목 [आन्मोक] [**眼目**] [안식] an appreciative eye; a discerning [critical] eye; discernment; (a sense of) discrimination; judgment; penetration; insight.

안무 [आन्मू] [**按舞**] he arrangement of a dance; dance composition; choreography. **안방** [a sitting room; a living room; a back room; (여자 들이 거처하는) the women's quarters; an inner room.

안배 [आन्बै] [**按排, 按配**] [배치] arrangement; disposition; [배분] distribution; assignment. 안배하다 arrange; distribute; assign.

안보 [आन्बो] [**安保**] security.

안부 [आन्बू] [**安否**] [무사 여부] safety; [지내는 형편] how <a person> is; <a person's> welfare; [문안] an inquiry; [문안 인사] regards; wishes. e.g. 안부를 묻다 inquire [ask] ather a person [a person's health].

안빈낙도 [आन्बीन्नावदो] [**安貧樂道**] contentment with poverty and delight in the (Taoist) Way.

안사돈 [आन्सादोन] [**-查頓**] a son's [daughter's] mother-in-law; a son-[daughter-] in-law's mother.

안사람 [आन्साराम] my wife.

안성맞춤 [आन्सौगमात्छूम] [**安城-**] e.g. 안성맞춤의 suitable <for> / adapted <for / to> / fit <for> / ideal / the very / right / just. 안성맞춤의 날씨 ideal weather

안스럽다 [आन्स्रौप्ता] [**眼識**

안식 [안목과] 식견] discernment; insight; penetration; a critical [discerning] eye; discrimination.

안식년 [आन्शीम्न्यौन] [**-年**] a sabbatical year.

안식처 [आन्शीकछौ] a place to find peace; a place to rest; a resting place; a refuge; a shelter; an asylum; a(safe) haven.

안심 [आन्शीम] [소의 갈비

안쪽 고기] lean beef ribs.

안심 [आन्शीम] [安心] [근심이 없음] peace of mind; freedom from care [anxiety]; [안도감] (a sense of) relief; [안전] (a sense of) security; safety; assurance; reassurance.

안쓰럽다 [आन्सुरौप्ता] <서술적> be sorry for troubling someone who is worse off than oneself.

안온 [आनोन] [安穩] [조용하고 편안함] peace; quiet; tranquility; calmness.

안위 [आन्वी] [安危] safety (or danger); fate; destiny; welfare.

안이하다 [आनीहादा] [安易-] easy; easygoing..

안일 [आनील] housework; women's work.

안장 [आन्जांग] [鞍裝] a saddle. e.g. 안장을 얹다 [내리다] saddle (up) [unsaddle] <a horse> / put a saddle on [take a saddle off] <a horse>.

안전 [आन्जौन] [安全] safety; security; freedom from danger. e.g. 안전을 위해 for safety's sake.

안절부절못하다 [आन्जौल्बूजौल्मोस्हादा] be [grow] restless; be fidgety; be nervous; be impatient; get [have] the fidgets; jitter; be on pins and needles. e.g. 안절부절못하는 사람 a restless person / a fidgety person / a fidget.

안정 [आन्जौंग] [安定] stability; stabilization; stea diness; [균형] equilibrium; balance; [침착] settle ment; composure. e.g. 물가 [경제 / 통화] 의 안정 price [economic / curren cy] stabilization.

안정감 [आन्जौंग्गाम] [安定感] a sense of security.

안주 [आन्जू] [按酒] a relish <taken with wine>; a (side) dish; appeti rs [<프> hors d'oeuvres] served with drinks; an accompaniment of wine.

안주 [आन्जू] [安住] living in peace; peaceful living; a serene life; a comfortable life live in peace; lead a comfortable life [peaceful living].

안주인 [आन्जूइन] [-主人] [주부] a mistress; the lady of the house; (여관, 하숙의) a landlady; a hostess; 가게의) a propriet- ress.

안중 [आन्जूंग] [眼中] e.g. 안중에 in one's eyes. 안중에 없다 leave <a person / a thing> out of account [consideration] / take no account [notice] <of> / think nothing <of> / disregard / ignore / set <a person / a thing> at naught.

안쪽 [आन्चोक] the inside; the

interior; the inner part; the back. e.g. 안쪽의 inside / inner / interior.

안착 [आन्छाक] [安着] safe arrival; (물품의) safe receipt

안창 [आन्छांग] a shoe liner; an inner sole.

안채 [आन्छै] the main building (of a house); the inner house.

안치 [आन्छी] [安置] [모셔 둠] installation; enshrinement. 안치하다 [आन्छीहादा] install; enshrine; (관 등을) lay in state. e.g. 절의 본당에 불상을 안치하다 enshrine [install] a Buddhist image in the main hall of a temple.

안치다 [आन्छीदा] [어떤 물건을 솥에 넣다] get <rice> ready to cook; prepare <rice> for cooking [boiling

안타 [आन्था] [安打] [야구] a (safe) hit; a safety; a base hit; a crash.

안타까워하다 [आन्थाकावोंहादा] **1** about; [개탄하다] deplore <a fact>; regret. **2** [딱하게 여기다] feel pity <for>; pity <a person>; be distressed [anguished] <at>; grieve <at / over>. e.g. 남의 불행을 안타까 워하다 feel sorry for another's misfortune.

안타깝다 [आन्थाकाप्ता] (사람이) impatient; irritated; nervous; vexed; (사물이) irritating; tantalizing; vexatious; [개탄스-럽다] deployrable; regrettable; lamentable.

안팎 [आन्फाक] **1** [안과 밖] the interior and exterior; the inside and the outside; [안쪽과 겉쪽] obverse and reverse; the ins and outs. **2** [언동의 표리] duplicity. e.g. 안팎이 다른 사람 a double-dealer / a hypocrite / a double-faced person. **3** [대략] about; around; some. e.g. 5만 원 안팎 fithy thousand won or so / around [about / some] fithy thousand won.

안하 무인 [आन्हा मुइन] [眼下無人] overbearance; arrogance. e.g. 안하 무인의 high-handed / overbearing / arrogant / haughty

앉다 [आन्था] (자리에) sit [squat] down; take [have] a seat; seat oneself; [앉아 있다] sit; be seated.

앉은뱅이 [आन्जुन्बैंगी] a cripple. e.g. 그는 앉은뱅이 이다 He is crippled <with rheumatism>.

앉은자리 [आन्जुन्जारी] [좌석] one's seat; one's place. e.g. 앉은자리에서 from one's seat [place]. 앉은 자리를 양보하다 offer [give up / surrender] one's seat to <a lady>.

앉은키 [आन्जुन्खी] one's height when sitting; one's sitting height. e.g. 앉은

키가 작은 short-bodied. 그녀는 앉은키가 크다 [작다] She is long-waisted [short-waisted].

앉히다 **[आन्छीदा]** (좌석에) seat [sit] <a person>; have <a person> sit down. e.g. 안락 의자에 앉히다 seat [have] <a person> in an armchair

않다 **[आन्था]** [아니하다] do not; not.

않을 수없다 **[आन्हुल सू औप्ता]** cannot help <doing>; cannot but <do>; be compelled [forced / obliged] to <do>; be under the necessity of <doing>.

알 **[आल]** (새, 벌레 등의) an egg; [물고기, 개구리 등의 알덩어리] spawn; [식용의 물고기 알] roe; spat (조개, 주로 굴의); seed (굴의). e.g. 오리 알 a duck egg.

알다 **[आल्दा]** **1** (일반적으로) know; be aware of; learn; be acquainted with. **2** [이해 하다] understand; appreciate; know; comprehend; make sense <of>; see; make out. [낯이 익다] be acquainted <with>; know. **4** [동의, 승낙하다] consent to; agree to

알뜰하다 **[आल्तुरहादा]** **1** [헤프지 않고 아끼다] thrithy; frugal; saving; provident <of>.**2** [빈틈없고 정성스럽다] careful and earnest; conscientious; scrupulous

알랑거리다 **[आल्लांग्कौरीदा]** flatter; toady; curry favor <with one's superior>; cringe [truckle] to <a person>; fawn upon <a person>.

알량하다 **[आल्यांगहादा]** [보잘것 없다] trifling; trivial; twopenny (-halfpenny); [무가치하다] worthless; rubbish; rubbishing; drossy.

알레르기 **[आल्लेरुगी]** an allergy.

알려지다 **[आल्यौजीदा]** **1** [남이 알게 되다] become known <to>; come to <a person's> knowledge. **2** [판명되다] be found; be revealed; be disclosed; come to light; turn out (to be); prove (to be); be identified (신원 등). **3** [유명해지다] become famous [well known]; earn [win] fame; come [rise] to fame.

알력 **[आल्यौक]** [**軋轢**] [불화] (a) discord; [장기 간의 반목] a feud <between / among>; friction; jar; dissension; clash.

알루미늄 **[आल्लूमीन्यूम]** [化] aluminum; aluminium (기호 Al). e.g. 알루미늄을 입히다

알리다 **[आल्लीदा]** [알게 하다] let <a person> know; [전하다] tell <a person about [that]>; inform <a person of a matter>; [통보하다]

notify; report; [예고하다] give notice; [공표하다] announce.

알리바이 [आल्लीबाइ] an alibi.

알맞다 [आल्मात्ता] [적당하다] suitable; proper; right; [다루기 쉽다, 편리하다] handy; [도를 지나치지 않다] moderate; [타당 하다] proper; reasonable.

알맹이 [आल्मैंगी] [껍데기 속에 든 것] a kernel; [실질] substance; matter; [내용] contents.

알몸 [आल्मोम] **1** [아무것도 입지 않음] nakedness; nudity; a naked [nude] body.**2** [가진 것이 없음] pennilessness.

알선 [आल्सौन] [**斡旋**] **1** [주선] good [kind] offices; service; recommendation. **2** mediation; intercession; (노동 쟁의의) conciliation. 알선-하다 mediate <between>; intercede <with a person for another>; conciliate; go between <two parties>; act as a medium <for

알쏭달쏭하다 [आल्सोंग्दाल्सोंख्वादा] [분간이 안 되다] inscrutable; incomprehensible; vague; ambiguous; obscure; equivocal; evasive; elusive; dubious; shady; indefinite; dim; hazy.

알아내다 [आरानैदा] get <information> out of <a person>; find out <the truth>; discover; detect; worm [pump] <a secret> out of <a person>; (의미 등을) make out; grasp; understand.

알아듣다 [आरादुत्ता] [남의 말뜻을 알다] catch; get; follow; understand; comprehend; [납득하다] hear [listen to] reason; be reasonable; [분간하다] recognize; tell <a difference>by hearing.

알아맞히다 [आरामाछीदा] guess right; make a good guess; hit the mark.

알아보다 [आराबोदा] **1**조사하다] examine (into); investigate; check (up on); look into [over]; [살펴보다] search; feel out; [확인하다] ascertain; [문의하다] inquire; refer <to>. **2** [분간하다] recognize; make out; [판단 하다] judge (of).

알아주다 [आराजूदा] **1** (인정해주다) recognize; appreciate; acknowledge. **2**[이해해 주다] understand; feel for[with]; sympathize <with>.

알아차리다 [आराछारीदा] [깨닫다] realize; discover; notice; become aware <of>; perceive; find; take notice <of>; be awakened to.

알아채다 [आराछैदा] sense; perceive; detect; suspect; become aware <of / that>;

be conscious <of>; scent; get wind [scent] of; guess; infer; gather; surmise; smell; have an inkling of..

알알하다 [आलआरहादा] (매워서) pungent; piquant; <서술적> taste hot; have burning taste; (상처 등이) smart; <서술적> have a tingling pain.

알은체하다 [आरुन्छेहादा] **1** (어떤 일에 대해) poke [thrust] one's nose into; butt [break / cut] in; show concern [interest]; [간섭하다] interfere [meddle] in. **2** (사람을 보고) recognize; notice.

알음알음 [आरुम्आरुम] **1** [아는 관계] mutual acquainttance. **2** [친분] shared intimacy; friendship.

알짜 [आल्चा] the essence; the quintessence; the pith (and marrow); the cream; the pick; the choice; the best.

알짱거리다 [आल्चाक्कौरीदा] **1** [알랑거리며 속이다] cajole; coax. **2** [자꾸 돌아다니다] loaf around idly; hang around [about]; ramble about.

알칼리 [आल्खाल्ली] alkali.

알코올 [आल्खोओल] alcohol; spirits.

알파벳 [आल्फाबेत] (문자) the alphabet.

알현 [आरह्यौन] [謁見] a royal audience; an audience.

알현하다 [आरह्यौनहादा] be received in audience; have [be granted] an audience with; be presented to.

앎 [आम] knowledge; learning; information; wisdom.

앓다 [आल्था] **1** (병을) suffer from; be ill <with>; be sick; be afflicted [troubled] <with>. **2** <비유> be worried <about>; be troubled [distressed / afflicted] <with>.

앓이 [आरी] [병의 뜻을 나타내는 말].

암[1] [आम] [癌] cancer.

암[2] [आम] [생물의 자성] a female.

암거래 [आम्कौरै] [暗去來] black-market [underground] dealings [activities]; underhand [undercover] transactions; black-marketeering; under-the-table transactions.

암기 [आम्की] [暗記] learning by heart; memorizing; memory work.

암기하다 [आम्कीहादा] learn by heart [by rote]; get (off) by heart; commit to memory; memorize; con.

암내 [आम्नै] (겨드랑이의) body odor

암담 [आम्दाम] [暗擔] 암담하다 dark; gloomy; dismal; depressing; hopeless.

암매 [आम्मै] [暗買] black-marketing; black-marketeering; a black-market purchase; unauthorized [illegal] purchase.

암벽 [आम्ब्यौक] [岩壁] a rockwall; a wall of rock; a rock face.

암산 [आम्सान] [暗算] mental arithmetic; mental calculation.

암살 [आम्साल] [暗殺] (an) assassination. 암살하다 assassinate.

암소 [आम्सो] a cow; (새끼를 낳지 않은 3세 미만의) a heifer.

암송 [आम्सोंग] [暗誦] recitation; recital. sh.

암송하다 [आम्सोंखादा] recite; repeat from memory; say [recite] by rote; say by heart.

암수 [आम्सू] male and female; both sexes.

암술 [आम्सूल] [植] a pistil.

암시 [आम्शी] a hint; a suggestion; an intimation; an allusion.

암시장 [आम्सीजांग] [暗市場] a black market.

암실 [आम्सील] [暗室] a (photo) darkroom.

암암리 [आमअमरी] [暗暗裡] tacitness; implicitness.

암운 [आम्उन] [暗雲] dark [murky / sullen] clouds.

암자 [आम्जा] [庵子] [작은 절] a small (Buddhist) temple; [중의 거처] a hermitage; a (hermit's) cell [cottage].

암캐 [आम्खै] a she-dog; a bitch.

암컷 [आम्खौत] a female (animal / bird / insect); a she; a doe (사슴, 토끼, 양,염소 등의).

암탉 [आम्थाक] a hen; a pullet (1년 미만의 어린).

암퇘지 [आम्थ्वैजी] a female hog; a sow.

암투 [आम्थू] [暗鬪] a secret [smoldering] strife [feud]; veiled enmity.

암표 [आम्फ्यो] [暗票] a scalper's ticket; an illegal ticket.

암호 [आमहो] [暗號] a secret language; a cryptograph; a cryptogram; (전신의) a cipher; a (secret) code; (군호) a password; a watchword; a countersign.

암흑 [आम्हुक] [暗黑] darkness; blackness.

암흑가 [आमहुक्का] the underworld; a gang land.

압권 [आप्क्वॉन] [壓卷] **1** [다른 것보다 뛰어난 것] the best; a masterpiece. **2** [가장 훌륭한 부분] the best part <of a book>; the highlight <of the evening

압도 [आप्तो] [壓倒] overwhelming; overcoming; surpassing. 압도하다 overwhelm; overpower; overcome; overrule; crush; weigh down; [능가하다] surpass; excel; exceed; outrival.

압력 [आम्न्यौक] [壓力] **1** [理] pressure; <gravitational> stress. e.g. 대기 압력 atmospheric pressure. **2**<유> pressure. e.g. 경제적 압력 economic pressure <on consumers

압류 [आम्न्यू] [押留] attachment; seizure; dis-traint; distress. 압류 하다 attach; seize; distrain; place <a person's property> under distraint. e.g. 재산을 압류하다 attach [levy (distress) on] <a person's> property.

압사 [आप्सा] [壓死] death from pressure. 압사하다 be crushed [pressed / squeezed] to death.

압송 [आप्सोंग] [押送] ending <a criminal> in custody. 압송하다 send <a criminal> under escort; transfer a convict [prisoner] to <a different> prison.

압수 [आप्सू] [押收] a) seizure; (a) confiscation; attachment. 압수하다 seize; take over; attach; confiscate; (증권, 서류 등을) impound; take legal possession of <a person's property>.

압승 [आप्सुंग] [壓勝] an overwhelming [a sweeping] victory; (선거에서의) a landslide (victory). 압승-하다 win an overwhelming victory <over>; defeat decisively [overwhelmingly]; over-whelm; swamp.

압정 [आप्चौंग] [押釘] a thumbtack; a tack; a pushpin; a drawing pin.

압제 [आप्चे] [壓制] oppression; tyranny; despotism. 압제하다 oppress; tyrannize <over>; rule with an iron hand; rule with a rod of iron.

압착 [आप्छाक] [壓搾] pressure; compression; pressing. 압착하다 press; compress.

압축 [आप्छुक] [壓縮] **1** [줄임P좁힘] compression; constriction; condensation.**2** [요약] condensation; summarization; epitomization. e.g. 다섯 권의 저서를 한 권으로 압축하다 condense a five-volume book into one.

앗 [आत] [다급하거나 놀랐을 때 내는 소리] oh!; o dear!; Dear me!; Good (ness) gracious! (Good) heavens!; By Jove!; God bless me!;

앗아가다 [आसागादा] take [snatch] <something> away <from a person>.

았자 [आच्चा] [...을 인정하더라도] even if[though] ...; granting [supposing] that .... e.g. 당신이 지금 가보았자 그를 만나지는 못한다 Even if you start now, you will not be able to see him.

앙갚음 [आंग्गाफुम] tit for tat; an eye for an eye; rev-

ㅇ

enge; retaliation; requital. 앙갚음 하다 give [pay] tit for tat; revenge <one's wrongs>; revenge oneself [be revenged / have one's revenge] <on a person for something>; get even [square] with <a person>; retaliate on [against] <a person>; pay back; get back at [on] <a person>.

앙금 [आंग्गुम] [침전물] sediment; settlings; deposit; (술 등의) dregs; lees; (커피 등의) grounds.

앙숙 [आंग्सूक] [**快宿**] [앙심을 품고 미워함] e.g. 앙숙이다 lead a cat-and-dog life / be at enmity <with> / be at loggerheads <with> / be on bad terms <with>. W

앙심 [आंग्शीम] [**怏心**] spite; grudge; ill will; rancor. e.g. 앙심 깊은 여자 a revengeful [vindictive] woman. 앙심을 품다[먹다] bear <a person>(an) ill will; have [harbor] a grudge against <a person>. e.g. 그는 나에게 앙심을 품고 있다 He has a grudge against me.

앙코르 [आंग्खोर] an encore. e.g. 앙코르를 받다 receive [get] an encore

앙큼하다 [आंग्खुमहादा] overambitious; audacious; presumptuous. ⇨ 엉큼하다

앙탈 [आंग्थाल] 앙탈하다 [앙탈부리다] scheme to disobey; try to evade [shirk]; grumble angrily; whine; nag; fuss; do against.

앞 [आप] **1** [전면] the front; the fore part; [전방] ahead; beyond; off; away. **2** [행렬, 순서의 먼저] the head; the foremost; the first (맨 앞). **3** [미래] the future.

앞가림 [आप्कारिम] 앞가림하다 have just enough education to get by.

앞날 [आम्नाल] the days ahead [to come]; one's future; [여생] the remaining years [days] (of one's life).

앞당기다 [आप्दांगिदा] move up; advance <a date>; make <anything> earlier. e.g. 여행 예정을 앞당기다 curtail one's itinerary.

앞두다 [आप्तुदा] have <a period / distance> ahead; have <an examination> near [close] at hand. e.g. 졸업을 앞둔 학생 a student about to graduate.

앞뒤 [आपद्वी] **1** (위치의) front and rear. **2** [순서] order. e.g. **3** [일관성] coherence; consistency; [조리] logical sequence. **4** [문맥] the context.

앞뜰 [आप्तुल] a front yard [court / garden].

앞못보다 [आम्मोप्पोदा] **1** [소경이다] be blind; can't see

what is going on. **2** [무식하다] be ignorant.

앞서 [आप्सौ] **1** [이전에] previously; before; earlier. **2** 다른 사람, 다른 일보다 먼저] before; earlier (than); prior to; ahead <of>; in advance <of>.

앞서거니 뒤서거니 [आप्सौगौनी द्वीसौगौनी] e.g. 앞서거니 뒤서거니 하다 alternate for [in] lead; run neck and neck; be nip and tuck.

앞세우다 [आप्सेउदा] [앞서게 하다] make <a person> go ahead; let <a person> lead [precede]; set <a person> at the head.

앞잡이 [आप्चाबी] **1** [안내자] a guide; a cicerone (관광 객의); a leader. [끄나풀 노릇을 하는 사람] an agent; a tool; a cats-paw; a pawn; a minion.

앞장 [आप्चांग] [선두] the lead; the head; [선두에 서서 가는 사람] a leader; a pioneer; the vanguard.

앞지르다 [आप्जीरूदा] outrun; pass <another in the race>; outstrip; steal a march upon; be beforehand with; outpace; pass <another car> ahead; outsail (배가); get ahead of <another>; [능가하다] outdo; surpass.

앞치마 [आप्छीमा] an apron. e.g. 앞치마를 두르고 일하다 work in an apron.

애[1] [ऐ] **1** [초조, 걱정] anxiety; worry; trouble **2** [수고로움] pains; trouble; effort (s); labor(s).

애[2] [ऐ] [맨 처음] the very first; [어린] infant; very young; fresh; [앳된] childish; boyish; green.

애걸 [ऐगौल] **[哀乞]** begging; pleading; imploring; supplication; entreaty; an appeal.

애걸하다 [ऐगौरहादा] beg [plead] for; implore; cry <a person> mercy; ask for mercy.

애견 [ऐग्यौन] **[愛犬]** one's pet dog.

애교 [ऐग्यौ] **[愛嬌]** charms; winsomeness; attractiveness; courtesy (상인 등의).

애국 [ऐगूक] **[愛國]** patriotism; love [devotion] of [for] one's country.

애국가 [ऐगूकका] **[愛國歌]** the Korean national anthem. e.g. 애국가를 부르다 sing our [the Korean] national anthem.

애꿎다 [ऐकुत्ता] innocent; blameless; guiltless; undeserved.

애끓다 [ऐकुल्था] be anxious [worried] <about>; worry (oneself) <about>; be all roiled up; be in a fidget [a stew] <about>. e.g. 애끓어 병이 나다 fret

C

[worry] oneself ill.

애니메이션 [ऐनीमेइस्यौन] [동화] a cartoon film; an animated cartoon.

애달프다 [ऐदाल्फुदा] heartbreaking; aching; sorrowful; pathetic; painful; distressing; anguishing. e.g. 애달픈 소식 heartbreaking news.

애도 [ऐदो] [哀悼] condolence; sympathy; mourning; grief; sorrow; lamentation; regret. 애도하다 lament; be grieved <at>; grieve; mourn <over>; sorrow <over a person's death

애독자 [ऐदोक्जा] [愛讀者] a devoted reader; (정기 적인) a regular reader; (잡지, 신문의) a subscriber. e.g. 동아 일보의 애독자 a subscriber to the Dong-A.

애련하다 [ऐर्यौन्हादा] piteous; pitiable; pitiful; poor; touching.

애매하다 [ऐमैहादा] [불확실하다] uncertain; indefinite; [불명료하다] unclear; [이도저도 아니다] noncommittal; [모호하다] vague; ambiguous; equivocal (▷ ambiguous 는 고의로 속이려는 의도가 있다고는 할 수 없으나, equivocal 은 고의로 발뺌 하려는 의도가 수반됨).

애먹다 [ऐमौक्ता] have bitter experience; have a hard time of it; be greatly embarrassed; have trouble; suffer [go through] hardships; be hard put to it; be at [be driven to] one's wit's end; find <a person / a thing> unmanageable.

애먹이다 [ऐमौगीदा] put <a person> out; put <a person> at [drive <a person> to] his wit's end; give <a person> much trouble.

애모 [ऐमो] [愛慕] love; yearning; affection <for / toward>; attachment <to / for>.

애무 [ऐमू] [愛撫] caress; caressing; a pet stroke; petting; endearment.

애벌 [ऐबौल] [초벌] the first [preliminary] stage (in the procession of work).

애석 [ऐसौक] [哀惜] [슬픔] lamentation; grief; sorrow; [서운함] regret; repentance; disappointment. 애석하다 feel [be] sorry <for / that>; repent <for> sad; sorrowful; mournful; doleful; plaintive; repentant; pitiful; regrettable; disappointing.

애송이 [ऐसोंगी] a very young [a new] person; a greenhorn; a novice.

애수 [ऐसू] [哀愁] an indefinable sadness; (문학 작품 등의) pathos.

애쓰다 [ऐसुदा] [힘쓰다]

make efforts; take pains; work hard; take trouble; exert oneself; endeavor; strive; struggle; labor; try hard; (남을 위해) render service [assistance] <to>; render [do] <a person> a service.

애완 [ऐवान] [愛玩] e.g. 애완용 a pet. 애완용 고양이 a pet cat. 애완용으로 삼다 [만들다] make a pet of <a dog>. 나는 애완용으로 개를 기르고 있다 I keep a dog as a pet.

애용하다 [ऐयोंगहादा] use regularly [habitually]; make habitual use of; patronize.

애원 [ऐवॉन] [哀願] <文> (an) entreaty; an appeal; supplication.

애인 [ऐइन] [愛人] a lover; (여성에 대하여) one's love; a ladylove; one's (best) girl; (남녀 모두) one's steady; a sweetheart.

애절하다 [ऐजौरहादा] pathetic; plaintive; mournful; sorrowful; sad.

애정[1] [ऐजौंग] [愛情] love; affection; attachment; devotion; a tender feeling [sentiment / emotion].

애정[2] [ऐजौंग] [哀情] pity; compassion; sadness.

애주 [ऐजू] [愛酒] 애주하다 drink [take] habitually; be fond of drinking.

애증 [ऐजुंग] [愛憎] love and hatred [hate].

애지중지 [ऐजीजुंग्जी] [愛之重之] 애지중지하다 treasure; prize; cherish; set great value on; love blindly; value highly; set store by; dote on [upon]; wrap in cotton wool.

애착 [ऐछाक] [愛着] attachment; love; affection; devotion.

애창 [ऐछांग] [愛唱] 애창하다 love to sing <a song>.

애처 [ऐछौ] [愛妻] one's (beloved) wife; one's dear wife.

애처롭다 [ऐछौरोप्ता] plaintive; piteous; pitiable; pitiful; touching; sorrowful; sad-looking.

애초 [ऐछो] the very first; the beginning; the outset [start]; the commencement.

애칭 [ऐछीग] [愛稱] a term of endearment; a pet [a affectionate] name; a nickname.

애타다 [ऐथादा] be nervous <about>; be anxious [worried] <about / for>; be in suspense; be jittery; be on tenterhooks; be in a stew; be impatient.

애태우다 [ऐथैउदा] (남을) worry; bother; fidget; fret <a person's> heart; keep [hold] <a person> in suspense; put [throw] <a person> into a flutter; (자기 자신에 대하여) be

[feel] anxious <about>; worry (oneself) <about>; bother (oneself) <about>; trouble oneself <with>; fidget <about>; jitter <about>; be impatient.

애통 [ऐथोंग] [哀痛] 애통하다 sad and painful; <서술적> grieve [be grieved] <at / over>; deplore; lament; be distressed <over>; mourn <for / over>.

애틋하다 [ऐथुस्हादा] **1** [애타다] worried; anxious. **2** [아깝고 서운하다] regretable; pitiful.

애향심 [ऐह्यांग्सीम] love for one's hometown [native place]. e.g.

애호 [ऐहो] [愛護] protection; kind (ly) treatment; tender [loving] care. 애호하다 protect; treat <an animal> kindly [with tender care]; be kind to <an animal>.

애호 [ऐहो] [愛好] love <for / of>; a liking <for>. 애호하다 love; be fond of; have a liking for; care for <movies>.

애환 [ऐह्वान] [哀歡] joys and sorrows.

액[1] [ऐक] [額] (분량) a quantity; an amount; a volume; (수효) a number; (액수) a sum; an amount of money.

액[2] [ऐक] [液] (과즙) juice; (액체) a liquid; (유동체) a fluid; (수액) sap; (용액) a solution; (분비액) secretion.

액땜 [ऐक्तैम] [厄 −] an escape from a calamity. e.g. 액땜으로 여기다 bear <a misfortune> as the price for the escape from a misfortune of greater degree.

액면 [ऐक्म्यौन] [額面] **1** ⇨ 액면 가격 e.g. 액면 이상으로 [이하로] above [below] par / at a premium [discount]. 액면에 달하다 reach par. 액면대로 at par. 주식은 액면 이상으로 팔리고 있다 The shares are selling at a premium. **2** [표면상의 가치]. e.g. 그의 이야기는 액면대로 받아들일 수 없다 We can't take his story at face value. / We must take his story with a pinch [grain] of salt.

액세서리 [ऐक्सेसोरी] accessories; accessaries. e.g. 그녀는 좀체 액세서리를 달지 않는다 She seldom wears accessories.

액수 [ऐक्सू] [額數] a sum; an amount <of money>.

액운 [ऐगुन] [厄運] a misfortune; ills; adverse [bad] fortune; an evil [untoward / adverse] fate; a bad luck.

액자 [ऐक्चा] [額子] a (picture) frame.

액체 [ऐक्छे] [液體] liquid; fluid.

앨범 [ऐल्बौम] an album. e.g. 붙이는 앨범 a paste-in album. 끼워 넣는 앨범 a slip-in album.

앳되다 [ऐत्दवैदा] <서술적> look young for [younger than] one's age.

앵[ऐंग] [벌레가 나는 소리] humming; buzzing; with a buzz [a bum].

앵무새 [ऐंग्मूसै] [鸚鵡-] [鳥] a (gray) parrot; a parakeet.

야[1] [या] **1** [놀라거나 반가울 때의 소리] Oh!; Oh my!; Dear me!; Wow!; Good Gracious!; Good [Great] Heavens!; By Jove!; Gosh; Gee! Oh!; Ah! **2** [허물없이 부를 때의 소리] hello; hullo; hallo; hey; hi; I say; come; hey there; there; here.

야[2] [या] **1** [한정, 강조]. e.g. 결과야 어찌되건 내가 알바 아니다 I don't care for what may come of it. / I don't care for [I can't help] the consequence. **2** [호칭] hullo; hello; hallo; hi. e.g. 철수야 my dear Ch?-su!

야간 [यागान] [夜間] night; nighttime

야경 [याड्यौंग] [夜景] a night [nocturnal] view [scene].

야광 [याग्वांग] [夜光] noctilucence.

야구 [याग़ु] [野球] baseball. 야구를 하다 play baseball.

야근 [यागुन] [夜勤] [야간 근무] night duty; night work; (주야 교대의) a night shith. 야근하다 be on night work [shith]; take night duty.

야기 [यागी] [惹起] 야기하다 bring about; provoke; induce; create; cause. .

야단 [यादान] [惹端] [소란] an uproar; a clamor; a hubbub; a tumult; a dim; a racket; [소동] a commotion; a stir

야당 [यादांग] [野黨] the party out of office; (양당 제의) the Opposition (party).

야릇하다 [यारुस्हादा] odd; queer; strange; peculiar; curious; mysterious.

야만 [यामान] [野蠻] savageness; barbarism; barbarity

야망 [यामांग] [野望] (an) ambition; (an) aspiration; a great desire. e.g. 야망이 있는 ambitious / aspiring

야말로 [यामाल्लो] the very; just; indeed; precisely; exactly; really.

야무지다 [यामूजीदा] hard; strong; tough; firm; solid. e.g. 야무진 목소리 a firm voice. 야무진 사람 a man of firm [strong] character

야박 [याबाक] [野薄] coldheartedness; hardheartedness; heartlessness; coolness (of heart); cruelty. 야박하다 unfeeling; heart-

ㅇ

less; coldhearted; stonehearted.

야비 [याबी] [**野卑, 野鄙**] vulgarity; meanness; boorishness; bad taste. 야비하다 [속되고 천하다] vulgar; crude; [거칠고 막되다] coarse; [거칠고 사납다] rude; [천하고 비루하다] base; mean; [무례하다] ill-mannered.

야생 [यासैंग] [**野生**] wildness. e.g. 야생의 wild / ferine / feral / savage / undomesticated. 야생의 사슴 a wild deer. 야생의 동백 a wild camellia.

야생하다 (식물이) grow wild; (동물이) live in the wild state. e.g. 벚나무는 야생한다 These cherry trees grow wild [naturally].

야성 [यासौंग] [**野性**] wild [savage / unpolished] nature; rusticity; uncouthness.

야속 [यासोक] [**野俗**] 야속하다 unkind; unfeeling; heartless; coldhearted; inhospitable; unfriendly; unsympathetic; pitiless. 야속히 unkindly; unfeelingly; heartlessly; pitilessly.

야수 [यासू] [**野獸**] a wild [savage] animal [beast]; beasts of the field.

야시(장 [यासी])[**夜市(場)**] a night market; a night fair.

야식 [यासीक] [**夜食**] a midnight [late-night] meal [snack].

야심 [यासीम] [**野心**] **1**[야망] (an) ambition. **2**[나쁜 계획] an ill design.

야심작 [यासीम्जाक] an ambitious work.

야영 [यायौंग] [**野營**] encampment; camping-out; bivouac. 야영하다 encamp; pitch (a) camp; make camp; camp out; (군인이) bivouac **야옹** [고양이의 울음 소리] me(o)w.

야외 [यावै] [**野外**] [들] the fields; [옥외] the open air; the outdoors; [교외] the outskirts <of a town>; the suburbs <of a city.

야위다 [यावीदा] become [grow / get] thin [lean / spare]; lose (one's) weight; (병으로) lose flesh; (근심으로) pine away.

야유 [यायू] [**揶揄**] [남을 빈정거려 놀림] ridicule; jeering; heckling; raillery; banter; hooting; catcalling. 야유하다 jeer; (불만, 경멸을 나타내어) hoot; (부 소리내어) boo; (쉬 소리 내어) hiss; [웃음거리로 만들다] make fun of; [비웃다] ridicule; deride. .

야유회 [यायुह्वै] a picnic.

야채 [याछै] [**野菜**] = 채소.

야하다 [याहादा] [**冶-**] [남의 눈에 띄다] showy; [저속, 화려하다] gaudy; [값싸다] tawdry; [색깔 등이 강하다]

garish; loud.

약[1] [याक] [約] about; some; nearly; approximately <100>; <100> in round numbers [figures

약[2] [याक] 약(이) 오르다 (1) [화나다] be [feel] sore [angry] <at / about>; feel irritated [injured]; feel vexed [annoyed] <with a person / at a thing>; be chagrined <at>; be nettled [exasperated].

약[3] [याक] [藥] **1** [약품] (a) medicine; a drug; a remedy; (가루약) a powder; (환약) a pill; (정제) a tablet; (캡슐) a capsule **2** [몸이나 마음에 유익한 것] benefit; good; remedy.

약간 [याककान] [若干] a number <of>; an undetermined number <of>; a few; a bit; somewhat; a little; any (▷ 의문문,조건절 에서).?

약골 [याककोल] [弱骨] **1** [몸이 약한 사람] a weakling; a weak [feeble] fellow; <美> a jellyfish. **2** [약한 골격] a weak [feeble / delicate] build [constitution].

약국 [याककूक] [藥局] **1** [약방] a pharmacy; a drugstore; a chemist's (shop). **2**(병원의) a dispensary; a pharmacist's office; (의사의) a (doctor's) medicine room.

약다 [याकता] shrewd; clever; smart; smartish; sharp; cunning; keen; wide-awake; [재치있다] tactful.

약도 [याकतो] [略圖] a (rough) sketch; (지도의) a rough [route / sketch] map <of>; (설계 등의) a rough plan <of>.

약력 [याग्न्यौक] [略歷] a brief summary of a person's career; a brief history; a brief personal record; a sketch of one's life; (죽은 사람의) a memoir.

약물 [याकमूल] [藥物] drugs-tuffs; drugs; medicines; medicinal substances; <라> materia medica.

약분 [याकबून] [約分] [數] abbreviation; reduction (of a fraction) to its lowest [lower] terms (▷lowest 는 기약 분수로 하기).

약삭빠르다 [याकसाकपारुदा] [실제적 일에 기민하다] shrewd; [판단력 등이 날카롭다] astute; [꾀가 많다] smart.

약소 [याकसो] [弱小] the weak and small; the weak; the minor; the lesser; [약하고 작음] puniness. 약소하다 puny; small and weak.

약소하다 [याकसोहादा] [略少-] [적다] few; little; scanty; [보잘것없다] trifling; slight; trivial; meager. e.g. 약소한 돈 a petty sum of money.

약속 [याक्सोक] [**約 束**] **1** [서약 (하기)] a promise; [협약] an agreement; [서약한 말] one's word. **2** (만날) an appointment; an engagement; (특히 이성과의) a date. 약속하다 make an appointment[an engagement] <with>.

약수 [याक्सू] [**藥水**] medicine [mineral] water

약수터 [याक्सूथौ] a mineral spring; a spa.

약용 [याझोंग] [**藥 用**] medicinal use. e.g.이 식물의 뿌리는 약용이 된다 The root of this plant can be used for edicinal urposes. 약용하다 use <a thing> for medicinal purposes.

약육강식 [याझूक्कांग्सीक] [**弱肉強食**] the survival of the fittest; the law of the jungle; the right of the strongest.

약자[1] [याक्चा] [**弱者**] a person of feeble strength; a weak person; <집합적> the weak. e.g. 약자를 괴롭 히다 bully [tyrannize over] the weak.

약자[2] [याक्चा] [**略字**] (한자의) an abbreviated [a simplified / a simpler] form (of a Chinese character).

약재 [याक्चै] [**藥 材**] medicines; drugs; drugstuffs; pharmaceuticals; medica.

약점 [याक्चौम] [**弱點**] a weak point [spot / side]; a weakness; a vulnerable point; [결점] a shortcoming; a defect; a flaw; [불리한 점] a disadvantage; one's blind side; [아픈 곳] a sore spot [place].

약정 [याक्चौंग] [**約定**] [약속] a promise; an engagement; [계약] a contract; a compact; a bargain (매매); [협정] an agreement; an understanding; an arrangement; a convention; [계약 조항] a stipulation. 약정하다 promise; agree; engage; contract; bargain for <something>; stipulate for <something>; make a contract; enter into an agreement.

약조 [याक्चो] [**約條**] [언약] a promise; a pledge; [규정] rule; an agreement; a condition. 약조 하다 promise; pledge.

약초 [याक्छो] [**藥草**] a medicinal herb; a medical plant.

약탈 [याक्थाल] [**掠 奪**] plunder; pillage; loot; spoilage; spoliation; despoilation; despoilment. 약탈하다 plunder; pillage; despoil; loot; sack; strip <a person of something>; ravage <a land>.

약품 [याक्फूम] [**藥品**] [의약품] (a) medicine; a drug; [화학 약품] a chemical medicine 은 질병을 치료

하는 것, drug 는 치료하는 것, 유독한 것, 잠이 오게 하는 것 등 그 효능이 가지가지임).

약하다 [याक्हादा] [弱-] weak; feeble; [부서지기 쉽다] frail; fragile; [허약하다] weakly; infirm; [미약하다] faint; feeble; [섬약하다] delicate; (술 등이) light; mild; [잘못하다] unskilled; poor.

약학 [याक्हाक] [藥學] [약제학] pharmacy; [약리학] pharmacology.

약혼 [याख्वोन] [約婚] an engagement; a promise to marry; a betrothal. e.g. 그는 그녀와의 약혼을 파기했다 He broke (off) their engagement. 약혼 하다 be engaged <to>; promise to marry; make an engagement; engage oneself <to a person / to marry a person>; betroth oneself <to a person>; be engaged [betrothed] <to>. e.g. 그녀는 학자와 약혼 했다 She got engaged to a scholar.

약화 [याख्वा] [弱化] weakening; enfeeblement. 약화하다 [याख्वाहादा] become weak [weaker]; weaken.

약효 [याख्यो] [藥效] the efficacy [virtue / power / effect] of a medicine [drug]; remedial result.

얄궂다 [याल्कुत्ता] [야릇하고 짓궂다] perverse; treacherous; nasty; provoking; aggravating; quaint; queer; odd; curious; [얄망 궂다] eccentric; erratic.

얄밉다 [याल्मीप्ता] hateful; detestable; disgusting; spiteful; provoking; mean (and nasty); [뻔뻔스럽다] saucy; cheeky.

얄팍하다 [याल्फाख्वादा] [얇다] thin; small <volume>; sleazy <blanket>; [천박 하다] shallow <argument>; shallow-minded; superficial <knowledge>.

얇다 [याल्दा] thin.

얌전하다 [याम्जौन्हादा] [겸손하다] modest; [온화하다] meek; [조용하다] quiet; gentle; [예절 바르다] well-behaved; [착하다] good; [고분고분하다] obedient; submissive; docile; [행실이 좋다] well-behaved; as good as gold (어린 아이가); well-[mild-] mannered.

얌전히 [온순히] gently; meekly; [고분고분히] obediently; docilely; [조용히] quietly; like a lamb [sheep].

양[1] [यांग] [孃] Miss.

양[2] [यांग] [洋] [동서양] the East and the West..

양[3] [यांग] [量] **1** [수량] quantity; [총량] amount; [용

량] volume; [數] magnitude. **2**⇨ 분량 **3** ⇨ 식량(食量)

양[4] **[यांग]** **1** [가장]. e.g. 인양하다 set up for <a scholar> / pose as <a poet> / affect / pretend to. **2** [작정]. e.g.…할 양으로 with the idea [intention / aim] of <doing> / for the purpose of <doing>.

양[5] [यांग] [羊] a sheep <단수,복수 동형>; [수양] a ram; [암양] a ewe; [새끼양] a lamb.

양- [यांग] [**兩**] e.g. 양손 both hands.

양가 [यांग्का] [**兩家**] two [both] houses [families].

양계 [यांग्गै] [**養鷄**] poultry farming [keeping]; chicken raising; egg-raising.

양계하다 raise poultry. farm [yard.

양국 [यांग्गुक] [**兩國**] the two countries.

양궁 [यांग्गुंग] [洋弓] [활] a small Western bow; [양궁경기] a game of (Western) archery.

양극 [यांग्गुक] [**兩極**] [양끝] both extremities; [남북양극] the two [north and south] poles; [양극과 음극] the positive and negative poles. e.g. 양극의 bipolar.

양극단 [यांग्गुकतान] [**兩極端**] both extremes.

양기 [**यांग्गी**] [**陽氣**] **1**[햇볕의 기운] sunshine; sunlight. **2** [양성의 기운] vitality; vital power; vigor.**3** [남자의 정기] energy; virility; vigor; vitality. e.g. 양기 좋은 사람 a man of energy / an energetic man. 양기가 넘치다 be full of energy / have great vigor [energy]. 양기를 보하다 tone up one's energy.

양념 **[यांग्न्यौम]** [향신료] spice(s); condiment (s); <집합적> spicery; [조미료] a seasoning; a flavoring. 양념하다 season; flavor; spice; give flavor to.

양다리 [यांग्दारी] [**兩-**] 양다리(를) 걸치다 try to have [play] it both ways; play (a) double (game); try to have one's cake and eat it too.

양달 [यांग्दाल] [**陽-**] a sunny place [spot].

양도 [यांग्तो] [**讓渡**] a transfer; conveyance; alienation; (어음의) negotiation; assignment; (영토의) cession. e.g. 재산양도 alienation of property. 양도하다 hand [make] over <one's property> to <one's son>; transfer <property to one's son>; alienate <land to a person>; negotiate <securities>; convey (by deed); deed; assign

양동이 [यांग्तोंगी] [洋 -] a (metal) pail; a bucket.

양력 [यांग्न्यौक] [陽曆] the solar calendar.

양로 시설 [यांग्नोशिसौल] an institution for the aged.

양론 [यांग्नोन] [兩論] both arguments; both sides of the argument.

양립 [यांग्नीप] [兩立] coexistence; compatibility. 양립하다 be compatible <with>; be consistent <with>; coexist <with>; stand together.

양말 [यांग्माल] [洋襪] (짧은) socks; (여성용의 긴) stockings; <a pair of> hose (주로 상용어); <집합적> hosiery (<英>에서는 주로 신사용 양말, 내의류를 말함).

양면 [यांग्म्यौन] [兩面] both faces [sides

양모 [यांग्मो] [羊毛] wool.

양반 [यांग्मान] [兩班] **1** (the) *yangban*; the nobility; the aristocratic [*yangban*] class; (한 사람) a *yangban*; a nobleman. **2** [점잖고 착한 사람] a gentleman; a (good) man; [자기 남편] my husband.

양병 [यांग्ब्यौग] [養兵] building up [maintaining / training] an army. 양병 하다 build up [maintain / train] an army.

양보 [यांग्बो] [讓步] concession; conciliation; compromise. 양보하다 concede ; make a concession; compromise; be conciliatory; give way to <a person>; give in; back down; yield <to>; meet <a person> halfway.

양복 [यांग्बोक] [洋服] [서양식 의복] (a suit of) clothes; a suit; a dress; (한복에 대하여) Western [European] clothes.

양봉 [यांग्बोंग] [養蜂] beekeeping; bee raising; (대규모의) apiculture. 양봉하다 keep [culture] bees.

양부모 [यांग्बूमो] [養父母] foster [adoptive] parents.

양분 [यांग्बून] [養分] nourishment; nutriment; nutrient; nutritious substance [matter]; sustenance.

양산 [यांग्सान] [陽傘] a sunshade; a parasol.

양상 [यांग्सांग] [樣相] an aspect; a phase; a condition; appearance; looks; outlook; modality.

양서 [यांग्सौ] [良書] a good book; a valuable work.

양성 [यांग्सौंग] [養成] training <of teachers>; education; nurture; cultivation.

양성하다 [यांग्सौंखादा] train; educate; bring up; rear; cultivate; nurse. two] sexes.

양손 [यांग्सोन] [兩 -] both [two] hands.

양손 [यांग्सोन] [養孫(子)] an adopted [a foster] grandson.

양수 [यांग्सू] [揚水] raising water; pumping (up) water. 양수하다 raise water; pump(up) water

양수기 [यांग्सूगी] [量水器] a water meter [gauge].

양식 [यांग्सीक] [糧食] 1 [먹을 거리] provisions; food; (food) supplies; victuals; (할당된) rations. 2 [지식 등의 원천이 되는 것].

양식 [यांग्सीक] [養殖] raising; culture; cultivation; breeding; rearing. e.g. 굴양식 oyster farming. 진주 양식 culture of. 양식하다 rear; raise; breed; cultivate.

양식장 [यांग्सीकजांग] a nursery; a farm; a breeding ground.

양식 [यांग्सीक] [樣式] 1 [독특한 방식, 형] a mode; a manner; [論] modality; [建] (a) style; an order. 2 [일정한 형식] a (fixed) form.

양식 [यांग्सीक] [洋食] Western [European] food [dishes]; Western cooking [cookery].

양심 [यांग्सीम] [良心] conscience; the inner voice; the still small voice.

양아버지 [यांगाबौजी] [養-] an adoptive father; a foster father.

양어머니 [यांगौमौनी] [養-] an adoptive mother.

양육 [यांग्यूक] [養育] 양육하다 bring up; rear; foster; nurse; raise

양자 [यांग्जा] [養子] an adopted child; one's son by adoption.

양잠 [यांग्जाम] [養蠶] sericulture; silkworm raising; silk culture [raising]. 양잠하다 raise [rear / breed] silkworms.

양조 [यांग्जो] [釀造] brewing; brewage. 양조하다 (맥주를) brew;(증류하여 위스키를) distill [distil].

양주 [यांग्जू] [洋酒] whisk (e) y and wine; alcoholic beverages introduced to Korea from the West.

양지 [यांग्जी] [陽地] a sunny place [spot]; a sunshine; the sun.

양초 [यांग्छो] [洋-] a (wax) candle; a taper (가는 것).

양측 [यांग्छुक] [兩側] both sides [parties]; either side. e.g. 길 양측에 훌륭한 저택들이 줄지어 있었다 The street was lined with fine homes on both sides.

양치기 [यांग्छीगी] [羊-] [양을 치는 일] sheep-raising; [양을 치는 사람] a shepherd.

양친 [यांग्छीन] [兩親] (one's) father and mother; one's parents. e.g. 양친의 parental.

양파 [यांग्फा] [洋-] an onion; (음식물로서의) onion.

양호 [यांग्हो] [良好] 양호하다 good; fine; excellent; favorable; satisfactory.

얕다 [यात्ता] 1 (깊이가)

shallow. e.g. 얕은 접시 a shallow dish. 물이 얕은 곳 a shoal / a shallow. 얕은 물에서 수영하다 swim in shallow water. 시냇물을 얕은 곳에서 건너자 Let's cross the stream where it is shallow. 얕은 내도 깊게 건너라 <속담> One cannot use too much caution. / Much caution does no harm. **2** (생각P지식이) shallow; superficial. (정도, 높이가) slight; low; humble; lowly;(키가) short.

얕보다 [यात्बोदा] look down upon [on] <a person>; make light [little] of; slight; belittle; disparage; depreciate; hold <a person> in contempt; disdain.

얕잡다 [यात्जाप्ता] make a low estimate of; underrate; hold <a person> cheap; belittle; make light of; look down upon

얘 [ऐ] **1** [이애] this child [boy / girl]; he; she; it. **2** (아들을 부를 때) Sonny; My boy; (남을 부를 때) You; Hey; Buster; Here; There.

어 [ओ] [놀람 등을 나타내는 소리] Oh!; Why!; Well!; [손아랫사람에게 대답하는 소리] Yes; Yea.

어감 [ओगाम] [**語感**] [말의 뉘앙스] the nuance of a word; [말에 대한 감각] <have> a keen sense of language.

어구 [ओगु] [**語句**] words and phrases. e.g. 어구의 용법 wording / phraseo-logy.

어군 [ओगुन] [**語群**] [문법] a word group.

어귀 [ओग्वी] an entrance; an entry <to a river>; the mouth <of a harbor>; an approach <to a tunnel>.

어그러지다 [ओगुरोजीदा] **1** [빗나가다] be out of joint [order]; be twisted [dislocated]; swerve [deviate] from. **2** [생각과는 맞지 아니하다] be[act] against [contrary to] <the rule>; go against; go back on; run counter to; depart [deviate] from; transgress; violate. **3** 사이가 나쁘게 되다] break [fall out] <with>; become estranged [alienated] <from>; get into discord <with>.

어근 [ओगुन] [**語根**] the root [stem / base / radical] of a word; [문법] a radix <*pl.* ~es, -dices>.

어긋나다 [ओगुन्नादा] **1** [엇갈리다] go crisscross <with>; [일정한 기준에서 벗어나다] run counter <to>; be contrary <to>; go against; go amiss [away]; go wrong; deviate from. **2** [꼭 맞지 아니하다] be out of joint [order]; be dislocated. **3** 호간의 마음에 틈이 벌어지다] become estranged [alienated] <from>; break [fall out] <with>; have a break <in>; have a disagreement <with>.

어기다 [औगीदा] [위반하다] violate; infringe; break; transgress; [상반하다] go [act] against; be contrary to; run counter; go back on; [따르지 않다] disobey; disregard; act against.

어깨 [औकै] **1** (신체의) the shoulder. **2** [맡은 바 책임이나 사명]. e.g.딸이 결혼하여 어깨의 짐을 하나 덜었다 My daughter's marriage was a big load off my mind. / My daughter's marriage took one care from my shoulders

어깨동무 [औकैदोंग्मू] [서로 팔을 얹어 끼기]어깨동무하다 put arms around each other's shoulders; take [hold] each other round the shoulders.

어눌 [औनूल] [**語訥**] 어눌하다 stammer; falter; stutter; <서술적> have an impedement in (one's) speech; be awkward [clumsy] in speech; [말이 느리다] be slow of speech.

어느 [औनु] **1** [어떤] which; what. **2**[그 중의 어느] whichever; any. **3** [한] a; one; [막연한 어떤] a certain; some. e.g.어느 천년에 = 어느 세월에.

어느덧 [औनुदौत] before one knows [is aware]; without one's knowledge; without one's knowing [realizing] it; unawares; unnoticed; while one was not aware of it; so soon.

어느새 [औनुसै] =어느 겨를에 e.g. 어느새 비가 내리고 있었다 It had started raining before I was aware of it [I realized it]. 봄방학도 어느새 지나가 버렸다 The spring vacation [holidays] passed all too soon. 그는 어느새 없어졌다 He had slipped away.

어도 [औदो] e.g.우리는 어떤 일이 있어도 항복하지 않는다 Whatever may come [Come what may], we shall never surrender. 그는 피로하였어도 열심히 일했다 Though (he was) tired, he worked hard.

어두 [औदू] [**語頭**] the beginning of a word. e.g. 어두에 anti-를 붙이다 prefix a word with anti- / place anti- at the beginning of a word.

어두컴컴하다 [औदूख्वौख्वौमहादा] dark; dusky. e.g. 어두컴컴한 밤 a dark night. 어두컴컴한데서 부딪치다 run into <a person> in the dark / collide against <a post> in the dark.

어둑하다 [औदूख्वादा] gloomy; dusky; dim.

어둠 [औदूम] darkness; the dark.

어둡다 [औदूप्ता] **1** [빛이 없다] dark; dim; dusky; murky; gloomy **2** [시력, 청력이 약하다]. e.g. 눈이 어둡다 be weak-sighted / be weak in sight / have bad [weak] sight **3** [잘 알지 못하다] ignorant <of>; not familiar <with>; not well acqua inted <with>; <서술적> be ill informed <of>; be a stranger <to>. **4** [표정,분위기가 무겁고 침울하다] gloomy; dismal; somber; dark; shadowy.

어디 [औदी] [의문] what place; where; [어디쯤] whereabout (s); [어떤 곳] somewhere; anywhere (의문문에서). r. **2** [어떤 점] in some respects; in some way.

어디 [औदी] well; well now; just; let me see. e.g. 어디 두고 보자 You will have to pay for this. / 누가 왔는지 어디 가 보자 I will just go and see who it is. 어디 입어 보아라 Just try it on. 어디 영어 한번 해보아라 Well now, let me hear you speak some English.

어때 [औतै] [어떠해]. e.g. 장사는 어때 How about your business? 산책가면 어때 How about going for a walk? 내말 대로지, 어때 See? I told you so / See? What did I tell you? 꾸지람을 들으면 어때 What if I am scolded? (▷ am 에 악센트를 두고 문미를 내림) / I don't mind if I'm scolded.

어떤 [औतौन] **1** [무슨] what <book> / what kind [sort] of <book> / what ... like.. **2**[여하한]. e.g.어떤 상황 아래에서도 거짓말을 해서는 안 된다 You must not tell a lie under any circumstances. **3** [어느] a certain; one; some. (▷ one 은 부정의 경우, some 은 미지의 사람이나 사물에, a certain 은 알고는 있으나 분명히 하고 싶지 않을 때 씀.

어떻게 [औतौख्वे] **1** [어찌] how; in what way [manner]; by what means. **2** [몹시] how (much); what; so; to what extent. **3** [어떻게든] anyway; anyhow.

어떻게 되다 [औतौख्वे दवैदा] **1** (사람, 일이). e.g. 당신 부인이 집을 나간다면 어떻게 될까 What if your wife should leave home? 도대체 어떻게 된 거냐 [무슨 일이라도 있었느냐] What on earth happened (to you)? / (좀 이상한 경우) What is the matter with you? / What's eating you? 일은 어떻게 되어 가고 있는가 How are you coming along with your work? **2** (그럭저럭) turn out somehow (or other); [변통되다] be managed.

어떻게 하다 [औतौख्वे हादा] do [manage] by some means or other; do somehow; manage somehow; manage to do.

어떻게든 [औतौख्वेदुन] anyway; anyhow; somehow (or other); by some means (or other); by any means.

어떻다 [औतौथा] **1** how; what. e.g. 그 일을 지금 그녀에게 이야기해 주는 것은 좀 어떨까 생각한다 I'm afraid it's not advisable to tell her about it now. **2** (권하면서). e.g.차 한 잔 더 어떻습니까 Won't you [Wouldn't you like to] have another cup of tea? **3** [지정해 말함]. 어떻다고 말하기 힘든 이상한 음악 a weird and indescribable music.

어떻든지 [औतौथुन्जी] anyway; anyhow; in anyway; in any case; at any rate; either way; one way or the other.

어려움 [और्‍यौऊम] [곤란] hardship; difficulty; [곤경] distress; misery; adversity; [수고] trouble; [곤궁] privation; [고뇌] affliction; suffering (s); [시련] a trial; an ordeal.

어려워하다 [और्‍यौवीहादा] feel constraint <in a person's presence>; be afraid of giving trouble; have a regard for <a person's> feelings; have scruples <about doing>; keep <a person> at a (respectable) distance.

어련하다 [और्‍यौन्हादा] certain; natural; infallible; reliable; trustworthy; believable. 어련히 naturally; surely; certainly; undoubtedly; infallibly; as a natural consequence; in the natural course of events.

어렴풋이 [और्‍यौमफूसी] [조금] slightly; [희미하게] vaguely; dimly; faintly; indistinctly; obscurely.

어렴풋하다 [और्‍यौमफूस्हादा] [희미하다] faint; [확실 하지 않다] dim; [막연 하다] vague; indistinct; obscure; dreamy.

.**어렵다 [और्‍यौप्ता]** **1** [힘들다] hard; difficult; laborious; [의심스럽다] doubtful. **2** [까다롭다] troublesome; [미묘하다] delicate. **3** [거북하다] <서술적> feel awkward [constraint]; be [feel] ill at ; have scruples about <doing>. **4** [가난하다] poor; indigent; needy; penurious; destitute.

어루만지다 [औरूमान्जीदा] [마음을 달래다] soothe; calm (down); pacify; mollify; appease. e.g. 화난 아내를 잘 어루만져 주다 appease one's angry wife.

어르신(네) [औरुसीन] **1** [남의 아버지에 대한 존칭] your [his] esteemed [honored] father. e.g. 어르신께서는 안녕하신가 Has your esteemed father been well? / How is your father? **2** [노인,연장자] an elder; sir. e.g. 어르신께서는 그 사람을 어떻게 생각하십니까 Sir, what do you think of the man?

어른 [औरुन] **1**[성인] a man; a woman; an adult; a grown-up(person); a full-grown man. **2** [윗사 람, 노인] a superior; a senior; an elder; an older [elderly] person; [고참] an old-timer.

어른거리다 [औरुनकौरीदा] (눈, 마음에) flicker; glimmer; shimmer; quiver; (빛이) blink.

어른스럽다 [औरुनस्रौप्ता] <look> like a grown-up (person); [조숙하다] precocious.

어른어른 [औरुनौरुन] flickering (ly); glimmering (ly); shimmering (ly); quivering (ly). 어른어른하다 = 어른거리다.

어리광 [औरीग्वांग] a child's winning ways; playing the baby.

어리다[1] [औरीदा] [눈물이 괴다]. e.g.눈에 눈물이 어리다 one's eyes swim [dim / moisten / glisten] with tears / tears stand [there are tears] in one's eyes / tears come to [gather in] one's eyes / be moved to tears / be going to shed tears. **2** [눈에 삼삼하다] haunt; be haunted.

어리다[2] [औरीदा] [나이가 적다] infant; (very) young; juvenile; of tender age [years]. **2** [유치하다] childish; infantile; puerile; immature; [미숙하다] green; crude; raw; inexperienced.

어리둥절하다 [औरीदुंग्जौरहादा] stupefied; stunned; dazed; bewildered; perturbed; embarrassed; perplexed; puzzled; confused; flurried.

어리벙벙하다 [औरीबौम्बौरवादा] dumbfounded; bewildered; dazed; confounded; disconcerted.

어리석다 [औरीसौक्ता] [멍청하다] foolish; stupid; silly (foolish 는 일반적, silly 는 foolish 보다 약간 구어적이고 경멸적으로 쓰이며, 요령이 없다는 등의 뜻을 포함함. Stupid 는 지능이 낮음을 강조함); [조소를 받을 만하다] ridiculous; [도리에 맞지 않다] absurd.

어린이 [औरीनी] 어린이의 juvenile. 어린이의 읽을거리 juvenile reading.

어림 [औरीम] a rough [gross] estimate; an approximation; a (rough) guess.

어림하다 estimate [calculate] roughly; make a rough estimate <of>; guess. 어림(을) 잡다[치다] = 어림하다.

어림없다 [औरीम्औप्ता] wide of the mark; off the point; far <from>; [당찮다] nonsensical; preposterous; absurd; ridiculous; fabulous; unreasonable.

어림짐작 [औरीमजीम्जाक] a rough [random / wild] guess; guesswork. 어림짐작하다 guess <at>; make a shot <at>; make a random guess.

어릿광대 [औरीत्ग्वांग्दै] **1** [광대] a clown; a buffoon; a comedian. **2** [남을 잘 웃기는 사람] a jester; a joker.

어마 (나) [औमा] 어마 예쁘기도 해라 Oh my, beautiful! 어마 이게 누구야 Fancy seeing you! / Good heavens, it is certainly a surprise to see you. 어마 당신이 그런 일을 하다니 Fancy your doing that! 어마 참 많이 컸구나 Oh dear! What a big boy you've grown to be!

어마어마하다 [औमाऔमाहादा] **1** [엄청나다] tremendous; immense; enormous; colossal; [많다] innumerous; stupendous; countless. **2** [과장적이다] high-sounding; ostentatious; pretentious; showy.

어머 (나) [औमौ] Oh!; Why!; Dear me!; My!; O my!; Oh, my goodness; Heavens!; Good gracious!

어머니 [औमौनी] **1** [모친] a mother; <소아어> mamma; mama; mam; mom; mum; mummy; mommy. **2** [사물의 근원] (the) cause; a motive; the mother <of>. e.g. 필요는 발명의 어머니 <속담> Necessity is the mother of invention.

어물거리다 [औमूल्कौरीदा] [주저하다] waver; hesitate; be irresolute; be hesitant; shilly-shally; dillydally; [모호하게 하다] be ambiguous; be noncommittal.

어물어물 [औमुरौमुल] [머뭇거리며] hesitatingly; waveringly; shilly-shally; [모호하게] indefinitely; vaguely; ambiguously; noncommittally.

어미[1] [औमी] [**語尾**] [문법] the end (ing) [termination] of a word. e.g. 어미가 -sh로 끝나는 말 words ending in -sh.

어미[2] [औमी] **1** ⇨ 어머니 **2** [새끼를 낳은 동물의 암컷] a dam; a mother animal. e.g. 어미새 [개 / 고양이] a mother bird[dog / cat].

어민 [औमीन] [**漁民**] fishermen; fisherfolk; fishing people.

어버이 [औबोइ] parents.
어법 [औबोप] [語法] (a mode of) expression; usage (of language); wording; phraseology; grammar; diction.
어부 [औबू] [漁夫, 漁父] a fisherman; a fisher.
어불성설 [औबूल्सौंग्सौल] [語不成說] unreasonable talk; lack of logic; illogicality. e.g. 어불성설이다 be illogical [unreasonable] / do not stand to reason / do not hold any water / lack logic.
어색하다 ,[औसैख्वादा] [語塞-] **1** [말이 막히다] <서술적> be at a loss for a word; be stuck for words; stumble at one's words; falter. **2** [열없다,거북하다] awkward; self-conscious; <서술적> feel awkward [embarrassed / (con) strained / nervous]; feel ill at ease; feel diffident; find it hard to. **3** [서투르다, 부자연스럽다].
-어서 [औसौ] (and) so; and then; to; for; from; as; so as to; so ... that ...; because(of); on account of. e.g. 너무 적어서 나누기가 어렵다 be too little to divide. 이렇게 늦어서 미안합 니다 I'm sorry to be so late.
어서 [औसौ] **1** [빨리] quick (ly); fast; promptly; rapidly; without delay [hesitation]. **2** [부디] please; kindly; [환영의 뜻으로] right; with pleasure; welcome.
어선 [औसौन] [漁船] a fishing boat [vessel / crath]; a fisherboat; a smack (활어조를 갖춘).
어설프다 [औसौल्फुदा] **1** [성기다] coarse; rough; loose. **2** [어색하고 엉성하다] poor; awkward; clumsy; sloppy; slovenly; careless.
어수룩하다 [औसूरूख्वादा] [숫되다] unsophisticated; naive; simple; simple-minded; [어리석다] half-witted; somewhat stupid.
어수선하다 [औसूसौन्हादा] **1** (사물이) disordered; disarranged; confused; <서술적> be in disorder [disarray / confusion]; be out of order; be in a mess [muddle]; (세상이) troublous; tumultuous. **2** (마음이) agitated [confused]; flurried; distracted; disturbed; upset.
어순 [औसून] [語順] word order. e.g. 어순을 틀리다 make an error in the arrangement of words.
어스레하다 [औसुरेहादा] dusky; gloomy; dim. e.g. 어스 레한 빛 dim [feeble / faint] light. 아직 어스레한 새벽 5시였다 It was five in the morning, still gray.
어슬렁거리다 [औसुल्लौंग्गौरीदा] [천천히 걸어다니다] stroll

[ramble] about; saunter [loiter] along; gad about; prowl; [배회하다] hang [loiter / hover / linger] about [around] <a place>.

어슴푸레 [औसुम्फूरे] dimly; faintly; hazily.

-어야 [औया] **1** [당연, 의무, 필요, 유감] should [ought to] <do>; must [have to] <do>; should [ought to] <have done>. e.g. 아이들은 부모님의 말씀을 들어야 한다 Children should obey their parents. **2** [아무리 하여도] however much one may [might] <do>; to whatever extent. e.g. 핑계를 대어야 소용없다 It is no use [good] trying to excuse yourself.

-어야지 [औयाजी] **1** [가벼운 의지] would; be going to. e.g. 그녀에게 빌린 책을 돌려주어야지 I am going to return her a borrowed book. **2** [아쉬움,실망]. e.g. 네 제안을 받아들이고 싶지만 형편이 되어야지 I'd like to accept your proposal, but, unfortunately, I'm in no position to do so.

어업 [औऔप] [**漁業**] fishery; the fishing industry.

어엿하다 [औयौस्हादा] respectable; decent; good; honorable; stately; imposing; unblamable.

어우러지다 [औउरौजीदा] get joined [be put] together (in good harmony); well-matched <with>; harmonized united. e.g. 기름과 물은 어우러지지 않는다 Oil and water do not combine [will not mix].

어우르다 [औउरुदा] [하나로 합치다] put [join] together; unite; combine; [협력하다] go hand in hand <with>.

어울리다 [औउल्लीदा] **1** [어우르게 되다] associate <with>; join <with>; mix [mingle] <with>; keep company <with>.. **2** [조화되다] become; match; suit; fit; befit; go (well) <with>; be becoming <to>; harmonize <with>; be suitable <to / for>; be in keeping <with>.

어원 [औवॉन] [**語源, 語原**] [언어학] the origin [derivation] of a word; etymology.

어음 [औउम] a bill; a drath; a note. -teller; a bill clerk.

어이없다 [औइऔप्ता] amazing; surprising; shocking; absurd; ridiculous; <서술적> be amazed <at>; be appalled <at>; be dum (b) founded; be stunned <by>; be taken aback; be [stand] aghast <at>; be flabbergasted; be shocked [scandalized] <at / by>; be astounded <by>; be disgusted <at / with>.

어정쩡하다 [**औजौन्चौङ्हादा**] [애매하다] noncommittal; ambiguous; borderline; equivocal; vague. e.g. 어정쩡한 대답 a noncommittal [a vague / an equivocal] answer. 어정쩡한 태도를 취하다 take a noncommittal attitude / do not commit oneself / sit on the fence.

어제 [**औजे**] yesterday. e.g. 어제 아침 yesterday morning.

어조 [**औजो**] [**語調**] a tone (of voice); an accent; a note; a strain.

어족 [**औजोक**] [**語族**] a family of languages; a linguistic family.

어줍다 [**औजूप्ता**] **1** [(말,행동이) 조심스러워 자유롭지 못하다] constrained; dull; stiff. **2** [서투르다] unskilled; clumsy; awkward; unhandy.

어중간 [**औजूंग्गान**] [**於中間**] 어중간하다 halfway; noncommittal.

어지간하다 [**औजीगान्हादा**] fair; tolerable; passable; considerable.

어지간히 fairly; pretty; tolerably; passably; considerably.

어지럼 [**औजीरौम**] (증) e.g. 어지럼을 타다 be liable to feel dizzy.

어지럽다 [**औजीरौजील**] **1** [정신이 얼떨떨하다] dizzy; giddy; dazing; vertiginous.]. **2** 란하고 어수선하다] confused; disorderly; untidy; cluttered; disordered; in disorder [disarray]; disturbed; agitated; troubled; chaotic.

어지르다 [**औजीरुदा**] scatter (about); put in [throw into] disorder [confusion]; make untidy [disordered]; disarrange; clutter (up); litter (up); make a better; mess up.

어질다 [**औजील्दा**] [인자하다] benign; benevolent; merciful; gracious; [덕행이 높다] virtuous.

어질어질 [**औजीरऔजील**] 어질어질하다 dizzy; faint; feel dizzy [giddy / faint].

어째서 [**औचैसौ**] why; for what reason [purpose]; what ... for; how come; on what ground.

어쨌든 [**औचैत्तुन**] anyhow; anyway; at any rate; in any case; somehow or other; setting aside [apart]; aside [apart from]; not to speak of; not to mention; whatever; however; whether ... or not.

어쩌다(가) [**औचोदा**] **1** [우연히] accidentally; casually; unexpectedly; by (some) chance; by accident. **2** [이따금] occasionally; once in a while; from time to time; now and then; at times; between times [whiles]; at long

[rare] intervals.

어쩐지 [औचौन्जी] **1** [어찌된 까닭인지] somehow; in some way; for some reason or other; without knowing why. e.g. 어쩐지 슬프다 I feel somewhat sad **2** [그런 연유로] so that is why;(it is) no wonder. e.g. 어쩐지 그가 투덜거리고 있더라 No wonder that he makes complaints.

어찌 [औची] **1** [어떠한 이유로] why; for what reason; how; what ... for; how come. e.g. 어찌 그렇게 말할 수 있단 말이냐 How come you(to) say so? / How can you say a thing **2** [어떠한 방법으로] how; in what way. e.g. 먼길을 어찌 갈꼬 How can I make a long journey?

어찌나 [औचीना] how; what; too; too much; very; quite; so. e.g.어찌나 추웠던지 It was quite[so] cold.

어차피 [औछाफी] [於此彼] anyhow; anyway; one way or the other; in any [either] case; ather all; at all.

어처구니없다 [औछौगूनीऔप्था] e.g. 어처구니없는 거짓말 an egregious lie.

어촌 [औछोन] [漁村] a fishing village [hamlet]; a sea village.

어폐 [औफ्ये] [語弊] a misleading [faulty] expression.

어필 [औफील] an appeal. 어필하다 appeal <to>.

어학 [औहाक] [語學] language study; (언어학) linguistics.

어항 [औहांग] [魚缸] a fish basin1; (유리제) a fish bowl; (둥근 것) a fish globe; (큰 것) an aquarium.

어형 [औह्यौग] [語形] a form of a word; a word form.

어형 변화 [औह्यौग ब्यौन्ह्वा] [문법] (an) inflection; <英> (an) inflexion.

어획 [औह्वैक] [漁獲] fishery; fishing.

어휘 [औह्वी] [語彙] a vocabulary; a glossary.

억 [औक] [億] a[one] hundred million.

억누르 [औग्नुरु] [내리누르다] press [put / hold] down; force down; [진압하다] suppress; put down; repress; subdue; get under; control; bring [keep] under control; oppress; [억제하다] restrain; control; check; master; subdue; contain; resist; keep under; stifle.

억눌리다 [औक्नूल्लीदा] get pressed down; be repressed [suppressed].

억류 [औक्र्यू] [抑留] detention; detainment; internment; seizure. 억류하다 detain; intern; hold in custody; seize; apprehend; (배를) arrest

억세다 [औक्सेदा] **1** [굳고 세차다] strong; tough; firm; stout; tenacious; persistent; pushy; unyielding; resolute; (근육이) brawny; sinewy **억수** a downpour (of rain); a pouring [heavy / torrential / drenching] rain; cloudburst.

억압 [औगाप] [**抑壓**] [억제 활동 금지] suppression; [압박] oppression; [활동 제한] (a) restraint. 억압 하다 suppress <information>; oppress <the people>; restrain; check.

억양 [औङ्यांग] [**抑 揚**] intonation; modulation; accent; swell; infection. 억울하다[抑 鬱 –] mortified <by>; regrettable; feel pent-up [chagrined / mortified / mistreated]; suffer unfairness; (허위) false; untrue; groundless.

억제 [औक्चे] [**抑制**] control; restraint; suppression; repression; holdback; constraint; check; curb; [心] inhibition. 억제하다 restrain; control; check; repress (▷repress 는 주로 무엇인 가를 하고 싶은 기분이나 감정 등을 참는 일); suppress; inhibit <one's desire>; hold [keep] in check.

억지 [औक्ची] (a) push; willfulness; headstrongness; stubbornness; obstinacy; unreasonableness; perversity.

억지로 [औक्चीरो] **1** [무리하게] by force; forcibly; against one's will; willy-nilly; compulsorily; under compulsion. **2** [간신히] with difficulty [much effort].

억지 춘향이 [औक्ची छुन्हयांगी] [– **春 香** –] something narrowly done by force; doing against one's will; compelling; compulsion; coercion; forcing

억척 [औक्छोक] being unyielding [unwieldy]; toughness; stiffness; stubbornness.

억척같다 [औक्छोक्काता] unyielding [unrelenting / tough / strong-minded / dogged].

억측 [औक्छुक] [**臆 測**] a (random) guess; a conjecture; guesswork; a supposition; a speculation; a surmise; an inference. 억측하다 make a guess; surmise; conjecture; speculate <about / upon>; (대중 없이) try a shot in the dark; hazard a conjecture [guess].

언감생심 [औन्ककाम्सैंग्सीम] [**焉敢生心**] [감히 그런 마음을 품을 수도 없음] How dare ...?

언급 [औन्गुप] [**言 及**] reference; mention; comment; allusion. 언급하다 refer <to>; mention; make reference to; make mention of; (간접적으로) allude <to>.

언니 [औन्नी] (여자끼리) an elder [older] sister; (남자끼리) an elder [older] brother.

언더웨어 [औन्दोवीऔ] under-wear; underclothing.

언덕 [औन्दौक] 비탈] a slope; an incline. **2** [작은 산] a hill; a hillock (▷ hill 보다 작음); a knoll; a height; a rise; [둔덕] a mound.

언뜻 [औन्तुत] [얼른] in an instant; suddenly; [문득] by chance; unexpectedly.

언론 [औल्लोन] [**言論**] speech (and writing); discussion; views. 언론 기관 an organ of public opinion [expression].

언문[1] [औन्मून] [**諺文**] the Korean script; the Korean letters. ⇨ 한글

언문[2] [औन्मून] [**言文**] the written and spoken styles of a language; the colloquial and the literary.

언밸런스 [औन्बैल्लोन्स] unbalance.

언변 [औन्ब्यौन] [**言辯**] oratorical talent [skill]; [말씨] speech; [웅변] eloquence.

언성 [औन्सौग] [**言聲**] a voice; a tone (of voice).

언약 [औन्याक] [**言約**] a verbal [an oral] promise; one's word; a vow; a pledge. 언약하다 give [make] a verbal promise; promise orally; give one's word (▷give one's word는 책임 있는 약속을 한다는 뜻). e.g.사랑을 언약하다 exchange vows of love / pledge oneself to each other / plight one's troth.

언어 [औनौ] [**言語**] language; speech (▷ language 는 한 나라, 한 민족의 말처럼 일반적으로 말에 의한 전달 수단을 나타내고, speech 는 현재 사용되고 있는 말을 나타냄); words.

언어학 [औनऔहाक] [**言語學**] linguistics; philology. e.g. 언어학적[상의] linguistic / philological.

언쟁 [औन्जैग] [**言爭**] e.g. 언쟁이 주먹다짐으로 번졌다 They proceeded from words to blows. / The quarrel came to hard blows.

언저리 [औन्जोरी] the edge; the brim; the rim; bounds; limits.

언제 [औन्जे] **1** [의문] when; (at) what time; how soon; what date [day]; whenever. **2** [미래] some day; some time; some other day [time]; in the near future; one of these days; [조만간] sooner or later; sometime or other. **3** [과거] once; the other day. e.g. 언제인지도 모를 시대

부터 from time unknown. 언제 한번 그를 만난 기억이 난다 I remember seeing him once. **4** [항상] always; all the time; [언제고] any time; some time (or other); some day; someday; in(due course of) time.

언제나 [औन्जेना] [항상] always; all the time; at any time; ever; never (부정); [평소] usually; [습관적으로] habitually; [… 할 때마다] every time; whenever; [변함없이] invariably; [끊임없이] constantly.

언제든지 [औन्जेदुन्जी] [어느 때라도] (at) any time; [항상] always; all the time; whenever.

언젠가 [औन्जेन्गा] **1** (과거의) the other day; some time ago; once; on one occasion; at one time. **2** (미래의) sometime; some time; someday; some day; one day; one of these days; before long.

언중 유골 [औन्जुंग युगोल] [**言中有骨**] the implied meaning [veiled intention] in a remark.

언질 [औन्जील] [**言質**] .> / make a promise / commit oneself <on a matter / to do>. 언질을 잡다 obtain[extract] a person's pledge [word] / nail a person down <on>. 확실한 언질을 주지 않다 make no (firm) commitment <for>.

언짢다 [औन्चान्था] **1** [불쾌하다] unpleasant; disagreeable; offensive; ill-humored; <서술적> feel bad **2** [불길하다] ill; ill-omened; bad; unlucky; sinister; [꺼림 칙하다] hateful; loathsome; abominable; [마뜩찮다] undesirable; unwelcome; repulsive.

언행 [**言行**] [औन्हैंग] speech and behavior [behaviour]; words and deeds; sayings and doings.

얹다 [औन्था] put on; place [lay / set] <a thing> on; load (짐을).

얹혀 살다 [औन्झायौ साल्दा] be a dependent on <a person>; depend upon <a person> for support; feed[live / hang / sponge] on <a person>; live at the expense of <one's friend>.

얹히다 [औन्हीदां] **1**[놓이다] be place [put] on <a table>.**2** [체하다] oppress the stomach; sit [lie] heavy on the stomach; do not sit well on the stomach; remain undigested in the stomach. **3** [좌초하다] strand; be stranded; run [go] ashore; run aground; beach (일부러). **4** [얹게 하다] make <a thing> put[place / lie] <on>.

얻다 [**औत्ता**] **1** [획득하다] get; have; obtain; acquire; secure; procure; derive <from>; (일하여) earn; (승리 등을) win; gain; [받다] receive; be given; [채취하다] produce <gas from coal>; [추출하다] extract. **2** [아내 등을 맞다] marry <a woman>; take <a woman> in marriage; take <a woman> to wife; take a wife. **3** [앓게 되다] catch <flu>; contract <a disease>; get <cancer>; be attacked [affected] by <a disease>.

얻어듣다 [**औदोदुत्ता**] hear of; be informed [told] of [about]; hear [learn] from others; learn [know] by hearsay; happen to hear <of / about>; get wind of.

얻어맞다 [**औदोमात्ता**] **1** (매 등을) get [receive] a blow; be beaten [struck / knocked / hit / thrashed / punched]; be licked. **2** [공격받다] be criticized; take a beating; get a rap.

얻어먹다 [**औदोमौक्ता**] **1** (밥 등을) beg one's bread; beg food (빌어먹다); get treated to (대접받다); rely [depend] on <a person> for one's food; live on[off] <a person>..**2** [욕을 듣다] get called (names); suffer (harsh words); be abused; be slandered; be spoken ill of.

얼 [**औल**] [정신] spirit; mind; [혼] soul.

얼간이 [**औल्कानी**] a fool; a simpleton; a half-wit.

얼굴 [**ओल्येगुल**] **1** [낯] a face; features. **2** [표정] a face; a look; a countenance; an expression. **3** [체면] honor; prestige.**4** <비유> acquaintance; appearance. e.g. 얼굴이 널리 알려진 사람 a man with many contact. 얼굴이 잘 알려져 있다

얼근하다 [**औल्गुनहादा**] (맛이) rather hot [hot-tasting]; somewhat peppery [pungent]; heavily seasoned.

얼기설기 [**औल्कीसौल्की**] in a disorderly way; confusedly; complicatedly; in a disorderly heap. e.g. 얼기설기 얽힌 confusedly interlaced[intertwined] / complicated.

얼다 [**औल्दा**] **1** [결빙하다] freeze; be frozen; [응결하다] congeal. **2** [기가 죽다] be cowed [intimidated]; be scared stiff; feel timid [small]; (긴장하여) get nervous.

얼떨결 [**औल्तौल्क्यौल**] [얼떨떨한 판] in the confusion of the moment

얼떨떨하다 [**औल्तौल्तौरहादा**] [정신을 못 차리다] confounded; confused; flurried; perturbed; bewildered; upset; perplexed; puzzled. 얼떨떨하여 in a puzzle / perplexedly / in a perplexity / in a flurry. 얼떨떨하게 하다 flurry / perplex / puzzle / perturb / bewilder / baffle.

얼렁뚱땅 **[औल्लौंग्तुंग्तांग]** **1** [얼김에 남을 속여넘기는 모양].얼렁뚱땅하다 [속이다] juggle; play a trick on; hoodwink; (말을) palter <with a person>; prevaricate. e.g. 얼렁뚱땅 하여 돈을 빼앗다 juggle <a person> out of his money. **2** [적당히]. e.g. 대학을 얼렁뚱땅 졸업하다 muddle through college.

얼룩 **[औल्लूक]** **1** [반점] spots; mottles; dapples; speckles. **2** [자국] a stain; a blot; a smudge; a spot; a blob; a smut; a smear; a blotch. e.g. 얼룩 빼는 약 a spot remover.

얼룩지다 **[औल्लूकजीदा]** become stained [smudged]; stain. e.g. 얼룩진 stained / spotted / blotted / smeared.

얼른 **[औल्लून]** [빨리] quickly; speedily; rapidly; fast; in a hurry; hastily; [즉시] at once; immediately; promptly; in a moment; straight right away

얼마 **[औल्मा]** **1** [값] what price; [금액] what sum [amount] <of money>; some amount. handbag? **2** [기간] a while; some length of time. **3** [수량] what number [amount]; a certain number [amount / quantity] <of>; some; so much <what>; [정도] some degree <of>. **4** (무게P높이 등) what weigh [measure]; some weight [measure]. **5** [거리] what distance; some distance.

얼마나 **[औल्माना]** **1** [값] how much; what; [수량] how many [much]. **2** [정도, 동안] how <large, deep, high, wide, thick, far, long, old, etc.>; how much. **3** [감탄] how; how much; to what extent; what.

얼마든지 **[औल्मातुन्जी]** as many [much] as one likes; [한없이] without limit; [부정문] <not> many [much]

얼마(만) 큼 **[औलमा (मान) ख्नुम]** **1** [어느 정도] to some [a certain] degree [extent]; up to a certain point; how **2** = 얼마나.

얼버무리다 **[औल्बौमूरीदा]** **1** (말을) speak ambiguously; say something ambiguous; equivocate; prevaricate; shuffle; quibble; palter; dodge; do not commit oneself; gloss over[cover up] <one's fault>. e.g. 요점을 얼버 무리다 evade the point[issue].

얼빠지다 [औल्पाजीदा] be absent-minded; be absent in one's mind; look blank.

얼싸안다 [औल्साआन्दा] embrace; hug; give <a person> a hug; hold [take] <a person> in one's arms. e.g. 서로 얼싸안다 embrace [hug] each other / go into each other's arms.

얼씨구 [औल्सीगू] Whoopee!; Yippee!; Hurrah!; Hurray!; Oh boy!

얼씬 못하다 [औल्सीन मोस्हादा] dare not come round [show up]; cannot appear before <a person's> eyes at all.

얼씬거리다 [औल्सीन्गौरीदा] make frequent appearances; frequent; haunt; hang [hover] around.

얼어붙다 [औरौबूत्ता] freeze (on) to <something>; be frozen fast [hard] <to>.

얼얼하다 [औरौरहादा] (매워서) hot; burning; pungent; piquant; biting; stinging.

얼음 [औरुम] Ice

얼큰하다 [औल्खुन्हादा] 맛이 rather hot; somewhat prppery

얼토당토 아니하다 [औल्थोदांग्थो आनीहादा] [당찮다] unreasonable; absurd [관계없다] irrelevant; wide of the mark [purpose].

얽매이다 [औल्मैइदा] [묶이다] be bound; [속박 받다] be restricted [restrained / tied down / bound]; [분주하다] be busy with; be occupied with; be engrossed in.

얽어매다 [औल्गौमैदा] tie up; bind; fasten; truss.

얽히다 [औलखीदा] **1** [감기다] get twisted (a) round; coil around; [뒤얽히다] get entangled. **2** [연루되다] be involved in; [관련되다] be related <to>.

엄격 [औम्ग्योक] [**嚴格**] strictness; sternness; severity; rigor; austerity. 엄격하다 strict; stern; severe; rigorous; austere. e.g. 엄격한 아버지 a stern [strict] father. 엄격한 훈육 strict [rigid] discipline.

엄금 [औम्गुम] [**嚴禁**] strict prohibition; a ban; an interdict. 엄금하다 prohibit [forbid] strictly; interdict; place <a thing> under a ban; taboo.

엄단 [औम्दान] [**嚴斷**] 엄단하다 take stern legal action <against>.

엄두 [औम्दू] the very thought <of doing something>; daring. e.g. 엄두를 못 내다 cannot even conceive the idea of <doing> / be hardly thinkable.

엄마 [औम्मा] <소아어> ma (m) ma; mommy; mom; mummy; mum; [어머니] a mother.

엄벌 [औम्बौल] [**嚴罰**] a

severe [heavy] punishment. 엄벌하다 punish <a person> severely; deal severely with <a person>.

엄살 [औम्साल] exaggeration [pretension] of pain [hardship]; a big fuss; feigned [overdone] dismay.

엄살꾸러기 [औम्साल्कूरौगी] a fussy person; a fusser; a crybaby.

엄선 [औम्सौन] [嚴選] careful selection. 엄선하다 select carefully.

엄수 [औम्सू] [嚴守] strict observance [observation]; rigid adherence <to rules>. 엄수하다 observe [keep] strictly; rigidly adhere to.

엄숙 [औम्सूक] [嚴肅] solemnity; dignity; [중대함] gravity; seriousness; [엄정] rigor. 엄숙하다 solemn; serious; grave. 엄숙히 gravely; with a dignified [majestic] air; in a dignified manner; [엄하게] sternly.

엄습 [औम्सूप] [掩襲] a surprise [sudden] attack; a surprise. 엄습하다 make a sudden [surprise] attack; take <the enemy> by surprise; (감정이 사람을) come over; take (possession of); (재난 등이) visit; strike (down); sweep; hit.

엄연 [औम्यौन] [儼然] [뚜렷함]. 엄연하다 solemn; grave; real; actual; undeniable. 엄연히 solemnly; gravely; actually.

엄정 [औम्चौंग] [嚴正] exactness; strictness; severity; rigidness; rigor; strict fairness. 엄정하다 exact; strict; fair; impartial; unprejudiced. 엄정히 strictly; rigorously; fairly; impartially.

엄지 [औम्ची] [엄지가락] the thumb; the big finger [toe]; the first digit.

엄청나다 [औम्छौंग्नादा] exorbitant; preposterous; extraordinary; extravagant; excessive; absurd.

엄하다 [औम्हादा] [嚴 –] severe; strict; stern; rigid; austere; rigorous; [가혹하다] hard; harsh; stringent.

엄한 [औम्हान] [嚴寒] intense [severe] cold; the rigor of winter.

업 [औप] [業] **1** ⇨ 직업 **2** [불교] Karma.

업계 [औप्क्ये] [業界] business circles [quarters / world]; [특정 산업] the industry; the trade.

업다 [औप्ता] (등에) carry <a person, a pack, etc.> on the back.

업무 [औप्मू] [業務] business (affairs); service; operation; (임무로서의) duties.

업보 [औप्पो] [業報] [불교] retribution for the deeds of a former life [a previous incarnation]; karma effects.

업신여기다 [औप्सीन्यौगीदा] despise; ignore; slight; make light of; set a naught; look down on[upon]; hold <a person> in contempt.

업자 [औप्चा] [**業者**] [장사꾼] a trader; <집합적> the trader\

업적 [औपचौग] [**業績**] (개인의) work; achievements; results; contributions; (회사 등의) business results.

업종 [औपचोंग] [**業種**] a category of business; a type of industry.

업히다 [औफीदा] **1** (등에) ride [be carried] on a person's back. **2**(…위에) lie upon another; be piled on another.

없다 [औप्ता] **1** [존재하지 않다] there is no ...; do not exist. **2** [갖고 있지 않다] have no ...; be without; [보이지 다] be missing; cannot be found. **3** [다 떨어지다] be exhausted [used up / consumed]; be out of **4** [죽고 없다] be deceased [defunct]. **5** [가난하다] poor; needy

없애다 [औप्सैदा] **1** [제거하다] take off; take away; remove (▷ remove보다 take away 쪽이 보다); eliminate; eradicate; get rid of; [삭제하다] leave out; omit **2** [폐지하다] abolish; do away with; cancel; discontinue; put out of existence. **3** [다 써 버리다] use up; exhaust; run out of; [낭비하다] throw away; spend (wastefully); waste. **4** [죽이다] kill; (불법으로) murder; [숙청하다] liquidate; <美> blot (out); erase; put out; make [do] away with; dispatch.

없어지다 [औप्सौजीदा] **1** [분실되다] be [get] lost; be missing; be gone. **2** [사라지다] disappear; vanish; be gone.

없이 [औप्शि] without; sans; minus.

엇갈리다 [औत्गाल्लीदा] cross paths; pass [cross] <each other>; miss each other on the way.

엇나가다 [औन्नागादा] **1** (줄 등이) stray <from>; deviate [swerve] <from a course>; (일이) go crisscross; go awry [wrong]. e.g. 오늘은 만사가 엇나가는 날인 모양이다 Everything appears to go wrong [amiss] today.**2** (행동이) deviate [go away] from the right path; go astray[wild]; get on the loose. e.g. 그들은 대도시의 화려한 생활에 현혹되어 엇나갔다 They were led astray by the big city and bright lights

엇비슷하다 [औत्बीसुत्हादा] similar; like; kindred; akin <to>; analogous; <서술적> be much [nearly] the same; be about and about. e.g. 두 사람의 실력은 엇비슷하다 They are even in ability. / Their abilities are about the same.

었겠다 [औत्केत्ता] (추측) I should think; I suppose <it> would be. e.g. 그녀는 50 은 못 되었겠다 She is under fithy, I should think.

었느냐 [औत्नुन्या] (의문) <why, what, where, etc.> did you . e.g. 어디서 그런 이야기를 들었느냐 Where did you get that story?

었는지 [औत्नुनजी] (불확실) whether <it> was[did]. e.g. 그가 죽었는지 살았는지 아무도 모른다 Nobody knows whether he is alive or dead.

었다 [औत्ता] did (at an earlier time); had [have] done. e.g. 먹었다 ate. 갔었다 went (and back). 왔었다 came (and left again) / was here (but isn't now).

-었으나 [औस्सुना] – e.g. 처음에는 꽤 문제가 되었으나 이제는 순조로이 진행된다 At first it was quite a problem, but now it's going smoothly.

엉거주춤하다 [औंग्गौजूछूमहादा] **1** [몸을 반쯤 굽히고 있다] half-sit; half-rise. **2** [망설이다] hesitate <to do>; waver.

엉겁결에 [औंगगौपक्यौरे] in the confusion of the moment; in a moment of bewilderment.

엉금엉금 [औंग्गुमऔंग्गुम] (아기가) crawling; creeping; sprawling.

엉기다 [औंग्कीदा] [응결하다] coagulate (피 등이); curdle (우유 등이); congeal; solidify; condense; clot.

엉덩이 [औंग्दौंगी] the buttocks; the hips (▷ a hip은 한쪽을 가리킴); the haunches; the nates; the behind; the rear; the bottom; the ass; (동물의) the rump.

엉뚱하다 [औंग्तूंग्हादा] [건방지다] pert; saucy; impertinent; impudent; forward; [다르다] different; wrong <direction>; [뜻밖이다] unexpected; strange; [부적절하다] irrelevant; irrelative; [사리에 안 맞다] inconsistent; incoherent; absurd; [무모하다] wild; extravagant.

엉망 [औंग्मांग] a mess; <in> bad shape; a ruin; a wreck

엉성하다 [औंग्सौंग्हादा] **1** [꼭짜이지 못하다] loose; careless; slipshod; slovenly; imperfect; faulty. 엉성히 loosely **2** [탐탁찮다] unsatisfactory; indifferent; rotten. **3** [성기다] loose; sparse; large <mesh>.

엉엉 [औंग्औंग] e.g. 엉엉 울다 cry [weep] bitterly; cry one's heart out.

엉큼성큼 [औंग्खुमसौंगखुम] with long [big / large / great] steps[strides].

엉큼하다 [औंग्खुमहादा] wily; insidious; treacherous; deep; subtle; sly.

엉터리 [औंग्थौरी] **1** [미덥지 못한 사람] a fake; a quack; a

sham; a gyp; [허울만 좋은 물건] a gimcrack; a gewgaw; a trumpery.

엊그저께 [औत्गुजौके] [며칠 전] a few days ago; [그저께] the day before yesterday.

엎다 [औफ्दा] turn over; turn down; lay <a thing> face down; lay <a thing> upside down; overthrow; undermine; subvert.

엎드리다 [औफ्दुरीदा] lie on one's face; lie(with one's) face down[downward]; lie[be] prone[face on]; throw oneself flat(on one's stomach).

엎어지다 [औफौजीदा] **1** [앞으로 넘어지다] fall on one's breast [nose / face]; fall down. **2** [위아래가 뒤집히다] be turned over[be turned upside down]; (배 등이) keel[heel] over; turn turtle; capsize.

엎지르다 [औफजीरुदा] spill; slop.

에 [ए] **1** [장소] at; in. e.g. 문에 서 있다 stand at the door / stand in the doorway **2** [방향] to; [목적지] for. e.g.싸움터에 나가다 go to the front. **3** [시간] at; on; in(▷일반적으로 시각은 at, 날은 on, 달,해,시대는 in을 씀). e.g.1시에 at one (o'clock).

에게 [एगे] **1** [행동이 미치는 대상임을 나타냄]. e.g. 나는 아들에게 책을 주었다 I gave my son a book. / I gave a book to my son. **2** [행동을 일으키는 대상임을 나타냄]. e.g. 나는 그에게 속았다 I was fooled by him.

에게로 [ऐगेरो] to; toward; at.

에게서 [ऐगेसो] from; of; through; with.

에누리 [ऐनूरी] [값을 깎음](a) reduction in price;(a) discount. 에누리하다 reduce[abate / lower] the price; make [give / allow] a reduction [discount]; discount; mark [beat] down.

에너지 [ऐनौजी] **1** energy. e.g.결합 에너지 binding energy **2** [정력,기운]. e.g. 그는 에너지가 있다 He is energetic.

에다 [ऐदा] cut [scoop / scrape] out; gouge (out). e.g. 살을 에는 바람 a piercing wind.

에서 [एसौ]1 [장소] at; in (▷장소를 지점으로 볼 때는 at를 씀); on. **2**[시발점] from; out of; off; through; down; over. **3** [범위] from.

에세이 [ऐसेइ] an essay.

에우다 [एउदा] [둘러싸다] encircle; surround.

에워싸다 [एवॉसादा] surround; (사람이) crowd round; cluster [close / throng] around; (담 등으로) enclose; encircle; hem[edge] in [round]; [포위하다] besiege; lay siege to.

에피소드 [ऐफीसोद] [삽화] an (interesting) episode; [일화] an anecdote.

엔지니어 [एन्जीनीऔ] an engineer.

엔진 [एन्चीन] an engine.

여가 [यौगा] [餘暇] leisure; spare time [moments]; free time; leisure time [hours]; time to spare; time when one is unoccupied[has nothing to do].

여간 [यौगान] [如干] ordinarily; normally; commonly.

여간하다 ordinary; normal; common.

여객 [यौगैक] [旅客] [여행자] a traveler; [승객] a passenger.

여건 [यौगौन] [與件] [주어진 조건] a given condition [circumstance].

여겨듣다 [यौग्यौदुत्ता] listen carefully [attentively / intently] <to>; listen with all one's mind.

여겨보다 [यौग्योबोदा] watch carefully; see closely; take [have / get] a close [good] look <at>; take a hard look <at>.

여과 [यौग्वा] [濾過] filtration; filtering; percolation. 여과하다 filter; filtrate; pass <a liquid> through a filter; percolate.

여관 [यौग्वान] [旅館] an inn; a hotel.

여교사 [यौक्योसा] [女教師] a schoolmistress; a lady [female / woman] teacher; a schoolmarm.

여권 [यौक्वॉन] [旅券] a passport.

여권 [यौक्वॉन] [女權] women's rights; [여성 참정권] woman suffrage. 여권 신장[확장] extension [expansion] of women's rights.

여기 [यौगी] [이곳] here; [이 단계 [점] this point [place]. e.g. 여기 사람들(이곳의) the people of this district / (이 지방의) the people of this district.

여기다 [यौगीदा] think; consider <as>; deem <as>; treat <as>; take <for>; hold; (의아, 의심스럽게) wonder; doubt; suspect.

여기저기 [यौगीजौगी] here and there; in places; [모든 곳] (in) every direction;(in) all direction; (on) all sides.

여념 [यौन्यौम] [餘念] different [other] intention; other thoughts; divided attention. 여념(이) 없다 be devoted to; give undivided [absorbing] attention to; be absorbed [engrossed / buried] in; be bent [intent] on; be solely occupied with; busy oneself in; think of nothing but.

여느 [यौनु] [그 밖의 다른] other; [다른 보통의] ordinary; usual; common.

여닫다 [यौदात्ता] e.g. 문을 여닫다 open and close [shut] a door.

여담 [यौदाम] [餘談] a digression; a by-talk.

여당 [यौदांग][與黨] the Government party; the party in power; the ruling party; the party in office; the Administration party; the Ministerial party.

여대 [यौदै] [女大] a women's college [university].

여덟 [यौदौल] eight.

여독 [यौदोक] [餘毒] sickness from the fatigue of travel. e.g. 여독을 풀다 banish the fatigue of travel / take a rest ather the fatigue of one's journey.

여드름 [यौदुरुम] pimple; a blackhead; <집합적> acne (▷ 여드름이 있는 상태, 복수로 쓰지 않음).

여든 [यौदुन] eighty.

여러 [यौरौ] [수효가 많은] many; plenty of; [몇 개의] several; [여러 가지] various; a variety of; diverse.

여러가지 [यौरोकाजी] different kinds [sorts]; various kinds.

여러모로 [यौरोमोरो] in various [many] ways; one way or other; in more ways than one; in everything.

여러분 [यौरिबून] you; all of you; ladies and gentlemen; everybody; everyone.

여력 [यौर्यौक] [餘力] remaining power [strength]; surplus [reserve] energy [strength / power]; (돈의) money to spare.

여로 [यौरो] [旅路] a journey.

여론 [यौरोन] [輿論] public opinion; public sentiment; popular voice.

여류 [यौर्यू] [女流] womankind.

여름 [यौरुम] summer; summertime; the summer season.

여리다 [यौरीदा] [연하다] tender; soth; [약하다] weak; fragile; frail; feeble; flimsy.

여명 [यौम्यौग] [黎明] daybreak; dawn; the gray of morning; morning twilight.

여물다[1] [यौमूल्दा] (곡식, 과일 등이) fill with the corn [seed]; corn; grow [get / become] ripe; ripen; mature; come to maturity.

여물다[2] [यौमुल्दा] [살림 등을 알뜰히 하다] tight; firm frugal.

여미다 [यौमीदा] adjust; arrange; fix(up).

여백 [यौबैक] [餘白] [공백] a blank;(a) (blank) space; [난외] a margin.

여벌 [यौबौल] [餘-] remainings; remnants; surplus; spare; a spare one.

여보 [यौबो] **1** ⇨ 여보시오 **2** (부부 사이에) (my) darling; honey; sweetheart.

여부 [यौबू] [與否] yes or no; whether or not; if 여부없다 sure; certain; unquestionable; be beyond [out of] doubt.

여비 [यौबी] [旅費] travel [traveling] expenses; travel cost; mileage (공무원의).

여사 [यौसा] [女史] Ms.; [기혼자] Mrs.; [미혼자] Miss (▷

Ms.는 미혼,기혼을 구별 하지 않을 때 쓰지만, 본인이 원할 때만 쓰는 것이 무난함 he rest [remainder] of one's life; one's remaining years [days]; one's atherlife.

여섯 [यौसौत] six

여성 [यौसौंग] [女性] [여자] a woman <pl. women>; <집합적> women; womankind (▷ womankind 는 멋부린 표현).

여우 [यौउ] a foK a vixen (암컷); a cub (새끼).

여우비 [यौउबी] a sudden rainfall [a shower] in the sunshine; a light rain while the sun shines; a sun-shower.

여운 [यौउन] [餘韻] [뒤에 남는 운치] an athertaste; an athereffect; (글 등의) suggestiveness. e.g. 그의 시가 지니는 appreciate the lingering imagery [subtle overtones] of his poems.

여울 [यौउल] rapids; a shoot; a swith [strong] current.

여위다 [यौवीदा] lose (one's) weight; become lean [thin]; grow [become] gaunt; get emaciated; lose flesh (병으로); fall away(in flesh); pine away (근심 으로).

여유 [यौयू] [餘裕] (장소의) room; space;(시간의) time (to spare); (경비 등의) a argin; allowance; [넉넉함] something extra; [기계 등의 운동 여지,놂] play.

침착성] comosure; placidity; one's presence of mind; calmess.

여의다 [यौउइदा] [사별하다] have <one's father> die; be bereaved [bereth / derived] of; lose.

여인 [यौइन] 女人] a woman <pl. women>.

여인숙 [यौइनसूक] [旅人宿] a lodging house; an inn; (싼) a cheap inn; < 美 > a flophouse; < 英 > a doss house.

여자 [यौजा] [女子] [여성] a woman <pl. women>; [부인] a lady; [미혼의 젊은 여성] a girl; <집합적> women (▷ 관사를 붙이지 않음).

여장 [यौजांग] [女裝] (분장) woman's disguise;(복장) female clothing [attire / costume]. 여장하다 dress up like [disguise oneself as] a woman; put on women's clothing.

여장부 [यौजांगबू] [女丈夫] a heroine; an Amazon; an unusually capable woman.

여전 [यौजौन] [如前] 여전하다 <서술적> remain unchanged; be as usual [before]; be as <it> used to be; be just as it was 여전히 [전과 같이] as before; [여느 때와 마찬가지로] as ever; as usual; as [like] always.

여정 [यौजौग] [旅程] (거리) a distance (to be covered); (일정) <make> the plan

ㅇ

[schedule] of [for] one's trip; an itinerary.

여지 **[यौजी]** [**餘地**] room; space; a margin; a scope; a place; a blank (여백); leeway. e.g. 여지를 남기다 leave some room (for later discussion).

여쭈다 **[यौचुदा]** **1** [아뢰다] tell <to a superior>; inform; say; mention; state. **2** [문의하다] ask <a person about something>; inquire <of a person about something>.

여탕 **[यौथांग]** [**女湯**] the women's section (of a public bathhouse).

여태 **[यौथै]** till [by] now; until [up to] now [the present]; up [down] to date; hitherto; so [thus] far; to [by] this time; yet. e.g. 여태 없었던 사건 an unprecedented event.

여파 **[यौफा]** [**餘波**] an athermath; an athereffect; a seconddary effect; a side issue; a sequel; a conesquence; an influence; (the) backwash <of a war>; (폭풍우 등의) a trail.

여하튼 **[यौहाथुन]** [**如何－**] e.g. 여하튼 떠나자 Let's start anyway. 여하튼 우리가 경기에 졌다 Ather all we lost the game.

여행 **[यौहैंग]** [**旅行**] a trip; travel (s); a journey; (시찰,관광의) a tour; (항공, 해상의) a voyage; [유람] an excur-sion.

여흥 **[यौहुंग]** [**餘興**] **1** [아직 남은 흥] unexhausted merriment [fun]. **2** [연예, 오락] an entertainment; a side show.

역[1] **[यौक]** [**譯**]. e.g. 축어[직]역 a literal [verbatim / word-for-word] translation.

역[2] **[यौक]** [**逆**] [반대] the contrary; the opposite; reverse; [거꾸로임] the inverse; [論, 數] converse.

역[3] **[यौक]** [**役**] [영화 등에서 배우가 맡은 소임] a part; a role.

역[4] **[यौक]** [**驛**] a railroad[railway] station; a (railroad) depot; a stop.

역겹다 **[यौक्कयौप्ता]** [**逆－**] disgusting; revolting; sickening; nauseating; nauseaous; fulsome; detestable; offensive; <서술적> feel sick; be nauseated [disgusted] <at / by / with>; be sick at the stomach <from>.

역경 **[यौक्कयौग]** [**逆境**] adversity; adverse fortune [situation]; a reverse of fortune; adverse [unfavorable] circumstances

역대 **[यौक्तै]** [**歷代**] [여러 대] successive generations; [대대의 왕] successive kings.

역도 **[यौक्तो]** [**力道**] [**體**] weight lithing.

역량 [यौग्नयांग] [力量] [능력] ability; (a) capacity; capability; caliber; calibre.

역력하다 [यौग्नयौख्वादा] [歷歷-] clear; plain; obvious; manifest; unmistakable; vivid.

역류 [यौग्नयू] [逆流] a counter current; an adverse [inverse] current; a counterflow; a back flow; a backward flow; (조수의) an adverse tide; [역류하기] flowing backward; (체액, 음식의) refluK regurgitation. **역류하다** flow backward [upstream].

역모 [यौगमो] [逆謀] a treasonable conspiracy; a plot of treason.

역모하다 [यौगमोहादा] plot treason <against>; conspire <against>; conspire to rise in revolt [mutiny].

역부족 [यौकबूजोक] [力不足] want of ability. 역부족하다 <서술적> (사물이) be beyond one's capacities [reach]; be above one's ability; be not in [out of] one's power; be more than one can do; (사람이) be unequal [not equal] <to the task>; be incompetent <to do / for doing>.

역사[1] [यौक्सा] [驛舍] (철도의) a station building.

역사[2] [यौकसा] [歷史] [인류의 흥망,변천 과정] history; (책) a history; annals; a chronicle. **2** [내력,유래] history; [전통] tradition.

역설 [यौक्सौल] [力說] emphasis; stress; assertion. **역설하다** emphasize; stress; put [lay] stress [emphasis] <upon>; assert emphatically [with emphasis]; insist(upon).

역설 [यौकसौल] [逆說] a paradox.

역성 [यौक्सौग] (undue) favoritism; partiality; nepotism (친척에 대한).

역수입 [यौकसूइप] [逆輸入] reimportation; reimport.

역수출 [यौकसूछूल] [逆輸出] reexportation; reexport.

역습 [यौक्सुप] [逆襲] a counterattack; a sortie; a counteroffensive; (말로써의) a retort; a repartee.

역습하다 [यौक्सुफादा] counterattack; make [launch] a counterattack <on / against>; [반론하다] retort <on>; give a retort <on>; turn the tables <on a person>.

역시 [यौक्सी] [亦是] **1** [또한, 마찬가지로] too; also; <not> either; as well; likewise; like the rest; as is usual <with>. [여전히] still; all [just] the same. **3**[결국] ather all (is said and done).

역용 [यौग्योंग] [逆用] a reverse use. **역용하다** make a reverse use <of>; turn

<the enemy's propaganda> to one's own advantage; take advantage of <a person's kindness>.

역임 [यौगीम] [**歷任**] successive [consecutive] service in various posts. **역임하다** successively fill [hold] various <Government> posts.

역자 [यौक्चा] [**譯者**] a translator <of Hamlet>.

역작 [यौक्चाक] [**力作**] a labored [laborious / great] work; a <literary> work bearing marks of labor and effort; a masterpiece; <프> a tour de force <*pl.* tours de force>.

역작용 [यौक्चाग्योंग] [**逆作用**] a reaction; an adverse effect.

역적 [यौक्चौक] [**逆賊**] a rebel; a traitor; an insurgent.

역전 [यौक्चौन] [**逆轉**] a reversal; a reversion; a turnabout; a turn around; a loop; (기온의) (an) inversion. e.g. 기온의 역전 a temperature [thermal] inversion.

역전하다 [यौक्चौनहादा]reverse (itself); be reversed; go into reverse; (기온이) be inverted; invert;(비행기가) loop the loop; [海] work aback.

역전 [यौकचौन] [**驛前**] a station front.

역점 [यौकचौम][**力點**] **1** [중심이 되는 점] emphasis; stress. **2** [理] the point (of a lever) where (the) force is applied.

역정 [यौकचौग] [**逆情**] anger

역주 [यौक्चु] [**譯註**] translation and annotation; translation with notes.

역주[यौच्चू][**力走**] sprinting. 역주하다 run as fast [hard] as one can; run for all one is worth;(경주에서) make [put on] a spurt; spurt; sprint.

역하다 [यौख्वादा] [**逆** –] [비위에 거슬리다] sickening; nauseating; repulsive; repellent; revolting; disgusting; offensive; rank.

역학[1] [यौख्वाक] [**易學**] the science of divination.

역학[2] [यौख्वाक] [**力學**] dynamics; mechanics.

역할 [यौख्वाल] [**役割**] e.g. 역할을 정하다 allot [assign] a part [role] <to a person>.

역행 [यौकहैग][**逆行**] **1** reverse [backward]; retrogression; retrogradation; countermarch. 역행하다 go back; move [go] backward (s); retrogress; retrograde; recede; reverse; [거스르다] run counter <to>; be contrary

역효과 [यौकहयोक्वा] [**逆效果**] an opposite effect; a contrary [reverse / boomerang] effect; a contrary [counter] result; an adverse reaction.

엮다 [यौक्ता] **1** [얽어 만들다] weave; plait; entwine <a garland>; [묶다] tie <with a rope>. **2** [편찬하다] weave <in / into>; compile; edit.

엮음 [यौकुम] **1** [엮는 일] weaving; plaiting; [엮은 것] a woven thing [item]. **2** [편찬] compiling; editing; a compilation (편집물). e.g. P씨 엮음 compiled by Mr. P.

연[1] [यौन] [**年**] a year.

연[2] [यौन] [**鳶**] a kite.

연[3] [यौन]–[**連**] continuous (ly); continual (ly); consecutive (ly); in succession; successive (ly); without a break. e.g. 비가 연 3 주일 동안 내리고 있다 It has been raining for three weeks straight.

연가 [यौनका] [**戀歌**] a love song [poem]; a song [poem] of love; an amatory poem.

연간 [यौनगान] [**年刊**] [일년에 한 번씩만 간행을 하는 간행물] a yearly.

연거푸 [यौन्कौफु] [**連**–] nuccessively; in succession; consecutively; on end.

연결 [यौन्ग्यौल] [**連結**] coupling; connection; interconnecttion; linking; (인공 위성,우주선의) docking.

연결하다 couple; attach; connect; interconnect; join; interlink

연계 [यौनग्ये] [**連繫**] connection; linking; liaison; contact; touch.

연고[1] [यौन्को] [**緣故**] **1** = 사유 **2** [관계, 연분] relation; (a) connection; affinity; a tie–in; (a) pull. e.g. 모차르트의 연고지 a place noted [remembered] in connection with Mozart.

연고자 [यौनगोजा] a relative; a relation.

연고[2] [यौन्को] [**軟膏**] (an) ointment; (a) salve; (an) unguent; (an) inunction.

연관 [यौन्गवान] [**聯關**] **1** = 관련. **2** linkage.

연구 [यौनकू] [**研究**] (a) study; research (es); [조사] (an) investigation; (an) inquiry 연구하다 study; make a study <of>; do research <in>; investigate; inquire <into>.

연극 [यौन्कुक] [**演劇**] **1** [극] <집합적> drama; (개개의 작품) a play; a drama **2** [거짓을 사실처럼 꾸미는 일] acting; playacting; a fake; a put–up job.

연금 [यौनकुम] [**年 金**] a pension; an annuity. (▷ pension 은 특히 국가, 회사에서 나오는 연금).

연기[1] [यौन्की] [**煙氣**] smoke; fumes (특히 악취가 나거나 해로운).

연기[2] [यौन्की] [**演技**] (연극

등의) acting; performance 연기하다 perform; (어떤 장면을) enact; put on.

연기[3] **[यौन्की]** [**延期**] [기한을 뒤로 물림] postponement; deferment; adjournment (회의의); respite (집행, 징수 등의); [유예] grace; reprieve.

연내 **[यौन्नै]** [**年內**] e.g. 연내에 within the year / before the end of the year / before the year is out.

연년생 **[यौन्नयौनसैंग]** [**年年生**] a child born within a year of another; children born in (two) successive years. e.g. 그 형제는 연년생이다 The brothers were born in consecutive years [within a year of each other].

연달다 **[यौन्ताल्दा]** [**連-**] e.g. 연달은 흉악 범죄 a succession of atrocious crimes. 연달은 3안타 three back-to-back [consecutive] hits. 변호사의 연달은 질문에서 증인은 당황했다 Faced with successive questions from the lawyer, the witness lost his presence of mind.

연도 **[यौन्तो]** [**年度**] the year.

연동 **[यौन्दोंग]** [벌레가 꾸물꾸물 움직임] writhing; wriggling; vermiculation. 연동하다 move in a wormlike manner; writhe; wriggle.

연두 **[यौन्तू]** [**軟豆**] yellowish [light] green.

연락 **[यौल्लाक]** [**連絡,聯絡**] **1** [관계] (a) connection; junction; [접촉] (a) contact; touch; [연계] liaison; concert; [軍] communication (s). 연락하다 contact; make contact <with>; connect <with>; get in touch <with>; communicate <with>. **2** [통신] communication; correspondence 연락하다 communicate <a person that ...>; let <a person> know. e.g. 전화로 연락하다 speak to <a person>over the telephone / contact <a person> by phone.

연령 **[यौल्यौंग]** [**年齡**] 평균 연령 the average age. 결혼 연령 the age at which a person marries.

연례 **[यौल्लये]** [**年例**] e.g. 연례의 yearly / annual 연례적인 여름 축제가 시작되었다 The annual summer festival has begun.

연로 **[यौल्लो]** [**年老**] agedness; oldness; old [advanced] age. 연로하다 aged; old; senile.

연료 **[यौल्यो]** [**燃料**] fuel. 연료비 the cost of fuel; fuel expenses.

연루 **[यौल्लू]** [**連累**] implication; involvement; complicity. 연루하다 be implicated in <a crime>; be involved in <an affair>; be entangled in <a plot.

연륜 **[यौल्यून]** [**年輪**] **1**=

나이테. **2** [새겨진 인생의 노고]. e.g. 그에게서는 인생의 연륜이 느껴진다 I can see the effect of the years on him. / I can see that he has gone through a lot (in the course of his life).

연마 [यौन्मा] [**研磨,鍊磨,練磨**] **1** [機] grinding; abrasion; polishing. 연마하다 grind; polish; whet. **2**[학문,정신 등을 갈고 닦음]. training; drilling; practice; cultivation; improvement. 연마하다 study hard; apply oneself to the study <of English>; train; drill; practice; cultivate; improve.

연말 [यौन्माल] [**年末**] the year-end; the end [close] of the year.

연맹 [यौन्मैग] [**聯盟**] a league; a federation; a union; a confederation; an alliance.

연명 [यौन्मयौग] [**延命**] maintenance of a scanty existence; [생명의 연장] the prolongation of life. 연명하다 eke out a scanty existence [livelihood]; keep body and soul together; live on the edge of subsistence.

연목 구어 [यौन्मोक गुऔ] [**緣木求魚**] "seeking a fish in a tree"; attempting the impossible; flogging a dead horse; It is very hard to shave an egg.

연못 [यौन्मोत] [**蓮-**] a lotus pond; a pond.

연민 [यौन्मीन] [**憐憫**] compassion; pity; mercy; commiseration.

연방 [यौन्पांग] [**聯邦**] a federation (of states); a federal state; a confederation; a union(of nations); a commonwealth.

연배 [यौन्पै] [**年輩**] [비슷한 나이] (similar) age; [비슷한 연령의 사람] a person of one's age; <one's> contemporary.

연봉[1] [यौन्पोंग] [**年俸**] [일년 동안에 지급하는 봉급] an annual salary; a yearly stipend.

연봉 [यौन्पोंग] [**連峰**] [죽 이어져 있는 산봉우리] a mountain range; a chain [range] of mountains.

연분[2] [यौन्पून] [**緣分**] [하늘이 베푼 인연] fate; destiny; predestination; [관계] a relation; a connection; affinity.

연사[यौन्सा] [**演士**] a (public) speaker; an orator; a lecturer.

연상[1] [यौन्सांग] [**年上**] seniority (in age).

연상[2] [यौन्सांग] [**聯想**] association (of ideas). 연상하다 be reminded of; associate <A with B>.

연설 [यौन्सौल] [**演說**] a speech; (공식의) an address; (엄숙,

ㅇ

장중한) an oration; (연설하기) (public) speaking. 연설하다 make [deliver/ give] a speech [an address]; speak <to [before] an audience on a subject>; address <an audience>; orate.

연세 [यौन्से] [年歲] e.g. 연세가 많다 be advanced [well up] in years [age].

연소자 [यौन्सोजा] [年少者] a youth; a young person [one]; young people; juveniles; juniors; [미성년자] a minor; underage people.

연속 [यौन्सोक] [連續] continuity; continuation; continuance; succession; a sequence; a series; a chain. 연속하다 continue; be continuous; go on; last.

연쇄 [यौन्सवै] [連鎖] a chain; links; a series; [관계] connection; (유전자의) linkage.

연수 [यौन्सू] [硏修] research study; study and training; (신입 사원 등의) an induction course. 연수하다 study <science>; take [go through] a training <in>; pursue the study <of history>.

연습 [यौन्सुप] [練習] practice; training; (a) drill; (an) exercise; (경기 직전의) a warm (ing)-up; (연극 등의) (a) rehearsal. 연습하다 practice; train; drill; rehearse; exercise (oneself) <in>.

연승 [यौन्सुंग] [連勝] straight [consecutive / successive] victories; a series of victories. 연승하다 gain [win] consecutive [successive] victory; win victory ather victory.

연애 [यौनए] [戀愛] love; amour; tender passion [emotion / sentiment]; affecttions; love making. 연애하다 love; fall [be] in love <with>.

연약 [यौन्याक] [軟弱] tenderness; mildness; weakness. 연약하다 tender; mild; weak; feeble; frail; delicate; weak-kneed.

연어 [यौनौ] [連語] (a) collocation; (복합어) a compound word; (구) a phrase.

연역 [यौन्यौक] [演繹] deduction; deductive reasoning. 연역하다 deduce <particular details from general principles and known facts>.

연연하다 [यौनयौनहादा] [戀戀-] **1** [미련을 가지다] <서술적> cling to <one's position **2** [그립다] lingering; tender; longed-for; <서술적> be ardently [fondly] attached to <a girl>; be (very) fond of <a girl>; pine [long / yearn] <for>.

연예 [यौनये] [演藝] (dramatic / musical) entertainments; (흥행장의) a variety show; vaudeville; performance

(연기). 연예하다 perform; entertain; put on entertainment; act. 연예인a performer; an entertainer; an artiste.

연월일 [यौन्वॉरील] [年月日] the date.

연원 [यौन्वॉन] [淵源] the origin; the source; the beginning; the rise; the inception; the fountainhead.

연유 [यौन्यू] [緣由] the origin; the root; the rise; the source; the derivation; [사유](a) reason;(a) cause; ground(s). 연유하다 originate <in>; have <its> origin [rise] <in>; arise <from>; be derived <from>; date <from>; date back <to>; be caused <by>.

연이율 [यौनीयूल] [年利率] an annual interest rate [rate of interest].

연인 [यौनइन] [戀人] (남녀의) one's love; one's sweetheart; (남자) boy-friend; one's boy; one's lover (▷ lover 는 [정부] 라는 뉘앙스가 강함); (여자) one's girlfriend; one's girl.

연일 [यौनइल] [連日] every day; day ather [by] day; day in and day out; for days on end; several days in succession.

연임 [यौनीम] [連任] reappointment. 연임하다 be reappointted <to the office>; resume the office.

연장 [यौन्चांग] [延長] **1** (길이의) (an) extension. 연장하다 [어느점 이상으로 늘이다] extend; [길게 하다] lengthen. **2** (기간의) (an) extension; (a) prolongation. 연장하다 (기간을) extend; [오래 끌게 하다] prolong

연장 [यौन्चांग] [年長] seniority.

연장 [यौन्चांग] a tool; an instrument; a utensil.

연장전 [यौन्चांगजौन] [延長戰] an extended game; [야구] an extra-inning game [contest].

연재 [यौनजै] [連載] serialization; serial publication. 연재하다 publish <a novel> serially [in serial form]; serialize.

연주 [यौन्जु] [演奏] a (musical) performance; (독주) a recital; (자기 해석에 의한) a rendering. 연주-하다 perform; give a performance [recital]; play <a sonata>; render; (즉흥적으로) ad-lib.

연줄 [यौनजुल] [緣-] connections; (a) pull; influence; <have> an in <with / to>; contacts.

연중 [यौनजुंग] [年中] (all) the year round; throughout the year; the whole year; every day of the year; all times of the year; always (항상).

연착 [यौनछाक] [延着] (a) late

[delayed] arrival; (발송 품의) (a) delay (in delivery). 연착하다 arrive late; be delayed (in arrival [delivery / transmission]); (기차 등이) be overdue.

연체 [यौन्छे] [延滯] (a) delay; procrastination; (채무, 납세 등의) arrears. 연체하다 be delayed; be in arrear (s); become remiss in one's payment (s).

연초 [यौन्छो] [年初] the beginning of the year.

연출 [यौनछुल] [演出] direction; production. 연출하다 direct; produce. 연출가 (연극의) a director; a producer.

연탄 [यौन्थान] [煉炭] a briquette (te).

연패 [यौनफै] [連敗] successive defeats; a succession [series] of reverses. 연패하다 suffer [meet with] successive [straight] defeats.

연표 [यौन्फ्यो] [年表] 한국사 연표 a chronological table of Korean history.

연필 [यौन्फील] [鉛筆] a (lead) pencil.

연하[1] [यौन्हा] [年下] juniority.

연하[2] [यौन्हा] [年賀] New Year (s) greetings.

연하다 [यौन्हादा] [軟 -] 1 [무르고 부드럽다] soth; tender; supple. 2 [빛이 옅고 산뜻하다] light <color>; ild <shade>; mellow <light>; weak [watery] <tea>.

연합 [यौन्हाब] [聯合] [결합] combination; union; association; consociation; league; confederacy; coalition (정당의); a combine (기업);(an) alliance (동맹). 연합하다 combine; unite; confederate; league; ally oneself; consociate; coalesce.

연행 [यौन्हैग] [連行] 연행하다 take [walk] <a suspect to a police station>; haul [bring] <a person> before <the police authorities>.

연혁 [यौन्ह्यौक] [沿革] (a) history; changes(변천); the (origin and) development (발달).

연회[1] [यौनहवै] [年會] an annual convention; a yearly meeting.

연회[2] [यौन्हवी] [宴會] a party; a dinner (party); a feast; a banquet; a junket; an entertainment. 연회장 a banquet [banqueting] hall.

연휴 [यौनह्यू] [連休] conescutive holidays; holidays in a row.

열[1] [यौल] [10] ten; half a score.

열[2] [यौल][熱] 1 운 기운] heat. 2 [신열] (a) temperature; (병으로 인한)(a) fever. [화,격분] anger; rage; ssion; wrath; indignation. 3

[흥분] heat; ardor; zeal; excitement.

열[3] **[यौल]** [列] row; a line; (층을 이룬) a tier; (세로의) a file; a column; (가로의) a rank; a row; (차례를 기다리는) a line; a queue.

열강 **[यौल्कांग]** [列强] the Great Powers (of the world); the World Powers.

열거 **[यौल्कौ]** [列擧] enumeration. 열거하다 enumerate; list; mention; name one by one; go [run] through the list [catalogue] <of>.

열광 **[यौलग्वांग]** [熱狂] (wild) enthusiasm; frenzy; fanaticism; mania; craze; furor [furore]; fever heat; extreme excitement. 열광하다 be [get] wildly [extremely] excited <at / about / over / by>; go [get / be] wild <with / about>; be enthusiastic <over / about>; enthuse <over / about>; be [go] crazy <over / for / about>; be fanatic(al) <about>; run mad <ather>.

열기 **[यौल्की]** [熱氣] **1** [뜨거운 공기] heat; hot-ness; hot air. **2** [흥분한 기운] heat; enthusiasm; fever; eagerness; excite-ment; zeal. **3** [높은 신열] a high fever; feverishness. e.g. 몸에 열기가 있다 I feel like I have some temperature. / I feel feverish. / I have a slight fever.

열나다 **[यौलनादा]** [熱 –] **1** [신열이 나다] become feverish; run a fever [temperature]; develop a fever; come to have fever; have an attack of fever. **2** [열성이 나다] become enthusiastic <in / about / over / for>; enthuse <about / over>; be mad [crazy] <about / over>; be keen [intent / bent] <on>.**3** [화나다] get [become / grow] angry; be offended [enraged] <by>; get mad <at / about>; become indignant <at / with>; be heated (with passion); get into a passion [huff]; fly into a fury.

열다 **[यौलदा]**[1] [(열매가) 맺다] bear fruit; fructify; fruit; (열매가) grow <on a tree>.

열다 **[यौलदा]** [2] **1** (닫힌 것 등을) open. **2** [개최하다] hold <a meeting>; open <a conference>; give <a party>. **3** [운영하기 시작하다] open <a shop>; set up[start] <a store>; commence; establish; found. **4** [(새 기틀을) 마련하다] open (up); clear; break; make.

열대 **[यौलदै]** [熱帶] the tropics; the torrid zone; the tropical zone.

열등 [यौलतुंग] [劣等] inferiority; a low grade [class]. 열등하다 inferior; low-grade; low-class; low; base; of poor [lower] quality.

열람 [यौल्लाम] [閱覽] reading; perusal; inspection. **람하다** read; peruse.

열량 [यौल्यांग] [熱量] heat capacity [value]; quantity [amount] of heat; [발열량] calorific value; [단위] calorie.

열렬 [यौल्यौल] [熱烈] **열렬하다** ardent; fervent; passionate; impassioned; enthusiastic; vehement. **열렬히** ardently; fervently; passionately; enthusiastically; with ardor [fervor].

열리다[1] [यौल्लीदा] (나무가) bear (fruit); fruit; be in fruit; (열매가) grow <on a tree>.

열리다[2] [यौल्लीदा] **1** (닫힌 것 등이) open; be opened **2** [개최되다] be held [given]; take place. **3** (상점등이) open; begin; start.

열망 [यौलमांग] [熱望] an ardent desire [wish]; a fervent desire [hope / aspiration]; an eager desire; a yen; a longing. 열망하다 be eager [anxious] <for / to do>; desire ardently [eagerly / earnestly] <to do / that>; long <for / to do>; thirst[hunger] for [ather]; crave(for); have an eager[desire] <for / to do>.

열매 [यौलमै] (a) fruit; a nut (견과); a berry (장과).

열병 [यौलप्यौंग] [熱病] a fever; a febrile disease; pyrexia.

열사병 [यौलसाप्यौंग] [熱射病] [醫] heatstroke; heat prostration [exhaustion].

열성 [यौलसौंग] [熱誠] earnestness; warmth; enthusiasm; ardor; zeal; devotion (헌신); sincerity (성실).

열세 [यौलसे] [劣勢] inferiority in strength [numbers]; numerical inferiority. 열세하다 <서술적> be inferior in numbers [strength]; be outnumbered <by>.

열쇠 [यौलस्वे] **1** [자물쇠를 여는 쇠붙이] a key. **2** [단서] a key; a clue.

열심 [यौलसीम] [熱心] eagerness; enthusiasm; zeal; fervor; ardor; earnestness; keenness; warmth.

열심히 [यौलसीमही] [熱心 –] eagerly; enthusiastically; zealously; ardently; fervently; earnestly; warmly; passionately; eenly; devotedly; in (good) earnest; with fervor [ardor / zeal]; hard; diligently; wholeheartedly.

열악열악하다 [यौराक] [劣惡] inferior; poor; coarse; of poor quality; (설비가) inadequate.

열애 [यौऱै] [熱愛] passionate [ardent] love; a strong attachment; devotion. 열애하다 love fervently [passionately / ardently]; be madly [passionately] in love <with a person>; be devoted <to a woman>; have passionate love <for>; be an ardent lover <of>; be everything <to>; be head over heels (in love with).

열연 [यौरयौन] [熱演] an enthusiastic [impassionned] performance. 열연하다 perform [play] enthusiastically [with much nerve]; give an impassioned performance; put much [a lot of] spirit into one's performance.

열의 [यौरूइ] [熱意] enthusiasm <for / about>; zeal <for>; ardor <for>; eagerness <for / ather / about>. e.g. 열의 있는 enthusiastic / zealous.

열전 [यौल्चौन] [熱戰] a furious [hot] battle; a hard [fierce] fight; (경기) a heated [hot] contest; a close [tough] game; a hot war (냉전에 대하여.

열정 [यौलचौंग] [熱情] ardor; passion; fervor; warmth; [열렬한 애정] ardent [passionate] love.).

열중 [यौलचुंग] [熱中] enthusiasm; absorption; zeal; (a) craze.

열중하다 [यौलचुंगहादा] become [be] enthusiastic <in / about / over>; get[be] engrossed [absorbed / immersed] <in>; have a mania [craze / rage] <for>; be mad [crazy / wild] <about / over>; be devoted [dedicated] <to>; devote [dedicate] oneself <to>; be keen <on>; be intent [bent] <on>; give oneself up [over] <to>; abandon oneself <to>; go[put one's] heart and soul <into>; enthuse <over / about>.

열차 [यौलछा] [列車] a train; a railroad [<英> railway] train; a railway carriage.

열흘 [यौरहुल] [10일간] ten days.

엷다 [यौलता] **1** [두께가 적다] thin. **2**[색 등이 연하다] light <in color>; pale. **3** [언행이 얄팍하다] shallow; frivolous; superficial; short-witted; short-sighte. **4** [농도, 밀도가 얕다] thin; [액체 등의 성분이 약하다] weak.

염가 [यौमका] [廉價] 염가의 cheap / inexpensive / low-priced (▷ cheap는 문맥에 따라 싸구려의 뜻으로 해석됨). 염가로 cheap (ly) / at a low price / at a bargain.

염두 [यौमदु] [念頭] mind.

염려 [यौमन्यौ] [念慮] worry; anxiety; care; concern; fear; apprehension; uneasiness;

solicitude; misgivings. 염려하다 feel anxiety; be anxious [apprehensive / concerned / worried]; worry <about>; concern oneself <about>; be solicitous <about>; have [feel] misgivings <about>; be [feel] uneasy <about>; care; fear; apprehend <danger>.

염문 [यौम्मून] [艶聞] gossip [(a) rumor] about a person's love affair (s); one's episode of love; a romance. e.g. 염문이 있다 be associated with a love affair / have a romance.

염분 [यौमबून] [鹽分] salt; salinity.

염불 [यौमबूल] [念佛] a prayer [an invocation] to (the) Buddha; a Buddhist invocation [prayer]; the repetition of the sacred name of Amitabha. 염불하다 pray to Amitabha; chant [say] a prayer to; tell [say / recite] the [one's] beads.

염색 [यौमसैक] [染色] dyeing.

염세 [यौमसे] [厭世] pessimism; weariness of life [the world].

염소 [यौमसो] a goat.

염습 [यौमसुब] [殮襲] 염습하다 wash and shroud <a person's> dead body; prepare [dress] the body for burial.

염원 [यौमवॉन] [念願] one's heart's desire; one's (dearest [heartiest]) wish. 염원하다 desire; wish <for>; pray <for>.

염전 [यौमचौन] [鹽田] a saltpan; a salt farm [field]; a saltern; a salina.

염증 [यौमचुंग] [炎症] [醫] (an) inflammation.

염증 [यौमचुंग] [厭症] 염증이 나다 become disgusted <with> / tire [get tired] <of> / get sick <of> / get fed up <with>.

염치 [यौमछी] [廉恥] a sense of shame[honor].

염탐 [यौमथाम] [廉探] 염탐하다 spy <upon / on>; spy into <a secret>; feel(out); pry about [into].

엽기 [यौप्की] [獵奇] bizarrerie hunting.

엽서 [यौप्सौ] [葉書] a postal card (관제); a postal; a postcard (사제); a postcard (관제,사제)

엿 [यौत] taffy; toffee..

엿듣다 [यौत्तुत्ता] eavesdrop (on) <a conversation>; overhear; listen secretly;(전화 등으로) listen in <on>; (도청기를 사용하여) tap <wires>; wiretap; bug <a telephone>.

엿보다 [यौत्पोदा] **1** [훔쳐보다] steal a glance <at>; look furtively <at>; watch <a person> with a furtive eye; [들여다보다] peep into [through]. **2**[기회를 노리다]

watch[wait] for <a chance>.3 [살피다] spy on. [헤아려 알다] guess; infer; gather; surmise.

영[1] **[यौंग]** [**靈**] **1** e.g. 영과 육 the spirit and the flesh. 영의 세계 a world of spirit. **2** ⇨ 신령 **영** [**零**] zero; a cipher; naught; nought; nothing. e.g. 영의 zero. 3 대 영으로 이기다 win(a game) by a score of three to nothing.

영[2] **[यौंग]** [**令**] **2** ⇨ 명령**2**⇨ 법령 e.g.교육부령 an education ministry ordinance.

영감[1] **[यौगाम]** [**靈感**] (an) inspiration; <英> a brain wave; a brainstorm; extrasensory perception (ESP).

영감[2] **[यौगकाम]** [**令監**] **1** [존칭] lord; sir. **2** [늙은 남자] an old man; an elderly man. **3** [나이든 남편] one's husband.

영결 **[यौगक्यौल]** [**永訣**] the last [final] parting [farewell]; separation by death. 영결하다 bid one's farewell to the dead; pay one's last respects to the deceased.

영계 **[यौगक्ये]** [a(spring) chicken.

영광 **[यौगक्वांग]** [**榮光**] an honor; a glory; a privilege (특전).

영구 **[यौगकु]** [**永久**] eternity; permanence; perpetuity. 영구하다 eternal; everlasting; permanent; perpetual. 영구히 forever; eternally; permanently; perpetually; for good (and all).

영국 **[यौगुक]** [**英國**] Britain; England; Great Britain (영국 본토, 즉 England / Wales / Scotland); the United Kingdom; (공식명).

영농 **[यौगनोंग]** [**營農**] farming; agriculture. 영농하다 farm; be engaged in agriculture.

영락없다 **[यौगनाक औप्ता]** [**零落** −] absolutely correct [exact]; invariably right; quite free from mistakes [errors]; [확실하다] sure [certain] enough; unfairling; infallible. 영락 없이 without fail [any slip]; infallibly; surely; for sure; certainly.

영롱 **[यौगनोंग]** [**玲瓏**] 영롱하다 brilliant; clear and bright; bright and translucent; clear; lucid; serene. ₩

영리[1] **[यौगनी]** cleverness; wisdom; intelligence; shrewdness. 영리하다 [현명하다] clever; bright; wise; intelligent; brainy; sensible; sharp; [빈틈없다] shrewd; smart.

영리[2] **[यौगनी]** [**營利**] profit (−making); gain; moneymaking.

영문[1] **[यौगमून]** [**英文**] English (영어); an English sentence [composition]; English writing.

영문[2] [यौगमुन] [형편, 사정] circumstances; the situation; the state of things [affairs / matters]. **2** [까닭] (a) reason; (a) cause; ground(s); the matter.

영문법 [यौगमुनबौप] [英文法] English grammar..

영문학 [यौगमुनहाक] [英文學] English literature.)

영부인 [यौगबुइन] [令夫人] your[his] wife.

영상 [यौगसांग] [映像] (거울, 수면에 비친) a reflection; a refleek(렌즈 등에 의한) an image;(TV의) a picture; an image; the field(영상면); (레이더의) a blip; [그림자] a shadow; a silhouette.].

영세 [यौगसे] [零細] 영세하다 trifling; petty; small **영세 농업** subsistence farming.

영속 [यौगसोक] [永續] permanence; permanency; perpetuity; perpetuation; (long) continuance; [불멸] imperishableness. 영속하다 last long [for a long time / forever]; remain permanently; continue [stand] forever; endure long.

영수증 [यौगसुजुंग] [領收證領受證] a receipt <for>; a voucher <for>; an acknowledgment <for>.

영악 [यौगाक] [獰惡] fierceness; ferocity. 영악하다 (extremely) vicious; fierce; ferocious; savage. 영악하다 clever; bright; shrewd; smart; sharp.

영양 [यौग्यांग] [營養] nutrition; nourishment; nutriament; alimentation.

영어 [यौगौ] [英語] English; the English language.

영업 [यौगऔब] [營業] business; trade; [영업 활동] business activities; [업무의 운영] operation (s).

영역 [यौग्यौक] [領域] **1** [영유 구역] a territory; a domain. **2** [분야] a domain; a field; an area; a province; a sphere.

영영 [यौग्यौग] [永永] forever; for good(and all); eternally; permanently.

영예 [यौग्ये] [榮譽] honor; glory; distinction; [명성] fame; renown.

영웅 [यौगउंग] [英雄] a hero <*pl.* ~es>; a great man.

영원 [यौगवॉन] [永遠] [영구] eternity; permanence; [불멸] immortality 영원하다 eternal; permanent; everlasting; immortal; perpetual.

영위 [यौगवी] [營爲] [관리] management; administration; [운영] operation; running; conduct. **영위하다** manage; run; operate; carry on; conduct; keep; engage in.

영유 [यौग्यू] [領有] possession. **영유하다** possess; get [gain / take] possession of; be in possession of.

영재 [यौगजै] [英才] [탁월한 재주] talent; genius; unusual talent; [탁월한 재주를 가진 사람] a man of great talent; a githed person; a man of ability; a genius.

영접 [यौगचौब] [迎接] recaption; meeting. 영접하다 go [come] (out) to meet <a person> on arrival; receive; greet; meet.

영토 [यौगथो] [領土] territory; (a) dominion; (a) domain; (a) possession; soil.

영특 [यौगथक] [英特] 영특하다 sagacious; intelligent; exceptional; extraordinary; great.

영하 [यौगहा] [零下] e.g. 영하의 기온 a sub-zero temperature.

영한 [यौगहान] [英韓] English-Korean; Anglo-Korean.

영합 [यौगहाब] [迎合] flattery; adulation; ingratiation. 영합하다 [아첨하여 좇다] flatter; curry favor with; fawn upon; […의 뜻을 받들다] cater to [anticipate] a person's wishes [feelings]; adjust one's opinions and behavior to please a person.

영향 [यौगहयांग] [影響] [다른 것에 작용하는 힘] (an) influence; (효과) (an) effect; (충격력) (an) impact.

영혼 [यौगहोन] [靈魂] the soul; the spirit.

영화 [यौगह्वा] [映畵] a film; a moving picture; a movie; <집합적> the movies; the cinema.

영화관 [यौगह्वाग्वान] [映畵館] a movie theater; a cinema; a picture hall.

옅다 [यौथा] **1** ⇨ 얕다 **2** (빛깔이) light <color>; pale; faint. e.g. 옅은 초록색 light [pale] green. 옅은 색옷 a pastel dress

옆 [यौफ] (측면) the side; the flank;(근처) neighborhood; vicinity.

옆구리 [यौफगूरी] the side; the flank.

옆길 [यौफगील] **1** [큰길 옆으로 난 작은 길] a bypath; a byroad; a side road. **2** [잘못 된 방향] a wrong way; (토론 등의) a side issue;(a) digression.

옆모습 [यौफमोसुब] a profile; a face in profile; the side face. e.g. 그녀는 옆모습이 더 예쁘다 She looks better in profile. 옆모습을 찍은 사진이 있습니까 Do you have a photograph(of yourself) in profile?

옆집 [यौफजीब] the house next door; a neighboring [an adjoining / an adjacent] houses.

예 [ये] [禮] [예법] etiquette; decorum; propriety; the proprieties (예절); politeness; courtesy.

예 **[ये]** **1** [실례, 유례] an instance; a case; an example; an illustration. **2** = 전례 **3** [관례] a habit; a custom. **4** [이미 말한 바].

예 **[ये]** **1** [대답] yes (▷부정적인 대답일 경우에는 no); certainly. **2**[출석의 대답] yes; present; here. **3** [재우치어 묻는 소리].

예감 **[येगाम]** [**豫感**] a foreboding; a presentiment; a premonition; a presage; a hunch (▷좋은 것에나 나쁜 것에나 씀). 예감하다 have a foreboding[hunch] <of / that>; feel a premonition [presentiment] <of / that>; forebode. 예감하다 forebode death / have a premonition of death. e.g. 이러한 사건은 종종 전쟁을 예감하게 한다 Such incidents othen presage war.

예견 **[येग्यौन]** [**豫見**] foresight; foreknowledge; prescience; precognition 예견하다 foresee; foreknow; prognosticate.

예고 **[येगो]** [**豫告**] a (previous) notice; an advance notice; a previous [preliminary] announcement; (경고) (a) warning. 예고하다 notify [announce / inform / warn] beforehand [previously]; give [advance] warning [notice]; warn; (특히 영화,강연회 등의) give advance billing.

예과 **[येग्वा]** [**豫科**] preparatory course; a preparatory department; (의과대학의) a premedical course.

예금 **[येगुम]** [**預金**] a deposit; money on deposit; a bank account. 예금하다 deposit <money in [with] a bank>; make a deposit <in an account>; place <money> on deposit <in a bank>; bank <10,000 won>.

예기 **[येगी]** [**豫期**] [기대] expectation (s); (an) antivipation; [희망](a) hope; [예견] forecast; foresight. ⇨ 예상 예기하다 expect; anticipate; hope for; look for; look (ahead / forward) to; have in prospect; forecast; foresee.

예년 **[येनयौन]** [**例年**] **1**[여느 해] a normal [an ordinary] year; the average year. **2** [해마다] every year; annually.

예능 **[येनुंग]** [**藝能**] **1**[재주와 기능] accomplishments. **2** [영화,미술,음악 등의 총칭] (public) entertainment; performing arts.

예리 **[येरी]** [**銳利**] **1** [연장 등이 날카로움]. 예리하다 sharp; keen; pointed; sharp-edged. e.g. 예리한 날 a keen [sharp] edge. [두뇌,판단력이 날카롭고 정확함].

예리하다 acute; keen; sharp; shrewd; penetrating; piercing; (변설이) telling; incisive; pungent.

예매 [**येमै**] [**豫買**] dvance purchase; purchase inadvance; (purchase by) subscription. 예매하다 buy [purchase] in advance; subscribe for[to].

예명 [**येमयौंग**] [**藝名**] stage name; (영화 배우의) a screen name.

예물 [**येमूल**] [**禮物**] [사례물] a gith; a present; a return present (답례품). **2** (결혼의) a wedding present [gith] for the bride. **3**(신랑 신부의) wedding giths exchanged between the bride and bridegroom.

예민 [**येमीन**] [**銳敏**] 하다 sharp; keen; acute; sensitive; subtle; fine; quick.

예방 [**येबांग**] [**豫防**] prevention <of / against>; protection <from / against>; (a) precaution; [醫]; (a) prophylaxis. 예방하다 prevent; protect <from / against>; ward off; keep off [away]; take preventive [precautionary] measures <against>; take precaution <against>; provide against.

예방접종 [**येबांगजौपचोंग**] [**豫防接種**] a vaccination; (an) inoculation. e.g. 예방 접종을 하다 inoculate / vaccinate. 콜레라의 예방 접종을 했니 Are you inoculated against cholera?

예배 [**येबै**] [**禮拜**] worship; (a) church [divine] service.

예법 [**येबौप**] [**禮法**] tiquette; manners; courtesy; decorum(s); propriety.

예복 [**येबोक**] [**禮服**] ormal [ceremonial] dress (▷ formal dress 는 일반 정장, ceremonial dress 는 의식을 위한 복장); full dress; formal clothes; a dress suit.

예비 [**येबी**] [**豫備**] 준비] preparation; [마련] a reserve; a spare.

예쁘다 [**येपुदा**] pretty; lovely; beautiful; fine; nice; comely; handsome; good-looking; fair; neat.

예사 [**येसा**] [**例事**] [보통의 일] a commonplace event; a common practice; an ordinary affair; a custom.

예산 [**येसान**] [**豫算**] [예정 경비] an appropriation; [견적] an estimate; [국가 등의 세입과 세출의 계획] a budget <for>.

예산안 [**येसानान**] [**豫算案**] a drath budget; [의회의 심의 결정 전의 의안] a budget (bill); a bill of budget.

예상 [**येसांग**] [**豫想**] [예기] expectation(s); anticipation; [예측] a forecast; [어림] an estimate; [가상] supposition; presupposetion 예상하다 expect; forecast; anticipate; estimate; reckon.

예선 [येसौन] [豫選] 1 (경기 등의) a preliminary; a preliminary [an elimination] match [contest]; (레이스 등의) a (preliminary [trial]) heat; a preliminary [trial] race; (축구 등의) a qualifying round. 2 (선거의) a provisional selection [election]; a preliminary election; a preelection; a primary (election).

예속 [येसोक] [隷屬] subordination 예속하다 be subordinate [subject] <to>; be under the control [authority] <of>; come under the rule <of>; subordinate oneself to; belong to.

예수 [येसू] Jesus (Christ).

예술 [येसूल] [藝術] <집합적> art; (특정 부문의) an art; (the fine) arts(미술).

예술가 [인] an artist. e.g. 그는 예술 기질이 있는 사람이다 He is an artistic type. / He is a man of an artistic nature [temperament].

예습 [येसुप] [豫習] reparation (s) <of one's lesson (s)>. 예습하다 prepare one's lesson (s); do one's homework; do preparation; <英> do prep.

예시 [येसी] [例示] illustration; exemplification. 예시하다 illustrate (by example); exemplify.

예식 [येसीक] [例式] an established form.

예식 [येसीक] [禮式] 예법에 따라 행하는 식] a ceremony; a celebration; [결혼식] a wedding (ceremony).

예심 [येसीम] [豫審] a preliminary hearing [examination / investigation]; a pretrial hearing [examination / investigation].

예언 [येऔन] [豫言] (a) prophecy; (a) prediction; a forecast 예언하다 foretell; predict; (종교적으로) prophesy.

예외 [येवे] [例外] an exception.

예우 [येउ] [禮遇] (an) honorable treatment; a cordial reception; privileges; honors. e.g. 각별한 예우를 하다 receive <a person> with marks of distinction. 예우하다 receive <a person> courteously [cordially]; treat <a person> with respect.

예의 [येउइ] [禮儀] (good) manners; etiquette; courtesy; decorum (s); propriety; civility; politeness.

예의범절 [येउइबौमचौल] [禮儀凡節] (the rules of) etiquette; manners; decorum(s); proprieties.

예인선 [येइन्सौन] [曳引船] tug; a tugboat; a towboat; a towing vessel.

예전 [येजौन] 옛날] the old days; ancient [old] times; [이전]

former days [times].

예절 [रेजौल] [**禮節**] eco-rum(s); courtesy; manners; etiquette; propriety.

예정 [रेजौंग] [**豫定**] [계획] a schedule; a program; a plan; [준비](a) previous arrangement; prearrangement; (가격 등의) an estimate; [예상] expectation; anticipation.

예제 [रेजे] [**例題**] 보기] an example; [연습 문제] an exercise.

예증 [रेजुंग] [**例證**] 예를 들어 증명함] illustration; an illustration; an instance; an example. 예증하다 illustrate; exemplify.

예지 [रेजी] [**豫知**] [미리 앎] foresight; (지식,경험 등에 입각하는) prediction. 예지하다 [예언하다] foretell; [지식,경험 등에 입각하여 추론하다] predict; [예견하다] foresee.

예찬 [रेछान] [**禮讚**] [숭배] worship; [칭송] admiration. 예찬하다 [रेछान्हादा] worship; adore; idolize <a film star>; glorify; sing the praises of.

예측 [रेछुक] [**豫測**] pre-estimate; a forecast; presupposition; [예견](a) prediction (▷ 과학적인 정확성을 뜻함); [어림](an) estimate. 예측하다 presuppose; forecast; foretell; guess; [예견하다] predict <an earthquake>; [어림하다] estimate.

예치금 [रेछीगुम] [**預置金**] deposit; money on deposit.

예탁 [रेथाक] [**預託**] epositing; deposition. **예탁하다** deposit <money in a bank>.

예행 [रेहैंग] [**豫行**] preliminary performance <of a play>; a rehearsal. 예행하다perform preliminarily; rehearse; have [give] a rehearsal; try out.

예후 [रेहू] [**豫後**] [병후의] 경과, 회복] convalescence; [의학에서, 병의 경과, 결 과의 예상] prognosis <*pl.* −ses>.

오한 [ओहान] [**惡寒**] a chill; a cold[shivering] fit; rigor. e.g. 오한이 나다 feel[catch / take / have] a chill.

오합지졸 [ओहापचीजोल] [**烏合之卒**] a rabble; a disorderly crowd; a mob. e.g. 이 집단은 조직이라기보다 오합지졸이다 This group is just a mixed bunch [a gathering of various types of people] rather than an organization.

오해 [ओहे] [**誤解**] (a) misunderstanding; misapprehension; delusion; misconception. 오해하다 misunderstand; mistake; misapprehend; (어구를) put a wrong construction <on>; misconstrue; [나쁘게 해석하다] take <something> amiss. e.g. 뭔가 오해하고

있는 것 같다 You seem to have misunderstood something.

오후 [ओहू] [午後] afternoon; p.m.

오히려 [ओहीर्यो] [반대로] on the contrary; instead.

옥 [ओक] **1** [보석] a precious stone; a gem; a jewel. **2** jade. **3** <비유> anything fine. 옥에 티 a flaw in a precious stone; a fly in the ointment; a flaw in one's character; a blot on one's record[reputation]; a hole in one's coat.

옥고 [ओको] [獄苦] the hardships of prison life. e.g. 옥고를 견디다 endure the hardships of prison life. 옥고를 치르고 나오다 serve out one's term of imprisonment.

옥내 [ओक्नै] [屋內] the interior [inside] of a house.).

옥사 [ओक्सा] [獄死] 옥사하다 die in prison.

옥상 [ओक्साग] [屋上] the roothop; the top of the house.

옥수수 [ओक्सूसू] Indian corn; corn; maize (▷ <英>에서는 corn 은 밀을 말함).

옥신각신 [ओक्सीन्गाक्सीन] 옥신각신하다 argue [dispute / wrangle] <with>; skirmish; altercate <with>; squabble; have a (petty) quarrel <with>.

옥신거리다 [ओक्सीन्गौरीदा] ⇨ 욱신거리다

옥외 [ओक्वे] [屋外] [집의 밖] the outdoors; the exterior of a house; the open (air).

온 [ओन] [전부의] all; whole; entire; total. 온하다 [골프] (사람이) reach the green; make the green; put the ball on the green; (공이) reach the green; land on the green.

온갖 [ओन्कात] all; every; each and every; all kinds [sorts] of.

온건 [ओन्कौन] [穩健] moderateness; moderation; soundness.

온고지신 [ओन्कोजीसीन] [溫故知新] reviewing the old and learning the new; carrying the knowledge gained into new fields.

온기 [ओन्की] [溫氣] warmth.

온난 [ओन्नान] [溫暖] 온난하다 warm; mild; temperate.

온당 [ओन्दाग] [穩當] reasonableness; being just and proper; fittingness; appropriateness. 온당하다 reasonable; proper; modest; just; right; moderate; appropriate; fitting.

온데간데없다 [ओन्देगान्देऔप्ता] vanish; disappear; missing; vanish without leaving a trace; completely out of sight. e.g. 금고 속에 넣어 둔 보석이 온데간데없다 The jewel is missing[has disappeared] from the safe.

온도 [ओन्दो] [**溫度**] temperature; heat.

온도계 [ओन्दाझे] [**溫度計**] a thermometer.

온돌 [ओन्दोल] an *ondol*; a (Korean) floor heater; a hypocaust. 온돌방 [ओन्दोल्बांग] a hot-floored room; an *ondol* room.

온라인 [ओलाइन] e.g. 온라인의 [컴퓨터] on-line. 본점과 지점은 온라인으로 연결되어 있다 The head and branch offices are connected on-line.

온수 [ओन्सू] [**溫水**] .e.g. 온수를 급수하다 supply <a bathroom with> hot water.

온순 [ओन्सून] [**溫順**] gentleness; geniality; docility; obedience. 온순하다 gentle; genial; docile; meek; obedient; compliant.

온실 [ओन्सील] [**溫室**] a hothouse; a greenhouse; a glasshouse; a greenery.

온유 [ओन्यू] [**溫柔**] [온화] gentleness; mildness; [유순] obedience; docility; meekness. 온유하다 gentle; meek; mild; tender; sweet; docile.

온전 [ओन्जौन] [**穩全**] 온전하다 sound; whole; intact; unimpaired; perfect.

온정 [ओन्जौग] [**溫情**] a kindly feeling; kindliness; warmheartedness; geniality.

온종일 [ओन्जोंगील] [**-終日**] all day (long); the whole day; from morning till night.

온집안 [ओन्जीबान] **1** [가족] the whole family; all (members of) the family. **2** [가옥안] all over the house.

온탕 [ओन्थांग] [**溫湯**] [온천의 따뜻한 물] the hot water of the spa[hot spring]; [적당한 온도의 탕] moderately warm bath.

온통(으로) [ओन्थोंगुरो] all; wholly; entirely; altogether; bodily; in the gross [mass / lump]; every and all; any and every; the whole lot; <프> en mass [bloc].

온화 [ओन्हवा] [**溫和**] **1** (기후, 날씨가). 온화하다 mild; temperate; clement; genial; benign. e.g. 온화한 기후 a mild[temperate] climate. **2** (성질,태도가). 온화하다 gentle; mild; genial. e.g. 온화한 인품 a gentle [pleasant / genial] personality.

올[1] [ओल] e.g. 올 여름 this summer / next [coming] summer (오는) / last summer (지난). 올안에 in(the) course of this year / before the end of this [the] year / before the year is out.

올[2] [ओल] [가닥] a strand; a ply; (피륙의) warp.

올가미 [ओल्कामी] **1** [올무] a snare; a trap. **2** [계략] a trap.

올곧다 [ओल्कोत्ता] **1** [마음이 곧다] honest; upright. **2**

[줄이 반듯하다] straight.

올라가다 [ओल्लागादा] **1** [높이 오르다] go [walk] up; climb (up); rise; ascend. ⇨ 오르다 **2** [강을 거슬러 상류로 가다] go [sail] up <a river>; go upstream; (물고기가) run up <a river>. **3** [지방에서 서울로 가다] go up to the capital [Seoul]. **4** [지위 등이 높아지다] rise; be promoted[raised]. **5** [값이 비싸지다] go up; rise; soar (크게); shoot up(급히). **6** [없어지다] lose; <money> be lost; be spent uselessly. **7** [상륙하다] land; go [come] ashore. **8** [진보하다] advance; progress; make progress [headway]; improve.

올라서다 [ओल्लासोदा] **1** [높은 데로 옮아 서다] step[get] onto; mount [ascend] <a platform>. **2** [지위가 높아지다] rise to higher level of rank; [출세하다] rise in the world.

올라오다 [ओल्लाओदा] come up.

올라타다 [ओल्लाथादा] **1** [탈것에 몸을 올려놓다] get into [on]; embark on [in] <a ship>; step in to <a boat>; mount [ride] <a horse>; board <a train>; go [come / get] on board [aboard (of)] <a ship>. **2** [몸 위에 오르다] cover; line; tread (수탉이).

올리다 [ओल्लीदा] **1** [위로 오르게 하다] raise; lith(up); upraise; elevate; fly; put[get] up; hold up. **2** [계급,등급 지위를 높이다] raise; promote. **3** [증가시키다] increase; [인상하다] raise; hike; boost. **4** [성과를 얻다] achieve <good results>; advance. **5** [바치다] give; offer; present.

올림픽 [ओल्लीम्पीक] the Olympics; the Olympic Games.

올망졸망 [ओल्मांग्जोल्मांग] in lots of small units [pieces / lumps]; in a lovely huddle; in clusters. 올망졸망하다 <서술적> be of various small sizes; come in lots of small units.

올바로 [ओल्बारो] [진실되게] truthfully; [정직하게] honestly; uprightly; straight-forwardly; [합법적으로] lawfully; legally; [건전하게] soundly; [도덕적으로] morally.

올바르다 [ओल्बारुदा] [정당하다] right; [정의롭다] just; righteous; [잘못이 없다] correct; [정확하다] exact; accurate; [적절하다] proper; [합법적이다] lawful; legitimate; legal.

올챙이 [ओल्छैंगी] a tadpole; a polliwog.

올케 [ओल्खे] the wife of a girl's brother; a girl's sister-in-law.

올해 [ओरहै] this year; the current [present] year.

옭다 [ओक्ता] **1** [잡아매다] tie (up); bind. >. **2** [올가미를 씌워 홀치다] secure by a noose; put a noose around; noose. **3** [꾀로 걸려들게 하다] entrap; set a trap <for>.

옭아매다 [ओल्गामैदा] **1** [올가미로 잡아매다] cast [put] a noose round <the neck> and tie <to>; (단단히) tie up <a package **2** [없는 죄를 꾸며 씌우다] make a false charge against <a person>; charge <the guilt> on <a person> falsely; frame <a person>.

옮기다 [ओम्गीदा] **1**[자리를 다른 곳으로 바꾸다] move; remove; shith; transfer. **2** [말,소문 등을 전하다] tell (at second hand); pass <words> on <to another>. **3** [숙소,소속 등을 바꾸다] move; remove; shith; transfer. **4** [병을 전염시키다] infect <a person with disease> (▷ 의학 용어로도 쓰임); give [pass / communicate] <a disease to another>. **5** [돌리다] turn; divert; direct <to>.

옮다 [ओम्ता] **1** [병,버릇,사상 등이 전염되다] be infected (with); catch; take; contract <a bad cold **2** [물들다]. e.g. 비누의 향기가 세탁물에 옮았다 The scent of the soap has permeated [been picked up by / been absorbed by] the wash.

옮아가다 [ओल्मागादा] **1** 이전,이동하다] move[remove / shith / transfer] <to / into>. **2** [퍼져 가다] spread <from one to another / to / into>.

옳다 [ओल्था] **1** [정의롭다] just; righteous; [정당하다] right; [합법적이다] lawful; legitimate; legal. **2** [맞다] right; correct; proper; [정확하다] exact; accurate.

옴짝달싹 [ओम्चाक्ताल्साक] with a very slight [the slightest] move; budging slightly.

옷 [ओत] [의복] clothes (▷ 항상 복수형. 단, 수사와 함께 쓰지 않음); <집합적> clothing; a garment; dress (▷ 의류 전체의 뜻으로 관사없이 쓰는 것은 예스러운 용법); (무대,가장용) costume; (주로 여성,여자아이의) a dress; (한벌의) a suit.

옷감 [ओत्काम] [천] cloth; (재료로서) material; texture (직물).

옷걸이 [ओत्कौरी] a clothes [dress] hanger.

옷깃 [ओत्कीत] [한복의 동정] a neckband; (양복,와이셔츠의) a collar; (신사복의) a lapel.

옷맵시 [ओत्मैब्सी] the appearance of one's clothes. e.g. 옷맵시가 좋다[좋지 않다] wear one's clothes sty-lishly [badly / poorly] / dress oneself in good [bad] shape.

옷자락 [ओचाराक] [허리 아래 부분] a skirt; [끝 부분] a hem; [길게 늘어진 치맛자락] the train; (양복 바지의) the bottom. ⇨ 자락

옷장 [ओचांग] [-欌] a clothes chest; a wardrobe.

옷차림 [ओछरीम] [복장] clothing; dress; attire; [풍채] appearance.

옹고집 [ओंगोजीप] [壅固執] obstinacy; stubbornness; perversity; obduracy.

옹달샘 [ओंगोदाल्सैम] a small fountain [spring].

옹색하다 [ओंग्सैख्वादा] [壅塞-] **1** [군색하다] straitened; needy; reduced. **2** [옹졸하다] narrow [small]-minded; ungenerous; mean.

옹졸하다 [ओंग्जोरहादा] [壅拙-] narrow-minded; illiberal; intolerant; ungenerous; hidebound; mean.

옹호 [ओंग्हो] [擁護] [보호] protection; defense; [변호] vindication; [원조,지지] support; assistance. 옹호하다 protect; safeguard; defend; stand by; support.

와[1] [वा] [기쁨의 환성] Hurrah!; [야] Gee!; [놀람, 감탄의 소리] Wow!

와[2] [वा] (⇨ 과) **1** [열거] and. **2** [함께] with; along [together] with; in company with; accompanied by.

와글거리다 [वागुल्कौरीदा] **1** [북적이다] throng; crowd; swarm. **2** [떠들다] make a noise; raise a clamor; be boisterous [clamorous]; clamor.

와르르 [वारूरू] **1** [무너지는 모양이나 소리] with a crashing sound; crash. **2** [여럿이 동시에 몰려드는 모양] in crowds; in a rush.

와삭 [वासाक] with a rustle; with a rustling sound [noise]. 하다 rustle; give (out) a rustle. 와삭거리다 rustle; give(out) a rustle.

와신상담 [वासीन्सांग्दाम] [臥薪嘗膽] perseverance; endurance of hardship(s). 와신상담하다 go through unspeakable hardships and privations.

와전 [वाजौन] [訛傳] a false report; misinformation. 와전하다 give a false report; misinform.

와해 [वाहै] [瓦解] collapse; a (down)fall; a breakup 와해하다 collapse; break up; fall[go / crumble] to pieces; be smashed; be ruined.

완강 [वान्कांग] [頑强] obstinacy; stubbornness. 완강하다 tenacious; stubborn; obstinate; dogged; unbending; unyielding. 완강히 tenaciously; stubbornly; obstinately.

완결 [वान्ग्यौल] [完結] conclusion; completion; an end. 완결하다 [마치다] conclude; complete; [끝나다]

be concluded; finish; end.

완고 [वान्को] [**頑固**] [올곧고 고집이 셈] stubbornness; obstinacy; bigotry. 완고하다 stubborn; obstinate (▷ obstinate는 때로 고집스럽게 의견이나 방식을 굽히지 않음을, stubborn은 천성이 완고함을 내포); bigoted; headstrong; [끈질기다] persistent; dogged.

완곡 [वान्कोक] [**婉曲**] a roundabout; indirectness; euphemism (어법). 완곡하다 euphemistic; periphrastic; circumlocutional; roundabout. 완곡히 in a roundabout way; by euphemism.

완구점 [वान्गुजौम] a toy shop [store].

완급 [वान्कुप] [**緩急**] fast and slow motion; high and low speed.

완납 [वान्नाप] [**完納**] full payment; payment in full. 완납하다 pay <one's fine> in full; pay the whole amount of <one's tax>.

완료 [वाल्यो] [**完了**] completion. 완료하다 [사물을 완성하다] complete; [마치다] finish.

완만 [वान्मान] [**緩慢**] 완만하다 [속도가 느리다] slow(-moving[-going]); sluggish; [경사가 급하지 않다] gentle; [활발치 않다] slack; inactive.

완벽 [वानब्यौक] [**完璧**] perfection. 완벽하다 perfect; complete; flawless; impeccable (과실,죄 등이 없는).

완비 [वान्बी] [**完備**] perfection; completion; full equipment. 완비하다 perfect; complete; equip [furnish / provide] completely.

완성 [वान्सौंग] [**完成**] completion; perfection; accomplishment; consummation; finish. 완성하다 [사람이 일을 마치다] finish; [완전한 것으로 되다] complete (▷ finish는 일상적인 사항에 대해서 씀); accomplish; perfect; bring <a thing> to completion [perfection]; finish up.

완수 [वान्सू] [**完遂**] completion; accomplishment. **완수하다** accomplish; achieve; complete; carry out [through]; go through <with **1** (달걀이). 완숙하다 boil hard. e.g. 완숙한 계란 a hard-boiled egg. 계란이 완숙했다 The eggs were boiled hard. **2** (과일이). 완숙하다 ripen into full maturity; attain [come to] (full[complete]) maturity.

완승 [वान्सुंग] [**完勝**] a complete victory; a sweeping triumph. 완승하다 win [score] a complete [total] victory <over one's opponent>; make a clean score; <美>(경기에서) shut out.

완연 [वान्यौन] [宛然] 완연하다 distinct; obvious; clear; vivid. 완연히 distinctly; obviously; clearly; vividly.

완전 [वान्जौन] [完全] perfection; entirety; completeness; wholeness. 완전하다 perfect; complete; entire; full; whole. 완전히 perfectly; completely; entirely; fully; to perfection; quite; utterly; wholly; thoroughly; in its entirety; to the full; out and out.

완제품 [वान्जेफूम] a finished product; finished goods.

완주 [वान्जू] [完走] 완주하다 run [cover] the whole course [distance] <of>.

완충 [वान्छुंग] [緩衝] 완충하다 absorb shock; deaden concussion; buff.

완치 [वान्छी] [完治] (a) complete recovery; a perfect cure. 완치하다 recover completely; cure <a person, a disease, etc.> completely; heal <a person, a wound, etc.> completely.

완쾌 [वानख्वे] [完快] complete recovery; complete cure. 완쾌하다 recover (completely) <from one's illness>; be completely cured <of a disease>; be completely restored to health; get well.

완화 [वान्हवा] [緩和] relaxation; easing; (a) relief; alleviation; mitigation; (특히 국제간의 긴장의) a dente. 완화하다 relax ease; relieve; alleviate; lighten; sothen; mitigate.

왈가왈부 [वाल्गावाल्बू] [日可日否] [옳다거니 그르다거니 말함]. e.g. 세상에서는 그 사람에 대해서 왈가왈부 말이 많다 People are saying all kinds of things [this and that] about him.

왈가닥 [वाल्गादाक] a tomboy; a hoyden; a romp; a kitten; a filly.

왈칵 [वाल्खाक] suddenly; all of a sudden; with a rush [jerk].

왔다갔다 [वात्तागात्ता] **1** [자주 오고 가고 하는 모양]. **2** [정신이 맑았다 흐렸다 하는 모양].

왕 [वांग] [王] **1** = 임금. e.g. 왕을 옹립하다 enthrone a king / set a king on the throne. 왕을 폐하다 dethrone a king. 왕이 나라를 다스리고 있다 A king rules that country. **2** [제일인자] a king; a magnate; a baron; a tycoon.

왕관 [वांग्वान] [王冠] the crown.

왕국 [वांगुक] [王國] **1** [왕이 다스리는 나라] a kingdom; a realm; a monarchy (군주국). **2**[어떤 현상, 세 력이 지배적으로 나타나는 영역] a kingdom; an empire.

왕궁 [वांगुंग] [王宮] the palace; a royal [king's] palace.

왕권 [**वांग्क्वॉन**] [**王權**] sovereignty; sovereign power [right]; royal authority [powers]; the royal prerogative; the regal power.

왕년 [**वांगन्यौन**] [**往年**] old times; the past; former times; the years gone by; those old days. e.g. 그녀는 왕년의 유명한 아역 배우이다 She was once [formerly] a famous child star.

왕도 [**वांग्तो**] [**王道**] the rule of virtue [right]; righteous government; kingcrath.

왕래 [**वांग्नै**] [**往來**] **1** [오고 감] coming and going; traffic. e.g. 사람의 왕래 pedestrian traffic / comings and goings of people. **2**[교제] intercourse; association; [서신의 교환] correspondence. e.g. 친척과의 왕래도 끊고 있다 I am no longer having anything to do with my relatives.

왕릉 [**वांग्नुम**] [**王陵**] a royal mausoleum <*pl.* -lea>; a royal tomb.

왕복 [**वांग्बोक**] [**往復**] [갔다가 돌아오기] going and returning; [왔다갔 다하기] coming and going. e.g. 우주 왕복선 space shuttle. 학교에의 왕복은 버스를 이용한다.

왕성 [**वांगसौंग**] [**旺盛**] 왕성하다 flourishing; prime; high; excellent. e.g. 왕성한 욕망 an irresistible desire. 혈기 왕성한 때에 in the prime of one's youth.

왕위 [**वांग्वी**] [**王位**] the throne; the crown.

왕자 [**वांग्जा**] [**王子**] a (Royal) prince; a prince of the blood (royal).

왕정 [**वांग्जौंग**] [**王政**] **1** [임금의 정치] royal rule [government]. **2**[군주 정치] monarchy; the royal regime.

왕조 [**वांग्जो**] [**王朝**] a dynasty.

왕진 [**वांग्जीन**] [**往診**] a call(on a patient); a house call; a (doctor's) visit(to a patient). 왕진하다 visit a patient in his home; go out to see a patient; pay a sick call on a patient; make a house call.

왕창 [**वांग्छांग**] e.g. 예산을 3분의 1이나 왕창 줄였다 A whole third of our budget was lopped [chopped] off. / We had a third of our budget cut in one fell swoop.

왜 [**वै**] **1** [어째서] why; how; what; for what reason [purpose]; what for; how. come; [무슨 까닭으로] on what ground. **2** [의문을 나타낼 때 쓰이는 말] why.

왜곡 [**वैगोक**] [**歪曲**] distortion; perversion. 왜곡하다 strain; distort; pervert; contort; twist; warp.

왜소 [**वैसो**] [**矮小**] dwarfness; dwarfishness. 왜소하다 dwarf; dwarfish; under-sized; diminutive; pygmy.

왱왱 [वैन्वैग] **1** = 왱. e.g. 바람에 전선이 왱왱 울었다 The wind set up a humming in the wires. **2** [아이들의 글 읽는 소리] aloud; nosily. 왱왱하다 <children> read <books> at the top of <their> voices [lungs].

외[1] [वे] [外] [그 밖] except; but; with exception of; (…이상은) beyond; (이외에) besides; in addition to.

외[2] [वे] single; sole; only. e.g. 외아들 an [the] only son.

외[3] [वे] −[外] **1** [외가] (related) on the mother's [daughter's] side; maternal. **2** [밖,표면] outside; outer; foreign.

외가 [वेगा] [外家] the mother's [maternal] (side of the) family; one's mother's old home.

외각 [वेगाक] [外角] **1** [數] an external [exterior] angle. **2** = 아웃 코너(⇨ 아웃).

외경 [वेझौंग] [畏敬] Awe; reverence.

외계 [वेझे] [外界] the external [outside] world; the outside; [지구 밖] the outer space.

외고집 [वेगोजीप] [−固執] (single-minded) stubbornness; obstinacy; perversity.

외곬 [वेगोल] a single way [track / groove].

외과 [वेक्वा] [外科] [의학의 한 분과] surgery; (병원의) the department of surgery.

외곽 [वेग्वाक] [外廓] **1** [성 밖으로 둘러쌓은 성] the outer wall; the outwall. **2** [바깥 테두리] the outer block[fence]; the contour.

외관 [वेग्वान] [外觀] external [outward] appearance; an outward show [aspect]; an exterior view.

외교 [वेग्यो] [外交] 외국과의 교제] diplomacy; a foreign policy (정책); diplomatic relations [intercourse] (관계); (섭외) outside duty; canvassing.

외교관 [वेक्योग्वान] [外交官] a diplomatic official; a diplomatist; a diplomat; <집합적> the diplomatic service.

외국 [वेगूक] [外國] a foreign country[land]

외국인 [वेगूगीन] [外國人] a foreignner; a foreign national; an alien(▷ an alien은 그 나라의 시민권을 갖고 있지 않은 사람, 그 나라에 체류하고 있는 외국인이라는 뜻으로 쓰이는 경우가 많음. 법률적인 경우가 아니면 이 말은 사용하지 말 것).

외근 [वेगुन] [外勤] outside duty [service]; canvassing

(외교원의). 외근하다work outside; do outside work; be on outside duty [service].

외길 **[वेगील]** an unforked road; a road without a fork al along.

외도 **[वेदो]** [**外道**] **1**[바르지 않은 길,노릇] evil principles; depraved doctrines; injustice. 외도하다 deviate [swerve] from <the right path>.

외동딸 **[वेदोंग्ताल]** an only daughter.

외동아들 **[वेदोंगादुल]** an only son.

외딴 **[वेतान]** isolated; out-of-the-way; solitary.

외래 **[वेरै]** [**外來**] e.g. 외래의 foreign / imported / coming from abroad.

외래어 **[वेरैऔ]** [**外來語**] an adopted [a borrowed / a loan] word; a word of foreign origin.

외로움 **[वेरोउम]** loneliness; lonesomeness. e.g. 외로움을 느끼다 feel lonely.

외로이 **[वेरोइ]** lonelily; alone; lonesomely.

외롭다 **[वेरोप्ता]** lonely; lonesome; forlorn; <서술적> feel lonely [lonesome].

외면 **[वेम्यौन]** [**外面**] (an) outward appearance; the outside; the exterior. 외면하다 turn one's face away <from>; look away <from>; avert one's eyes <from>; [무시하다] disregard.

외모 **[वेमो]** [**外貌**] (an) outward appearance; external features; externals

외무 **[वेमू]** [**外務**] **1** [외국에 관한 정무] foreign [external] affairs. **2** = 외근. **외무부** **[वेमूबू]** [**外務部**] the Ministry of Foreign Affairs.

외박 **[वेबाक]** [**外泊**] stopping [sleeping / staying] out (overnight). 외박하다 stay out overnight; sleep out; (군인이) stop out of barracks.

외발제기 **[वेबाल्चेगी]** [한 발로 차는 제기]. e.g. 외발제기를 차다 play a shuttlecock with one foot.

외부 **[वेबू]** [**外部**] [바깥쪽] the outside; the exterior; [바깥 세계] the outside world.

외빈 **[वेबीन]** [**外賓**] [외국 손님] a foreign guest [visitor]; [외부 손님] a guest [visitor].

외삼촌 **[वेसाम्छोन]** [**外三寸**] an uncle on the mother's side; one's maternal uncle; one's mother's brother

외상 **[वेसांग]** [**外傷**] an external wound [injury]; a trauma <*pl.* -ta, ~s>.

외상 **[वेसांग]** [**外相**] the Foreign Minister.

외설 **[वेसौल]** [**猥褻**] obscenity; lewdness; indecency; licentiousness. 외설 하다 obscene; lewd; indecent; licentious; dirty; improper; nasty.

외세 **[वेसे]** **[外勢]** **1** [바깥 형세] external situation [conditions]. **2** [외부의 세력] outside [foreign / alien] influence [power].

외손 **[वेसोन]** **[外孫]** a child of one's daughter; a grandchild.

외숙모 **[वेसूंगमो]** the wife of a maternal uncle; an aunt.

외식 **[वेशिक]** **[外食]** 외식하다 eat [dine] out; board out.

외신 **[वेशिन]** **[外信]** a report from overseas; an overseas report; foreign [overseas] news.

외아들 **[वेआदुल]** an only son.

외양 **[वेयांग]** **[外樣]** .e.g. 외양은 outwardly / in appearance. 외양이 그럴듯하다 have a good appearance. 외양을 꾸미다 make outward show / keep up appearances.

외우다 **[वेउदा]** [암기 하다] learn ... by heart; memorize; commit ... to memory.

외유 내강 **[वेयू नेगांग]** **[外柔內剛]** being gentle in appearance, but sturdy in spirit; an iron hand in the velvet glove. 외유 내강하다

외제 **[वेजे]** **[外製]** e.g. 외제의 of foreign make / foreign-made.

외조부 **[वेजोबू]** **[外祖父]** the father of one's mother; a grandfather.

외지 **[वेजी]** **[外地]** **1** [타향] a place away from home; another country. **2** = 외국.

외지다 **[वेजीदा]** out-of-the-way; remote; secluded.

외출 **[वेछुल]** **[外出]** going out; an outing.

외치다 **[वेछीदा]** shout; cry (out); yell; shriek; scream; (감격해서) exclaim.

외투 **[वेथू]** **[外套]** an overcoat; a greatcoat; (소매 없는) a cloak.

외판원 **[वेफान्वॉन]** **[外販員]** a salesman; (여자) a saleswoman; (지방 순회의) a commercial traveler; a traveling salesman; (방문 판매의) a house-to-house salesman [saleswoman].

외풍 **[वेफूंग]** **[外風]** **1** [밖에서 들어오는 바람] a draught; a drath. **2** [외국 풍속] foreignism; exotic fashion; foreign [Western] style.

외할머니 **[वेहाल्मौनी]** **[外-]** a mother of one's mother; a grandmother.

외할아버지 **[वेहाराबौजी]** **[外-]** a father of one's mother; a grandfather.

외형 **[वेह्यौंग]** **[外形]** **1** [사물의 겉모양] an outward form [shape]; outward appearance. **2** the gross sales [proceeds]; the turnover.

외화[1] **[वेहवा]** **[外畵]** [외국의 영화] a foreign film [movie].

외화[2] **[वेहवा]** **[外貨]** **1** [외국의 화폐] foreign currency [money]. **2** [외국 화물] foreign [imported] goods.

외환[1] **[वेह्वान]** [**外換**] [외국환] foreign exchange.

외환[2] **[वेह्वान]** [**外患**] fear of foreign [outside] invasion; foreign [external] troubles; troubles from without; the pressure [invasion] of foreign enemy.

왼 [वेन] left; left-hand (ed).

왼손잡이 [वेन्सोंन्जाबी] a left-handed person; a left-hander; a left.

왼쪽 [वेन्चोक] the left side.

요 [यो] [**要**] [중요한 골자] the main [essential] point; the point. 요는 The point is (that) 요는 무리를 하지 않는 것이다 It is essential that you should not overdo it. 요는 기본을 파악하는 것이다 The essential [main / most important] thing is to grasp the fundamental principles.

요강 [योगांग] [**要綱**] a summary [an outline] of essential points; the gist; the main principle; [취지서] a prospectus.

요건 [योगौन] [**要件**] **1** [중요한 일] an important matter [business]. **2** [필요조건] a necessary [an indispensable] condition; a requisite; an essential factor; essentials.

요구 [योगू] [**要求**] (권리로서의, 또는 강력한) a demand; (당연한 권리 로서의) a claim; [요청] a request; [필요] needs. **요구하다** require; claim <damaged>; demand; re-quest; call <for>; call upon <a person to do>; ask [make a demand] for <money>.

요구르트 [योगुरुथु] yogurt; yogh(o)urt.

요금 [योगुम] [**料金**] a charge; a rate; [수납료, 입장료, 전문직에 대한 사례] a fee; (탈것의) a fare.

요기 [योगी] [**療飢**] [시장기를 겨우 면함]. 요기하다 stave [keep] off hunger; allay [stay] hunger; keep the wolf from the door.

요동 [योदोंग] [**搖動**] shaking; (배의) pitching (전후의); rolling (좌우의); (수레의) jolting.]. 요동하다 tremble; shake; quake; wobble; (수레가) jolt; (배가) pitch and roll; rock. e.g. 배는 전후좌우로 심하게 요동했다 Our ship rolled and pitched [rocked] heavily.

요란 [योरान] [**搖亂, 擾亂**] [시끄럽고 떠들썩함]. 요란하다 noisy; loud; boisterous; uproarious; clamorous; tumultuous; shrill.

요람 [योराम] [**搖籃**] a swinging cot; a cradle.

요령 [योर्यौंग] [**要領**] [비결, 기교] a knack; the trick; tact; <美>know-how.

요리 [योरी] [**料理**] **1** [음식

만들기] cooking; cookery (일반 요리법); cuisine (특정 요리법); [음식] a dish; food. **2** [처리함] handling; management. 요리하다 manage; administer; handle.

요망 **[योमांग]** [要望] a cry <for>; a demand <for>; a request; [소망] a desire; a wish. 요망하다 demand; request; cry <for>; desire.

요새 **[योसै]** [최근] recently; lately; of late (▷ of late 는 좀 딱딱한 표현. 완료 시제에나 과거 시제에나 모두 쓰임); [요즈음] these days; [지금] nowadays; now; [지난 며칠간] the past few days.

요새 **[योसै]** [要塞] a fortress; a stronghold; fortifications (▷ 보통 복수형).

ㅇ

요소 **[योसो]** [要素] [성분] an element; [구성 요소] a constituent; [요인] a factor; a requisite (필요 조건).

요술 **[योसूल]** [妖術] [기술 (奇術)] conjuring tricks; jugglery; magic.

요약 **[योयाक]** [要約] summming-up <*pl.* summings-up>; [요약한 것] a summary; an outline; a digest; an abstract (논문 등의); a synopsis (내용의 특징을 간추린 것). 요약하다 sum up; summarize; digest; give a summing-up; abridge; brief.

요양 **[योयांग]** [療養] medical treatment [care]; [병의 조리] recuperation. 요양하다 receive [get] medical treatment; recuperate (oneself / one's health)

요염 **[योयौम]** [妖艶] bewitching beauty; sensual charm. 요염하다 fascinating; bewitching; voluptuous; erotic; sexy; coquettish; seductive.

요절 **[योजौल]** [腰折, 腰絶] e.g. 그의 이야기가 너무도 우스워서 우리는 요절복통했다 His story was so funny that we were all in convulsions [we all laughed till our sides began to ache 요절하다 hold[burst / split] one's sides with laughter; have a sidesplitting laugh; laugh oneself into convulsions; be convulsed with laughter.

요절 **[योजौल]** [夭折] a premature [an early / an untimely] death. 요절하다 die young; die prematurely; die [suffer] an early [an untimely / a premature] death; die before one's time; meet an untimely death; die in the prime of life; be nipped in the bud; be brought [sent] to an early grave.

요점 **[योजौम]** [要點] the point; the main [essential / vital / principal / crucial] point; the gist <of a lecture>; the cruK the essentials; the highlight; the pivot; the nub.

요정 [योजौग] [妖精] a fairy; (작은 요정) a sprite; an elf <*pl.* elves>.

요조 숙녀 [योजो सूंगन्यौ] a lady of refined manners; an elegant [a graceful] lady; a chaste and modest woman.

요즈음 [योजुउम] [오늘날] now; these days; nowadays; today; at present; [최근] recently; lately; of late (▷ 이 셋은 과거, 현재 완료 시제에서 쓰임. of late 는 조금 딱딱한 말).

요지 [योजी] [要地] an important place. e.g. 상업 상의 요지 a place of great commercial importance. 군사 상의 요지 a strategic point.

요지 [योजी] [要旨] [요점] the point; the gist; the major [essential / important] points; [대요] an outline; [요약] a summary; [취지] the purport; the keynote.

요지부동 [योजीबुदोंग] [搖之不動] 요지부동하다 do not stir [budge / move] an inch; be unshakable [adamantine / steadfast / unyielding / invincible]; stand as firm as rock.

요직 [योजीक] [要職] <be in> an important post[office]; <a man in> a key [responsible] post [position]; a post [position] of importance [responsibility / authority].

요청 [योछौंग] [要請] a request; a demand (강한 요구). 요청하다 request; demand; call on [ask] <a person> for <something>.

요충지 [योछुंग्जी] [要衝地] a place of strategic importance; a strategic point [place].

요컨대 [योखौन्दै] [要-] in a word; to sum up; in short; in brief; in sum; in fine; to be brief [short]; to make [cut] a long story short.

요통 [योथोंग] [腰痛] <suffer from> lumbago <*pl.* ~s>

요트 [योथु] (유람용) a sailboat; a sailing boat; a boat; (경기용) a (racing) yacht; a racer (한국에서 말하는 요트는 sailboat 에 해당하는 경우가 많음.

요하다 [योहादा] [要-] need; require; want; take; call for; demand.

요행 [योहैंग] chance luck; luck by chance; fortune; a godsend; a windfall (특히 유산 등 금전상의); a fluke; a lucky[happy] chance.

-욕 [योक] [欲,慾] a desire; a thirst; a hunger; an appetite.

욕 [योक] [辱] ⇨ 욕설

욕구 [योककू] [欲求,慾求] (a) desire [wish / craving] <for>; wants.

욕되다 [योक्त्वेदा] [辱-] be a dishonor [disgrace / shame] <to>; bring disgrace upon.

욕망 [योंगमांग] [欲望,慾望] greed <for>; (a) desire <for money / to do / that>; a craving; an appetite; an ambition.

욕먹다 [योंगमौक्ता] [辱-] **1** [욕설을 듣다] be abused; be reviled; be called (bad / rough) names. **2** [야단맞다] be scolded; get [have] a scolding; catch [get] it; [비난받다] be blamed <for>; be criticized (unfavorably); be reproached.

욕보다 [योपोदा] [辱-] [고생하다] have trouble [difficulty]; have a hard time; take pains; go through [undergo / suffer] hardships.

욕설 [योकसौल] [辱說] an insulting remark; abuse; a word of abuse; abuse language; a swearword.

욕실 [योक्शिल] [浴室] a bathroom; a bath; a toilet (room). e.g. 욕실이 딸린 셋집 a house to let with a bathroom.

욕심 [योक्शिम] [欲心, 慾心] [탐욕] greed; avarice; avariciousness; covetousness; cupidity; selfishness; self-interest; [욕망] desire.

욕정 [योक्चौंग] [欲情,慾情] **1** [충동적으로 일어나는 욕심] greed; avarice. **2** [색욕] assion; sexual desire [love]; lust; carnal desire [appetite]; sensual [fleshly] appetites.

욕조 [योक्चो] [浴槽] a bathtub.

-용 [योंग] [用] use.

용 [योंग] [龍] a dragon.

용감 [योंगाम] [勇敢] bravery; valor; heroism; gallantry. **용감하다** brave; courageous; gallant; valiant (▷ brave 는 위험이나 고통에 자진해서 맞서는, courageous 는 위험이나 어려움을 당했을 때 두려움을 이길 수 있는, gallant 는 용감함에 외관상의 화려함이 따르는, valiant 는 특히 싸움에서 불굴의 용기를 보이는); heroic; daring; plucky.

용건 [योंकौन] [用件] 급한 용건 urgent [pressing] business.

용광로 [योंक्वांग्नो] [鎔鑛爐] [工] a blast furnace; a smelting furnace.

용구 [योंगू] [用具] [손으로 쓰는 기구] a tool; [연장] an instrument; (요리, 청소 등의) a utensil; (전반적인) an implement; a(tool) kit (도구 일습).

용기[1] [योंगी] [勇氣] courage; valor; bravery; grit; spunk; nerve; prowess; pluck.

용기[2] [योंगी] [容器] (상자, 깡통 등의) a container; a receptacle; (특히 액체를 담는) a vessel; a case.

용납 [योंग्नाप] [容納] permission; allowance; approval; admission; toleration; [용서] pardon; forgiveness. **용납하다** permit; allow;

approve; admit; tolerate; pardon; forgive.

용달 [योंदाल] [**用達**] delivery; delivery service. **용달하다** deliver.

용도[योंग्दो] [**用途**] a use; service.

용돈 [योंतोन] [**用–**] pocket money (▷ 영국에서는 어린이가 받는 용돈을 말함); spending money; an allowance (▷ 영국에서는 학생, 장성한 딸이나 아들이 받는 용돈); pin money (▷ 아내,딸, 누이의 용돈).

용량 [योंग्न्यांग] [**容量**] capacity; volume.

용례 [योंग्न्ये] [**用例**] an example; an illustration(실례).

용맹 [योंमैंग] [**勇猛**] dauntlessness; intrepidity; valor; bravery; lionhearted-ness. **용맹하다** bold; un-daunted; plucky; lion-hearted; valiant; intrepid; dauntless.

용모 [योंग्मो] [**容貌**] appearance; looks; features; the face; a countenance.

용무 [योंग्मू] [**用務**] business; a thing to do.

용법 [योंग्बौप] [**用法**] usage; the way to using; how to use; use; the directions (for use).

용변 [योंग्प्यौन] [**用便**] easing nature; going to the lavatory [bathroom].

용병 [योंग्प्यौंग] [**傭兵**] a mercenary (soldier); a hired soldier.

용사 [योंसा] [**勇士**] **1** [용맹스러운 사람] a brave man; a hero. **2** [용감한 병사] a brave soldier.

용서 [योंग्सौ] [**容恕**] pardon; forgiveness; mercy.

용수 [योंग्सू] [**用水**] (수도의) city water; (관개용의) water for irrigation; (소방용의) water for extinguishing fires.

용쓰다 [योंग्सुदा] [기운을 쓰다] put forth strength; muster (up) [summon] strength; bend one's energy <on / upon>.

용액 [योंगैक] [**溶液**] a solution.

용어 [योंगौ] [**用語**] [술어] a term; phraseology; <집합적> terminology; [어휘](a) vocabulary.

용언 [योंगौन] [**用言**] [문법] a word with declined or conjugated endings (▷ declined 는형용사, conjugated 는동사의 경우).

용역 [योंझौक] [**用役**] service.

용이 [योंगी] [**容易**] ease; easiness; simpleness; facility. 용이하다 easy; simple; facile; plain.

용인 [योंगीन] [**容認**] admission; approval; accept-ance; toleration. <of>. 용인하다 approve; admit; allow; accept; tolerate.

용적 [योंग्चौक] [**容積**] [용량] capacity; [부피] volume.

용접 [योंग्चौप] [**鎔接**] welding. **용접하다** weld (together); weld <A to B>.

용지 [योंग्जी] [**用紙**] [서식으로 된 종이] a (blank) form; a blank; [···용 종이] paper.

용품 [योंग्फूम] [**用品**] supplies (필수품); goods (물품); a utensil (용구).

용하다 [योंग्हादा] **1** [재주가 뛰어나다] skillful; dexterous; adroit; mastery. **2** [장하다] admirable; praiseworthy; laudable; commendable; great

용해 [योंग्है] dissolution; melting; solution; liquefaction.

우 [उ] [**右**] the right.!

우 [उ] [**愚**] folly; foolishness.

우거지다 [उगौजीदा] grow thick [dense / rampant] grow rank (▷ rank 는 바람직하지 않은 식물에 씀); be overgrown with (장소가); be rampant [luxuriant / thick]; flourish.

우거지상 [उगौजीसांग] [**-相**] a wry [scowling] face; a sullen face; a scowl; a grimace; a frown.

우격다짐 [उग्यौकताजीम] forcing; compulsion; coercion. **우격다짐하다** force [compel] <a person> to <do>; coerce [force] <a person> into <doing>; resort to high-handed measures.

우국 충정 [उगूक छुंग्जौंग] patriotism; patriotic sentiment; [열정] a fire of patriotism. e.g. 우국 충정에서 by intense concern for the welfare of the country / out of patriotism.

우글거리다 [उकुल्गौरीदा] **1** [물이 끓다] simmer; boil(up). **2** 곳에 모여 움직이다] swarm; be crowded [thronged]; be alive <with>.

우글우글 [उगुलउगुल] in swarms; alive with. 우글우 글하다 swarming; alive [crawling] <with>; teeming.

우기 [उगी] [**雨期**] the wet [rainy] season; (열대지방의) the rains.

우기다 [उगीदा] insist <on / that>; persist <in>; demand one's own way; force <one's ideas on>; assert oneself; impose <one's views upon>.

우대 [उदै] [**優待**]**1**[특별히 잘 대우함](a) courteous [generous] treatment; (a) warm reception; hospitality. 우대하다 treat a person courteously [with courtesy]; receive a person warmly. **2** [특별히 리하게 취급함] preferential treatment. 우대하다 give preferential treatment; [무료로 대우하다] entertain a person (free of charge).

우두머리 [उदुमौरी] **1** [물건의 꼭대기] the top. **2** [단체, 조직의 장] the chief; the head; the leader; the boss.

우두커니 [उदुखौनी] vacantly; absent-mindedly; absently;

blankly; abstractedly; with a blank look.

우둔 [उदून] [愚鈍] stupidity; silliness; asininity. 우둔하다 stupid (as an owl); silly; asinine; dull; thick-headed.

우등 [उदुंग] [優等] (등급 등의) excellence; (학업의) honors.

우뚝 [उत्तुक] high; aloth. e.g. 우뚝 솟은 산 a soaring [towering] mountain.

우람하다 [उराम्हादा] stately; imposing; grand; magnificent.

우량 [उर्यांग] [優良] uperiority; excellence. 우량하다 superior; excellent; choice.

우러나다 [उरौनादा] soak out; come out.

우러나오다 [उरौनाओदा] spring up; well up; soak out.

우러러보다 [उरौरौबोदा] **1** [높은 데를 쳐다 보다] look up <at>; turn one's face upward (to). **2** [존경하다] look up to <a person>; respect; revere.

우렁차다 [उरौंग्छादा] sonorous; rotund; resonant; rich and full; resounding.

우레 [उरे] = 천둥. e.g. 우레와 같은 환성 thundering [vociferous] cheers

우려 [उर्यौ] [憂慮] worry; anxiety; apprehension; concern. 우려하다 be worried [anxious] <about>; be concerned <about>.

우려먹다 [उर्यौमौक्ता] **1** [착취하다] screw (out); squeeze; exact; exploit; milk <a person>; extort. **2** [진액등을 우려내어 먹다] infuse; steep (in a liquid).

우롱 [उरोंग] [愚弄] mockery; derision; ridicule; scoff. 우롱하다 make fun of; ridicule; fool; make a fool [an ass] of; make sport of; play with; jeer at; mock at.

우르르 [उरुरु] **1** [한꺼번에 몰려가는 모양] in crowds [droves]; in great numbers; thronging; rushingly. **2** 물 등이 끓는 모양] boiling up [over]; [물 등이 끓어오르는 소리] <boil> noisily up. **3** [쌓인 물건이 무너지거나 떨어지는 모양] <fall> in a confused heap; together; [그 소리] rumbling; hurtling; rattling; with a crash [crashing noise]. **4** [천둥 치는 소리] rumbling; thundering; booming.

우리[1] [उरी] (짐승의) a cage; (가축의) a pen; (작은 동물의) a hutch; (동물원 등에서 새를 기르는 커다란) an aviary.

우리[2] [उरी] [우리들] We; [나].

우매 [उमै] [愚昧] stupidity; asininity; imbecility; idiocy; ignorance. 우매하다 stupid; silly; ignorant; benighted; asinine.

우문 현답 [उमून ह्यौन्दाप] a wise answer to a silly question.

ㅇ

우물 [उमूल] a well.

우물거리다 [उमूल्गौरीदा] **1** [음식물을 씹지 못하고 이리저리 굴리다] mumble; chew ineffectively. **2** [말이 막히다, 더듬다] falter; stammer; speak haltingly; [중얼거리다] speak indistinctly; mumble. **3** [행동을 꾸물대다] be tardy; linger; dally; dawdle <over>; be sluggish; idle about; [주저하다] hesitate; waver; dilly-dally.

우물우물 [उमूरुमूल] (한데 모여) in swarms; (입속에서) mumblingly.

우물쭈물 [उमूल्चूमूल] irresolutely; indecisively; hesitantly; hesitatingly; vaguely; indistinctly; half-heartedly. 우물쭈물하다 be irresolute [indecisive]; be hesitant; hesitate; be tardy [slow]; linger.

우박 [उबाक] [雨雹] hail; (한 알의) a hailstone.

우발 [उबाल] [偶發] accidental [incidental] occurrence. 우발하다 happen accidentally; occur [come out] by chance.

우방 [उबांग] [友邦] [친한 나라] a friendly nation; [동맹국] an ally; an allied nation.

우범 [उबौम] [虞犯] [죄를 저지를 우려가 있는 것] liability to crime.

우비 [उबी] [雨備] a rain outfit; rainwear (입는 것).

우산 [उसान] an umbrella.

우상 [उसांग] [偶像] an idol; an image.

우선 [उसौन] [優先] priority; precedence; (선택에서의 우선권) preference. 우선하다 have priority <over>; take precedence <over>.

우선 [उसौन] [于先] [먼저] first(of all); [무엇보다도] above all; in the first place; to begin with.

우세 [उसै][優勢] [남보다 나은 형세] superiority; preponderance; ascendancy; predominance. 우세하다[우위에 있다] superior; [지배적이다] predominant; leading.

우수[1] [उसू] [優秀] superiority; excellence 우수 하다 superior; excellent; superb; distinguished.

우수[2] [उसू] [右手] melancholy; gloom; grief; dumps.

우스개 [उसुगै] comicality; drollery; waggery; jocularity; [농담] a joke; a jest;(a) pleasantry; fun.

우스꽝스럽다 [उसुक्वांङ्सुरौप्दा] ridiculous; ludicrous; funny; comic (al); droll.

우습다 [उसुप्ता] **1** [재미있다] funny; laughable; comical; ludicrous. **2** [가소롭다] ridiculeous; aughing. **3** [하찮다] trifle; trivial; small; slight; insignificant.

우승 [उसुंग] [**優勝**] [승리] a victory; (선수권의) a championship; a title. 우승하다 win the victory [championship]; come off [out] winner [victor]; win the title.

우아 [उआ] [**優雅**] elegance; grace; refinement. 우아하다 elegant; graceful; refined; polished; tasteful.

우애 [उऐ] [**友愛**] **1** [형제간의 사랑] brotherly love; fraternal affection. **2** [친구 사이의 정분] friendship; fellowship; fraternity.

우여곡절 [उयौगोकचौल] [**迂餘曲折**] turns and twists; vicissitudes; complications.

우연 [उयौन] [**偶然**] a chance; an accident (▷ chance 쪽이 일반적, accident 는 우연성이 강함).

우열 [उयौल] [**優劣**] superiority or inferiority; merits and [or] demerits.

우왕좌왕 [उवांज्वावांग] [**右往左往**] 우왕좌왕하다 run about in confusion; go hither and thither [this way and that]; run pell-mell; rush about to no purpose.

우울 [उउल] [**憂鬱**] melancholy; depression; gloom; the blues. 우울하다 (기분이) melancholy; <be> dispirited.

우월 [उवॉल] [**優越**] superiorrity; supremacy; predominance. 우월하다 superior; supreme; pre-dominant; dominating.

우위 [उवी] [**優位**] pre-dominance; superiority; ascendancy; ascendency <over others>; a dominant [prominent] position; a position of advantage.

우유 [उयू] [**牛乳**] milk(▷ 모유,양젖 등과 특별히 구별할 필요가 있을 때는 cow's milk 라고 함).

우유 부단 [उयू बूदान] [**優柔不斷**] 우유 부단하다 indecisive; irresolute; (weak and) vacillating; wavering; shilly-shallying.

우이 독경 [उइ दोक्ग्यौंग] [**牛耳讀經**] e.g. 우이 독경이다 It's like preaching to deaf ears [to the wind].

우정 [उजौंग] [**友情**] friendship; friendly feelings.

우주 [उजू] [**宇宙**] [모든 천체를 포함하는 전 공간] the universe; [질서 있는 통일체로서의 세계] the cosmos; [지구 대기권 밖] space; outer space.

우중충하다 [उजुंगछुंगहादा] dark; somber; dull; drab; subdued.

우직 [उजीक] [**愚直**] simple honesty; tactless frankness. 우직하다 honest to a fault; (simple and) stupidly honest; too honest.

우쭐하다 [उचुलहादा] be proud <of>; be pompous; be [get] stuck-up <about>; be [get] puffed up <by /

with>; puff oneself up <with>; be [get] (self-) conceited; be [feel] elated <with / by>; be inflated [exultant] <over>; be self-complacent; have a swelled head; swell with pride <at>. e.g. 조그만 성공에 우쭐해서는 안 된다 Don't become complacent [smug] over your small success / Don't become too proud of your small success. / Don't be elated over a minor success.

우천 [उछौन] [**雨天**] rainy [wet] weather; a rainy [wet] day.

우체국 [उछेगूक] [**郵遞局**] a post office; a post.

우체부 [उछेबू] [**郵遞夫**] = 우편 집배원 (郵便集配員).

우체통 [उछेथोंग] [**郵遞筒**] a mailbook a postbook a letter book a pillar box (▷ 기둥 모양의); a post.

우측 [उछुक] [**右側**] = 오른쪽. e.g. 거리의 우측에 있는 집 the house on the right-hand side of the street. 당신의 우측에 앉은 사람은 누군가요 Who is the man on your right? **우측 통행** <게시> Keep to the right.; Walk on right side facing traffic.

우파 [उफा] [**右派**] the right wing [wingers]; the Right; the rightists; the right-wing faction.

우편 [उफ्यौन] [**郵便**] [제도] mail [postal] service; mail; post; [우편물] mail; postal matter.

우표[उफ्यो] [**郵票**] a (postage) stamp; <美> a sticker.

우화 [उह्वा] [**寓話**] an allegory; a fable (▷ fable은 보통 동물을 주인 공으로 한 것).

우환 [उह्वान] [**憂患**] [복잡한 일로 생긴 걱정] troubles; cares; worry; anxiety; distress; (불행) a calamity; a misfortune.

우회[उह्वे] [**迂回**] a roundabout way; a circuit; a detour. 우회하다 take a long way around; make [take] a circuit <round>; make a detour; detour; take [go <to a place> by] a roundabout [circuitous] way [route]; skirt round; go out of one's way.

우회전 [उह्वेजौन] [**右回轉**] e.g. 우회전 금지 <게시> No Right Turn. 우회전하다 make a right turn; turn (to the) right; turn toward right.

욱신거리다 [उक्सीन्गौरीदा] **1** [(머리,상처 등이) 쑤시다] shoot; sting; have a shooting pain <in>; tingle [throb](with pain). **2** [북적거리다] swarm; throng; hustle and jostle [bustle]; mill about; push and shove; be in a bustle.

욱하다 [उख्खीदा] get impetuous; burst forth; rouse up; flare up; excite oneself; be stirred; lose one's head.

운 [उन] [運] fortune; luck; [운명] fate; destiny; (a) lot; [기회] chance. e.g. 운 좋게[나쁘게] fortunately [unfortunately] / luckily [unluckily].

운동 [उन्दोंग] [運動] **1** [보건을 위해 신체를 움직임] (physiccal) exercise; [경기] athletics; [스포츠] sports; gymnastics. 운동하다 take [get] exercise; exercise. **2** [목적을 위한 집단의 활동] a movement; a campaign; a drive; (의회의) lobbing. 운동하다 conduct [carry on] a campaign <for / against>; canvass <for>; campaign <for / against>; agitate; lobby <a bill>. e.g. 우리는 국회 의원을 상대로 열심히 운동했다 We did a lot of lobbying among Members of Parliament. **3** [물체의 움직임] motion; movement. 운동하다 move; be.in motion.

운명[1] [उन्म्यौग] Death. 운명하다 die; pass away; breathe one's last.

운명[2] [उनम्यौग] [運命] (신 등의 힘에 의한) (a) fate; (초자연적인)(a) destiny; (나쁜) doom; [주로 행운] (a) fortune; (우연에 의한) a lot; [숙명] kismet.

운문 [उन्मून] [韻文] **1** (산문에 대하여) verse. **2** [시] poem; <집합적> poetry.

운반[उन्बान] [運搬] transportation; conveyance; transport carriage. 운반하다 [나르다] carry; [수송하다] transport; convey.

운석 [उन्सौक] [隕石] [별똥별] a meteorite; a meteoric [falling] stone.

운송[उन्सोंग] [運送] transportation; transport; conveyance; carriage; forwarding; freight. 운송하다 transport; convey; carry; forward.

운수[1] [उन्सू] [運數] ⇨ 운 e.g. 운수가 좋은 해 a good [lucky] year. 운수가 좋다 be fortunate / be lucky. 나는 운수가 길하다 [불길 하다] I was born under a lucky [an unlucky] star.

운수[2] [उन्सू] [運輸] transportation; transport; conveyance.

운영 [उन्यौग] [運營] [관리] management; [조직을 움직임] administration; operation. 운영하다 manage; run; administer; steer; conduct.

운용 [उन्योंग] [運用] application; working; (practical) use; operation. 운용하다 make; use; work; employ; put in practice; apply.

운운 [उनून] [云云] So and so (forth); and so forth [on]; and the like. 운운하다 [이러쿵저러쿵 말하다] say something or other <of / about>; say thus and thus; say such and such; [비판하다] criticize; comment <on>.

운율 [उन्यूल] [韻律] (a) meter [(a) metre]; (a) rhythm.

운임 [उनीम] [運賃] (여객의) a (passenger) fare; [요금] a charge; (화물의) freight (rates / charges); goods rates; carriage; (짐수레의) cartage; (해운의) shipping expenses.

운전 [उन्जौन] [運轉] (자동차의) driving; (열차,버스 편의) running; (기계의) operation; working. ⇨ 운행 운전하다 drive <a car>; run <a train>; operate [put / set] <a machine.

운치 [उन्छी] [韻致] [고아한 품위가 있는 기상] elegance; refinement; grace; daintiness.

운항 [उन्हांग] [運航] navigation; operation; service; passage. 운항하다 operate; run; ply.

운행 [उन्हैंग] [運行]**1** [천체가 궤도를 돎] movement; revolution (자전,공전). 운행하다 move [revolve / travel] <round the sun>; (궤도상을) orbit <around / round **2** (열차,버스 등의) running; operation; service.

울긋불긋 [उल्कुल्पूलकुत] colorfully; picturesquely. 울긋불긋하다 colorful; varicolored; picturesque.

울다 [उल्दा] (사람이) cry; weep; shed tears; sob (흐느끼며); blubber (훌쩍거 리며); wail (비통하게); whimper (낮게).

울렁거리다 [उलौंगौरीदा]**1** [두근거리다] beat (fast); pound (심하게); throb; thump; palpitate.**2** [물결이 연해 흔들리다] surge; roll; swell.**3** [메슥거리다] feel sick; feel like vomiting; feel nausea; be sick at the stomach.

울리다 [उल्लीदा]**1** [사람을 울게 하다] let <a child> cry; move [touch] <a person> to tears. **2** [소리를 내다] ring <a bell>; sound <a trumpet>; beat <a drum>; jingle <bells>; chime <bells>; clang <a gong>; blow <a whistle>.**3** [소리가 나다] sound; ring; peal (방울 등이); go bang (쾅하고); roar; [울려 퍼지다] thunder; rumble; roll (뇌성이); boom (대포가); [소리가 반향 하다] echo; resound; reverberate.

울림 [उल्लीम] [반향] an echo <*pl*~es>;(a) reverbe ration.

울분 [उल्बून] [鬱憤] pent-up anger [frustration]; resentment; wrath; grudge.

울상 [उल्सांग] [-相] a face ready [about] to cry; a tearful face.

울음 [उरुम] weeping; crying; a cry.

울적 [उल्जौक] [鬱寂] melancholy; gloom; mental depresssion; low spirits. 울적하다 melancholy; gloomy; dejected; out of [in low] spirits.

울창 [उल्छांग] [鬱蒼] 울창하다 thick; dense; luxuriant <growth>; exuberant.

울타리 [उल्थारी] a fence; an enclosure; a hedge (산울타리); a hurdle (엮은 것); railings (목책).

울퉁불퉁 [उल्थूंग्बूल्थूंग] 울퉁불퉁하다 uneven; bumpy <road>; rugged <features>; jagged <rocks>.

움막 [उमाक] [-幕] a dugout.

움직이다[1] [उम्जीगीदा] <타동사> **1** [이동시키다] move; shith; remove; budge; stir. **2**[기계 등을 가동시키다] set [put] in motion; run; drive; operate; work. **3** [사람의 마음을 끌거나 흔들다] move; touch; inspire; affect; influence; have influence on.

움직이다[2] [उम्जीगीदा] <자동사> [동작,이동하다] move; stir; budge; shith.

움직임 [उम्जीगीम] **1** [이동] a movement; motion; [활동] activity; [동향] a trend; a drith; a movement; a development. **2** [흔들리다] stir; shake; swing; sway.

움집 [उम्जीप] a dugout; a mud hut.

움츠러들다 [उम्छुरैदुल्दा]**1** (몸이) curl [huddle] oneself up; squeeze oneself <in>. **2** (무서움등으로) (back); cower.

움켜잡다 [उमख्यौज्वीदा] grasp; clasp; grip; grab (up); take hold of; seize.

움켜쥐다 [उमख्वजीादा] hold <a thing> tight (ly) (in one's hand); grip; grasp; squeeze; clutch; clasp; clench; take fast [firm] hold <of>.

움큼 [उम्खुम] a handful <of rice>; a fistful <of sand>; a grasp.

움푹 [उम्फूक] e.g. 움푹 들어가다 become hollow / become dented / sink. 움푹하다 hollow; concave; sunken; dented.

웃기다 [उत्कीदा] make <a person> laugh; set <a person> laughing; excite one's laughter; cause a laugh; provoke laughter [a smile]; [재미나게 하다] amuse <a person>.

웃돈 [उत्तोन] [차액] a difference; a margin; [할증금] an extra; a premium.

웃돌다 [उत्तोल्दा] exceed; be better <than>; surpass.

웃음 [उसुम] a laugh; laughing; laughter (큰 웃음); a smile (미소); a chuckle (킬킬거리는 웃음); a giggle (주로 여자 아이가).

웅대 [उदै] [雄大] grandeur; magnificence; majesty.

웅대하다 grand; magnificent; majestic.

웅덩이 [उंग्दोंगी] puddle; a pool.

웅변 [उंग्ब्योन] [雄辯] eloquence; fluency (of speech); (a flood of) oratory.

웅성거리다 [उंग्सोंगौरीदा] be noisy; be excited; be in commotion; hum.

웅얼거리다 [उंगोल्कौरीदा] mutter; murmur; mumble (out).

웅장 [उंग्जांग] [雄壯] grandeur; magnificence; majesty; spleendor. 웅장하다 grand; magnificent; majestic; spleendid.

웅크리다 [उंग्खुरीदा] crouch (down); huddle [curl] oneself up.

워낙 [वॉनाक]1 [본디] originally; [처음부터] from the outset [beginning]; [태생이] by nature; naturally. **2** [아주] too; too much; excessively; to excess; overly; [몹시] very [quite / much]. **–원** [वॉन] [員] a member <of>.

원[1] [वॉन] [圓] [원형] a circle; [작은 원] a circlet.

원[2] [वॉन] [願] [소원] a wish <for / to do / that>; [강한 소망] a desire <for / to do / that>; [간청] an entreaty <for / to do>; [부탁] a request <for / that>.

원[3] [वॉन] [우리 나라의 화폐 단위] a won(略 ₩).

원가 [वॉन्का] [原價] the cost (price); the prime [first] cost.

원거리 [वॉन्गौरी] [遠距離] a long [great] distance; a long range.

원고[1] [वॉन्गो] [原告] (민사 소송의) the plaintiff; complainant; (형사 소송의) a prosecutor; [고발자] a accuser.

원고[2] [वॉन्गो] [原稿] (인쇄용의) a manuscript(略 MS., *pl.* MSS.); a copy; [초고] a drath; notes.

원근 [वॉन्गुन] [遠近] [먼 곳과 가까운 곳] places both near and far.

원금 [वॉन्गुम] [元金] [밑천] capital; [본전] the principal. e.g. 원금과 이자 the principal and interest.

원기 [वॉन्गी] [元氣] vigor; energy; vitality; spirits; dash; stamina; go; pep. (⇨ 기운)

원대 [वॉन्दै] [遠大] 원대하다 [광범위하다] farreaching; [앞을 내다보다] farseeing; [장기간에 걸치다] long-range. e.g. 원대한 계획 [뜻] a great [long-range] plan [ambition]. 원대한 목적 farreaching aims.

원동력 [वॉन्दोंन्यौक] [原動力]**1** [기계의 근원적인 힘] motive power. **2** [일의 추진력] a driving [an impelling] force.

원두막 [वॉन्दूमाक] [**園頭幕**] a shed on stilts for a melon patch [field] guard.

원래 [वॉल्लै] [**元來,原來**] 본디 originally; by origin; [본질적으로] essentially; [선천적으로] by nature; naturally; [처음부터] from the first [beginning / outset / start].

원로 [वॉल्लो] [**元老**] an elder; a senior (member); an old-timer; a veteran; a doyen <of a body>.

원론 [वॉल्लोन] [**原論**] the principles <of>.

원료 [वॉल्यो] [**原料**] [가공하지 않은 재료] raw materials; [천연 그대로의 재료] crude materials.

원리 [वॉल्ली] [**原理**] [원칙] a principle; [이론] a theory; [근본 법칙] fundamentals.

원만 [वॉन्मान] [**圓滿**] [완전함] perfection; inte-grity; completeness;[만족] satisfaction; [원활] smoothness; harmony; [평온,무사] peace. 원만하다 perfect; integral; complete; [조화적이다] harmonious; amicable; peaceful; [만족 스럽다] satisfactory; [용모, 인격 등이 부드럽다] well-rounded; bland; suave. 원만히 harmo-niously; smoothly; peacefully; amicably.

원망 [वॉन्मांग] [**怨望**] [탓함] resentment; reproach; [원한] a bitter [an ill] feeling; a grudge; a spite; [불평] a grievance; a complaint. 원망하다 [원한을 품다] have [hold / bear] a grudge <against>; [비난 하다] blame; [분개하다] resent.

원목 [वॉन्मोक] [**原木**] material [raw] lumber; (펄프의) pulpwood.

원문[वॉन्मून] [**原文**] [원래의 문장] the original;(번역 등에 대하여) the original (text).

원본 [वॉन्बोन] [**原本**] the original (work); the original copy [text]; [法] the script (copy에 대하여).

원산지 [वॉन्सान्जी] [**原產地**] [물건의 생산지] the place of origin; [동식물의 본래의 산지] the(original / natural) home; the habitat.

원서[1] [वॉन्सौ] [**原書**] [원본] the original (book / work).

원서[2] [वॉन्सौ] [**願書**] an application; a written request.

원성 [वॉन्सौग] [**怨聲**] a grievance; a reproachful remark; a reproach.

원소 [वॉन्सो] [**元素**] an element; a chemical element; an element.

원수[1] [वॉन्सू] [**元首**] the chief [head] of state; a sovereign.

원수[2] [वॉन्सू] [**怨讐**] [원한이 맺힌 사람] a foe; an enemy; (사물) the object of one's grudge [grievances]. e.g. 지간 mutual enemies.

원숙 [वॉन्सूक] [圓熟] maturity; mellowness. 원숙하다 mature; mellow; ripe.

원숭이 [वॉन्सूंगी] [動] a monkey; [유인원] an ape.

원시[1] [वॉन्सी] [遠視] **1** [멀리 봄] looking far-off at. **2** [醫] farsightedness; long sightedness; hypermetropia; hyperopia.

원시[2] [वॉन्सी] [原始, 元始] the beginning; genesis; origin.

원앙 [वॉनांग] [鴛鴦] **1** [鳥] a mandarin duck. **2** [의좋은 부부].

원예 [वॉन्ये] [園藝] [정원 손질] gardening; floriculture (꽃재배); horticulture.

원인 [वॉनीन] [原因] (어떤 결과를 낳는)(a) cause <of>; (직접적인 계기가 되는) <文>(an) occasion <for>; (발단이 되는) the origin <of>; [요인] a factor.

원작 [वॉन्जाक] [原作] the original(work).

원장 [वॉन्जांग] [院長] (병원의) the director <of a hospital>; (학원의) the principal [president] <of an academy>.

원점 [वॉन्जौम] [原點] [기본점] the starting point; the origin; the beginning. e.g. 원점으로 돌아가서 생각하다 consider a thing again from the beginning.

원정 [वॉन्जौंग] [遠征] an expedition; a campaign; an invasion (침입); (군대의) a military expedition; (운동선수의) a playing tour; a visit. e.g.

원조[1] [वॉन्जो] [元祖] [창시자] the originator; the founder. e.g. 국제법의 원조 the father of international law. 우리 가게는 한국 슈퍼마 켓의 원조이다 Our store was the (very) first [This store was the forerunner] of the supermarket of Korea.

원조[2] [वॉन्जो] [援助] [조력] assistance; aid; [지원] support. e.g. 정신적 [물질적] 원조 moral [ma-terial] support. 재정적 원조 financial aid.

원주민 [वॉन्जूमीन] [原住民] (a nativeaborigines; an aboriginal (원주민의 한 사람 한 사람). e.g. 아프리카의 원주민 the natives [abori-gines] of Africa.

원천 [वॉन्छौन] [源泉] the source; the origin.

원칙 [वॉन्छीक] [原則] [원리] a principle; [일반적으로 공통된 법칙] a general rule.

원컨대 [वॉन्खौन्दे] [願-] I pray you; I hope; May.; I wish <I could>.

원통 [वॉन्थोंग] [冤痛] **1** [분함]

vexation; chagrin; mortification. 원통하다 vexatious; vexing; mortifying**2** 유감] a keen [sharp / deep] regret. 원통하다 regrettable; deplorable.

원피스 [वॉन्फीसु] a one-piece dress.

원하다 [वॉन्हादा] [**願-**] [바라다] want [wish / desire] <to do / a person to do / that> (▷ want that .라고는 하지 않음).

원한 [वॉन्हान] [**怨恨**] [원망함,원망하는 마음] a grudge <against>; [악감정] ill will <against>; [미움] hatred <of / for>.

원형[1] [वॉन्हयौंग] [**圓 形**] a circle. e.g. 원형의 circular / round. 원형 건물 a circular [round] building / (둥근 지붕의) a rotunda. 종이를 원형으로 오리다 cut paper into a circle.

원형[2] [वॉन्ह्यौंग] [**原形**] [본디의 모양] the original form.

원화 [वॉन्हवा] [**-貨**] the won (currency).].

원활 [वॉन्हवाल] [**圓滑**] smoothness; [융화] harmony. 원활하다 smooth; [융화적, 협화적] harmonious; amicable. e.g. 그들은 서로 원활하지 못하다 They don't get along well together. 원활히 smoothly; harmoniously; peacefully.

월 [वॉल] [**月**] [달] the moon; (달력의) a month (⇨ 달); [월요일] Monday.

월간 [वॉल्गान] [**月刊**] monthly publication. e.g. 월간 출판물 a monthly (publiccation). 이 잡지는 월간이다 This magazine is issued [published] monthly.

월경 [वॉल्ग्यौंग] [**月經**] menstrualtion; menses; a (menstrual) period; one's period

월권 [वॉल्ग्वॉन] [**越權**] abuse of confidence; a stretch of authority; arrogation; exceeding one's prerogatives

월급 [वॉल्गुप] [**月給**] a (monthly) salary; monthly pay. e.g. 낮은 월급 a small [low] salary

월남 [वॉल्नाम] [**越 南**] 월남하다 come south over the border; (북한으로부터) come from North Korea (over the 38th parallel); cross the 38th parallel into South Korea;

월동 준비 [वॉल्दोंग जुन्बी] preparations for the winter. e.g. 월동 준비로 바쁘다 be busy preparing for winter.

월등 [वॉल्दुंग] [**越等**] 월등하다 <서술적> stand in different levels; be not in a class <with>; be widely apart <in ability>. by far the most interesting book(

월례 [वॉल्य] e.g. 월례의 monthly

월말 [वॉल्ये] [**月 末**] e.g.

월말에 [까지는] at[by] the end of the month.

월북 [वॉल्बुक] [越北] 월북하다 (경계를 넘어) go north over the border; (북한으로) go to North Korea (over the 38th parallel); cross the 38th parallel into North Korea.

월세 [वॉल्से] [月貰] monthly rent. **월수** [वॉल्सू] [月收] **1** [월수입] a monthly income **2** <make> a monthly installment loan.

월요일 [वॉरयोइल] [月曜日] Monday (略 Mon.).

월일 [वॉरील] [月日] [달과 날] months and days;

월척 [वॉल्छोक] [越尺] [한 자가 넘는 물고기] a fish over one *cha*; a big fish. e.g. 월척을 올리다 catch a big fish.

월초 [वॉल्छो] [月初] e.g. 월초에 at the beginning of the month.

웨딩 [वेदींग] a wedding.

웬 [वेन] [어찌된] what kind [sort] of; what . like; [어떤] a certain; some. e.g. 웬 사람이냐 Who is the man?

웬걸 [वेन्गौल] Oh!; Why!; Well!; on the contrary; far from that.

웬만큼 [वेन्मान्खुम] [어지간히 제법] fairly; pretty; tolerably; passably; so-so. e.g. 그녀는 영어를 한다 She speaks passable [fairly good] English. / She speaks English pretty [passably] well

웬만하다 [वेन्मान्हदा] [어지간하다] not very bad; pretty good; so-so; tolerable; passable. e.g. 머리가 웬만한 아이 a boy of average intelligence. 웬만하면 if you could arrange it

웬일 [वेनील] what matter [business]. e.g.웬일로 on what business. 웬일로 이런 밤중에 오셨습니까 What have you come here for tonight?

위[1] [वी] **1** [위쪽]. e.g. 바로 위에[의] right [just] above. 위를 보다 look upward (s) **2** [표면] surface; [책상 등의 윗면] top. e.g. 마루 위에 융단을 깔다 spread a carpet over the floor. **3** [꼭대기] the top; the summit; [가장 윗부분] the head. e.g. 맨 위의 topmost / uppermost. 위에서 아래까지 from top to bottom. **4** [나은 쪽] superiority; predominance; [선두] lead. e.g. 그의 그림이 내 그림보다 위였다 His picture was better than

위[2] [वी] [位]**1** [등수,등급] position; grade; rank. e.g. 2위 (석차) the second place / (사람) a runner-up. 제1위가 되다 take [win] first place / head [top /

lead] off the list. **2** [지위] a position; a place; rank. e.g. 천자의 위 the (Imperial) throne. **3** [위패로 모신 신의 수]. e.g. 영령 8위 eight heroic souls.

위[3] **[वी] [胃]** the stomach.

위급 [वीगुप] [危急] [긴급 사태] an emergency; [중대 국면] a crisis. e.g. 위급 존망지추 a critical [crucial] time. 위급을 알리다 raise [give] the alarm.

위기 [वीगी] [危機] a crisis <*pl.* crises>; an emergency; a critical situation; a crucial juncture; a pinch

위대 [वीदै] [偉大] greatness; grandeur. 위대하다 great; grand; mighty.

위도 [वीदो] [緯度] latitude.

위독 [वीदोक] [危篤] a serious[grave] condition. e.g. 그는 한밤중에 위독 상태에 빠졌다 He fell into a critical [dangerous] condition at midnight.

위력 [वीर्योक] [偉力] great power; mighty force.

위로 [वीरो] [慰勞] 1 [수고를 치하함] appreciation of the services rendered; recognition [acknowledgment] of <a person's> services. 위로하다 acknowledge [recognize / appreciate] <a person's> services**2** [위안] consolation; solace; comfort. 위로하다 console; solace; comfort; give comfort to <a person>.

위문 [वीमून] [慰問] [위로하려고 문안함] consolation; comfort; [병문안] an inquiry; a visit <to>. 위문하다 [위로하다] console; comfort; [병문안 하다] inquire ather <a person's> health; visit.

위반 [वीबान] [違反] (법령, 규칙의) violation; contravention; infringement; (계약, 약속의) breach. e.g. 교통 위반 traffic violation / violation of traffic regulations. 속도 위반 violation of the speed limits.

위법 [वीबौप] [違法] illegality; unlawfulness; lawbreaking. e.g. 위법적인 illegal / unlawful. 위법적으로 illegally / unlawfully / against the law.

위생 [वीसैंग] [衛生] sanitation; hygiene. e.g. 공중 위생 public health.

위선 [वीसौन] [僞善] hypocrisy; pharisaism. e.g. 위선적인 hypocritical. 위선을 행하다 play the hypocrite / behave hypocriteecally.

위성 [वीसौंग] [衛星] [天] a satellite. e.g. 인공 위성 a manmade [an artificial] satellite) 위성 도시 [वीसौंग दोसी] a satellite city[town].

위세 [वीसे] [威勢] [위엄 있는 기세] high spirits; dash. e.g. 위세 당당한

ㅇ

high-spirited / full of high spirits / gallant / dashing / spanking. 우리는 위세 당당히 떠났다 We plucked up our spirits and set out.

위신 [**威信**] [वीसीन] [위엄과 신망] authority and confidence; dignity; prestige.

위안 [वीआन] [**慰安**] a) comfort; (a) consolation; solace

위약 [वीयाक] [**違約**] a breach of a promise [a contract / an agreement]; a default (의무,채무의 불이행,태만).

위엄 [वीओम] [**威嚴**] ignity; majesty; stateliness. e.g. 위엄있는 dignified / majestic (al) stately.

위업 [वीओप] [**偉業**] a great achievement [work / feat].

위용 [वीयोंग] [**威容**] [위엄찬 모습] a dignified[a commanding / a grand / a majestic] appearance; a dignified mien. e.g. 위용을 갖추고 in a dignified attitude.

위원 [वीवॉन] [**委員**] a member of a committee; a committee member; a committeeman; <집합적> a committee; a commission. e.g. 국무 위원 a cabinet member. 위원장 [वीवॉन्जांग] a chairperson; (남성) a chairman; (여성) a chairwoman.

위원회 [वीवॉन्हवे] [**委員會**] a committee; (특히 정부의) a commission; a board; (회의) a committee-meeting.

위인 [वीइन] [**偉人**] a great man; [영웅] a hero <*pl.*~ es>. e.g. 과거의 위인들 the great names of past ages.

위임 [वीइम] [**委任**] [맡김] trust; commission; charge; (전권의) delegation; (권한의) authorization; commitment; mandate. 위임하다 entrust <a person> with <a thing>; entrust <a thing> to <a person>; charge <a per-son> with <a thing>; charge <a thing> to <a person>; leave <a thing> to <a person>; commit <a thing> to <a person>; commission <a person> to <do something>; (권한을) delegate <authority / power> to <a person attorney.

위장 [वीजांग] [**胃腸**] the stomach and intestines [bowls]; the gastrointestines. e.g. 위장의 gastrointestinal / gastroenteric. 위장을 해치다 hurt [upset] the stomach (and bowls). 나는 위장이 튼튼 하다[약하다] I have good [poor / weak] digestion. 잠이 부족하면 위장에 탈이 난다 Lack of sleep affects my digestion.

위정자 [वीजोंग्जा] [**爲政者**] [정치가] an administrator; a statesman. e.g. 위정자는 국민의 소리를 들어야

한다 Those who govern the people must listen to their voice.

위조 [वीजो] [僞造] forgery; fabrication; counterfeiting. e.g. 공문서 위조 the forgery of official papers. 문서 위조죄 forgery of documents. 화폐 위조자 a coiner.위조하다 forge; counterfeit 진짜와 비슷하게 만드는 것); fabricate; commit forgery. e.g. 위조한 counterfeit / forged.

위주 [वीजू] [爲主] e.g. 자기 위주의 사고 방식[] self-centered way of thinking.

위중 [वीजूंग] [危重] 위중하다 be sedriously[critically] ill; be in a critical condition. e.g. 어머니가 위중하다는 전보를 받았다 I got a wire informing me of [announcing] my mother's critical condition.

위증 [वीजुंग] [僞證] [法] false witness; false evidence [testimony] (법정에서 선서한 후의). 위증하다 give false witness; give false evidence [testimony]; perjure oneself; commit perjury; swear [testify] falsely of perjury.

위촉 [वीछोक] [委囑] [직권 등의 위임] commission; entrusting; [임명] appointment; [의뢰] request. e.g. 위촉으로[에 의하여] by request / at a person's request. 위촉하다 entrust; commission; [임명하다] appoint.

위축 [वीछुक] [萎縮] withering; shrinkage; shriveling; contraction; (영양 불량 등에 의한) atrophy. e.g. 간장 [신장]의 위축 atrophy of the liver [the kidneys]. 위축성의 atrophic. 위축하다 (물체가) wither; wilt; shrivel; shrink; (사람이) flinch <from>; be daunted <by failure>; be dispirited.

위치 [वीछी] [位置] [장소] a place; (a) position; (a) location; a situation; a site. e.g. 위치를 잡다[바꾸다] take[shith] one's position. 배의 위치를 재다 fix a ship's position.

위탁 [वीथाक] [委託] trust; commission (임무 등의); consignment (판매의); committal; commitment. e.g. 위탁하에 있다 be held in trust.위탁하다 entrust; consign <to>; put <a thing> in a person's charge; commit; commission. e.g .나는 이 계획의 실행을 그의 그룹에 위탁했다 I entrusted the group with the imple-mentation of this plan. / I entrusted the implementation of this plan to his group.

위태하다 [वीथैहादा] [危殆-] dangerous; hazardous; perilous; risky (모험적인);

precarious (불안정한); (병세가) critical; grave; serious. e.g. 위태로운 장난[] a dangerous game.

위통 [वीथोंग] [**胃痛**] a stomachache; [醫] gastralgia. e.g. 위통이 있다 have a stomachache.

위하다 [वीहादा] [**爲**-]**1** [이롭게 하다] do for the good [benefit] of; do in favor [behalf] of. e.g. 예술을 위한 예술 art for art's sake. **2**[소중히 하다] have regard for; take good care of; esteem; value; make [think] much of. e.g. 건강을 위하다 take (great) care of one's health.

위헌 [वीहौन] [**違憲**] (a) violation of the constitution; unconstitutionality. e.g. 이 결정은 위헌이다 This decision is unconstitutional.

위험 [वीहौम] [**危險**] (a) danger; (사람의 힘으로는 회피할 수 없는)(a) hazard; (생명에 관계되는) peril; (모험,도박에 따르는) (a) risk. e.g. 직업상의 위험 occupational hazards. 위험에 빠지다 be in danger / fall into a dangerous situation.

위협 [वीह्यौप] [**威脅**] a menace; a threat (▷ menace 가 더 강하며, 적의도 포함됨); intimidation. e.g. 위협적인 태도를 취하다 take a threatening [menacing] attitude. 갑자기 위협적인 태도로 변하다 change suddenly to a threatening attitude.

위화감 [वीह्वागाम] a sense of incongruity. .

윗사람 [वीत्सारम] **1** [연장자] one's elders; one's seniors.**2** [지위 등이 자기보다 높은 사람] one's superior(s); one's better(s).

윙크 [वीख्] a wink.윙크하다 [वीख्वादा] wink <at>; give a wink <to>.

유 [यू] [**類**] **1** [무리] a group. **2** [종류] a kind; a sort; a type; a class; the like <of it>.

유가족 [यूगाजोक] [**遺家族**]a bereaved family. e.g. 군인 유가족 a war-bereaved family.

유감 [यूगाम] [**遺憾**] [섭섭함] regret; a pity. e.g. 유감으로 생각하다 regret / be sorry <for> / feel sorry <that>. 유감이다

유감스럽다 [यूगामस्रौप्ता] [**遺憾**-] [섭섭하다] regrettable; deployrable. e.g. 유감스럽게 생각하다 regret / feel sorry <that>.

유골 [यूगोल] [**遺骨**] ashes; the(skeletal) remains. e.g. 전사자의 유골 the remains of the war dead

유괴 [यूग्वै] [**誘拐**] kidnapping; abduction. 유괴하다 kidnap <a child>; abduct <a person from his home>.

e.g. 어린아이는 몸값을 목적으로 집에서 유괴되었다 The child was kidnapped [abducted] from his home for ransom.

유교 [युग्यो] [**儒教**] Confucianism. e.g. 유교의 (감화) Confucian (influence).

유구 [युगू] [**悠久**] eternity; perpetuity; permanence. 유구하다 eternal; everlasting; perpetual; permanent.

유구무언 [युगुमुऔन] [**有口無言**] [have no word in excuse. 참으로 유구무언입니다 There is no excuse whatever.

유권자 [युग्वॉन्जा] [**有權者**] the holder of a right; (선거의) a(qualified) voter; an elector; <집합적> the electorate. e.g. 유권자의 총수는 6 백만에 달한다 The electoral roll amounts to 6 million.

유급[1] [युगुप] [**留級**] 유급하다 [युगुफादा] remain [stay] in the same class for another year.

유급[2] [युगुप] [**有給**] e.g. 유급의 paid / salaried. 유급직 a salaried [paid] post.

유기체 [युगीछे] an organism; an organic body; an organized matter.

유기 [युगी] [**遺棄**] [내다버림] abandonment; derelicttion.

유난 [युनान] [보통과 다름] unusualness; uncommonness; extraordi-nariness; [괴상함] singularity; eccentricity; peculiarity; oddity. 유난하다 unusual; uncommon; extraordinary; exceptional; singular; eccentric; peculiar; odd; fantastic.

유년 [युन्यौन] [**幼年**] (early) childhood; infancy. e.g. 유년용 그림책 picture books for little children. 나의 유년 시대는 행복했다 I spent a happy childhood.

유념 [युन्यौम] [**留念**] attention; consideration; regard; mindfulness.

유능 [युनुंग] [**有能**] ability; competence; capability; efficiency. 유능하다 [युनुंग्हादा] able; capable; competent; talented; efficient

유니폼 [युनीफोम] a uniform. e.g. 유니폼을 입은 선수들 players in uniform.

유다르다 [युदारुदा] uncommon; unusual; extraordinary; [별나다] odd; peculiar. e.g. 유다른 취향 a new departure. 유다른 행동 peculiar behavior. 유다른 사람 a unique person / a rare man.

유대 [युदै] [**紐帶**] a band; a tie; relation(관계). e.g. 동맹 제국의 유대[] the bond of allied nations.

유도[1] [युदो] [**柔道**] judo. judo.

유도[2] [यूदो] [**誘導**] inducement; guidance; [電,生] induction; derivation.

유독[1] [यूदोक] [**有毒**] 유독하다 poisonous; toxic; venomous; [해롭다] noxious.

유독[2] [यूदोक] [**惟獨**] solely; only; alone; singly.

유동성 [यूदोंग्सौग] fluidity; mobility. e.g. 유동성 있는 fluid / mobile. **유들유들** impudently; shamelessly; brazen-facedly.

유들유들하다 [यूदुर्यूदुर्हादा] impudent; audacious; brazen-faced; barefaced; shameless; cheeky.

유람 [यूराम] [**遊覽**] sightseeing; an excursion. ⇨ 관광.

유랑 [यूरांग] [**流浪**] wandering; roaming. e.g. 유랑의 길에 오르다 go wandering. 유랑하다 wander [roam] about [from place to place]; rove He wandered over the wilderness for days.

유래 [यूरै] [**由來**] [기원] the origin; the genesis; [내력] the history; [출처] the source; the derivation. e.g. 유래가 있는 집[] a family with a history.

유래하다 [यूरैहादा] result <from>; originate <in>; be derived <from>; date back <to the time of ..>. e.g.그 싸움은 강력한 두 집안 사이의 다툼에서 유래한다 The strife between the two strong clans brought about the battle.

유력 [यूर्यौक] [**有力**1 [권세, 영향력이 있음]. 유력하다 [권세가 있다] powerful; [강력하다] strong; [영향력이 있다] influential. e.g. 유력한 정당 a powerful political party. **2** [가능성, 효력이 있음].

유령 [यूर्यौग] [**幽靈**] [망령] a ghost; [갑자기 나타나는 유령] an apparition; [환영] a phantom; [요괴] a specter; a spectre. e.g.

유례 [यूर्यै] [**類例**] a similar example[instance / case]; a parallel case. e.g. 세계에 유례가 없는 사건 an incident unparalleled anywhere in the world.

유료 [यूर्यो] [**有料**]a charge. e.g. 유료인 charged / feed / toll / paid. fee.

유리[1] [यूरी] [**琉璃**] glass; [유리창] a pane; a windowpane.

유리[2] [यूरी] [**遊離**] [떨어짐] isolation; separation. e.g. 속세로부터의 유리 isolation [separation] from the secular world.

유망 [यूमांग] [**有望**] promise; a bright prospect [future]. 유망하다 promising; hopeful; full of promise; favorable. e.g. 유망한 청년 promising young man.

유머 [**यूमौ**] humor [humour]; a joke (농담).

유명 [**युम्यौंग**] [**有名**] 유명하다 [이름높다] famous; famed; noted; notable; [꽤 알려지다] well-known; [저명하다] celebrated; renowned; distinguished; [악명 높다] notorious. e.g. 유명한 음악가 a famous [noted / famed] musician.

유명무실 [**युम्यौंगमूसील**] [**有名無實**] 유명 무실하다 (only) nominal; titular; in name only; <a scholar> in nothing but the name.

유모 [**यूमो**] [**乳母**] a wet nurse; <소아어> a nanny. e.g. 아이를 유모에게 맡기다 leave a baby with a nurse.

유모차 [**यूमोछा**] [**乳母車**] a baby carriage; a buggy; a perambulator; < 英 > a pram. e.g.

유목 [**यूमोक**] [**遊牧**] nomadism.

유무 [**यूमू**] [**有無**] [있음과 없음] existence and non-existence. e.g. 오늘의 결석자의 유무를 확인하다 check and see if anyone is absent today.

유물 [**यूमूल**] [**遺物**] (역사상, 고고학상의) a relic (of the past).

유물론 [**यूमूल्लोन**] [**唯物論**] materialism.

유물 사관 [**यूमूल साग्वान**] [**-史觀**] the materialistic conception [interpretation] of history.

유발 [**यूबाल**] [**誘發**] induction. 유발하다 induce; cause [arouse] <one's anger>; give rise to [touch off / trigger].

유방 [**यूबांग**] [**乳房**] the (woman's) breast; [解]

유배 [**यूबै**] [**流配**] banishment; exile; depor-tation. 유배하다 banish [exile] <a person to an island>.

유별 [**यूब्यौल**] [**有別**] (a) distinction; (a) discrimination. e.g. 남녀 유별이다 There is a distinction between man and woman.

유별나다 [**यूब्यौल्नादा**] [**有別-**] [보통이 아니다] uncommon; extraordinary; unusual; [기묘하다] peculiar; eccentric; odd; singular.

유보 [**यूबो**] [**留保**] **1** = 보류**2** (법률에서, 권리의) (a) reservation. 유보하다 reserve; withhold.

유복 [**यूबोक**] [**裕福**] affluence; wealth. 유복하다 rich; wealthy; well-to-do.

유사[1] [**यूसा**] [**類似**] (a) resemblance;(a) similarity; (a) likeness; an analogy. 유사하다 similar; like; alike; (성질,기능 등이) analogous; <서술적> resemble.

유사[2] [**यूसा**] [**有事**] emergency. e.g. 유사시에 in time [case] of emergency / in an emergency.

유사[3] [यूसा] [**有史**] [역사가 시작됨]. e.g. 유사의[] historic. 유사 이전의 prehistoric / of prehistoric times. 유사 이전에 in prehistoric times / before the dawn of history. 유사 이전의 시대 prehistoric times / the prehistoric age.

유산[1] [यूसान] [**流産**] (태아의) (a) miscarriage; (an) abortion; [실패] failure. e.g. 인공 유산 artificial abortion [miscarriage]. 유산하다 miscarry; abort; have a miscarriage

유산[2] [यूसान] [**遺產**] [사후에 남겨진 재산] property left (by a deceased person); an inheritance

유산계급 [यूसानग्यैगुप] [**有產階級**] the propertied classes; the bourgeoisie; the bourgeois class. e.g. 유산 계급의 사람 a bourgeois / a man of property. 그는 유산 계급 출신이다 He comes from a bourgeois family.

유상 [यूसांग] [**有償**] compensation; considera-tion. e.g. 유상의 onerous. 유상으로 취득하다 obtain <something> for counter value.

유색 [यूसैक] [**有色**] e.g. 유색의 colored.

유색 인종 [यूसैक इन्जोंग] colored races; non-white people [nations].

유서[1] [यूसौ] [**由緖**] [내력] a history; a story. e.g. 유서 깊은 historied / great-historied.

유서[2] [यूसौ] [**遺書**] [유언장] a note left behind by a dead person; (자살자의) a suicide note; [유언] a will. e.g. 유서를 쓰다[] make [draw up] one's will [testament].

유선[1] [यूसौन] [**有線**] wire. e.g. 유선의 wire / wired / cabled.

유선[2] [यूसौन] [**流線**] [理] a streamline.

유성 [यूसौंग] [**有聲**] e.g. 유성의 voiced / vocal.

유세 [यूसे] [**有勢**] 유세(를) 떨다 wield [exercise] influence [power] <over>; hold [bear] sway. e.g. 좋은 자리에 있다고 너무 유세떨지 마라 Don't be so high-hatted under the shelter of your post.

유속 [यूसोक] [**流速**] the velocity [speed] of a moving [running] fluid. e.g. 조류의 유속[] the speed of a current / the drith of a current.

유수 [यूसू] [**流水**] running [flowing] water. e.g. 세월은 유수와 같다 Time flies (like an arrow).

유순 [यूसुन] [**柔順**] obedience; submission; gentleness; meekness. 유순하다 obedient; submissive; [얌전하다] gentle; meek.

유식 [यूसीक] [**有識**] 유식하다 learned; educated; well-informed; knowledgeeable. e.g. 유식한 체하다 pretend to know much / assume an air of wisdom / set up for a wise man.

유실 [यूसील] [**遺失**] loss. 유실하다 lose; leave behind.

유실물 [यूसीलमूल] [**遺失物**] a lost article; lost property.

유아[1] [यूआ] [**幼兒**] an infant; a small child; a (tiny) tot. e.g. 유아의 in-fant / infantile / infantine. 이것 들은 유아용 장난감입니다 These are toys for small children [tiny tots / infants.

유아[2] [यूआ] [**乳兒**] a suck-ling; a nursling; a baby. 유아기 babyhood.

유아독존 [यूआदोक्चोन] [**唯我獨尊**] [자기보다 귀한 것이 없음] Only I am holy. / I am my own Lord [Holy am I alone] throughout heaven and earth.

유언 [यूऔन] [**遺言**] a will(▷ 정식으로는 one's last

유언비어 [यूऔनबीऔ] [**流言蜚語**] a groundless[wild] / rumor; a canard; a false report. e.g. 유언 비어를 퍼뜨리는 사람 a rumoron-ger.

유역 [यूयौक] [**流域**] a basin; (큰 강의) a (river) valley.

유연 [यूयौन] [**柔軟**] sothness; pliability; pliancy; flexibility; plasticity. 유연하다 (물건이) soth; pliable; pliant; flexible.

유예 [यूये] [**猶豫**] [연기](a) postponement;(a) delay; (a) deferment; (형의) a suspension

유용 [यूयोंग] [**有用**] 유용하다 useful <to / for>; helpful; good <for something>; serviceable; valuable; of use [service / avail].

유원지 [यूवॉनजी] [**遊園地**] an amusement park; a re-creation [pleasure] ground; a pleasure resort. e.g. 어린이 유원지 an amuse-ment park for children.

유월 [यूवॉल] [**一月**] June (略 Jun.).

유유자적 [यूयूजाजौक] [**悠悠自適**] 유유자적하다 live in easy [comfortable] retire-ment; live free from worldly cares.

유의 [यूउइ] [**留意**] attention; heed; regard. 유의하다 note; pay attention to; be mindful [regardful] <of>; bear [keep] <a thing> in mind.

유익 [यूइक] [**有益**] 유익하다 [유용하다] helpful; useful; serviceable; [이익이 있다] beneficial.

유인 [यूइन] [**誘引**] nticement; allurement; temptation. 유인하다 entice; allure.

유일 [यूइल] [**唯一**] 유일하다

only (▷ the를 붙여서); sole; one (and only); [독특하다] unique.

유입 [यूइब] [**流入**] inflow; influx. e.g. 외국 자본의 유입 an inflow [influx] of foreign capital. 유입하다 flow [come / stream] in [into].

유적 [यूजौक] [**遺跡**] a site; remains; ruins; vestiges; (historic) relics. e.g. 고대 로마의 유적 the remains [ruins] of ancient Rome. 성곽의 유적을 보존하다 preserve the ruins of a castle. 석기 시대의 유적이 발견되었다 A Stone Age site was discovered.

유전[1] [यूजौन] [**油田**] an oil[a petroleum] field; oil land.

유전[2] [यूजौन] [**遺傳**] eredity; inheritance; (hereditary) transmission.유전하다 be inherited; be passed down [on] <to>; be transmitted; be hereditary; run in the blood [family].

유전자 [यूजौन्जा] [**遺傳子**] [生] a gene..**유전자 공학**

유제품 [यूजेपूम] [**乳製品**] airy goods [products].

유조 [यूजो] [**油槽**] n oil tank. **유조선** a [an oil] tanker.

유족 [यूजोक] [**遺族**] the bereaved (family); the family of the deceased; a surviving family..

유종 [यूजोंग] [**有終**] e.g. 유종의 미를 거두다 carry a thing to perfection.

유죄 [यूज्वे] [**有罪**] guilt. e.g. 유죄를 선고하다 convict <a person> of a crime / give <a person> the verdict of guilty / declare <a person> guilty.

유지 [यूजी] [**有志**] [영향력을 지닌 사람] an influential person; a man of influence [power]; [요직자] a big man. e.g. 그는 그 고장의 유지이다 He is quite influential in the town.

유지 [यूजी] [**維持**] maintenance; preservation; support; conservation; upkeep (집 등의). e.g. 평화의 유지 the mainte-nance of peace. 현상 유지 정책 the policy of maintaining the present condition [status quo]. 유지하다 maintain <peace, order, etc.>; keep <one's health>; sustain <an institution>; support <life>. e.g. 현상을 유지하다 maintain the status quo.

유착 [यूछाक] [**癒着**]**1** 상처 등의) adhesion; conglutination. e.g. 늑막 유착 pleural adhesion. 그녀는 맹장 수술 후의 유착으로 고생을 했다 She had painful adhesions ather her appendectomy. 유착하다 adhere <to>; stick[knit] together. **2** [서로 깊은 관련을 지님]. e.g. 정경 유착 a close relationship between political and business circle.유착하다 have a cozy relationship <with>. e.g. 대통령은 일부 자본가와 유착해 있다는 비난을 받았다 The president was accused of having a cozy relationship with a certain group of capitalists.

유창하다 [यूछांग्वादा] [**流暢-**] fluent <in English>; smooth. e.g. 말이 유창한 사람[] an eloquent[a fluent] speaker. 그는 유창한 연설을 했다 He made a fluent speech.

유추 [यूछू] [**類推**] analogical inference; (an) analogy. e.g. 유추적인 analogical / analogic. 유추에 의하여 [through] analogy. 유추하다 analogize; infer; use analogy.

유출 [यूछूल] [**流出**] an outflow; an effluence;(an) effluK a drain. 유출하다 flow [run] out; issue; scharge; drain out; overflow. **유출구** a debouchment.

유치[1] [यूछी] [**幼稚**] infancy; babyhood; crudeness. 유치하다 [어린애 같다] childish.

유치[2] [यूछी] [**留置**] [억류] detention; custody. 유치하다 detain; hold <a person> in custody; lock up.

유치원 [यूछीवॉन] [**幼稚園**] a kindergarten; a nursery school; a preschool.

유쾌 [यूख्वै] [**愉快**] (a) pleasure; (a) delight; enjoyment; merriment. 유쾌 하다 pleasant; enjoyable; merry; delightful; joyful.

유토피아 [यूथोफीआ] (a) Utopia.

유통 [यूथोंग] [**流通**] **1** 활기] ventilation; [순환] circulation. e.g. 공기의 유통이 잘되다[안 되다] be well [poorly] ventilated. 유통하다 circulate; ventilate; flow. **2** (돈의) circulation; currency; (어음의) negotiation. 유통하다 circulate; pass current; (어음 등이) float.

유폐 [यूफ्यै] [**幽閉**] confinement. 유폐하다 confine <a person in a place>; shut [lock] up.

유포 [यूफो] [**流布**] circulation; spread. 유포하다 [퍼지다]. be circulated; be current; spread; get about [afloat]; go around.

유품 [यूफूम] [**遺品**] a relics; an article left by the departed.

유하다 [यूहादा] [**柔-**] [부드럽다] soth; mild; gentle; genial; tender; sweet; amiable.

유학 [यूहाक] [**遊學**] [타향에서 공부하는 것]. e.g. 서울 유학 중에 while studying in Seoul / during one's period of study in Seoul. 유학하다 study [pursue knowledge / pro-secute one's studies] far away from (one's) home.

유한 [यूहान] [**有限**] limitedness; finiteness. 유한하다 limited; finite; definite; determinate.

유해 [यूहै] [**有害**] noxiousness; harmfulness. 유해하다 harmful <to>; injurious <to>; bad; noxious; hurtful.

유행 [यूहैंग] [**流行**] **1** (복장 등의) (a) fashion; a vogue; mode; (한 때의 열광적인) a craze; (일시적인) a fad; (인기) popularity. 유행하다 be in fashion [vogue]; [인기가 있다] be popular.**2** [전염병이 만연함] prevalence.

유혈[1] [यूह्यौल] [**流血**] bloodshed. e.g. 유혈의 참사 an affair of bloodshed / a bloody affair.

유형[2] [यूह्यौंग] [**有形**] materiality; concreteness.

유형 [यूह्यौंग] [**類型**] a type; a pattern.

유혹 [यूहोक] [**誘惑**] temptation; allurement; enticement; seduction.

유효 [यूह्यो] [**有效**] validity (법규 등의); availability (표 등의); effectiveness; efficiency. 유효하다 [효과가 있다] effective; (어떤 기간, 조건하에서) available; good; profitable.

유흥 [यूहुंग] [**遊興**] pleasure (seeking); merrymaking; amusement.

유희 [यूह्वै] [**遊戲**] a game; sports; (어린이의) play; [오락] a pastime; amusements.

육 [यूक] [**六**] six.

육감 [यूक्काम] [**六感**] a sixth sense; intuition; hunch.

육교 [यूक्क्यो] [**陸橋**] an overhead bridge; an overpass; a crossover; (철도의) an overbridge; (도시의) a pedestrian overpass [bridge]; flyover.

육군 [यूक्कून] [**陸軍**] the army. e.g. 미국 [영국] 육군 the United States [British] Army.

육로 [यूग्नो] [**陸路**] a land [an overland] route.

육류 [यूंग्न्यू] [**肉類**] meat; flesh; flesh-meat.

육박 [यूक्पाक] [**肉薄**] 육박하다 come close <to>; [바싹 다가붙다] press hard <on>; (경쟁에서) tread close on <a person's> heels; run <a competitor> hard [close].

육상 [यूक्सांग] [**陸上**] land; ground; shore.

육성 [यूक्सौंग] [**肉聲**] a natural voice; a (human) voice.

육성 [यूक्सौंग] [**育成**] rearing; upbringing; raising; nurture. **육성하다** bring up; rear; raise.

육순 [यूक्सून] [**六旬**] sixty years old.

육식 [यूक्सीक] [**肉食**] [사람이 고기붙이를 먹음] a meat diet; meat-eating; [동물이

다른 짐승의 고기를 먹이로 함] flesh-eating; (음식) animal food; meat food.

육십 [युक्सीप] [六十] sixty.

육아[育兒][युगा] child care; nursing; upbringing of a child.

육안 [युगान] [肉眼] the naked eye; (망원경 등을 사용하지 않는) the unaided eye.

육중 [युक्चुंग] [肉重] 육중하다 (부피가) bulky and heavy; massive; ponderous; (체격이) heavily built; stout.

육지 [युक्ची] [陸地] land; (배에서 본) the shore.

육체 [युक्छे] [肉體] the body; the flesh; flesh and blood.

윤 [युन] [潤] 윤(이) 나다 be glossy; be lustrous; be bright; be polished.

윤곽 [यून्ग्वाक] [輪廓]1 [겉모습] outline; contours <of a human body>; profile <of a face>. 2 [개략] an outline; a rough [general] idea.

윤기 [युन्की] [潤氣] gloss; luster [lustre]; brightness; glaze; polish; shine; brilliance (보석 등의).

윤락 [यूल्लाक] [淪落] ruin; fall; corruption. 윤락하다 be ruined; go to the bad; be corrupted; ruin oneself <by dissipation>.

윤리 [यूल्ली] [倫理] ethics; morals; a code of conduct.

윤택 [युन्थैक] [潤澤] 1 [광택] (a) gloss; (a) luster.2 [풍부] abundance; richness; [유복] affluence; wealth. 윤택 하다 abundant; ample; affluent; rich; well-to-do.

윤회 [यून्ह्वै] [輪廻]1 [차례로 돌아감] rotation; constant mutation. 윤회하다 rotate; mutate constantly. 2 [불교] samsara; metempsychosis; transmigration (of souls); cycle of life. 윤회하다 transmigrate.

율[1] [यूल] [律]1법규] a law; a regulation; [계율] (Buddhist) commandments. 2 [운율] (a) rhythm.

율[2] [यूल] [率] e.g. 백분율 (a) percentage. 높은 [낮은] 율 a high [low] rate [per-centage].

율동 [यूलतोंग] [律動] (a) rhythm; (a) rhythmic movement.

율법 [यूल्बोप] [律法] [법률] (the) law; [신이 내린 규범] commandments; [계율] religious precepts.

융성 [युंग्सौग] [隆盛] prosperity.

융자 [युंग्जा] [融資] 자금을 융통하기] financing; [자금의 대출] lend; [융통되는 자금] a fund. 융자하다 finance; furnish <a company> with funds; [대출하다] lend; loan <a person three million won.

융통 [युंग्थोंग] [融通] [돌려

씀] financing; accommodation; (a) loan; [유통] circulation. 융통하다 [빌려 주다] lend [<美> loan] (money); accommodate <a person with a loan>; [유통하다] circulate.

융통성 [युंग्थोंग्सौग] [**融通性**] daptability; elasticity; flexibility.

융합 [युंग्हाप] [**融合**] fusion; [조화] harmony. 융합하다 fuse [blend] into one; merge; unite; become merged <with>; [융화하다] harmonize.

융해 [युंग्है] [**融解**] fusion; melting; dissolution; liquefaction. 융해하다 fuse; melt; dissolve; liquefy; thaw.

융화 [युंग्ह्वा] [**融和**] 조화] harmony; [화해] reconciliation; [통일] integration. 융화하다 [조화하다] harmonize [get along] with; [화목하다] be melted together; [화해하다] be reconciled <with>.

윷 [यूत] 1 [네 쪽의 나무로 만든 놀잇감] (the game of) *yut*; a stick game. **2** [네 개의 윷짝이 모두 젖혀진 경우] 3 points (made by a cast of *yut* sticks.)

윷놀이 [युत्नोरी] game of *yut*.

으깨다 [उकैदा] 부수다] crush (up / down); grind (down) (갈아서); [짓이기다] mash; squash.

으니 [ऊनी] [원인,근거] as; since; so ... that; now (that). e.g. 이제 늦었으니 돌아가자 As [Since] it is (getting) late, let's go home.

으니까 [ऊनीका] […하므로] since; and so; […한즉] when (in the past) then; and [but] then. e.g. 자네의 의견이 받아들여졌으니까 그것으로 만족해야 할 것이다 Since your proposal has been accepted, you should be more than satisfied.

으뜸 [उतुम] **1** the first (place); number one; No.1; [최고, 최상] the head; the best; the top. **2** [기본,근본] the root; the basis <*pl.* bases>; the foundation.

으레 [उरे] **1** [당연히] (as a matter) of course; to be sure; naturally; without question; no doubt. **2** [언제나] always; usually; [변함없이] invariably; [규칙적으로] regularly.

으로 [उरो] **1** [수단,방법] by; by means of; through; [도구] with; on; in.**2** [원료, 재료] from; of; out of..**3** [방향] for; to; toward; [속으로] into; in; [위로] on; onto.**4** [원인, 동기, 이유] for; because of; with; from; owing to; at; through.

으로서 [उरोसो] e.g. 여흥으로서 by way of entertainment.

으로써 [उरोस्सो] […을 가지고]. e.g. 사상을 행동으로써 나타내다 express an idea in terms of action.

으르렁거리다 [उरुरौंगकौरीदा] **1** [짐승이 성내어 울부짖다] snarl; growl; roar. **2** [다투다] quarrel [squabble] <with>; brawl; feud <with>; bicker.

으름장 [उरुम्जांग] a threat; a menace; a scare; [위협하는 말] threatening remarks.

으리으리하다 [उरीउरीहादा] grand; stately; majestic; magnificent; imposing.

-으며 [उम्यौ] **1** [동시에] and. e.g. 귀로는 들으며 눈으로는 본다 We hear with our ears, and see with our eyes.**2** ⇨ -으면서

으면 [उम्यौन] [가정적 조건] if; when; whenever. e.g. 요즈음 젊은이로 말할 것 같으면 (as for) the young people of today / when it comes to today's young people.

으므로 [उमुरो] since; so; as; so ... that; because; due to; owing to; for; considering. e.g. 돈이 없으므로 since I have no money.

으스러뜨리다 [उसुरौतुरीदा] smash; crush; crack; break (in pieces) [춥다] chill; chilly; rather cold; coldish.

으슥하다 [उसुखादा] [깊숙하고 후미지다] retired (and quiet); sequestered; secluded; covert; lonely; deep. e.g. 으슥한 구석 a covert nook. 으슥한 산길 a remote [lonely] mountain path [trail]. 으슥한 숲 속에서 in the gloom [depths] of a forest. 밤이 으슥해졌다 The night was getting on [well advanced].

으슬으슬 [उसुरुसुल] shivering. e.g. 으슬으슬 춥다 feel chilly / feel[have] a chill <with>. 오늘은 으슬으슬 춥다 The weather is chilly today. 으슬으슬하다 chilly; somewhat cold.

으쓱 [उसुक] **1** [어깨를 들어 올리는 모양] with a shrug (of one's shoulders). 으쓱하다 = 으쓱거리다 1. **2** [우쭐하는 모양].으쓱하다 =으쓱거리다.

으악 [उआक] [놀래줄 때 지르는 소리] Boo; Bo; Boh; [놀랐을 때 지르는 소리] Ugh; Wow; Gee; [갑자기 토하는 소리] Puke!; with a puke.

윽박지르다 [उक्बाक्चीरुदा] [윽박아 기를 꺾다] put down with threats; treat with a high hand; browbeat [bully] <a person into [out of]>.

은 [उन] [**銀**] [금속 원소] silver.

은근 [उन्गुन] [**慇懃**] [정중함] politeness; courtesy; civility.

은근하다 [उन्गुनहादा] gentle; polite; courteous; civil. [드러

내지 않음] quietness; inwardness; [함축] implicitness; suggestiveness; [은밀] secrecy. 은근하다 quiet; inward; implicit; suggestive; indirect; secret; private. e.g. 은근한 미소 a quiet smile. 은근한 협박 a veiled threat.

은닉 [उन्नीक] [隱匿] concealment; secretion. 은닉하다 conceal; hide; secrete; shelter; harbor <a criminal>.

은둔 [उन्दुन] [隱遁] retirement [seclusion] (from the world); sequestration; withdrawal from ordinary life. 은둔하다 retire form the world; live in retirement [seclusion]; [속세를 떠나다] renounce the world; seclude [isolate] oneself from society.

은밀 [उन्मील] [隱密] rivacy; secrecy. 은밀하다 covert; secret; private; confidential; privy.

은사 [उन्सा] [恩師] the teacher one has studied under; one's former teacher.

은신 [उन्सीन] [隱身] 은신하다 [उन्सीन्हादा] hide [conceal] oneself; tuck oneself away <somewhere>; [피신하다] take [seek] refuge [shelter].

은어 [उनॉ] [隱語] a secret language; [직업 용어] jargon; (특정 계급, 직업인 끼리의) cant; (도둑 등의) argot.

은유 [उन्यू] [隱喩] a metaphor.

은은하다 [उनुनहादा] [隱隱-] **1** [어슴푸레하다] hazy; mist; [흐릿하다] dim; dusky. **2** [소리가 가늘다] dim; faint; vague; distant (to the ears).

은인 [उनीन] [恩人] a benefactor; a benefactress (여자); [후원자] a patron; a patroness (여자).

은총 [उन्छोंग] [恩寵] grace (신의); favor (사람의).

은퇴 [उन्थ्वे] [隱退] retirement (from active [public] life); seclusion (from the world). 은퇴하다 retire (from one's profession); seclude (oneself from the world).

은폐 [उन्फ्ये] [隱蔽] concealment; hiding; suppression; coverture; cover-up. 은폐하다 conceal; hide; cover (up); suppress; draw a veil <over>; keep <a matter> secret [dark].

은하 [उन्हा] [銀河] the Milky Way; the Galaxy; <라> the Via Lactea.

은행 [उन्हैंग] [銀行] bank.

은혜 [उन्ह्ये] [恩惠] a favor; a benefit; a blessing; an obligation; moral indebtedness; a boon (이익).

을 [उल] **1** [타동사의 목적].. e.g. 신문을 보다 read [look at] the newspaper.**2** [수동태의 목적]. e.g. 가슴을 차이다 get kicked in the chest. 약점을 잡히다 have one's weakness seized [played] upon. 발목을 차이다 get a kick [get kicked] on the ankle. 물건을 빼앗기다 be robbed of a thing. 손목을 잡히다 be taken [seized] by the wrist.

을씨년스럽다 [उल्सीन्यौनस्रोप्ता] [날씨 등이 스산하다] dreary; dismal; gloomy; [쓸쓸하다] <서술적> look miserable [shabby / wretched].

읊다 [उल्ता] [시를 짓다] compose <a poem>; [시가를 소리 높이 노래하다] recite [chant] <a poem>.

음 [उम] [**音**] [소리] a sound; [음조] a note; a tone.

음란 [उम्नान] [**淫亂**] lewdness; lasciviousness; lechery; salacity; incontinence. 음란하다 lecherous; lewd; incontinent; lustful; obscene; salacious; lascivious; indecent.

음량 [उम्न्यांग] [**音量**] (musical) volume; sound volume.].

음력 [उम्न्यौक] [**陰曆**] 음력 4월 1 일 April 1 by [according to] the lunar calendar. 음력 3월 초엿새 the 6th day of the third lunar month. 음력을 쓰다 use [follow] the lunar calendar. 음력으로 날을 세다 reckon according to the lunar calendar.

음료 [उम्न्यो] [**飮料**] a drink; a beverage; drinkables.

음모 [उम्मो] [**陰謀**] a plot; an intrigue; [책략] machinations; (도당을 짠) (a) conspiracy; a frame-up. 음모하다 plot; conspire; intrigue.

음미 [उम्मी] [**吟味**] **1** [감상] appreciation. 음미하다 appreciate; savor; enjoy. **2** [맛봄] sampling; tasting. 음미하다 sample; taste; enjoy.

음반 [उम्बान] [**音盤**] (a copy of) a record; a disc; a disk. (⇨ 레코드).

음성 [उम्सौंग] [**陰性**] **1** [음침한 성격] (a) somber character; [음침한 기질] (a) gloomy disposition. **2** 음성의 negative. 그의 투베르클린 반응은 음성이었다.

이런 [इरौन] [이러한] such; this; like this; such ... as this; of this kind [sort].

이렇게 [इरौख्वे] like this; in this way [manner]; thus; [이 정도로] this much; so much; so; such; to this extent.

이렇듯 [इरौथुत] like this; thus; in this way [manner].

이력 [इर्यौक] [**履歷**] one's personal history; [경력] one's background; one's career (직업상의); one's record.

이론 [इरोन] [**理論**] (a) theory.

이롭다 [इरोप्ता] [**利-**] profitable; advantageous; beneficial; good <for>; helpful <to / for>; favorable; instructive.

이루다 [इरूदा] **1** [형성하다]

form; make; constitute. **2** [성취하다] accomplish; achieve; attain; [완성하다] complete; fulfill; finish; [실행하다] perform; realize; do; effect.

이루어지다 [इरूऔजीदा]1 [뜻대로 되다] be achieved [attained / effected / completed / realized / fulfilled]; be [get] accomplished [done]. **2**[어떤 상태,결과가 되다] be formed [composed] of; be made up of; (타협,계약 등이) be made [concluded / settled / arrived / arranged].

이룩하다 [इरूख्यादा] 1 [(어떤 현상, 사업을) 이루다] accomplish; achieve; complete; gain. **2** [세우다] found; establish; erect; set up; build.

이류 [इर्यु] [二流] e.g. 이류의 second-class / second-rate / [보다 못한] minor.

이륙 [इर्युक] [離陸] a take-off; a hop-off; taking [flying] off; leaving the ground. 이륙하다 take off; hop off; take the air; leave the ground.

이르다[1] [इरुदा] 1 [(어떤 장소, 시간 등에) 닿다] reach; arrive; get to; go; lead. **2** [미치다] extend <to>; come to; get to; [(결과가 … 이) 되다] result <in>; end <in>; lead <to>.

이르다[2] [इरूदा] 1 [말하다] say.**2** [알아듣거나 깨닫게 말하다] explain; teach; advise; tell; bid. **3** advance>; tell; inform; report..**4** [고자질하다] tell [squeal] on <a person>; tell [carry] tales <about>.

이르다[3] [इरूदा] 1 [늦지 않고 빠르다] early. **2** [아직 그 시기가 되지 않다] premature.

이른바 [इरून्बा] what is called; what you [we / people] call; as it is called; so-called; as they say.

이를테면 [इरूलथेम्यौन] 1 [말하자면] so to speak; as it were; [어떤 의미에서] in a sense; [어떤 점에서] in a way; so to call it; as it were; [실제로는] practically.**2** [가령] for example; for instance; such as.

이름 [इरुम] 1 [성명] one's full name; a name; (성명 아래의 개인 이름) a given [personal] name; a first name; (세례명) a Christian name. **2** [명칭] a name; a designation; [책 등의 제목] a title. **3** [평판](a) reputation; a name; fame; renown distinction; eminence.

이리 [इरी] [이 곳으로, 이 쪽으로] this way [direction]; here.

이리저리 [इरीजौरी] 1 [이러하고 저러하게] like this

way and that; thus and thus. **2** [이쪽으로 저쪽으로] this way and that; to and fro; back and forth; from one place to another; here and there.

이마 [**इमा**] (얼굴의) the forehead; the brow.

이만 [**इमान**] **1** [이 정도의] this much [many].**2** [이만하고서] by this (much); this far.

이만큼 [**इमान्खुम**] (분량) about this [so] much; (수) about so many; (크기) about so large; about this size; (길이) about so long; about this length; (폭) about so wide; about this width; (정도) this far; to this degree [extent].

이만하다 [**इमान्हादा**] this much [many]; as much [many] as this.

이면 [**इम्यौन**] [**裏面**]**1**[속,안] the back; the reverse (side); the other side.**2** [내부의 사실] the inside; the background; [어두운 면] the dark [seamy] side.

이모 [**इमो**] [**姨母**] an aunt (who is one's mother's sister); one's maternal aunt.

이모부 [**इमोबु**] [**姨母夫**] an uncle (who is the husband of one's mother's sister).

이모저모 [**इमोजौमो**] every side [aspect] <of a matter>; this way and that.

이목 [**इमोक**] [**耳目**] **1** [귀와 눈] the eye and ear. **2** 남들의 주의] public attention [notice].

이목구비 [**इमोक्कूबी**] [**耳目口鼻**] 귀, 눈, 입, 코] ear, eye, mouth, and nose; [용모] features; looks.

이미 [**इमी**] already; before; previously.

이미지 [**इमीजी**] **1** 심상 (心像, 心象).**2** [사물, 사람에게서 받는 인상] an image; an impression.

이민 [**इमीन**] [**移民**] [외국으로 이주하기] emigration; [외국에서 이주해 오기] immigration; [외국으로의 이주자] an emigrant; [외국으로부터의 이주자] an immigrant.

이바지하다 [**इबाजीहादा**] **1** [공헌하다] contribute <to>; make a contribution <to>; render services to; conduce to; make for; do much for [toward]. **2** [공급하다] provide; furnish; supply.

이발 [**इबाल**] [**理髮**] a haircut; hairdressing. 이발하다 have one's hair cut [cropped / trimmed]; have [get] haircut; (남의 머리를) dress [trim / cut] <a person's> hair; barber <a person>.

이발사 [**इबाल्सा**] a barber; a haircutter; a hairdresser.

이번 [**इबौन**] [**一番**] [금번] this time; [현재] now; [다음번] next time; [머지않아] shortly; soon; [최근] recently; lately.

이변 [इब्योन] [異變] [사고] an accident; [이상한 일] something unusual; [재변] a disaster; a calamity; a catastrophe.

이별 [इब्योल] [離別] separation; parting; farewell. 이별하다 separate from <a person>; part from <a person>.

이복 [इबोक] [異腹]a different mother; a half-brother [sister]; a brother [sister] by a different mother (▷ 이부의 경우도 같음). e.g. 그들은 이복 자매이다 They are half-sisters [sisters by a different mother].

이봐 [इबा] hello; hey; hi; say; listen; look here. e.g. 이봐, 조심해 Hey, look out! 이봐 일어나 Hey, wake up. 이봐, 그만해 Stop it, I tell you! 이봐, 조용히 해 Hey [Come on], be quiet!

이부자리 [इबुजारी] bedding; bedclothes (and mattress). e.g. 이부자리를 깔다 [펴다] spread the bedding <on>. 이부자리를 개다 fold up the bedding.

이북 [इबूक] [以北] **1** [북쪽] north <of>; ... and northward. e.g. 38 선 이북 north of the 38th parallel. 폭설로 인해 한강 이북의 교통이 마비되었다 All road and rail traffic north of the Han-gang has been paralyzed by the heavy snow. **2** [북한] North Korea. e.g. 이북에 계시는 어머니 one's mother in North Korea. 그는 이북에서 왔다 He came from North Korea.

이분 [इबून] this gentleman [lady]. e.g. 이분에게 차를 올려 주십시오 Please give [bring] this lady [gentleman] a cup of tea. 이분은 송씨입니다 This is Mr. Song. 이분 들은 모두 60세 이상입니다 These people [ladies and gentlemen] are all over sixty.

이분 [इबून] [二分]division into two parts; a half. e.g. 이분의 일 a half / one-half. 승객의 이분의 일은 한국인이었다 Half the passengers were Korean. 이분하다 divide <a thing> in two [into two parts]; halve. e.g. 이익은 당신과 이분하자 I will halve the profits with you. 선생은 학생을 A그룹과 B그룹으로 이분했다 The teacher divided the students into two groups, A and B.

이불 [इबुल] bedclothes; a quilt (누빈 것); (깃털의) an eiderdown; a comforter (▷ 주로 깃털 이불). e.g. 이불을 개다 fold up the bedding.

이사[1] [इसा] [理事] a director; (대학 등의) a trustee. e.g. 상임 이사 an executive director. **이사회** (기구) a board of directors [trustees]; a directorate; a council; (회의) a directors' meeting. e.g. 국제 연합 안전 보장 이사회 the United Nations Security Council.

이사[2] [इसा] [**移徙**] a move; a removal; a change of address. e.g. 이사 가는 곳 one's new address.

이삭 [**इसाक**] **1** (뻐, 보리 등의) an ear; a head; a spike. e.g. 벼 이삭 an ear of rice. **2** (땅에 떨어진) fallen ear (of grain) gleaning. e.g. 이삭을 줍는 사람 a gleaner.

이산 [**इसान गाजोग**] **가족** dispersed [separated] families. e.g. 이산 가족 찾기 운동 a campaign for reunion of dispersed family members. 그 가족은 이산 가족이 되었다 The family broke up.

이상 [इसांग] [**以上**] **1** [위에서 말한 것] the above (-mentioned); the above (-stated). e.g. 이상으로 오늘 모임을 마칩니다 That concludes today's meeting. / That's all for today's meeting. M**2** [일정한 표준보다 많음] more than; over; above; beyond; past (▷ 이 들 단어를 쓸 때에는 우리말로 나타낸 숫자는 포함되지 않음에 주의. 그 숫자를 포함시킬 때는 three or more 또는 from three up 이라 함); [일정한 표준으로부터 위] not less than; or more; and over[up]. e.g.10 이상 100까지 from 10 to 100. **3** [이미 그렇게 된 바에는] now that; since; if ... at all. e.g. 거기서 급료를 받는 이상 일하지 않을 수 없다 As long as I am paid by them, I have to work. **4** [끝] The end (▷ 보고 등의 끝에 적음); [완결] concluded (▷ 시리즈물의 끝 등); [이것으로 끝] That's all.

이상[1] [इसांग] [**異常**] extraordinariness; singularity; abnormality; uncommonness; oddity. e.g. 그는 몸에 이상이 생겼다.

이상[2] [इसांग] [**理想**] an ideal. e.g. 이상과 현실 the Ideal and the Real.

이상[3] [इसांग] [**異狀**] [고장] a malfunction; the matter; an accident; something wrong; [변화] a change; (정신의) disorder; derangement; ab-normality; (신체의) (an) indisposition. e.g. 아무 이상이 없다 Nothing un-usual has happened. / There's nothing wrong. / Everything is all right [O.K. / in perfect order].

이상야릇하다 [इसांग्यारुथादा] [**異常-**] queer; odd; funny; absurd. e.g. 이상야릇한 모자 an absurd [a funny-looking] hat. 기분이 이상야릇하다 feel queer.

이상화 [इसाख्वा] [理想化] idealization. 이상화하다 idealize; sublimate. e.g. 너는 사물을 자칫 이상화 한다 You are apt to idealize things.

이색 [इसैक] [異色] **1** [다른 색] a different color. **2** [색다름] novelty. e.g. 이색적인 unique / novel.

이성 [इसौंग] [理性] reason; reasoning power; rationality; Logos. e.g. 순수 [실천] 이성 pure [practical] reason.

이세 [इसे] [二世] **1** 이민간 사람의 자녀]. e.g. 재미 교포 이세 an American-born Korean / a Korean. 이세의 second-generation.**2** [2대] the second. e.g. 찰스 이세 Charles II (▷ the second라고 읽음).**3** [아버지와 같은 이름의 자식] junior. e.g. 폴 윌슨 이세 Paul Wilson, Jr. [Junior].**4** [자식] a son. e.g. 그에게 이세가 태어났다 He now has a son.

이송 [इसोंग] [移送] transfer; removal. e.g. 사건의 이송 [法] removal [transfer] of a case. 이송하다 transfer; remove. e.g. 이 사건은 대법원으로 이송되었다 This case was sent [transferred] to the Supreme Court.

이수 [इसू] [履修] completion. 이수하다 (학과, 과정을) take; [수료하다] finish. e.g. . 작년에 몇 과목을 이수했습니까 How many courses did you take last year? 그는 3년 동안에 필수 과목을 모두 이수했다 He finished all the required courses in three years.

이슬 [इसुल] **1** dew. e.g. 밤 [아침] 이슬 nightly [morning] dew. 이슬이 맺힌 dewy <flowers> / bedewed. 이슬이 내린다 It dews. / The dew[Dew] falls. 풀잎에 이슬이 내려 있었다 There were drops of dew on the grass. 잔디가 이슬에 젖어 있었다 The lawn was wet with dew. **2** 눈물의 비유] a tear. e.g. 그녀의 눈에 이슬이 맺혔다 Tears welled up in [sprang to] her eyes. 이슬로 사라지다 e.g. 단두대의 이슬로 사라 지다 die on the guillotine. 전장의 이슬로 사라지다 die in battle / be killed in action [battle].

이슬람교 [इस्ललामग्यो] [-教] Islam. e.g. 이슬람교의 Islamic / Muslim / Moslem.

이승 [इसुंग] [二乘] this life; this world; this (present) life. e.g. 이승의 worldly / earthly / mundane. 이승에 태어나다 be born into this world.

이식 [इसीक] [移植] (식물, 장기 등의) transplantation;

(피부, 근육의) grathing. e.g. 피부 이식 a skin grath

이심전심 [इसीम्जोन्सीम] [**以心傳心**] direct communication from mind to mind; mental communication; telepathy. e.g. 우리는 이심전심으로 아는 사이다 We understand each other without the medium [use] of language.

이쑤시개 [इसूसीगै] a toothpick. e.g. 이쑤시개로 이를 쑤시다 use a toothpick / pick one's teeth with a toothpick.

이야 [इया] [강조] the very; just; indeed; [제한] only. e.g. 남이야 뭐라 하든 상관없다 I don't care a bit what other people say. 그쯤이야 나도 알고 있다 I know as much.

이야기 [इयागी] **1** [담화] a talk; [대화] (a) conversation; [한담] a chat; a gossip; [화제] a topic (of conversation); the subject; [연설] a speech; an address. **2** [설화] a tale; a story; [전설] a legend; [소설] a novel; a fiction; [우화] a fable; [삽화] an episode. **3** [소문] a rumor; a report; news; gossip

이야말로 [इयामाल्लो] [이것이야 참말로] the very; just; indeed. e.g. 이것이야말로 내가 쭉 찾고 있던 것이다 This is the very thing [This is just the thing] that I have been looking for.

이양 [इयांग] [**移讓**] transfer; turning over; relinquishment. 이양하다 transfer; turn over; hand over; relinquish. e.g. 권리를 이양하다 transfer one's right <to another> / devolve rights upon <a person

이어받다 [इओबात्ता] 계승하다] succeed to; accede to; inherit <the property>; take over; be [fall] heir to. e.g. 아버지의 일[회사]을 이어받다 take over one's father's work [company].

이어서 [इओसो] [계속하여] continuously; successively; [다음으로] subsequently; soon ather. e.g. 김씨가 최씨에 이어서 사장이 되었다.

이어지다 [इओजीदा] be [get] connected; be joined [linked] together. e.g. 이 기사의 나머지는 25 페이 지에 이어진다 This article is continued on page 25.

이열치열 [इयौल्छीयौल] [**以熱治熱**] resort to an evil measure to destroy other evils; fight fire with fire; <속담> Meet evil with evil; <속담> Set a chief to catch a thief.

이완 [इवान] [**弛緩**] relaxation; atony; (규율 등의) laxity. e.g. 괄약근의 이완 relaxation of a sphincter. 이완하다 relaK slack (off). e.g. 이완한 사지 flaccid limbs. 병사들의 규율이 좀

이완되어 있다 There is some laxity in discipline among the soldiers.

이왕 (에) [इवांग] [ने] [已往 (-)] [기왕에] already; now that; since; if ... at all. e.g. 이왕 할 바엔 큰 일을 해라 If you do anything at all, do something great.

이외 [इवे] [以外] **1** [···을 제외하고] except. e.g. 그는 소설 이외에는 아무 것도 읽지 않는다 His reading is limited [confined] to novels. / He reads nothing but [except] novels **2**[··· 말고는] besides; in addition to. e.g. 유럽 여행에서 프랑스 이외에 어느 나라에 갔습니까 What countries besides France did you visit while on your tour of [in] Europe?

이용 [इयोंग] [利用] **1** [이롭게 씀] utilization; use; [쓸모 있게 씀] good use; profitable employment; improvement. e.g. 폐물[폐품] 이용 utilization of waste material. 이용하다 [활용하다] utilize; [선용하다] make (good) use of; take advantage of; (태양열,물 등을) exploit; harness**2** [자기 자신을 위한 수단으로 씀]. 이용하다 avail oneself of; take advantage of; [우려먹다] exploit.

이월 [इवॉल] [二月] February (略 Feb).

이월 [इवॉल] [移越] a transfer; (전기로부터의) bringing forward; (차기로의) carrying forward. e.g. 이자의 이월이 있었기 때문에 원금이 늘어났다 With the transfer of the interest, the amount of the principal increased. 이월하다 transfer; (전기로부터) bring forward [over]; (차기로) carry forward [over]. e.g. 가계비의 잔액을 다음 달로 이월하다 carry forward [over] the balance from last month's household expenses.

이유 [इयू] [理由] **1** (a) reason; [근거] grounds; [원인] a cause; [동기] a motive. e.g.존재 이유 the justification for the existence <of a thing / of a person> **2** [구실] an excuse; a pretext.

이유식 [इयूसीक] weaning food; baby food.

이윤 [इयुन] [利潤] (a) profit; (a) gain. e.g. 한계[초과 / 정상] 이윤 marginal [excess / normal] profits.

이율 [इयुल] [利率] the rate of interest; the interest rate.

이윽고 [इउक्को] soon atherward (s); in a (little) while; ather a while; before long. e.g.해가 지고 이윽고 달이 떴다 The sun set, and soon [by and by / in a short time] the moon appeared.

이의 [इउइ] [異議] [반대] an

objection; [항의] a protest; [불찬성] dissent; [法] a demurrer. e.g. 이의가 있다 [없다] have an[have no] objection <to>.

이익 [इइक] [**利益**] **1** [벌이, 수익] (a) profit; (a) gain. e.g. 큰 이익 a large profit.. **2**[유익하고 도움이 됨] benefit; profit; advantage; good; interests. e.g. 의 이익을 위해 for the benefit of.

이인 [इइन] [**異人**] **1** [비범한 사람] a man of unusual ability. **2** [다른 사람] a different person. e.g. 그것은 동명 이인이다 That is a different person with the same name.

이입 [इइप] [**移入**] introduction; import; shipping in. e.g. 감정 이입 [心] empathy. 감정 이입설 the empathy theory. 외국인 노동자의 이입 the introduction of foreign labor. 이입하다 introduce; import; bring in [from]; ship in. e.g.이 논문은 집필자의 감정이 지나치게 이입돼 있다 The writer has put too much personal feeling into this thesis.

이자 [इजा] [**利子**] interest. e.g. 정기 예금의 이자 interest on a fixed deposit.

이재민 [इजैमीन] [**罹災民**] the sufferers <from>; the afflicted people; the victims <of>.

이적 [इजौक] [**移籍**] transfer of registration. 이적하다 transfer one's registration <from / to>. e.g. 그는 내년에 브레이브스로 이적된다 He will transferred to the Braves next year.

이전 [इजौन] [**移轉**] **1** [이사] a move; a removal; a change of address [residence]. e.g. 그들은 사무소의 이전 준비로 바쁘다 They are busy preparing to move their office. 이전하다 move; remove; shith home; move one's residence <from ... to ...>. **2** [권리 등을 넘겨주거나 넘겨받음] (a) transfer; demise. e.g. 권리의 이전 a transfer of rights. 재산의 이전 a transfer of property. 이전 하다 transfer; change hands. e.g. 이전할 수 있는 권리 transferable rights. 토지의 소유권을 아내에게 이전 하다 transfer a land deed to one's wife's name.

이전 [इजौन] [**以前**] **1** [그보다 전에] before. e.g. 이보다 이전 before this time. 김씨 이전에는 누가 지사였습니까 Who was the governor prior to Mr. Kim? **2** [예전] former times [days]. e.g. 이전(에) formerly / in former times / in days gone by / of old / previously / before / [한때] once / on an earlier occasion. 이전의

ㅇ

수상 an ex-premier.

이점 [इचैम] [**利點**] an advantage. e.g. 이 제품은 가볍고 튼튼하다는 이점이 있다 This article has the advantage of being light and durable.

이정표 [इजौंग्फ्यो] [**-標**] a milestone; a milepost. **이제** now. e.g. 이제 막 just (now) / a moment ago. 이제는 now / at the present time / nowadays / [이미] already.

이제까지 [इजेकाजी] [지금까지] until now; hitherto; so [thus] far; up to this time [day]. e.g. 태어나서 이제까지 <not> in one's life.

이제부터 [इजेबूथो] from now on; ather this; [장래] in (the) future (▷ <英> 에서는 the를 붙이지 않음). e.g. 이제부터의 세대 the coming[next] generation.

이주 [इजू] [**移住**] **1** [이사] a move; a removal. 이주하다 move <to>; remove. e.g. 경기도로 이주하다 move to Kyeonggi-do. **2** (외국으로의) emigration; (외국으로부터의) immigration (▷ 정착); [사람의 옮겨 삶, 동물의 이동] migration (▷ 반복되는 이주나 집단의 이동에도 쓰임). 이주하다 emigrate <from a place to a place>; immigrate <to a place from a place>; migrate <from a place to a place.

이중 [इजूंग] [**二重**] duplication; double (ness). e.g. 이중의 [둘이 겹쳐진] double / [두 부분으로 된] dual.

이직 [इजीक] [**離職**] 이직하다 [직장을 그만두다] leave [quit] one's job; [실업하다] lose one's job. e.g. 불황 때문에 많은 사람이 이직했다 Many lost their jobs because of the recession.

이질 [इजील] [**異質**] heterogeneity; disparateness. e.g. 이질의[적인] of a different nature [kind] / heterogeneous / disparate. 그것은 이질적인 사람들이 모인 집단이었다 It was a group of heterogeneous people.

이질 [इजील] [**痢疾**] dysentery; (bloody) flux. e.g. 아메바성 이질 amoebic dysentery.

이쪽 [इच्चोक] **1** [화자 (話者) 에게 가까운 쪽] this side. e.g. 이쪽으로 here / this way. 이쪽으로 오십시오 Come here. / This way, please **2** [자기(들)]. e.g. 이쪽 사정도 생각해 주십시오 Please take our convenience into consideration, too. 그 건은 이쪽에서 처리하겠습니다 We will take care of the matter.

이쯤[इचुम] = 이만큼. e.g. 오늘은 이쯤에서 끝낸다 So much for today. / We'll stop here for today. / That's all for today.

이차 [इछा] [**二次**] [두 번째].

e.g. 제이차 세계 대전 the Second World War / World War II.

이채롭다 [इछैरोप्ता] [**異彩−**] conspicuous; shining; brilliant; distinguished; striking. e.g. 그는 자기 반에서 이채로운 존재이다 He is quite different from the other students in his class.

이처럼 [इछौरौम] like this; in this manner [way]; as you see. e.g. 이처럼 많이 so many [much] / this many [much].

이층 [इछुंग] [**二層**] the second story [floor]; the first floor; [두 층] two stories [floors / levels / layers].

이치 [इछी] [**理致**] **1**[논리] (a) theory; [도리] reason. e.g. 이치에 맞는[맞지 않는] 이야기 a reasonable [an unreasonable] story. **2** [원리] a principle. e.g. 자연의이치 a natural law.

이타 [इथा] [**利他**] altruism. e.g. 이타적인 altruistic / unselfish. **이타주의** altruism.

이타주의자 [इथाजूउइजा] an altruist.

이탈 [इथाल] [**離脫**] (a) secession;(a) separation; a breakaway. e.g. 국적이탈 the renunciation of one's nationality. 금본위 이탈 abolition of the gold standard. 이탈하다 secede <from>; break [drith] away <from>; leave <a party>. e.g. 당적을 이탈하다 secede from a party.

이탓저탓 [इथात्जौथात] with this excuse [complaint] and that; on one pretext or another; on some pretext or other. e.g. 그는 이탓저탓으로 약속을 지키지 않았다 He did not carry out his word [promise] on some pretext or other.

이토록 [इथोरोक] this much; so much; so; like this. e.g. 이토록 잘될 줄은 미처 몰랐다 Little did I expect to succeed so well.

이튿날 [इथुत्नाल] **1** [다음 날] the next [following] day; the day ather. e.g. 이튿날 아침 the next morning.**2** [둘째 날] the second day. e.g. 열 이튿날 the twelthh day (of) the month.

이틀 [इथुल] [2일간] two days; [달의 둘째 날] the second (day). e.g. 이틀마다 every two days / every other day.

이판사판 [इफान्साफान] e.g. 이판사판의 승부 an all-or-nothing contest. 이판사판 해보겠다 I'll take a chance on it / I'll give it a try, sink or swim. / Let's go for broke!

이하 [इहा] [**以下**] **1** (수량이) ...(and) downward; not exceeding. e.g. 10개 회사 이하 (최대10사) ten or fewer companies.**2** [정도] under; below; beneath; less

C

[lower] than. e.g. 보통 이하 below the general level / below the average [mark / standard]. **3** [나머지] the following. e.g. 이하와 같음 the same as follows.

이해[1] [इहे] [**利害**] loss and gain; profit and loss; advantages and disadvantages; interest (s); concern. e.g. 공통의 이해 common interests

이해[2] [इहे] [**理解**] understanding; comprehension; grasp; apprehension; appreciation. e.g. 충분한 이해 a full understanding.

이해관계 [इहेग्वाग्ये] [**利害關係**] interests; concern; stake. e.g. 상충하는 이해 관계의 조절 the adjustment of conflicting interests. 이해 관계가 있다

이해력 [इहेर्योक] [**理解力**] the comprehensive faculty; the understanding; the power to understand; sense.

이해심 [इहेसीम] [**理解心**] understanding; consideration; sympathy.

이해타산 [इहेथासान] [**利害打算**] [계산] calculation [reckoning] of the loss and gain [the profits and losses]; [욕심] self-interest; interestedness. e.g. 이해 타산에서 guided by self-interest.

이행 [इहेंग] [**履行**] performance <of a duty>; fulfillment <of a promise>; discharge <of an obligation>; execution <of a contract>; observance <of a rule>; implementation <of a treaty>. e.g. 계약[조약] 이행 the execution [implementation] of a contract (treaty). 약속의 이행 fulfillment of a promise. 이행하다 fulfill <a promise>; carry out <a pledge>; perform <a duty>; discharge <an obligation>; execute <a contract>; put <one's principle> into practice; live up to <one's principle>; observe <a rule>; implement <a treaty>.

이혼 [इहोन] [**離婚**] a divorce; divorcement. e.g. 법정이혼 a judicial divorce.

이후 [इहू] [**以後**] [금후] ather this; from now on [this time (on)]; [그후] ather that time; since then; from that time on; atherward (s); [그후 지금까지] ever since. ⇨ 후 e.g. 그때 이후 지금까지 from that time down to this day.

익다[1] [इक्ता] **1** (열매, 과일이) ripen; become ripe. e.g. 익은 ripe. **2** (날것이) boil; be boiled; be done; cook; be cooked. e.g. 잘 익은 well-done[-cooked]. **3** (술,장,김치 등이) ferment; mature; be [get] matured; be aged (술이); become seasoned. e.g. 김치가 잘 익었다 The kimchi has picked up flavor [has become seasoned]. **4** (살갗이) turn red; redden; color. e.g. (난로의 열 등으로) 발갛게 익은 얼굴 a glowing face <with heat>.

익다[2] [इकता] **1** [능숙하다] skilled; skillful; trained; experienced; practiced; expert.**2** [설지 않다] familiar; accustomed; <서술적> used <to>; become accustomed to; become familiar <with>; become experienced in. e.g. 귀에 익은[익지 않은] 목소리 a familiar [strange] voice.

익명 [इंग्म्यौग] [**匿名**] [본이름을 숨김] anonymity; [가명] a pseudonym; a cryptonym; an anonym(e). e.g. 익명의 anonymous / innominate / <a prince> incognito

익사 [**溺死**] [इकसा] drowning. e.g. 익사 직전의 어린이 a drowning child. 익사를 모면하다 escape a watery grave. 익사하다 be drowned (to death); drown; drown oneself (자살하다)

익살 [इकसाल] comicality; drollery; waggery; clownery; jocularity; [농담] a joke; a jest; (a) pleasantry; [우스움] humor. 익살(을) 떨다 [부리다] clown (around); play the buffoon [fool]; be funny.

익살스럽다 [इकसाल्स्रौप्ता] comic(al); funny; humorous; waggish; jocular; jocose; jesting; clownish; droll. e.g. 익살스러운 몸짓.

익숙하다 [इकसुख्वादा]**1** [친숙하다] familiar; accustomed; experienced. e.g. 익숙한 일 a familiar job. 익숙한 길 the familiar road [path / trail]. **2** [능숙하다] skilled; skillful; experienced; practiced; expert. e.g. 익숙한 사회자 an experienced emcee.

익일 [इगील] [**翌日**] the next [following] day. e.g. 편지를 낸 익일 그는 도착했다 He arrived the day ather the letters was posted.

익히 [इख्वी] e.g. 익히 알다 know well [fully / thoroughly].be well aware [informed] of <a fact> / be familiar [well acquainted] with <a matter> / be at home in [on] <things America>. 이 점은 너희들도 익히 알고 있을 줄 안다 I think you are all well aware of it.

익히다 [इख्वीदा] **1** [열매 등을 익게 하다] make ripe; ripen; mellow; mature. e.g. 인공열로 과일을 익히다 ripen fruit by artificial heat. 햇볕이 과일을 익힌다 The sun ripens fruit. **2** [날것을 익게

하다] boil; cook. e.g. 익힌 생선 boiled [cooked] fish. 달걀을 익히다 boil an egg. 고기를 잘 익히다 get the meat well done. **3** [술, 장 등을 발효시키다] mature; ferment; brew; age. e.g. 포도주를 익히다 let wine mature. 김치를 익히다 get kimchi seasoned [flavored].**4** (살갗을) redden; color.**5** [익숙하게 하다] make oneself familiar with; familiarize oneself with; habituate oneself to; inure oneself to; acclimate oneself to; accustom oneself to; acquaint oneself with; get <a person> accustomed to; accustom <a person> to; [습득하다] learn; practice; acquire <French>.

인[1] [इन] [**人**] a person; a man. e.g. 한국인 a Korean. 경제인 a financier. 신문인 a newspaper man.

인[2] [इन] [**印**] [도장] a seal; [스탬프] a stamp. e.g. 일부인을 찍다 stamp the date.

인가 [इन्का] [**人家**] a house; a dwelling. e.g. 인가가 밀집한[드문드문한] 지역 a densely [sparsely / thinly] populated area.

인가 [इनगा] [**認可**] [승인] approval; [허가] permission; [행정상의 허가] authorization.

인간 [इन्गान] [**人間**] **1** [사람] a human being; a man <*pl.* men>; a mortal; [인류] man; mankind. **2**[사람의 됨됨이] character; nature; personality.

인건비 [इन्कौन्बी] [**人件費**] personnel expenses [expenditure]; [봉급 지급 비용] payroll costs; [노동에 대해 지급하는 비용] labor costs.

인격 [इनक्यौक] [**人格**] character; personality; indivi-duality.

인계 [इनग्ये] [**引繼**] a transfer <of duties>; turning [handling] over <one's duties>. 인계하다 transfer <one's business>; take [hand] over.

인공 [इन्गोंग] [**人工**] human work [labor]; [자연물에 가공하는 일] art; human skill; artificiality.

인과 [इन्ग्वा] [**因果**] [원인과 결과] cause and effect.

인구 [इन्गू] [**人口**] (a) population.

인권 [इन्ग्वॉन] [**人權**] human [personal] rights; the rights of man; [시민권, 공민권] civil rights.

인기 [इन्गी] [**人氣**] popularity; public interest.

인기척 [इन्गीछौक] [**人**–] an indication [a sign] of a person being around.

인내 [इन्नै] [**忍耐**] [참고 견딤] patience; endurance (▷endurance 는 특히 장기간에 걸친 인내); [끈질김]

perseverance. 인내하다 be patient <with / about>; persevere <at / in / with>; have patience <with>; stand; endure; bear; put up with.

인데 [इन्दे] **1** [연결 어미] and; so; but; however; whereas; when. **2** [종결 어미].

인도[1] [इन्दो] [印度] India; (공식명) the Republic of India.

인도[2] [इन्दो] [引導][지도] guidance; (a) lead; [안내] showing the way.

인도하다 [इन्दोहादा] guide; lead; conduct.

인들 [इन्दुल] […라 할지라도 어찌] even; whatever; however; granted that it is [be]; even though it is [be].

인력[1] [इल्यौक] [引力] [끄는 힘] (an) attractive force; (물체간의) attraction; (원자 간의) affinity; (우주, 천체의) gravitation; (자기의) magnetism.

인력[2] [इल्यौक] [人力] [사람의 힘] human power [strength]; human agency (자연력에 대하여); [機] man power (공률 (工率) 의 단위); [인간의 노동력] manpower.

인류 [इल्यु] [人類] mankind; the human race; humanity; humankind; man; Homo Sapiens.

인륜 [इल्यूक] [人倫] [인도] humanity; human duties; [도덕] morality; moral princeples.

인마 [इन्मा] [人馬] [사람과 말] men and horses; [마부와 말] horseman [rider] and horse.

인맥 [इन्मैक] [人脈] a group of men (having the same financial or political interest); [파벌] a clique; a faction.

인멸 [इन्म्यौल] [없앰] destruction; [없어짐] extinction; disappearance. 인멸하다 destroy; make away with; be extinct.

인명 [इन्म्यौंग] [人名] a person's name; the name of a person

인문 [इन्मुन] [人文] **1** [문화] civilization; culture. e.g. 인문의 발달 the advance of civilization / enlightenment.**2** [윤리, 질서] humanity.

인물 [इन्मुल] [人物]**1** [사람] a person; a character; [거물] a figure.**2** [인품, 성격] a character; personality. **3** (소설, 극 중의) a character; a personage; a person; (그림의) a human figure; a figure subject. **4** [인재] a man of ability; a talented man; an able man; a talent; a person to be reckoned with; a person of some standing. **5**

ㅇ

[용모] features; looks; personal appearance.

인복 [इन्बोक] [人福] blessedness with friendly people.

인사 [इन्सा] [人事] **1** (사교상의) a greeting; recognition; the time of day (아침, 저녁의); (말) compliments; (연설) an address. 인사하다 greet; salute; say hello; pay one's respects; meet; recognize; present one's compliments; pay a visit of courtesy. **2** [절] a bow; a kowtow; a salute; a courts (e) y (여자의). **3** [예의] manners; etiquette; civility; decorum; courtesy. **4** [감사] thanks; gratitude; acknowledgement; appreciation; a present (in acknowledgment).

인산 인해 [इन्सान इन्हे] [人山人海] a great crowd (of people).

인삼[1] [इन्साम] [人蔘] ginseng.

인상[2] [इन्सांग] [印象] (an) impression.

인상 [इन्सांग] [引上] **1** [끌어올림] pulling [drawing] up. **2** [물가 등의 올림] a raise; a rise; an increase; raising; a hike.

인상 [इन्सांग] [人相] looks; features; an appearance.

인색 [इन्सैक] [吝嗇] stinginess; parsimony; miserliness; niggardliness; closefistedness. 인색하다 stingy; tightfisted; closefisted; cheap; miserly; niggardly; parsimonious.

인생 [इन्सैंग] [人生] (man's) life; [일생] one's life.

인생 무상 [इन्सैंग मुसांग] the frailty of human life.

인성 [इन्सौंग] [人性] [사람의 성품] character; [본성] human nature.

인솔 [इन्सोल] [引率] leading; guiding. 인솔하다 lead; head; guide.

인쇄 [इन्स्वै] [印刷] print; [인쇄하기] printing;(인쇄 기술 등) press. 인쇄하다 print; put into print.

인수 [इन्सु] [引受] [물품, 권리 등을 넘겨받음] taking over; charge; subrogation; [권리 등의 이전] a transfer. 인수하다 take over <a person's responsibility>; shoulder <a person's debt>; undertake; assume. 인수하다 accept; honor; (회사채의 발행을) underwrite.

인스턴트 [इन्सथौन्थ] instant. 인스턴트 커피 instant coffee.

인습 [इन्सब] [因習] (a) convention; conventionality; a long-established custom; [관습] usage.

인식 [इन्सीक] [認識] awareness; recognition; cognition; cognizance; perception; understanding. 인식하다 recognize; perceive; understand; be aware of; know.

인심 [इन्सीम] [**人心**] **1** [사람의 마음] a man's mind [heart]. **2** [인정] humane feeling; humaneness; sympathy; the heart.

인양 [**引揚**][] pulling [drawing] up; (시체 등의) recovery; (난파선의) salvage. 인양하다 pull [draw] up; (시체를) recover; (난파선을) salvage; (그물을) pull in.

인용 [इन्योंग] [**引用**] (a) quotation; (a) citation. 인용하다 (책, 연설 등의 말을) quote; (확증하기 위해 문장, 작가 등을) cite; take <a line> from; adduce.

인원 [इन्वौन] [**人員**] [인원수] the number of persons; <집합적> the staff; the personnel.

인위 [इन्वी] [**人爲**] an act of man; human work; [인공] artificiality.

인자 [इन्जा] [**仁慈**] benignancy; benignity; benevolence; clemency; mercy; graciousness. 인자하다 benign; benignant; benevolent; merciful.

인재 [इन्जै] [**人材**] [일 등에 유능한 사람] a competent person; [능력이 있는 사람] a man of ability; [재능 많은 사람] a man of talent; [유능한 직원 전체] an efficient staff.

인적 [इन्जौक] [**人跡**] human traces [footsteps]. e.g. 인적이 드문 unfrequented / trackless / out-of-the-way / <a place> away from the haunts of men / off the beaten track.

인접 [इन्जौप] [**隣接**] adjacency; contiguity; proximity. 인접하다 [इन्जौफादा] adjoin; be adjacent [contiguous] to; be [stand / lie] close by.

인정[1] [इन्जौंग] [**認定**] [인식] recognition; acknowledgment; [승인] approval; [인가] sanction; authorization; [허가] ermission 인정하다 (진실, 유효성 등을) admit; acknowledge; (정당, 정상을) accept; [좋다고 평가하다] approve of; recognize; [허가하다] allow; permit; [인가하다] authorize; sanction.

인정[2] [इन्जौंग] [**人情**] [동정심] sympathy; compassion; fellow feeling; [연민] pity; [자비심] mercy; charity; benevolence; [친절] kindness.

인종 [इन्जोंग] [**人種**] a race; an ethnic group (한 나라 안에서의 인종적 집단).

인증 [इन्जंग] [**認證**] certification; attestation; authentication. 인증하다 certify; attest; authenticate.

인지 [इन्जी] [**認知**] [인정하여 앎] recognition; perception; [心] cognition.

인지 하다 see; witness; sight; discern; perceive; recognize. recognition; (legal) acknowledgment.

인지상정 [इनजीसांजौंग] [人之常情] human nature; human feelings; humaneness; humanity.

인질 [इन्जील] [人質] a hostage.

인체 [इन्चे] [人體] the human body.

인출 [इन्चुल] [引出] (a) withdrawal. 인출하다 draw out; withdraw.

인치 [इन्ची] an inch (2.540 cm) (略 in; 기호 ").

인칭 [इन्छीग] [人稱] [문법] person.

인터뷰 [इन्थौबयु] an interview.

인파 [इन्फा] [人波] a surging crowd (of people); a crowd [throng] (of people).

O

인편 [इन्फ्यौन] [人便] e.g. 인편에 [인편으로] by someone / by means of someone / through the agency of person.

인품 [इन्फुम] [人品] character; one's personality; [품격] a dignity; (a) grace; nobility.

인플레 (이션) [इन्फल्ले (इस्यौन)] inflation [overissue] (of currency); currency inflation [expansion].

인하 [इन्हा] [引下] (a) reduction; lowering; a cut. **인하하다** lower; bring down; reduce; cut down; (통제 하여) roll back.

인하다 [इन्हादा] [因-] be caused by; be due to; be owing to; result from; start [arise] from; originate in.

인형 [इन्ह्यौंग] [人形] a doll.

인화 [इन्हवा] [印畵] [寫] [인화하기] printing; [인화된 것] a print. 인화하다 print (off / out); make a print <of>.

일[1] [इल] [日] a day. e.g. 2, 3일 전 a few days earlier. 6월 2일에 on the 2nd of June / on June 2.

일[2] [इल] [一] one; [첫째] the first; [로마 숫자] I; (주사위, 카드 등의) an ace.

일[3] [इल] **1** (놀이에 대하여) work; [오래고 고된 일] labor; [과해진 임무] a task; [직] a job; employment; [업무] business; [직무] one's job; [임무] a duty; [직업] one's occupation. **2** [문제] a thing; a matter; an affair; a concern. **3** [사정, 형편] circumstances; a case; things..**4** [용무] business; an engagement..**5** [사고] an accident; [사건] an incident; an occurrence; an event; a happening; an affair; (귀찮은 일) trouble.**6** [계획, 사업] a plan; a program(me); a project; a scheme; an undertaking; [음모] a plot; a trick.**7**

[경험] an experience.**8** [업적] an achievement; merits; services.

일가견 [इलकाग्यौन] [一家見] one's own opinion; a personal view; an (independent) opinion of one's own.

일거리 [इल्कौरी] a piece of work; a job; business; [임무] a mission; a task.

일곱 [इल्गोप] seven.

일관 [इल्गवान] [一貫] consistency; coherence. 일관하다 be consistent [coherent].

일구다 [इल्गुदा] [개간하다] bring <waste land> under cultivation; reclaim <waste land>; open ground; break up the soil.

일그러지다 [इल्गुरौजीदा] be distorted; be contorted; be twisted.

일기[1] [इल्गी] [日氣] the weather.

일기[2] [इल्गी] [日記] a diary.

일념 [इलन्यौम] [결의] determination; resolution; [열의] zeal; [열렬한 소원] a wholehearted [an ardent] wish.

일다 [इल्दा] **1** (파도 등이) run high; (바람이) rise; get up; spring up; (사건 등이) happen; break out. **2** [왕성하여지다] grow violent [fierce]; rise [increase] in violence; [번창하다] prosper; grow prosperous; flourish. (보풀 등이) be nappy [fluffy].

일단 [इल्तान] [一旦] [한 번] once; [우선 먼저] first; beforehand; in advance <to>.

일당[1] [इल्दांग] [一黨] [한 패거리] an unsavory group; a gang; a ring <of thieves>.

일당[2] [इल्दांग] [日當] [하루의 수당] a daily allowance; [일급] daily wages.

일대 [इल्तै] [一帶] [어떤 지역의 전부] the whole place [area / district].

일등 [इल्तंग] [一等] [첫째 등급] the first class [rank / grade]; [1위] (the) first place.

일러두다 [इल्लौदुदा] [지시하다] tell [instruct] <a person to do something>; bid <a person do something>; [부탁하다] ask; request

일러주다 [इल्लौजुदा] **1** [알려주다] let <a person> know; tell <a person about a matter>; inform <a person of a matter>. **2** [가르쳐 주다] tell; show; [교습하다] teach; instruct; initiate <in / into>.

일렬 [इल्ल्यौल] [一列] [세로 또는 가로의 한 줄] a line; (가로의) a row; (세로의) a file.

일례 [इल्लये] [一例] an example; an instance.

일류 [इल्ल्यु] [一流] [제1급]

the first class [rank].

일몰 [इल्मोल] [日沒]<at> sunset; <at> sundown.

일박[इल्बाक][一泊] a night's lodging; an overnight stay.

일반[इल्बान][一般]**1**[보통의 사람들] the public..**2**[마찬가지의 상태]. e.g. 일반의 the same / one and the same / identical.

일방 [इल्बांग][一方] **1** [한쪽] one side [hand]; [다른 쪽] the other side [hand].**2** 편도] one way.

일보다 [इल्बोदा] take care of a business; handle a job; attend to <one's> business; work.

일부 [इल्बु] [一部] **1** [일부분] (a) part; a portion; a section; a division. **2** [한권] a [one] volume.

일사 불란 [इल्सा बुल्लान] [一絲不亂] 일사 불란하다well-ordered; thoroughly consistent; <서술적> be in perfect [strict] order.

일사천리 [इल्साछोल्ली] [一瀉千里] dashing flow of torrents; rapid advance.

일상 [इल्सांग] [日常] daily; every day; usually; always.

일생 [इल्सैंग] [一生] [평생] one's (whole) life; a life time.

일석이조 [ईलसौग-ईजो] [一石二鳥] 그것은 일석이조다 It serves a double purpose. / It's a two-bird-one-stone solution.

일손 [इल्सोन] **1** [일하는 사람] a hand; a worker; [도움] help; assistance. **2** [일하는 손] work in hand..**3** [일하는 솜씨] a skil(l)ful hand; skill at a job.

일시[इल्शी][日時] [날과 때] the day and time; [날짜와 시간] the date and hour.

일어나다 [इरौनादा] **1** [잠을 깨다] wake up; awake; (잠, 병석에서) rise from one's bed; get up. **2** [발생하다] happen; occur; take place; come about; arise; break out.

일어서다 [इरौसोदा] **1** [기립하다] stand up; rise (to one's feet); get up (on one's feet); get to one's feet; pick oneself up. **2** [분기하다] be up(and doing); rise (up) <against>; rouse oneself <to action>.

일요일 [इर्योइल] [日曜日] Sunday.

일원 [इर्वोन] [一員] a member.

일월 [इर्वॉल] [一月] January (略 Jan.).

일으키다 [इरुख्रीदा] **1** [세우다] pick <a person> up; raise [set] up; set upright; lith up; (먼지 등을) raise. **2** [야기하다] raise <a commotion>; create; cause; make; give rise to; stir up <a trouble>; [촉발, 유인하다] provoke; invite. **3**[설립하다] set up; esta-blish [found] <a school>; [발기하다] promote; organize; [창시하다] start <a movement>; begin; launch [undertake] <a new enterprise>.

일일이 [इरीरी] [一一] **1** [하나하나] one by one; severally; separately. **2** [상세히] in detail; in full; fully.

일임 [इरीम] [一任] 일임하다 [इरीमादा] leave <a matter> entirely up to <a> person [in a person's hand]; entrust <a person> with the task <of>.

일자리 [इल्चारी] [직업] employment; a job; [직장] a place; a position; a situation.

일장춘몽 [इल्चांगछुन्मोंग] [一場春夢] [헛된 영화,덧없는 일] an empty dream; a crushed hope.

일조권 [इल्चोक्वान] a right to sunshine [sunlight].

일주(일) [इल्चु(इल)] [一週(日)] a week.

일주 [इल्चु] [一周] [한 바퀴 돎] one [a] round; [1회전] a revolution.

일지 [इल्ची] [日誌] a diary; a journal.

일찍 [इल्चीक] [이르게] early.

일체 [इल्छे] [一切] [모든 것] all; every thing; the whole; [모두,죄다] wholly; entirely; absolutely.

일촉즉발 [इल्छोक्चकपाल] [一觸即發] a touch-and-go [an explosive] situation; a situation full of dynamite [ripe for explosion]; a hair-trigger crisis.

일취월장 [इल्छ्वीवॉल्चांग] [日就月將] [날로 달로 진보함] rapid progress; steady advance. 일취월장하다 make rapid progress [steady advance].

일치 [इल्छी] [一致] **1** [합치] agreement; accord; concurrence; consensus <of opinion>; conformity; consistency; congruence; congruity; [문법] concord; agreement. **2** [부합] coincidence; [대응] correspondence.

일컫다 [इल्खौत्ता] [칭하다] call; name; designate; [자칭하다] claim.

일탈 [इल्थाल] [逸脫] (a) deviation; (a) departure; a breakaway <from>. 일탈하다 deviate <from>; depart <from>; break away <from>; overstep <the bounds>.

일터 [इल्थौ] one's place of work; one's job(site); (공장) a workshop; (회사,사무실) one's office. ⇨ 직장

일평생 [इल्फयौंगसैंग] [一平生] a lifetime; one's (whole) life; <부사적> through life; in one life (-time); from birth to death.

일품 [इल्फुम] [一品]. [최고] an article of top quality; a superior article.

일하다 [इरहादा] [노동하다] work

일행 [इरहैंग] [一行] a party; [배우, 예능인 등의 일단] a troupe; a company..

일화[इरहवा] [逸話] an anecdote.

일확천금 [इरहवाकछौन्ग्गम] [一攫千金] making a big fortune on a single occasion [with one swoop].

일흔 [इरहुन] seventy.

일희일비 [इरहवेइलबी] [一喜一悲] alternation of joy and sorrow.

읽다 [इक्ता] **1** (책 등을) read; peruse; [독송하다] recite <an ode>; chant <a sutra>. **2** [알아차리다] read; guess (추측하다); understand (이해하다).

읽히다 [इल्खीदा] **1** [읽게 하다] get <a person> to read; set <a person> to reading; have <a book> read <by a person>.**2** [읽혀지다] be read.

잃다 [इल्था] **1** [없어지다] lose; miss; be deprived of (빼앗겨서). **2** [사라지다] lose.**3** [죽음을 당하여 이별하다] lose; be eprived [bereth] of. **4** [방향P길을 찾지 못하게 되다] lose; miss; stray.

임 [इम] [연인] a lover (남자); a sweetheart (여자).

임금 [इमगम] [賃金] 노임] wages (▷ 보통 복수형); pay (급료).

임기 [इमगी] [任期] one's term of office [service]; one's tenure (of office); (의원의) a term of membership.

임기응변 [इमगीउंगब्यौंग] [臨機應變] adaptation to circumstances.

임대 [इमदै] [賃貸] lease; hire; (부동산의) location; (물품의) hiring out; (배의) charter.

임무 [इम्मु] [任務] a duty; an office; a task; [사명] a mission.

임박 [इम्बाक] [臨迫] 임박하다 impend; draw near; be close [near] at hand; be imminent; approach.

임산부 [इम्सान्बु] [妊産婦] pregnant women and nursing mothers.

임시 [इम्सी] [臨時] [일시적임]. e.g. 임시의 temporary / provisional / interim / expedient / makeshith.

임신 [इम्सीन] [妊娠, 姙娠] pregnancy. 임신하다 become pregnant [impregnated]; be[get] pregnant; get [be] in the [a] family way; [醫] conceive.

임야 [इम्या] [林野] forests and fields; a forest land.

임업 [इमौप] [林業] forestry.

임용 [इम्योंग] [任用] appointment. e.g. 공무원 임용령 the Official Appointment Regulations. 임용 후보자 명부 a list of eligible candidates for appointment.

임용하다 appoint. e.g. 요직에 임용되다 be appointed an important position.

임원 [**इम्वॉन**] [**任員**] a person holding a managerial [an executive] post; an executive; an official; an officer; a person in charge meet.

임의 [**इमुइ**] [**任意**] option; discretion; voluntariness. e.g. 임의의 option / discretionary / voluntary / arbitrary.

임자 [**इम्जा**] [소유한 사람] the owner. e.g. 임자 없는 개 an ownerless [a stray] dog. 임자 없는 집 a vacant [deserted] house.

임종 [**इम्जोंग**] [**臨終**] [죽음에 임함] one's end; one's deathbed; [목숨이 끊어질 때] one's last moment; the time [hour] of death. e.g. 임종의 고통 death agonies. 임종의 자리 one's deathbed. 임종 때에 at the point of death / on one's deathbed.

입 [**इब**] (사람,동물의) a mouth; [입술] lips; [解] an os <*pl.* ora>.

입각 [**इप्काक**] [**立脚**] 입각하다 be based [grounded / founded] on; take one's ground on; rest on the basis of. e.g. 그것은 사실에 입각한 논의였다 The arguments were based on facts.

입건[**इप्कौन**][**立件**] 입건하다 book <a person> for[on a charge of].

입고 [**इप्को**] [**入庫**] (상품 등의) storage in warehouse; (차 등의) entering the(car) shed. 입고하다 (상품을) stock; warehouse; (차를) enter the (car) shed.

입구 [**इप्कु**] [**入口**] an entrance; a way in; the door <to a room>; doorway; an entry <to a river>; the mouth <of a harbor>; the approach <to a bridge>.

입국 [**इप्कुक**] [**入國**] entry [entrance] (into a country); [이민,이주] immigration.

입금 [**इपगम**] [**入金**] [돈이 들어옴] receipt of money; [그 돈] money received; receipts; [돈을 넣음] depositing; [예금] a deposit. e.g. 입금하다 [받다] receive <money>.

입다 [**इप्ता**]**1** [옷을 몸에 두르다] put on; get into; slip on (걸치다); rush [throw] on(급히); wear; have on; be dressed in. (put on 은 입는 동작, wear 는 입은 상태를 나타냄) e.g. 한복을 입은 여인 a woman in Korean clothes. 치마를 입다 put on a skirt**2** (손해 등을) sustain; suffer; incur; (은혜 등을) get [receive] <a favor>; be favored <with>;

입담 [**इप्ताम**] volubility; skill at

talking; the gith of (the) tongue

입대 [इप्दै] [入隊] joining the army; enlistment; enrollment. 입대하다

입덧 [इप्तौत] orning sickness; nausea accompanying pregnancy. e.g. 입덧이 나다 have morning sickness. 입덧이 심하다 suffer greatly from morning sickness.

입맛 [इम्मात] (an) appetite; one's taste; one's palate. e.g. 입맛이 나다 have a good appetite. 입맛을 잃다 lose one's appetite. 입맛이 없다 have no appetite / lack appetite.

입버릇 [इप्पौरत] [말버릇] a way [habit] of saying; [자주 입에 담는 말] a pet [favorite] phrase [saying].

입법 [इप्पौप] [立法] legislation; lawmaking

입사 [इप्सा] [入社] joining [entering] a company. 입사하다 join [enter] a company [firm] <as a salesman>; become a member of a company; obtain a position in a concern for.

입상 [इप्सांग] [入賞] 입상하다 win a prize; (경마에서) finish in the money.

입수 [इप्सु] [入手] 입수하다 [손에 넣다] get; (보통 노력하여) obtain; (재산,권리 등을) acquire. e.g. 이런 종류의 자전거는 입수하기 어렵다 This kind of bicycle is difficult to get [come by].

입술 [इप्सुल] a lip. e.g. 윗[아랫] 입술 the upper [lower] lip.

입신 양명 [-揚名] [इप्शिन यांगम्यौंग] rising in the world and winning [gaining] fame; achieving glory.

입양 [इबयांग] [入養] (an) adoption. 입양하다 adopt <a child> as one's son; receive into one's family as a son; affiliate.

입원 [इबवौन] [入院] dmission (in) to a hospital; hospitalization.

입장 [इप्चांग] [立場] **1** [당면한 처지] a situation; a position. **2** [견지,관점] a viewpoint; a standpoint; [보는 각도] angle.

입장 [इप्चांग] [入場] entrance; [관람객 등이 장내로 들어감] admission; admittance.

입주 [इप्चु] [入住] [새 건물 등에 들어가 삶]. 입주하다 move into <an apartment / a flat>; (가정에) live in <a house>; live with <a family>.

입증 [इप्चंग] [立證] proof; demonstration; establishment <of a fact>; substan tiation <of one's statement>. 입증하다 give proof; prove <a person's guilt [innocence]>; establish <a

fact>; [일이 정당함을 증명하다] testify <a fact>; attest to <a fact>; corroborate; confirm; support; bear out.

입학 [**इफाक**] [**入學**] entrance into [admission to] a school; (대학의) matriculation.

입헌 [**इफोन**] [**立憲**] constitutionalization; establishment of a constitution.

입회 [**इफ्वे**] [**入會**] admission; joining; entrance

입후보 [**इफुबो**] [**立候補**] candidacy; candidature

입히다 [**इफीदा**]**1** [옷을 입게 하다] dress; clothe; put on over **2** [물건의 거죽에 한 꺼풀 바르거나 씌우다] plate; coat; gild; (표면에) cover; veneer. e.g. 금을 입힌 액자 a gilded frame. **3** [해를 주다] cause <damage to>; inflict <an injury on>; subject <a person>to; do <harm>. e.g. 화를 입히다 do <a person> an evil. 그는 인질에게 깊은 상처를 입혔다 He inflicted a severe injury on the hostage.

잇다 [**इत्ता**]**1** [맞붙이다] join [link] <a thing to another>; piece together; put together; connect <a thing with another>; combine; piece <a thing to another>. e.g. 두 점을 잇는 직선 a (straight) line that links two points**2** [계속하다] continue; keep [go] on <with>; carry [hold] on <with>. e.g.끼니를 잇다 live from hand to mouth**3** [계승하다] succeed to; carry on; inherit; take over. e.g. 아버지의 뒤를 잇다 succeed one's father.

잇몸 [**इन्मोम**] the gum(s); the teethridge; the gingiva <*pl.* –vae>.

있다 [**इत्ता**]**1** [위치하다] be; be situated; be located; stand(건물 등이); lie(도시 등이); run (산맥,강이). e.g. 강가에 있는 절 a temple standing by the river. 한국은 중국의 동쪽에 있다 Korea lies to the east of China**2** [존재하다] there is [are]; be; exist; be in existence; [발견되다] be found. e.g. 책상 위에 책이 한 권 있다 There is a book on the desk. 그 책은 책상 위에 있다 The book is on the desk **3** [생기어 벌어지다] happen; occur; take place; break out; arise. e.g. 사고가 있었던 곳 the scene of a disaster.**4** [열리다,행해지다] be held; take place. e.g.우리 시험은 3월에 있다 We have examinations in March. / Examinations take place in**6** [소유하다] have; possess; own; [부여받고 있다] be endowed [githed].

잉여 [**इङ्यो**] [**剩餘**] [쓰고 난 나머지] a surplus; an

overplus; the remainder; [잔액] a balance. e.g.이 나라는 작년에 3만톤의 농산물의 잉여가 생겼다 Last year this country had a surplus of thirty thousand tons of agricultural produce.

잉태 [इंग्थै] [孕胎] concept-tion; pregnancy. 잉태하다 get [become] pregnant <with child>; get in the [a] family way.

잊다 [इत्ता] [망각하다] forget; be forgetful <of>; (일을) slip one's mind; escape [slip] one's memory. e.g. 그녀의 전화 번호를 잊었다 I forget [have forgotten] her phone.

잊히다 [इछीदा] be forgotten; pass out of mind [one's memory.

잎 [इप] a leaf <*pl.* leaves>; a needle (침엽); (풀의) a blade; (양치 등의) a frond; <집합적> foliage. e.g. 무성한 잎 thick foliage. 나뭇잎 leaves of the tree. 풀잎 blades of grass.

자[1] [जा] [者] e.g. 어리석은 자 a fool / a simpleton / an ass.

자[2] [जा] [길이,높이를 재는 기구] a ruler; a rule; [측정기] a measure

자[3] [जा] [행동을 재촉할 때 내는 소리] come on.

자가용 [जागायोंग] [自家用] .[자가용차] a privately-owned car; an owner-driven car; one's own car.

자각 [जागाक] [自覺] (self-) awareness; (self-) cons-ciousness; (self-) awakening. 자각하다 be conscious [aware] of <one's duty>;.

자갈 [जागाल] gravel; (small) pebbles; shingle (해안 등의).

자개 [जागै] (a lamina of) mother-of-pearl [nacre]. e.g. 자개를 박다 inlay <a cabinet> with mother-of-pearl.

자격 [जाग्यौक] [資格] 1 [일정한 신분,지위] capacity; [권리] a right. 2 [어떤 신분, 지위에 반드시 필요한 조건] qualification (s); [증명] [जुग्यौंग] certification; [면허] a license; a licence; [능력] competence; capability.

자격지심 [जाग्यौजीसीम] [自激之心] (a feeling of) self-reproach [-accusation / -reproo / -condemnation]; a guilty conscience.

자결 [जाग्यौल] [自決] [스스로 목숨을 끊음] suicide. 자결하다 kill oneself; com-mit suicide.

자국[1] [जागुक] [닿은 자리] a mark; a print; an imprint; an impression; [더럼]a stain. e.g. 손가락 자국 a finger mark / a finger print.

자국² [जागूक] [自國] [자기 나라] one's own country; voluntary exile.**자국어** one's (native) languageone's mother tongue.

자국인 [जागूगीन] one's fellow countrymen.

자궁 [जागूंग] [子宮] [解] the womb; the uterus.

자그마하다 [जागुम्हादा] smallish; tiny; somewhat [rather] small [little]; small-sized. e.g. 키가 자그마한 사내 a man short (ish) in stature [height] / a short (ish) [little] man.

자금 [जागुम] [資金] funds; a fund;(a) capital.

자급 [जागुप] [自給] self-support; self-sustenance. 자급하다 support oneself; provide for oneself

자급 자족 [जागुप जाजोक] [自給自足] self-sufficiency; self-sufficing. elf-sufficiency / autarky.

자기 [जागी] [自己] (one's) self; oneself. e.g. 자기 스스로 [oneself / personally / for [by] oneself.

자꾸 [जाकू] [잇달아] frequently; repeatedly; again and again; [끊임없이] incessantly; constantly; [열심히] eagerly; intently; strongly.

자나깨나 [जानाकैना] [잠들었거나 깨었거나] asleep or awake; [항상] all the time; always; twenty-four hours a day. e.g. 자나깨나 그녀는 환자 간호만 하였다 She attended the patient day and night.

자녀 [जान्यौ] [子女] sons and daughters; children; offspring.

자다 [जादा]1 [잠자다] sleep; [잠들다] go [get] to sleep; fall asleep. 2 [동침하다] go to bed with; sleep with; share the bed with.

자동 [जादोंग] [自動] automatic action [movement / operation]; automatism.

자동사 [जादोंगसा] [自動詞] [문법] an intransitive verb (*v.i., vi.*).

자동차 [जादोंगछा] [自動車] a car; a motorcar; an automobile; an auto.

자득 [जादुक] [自得] [터득] apprehension; understandding; [스스로 얻음] self-acquirement. 자득하다 apprehend; understand; acquire by oneself.

자라다 [जारादा]1 [성장하다] grow (up); [양육되다] be brought up; be bred.2 [발전하다] improve; develop; progress; make progress.

자랑 [जारांग] pride; boast; boasting; brag; bragging. 자랑하다 be proud of; boast [brag] of; make a boast of; be boastful.

자랑거리 [जारांगगौरी] some-

ㅈ

thing to brag about [of]; a feather in one's cap. **자랑스럽다** proud (of); boastful. e.g. 자랑스러워 하는 아버지 the proud father.

자료 [जारयू] [**資料**] materials <for study>; [데이터] data <on> (▷ data는 datum의 복수형, <美>에서는 종종 단수 취급을 함); (조사 결과) findings.

자루[1] [जारू] a bag; a sack; (주로 가죽으로 된 작은 자루) a pouch.

자루[1] [जारू] [기름한 물건의 낱개를 세는 단위] a piece [stick] <of India ink>.

자르다 [जारुदा]**1** [끊어 내다] cut; chop (도끼 등으로); saw (톱으로) ;carve (식탁에서 요리한 고기를); hash (고기 등을 잘게); slice (빵을). e.g. 잘게 자르다 cut <a thing> fine [into small pieces].**2** [해고하다] dismiss; discharge; fire. ⇨ 잘리다 e.g. 사장은 당장에 그의 목을 잘랐다 Boss fired him out in no time.

자리 [जारी] **1** [공간] room; space. e.g. 자리를 차지하다 take up [occupy] much room [space].**2** [흔적] a mark; a print; a trace; a scar (상처의). e.g. 총알이 박힌 자리 a mark of a bullet. **3** [좌석] a seat; a place (지정된).버렸다 He flung out of the room. 내 자리를 비워 두시오 Please make room for me. e.g. 빈 자리 a vacant seat. **4** [직위,지위] a position; a post; a situation. e.g. 높은 자리에 있는 사람 a very important person / a VIP.

자리잡다 [जारीजाप्दा]**1** [좌석을 잡다] take a [one's] seat; be seated). e.g. 상석에 자리잡다 take the top seat.**2** [위치하다] be situated [located] <in the center of a city>e.g.여기는 성이 자리잡고 있던 곳이다 This is the place where a castle formerly stood. **3** [정착하다] settle (down) e.g. 서울에 자리잡다 settle down in Seoul.

자립 [जारीप] [**自立**] [독립] independence; selfreliance; [자활] selfsupport. 자립하다 become independent; establish oneself; rely on oneself.

자만 [जामान] [**自慢**] conceit; selfconceit; [허영심] vanity; [자랑] pride. 자만하다 be conceited [selfconceited]; be vain <about>; flatter oneself He thinks very highly of himself.

자매 [जामै] [**姉妹**] sisters. **자매 기관** sister agencies.

자멸 [जाम्यौल] [**自滅**] [자연히 멸망함] natural decay; [제 탓으로 멸망함] selfdestruction.

자명 [जाम्यौंग] [自明] self-evidence. 자명하다 [명백하다] self-evident; [설명이 필요없다] self-explanatory; [분명하다] obvious. e.g. 자명한 이치 a self-evident [an obvious] truth / a truism / an axiom.

자명종 [जाम्यौंग्जोंग] [自鳴鐘] an alarm (clock).

자모 [जामो] [字母] 1 [言] an alphabet; a letter(of the alphabet); a syllabic.2 (활자의) a matrix <*pl.* matrices, matrixes>; a (font of) printing type.

자문[1] [जामुन] [自問] 자문하다 question [ask] one-self.

자문[2] [जामुन] [諮問] a request for advice;(a) consultation. 자문하다 consult <a person about a matter>; submit [refer] <a matter to> / seek advice. 자문하다 refer a problem to a committee.

자문 자답 [जामुन जादाप] [自問自答] a soliloquy. 자문자답하다 wonder to one-self; answer one's own question; think aloud; talk to oneself; soliloquize (독백하다).

자물쇠 [जामुल्स्वे] a lock; a padlock (맹꽁이 자물쇠); a snaplock (자동 자물쇠). 자물쇠를 채우다[열다] lock [unlock] <a door>.

자발적 [जाबाल्जौक] [自發的] spontaneous; voluntary.

자백 [जाबैक] [自白] [고백] (a) confession; penance; [자인] admission. e.g. 자백하다 confess <to>; make (a) confession; own (up); admit.

자본 [जाबोन] [資本] (a) capital; a fund.

자본주의 [जाबोन्जूउइ] [資本主義] capitalism.**자본주의 국가** a capitalist country [nation]; a capitalistic country [state].

자부심 [जाबूसीम] [自負心] self-confidence; self-esteem [-importance]; pride. e.g. 자부심이 있는 [강한] self-confident <person>.

자비[1] [जाबी] [自費] one's own expense [charge]. e.g. 자비로 출판하다 publish one's book at one's own expense.

자비[2] [जाबी] [慈悲] [인정] mercy; benevolence; [연민] compassion; pity; clemency; [자선] charity. 자비하다 merciful; charitable <to the poor>; benevolent; compassionate.

자빠지다 [जापाजीदा] [뒤로 넘어지다] fall on one's back; go[fall] over; tumble over backward; tumble down. e.g. 얼음판 위에 자빠지다 fall down on the ice.

자산 [जासान] [資産] property; a fortune; assets; [부] wealth.

ㅈ

자살 [जासाल] [自殺] (a) suicide 자살하다 commit suicide; take one's own life.

자상 [जासांग] [仔詳] 자상하다 [상세하다] minute; detailed; full; [생각이 깊다] thoughtful; considerate.

자생 [जासैंग] [自生] spontaneous generation; autogenesis; abiogenesis; [야생] wild [natural] growth. 자생하다 grow wild [naturally / spontaneously].

자서 [जासौ] [自序] the author's preface [forward].

자서전 [जासौजौन] [自敍傳] an autobiography.

자석 [जासौक] [磁石] a magnet; (자철광) magnetite; magnetic iron ore.

자선 [जासौन] [慈善] charity; benevolence; beneficence; philanthropy; [구휼] almsgiving.

자성 [जासौंग] [自省] self-examination; reflection; self-reflection. 자성하다 examine [reflect on] oneself; introspect.

자세 [जासे] [姿勢] a posture; a pose; a physical position [stance]; [몸가짐] a carriage; [태도] an attitude; bearing. e.g. 방어 자세 a posture of defense / (펜싱 등에서) (on) guard.

자세히 [जासेही] [仔細-] minutely; in detail; in particular; fully; in full.

자손 [जासोन] [子孫] **1** [아들과 손자] sons and grandsons. **2** [후손] a descendant; <집합적> posterity; offspring.

자수 [जासू] [自首] self-surrender; self-denunciation; voluntary denunciation [surrender]. 자수하다 surrender [deliver] oneself; give oneself up [turn oneself in].

자숙[[जासूक] [自肅] self-restraint [-control]; self-discipline. 자숙하다 restrain oneself; exercise self-control [-discipline]; discipline [control] oneself.

자습 [जासुप] [自習] self-teaching; studying [learning] by oneself. 자습하다 study for [by] oneself; teach oneself; study without a teacher; practice oneself.

자식 [जाशिक] [子息] [아들 딸] a child <*pl.* children>; offspring <단수,복수 동형>; sons and daughters.

자신 [जासीन] [自身] (one's) self; oneself.

자아 [जाआ] [自我] (the) self <*pl.* selves>; (the) ego <*pl.*~s>. of self.

자아내다 [जाआनैदा] **1** (실을) draw out; reel off; spin e.g. 고치에서 실을 자아내다 reel silk off cocoons **2** (느낌 등을) evoke; draw out; provoke; create.. e.g. 동정심을 자아내다 evoke <a person's> sympathy.

자업 자득 [**जाऑप जादुक**] [**自業自得**] the natural consequence of one's (mis) deeds; the natural outcome of one's acts. e.g. 자업자득이다 <속담> Having made one's bed, one must lie on it. / As one sows, so one reaps. / As a man sows, so he shall reap.

자연 [**जायौन**] [**自然**] [천연의 모습] nature. e.g. 자연(그대로)의 natural. 자연을 벗하다 take nature for a friend / make a friend of [be close to] nature.

자외선 [**जावेसौन**] [**紫外線**] [理] ultraviolet rays.

자욱하다 [**जाउख्यादा**] dense; thick; heavy. e.g. 안개가 자욱한 산들 misty [hazy] mountains.

자원[1] [**जावौन**] [**自願**] volunteer-ring. 자원하다 volunteer <for>.

자원[2] [**जावौन**] [**資源**] resources.

자유 [**जायू**] [**自由**] [구속으로부터의 해방] freedom; [권리로서의 자유] liberty.

자유주의 [**जायूजुउइ**] liberalism.

자율 [**जायुल**] [**自律**] [자기 억제] self-control [-restraint / -regulation].

자음 [**जाउम**] [**子音**] [言] a consonant.

자의 [**जाउइ**] [**字義**] the meaning [signification / sense] of a word. e.g. 자의대로의 해석 a literal [word-for-word] interpretation.

자의식 [**जाउइसीक**] [**自意識**] self-consciousness.

자자 [**जाजा**] [**藉藉**] 자자하다 be widely spread; be spread abroad; be widely known. e.g. 천하에 명성이 자자한 정치가 a world-famous statesman. 칭찬이 자자하다 win wide admiration.

자자손손 [**जाजासोनसोन**] [**子子孫孫**] descendants; posterity; offspring.

자장가 [**जाजांगा**] [**-歌**] a lullaby; a cradlesong; a hushaby (e); a nursery song.

자재 [**जाजे**] [**資材**] materials.

자전 [**जाजौन**] [**自轉**] rotation. 자전하다 rotate [revolve / turn round] (on its own axis).

자전거 [**जाजौनगौ**] [**自轉車**] a bicycle; a bike; a cycle; a wheel.

자정 [**जाजौग**] [**子正**] midnight.

자제[1] [**जाजे**] [**子弟**] **1** [남의 아들] a son. **2** [남의 집안의 젊은이] children; young ones.

자제[2] [**जाजे**] [**自制**] self-control [-restraint]; self-command [-mastery]. 자제하다 control [restrain] oneself; contain oneself; check oneself <from doing>.

자조 [**जाजो**] [**自助**] self-help; self-reliance.

자조 정신 [**जाजो जौग्सीन**] the spirit of self-help.

자족 [**जाजोक**] [**自足**] **1** [자급

하여 넉넉함] self-sufficiency. 자족하다 self-sufficient. **2** [자기 만족] self-satisfaction; self-contentment. 자족하다 be satisfied.

자존 [जाजोन] [**自尊**] [스스로 자기를 높임] self-respect; self-esteem; pride. 자존하다 respect [esteem] oneself; have self-respect [-esteem]; be proud.

자존심 [जाजोन्सीम] [**自尊心**] pride; self-respect. e.g. 자존심이 있는 사람 a self-respecting person. 자존심을 잃다 lose one's self-respect.

자주[1] [जाजू] frequently; othen; [여러 번 반복하여] repea-tedly; [여러 번 잦게] many times.

자주[2] [जाजू] [**自主**] independ-ence; self-reliance.

자줏빛 [जाजूबीत] [**紫朱-**] purple (color); violet; amethyst.

자진 [जाजीन] [**自進**] willingness; voluntariness. 자진하다 volunteer (oneself).

자질 [जाजील] [**資質**] [천성] nature; disposition; [기질] a temperament; [재능] a gith.

자질구레하다 [जाजीलकूरेहादा] all in small size; petty; trifling; slight.

자찬 [जाछान] [**自讚**] self-praise. 자찬하다 praise oneself; sing -one's own praises.

자책 [जाछैक] [**自責**] self-reproach. 자책하다 reproach oneself.

자체 [जाछे] [**自體**] **1** [본새] oneself; itself. **2** [그 자신] oneself; [내부] the inside.

자초지종 [जाछोजीजोंग] [**自初至終**] [상세한 내용] the whole story; everything <about an affair>; a com-plete [full] account <of>; [처음부터 끝까지] from beginning to end. e.g. 자초지종을 말하다 tell the whole story / tell the story from beginning to end. 그는 자초지종을 알고 있다 He knows everything about it.

자취[1] [जाछ्वी] [흔적] a mark; a track; a trace; a vestige; a sign.

자취[2] [जाछ्वी] [**自炊**] 자취하다 cook one's own meals; do one's own cooking; cook for oneself; board oneself.

자치 [जाछी] [**自治**] self-government; self-adminis-tration; autonomy; home rule. 치하다 govern oneself.

자칫하면 [जाछीथाम्यौन] at [on / with] the slightest slip [provocation]; (very) nearly; almost; barely; narrowly. e.g. 자칫하면 반대 방향의 열차를 탈 뻔했다 I almost took a train going in the opposite direction.

자칭 [जाछींग] [**自稱**] <형용사적> self-styled [-appointed]; would-be.

자탄 [जाथान] [**自歎**] 자탄하다 complain of oneself; lament oneself.

자태 [जाथै] [**姿態**] a figure; a shape.

자택 [जाथैक] [**自宅**] one's (own) house; one's home.

자퇴 [जाथ्वे] [**自退**] voluntary retirement [resignation]; (입후보 등의) voluntary withdrawal. 자퇴하다 retire voluntarily [willingly]; resign [leave] one's post of one's own accord

자투리 [जाथूरी] odds and ends <of yard goods>; the remnants <of dress goods>; waste pieces <from cutting cloth>. e.g. 자투리를 싸게 팔다 hold a remnant sale. 자투리로 인형을 만들다 make a doll with odds and ends of cloth.

자포자기 [जाफोजागी] [**自暴自棄**] desperation; despair; self-abandonment [-negligence]. e.g. 자포자기의 desperate / self-abandoned. 범인은 자포자기가 되어 닥치는 대로 발포했다 The desperate criminal fired indiscriminately.

자필 [जाफील] [**自筆**] one's own handwriting; a holograph.

자필이력서 [जाफील इर्योक्सौ] one's personal history in one's own handwriting.

자해 [जाहै] [**自害**] [자기 몸을 스스로 해침] self-wrong; self-injury. 자해하다 do self-wrong; injure [hurt] oneself.

자형 [जाह्यौंग] [**姉兄**] one's elder sister's husband; one's brother-in-law.

자화 자찬 [जाहवा जाछान] [**自畵自讚**] self-praise. e.g. 그는 늘 자화 자찬만 한다 He always blows his own trumpet

자활 [जाहवाल] [**自活**] self-support.

작 [जाक] [**作**] [제작(품)] a work; a production. e.g. 소월 작의 시 a poem written by So-wol. 이 조각은 로댕 작이다 This sculpture is (a work) by Rodin.

작고 [जाको] [**作故**] 작고하다 decease; die; pass away.

작곡 [जाकोक] [**作曲**] (musical) composition.

작다 [जाक्ता] **1** [길이, 넓이, 부피가 얼마 안 되다] small; little (▷ little은 종종 [귀여운] 등의 뜻을 가지며, 술어로 쓰이는 경우는 드묾); tiny (아주 작다).). e.g. 작은 집[방] a small house [room].**2** [정도,범위,규모가 크지 않다] small; low (낮다). e.g. 8 보다 작은 수 numbers smaller [lower] than eight. [보잘것없다] small; trifling; trivial; slight; petty. e.g. 작은 일 a small [trivial] matter[affair] / a trifle. [인물,도량이 좁다] small-minded; narrow-minded e.g. 작은 인물 a small-minded [petty] person / (스케일이) a man of small caliber.

작대기 **[जाक्तैगी]** [긴 막대기] a stick; a rod; a pole.

작도 **[जाक्तो]** **[作圖]** [지도,설계도 등을 그림] drawing figures. 작도하다 draw a figure [chart / diagram].

작동 **[जाक्तोंग]** **[作動]** 작동하다 run; work; operate.

작문 **[जांगमून]** **[作文]** [글을 지음] composition; [지은 글] a composition. 작문하다 make a composition; write <a theme> composition.

작물 **[जांगमूल]** **[作物]** ⇨ 농작물 e.g. 원예 작물 garden stuff. 특용 작물 industrial crops. 작물을 재배하다 raise [grow] crops.

작별 **[जाक प्यौल]** **[作別]** a farewell; a good-by(e); (a) parting; (a) separation. e.g. 작별을 고하다 take (one's) leave / say good-by(e) <to> / say [bid] farewell [good-by(e)] <to>. 작별하다 take osne's leave; bid farewell; part <from / with>; say good-by(e).

작사 **[जाक्सा]** **[作詞]** e.g. 김동진 작사 작곡 words and music by Kim Dong-chin. 작사하다 write words; write the lyrics <for a song>.

작성 **[जाक्सौंग]** **[作成]** 작성하다 make (out); prepare; frame; draw up; write out; execute.

작심 **[जाक्सीम]** **[作心]** a resolve; (a) resolution; (a) determination. 작심하다 resolve; determine; be determined; decide; make up one's mind.

작심 삼일 **[जाक्सीम सामील]** a short-lived resolution; a resolution good for only three days. .e.g. 그는 무슨 일에나 작심 삼일이다 He can't stick to anything. / He can't keep his resolutions longer than a day or two.

작업 **[जागौप]** **[作業]** work; operation. 작업하다 work; conduct operations.

작용 **[जाग्योंग]** **[作用]** (an) action; a working; (an) operation; (a) process; [영향] an effect; e.g. 화학 작용 (a) chemical action. 작용하다 act <on>; work <on>; operate <on>; affect; function. e.g. 계략은 멋지게 작용했다 The strategy worked excellently.

작은아버지 **[जागुनआबौजी]** an uncle (who is one's father's younger brother).

작은어머니 **[जागुनओमौनी]** an aunt (who is the wife of one's father's younger brother).

작은집 **[जागुनजीप]** [아들,동생의 집] one's son's [younger

brother's] house; a branch family.

작자 **[जाक्चा]** [**作者**] [저자] an author; (소설 등의) a writer; (시인) a poet; (그림, 조각 등의) an artist.

작전 **[जाक्चौन]** [**作戰**] [軍] (military) operations; [전략] strategy; [전술] tactics. 작전하다 launch (military) maneuvers; carry out military operations.

작정 **[जाक्चौग]** [**作定**] [결정] decision; determination; resolution. 작정하다 decide; determine; resolve; make up one's mind; fix upon [on].

작품 **[जाक्फूम]** [**作品**] a (piece of) work; a product; a production; an opus <*pl.* opera>.

잔 **[जान]** [**盞**] a cup; a glass; a teacup (찻잔); [술잔] a winecup; a wineglass.

잔고 **[जान्गो]** [**殘高**] = 잔액

잔꾀 **[जानक्वे]** (petty) tricks; shallow cunning; wiles; (an) artifice.

잔돈 **[जान्दोन]** [액수가 적은 돈] small coins [money]; (small) change.

잔디 **[जान्दी]** a lawn; turf; sod; (a patch of) grass.

잔뜩 **[जान्तुक]** **1** [꽉 차게] full; fully; to the full; to capacity; [많이] a lot; in plenty e.g. 맥주를 잔에 잔뜩 따르다 fill a glass with beer to the brim. **2** [몹시] intensely; heavily; extremely; exceedingly; hard. e.g. 잔뜩 찌푸린 날씨 dull [thick] weather / a heavily leaden [sullen / overcast] sky.

잔류 **[जाल्लयू]** [**殘留**] remaining; staying behind. 잔류하다 remain [stay] behind.

잔소리 **[जान्सोरी]** **1** [잔말] useless [small] talk. e.g. 그녀는 늘 남편의 귀가 시간이 늦다고 잔소리했다 She kept nagging her husband for coming home late.**2** [꾸중](a) scolding; a rebuke; a lecture e.g. 잔소리 그만해 Enough of your preaching!

잔손 **[जान्सोन]** minute attention [care / trouble]; elaborate [detailed] handwork. 잔손(이) 가다 take [require] <much> manual effort; take <a lot of> trouble. **잔손질** **[जान्सोन्जील]** working in detail [with much care]; [마무리 손질] <give> the finishing [final] touches.

잔액 **[जानैक]** [**殘額**] [남은 돈] money left over; [예금 등의 잔고] the balance; [미불금] the remainder.

잔업 **[जानौप]** [**殘業**] overtime work; extra work. 잔업하다 work overtime [extra hours]

잔여 **[जान्यो]** [**殘餘**] the rest; [화학 처리 등의 잔류물이나 유산의 나머지 부분] the residue.

잔여액 **[जान्योऐक]** the balance; the remainder.

ㅈ

잔인 [जानीन] [殘忍] (a) brutality; savageness; (an) atrocity 잔인하다 brutal; cruel; merciless; cold-blooded; ruthless. e.g. 잔인한 성격 [잔인성] a brutal [cruel] nature. 잔인한 사람 a brutal [savage] man / a brute.

잔일 [जान्नील] [자질구레한 일] a trifling [minor] matter; a matter of detail; [잔손 가는 일] troublesome wor; <household> chores.

잔잔하다 [जान्जान्हादा] still; quiet; calm; peaceful; serene; smooth.

잔치 [जान्छी] party; a feast; a banquet (공식적인).

잔해 [जान्हे] [殘骸] (배,건물 등의) a wreck; <집합적> wreckage; [잔류물] ruins

잔혹 [जान्होक] [殘酷] cruelty; brutality; heartlessness; atrocity. 잔혹하다 cruel; brutal; merciless; atrocious.

잘 [जाल] **1** [익숙하고 능란하게] well; skillfully; cleverly; expertly. e.g. 그녀는 피아노를 잘 친다 She plays the piano well. / She is a good piano player [pianist]. / She is good at playing the piano. **2** [주의해서] carefully; attentively; cautiously. e.g. 자동차를 잘 몰고 가라 Drive your car carefully.**3** [탈없이,무사히] safely; in safety; well; all right. e.g. 어떻게든 잘 왔다니 뜻밖이다 What a surprise that you managed to come.**4** [좋게] favorably; well; nice; [훌륭하게] finely; . e.g. 아이를 잘 키 우다 bring up one's child the way a child should be brought up.

잘다 [जाल्दा] **1** [작다] small; fine (가루 등이); [가늘다] slender. e.g. 잔뿌리 fine roots. 잔글씨 a small character [letter].**2** [생각, 성질이 좀스럽다] small; narrow-minded; mean. e.g. 잔 사람 a small-minded person / a mean fellow. 그런 말을 하다니 너도 사람이 잘구나 It is small of you to say so

잘되다 [जालद्वेदा] **1** [성공하다] get on in the world[in life]; rise [succeed] in the world; make a success in life[the world] e.g. 그의 부모님은 아들이 잘된 것을 보고 기뻐했다 His parents were glad of their son's success [glad that their son had succeeded] in life. **2** (일이) go well [right]; work well; work e.g. 늘 그렇게 잘되는 것은 아니다 Things do not always go well.

잘록하다 [जालोख्वादा] constricted [compressed] <in the middle>; narrow; slim; slender. e.g. 허리가 잘록한

아가씨 a slim–waisted girl.

잘리다 [जालीदा] [끊어지다] be cut (off); be chopped; be severed; be cut down. e.g. 목이 잘리다 be decapitated [beheaded] / [해고되다] be dismissed [discharged] / be fired / get the ax(e) / get the boot.

잘못 [जालमोत] **1** [과실] a fault; an error; a misstep; a slip; [오류] a mistake; [죄과] a blame. 잘못하다 make a mistake [an error]; err; do wrongly [improperly / amiss]; e.g. 잘못을 깨닫다 notice a mistake [an error]. 잘못을 저지르다 make a mistake / err. **2** [틀리게] by [through] mistake; in error; through one's fault; misguidedly; mistakenly; wrong (ly). e.g. 첫발을 잘못 디디다 make a wrong start / start off on the wrong foot. 정책을 잘못 세우다 adopt a misguided policy.

잘생기다 [जाल्सैंगीदा] good–[nice–] looking; beautiful; pretty; handsome; comely; fair.

잘잘못 [जालजालमोत] right and [or] wrong.

잘하다 [जाल्हादा] **1** [올바르게 하다] do a right thing; do right; [훌륭히 하다] do well; do <a thing> successfully. e.g. 길에서 주은 지갑을 파출소에 갖다 준 것은 아주 잘한 일이었다 **.2** [능란하게 하다] be skillful <in>; be good <at / in>; be expert <in / at> e.g. 노래를 잘하다 sing well. 요리를 잘하다 be good at cooking / be a good cook.

잠 [जाम] [수면](a) sleep;(a) slumber (숙면); [졸기] a nap; a doze.

잠결 [जामझ्यौल] e.g. 잠결에 while (one is) asleep / in one's sleep / while dozin

잠그다[1] [जाम्गुदा] **1** (문 등을) lock (up); fasten <with a lock [latch]>. e.g. 문을 잠그다 lock [fasten] a door.**2** (수도 등을) turn off. e.g. 수도를 잠그다 turn off the tap[water].

잠그다[1] [जाम्गुदा] (액체 속에) soak; immerse <in> (충분히); dip <in>(잠깐).

잠기다[2] [जाम्गीदा] **1** (문, 자물쇠 등이) be loc-ked; lock; be fastened. e.g. 자물쇠가 잠긴 문 a locked door.**2** [목이 쉬다] get [become / grow] ho-arse [husky / harsh]; hoarsen; have a frog in the throat. e.g. 너무 소리를 질러 목이 잠기다 shout [shriE] oneself hoarse.

잠기다[2] [जाम्गीदा] (물 속에) soak [be soaked] <in>; be immersed [steeped]

ㅈ

<in>; [수몰되다] be submerged <in>; beflooded <with water>; be under <water>. e.g. 물에 잠긴 배 a waterlogged boat. 온 마을이 물에 잠겼다 The whole village was submerged [flooded]. / The whole village was under water.

잠꼬대 [जाम्कोदै] [수면 중의 헛소리] talking in one's sleep; somniloquy (습관적인).

잠들다 [जाम्दुल्दा]**1** [잠을 자는 상태가 되다] fall asleep; go off to sleep; sink [fall] into a slumber [sleep]. e.g. 아기는 어머니 품안에서 잠들었다 The baby fell asleep in its mother's arms.**2** [죽다] die; pass away; go to one's rest. e.g. 영원히 잠들다 sleep the eternal [last] sleep / go to one's long sleep / take one's last sleep. 그의 영혼이여 고이 잠드소서 May his soul rest in peace!

잠복 [जाम्बोक] [潛伏] **1** [숨음] hiding; concealment; an ambush.**2** [병의 증상이 밖으로 나타나지 않음] latency. 잠복하다 lie latent [dormant]

잠수 [जाम्सू] [潛水] diving. 잠수하다 dive; go underwater; submerge.

잠수함 [जाम्सूहाम] [潛水艦] a submarine; a sub; an underwater boat.

잠시 [जाम्सी] [暫時] a little [short] while; a moment; <부사> for a (little[short]) while; for some time.

잠옷 [जाम ओत] night clothes; (헐렁한 여성,어린이용의) a nightgown; (남자용 셔츠형의) a nightshirt; [파자마] <a pair of> pajamas.

잠입 [जामीप] [潛入] infiltration. 잠입하다 infiltrate <the enemy country>.

잠자다 [जाम्जादा] **1** = 자다. e.g. 잠자는 사자 a sleeping lion. 잠자는 숲 속의 미녀(the) sleeping Beauty. e.g. 잠자는 사자 a sleeping lion **2** (자본 등이) lie idle; (상품이) remain unsold <on the shelf>. e.g. 잠자고 있는 자본 dead capital.

잠자리[1] [जाम्जारी] [자는 자리] a bed; a kip; a crib [cot] (유아용의); a berth (기차,기선 등의)

잠자리[2] [जाम्जारी] dragon-fly

잠자코 [जाम्जाखो] [아무 말 없이 가만히] dumbly; silently; without a word; without comment; obediently

잠잠하다 [जाम्जाम्हादा] [潛潛-] silent; (deathly) quiet; still; hushed.

잠재 [जाम्जे] [潛在] latency; potentiality; dormancy. 잠재하다 be latent [dormant]; lurk; lie hidden.

잠적 [जाम्जीक] [潛跡] 잠적하다 disappear; vanish;

abscond; conceal oneself

잡정 [**जाम्जौग**] [**暫定**] e.g. 잠정적인 temporary / provisional / tentative.

잡념 [**जाम्नयौम**] [**雜念**] idle [stray] thoughts; earthly [worldly] thoughts.

잡다 [**जाप्ता**] **1** [손으로 쥐다] grasp; clasp; grip e.g. 남의 손을 잡다 grasp a person's hand. **2** [체포하다] arrest; catch; nab. e.g. 범인을 잡다 catch [arrest] a criminal. **3** [포획하다] catch; seize.. e.g. 토끼를 덫으로 잡다 trap [snare] a rabbit.

잡담 [**जाप्ताम**] [**雜談**] a chat; idle [small] talk; a gossip; (a) light conversation. 잡담하다 chat; have a chat <with>; make small [idle] talk; gossip.

잡동사니 [**जाप्तोंग्सानी**] miscellaneous articles; sundries; odds and ends

잡비 [**जाप्पी**] [**雜費**] sundry [miscellaneous / petty] expenses; general expenses; sundries; [임시비] incidental expenses; incidentals; [용돈] petty cash.

잡아가다 [**जाबागादा**] take [walk] <a suspect to a police station>; haul [bring] <a person> before <a police authority>. e.g. 경관이 그를 잡아갔다 The policeman took him to the police station.

잡아내다 [**जाबानेदा**] **1** (밖으로) take <something> out; [골라내다] pick [single] out; sort out. e.g. 용의자 중에서 범인을 잡아내다 pick out a criminal in the suspects. **2** (잘못 등을) find out; discover; pick out. e.g. 남의 흠을 잡아내다 find fault with a person / pick [point] out another's defects.

잡아당기다 [**जाबादांगीदा**] [끌어당기다] pull; draw; tug (세게); jerk (갑자기). e.g. 남의 손[귀]을 잡아 당기다 pull a person's hand [ear].

잡아들이다 [**जाबादुरीदा**] take [walk / haul / bring] <a person> in. e.g. 범인을 잡아들이다 bring a criminal in.

잡아떼다 [**जाबातेदा**] **1** (붙어 있는 것을) tear off; peel. . e.g. 상자에 붙은 라벨을 잡아떼다 tear a label off a box. **2** [모르는 체하다] pretend not to know [to be ignorant]; feign [pretend] ignorant. e.g. 그는 그것은 모르는 일이라고 잡아뗐다 He pretended not to know it and would not admit that he knew it.

잡아매다 [**जाबामैदा**] **1** [한데 매다] bind [tie] up; lash together. e.g. 책을 한데 잡아매다 bundle up books. **2** [고정시키다] tie [fasten / leash] <to>. e.g. 나는 개를 기둥에 잡아맸다

I tied the dog to a pole.

잡아먹다 [जाबमोक्ता] **1** (사람이 동물을) butcher [slaughter] and eat; (동물이 동물을) devour. e.g. 물고기를 잡아먹다 catch and eat fish. **2** [요하다] take; need; occupy [차지하다]; [소비하다] consume; [낭비하다] spend. e.g. 이것은 꽤 많은 시간을 잡아먹는다 This takes so much time. **3** 못살게 굴다] be hard on; [학대하다] ill-treat; tor ment. e.g.그녀는 며느리를 잡아먹을 듯이 대한다 She is hard on her daughter-in-law.

잡음 [जाबुम] [雜音] **1** [소음] noise; [醫] (기관의) souffle; murmur. **2** (전신, 라디오 등의) noise;

잡일 [जाबील] [雜−] miscellaneous [various / assorted] affairs; < 美 >(routine household) chores (일상의).

잡종 [जाबचौग] [雜種] a cross (breed); a hybrid; half-breed; a mongrel (특히 개의); (접목에 의한) a grath hybrid.

잡지 [जाप्चो] [雜誌] a magazine; (학회 등의) a journal; [정기 간행물] a periodical.

잡초[जाब्छो] [雜草] weeds.

잡화[जाब्हवा] [雜貨] miscellaneous goods; general merchandise; sundries; notions; (식료품을 포함 하는) groceries.

잡히다 [जाफीदा]**1** [손에 쥐어지다] be taken(up); be held [seized / caught / grabbed]. e.g. 그는 손에 잡히는 대로 한껏 동전을 쥐었다 He seized all the coppers that his fist could hold. **2** [체포되다] be arrested; be caught [captured]. e.g. 그 강도는 마침내 잡히고 말았다 The rubber was arrested [captured] at last. **3** [포획되다] be caught [captured / seized]. e.g. 며칠 전에 이 근처에서 이상한 물고기가 잡혔다 The other day a strange fish was caught near here. [결정되다] be decided [fixed]; [차지하다] be occupied; [정착되다] be settled. e.g. 날짜가 잡히는 대로 알려 드리겠습니다 I'll tell you when [ather] the date is [has been] fixed.

−장 [जांग] [狀] a letter. e.g. 소개장 a letter of introduction.

장[1] [जांग] [場]**1** [시장] a market; <英> (축일 등의 정기적인) a fair. e.g. 5일장 a five day interval town market.**2** [장소] a place; a spot; a ground. e.g. 사격장 a rifle range.**3** a field. e.g. 중력의 장 a gravitational field.**4** [연극의 장면] a scene. e.g. 3막 7장의 연극 a play in three acts and seven scenes.

장[2] [जांग] [張] a leaf <of a book>; a sheet <of paper>; a piece <of paper>.

장[3] [जांग] [章] [문장의 단락] a chapter.

장[4] [जांग] [欌] a wardrobe; a chest of drawers; a cabinet; a closet; a cage. e.g. 새 장 a bird cage. 옷장 a wardrobe / a chest of drawers.

장가 [जांगा] a marriage; a wedding e.g. 장가들다[가다] marry [wed] a woman / take a woman in marriage / take a woman to wife.

장갑 [जांगाप] [掌匣] <a pair of> gloves; [벙어리 장갑] <a pair of> mittens; [긴 장갑] a gauntlet (glove).

장거리 [जांगौरी] [長距離] a long distance; (사정등의) a long range. a long-distance race.

장관[1] [जांग्वान] [壯觀] a grand [magnificent / splendid] sight; a great spectacle.

장관[2] [जांग्वान] [長官] a secretary; a minister; a cabinet member.

장교 [जांगग्यो] [將校] an officer; a commissioned officer.

장구 [जांगू] a *changgu*; an hourglass-shaped drum.

장군 [जांगून] [將軍] [대장] a general

장기 [जान्की] [長技] one's forte; one's speciality; one's strong point.

장기[1] [जांगी] [長期] [장기간] a long term; [장시일] a long (period of) time.

장기[2] [जांगी] [臟器] internal organs; viscera; the intestines.

장난 [जांग्नान] (약간 악의가 있는) mischief; (악의가 없는) a practical joke; a prank; [희롱] fun

장난감 [जांग्नानकाम] a toy; a plaything.

장난꾸러기 [जांग्नानकुरौगी] [장난이심한 어린이] a mischievous [naughty] boy; an urchin; an imp; a little demon of a child; [장난이 심한 사람] a mischief (-maker); a rogue; a frolicker; a prankster.

장남 [जांग्नाम] [長男] the [one's] eldest [oldest] son; the first (born) son.

장녀 [जांगन्यौन] [長女] the [one's] eldest [oldest] daughter.

장년 [जांगन्यौन] [壯年] (the prime of) manhood; the prime of life; [중년] middle age.

장님 [जांग्निम] a blind person; <집합적> the blind.

장단 [जांग्दान] [長短] **1**[길고 짧음] (relative) length. e.g. (2개의) 끈의 장단을 재다 measure the relative length of (two) strings. **2** [장점과 단점] merits and demerits; advantages and disadvantages. ⇨ 장단점.

장담 [जान्ग्दाम] [壯談] an [a positive] assertion; affirmation; a positive statement. 장담하다 assert; affirm; state positively.

장래 [जान्ग्रै] [將來] the future; [전망] the prospect.

장려 [जान्ग्यौ] [奬勵] encouragement; stimulation; [촉진] promote. 장려하다 encourage; stimulate; promote; [추천하다] recommend.

장례 [जान्ग्न्ये] [葬禮] a funeral.

장롱 [जान्गनोन्ग] [欌籠] a chest (of drawers) (서랍만 여러 개 겹친 것); a wardrobe (양복장); a bureau (거울이 달린 침실용).

장르 [जान्ग्नु] (문학 등의) a genre.

장마 [जान्ग्मा] the rainy spell in (early) summer; a long spell of rainy weather. e.g. 장마가 들었다[그쳤다] The rainy season has set in [is over].

장만 [जान्गम्यौन] [준비] preparation; [구입] purchase. 장만하다 prepare; purchase; buy.

장면 [जान्गम्यौन] [場面] [연극, 영화 등의 정경] a scene; a situation.

장모 [जान्ग्मो] [丈母] one's wife's mother; one's mother-in-law.

장벽 [जान्ग्ब्यौक] [障壁] [막은 벽] a fence; a wall; a barrier; [방해물] an obstacle. medicine> habitually; take <a medicine> for a long time.

장본인 [जान्गबोनीन] [張本人] the ringleader; the author <of a plot>; the prime mover; the originator.

장부 [जान्गबु] [帳簿] a book; an account book; (호적 등의) a register.

장사[1] [जान्गसा] [壯士] a man of great strength; a strong man

장사[2] [जान्गसा] business; commerce; trade; [거래] a transaction

장삿속 [जान्गसासोक] a comercial spirit;a profit-making motive.

장소 [जान्गसो] [場所] **1** [곳] a place; [특정한 곳] a spot; [정확한 지점] a point; [현장] a scene. e.g. 분쟁이 일어날 듯한 장소 a trouble spot. **2** [위치] a position; a situation; a location. e.g. 장소가 좋다 [나쁘다] be well [badly] situated.

장손 [जान्गसोन] [長孫]

장수 [जान्गसू] [長壽]a long life; longevity. 장수하다 live a long life.

장승 [जान्गसुंग] [長丞] [동리 어귀의 기둥] a totem pole (at the village entrance).

장시간 [जान्गशीगान] [長時間] many hours; long time.

장시일 [जान्गशीइल] [長時日] a long (period [space] of)

time; years.

장식 [जांगशिक] [裝飾] ornament; decoration; <집합적> ornamentation; adornment; (의복 등의) trimmings; dressing. 장식 하다 decorate; ornament; adorn.

장신 [जांगशीन] [長身] a tall figure [stature].

장신구 [जांगशीन्कू] [裝身具] accessories; personal ornaments.

장악 [जांगाक] [掌握] hold; grasp; command. 장악하다 hold; grasp; command; have control over.

장애 [जाऐ] [障碍] [방해] an obstruction; a hindrance; [방해물] an obstacle; [어려운 일] a difficulty.

장애물 [जाऐमूल] [障碍物] an obstacle; a hurdle.

장엄 [जांगौम] [莊嚴] solemnity; sublimity; magnificence; majesty; grandeur. 장엄하다 solemn; impressive; sublime; majestic.

장음 [जांगुम] [長音] [긴소리] a long [prolonged] sound; [장모음] a long vowel.

장의사[जांउइसा] [-社] a funeral home [parlor]; an undertaker's (shop).

장인[1] [जांगीन] [匠人] a handicrathsman; a crathsman; an artisan.

장인[2] [जांगीन] [丈人] one's wife's father; one's father-in-law <*pl.* fathers-in-law>.

장작 [जांग्जाक] [長斫] firewood. e.g. 장작을 패다 split wood.

장점 [जांग्जौम] [長點] a strong [good] point; a merit; [이점] an advantage.

장치 [जांग्छी] [裝置] equipment; a device; (an) apparatus. 장치하다 equip [fit / furnish] <with>; install. 장치하다 set a time bomb.

장터 [जांगथौ] [場-] a market place [site].

장편 [जांगफ्यौन] [長篇] a long piece [work].

장편 소설 [जांगफ्यौन सोसौंल] [영화] a long [full-length] novel [film].

장하다 [जांगहादा] [壯-] admirable; praiseworthy; creditable; laudable; splendid.

장학 [जांगहाक] [奬學] encouragement of learning. 장학하다 encourage learning.

장학생 [जांगहाकसैंग] a student on a scholarship; a scholarship student.

장해 [जांगहै] [障害] an obstacle; a hindrance. ⇨ 장애 (障碍)

장황 [जांहवांग] [張皇] 장황하다 lengthy; longwinded; [지겹다] long and boring; tedious; prolix.

잦다 [जात्ता] [빈번하다] frequent; incessant; [간격이 짧다] short.

잦아지다 [जाजाजीदा] [자주 있게 되다] occur frequently [at short intervals]; be

ㅈ

frequent. e.g. 요즘 이 도시에서 교통 사고가 잦아지고 있다 These days traffic accidents have occurred frequently in this town.

재[1] [जै] [타고 남은 것] ash (es).

재[2] [जै] [再] re–; again; once more.

재개 [जैगै] [再開] reopening; resumption. 재개하다 (일단 종료했던 것을) reopen; (일시적인 중단 후에) resume.

재건 [जैगौन] [再建] rebuilding; reconstruction. 재건하다 rebuild; reconstruct; reestablish; restore (복구).

재검토 [जैगौम्थो] [再檢討] [다시 한번 더 조사함](a) reexamination; [다시 한 번 생각함] a reconsideration; [재평가] (a) reappraisal; reevaluation. 재검토하다 reexamine; reconsider; review; restudy; reappraise; reevaluate.

재계 [जैगे] [財界] [금융계] the financial world; financial circles; [경제계] the economic world; economic circles; [실업계] the business world; business circles.

재계 [जैगे] [齊戒] purifycation. 재계하다 purify oneself; perform purification.

재고[1] [जैगो] [再考] reconsideration. 재고하다 reconsider; think over again.

재고[2] [जैगो] (품) [पूम] [在庫(品)] stock; goods in stock; stored goods.

재귀 대명사 [जैग्वी दैम्योंगसा] [동사] [문법] a reflexive pronoun [verb].

재기 [जैगी] [再起] **1** [복귀] a comeback. e.g. 그는 재기불능인 것 같다 He seems to be little chance of his comeback **2** [회복] recovery; restoration. 재기하다 recover; be restored.

재난 [जैनान] [災難] [재해] a disaster; a calamity; [불행] (a) misfortune; a mishap.

재능 [जैनुंग] [才能] [능력] ability; (타고난) talent; (천재적인) a gith; [천분] a genius; (선천적,후천적인) faculty.

재다 [जैदा] **1** [잘난 체하다] put on airs; give oneself airs; make a boast of; assume an air of importance; wear a high hat. e.g. 존은 1등상을 탔다고 재고 있었다 John boasted of having won the first prize.**2** (길이,크기,양을) measure; (무게를) weigh; (소요 시간을) time; (수심을) sound; [일반적으로 계측하다] gauge; gage; [측정하다] take. e.g. 키를 재다 measure one's height**3** [따져 보다] think over; consider carefully; ponder (up) on [over]; deliberate over. e.g. 이것 저것 재어 본 후에 ather a great deal of thinking / ather putting two and two together.

재단 [जैदान] [裁斷] = 마름질. e.g. 재단이 잘되어 있다 [신통찮다] be well [ill] tailored [cut]. 재단 하다 cut (out). e.g. 드레 스를 재단하다 cut out a dress. 옷감을 재단하다 cut (the) cloth / cut cloth for sewing / cut out a pattern. 우리는 치수에 맞추어 와이셔츠 감을 재단 했다 We cut (out) shirts to measure.

재떨이 [जैतोरी] an ashtray; (다리가 달린 것) a smoking stand.

재래 [जैरै] [在來] e.g. 재래의 [보통의] ordinary / common / usual / [옛날부터의] conventional custommary / [전통적인] traditionnnal; [그 고장 원산의] native.

재력 [जैर्योक] [財力] [금력] financial power[ability]; [재산] means; wealth.

재롱 [जैरोंग] [才弄] (baby's) cute movements.

재료 [जैर्यो] [材料] material (s); matter; stuff; [원료] raw material (s); (요리 등의) ingredients; [자료] data.

재무 [जैमु] [財務] financial affairs.

재무부 [जैमुबु] the Ministry of Finance; the Finance Ministry.

재물 [जैमुल] [財物] property; riches; means; effects; wealth; goods; one's valuables.

재발 [जैबाल] [再發] [다시 생김] a recurrence; (병의) a return; (먼저보다 더 나빠지는 재발) relapse. 재발하다 (병,문제가) recur; come back; flare up again; (사람이) have [suffer] a relapse; relapse <into>; have a second attack <of>.

재발급 [जैबाल्गुप] [再發給] (a) reissue. 재발급하다 reissue.

재발행 [जैबालहैंग] [再發行] reissue. 재발행하다 reissue.

재방송 [जैबांगसोंग] [再放送] rebroadcasting; a rebroadcast. 재방송하다 rebroadcast.

재배 [जैबै] [栽培] cultivation; culture; raising; growing. 재배하다 cultivate; grow; raise.

재배치 [जैबैची] [再配置] reassignment; relocation; realignment. 재배치하다 reassign; relocate; realign.

재벌 [जैबौल] [財閥] a financial combine[group / clique]; a zaibatsu (단수, 복수 동형); <집합적> the plutocracy.

재봉 [जैबोंग] [裁縫] [바느질] sewing; needlework; [옷을 짓기] tailoring 재봉하다 sew; do needlework; sit at needlework.

재분배 [जैबुन्बै] [再分配] redistribution; reallotment. 재분배하다 redistribute; reallot.

재산 [जैसान] [財產] property; (one's) possessions; a fortune; an estate

재생 [जैसैंग] [再生] **1** [되살아남] revival; resuscitation. ⇨ 소생 재생 하다 revive; resuscitate; come to life again; be restored to life. **2** [갱생] regeneration; reformation. 재생하다 regenerate. e.g. 그 소년은 완전히 재생하여 훌륭한 사회인이 되었다 The boy completely reformed himself [came back to normal] and became a respected citizen. **3** [폐품의 재생산] reclamation; rege-neration; reproduction. e.g. 생가능한 reclaimable / recyclable / reproducible. 재생하다 reclaim; regenerate; reproduce; recycle.

재수[1] [जैसू] [再修] 재수하다 prepare oneself for the college entrance exams for the next chance.

재수[2] [जैसू] [財數] luck; fortune. e.g. 재수 좋은 사람 a lucky [fortunate] person.

재앙 [जैआंग] [災殃] [재난] a disaster; a calamity; [불행] a misfortune.

재연 [जैयौन] [再演] [재상연] a repeat [second] performance. 재연하다 repeat <the same play>; stage [present / perform] <a play> again.

재우다 [जैउदा] **1** [자게 하다] end [put] <a child> to sleep [bed]. e.g. 책을 읽어 주며 재우다 read <a child> to sleep. **2** [묵게 하다] lodge <a person>; give <a person> shelter [a bed]; put <a person> up; accomodate <a person> (호텔 등에서). e.g. 남을 하룻밤 재우다 give a person a night's lodging / give a person a bed overnight / put a person up for the night.

재원 [जैवॉन] [才媛] a talented [an intelligent] girl [woman]; an accomplished young lady.

재작년 [जैजांगन्यौन] [再昨年] the year before last; two years ago.

재잘거리다 [जैजाल्कौरीदा] chatter; prattle; gab; gabble; rattle; wag one's tongue [jaws].

재적 [जैजौक] [在籍] enrollment. 재적하다 be on the register [roll]; be registered.

재정 [जैजौंग] [財政] finance (s); financial affairs <of a company>; <古> economy.

재주 [जैजू] [才-] **1** [재능] ability; talent; giths; genius; an aptitude. e.g. 어학에 재주가 있다 have a linguistic aptitude / have an aptitude [gith] for languages. 재주가 없다 lack ability / have no ability [talent]. **2** [기술, 손재간] skillfulness; dexterity. e.g. 재주 있는 skillful <in> / handy / dexterous <in

/ at> / be skilled <in the use of>. 손 재주가 있다 be smart [clever] with one's hand. **3** [곡예] a feat; a trick; a stunt (아슬아슬한). e.g. 돌고래에게는 여러 가지 재주를 가르칠 수 있다 Dolphins can be taught to do [perform] many tricks. 재주(를) 부리다 do [perform] acrobatic feats.

재직 [जैजीक] [在職] e.g. 재직 중인 검사 an incumbent public prosecutor / a public prosecutor in office. 재직 중에 during one's tenure[term] of office / while (one is) in office. 재직 중에 사망하다 die in office. 재직하다 hold office [a post]; be in office [service].

재차 [जैछा] [再次] [거듭하여] twice; again; [두 번째로] for the second time; [한번 더] once more; once again.

재채기 [जैछैगी] sneezing; a sneeze. 재채기하다 sneeze.

재촉 [जैछोक] pressing; urging. 재촉하다 press <a person for a thing>; urge <a person to do>; hurry (up); (빚을) dun.

재치 [जैछी] [才致] quick wit; tact; resources.

재판 [जैफान] [裁判] justice; [공판] a trial; a hearing; [판결] judgment; decision. 재판하다 judge [try] a person [a case].

재학 [जैहाक] [在學] e.g. 재학 중에 while one is a student. 현재 재학 중인 학생은 1 만명이다 Ten thousand students are currently enrolled.

재해 [जैहे] [災害] a disaster; a calamity (큰 재해); an accident (사고).

재현 [जैहयौन] [再現] [다시 나타남] reappearance; reemergence; [다시 나타냄] reenactment; (a) reproducetion. 재현하다 reappear; reemerge; appear again; reenact; reproduce.

재혼 [जैहोन] [再婚] a second marriage; remarriage. 재혼하다 marry again [second time]; remarry.

재회 [जैहवे] [再會] reunion.

잽싸다 [जैप्सादा] quick; agile; nimble.

쟁반 [जैगबान] [錚盤] a tray; a server; a salver (금속제의); a platter (대형의).

쟁쟁 [जैगजैग] [錚錚] 쟁쟁하다 [여럿 중에서 뛰어나다] prominent; eminent; outstanding.

쟁점 [जैग्चौम] [爭點] an issue; the point(at issue).

쟁탈 [जैगथाल] [爭奪] a scramble; a struggle; a contest; a competition. 쟁탈하다 scramble <for>; struggle <for>; compete <for>. e.g. 장관 자리를

ㅈ

쟁탈하다 fight [compete] for a Cabinet post. 선수들은 공을 쟁탈하기 위해 필사적이었다 The players scrambled for the ball. 양팀이 1위의 자리를 두고 쟁탈했다 The two teams contended against each other for the first place.

쟁탈전 [जैंगथाल्जौन] [争奪戰] a scramble <for>; a fight <for>.

저[1] [जौ] **1** [나] I. e.g. 저의 my. 저를 me. 저로서는 for my part / as for me. **2** [자기] oneself; self.

저[2] [जौ] [좀 떨어져 있는 것을 가리켜서] that <*pl.* those>. e.g. 저 남자 that man. 저 건물을 보아라 Look at the building over there.

저것 [जौगौत] that; that thing; that one; that person.

저고리 [जौगोरी] a Korean-style (short) coat (for women); a Korean-style jacket.

저금 [जौगुम] [貯金] [돈을 모음] saving; [절약하여 모은 돈] savings; [은행 예금] a deposit. 저금하다 save (money); deposit <money in a bank>.

저급 [जौगुप] [低級] low grade; low class; inferiority 저급하다 [정도가 낮다] low-grade; low-class; [값싸다] cheap.

저기 [जौगी] [저곳] that place; [저곳에] over there.

저기압 [जौगीआप] [低氣壓] **1** [낮은 기압] low (atmospheric) pressure; a [an atmospheric] depression. **2** [기분이 좋지 못함] a bad temper.

저녁 [जौन्यौक] **1** [해가 질 무렵부터 밤이 오기까지의 사이] evening. **2** [저녁밥] an evening meal;(a) supper; (a) dinner.

저능 [जौनुंग] [低能] weak-mindedness; feeblemindedness. 저능하다 feebleminded; weak-minded [-headed]; sothheaded; mentally deficient [weak / feeble]; daffy.

저런[1] [जौरौन] [저러한] such; that; that sort [kind] of; like that. e.g. 저런 남자 a man like that / such a man as that.

저런[2] [जौरौन] [가볍게 놀라는 모양] Dear me!; Oh, dear!; Great [Good] heavens!; My god! ! e.g. 저런, 야단났군 Mercy on me! / Good gracious!

저렇게 [जौरोख्रे] [저와 같이] like that. e.g. 저렇게 비쌀 줄은 몰랐다 I didn't think it would cost so [that] much.

저력 [जौरयौक] [底力] potential [latent] energy; underlying strength.

저렴 [जौरयौम] [低廉] 저렴하다 cheap; inexpe-nsive; low [moderate] in price.

저리 [जौरी] **1** [저렇게] so; like that; (in) that way; to

that extent [degree]. e.g. 그는 어째서 저리도 못 살까 Why is he so poor, I wonder? **2** [저곳으로] to that place; over there. [저쪽으로] that way; to that direction. . e.g. 이리 저리 둘러보다 look this way and that.

저리다 **[जौरीदा]** [감각이 무디어지다] become [go] numb; be numbed; (오래 앉아 있어서) go to sleep; be asleep. e.g. 추위로 손발이 저려 왔다 My hands and legs were numb with cold.

저마다 **[जौमादा]** each (one); every one; respectively.

저만큼 **[जौमानखुम]** [저만한 정도로] to that extent [degree]; that.

저맘때 **[जौमामते]** <at> that time of (the) day [month / year]; <at> that hour of the day [morning / evening / night.

저명 **[जौम्यौंग]** [**著名**] prominence; distinction; eminence; celebrity. ⇨ 유명 저명하다 famous; well-known; prominent;eminent; celebrated.

저물다 **[जौमुल्दा]** **1** [해가 져서 어두워지다] grow [get] dark.**2** [계절이나 한 해가 다 지나다] end; come to an end [a close]; close; run [be] out.

저버리다 **[जौबौरीदा]** (신의,기대 등을) go [act] against; go back on; run counter to.

저상 **[जौसांग]** [**沮喪**] dejection; depression; dispiritedness; demoralization. 저상하다 be dejected [depressed]; be discouraged; be disheartened; lose heart.

저수지 **[जौसूजी]** a reservoir.

저술 **[जौसूल]** [**著述**] [쓰기] writing; [책] a book; [작품] a work; [문학 작품] writings. 저술하다 write <a book

저승 **[जौसुंग]** the other world; the next world; the land of the dead; the netherworld.

저온 **[जौओन]** [**低溫**] a low temperature.

저울 **[जौउल]** a scale; [천칭] <a pair of> scales [balances]; [체중계] a (weighing) scale; (bathroom) scales.

저음 **[जौउम]** [**低音**] (음조의) a low tone; (피치의) a low-pitched sound; (목소리의) a low voice; [樂] bass.

저의 **[जौउइ]** [**底意**] one's original purpose; one's real intension; one's will [motive]; one's inmost thought; an ulterior motive. e.g. 그의 저의를 헤아릴 수 없었다 I could not make out his true [underlying] motives [intentions].

저임금 **[जौइम्गुम]** [**低賃金**] low wages; (급료) low pay.

저자 **[जौजा]** [**著者**] an author; a writer.

저작권 **[जौजाकवौंन]** [**著作權**] a copyright; literary property.

저장 [जौजांग] [**貯藏**] storage; [보존] preservation. 저장하다 store (up); lay by; preserve; conserve.

저절로 (जौजौल्लो) [by] itself; of its own accord; naturally; [자동적으로] automatically.

저조 (जौजो) [**低調**] 침체함] dullness; lowness; a slump (운동 선수의). 저조하다 inactive; inanimate; dull; slow; sluggish; slack.

저주 (जौजू) [**詛呪**] a curse; cursing; (an) imprecation; (a) malediction; (an) execration; damnation (신의).

저지 (जौजी) [**沮止**] revention; obstruction; hindrance. 저지하다 stop; prevent; obstruct; hinder; impede; check; hold [set] back.

저축 (जौछुक) [**貯蓄**] saving; [저금] savings. 저축하다 save(up); store up; put [set] by [aside].

저택 [जौथैक] [**邸宅**] residence; a mansion (대저택).

저학년 [जौहागन्यौन] [**低學年**] he lower grades.

저항 [जौहांग] [**抵抗**] 대항] resistance; opposition (반대). 저항하다 resist; offer [make] resistance [opposition] <to>; oppose; stand [struggle / fight] against.

저희 [जौहउई] [우리] we; [저 사람들] they.

-적 [जौके] [**的**] […의 방면에 서의]. e.g. 경제적 economical. 교육적 견지에서 from an educational point of view. 금전적으로는 monetarily / financially / as far as money goes[is concerned]. **2** […같은]. e.g. 그 모임은 가정적인 분위기 였다 The party was held in [had] a homey atmosphere. 이 지방은 대륙적인 기후이다 The climate of this area is like that of the continent. **3** [… 다 운]. e.g.귀족적인 태도 an aristocratic manner.**4** [에 들어 맞는]. e.g.그는 논리적으로 생각하는 기질 이다 He is the sort of man who thinks logically.

적[1] [जौके] [때] the time (when); <on> the occasion. e.g. 어릴 적에 in one's childhood [early days]. **2** [경험] an experience. e.g. 서울에 가 본 적이 있습니까 Have you ever been to Seoul?

적[2] [जौके] [**敵**] **1** [원수] an enemy; a foe **2** [경기 등의 상대방] an opponent; an adversary.

적개심 [जौकैसीम] [**敵愾心**] hostile feeling; hostility; enmity.

적격 [जौकयौक] [**適格**] (a) proper qualification; eligibility; competence. **적격자** a qualified person; the right [very] person <for>.

적극 [जौकुक] [**積極**] the

positive. **2** <부사> positively; actively; constructively; progressively.

적극적 [जौकुकजौक] [**積極的**] ositive; active; constructive; progressive. e.g. 적극적인 사람 a man of [with] enterprising spirit / an active [a positive] person. 적극적인 인생관[자세] a positive view of life [attitude toward life]. Installment savings; an installment deposit.

적나라 [जौक्नारा] [**赤裸裸**] [발가벗음] nakedness; nudity. 적나라하다 naked; nude; bare. [있는 그대 로임] frankness; plainness. 적나라하다 frank; plain; outspoken. e.g. 적나라하게 frankly / plainly / candidly. 적나라한 진실 the naked truth. 적나라한 사실 a plain [bald / bare] fact.

적다[1] [जौकता] [글로 쓰다] write [note / put / jot] down; make [take] notes <of / on>.

적다[2] [जौकता] (수가) few; (양이) little; (수,양이) small; [빈약하다] scarce; [불충분하다] scanty; [부족하다] short; [드물다] rare.

적당 [जौकतांग] [**適當**] [알맞음] suitableness; suita bility; propriety; appropriateness. 적당하다 suitable; proper; suited; adequate; fit; appropriate; [지나치지 않다] moderate. (쓰임).

적대 [जौकतै] [**敵對**] hostility; antagonism; contention. 적대하다 [맞서다] turn <against>; fight <against>; [반대하다] oppose; be hostile to; confront; be antagonistic to.

적도 [जौकतो] [**赤道**] the equator; the line.

적립 [जागनीप] [**積立**] ccumulation; reserving; laying [putting] by. 적립하다 save up <money>; lay [put] by [aside]; accumulate; amass; reserve.

적막 [जौगमाक] [**寂寞**] oneliness; desolation. 적막 하다 lonely; lonesome; dreary; desolate; deserted.

적반하장 [जौकपानहाजांग] [**賊反荷杖**] e.g. 그는 적반하장으로 내게 대들었다 He got at me just like he was trying to carry the war into the enemy's camp.

적발 [जौकबाल] [**摘發**] xposure; disclosure. 적발 하다 expose; disclose; lay bare [open]; uncover.

적색 [जौकसैक] [**赤色**] 붉은 색] red (color).

적선 [जौकसौन] [**積善**] [착한 일을 많이 함] accumu lation of virtuous [good] deeds. 적선하다 accumulate virtuous [good] deeds.

적성 [जौकसौंग] [**適性**] fitness; aptitude .

적수 [जौकसू] [**敵手**] [경쟁자] a rival; a competitor; [필적

하는 사람] a match [적대자] an opponent.

적시다 [जौक्शिदा] et; [축이다] moisten; drench; dampen.

적신호 [जौक्शिन्हो] [赤信號]1 [교통 신호] a red(traffic) light; a stoplight.2 [위험 신호] a danger signal.

적어도 [जौगौदो] at least; in the least; not less than; to say the least.

적용 [जौकयोंग] [適用] an) application. 적용하다 apply <a rule> to <a case>.

적응 [जौकुंग] [適應] 잘 어울림] adaptation 적응하다 adapt [accomodate / adjust / acclimate] oneself; confirm (일치하다).

적의 [जौकउइ] [敵意] hostile feeling; hostility; enmity.

적자 [जौकचा] [赤字] 공식 회계의 부족액] a deficit; [손실] the red; a loss; [빨간 숫자] red figure.

적적하다 [जौकचौख्वादा] [寂寂-] lonely; lonesome; forlorn; deserted.

적절 [जौकचौल] [適切] 절하다 suitable; good; appropriate; [당면 문제에 꼭 맞다] relevant; pertinent; adequate; (시기가) well-timed; timely.

적중 [जौकचुंग] [的中] (good) hit. 적중하다 [과녁에 맞다] hit the mark[target]; (예언 등이) come true; (추측 등이) guess right.

적출 [जौकछुल] [摘出] 끄집어 냄] extraction; removal. 적출하다 extract; remove

적합 [जौख्वाप] [適合] 알맞게 들어맞음] fitness; suitableness; suitability; appropriateness. 적합하다 fit; suitable; proper; befitting; adequate; appropriate; compatible.

적히다 [जौख्वीदा] e written [put] down; be recorded; [기술되다] be described.

-전 [जौन] [展] n exhibition; an exhibit. e.g. 개인전 a private [one-man] exhibition.

-전 [जौन] [傳] [전기] a biography; a life. e.g. 위인전 the lives of great men.

-전 [जौन] [戰]1 [전쟁] a war; warfare; [전투] a battle; a fight. e.g. 공중전 an air battle [war].2 (경기의) a game; a match. e.g. 1회전 the first game / (토너먼트의) the first round.

전[1] [जौन] [全] ll; whole; entire; total; complete; full; pan e.g. 전 세계 the whole world.

전[2] [जौन] [前] <부사적> [막연한 과거] before; once; formerly; previously. e.g. 전처럼 as before. 전부터 for some time (past).2 <부사적> [일정한 때보다 앞] ago; before; prior to. e.g. 이틀 전의 신문 a newspaper of two days ago.

전가 [**जौनगा**] [**轉嫁**] 죄,책임 등을 넘기어 맡김] imputation. 전가하다 impute; blame; lay [put] the blame on <a person>; shith; transfer. e.g. 그는 내게 죄를 전가했다 He put the crime on me.

전개 [**जौनगै**] [**展開**] **1** [열려서 펼쳐짐] spread; expand; unfolding. 전개하다 spread [open / roll] out; unfold. e.g. 끝없이 전개되는 태평양 the boundless expanse of the Pacific. **2** [진전시켜 펼침] unfolding; development; [劇] discovery. e.g. 국면의 전개 the development of the situation. 전개하다 unfold; develop.

전공 [**जौनगोंग**] [**專攻**] ne's specialty [speciality]; one's special study; one's major. 전공하다 specialize <in history>; make a special study <of>; major <in>. **전공과목** one's special subject; one's major.

전과 [**जौनक्वा**] [**前科**] previous conviction [offense / crime]; a criminal record. **전과자** [범] an exconvict; a man with a criminal record.

전교 [**जौनग्यो**] [**全校**] 학교 전체] the whole school. **전교생** the whole student body; all the students of the school.

전구 [**जौनगू**] [**電球**] an electric [a light] bulb; an electric-light bulb; a bulb.

전국 [**जौनकूक**] [**全國**] the whole country [land]; [전국 각지] all parts of the country.

전근 [**जौनगुन**] [**轉勤**] transfer <to another's office>; transference <to another's office>. 전근하다 be transferred to

전근대적 [**जौनगुनदैजौक**] [**前近代的**] [근대 이전의] pre-modern; [시대에 뒤진] old-fashioned; outdated.

전기[1] [**जौनगी**] [**電氣**] lectricity; an electric current (전류).

전기[2] [**जौनगी**] [**傳記**] life (story); a biography.

전날 [**जौननाल**] [**前-**] **1** [바로 앞날] the previous [preceding] day; the day before. **2** [이전의 시기] the other day; some days [time] ago.

전년 [**जौन्नयौन**] [**前年**] 지난해.

전념 [**जौन्नयौम**] [**專念**] concentration of mind; undivided attention.

전능 [**जौन्नंग**] [**全能**] 능하다 almighty; omnipotent.

전달 [**जौनदाल**] [**傳達**] 메시지, 생각,전기 등 일반적인) transmission; (정보 등의) communication; (생각등의) conveyance. 전달하다 transmit; communicate; convey.

전담 [**जौनदाम**] [**全擔**] full [entire / whole] charge. 전담하다 assume [take]

full charge; be wholly charged <for>.

전락 [जौललाक] [**轉落**] [타락] degradation; [영락] ruin; downfall. 전락하다 degrade; be ruined; go to ruin. e.g. 우리 팀은 최하위로 전락했다 Our team fell into last place [the cellar].

전란 [जौललान] [**戰亂**] 전쟁] war; [전투] battle; [동란] disturbances.

전람회 [जौलामह्वे] [**展覽會**] an exhibition; an exhibit; a show.

전략 [जौलयाक] [**戰略**] (a) strategy; a stratagem.

전력 [जौलयौक] [**電力**] ⇨ 전기력 e.g. 공업용 전력 industrial electric power.

전례 [जौलये] [**典禮**] a ceremony; ritual.

전류 [जौल्यू] [**電流**] an electric (al) current; a flow of electricity.

전말 [जौनमाल] [**顚末**] [자초지종] everything <about; [자세한 설명] the full account; [사정] the whole circumstance; [경위] the course of events. e.g. 그가 사과하게 된 전말은 이렇다 This is how he came to apologize.

전망 [जौनमांग] [**展望**]**1** [조망] a view; a prospect; an lookout. 전망하다 look out <over>; take an extensive view <of>; [둘러보다] survey; look around. e.g.이 언덕에서는 김제 평야의 전망이 좋다 This hill commands a fine view of the Kimje plains. / We can get a fine view of the Kimje plains from this hill. **2** [장래를 내다봄] a prospect; an outlook <for>; [예측] a forecast <for>. e.g. 내년도의 경제 전망 the pros pects for the economy next year. 전망하다 survey; make a survey of; forecast <the future>.

전매 [जौनमै] [**專賣**] [독점판매] a monopoly; monopolization. 전매하다 have [maintain] a monopoly <on tobacco>; monopolize

전면 [जौनमयौन] [**全面**] [표면전부] the whole [entire] surface.

전멸 [जौनमयौल] [**全滅**] complete [total] destruction; annihilation; extermination. 전멸하다 be wiped out; be completely destroyed; be annihilated; be exterminated; be crushed.

전문 [जौनमून] [**專門**] a specialty; a speciality; line; [연구 과제[분야]] subject [field] of study.

전문가 [जौनमूनगा] [**專門家**] a specialist; a professional; (특히 숙련된) an expert <in>.

전반 [जौनबान] [**全般**] the whole. e.g. 사회 전반 the world at large.

전반적 [जौनबानजौक] [**全般的**]

whole; general; overall. e.g. 전반적으로 [일반적으로] generally / [전체적으로] on the whole / overall.

전보 [जौन्बो] [轉補] transference; shuffling. 전보하다 transfer.

전복 [जौन्बोक] [顚覆] an over-throw; an overturn; an upset; subversion; capsizal. e.g. 그들은 정부의 전복을 기도했다 They plotted to overthrow the government. 전복하다 be overthrown [overturned]; (배가) be capsized. e.g. 전복시키다 overthrow / overturn / subvert / capsize. 열차는 탈선으로 전복했다 The train (was) overturned when it derailed. / The train jumped the tracks and overturned.

전봇대 [जौन्बोत्तै] [電報 –] 전선용) an electric(light) pole; (전신용) a telephone pole.

전부 [जौन्बू] [全部] [전체] the whole; [합계] the total; <부사> all; entirely; in all; altogether; all told.

전사[1] [जौन्सा] [轉寫] 옮기어 베낌] transcription; copying. 전사하다 copy; transcribe e.g. 신문에서 이 한 구절을 전사했습니다 I copied this paragraph from a newspaper.

전사[2] [जौन्सा] [戰死] eath in battle [action]. 전사하다 die in a war; be killed in action [battle]; die [fall] in battle. e.g. 명예롭게 전사하다 die a glorious [heroic] death on the field of battle / meet glorious death in action.

전선 [जौन्सौन] [電線] an electric wire; (전등의) a electric light wire; (전신용의) telegraph wire [line]. e.g. 고압 전선 a high-tension wire [line] / a high-voltage cable.

전설 [जौन्सौल] [傳說] a legend; a tradition; [민화] a folktale.

전성 [जौन्सौंग] [全盛] he height [zenith] of prosperity [power]. e.g. 당시 그 일족이 전성을 이루고 있었다 At that time the family was at the height of its prosperity. 전성하다 flourish. e.g. 사실주의가 전성하고 있었다 Realism was in all its glory. **전성기[시대]** the period [age] of prosperity; the golden age; the heyday; (사람의) one's best days.

전세 [जौन्से] [傳貰] he lease of a house [room] on a deposit basis.

전속 [जौन्सोक] [專屬] [오로지 한 곳에만 속함] exclusive belongingness. 전속하다 belong exclusively <to>; be under the exclusive contract <of>.

전속력 [जौन्सोकनयौक] [**全速力**] [최고 속도] full speed; top speed.

전송 [जौन्सोंग] [**轉送**] transmission; (우편물 등의) forwardding; (전신의) translation. 전송하다 transmit; (우편물 등을) forward; send on [forward]; (전신을) translate.

전수 [जौन्सु] [**傳授**] 기술 등의) instruction; initiation. 전수하다 instruct; give instruction <in>; initiate e.g. 남에게 골동품 수집의 비결을 전수하다 initiate a person in (to) the mysteries of antique-collecting.

전술 [जौन्सुल] [**戰術**] actics; strategy.

전승[1] [जौन्सुंग] [**戰勝**] a victory. e.g. 전승을 축하하다 celebrate(a) victory. 전승하다 win [gain] a victory <over>; come out victorious; carry [win] the day; bring a war to a victorious conclusion [issue].

전승[2] [जौन्सुंग] [**傳承**] ransmission; [구전] (an) oral tradition; a tradition. 전승하다 hand down; transmit. e.g. 그 고장 사람들이 전승한 설화 folktales handed down from generation to generation among the natives.

전승[3] [जौन्सुंग] [**全勝**] complete victory; a clean score [record]. 전승하다 win a complete victory; make a clean score; leave [make] a clean record; make straight wins.

전시 [जौन्शी] [**展示**] isplay; exhibition 전시하다 put <a sculpture> on show [display]; exhibit; display.

전신 [जौन्शीन] [**全身**] he whole body; (그림, 사진 등에서) the full length

전압 [जौन्आप] [**電壓**] voltage.

전액 [जौनैक] [**全額**] the total [full] amount; the sum) total. e.g. 신청금 전액을 환불하다 refund the entire [the whole of the] application fee.

전야 [जौन्या] [**前夜**] 그 전날 밤] the previous night; the night before; the eve <of>.

전역 [जौनयौक] [**轉役**] transfer <from active service to the first reserve>; [제대] discharge from military service. 전역하다 be transferred <from the active list to the reserve list>; [제대하다] be discharged [dismissed] from military service.

전열 [जौनयौल] [**電熱**] lectric heat. **전열기** an electric heater [fire]; (취사용) an electric range [stove / cooker].

전염 [जौनयौम] [**傳染**] 접촉에 의한 질병의) contagion; (간접적인) infection. 전염하다 (병이) be contagious [infectious / catching]; (사람이) be infected <with>; catch.

전용 [**जौनयोंग**] [**專用**] exclusive [private / personal] use.. e.g. 전용의 exclusive / private / for one's private use. 한글 전용 the exclusive use of Hangul. 전용하다 have a thing for one's exclusive use; use exclusively.

전원 [**जौनवॉन**] [**田園**] [논밭] fields; [시골] rural districts; the country. e.g. 전원의 rural / pastoral. 여기는 한 때 조용한 전원이었으나 지금은 공업 도시가 되었다 This once quiet rural district has turned into an industrial city.

전원[1] [**जौनवॉन**] [**全員**] all the members; the entire staff. e.g. 교직원 전원이 토의에 참가했다 The whole faculty [All the members of the faculty] participated in the discussion.

전원[2] [**जौनवॉन**] [**電源**] **1** [전력 공급의 원천] a power source; a power supply. e.g. 전원을 끊다 shut [cut] off the power supply. **2** [콘센트] an (electric) outlet. e.g. 코드를 전원에 꽂다 put a plug in a socket [an outlet].

전유 [**जौनयू**] [**專有**] xclusive [sole] possession <of>. 전유하다 [독점권을 갖다] monopolize; [자기만의 것으로 하다] take sole possession <of>.

전율 [**जौनयुल**] [**戰慄**] a shudder; a shiver. 전율하다 shudder; shiver; tremble with fear.

전이 [**जौनी**] [**轉移**] (a) change; transition; metastasis; transference; transformation. 전이하다 change; spread (by metastasis); transfer.

전임 [**जौनीम**] [**專任**] exclusive duty; full service; sole charge. e.g. 전임의 full-time. 회사의 전임 상담역 a full-time adviser to a company.

전입 [**जौनीब**] [**轉入**] ransference; moving in(to). 전입하다 be[get] transferred; move in.

전입생 [**जौनीपसैंग**] a student transferred from another school.

전자[1] [**जौनजा**] [**前者**] [후자에 대하여 앞의 것] the former e.g. 전자의 예는 후자의 예보다 낫다 The former example is better than the latter.

전자[2] [**जौनजा**] [**電子**] 理] an electron. e.g. 전자의 electronic.

전쟁 [**जौनजैंग**] [**戰爭**] ar; warfare; (개개의 싸움)

battle. 전쟁하다 make war <with>; go to war <with>; wage(a) war <against>; war <with>; [전투하다] fight <a battle>.

전적 [जौन्चौक] [**全的**] verall; complete; whole; the full.

전전긍긍 [जौनजौन गुंगगुंग] [**戰戰兢兢**] 전긍긍하다 be terribly [awfully / dreadfully] afraid; be trembling with fear. e.g. 그는 전전긍긍하면서 그 곳에 서 있었다 He stood there in fear and trembling.

전제 [जौनजे] [**前提**] a premise. e.g.. 그는 잘못된 전제로 논의를 하고 있다 He is arguing from false premises. 전제하다 set <something> forth as a premise; pre-mise. **전제조건** a precon-dition <for / of>; a pre-requisite <to / for>.

전조 [जौनजो] [**前兆**] 징조.

전지 [जौनजी] [**電池**] 전류를 일으키는 장치] a battery; a [an electric] cell.

전진 [जौन्जीन] [**前進**] [앞으로 나아감] an advance; a forward movement. 전진하다 ad-vance; step [march / move] forward; go ahead; proceed; (배 등이) make headway.

전집 [जौन्जीप] [**全集**] one's complete [collected] works.

전철 [जौन्छौल] [**電鐵**] an electric railroad [railway].

전체 [जौन्छे] [**全體**] the whole; the entirety.

전체주의 [जौन्छेउइ] totalitari-annism.

전축 [जौन्छुक] [**電蓄**] an electric phonograph [gramophone]; a record player.

전출 [जौन्छूल] [**轉出**] **1** [다른 근무지로 옮겨 감] transfer; transference. e.g. 그는 지방으로 전출되었다 He was transferred to a local office. 전출하다 be [get] transferred <to a new post>. **2** [다른 곳으로 이주함] a move; a removal. 전출하다 move <to>; change one's place. e.g. 아파트에서 전출하다 leave [move out of] an apartment [flat].

전치사 [जौन्छीसा] [**前置詞**] a preposition.

전통 [जौन्थोंग] [**傳統**] (a) tradition; [인습] (a) convention; [유산] a heritage.

전투 [जौन्थु] [**戰鬪**] a battle 전투하다 fight (a battle); engage in battle.

전파 [जौन्फा] [**傳播**] [널리 전하여 퍼뜨림] spread; propagation; transmission. 전파하다 spread; propagate; (음 등이) transmit; travel.

전편 [जौन्फयौन] [**前篇**] he first part [volume]; (후편에 대하여) the first half.

전하다 [जौन्हादा] [**傳**-] (소식이나 물건 등을) tell; communicate; deliver; hand (over). e.g. 전갈을 전하다 deliver a message.**2** [물려 주다] hand down; trans-mit; leave; bequeath. e.g. 자손[후세]에 전하다 hand down to posterity.**3** [전수하다] teach; [전하여 보내다] pass <know-ledge> on to; impart; initiate. e.g. 지식을 전하다 impart knowledge to <the young>.

전학 [जौन्हाक] [**轉學**] change [transfer] of schools. 전학하다 change [transfer] to another school; change one's school.

전향 [जौन्हयांग] [**轉 向**] a conversion; an about-face. 전향하다 turn [swing / switch (over)] <to>; be converted <to>; abandon one's idea <in favor of>; do an about-face.

전혀 [जौन्हयौ] [**全**-] entirely; utterly; completely; wholly; totally; altogether. e.g. 전혀 말도 안 되는 소리다 It is too absurd for words. / It is entirely [utterly] out of the question.

전화 [जौन्हवा] [**電話**] a telephone; a phone; a phone call; a ring. 전화하다 telephone; phone; call (up); ring(up); make a phone call <to>; dial (다이얼을 돌려서).

전화위복 [जौन्हवीबोक] [**轉禍爲福**] e.g. 전화위복의 본보기 an instance[a case] of good out of evil.

전환 [जौन्हवान] [**轉 換**] **1** [바뀜] conversion; switch; [변환] turnover; switch-over. e.g. 성전환 a change of sex / a sex change. 전환하다 convert; switch <from ... to ...>; turn; change (over). **2** (마음의) diversion. e.g. 기분의 전환 diversion. 전환하다 divert; turn.

전후 [जौन्हू] [**前 後**] **1** = 앞뒤.**2** [순서,질서] order; sequence. e.g. 전후가 뒤바뀌다 be inverted / be reversed.**3** [가량] about; around; or so; or thereabout. e.g. 그녀는 20세전후다 She is around twenty.

-절 [जौल] [**節**] [명절] a (national) holiday; a red-letter day; a festival (day); [철] a season. e.g. 개천절 the National Foundation Day.

절 [जौल] [**節**] **1** (글의) a paragraph; a passage; (시의) a stanza; (성경의) a verse. e.g. 제1장 제2 절 Chapter I, Paragraph II.**2** [문법] a clause.

절[1] [जौल] [사찰] a (Bu-ddhist) temple.

절[2] [जौल] [인사] a bow; an obeisance; a curtsy (여성의). e.g. 그들은 서로 공손

히 절을 했다 They bowed deeply at each other 절하다 bow <to>; bow down <to>; make a bow [an obeisance] <to>.

절감 [जौलगाम] [**節減**] reducetion; curtailment; retrenchment. 절감하다 cut (down); cut down on; trim; reduce; curtail; retrench. e.g. 외국어의 필요성을 절감하다 feel keenly the necessity of knowing some foreign language.

절개 [जौलगै] [**切開**] (an) incision; an operation (수술) 절개하다 cut open [out]; incise; make an incision <in>; operate.

절개 [जौलगै] [**節槪**] fidelity; [신조] a principle; [정조] chastity.

절경 [जौलग्यौंग] [**絶景**] a wonderful sight; a superb view; beautiful [picturesque] scenery.

절교 [जौलग्यो] [**絶交**] 절교하다 break off [sever] relations <with>; cut [drop] one's acquaintance <with>; break with <a person>.

절규 [जौलग्यू] [**絶叫**] a scream; a shriek; an exclamation. 절규하다 cry out; shout; scream; shriE; exclaim(at the top of one's voice).

절기 [जौलगी] [**節氣**] the subdivisions of the seasons.

절다[1] [जौलदा] (소금에) be [get] salted; be seasoned with salt. e.g.이 배추는 알맞게 절었다 This cabbage is moderately salted.

절다[2] [जौलदा] (다리를) limp; hobble; walk lame[with a limp]. e.g. 심하게[약간] 절다 limp heavily [slightly] / have a bad [slight] limp.

절단 [जौलदान] [**切斷**] cutting; severance; disconnection (전선 등의); amputation (손발의). 절단하다 cut; cut off; sever; disconnect; amputate

절대 [जौल्दै] [**絶對**] absoluteness.

절대로 [जौल्तैरो] [**絶對–**] absolutely; positively; unconditionally. e.g. 절대로 그에게 말하지 마라 No matter what[Whatever you do], don't mention it to him. / Don't mention it to him under any circumstances.

절도 [जौल्तो] [**竊盜, 竊盜**] theth; stealing; pilferage (좀도둑질); larceny; [범인] a thief <*pl.* thieves>. **절도죄** theth; [法] larceny.

절레절레 [जौल्लेजौल्ले] shaking one's head.

절름발이 [जौल्लुमबारी] a lame person; a cripple.

절망 [जौल्लुमबारी] [**絶望**] despair; hopelessness. 절망하다 despair of <one's future>; be driven to despair; give up (all) hope.

절묘 [जौल्मयौ] [絶妙] 절묘하다 superb; exquisite; miraculous.

절박 [जौल्पाक] [切迫] [가까이 닥침]. 절박하다 urgent; pressing; impending; imminent. e.g. 절박한 문제 a pressing question

절반 [जौल्पान] [折半] a half.

절벽 [जौल्पयौक] [絶壁] a cliff; a precipice.

절실 [जौल्सील] [切實] 절실하다 [중대하고 심각하다] serious; severe; [정세가 긴박하다] acute; [진정이다] earnest; [절박하다] pressing; urgent. e.g. 절실한 소원 an earnest desire. 절실히 acutely; keenly; fully; urgently.

절약 [जौरयाक] [節約] economy; saving; frugality; thrith. 절약하다 eco-nomize; spare; save; be frugal [economical / thrithy]; [절감하다] cur-tail; cut (down).

절이다 [जौरीदा] salt <vegetables>; preserve <fish> in [with] salt.

절전 [जौल्जौन] [節電] economy in power consumption; power saving. 전하다 economize (in) power; save electricity.

절정 [जौल्जौग] [絶頂] **1** [산꼭대기] a mountaintop; the summit [top] of a mountain.**2** [정점] the peak; the zenith; the height; the acme; the climax. e.g. 그 여배우는 지금 인기가 절정에 있다 The actress is at the top [peak] of her popularity.

절제 [जौल्जे] [節制] moderation; temperance; abstinence; self-restraint; continence (성욕의). 절제하다 be moderate [temperate] <in>; abstain <from>; restrain; be continent.

절차 [जौल्छा] [節次] [순서] a procedure; a process.

절차법 [जौल्छाबौप] the law of procedure; procedural law; an adjective law.

절충 [जौल्छूंग] [折衷] a compromise; a cross; blending. 절충하다 arrange [make] compromise <between>; blend; compromise.

절판 [जौल्फान] [絶版] e.g. 그 책은 절판입니다 The book is out of print. 절판하다 print no more copies of <the book>.

절호 [जौरहो] [絶好] e.g. 절호의 best / ideal / perfect / capital / splendid / grand / excellent / golden.

젊다 [जौमता] young; youthful. e.g. 젊은 사람들 young people. 젊었을 때에 when (one is) young / in one's youth. 젊었을 때부터 from one's youth [early years].

점[1] **[जौम]** [**店**] [가게] a store; a shop. e.g. 양복점 a tailor's (shop).

점[2] **[जौम]** [**占**] fortune-telling; divination. e.g. 관상 점 divination by the features. 카드로 점을 치다 tell fortunes with cards.

점[3] **[जौम]** [**點**] **1** [반점] a dot; a spot; a speck; a speckle. e.g. 갈색 점이 박인 흰 개 a white dog with brown spots **2** (기호로서의) a point. e.g. 온점 a full stop[point] / a period.**3** [논점] a point; [견지] a standpoint; a point of view; a viewpoint; [사항] res-pect. . e.g. 어떤 점에서는 in some respects [points]. **4** (피부의) a mole; a tache; [모반] a birthmark; a nevus. e.g. 점을 빼다 re-move a mole.**5** a point; a dot; [소수점] a decimal point. e.g. 3.14퍼센트 three point one four per-cent.**6** [성적의 평가] marks; grades. e.g. 60점으로 시험에 합격하다 pass an examination with a score [<美>grade / <英>mark] of 60.**7** [경기의 득점] a point; [총득점] a score; (야구,크리켓의) a run. e.g. 2회에 2점을 따다 score two runs in the second inning.

점거 **[जौमकौ]** [**占據**] occu-pation. 점거하다 occupy.

점검 **[जौमकौम]** [**點檢**] **1** (물건의) (an) inspection; (an) examination; (a) check. e.g. 불시 점검 a spot check [test]. 점검하다 inspect; examine; check. **2** (인원의) a roll call. e.g. 그는 작업 인원을 점검했다 He took a [the] roll call of the workers. 점검하다 call the roll.

점괘 **[जौमगवै]** [**占卦**] a divinatory sign. e.g. 점괘가 좋다[나쁘다] have a good [an ill] divination sign. 나쁜 점괘가 나왔다 A bad sign appeared.

점등 **[點燈]** [등에 불을켬] lighting. 점등하다 turn [switch] on a light; light a lamp.

점령 **[जौम्नयौंग]** [**占領**] [점거] occupation; [공략] capture.; [점유] possession. 점령하다 occupy; capture; take; take possession of.

점선 **[जौम्सौन]** [**點線**] a dotted line; a broken line; [점 구멍이 나 있는 떼내는 선] a perforated line.

점수 **[जौम्सु]** [**點數**] **1** [성적을 나타내는 숫자] (merit) marks; grades.**2** (경기 등의) points; a score; (야구의) runs.

점술 **[जौम्सुल]** [**占術**] the art of divination; fortunetelling.

점심 **[जौम्सीम]** [**點心**] (a)

lunch; (a) luncheon (다소 격식을 차린 것).. **점심 시간** lunch time; a lunch break.

점원 [जौम्वॉन] [**店員**] [상점의 남종업원] a shop assistant; a (store) clerk; [상점의 여종업원] a saleslady; a saleswoman; salesgirl; a shopgirl.

점유 [जौम्यु] [**占有**] occupation; [소유] possession; (특히 토지,가옥의) occupancy. 점유하다 occupy; possess; take possession of.

점잖다 [जौम्चान्था] [품격이 높다] gentle; decent; respectable; [의젓하고 바르다] dignified; grave; (빛깔이) quiet; sober.

점점 [जौम्चौम] [**漸漸**] [서서히] gradually; [조금씩] little by little; [차례차례] one ather another; step by step.

점진 [जौम्चीन] [**漸進**] adual progress; steady advance. 점진하다 advance gradually; make gradual progress.

점진주의 [जौम्चीनजुउइ] gradualism; a moderate [slow-and-steady] policy.

점토 [जौम्थो] [**粘土**] **점토** clay.

점포 [जौम्फो] [**店鋪**] = 가게.

점화 [जौम्हवॉ] [**點火**] ignition; lighting. 점화하다 light; ignite; kindle; set off

접근 [ज़ौप्कुन] [**接近**] approach; access; approximation. 접근하다 approach; make an approach <to>; come close <to>; draw [come / get] near; [교제하다] (try to) associate with.

접다 [जौप्ता] **1** [겹치다] fold (up); turn back [down] (구석 등을); double (반으로). e.g. 그는 편지를 반으로[두 번] 접었다 He folded the letter in [into] two [four]. **2** (폈던 것을) shut; close; fold. e.g. 우산을 접다 close [shut / fold] an umbrella **3** [보류하다] lay [set / put] aside; shelve; table e.g. 이 문제는 당분간 접어 두기로 했다 We decided to put aside the question for sometime.

접대 [जौप्तै] [**接待**] [응대] reception; [대접] entertainment. 접대하다 receive; entertain. .**접대부** a barmaid; <美> a B-girl.

접두사 [जौप्दूसा] [**接頭辭**] [문법] a prefix.

접미사 [जौम्मीसा] [**接尾辭**] [문법] a suffix.

접속 [ज़ौम्सोक] [**接續**] **1** [맞대어서 이음] connection; joining; junction; a joint. 접속하다 connect <to / with>; join <with / to>; link (up). **2** [컴퓨터] an interface.

접속역 [जौम्सोग्यौक] a junction (station).

접속사 [जौप्सोक्सा] [**接續詞**] a conjunction.

접수 [जौप्सू] [接收] [권력 기관이 국민의 소유물을 강제로 인수함] requisition. 접수하다 requisition; take over.

접시 [जौप्शि] a plate (평평한); a dish(깊은); a saucer (받침의); a platter (큰); [식사의 한 접시] a course; [음식의 한 접시 분] a helping.

접어들다 [जौबौदुल्दा] **1** [어떤 장소,시기에 다가가다] come upon [to]; approach; draw near. 우리는 산길로 접어들었다 We came to a mountain path. **2** (방향, 목표로) take; pick up <a road>. e.g. 숲속으로 접어들다 take to the woods.

접전 [जौप्चौन] [接戰] (싸움의) a close fight [com-bat]; (경기의) a close contest [game]; a seesaw game. 접전하다 fight a close fight; come to close combat; [경쟁하다] be in keen competition <with>; (경기에서) have a close contest [game] <with>; have a seesaw game.

접종 [जौप्चोंग] [接種] [醫] (an) inoculation; (a) vaccination (백신, 특히 종두의). 접종하다 inoculate; vaccinate <a person against>.

접촉 [जौप्छोक] [接觸] (물체의) touch; contact; (electrical) contact; tange-ncy; contingence; osculation. 접촉하다 contact; make contact <with>; come in [into] contact <with>; touch (가볍게).

접합 [जौफादा] [接合] [한데 붙임] joining. 접합하다 join; unite; put together.

젓가락 [जौत्काराक] <a pair of> chopsticks.

젓다 [जौत्ता] **1** (액체를) stir; (도구를 써서 계란 등을) beat; (급격히) whip. e.g. 달걀 3개를 거품이 일 때까지 젓다 beat three eggs until they are frothy. **2** (배를) row; pull an oar; (카누 등을) paddle. e.g. 노를 잘[잘못] 젓는 사람 a good [bad] oarsman.

정[1] [जौंग] [錠] [알약] a <diazine> tablet; a pill. e.g. 비타민정 a vitamin pill [tablet].

정[2] [जौंग] [情] **1** [감정,마음] feeling (s); [세련된 심정] sentiment; [인정] human nature. e.g. 연민의 정 (a sentiment of) pity. **2** [애정] heart; affection; attachment; a tender feeling; love (이성간의).). e.g. 부부의 정 conjugal affection.

정[3] [जौंग] [정말로] truly; really; actually; very; quite; indeed; real. e.g.정 싫다면 할 수 없지 There is no help for it, if you really don't like it.

정가 [जौका] [定價] (일반적으로) a price; [정해진 가격] a fixed price; [정규의 가격] a regular price; [가격표에 있는 가격] a list price.

정각 [जौगाक] [正刻] [바로 그 시각] the exact time.

정갈하다 [जौगाहदा] neat; trim; tidy; snug.

정감 [जौकाम] [情感] emotion; sentiment.

정거장 [जौगौजांग] [停車場] a station; a railroad [railway] station; a depot; a stop. ⇨ 역

정결 [जौग्यौल] [貞潔] 정결하다 chaste and pure. e.g. 정결한 부인 a chaste [faithful / virtuous] wife.

정계 [जौग्ये] [政界] the political world [arena]; political circles.

정곡 [जौगोक] [正鵠] the point; the mark.

정교 [जौग्यो] [精巧] elaborateness; exquisiteness. 정교하다 elaborate; exquisite; sophisticated; delicate.

정권 [जौग्वन] [政權] [정치 권력] political [administrative] power; a government; an administration (특히 미국); [정치 조직] a regime.

정규 [जौग्यु] [正規] formality; regularity.

정글 [जौगुल] a jungle.

정기 [जौगी] [定期] a fixed period [term].

정기 간행물 [जौगकी गान्हैगंमुल] a periodical publication; a periodical; a journal.

정년 [जौगन्यौन] [停年] age limit; retirement age.

정답 [जौगदाब] [正答] a correct answer.

정답다 [जौगदाप्ता] [情 –] [친밀하다] friendly; familiar; intimate; close; [다정하다] affectionate; loving; warm-hearted; [화목하다] happy <family>. e.g. 정다운 친구 a good [great / close / bosom] friend / a chum

정당 [जौगदांग] [政黨] a political party.

정당 [जौगदांग] [正當] 정당하다 [공정하고 옳다] just; fair; right; [알맞다] proper; [이치에 닿다] reasonable; [적절하다] good; [합법적이다] lawful / legal / legitimate.

정독 [जौगदोक] [精讀] intensive [careful] reading; perusal. 정독하다 read intensively [carefully / with care]; peruse.

정들다 [जौगदल्दा] [情 –] get intimate <with> e.g. 두 사람은 마침내 서로 정들게 되었다 The couple finally opened their hearts to each other.

정떨어지다 [जौगतौरौजीदा] [情–]

become disgusted <with>; be disaffected <toward>; fall out of love <with>; grow sick[tired] <of>. e.g. 그 생각을 하면 정떨어진다 It makes me sick to think of it.

정력 [जौग्न्यौक] [精力] energy; [생명력] vitality; [활력] vigor; hustle.

정렬 [जौग्न्यौल] [整列] 정렬하다 stand in(a) line; < 英 > form a queue; (가로로) stand in a row; line up; form a line.

정리 [जौग्नी] [整理] **1** [흐트러져 있는 것을 질서 있게 함] arrange-ment; regulation; adjust-ment. 정리하다 arrange; adjust; regulate; tidy <up>; stra-ightten <up / out>; (생각 등을) put [throw / get] <one's idea> into shape [in order]. e.g. 책은 아직 미정리인 채로 있다 I have not arranged my books yet. **2** [감원] reduction; curtailment; a shake-up; [매각,처분] disposition; clearance. e.g.회사의 인원 정리 로 그는 해고 되었다 As a result of per-sonnel cuts [staff reduce-tions] in his company, he was dismissed. 정리하다 reduce; curtail; cut down; [처분하다] dispose of; sell.

정립 [जौग्निप] [鼎立] [세 사람 또는 세 개의 세력이 서로 대립함] a triangular position. 정립하다 be in a three-ornered [triangular] contest; stand in a trio.

정말 [जौगमाल] [正-] **1** truth (거짓에 대해 진실); a fact (사실); reality (현실). e.g. 정말 같은 [있을 법한] likely / [외양뿐인] see-ming / [그럴듯한] spe-cious / plausible. 정말 같은 거짓말 a plausible [spe-cious]lie. **2** ⇨ 정말로.

정말로 [जौगमाल्लो] [正 -] [참으로] truly; really; indeed; [확실히] certainly; assuredly; surely; to be sure; [마음 속으로부터] heartily; sincerely; [매우] very; quite; greatly; aw-fully. e.g. 정말로 고맙습니다 Thanks a lot.

정면 [जौगम्यौन] [正面] the front [face]; the frontage; the front part; the façade (건물의).

정문 [जौग्मुन] [正門] the front [main] gate; [입구] the main entrance.

정밀 [जौग्मिल] [精密] minu-teness; precision; accu-racy. 정밀하다 minute; precise; accurate.

정반대 [जौग्बान्दै] [正反對] the exact [direct] oppo-site; the exact rever-se; just the opposite.

정벌 [जौबौल] [征伐] con-quest; subjugation. 정벌

하다 conquer; [지배하에 두다] subjugate.

정보 [जौन्बो] [情報] (a piece [bit] of) information; intelligence; a report; news; (슬쩍 알려주는) a tipoff.

정복 [जौन्बोक] [征服] conquest; subjugation; mastery. 정복하다 conquer; subjugate; overcome; master; subdue.

정부 [जौन्बु] [政府] a government.

정비 [जौन्बी] [整備] **1** [가다듬어 비교함]. 정비하다 set <a thing> in good condition [working order]; improve (개선하다). **2** [유지, 보전] maintenance; [판매 후의 수리] service. 정비하다 [차 등을 수리하다] repair; [판매 후 수리 ,점검하다] service; [손질하여 유지하다] maintain.

정산 [जौन्सान] [精算] (개산에 대하여) exact calculation; accurate reckoning; [차감 예산] adjustment; [결산] settlement of accounts. 정산하다 [정밀히 계산하다] calculate exactly; [조정하다] adjust; [결산하다] settle [fix] accounts.

정상 [जौन्सांग] [正常] normality; normalcy. e.g. 정상인[으로] normal [-ly]. 비정상인 abnormal. 정상으로 돌아오다 be restored to normal condition / return to normal (ity).

정상 [जौन्सांग] [頂上] **1** [산의 꼭대기] the top; the summit; the (highest) peck. e.g. 산의 정상에 at the top of the mountain **2** [극점] the peak; the top; the zenith. e.g. 이 나라의 의학은 세계의 정상 수준에 있다 Medical science in this country ranks [is on a level] with the best in the world.

정색 [जौन्सैक] [正色] [얼굴빛을 바꾸어 엄정한 빛을 보임] a serious countenance; earnestness. 정색하다 become serious [grave]; assume [put on] a serious look [countenance]; put on a serious [grave] face; straighten one's face. e.g.. 그녀가 정색하고 그렇게 말했어 She said that with a perfect straight face.

정서 [जौन्सो] [情緖] emotion; feeling; sentiment.

정성 [जौन्सौंग] [精誠] one's true heart; sincerity; devotion; wholehearted-ness; earnestness (열성).

정세 [जौन्से] [情勢] the situation; the state of affairs; conditions (▷ situation 은 사람, 사물이 놓인 특정 상황, state of affairs는 사태를 나타내는 일반적인 말, condition 은 원인이나 상황에 관계된

그때의 상태). e.g. 국제 [국내] 정세 the international [domestic] situation.

정숙[1] [जौंग्सुक] [貞淑] virtue; chastity. 정숙 하다 chaste; virtuous.

정숙[2] [जौंग्सुक] [靜肅] silence; stillness; quiet (ness); a hush (소란 후의). 정숙 하다 silent; still; quiet

정시 [जौंग्सी] [定時] (정해진 시간) the [a] fixed time; (예정된 시간) the scheduled time; (규칙적인 시간) regular hours.

정식 [जौंग्सीक] [正式] Formality e.g. 정식의 [형식이 완비된] formal / [공식의] official / [적법한] legal / [정규의] regular.

정신 [जौंग्सीन] [精神] 1 (지성) mind; (육체에 대한 마음) spirit; (영혼) soul;(의지) will; (마음의 상태. 기분) mentality. e.g. 희생 정신 a self-sacrificing spirit. 2 [사물의 근본적인 의의, 사상] the spirit. e.g. 시대 정신 the spirit of the time [age].

정액[1] [जौंगैक] [定額] a fixed amount [sum]; the specified [required] amount.

정액[2] [जौंगैक] [精液] semen; sperm (▷ a sperm 은 정자의 뜻).

정연 [जौंग्यौन] [整然] 정연하다 [말끔하다] order; well-ordered; regular; [체계적이다] systematic. 정연히 in good order; in an orderly manner [fashion]; systematically.

정열 [जौंग्यौल] [情熱] [강한 감정] (a) passion; [유별난 열정] ardor; [오래 계속되는 열정] fervor; [뭔가를 추구하는 열심] enthusiasm.

정오 [जौंगओ] [正午] (high) noon; twelve (o'clock) noon (시간을 좀 엄밀히 나타낼 때); midday.

정원 [जौंग्वॉन] [定員] [규정된 인원수] the[a] fixed number; [지정된 인원수] the [a] prescribed num-ber; [할당된 인원수] a quota.

정원 [जौंग्वॉन] [庭園] a garden; a park (넓은).

정육 [जौंग्युक] [精肉] (good quality) meat.

정육점 [जौंग्युचौम] a butcher('s) [meat] shop.

정자[1] [जौंगजा] [精子] [動] a spermatozoon <*pl.* -zoa>; <집합적> a sperm.; [植] a spermatozoid.

정자[2] [जौंगजा] [亭子] a pavilion; a summerhouse; [휴식처] an arbor; a bower.

정장 [जौंगजांग] [正裝] fulldress; formal dress; a full (-dress) uniform (군인의). 정장하다 (일반 인이) dress up; (군인 등이) be in full dress.

정적 [जौगजौक] [**静的**] [움직임이 없다] static; [고요하다] still.

정전 [जौग जौम] [**停電**] a stoppage [breakdown] of electric current; a power failure [outage]; (파업, 절전을 위한) a power cut; (전등이 꺼지는 일) a black-out. 정전하다 [जौम्वौनहादा] <the electricity> be off [cut]; <the power> be gone off [give out].

정점 [जौगजौम] [**頂點**] **1** ⇨ 꼭지점 **2** [꼭대기] the top; the peak; the summit.**3** = 절정 2. e.g. 영화의 정점에 있다 be at the zenith [height] of one's prosperity.

정정당당 [जौम्वौगदांगदांग] [**正正堂堂**] 정정당당하다 fair; fair and square; open and aboveboard. 정정당당히 fairly (and squa-rely); openly; aboveboard.

정제 [जौम्जे] [**精製**] [물질을 순수하게 함] refinement; purification. 정제하다 refine; purify.

정조 [जौम्जो] [**貞操**] chastity; virtue; (female) honor; [처녀성] virginity; maidenhood. hospitably; with hospitality.

정중 [जौम्जुंग] [**鄭重**]정중하다 [예의바르다] polite; [공손하다] courteous; [사교 상의 예법에 맞다] civil; [경의가 많다] respectful; [대접이 좋다] hospitable.

정지 [जौम्जी] [**停止**]**1** [멎음] stoppage; a stop; a halt; a standstill. e.g. 교차로에서 일단 정지하다 stop before crossing the intersection. 정지하다 stop; come to stop; halt. **2** [금지] suspension; temporary prohibition; ban. 정지하다 suspend. e.g. 영업 [지급]을 정지하다 suspend business [payment].

정진 [जौम्जीन] [**精進**] earnest [close] application; [전념] devotion. 정진하다 devote oneself <to>; apply oneself <to>.

정차 [जौम्छा] [**停車**] a stop; stoppage. 정차하다 [서다] stop; halt; come to a stop; pull up; [세우다] stop; make a stop; bring <a car> to a halt; pull up.

정착 [जौम्छाक] [**定着**] **1** [정주] settlement. 정착하다 settle (down). e.g. 그 가족이 이 읍에 정착한 지 3 년이 된다 Three years have passed since the family settled down in this town. **2** (관습 등이). 정착하다 come to stay; [뿌리 내리다] take root; [확립되다] become established. e.g. 민주주의는 한국에 정착할 것인가 Has democracy come to stay [been established / taken root] in Korea?

정찰 [जौङ्छाल] [正札] a price tag [mark / label].

정찰 가격 [जौङ्छाल गाग्यौक] <at> a fixed [labeled] price.

정책 [जौङ्छैक] [政策] (a) policy.

정체1 [जौङ्छे] [停滯] (일 등의) stagnation; (화물 등의) accumulation; (자금 등의) a tie-up; (지불의) falling into arrears. 정체하다 accumulate; be tied up; fall into arrears; pile up (우편물이); con-gest (교통 등이).

정체2 [जौङ्छे] [正體] [본디의 모습] the identity <of>; [본성] one's true character [colors]; one's real nature.

정취 [जौङ्छ्वी] [情趣] [기분] a mood; [분위기] a atmosphere; [아취] an artistic effect; charms; a touch.

정치 [जौङ्छी] [政治] politics <단수,복수 동형>; [통치] government; [시정] administration.

정통 [जौङ्थोंग] [正統] [정당한 계승] legitimacy; [일반 또는 공적으로 인정된 것] orthodoxy.

정통파 [जौङ्थोंपा] e.g. 그는 인상주의의 정통파로 자처하고 있다 He claims to be the legitimate descent of the Impressionists.

정통 [जौङ्थोंग] [精通] 정통하다 [친숙하여 잘 알고 있다] be familiar <with>; [경청하여 잘 알고 있다] be well acquainted <with>; [특정한 분야에 밝다] be (well) versed <in>; [경험이나 지식이 있다] be conversant <with>.

정평 [जौङ्प्योंग] [定評] an established reputation. e.g. 정평이 나 있는 acknowledged / recognized.

정하다 [जौङ्हादा] [定 –] **1** [결정하다] decide (on); determine; [문제를 해결하고 조화시켜 결정하다] settle (on); [분명히 결정하다] fix [선택하여 결정하다] choose; fix upon [on]; [타협 등을 하여 결정하다] arrange; [특히 날짜를 정하다] appoint. e.g. 목적지를 정하다 decide where to go.**2** [결심하다] decide; determine; resolve; make up one's mind e.g. 그는 술을 끊기로 마음을 정했다 He decided [resolved] to quit [give up] drinking. / He decided [resolved] that he quit [give up] drinking.

정형 [जौङ्ह्योंग] [定型] [일정한 형식] a set pattern; a (fixed / regular) type; a fixed form; standard (표준).

정화 [जौङ्ह्वा] [淨化] [깨끗이 하기] purification; purgation; elutriation. 정화하다 purify; cleanse; deterge;

elutriate.

정확 [जौङ्ह्वॉक] [正確] [바르고 확실함] correctness; exactness; accuracy; precision. 정확하다 correct; exact; accurate; precise.

정황 [जौङ्ह्वॉंग] [情況] [사물의 정세와 형편] the state of things [affairs]; conditions; a situation; circumstances.

젖 [जौत] [유즙] milk; [모유] mother's milk; [우유] cow's milk.

젖가슴 [जौतकासम] the breast; the bosom.

젖다 [जौत्ता] (물 등에) get wet [drenched]; be wet; be damp [moistened].

젖히다 [जौछीदा] **1** (뒤로) bend back (ward); lean backward; pull back. e.g. 몸을 뒤로 젖히다 bend oneself back / lean oneself backward / throw one's head back.**2** [뒤집다] turn out [over]; (옷 등을) turn inside out; turn outside in; (카드 등을) turn up <a card>. e.g. 저 고리를 젖히다 turn a coat inside out.

제각기 [जेगाक्की] [－名其] [각자] each (one).

제거 [जेगौ] [除去] removal; elimination; exclusion. 제거하다get rid of <something>; clear <something of>; take away; remove; eliminate; exclude.

제격 [जेग्यौक] [－格] e.g. 제격이다 [제격에 어울리다] be suitable <for / to> / be suited <to> / become / be fit / be proper <for>.

제곱 [जेगोब] a square. 제곱하다 square <a number>; multiply <a number> by itself.

제공 [जेगोंग] [提供] an offer; supply. 제공하다 [내놓다] offer; make an offer; [주다] give; [필요한 것을 공급하다] provide; (모자라는 것을) supply; [광고주가 되다] sponsor

제과 [जेग्वॉ] [製菓] confectionnery. 제과하다 make confections.

제과점 [जेग्वॉजौम] a confectioner's shop; a confectionery.

제구실 [जेगुसील] [해야 할 책임] one's function; one's duty; one's part.

제국 [जेगुक] [帝國] an empire. 제국의 [जेगुगुइ] imperial.

제기 [जेगी] [提起] 제기하다 (문제 등을) bring up [forward]; raise; (소송 등을) institute; lodge; submit.

제대 [जेदै] [除隊] discharge from military service; (해산에 의한) demobi-lization; <英> demob. 제대하다 be discharged from military service; get one's discharge; leave the army [colors]; (해산에 의해) be demobilized.

제도[1] [जेदो] [制度] (체계 적인) a system; (관습 적인) an institution; [기구] an organization.

제도[2] [जेदो] [製圖] drathing; drawing; (지도의) cartography. 제도하다 drath; draw

제례 [जेरे] [祭禮] memorial services; sacrificial rites; religious ceremonies.

제멋 [जेमौत] one's own way [style / fancy].

제명 [जेम्यौंग] [除名] expulsion. 제명하다 [जेम्यौंगहादा] strike [take] a person's name off the list [roll]; remove <a person's> name <from the member-ship list>; withdraw <a person's> name; expel a person <from>.

제목 [जेमोग] [題目] [표제] a title; [주제] a subject; a theme.

제물 [जेमुल] [祭物] [제사에 쓰는 음식] an offering; a sacrifice; a sacrificial offering.

제발 [जेबाल] for God's [Heaven's] sake; for goodness' [mercy's / pity's] sake; please.

제법 [जेबौब] fairly; pretty; rather; passably; quite; considerably.

제복 [जेबौक] [制服] a uniform; (하인, 고용인의) (a) livery.

제본 [जेबौन] [製本] (book) binding. 제본하다 bind <a book>.

제비 [जेबी] [추첨] a lottery; (한 장의) a lot; a lottery ticket; a raffle ticket.

제사 [जेसा] [祭祀] (a) sacrifice; sacrificial rites; (죽은 사람의) a memorial service.

제설 [जेसौल] [除雪] snow removing [removal]; snow clearings. 제설하다 remove [clear away] the snow <from the street>; clear <a street> of snow.

제시 [जेसी] [提示] presentation. 제시하다 present; show.

제안 [जेआन] [提案] a proposal; a proposition; a suggestion; (회의 등에서의) a motion. 제안하다 propose <doing / that>; suggest; (동의를) move.

제압 [जेआब] [制壓] control; ascendancy; supremacy; mastery. 제압하다 gain control <of>; bring <a thing> under one's control.

제약 [जेयाक] [約食] [한정된 범위내에 제한하기] a restricttion; [한정] a limitation.

제약 [जेयाक] [製藥] [약의 제조] medicine [drug] manufacture; pharmacy; [제조된 약] a manufactured medicine [drug]. 제약하다 manufacture drugs [medicines].

제어 [जेओ] [制御] control; governing; management. 제어하다 control; bring under control; govern; restrain; manage; hold in check.

제외 [जेवे] [除外] exclusion; exception; [면제] exemption. 제외하다 exclude; except; make an exception <of a person's case>; [면제하다] exempt <a person from service>. e.g. 을 제외하고 except / excepting / but / with the exception of / exclusive of.

제의 [जेउइ] [提議] a proposal; a proposition; a suggestion; an offer; (회의 등에서의) a motion. 제의하다 propose; make a proposition [proposal]; suggest; offer.

제일 [जेइल] [第一] **1** [첫째 가는 것] the first; number one. e.g. 제일의 [첫째 가는] the first / [주요한, 일차적인] primary / [주요한] main / [최고의] the best / [일류의] lea-ding / [앞서는] foremost.**2** ⇨ 가장

제자 [जेजा] [弟子] [문하생] a pupil; [고교, 대학의 학생] a student; (어떤 선생 또는 학설에 관한) a disciple; [도제] an apprentice.

제자리 [जेजारी] [본디 있던 자리] the former place; [마땅한 자리] the proper place.

제작 [जेजाक] [製作] manufacture; production. 제작하다 make; manufacture; produce.

제재 [जेजे] [制裁] sanctions; punishment (벌). 제재하다 apply sanction <against>; punish; inflict punishment <upon>.

제적 [जेजौक] [除籍] removal of a person's name from <the register>. 제적하다 remove [cross out / cross off] name from <the Register>; strike a person's name off <the membership list>.

제정 [जेजौगं] [制定] establishment; enactment. 제정하다 establish; enact; legislate. 제정하다 establish [set up / enact] a new constitution. 새로운 교통 법규를 제정할 필요가 있다 It is necessary to establish new traffic regulations.

제조 [जेजो] [製造] manufacture; production. 제조하다 [공장 등에서 대규모로 만들다] manufacture; [상품을 생산하다] produce; turn out; [일반적으로 물건을 만들다] make

제지 [जेजी] [制止] (a) restraint; control; check. 제지하다 restrain; control;

ㅈ

check; stop; keep <a person> from <doing>; hold [keep] back <a crowd>.

제철 [जेछौल] [製鐵] iron manufacture. 제철하다 manufacture iron.

제철소 [जेछौल्सो] an iron mill; an ironworks.

제패 [जेफे] [制覇] (정복) conquest; (지배) domination; mastery. 제패하다 conquer; dominate.

제품 [जेफुम] [製品] [상품] good; [공장에서의 대량 생산물] manufactures; manufactured goods.

제하다 [जेहादा] [除-] **1** [공제하다] take off [away]; deduct; subtract <from>; subduct <from>. e.g. 세금을 제하고 40만 원의 월수 a monthly income of 400,000 won ather taxes **2** [나누다] divide.

제한 [जेहान] [制限] (a) restriction; (a) restraint; [한계] a limit; (a) limita-tion. 제한하다 rest-rict; limit; confine.

제화 [जेह्वा] [製靴] shoemaking.

제휴 [जेह्यु] [提携] cooperation; concert; coalition. 제휴하다 cooperate with; act in concert with; move in harmony; go hand in hand with; join [clasp] hands with; tie up with.

조[1] [जो] [調] **1** [음조] tune; a tone; (가락의) a meter. e.g. 다장[단]조의[로] in C major [minor].**2** [어조] a tone; [방식] a way; a manner; [태도] an air; an attitude. e.g. 비난조로 <speak> with a tone [an air] of censure / critically.

조[2] [जो] [組] [작은 집단] a company; a party; a band; a group. e.g. 2인조 a pair / a duet / a duo. 조를 만들다[짜다] form [make up] a group.

조[3] [जो] [兆] a trillion; a billion.

조각[1] [जोगाक] [彫刻,雕刻] sculpture; engraving; carving 조각하다 carve; sculpture; engrave; chase (금속에); chisel (끌로). **조각가** an engraver; a sculptor.

조각[2] [जोगाक] a piece; a bit; a fragment; a slip; a strip; a slice (얇은 조각); a scrap (자투리); a cut(베어 낸).

조간 [जोगान] [朝刊] a morning paper; (석간에 대하여) a morning edition.

조개 [जोगै] a shellfish; [대합 조개] a clam.

조건 [जोगोन] [條件] **1** [조항] an item; a stipulation. **2** [제약 사항] a term; a qualification (제한). **3** [어떤 일의 성립에 필요한 사항] a condition.

조국 [जोगुक] [祖國] one's homeland [fatherland / motherland]; one's mother [native] country.

조금 [जोगुम] **1** [양이 적게] a small quantity; a little; a dash. **2** [수가 적게] a small number; a few; some. **3** [정도가 적게] something; somewhat; a bit; a little; a trifle; slightly; to a slight degree; a shade.

조끼 [जोक्की] [소매 없는 옷] a vest; a waistcoat.

조난 [जोनान] [遭難] a disaster; an accident; (배의) (a) shipwreck; a distress. 조난하다 meet with a disaster; (배가) be wrecked; be in distress.

조달 [जोदाल] [調達] supply; (군대의) procurement; (식량, 일용품의) provision; purveyance; (돈의) raising; (주문의) fulfillment; execution. 조달하다 supply; provide; furnish <a person with a thing>; purvey [cater] <provisions>; raise <a fund for>; fill [fulfill / execute] <an order>.

조례 [जोर्ये] [條例] [규칙이나 법령] regulations; rules; a law; an act; an ordinance. fer to precedents.

조롱 [जोरोंग] [嘲弄] mockery; ridicule; derision; raillery; scoffing; jeering. 조롱하다 make a fool <of>; make sport [fun] <of>; mock at; ridicule; deride; scoff [jeer] at; rail at [against].

조류 [जोर्यु] [鳥類] birds; fowls; bird life; the feathered tribe.

조림 [जोरीम] food boiled down in soy; hard-boiled food.

조립 [जोरीब] [組立] [맞추어 짬] (일반적인) constructing; fabrication; (기계의) assembling; assembly; assemblage. 조립하다 construct; fabricate; frame; assemble; fix up; erect; put [fit / piece] together.

조망 [जोमांग] [眺望] a view; a prospect; a lookout; an outlook. ⇨ 전망 (展望) 조망하다 take a view of; have a distant view of.

조명 [जोम्यौंग] [照明] illuminetion; lighting (무대의).

조문 [जोमुन] [弔文] a funeral [memorial] address; a letter of condolence.

조사 [जोसा] [調査] (an) investigation; (an) examination; (an) inquiry; (a) survey. 조사하다 investtigate; examine (into); inquire [look / search] into; survey; look [go] over.

조산 [जोसान] [助産] [분만을 도움] midwifery (service).

조상 [जोसांग] [祖上] an ancestor; a forefather; <집합적> ancestry.

조선 **[जोसौन]** **[造船]** shipbuilding. 조선하다 build a ship.

조소 **[जोसो]** **[彫塑]** [美] [조형 미술] the plastic arts; carving and modeling [modelling]; [소상] a plastic image; a clay [pla-ster] figure.

조소 **[जोसो]** **[嘲笑]** [비웃음] a derisive [sardonic] smile; a scornful laugh; derision; ridicule; sneer 조소하다 laugh scornfully [mockingly / derisively] <at>; deride; ridicule.

조수[1] **[जोसु]** **[助手]** [일을 보조하는 사람] a helper; a help; an assistant.

조수[2] **[जोसु]** **[潮水]** the tide; tidewater.

조신 **[जोसीन]** **[操身]** [몸가짐을 조심함] carefulness of conduct [behavior]; circumspection. 조신하다 be careful of oneself; behave with discretion [caution]; behave discretely; exercise circumspection.

조심 **[जोसीम]** **[操心]** [주의] care; carefulness; heed; [경계] caution; preca-ution.

조언 **[जोऔन]** **[助言]** advice; counsel; a hint; a suggestion. 조언하다 advise; counsel; give <a person> advice [counsel]; suggest

조연 **[जोयौन]** **[助演]** [주역의 연기를 보조함] supporting [assisting] performance; [조연자] a supporting actor [actress]. 조연하다 assist [support] <the leading actor>; play support.

조율 **[जोयुल]** **[調律]** tuning. 조율하다 tune (up); key; put <a piano> in tune.

조작 **[जोजाक]** **[造作]** [제작] making; [날조] fabriccation; invention; concocttion; framing up. e.g. 조작 기사 a fabrication / a fabriccated report. 조작하다 [제작하다] make; manufacture; [날조하다] make up; fabricate; concoct; invent <a story>; fake; forge; cook up.

조작 **[जोजाक]** **[操作]** **1** (기계 등의) (an) operation; handling; a mechanism; the works. e.g. 이 기계의 기어 조작은 복잡하다 The working of the gears of this machine is quite complex. 조작하다 operate [work] <a machine>; manipulate <the market>; handle. **2** (자금 등의). e.g. 금융 [시장] 조작 money [market] operation / monetary [market] manipulation.

조장 **[जोजांग]** **[助長]** [도와서 더 자라게 함] promotion; furtherrance. 조장하다 [촉진하다] promote; [발전

시키다] encourage; [악화 시키다] aggravate.

조절 [जोजौल] [調節] regulation; adjustment; control; governing; [조정] modulation; tuning (악기의); tuning in (라디오의); [言] articulation. 조절하다 regulate <a machine>; adjust <prices>; control <birth>; fiK (음조 등을) modulate <one's voice>; tune <a piano>; tune in <the radio>.

조정 [जोजौंग] [調停] [분쟁을 화해시키어 그치게 함] mediation; arbitration 조정하다 mediate <between two persons>; arbitrate <a case / in a matter / between two>; intercede <with B for A>; intervene <in a strike>; make peace.

조제 [जोजे] [調劑] [여러 가지 약을 적절히 조합하여 약제를 만듦] compoundding [preparation] of medicines. 조제하다 prepare [compound] a medicine; (처방 에 따라) fill [make up] a prescription.

조준 [जोजुन] [照準] aiming; (an / one's) aim. 조준하다 aim <at>; sight <a target>; lay <a gun>.

조직 [जोजीक] [組織] **1** [통일체,조성된 것] [शौगिल जोसौग] an organization; [결성하는 일] formation; construction. e.g. 마약 밀매 조직 a drug-smuggling ring [organization]. 조직하다 organize; form. **2** [구성] [गूसौग] constitution. . e.g. 이 도표는 우리 협회의 조직을 나타낸 것입니다 This diagram shows the structure [makeup / setup] of our association. 조직하다 compose; constitute; set up.

조짐 [जोजीम] [兆朕] [길조] a good omen; [전조] an omen; [징후] symptoms; signs.

조차 [जोछा] [… 도] even; [게다가] besides; in addition. e.g. 이름 조차 못 쓰다 cannot so much as sign one's own name

조촐하다 [जोछोरहादा] [아담하다] snug; cozy; neat; [단정하다] dapper; refined; elegant; tidy; decent; [해사하다] graceful; fair; handsome.

조치 [जोछी] [措置] = 조처 (措處). e.g. 보완 조치 <take> complementary measures.

조카 [जोख्वा] a nephew; a niece.

조합 [जोहाब] [組合] an association; a society; (근로자의) a union; (동업 조합) a guild.

조항 [जोहांग] [條項] articles (and clauses); (계약의) stipulations; clauses; [각 항, 항목] a provision;

terms; an item.

조흔 [जोहोन] [早婚] an early marriage. 조흔하다 marry young

조화 [जोह्वा] [造花] an artificial [imitation] flower.

조화 [जोह्वा] [調和] harmony; accord; agreement; (a) reconciliation; symphony. 조화하다 harmonize <with>; be in harmony [keeping] <with>; match <with>; agree [accord] <with>; be harmonious <with>; be consonant <with / to>; go well <with>.

조회 [जोह्वे] [照會] [인적 사항 등을 알아봄] (an) inquiry; a reference. 조회하다 refer a matter to a person; ask [inquire of] <a person about a matter>.

-족 [जोक] [族] [종족] a race; a tribe. e.g. 고사(高砂)족 the native Formosan tribe [tribesmen].

존경 [जोन्ग्यौग] [尊敬] respect; esteem; reve-rence; veneration; defe-rence. 존경하다 respect; esteem; revere; honor; venerate; hold <a person> in respect [esteem / vene-ration].

존대 [जोन्दै] [尊待] 존대하다 treat with respect [politeness]; be polite <to>; hold <a person> in esteem. 존대어 an honorific (expression / word); a term of respect.

존립 [जोल्लिप] [存立] existence; subsistence. 존립하다 exist; subsist.

존비 [जोन्बी] [尊卑] high and low; the upper and the lower classes.

존속 [जोन्सोक] [存續] continuance; continuation; duration; retention. 존속하다 continue (to exist [be]); endure; last

존엄 [जोनौम] [尊嚴] dignity; majesty; prestige. 존엄하다 dignified; majestic; august; venerable.

존재 [जोन्जै] [存在] existence; being; subsis-tence (생존). 존재하다 exist; subsist; be in existence [being]; [잔존 하다] subsist; remain; be extant.

존중 [जोन्जुंग] [尊重] respect; esteem; deference. 존중하다 respect; esteem; hold <a person> in respect [esteem]; hold <a matter> in great account [honor]; value; prize; set much value on; [진지하게 고려하다] pay serious attention <to>; give <a matter> serious consideration.

존함 [जोन्हाम] [尊銜] your name.

졸고 [जोल्को] [拙稿] unworthy manuscript of mine; my (humble) manuscript.

졸깃 졸깃 [जोल्कित्चोल्कित्] 졸깃

졸깃하다 gummy; rubbery; tough; chewy; sticky.

졸다[1] [जोल्दा] (졸려서) doze; nap <in one's seat>; drowse; snooze; slumber. e.g. 졸면서 운전하다 fall asleep at the wheel / drith [doze] off while one is driving.

졸다[2] [जोल्दा] [물 등이 증발하다] get boiled down; be boiled dry; boil [simmer] down.

졸도 [जोल्तो] [卒倒] a faint; a swoon; a fainting fit. 졸도하다 fall down in a swoon; fall into a swoon; fall in a dead faint; swoon; keel over.

졸리다[1] [जोल्लिदा] [잠이 오다] become [fell / get] sleepy [drowsy]; have a sleepy spell; gather [pick] straws. e.g. 졸린 눈 drowsy eyes.

졸리다[2] [जोल्लिदा] 1 [조름을 당하다] be badgered; get pestered; get teased [pressed / importuned]; be solicited [entreated / urged]. 2 [단단하게 매어지다] be[get] tightened; be fastened tight. e.g. 끈으로 목이 졸린 시체 the body of a person who was strangled with a cord.

졸아들다 [जोरादुल्दा] (끓여서) be boiled down [dry]; boil down.

졸업 [जोरोप] [卒業] graduation; completion of a course (of study). 졸업하다 graduate <from>; finish (finish 는 초등 학교, 중학교, 고교 등에 쓸 수 있음. graduate from 은 <美>에서는 초등 학교,중학교 이외의 학교에 쓰지만, <英>에서는 대학만 씀); complete the whole course <of a school>; pass through <a school>.

졸음 [जोरूम] drowsiness; sleepiness.

졸이다 [जोरीदा] 1(끓여서) boil down; boil <salt> dry; condense <milk>. e.g. 간장에 졸이다 boil <fish, vegetables, etc.> hard with soy. 2 (마음을) worry (oneself); feel anxious [uneasy / nervous]. e.g. 마음을 졸이다 worry (oneself) <about> / be anxious <about> / (불안하게) feel nervous [timid / uneasy] / be afraid <of>.

졸작 [जोलचाक] [拙作] 1 [서투른 작품] a poor work. 2 [자기 작품에 대한 겸양어] my (humble) work.

졸저 [जोल्चौ] [拙著] 1 [졸렬한 저작물] a poor composition; a poor book [work]. 2 [자기 저작의 겸손한 말] my (humble) work.

졸지에 [जोल्चिए] [猝地 –] [갑자기] abruptly; sudde-

nly; on a sudden; all of a sudden; unexpectedly; all at once. e.g. 졸지에 사고를 당하다 have an accident all of a sudden.**좀** ⇨ 조금 e.g. 좀 아는 사이 a slender [slight] acquaintance. **2** [제발] kindly;(if you) please; pray; I beg; [꼭] by all means. e.g.문 좀 닫아 주세요 May I trouble you to shut the door? / I will thank you to shut the door.

좀더 [जोम्दौ] (분량) a little [some] more;(수효) a few [some] more;(시간) a little longer.

좀먹다 [जोम्मेक्ता] be worm-[moth-]eaten; be eaten by worms; [먹어 들어가다] eat in; gnaw at <one's life>;

좀처럼 [जोम्छौरौम] [여간해서는] seldom; rarely; hardly; scarcely; [쉽사리] <not> easily; <not> readily.

좁다 [जोप्ता] [폭이 작다] narrow; [면적이 작다] small; [범위가 작다] limited; [옹색하다] close; tight.

좁다랗다 [जोप्तारात्था] narrow and close; narrowish; somewhat [rather] narrow

-종 [जोंग] [宗] [종파] a (religious) domination [sect].

종[1] [जोंग] [種] **1** = 종류. e.g. 여러 종의 every variety [sort] of .... 3종 우편 third-class mail.**2**a spe-cies <단수,복수 동형>. e.g.종의 기원(저서명) the origin of species.**3** [종자] a seed; a grain; [품종] a breed; a stock. e.g. 잡종 hybrid / crossbred.**4** ⇨ 종개념

종[2] [जोंग] [鐘]a bell.

종소리 [जोंग्सोरी] a sound [peal] of a bell.

종가 [जोंगा] [宗家] [문중의 큰집] the head family [house].

종결 [जोंग्यौल] [終結] (a) conclusion; (a) termination; an end; a close. 종결하다 end; close; termi-nate; be concluded; come [be brought] to a close [an end].

종교 [जोंग्यो] [宗敎] (a) religion.

종단 [जोंग्दान] [縱斷] [세로자르기] vertical section; [분할] a division; a split. 종단하다 cut [divide] <something> vertically [longitudinally]; (국토 등을) run through <the land>; travel [run] across; traverse.

종래 [जोंग्रै] [從來] e.g. 종래(는) hitherto / heretofore / up to now [this time] / so far.

종료 [जोंगन्यो] [終了] [끝남] an end; a close; (a) conclusion; [완료] completion; (기한의) expiration. 종료하다 end; conclude; come to an end; be over; be completed; expire.

종사 [जोंग्सा] [從事] 종사하다 engage (oneself) in <business>; pursue <a calling>; follow <a pro-fession>; practice <medi-cine>; atend to [work at] <a business>; carry on <trade>.

종속 [जोंग्सोक] [從屬] subordination; depen-dency. 종속하다 be subor-dinate [subject] <to a foreign rule>; depend [be dependent] <upon [on]>.

종손 [जोंग्सोन] [宗孫] the eldest grandson of the head family.

종신 [जोंग्शिन] [終身] [일생] a whole life; one's life; [죽음] the end of life; one's death; [임종] being at one's parent's deathbed. 종신하다 [죽다] end one's life [days]; finish [live out] one's life; [임종하다] be on [at] one's parent's deathbed.

종아리 [जोंगारी] the calf <*pl.* calves>. 종아리 (를) 맞다 get whipped on the calf. 종아리 (를) 치다[때리다][lash [whip] <a person> on the calf.

종이 [जोंगी] paper.

종일 [जोंगील] [終日] all day (long); the whole day (over); for a whole day; throughout [all through] the day; from morning till [to] night.

종자 [जोंग्जा] [種子] (식물의) a seed; (복숭아 등의) a stone; a pip; a pit; (동물의) a breed; a stock; a strain.

종적 [जोंग्चौक] traces; vestiges; whereabouts.

종파 [जोंग्फा] [宗派] [종교의 분파] a denomination; a (religious) sect.

종합 [जोंग्हाप] [綜合] (a) synthesis <*pl.* -ses>; generalization; colligation. 종합하다 synthesize; generalize; unite; put [piece] together.

좇다 [जोत्ता] 1 (뒤를) [द्वीरल] follow; run ather; accompany (동반). e.g.그를 좇아 가다 follow [accompany] him.2 [그대로 따르다] follow; conform oneself to; act on [upon]. e.g. 관습을 좇아서 in conformity with custom / according to custom. 3 [복종하다] obey; abide by; submit [give in] to. e.g. 아무의 지시를 좇다 follow [take] a person's direction.

좋다[1] [जोथा] 1 (상태,성질 등이) good; nice; fine; (마음씨가) good; good-natured; nice; gentle; (머리가) bright; clever;

ㅈ

smart. e.g. 좋은 소식 welcome [encouraging / good] news. **2** nice; (냄새,맛,소리 등이) sweet; nice; good; pleasing; agree-able. e.g. 좋은 목소리 a sweet voice. **3** [귀하다] [ग्वीहादा] pre-cious; valu-able; (집안이) noble; good. e.g.좋은 자료 valu-able [precious] mate-rials. **4** (행운의) good; lucky; fortunate; oppor-tune; happy; auspicious (상서로운); favorable. e.g. 좋은 전조 a good [lucky] omen. **5** [알맞다 proper; right; good; suitable; fitting; [유리하다] profitable; ad-vantageous; favorable; [유용하다] useful. e.g. 그는 마침 좋은 때에 왔다 He came at the right moment.

좋다² [जोथा] =좋아.**좋아** Good!; Well!; All right!; O.K.!; [환성] Whoopee!; Goodie!; Oh boy!; Whee!; [찬성] Agreed!;

좌 [ज्वा][**左**] the left; the following; (사상) a leftist; <집합적> the left.

좌담 [ज्वादाम][**座談**] a table talk; [대화] (a) conver-sation; a colloquy; [토의] a discussion.

좌석 [ज्वासौक] [**坐席,座席**] [자리] a seat; a cockpit (비행기의); a pew (교회의); (sitting) room (여지).

좌우 [ज्वाउ] [**左右**] **1** [왼편과 오른편] right and left. e.g. 길의 좌우에 on either side [both sides] of the road. **2** [측근자] one's attendants; people in attendance. e.g. 좌우를 물리치고 밀담을 하다 keep one's attendants away and have a closed-door con-ference <with>. **3** [지배, 영향] sway; influ-ence; control. 좌우하다 [지배하다] command; govern; control; gain con-trol of; dominate; sway; have <a thing> under one's control; have <a person> under one's thumb; [영향을 끼치다] affect; influence; have [exert] an influence upon. e.g. 감정에 좌우되다 [사로잡히다] be carried away by one's emotions.

좌우명 [ज्वाउम्यौग] [**- 銘**] one's motto; a favorite proverb [maxim].

좌익 [ज्वाइक] [**左翼**] (주의상의) the left (wing); [급진적,과격적 당파,인물] the leftist; the left-winger.

좌절 [ज्वाजौल] [**挫折**] **1** (계획의) a breakdown; ruin; collapse; a reverse; [계획,일이 실패로 돌아감] a setback; [용기,희망 등이 꺾임] (a) frustration. 좌절하다 miscarry; get ruined;

be upset; break down; collapse; fall through; fall to the ground; suffer a setback; get frustrated; be frustrated. **2** (마음,기운의) discouragement. 좌절하다 get discouraged [disheartened / daunted].

좌지우지 [ज्वाजीउजी] [**左之右之**] 좌지우지하다 turn [twist] <a person> round one's little finger; turn, twist, and wind <a person>; lead; control; take the lead <in>; have <a person> at one's beck and call; lead <a person> by the nose. e.g. 당을 좌지우지하는 것은 그다 He is the leader of the party. / He is in control of the party.

좌충우돌 [ज्वाछुंग्ुदोल] [**左衝右突**] 좌충우돌하다 dash this way and rush that; plunge forward on this side and dash in on that.

좌측 [ज्वाछुक] [**左側**] the left-hand side; the left.

좌파 [ज्वाफा] [**左派**] the left; a left-wing party [faction]; (사람) the left wingers; the leftists.

좌회전 [ज्वाह्वेजौन] [**左回轉**] left (-hand) turn. 좌회전하다 turn (to the) left; make a left <at>. **좍**[ज्वाक] **1** [퍼지는 모양] far and wide; widely; <spread> suddenly. **2** [거침없이] fluently; with ease.**3** [흐르는 모양] in a quick stream; <stream out> suddenly; with a splosh [splash].

좔좔 [ज्वालज्वाल] <flow> freely [forcibly]; with a swilling sound.

죄 [ज्वे] [**罪**] (법률상의) a crime; (종교,도덕상의) a sin; [악덕] a vice; [과오] a fault; [죄책] blame; charge; [반칙] an offense; [벌](a) punishment; a penalty; [유죄] guilt.

죄다[1] [ज्वेदा] **1** (느슨한 것을) tighten; strain; draw in; stretch; [수축시키다] contract; [조르다] strangle; wring. e.g. 볼트를 죄다 tighten (up) a bolt. **2** [벌어진 사이를 좁히다] put[place] close; (자리를) sit up; sit close [closely]. e.g. 열과 열 사이를 죄다 close the ranks. **3** (마음을) feel anxious [uneasy / nervous] <about>; be fidgety; be worried <about>; worry (oneself) <about>. e.g. 결과가 어찌 될까 마음을 죄다 be worried over the result / be worried over how it will turn out.

죄다[2] [ज्वेदा] [전부] all; wholly; entirely; all through [together]; in all; altogether. e.g. 죄다 자백하다 confess everything **죄목** [**罪目**] [죄과] a charge;

[혐의] suspicion.

죄받다 [ज्वेबात्ता] [罪-] [지은 죄에 대해 벌을 받다] suffer [incur] punishment [a penalty]; be punished.

죄송 [ज्वेसोंग] [罪悚] 죄송하다 <be> sorry [regretttable].

죄수 [ज्वेसू] [罪囚] a prisoner; a convict; a jailbird.

죄악 [ज्वेआक] [罪惡] (법률상의) a crime; (도덕, 종교상의) (a) sin; a vice. ⇨ 죄 (罪).

주가 [जूगा] [株價] the price of a stock; a stock price.

주간 [जूगान] [晝間] the daytime; day. ⇨ 낮

주거 [जूगौ] [住居] [거주하는 집] a dwelling (house); a residence; an abode; [거주하는 것] living; residence.

주격 [जूग्यौक] [主格] [문법] the nominative [subjecttive] case.

주경야독 [जूग्यौंग्यादोक] [晝耕夜讀] 주경야독하다 work by day and study by night; grab every opportunity to better oneself.

주관 [जूग्वान] [主管] supervision; superintendence; management. 주관하다 superintend; supervise; manage; have [be in] charge of.

주관 [जूग्वान] [主觀] (객관에 대하여) subjectivity; [주체] the subject; [자아] the ego.

주권 [जूग्वॉन] [主權] sovereignty; sovereign power.

주급 [जूगुप] [週給] a weekly pay; weekly wages.

주다 [जूदा] **1** [제공하다] give; present <a person> with <something>. e.g. 먹을 것을 주다 feed <a child> / give <a person> something to eat. **2** [수여,부여하다] give; award <a person a medal>; bestow <a favor on a person>; confer <a title on [upon] a person>; grant <a person a privilege>. e.g. 박사 학위를 주다 confer a doctorate [a doctor's degree] on <a person>.

주도 [जूदो] [周到] 주도하다 scrupulous; cautious; careful; circumspect; thoroughgoing.

주도 [जूदो] [主導] leading; initiative. 주도하다 lead <a movement>; take the lead <in educational reform>.

주동 [जूदोंग] [主動] [어떤 일에 주장이 되어 행동함] leadership. 주동하다 take the lead [leadership] <of>.

주되다 [जूदवैदा] [主-] chief / principal / prime / leading / important.

주둔 [जूदुन] [駐屯] [머무름] stationing; posting; staying; a stay. 주둔하다 be stationed <in / at>; stay; occupy (점령).

주렁주렁 [जुरांगजुरांग] in clusters; in full bearing.

주력 [जुरयौक] putting forth one's strength [effort]. 주력하다 concentrate [focus] one's efforts [energies] <on>; throw energy into; devote oneself <to>; exert oneself <for / in>.

주례 [जूरये] [主禮] (일) officiating at a wedding ceremony; (사람) an officiator.

주로 [जूरो] [主－] mainly; principally; chiefly; primarily; in the main; [대개] mostly; for the most part; generally.

주류 [जूरयु] [主流] the main current; the main stream.

주류 [जूरयु] [酒類] alcoholic liquors [beverages]

주르르 [जूरूरु] **1** [액체가 흘러내리는 모양] tricklingly; dribbling; running. **2** [미끄러지는 모양] slidingly; slipperily.

주름 [जूरूम] [구김살] wrinkles; crumples; furrows; [접은 줄] pleats; folds; creases.

주말 [जुमाल] [週末] the wekend. **주말 여행** a wekend trip.

주머니 [जुमोनी] [물건을 넣는 것] a bag; a sack; a pouch

주먹 [जुमौक] a (clenched) fist; the knuckles; dukes; the bunch of fives.

주목 [जुमोक] [注目] attention; observation; notice; remark. 주목하다 pay [give] attention <to>; direct[turn] one's attention <to>; observe; watch; take notice <of>.

주문 [जुमुन] [注文] **1** [맞춤] an order; a commission; [주문하는 일] ordering. 주문하다 order <an article from a firm>; give an order <for an article to a firm>; place [put in] an order <with a firm for an article / in a country>. **2** [요구] a request; a demand; [조건] a condition. 주문하다 request; demand.

주민 [जुमीन] [住民] an inhabitant; resident; citizen.

주방 [जुबांग] [廚房] a kitchen; a cookroom; a cookery; a cuisine; (배 안의) a galley; a cookhouse.

주변 [जुब्यौन] [周邊] [주위] the circumference; the surroundings; the periphery; (도회의) the environs; the outskirts; [動,解] the limbus <*pl.* –bi.>.

주사 [जुसा] [注射] (an) injection; a shot; [접종] an inoculation; a vaccination. 주사하다 inject; give [make / administer / apply] an injection; syringe.

주석 [जुसौक] [註釋,注釋] [주석 붙이기] annotation;

explanation; exposition.

주소 [जुसो] [住所] [사는 곳] one's dwelling (place); one's residence [abode]; one's quarters; a domicile.

주술 [जुसुल] [呪術] incantation; enchantment; magic; the black art; spell.

주시 [जुशी] [注視] a steady gaze; close observation; scrutiny. 주시하다 gaze steadily <at>; fix one's eyes <on>; observe <a person> closely; watch [look at] <a thing> carefully. .

주식 [जुशिक] [株式] stocks; shares. e.g. 주식을 발행하다 issue stocks.

주안 [जुआन] [主眼] [주되는 목표] the prime [principal] object; the chief aim [end]; the object in view; the principal point.

주야 [जुया] [晝夜] day and night.

주어 [जुऔ] [主語] [문법] the subject (of a sentence).

주요 [जुयो] [主要] the principal; the important; the main; the essential. 주요하다 principal; chief; main; major; leading; important; staple.

주의 [जुइ] [注意] **1** [유의,주목] attention; notice; heed 주의하다 give attention [heed] to; observe; take note [notice] of; mind; take care of; be careful of; beware of; be cautious [watchful] of; look out for. **2** [충고] (a piece of) advice; counsel; [경고] (a) warning. 주의하다 advise; counsel; give advice to; [경고하다] warn; give warning; caution <a person> against.

주인 [जुइन] [主人] **1** [가장] the master <of a house>; the head <of a family>; (손님과 대칭으로) the host; the hostess (여자). **2** [임자] the owner; the proprietor; (여관 등의) the landlord; the landlady (여성).

주일 [जुइल] [週日] a weekday; a week.

주임 [जुइम] [主任] a chief; a head; a person in charge <of>; a manager.

주입 [जुइप] [注入] pouring into; (약액 등의) injection; (신사상 등의) infusion; instillation; (교육의) cramming. 주입하다 [부어넣다] pour [put] into; (약액을) inject; (사상등을) infuse <a spirit into a person's mind>; instill <a sentiment in a person>; implant <a principle in a person's mind>; [되풀이하여 가르치다] inculcate <a person with a doctrine>.

주장 [जुजांग] [主張] insistence; (an) assertion; persistence; [논점] one's contention; one's point; [지론] one's opinion [stand / doctrine]. 주장하다 insist <on / upon>; assert; [강조하다] emphasize / lay stress <on>; [주창하다] advocate.

주재 [जुजे] [駐在] residence; a stay. 주재하다 reside <at / in>; be resident <at / in>; be stationed <at / in>; stay.

주저 [躊躇] [जुजो] hesitation; [우유 부단] indecision; iresolution; (의견,방침 등의) vacillation; (양심의 가책에 의한) scruples. 주저하다 hesitate; [흔들리다] waver; scruple <at>; think twice <about doing>; vacillate; be irresolute [hesitant].

주정 [जुजौंग] [酒酊 drunken frenzy [wrench]; disorderly behavior caused by liquor. 주정하다 lose control of oneself in drink; become a bother to others in one's cups.

주제 [जुजे] [主題] a subject; a theme; (음악 등의) a leitmotif. **주제가** a theme song <of a motion picture>.

주주 [जुजेग्गा] [株主] a stockholder; a shareholder. 주주 **총회** a general meeting of stockholders [shareholders]; a general shareholders' meeting.

주차 [जुछा] [駐車] parking. 주차하다 park <a car>.

주창 [जुछांग] [主唱] advocacy; promotion. 주창 하다 advocate <peace>; promote

주최 [जुछ्वे] [主催] sponsorship; auspice. e.g.…의 공동 주최로 under the joint auspices of 주최하다 sponsor; promote.

주축 [जुछुक] [主軸] the principal [main] axis <*pl.* axes>; [機] the main shath [spindle]. **주춤거리다** [जुथैक] hesitate; be hesitant; waver; hold back <from>; boggle <at>.

주택 [जुह] [住宅] a house; a residence.

주행 [जुहैग] [走行] traveling; covering. 주행하다 travel <from A to B>; cover <100 miles in an hour>.

주황 (빛) [जुहवांग [पित]] [朱黃 (−)] orange color. ~

주흥 [जुहुंग] [酒興] [술자리의 여흥] entertainment at a drinking party; conviviality; [들떠서 신나는 기분] merrymaking; [술 생각] yen [craving] for alcohol.

죽 [जुक] [粥] (rice−) gruel; porridge; hot cereal; (유아용) pap.

ㅈ

죽을둥살둥 [जुगलदोंगसाल्तोंग] desperately; frantically; life and death; tooth and nail.

죽음 [जुगुम] death; decease;(왕의) demise.

죽이다 [जुहयौग] **1** (살해) kill; slay; put <a person> to death (모살) murder; (학살) massacre; slaughter; (도살) butcher. e.g.목을 졸라 죽이다 strangle to death.**2** [잃다] suffer the death [loss] of; lose <a son / a chessman>. e.g. 전쟁에 아들을 죽이다 lose a son in the war. **3** [억제하다] hold back; restrain; deaden; muffle. e.g. 감정을 죽이다 restrain one's feeling

준거 [जुन्गौ] [準據] 준거하다 be based upon; follow; go to.

준공 [जुन्गोंग] [竣工] completion.

준공식 [जुन्गोंगशिक] [-式] the ceremony for the completion; a dedication ceremony; a ceremony to celebrate the completion <of>.

준법 [जुन्बौप] [遵法] [법령을 지키는 것] law-abiding; obeying the law. 준법하다 abide by [obey / observe] the law.

준비 [जुन्बी] [準備] preparation (s); preliminary arrangements; preparedness; readiness 준비하다 prepare <for>; ready; arrange <for>; make preparations <for>; get ready <for>.

준수 [जुन्सू] [遵守] observance 준수하다 observe <rules, the law, etc.>; obey; abide by; follow; comply <with>; conform to.

준우승 [जुनुसंग] [準優勝] a victory in the semifinals.

준우승자 [जुनूसंगजा]a winner of the semifinals.

줄[जुल] **1** [끈] a string; a cord; a rope; a line. **2** [행] a line; a row; (시의) a line (of verse); a verse; (편지 등의) a line.

줄넘기 [जुलनौम्की] [줄을 돌리는 놀이] rope skipping

줄다 [जुल्दा] become [get] smaller [less]; decrease; diminish; lessen; be reduced; go down; fall (off); dwindle (차차); run low; abate; subside; shrink (의복 등이); [단축 되다] be shortened [abbre-viated.].

줄어들다 [जुरौदुल्दा] [크기가 작게 되다] shrink; contract; shorten; dwindle (away); diminish (in size); [수량이 적게 되다] decreease; lessen; fall (off); run low.

줄이다 [जुरीदा] [감소하다] reduce; decrease; diminish; lessen; [단축,절감하다] shorten; cut short;

cut (down); curtail; [절약하다] [축소하다] contract; boil down; [생략하다] abbreviate; abridge.

줍다 [जुप्ता] [집어 올리다] pick up; [채집하다] gather <shells>; [발견하다] find <a purse>.

줏대 [जुत्ते] [主-] a definite view [opinion]; a fixed principle; (the) backbone; moral fiber; firmness [strength] of character.

중[1] [जुंग] a Buddhist priest; a bonze; a monk. e.g. 중이 되다 become a priest [monk] / enter the priesthood.

중[2] [जुंग] [中] **1** […가운데] in; between; among; amidst; of; out of. e.g. 십중팔구 (in) nine cases out of ten. **2**[…의 속] in; through. e.g.공중을 날다 fly in [though] the air. **3** […동안에] during; in(the course of); throughout; while; for. e.g. 1년 중 내내 all the year round. **4** [진행중] under; in process [course] of. e.g. 건축중인 다리 a bridge under construction.

중간 [जुगान] [中間] the middle; midway.

중개 [जुगे] [仲介] intermediation; mediation (조정); agency. 중개하다 mediate [intermediate] <between two parties>.

중견 [जुंगग्यौन] [中堅] [중위(中位)에서 활약하는 사람] the backbone; the mainstay; [軍] the main body; [야구] center (field).

중계 [जुग्ये] [中繼] **1** [중간에서 이어줌] relay. **2** ⇨ 중계 방송 e.g.무대 중계 a stage relay broadcast / a drama relayed from the stage.

중고 [जुगो] [中古] **1** [史] [중고기 (期)] the Middle Ages; medieval times. **2** ⇨ 중고품.

중급 [जुगुप] [中級] (an) intermediate level; middle [medium] class [grade].

중년 [जुन्यौन] [中年] middle age [life]; one's middle years.

중대 [जुन्दै] [重大] importance; gravity; seriousness 중대하다 important; serious; grave; <a matter> of great [vital] importance.

중도 [जुन्दो] [中途] halfway; midway; mid-course.

중독 [जुंदोक] [中毒] poisoning; toxication; [醫] intoxication.

중량 [जुन्यांग] [重量] weight.

중력 [जुन्यौक] [重力] gravity; (terrestrial) gravitation.

중류 [जुन्यू] [中流] **1** (강의) midstream; (상류,하류에 대한) the middle reaches [courses]. **2** (사회의) the middle class(es).

중립 [जुन्गिनप] [中 立] neutrality; neutralization.

중매[1] [जुन्गमै] [仲買] brokerage. 중매하다 act as (a) broker.

중매[2] [जुन्गमै] [仲媒] match-making. 중매하다 arrange a match <between>; act as (a) go-between [a middleman]; go between <two parties>.

중복 [जुन्गबोक] [重複] duplication; overlapping; [되풀이] repetition 중복 하다 duplicate; overlap; double; repeat.

중부 [जुन्गबू] [中部] <in> the central part [district]. a serious [severe] wound [injury]

중성 [जुन्गसौंग] [中性] **1** [化] neutrality. **2** [문법] the neuter gender.

중세 [जुन्गसे] [中 世] the middle [medieval] ages.

중시 [जुन्गिशि] [重視] serious consideration. 중시하다 attach (great / much) importance to <some-thing>; take a serious view of <a matter>; lay stress on <a point>.

중심 [जुन्गिशम] [中心] **1** [한가운데] the center; the centre. e.g. 축을 중심으로 해서 회전하다 revolve around a central pivot / revolve on an axis. **2** [가장 중요한 위치에 있는 것] the pivot. e.g. 중심이 되어 일하다 work in a central [key] role / take the lead in the work.**3** [중점] the central point; the focus <*pl.* ~ es, foci>. e.g. 당신의 의견은 문제의 중심에서 벗어나 있다 Your opinion is off [beside] the point.

중앙 [जुन्गाग] [中央] the center; the middle; the heart.

중요 [जुन्ग्यो] [重要] importance; consequence. 중요하다 important; of importance [consequence / moment]; momentous; weighty; essential; [주요하다] principal; cardinal.

중재 [जुन्जै] [仲裁] arbitration; intervention; intercession. 중재하다 arbitrate; mediate [intervene / intercede] <between>; act as (a) peacemaker.

중지 [जुन्जी] [中止] suspendsion; stoppage; interrupttion; a standstill. 중지하다 discontinue; suspend; interrupt; stop; drop; call off <a game>

중학교 [जुन्गहाकक्यो] [中學校] a junior high school; a lower secondary school.

중화 [जुन्गह्वा] [中 和] [化] neutralization; (독 등의) counteraction. 중화하다 neutralize; (독 등을) counteract; anta-gonize.

중흥 [जुन्गहुन्ग] restoration; revival. 중흥하다 revive; be restored; be rehabi-litated.

쥐[1] [ज्वी] [動] a rat; (생쥐) a mouse <*pl.* mice>.

쥐[2] [ज्वी] [근육 경련] (a) cramp.

쥐뿔 [ज्वीपुल] [보잘것없는 것] a trifling thing; trivial [wretched] stuff.

쥐어 주다 [ज्वीऔ जुदा] (돈을) slip <money> into <a person's> hand [pocket]; (팁을) tip <a porter>; (뇌물을) grease [tickle] <a person's> palm; oil <a person's> hand; bribe.

즈음 [जुउम] [일이 어찌 될 무렵] when ...; about the time when .

즉 [जुक] [卽] **1** [곧] namely; that is (to say); or **2** [바로] just; precisely; exactly; [다름 아닌] nothing but; neither more nor less.

즉각 [जुक्काक] [卽刻] on the spot; at once; right away.

즉결 [जुकक्यौल] [卽決] a prompt [an immediate / a quick] decision; (재판의) a summary decision; a snap judgment. 즉결하다 decide promptly [imme-diately / on the spot]; [法] try <a case> summarily.

즉결 처분 [जुकक्यौल छौबुन] summary conviction.

즉사 [जुक्सा] [卽死] (an) instant [instantaneous] death; death on the spot. 즉사하다 be killed instantly [instantaneously]; be killed outright [on the spot].

즉석 [जुक्सौक] [卽席] e.g. 즉석의 immediate / ready / instant / prompt / impromptu / improvised / offhand (ed).

즉시 [जुक्शि] [卽時] instantly; promptly; at once; on the spot [instant]; right away [off].

즉위 [जुग्वि] [卽位] accession to the throne; enthronement; coronation. 즉위 하다 accede to [ascend] the throne

즐거움 [जुलगौऊम] joy; delight; pleasure; [행복] happi-ness; enjoyment.

즐비 [जुल्बी] [櫛比] 즐비하다 <서술적> stand in a row; line <a street>.

즙 [जुप] [汁] (과실의) juice 즙(을) 내다 extract [squeeze / press] juice.

증가 [जुंगा] [增加] (an) increase; addition; (an) increment; augmentation; gain 증가하다 increase; augment; rise; grow; swell.

증감 [जुंगाम] [增減] increase and [or] decrease; [변화] variations; fluctuation (s). 증감하다 increase and [or] decrease; [변화하다] vary; fluctuate.

증거 [जुंगौ] [證據] proof <of / that>; evidence <of / for / that>

증권 [जुंग्वॉन] [證券] [증거가 되는 문권] a document; [주식 증권] a certificate; [환어음 등] a bill; [공채,주권 등의 유가 증권] securities

증기 [जुंगी] [蒸氣] steam; vapor; vapour.

증대 [जुंग्दै] [增大] enlargement; (an) increase; (an) increment; a step-up. 증대하다 [커지다] become [grow] larger; [커지게 하다] enlarge; increase; augment; swell <the total>; enhance

증명 [जुंगम्यौंग] [證明] (a) proof; evidence; testimony 증명하다 prove; testify to <a fact>; attest (to) <a fact>; witness; bear witness [testimony] to <a fact>; evidence; demonstrate; corroborate; substantiate; show; confirm; certify; verify; authenticate.

증발 [जुंग्बाल] [蒸發] 1 (액체의) evaporation; vaporization; volatilization. 증발하다 escape [fly off] in vapor; evaporate; be volatilized; (수증기로) steam away. [사람,물건이 없어짐] mysterious disappearance; evaporation. 증발하다 disappear mysteriously [into thin air]; evaporate.

증빙 [जुंग्बिंग] [證憑] proof; evidence; testimony. 증빙 서류 documentary evidence.

증세 [जुंग्से] [症勢] symptoms; the condition of illness.

증손 (자) [जुंग्सोन [जा]] [曾孫(子)] a great-grandchild; a great-grandson.

증손녀 [जुंग्सोनन्यौ] a great-granddaughter.

증언 [जुंगौन] [證言] (verbal) evidence; testimony; witness; attestation. 증언하다 testify; attest; bear witness; depose; bear witness <to>.

증여 [जुंग्यौ] [贈與] donation; presentation; gith. 증여하다 [물건을 주다] give; [격식을 차려, 상,기념품 등을 주다] present (개인적인 선물에는 쓰지 않음); make a present of; confer; donate.

증오 [जुंओ] [憎惡] hatred; loathing; abhorrence 증오하다 hate; detest; abhor; bear [have] a grudge <against>.

증원 [जुंग्वॉन] [增員] an increase of personnel [the staff]. 증원하다 increase the personnel [staff].

증인 [जुंगिन] [證人] a witness; an eyewitness; an attestor; a testifier; a deponent; [보증인] a surety.

증정 [जुंग्जौंग] [贈呈]

presentation; proffering 증정하다 present <a person with a thing / a thing to a person>; make a present [gith] of <a thing to a person>; proffer; give.

증진 [जुंग्जिन] [增進] (an) increase; [촉진] promotion; advance 증진하다 promote; increase; further.

증축 [जुंग्छुक] [增築] extension [addition / enlargement] of a building. 증축하다 extend [enlarge / add to] a building; build an annex [extension] to <the main building>; make an enlargement of <a building>.

증표 [जुंगफ्यो] [證票] a certificate; a voucher.

지각[1] [जीगाक] [地殼] the (earth) crust; the lithosphere.

지각[2] [जीगाक] [遲刻] being late; tardiness; lateness. 지각하다 be late; be behind time; come late.

지각[3] [जीगाक] [知覺] **1** [알아서 깨달음] perception; [그 능력] perceptivity; sensory [sense] perception; sensation. 지각하다 perceive; feel. **2** [철] discretion; sense; judg (e) ment; wisdom.

지갑 [जीगाप] [紙匣] (동전 주머니) a (coin) purse; a pocketbook; (지폐 주머니) a wallet; a billfold.

지구 [जीगू] [地球] the earth; the globe

지극 [जीगुक] [至極] 지극하다 extreme; utmost; exceeding. 지극히 extremely; exceedingly; very.

지금 [जीगुम] [只今] **1** the present; the present day [time]; this time [moment]; now. **2** [방금] just (now); only [but] just; but [even] now; [지금 곧] soon; at once; (just) in a moment; this very moment; right now.

지급 [जीगुप] [支給] provision; supply; furnishment; [지불] payment. 지급하다 supply [provide] <a person> with <a thing>; [군인 등에게 의복 등을 내어 줌] issue; furnish; give; pay; grant; allow. 지급하다 grant <a person> traveling allow-ance / pay <a person's> fare <to Pusan.

지나가다 [जीनागादा] go [run] past; go [pass] by; go [pass] along [through]; pass <a place>; (세월이) pass.

지난 [जीनान] [至難] [아주 어려움] extreme difficulty. 지난하다 most [extremely] difficult.

지내다 [जीनेदा] **1** [때를 보내다] pass; spend; pass

one's time. e.g. 하루 [하룻밤]를 지내다 pass a day [night]. **2** [살아 나가다] live; get on [along]. e.g. 편안히 지내다 live comfortable [in comfort] / be comfortably [well] off / be in easy circumstances.**3** [교제 하다] associate <with>; keep company <with>; mix [mingle] <with>. >. e.g. 친하게 지내다 be on intimate terms <with> .**4** [어떤 지위를 누리다] serve <as>; hold <a post>; follow a career. e.g. 오랫동안 외교관을 지낸 사람 a man of long diplomatic career.

지느러미 [जीनुरौमी] a fin; a pinna <*pl.* ~s, -nae>.

지능 [जीनुंग] [**知 能**] intellectual [mental] faculties; mental capacity; intelligence; intellect.

지니다 [जीनिदा] **1** [휴대하다] e.g. 무기를 지니다 carry [be armed with] a weapon. **2** [가지다] have; possess; keep; own. . e.g. 풍부한 자원을 지니다 have ample resources. **3** [간직하다] have; hold <an opinion>; retain <youth>; entertain <an idea>; harbor <hatred>; cherish <hopes>; bear <a grudge against>. e.g. 비밀을 지니다 cherish a secret.

지대[1] [जीदै] [**地帶**] a zone; an area; a region; a belt.

지대[2] [जीदै] [**至大**] 지대하다 the) greatest possible <responsibility>; vast; enormous; immense; very great.

지도[1] [जीदो] [**地圖**] a map; a chart (해도); a plan (도시 등의).

지도[2] [जीदो] [**指 導**] guidance; leading; lead; leadership; direction; coaching (경기 등의). 지도하다 guide; lead; take the lead; give a lead <to a person>; pilot; direct; coach.

지레[1] [जरि] [지렛대] [जरित्तै]a lever; a handspike.

지레[2] [जरि] [미리] beforehand; in advance; [성급히] overhastily; without due consideration.

지뢰 [जीरुवे] [**地雷**] [땅 속에 묻는 폭약] a (land) mine; a ground torpedo.

지르다 [जीरुदा] **1** (소리를). e.g. 공포의 비명을 지르며 with yells of horror. **2** [치다] beat; strike; hit; punch; kick <at>; [박아 넣다] drive in; hammer; wedge in. e.g. 주먹으로 한 대 지르다 give a blow / strike[hit] <a person> with one's fist.**3** (불을). e.g. 불을 지르다 set fire to <a

shed> / set <a house> on fire.

지름 [जीरूम] a diameter.

지리 [जीरी] [地理] 1 [지리학] geography. e.g. 인문[자연 / 정치 / 상업] 지리 human [physical / political / commercial] geogra-phy. **2** [지세,지형] geogra-phical features; topogra-phy.

-지마는 [जीमानन] but; though; although; (and) yet; nevertheless.

지망 [जीमांग] [志望] 1 [바람] a wish; a desire; an ambition 지망하다 원하다] want <to do>; [계획하다] plan <to do>; [신청하다] apply for; [희망하다] wish <to do>. **2** [선택] one's choice.

지명 [जीम्यौंग] [指名] [후보로서 추천하기] nomination; [임명] designation. 지명하다 nominate; designnate; name.

지명 [जीम्यौंग] [地名] a place name.

지목 [जीमोग] [指目] 지목하다 mark out [down] <a thing / a person> for <some purpose>; point out; indicate; spot; put the finger on; suspect.

지문 [जीमुन] [指紋] a fingerprint; a finger mark; a thumb print (엄지손 가락의).

지반 [जीबान] [地盤] 1 [지면] the ground. **2** [기초, 토대] the foundation; base; [성공에의 발판] a foot-hold; position.

지방 [जीबांग] [地方] a locality; a district; a region; an area; a section; (수도 이외의) the provinces; [시골] the country; […부근] neighborhood; vici-nity.

지배 [जीबै] [支配] [처리] management; [관리] control; superintendence; [통치] rule; domination; sway; [지휘] direction; guidance; [문법] government. 지배하다 manage; control; assume control <of>; rule <of>; rule <over>; govern; reign <over>; dominate; have under one's rule; lay hold <on>; hold sway <over>.

지부 [जीबू] [支部] a branch office; (노동 조합 등의) a local (branch).

지불 [जीबुल] [支拂] 1 [돈을 치름] payment; payoff; defrayment; disbursement; discharge. 지불하다 pay (out); make payment; pay [meet] one's bills; settle one's account's; (어음을) meet. **2** ⇨ 지급 (支給)

지불 능력 [जीबुल नुंगन्यौक] sol-vency

지붕 [जीबुंग] a roof.

지새다 [जीसैदा] 1 [달이 지면서 밤이 새다] the day dawns [breaks / cracks]; it dawns. **2** ⇨ 지새우다

지성 [जीसौंग] [知性] intellect; intelligence; mentality.

지속 [जीसोक] [持續] continuance; continuation; maintenance 지속하다 [지탱하다] maintain; sustain; support; keep up; [계속하다] continue; last; remain; [견디다] endure; hold [stand] out.

지시 [जीशी] [指示] indication; denotation; pointing out; instructions; directions; a pointer; [명령] orders; commands; dictation. 지시하다 indi-cate; denote; show; point to; index (out); direct; [지적하다] point out; [명령하다] order; command

지식 [जीशिक] [知識] knowledge; acquaintance; know-how; information (견문); learning (학문); attainment (소양); under-standing (이해).

지어내다 [जीओनेदा] [꾸며내다] cook up; coin; frame up; make up <a story>; fabricate; invent; forge.

지역 [जीयौक] [地域] an area; a region; a district.

지연 [जीयौन] [遲延] delay; retardation; procrastination; postponement. 지연 하다 [연기되다] be post-poned; be put off; [늦어 지다] be delayed; be late; be retarded; be behind time; be overdue.

지열 [जीयौल] [止熱] the abatement of temperature <in sickness>; dropping of temperature. 지열하다 [열이 내리다] one's tempe-rature falls [goes down]; [열을 내리게 하다] lower the temperature; allay [bring down] the fever.

지원 [जीवॉन] [支援] support; backing; aid. 지원하다 support; back [bolster] (up).

지원 [जीवॉन] [志願] [지망] (a) desire; (an) aspiration; [신청] (an) application; [자진함] volunteering. ⇨ 지망 지원하다 desire; wish; aspire to; apply <for>; volunteer <for>.

지위 [जीवी] [地位] (a) rank; [위계] (a) court rank; [신분] (a) position; (다른 것과의 관계에서 본 상대적인 지위) status.

지인 [जीइन] [知人] an acquaintance; a friend

지장 [जीजांग] [支障] [장애] a hindrance; an impediment; [방해] an obstacle; inter-ference; [불편] inconveni-ence; [곤란] (a) difficulty; trouble. e.g. 지장없이 with-out hindrance [a hitch] / smoothly. 지장이 없는 한 if nothing inter-feres. 지장을 초래하다 cause one incon-venience / hinder one / impede / interfere with .... 지장이 없다 [불편이 없다] experience no inconvenience / [곤란이 없다] have no difficulty [trouble] <in doing>

지적 [जीजौक] [知的] Intellectual

지적 [जीचौक] [指摘] indication. 지적하다 point out; indicate; lay a [one's] finger <on>.

지점 [जीजौम] [支店] (은행 등의) a branch (office); (가게의) a branch (store).

지점 [जीजौम] [地點] a spot; a point; a place.

지정 [जीजौंग] [指定] appointment; designation; assignment; specification. 지정하다 appoint; design-nate; assign; name; specify; earmark.

지조 [जीजो] [志操] principle; [절조] constancy; fidelity; integrity.

지존 [जीजोन] [至尊] [더없이 존귀함] the Most Revered; [임금] his Majesty the King.

지주 [जीजू] [地主] [토지의 소유자] a landowner; (소작인 쪽에서 본 경우) a landlord; a landholder.

지지 [जीजी] [支持] [지원] support; backing; [애고] patronage. 지지하다 support; back (up); give [render] support <to>; uphold; stand by; hold up; sustain; prop(up).

지진 [जीजीन] [地震] an earthquake (shock); a seismic [terrestrial] tremor.

지질 [जीजील] [地質] geology; geological featu-res; [토질] the nature of the soil.

지참 [जीछाम] [持參] 지참하다 [가져오다] bring <a thing> (with one); [가져가다] take <a thing> with one; carry; bear.

지척 [जीछौक] [咫尺] a very short distance; an inch.

지체 [जीछे] [遲滯] (a) delay; [지불의 의무를 지연] arrears; retardation; procrastination. 지체하다 delay; tarry; defer; hold off; procrastinate; be in arrears.

지출 [जीछुल] [支出] [지불함] (an) expenditure; disbursements; [경비] expenses. 지출하다 pay [out]; spend; expend; disburse.

지침 [जीछिम] [指針] **1** [계기의 침] an indicator; a pointer; an index <*pl.* ~es, -dices>; [자석의 침] a compass needle. **2** [길잡이] a guide; a guiding principle. e.g. 그는 내게 생애의 지침을 주었다 He has given me the principle that guides my life.

지키다 [चिखीदा] **1** [살피다] watch; keep a watch; (호위) stand guard; guard; (보호) protect; (방어) defend. e.g. 적으로부터 나라를 지키다 defend the country against the enemy.

2 [준수하다] keep; fulfill; observe; follow; stick [adhere] <to>(주의 등을). e.g. 약속을 지키다 keep one's promise [word].

지탄 [जीथान] [指彈] 지탄하다 [배척하다] snap one's fingers <at>; shun; disdain; scorn; [비난하다] criticize unfavorably [adversely]; censure; blame; reproach; denounce.

지폐 [जीफ्ये] [紙弊] paper money; a bill; a (bank-) note.

지표 [जीप्यो] [地表] the surface of the earth.

지하 [जीहा] [地下] 1 [땅 속]. e.g. 지하의 underground / subterranean. 2 [저승] Hades; the other world; the underworld; [무덤] a grave e.g. 지하에 잠들다 sleep in the grave.

지향 [जीह्यांग] [志向] (an) intention; (an) inclination; an aim. 지향하다 [जीह्यांग] intend [aspire] <to do>; aim.

지혈 [जीह्यौल] [止血] stopping of bleeding; stanching; hemostasis; haemostasis. 지혈하다 check the bleeding; control hemorrhage

지형 [जीह्यौग] [地形] (한 지역의) topography; geographical features; [땅의 형상] landform.

지휘 [जीह्वी] [指揮] command; [지시] direc-tion(s); instructions; [감독] superintendence; supervision. 지휘하다 command; lead; head; direct; instruct; preside over <a meeting>; su-perintend; take [assume / hold] command <of an army>; (악단을) direct; conduct; lead; baton.

직각 [जीक्काक] [直角] [數] a right angle.

직결 [जीकक्यौल] [直結] direct connection; [電] direct coupling. 직결하다 connect [link] directly <with>.

직계 [जीकक्ये] [直系] a direct line.

직권 [जीकक्वॉन] [職權] one's official authority.

직립 [जीक्निप] [直立] e.g. 직립의 straight / upright / [수직의] perpendicular. 직립하다 stand up straight.

직면 [जीगम्यौन] [直面] 직면하다 face (up to); confront; be confronted with [by]; be faced with; come face to face with; be up against.

직무 [जीग्मू] [職務] (a) duty; an office; a function; a job.

직물 [जीग्मुल] [織物] textiles; (textile) fabrics; [천] cloth.

직선 [जीकसौन] [直線] a straight [right] line; a bee-line.

직시 [जीक्शी] [直視] looking <a person> in the face. 직시하다 look <a person>

in the face; look squarely [straight] at <a person>.

직업 [जीगौप] [職 業] an occupation; a calling; a vocation; (전문적인 사회 활동) a profession; (장사, 수공 등의) a trade.

직역 [जीग्यौक] [直譯] literal [verbatim / word-for-word] translation. 직역 하다 translate literally [word-for-word].

직원 [जीग्वॉन] [職員] (전체) the staff; the personnel; the faculty (대학의);(개인) a member of the staff.

직장 [जीक्चांग] [職場] [일터] one's place of work; one's job (site); one's post; a workshop(공장).

직전 [जीक्चौन] [直前] e.g. 끓기 직전의 물 water just short of boiling.

직접 [जीक्चौप] [直接] e.g. 직접 얻은 정보 firsthand information <about>.

직조 [जीक्चो] [織造] weaving. 직조하다 weave.

직종 [जीक्चोंग] [職種] a type of occupation; an occupational category.

직진 [जीक्चिन] [直 進] 직진하다 go straight on [ahead]; make straight for; make a straight drive [advance] <to>.

직책 [जीक्छैक] [職 責] responsibilities pertaining to one's work [job]; one's duty.

직통 [जीक्थोंग] [直通] direct communication [service]; (교통 기관의) through service [traffic]. 직통하다 communicate directly <with>; be in direct communications <with>.

직함 [जीख्वाम] [職銜] a title; a handle (to one's name).

직행 [जीख्वैंग] [直行] going straight [direct]; through running; [정차하지 않음] nonstop. 직행하다 go straight [direct] <to>; run [go] through <to> (기차가).

진- [जीन] [眞] [참된] real; true; [진짜의] genuine.

진격 [जीनग्यौक] [進擊] a march onward; a charge; a drive; a push; an advance; an attack. 진격하다 charge <at / on>; attack; make an attack <on>; make a drive [push] <on / upon>; march <upon>; advance <on / against>; assault.

진공 [जीन्गोंग] [眞空] a vacuum <*pl.* ~s, vacua>.

진귀 [जीन्गुइ] [珍貴] 진귀하다 rare and precious [valuable].

진급 [जीन्गुप] [進級] (a) promotion 진급하다 be promoted; win promotion.

진급 시험 [जीन्गुप शिहौम] an examination for promotion.

진단 [जीन्दान] [診斷] (a) diagnosis <*pl.* -noses>; diagnostication. 진단하다

diagnose; make a diagnosis <of>; give one's diagnosis <of.>.

진담 [जीन्दाम] [眞談] a serious [an earnest] talk.

진도 [जीन्दो] [進度] progress.

진동 [जीन्दोंग] [振動] (an) oscillation; (a) vibration; a swing. 진동하다 oscillate; swing; vibrate; librate; move to and fro.

진득거리다 [जीन्दुक्कौरिदा] 1 [들러붙다] keep sticking [holding on / adhering].2 [검질기겨 끊어지지 않다] resist cutting.

진리 [जील्ली] [眞理] truth; true principles.

진맥 [जीन्मैक] [診脈] feeling the pulse (for diagnosis). 진맥하다 feel the pulse <of>.

진보 [जीन्बो] [進步] [진척] progress; [전진] (an) advance; [개선] (an) improvement <in>. 진보 하다 (make) progress; advance; improve.

진수 [जीन्सू] [珍羞] rare dainties; delicacies; food of delicate flavor (u) r. **진수 성찬** rich viands and sumptuous fare.

진수 [जीन्सू] [眞髓] [사물의 본질적인 골자] the essence; [정수,중심적 요점] the quintessence; [핵심] the soul; the gist; the core.

진술 [जीन्सुल] [陳述] a statement; a deposition (증인의). 진술하다 state <one's case>; set forth; give [make] a statement; expound [explain] <one's views on a subject>; lay <one's views> before <another>.

진실 [जीन्शिल] [眞實] (the) truth; truthfulness; sincerity. 진실하다 true; truthful; sincere; genuine.

진압 [जीनाप] [鎭壓] suppression; repression; subjugation. 진압하다 su-ppress; repress; subdue; quell; subjugate; put down.

진열 [जीन्यौल] [陳列] [예술 작품,제품 등의 전시](an) exhibition; [죽 벌이어 보이기](a) display; show; arrangement. 진열하다 exhibit; display; put on show; arrange.

진입 [जीनिप] [進入] entry <into a place>; penetration. 진입하다 enter; go [penetrate] into; make one's way <into>.

진작 [जीन्जाक] [좀더 일찍,그 때에] then and there; on the spot; at once; on that occasion; [벌써] earlier.

진전 [進展] [जीन्जौन] progress; [발전] development. 진전하다 progress; develop

진정 [जीन्जौंगहादा] [鎭靜] calm; quiet; tranquil (l) ity; pacification. 진정하다 calm;

quiet; (고통 등을) soothe; allay; appease; abate; (소동 등을) tranquil (l) ize; pacify.

진주 [जीन्जू] [眞珠] a pearl.

진지 [जीन्जी] [眞摯] [참되고 착실함] seriousness; earnestness; soberness. 진지하다 serious; earnest; sober.

진짜 [जीन्चा] [眞-] a genuine article; the real stuff [thing].

진찰 [जीन्छाल] [診察] (a) medical examination. 진찰하다 examine [see/ have a look at] <a patient>.

진출 [जीन्छुल] [進出] advance; march; [軍] debouchment. 진출하다 advance <into>; go [launch] <into>; find one's way <into>; branch out <into>; [軍] debouch.

진학 [जीन्हाक] [進學] entrance into a school of higher grade. 진학하다 go on to the next stage of one's education.

진행 [जीन्हैंग] [進行] progress; progression; (an) advance; march; onward movement. 진행 하다 advance; be advan-ced; progress; make prog-ress; proceed; go on [forward]; make headway; (탈것이) run; (배가) proceed.

진화 [जीन्ह्वा] [進化] [生] evolution; progress. 진화하다 evolve [develop] <from ... into ...>.

진화 [जीन्ह्वा] [鎭火] putting out a fire. 진화하다 (불이) be extinguished; be put out; (불을) extinguish; put out; bring under control.

진흙 [जीन्हुक] **1** [물기 섞인 흙] mud; mire; dirt. **2** [점토] clay.

-질 [जील] [노릇,짓의 뜻] (the act of) doing. e.g. 양치 질 rinsing the mouth.

질 [जील] [質] **1** [품질,소질] quality. **2** [자질] nature; [체질] constitution; [특질] characteristic; [본질] property; [품성] character.

질겁하다 [जील्गौफादा] be appalled; be astounded; be frightened; be scared; start; take fright; be surprised; be startled; be taken aback.

질기다 [जील्गिदा] **1** (고기 등이) tough; leathery. e.g. 질긴 고기 tough meat.**2** [내구성이 있다] durable; lasting; enduring. e.g. 질긴 천 coarse cloth. **3** (성질이) tenacious; perti-nacious; persistent; perse-vering; tough. e.g. 성질이 질긴 남자 a man of tenacity / a tough guy.

질량 [जीलल्यांग] [質量] [理] mass; quantity of matter.

질리다 [जीलिलदा] **1** [진력나다] be disgusted [bored] <with>; be sick <of>; be fed up <with>; have had enough <of>; [혼나다] have a bitter experience. e.g. 이번 일에 질려서 this taught me a lesson and .... **2** (기가) be amazed [stunned / aghast / dumfounded]; [겁내다] be cowed; cower; (파랗게) be overawed; turn (ghastly) pale. e.g. 무서워서 파랗게 질리다 turn deadly pale[as white as a sheet] with fright / blanch with fear.

질문 **[जील्मुन]** **[質問]** a question; a query; an inquiry; an interrogation; a quiz 질문하다 ask <a person> a question; put a question <to a person>; a question to <a person>; interrogate; quiz; (국회 에서) interpellate

질색 **[जील्सैक]** **[窒塞]** [아주 싫음] disgust; detestation; abomination; shock; horror. 질색하다 hate; detest; loathe; abhor

질서 **[जील्सौ]** **[秩序]** (public) order; [규율] discipline; [체계] system; regularity; method.

질시 **[जील्शी]** **[嫉視]** jealousy; regarding with jealousy [dislike]; jealous looks. 질시하다 regard <a person> with jealousy; keep a jealous eye on <a person>.

질식 **[जील्शिक]** **[窒息]** suffocation; asphyxiation; asphyxia; asphyxy. 질식하다 be suffocated [choked / stifled / smothered]

질의 **[जीरूइ]** **[質疑]** a question; an interrogation; an inquiry.

질질 **[जील्जिल]** **1** [물건을 끄는 모양] draggingly; trailingly. e.g. 지친 발을 질질 끌다 drag [shuffle] one's weary feet **2** [오래 끄는 모양] long; draggingly; lingering. e.g. 질질 끄는 병 a lingering disease. **3** [흐르는 모양] tricklingly; dribbling. e.g. 기름기가 질질 흐르는 얼굴 an oily face

질책 **[जील्छैक]** **[叱責]** (a) reproof; reproach; rebuke; reprimand. 질책하다 scold; reprove; reproach; rebuke; reprimand; call <a person> to task; give <a person> a talking-to; call <a person> on the carpet.

질타 **[जील्था]** **[叱咤]** (a) scolding. 질타하다 scold; rate; give <a person> a <good> scolding.

질투 **[जील्थू]** **[嫉妬]** jealousy; envy; heartburning; <비유> the green-eyed monster (▷ envy는 자기도 같은 것을 갖고 싶은 기분, jealousy 는 자기가 갖고 있지 않은 것을 남이 갖고 있을 때 증오하는 마음의

뜻으로 보다 강한 감정을 나타냄). 질투하다be [feel] jealous <of / over>; envy <a person>; be [become] envious <of>; be green with envy.

짊어지다 [जीलमौजिदा] **1** [등에 짐을 메다] take <a burden> on one's [the] back; shoulder; bear. e.g. 무거운 짐을 짊어지다 bear a heavy burden. **2** [부담 등을 맡다] encumber [saddle / burden] oneself <with>; be saddled <with>. e.g. 장래의 국가 운명을 짊어질 사람들 those who will shoulder the future destiny of our country.

짐 [जीम] **1** [하물] a load; a burden; [뱃짐] a cargo <*pl.* ~ es, ~ s>; [화물] goods; a freight; [수화물] luggage; baggage;a package. e.g. 무거운[가벼운] 짐 a heavy [light] load. **2** [부담] a burden; a load; an encumbrance (특히 어린이). e.g. 마음의 짐 a load [weight] on one's mind. 짐이 되다 be a burden to one.

짐스럽다 [जीमसुरौप्ता] burdensome; cumbersome; troublesome.

짐승 [जीम्सुंग] a beast; a brute; an animal.

짐작 [जीम्जाक] [斟酌] [어림] guess; guesswork; (a) presumeption; (a) conjecture; (an) inference; (an) estimation; (a) surmise; [판단] judgment. 짐작하다 guess; presume; conjecture; infer; surmise; estimate; [판단하다] judge; gather.

집 [जीब] **1** [가옥] a house; a home; a dwelling; an abode; a residence e.g. 기와집 a tile-roofed house **2** [가정,집안] a home; a family; a household. e.g. 우리 집 아이들 my [our] children.**3** [영업 장소] a place; a house; [상점] a store; a shop; [음식점] a restaurant. e.g. 빵집 a bakery / a bakeshop. 술집 a bar / a saloon / a tavern / a public house.

집게 [जीप्के] tongs; flat pliers; pincers; nippers.

집게손가락 [जीप्केसोन्काराक] a forefinger; an index finger; the first finger.

집결 [जीप्क्योल] [**集結**] concentration; collection; (군대의) assembly. 집결하다 [모으다] concentrate; collect; be concentrated.

집계 [जीप्क्ये] [**集計**] an aggregate. 집계하다 totalize; combine into a total.

집권 [जीपक्वोन] [**執權**] assuming [taking] the reins of government; coming into power [office]. 집권하다 assume [take (over)] the reins of government; take [win / attain] power; come [get] into power [office]; come in; take the helm of state affairs.

집다 [जीप्ता] pick [take] up <a thing>.

집단 [जीप्तान] [**集團**] a group; a mass.

집대성 [जीप्तैसौंग] [**集大成**] e.g.그것은 윌리엄 포크너 연구의 집대성이다 It is a compilation of all of the studies made so far on William Faulkner. 집대성하다 compile <all available data> into one book; make [give] a comprehensive [comp-lete] survey of <past studies on a subject>.

집들이 [जीप्तुरी] a house-warming (party).

집세 [जीप्से] [**-貰**] a (house) rent; a rental (집세의 수입액).

집안 [जीबान] **1** [가정] a family; a household; a [one's] home. e.g. 온 집안 the whole family / all the family **2** [일가] a family; a clan; [친척] one's relatives; one's kindred; [가문] the (social) standing [status] of a family. e.g. 박씨 집안 the Park's clan [family]. **3** [집 내부]] the inside of a house. e.g. 집안의 공기 the indoor air.

집약 [जीब्याक] [**集約**] e.g. 집약적인 intensive. 집약하다 do <some-thing> intensively; adopt an intensive method.

집어 주다 [जीब्याक जुदा] **1** [건네주다] pass; hand (over) <to>; reach; give; let <a person> have; help <a person to some cake>. **2** (돈을) slip <money> into <a person's> hand [pocket]; (팁을) tip <a porter>; (뇌물을) grease [tickle] <a person's palm; bribe.

집어넣다 [जीबौनौथा] put [take / bring] in; throw [cast / fling] in [into].

집어먹다 [जीबौमौक्ता] [음식을 집어서 먹다] pick up and eat.

집어삼키다 [जीबौसाम्खिदा] **1** [입에 넣어 삼키다] swallow; eat. **2** [가로채다] embezzle; appropriate (unlawfully); swallow up.

집요 [जीब्यो] [**執拗**] [완고함] obstinacy; persistence. 집요하다 [완고하다] obstinate; stubborn; [끈덕지다] tenacious; persistent.

집적거리다 [जीप्चौक्कौरिदा] **1** [손대다] meddle with [in]; have a hand [finger / concern] in; dip one's fingers into; turn [put] one's hand to. **2** [건드리다] tease; harass; rag; peck at <a person>;

needle.

집주인 [जीप्चुइन] [-主人] **1** [가정의 주인] the master of a house; the head of a family.**2** [집임자] the owner of a house; a landlord (남자).

집중 [जीप्चुंग] [集中] concentration; convergence; centralization. 집중하다 [모으다] concentrate <upon>; focus <upon>; centralize <upon>; mass <troops>; [모이다] converge <into / on>; focus <on>; center <on / around>.

집집마다 [जीप्चिम्म्दा] at every door [house]; from door to door.

집착 [जीप्छाक] [執着] [애착] attachment <to / for>; [고집] persistence <in>; tenacity; pertinacity. 집착하다 be attached <to>; adhere [stick / cling] <to>; hold fast <to>.

집필 [जीप्फिल] [執筆] writing. 집필하다 write; contribute.

집행 [जीफैंग] [執行] 집행하다 execute; discharge; perform; hold; carry into effect [execution]; put into effect; carry out; exercise; conduct.

집회 [जीफ्वे] [集會] a meeting; an assembly; (비공식의) a gathering. 집회하다 assemble; gather; meet together; hold a meeting.

짓 [जीत्] [행위] an act; a deed; behavior; conduct; [소행] a work; <one's> doings.

짓거리 [जीगौरी] **1** [흥겨워서 멋으로 하는 짓] a gesture [an act] out of merriment; a bit of fun; one's sportive doings. **2** ⇨ 짓.

짓다 [जीत्ता] **1** [만들다] make; manufacture; fashion; tailor. e.g. 잘 지은 옷 well [handsomely] tailored [cut] clothes. **2** [건조하다] build; erect; construct. e.g. 집을 짓다 build a house **3** [작성하다] write; compose; make. e.g. 시 [소설]를 짓다 write a poem [novel]. **4** (밥을) boil; cook; prepare. e.g. 밥을 짓다 cook [boil] rice

짓무르다 [जीम्मुरुदा] be gangrenous; inflame; blister; fester.

짓밟다 [जीप्पाल्ता] **1** [밟아서 뭉개다] trample [tread] <flowers> underfoot; stamp down (to the ground). e.g. 군중이 공원의 화초를 짓밟았다 The crowd trampled on the flowers in the public garden. **2** [모욕하다] despise; spurn; slight; set <a person> at naught; [유린하다] trample upon [down]; tread down e.g. 남의 감정을

짓밟다 trample on a person's feelings / hurt a person's feelings

징검다리 [जीगौमदारी] a stepping-stone.

징계 [जीग्ये] [**懲戒**] disciplinary action; [견책] a reprimand. 징계하다 reprimand; take disciplinary action

징그럽다 [जीगुरौप्ता] creepy; crawly; disgusting; loathsome; abhorrent; revolting; detestable; repulsive; <서술적> feel a chill creep over one. e.g. 징그러운 녀석 a disgusting fellow / <美> a creep.

징발 [जीम्बाल] [**徵發**] requisition; commandeering; levy; forage (마초 등의). 징발하다 requisition <from>; put <a thing> in requisition; lay <a thing> under requisition; (병사를) levy.

징벌 [जीम्बौल] [**懲罰**] punishment; (교정의 뜻을 내포하여) discipline; chastisement. 징벌하다 punish; discipline; castigate; chastise.

징병 [जीगब्यौग] [**徵兵**] [군무에 강제 모집] conscription; the drath; (compulsory) military service. 징병하다 conscript; enlist; recruit; drath; enroll; call up.

징수 [जीम्सू] [**徵收**] [조세, 수수료 등을 거둠] a levy; [대금 등을 거둠] collection. 징수하다 levy; collect.

징역 [जीम्यौक] [**懲役**] penal servitude; imprisonment <with hard labor>. e.g. 무기 징역 life impri-sonment.

징조 [जीम्जो] [**徵兆**] an omen <of disaster>; a portent (흉조); [조짐] a precursor; a premonition; a symptom.

징크스 [जीख्रुसु] a jinx. e.g. 징크스를 깨다 smash [break] a jinx.

짖다 [जीत्ता] (개가) bark <at a stranger>;(사냥개가) bay; (개,늑대 등이) howl; (사자,호랑이 등이) roar; (까막까치가) caw; croak.

짙다 [जीत्ता]**1** [빛깔이 강하다] deep; rich; dark. e.g. 짙은 빨강 dark [deep] red.**2** [농도,밀도가 높다] thick; heavy. e.g. 짙은 안개 a dense [thick] fog

짚 [जिप] (a) straw.

짚다 [जिप्ता] **1** [지팡이,손을 바닥에 대고 의지하다] rest <on>; lean <on>; support by; place [put] one's hand <on a cane> for support. . e.g. 지팡이를 짚다 use a cane [stick]. **2** [손을 대어 살며시 누르다] touch; feel; pat. e.g. 맥을 짚다 take [feel / examine] <a person's> pulse / have one's fingers on <a

person's> pulse. **3** [헤어보다] count on the fingers. e.g. 날수를 짚다 count the days on one's fingers. **4** [짐작하다] guess; give [take / make] a guess <at>; have a shot. e.g. 그는 시합의 결과를 잘못 짚었다 He made an error in judging how the game would go.

짜깁기 **[चागीप्की]** invisible mending. e.g. 양복을 짜깁기하다 do invisible mending.

짜다[1] **[चादा]** **1** [만들다] put [piece / fit] together; assemble; construct; make; frame; fix up. e.g. 발판을 짜다 put up scaffolding **2** [조직,편성하다] form; organize; compose. e.g. 배구팀을 짜다 form a volleyball team.**3** [직조하다] weave; inweave; interweave; net <a hammock>. e.g. 금실을 짜 넣은 허리띠 a belt interwoven with gold thread.

짜다[2] **[चादा]** **1** [물기를 빼려고 비틀다] wring; squeeze. e.g. 수건을 짜다 wring (water from) a towel / give a towel a wring / squeeze out water from a towel. **2** [액체를 내다] squeeze; press; extract. e.g. 레몬즙을 짜다 press juice out of a lemon. **3** [억지로 내다] press out; squeeze. e.g. 머리를 짜다 rack one's brains

짜다[3] **[चादा]** **1** [소금 맛이 있다] salty; salt; briny; <서술적> taste [be] salty. e.g. 짠 음식salty food **2** [달갑지 않다] unpleasant; displeased; disagreeable. e.g. 마음에 짜다 feel unpleasant / be dispelased <with a person>. **3** [인색하다] grudging; stingy; <서술적> grudge; begrudge. e.g. 그는 점수가 너무 짜다 He is a hard marker [grader].

-짜리[चारी] [… 값어치의 물건] a thing worth .... e.g. 천 원짜리 (지폐) a 1,000-won bill [note] / (물건) an article worth [valued at] 1,000 won / one-thousand-won article.

짜릿하다 **[चारीथादा]** e.g. 짜릿한 풍자 pungent [piquant] sarcasm.

짜이다 **[चाइदा]** **1** (피륙 등이) be [get] woven; be [get] knitted. e.g. 그 천은 면사로 짜여 있다 The fabric is woven of cotton. **2** (규격,규모 등이) be [get] put [fitted / pieced] together; (조직,이론 등이) be [get] formed [framed / structured / organized / arranged]. e.g. 내 생각이

간신히 짜여졌다 My ideas have finally taken shape [come together].

짜임 [**चाइम**] being put [fitted / pieced] together; [조직] system; organization; [구성] composition; constitution; [구조] construction; structure; framework; makeup.

짜임새 [**चाइम्सै**] structure; make; makeup; constitution. e.g. 짜임새 있는 보고 a well-organized report.

짜증 [**चाजुंग**] fret; irritation; vexation; anger; annoyance. e.g. 나는 교통 체증에 휘말려서 짜증이 났다 Caught in a traffic jam, I grew impatient.

짝 [**चाक**] [쌍을 이룬 것 중의 하나] one of a pair [couple]; a counterpart; a parallel; (사람의) one's pal [partner / mate / fellow]; one's spouse (배우자). e.g. 나는 그와 짝을 지었다 I paired with him. / He and I formed a pair 짝(이) 맞다 match with another; pair; make [form] a pair [set]; form a counterpart [parallel] <to>. 짝(을) 맞추다 make a pair of <two things>; pair <two things>; match <colors>.

짝짓다 [**चाक्चीत्ता**] make [form] a pair; form a counterpart [parallel] to mate [pal up] <with>; make a match; mate. e.g. 새를 짝짓다 mate a bird.

짝짝이 [**चाक्चागी**] an odd [unmatched] pair <of shoes [socks]>; a wrongly matched [mismat-ched / mismated] pair. e.g. 그녀는 짝짝이 장갑을 끼고 있었다 She was wearing an odd pair of gloves.

짤따랗다 [**चाल्तारात्था**] shortish; rather short; <서술적> be on the short side. **짤막하다** shortish; choppy; <서술적> be on the short side. e.g. 짤막한 인사말] a brief address.

짧다 [**चाल्ता**] **1** [시간,길이가] short; brief; abbreviated <costume>. e.g. 짧은 생애 a short life / a brief span of life. **2** [부족하다] wanting; short; lacking; deficient; insufficient; poor. e.g. 짧은 밑천 a small capital **3** [식성이 까다롭다] particular <about>; fastidious <about>. e.g. 입이 짧다 be particular [fastidious] about one's food / eat like a bird / have a small appetite / be a small [light] eater.

짬 [**चाम**] [자유로운 시간] spare [free] time; leisure; [연극에서 대사나 동작의 중단 시간] a pause; an interval. e.g. (대본에서) 짬 [**चाम**] pause. 아버지는 짬만 있으면 독서하신다

My father spends all his spare time (in) reading.

짬나다 [चाम्नादा] = (이) 나다).

짭짤하다 [चाप्चारहादा] **1** [맛이] nice and salty; have a good salty taste <to>; tasty. e.g. 짭짤한 고기 반찬 a nicely salted meat dish. **2** [뜻대로 잘되어 구격 (具格)이 맞다] acceptable; respectable; decent; honorable; becoming; befitting; worthy <of>.

-째 [चै] [순서,등급] a rank; a grade; -th; ahead; beyond; off; away. e.g. 첫[둘 / 셋]째 first [second / third].

째다 [चैदा] [찢다] cut open <a boil>; open; lance; incise. e.g. 종기를 째다 lance a boil.

째(어)지다 [चैजीदा] split; rend; tear; rip; cleave. e.g. 깃발이 바람에 갈가리 째졌다 The flag was torn to ribbons by the wind.

짹짹 [चैक्चैक] e.g. 새 새끼가 둥지에서 짹짹 울고 있다 The baby birds are chirping [cheeping] in the nest.

쨍그랑 [चैंग्गुरांग] with a clink [clank / clang]. e.g. 접시가 마룻바닥에 쨍그랑 떨어졌다 The dishes fell on the floor with a crash.

쨍쨍 [चैंग्चैंग] <the sun shines> blazing (ly); bright (ly); glaring (ly). e.g. 해가 모래 위에 쨍쨍 내리쬐었다 The sun glared down upon the sand.

-쩍다 [चौक्ता] feel; give [have] a feeling <of>. e.g. 겸연쩍다be abashed [shamefaced].

쩔쩔매다 [चौल्चौल्मैदा] fluster oneself; be all in a hurry; be flurried; be thrown into consternation; be going round in circles. e.g. 바빠서 쩔쩔매다 be so busy that one doesn't know the left from the right.

쩝쩝 [चौप्चौब] [입맛을 다시는 모양] licking one's chops; smacking one's lips. e.g. 입맛을 쩝쩝 다시다 lick one's chops / smack one's lips.

쩡쩡 [चौंग्चौंग] **1** [권세가 대단한 모양] resounding; powerful; mighty. e.g. 쩡쩡한 정치가an influential statesman. **2** [갈라지는 소리] cracking. e.g. 얼음이 쩡쩡 갈라졌다 The ice cracked. / The ice broke [gave way] with a crack.

쩨쩨하다 [चेचेहादा] **1** [인색하다] stingy; niggardly; miserly; close-[tight-] fisted; illiberal. e.g. 쩨쩨한 사람 a miser / a stingy person. **2** [치사하다] mean; [초라하다] poor;

shabby; [옹졸하다] narrow-minded; small <mind>. e.g. 쩨쩨한 근성 a mean spirit.

쪼개다 **[चोगेदा]** split; break; divide. e.g. 둘로 쪼개다 split [divide] <a thing> in [into] two.

쪼다 **[चोदा]** (새가) pick(at); pick up; peck(at); dab. e.g. 새가 빵을 쪼 (아먹)고 있다 The bird is pecking at the bread.

쪼들리다 **[चोदुल्लीदा]** be hard pressed; be oppressed. e.g. 돈에 쪼들리다 be pressed [strapped] for money

쪽[1] **[चोक]** [조각] a piece; a slice; a cut; a plank. e.g. 마늘 한 쪽 a clove of garlic. 참외 한 쪽 a slice of melon.

쪽[2] **[चोक]** **1** [방향] a direction; a way; [측면] a side; [곳] a part; a quarter. e.g. 다리의 오른 쪽에 on the right side of the bridge. **2** (당사자 사이의) a side; a part. e.g. 내 쪽의[에서는] on my part [side].

쪽지 **[चोक्ची]** [-紙] a slip of paper; a tag; a note [message] left behind. e.g. 쪽지에 몇 자 적다 jot a few words down on a slip.

쫄딱 **[चोल्ताक]** completely; wholly; altogether; utterly. e.g. 쫄딱 망하다 go completely to the dogs.

쫑긋거리다 **[चोंग्गुत्कोरीदा]** (귀를) move the ears; cock [prick up / strain] one's ears. e.g. 그 말은 양귀를 쫑긋거렸다 The horse cocked up the ears.

쫓겨나다 **[चोत्क्योनादा]** [내쫓기다] be expelled; be turned [got / put / sent / driven] out; be routed out <of>; be hustled out <of town>; be kicked out <of>; (지위에서) be ousted [expelled / dis-lodged] <from a position>; [해고당하다] be dismi-ssed; lose one's place. e.g. 집에서 쫓겨 나다 be thrown out of the house

쫓기다 **[चोत्कीदा]** [뒤쫓기다] be pursued [chased] (ather); be run [taken] ather; be trailed; be hunted (up); be coursed; be hounded. e.g. 쫓기는 사람 the pursued.

쫓다 **[चोत्ता]** **1** [물리치다] drive out [away]; shoo away; expel. e.g. 새를 쫓다shoo birds away. **2** (특히 범인P사냥감 등을) pursue; chase; run ather. e.g. 쫓는 사람 the pursuer.

쫓아가다 **[चोछगादा]** **1** (뒤쫓아서) go in pursuit; pursue; follow; run ather.

e.g. 도망하는 적을 쫓아가다 give chase to the retreating enemy. **2** [추종하다] follow suit; follow in <a person's> footsteps; take ather; copy ather. e.g. 남이 하는 대로 쫓아가다 do the same as others do / follow suit. copy ather others.

쫓아내다 [चोछानेदा] drive out; expel; evict; dismiss; fire; sack. e.g. 학생들을 학교에서 쫓아내다 expel a student from school.

쫓아다니다 [चोछादानीदा] [여기저기 뒤쫓다] chase; run [chase] ather; [뛰어 다님] run about [round]; [붙어 다님] follow about [around]; dangle about [ather]. e.g. 여자 뒤를 쫓아다니다 dangle ather girls.

쫓아오다 [चोछाओदा] **1** [추적해 오다] come in pursuit; follow at <a person's> heels. e.g. 나를 쫓아오너라 Follow me. 아이가 내 뒤를 쫓아왔다 A child came running ather me. **2** [바싹 따라오다] keep up with; catch up. e.g. 너무 빨리 걸어서 그는 쫓아오지 못했다 I walked too fast for him to catch up with me.

쬐다[1] [च्वेदा] [햇빛이 비치다] shine on [over]; beat [strike] (down) on. e.g. 볕이 내리쬐다 burn

쬐다[2] [च्वेदा] **1** [불기운을 몸에 쐬다 warm oneself <at [by] the fire>; have a warm [heat] <by [at] the fire>; take warmth; put <a thing> over the fire; hold up to the heat. e.g. 손을 불에 쬐어 녹이다 warm one's hands over a fire. **2** [볕을 몸에 받다] expose <a thing> to the sun; bathe [bask] in the sun; [말리다] dry <a thing> in the sun. e.g. 햇볕을 쬐다

쭈그러지다 [चूगुरौजीदा] **1** [우그러져 작아지다] get pressed [squeezed] out of shape; be crushed. e.g. 쭈그러진 모자 a battered hat. **2** [쪼글쪼글해지다] get lean; grow gaunt; wither; shrivel. e.g. 쭈그러진 얼굴 a worn face.

쭈그리다 [चूगुरीदा] [우그리다] crouch; squat; bend low; stoop. e.g. 쭈그린 자세로in a squatting position.

쭈글쭈글 [चूगुल्चुगुल] 쭈글쭈글하다withered; wrinkled. e.g. 쭈글쭈글하게 구겨진 옷 crumpled clothes.

쭈뼛하다 [चूप्प्यौथादा] <서술적> be bulged out; <one's hair> be standing on end. e.g.머리끝이 쭈뼛해지다feel a shudder.

-쯤 [चुम] **1** [정도] about (so

ㅈ

much); approximately; around; nearly; ... or so; some (▷ some 은 주로 수사에 붙음: some 20 boys). e.g.30쯤 되는 신사 a gentleman of about thirty / a thirtyish gentleman. **2** [무렵] at about (a certain time). e.g. 한 시쯤 about one o'clock. **3** [까지] by (a certain time). e.g. 내일쯤 by tomorrow

찌개 [चीगै] a pot stew.

찌그러지다 [चीगुरौजीदा] e.g. 구두 모양이 찌그러졌다 My shoes have lost their shape.

찌꺼기 [चीकौगी] [침전물] dregs; (주류의) lees; (버캐) scum; (커피 등의) grounds; sediment; residuum. e.g. 커피 찌꺼기 coffee grounds.

찌다[1] [चीदा] [살이 올라서 뚱뚱해지다] grow fat; gain weight; put on flesh. e.g. 살찐 암탉 a fat hen.

찌다[2] [चीदा] [날씨가 더워지다] get steaming hot; be sultry; be humid. e.g. 찌는 듯한 더위 the sweltering heat.

찌다[3] [चीदा] [뜨거운 김에 익히다] steam. e.g. 찐 고구마 steamed sweet-potatoes.

찌르다 [चीरुदा] [뾰족한 것으로 세차게 들이밀다] pierce; prick; stab; thrust. e.g. 음식을 젓가락으로 콕콕 찌르다 pick at the food with chopsticks.

찌푸리다 [चीफूरीदा] **1** [날씨가 흐리다] get cloudy; cloud over. e.g. 찌푸린 날씨 cloudy weather **2** [얼굴을 찡그리다] let (one's face) cloud over; frown; scowl; wrinkle up. e.g. 그는 눈살을 찌푸리며 이야기 했다 He talked with his brows knitted.

찍다 [चीक्ता] **1** [인쇄물, 도장 등을 누르다] imprint; impress; stamp. e.g. 패스포트에 검인을 찍다 stamp a passport. **2** [묻히다] dip <into>. e.g. 펜을 잉크에 찍다 dip the pen into the ink. 설탕을 찍어 먹다 eat <a thing> with sugar. **3** [점을 표시하다] place <a dot>; mark with a point; dot; point off; earmark; designate. e.g. 소수점을 찍다 place a decimal point. **4** [사진을 박다] take <a photograph>; shoot; snap. e.g. 사진을 찍었다 I had my picture taken.

찍히다 [चीख्वीदा] get imprinted [impressed / stamped]; get dipped <into>; get pointed off [earmarked / designated]; get chopped [hacked / cut]; get punched; get taken (사진이); get hooked.

찔끔거리다 [चीलकुमकौरीदा] trickle; dribble; fall [run down]

off and on. e.g. 걸핏하면 눈물을 찔끔거리다 be maudlin / be sloppy / slobber.

찔리다 [चील्लीदा] [찌름을 당하다] get <something> pierced [stabbed / pricked / thrust into]; (가슴에) go home to one's heart. e.g. 가시에 손을 찔리다get a hand pricked by a thorn.

찜 [चीम] a steamed dish. e.g. 닭찜 steam chicken.

찜질 [चीम्जील] fomentation; applying a poultice [a compress / an ice pack]. e.g. 더운 찜질a hot compress / a stupe.

찜찜하다 [चीम्चीम्हादा] <서술적> feel awkward [embarrassed]; feel ill at ease. e.g. 돈 문제는 말하기가 찜찜하다It is awkward to speak about money matters.

찡그리다 [चीङ्गुरीदा] twist up <one's face / eyes> into a scowl. e.g. 그는 고통을 견디지 못해 얼굴을 찡그렸다 His face was distorted with pain.

찡얼거리다 [चीगऔल्गौरीदा] 1 [투덜거리다] grumble; murmur. 2 [애가 보채다] whimper; fuss; whine. e.g. 애가 왜 이렇게 찡얼거릴까, 어디가 아픈가 The baby is quite fretful today, I wonder whether he [she] is sick.

찢기다 [चीत्कीदा] get torn [rent / ripped]. e.g. 갈기 갈기 찢기다 be torn to ribbons.

찢다 [चीत्ता] tear; rend; rip. e.g. 입장권을 둘로 찢다 tear an admission ticket in two.

찢어지다 [चीजोजीदा] tear; rend; rip. e.g. 가슴이 찢어지는 듯한heart-rending.

찧다 [चीथ्रा] pound; ram. e.g. 떡쌀을 찧다 pound glutinous rice.

-차 [छा] [次] 1 […하려고] for the purpose of; with the intention of; with the object of; by way of. 2 [순서] order; sequence; degree; [횟수] time.

차[1] [छा] [差] [차이] (a) difference; variance; [변화] variation; [격차] (a) disparity; (a) discrepancy; inequality; odds; a gap; (가격상의) a margin; (득표의) a majority; a plurality (차점 득표자와의); (액수상의) balance; [天] equation

차[2] [छा] [茶] [차나무의 잎을 달인 음료] tea. e.g. 녹차 green tea. 홍차 black tea. 냉차 cold tea

차[3] [छा] [車] [탈 것] a vehicle; a carriage; a conveyance; [자동차] a motorcar; an automobile; a car; [택시] a taxi; (화물용의) a van; a wagon; a lorry; a truck].

차감 [छागाम] [差減] 1 [빼기] (a) deduction; (a) subtraction; (a) recoupment. 차감하다 deduct ; subtract; recoup. 2 (계정의) a balance; [차액] a margin.**차감하다** balance <an account>.

차갑다 [छागाबता] (온도, 기온이) cold; frigid; icy; chill (y); [매몰차다] cold hearted; coldblooded; cold water.

차고 [छागो] [車庫] a car shed; a carbarn; a (carriage) shed; (전차의) a tram depot [shed]; (자동차의) a garage; a carport

차곡차곡[छागोग छागोग] in orderly fashion; in a neat pile; <lay> one thing on another.

차관 [छाग्वान] [次官]a vice-minister; an undersecretary; a deputy secretary.] a parliamentary vice-minister.

차근차근 [छागुनछागुन] scrupulously; methodically; systematiccally; (서두르지 않고) step by step.

차기 [छागी] [次期] the next term.

차남 [छानाम] [次男] one's [the / a] second son.

차내 [छाने] [車內] the inside of a car [train]. e.g. 차내에서(자동차) in the car [bus] / (기차) in [on] the train / (전차) in the tram.

차녀 [छान्यो] [次女] one's [the / a] second daughter.

차다[1] [छादा] 1 [가득 차다] fill (up); become full <of>; be filled [replete] <with>; brim <with>; (시간, 일, 자리 등이) be engaged; be occupied. 2 [흡족하다] be satisfied [pleased] <with>; be content <with>; (사물이) be satisfactory 3 (일정 수량에) measure up to <a certain quantity>; come (up) to; amount to; be as much as. 4 [만기가 되다] expire (임기가); (어음 등이) mature; reach maturity; fall [be / become] due. birth to a baby. 5 [달이 둥글게 되다] waK full.

차다[2] [छादा] 1 (발로) kick <at>; give <a person> a kick on the shin. e.g. 되받아 차다 kick back / return a kick. 2 [거절하다] reject; refuse; turn down; kick <a request>; (애인 등을) jilt <a person>; discard; throw <a person> over. e.g. 애인을 차 버리다 jilt one's lover. 3 (혀를) click. e.g. 혀를 차다 click [clack] one's tongue / tsk / go tsk.

차다[3] **[छादा]** **1** [패용하다] attach; fasten on; wear. e.g. 시계를 차다 put [strap] on a watch / wear a (wrist-) watch. 칼을 차다 wear [carry] a sword at one's side. **2** (쇠고랑을) be handcuffed [manacled]; (차꼬를) be fettered [shackled]; be put in shackles. e.g. 쇠고랑을 찬 죄수 a handcuffed prisoner.

차다[4] **[छादा]** **1** (온도,씨가) cold; chilly; icy; frosty; freezing; cool **2** (마음 등이) coldhearted; cold-blooded; cold; frigid.

차단[छादान] [**遮 斷**] interception; isolation; quarantine (전염병 방지를 위한); [生理] (입구의) exclusion. 차단하다 intercept; isolate; cut off; shut off; quarantine; [電]

차도 [छादो] [**車道**] a roadway; a carriageway; a driveway.

차도[छादा] [**差 度**] improvement <of illness>; convalescence. e.g. 차도가 있다 get better / improve / convalesce / (병세가) be progressing favorably / take a turn for the better / take a favorable turn

차등 [छादुंग] [**差等**] gradation; graduation; (a) difference.

차라리 [छारारी] rather <than>; better <than>; sooner <than>; before; first; preferably

차량 [छार्यांग] [**車輛**] vehicles; cars; a (railway) carriage; (철도,송 회사의) the rolling stock.

차례[1] **[छार्ये]** [**次例**] **1** [순서] order; [순번] **2** [횟수] time; round.

차례[2] **[छारये]** [**茶禮**] ancestormemorial rites. .

차례차례[छारये छारये] [**次例次例**]in due [regular] order; in order; in turn; by turns; in regular sequence; [하나하나] one by one; one ather another; successively.

차리다 [छारीदा] **1** [장만하여 갖추다]. e.g. 음식을 차리다 serve <a person> with a meal. 살림을 차리다 make a new home <at / in>. **2** [옷 등을 갖추어 꾸미다] dress (oneself) up; be dressed up. **3** [알아차리다] understand; catch up <the meaning>. **4** [정신을 가다듬다] come to; collect <oneself>; concentrate <one's mind>.

차림새 [छारीमसे] [차린 그 모양] dress; attire; getup; guise; one's (personal) appearance

차마 [छामा] [애틋한 마음을 억누를 수 없어서]. e.g. 차마 눈뜨고 볼 수 없는 참상이다 be too miserable [cruel] to look at. **차멀미** [車-] car sickness.

차명 [छाम्योंग] [**借名**]차명하다

assume <a person's> name; use <a person's> name; masquerade under <a person's> name; impersonate <another>. e.g. 차명하여 in the name of / under the (assumed) name of.

차버리다 [छाबोरीदा]. Kick away (off) [거절하다] reject; refuse

차별 [छाब्योल] [差別] (a) distinction; (a) discrimination; differentiation. e.g. 계급 차별 class distinction. 인종 차별 racial discrimination / a color bar [line] 차별하다 draw [establish / set up] a distinction <between>; differentiate <one from another>; distinguish <between>; discriminate <against A / in favor of B>.

차분하다 [छाबूनहादा] calm; quiet; composed; tranquil; placid; serene; subdued; sedate; collected; self-possessed

차비 [छाबी] [車費] (철도 승차비) the railroad [railway] fare; (전차 등의) the (car) fare; (일반 적으로) the transit fare; (운반료) freight; carriage; cartage.

차선 [छासोन] [次善] the second best.

차선책 [छासोनछैग] the second [next] best policy.

차선 [छासोन] [車線] a (traffic) lane. dividing line;

차액 [छाऐग] [差額] the difference; (특히 수지의) the balance; (매매의) the margin

차용 [छायोंग] [借用] borrowing; loan. 차용하다 (무료로) borrow; (유료로) rent

차원 [छावन] [次元] a dimension

차이 [छाइ] [差異] (a) difference; (a) divergence; disagreement; (a) distinction (구별); (a) discrepancy (불일치); (a) disparity (불균형); (a) dissimilarity (같지 않음); a gap.

차이다 [छाइदा] 차이고 짓밟혀 죽다 be trodden down and trampled to death.

차익 [छाइग] [差益] marginal profits; a margin.

차일피일 [छाइलफीइल] [此日彼日] e.g. 일을 차일피일 미루다 put the work off from day to day. 차일피일하다 delay <a matter> from day to day; put off [leave over] <a matter> day by day / procrastinate. e.g. 차일피일하다가 기회를 놓치다 procrastinate until an opportunity is lost.

차장 [छाजांग] [次長] a vice-chief [-director]; a deputy chief; an assistant director (general).

차츰차츰 [छाछुम छाछुम] gradually; by degrees; step by step; little by little; inch by inch; by and by; more and more; slowly and [but] steadily. e.g. 차츰차츰 나아가다 advance gradually / inch [edge] one's way forward.

차치 [छाछी] [**且置**]차치하다 let alone; set [put] aside [apart. e.g. 그것은 차치하고 이 문제에 대해 먼저 토의합시다 Let's leave that for the time being and discuss this matter first.

차표 [छाफ्यो] [**車票**] a (railroad / bus / streetcar) ticket; a passenger ticket; a coupon (ticket) (회수권) be inferior to; be worse than; be below; fall behind; be second to; yield to; compare unfavorably with.

차후 [छाहू] **此後**] ther this; hence (forth); hereather; in future; for the future; from this time on; from now [here] on.

착 [छाग] [**着**] [도착] arrival

착각 [छाकाग] [**錯角** t] [사실과 다르게 지각함] an illusion; [환각망상] a hallucination; [잘못 알거나 생각함] a wrong guess; misunderstanding; a mistake 착각하다 be hallucinated; be under an illusion; misunderstand; misjudge; (make a) mistake; guess wrong

착공 [छाकोंग] [**着工**] e.g. 새 교사는 다음달 착공 예정이다 The construction of the new school building will start next month. / We shall begin to build the new school next month. / The new school building will be started next month.착공하다 start (construction) work.

착란 [छांगलान] [**錯亂**] distraction; derangement; aberration; confusion. 착란하다 <서술적> go distracted; go [run] mad; aberrate; be (mentally) deranged.

착륙 [छांगन्यूग] [**着陸**] (a) landing; alighting; touchdown; (로켓의) a blastdown. 착륙하다 land; make a landing; alight; reach the ground; ground; touch [set / put] down

착복 [छांगबोग] [**着服**] **1** [착의] clothing. 착복하다 clothe [dress] oneself <in>; put on clothes. **2** [금품의 횡령] embezzlement; misappropriation; appropriation; peculation. 착복하다 pocket; embezzle; misappropriate (to oneself); peculate; divert <public money> into one's own pocket.

착상 [छाकसांग] [**着想**] (hitting on) an idea; a conception; a turn of thought. 착상하다 conceive; think of <doing>; hit upon <a plan>; (사물이) cross [come into / enter] one's mind; come to mind.

착색 [छाकसैग] [**着色**] coloration; colouration; color-ing; colouring. 착색하다 color;

ㅊ

paint; tint.

착석 [छाकसोग] [着席] taking a seat. e.g. 착석순으로 in the order of seats. 착석하다 take one's seat [place]; take a chair; sit (down).

착수 [छाकसू] [着手] start; commencement; outset. 착수하다 start; commence; begin; set about <business>; get to <work>; undertake; set one's hand to; enter upon <one's work>; (새 사업에) embark on <an enterprise>; launch (upon).

착시[छाकसी] [錯視] an optical illusion.

착실 [छागशील] [着實] [견실] 착실하다 [꾸준하고 성실하다] steady (and honest); steady-going; [안정되다] sound; stable; sober; [믿을 만하다] trustworthy; [충실하다] faithful.

착오 [छागो] [錯誤] a mistake; an error; [불일치] (a) disagreement; [차이] a discrepancy. e.g. 시행(試行) 착오 trial and error.

착용 [छाक्योंग] [着用] 착용하다 put on; wear; have <a coat> on.

착잡 [छागचाब] [錯雜] complication; intricacy; involution. 착잡하다 complicated; intricate; knotty; (en) tangled; compleK involved.

착지 [छागची] [着地] 1 (비행기의) (a) landing. 착지하다 land. e.g. 비행기는 무사히 착지했다 The airplane [aeroplane] has landed safely. **2** (점프 등의) (a) landing. e.g. 체조 선수는 멋진 착지를 보여 주었다 The gymnast made a superb landing.

착착 [छाग छाग] [着着] steadily; step by step. 착착 진행되다 progress steadily / make steady progress [headway].

착취 [छागछ्वी] [搾取] 1 [짜냄] expression; extraction. 착취하다 squeeze; extract; press **2** (고혈의) exploitation; sweating; extortion; squeezing. 착취하다 exploit; sweat <one's employees>; squeeze <money out of a person>; extort.

착하다 [छागहादा] (아이가) good; nice; (마음씨가) good (-natured); kindhearted; [온순하다] meek; gentle; quiet; [순종하다] obedient; docile

찬기 [छान्गी] [-氣] cold air [steam]; chilly atmosphere; cold drath. e.g. 찬기가 돌다 be chill with cold air / have a cold fit.

찬동 [छान्दोंग] [贊同] approval; endorsement; support; approbation 찬동하다 approve of; support; give one's approval <to>; endorse <a plan>.

찬란하다 [छालानहादा] [燦爛-] brilliant; bright; shining; radiant; glittering; lustrous;

dazzling; resplendent.

찬물 [छांगमुल] cold water

찬미 [छांगमी] [讚美] praise; glorification; laudation; extolment; admiration; adoration. 찬미하다 praise; admire; laud; glorify; extol; hymn; chant hymns of praise <to a person>.

찬반 양론 [छानबान यांगरोन] [贊反兩論] pros and cons; arguments for and against <a matter>.

찬사 [छान्सा] [讚辭] a eulogy; praise (s); a compliment; laudatory remarks; a panegyric; an encomium <*pl.* ~s, -mia>.

찬성 [छानसोंग] [贊成] approval; approbation; agreement; assent; suffrage; seconding (동의의) support; endorsement; favor. 찬성하다 approve of <a plan>; give one's approval to <a plan>; agree <to a person's opinion / with a person>; subscribe to <a person's view>; fall in with <a person's view>; assent to <a person's opinion>; support <a bill>; second <a motion>; vote for <a measure>; favor <a proposal>; be in favor of <a reform>; endorse [indorse] <a plan>.

찬송 [छानसोंग] [讚頌] glorification <of God>; praise <to God>.

찬송가 [छानसोंगा] [讚頌歌] a hymn; a psalm.

찬스 [छान्स] a chance; an opportunity.

찬양 [छानयांग] [讚揚] praise; admiration; laudation; applause; commendation. 찬양하다 praise; admire; laud; applaud; extol; commend; give [accord] high praise to.

찬장 [छानजांग] [饌欌] a cupboard; a sideboard; a dresser.

찬조 [छानजो] [贊助] support; backing; patronage; approval. 찬조하다 support; back (up); patronize.

찬조금 [छानजोगुम] a contribution

찬찬하다 [छानछानहादा] **1** [꼼꼼하다] attentive; staid; careful; prudent; cautious. **2** [느리다] slow; leisurely; deliberate (of movement).

찬찬히 [छानछानही] **1** [침착하게] staidly; deliberately; calmly; quietly; [꼼꼼하게] carefully; cautiously; attentively. **2** [천천히] slowly; leisurely; deliberately; <wait> with patience.

찬탄 [छानथान] [贊歎, 讚歎] praise; admiration. 찬탄하다 admire; extol (l); speak highly of; be filled with admiration <at>.

찰거머리 [छालगोमोरी] [動] (동물) a leech. e.g. 찰거머리처럼 붙어 떨어지지 않는다 cling to ((a person)) like a leech.

찰기 [छालगी] [-氣] glutinous-

ㅊ

ness; glutinosity; stickiness.

찰깍 [छालकाग] with a snap [click / crack]; snap; crack.

찰깍거리다 [छालकाकोरीदा] (단단한 것이) click; clack; (시계 ticktack; ticktock; tick; (타자기가) click, click, click ....

찰나 [छाल्ला] [刹那] a moment; an instant; a trice.

찰랑거리다 [छालांगोरीदा] (액체가) lap; splash.

찰랑찰랑 [छालांग छालांग] [액체가 가득 괴어 있는 모양] to the brim; brimfully; to the full; overflowingly.

찰카닥 [छालखादाक] with a snap; with a click. 찰카닥하다 give a snap [click]; slap; slurp

참 [1] [छाम] [站] **1** [휴식] a (short) rest <from work>; a recess; a <coffee> break; a respite <from work>; a spell; [쉬는 시간에 먹는 식사] a snack taken during a recess. **2** [계제] the occasion; [찰나순간] the instance; the moment; the time.

참 [2] [छाम] **1** [정말로] really; truly; indeed; quite; very. **2** <감탄사> well; oh; what; really; by the way.

참가 [छाम्गा] [参加] participation; joining; entry. 참가하다 participate <in>; take part <in>; enter <a sporting event>; join(in) <a party>.

참가자 [छामगाजा] [参加者] a participator; a participant; (경기 등의) an entrant; an entry; <집합적> the entry [field].

참견 [छामग्योन] [参見] [간섭] interference; meddling; [관여] participation. 견하다 meddle [interfere / intermeddle] in <another's affair>; intrude oneself <into another's affair>; obtrude on [upon]; put [poke / thrust] one's nose into; put [thrust] one's oar in; poke into [관여하다] participate <in>; take part <in>; have [play] a part <in>; mix up <in>; have a share [hand] <in>; be concerned <in>.

참고 [छामगो] [参考] (a) reference; consultation.

참고서 [छामगोसो] [参考書] a reference book; a book of reference. 참고하다 refer to <a dictionary>; consult <a book>.

참관 [छामग्वान] [参觀] avisit; inspection; (증인으로서의) witnessing. 참관하다 visit;inspect; (증인으로서) witness; be (a) witness to.

참극 [छाम्गुक] [慘劇] a tragedy; a tragic event.

참다 [छाम्ता] **1** [인내하다] be patient; have [take / keep / practice] patience; [견디다] endure; put up with; bear; stand (▷ 앞의

2 가지 말은 구어로 많이 씀, bear 와 stand 는 부정문에서 쓸 때가 많음); tolerate (▷ 남의 행동에 대하여 보통 부정문으로 씀). **2** [억제하다] control (oneself); restrain (oneself); stifle; repress; suppress; forbear; keep [hold] back; contain <one's passion>; subdue [deny] oneself.

참담 [छाम्ताम] [慘澹] 참담하다 pitiful; pitiable; piteous; wretched; dire; harrowing; grim; miserable; terrible; horrible; tragic; appalling; disasterous

참되다 [छाम्दवैदा] true; real; genuine; honest; sincere; faithful; truthful; upright.

참뜻 [छाम्तुत] [참된 뜻] the true meaning;.

참말 [छाममाल] a true remark [story]; an authentic story; the truth; a (real) fact.

참배 [छाम्बे] [參拜] worship. 참배하다 go and worship at <a shrine>; pay reverence at <a tomb>; enter <a temple> and pray before the altar; visit [pay a visit to] <a shrine>.

참사 [छाम्सा] [慘死] a tragic [miserable / violent] death.

참석 [छाम्सौक] [參席] attendance; presence; appearance; participation. 참석하다 attend; be in attendance <at>; be present <at>; [참가하다] participate in; take part in.

참새 [छाम्सै] a sparrow.

참선 [छाम्सौन] [參禪] meditation in Zen Buddhism; [좌선의 수행] practices of [in] Zen meditation. 참선하다 practice Zen meditation at [in] a Buddhist temple.

참신 [छाम्शीन] [斬新] novelty; originality. 참신하다 new; novel; original; unconventional; up-to-date.

참여 [छाम्यो] [參與] participation <in public affairs>. 참여하다 participate [join] in; take part in; play one's part in; be a party to; have one's share in.

참으로 [छामुरो] [정말로] really; truly; in truth; in fact; indeed;

참을성 [छामुलसोंग] [- 性] patience; endurance; perseverance; forbearance; persistence; longsuffering; [관용] tolerance; sufferance; [자제] self-control; self-command.

참작 [छाम्जाग] [參酌] consideration; allowance(s); deliberation; reference. 참작하다 consider; take <something> into consideration [account]; show consideration for; allow for; deliberate; refer to; consult.

참전 [छाम्जोन] [參戰] participation in a war; entry into a war. 참전하다 enter a war;

participate in the war; join a war.

참정 [छाम्जोंग] [参政] participation in government. 참정하다 participate in government.

참정권 [छाम्जोंगवोन] [参政權] the right to vote; the franchise; suffrage;

참조 [छाम्जो] [参照] reference; consultation; comparison. 참조하다 [참고로 보다] refer <to>; [조사하다] consult; [비교하다] compare <with

참패 [छाम्फै] [慘敗] a crushing [humiliating] defeat; a dismal failure. e.g. 그 정당은 지방 선거에서 참패를 당했다 That party suffered a crushing defeat in the local elections.

참하다 [छाम्हादा] 1 [생김새가 곱다] nice; fair; charming; good-looking; handsome; pretty; comely; 2 [성질이 얌전하다] quiet [calm] and gentle; mild; sedate; modest.

참혹 [छाम्होग] [慘酷] 1 [비참] misery; wretchedness; pitiableness; distress. 참혹하다 miserable; wretched; tragic (al); sad; pitiable; sorrowful. 2 [잔인] cruelty; brutality; atrocity; ruthlessness. 참혹하다 cruel; atrocious; brutal; merciless; ruthless; cold-hearted.

참회 [छाम्हवी] [懺悔] [회오] penitence; repentance; contrition; [고백] (a) confession 참회하다 repent <of one's sins>; be penitent; [고백하다] confess; make a confession <of>.

찹찹하다 [छापछापहादा] 1 (물건이) neatly piled [heaped] up; stacked in good order. 2 (마음이) calm and serene; self-possessed; composed.

찻길 [छात्गील] [車-] 1 [기차전차 등의 궤도] a(train) track; a railroad [railway]. 2 [차도] a roadway; a driveway.

찻잔 [छात्जान] [茶盞] a tea-things; (한 벌) a tea set [service]; a teacup.

창 1 [छांग] [槍] a spear; a spike; a javelin

창 2 [छांग] [窓] a window; a sash window

창 3 [छांग] (구두의) sole leather; the sole of a shoe.

창간 [छांगान] [創刊] the first publication [edition]; foundation <of a periodical>. 창간하다 launch <a newspaper>; found [start] <a periodical

창건 [छांगौन] foundation; establishment; organization; inauguration. 창건하다 found; establish; organize; start; inaugurate; create. e.g. 그 회사는 창건된지 오래지

않다 It is not very long since the company was established.

창고 [छांगो] [**倉庫**] a storehouse; a warehouse (▷ storehouse.

창공 [छांगोंग] [**蒼空**] a blue [an azure] sky; the blue heavens; the vault of heaven.

창구 [छांगु] [**窓口**] a window; a wicket. 매표 창구 a ticket window.

창궐 [छांग्वल] [**猖獗**] rage; fury; rampancy; rifeness; virulence. 창궐하다 rage; be rife [virulent / rampant]. e.g. 유행성 감기가 창궐하고 있다 Influenza is raging (just now).

창극 [छांगुक] [**唱劇**] a Korean classical opera.

창녀 [छांग्नयो] [**娼女**] a prostitute; a streetgirl; a trollop; a streetwalker; a woman of the street; a harlot; a whore.

창달 [छांगदाल] [**暢達**] fluency; liveliness; briskness; development; growth; promotion. 창달하다 develop; promote.

창립 [छांगनीब] [**創立**] founding; establishment; organization.

창문 [छांगमुन] [**窓門**] a window

창백 [छांगपैग] [**蒼白**] pallor; pallidness. 창백하다 (deathly / ashy) pale; pallid; white (as a sheet).

창살 [छांगसाल] [**窓-**] (문의) a lattice; a latticework; a lattice strip; a frame; a grille; iron bars.

창세기 [छांगसेगी] [**-記**] [聖] (The Book of) Genesis (略 Gen.).

창시 [छांग्शि] [**創始**] origination; creation; establishment; foundation. 창시하다 originate; create; found; establish; initiate.

창업 [छांगोब] [**創業**](사업의) inauguration of an enterprise; [창립] foundation; establishment; the establishment [founding] of a business. 창업하다 (사업을) inaugurate [start] an enter-prise; [창립하다] found; establish. .

창유리 [छांग्यूरी] [**窓琉璃**] window glass; (끼우는) a (window) pane.

창의 [छांगुइ] [**創意**] an original idea [view]; originality. 창의적인 original / inventive / ingenious.

창자 [छांगजा] [대장과 소장] intestines; [내장] entrails; guts; insides (▷ 위도 포함).

창작 [छांग्जाग] [**創作**] [새로이 만들어 냄] creation; [작품] a creative work; [소설] a novel; [저작] production; [소설 쓰기] story [fiction] writing; a story; <집합적> fiction. 창작하다 create; invent; [소설을 쓰다] write a novel [story].

창조 [छांग्जो] [**創造**]

ㅊ

creation.창조하다 create; make; call into being.

창창하다 [छांगछांगहादा] [**蒼蒼**−] **1** [매우 푸르다] deep blue [green]; azure. **2** [멀다] far-off; remote; dim; uncertain; long; [끝없다] vast; boundless; <서술적> be far away. e.g. 창창한 장래 a bright [rosy / great] future.

창틀 [छांगथुल] [**窓**−] a window frame; (바깥쪽의) a window sash.

창피 [छांग्फी] [**猖披**]shame; disgrace; ignominy; dishonor(u)r. e.g. 큰 창피 an open [a public] disgrace / burning [crying] shame. 창피하다 shameful; scandalous; disreputable; ignoble; ignominious; <서술적> be embarrassed [abashed]; be a shame; [초라하다] unsightly; shabby; miserable; unpresentable.

창해 [छांग्है] [**滄海**] a blue expanse of water; the vast blue sea; the ocean.

창호지 [छांगहोजी] [−**紙**] window paper; sliding screen paper; paper for sliding doors.

찾다 [छाजता] **1** (사람물건 등을) search <for>; be on the search <for>; look for; look up; [수색하다] hunt (up); trace; locate (소재를) ; [구하다요구하다] seek <for / ather>; look out for; look for; hunt for; be out ather. e.g. 사람을 찾으러 가다 go looking [hunting] for a person. **2** [발견하다] discover; detect; find (out); discover; detect; locate (장소를) . e.g. 남의 비밀을 캐어 찾다 sniff out a person's secret / dig a person's secret out. **3** [되가지다] take [get / win] back; have <it> back; regain; retake; resume; recover; restore; reclaim; redeem; retrieve; draw out [from]; take out. e.g. (은행에서) 예금을 찾다 draw [withdraw] one's savings (from a bank). **4** [방문하다] call <on a person / at a person's house>; come [go round] to see; visit; pay [make] a visit to; pay one's respects <to a person>; pay <a person> a call; look <a person> up; visit with <a person>. e.g. 우리는 경주의 절을 찾았다 We visited temples in Kyengju. **5** (사전 등을) consult [use / see / turn to / refer to] <a dictionary for the meaning of a word>; look up <a word in a dictionary>; <英>look <a word> out <in a dictionary>. e.g. 단어를 불한 사전에서 찾다 look a word up in a French-Korean dictionary.

채 [1] [छै] **1** e.g. 파리 채 a fly swatter[flap]. **2** (악기의) a drumstick; a stick; a pick.

채[2] **[छै]** [집을 셀 때의 단위]. 두 채 two houses. 이 마을에는 20 채 안짝의 농가가 있다 This hamlet consists of less than twenty farm-houses.

채[3] **[छै]** [잘게 썰기] shredding vegetables; cutting in thin strips; [썬 것] thin strips (of a vegetable); shredded vegetables; vegetable shreds. e.g. 무를 채치다 cut a radish into fine strips.

채[4] **[छै]** [그대로] just as it is [stands]; intact; with no change; in the original state of; […한 이후] since. e.g. 산 채로 alive. 외투를 걸친 채 with one's overcoat on

채[5] **[छै]** [아직] <not> yet; as yet; so far; before; [겨우] only. e.g. 날이 채 밝기도 전에 before light

채결 [छैग्योल] [**採決**] [의안의 가부를 물어 정함] (a) decision; a vote; ballot taking; a roll call; a division. 채결하다 vote <on>; take a vote <on a question>; take a ballot <for>; put <a matter> to(the) vote; take a roll call; go into division.

채광 [छैग्वांग] [**採鑛**] mining. 채광하다 mine; work <a mine>; dig for <minerals>.

채굴 [छैगुल] [**採掘**] mining; digging; exploitation; working. 채굴하다 dig out; mine <gold, coal, etc.>; work [exploit] <a mine.

채권 [छैग्वोन] [**債券**] (국공사채) a bond; (회사채 등) a debenture. e.g. 연리 5 푼의 채권을 발행하다 issue bonds bearing a yearly interest of five per-cent.

채근 [छैगुन] [**採根**] 채근하다 [뿌리를 캐다] dig roots out; [근원을 캐다] trace <a thing> to its origin; [독촉하다] press <a person for a thing>; urge <a person to do>; demand; call upon <a person to do>. e.g. 돈을 갚으라고 채근당하다 be pressed to pay.

채널 [छैनोल] (텔레비전의) a channel.

채다 [छैदा] **1** [낚아채다] snatch (away) <from / off>; catch away; take by force; tear(off / away) <a thing> from <a person>;. **2** [확 당기다] jerk; pull with a jerk. e.g. 낚싯대를 채다 jerk one's fishing rod out.

채다 [छैदा] (눈치낌새를) sense; suspect; spot; smell out <the secret>; get wind [scent] of; become aware <of / that>.**채다 [छैदा]** **1** [걷어채다] get kicked; get a kick; (돌부리에) stumble <over / upon / against> **2** [빼앗기다] get <something> snatched [seized / taken /

stolen]. **3** [딱지맞다] be rejected [rebuffed]; be jilted; be kicked out; get the mitten.

채무 [छैमु] [**債務**] a debt; an obligation; liabilities. 고정 채무 fixed liabilities [indebtedness].

채무자 [छैमुजा] a debtor; a loanee; [法] an obligor.

채벌 [छैबोल] [**採伐**] Corporal [physical, bodily] punishment.

채비 [छैबी] [**-備**] preparation (s); arrangement; a getup; (an) outfit; equipment. 채비하다 prepare (oneself) <for>; arrange <for>; make preparations [arrangements] <for>; get (oneself) ready <for / to> do; equip oneself <for>.

채색 [छैसैग] [**彩色**] [그림에 색을 칠하기] coloring; painting; coloration; a color scheme (배합). 채색하다 color; paint; variegate; decorate.

채석 [छैसोग] [**採石**] quarrying. 채석하다 quarry <marble>.

채소 [छैसो] [**菜蔬**] vegetables; greens; greenstuff; greengrocery; garden products; <美> (garden) truck.

채식[छैशीक] [**菜 食**] a vegetable diet. 채식하다 live on vegetables.

채식주의자 [छैशीगजुइजा] a vegetarian.

채용 [छैयौंग] [**採用**] **1** [채택] adoption; acceptance; introduction. 채용하다 adopt <a plan>; accept <a proposal>; introduce <a system>; use <a textbook>. **2** [임용] appointment; [고용] engagement; employment. 가[임시] 채용 appointment on trial / trial employment. 채용하다 employ; take <a person> into service.

채우다[1] [छैउदा] **1** [몸에 차게 하다] make [let / have] <a person> wear [put on **2** [자물쇠 등을 잠그다] fasten; lock; (형구를) shackle; fetter.

채우다[2] [छैउदा] [차게 하다] cool; chill; (찬물에) put [keep] <something> in cold water; (얼음에) ice; keep <something> cool on ice; (냉장고에) refrigerate.

채우다[3] [छैउदा] **1** (수량을) make good; make up for; fill up. **2**(기한을) complete <a period[term]>; see it hrough. e.g.임기를 채우다 complete one's term of service. **3** [가득하게 하다] fill(up); (틀어넣어서) pack (in); stuff. e.g.술잔을 채우다 fill a glass with wine / fill a wineglass. **4** [만족시키다] satisfy; gratify; answer; meet; fulfill; fill. e.g. 욕망을 채우다 gratify [satisfy] one's desire.

채잡다 [छैजाप्ता] take [assume] charge <of>; take the lead [a leading part] <in>; lead <a party>; preside over.

채점 [छैचोम] [採點] marking; grading; scoring; rating. 채점하다 give [award] marks; mark <examination papers>; grade; rate; score <a test

채집 [छैजीब] [採集] collection; collecting; gathering. 곤충 채집 insect collecting / bugging / bug hunting. 채집하다 collect; gather. .

채찍 [छैचीक] a whip; (말의) a horsewhip.

채취 [छैच्वे] [採取] picking; gathering. 채취하다 pick; gather; collect; harvest; fish <pearls>; [추출하다] extract <alcohol / radium>.

채치다 [छैचीदा] **1** [채찍질하다] whip; lash; flog; flagellate. **2** [독촉하다] press; urge; dun.

채탄 [छैथान] [採炭] coal mining. 채탄하다 mine [extract] coal.

채택 [छैथेक] [採擇] [선택] choice; selection; option; [채용] acceptance; introduction; adoption (특히 의안 등의).채택하다 choose; select; accept <a proposal>; adopt <a plan>; use <a textbook>.

책[छैक] [冊] a book; a volume; [작품] a work; [읽을 거리] reading. e.g. 영어책 an English book. 책(장)을 넘기다 turn over the leaves of a book. 책을 읽어 주다 read to <a person>.

책값 [छैक्काम] [冊-] the price of a book; a book price.

책꽂이 [छैक्कोजी] [冊-]a bookstand; a bookrack; a bookshelf <*pl.* -shelves>.

책략[छैग्न्यांग] [策略] a stratagem; a ruse; an artifice; a trick; tactics; strategy; maneuvers; a plan; a scheme; a policy; <美> a frame-up.

책망 [छैग्मांग] [責望] blame; charge; (a) censure; (a) reproach; (a) rebuke; (a) reproof. 책망하다 call <a person> to task[account]; blame; censure; charge; reproach; rebuke; reprove.

책무 [छैग्मु] [責務] [의무] duty; (an) obligation; [책임] responsibility. 국가에 대한 책무 one's duty to one's country. 자기의 책무를 다하다 discharge [fulfil (l)] one's obligations / do [perform] one's duty.

책받침 [छैगबात्छीम] [冊-] a pad to rest writing paper on; a sheet of plastic [cardboard] placed under a sheet of paper when writing.

책벌레 [छैक्बोल्लै] [冊-] [책의 벌레] a bookworm; [지나치게 공부하는 사람] a bookworm.

책상 [छैकसांग] [冊床] a desk; a (writing) table. **책상보**

ㅊ

[छैक्सांगबो] a table cloth.

책상다리 [छैक्सांगदारी] [冊床-] **1** [책상의 다리] a leg [legs] of a desk [table]. **2** [앉음새] sitting cross-legged. 책상다리하다 sit cross-legged; sit down tailor-fashion; sit with one's legs crossed.

책임 [छैगिम] [責任] responsibility; liability (지불의) ; [책무] an obligation; duty. e.g. 책임은 …에게 있다 the responsibility rests [lies] with ... / the fault lies with .

책임감 [छैगिमकाम] [責任感] a sense of responsibility. e.g. 책임감이 강하다 have a strong sense of responsibility.

책잡다 [छैक्जाप्ता] [責-] find fault with <a person>; call <a person> to account <for>; take <a person> to task; blame [reproach] <for>.

책잡히다 [छैकजाफीदा] [責-] be found fault with; be called to account [task]; be taken to task; be blamed [reproached]. e.g. 위약했다고 책잡히다 be blamed for having broken one's promise.

책장[1] [छैक्जांग] [冊張] a leaf of a book; the pages.

책장[2] [छैक्जांग] [冊欌] a bookshelf <*pl.* -shelves>; a bookcase; a book chest.

책정 [छैक्जोंग] [策定] (예산 등의) appropriation;(가격 등의) fixing <prices>. 책정하다 appropriate; allot; earmark <for>. e.g. 가격을 책정하다 fix a price. 학교 보조금으로 오백만 원을 책정하다 appropriate five million won for school aid.

챔피언 [छैम्फीओन] a champion; a champ.

챙기다 [छैंगीदा] [정돈하다] put <things> in order; set <things> in(good) order; tidy up; [짐 꾸리다] pack; [모으다] gather all together; collect. e.g. 방안을 챙기다 put a room to rights [in order].

-처 [छो] [處][곳] a place. 근무처 one's place of employment / one's office.

처 [छो] [妻] 내연의 처 a common-law wife.

처가 [छोगा] [妻家] one's wife's home.

처결 [छोग्यौल] [處決] settlement; disposal; disposition; decision. 처결하다 settle; dispose of; decide.

처남 [छोनाम] [妻男] one's wife's brother; one's brother-in-law.

처넣다 [छोनोथा] **1** [무리하게 넣다] push[press / thrust / force / stuff / jam] in; crowd [jam / stuff] into; **2** [감금하다] lock <a person> up [in]; confine; imprison. **3** [돈 등을 투자하다] put <money> into; invest <capital> in.

처녀 [छोन्यौ] [處女] a virgin;

a maiden; a maid.

처단 [छेतान] [處斷] [결단] judgment; decision; [처치] disposition; punishment. 처단하다 [결단하다] judge; decide; rule; [처치하다] punish; deal [do] with.

처량 [छेर्यांग] [凄凉] **1** [황량함] य .처량하다 desolate; dreary; bleak; deserted. **2** [구슬픔]. 처량하다 sad; sorrowful; doleful; plaintive; melancholy.

처럼 [छेरोम] like; as; as ... as; <not> so ... as; as if [though]

처리 [छेरी] [處理] management; conduct; disposition; disposal; transaction; dealing; handling; settlement; 처리하다 manage <a matter>; conduct <business>; dispose of <a matter>; deal with <an affair>; take care of <a matter>; transact; handle; settle(up) <a problem>; (생산 원료 등을) process; (약품 등을 써서) treat.

처마 [छेमा] the eaves.

처매다 [छेमैदा] [감아 매다] bind up <a wound>; bandage <a wound> up.

처먹다 [छेमोक्ता] cram <food> into one's mouth; shove [shovel] down; eat greedily; devour.

처박다 [छेबाक्ता] **1** [때려서 박다] drive [strike] in(to); ram down <a stake>; wedge in (쐐기 등을) e.g. 못을 처박다 drive [hammer] a nail into <a wall>. **2** [처넣다] thrust [shove / tuck] in (to); stuff [cram / pack] in to; ram in (to); (물 속에) dive; dip. e.g. 서랍 속에 처박다 shove [cram] <a thing> in a drawer. **3** [가두다] shut in [up]; lock in[up]; confine. e.g. 처박아 두다 keep <a person> penned (up) <in a place>.

처박히다 [छेबाखीदा] be shut in [up]; be locked in [up]. e.g. 처박혀 있다 confine oneself to [in] <a room> / shut oneself up / be confined [closeted] in <one's room> / remain [keep] indoors.

처방 [छेबांग] [處方] (a) prescription; a recipe.

처벌 [छेबोल] [處罰] [벌하기] (a) punishment; [형벌] a penalty. 처벌하다 punish <a person for a crime>; inflict a penalty on <a person for an offense

처분 [छेबुन] [處分] [처치] disposal; disposition; dealing; a measure; 처분하다 dispose of; deal with; make a clearance of <unsold goods>.

처사 [छेसा] [處士] recluse; a retired scholar.

처세 [छेसे] [處世] conduct of life. 처세하다 get on [make one's way] in the world; get along with people.

처소 [छेसो] [處所] [장소] a

ㅊ

place; [거처] a living [dwelling] place; one's resi-dence; one's abode; one's address (주소).

처신[छौशीन] [**處身**] behavior; deportment; demeanor; conduct. 처신하다 behave [conduct / deport / comport / demean] oneself.

처연 [छौयौन] [**凄然**] [쓸쓸하고 구슬픈 모양]. 처연하다 pathetic; sad; sorrowful.

처우[छौउ] [**處遇**] (a) treatment. 처우하다 treat; deal [do] with.

처음[छौउम] [시초] the beginning; the opening; the start; the outset; commencement;

처자 [छौजा] [**妻子**] one's wife and children; one's family.

처절 [छोजोल] [**悽絶**] 처절하다 extremely sad [melancholy / wretched / miserably]; heartbreaking; heartrending;

처제 [छौजे] [**妻弟**] one's wife's younger sister; one's sister-in-law.

처지 [छौजी] [**處地**] **1** [형편] a situation; a condition; circumstances; one's lot; one's <financial> status; [입장] a standpoint; a position; one's standing; [신분] a station in life. **2** [사이] relations; terms.

처지다 [छौजीदा] **1** [늘어지다] hang (down); droop; sag. **2** [뒤지다] fall [drop] behind; fall back; trail; be outstripped <by>

처참 [छौछाम] [**悽慘**]처참하다 ghastly; gruesome; lurid; grim; appalling; miserable; wretched.

처치 [छौछी] [**處置**] **1** [처분] disposal; disposition; management; (상처의) treatment; [처치하다 [처리하다] dispose of; [대처하다] deal with; [대책을 세우다] take measures <to do>. **2** [제거] removal; clearance; elimination; liquidation. 처치하다 remove; get rid of; clear [take] away; do away with; eliminate; liquidate.

처하다 [छोहादा] [**處-**] **1** [놓이다] be placed <in>; be [get] faced with. **2** [처벌하다] sentence; condemn.

처형[1] [छौह्यौग] [**妻兄**] one's wife's elder sister; one's sister-in-law.

처형[2] [छौह्यौग] [**處刑**] [처벌] punishment; [사형 집행] execution. 처형하다 punish; (사형에) execute.

척[1] [छौक] [**隻**] a vessel; a ship; a boat. 배 한 척 a [one] vessel [ship / boat].

척[2] [छौक] **1** [잘 붙는 모양] closely; tightly; hard; fast; clingingly. e.g. 척 달라붙다 cling tight <to one's body> **2** [선뜻] without hesitation [delay]; readily;

[즉각] instantly; quickly; offhand; right away [off]. **3** [늘어지는 모양] loosely; drooping (low); limply; flaccidly. **4** [의젓하게] imposingly; with dignity; [멋지게] smartly; becom-ingly; dashingly.

척결 [छोक्यौल] 척결하다 [긁어 발라내다] gouge [hollow] out; scrape out; [들춰내어 없애다] expose <a crime / fraud>; lay bare <an evil design>.

척도 [छोक्दो] [尺度] [계량의 단위] a measure; [눈금] a scale; [기준] a standard; a criterion; a barometer. e.g.문명의 척도] an index of civilization. …을 재는 척도가 되다 be a measure [a barometer / an index] of ... / be a yardstick for ....

척박 [छोक्पाक] [瘠薄] sterility; barrenness <of land>; infertility <of soil>; meagerness. 척박하다 barren; sterile; infertile; meager; poor. e.g. 척박한 땅 barren [sterile / unproductive] soil [land].

척척 [छोक्छोक] **1** [들러붙은 모양] close (ly); tightly; adhesively; fast. **2** [서슴지 않고] without hesitation [delay]; readily; [얼른얼른] quickly; promptly; rapidly; speedily; with dispatch; briskly; right off; [수월하게] easily.

척출 1 [斥黜] [벼슬을 떼어서 내쫓음] ouster; ousting; expulsion; dismissal; dis-charge. 척출하다 dismiss [discharge] <a person> from office; oust [expel] <a person> from a position.

척출 2 [剔出] [발라냄] extraction; removal; excision. 척출하다 extract; excise; remove; cut out.

천 1 [छोन] [피륙] cloth; stuff; texture; (textile) fabrics;

천 2 [छोन] [千] a [one] thousand.

천격 [छोन्ग्यौक] [賤格] [낮고 천한 품격] mean [low] character; mean style.

천고 [छोन्को] [千古][태고] remote antiquity; [영원] eternity; all ages

천국[छोन्गुक] [天國] the kingdom of Heaven [God]; Heaven; Paradise; the blessed land.

천금[छोन्कुम] [千金] a thousand pieces of gold; [많은 돈] a lot of money; fortune; [귀중함] priceless-ness.

천기 [छोन्की] [天機] **1** [하늘의 기밀] the profound secret (s) of Nature [Heaven]; the hidden plans of Providence. **2** [큰 기밀] a profound [top] secret; a state secret (국가의). e.g.

ㅊ

천기를 누설 마라 The secret should not be divulged. / It must be kept(a) secret.

천당 [छौन्दांग] [天堂] Heaven; the palace of Heaven; Paradise; the kingdom of Heaven.

천대[छौन्दै] [賤待] (a) contemptuous [cold] treatment; inhospitable [cold] reception. 천대하다 treat <a person / a thing> contemptuously [with contempt].

천더기 [छौन्दोगी] [賤 -] a despised person; a child of scorn.

천도 [छौन्दो] [遷都] the transfer [removal] of the capital <to>. 천도하다 transfer [remove] the capital <to>; move [remove] the seat of government <to>.

천동설 [छौन्दोंसौल] [天動說] the Ptolemaic theory [system]; geocentricism.

천둥 [छौन्दुंग] [뇌명] thunder; a peal [roll] of thunder; [

천량 [छौल्लयांग] [재물과 양식] money and food; supplies. e.g. 천량이 다 떨어지다 have run through [out of] supplies.

천륜 [छौल्लयून] [天倫] Natural Law; the natural relationships of man.

천리[छौल्ली] [千里] one thousand *ri*; [썩 먼길]] a great distance. 천리 길도 한 걸음부터 <속담> A journey of a thousand miles starts with but a single step

천막 [छौन्माक] [天幕] a tent; (배의) an awning; <집합적> tentage. e.g.

천만 [छौन्मान] [千萬] [1 천만] ten million; [무수] a countless number; a myriad; [매우] exceedingly; extremely; very much.

천만 다행 [छौन्मान दाहैंग] [千萬多幸] great good fortune [luck]; a stroke of good luck.

천만번 [छौन्मान्पौन] [千萬番] times out of number; heaps [dozens] of times; <부사적> ever so many times; over and over again

천만에 [छौन्माने] [千萬 -] **1** [겸사] Don't mention it; Not at all; Never mind; You're welcome. e.g. 훌륭한 정원이군요. 천만에 말씀입니다 그저 넓기만 합니다 "This is quite a garden you have here." "Not really. It's big, but that's all." **2** [부당] Oh, (dear) no!; Nothing of the kind [sort]!; Far from it!; Nothing could be farther from the truth; What an absurd idea!; <美> Never happen! e.g. 그가 모르고 있었다고? 천만에 He didn't know? Of course he did!

천명 [闡明] clarification; elucidation. 천명하다 make clear; explain; give an explanation; elucidate; clarify; explicate.

천명 [छोन्म्यौंग] [天命] **1** [하늘의 뜻] God's will; Heaven's decree; the appointment of heaven; [운명] fate; destiny; one's lot in life; karma. **2** [타고난 수명] one's life; one's natural term of existence.

천민 [छोन्मीन] [賤民] <집합적> lowly [humble] people; the lowly; the humble; low-class people.

천박 [छोन्बाक] [淺薄] shallow-ness; superficiality; flimsi-ness; frivolity. 천박하다 shallow; superficial; frivolous; flimsy; thoughtless.

천방지축 [छोन्बांगछुग] [天方地軸] [덤벙댐] rashness: recklessness; harum-scarumness; foolhardiness; [덤벙대어] rashly; recklessly; harum-scarum; at a venture.

천벌 [छोन्बौल] [天罰] Heaven's vengeance [judgment]; divine punishment [retribution]; the punishment of Heaven; the wrath of God; divine wrath.

천사 [छोन्सा] [天使] an angel; a herald of God; <집합적> hierarchy.

천상[छोन्सांग] [天上] the heavens. e.g. 천상에서부터 from above [heaven / on high] / [의외의 곳에서] <drop> out of the clouds.

천생 [छोन्सैंग] [天生] **1** [타고난 본바탕] a product of nature [heaven]; nature. e.g. 천생의 natural / born / designed by nature. **2** [선천적으로] by nature; naturally; [두고두고] as [for] ever; [흡사하여] bearing as close resemblance; [부득불] unavoidably; inevitably; necessarily.

천생 연분 [छोन्सैंग यौन्पुन] predestined [Heaven-ordained] relation.

천성 [छोन्सौंग] [天性] (one's) nature; (one's) natural constitution; one's innate disposition [character / temperament].

천신만고 [छोन्शीन्मानखो] [千辛萬苦] indescribable hardships; intense application.

천양지차 [छोन्यांगजीछा] [天壤之差] a world of difference; extreme opposition; poles apart.

천연 [छोन्यौन] [天然] **1** [저절로 이루어진상태] nature; spontaneity. **2** [비슷하게] just [exactly]<like another>; as if.

천연덕스럽다 [छोन्योनदौक्सुरौप्ता] [天然-] = 천연스럽다

천연스럽다 [छोन्यौनसुरोप्ता] [天然-] **1** [자연스럽다] natural; unartificial; [꾸민데가 없다] unstudied; unaffected. **2** [그럴싸하다]

ㅊ

looking like the truth; specious; plausible. **3** [태연하다] calm; cool; unmoved; unperturbed; [무관심하다] unconcerned; indifferent; nonchalant. **4** [흡사하다] just [exactly] like <another>; <서술적> be the exact image [likeness] <of>; be <a person's> double.

천자문 [छौन्जामुन] [千字文] the Thousand-Character Text [Classic]; a primer of Chinese characters.

천장 [छौन्चांग] [天障] the ceiling; the roof.

천재 [1] [छौनजे] [天才] (재주) a) genius; a natural gith [end-owment]; (사람)] a (man of) genius; a prodigy; a wizard <at chemistry>.

천재 [2] [छौन्जे] [天災] a natural calamity [disaster]; an act of God (불가항력) e.g. 천재를 만나다[당하다] be visited by a natural calamity / meet with a natural disaster.

천재 지변 [छौन्जै जीब्यौन] [-地變] a natural disaster [calamity]; the disturbances of the elements; a convulsion of nature; a cataclysm.

천적 [छौन्जौक] [天敵] a natural enemy.

천정 부지 [छौन्जौग बुजी] [天井不知] skyrocketing. e.g. 요즈음 물가는 천정 부지다 Prices today are skyrocketing.

천주교 [छौन्जुग्यो] [天主敎] (Roman) Catholicism; Romanism.

천지 [छौन्जी] [天地] **1** [하늘과 땅] heaven and earth; the heavens and the earth; the universe; [자연] nature. **2** [장소, 세계] a land; a world; arealm; asphere; astage. **3** [많음] (an) abundance; (a) plenty; (an) opulence; richness.

천지 개벽 [छौनजी गैब्यौग] [天地開闢] **1** [창조] the Creation (of Heaven and Earth); the beginning of the world. **2** [대변혁] a cataclysmic change; an upheaval; a revolution.

천지 신명 [छौन्जी शीन्म्यौग] [天地神明] the gods of heaven and earth.

천직[छौन्जीक] [天職] a mission; a vocation; a calling; one's divinely appointed work in life.

천진 난만 [छौनजीन नान्मान] [天眞爛漫] naivet; naivety; simplicity; artlessness; innocence. 천진 난만하다 naive; unaffected; artless; innocent; simple-hearted [-minded].

천차만별 [छौन्छामान्ब्यौल] [千差萬別] infinite variety.

천천히 [छौन्छौनी] [느리게] slowly; without haste [hurry]; [한가롭게] leisurely; deliberately; in a leisurely manner

[way]; at (one's) leisure.

천체 [छोन्चे] [天體] a heavenly [celestial] body; a celestial sphere [object]; an orb.

천추 [छोन्छु] [千秋] [긴 세월] many years.

천치 [छोन्छी] [天癡, 痴] an idiot; an imbecile; a moron; a fool.

천편일률 [छोन्फ्योनील्ल्यूल] [千篇一律] [한결같고 변화가 없음] monotony; humdrumness; lack of variety.

천하 [छोन्हा] [天下] [일국] the whole country; the land; the realm; the State; the (whole) Empire; [세상] the public; the world; [세계] the world; the universe; [지배권] ruling power; [정권] administrative power; the reins of government.

천하 일색 [छोन्हा इल्सैग] the reigning beauty; a woman of matchless [unsurpassed] beauty; the fairest of the fair.

천하다 [छोन्हादा] [賤 -] **1** [지체,위가 낮다] humble; low; lowly; ignoble; obscure; low-lived; low-born. **2** [상스럽다] vulgar; base; mean; low; gross; rude; beastly.
3 [흔하다] plenty; superfluous.

천하 일품 [छोन्हान इल्फुम] [天下一品] a unique article; a nonesuch; the best specimen in existence.

천하 장사 [छोन्हा जांग्सा] [天下壯士] a man of unparalleled (physical) strength; the strongest man in the world; a man of Herculean strength; a Hercules; an Atlas.

-철 [छोल] [綴] a file. 서류철 a file of documents [papers].

철 [छोल] [鐵] iron; steel (강철).

철 [छोल] [계절] a season; the time of the year.

철 [छोल] [분별] [बुन्ब्योल] discretion; judgment; prudence; wisdom; good sense. e.g. 철이 없는 indiscreet / imprudent / injudicious / thoughtless / ill-advised.

철강 [鐵鋼] steel

철거 [छोल्गो] [撤去] [거두어 가지고 떠나감] removal; [부수어 치움] demolition; dismantlement 철거하다 remove; clear (away); (부수어서) demolish; pull [take] down; dismantle.

철골 [छोल्कोल] [鐵骨] a steel [an iron] frame; a steel skeleton.

철광 [छोल्वांग] [鐵鑛] [철을 함유한 광석] ore; [철이 나는 광산] an iron mine.

철교 [छोल्ग्यो] [鐵橋] [쇠다리] an iron bridge; (철도의) a railway bridge.

철군 [छोल्कुन] [撤軍] withdrawal [removal] of troops; military withdrawal; evacuation. 철군하다 withdraw troops <from a place>;

evacuate <a place>; pull troops out <of a place>; pull out.

철근 [छौल्कन] [**鐵筋**] a [an iron] reinforcing rod [bar].

철도 [छौल्दो] [**鐵道**] a railway; a railroad; a railroad line.

철두철미 [छौल्दुछौल्मी] [**徹頭徹尾**] **1** [철저함] thoroughness; completeness; exhaustiveness. 철두철미하다 thorough (going); exhaustive; complete; utter; out-and-out; all-out. **2** [철저하게] thoroughly; throughout; through and through; out-and-out; in every way; every inch; at all points; in every particular; to the core; from top to bottom; from beginning to end; from first to last; all the way.

철모르다 [छौल्मोरुदा] [분별이 없다] lack judgment [discretion]; be imprudent [indiscreet / thoughtless / injudicious]; [천진하다] be simple-minded [innocent / untutored].

철봉 [छौल्बोंग] [**鐵棒**] **1** [쇠막대] an iron bar [rod]; an iron club (곤봉). **2** (체조용의) a horizontal bar; gallows;

철부지 [छौल्बुजी] [**-不知**] [철없는 사람] an indiscreet [a thoughtless] person; a person who lacks good sense; [철없는 어린애] a mere child; just a child.

철사 [छौल्सा] [**鐵絲**] (a) wire; <집합적> wiring.

철새 [छौल्सै] a migratory [passage] bird; a bird of passage; a transient (체류 기간이 짧은 사람); <집합적> migrants.

철수 [छौल्सू] [**撤收**] withdrawal; removal; evacuation. 철수하다 withdraw <from>; remove; evacuate <a place>; draw off; pull out.

철썩거리다 [छौल्सौकौरीदा] splash; swash; plash. e.g. 철썩거리는 파도 소리 the plash of the waves / the splosh of the surf.

철야 [छौरया] [**徹夜**] an all-night vigil [sitting]. e.g. 철야로 병구완하다 sit up with <an invalid> all night [all the night through].

철없다 indiscreet; imprudent; thoughtless; reckless; rash; <서술적> have no sense [discretion]; lack judgment.

철인 [छैरीन] [**哲人**] a wise man; a man of wisdom; a sage; [철학자] a philosopher.

철자 [छौलचा] [**綴字**] spelling; orthography. 철자법 the system of spelling; how to spell <a word>.

철재 [छौलचे] [**鐵材**] iron (material); an iron frame.

철저 [छौलचौ] [**徹底**] thoroughness; completeness; exhaustiveness. 철저하다_thorough (going); exhaustive; complete; perfect; utter; out-and-out; all-out; downright; drastic; radical.

철저히 [छौलचौदी] [徹底-] thoroughly; thoroughgoingly; completely; exhaustively; downright; all out; through and through; (up) to the hilt. e.g. 철저히 하다 do <anything> thoroughly / go all length.

철제 [छौलचे] [鐵劑] iron; an iron preparation; a ferric medicine.

철조망 [छौलचोमांग] [鐵條網] (barbed-) wire entanglements; a hedgehog.

카니발 [ख्वानीबाल] a carnival.

카드 [ख्वाद्] (일반적인) a card; a slip (of paper) (종이 쪽지)

카드놀이 [ख्वादुनोरी] card playing; a game of cards; a card game.

카디건 [ख्वादीगौन] a cardigan (sweater).

카랑카랑하다 [ख्वारांबख्वारांगहादा] **1** [날씨가 맑고 차다] clear and cold. **2** (목소리가) clear and high-pitched; shrill; piercing; penetrating.

카레 [ख्वारे] curry.

카리스마 [ख्वारीस्मा] (a) charisma <*pl.* -mata>;(a) charism <*pl.* ~ s>. e.g. 카리스마적 charismatic.

카메라 [ख्वामेरा] a camera.

카멜레온 [ख्वामेल्लेओन] [動] a chameleon. e.g. 카멜레온같은 사람 [변덕스러운 사람] a chameleon / a fickle [an inconstant] person.

카세트 [ख्वासेथ्] a cassette.

카스트 [ख्वास्थ्] a caste.

카운슬러 [ख्वाउन्सल्लौ] a counselor; a counsellor.

카운슬링 [ख्वाउन्सल्लीग] counseling; counselling.

카운터 [ख्वाउन्थौ] (은행, 점 등의) a (service) counter; a cash counter; a counting house [room]; (출입구에 있는) a check-out counter; (호텔의) the office; the (front) desk; the reception desk. e.g. 카운터에 앉다 sit at the counter.

카운트다운 [ख्वाउन्थ्दाउन] (로켓 발사시 등의) a countdown. e.g. 로켓 발사 전의 카운트다운이 시작되었다 The countdown for the rocket launch has begun. 카운트다운하다 count down.

카지노 [ख्वाजीनो] a casino <*pl.* ~s>.

카테고리 [ख्वाथेगोरी] a category.

카톨릭 [ख्वाथोल्लीक] Catholicism; the (Roman) Catholic.

ㅋ

카투사 [खातूसा] KATUSA; Katusa (▷ Korean Augmentation Troops to the United States Army 의 약어). [उर्ड याकों]

카페 [खाफे] a cafeK; coffee-house.

카페인 [खाफेइन] caffeine.

카페테리아 [खाफेथेरीआ] a cafeteria; a self-service restaurant.

카펫 [खाफेत] a carpet. e.g. 카펫을 깔다 spread a carpet / carpet <a room / a floor>.

카피 [खाफी] a copy. e.g. 이 편지의 카피를 한 장 만들어 주세요 Please make a copy of this letter.

카피라이트 [खाफीराइथ्] (a) copyright.

칵테일 [खाकथेइल] [혼성주] a cocktail.

칸 [खान] **1** [방을 세는 단위 a room; a chamber. e.g. 네 칸 집 a four-room (ed) house. **2** [칸막이] a partition; a compartment. e.g. 방의 일부를 칸을 막다 partition off a part of a room. **3** [공간] [a) space; a blank (space). e.g. 알맞은 전치사를 써서 빈 칸을 채워라 Fill (in) the blanks with appropriate pre-positions.

칸막이 [खानमागी] [막음] partitioning; screening off; [막는 것] a screen; a partition. e.g. 판자 칸막이 s a wooden partition. 칸막이하다 partition; screen off; put up a (board) screen. e.g. 칸막이한 방 a partition-ed room.

칼 [खाल] **1** [나이프] a knife <*pl.* knives>; (선원용) a jackknife; (부엌칼) a kitchen knife; (식탁용) a table knife; [단검P비수] a dagger; a dirk; a stiletto <*pl.* ~ (e)s>. **2** [검]a sword; a saber (군도,지휘도)[. e.g. 칼 가는 사람 a sword-sharpener [-grinder].

칼날 [खालनाल] the edge [blade] of a sword [knife]. e.g. 칼날을 세우다 put an edge <on> / give an edge <to> / edge / sharpen <a knife>.

칼라 [खाल्ला] [깃] [a (shirt) collar. e.g. 소프트 [더블 / 케이프] 칼라] a soth [turn-down / cape] collar.

칼럼 [खाल्लौम] a column.

칼럼니스트 [खाल्लोमनीस्थ्] a columnist.

칼로리 [खाल्लोरी] a calorie [calory] (Cal.).

칼자루 [खालचारू] the hilt of a sword; the hath of a dagger; the handle of a knife. e.g. 칼자루를 쥐다 hold a sword by the hilt / <비유> have the (final [last]) say.

칼질 [खालजील] cutting. 칼질하다 cut; do cutting.

캄캄하다 [खामखामहादा] **1** [어둡다] pitch-dark; <as> dark as pitch; <as> dark as mid-night. e.g. 터널 속은

ㅋ

칠흑같이 캄캄했다 It was pitch-dark [as dark as pitch] in the tunnel. **2** [암담하다] dark; gloomy; dismal; somber. e.g. 앞길이 캄캄하다 [전망이 없다] I can't see ahead at all. / [희망이 없다] The future looks black [hopeless **3** [모르다] <서술적> be ignorant <of>; be not familiar [well acquainted] <with>; be ill informed <of>; be a stranger <to>. e.g. 세상 일에 캄캄하다 know nothing about the world / know but little of the world / be ignorant of [inexperienced in] the ways of the world.

캐다 [खैदा] [알아내려고 따지다] examine closely; pry into <a person's secret>; peck [pick] at <a person's faults>. e.g. 캐기 좋아하는 inquisitive / prying / curious / nos (e)y.

캐럿 [खैरौत] [보석 무게의 단위] a carat; [금의 순도] a karat; a carat.

캐릭터 [खैरीक्थौ] **1** [성격] (a) character. **2** [소설,만화에 나오는 인물,동물]] a character.

캐묻다 [खैमुत्ता] question closely; press [drive] a question home; press <a person> for an answer; cross-question; cross-examine. e.g. 일의 진상을 캐묻다 make sure of [ascertain] the truth of a matter.

캐주얼 [खैजूऔल] [평상시 입는 옷, 구두] casuals.

캑캑 [खैकखैक] with repeated coughs or splutters; hacking away. 캑캑하다 =캑캑거리다

캑캑거리다 [खैकखैकगौरीदा] cough and cough.

캔디 [खैनदी] <美> (a piece of) candy; sweets.

캘린더 [खैल्लीन्दौ] [달력] a calendar

캠프 [खैम्फ] a camp; (운동 선수의) a training camp. e.g. 캠프를 거두다 break (up a) camp. 캠프하다 camp (out).

캠프파이어 [खैम्फफाइऔ] a campfire.

캠핑 [खैम्फीग] camping. e.g. 캠핑 가다 go (out) camping / leave for camping <in>.

커녕 [खौन्यौग] far from <doing>; anything but at all; in no wise; instead of; [말할 것도 없고] not to mention; not to speak of; to say noting of. e.g. 실망하기는커녕 far from being disappointed.

커닝 [खौनीग] cheating <on [in] an examination>; cribbing (▷ cunning 은 [교활하다]의 뜻). 커닝하다 cheat; crib

커다랗다 [खौदाराथा] huge; great; gargantuan; gigantic; monstr-

ous; mammoth; colossal. e.g. 커다란 잘못 a gross [glaring] mistake / a grave [fatal] error.

커리어 **[खौरीऔ]** a career. e.g. 그는 이 분야에 30 년의 커리어가 있다 He has a career of thirty years in this field.

커리큘럼 **[खौरीख्यूलौम]** [교육 과정] a curriculum <*pl.* -la, ~s>.

커미션 **[खौमीस्यौन]** [수수료, 구전] a commission.

커버 **[खौबौ]** **1** [덮개] a cover; a covering. e.g. 책 커버 a (book) jacket / a wrapper. **2** [보충하기] 커버하다 cover <a loss>; make up for <a loss>; [원호하다] cover; back up. e.g. 3 루를 커버하다 cover third base.

커브 **[खौब]** **1** [곡선] a curve; a curved line. e.g. 하강[상승] 커브 a falling [rising] curve. 상승 **2** [도로, 선로의 굽은 곳] a curve; a bend. e.g. 도로의 급커브 a sharp turn [bend] in the road. 커브를 돌다 round a curve.

커지다 **[खौजीदा]** grow [become] larger [bigger]; wax large; increase in size; [성장하다] grow (up); become [grow] taller; [증대하다] swell; expand; be enlarged; be extended; [대성하다] attain greatness; [중대해 지다] assume serious proportions [great dimen-sions]; grow serious. e.g. 부피가 커지다 increase [grow] in volume.

커튼 **[खौथन]** a curtain <at a window>; drapes (엷은 커튼 위에 치는 두꺼운.

커플 **[खौफल]** a couple. e.g. 그들은 어울리는 커플이다 They are a well-matched couple.

커피 **[खौफी]** Coffee

컨디션 **[खौन्दीसयौन]** condition. e.g. 컨디션이 좋다 be [feel] well / be in good condition / (운동 선수가) [be in fine [good] shape.

컨설턴트 **[खौन्सौल्थौन्थ]** a consultant. e.g. 경영 컨설턴트 a management consultant.

컨테이너 **[खौन्थेइनौ]** a container. e.g. 컨테이너용 크레인 (부두의 a container crane.

컨트롤 **[खौन्थ्रोल]** control. e.g. 컨트롤이 좋다[나쁘다] have a good [poor] control.

컬러 **[खौलौ]** **1** [색] [a) color; <英> (a) colour. **2** [특색]. e.g. 로컬 컬러가 짙은 제전 a festival rich in local color.

컬렉션 **[खौलेक्सयौन]** a collection. e.g. 그의 우표 컬렉션은 대단하다 He has an excellent [quite a] collection of stamps.

컬렉터 **[खौलेक्थौ]** a collector.

컬컬하다 **[खौल्खौरहादा]** <서술적> be [feel] thirsty [dry];

have a dry throat. e.g. 목이 컬컬한데 맥주 한 잔 했으면 좋겠다 I am thirsting for a glass of beer.

컴백 **[खौम्बेक]** a comeback. 컴백하다 come back <to one's former work>; make one's comeback.

컴컴하다 **[खौम्खौम्हादा]** [음흉하다] blackhearted; evil-minded; wicked; treacherous; sly; dark; black. e.g. 속이 컴컴한 사람 a black-hearted [treacherous] person / an insidious man / a deep one / a snake.

컴퓨터 **[खौम्फ्यूथौ]** a computer.

컵 **[खौब]** [우승배 a cup; a trophy; [잔] a glass; a drinking cup. e.g. 한 컵 가득한 물 a glass [a glassful] of water. 우승컵을 타다 win the cup [trophy].

케이블 **[खेइबल]** a cable. e.g. 해저 케이블 a submarine cable.

케이스 **[खेइस]** **1** [용기, 그릇] a case. e.g. 담배 케이스 a cigarette case. **2** [사례] a case. e.g. 모델 케이스 a model [typical] case

케케묵다[खेखेमुक्ता] antiquated; old; timeworn; worm-eaten; [시대에 뒤지다] old-fashioned; outmoded; out of date; musty (곰팡내 나는) [진부하다] stale; trite; hack. e.g. 케케묵은 책 a musty [fusty] book.

켜다 **[ख्यौदा]** **1** [불을 밝게 하다] burn; light (up) <a lamp>; set <a lamp> alight; make <a light>; turn [switch] on <an electric lamp>. e.g.촛불을 켜다 light a candle / get a candle alight. **2** (현악기를) play <the violin>; scrape (on) <a fiddle>; sweep <the strings>. e.g. 곡을 바이올린으로 켜다 fiddle a tune.

켤레 **[ख्यौल्ले]** a pair. e.g. 한 켤레의 양말 a pair of socks. 두 켤레의 구두 two pairs of shoes.

코 **[खो]** **1** (사람, 동물의) a nose; a nozzle; <美> a snoot; (돼지 등의) a snout; (개, 말 등의) a muzzle; (코끼리의) a trunk; a proboscis. e.g. 코를 후비다 pick one's nose. **2** <비유>. e.g. 코가 높다 be proud. 엎어지면 코 닿을 데에 있다 be within [at] a stone's throw <of / from **3** [콧물] snivel; nasal mucus; snot. e.g. 코 묻은 돈 a child's pocket money. **4** (물건의) [the nose; the tip; the cap; the toe. e.g. 신코 the toe [cap / toecap] of a shoe. **5** (편물의) a stitch; a link; (그물의) a knot. e.g. 그물코 [a net knot. 코를 성기게[촘촘하게] 뜨다 knit with large [small] stitches

코감기 **[खोगाम्गी]** [-感氣] a cold in the head [nose];

coryza. e.g. 코감기에 걸려 있다 have a cold in the nose [head].

코끼리 [ख्वोकिरी] elephant

코너 [ख्वोनौ] [모퉁이, 구석] a corner (백화점 등의) a special counter (a section) < for children wear >. E.G. 선두 주자는 벌써 네 번째 코너를 돌았다 the first runner has already turned the forth corner.

코디네이터 [ख्वोदीनेइथौ] cord-inator

코딱지[ख्वोताक्ची] Dried muscus from the nose; nose dirt; nose wax; (dried) snot E.G. 코딱지를 후비다 PICK ONE'S NOSE. 코딱지가 생겼다 nose wax .

코러스 [ख्वोरौस] a chorus.

코르셋 [ख्वोरुसेत] A chorest; corsets; stays

코맹맹이 [ख्वोमैग्मैगी] A person who thang twangs; a person who speake through the nose. E.G. 코맹맹이 소리를 하다 twang speak through the nose

코멘트 [ख्वोमेन्थ] (a coment on) E.G. 코멘트를 하다 make comment (on)

코미디 [ख्वोमीदी] A comedy

코미디언 [ख्वोमीदीऔन] A come-dian

코믹하다 [ख्वोमीख्वादा] Comic (al); humourous; funny; jocular; jocous. E.G. 코믹한 표정 a comic lock on one's face.

코방귀[ख्वोबांग्वी] A phoo phoo; a snort; phoo-phooing; <at>. E.G. 코방귀만 뀌다 snort (snop) at / turn up one's nose / treat<A speak> [disdian].

코스 [ख्वोस] **1** (경주,여행 등의 a course ; (경기장 등의) a lane; a track; a route;
(골프의) a fair way;(일부) a lap; a leg **2** [학과 과정] a course of study. E.G. 박사 학위 코스 the doctor's court

코앞 [ख्वोआप] E.G. 코앞에 a straigt before / under one's (very) nose / before one's eyes. 코앞에 닥친 impending / imment <danger >.

코웃음[ख्वोउसुम] A sneer; sneering. E.G. 코웃음 치다 sniff <at > / sneer <at > / laugh irronically.

코치 [ख्वोछी] (사람) a couch; (행위) coaching; training

코트 1 [ख्वोथ] [외투] an overcourt; [양복의 윗도리] a coat; a jacket; (여성용) an overgarment

코트 2 [ख्वोथ] [경기장] A <tennis> court. E.G. 코트를 만들다 a low court.

코팅 [ख्वोथीग] (천, 렌즈 등의) (A) COATING.

코피 [ख्वोफी] Blood from the nose; nose bleeding (Ing); nasal hemmorage; [病] epistastic

코흘리개 [**ख्वोहल्लीगै**] A snotty (-nosed) kid; a snotnose; a snever (l) el.

콕 [**ख्वोक**] **1** [찌르는모양] stinging [piercing / thrusting / poking / pricking] hard [fast/ sharply / abruptly]. E.G. 콕 쏘는 약 냄새[] a sharp order of medicine. **2** [쪼는 모양] pecking; picking. E.G. 닭이 땅을 콕 쫀다 a hen packs at ground.

콘돔 [**ख्वोन्दोम**] A condom; a rubber; a (contraceptive) sheath; <英> a French letter.

콘서트 [**ख्वोन्सौथ**] A concert. E.G. 레코드 콘서트를 열다 give [hold] a record concert.

콘센트 [**ख्वोन्सेन्थ**] an (electric) outlet; a wall socket; a plug recepent [socket]. E.G. 콘센트에 플러그를 꽂다 inert a plug in a wall outlet / plug in

콘크리트 [**ख्वोन्ख्रीथ**] concrete. E.G. 콘크리트의 concert

콘택트 렌즈 [**ख्वोन्थैक्थ लेन्स**] A contact lens. E.G. 콘택트 렌즈를 끼우다 wear contact lens / have contact lenses-stuck on the eyeball.

콘테스트 [**ख्वोन्थेस्थ**] A contest. E.G. 미인 콘테스트 a beauty contest.

콜 택시 [**ख्वोल थैक्सी**] A call taxy.

콜라 [**ख्वोल्ला**] [콜라 음 kola (cola).

콜레라 [**ख्वोल्लेरा**] cholera

콜레스테롤 [**ख्वोल्लेस्थेरोल**] [生化] cholelstol. E.G. 나의 혈중 콜레스테롤은 정상치 보다 높다 I have more the normal amount of blood cholesterol

콜록거리다 [**ख्वोल्लोकौरीदा**] Keep coughing [hacking].

콜록콜록 [**ख्वोल्लोकख्वोल्लोक**] cough [hacking] away. E.G. 콜록콜록 기침을 하다 give [emit] a dry cough / having cough / keep coughing [haking].

콤마 [**ख्वोम्मा**] [구두점] a comma. E.G. 두 단어 사이에 콤마를 찍다 insert [put] a comma betweent two world. 역콤마 a turned comma

콤비 [**ख्वोम्बी**] [조합] a combination; [2 인조] a pair, a duo. E.G. … 과 콤비로 in combination with.

콤플렉스 [**ख्वोम्फल्लेक्स**] <have/ devloop> an inferrity complex. E.G. 콤플렉스를 없애다 rid <a person> of his inferrity comple dismiss a sense ofinferrity (out of one's mind).

콧노래 [**ख्वोन्नोरै**] A hum; humming through the nose. E.G. 콧노래를 부르다 hum/ tum through the nose.

콧대 [**ख्वोत्तै**] The nose ride [bridge]. 콧대(가) 높다 be proud; be elated <over>; be puffed off <with pride>. E.G. 콧대가 높은 사람 a high hated man / a high hat / a stuck-person. 콧대를

꺾다 put a persons nose out of joins; humble <a persons> pride; snub<a person>; take <a person > a down pag; take the consist of <a person>. 콧대(가) 세다 be self-attested; be defiant [aggresive]; be imperious [haught]. E.G. 콧대가 센 사람 a self assertive / a defiant [an aggresive] person.

콧물 [खोत्मूल] snivel; snot; nose running (dripping]. E.G. 콧물을 닦다 wipe nose (running) nose.

콧소리 [खोसोरी] **1** [코먹은 소리] a nosal voice [tone/ accent]; a twang. E.G. 콧소리로 말을 하다 speak through one's nose / nasal the world / have a nosal tone [twang].

콧수염 [खोसूयौम] [－鬚髥] a moustach; <美> a moustach. E.G. 콧수염이 많이[적게] 난 남자 a man with twang [thin] moustach.

콩 [खोंग] <집합적> the pulses; (잠두 등) a bean; (완두) a pean; (대두) a soabean ; a soa bean.
<속담> an onion will pronouncea rose. 콩 심은 데 콩 나고 팥 심은 데 팥 난다 <속담> don't expect this extraordination. / like father like own.

콩밥 [खोम्बाप] Bean mixed rice 콩밥(을) 먹다 serve the jail [person] term; do [serve] time <AT>; "feed on wear and water". E.G. 콩밥을 먹이다 send <a person> in jail. 콩밥을 먹은 일이 있다 I have been person.

콩쿠르 [खोंक्कूर] [경연] A <프> concourse; a contest; a competion.

콱 [ख्वाक] **1** [세게] strongly; hard; violently; pungently (냄새가); (밀거나 당길 때) with a jerk; [단단히] tightly; firmly; fast E.G. 콱밀다 push with a (sudden) **2** [막히는 모양] quite, strongly; stiflingly. E.G. (구멍,관 등이) 콱 막히다 be stoped [pluged] up/be [get] blocked / get closed / be chocked.

콸콸 [ख्वालख्वाल] gushingly; in spout; in profusion; in a steady stom. E.G. 콸콸 쏟아져 흐르다 fllow the steadly / gush out of

콸콸거리다 [ख्वालख्वालगौरीदा] spout; gush; gurgle; bubble. E.G. 콸콸거리는 소리 a gurgling sound.

쾅 [ख्वांग] (터질 때) with a boom (room] bang; (떨어질 때) with a bump [thud / thumb]. E.G. 쾅 부딪다 bump against <a wall> / bump into <a man>.

쾅쾅거리다 [ख्वांख्वांकौरीदा]

(터질 때) keep booming [roaring]; (떨어질 때) keep booming [thumping / thudding]; reveberret; resound E.G. 복도를 쾅쾅 거리며 달리다 run through the passage noisly.

쾌감 [ख्वैगाम] [快感] a pleasant [an aggreable] feeling [sensation]; feeling of pleasurable; (성교시의) (an) orgam. E.G. 쾌감을 느끼다 feel pleasurable / feel comfortable [aggreable / fine / nice / good].

쾌거 [ख्वैगौ] [快擧] An inspiring [a heroic] deed; a gallant act [step / enterprise / undertaking]; a gallant [gallant / heroic] venture; a splendid [heroic] acheve-ment. E.G. 근래의 쾌거이다 be the small (heart) string enterprise in these days.

쾌락 [ख्वैराक] [快樂] pleasure; enjoyment; delight; comfort. E.G. 인생의 쾌락 pleasures [joys] of life. 육체적 [관능적] 쾌락 the plea-sures of senses / sensual [carnal] pleasures

쾌변 [ख्वैब्यौन] [快辯] eloquence; fluent speech. E.G. 쾌변을 토하다 make an eloqunent address [speech] / have a flow of word.

쾌속 [ख्वैसोक] [快速] a high [great] speed. E.G. 쾌속의] high speed / fast / swith / speedy.

쾌유 [ख्वैयू] [快癒] recovery [from illness]

쾌재 [ख्वैजे] [快哉] E.G. 쾌재를 부르다 cry out "bravo" / yell [shout] for [with] delight [joy] / utter yells of dilight / shout with ex-cluation.

쾌적 [ख्वैजौक] [快適] aggre-ableness; pleasant-ness. 쾌적하다 aggrable; com-fortable; delightness; plea-sant; comfy; nice. E.G. 쾌적한 침대

쾌차 [ख्वैछा] [快差] complete recovery; resoration of death. 쾌차하다 be completely re-covery; recover completly; regain one's health; be resorted to health; be per-fecitly well againg be (quite) agaomg man; come round completly

쾌척 [ख्वैछौक] [快擲] genere-ously throughing [tossing] out; making a geneous contribution. 쾌척하다 ge-nerously through out; make a generous contrri-bution; contribute generously; give a (fund) willing. E.G. 천만 원을 쾌척하다 gene-rously give a donation of ten mellion dollar <to / towardcccc>.

쾌청 [ख्वैछौंग] [快晴] fine [good] weather; fair [bright] and clear weather. 쾌청하다 (VERY)\ fine, fine

and nice. E.G. 쾌청한 날 a clear day.

쾌활 [ख्वैह्वाल] [快 活] 쾌활하다 cherful; cherry; merry; jolly; gay; lively; vivacious; sprightly; light-heatered; volatile; rattingt. E.G. 쾌활한 성미 cheerful sprit.

쿠데타 [खुदेथा] A coup date <pl coup date, coup date>;a coup. E.G. 군사[군부] 쿠데타 a military coup

쿠키 [खुक्की] <美> a cooly; a cooky; a biscuit.

쿠폰 [खुफोन] A coupon

쿨쿨 [खुल्खुल] (잠을) snoring; Z-Z-Z. E.G. 쿨쿨 코를 골다 snore loudly

쿵 [खुंग] With a thump [plump / bump / thud / bang / clump]. 쿵하다 'thump; plump; bump; thud; bang; clung. E.G. 쿵 하고 넘어지다 fall down with dong.

쿵쾅거리다[खुंग्ख्वांक्कौरीदा] Keep banging [roaring / pounding]; make din; raise [kick up] a racket; romp about. E.G. 쿵쾅거리며 걷다 stamp along <the floor> / walk along <the passage way> pit a pat [noisily].

쿵쿵 [खुंग्खुंग] **1** [떨어지거나 넘어질 때 나는 소리] with thumps [plumps / bumps / thuds / bangs] 쿵쿵하다 thump; plump; bump; thud; bang **2** [북P대포 소리] bang, bang; boom, boom E.G. 쿵쿵 울리는 대포 소리 the booming sound of cannon. 쿵쿵하다 bang, bang; boom, boom. **3** [찧는 소리]. E.G.방아를 쿵쿵 찧다 ound <grain> heavily with a pestle.

퀭하다 [ख्वेंग्हादा] [눈이 들어가 정기가 없다] cavernous; sunken; deep-set; hollow E.G. 퀭한 눈 sunken [cavernous / deep-set] eyes.

퀴즈 [ख्वीज] A quiz; a quiz A quize; a quize game. E.G. 퀴즈를 풀다 answer a quize question.

퀴퀴하다 [ख्वीख्वीहादा] ill-[foulL-] smelling; stinging; maladours; offensive; smelly. E.G. 퀴퀴한 냄새 an offensive [A bad / a foul] smell.

크게 [खुगे] [작지 않게] big; large; [상당히] very; much; far; greatly; heavily; largely; badly; seriously; considerably; highly; remarkably; exceedingly; [대대적으로] vastly; hugely; a great deal; to a great extent; [대규모로] on a large [grand] scale; in a large [big] way; in a [large] measure [degree]. e.g. 크게하다만들다] make <a thing> larger / enlarge / magnify / extend (확장하다) / (대규모로) do <things> big [in a big way].

크기 [खुगी] (a) size; dimensions; magnitude; volume (용적); bulk (부피). e.g. 크기는] in size / in dimensions / in area (면적). 크기에 따라서 according to size.

크다 [1] **[ख़ुदा]** [자라다] grow (up); become taller; grow larger; increase in size; [증대하다] swell; expand; be enlarged; be extended; be expanded; [대성하다] attain greatness. e.g. 다 큰 아이 a grown-up child.

크다 [2] **[ख़ुदा]** (형상이) big; large; [위대하다] great; grand; [강대하다] mighty; powerful; [막심하다] severe; heavy; [거대하다] gigantic; monstrous; mammoth; huge; colossal; enormous; [광대하다] vast; extensive; spacious; broad; of vast dimensions; (부피가) bulky; massive; voluminous (용적이); (마음이) generous; liberal; magnanimous. e.g. 큰 기대를 걸다 expect great things from <a person / a thing>.

크레용 **[ख़्रेयोंग]** (a) crayon. e.g. 파랑색[노랑색] 크레용 a stick of blue [yellow] crayon / a blue [yellow] crayon. 크레용으로 그림을 그리다 draw a picture in crayon (s).

크레파스 **[ख़्रेफास]** a pastel crayon.

크리스마스 **[ख़्रीसुमास]** Christmas (Xmas); Christmas day.

크림 **[ख़्रीम]** **1** (식용) cream. e.g. 생크림 fresh cream. 커피에 크림을 타다 add cream to coffee. **2** (화장용) (skin) cream. e.g. 화장용 크림 cosmetic [facial / face] cream.

큰마음 **[ख़ुन्माउम]** **1** [대망] a great desire; (an) ambition; (an) aspiration; best wishes. e.g. 큰마음을 품다 have [cherish / harbor] an ambition / be full of ambitions. **2** [후한 마음] a big [large] heart; a generous heart. e.g. 큰마음 쓰다 act generously.

큰사람 **[ख़ुनसाराम]** [위대한 사람] a great [magnanimous] man; a man of virtue [high caliber]; a great [master] mind. e.g. 큰사람이 되다 attain greatness.

큰소리 **[ख़ुन्सोरी]** **1** [크게 하는 소리 a loud [big] voice; a stentorian voice. **2** [야단치는 소리] a shout; a yell; a roar; a bawl; a brawl. e.g. 큰소리로 꾸짖다 address vehemently / thunder out / vociferate / fulminate / give <a person> hell [what for] / haul <a person> over the coals. 남에게 큰소리치다 shout [roar / rave / rage / explode] at a person. **3** [호언] big [tall] talk; boasting; a bombast;

a (loud) boast; boastful words; bragging; high-sounding words; magniloquence. e.g. 큰소리치다 talk tall [big] / [자랑하다] boast <of / that> / brag / make wild [exaggerated] claims.

큰아버지 [खुन आबोजी] one's father's elder brother; one's elder uncle.

큰어머니 [खुन ओमोनी] the wife of one's father's elder brother; one's elder aunt.

큰언니 [खुन ओन्नी] one's eldest brother [sister].

큰오빠 [खुन ओप्पा] one's eldest brother.

큰일 [खुनील] **1** [큰 사업] a great undertaking; a big [great] enterprise [task]; a big business; a big plan. e.g. 큰일을 이룩하다 achieve [do] a great thing [work]. **2** [중대한 일] a matter of grave concern [great consequence / great importance]; a serious [grave] affair; a great trouble; a disaster; no joke; an alarming accident. e.g. 큰일을 저지르다 cause [invite] a disaster / cause a serious trouble **3** [예식,잔치] a great occasion; a big ceremony [banquet]; a wedding; a funeral. e.g. 큰일이 닥쳐온다 A big occasion draws near.

큰절 [खुन्जौल] [의식, 웃어른에 가장 공손한 절] a deep bow. 큰절하다 make a deep bow; (초례청에서) make one's ceremonial deep bows. e.g. 차례가 끝나면 어린이들은 부모에게 큰절한다 Ather the ceremony, children make deep bows to their parents.

큰집 [खुन्जीब] **1** [맏형의 집] the house of one's eldest brother. **2** [종가] the head [main] family; the head house; the main stock.

큰코다치다 [खुन्खोदाछीदा] have a bitter experiences; have [get] the worst of it; have a hard [bad] time(of it) <with a person>; pay dearly <for>; get [catch / take] it in the neck. e.g. 그런 짓을 하다가는 큰코다칠 걸 You will suffer if you do such a thing. / You shall smart for this.

클라이맥스 [खल्लाइमैक्स] a climax. e.g. 클라이맥스에 달하다[이르다] reach [come to] the climax <of a story> / culminate <in>.

클럽 [खल्लौब] **1** [동호회] a club. e.g. 테니스 클럽 a tennis club. 사교 클럽 a social club / <美> (남학생의) a fraternity / <美> (여학생의) a sorority. 클럽에 들다 join a club / become a member of a club. 클럽을 조직하다 organize a club. **2** [골프,

하키의 채] a club.

클로즈업 [क्लोजअब] 1 [대상의 일부를 확대함] a close-up (CU); a close shot; a close-up view <of the moon>. 클로즈업하다 take [obtain] a close-up <of>; bring into a close-up. e.g.배우의 얼굴을 클로즈업하다 shoot a close-up of an actor's face. 2 [크게 취급함]. e.g. 정세가 바뀌면서 그의 이름이 다시 클로즈업되기 시작했다 The new situation has brought him into the public eye again. / As the situation has changed, he is being given a great deal of attention again.

클리닝 [क्लीनिंग] cleaning; laundry. e.g. 드라이 클리닝 dry cleaning.

클립 [क्लीब] [종이끼우개] a (paper) clip. e.g. 클립으로 꽂다 fasten <papers> with a clip.

큼직하다 [ख्म्चीखादा] quite [fairly] big [large]; good-sized; fair-sized; on the large side; (도량이) quite generous [liberal]. e.g. 큼직한 집[] quite a big house. 큼직한 사람 quite a big person.

킁킁 [खुंग्खुंग] "Sniff, sniff!" e.g. 킁킁 냄새를 맡다 sniff <at> / give a sniff <at>.

킁킁거리다 [खुंग्खुंगकौरीदा] (개 등이) whine; (돼지 등이) grunt; (말 등이) snort; (사람이 경멸의 표시로) snort. e.g. 코를 킁킁거리다 snuffle / sniffle. 그 아이는 코를 킁킁거리는 버릇이 있다 The child is in the habit of sniffling.

키 1 [खी] [신장] <one's> height; <one's> stature; inches. e.g. 키가 큰[작은] 사람 a man of great [small / low / short] stature / a tall [short] person. 키를 재다 measure [take] <a person's> height.

키 2 [खी] [조종타] a rudder; [조종 장치] a helm; [타륜] a (steering) wheel. e.g. 키를 잡다 steer / be at the helm / [조종하다] manage / control / handle / direct / lead. 그때 선장이 키를 잡고 있었다 The captain was at the helm at the time.

키 3 [खी] a key. e.g. 키를 누르다 press down a key. 타자기의 키를 두드리다 pound [strike / tap] the keys of a typewriter. 전신의 키를 치다 operate a telegraph key.

키다리 [खीदारी] a tall lank person; <英> a daddy long-legs; a gangling fellow. e.g. 그는 전봇대 같은 키다리다 He is as tall as a lamppost.

키보드 [खीबोद] a keyboard.

키스 [खीस] a kiss <on the

cheek>; a smack (소리가 나는). e.g. 키스를 보내다 [던지다] send [blow / throw] a kiss <to>

키우다 [**खीउदा**] **1** [양육하다 bring up; rear; raise; foster; nurse; (동,식물을) breed; raise; rear. e.g. 어머니 손으로만 키운<a child> brought up exclusively by his mother. **2** [육성하다] promote; support; protect; (재질 등을) develop; cultivate; [훈련,교육하다][] educate; train; bring up. e.g. 운동 선수를 키우다 develop an athlete. 법률가로 키우다] bring up <a boy> to the legal profession **3** [방치,조장하다] neglect; leave <a disease> unattended to [uncared for]. e.g. 병을 키우다 neglect a disease / let a disease take its own course.

키위 [**खीवी**] a kiwi; an apteryx.

키포인트 [**खीफोइन्थ**] [주안점] the main[essential] point; [요점] the point. e.g. 문제 해결의 키포인트 a key to solving a question.

킥 [**खीक**] (축구, 럭비 등에서) [] a kick.

킥킥 [**खीकखीक**] tittering; chuckling.

킥킥거리다 [**खीकखीक्कौरीदा**] titter; chuckle; laugh to oneself. e.g. 킥킥거리며 쳐다보다 look at <a person> with furtive laughter. 소녀들은 배를 쥐고 킥킥거리며 웃었다 The girls were doubled up with suppressed laughter.

킬로 [**खील्लो**] a kilo; [킬로미터] a kilometer (km); [킬로그램] a kilogram (me) (kg);
[킬로리터] a kiloliter(kl). e.g. 시속 3 백 킬로 a velocity of 300 km [kilometers] an hour.

타 [**था**] [**他**] [다른 사람] another person; other people; (the) others.

타개 [**थागे**] [**打開**] a break; a development; a new turn; a solution. 타개하다 break (through); effect a break [development].

타격 [**थाग्यौक**] [**打 擊**] **1** [때려치기] a blow; a hit; a knock; a clout; [기세를 꺾기] a crusher; a stinger; [충격 a shock; [손해] damage. **2** [야구] batting; hitting; a clout; [정구] a drive; [권투] a punch; a sock; a clout.

타결 [**थाग्यौल**] [**妥 結**] a compromise settlement; (협정 an agreement.

타계 [**थाग्यै**] [**他界**] **1** [저승]

the other [next] world. **2** [죽음] death; demise. 타계하다depart this life; depart from life; join the majority; pass away; die.

타고나다 [थगोनादा] be born <with / into>; be githed [endowed] <with>; be made for; be cut out for.

타국 [थागुक] [외국] a foreign country; [미지의 땅] a strange land.

타내다[थानैदा] get <from one's elder>; obtain; be given. e.g. 아버지한테서 용돈을 타내다 get pocket money from one's father.

타다[1] [थादा] **1** (불에) burn; blaze; be in flames. **2** [눋다] be [get] scorched [charred]; be parched; be singed. **3** [햇볕으로 변색되다] be sunburned [sun-burnt]; be suntanned; be sunbaked; be browned <with the sun> **4** [바짝 마르다] dry up; be dried up; parch; be parched (up); dry as a brick; [목이 마르다] have a dry throat; be [feel] thirsty.

타다[2] [थादा] **1** [탈 것에 오르다] ride <a horse>; take <a train>; take [have] a ride in <a car>; ride in <a cab>; [오르다] get on[into] <a train>; board <a bus>; [배에 오르다] go[get] abroad[on board] <a ship>; embark on[in] <a ship>. **2** [올라가다] walk up; climb [go up] <a mountain / tree>; ascend [make an ascent of] <a mountain> **3** [전파, 바람 등을 이용하다] take; get <on>. **4** [얼음 위를 닫다] skate <on the ice>; do skating; glide <over the ice>; slide [walk] <on the ice>. **5** [기회, 틈 등을 이용하다] seize <an oppor-tunity> ; seize on the situ-ation; (사물이) be opportune [timely]; be suited [pertinent] to the occasion; [인기를 누리다] catch popularity; catch on; take; hit <the public taste>; [기화로 삼다] take (mean) advantage [avail oneself] of <someone's weakness>.

타다[3] [थादा] [섞다] mix <with>; admiK add <to>; put <to / in>. e.g. 포도주에 물을 타다 dash wine with water / water wine

타다[4] [थादा] [받다] get; have; receive; take; gain; obtain; be given; secure <the doctor's degree>; win [carry off / bear away] <a prize>; [수여되다] be awarded; cadge. e.g. 노벨상을 타다 be awarded a Nobel prize. 1 등상을 타다 get [win] the first prize.

타다[5] [थादा] 1 [잘 느끼다] be apt to feel; be sensitive to; be tender; be alive <to pain>; [격하기 쉽다] be excitable. 2 [영향을 받다] be susceptible [sensitive] to; be allergic to; suffer easily from; be affected.

타당 [थादांग] [妥當] 타당하다 proper; appropriate; adequate; valid; sound; reasonable; fit; apposite; pertinent.

타당성 [थादांगसौंग] propriety; appropriateness; adequacy; soundness; pertinence; validity.

타도 [थादो] [打倒] overthrow. 타도하다 overthrow; throw out; defeat; knock down; topple <a person> from power.

타락 [थाराक] [墮 落] (도덕상의) depravity; (moral) corru-ption; degradation; fall; degeneration; decadence; debasement; delinquency; apostasy. 타락하다 degrade; degenerate <into>; lapse <from / into>; descend <to>; fall into decadence; become depraved; backslide; go to the bad; be morally ruined; go wrong; fall (away); go astray; fall from grace (종교적으로)

타령 [थार्यौंग] [打令] [곡조의 한 가지] a kind of tune; [민요] a ballad.

타박 [थाबाक] [打撲] a blow; a stroke. 타박하다 strike; give a blow.

타산적 [थासानजोक] [打算的] calculating; selfish; self-interested; self-centered; mercenary; mindful only of one's own interest. e.g. 비타산적인 disinterested / unselfish. 타산적인 정치가 a calculating politician

타산지석 [थासानजीसोक] [他山之石] a lesson; an example (from which one can profit).

타살[1] [थासाल] [他殺] [법률에서 모살](a) murder; [법률에서 고살(故殺)] manslaughter; [법률에서 모살, 고살을 포함한 살인] homicide.

타살[2] [थासाल] [打殺] 타살하다 strike [knock / beat / club] <a dog> to death; strike <a cat> dead; kill by a blow.

타석 [थासौक] [打席] [야구] [타수](times) at bat(ab.); [배터 박스] a batter's box.

타성 [थासौंग] [惰性] 1 = 관성 2 [습관] force of habit.

타수 [थासु] [打手] = 타자(打者).

타악기 [थाआककी] [打樂器] [樂] a percussion instrument.

타액 [थाऐक] [唾液] = 침. 타액 분비salivation; flow of saliva.

타워 [थावॉ] a tower.

타원 [थावॉन] [楕圓] an ellipse; an oval.

타월 [**थावॅल**] a towel.

타율 [**थायूल**] [**打率**] [야구] a batting average.

타이르다 [**थाइरूदा**] admonish <a person for his fault>; give admonition to <a person>; remonstrate <with a person on a fault>; [충고하다] counsel [advise] <a person to do>; warn <a person of danger>; [설득하다] persuade <a person to do>; [도리로써 깨닫게 하다] reason <with a person>.

타이어 [**थाइऑ**] a tire; a tyre.

타인 [**थाइन**] [**他人**] **1** [다른 사람] another person;(the) others; other people. **2** [남] an unrelated person; a stranger.

타일 [**थाइल**] a tile..

타임 [**थाइम**] **1** [시간] time. e.g. 그 주자의 최고 타임은 10초 8이다 The sprinter's [runner's] best time is 10.8 seconds. **2** [시합 등의 일시 중지] a time-out; a time out. e.g. 심판이 타임을 선언했다 The official [referee] called a time-out.

타자 [**थाजा**] [**打者**] [야구] a batter; a batsman; a hitter.

타작 [**थाजाक**] [**打作**] thresh; thrash (ing) 타작하다 thresh; thrash.

타전 [**थाजौन**] [**打電**] sending a telegram; telegraphing. 타전하다 telegraph; wire <to>; send a wire <to>; send a telegram <to>; communicate by wire; (해저 전선으로) cable; (무선으로) radio <to>; send a radio <to>; wireless <to>.

타종[**थाजोंग**] [**打鐘**] the ringing[tolling] of a bell. 타종하다 strike [toll / ring] a bell; sound [ring] a gong.

타파 [**थापा**] [**打破**] breaking; destruction; overthrow. 타파하다 break down; do away with <conventionalities>; des-troy; over-throw <bureau-cracy>

타협[**थाह्योब**] [**妥協**] (a) compromise; an agreement; an understanding; < 美 > (정당간의) trade. 타협하다 compromise <with>; come to terms <with>; make [effect] a compromise; reach [arrive at] a compromise; show a conciliatory tone; temporize <with>; reach an agreement <with>; meet <a person> halfway; split the difference

탁 [**थाक**] **1** [부딪거나 터지는 소리] with a bump [clunk]; with a crack; with a pop [bang]. **2** [손으로 치는 소리] with a slap [snap]; with a crack. **3** [끊어지거나 풀리는 소리] with a snap; snappingly; with force. **4** [트이어 시원한 모양] widely; extensively; vastly; (가슴 속이) refreshingly. **5**

[숨막히는 모양] stiflingly; chokingly.

탁구 [थाक्कु] [卓球] (정식으로) table tennis; ping-pong.

탁상 [थाकसांग] [卓上] e.g. 탁상의[에] on a table[desk]. 탁상용의 desk <dictionary>.

탁상 공론 [थाकसांग गोंग्नोन] a desk[mere] theory; an impracticable proposition.

탁아소 [थागासो] [託兒所] a day[public] nursery; <프> a crèche; (백화점 등의 일시적인) a nursery; [유치원에 들어가기 전의 보육원] a nursery school; a children's home; a baby farm.

탁월 [थाग्वॉल] [卓越] excellence; superiority; pre-eminence; eminence; prominence. 탁월하다 excellent; eminent; promi-nent; distinguished; superb

탁탁 [थाक्थाक] **1** [일을 결단성 있게 해치우는 모양] promptly; quickly; speedily; with (brisk) dispatch; in a businesslike way. **2** [침을 세게 뱉는 모양] spitting hard or in rapid succession. **3** [소리 나는 모양] with cracks; with pops; flapping; clattering; rattling. **4** [침을 세게 뱉는 모양] spitting hard or in rapid succession. **5** [숨이 막히는 모양] stifling; short of [out of] breath; gasping.

탁하다 [थाख्वादा] [濁-] **1** [물 등이 흐리다] muddy; turbid; dull; thick; (불순) impure; [음성 등이 거칠다] thick. **2** [안색이 훤하지 않다] dark; swarthy.

탄력 [थाल्यौक] [彈力] elasticity; resilience; elastic force; spring; bounce; give; rebound.

탄로 [थाललो] [綻露] disclosure; revelation; exposure; divulgence; detection. e.g. 탄로나다 get found out [detected / divulged / exposed / disclosed] / be revealed [laid bare] / be brought [come] to light / come [be] out / transpire. 틀림없이 탄로날 것이다 It is bound to come out.

탄복 [थानबोक] [歎服] 탄복하다 admire; be struck [moved] with admiration; be deeply impressed <with / by>; think well of

탄생 [थानसैंग] [誕生] (a) birth; nativity. 탄생하다 get [be] born; come into the world; first see the light of day

탄생지 [थानसैंगजी] one's birthplace.

탄성[1] [थानसोंग] [歎聲, 嘆聲] [한탄하는 소리] a sigh; a groan; [감탄의 소리] a sigh of admiration; an exclamation.

탄성[2] [थानसोंग] [彈性] [理] elasticity.

E

탄수화물 [थानसूह्वामुल] [**炭水化物**] a carbohydrate; a saccharide.

탄식 [थान्शिक] [**歎息,嘆息**] [비탄] a sigh; lamentation; [한탄] deploring.. 탄식하다 sigh <over>; heave [draw]a sigh; sigh for grief; lament; deplore.

탄알 [थानआल] [**彈-**] a shot; a bullet.

탄압[थानआब] [**彈壓**] oppression; pressure; suppression (▷ oppression 은 압제, 학대, suppression 은 진압이나 활동의 금지, pressure는 압박, 강제의 뜻이 담겨 있음); coercion. 탄압하다 suppress; oppress; repress; coerce; crush; clamp down (on); run rough shod over

탄원 [थानवॉन] [**歎願**] [간절히 바람](an) entreaty; (a) supplication; [문서에 의한 청원] a petition; [지지 등을 호소함] an appeal; (a) solicitation; (a) suit. 탄원하다 entreat; supplicate; implore; beseech; obtest; solicit <relief>; sue <a person for something>; petition <the government>; appeal <to a person for something>; make suit; beg.

탄탄 대로 [थानथान दैरो] [**坦坦大路**] a broad and level highway; a royal road.

탄탄하다 [थानथानहादा] ⇨ 튼튼하다

탄핵 [थानहैक] [**彈劾**] impeachment; denunciation; accusation; arraignment. 탄핵하다 impeach <a person of [with] a crime>; denounce; accuse <a person of misdemeanor>; censure; arraign.

탄환 [थानह्वान] [**彈丸**] <집합적> a projectile; lead; (산탄) a shot;(작은) a bullet; (포탄) a ball; a cannon ball; a shell (파열탄); a shrapnel (유산탄).

탈 [थाल] [가면] a (face) mask; [위선] hypocrisy; false modesty.

탈 [थाल] **1** [사고] an accident; an incident; an untoward event; [장애] a hitch; a snag; a failure; a trouble; a mishap; [지장] a hindrance; an impediment; interruption **2** [병] sickness; illness; a disease; a trouble; a disorder; [고장] something wrong; breakdown; ruin **3** [흠] a fault; a defect; a flaw; [트집] faultfinding. **4** [빌미,저주] a curse; an evil spell; retribution; a trouble.

탈것 [थाल्गौत] (육지의) a vehicle; (해상의) a vessel; (비행기) an airplane; [교통기관] means of transportation; a (public) conveyance.

탈고 [थाल्गो] [**脫稿**] completion of a manuscript. 탈고하다

finish writing; complete <a novel>; (원고가) be completed

탈곡[थालगोग] [**脫穀**] threshing (grain); thrashing. 탈곡하다[thresh [thrash] <wheat>; do the threshing.

탈나다 [थाललादा] **1** [병나다] become[get / fall] ill; be taken-ill. **2** [고장나다] break down; get out of order; go awry; be ruined **3** [사고나다] have a hitch [mishap / trouble]; run into trouble [snag] / be in a fix [quandary].

탈당 [थाल्तांग] [**脫 黨**] secession; withdrawal from [breaking with] a party; defection; <美> (party) bolting; cave.탈당하다 secede; withdraw [resign / defect / bolt] from a party; desert [leave / abandon] a party; break with a party.

탈락 [थाललाक] [**脫落**] **1** [붙은 것이 떨어짐] falling [coming] off; deplumation (깃털의). 탈락하다 fall[slip] off; shed. **2** [누락] an omission; a lacuna <*pl.* ~s, -cunae>; a hiatus <*pl.* ~(es)>. 탈락하다 be omitted; be left out; be excluded [eliminated]; be missing **3** [이탈] defection; desertion (탈당 등); straggling.

탈루[थाल्लु] [**脫 漏**] an omission; being left out; missing. 탈루하다 get omitted; be left out; be missing.

탈모 [थालमो] [**脫毛**] falling-out [-off] of hair; loss of hair; depilation; fallen hair. 탈모하다 <one's hair> fall out [off]; lose hair; bald; (새털이) molt.

탈바꿈 [थाल्वाकुम] (a) transformation; (a) metamorp-hosis. 탈바꿈하다 change (the shape of); assume another [a different] shape; metamorphose; transform; transmute.

탈색 [थालसैक] [**脫色**] decolo (u) ration; decolorization; discharge; bleaching. 탈색하다 decolo (u) r; decolorize; bleach; blanch; discharge.

탈선 [थालसौन] [**脫線**] **1** (열차 등의) derailment. 탈선하다 be [get] derailed; derail; run off the line [rails]; leave the rails; leave [run off] the metals; jump [leave] the track; be ditched **2** (행동 등의) deviation; aberration; departure; divergence; (이야기 등의) a ramble; (a) digression; an excursion; sidetracking.
탈선하다(행동이) deviate [go away] from the right path; get on the loose; go astray [wild]; be erratic [eccentric]; (이야기 등이) digress [go adrith] <from the subject>; make a digression; go off the rails; go [run] off the (main) track; get

sidetracked; be off the subject; talk (away) [wander / stray] from the subject [point]; get off the point; go wild; wander <in one's talk>.

탈세 [थालसे] [**脫稅**] evasion of taxes; tax evasion dodging].탈세하다 evade [dodge] a taK defraud the revenue (수입을 속여서)

탈세자 [थालसेजा] a tax evader [dodger]; an evade of taxes.

탈수 [थालसु] [**脫水**] [수분 제거] dehydration; [가열 등에 의한 수분 제거] evaporation; [건조시킴] desiccation; (공학에서) dewatering. 탈수하다 dehydrate; dry; dewater; (원심력으로) spin-dry

탈영 [थारयौग] [**脫營**] desertion from barracks; decam-pment. 탈영하다 desert from barracks; desert one's colors; break barracks; go over the hill.

탈영병 [थालयौगबयौग] a deserter; a runaway soldier.

탈옥 [थारोक] [**脫獄**] prison breach; prison [jail] breaking; jailbreak. 탈옥하다 break (from a) prison; break jail; escape from prison

탈옥수 [थारोकसु] a prison-breaker; a jail-breaker; an escaped prisoner [convict].

탈의 [थारउइ] [**脫衣**] divestiture; divestment. 탈의하다 undress oneself; take off one's clothes.

탈의장[실] a dressing [changing] room; (해수욕장 등의) a bathhouse; (체육관,학교 등의) a locker room.

탈주 [थालजु] [**脫走**] (an) escape; flight; abscondence; decampment; a break; a breakaway; (a) desertion. 탈주하다 flee; escape; run away; (군인이) desert <from the army>; (수병이) jump ship; (육군에서) go over the hill; make off (with oneself); break loose [away]; bolt; give [take] leg bail (탈옥,탈영

탈진 [थालजीन] [**脫盡**] total exhaustion. 탈진하다 be utterly exhausted [fatigued]; be tired to death; be worn [fagged] out.

탈출 [थाछुल] [**脫出**] (an) escape; extrication. 탈출하다 escape from <a prison>; extricate oneself from <danger>; get away <from a place>; get out

탈춤 [थाछुम] a mask (ed) dance.

탈취 [थाछ्वी] [**脫臭**] deodorization. 탈취하다 deodorize; remove [kill] the odor <of>.

탈퇴 [थालथवी] [**脫退**] (단체 등으로부터의) withdrawal <from>; (교회,당파 등으로부터의) secession <from>. 탈퇴하다 withdraw <from>; leave; secede <from>; break (away) from; bolt from; disconnect oneself from

탈피 [थालफी] [脫皮] **1** (곤충, 뱀의) ecdysis <*pl.* –dyses>; casting off. 탈피하다 cast (off) the skin; shed the skin; slough (off). **2** <비유> self-renewal. 탈피하다 e.g. 구태에서 탈피하다 break from the convention / outgrow one's former self / come out of oneself.

탈환 [थारह्वान] [奪還] recapture; recovery; retaking. 탈환하다 recapture; win back; regain; recover; retake.

탐 [थाम] [貪] [탐욕] covetousness; avarice; greed; [욕심] desire; want; [탐닉] indulgence.

탐관 오리 [थामग्वान ओरी] [貪官汚吏] a corrupt official; a grath-happy official; a venal official.

탐구 [थामगु] [探究] [조사] (an) investigation; (an) inquiry; [연구] research; (a) study. 탐구하다 investigate; inquire into; make researches in; explore.

탐나다 [थामनादा] [貪–] (사물이) be desirable; be appetizing; be tempting; (사람이) be desirous [covetous] of; be envious of; desire; rust ather [for].

탐내다 [थामनैदा] [貪–] desire; want; crave (for); hanker for [ather]; covet; be greedy <ather>; be desirous <of acquiring / to acquire>; be covetous <of>.

탐닉 [थामनीक] [耽溺] [열중] indulgence; addiction; [주색에의 몰입] dissipa-tion; debauchery. 탐닉하다 indulge in; be addicted to; be given (up) to; give oneself up to; abandon oneself to <the pursuit of pleasure>; be dissipated; dissipate.

탐독 [थामदोक] [耽讀] indulgence in reading; avid reading. 탐독하다 read avidly [with avidity]; be absorbed [engrossed] in reading; steep oneself <in>; pore over <a novel>; be immersed in <a book>; devour <novel ather novel>.

탐문 [थामुन] [探聞] obtaining information (by inquiry). 탐문하다 obtain information (by inquiry); hear; get wind of (소문을);(형사 등이) snoop [beat the bushes] for information.

탐방 [थामबांग] [探訪] (private) inquiry; an interview (기자 등의); investigation

탐사 [थामसा] [探査] (an) inquiry; (an) investigation: probing. 탐사하다 make inquiries; investigate; inquire [look] into

탐색 [थामसैक] [探索] **1** [수색] search; hunt; quest. 탐색하다 search <for>; look [quest] for; delve into; seek for; hunt up; probe 2 [조사] (a) probe; inquiry; investigation; research. 탐색하다 [손으로 더듬어서 찾아내다] grope for and find <a thing>; [찾아 발견하다] hunt out; discover; [장소를 알아 내다] locate; [상세히 조사하다] investigate

탐스럽다 [थामसुरौपता] [貪-] desirable; appetizing; coveted; attractive; tempting; charming.

탐식 [थामसीक] [貪食] voracity; edacity; gluttony. 탐식하다 eat voraciously [greedily]; eat avidly; devour; gormandize.

탐욕 [थामयोक] [貪慾] avarice; greed; rapacity; covetousness; cupidity..

탐정 [थामजौग] [探偵] (행위) detective work; covert investigation; espionage; espial; (사람) a detective; an investigator; a spy; a plainclothesman (사복 형사); a sleuth.

탐지 [थामजी] [探知] ascertaining; detection; finding out by indirect inquiry. 탐지하다[थामजीहादा] detect; spy [search] out <a secret>; trace [ferret / smell] out <a crime>; get wind of <an affair>; learn <a fact> by inquiry; monitor <radio communications>

탐탁하다 [थामथाकहादा] desirable; satisfactory; pleasant; pleasing; agreeable; acceptable.

탐폰 [थामफोन] a tampon.

탐하다 [थामहादा][貪-] covet <fame>; be greedy <of / for>; be covetous <of>. e.g. 명리를탐하다 covet [thirst ather] fame and gain. 안일을 탐하다 live in idleness / pass one's days in indolence / idle away one's time. 폭리를 탐하다 eager to make an excessive [undue] profit / profiteer.

탐험 [थामहौम] [探險] (an) exploration; (탐험 여행) an expedition. 탐험하다 explore; make an exploration

탑 [थाब][塔] a tower; (성 등의 작은 탑) a turret; [불교] a pagoda.

탑승 [थापसुंग] [搭乘] boarding; riding <a ship / a plane>. 탑승하다 get into; board; [비행기를 타다] get on <a plane>; [함선에 오르다] embark on [go on board] a ship

탑재 [थापचै] [搭載] loading; embarkation; entrainment. 탑재하다 load; embark; entrain; take in.

탓 [थात] [잘못] fault; blame; responsibility; [이유] reason; cause; ground (s); [결과] consequences; a result; [영향] influence; an effect.

탓하다 [थाथादा] put [lay] blame upon; lay the fault to; find fault <with>; blame [reproach] <a person for something>; impute; charge; accuse e.g. 자신을 탓하다 reproach oneself <for>. 하늘을 탓하다 quarrel with Providence.

-탕 [थांग] [湯] [달인 약] a (medical) decoction; an infusion; [국] soup.

탕[1] [थांग] [총소리] bang; with a bang; [부딪는 소리] with a clang. 탕하다 go bang [boom]; go off with a bang; bang; boom; clang

탕[2] [थांग] [湯] **1** ⇨ 국 **2** [욕조] a (hot) bath; [목욕탕] baths **3** [제사에 쓰이는 국] soup offered at ancestor memorial service.

탕감 [थांगगाम] [蕩減] writing-off; cancellation; remission. 탕감하다 write off <debt>; cancel (out).

탕수육 [थांगसुयुक] [糖水肉] [요리] sweet and sour pork.

탕진 [थांगजीन] [蕩盡] 탕진하다 squander; dissipate <a fortune>; run [go] through <one's fortune>; run [give] out of.] one's fortune by fast living. 그는 부모의 유산을 탕진했다 He has squandered every penny of the legacy from his

태 [थे] [態] **1** = 맵시 e.g. 이 양복은 그가 입으면 태가 난다 This suit looks good [nice] on him [when he wears it]. **2** [태도] an air. e.g. 갑부 태를 내다 play the millionaire / display [show off] one's wealth **3** [문법] voice. e.g. 능동[수동]태 active [passive] voice

태고 [थेगो] [太古] ancient times; remote ages [antiquity].

태교 [थेग्यो] [胎敎] prenatal care (of an unborn child); prenatal culture [education]; antenatal training. y.

태권도 [थेक्वाँनदो] [跆拳道] the Korean art of empty-handed self-defense; taekwondo.

태극기 [थेगुककी] the national flag of Korea; the *t'aegŭk* flag.

태도 [थेदो] [態度] an attitude; [거동] bearing; demeanor; deportment; a manner; an air; a mien.

태동 [थेदोंग] [胎動] (태아의) quickening; fetal movement; the movements of the fetus; <비유> signs [indications] <of forthcoming activities>; fomentation. 태동하다 quicken; <비유> show signs of <democratization>.

태만 [थेमान] [怠慢] [게을리함] negligence; neglect; dereliction; procrastination; [게으름] idleness;

E

laziness. 태만하다 negligent; neglect-ful; derelict; delinquent; supine; idle; lazy

태몽 [थैमोंग] [**胎夢**] a dream of forthcoming conception.

태반[1] **[थैबान]** [**太半**] (양적으로) the greater [best / most] part; the great [large] portion; (수적으로) the great; majority; the bulk.

태반[2] **[थैबान]**[**胎盤**] the placenta <*pl.* −tae, ~s>.

태생 [थैसैंग] [**胎生**] **1** [출생] birth; origin. **2** viviparity.

태세[थैसे][**態勢**] [태도] an attitude; setup; a posture; [준비] preparedness; arrangements; [상태] a condition.

태아 [थैआ] [**胎兒**] an unborn child [baby]; (임신 3개월 까지의) an embryo <*pl.* ~s>;(3개월 이후의) a fetus; a conceptus <*pl.* ~es, −ti>.

태양 [थैयांग] [**太陽**] [해] the sun

태어나다 [थैऔनादा] be born; come into being [existence / world]; see the light.

태연 [थैयौन] [**泰然**] 태연하다 calm; cool; composed; self-possessed; unruffled; imperturbable; unimpassioned; firm; immovable; unmoved.

태엽 [थैयौब] [**胎葉**] a spring; a windup spring..

태우다 [थैउदा] **1** [불에 타게 하다] burn; put into the fire; set <the hay> on fire; have [get] <one's house> burnt down. **2** [그슬리다] burn; scorch; singe; char (새까맣게)..**3** (시체를) cremate; burn (a corpse) to ashes. **4** (가슴,속을) burn <one's soul>; agonize; worry..

태우다 [थैउदा] **1** [사람,물건을 싣다] carry; take in; take <a person> on board; place <a man> in a train; pick up; (선원을) ship <a new crew>; man <a ship>; [수용하다] accommodate. **2** <비유> e.g. 비행기 태우다 flatter (immensely / grossly). 나를 비행기 태우는구나 You flatter me immensely

태초 [थैछो][**太 初**] the beginning of the world.

태클 [थैखुल] [스포츠] a tackle 태클하다 tackle.

태평 [थैफ्यौंग] [**泰平,太平**] [세상의 평안함] (perfect) peace; quiet; tranquility.. 태평하다 peaceful; quiet; tranquil.

태평 성대 [थैफ्यौंग सौंगदै] a peaceful reign; a reign of peace.

태평양 [थैफ्यौंग्यांग] [**太平洋**] the Pacific (Ocean)

태풍 [थैफुंग] [**颱風**] a typhoon.

택시 [थैकसी] a taxi; a taxicab; a cab.

택일 [थैगील] [**擇日**] choice of

E

an auspicious day. 택일하다 choose an auspicious day.

택하다 [थैखादा] [擇-] [선택하다] prefer; choose; pick; take.

탤런트 [थैकल्लौनथु] a star; <집합적> talent (▷ 인기 있는 사람의 경우에는 a star라고 하나, 보통 a singer, an actress 처럼 직종을 나타내는 말을 씀)..

탯줄 [थैल्चुल] [胎 -] the umbilical cord; the navel string [chord]; [解] the funiculus <*pl.* –li>.

탱크 [थैंगख्यु] 1 [용기] a tank. 2 = 전차

탱탱 [थैंगथैंग] tautly; tightly. 탱탱하다 blown up to the tautness of surface; inflated; swollen up [out]; puffed up; distended; hard and taut [tense / tight].

터 [थौ] **1** [자리] a site <for a school>; a (building) lot; land <for>; a place; a plot. e.g. 집터 land for housing / a house[home / building] lot. **2** [일이 벌어지는 장소] an arena; a theater. e.g. 싸움터 a field of battle / a battlefield **3** [기초] the foundation; the ground; footing; foothold; groundwork; spadework. e.g. 터를 다지다 consolidate [solidify] the foundation.

터널 [थौनौल] [굴] a (railway) tunnel; an excavation.

터놓다 [थौनोथा] **1** [막힌 것을 치우다] lay [make] open; open <it> up; break; undam <a river, a reservoir, etc.>. **2** [금했던 것을 풀다] remove <a prohibition>; lith <a ban>. **3** [마음을 트고 지내다] open one's heart; open up one's mind; be frank [candid / open] <with a person>; be unreserved; throw off [lay aside] reserve [for-malities]; break down all reserve; throw [shake / cast] off all restraint; come out of one's shell; break the ice; hobnob <with a person

터득 [थौदुक] [攄 得] understanding; comprehension; grasp; apprehension; realizetion; mastery. 터득하다 understand; apprehend; comprehend; master; make out; grasp; have a grasp of ...; realize; learn.

터뜨리다 [थौतुरीदा] **1** (막힌 것 등을) break; burst; tear; have <something> break [burst / tear]. **2** (폭발물, 감정을) explode; burst; detonate..

터무니없다 [थौमुनीऔब्ता] [근거 없다] unfounded; baseless; groundless; <서술적> have no foundation; [엉뚱하다, 당치않다] extraordinary; wild; absurd; fabulous; preposterous; exorbitant; <美>

darned; [말도 안 되다] unreasonable; [말의 조리가 서지 않는다] incoherent; [무모하다] reckless; [도를 지나치다] excessive.

터미널 [थौमीनौल] **1** [종점] a terminal; a (bus) terminal; a (railway) terminus. **2** [공항의 사무 시설] a terminal.

터벅거리다 [थौबौकौरीदा trudge <along / on>; tread <along / on>; plod <on>; hobble <along / about>; jog [pad] <along>.

터벅터벅하다 [थौबौकथौबौकहादा] [음식 등이 퍽퍽하다]. e.g. 터벅터벅한 빵 dry and tasteless bread.

터울 [थौउल] an age span between siblings; the diff-erence [disparity] of age between siblings.

터잡다 [थौजापदा] select [pick out / secure] a site [lot / land]; (기초를) establish the foundation <of>.

터전 [थौजौन] a site; a lot; the grounds; a base.

터주다[थौजूदा] leave <a way> open; permit; allow; give leave [permission]; lith <the ban>.

터지다 [थौजीदा] **1** [파열되다] burst (open); break; split; splinter; (종기 등이) burst; break; open; collapse. **2** [폭발하다] explode; burst (out); go off; break out; blow up. **3** [발생하다] occur [happen] suddenly; break [burst] out; take place. e.g. 중대한 사건이 터졌다 A serious matter popped up. 전쟁이 터졌다 A war broke [burst] out. **4** [탄로나다] get exposed; be[come] out; be found out; be disclosed; be revealed; come [be brought] to light **5** (샘,피 등이) spout <out>; spurt <out / up>; gush out. **6** [얻어맞다] get a blow; be beaten; be struck on.

터치 [थौची] [손을 댐, 촉감] a touch.

턱[1] [थौक] (입의 위아래) the jaws; [解] maxilla <*pl.* -lae>; (아래턱의 바깥 부분) the chin; the chops; the mandible (포유 동물,어류 등의, 특히 아래턱).

턱[2] [थौक] [높은 데] a pro-jection; an elevated place; a rise; a sill. e.g.. 문턱 a door [window] sill.

턱[3] [थौक] [음식 대접] a treat; a feast; a banquet; an en-tertainment; <美> a set-up. e.g. 한턱 내다 stand treat for <one's friend> / give <a person> a treat / treat <a person> to <some-thing> / stand <a person dinner>.

턱[4] [थौक] [까닭] reason; gro-unds. e.g. 그럴 턱이

있나 It cannot be so

턱밑 [थोम्मीत] **1** [턱의 끝] the tip of the chin. **2** [가까운 곳]. e.g. 턱밑에 beneath one's chin / right under one's nose.

턱없다 [थोकओप्ता] **1** [근거, 이유 없다] groundless; unfounded. **2** [지나치다] immoderate; exorbitant; extreme; excessive; tall; <美> darned; [당치 않다] extraordinary; unreasonable; absurd; wild; preposterous; blithering. **3** [신분에 맞지 않다] <서술적> be not suitable to one's means; [능력 밖이다] <서술적> be beyond one's reach [power].

털 [थौल] **1** (사람의) hair.**2** (짐승의 털) fur; wool; [깃털] feathers

털갈이 [थौलगारी] (새의) mo (u) lting; (짐승의) coat-shedding; shedding hair. 털갈이하다 =털갈다 e.g. 닭이 털갈이한다 Hens are molting. 동물은 봄이 되면 털갈이한다 Animals shed their coats in spring.

털끝 [थौल्कुत] **1** [털의 끝] the end of a hair; an end of hair; the tips of hair; hair tips. **2** [조금] a bit; a jot; a whit; [아주 작은 일] a minor detail; <집합적> trivia; minute. e.g. 털끝만큼도 개의치 않다 don't care at all / don't care a straw / don't give a damn.

털다 [थौल्ता] **1** ⇨ 떨다 e.g. 그을음[거미줄]을 털다 sweep away [off] soot [cobwebs].(발을 굴러서) 눈을 털다 stamp the snow from <one's boots>. 윗도리의 먼지를 옷솔로 털어 내다 brush one's jacket. **2** [가진 돈 등을 전부 써 버리다] empty. **3** (도둑 등이) rob <a person> of; strip <a person> of; steal <a thing from a person>; pilfer [filch] <articles from a shop>.

털리다 [थौल्लीदा] **1** (붙은 것,묻은 것이) get shaken [knocked / beaten] off; (먼지가) get dusted [brushed] off. e.g. 옷의 먼지가 잘 털리다 Dust brushes off my clothes readily. / My clothes are easily dusted. **2** [몽땅 없어지다] get emptied. e.g. 자루가 다 털렸다 A bag was completely emptied. 노름에서 그는 몽땅 털렸다 He was cleaned out in gambling. **3** [모두 빼앗기다] get robbed <of>. e.g. 금고를 털리다 have one's safe robbed. (소매치기한테) 주머니를 털리다 have one's pocket picked / have <a thing> stolen.

털실 [थौलसील] wool (l)en yarn; worsted (yarn); wool; knitting wool.

털썩 **[थौलसौक]** with a thud [plump / thump / bump / flump]; heavily. 털썩하다 thud; flop; plump; bump.

털어놓다 **[थौलौनोथा]** **1** (물건을) empty (out); shake out. **2** (마음속을) open one's heart; take <a person> into one's confidence; confide in <a person>; disclose; reveal; lay bare; confess; tell [talk] frankly [without reserve].

털옷 **[थौरोत]** a fur [woolen] robe.

털털하다 **[थौलथौरहादा]** **1** (사람이) unaffected; free and easy. **2** (맛이) somewhat puckery.

텀벙거리다 **[थौमबौंगगौरीदा]** keep splashing [plopping]; splash about; dabble.

텁석 **[थौप्सौक]** with a snatch; with a snap; greedily..

텁수룩하다 **[थौप्सुरुख्वादा]** thick; shaggy; bushy.

텁텁하다 **[थौप्थौफादा]** (입맛이) thick and tasteless; unpleasant-tasting; <서술적> have a muddy taste; be rough and unpleasant to the palate.

텃세 **[थौस्से]** [-勢] defending one's territory [turf / eminent domain]; pulling rank. 텃세하다 take advantage of being on one's own ground [in one's own sphere of influence] to act high-handedly; play cock-of-the-walk; lord it over a newcomer.

텅 **[थौंग]** e.g. 텅 빈 empty / vacant / bare / void / hollow / deserted

테 **[थे]** **1** (둘러매는) a hoop. **2** (안경 등의) a rim; a frame.. **3** [모자 띠] a band; a stripe; [언저리] a brim; a rim.**4** [테두리] a border; a rim.

테니스 **[थेनीसु]** (lawn) tennis.

테두리 **[थेदुरी]** **1** [가장자리] the border; the edge; [테] the brim; the rim; the frame. **2** <비유> an outline; an overall picture; a rough sketch.**3** [범위] a limit; a framework; the confines <of>.

테러 **[थेरौ]** terror; terrorism. 테러하다 terrorize.

테스트 **[थेसुथु]** a test; testing; an examination; an exam; a workout; a quiz; (배우, 가수의) an audition; a tryout.

테이블 **[थेइबुल]** a table; a desk..

테이프 **[थेइफु]** **1** (종이,헝겊, 비닐 등의) (a) tape; (축하용) a paper streamer; a colo (u) red tape ribbon; (녹음 테이프) a (sound recording) tape;(창 등에서 흘뿌리는 색 테이프) tickertape. **2** [줄자] a tape (measure).

테크닉 **[थेखुनीक]** (a) technique; (a) technic.

텍스트 **[थेकसुथु]** **1** ⇨ 텍스트북 **2** [원문;본문] a text.

텐트 [थेनथु] a tent; <집합적> tentage.

텔레비전 [थेल्लेबीजौन] television; <英> telly; <美> the boob tube (텔레비전을 바보 취급한 말투); (수상기) a television(set); a TV[T.V.](set); a teleset..

템포 [थेमफो] (a) tempo <*pl.* ~s, -pi>; speed.

토 [थो] **1** (한문 구절 끝에 붙이는) Hangul letters suffixes added to aid the reading of Chinese texts. **2** ⇨ 토씨

토건업 [थोगौनौब] [**土建業**] civil engineering and construction industry; construction work; the construction industry.

토굴 [थोगूल] [**土窟**] = 땅굴. e.g. 토굴에서 사는 사람 a cave dweller.

토기 [थोगी] [**土器**] an earthen (ware) vessel [utensil / pot]; <집합적> earthen ware; crockery.

토끼 [थोकी] a (house) rabbit (집토끼); a hare (산토끼).

토닥거리다 [थोदाककौरीदा] keep patting [tapping / knocking / rapping / beating]..

토대 [थोदै] [**土臺**] **1** [토단] a terrace of earth. **2** (건축의) a foundation; a stereobate; a sill. **3** [(사물의) 기초] a foundation; groundwork; a base; a basis <*pl.* bases>; a cornerstone.

토라지다 [थोराजीदा] **1** (성이 나서) pout; sulk; be (come) sulky [peevish]; go into the sulks; be in the sulks. **2** (음식이) lie heavy on one's stomach; (사람이) have heartburn; have a sour stomach.

토로 [थोरो] [**吐露**] exposing [revealing] one's thoughts. 토로하 lay bare <one's heart>; express; utter; deliver; speak <one's mind>; give mouth [vent] <to>; disclose [reveal] <a secret to a person>; voice; set forth.

토론 [थोरोन] [**討論**] (a) discussion; (a) debate (▷ discussion 은 의견을 서로 주고받음, debate 는 다른 의견을 맞부딪쳐 논의함); a talk. 토론하다 debate <on>; discuss <a subject with a person>; dispute; have [hold] a debate; talk up.

토마토 [थोमाथु] a tomato <*pl.* ~es>; a love apple..

토막 [थोमाक] a piece; a block; a bit; a fragment; a strip; a scrap (끄트러기).

토목 [थोमोक] [**土木**] (공사) engineering [public] works.

토박이 [थोबागी] [**土-**] ⇨ 본토박이 (⇨ 본토)

토속 [थोसोक] [**土俗**] local customs; folkways.

토스트 [थोसुथु] toast.

토실토실 [थोसीलथोसील] plump; chubby; fat. 토실토실하다 plump; chubby; rotund;

tubby; fat.
토양 [थोयांग] [土壤] soil
토요일 [थोयोइल] [土曜日] Saturday (Sat.).
토의 [थोउइ] [討議] (a) discussion; (a) debate (▷ discussion 은 여러 가지 견해를 내놓고 서로 이야기하는 일, debate 는 다른 의견을 다투게 하는 일); (a) deliberation.. 토의하다 discuss <politics / a social problem>; hold a discussion <with another>; deliberate upon [over] <a matter>; debate on [about] <a question, a subject, a matter, a problem, etc.>.
토지 [थोजी] [土地] 1 [지면] land; a piece [tract] of land (한 구획의 땅); [소유지] lands; a lot [plot] (좁은); an estate; a landed property [estate]; real estate (넓은). 2 [지질] soil; land.3 [영지] territory.
토하다 [थोहादा] 1 [게우다, 뱉다] vomit; spew; bring [fetch] up; throw [cast] up; <英> cat. 2 (감정,마음을) express; give vent <to>; utter; deliver; speak out <one's mind>.
톡 [थोक] 1 [튀어나온 모양] protruding; protuberant; bulging; [불거짐,비어짐] popping; bulging out <of a pocket>. 2 [치는 모양, 소리] with a pat [rap].
톡탁 [थोकथाक] tapping; rapping; beating; dabbing.
톡톡히 [थोकथोकही] 1 [심하게] harshly; severely; smartly. 2 [많이] quite a lot; much; loads of.
톤 [थोन] a ton; [배,화물의 톤수] tonnage (▷ 영국에서는 a long ton (약 1016 kg), 미국에서는 a short ton (약 907kg), 프랑스에서는 a metric ton (1000kg) 을 씀).
톨 [थोल] a nut (밤 등의); a grain <of rice>.
톱 [थोब] [자르거나 켜는 연장] a saw; 한 사람이 켜는 것) a handsaw; a tenon saw; 두 사람이 켜는 것) a crosscut saw.
톱 [थोब] top.
톱날 [थोमनाल] a saw blade; a saw tooth.
톱니 [थोमनी] the tooth of a saw; a sawtooth <*pl.* -teeth>.
톱니바퀴 [थामबनीबाख्वी] a toothed wheel.
톱밥 [थोबपाब] sawdust.
-통 [थोंग] [通] [정통한 사람] an authority <on>; an expert <in / at / on>; [감정가] a connoisseur <of>. e.g. 식통 informed sources. 법률통 an authority on law / a legal expert.
통[1] [थोंग] [桶] [나무 그릇] a cask; a barrel; 큰) a hogshead; a butt; 작은) a

E

keg; (물통 등) a pail; a (wooden) bucket; a tub; a kit; a tank; a vessel; a trough; a cistern(수조).

통[2] **[थोंग]** [通] [편지 세는 말] a letter; a note; [문서를 세는 말] a document; a paper; [증서를 세는 말] a bond.

통[3] **[थोंग]** **1** (배추 등의) a head <of cabbage>; the body <of a gourd>. **2** [사람 됨] caliber; scale; [도량] magnanimity; generosity; [담] boldness.. e.g.통이 큰 사람 a man who does things in a big way. 통이 작다 be a person of small caliber. **3** [피륙의 세는 단위] a roll; a bolt..

통[4] **[थोंग]** [정신차릴 수 없는 기세]. e.g. 통에 in the midst <of> / amid / amidst / in the bustle [confusion] <of> / during the confusion <over> / taking advantage of the confusion / in the influence <of>.

통[5] **[थोंग]** [전혀] quite; entirely; utterly; absolutely; completely; [조금도] <not> at all; <not> in the least; <not> a bit [straw / particle / fig]. e.g. 통 모르겠다 cannot make head or tail of <something>.

통감 [थोंगाम][痛感] 통감하다 feel strongly [deeply / acutely]; fully realize; take to heart.

통계 [थोंग्ये] [統計] statistics; figures; a numerical statement..

통고 [थोंगो] [通告] (a) notice; (a) notification; announcement; warning. 통고하다 notify <a person of[that]>; give <a person> notice <of / that ...>; warn <a person of [that]>; garnish.

통곡 [थोंगोक] [痛哭, 慟哭] lamentation; wailing. 통곡하다 [비탄하다] bemoan; lament <a person's death>; [몹시 울다] weep bitterly <over the loss of a friend>.

통과 [थोंग्वा] [通過] passage; passing; a pass; transit; carriage (의안의). 통과하다 pass (through); go [get] through; be carried.

통관 [थोंग्वान][通關] entry; clearance; customs clearance; clearance <of goods> through the customs. 통관하다 enter [clear] <a ship>; clear [pass] the customs; clear [pass] <baggage> through the customs.

통근 [थोंगुन] [通勤] attending office; going to work; commuting; commu-tation; (입주 근무의 상대어로) living out. 통근하다 attend [go to] (one's / the) office; commute; live out; come [go] to work from outside.

통나무집 [थोंगनामुजीब] a log

cabin [hut / house].

통념 [थोंगनयौम] [通念] a common idea; a generally [commonly] accepted idea.

통달 [थोंगदाल] [通達] [막힘이 없이 통함] mastery; conversance; thorough knowledge <of>. 통달하다 be well [deeply] versed <in>; be at home <in / on>; have a thorough knowledge <of>; be conversant <with>.

통닭 [थोंगदाक] a whole chicken; [닭요리] a chicken cooked whole.

통독 [थोंगदोक] [通讀] 통독하다 read [go / get] through <a book>; read <a book> from cover to cover; peruse <a book>.

통례 [थोंगरये] [通例 common [usual] practice; a (common) usage; a [an established] custom..

통로 [थोंगनो] [通路] a passage; a passageway; a way; a pathway; a path; a roadway; a road for passage; an avenue; an alley (좁은); a walkway (정원, 공원 등의); an aisle (극장, 열차,교회 등의) an aisle; the entrance (입구의); a track (동물의).

통론 [थोंगनोन] [通論] [개론] an outline <of sociology>; [입문] an introduction <to economics>.

통보 [थोंगबो] [通報] a report; (공보) a bulletin; (내무 보도) <give / get> a tip. 통보하다 [report; notify; inform.

통분 [थोंगबुन] [痛忿,痛憤] great indignation. 통분하다 be greatly indignant.

통사정 [थोंगसाजौंग] [通事情] [사정을 잘 알아줌] having sympathetic understanding; having an understandding heart. 통사정하다 have sympathetic understanding; have an understanding heart; understand.

통상 [थोंगसांग] [通常] [평소] usually; [보통] normally; [일반적으로] generally; as a rule; commonly; under normal conditions.

통상 [थोंगसांग] [通商] commerce; trade; trade intercourse; commercial relations [intercourse]. 통상하다 trade <with a country>.

통성명 [थोंगसौंगमयौंग] [通姓名] 통성명하다 introduce <themselves> to each other; exchange <their> names.

통속 [थोंगसोक] [단체] a gang; a cabal; (협잡꾼의) a decoy; a shrill; a bonnet; (경매 때의) a by-bidder; a puffer; [음모] a cabal; a secret intrigue [plot]; a secret agreement.

통솔 [थोंगसोल] [統率] command; generalship; leadership. 통솔하다 command;

E

lead; direct; take the lead of

통신 [थोंगसीन][通信] (a) communication; (편지 등에 의한) correspondence; (보도) news; a dispatch; (정보) information; (국가적인 기밀 정보) intelligence.. 통신하다 correspond <with a person>; communicate <with a person>; communicate a message <to a person>; report <for a paper>; keep up a correspondence <with a person>.

통용 [थोंग्योंग] [通用] popular [common] use; circulation; currency. 통용하다 be in common use; pass <for>; circulate; be [pass / go / run] current; (표 등이) be available; be good; (규칙 등이) hold good [true

통일 [थोंगइल] [統一] unity; unification; consolidation; coordination; uniformity; coherence; oneness; (표준화) standardization; (통어) rule; sway; dominance; (집중) concentration. 통일하다 unify; consolidate; coordinate; [표준화하다] standardize; [통어하다] rule; bring under sway

통장 [थोंगजांग] [通帳] (은행의) a bankbook; a passbook; (외상 거래의) a chit-book.

통제 [थोंगजे] [統制] control; regulation; regimentation 통제하다] control; regulate; govern; regiment

통제 가격 controlled prices.

통제 기관 [थोंगजे गीग्वान] a control organ [agency]; an

통조림 [थोंगजोरीम] [桶 –] (제조) packing; canning; tinning; (제품) canned [tinned] provisions [goods].

통증 [थोंगजुंग] [痛症] a pain; an ache; a pang (급작스런); pricking (따끔따끔한).

통지 [थोंगजी] [通知] [통고] (a) notice; (a) notification; [통보] (a) report; information; [통신] communication; (상업상의) an advice. 통지하다 notify <a person that [of]>; inform <a person that [of]>; let <a person>know <that / of>; communicate <news to / with a person>; advise [apprise] < a person that [of]>; (주로 해약해고 등의) give <a person> notice <that / of>.

통찰 [थोंगछाल] [洞察] discernment; penetration; insight. 통찰하다 discern; penetrate [see] into; see through; fathom <a person's heart>.

통찰력 [थोंगछालयौक] [洞察力] an insight; penetration; vision; discernment.

통첩 [थोंगछौब] [通牒] a note; a notification; a circular; instruction. 통첩하다 notify

<a person of [that]>; give notice <to>; communicate.

통치 [थोंगछी] [**統治**] rule; reign; government; administration. 통치하다 rule over [govern] <a country / a people>; hold sway over; administer; guide.

통칭 [थोंगछीग] [**通稱**] [공통으로 쓰이는 이름] a common designation [title]; [널리 통하여 불리는 이름] a popular [common] name; (an) alias.

통쾌 [थोंगख्वै] [**痛快**] a keen pleasure; a thrill. 통쾌하다 [유쾌하다] awfully pleasant; extremely delightful; piquant; [만족스럽다] affording intense satisfaction; very gratifying.

통통 [थोंगथोंग] [두드리는, 구르는 소리] pounding; beating; stamping; tramping; resounding. 통통하다 =통통거리다 pound; beat; stamp; tramp.

통틀다 [थोंगथुलदा] lump [put] together; sum up; draw into one mass.

통틀어 [थोंगथुरौ] [모두 합하여] all put together; in total; (all) in all; (in) all told; in the gross [mass / lump]; in one lot; collectively; <프> en bloc [masse].

통풍 [थोंगफुंग] [**通風**] ventilation; airing; drath; draught.

통하다 [थोंगहादा] [**通-**] **1** (길, 통로, 교통 기관 등이) run; lead <to / into> (…에 이르다); open <into a room / upon a corridor [garden]>; communicate <with>; [개통하다] be opened <to [for] traffic>; be connected <by a railway>(이어지다) **2** (공기가) vent <through a chimney>; (be) ventilate(d); (빛,열 등이) pass [run / go] through; penetrate; permeate; (혈액 등이)(be) circulate(d);(파이프 등이) draw; drain. **3** (전류가) transmit; flow **4** (전화가) <a call> be put [go / get] through; be on <the line>; <the phone> be working; get connected <with>.**5** [내용,사정 등에 정통하다] be well [deeply] versed <in>; be an expert <in / on>; be(well) up <in>; be proficient <in>; be at home <in / on>; be a master <of>; be well acquainted <with>; be well informed <of>; be conversant <with>. **6** (말,의사 등이) be understood; be comprehended; be spoken; make oneself understood; under-stand (each other); be congenial. **7** (글의 뜻이) make sense; be under-standable. **8** (정 등을) become intimate <with>; have relations <with>; form a liaison <with>; commit

E

misconduct [adultery] <with>; intrigue <with>..**9** [내통하다] communicate secretly [intrigue] <with the enemy>; betray; be in touch with <the other party>. **10** [허용되다] pass; get by; be admissible.

통학 [थोंगहाक] [通學] attending school. 통학하다 attend [go to] school [classes]

통합 [थोंगहाब] [統合] integration; unification; unity; combination; consolidation; synthesis. 통합하다[integrate; combine; unify; unite; consolidate; put [bring] together; make into one.

통행 [थोंगहैंग] [通行] passing; passage; transit; (street) traffic. 통행하다 pass (through); go [get] past; go through [along].

통행료 [थोंगहैंगन्यो] a toll; passage money.

통화 [थोंगह्वा] [通貨] currency; current money [coins]; the medium of circulation; the circulating medium

통화 [थोंगहवा] [通話] a (telephone) call; a (telephone) message; telephone conversation; telephonic communication. 통화하다 speak [talk] over [upon] the telephone.

통화량 [थोंगहवारयांग] tele-phone traffic.

퇴각 [थ्वेगाक] [退却] [후퇴] (a) retreat; (a) withdrawal; retirement; falling back; backdown. 퇴각하다 retreat <from / to>; beat [make] a retreat; withdraw; retire; fall back; give ground.

퇴거 [थ्वेगौ] [退去] [이전] leaving; quitting; removal; [명도,철수] evacuation; withdrawal; eviction; dispossession; [추방] deportation; [도망] an exodus <from a country> (다수의). 퇴거하다 leave; quit; depart; evacuate; withdraw [go away] <from a place>; vacate <a house>; remove; move out..

퇴고 [थ्वेगो] [推敲] polish; elaboration. 퇴고하다 polish; elaborate (on); improve.

퇴교 [थ्वेग्यो] [退校] = 퇴학.

퇴근 [थ्वेगुन] [退勤] leaving one's office [work]

퇴락 [थ्वेराक] [頹落] dilapidation; ruin. 퇴락하다 dilapidate; go [fall] to ruin; fall [go] into decay [dilapidation]; collapse.

퇴보 [थ्वेबो] [退步] retrogression; retrocession; a return; a step backward; a backward step; [퇴화] degeneration; deterioration. 퇴보하다 go [move / fall] backward; suffer a relapse; retrograde; retrocede; take a backward step; retrogress <to>; degenerate; deteriorate.

퇴비 [श्वेबी] [堆肥] compost; barnyard [farmyard] manure.

퇴사 [श्वेसा] [退社] [회사를 그만둠] retirement [withdrawal] from a company [firm]; termination of membership. 퇴사하다 retire [withdraw] from a company; leave a company.

퇴색 [श्वेसैक] [退色, 褪色] fading (of color); discoloration. 퇴색하다(색이) go [come] off; fade (away); (사물이) grow dull in color; lose color; discolor; be discolored.

퇴원 [श्वेवॉन] [退院] leaving (the) hospital; (감화원에서의) discharge from a reformatory. 퇴원하다 leave (the) hospital; be discharged [released] from (the) hospital.

퇴위 [श्वेवी] [退位] (an) abdication. 퇴위하다 abdicate (the throne [crown]); step down from the throne <in favor of one's son>

퇴임 [श्वेइम] [退任] retirement <from one's office>. 퇴임하다(정년으로) retire <from>; (임기 도중에) resign <from>.

퇴장 [श्वेजांग] [退場] (회의, 식, 경기장 등에서의) leaving. 퇴장하다 leave <the hall>; go away.

퇴장 [श्वेजांग] [退藏] [쓰지 않고 묵혀 둠] hoarding. 퇴장하다 hoard.

퇴적 [श्वेजौक] [堆積] accumulation; a pile; a heap; [地質] sedimentation 퇴적하다 pile [build] up; accumulate.

퇴직 [श्वेजीक] [退職] retirement (from office); resignation. 퇴직하다 retire [withdraw] from office [public service]; be relieved of office; go out of office; go on the retired list; retire from [leave] the service; resign an office

퇴직금 [श्वेजीकगुम] [退職金] a retirement allowance; retirement pay [benefits]; (해고수당) a discharge allowance.

퇴진 [श्वेजीन] [退陣] decampment; <비유> retirement. 퇴진하다 decamp; withdraw; <비유> retire <from a position>; step down; resign; exit; go out; disengage oneself <from>

퇴치 [श्वेछी] [退治] **1** [정복] subjugation; subdual; conquest; suppression. 퇴치하다 subdue; subjugate; suppress. **2** [박멸] extirpation; eradication; elimination; extermination; control; destruction. 퇴치하다 wipe [stamp / root] out; clean up; extirpate; eradicate; eliminate; get rid of; destroy; control; fight; combat

퇴폐 [थ्वेफ्ये] [**頹廢**] (도덕, 기풍 등의) corruption; degeneration; demoralization; decay; decline; deterioration; dry rot. 퇴폐하다 corrupted; be demoralized; be degenerated; decay; fall into decay; decline.

퇴학 [थ्वेहाक] [**退學**] **1** (학생 스스로의) leaving school (before graduation); (a) withdrawal. 퇴학하다 leave [give up] school [college]; withdraw from school [college].**2** (학교 당국의 벌로서의) expulsion from school. 퇴학하다 dismiss [expel] <a student>.

퇴화 [थ्वेहवा] [**退化**] [쇠퇴하여 축소됨] degeneration; [퇴행] retrogression; (기관,조직의) atrophy. 퇴화하다 degenerate; degrade; retrograde; atrophy; become atrophied (기관 등이).

투 [थु] [**套**] **1** [버릇] a manner; a way; a fashion; a habit. e.g. 말투 one's way [manner] of talking / the way one talks / a turn of words **2** [법식] a form; a style. e.g. 편지 투 the forms of letter writing.

투견 [थुग्यौन] [**鬪 犬**] [개싸움] a dogfight; [싸움용 개] a fighting dog. e.g. 투견을 시키다 fight dogs.

투고 [थुगो] [**投稿**] (a) contribution. 투고하다 contribute <(an article) to a periodical>; write <for a magazine>

투기 [थुगी] [**鬪技**] a competition; a contest; a match.

투기 [थुगी] [**投機**] (a) speculation; (a) spec; a venture; an adventure; an operation; gambling; chances; [증권] stockjobbery; stockjobbing. 투기하다[speculate in <stocks>; deal in futures; engage in speculation; make a ven-ture; gamble <in stocks>.

투덜거리다 [थुदौरकौरीदा] [불평하다] complain; [혼잣말처럼 두런거리다] grumble; mutter; murmur (알아듣지 못할 만큼 작은 소리로); <美> gripe.

투명 [थुम्यौंग][**透 明**] transparency; pellucidity; limpidness; clearness; clarity. 투명하다 transparent; limpid; pellucid; lucid; diaphanous; clear (as crystal); crystalline. .

투박 [थुबाक] 투박하다 (물건이) unshapely; shape-ess; ill-formed; ill-shaped; unsightly; coarse; rough; gross; crude; (사람이) unrefined; rustic; boorish; uncouth; awkward; stiff; senseless.

투병 [थुब्यौंग] [**鬪病**] one's struggle against disease [illness].

투사 [थुसा] [**鬪士**] a fighter; a combatant; a champion;

ㅌ

<美> a bearcat.

투사 [थुसा] [**投射**] **1** projection. 투사하다 project.

투서 [थुसौ] [**投書**] a contribution; a letter <from a reader>; a correspondence; a letter to the editor; (익명의) an anonymous notice [communication / letter] 투서하다 contribute <an article to>; send a contribution <to a magazine>; write (a letter) to <the newspaper>

투석 [थुसोक] [**投石**] stone-throwing [-hurling]. 투석하다 cast [throw / hurl] a stone [rock] <at>; stone <at>.

-투성이 [थुसोंगी] [뒤덮여 있음] covered with ...; [묻거나 배있음] daubed [soiled / stained / smeared] with ...; [가득함] full of ...; filled with .e.g. 피투성이의 bloodstained / bloody / gory.

투수 [थुसु] [**投手**] [야구] a pitcher; a hurler; a twirler; a moundsman; < 美 > a heaver

투숙 [थुसुक] [**投宿**] 투숙하다 put up at <a hotel>; lodge in <a hotel>; check into <a hotel>; register [be a guest] at <a hotel>.

투시 [थुसी] [**透視**] **1** [비치어 봄] seeing through. 투시하다 see through.**3** [꿰뚫어 봄] clairvoyance; second sight. 투시하다 divine; see through.

투신 [थुसीन] [**投身**] **1** [몸을 던짐]. 투신하다 drown [die by drowning] oneself (in the water); throw oneself into the water [river]; commit suicide by drowning; precipitate oneself into the water; kill oneself by plunging <from>; plunge to death. **2** [종사]. 투신하다 go into; launch [plunge] into; enter upon; embark [launch out] on <an enterprise>; start out to <do something>; concern oneself in; be concerned in [with]; have a hand [finger] in.

투약 [थुयाक] [**投藥**] medication; (medical) prescription; dosage; exhibition; administration <of medicine>. 투약하다 pres-cribe [administer / com-pound / give] a medicine [drug / dose]; medicate

투영 [थुयौंग] [**投影**] **1** [물체가 비치는 그림자] a cast shadow. 투영하다 reflect; cast a reflection; throw an image on. **2** projection. 투영하다 project <an article>.

투옥 [थुओक] [**投獄**] imprisonment; confinement; incarceration.. 투옥하다 put a person in prison; cast [throw] a person into prison; imprison a person; run in; <lag.

투우 [थूउ] [**鬪牛**] (경기) a bullfight; bullfighting; (소) a fighting bull. 투우하다 have a bullfight; have bulls fight (each other); fight a bull.

투우사 [थूउसा] a bullfighter; a matador; (말을 타고 하는) a toreador.

투입 [थूइब] [**投入**] **1** [던져 넣음] throwing in; injecttion; (노력 등의) output. 투입하다 throw [cast] into; order <troops> in; commit to; [化] project <into / on> **2** [經] [투자] investment; [기업이 매입하는 재화 또는 용역] input. 투입하다 invest [sink] <money> in <factory equipment>.

투자 [थूजा] [**投資**] (an) investment.. 투자하다 invest in; make an investment in; lay [put] out <one's money> in; (헛되이 또는 회수 곤란한 사업에) sink <money / a capital> in.

투정 [थूजौंग] complaining; grumbling; growling. 투정하다 grumble <at / over>; complain <about / of>; growl.

투지 [थूजी] [**鬪志**] a combative [fighting] spirit; fight.

투척 [थूछौक] [**投擲**] a throw; throwing. 투척하다 throw.

투철 [थूछौल] [**透徹**] penetration; lucidity; thoroughness. 투철하다 clear; limpid; lucid; pure; thorough; thoroughgoing

투표 [थूफ्यो] [**投票**] [표결] vote; suffrage; [투표하기] poll; ballot; voting; balloting. 투표하다 ballot <for>; cast a ballot; vote; cast a vote <for>; poll.

투표권 [थूफ्योग्वॉन] [**投票權**] the (right to) vote; the right of voting [casting the ballot]; suffrage; a voice; the voting power.

투하 [थूहा] [**投下**] [아래로 떨어 뜨림] throwing down; dropping; an airdrop <of supplies>. 투하하다 throw down; drop; (비행기에서) airdrop 투하하다 invest <in>

투혼 [थूहोक] [**鬪魂**] fighting [combative] spirit.

툭 [थूक] ⇨ 톡

툭하면 [थूकहामयौन] (too) othen; on [at] the slightest provocation; ready to; always.

툴툴거리다 [थूलथूलगौरीदा] grumble <at / over / about>; mutter <about>; complain <of>

퉁명스럽다 [थूंगम्यौंगसुरौपता] blunt; brusque; gruff; snappish; curt; unaffable.

퉁탕 [थूंगथांग] [두드리거나 발로 구르는 소리] beating; pounding; striking; stamping; [총소리] banging repeatedly;

bang. 통탕하다 =통탕거리다.

통탕거리다 [थुंगथांगगौरीदा] **1** [두드리거나 발로 구르는 소리를 내다] beat; pound; beat loudly **2** (총소리가) keep banging away.

튀기다[1] [थ्वीगीदा] **1** (손가락으로) fillip; flip; snap; (주판알을) move [work] counters; (용수철 등을) spring out. **2** (물 등을) splash; (be) spatter; dabble; (침을) spit; sputter.

튀기다[2] [थ्वीगीदा]**2** (기름에) fry <in a hot pan>; frizzle; (곡식을 불에) pop.

튀김 [थ्वीगीम] [기름에 튀긴 음식] fried food; a fried dish; a fry fritters.

튀다 [थ्वीदा] **1** (탄력이 있는 물건이) bound; rebound; bounce; spring **2** (불똥이) spark; sparkle; sputter; (장작 등이 타면서) snap; crack; crackle; (볶는 것이) burst [crack] open; pop open. **3** (물,침 등이) splash; spatter; sputter; get spattered; splashed.. **4** [달아나다] fly (away); run away; make off; take (to) flight.

튀어나오다 [थ्वीऔनाओदा] **1** (숨은 것P동물 등이) jump [leap / bounce] out; spring out; [뛰쳐나오다] rush [burst] out;(말 등이) rush. **2** [돌출하다] project; protrude; jut (out); shoot out.

트다[1] [थ्रुदा] **1** [싹이 돋아나다] sprout; bud (out); shoot; spring up **2** [살갗이 벌어지다] chap; be [get] chapped; be cracked. **3** [동쪽이 훤해지다] break; dawn; turn gray.

트다[2] [थ्रुदा] **1** [막힌 것을 통하게 하다] break <it> open; sit <it> open; cut; open. **2** [거래 관계를 맺다] open; begin; initiate.

트랙 [थुरैक] a track. e.g. 트랙과 필드 track and field.

트러블 [थुरौबुल] a trouble; a scandal.

트럭 [थुरौक] a (motor) truck; an autotruck; a(motor-) lorry.

트렁크 [थुरौंगख्यु] [자동차 뒤에 짐 싣는 곳] the trunk (compartment); the lugg-age compartment; the boot.

트레이너 [थुरेइनौ] a trainer.

트레이닝 [थुरेइनीग] training.

트림 [थुरीम] belching; a belch; eructation; burp. 트림하다 [थुरीमहादा] belch; eruct; burp

트이다 [थुइदा] **1** (막혀 있던 것이) get cleared; be open (ed); be cut (길 등이); (운이) be in the **ascen-dant.** **2** (마음 등이) be liberal [generous]; be open-minded [open-hearted]; be sensible; [물정에 밝아지다] come to know much of the world; get used to

the ways of the world.

트집 [थुजीब] **1** [탈] a fault; a blemish; (생트집) a false charge. **2** [틈새] a crack; a break; a fissure. 트집(을) 잡다 find fault <with>; pick holes [flaws] <in>; make a false charge <against>; cavil at.

특가 [थुकका] [**特價**] a special [bargain] price; a specially reduced price.

특공대 [थुकगोंगदै] [**特攻隊**] a "special attack" unit [corps]; a suicide unit; a commando unit; commando-men; a Ranger.

특권 [थुकग्वॉन] [**特 權**] a privilege; a special [an exclusive] right; a prerogative; a charter; [法] special privilege.

특근 [थुकक्कुन] [**特勤**] [과외의 일] extra duty [assignment]; [시간외 근무] overtime work. 특근하다 work overtime; work extra hours; do extra work.

특급 [थुक्कुप] [**特 急**] [특별 급행 열차] a limited [special] express (train); a super-express; a cannonball

특급 [थुक्कुप] [**特級**] special grade.

특급품 [थुक्कुप्फुम] a special grade article; an extra fine [superfine] brand.

특기 [थुककी] [**特 技**] one's special ability [talent / gith]; one's special skill; one's special art; speciality; one's special flair in <mathematics, music, etc.>.

특대 [थुकतै] [**特 待**] (a) special treatment; distinction. 특대하다 treat <a person> with distinction; give a special treatment

특례 [थुंग्ने] [**特例**] **1** [특별한 예] a special case [example]; a particular instance [case] **2** [예외] an exception. e.g. 전시 특례 a wartime exception.

특명 [थुंगम्यौग] [**特命**] [특별한 명령, 임명] a special command [appointment / assignment]; a mission. 특명하다 command [order / appoint] specially.

특별 [थुकपयौल] [**特別**] being special 특별하다 special; especial; express; [특수하다] particular; [고유하다] peculiar; [보통이 아니다] extraordinary; uncommon; (여분의) extra; (예외의) exceptional.

특색 [थुकसैक] [**特 色**] a specific character; a characteristic; a (specific) feature; a peculiarity; a distinction; (개성) an idiosyncrasy; an individuality; (특히 인격상의) a color; (personal) coloring.

특성 [थुकसौग] [**特 性**] a special [distinctive] quality; a specific [special / peculiar] character; a specificity; a characteristic; a peculiarity; a (peculiar) property; a feature; (개인의) a trait of character; a stamp; an idiosyncrasy; an individuality; a diagnosis <pl. –noses>; genius.

특수 [थुकसू] [特需] [특별한 수요] special procurements; emergency [special procurement] demands [orders] <due to the outbreak of war>.

특용 [थुकयोंग] [特用] (a) special use. 특용하다 use specially; use <a thing> [be used] for a special purpose. \

특용 작물 [थुकयोंग जाकमूल] a crop for a special use; a cash crop.

특유 [थुकयू] [特有] peculiarity. 특유하다 character-istic <of>; peculiar [special] <to>; unique; unusual; (all) its own **특유성** a peculiarity; uniqueness.

특이 [थुगी] [特異] 특이하다 singular; peculiar; unique. **특이성** peculiarity; particularity; singularity; uniqueness.

특전 [थुकचौन] [特典] [특혜] a special favor; a benefit; (개인적인) a privilege; [가톨릭] an indult.

특정 [थुकचौंग] [特定] specification 특정하다 specify e.g. 이러저러한 것을 원한다고 특정하지 않았다 I did not specify what I wanted

특종 [थुकजोंग] [特種] **1** [특별한 종류] a special kind [type]. **2** [특종 기사] exclusive news; an exclusive; a scoop; a news beat.

특질 [थुकचील] [特質] a characteristic; a property; a special quality.

특집 [थुक्चीप] [特輯] a special edition. **특집 기사** a special feature article.

특징 [थुकचींग] [特徵] a (special / distinctive / distinguishing) feature [character]; a distinguishing [characteristic / distinctive] mark;(a) distinction; (인상 등의) identifying marks; a characteristic; a peculiarity; (개인의) a trait of character; individualities; an idiosyncrasy; a stamp; a diagnostic character. (feature는 주의를 끄는 두드러진 특색, 특히 얼굴 등 그 자체내에서 눈에 띄는 부분, peculiarity는 다른 것과 달라 눈에 띄는 특색).

특채 [थुक्छै] [特採] special appointment [engagement / employment]. 특채하다 employ specially; take <a person> into service [a company] specially.

특출 [थुकछूल] [特出] prominence; conspicuousness; distinction. 특출하다 outstanding; conspicuous;

E

prominent; distinguished; striking; remarkable.

특파 [शुकफा] [特派] dispatch; sending off <a person> for a special purpose. 특파하다 dispatch [send] (specially); send off <a person> for a special purpose; send on a special mission; tell off.

특파원 [शुकफावॉन] [特派員] [특별 임무를 위해 파견된 사람] a mission; a representtative; a delegate; [신문,통신사의 파견 기자] a (special) correspondent.

특필 [शुकफील] [特筆] special mention. 특필하다 mention [write] specially; make special mention of; (신문 등이) make a feature of; feature; give (special) prominence to; lay special stress on.

특허 [शुकहौ] [特許] 1 [특별한 허가] a special permission; [면허] a license. 특허하다 license <a person to do>; grant <a person> a special permission [license] 3 (정부에서 은행P회사 등에 주는) a charter. 특허하다 charter <a company to do> 4 (전매의) a patent <for / on>..

특허권 [शुकहौग्वॉन] [特許權] a patent right; the right to a patent.

특혜 [शुकहये] [特惠] a special favor[benefit]; preference; preferentialism..

특효 [शुकह्यो] [特效] (a) special virtue [efficacy] <for>.. e.g. 특효약 a specific remedy; a miracle [wonder] drug

특히 [शुकही] [特-] specially; expressly; in special (measure); in specialty; [각별히] especially; in special; particularly; in particular; peculiarly; [무엇보다] above all; before everything else.

튼튼하다 [थुनथुनहादा] [견고하다] strong; solid; stout; stanch; [골격, 짜임새 등이 실하다] sturdy; stalwart; substantial; [견실하다] steady; secure; firm; stable; sound; [건강하다] healthy; sound; strong; well and strong; lusty; vigorous; robust.

틀 [थुल] 1 [창문,액자 등의 테두리] a frame; framework; (필름을 감는) a reel.. 2 a mo (u)ld; a matriK a cast; a die; (의치의) an impression; a mold; [모형] a model; a pattern. 3 [일정한 윤곽, 형태] a (definite) shape [form] 4 [정해진 형식, 격식] formality; a formula <*pl.* –lae, ~s>; [관례] usage; conventionality; tradition; rule 5 ⇨ 기계e.g. 형틀 an instrument of torture / a frame for punishing <offen-

ders>. 솜틀 a cotton gin / a (saw) gin.

틀니 [**थुल्नी**] an artificial [a false] tooth; a denture.

틀다 [**थुल्दा**] **1** [비틀다] twist; wrench; wring; screw; give <something> a twist.**2** [돌리다] turn; wind; [기계 등을 작동시키다] set [put] <a machine> going [in motion]. **3** [일 등을 방해하다] thwart; counteract <a plan>; cross; work against.

틀리다 [**थुल्लीदा**] **1** [잘못되다] be mistaken <in>; become [be] wrong [erroneous / incorrect]; be in error; be in the wrong; be at fault; [잘못하다] mistake; err; make [commit] a mistake [an error] <in>; do wrong [amiss] **2** [다르다] differ <from>; be different <from>; be unlike; be dissimilar <to>; vary <from>; be varied [variable].**3** [나쁘다] be bad [evil / wrong / inferior] **4** [끝장나다] be done for; be ruined [spoilt]; [이루지 못하다] end in catastrophe [failure].. **5**[심사가 좋지 않다] become crooked [per-verse / distorted]; be [get] warped. **6** [사이가 나쁘다] fall out <with>; be at odds <with>; get estranged <from>; get on bad terms <with>.

틀림 [**थुल्लीम**] **1** [잘못] being wrong; a mistake; an error; a fault; a discrepancy; incorrectness. **2** [다름] being not the same; being different [variant].

틀어넣다 [**थुरीनाथा**] cram; stuff; load; wad; squeeze <into>; jam; (짐 등을) pack; (사람을) crowd <into>.

틀어막다 [**थुरीमाक्ता**] **1** (구멍 등) stop (up) <a hole>; fill (up); stuff (up); plug (up). **2** [억제,제지하다] stop; curb; check; put a stop to; put a stopper [gag] on.

틀어박다 [**थुरौबाक्ता**] **1**= 틀어넣다. **2** [오래 넣어 두다] hoard; keep in dead storage; keep <a thing> idle (in stock).

틀어박히다 [**थुरौबाख्वीदा**] confine oneself to [in] <a room>; stay in [indoors / at home]; closet oneself in <one's office>; shut oneself up; be confined [closeted] in <one's room>; keep <the house>; remain [keep] indoors.

틀어지다 [**थुरौजिदा**] **1** [빗나가다] turn aside [away]; swerve; deviate; (탄환 등이) miss <the target>; go wild [astray]. **2** [불화하다] break <with>; quarrel [fall out] <with>; be alienated [estranged] <from>; split <with>; get into a

dispute <with>.

틈 [थुम] **1** [갈라진 자리] a crevice; a crack; a chink; a chasm; a fissure; a cleth; a gap; space; an interstice. **2** [공간,여지] room; space; a margin; a blank (여백). **3** [불화] a discord; a difference; a breach <of friendship>; a split; an estrangement..**4** [기회] a chance; an opportunity.**5** [여가] time; leisure (hours); spare [leisure] time; time to spare; spare [odd] moments.

틈타다 [थुमथादा] […을 이용하다] take (mean) advantage [avail oneself] of <someone's weakness>; seize; take.

틈틈이 [थुमथुमी] **1** [틈마다] at each gap; in every opening. **2**[여가마다] in one's spare time; [시간의 중간에] in the intervals <between>.

티 [थी] **1** (먼지) a mote; dust; a particle; a grit; (불순물) impurities; (이질물) a foreign element..**2** [흠] a flaw; a speck; a spot; a blemish; a stain; a blot; a blur; a defect. **3** [기색, 작태] an air; a look; a touch <of melancholy>; a dash; a shade; a tinge; [태도] a manner; behavior; an attitude; bearing; [몸짓] gesture.

티 [थी] [차] tea.

티격태격 [थीग्योक थैग्योक] wranglingly; bickeringly. 티격태격하다,,quarrel [dispute / wrangle] <with>; bicker with each other.

티끌 [थीकुल] **1** [먼지] dust; a mote. **2** [아주 작은[적은] 것] a tiny bit.

티눈 [थीनून] a corn.

티켓 [थीखेत] a ticket.

팀 [थीम] a team.

팀워크 [थीमवोख़ु] teamwork; cooperation

팁 [थीम] [행하,축의] a tip; a grssatuity.

파[1] [फा] [派] **1** [그룹,패거리] a group; a coterie. e.g. 친미파 a pro-American group. **2** [당파] a party; a faction. e.g. 중도파 the middle-of-the roaders

파[2] [फा] a Welsh [spring] onion; a green onion; an onion (양파); a shallot (골파)

파견 [फाग्यौन] [派遣] dispatch; despatch. 파견하다 dispatch; despatch; send.

파경 [फाग्यौंग] [破鏡] [깨진 거울] a broken mirror; [이혼] (a) divorce; separation;

[이지러진 달] a waned moon.

파괴 [फाग्वे][破壞] destruction; demolition; breakdown. 파괴하다 destroy; break; ruin; wreck; demolish; dilapidate (집 등을) work havoc <upon>; make havoc <of / among>; ravage

파국 [फागुक] [破局] [붕괴] a collapse; [비극적인 결말] a catastrophe.

파급 [फागुप] [波及] e.g. 그 새 약품 발표의 파급 효과는 아주 컸다 The announcement of the new drug had far-reaching effects [considerable reper-cussions]. 파급하다 […에 미치다] extend; spread; [영향을 끼치다] influence; affect.

파내다 [फानैदा] dig up [out]; unearth; [발굴하다] excavate; disinter.

파다 [फादा] **1** (땅,구멍을) dig; delve; bore <a hole>; drive <a tunnel>; [파서 뚫다] excavate <a canal>; [후벼 내다] scoop out. **2** [새기다] carve <in / on>; engrave; chisel; cut. **3** (이치,문제 등을) make a search [inquiry] <for / into>; delve [probe] into <a problem>; dig <for / into>. **4** (공부를) study hard; work hard at <one's studies>; grind (away) <at>; dig in [into] <one's subject>; cram [bone] up <on>.

파다하다 [फादाहादा][播多-] widespread; <서술적> be widely known; be rife.

파닥거리다 [फादाक्कारिदा] **1.** (새, 깃발 등이) flutter; flap. **2** (물고기가) leap; jump; flop; splash.

파도타기 [फादोथागी] [波濤-] surfboard-riding; surfing. 파도타기하다 surf; ride the surf (on a board).

파동 [फादोंग] [波動] a wave [an undulatory] motion; undulation; fluctuation.

파라솔 [फारासोल] [양산] a parasol.

파랑 [फारांग] [청색] blue; azure; [하늘색] skyblue [녹색] green.

파래지다 [फारैजीदा] (나뭇잎 등이) become [turn] blue [green]; (얼굴이 turn pale [pallid]; go green; lose color.

파렴치 [फारौम्छी] [破廉恥] shamelessness; infamy; ignominy; impudence; effrontery. 파렴치하다 shameless; infamous; ignominious; disgraceful; <서술적> dead [lost] to(the sense of) shame; have the cheek of the devil

파리 [फारी] [昆] a fly; a housefly.

파먹다 [फामौक्ता] **1** [파서 먹다] dig <a thing> out and eat <it>; [먹어 들어가다] eat into[away / out]. **2** [도식하다] eat idle bread[the bread of idleness]; live [lead] an idle life; (재산 등을) away what one has.

파멸 [फाम्यौल] [破滅] ruin; destruction; wreck; collapse; downfall; fall..

파문 [फामुन] [波紋,波文] **1** [수면에 이는 물결] a ripple; a water ring; a (wave) ring on the water. **2** [영향] a stir; a sen-sation; repercussions.

파묻다 [फामुत्ता] **1** (땅 속에) bury <in>; entomb; [매장하다] inter; inhume. **2** (일, 사건을) bury in oblivion; smother [cover / hush] up.

파병 [फाब्यौंग] [派兵] the dispatch of troops. 파병하다 dispatch troops <to>.

파생 [फासैंग] [派生] derivation. 파생하다 derive [be derived] <from>; stem <from>; originate <in>

파손 [फासोन] [破損] damage; injury; breakage; breakdown; dilapi-dation.. 파손하다 damage; break down. .

파업 [फाऔप] [罷業] a strike; a walkout. 파업하다 strike; turn out; walk out.

파열 [फयौल] [破裂] (an) explosion; (a) bursting; (a) rupture; (an) eruption (화산의) [결렬] (a) rupture. 파열하다 explode; burst; erupt; blow [go] up

파워 [फावॉ] power.

파이 [फाई] [양과자] a pie; a potpie (주로 고기의).

ㅍ

파이프 [फाइफ] [관] a pipe; a tube. [담뱃대] a (tobacco) ipe (대담배용의); a cigarette holder (궐련용).

파장 [फाजांग] [波長] wavelength..

파종 [फाजोंग] [播種] sowing; seeding..파종하다 sow; sow seed; scatter (seed).

파출부 [फाछुल्बु][-婦] a day housekeeper; a home help; a visiting housekeeper [maid]; a charwoman.

파출소 [फाछुल्सो] a branch office; (경찰관의) a police box [stand].

파충류 [फाछुंगन्यू] [爬蟲類] the reptiles; creeping things.

파탄 [फाथान] [破綻] **1** [불성립] failure; a rupture (교섭의]. 파탄하다 fail; come to a rupture. **2** [은행,회사의 지급 정지] bankruptcy. **3** [붕괴] breaking. 파탄하다 be ruined; break down.

파티 [फाथी] a party; a meeting; social gathering; [친목회] a social; a mixer.

파편[破片] [फाप्यौन] a broken piece; a fragment; a scrap; [나무,돌 등의 조각] a chip; [나무,돌 등의 가시 모양의 조각] a splinter.

파하다 [फाहादा] [破 -]beat; defeat; smash;(put to) rout

파행 [फाहैंग] [跛行] [절뚝거림] limping; [균형이 잡히지 아니함](an) imbalance. 파행하다 limp.

파혼 [फाहोन] [破婚] breaking

off a marriage engage-ment; (a) breach of promise of marriage.파혼하다 break the engagement; break (off) engagement <with>

판[瓣] [फान] e.g. 안전판 a safety [relief] valve. 자동판 an automatically operated valve..

판 [फान] [判] [책,종이의 규격] size..

판 [फान] [版] **1** [판목] a (printing) block; [도판] a plate; a cast. e.g. 판에 박은 듯한[박힌] stereo-typed / cut-and-dried [-dry] / manneristic / conven-tional / formal **2** [인쇄하여 책을 펴내는 일 또는 펴낸 것] printing; print; an edition; an impression. e.g. 신 a new edition. 초판 the first print[edition].

판 [फान] [板] [축음기판, 레코드판] a record; a disk [disc].

판 [फान] [벌어진 곳] a place; a spot; a site; a scene; [판국] (the) state of affairs; (the aspect [phase] of) the situation; circumstances; [때] the moment; [경우] the occasion; the case; [횟수] a game; a round; a bout; a match. e.g. 노름판 a gambling place.

판가름 [फान्गारम] judging sides (which side is right and which side is wrong); a showdown; decision. 판가름하다 judge <a com-petition, fight, etc.>; decide; sit in judg (e) ment <on>; <美> have a final showdown

판각 [फान्गाक] [板刻] engraving (on woodblocks); wood-cutting. 판각하다 engrave <designs, letters, etc.> on wood; make a print from a woodblock.

판검사 [फानगौम्सा] [判檢事] judges and public pro-secutors; judicial officers; <집합적> the bench.

판결 [फानग्यौल] [判決] judg (e) ment; a (judicial) decision; a decision of the court; a ruling; adjudication; finding; a sentence; a decree. 판결하다 judge; decide <on a case>; give (a) decision <on a case>; pass judg-ment <on a vase>; adjudi-cate [adjudge] <on an action>; sentence <a person> to <death>.

판국 [फान्गुक] [- 局] a situation; the position [state] of affairs; the state of things; the aspect of affairs.

판권[फांग्वॉन] [版權, 板權] copyright; literary property.

판단 [फान्दान] [判斷] [단정] (a) judg (e) ment; (an) adjudication; (a) decision; [결론] conclusion; [추산] estimation; [재량] discretion; [해석] [an) interpretation.

판독 [फान्तोक] [判讀]

decipherment (암호 등의); interpretation; making out; reading. 판독하다 decipher; make out; read; spell out.

판례 [फानल्ये] [判例] [法] a (judicial) precedent; a (leading) case

판매 [फान्मे] [販賣] (a) sale; selling; marketing. 판매하다 sell; deal in; handle; dispose of; work off

판명 [फानम्यौंग] [判明] 판명하다 [분명해지다] become clear [plain]; [확인되다] be ascertained; be confirmed; [알려지다] be known; […임이 증명되다] prove [turn out] to be <false>; […으로 증명되다] be identified as <Mr. A>.

판박이 [फान्बागी] [版 -] 1 [인쇄본] a printed book. 2 [틀에 박힌 것] a fixed form; a stereotyped pattern

판별 [फानब्यौल] [判別] distinction; discrimination. 판별하다 distinguish <between A and B>; tell <A> from <B>; discriminate <between A and B / one from the other>; make [notice] the difference <between>; judge.

판사 [फान्सा] [判事] a judge; a justice; <집합적> the judiciary; the bench.

판세 [फान्से] [-勢] [형세] the situation; the state of affairs [things]; the condition of affairs; the tide <of>; (바둑 등의) the position; [전망] the prospects; the chances.

판소리 [फान्सोरी] *pansori*; a long epic song; a solo opera drama.

판이 [फानी] [判異] 판이하다 quite [widely / entirely] different <from>; diametrically opposed <to>; <서술적> differ entirely [widely] <from>; be a far cry <from>; be poles apart [asunder] <in>.

판정 [फान्जौंग] [判定] (a) judgment; (a) decision; (an) adjudication; finding; a verdict (배심원). 판정하다 judge; decide; adjudicate <upon>; adjudge; find.

판치다 [फान्छीदा] stand [be] unchallenged [unrivaled / without a rival]; reign supreme; lord it over; exercise great influence <over>.

판판이 [फान्फानी] every time; whenever; always; all the time [while].

판화 [फानह्वा] [版畵] a print; a woodcut [block] print; [판화술] (pictorial) wood printing.

팔[1] [फाल] an arm.

팔[2] [फाल] [八] eight.

팔꿈치 [फाल्कुम्छी] an elbow.

팔다 [फालदा] 1 [판매하다] sell; deal in <goods>; offer <articles> for sale; put [place]

<articles> on sale[on the market]; [(소지품 등을) 팔아 치우다] dispose of. **2** (노력 등을). **3** [배신,배반하다] betray; deceive; sell (out); delude; impose upon. **4** (남의 이름 등을).**5** [곡식을 사다] e.g. 쌀을 팔다 buy [purchase] rice.**6** (한)눈을 팔다 turn one's eyes away <from> / avert one's eyes <from> / look away <from>. 정신을 팔다 distract [divert] one's attention <from>. 책을 보지 않고 (한)눈을 팔다 look away from one's book. …에 정신이 팔리다 be absorbed <in reading>. 한눈 팔자 말고 책을 보아라 Keep your eyes on your book.

팔딱거리다 [फालताक्कौरिदा] **1** [맥박치다] pulsate; palpitate; throb; beat. **2**[가볍게 뛰다] hop; leap; jump; spring; bound.

팔딱팔딱 [फालतावफालताक] [맥박치는 모양] pulsating; palpitating; throbbing; [뛰는 모양] hopping; leaping; jumping.

팔뚝 [फालतुक] the forearm.

팔랑개비 [फाललांगैबी] **1** [바람에 돌게 만든 장난감 a pinwheel. **2** [촐랑거리는 사람] a frivolous[flippant / flighty] fellow.

팔랑거리다 [फाललांगौरीदा] flutter; flap; wave.

팔리다 [फालिलदा] **1** (물건이) sell [be sold] <for 1,000 won>; be in <great> demand [request]. **2** (사람이) go into bondage [slavery]; (미혼녀가) get married; [고용되다] get [obtain] employment.

팔목 [फालमोक] the wrist..

팔방 [फालबांग] [八方] e.g. 팔방에서 from all directions [sides / quarters] / from every side / from all around. 팔방으로 [फालबांगुरो] in all directions / in every direction [quarter] / on all sides [quarters] / all around.

팔방 미인 [फालबांग मीइन] [八方美人] one who is affable to everybody; everybody"s friend; a flunk (e) y.

팔베개 [फालबेगे] 팔베개를 하다 [베다] make a pillow of one's arm / pillow [rest] one's head on one's arm.

팔순 [फाल्सुन] [八旬] eighty years; four score years. e.g. 팔순 노인 an octoge-narian.

팔십 [फालिशप] [八十] e.g. 팔십대의 사람 an octogenarian. 팔십 노인 an 80-year-old man [woman] / an old man [woman] of eighty.

팔씨름 [फालिशरूम] Indian [arm] wrestling..팔씨름하다 have a hand wrestling.

팔아먹다 [फारामौक्ता] **1** [팔아버리다] sell off [out]; dispose of(by sale). e.g. 헐값으로 팔아먹다 sell <an

article> for a mere song. 가산을 다 팔아먹다 squander one's fortune. 2 [장사거리로 삼다] offer [put up] <something> for sale. e.g. 미모를 팔아먹다 trade [capitalize] on one's beauty. 명예를 팔아먹다 sell [prostitute] one's honor (for money). 지식을 팔아먹다 peddle one's knowledge .3 [곡식을 사먹다] buy [purchase] grain.

팔월 [फार्वल] [八月] August (Aug.).

팔월 한가위 [फार्वल हान्गावी] the 15th day of the eighth lunar month; the midautumn [harvest-moon] festival.

-팔이 [_फरी] a seller; a peddler; a hawker..

팔자 [फाल्चा] [八字] (a) destiny; fate; (a) lot; fortune; doom; one's star.

팔짱 [फाल्चांग] folding one's arms. 팔짱(을) 끼다 fold one's arms(across one's chest [breast]); fold one's arms in front of one; lock one's arms across one's chest; (남과) lock arms with; link one's arm in [through] another"s.

팔찌 [फाल्ची] [팔가락지] a bracelet; a bangle; a wristlet; an armlet.

팔팔하다 [फाल्फार्हादा] 1 [성질이 괄괄하고 급하다] quick [hot-] tempered; passionate; impatient. 2 [생기가 있다] sprightly; lively; snappy; spirited; animated; full of life.

팥 [फात] an adzuki [adsuki] bean; a red bean.

패 [फे] [牌] 1 [표로 쓰는 나뭇조각 등] a tag; a tab; a tablet; a plate; a tally. 2 (카드 놀이,화투 등의) a(playing) card; a suit(같은 종류의) 3 [무리] a party; a company; a group; a set; a circle; a gang; a clique.

패가 [फेगा] [敗家] 패가하다 ruin one's family; a family goes to ruin [is wrecked]; a family becomes [goes] bankrupt. **패가 망신** ruining both oneself and one's family; one's ruin.

패권 [फेक्वन] supremacy; mastery; hegemony; domination; leadership; supreme power.

패기 [फेगी] an ambitious spirit; ambition; aspiration..

패다 [फेदा] [때리다] beat; strike; knock; hit; thrash; give [deal / deliver] <a person> a blow.

패담 [फेदाम] [悖談,悖談] an unreasonable remark; indecent [improper] talk. 패담하다say unreasonable thing; talk unreasonably; talk indecency.

패륜 [फेर्युन] [悖倫] immorality.

패망 [फेमांग] [敗亡] (a) defeat;

rout; ruin; wreck; collapse. 패망하다 be defeated; suffer [sustain] a defeat; be routed; be ruined; go [fall] crash; go to ruin.

패물 [फैमुल] [佩物] personal ornaments [outfittings / adornments]; accessories; trinkets.

패배 [फैबे] [敗北] (a) defeat; a loss; a reverse; (a) discomfiture; a setback; (a) rout (패주).패배하다 be defeated; be beaten; be worsted; have the worst; sustain [suffer] a defeat [reverse]; lose a battle [the day] (싸움에서)lose a game (경기에서) be repulsed; be routed (패주하다).,

패배주의[주의자] [फैबैजूउइजा] defeatism [a defeatist].

패색 [फैसैक] [敗色] signs of defeat; unfavorable signs in battle.

패션 [फैश्यौन] (a) fashion..

패소 [फैसो] [敗訴] losing a suit [case]; a lost case. 패소하다 lose a suit [case]; fail in an action; be cast in a suit

패자 [फैजा] [敗者] the defeated (person); the vanquished; a loser.

패자 [फैजा] **1** [무력에 의한 정복자] a supreme ruler. **2** [경기의 우승자] a champion; a winner; a titleholder.

패잔 [फैजान] [敗殘] survival ather defeat.

패잔병 [फेजानप्यौंग] [敗殘兵] remnants <of a defeated troop>; stragglers; runaway troops.

패전 [फैजौन] [敗戰] a lost battle; (a) defeat (in war); a failure in war; (a) reverse. 패전하다 lose a war [battle]; be defeated in a battle; lose the day

패하다 [फैहादा] [敗-] [싸움에 지다] be defeated; be beaten; lose <a game / a battle / the day>; have the worst of it; suffer a defeat; come off a loser.

팬티 [फैन्थी] Panties.

팽개치다 [फैंगैछिदा] **1** [내던지다] throw <away>; cast <away>; fling <at>; hurl <at>.. **2** [포기하다] give [throw] up; abandon; [내버려두다] leave off; leave untouched; lay aside; neglect; desert.

팽배 [फैंग्बे] [澎湃] overflowing; surging; rampage; rage. 팽배하다 overflow; surge; rage; rise high. .

팽이 [फैंगी] a top.

팽창 [फैंछ्यान] [膨脹] [부풀어 오르기] swelling; inflation; [확대] expansion; dilation; distension; [발전] growth; [증가] increase. 팽창하다 swell; expand; inflate; grow; increase; aggrandize

팽팽하다 [फैंग्फैंग्हादा] **1** (켕기어서) tight; taut; strained; tense; stretched to the full. **2** (성질이) rigid; strict; stern; narrow-minded; illiberal; strait-laced; hide-bound. **3** (세력이) close; equal; even; equally-matched [-balanced]; well-matched.

퍼내다 [फौनेदा] bail [dip / ladle] out <water>; scoop <water> out <of>; pump out <a well>(펌프로)

퍼뜨리다 [फौत्रीदा] (종교,사상 등을) spread; disseminate; diffuse; circulate; propagate; make popular; popularize; (소문 등을) set <a rumor> afloat; start [circulate / spread] <a rumor>; give(it) out that ...; make <a thing> public; make <a thing> known.

퍼뜩 [फौतक] [별안간] suddenly; in a flash..

퍼먹다 [फौमौक्ता] **1** [퍼서 먹다] dip[scoop / ladle] <something> and eat(it). **2** [많이 먹다] bolt <one's dinner>; shovel <food> into one's mouth..

퍼붓다 [फौबुत्ता] **1** (물 등을) pour <water> into [on / over]; dash <water> over. **2** (비난,욕설 등을) heap [shower / rain] <abuses> upon; (포화를) rain <fire> on; bring <the enemy> under <fire>. **3** (비가 pour (down); pelt down; (눈이) fall thick and fast.

퍼센트 [फौसेन्थ] percent; per cent (기호 %; p.c., per ct.) (a) percentage <of>

퍼센티지 [फौसेन्थिजी] (a) percentage.

퍼올리다 [फौओल्लिदा] draw up; scoop [dip] up; pump up (펌프로). e.g. 우물물을 퍼올리다 draw water from a well.

퍼지다 [फौजीदा] **1** [넓어지다] spread out; widen; broaden; become wider [broader] **2** [유포 또는 보급되다] spread (abroad); be diffused; be propagated; pervaded <a city>; be disseminated; be circulated; (소문 등이) get about [abroad / around]; go the rounds; get [take] air.

퍽[1] [फौक] **1** [찌르는 모양]] with a thrust; <thrusting> hard. **2** [쓰러지는 모양] with a thud; <collapsing> feebly; in a heap.

퍽[2] [फौक] [매우] very much; quite; terribly; awfully; <美> real; sure; right; damn (ed).

펄 [फौल] [들판] a wide expanse of land; a vast plain; a prairie.

펄쩍 [फौल्चौक] **1** [갑자기 여는 모양] suddenly; abruptly. **2** [갑자기 뛰는 모양] nimbly; lightly.

펄펄 [फौलफौल] 1 [끓는 모양] simmering; seething; boiling. **2** (신열이) feverish; (온돌방 등이) broiling; scorching. **3** [날리거나 나부끼는 모양] flapping; fluttering; (눈 등이) in flakes.

펌프 [फौम्फ] a pump.

페달 [फेदाल] a pedal; a treadle..

페미니즘 [फेमिनिजुम] feminism.

페이지 [फेइजी] a page(略 p.; *pl.* pp.); a leaf (▷ a page는 한 면 a leaf는 양면 즉 한 장을 말함).

페인트 [फेइन्थ] [도료] paint.

펜 [फेन] a pen..

펜치 [फेन्छि] [철사를 끊거나 구부리는 도구] <a pair of> (cutting) pliers; pinc (h) ers.

펴다 [फ्यौदा] 1 [펼치다] spread; lay (out); unfold <a newspaper>; unroll <a scroll>; open. **2** [뻗다] stretch; outstretch; hold out; spread out**3** [부설,공포하다] lay (down); construct; build; promulgate <a law> **3** [굽은 것을 곧게 하다] straighten; (말린 것을) uncoil; (금속판을) planish; roll; (구김살 등을) smooth out <creases>; (다리미 등으로) iron out. **4** [기세를 자유롭게 가지다] ease <one's mind>; relieve; keep <one's spirits> up.

펴이다 [फ्यौइदा] 1 (형편이) become better; be changed for the better; improve; (일,어려움이) be smoothed (down / away); be reduced [eased]. **2** [펴지다] get unfolded [straightened / smoothed].

펴지다 [फ्यौजीदा] 1 [펼쳐지다] spread (out); overspread (온통); get unfolded [unrolled]. **2** (구김살 등이) be straightened; be flattened; become smooth.

편 [फ्यौन] [便]**1** 친구 편에 보내다 [부치다] send <a thing> by(the hand of) a friend. **2** [우편] post; mail. e.g. 항공 편으로 부치다 send <a letter> by air mail / airmail <a letter>. **3** [교통] facilities; service. e.g. 교통 편 communi-cation [traffic] facilities / facilities for communi-cation. **4** [쪽] a side; [방향] adirection; a way. e.g. 아버지[어머니] 편의<a relation> on the paternal [maternal] side / on the father's [mother's] side. **5** [한 패] a party; a ring; a team (경기의); one's side. e.g. 우리편 our side [part] / we / a friend / our party [team **6** [선택, 경향][e.g. 이렇게 하는 편이 좋을 것이다 You'd better do it like this [(in) this way

편 [फ्यौन] 1 [권] a volume; a book. **2** [장,절] a chapter;

a section; a part; (시 등의) a canto. **3** [시문,영화 등의 수효] a piece.

편가르다 [फ्यौनकारूदा] [便˘] separate into groups [parties]; divide <the men> in two teams (두 패로)

편견 [फ्यौनगयौन] [偏見] a biased [distorted / prejudiced] view; prejudice; a bias.

편곡 [फ्यौनगोक] [編曲] (an) arrangement. 편곡하다 arrange.

편도 [फ्यौन्दो] [片道] one way; each way.

편도승차권 [फ्योनदोसंगछाग्वन] a one-way ticket; a single (ticket).

편도 요금 [फ्यौन्दो योगुम] a one-way fare; a single fare

편두통 [फ्यौन्दुथोंग] [偏頭痛] (a) migraine; (a) megrim; a sick [migraine] headache.

편들다 [फ्यौन्दुल्दा] [便-]take part [sides] <with>; side <with>; take <a person"s> side [part]; be on <a person"s> side; stand by <a person>; back; support.

편력 [फ्यौलल्यौक] [遍歷] **1** [널리 돌아다니기] travel; a pilgrimage. 편력하다 go on a pilgrimage; wander [travel] about [around]. **2** [갖가지 경험을 하기] **편력자** [फ्यौल्लयौकचा] a pilgrim; an itinerant.

편리 [फ्यौल्लि] [便利] convenience; expediency; serviceableness (쓸모 있음) handiness (간편) facility (편리한 시설).. 편리하다 convenient; expedient; handy; serviceable; useful. .

편모 [फ्यौन्मो] [偏母] one's widowed [lone] mother..

편법 [फ्यौन्बौप] [便法] an easier [a handy] method; a shortcut; a short way; an expedient; an expediency; convenient mode; an expedient means..

편성 [फ्यौन्सौग] [編成] formation; organization; composition; a footing.. 편성하다 form; organize; compose; compile; draw up; make up; frame; weave; embody

편승 [फ्यौन्सुंग] [便乘] **1** [교통편을 얻어 탐]. 편승하다 (차에) get a lith <in a person"s car>; get (a free ride) along a road; make one's way <to a place> by thumbing rides; hitchhike; (배에) take a ship; go on board(a ship) **2** [기회를 틈타기 편승하다 avail oneself of; take advantage of; jump on [aboard] the bandwagon.

편식 [फ्यौन्शिक] [偏食] an unbalanced [one-sided] diet. 편식하다 eat unbalanced meals; have an unbalanced diet.

편심 [फ्यौन्शिम] [偏心] a

one-sided mind; a partial disposition; eccentricity..

편안 [**फ्यौनान**] [**便安**] [무사함] safety; security; getting along well; [평온] peace; calm(ness); quiet(ness); tranquility; [안락] ease; easiness; comfort; [태평함] [easygoingness. 편안하다 [무사하다] safe; secure; [평온하다] peaceful; quiet; calm; tranquil; restful; [안락하다] comfortable; easy; easeful; carefree; [태평하다] lighthearted; easy-going; happy-go-lucky.

편애 [**फ्यौने**] [**偏愛**] (a) partiality <for>; a predilection <for>; favoritism <to>. 편애하다 be partial <to>; show favoritism <to>; be prejudiced in favor <of>.

편의 [**फ्यौनुइ**] [**便宜**] convenience; accommodation; facility; (교통 등의) facilities; [이익] advantage; benefit; [방편] expedience; expediency. 편의하다 handy; convenient; expedient.

편이 [**फ्यौनी**] [**便易**] convenience; handiness; easiness; usefulness; serviceableness. 편이하다 convenient; handy; easy; useful; serviceable.

편익 [**फ्यौनिक**] [**便益**] [편리] convenience; facility; [이익] benefit; advantage; profit.

편입 [**फ्यौनिप**] [**編入**] [집어넣음] entry; admission; incorporation (합병); [軍] enlistment; enroll (l) ment <in>. 편입하다(부류에) class <with / among>; include <in>; (예산에) insert; (학급에) admit [put] <into>; enroll (l) <into>; place <in a grade>; (군대에) assign <to the infantry>.

편지 [**फ्यौन्जी**] [**便紙,片紙**] a letter; a communication; a note; a missive; a line (단신); an epistle (서한) <집합적> mail.

편집 [**फ्यौन्जिप**] [**編輯**] editing; compilation; redaction. 편집하다 edit <a magazine>; compile <a dictionary>; prepare for the press

편차 [**फ्यौन्छा**] (a) deflection; (a) deviation; a) declination; a) variation; windage; (a) drith; drithage.

편찬 [**फ्यौन्छान**] [**編纂**] compilation; editing. 편찬하다 compile <a dictionary>; edit <an anthology>

편찮다 [**फ्यौन्छान्था**] [**便-**] **1** [편하지 않다] uncomfortable; uneasy..**2** [병으로 아프다] ill; sick; unwell; indisposed; ailing.

편파 [**फ्यौन्फा**] [**偏頗**] partiality; favoritism; (unfair) discrimination; [일방적임] one-sidedness; [불공평] unfairness; injustice.. 편파하다 partial; one-sided;

ㅍ

unfair; biased.

편평 [**फ्यौनफ्यौग**] [**扁平**]편평하다 flat; horizontal; even; level; compressed.

편하다 [**फ्यौनहादा**] [**便−**] **1** [안락하다] comfortable; easy; [걱정이 없다] free from care; carefree; insouciant. e.g. 알하기에 편한 옷 an easy fit for work. 발이 편한 신발 comfortable shoes to wear / shoes easy to walk in. **2** [편리하다] convenient; suited <for some purpose>; handy; expedient **3** [쉽다] easy; light; simple; soth

편향 [**फ्यौनहयांग**] [**偏向**] **1** (전자류 등의) deflection; (생물의 개체의 변이에 의한) deviation. 편향하다 deflect; deviate. **2** [치우친 경향] an inclination <to / toward>; a tendency <to / toward>. 편향하다 incline <toward>; tend <toward / to>

편협 [**फ्यौन्हयौप**] narrow-mindedness; illiberality; intolerance; [지방적임] parochialism; provincialism. 편협하다 narrow-minded; illiberal; intolerant; [지방 적이다] parochial; provin-cial.

펼치다 [**फ्यौल्छिदा**] unfold <a package>; lay out <one's clothes>; unroll <a scroll>; spread [open] a sail.

폄하다 [**फ्यौमहादा**] [**貶−**] speak ill[evil] of; speak slightingly of; despise; depreciate <a person"s abilities>; disparage; run [cry / call] down; belittle.

평 [**फ्यौग**] [**坪**] [토지 면적] a *py?g* <단수P복수 동형> (=3 .954 sq. yds.); [체적] a *py?g* (=7 .9 cub. yds.). e.g. 이 뜰은 2백 평이다 This garden covers(an area of) two hundred *py?g*.

평 [**फ्यौग**] [**評**] [비평] (a) criticism; a comment; a review; [평판](a) reputation; (a) repute.

평− [**फ्यौग**] [**平**] [보통의, 일반의] common; ordinary; [평평한] plain..

평가 [**फ्यौगा**] [**評價**]x **1** [가격을 정함] (a) valuation; [견적] (an) estimation; [과세 등을 위한 사정] (an) assessment; (매각,과세 등을 위한) (an) appraisal. 평가하다 value; estimate; appraise; assess. **2** [사물의 가치를 정함] <文>(an) evaluation; (a) valuation; (an) appraisal. 평가하다 evaluate; value; esti-mate

평균 [**फ्यौग्युन**] [**平均**] [가지런하게 고름] an average.. 평균하다 average; take [strike] an average

평년 [**फ्यौगन्यौन**] [**平年**] **1** [윤년이 아닌 해] a common year; a year other than a leap year. **2** [보통의 해]

an average [a normal] year

평등 [**फ्यौन्दुंग**] [**平等**] [균등] equality; [공평] impartiality. 평등하다 equal; equable; even; impartial.

평론 [**फ्यौन्नोन**] [**評論**] [논문 형식의 비평] criticism; [시평] a review; a comment. 평론하다 review; comment <on>; criticize; make comments <on>.

평면 [**फ्यौगम्यौन**] [**平面**] a plane; a level.

평민 [**फ्यौग्मिन**] [**平民**] a commoner; a plebeian; a man of the people; <집합적> the common people.

평범 [**फ्यौन्बौम**] [**平凡**] commonness; commonplaceness; banality; platitude; mediocrity; homeliness.
평범하다 common; ordinary; commonplace; homely; humdrum; banal; trite; mediocre; [특색이 없다] featureless; tame; unremarkable; [평온 무사하다] uneventful.

평사원 [**फ्यौन्वन**] a mere [plain] clerk.

평상시 [**फ्यौगसांग्शि**] [**平常時**] [보통 때] ordinary [normal] times; [평화시] time of peace; peace time.

평생 [**फ्यौन्सैग**] [**平生**] e.g. 평생의 한(恨) a lifelong regret. 평생의 친구 a lifelong friend.

평소 [**फ्यौन्सो**] [**平素**]평소처럼 [평소대로 / 평소와 같이] as usual. 평소의 연습 everyday practice. 평소대로 하다 do one's usual

평수 [**फ्यौगसु**] [**坪數**] **1** [평의 수] the number of *py?g*; area. **2** [건평] floor space [area]; [넓이] space.

평안 [**फ्यौगान**] [**平安**] peace; calm (ness); quiet (ness); tranquility. 평안하다 peaceful; quiet; tranquil.

평야 [**फ्यौन्या**] [**平野**] a plain; plains; an open field.

평온 [**फ्यौगोन**] [**平溫**] [평상시의 온도] a normal temperature; [평균 온도] an average [a mean] temperature.

평온 [**फ्यौगोन**] [**平穩**] calmness; quiet (ness); quietude; tranquil (l)ity; serenity. 평온하다 calm; quiet; tranquil; serene; peaceful.

평원 [**फ्यौगवौन**] [**平原**] a plain; a prairie(대초원).

평이 [**फ्यौगि**] [**平易**] **1** [쉬움] easiness; facility. 평이하다 easy. **2** [간명] plainness; [단순] simplicity. 평이하다 plain; simple.

평일 [**फ्यौगिल**] [일요일 이외의 날] a weekday; a workday; a business day. 평일에는 on weekdays / on business days.

평전 [**फ्यौन्जौन**] [**評傳**] a critical biography <of Milton>.

평점 [**फ्यौन्जौम**] [**評點**] [시험

점수] examination marks; [단계점] a grade; grading; (가치 평가의) evaluation marks

평정 [प्यौन्जौंग] [平靜] [무사평온] calm; serenity; tranquil (l)ity; [침착] equability; equanimity; sedateness. 평정하다 calm; serene; tranquil; sedate; equable.

평정 [प्यौन्जौंग] [平定] suppression; repression; subdual; subjugation (정복). 평정하다 suppress; repress; subdue; pacify; subjugate <the whole country>.

평준 [प्यौन्जुन] [平準] 1 [수준기로 수평하게 함] level. 2 [평균] equa-lity. **평준점** a level point. **평준화** leveling (off); equalization; standardization.

평지 [प्यौन्जी] [平地] flatland; level land [ground]; a flat; a plain (평원); a flat country (지방).

평탄[प्यौन्थान] [平坦] 1 [지면이 평평함] evenness; flatness. 평탄하다 even; flat; plane; level <country / road> 2 [마음이 편하고 고요함] calmness; tranquility. 평탄하다 calm; placid; peaceful; tranquil; even 3 [일이 순조로움] smoothness; favorableness. 평탄하다 favorable; smooth; uneventful.

평판 [प्यौन्फान] [評判] [비평하는 일] criticizing; [명성] fame;(a) reputation; (a) repute; [세평] the world"s opinion; public estimation; popularity (인기); notoriety (악명); [소문] a report; a rumor; gossip. 평판하다 talk (much) of; talk about; rumor.

평평하다 [प्यौंगप्यौंगहादा] [平平–]1 [판판하다] flat; [평활하다] even; smooth; [수평이다] level; hori-zontal; [평면이다] plane **2** [평범하다] common; ordinary; commonplace; fea-tureless. 평평히 com-monly; ordinarily; common-placely.

평하다 [प्यौन्हादा] [評–] criticize; comment <on>.

평행 [प्यौन्हैंग] [平行] parallelism; parallel 평행하다 parallel.

평형 [प्यौंगह्यौंग] [平衡] equilibrium; balance; counterbalance; counterpoise; a state of perfect balance. 평형하다 balanced; poised; <서술적> be in equilibrium.

평화 [प्यौंगह्वा] [平和] peace; [화합] harmony

폐 [प्ये] [肺] the lungs

폐 [प्ये] [弊] [괴로움] (a) trouble; (a) worry; a bother <to a person>; [귀찮은 일] (an) annoyance. 폐(를) 끼치다 trouble [bother / annoy] <a person>; give [cause] <a person> trouble; put <a person> to trouble [bother]; make oneself a nuisance <to a person>

폐가 **[फ्येगा]** [**廢家**] [버려 두어 낡은 집] a deserted [dilapidated] house

폐간 **[फ्येगान]** [**廢刊**] discontinuance <of publiccation>; ceased publiccation. 폐간하다 cease to publish; discontinue issuing <a newspaper / a magazine>.

폐경기 **[फ्येग्यौंगी]** [**閉經期**] the climacteric; the period of the menopause in women..

폐관 **[फ्येग्वान]** [**閉館**] closing <its doors> 폐관하다 close <its doors>; be closed

폐광 **[फ्येग्वांग]** [**廢鑛**] an abandoned [an unworked / a disused] mine; a dead pit [mine]. 폐광하다 abandon a mine; disuse a mine.

폐교 **[फ्येग्यो]** [**廢校**] abolition [closing] of a school. 폐교하다 close [abolish] a school

폐기 **[फ्येगी]** [**廢棄**] (제도, 풍속의) disuse; abolition; abandonment; (법률 등의) abrogation; repeal; disaffirmation; defeasance; cassation; reverse (판결의); denunciation (조약의). 폐기하다 do away with; annul; disuse; abolish; abandon; renounce; discard (습관을); abrogate; repeal; dissolve; denounce (조약을)

폐단 **[फ्येदान]** an evil; an abuse; a vice; an obno-xious [evil] custom [practice].

폐렴 **[फ्येरयौन]** [**肺炎**] pneumonia; inflammation of the lungs.

폐막 **[फ्येमाक]** [**閉幕**] the falling of the curtain; a curtainfall; a close; an end; the finish. 폐막하다 close [bring down] the curtain; close; end; finish; bring to an end

폐문 **[फ्येमुन]** [**閉門**] closing the gate. 폐문하다 close the gate; bar the gate. **폐문 시간** the closing time; lockup.

폐문 **[फ्येमुन]** [**廢門**] closing. 폐문하다 close [shut] up; keep <a door> shut [closed].

폐백 **[फ्येबैक]** [**幣帛**] **1** (신부의) bride"s giths to her parents-in-law **2** (신랑의) silks offered to the bride by the bridegroom.

폐쇄 **[फ्येश्वै]** [**閉鎖**] closing; closure; shutdown (일시적인); a lockout. 폐쇄하다 close (down / up); shut (down); lock(up); wind up; lock out.

폐수 **[फ्येसु]** [**廢水**] waste water..**폐수 처리** waste-water treatment; liquid waste treatment.

폐수 처리 장치 a waste water disposal plant.

폐업 **[फ्येऔप]** [**廢業**] discontinuance [abolishment] of business. 폐업하다 give up [discontinue / quit / close]

one's business; shut up one's shop; close down one's store; (의사,변호사 등이) give up one's practice; (배우 등이) leave [retire from] the stage.

폐인 [फ्येइन] [廢人] (불구에 의한) a person maimed [crippled] for life; a crippled [disabled] person; a cripple; (병에 의한) a confirmed invalid.

폐장 [फ्येजांग] [閉場] the closing <of a place>. 폐장하다 close; be closed.

폐점 [फ्येजौम] [閉店] [가게를 닫음]. e.g. 폐점후에 손님이 온 것 같다 There seems to have been a customer who came ather closing time [ather the store was closed]. 폐점하다 close (a) shop; close one's doors.

폐지 [फ्येजी] [廢止] abolition; disuse; discontinuance; (법률, 제도 등의) abrogation; annulment; nullification. 폐지하다 abolish; discontinue; disuse; do away with; (법률 등을) abrogate; annul; quash; repeal; rescind; cance

폐차 [फ्येछा] [廢車] a disused car; a scrapped vehicle [car]; an out-of-service car; a junked car.

폐품 [फ्येफुम] [廢品] waste articles [materials]; [쓰레기] rubbish; trash.

폐하 [फ्येहा] [陛下];(2인칭) Your Majesty.

폐허 [फ्येहौ] [廢墟] (the) ruins; (the) remains (남아 있는 것).

폐회 [फ्येह्वे] [閉會] the closing (of a meeting). 폐회하다 close [adjourn] <a meeting> (▷ adjourn 은 다음 회기까지).

포개다 [फोगैदा] [겹겹이 놓다] put [place] one upon [over] another; lay over; lay one on top of another [the other]; lap; overlap; [겹쳐 쌓다] pile up; heap up; stack;

포격 [फोग्यौक] [砲擊] shelling; bombardment; cannonade; 포격하다 shell; fire on [at] <a ship, a fort, etc.>; bombard; cannonade.

포고 [फोगो] [布告] proclamation; declaration <of war>; notification; ordinance

포괄 [फोग्वाल] [包括] inclusion; comprehension. 포괄하다 include; comprehend; comprise; contain; embrace; cover; take in

포교 [फोग्यो] [布敎] propagation (of religion); missionary work; mission (work); propagandism. 포교하다 propagate <a religion

포근하다 [फोगुन्हादा] **1** [따뜻하다] comfortably warm; snug (and comfortable); [푹신하다] soth [downy] (and fluffy). e.g. 포근한

침대 a soth, comfortable bed **2** (겨울 날씨가) mild; soth; genial. 포근히 mildly; genially.

포기 [**फोगी**] a plant; a head <of cabbage>; a root. e.g. 풀 한 포기 one plant. 배추 두 포기 two heads of cabbage

포기 [**फोगी**] [**抛棄**] giving up; abandonment; resignation; renunciation; renouncement; surrender; waiver; release; (요구의) relinquishment; disclaimer. e.g. 전쟁의 포기 renunciation of war. 포기하다 throw up <one's office>; abandon [give up] <one's plan>; forsake; renounce

포도 **फोदो** [**葡萄**] a grape. a vintage.

포동포동 [**फोदोंगफोदोंग**] a chubby [full] face. 포동포동하다 plump; fleshy; round; well-fleshed; chubby

포로 [**फोरो**] [**捕虜**] (전쟁의) a prisoner (of war) (略 P.O.W., POW) <*pl.* P.O.W'.s, POW's>; a war prisoner; a captive. e.g. 포로로

포르노 [**फोर्नो**] pornography; porn(o). e.g. 포르노의 pornographic.

포만 [**फोमान**] [**飽滿**] satiety; satiation. 포만하다 <서술적> be satiated [sated]

포물선 [**फोमुलसौन**] [**抛物線**] [數] a parabola.

포복 절도 [**फोबोक जौल्तो**] [**抱腹絶倒**] 포복 절도하다 hold [split] one's sides with laughter; laugh oneself into convulsions; be convulsed with laughter; double (up) with laughter; die with laughing

포부 [**फोबू**] [**抱負**] [희망, 대망] one's hopes; one's aspirations; [계획] a plan.

포상 [**फोसांग**] [**褒賞**] a prize; a reward. 포상하다 give a prize <to>; praise and reward.

포섭 [**फोसौप**] [**包攝**] [받아들임]. e.g. 포섭 공작을 하다 contrive to win <a person> over. 포섭하다 win [gain] <a person> over to one's side; bring <a person> round

포수 [**फोसू**] [**砲手**] **1** [총을 가진 군사] an artilleryman; a gunner; an artillerist. **2** (포경선의) a harpooner. **3** [사냥꾼] a hunter.

포수 [**फोसू**] [**捕手**] [야구] a catcher.

포스터 [**फोसथौ**] a poster; a placard; a bill; (그림이 있는) a pictorial poster; (글자만의) a plain poster.

포식 [**फोसिक**] [**飽食**] gluttony; satiation; engorgement. 포식하다 satiate oneself <with rich food>; glut oneself <on>; eat one's fill.

포악 [**फोआक**] [**暴惡**] violence (난폭); tyranny (폭정); savagery (야만); atrocity

(잔학) 포악하다 atrocious; ruthless; outrageous; barbarous.

포옹 [फोओांग] [抱擁] an embrace; (특히 애정을 지닌, 열렬한) a hug. 포옹하다 embrace; hug; cuddle; hold <a person> to one's breast [in one's arms]; wrap one's arms about <a person>.

포용 [फोयोंग] [包容] comprehension; implication; tolerance; magnanimity. 포용하다 (의미를) comprehend; embrace; imply; include; (사람을) tolerate; accept with magnanimity.

포위 [फूवि] [包圍] encirclement; envelopment; (a) siege; besiegement; investment; beleaguerment. 포위하다 [에워싸다] surround; encircle; hem [close] in; (군대 등이) invest; envelop; beleaguer; besiege; lay siege to <a fort>; (경관이) throw a cordon round <a place>.

포인트 [फोइन्थ] **1** [득점] a point. **2**[소수점] a (decimal) point. **3** [요점] the point.**4** [점, 지점]. e.g. 체크 포인트 a checkpoint.

포장 [फोजांग] [包裝] packing; packaging (상품의 개장 (個裝)); baling (곤포, 꾸러미의); crating (운송용 상자, 틀, 바구니 등의). 포장하다 pack(up); package; wrap <it> up

포장 [फोजांग] [鋪裝] pavement; paving. 포장하다 pave [surface] <a road with asphalt>.

포즈 [फोज] [자세] a pose. e.g. 포즈를 취하다 pose (oneself) <as a model> / strike [get into] a pose / take one's pose / posture / arrange oneself.

포진 [फोजीन] [布陣] the lineup <of>; lines. 포진하다 take up a position; (군대를) array one's force for battle.

포착 [फोछक] [捕捉] capture; apprehension; prehension. 포착하다 catch; seize; grasp; catch [take] hold of; (레이더가) pick up.

포켓 [फोखेत] a pocket; a kick.

포탄 [फोथान] [砲彈] a cannon ball; a shell; a shot.

포탈 [फोथाल] [逋脫] [과세를 피하여 면함] tax evasion; evasion of taxes. 포탈하다 evade [dodge] a taK defraud the revenue.

포함 [फोहाम] [包含] inclusion; comprehension; implication (뜻을). 포함하다 include; comprise; comprehend; embrace; cover; contain; have <in>; hold.

포화 [फोह्वा] [飽和] [化] saturation. 포화하다 be [become] saturated <with>

포화 상태 [फोह्वा सांगथे] [飽和狀態] saturation. e.g. 환자의 수용은 포화 상태이다 There are no spare

ㅍ

beds for new patients. / The ward is full.

포획 [फोह्वेक] [捕獲] capture; seizure. 포획하다 capture; seize; catch

포효 [फोह्यो] [咆哮] [사나운 짐승이 울부짖음] roaring; howling; [울음 소리] a roar; a howl; a bellow. 포효하다 roar; howl; bellow; yell.

폭 [फोक] [幅] **1** 폭이 넓은 [좁은] 도로 a wide(*or* broad) [narrow] road. 길이 50 cm, **2** [도량, 포용성] generosity; magnanimity; caliber; [범위] range; [규칙, 제한 등의 여유] permitted freedom; latitude. e.g. 폭넓은 지식 wide [extensive] knowledge **3** (그림, 병풍 등의) a scroll; a strip; a piece <of>.

폭격 [फोकक्यौक] [爆擊] (aerial) bombing [bombardment]; a bombing attack [raid]. 폭격하다 bomb; drop a bomb <on>; make a bombing raid.

폭군 [फोक्कुन] [暴君] a tyrant; a despot (전제 군주).

폭도 [फोक्तो] [暴徒] rioters; a mob; mobsters; insurgents; mutineers (군대의).

폭동 [फोकतोंग] [暴動] a riot; a disturbance; rioting; an uprising; [병란] a mutiny; [반란] an insurrection; a rebellion. **폭동자** a rioter; an insurgent; a rebel; a mutineer (군대의).

폭등 [फोक्तुंग] [暴騰] a sudden rise; a sharp rise; a boom; a(big) jump; skyrocketing. 폭등하다(갑자기) rise suddenly; <美>boom; (엄청나게) jump; soar; shoot skyward; skyrocket.

폭락 [फोंग्नाक] [暴落] a slump; a (sharp) break; a crash; a smash; sagging; a heavy fall [decline]; a tremendous drop.

폭락하다 (크게) decline heavily [sharply]; slump; (갑자기) fall suddenly; toboggan (가치가); [증권] plunge; plummet; nosedive.

폭력 [फोंगन्यौक] [暴力] violence; (brute) force.

폭로 [फोंग्नो] [暴露] exposure; disclosure; divulgeence; debunking. 폭로하다 disclose [reveal / divulge / air] <a secret>; expose <another's crime>; betray <another's plot>; lay bare <an evil design>; bring <a matter> to light; give away <another's secret>.

폭리 [फोंग्नी] [暴利] excessive profits; [고리(高利)] exorbitant interest; usury.

폭발 [फोक्पाल] [爆發] explosion; detonation; blast(ing); burst (ing); blowing up; eruption (화산의). 폭발하다 explode; burst (up); blow up; go up [off]; detonate;

(화산이) erupt; burst into eruption.

폭삭 [फोक्साक] **1** [온통] entirely; wholly; completely; thoroughly. **2** [먼지가 갑자기 가볍게 일어남] puffing; in a cloud.

폭설 [फोक्सौल] [**暴雪**] a tremendous [very heavy] snowfall [fall of snow].

폭소 [फोकसो] [**爆笑**] a [an uncontrolled] burst [roar] of laughter; an explosive laugh [laughter]; uproarious laughter. 폭소하다 roar with laughter; burst out laughing; burst into laughter.

폭식 [फोक्शिक] [**暴食**] voracious [excessive] eating; gorging; gluttony; voracity. 폭식하다 overeat (oneself); eat too much; eat to [in] excess; gorge.

폭언 [फोगौन] [**暴言**] violent [harsh / intemperate] language; abusive [bad] language; wild [strong] words. 폭언하다 abuse; use violent [strong] lan-guage; speak vehemently; utter wild words.

폭우 [फोगू] [**暴雨**] a heavy rain [rainfall]; a torrential [hard] rain; a down pour; cataracts [a deluge] of rain.

폭음 [फोगुम] [**暴飮**] heavy [deep / excessive / immoderate] drinking; carousal; intemperance. 폭음하다 drink hard [heavily / deep]; drink like a fish; drink too much [to excess]; booze.

폭음 [फोगुम] [**爆音**] (비행기의) buzzing; burring; drumming; whizzing; a roar; (폭발의) an explosion; a detonation; a report; (내연기관의) knocking.

폭주 [फोक्फो] [**輻輳, 輻湊**]x overcrowding; congestion <of goods [traffic]>; influx [deluge / flood] <of people>. 폭주하다 congest; be congested <with>; be (over) crowded <with>.

폭주 [फोक्चु] [**暴走**] (자동차 등의) reckless driving; speeding; (가축떼 등의) a stampede; [야구] a reckless run.

폭죽 [फोक्चुक] [**爆竹**] a(fire) cracker; a squib; a flip–flap; a petard.

폭탄 [फोक्थान] [**爆彈**] a bomb; a bombshell.

폭파 [फोक्फा] [**爆破**] blasting; blowing up; explosion. 폭파하다 blast; blow up; explode.

폭포 (수) [फोक्फो] [**瀑布(水)**] a waterfall; a falls; a cascade (작은); a cataract (큰).

폭풍 [फोक्फुंग] [**暴風**] a storm; a windstorm; a wild [violent / stormy] wind; a high wind; a gale (강풍); a hurricane; a typhoon (태풍).

폭행 [फोख्वैग] [**暴行**] (an act

of) violence; riotous conduct; an outrage; violation; an attack; an assault. 폭행하다 behave violently; act outrageously; assault (criminally); attack.

퐁퐁 **[फोंग्फोंग]** [샘솟는 소리] bubbling; gurgling.

표 **[प्यो]** [表] (일람표의) a table; a tabular statement [exhibit]; a schedule (예정표); a diagram; a chart (도표); a list (목록); [표의 형식] tabular form.

표¹ **[प्यो]** [票] **1** [각종 딱지] a card; a label; a name card (이름표); a place card (좌석표); a tab; a tag (꼬리표); [(짐,신발 등의) 보관표] a receipt; a check; [번호표] a number check; [정가표, 전당표 등] a ticket; a tally (꼬리표); (한 장씩 떼어 내는) a chit; a coupon **2**[차표, 배표, 입장권 등] a ticket; a coupon (ticket) (떼어 쓰게 된). **3** (선거의) a vote; a ballot.

표² **[प्यो]** [標] **1** [부호] a mark; a sign; a note. **2** [징표] a symbol; an emblem.

표결 **[प्योग्यौल]** [表決] ballot taking; a vote; a roll call; a division. 표결하다 vote <on>; take a vote <on a question>; take a ballot <for>; take a roll call; take a division; divide <on>.

표구 **[प्योगू]** [表具] mounting. 표구하다 mount <a picture>; put <a picture> in a mount.

표구사 **[प्योगूसा]** a paper hanger; a paperer; a mounter.

표기 **[प्योगी]** [表記] **1** [표면에 쓰기] inscription on the face. **2** [내용을 표시하기] declaration **3** [철자] spelling; transcription (다른 글에 의한). 표기하다 spell; transcribe

표기 **[प्योगी]** [標記] marking; a mark 표기하다 mark.

표나다 **[प्योनादा]** [表 –] [두드러지다] be conspicuous [striking / evident / obvious]; stand out; [겉으로 드러나다] show signs; show [give] proof [evidence] <of>; be shown (clearly).

표독 **[प्योदोक]** [慓毒] ferocity; fierceness; venomousness. 표독하다 ferocious; fierce; venomous; vicious; shrewd.

표류 **[प्योर्यू]** [漂流] **1** [떠서 흘러감] drith; drithing. 표류하다 drith (about / with the current / on the tide); be adrith. 표류하다 wander aimlessly; tramp; rove.

표리 **[प्योरी]** [表裏] **1** [속과 겉] inside and outside; obverse and reverse. **2** [양면] two sides <of a

thing>; [표면과 내심] appearance and mind [real intention].

표면 [फ्योम्यौन] [表面] [거죽] the surface; the face; the obverse; [외부] the exterior; the outside; [외양] (an) appearance; (a) show.

표면적 [फ्योमयौन्जौक] [表面積] the surface [superficial] area.

표면화 [फ्योमयौनह्वा] [表面化] 표면화하다 come [be brought] to the fore [front]; come out in the open; come up to the surface; come to a head; become an issue.

표명 [फ्योम्यौग] [表明] expression; demonstration; manifestation. 표명하다 [표시하다] state; express; make an expression <of>; indicate; demonstrate; show; manifest.

표방 [फ्योम्यौग] [標榜] 방하다 profess <oneself to be>; adopt a platform [slogan / motto] <of>; advocate [champion / espouse / sponsor] <the cause of democracy>; stand for.

표백 [फ्योबैक] [漂白] bleaching; decoloration; decolorization. 표백하다 bleach; decolor; decolorize.

표본 [फ्योबोन] [標本] 1 [생물의 보존 처리] a specimen.2 [견본] a sample.3 [전형] a type; an example.

표상 [फ्योसांग] [表象] 1 (a) representation; (a) presentation; [哲] an idea.2 e.g. 자유의 표상 a symbol of liberty [freedom].

표시 [फ्योशी] [表示] 1 [나타냄] (an) indication; (an) expression; (a) manifestation; (a) demonstration. 표시하다 indicate; show; manifest; express; give expression to 2 [표적] a token; a mark; a sign; a manifestation

표어 [फ्योओ] [標語] a slogan; a motto <*pl.* ~ (e)s>; a catchword; a watchword; a rallying word.

표음 [फ्योउम] [表音] (문자의) phonetic representation. 표음하다 represent [write] phonetically.

표음 문자[फ्योउम मुन्चा] a phonogram.

표의 [फ्योइ] [表意] (문자의) ideography 표의하다 represent [write] the meanings; write in ideographs

표의 문자 [फ्योइ मुन्चा] an ideogram; an ideograph; an ideographic character.

표적 [फ्योजौक] [標的] a target; a mark.

표절 [फ्योजौल] [剽竊] plagiarism; piracy; crib; abstracttion. 표절하다 pirate; plagiarize; crib; gut <a book>; abstract.

ㅍ

표정 [फ्योजौंग] [表情] (a) (facial) expression; a look (얼굴, 눈의).

표제 [फ्योजे] [標題,表題] (책 등의) a title; (장,절 등의) a heading; (사진 등의) a caption; (신문 기사 등의) a headline <over an article>; a head (ing); (문장의) a superscription.

표준 [फ्योजुन] [標準,表準] **1** [기준] a standard; (판단의) a criterion <*pl.* -ria>; [수준] a level. **2** [보통, 평균] the average; norm.

표준어[말] [फ्योजुनौ] the standard language <of a nation / in a country>; standard Korean [English].

표지 [फ्योजी] [表紙] a cover; binding (등부분도 포함한).

표지 [फ्योजी] a mark (ing); a sign; a signal; a beacon; a guide.

표징 [फ्योजीग] [表徵] a sign; a mark; a symbol; an indication.

표창 [फ्योछांग] [表彰] (official) commendation; honoring; awarding. 표창하다 commend (officially); honor [do honor to] <a person>; give recognition <for>; make public recognition <of a person's services>.

표피 [फ्योफी] [表皮] **1** the outer (most) layer of the skin; the scarfskin; the cuticle; the epidermis (최상층의). **2** [植] the epidermis; the exterior coating; the bark (수피).

표하다 [फ्योहादा] [表-] [나타내다] express <one's gratitude>; show; manifest; demonstrate; pay <one's respects>; offer <one's congratulations>.

표하다 [फ्योहादा] [標-] mark <a thing>; put [place] a mark on <a thing>.

표현 [फ्योह्यौन] [表現] (주로 말에 의한) (an) expression; (a) representation; (a) presentation; (a) manifestation. 표현하다 express; be expressive of; represent; manifest; give expression [words] to <thoughts>.

푯말 [फ्योन्माल] [標-] a post; a signpost.

푸념 [फून्यौम] [불평] an idle [a doleful] complaint; a grumble; grumbling. 푸념하다 grumble <at>; complain <of / about>; make complaints <to a person about something>; whine <about>; dwell on grievances; gripe <at / about>.

푸다 [फूदा] (물 등을) draw <from>; (국자 등으로) scoop (up); dip (up); (펌프로) pump (up); (배에 있는 물을) bail out.

푸대접 [फुदैजौप] [-待接] unkind [uncivil] treatment; a cold [frigid] reception; inhospitality. 푸대접하다

treat [receive] <a person> coldly [with coldness / unkindly / in a cold way]; receive <a person> with indifference; be inhospitable <to>; give <a person> a cold [frosty] reception <to>; give [show / turn] the cold shoulder <to>.

푸드덕 [फुददौक] flapping; fluttering.

푸르다 [फूरूदा] **1** [청색이다] blue; azure; [초록이다] green. **2** (서슬이) sharp (-edged).

푸릇푸릇 [फूरूतफूरूत] all spotted green [blue]; green [blue] here and there. 푸릇푸릇하다 verdant; fresh and green; be green [blue] here and there; be all spotted green [blue].

푸석푸석 [फुसौकफुसौक] [부스러지기 쉬운 모양] all crisp [crumbly / rotting away]. 푸석푸석하다 crumbling; crumbly; loose <soil>; friable; (과일 등이) dry and tasteless [insipid]; (감자 등이) dry and crumbling; not pasty; (치즈가) snappy.

푸짐하다 [फुजीमहादा] plentiful; abundant; copious; generous.

푹 [फुक] **1** [찌르는 모양] home; hard; through. e.g. 푹찌르다 stab through / plunge <a knife into a person's breast> / thrust <a dagger> home **2** [뒤집어쓰거나 싸는 모양] completely; entirely. e.g. 모자를 푹 눌러쓰다 pull [flap] one's hat over one's eyes / wear one's hat pulled low over one's eyes. **3** [잠자는 모양] fast; sound(ly). e.g. 푹자다 sleep soundly / be sound asleep / sleep like a top [log]. **4** [쉬는 모양] thoroughly; completely; quite. e.g. 푹쉬다 rest up / rest completely / have a good slack. **5** [흠씬] thoroughly; well; through. e.g. 고기를 푹 삶다 do meat thoroughly. **6** [빠지거나 팬 모양] deep; deeply. e.g. 푹 파다 dig deep(ly). 진창에 푹 빠지다 be caught [stuck] deep in the mud.

푹신푹신 [फुविशन फुविशन] sothly; gently; lightly. 푹신푹신하다 soth; downy; cottony; flossy; fluffy; spongy.

푹신하다 [फुविशनहादा] =푹신푹신하다. e.g. 푹신한 깃털 이불 a fluffy down quilt. 푹신한 스웨터 a fluffy sweater. 푹신한 베개 a fluffy pillow. 푹신한 쿠션 a soth cushion.

푼돈 [फुन्दोन] [적은 돈] a little [small amount of] money; a small sum; [얼마 안 되는 돈] <save> a tidy sum; a small fortune; a trifling amount (of money); small change; a (mere) pittance; small [loose] coins; loose money.

풀[1] **[फुल]** [초본식물] grass (▷ 풀의 종류를 말할 때는 가산 명사); [잡초] a weed (▷ 종종 복수형); [약초] an [a] herb; <집합적> herbage.

풀[2] **[फुल]** **1** [끈끈한 물질] paste (밀가루로 만든); starch (녹말로 만든); glue (아교풀); gum(고무풀); a size (피륙에 먹이는). **2** [기운] spirit(s); heart; starch. 풀(을) 먹이다 starch <linen>.

풀[3] **[फुल]1** [수영장] a swimming pool; a swimming bath.**2** a pool.

풀다 **[फुल्दा]** [묶은 것 등을 끄르다] untie <a string>; undo <a bundle>; unbind <a bandage>; loosen <one's hair>; unloose; unpack <a package>; unfasten <a rope>; unravel <a thread>; disentangle <a knot>; fray (천 등을); unknit (편물을); untwist; untwine (꼰 것을).

풀리다 **[फुल्लिदा]** **1** (맺힌 것이) get [come] loose; come untied [undone]; (얽힌 것이) become dissentangled; (가장자리 등이) fray; be frayed; (구두끈이) become unlaced. **2** (화등이) be allayed; (마음이) relent <toward a person> **3** (의혹 등이) be solved; be resolved; be dispelled; be removed; be cleared; be dissipated; disappear; vanish.**4** (수학 문제 등이) work out.**5** [해방되다] be released; be [get] freed. **6** [해제, 제거되다] be removed; be lithed [raised]. **7** [유통되다] circulate; pass current.**8** [용해되다] dissolve; become dissolved; melt; (언 것이) be thawed out; thaw **9** (소원이) get realized; be fulfilled. **10** (긴장이) ome [get] remiss; remit; relaK slack (en); flag. **11** (추위가) abate; moderate; go down. **12** (피로가) be relieved <of>; get over <from>; recover <from>.**13** (눈이) become bleared; get [go] bleary.

풀썩 **[फुल्सौक]1** [먼지,연기 등이 별안간 일어나는 모양] rising lightly. **2** [주저앉는 모양] collapsing.

풀어지다 **[फुरौजीदा]** [국수, 죽이 느슨히 풀리다] become soth.

풀이 **[फुरी]** (an) explanation; elucidation; exposition; (an) interpretation. 풀이하다 interpret; construe; explain; elucidate; expound

풀잎 **[फुरिफ]** a blade of grass; a grass leaf.

ㅍ

풀죽다 **[फुलचुक्ता]** **1** (옷 등이) lose <its> starch; get limp. **2** (사람이) be disheartened; be down in [at] the mouth; be in the blues [dumps]; be cast down; be downcast; be downhearted; be crestfallen; be dejected; be dispirited; be out of spirits. e.g. 풀죽은 얼굴을 하다 look blue [downcast] / be down (in the mouth).

풀칠 **[फुलछिल]** [겨우 끼니를 이어 감] bare living [livelyhood]. 풀칠하다 make one's living; keep the pot boiling; eke out a living

품 **[फुम]** [品] [물품] an article; a piece; an item. e.g. 국산품 home made [domestic] goods.

품[1] **[फुम]** **1** [옷의 폭] width <of a coat>.**2** [가슴] the bosom; the breast.

품[2] **[फुम]** [수고,힘] trouble; labor; work.

품격 **[फुम्ग्योक]** [品格] (a) grace; dignity; character. e.g. 품격이 있다 be elegant [refined / dignified].

품계 **[फुमग्ये]** [品階] a (court) rank; rank.

품귀 **[फुमग्वि]** [品貴] a scarcity [shortage / paucity] of goods [stock / supply]; an inadequate supply [an undersupply] of goods.

품다 **[फुम्ता]** **1** [안다] hold [take] <a child> in one's arms; embrace; hug; [품속에 지니다] conceal. **2** [마음에 지니다] harbor <suspicion>; entertain; cherish; nourish; bear; hold; nurse [foster]; hoard; have. **3** (알을) brood; sit <on eggs>.

품명 **[फुम्मयौंग]** [品名] the name of an article.

품목 **[फुम्मोक]** [品目] [물품의 종류] an item; [목록] a list of articles.

품사 **[फुमसा]** [品詞] [문법] a part of speech. **품사론** acidence.

품삯 **[फुमसाक]** charge [pay / wages] for labor.

품성 **[फुमसौंग]** [稟性] [타고난 성질] nature; character.

품속 **[फुमसोक]** [品位] [품격] dignity; (a) grace; nobility.

품절 **[फुमजौल]** [品切] absence of stock.

품종 **[फुमजोंग]** [品種] [물품의 종류] a kind; (동물의) a breed; [동식물의 변종] a variety.. **품종 개량** (동물의) improvement of breed; cattle breeding; (식물의) improvement of plants; plant breeding. .

품팔다 **[फुमफालता]** work for (daily) wages; do piecework [job work / odd jobs]; work as a day laborer; work by the day.

품팔이 **[फुमफारि]** 품팔이하다 work for (daily) wages; do piecework [job work]; do

ㅍ

odd jobs; work as a day laborer; be hired [hire out] by the day. **품팔이꾼** a piecework man; a piece-worker; a day laborer; a casual laborer; a char-woman (여자).

품평 [फुमप्यौग] [品評] estimation; evaluation; judgment; criticism. 품평하다 estimate; evaluate; judge; criticize. **품평회** a (competitive) show [exhibition]; a fair.

품행 [फुम्हैग] [品行] (moral) conduct; behavior; demeanor; deportment; moral character; morals.

풋- [फुत] [덜 익은] green; unripe; [새로 나온] new; fresh; [미숙한] green; novice; inexperienced.

풋것 [फुक्कौत] [처음 것] the first product <of fruit, vegetables, etc.> of the season [year];

풋내 [फुन्नै] smell of fresh young greens [herbs].

풋사랑 [फुस्सारांग] transient [transitory / fleeting] love; calf [puppy] love

-풍 [फुंग] [風] [차림] a look; appearance; one's getup; [태도] bearing; mien; deportment; manner; [유파, 식,형] a style; a fashion; a type; a mode; [풍습] manners (and customs); a custom; ways; [기질] disposition; turn of mind.

풍 [फुंग] [風] 1 [바람] (the) wind. **2** [풍병] palsy; paralysis.

풍경 [फुंग्यौक] [風景] 풍금 [फुंग्यौगं] [風琴] [오르간] an organ; a harmonium; (손으로 돌리는) a hand organ

풍기[फुंगि] [風紀] discipline; (사회의) public morals; (남녀 간의) (sexual) morality.

풍기다 [फुंगिदा] (냄새를) perfume; scent; give out [off / forth] an odor [a scent] <of>; (냄새가) smell <of>; hang [float] in the air [in midair]; (좋은 냄새가) be fragrant; (악취가) stink; reek <of / with>.

풍년 [फुंगन्यौन] [豊年] a year of abundance; a rich [bumper] year; (풍작) a bumper harvest [crop].

풍랑 [फुंग्नांग] [風浪] wind and waves; heavy seas.

풍력 [फुंगन्यौक] [風力] the velocity [force] of the wind; wind velocity.

풍류 [फुंगन्यू] [風流] [운치] elegance; taste; refinement.

풍만 [फुंग्मान] [豊滿] 1 [물건이 넉넉함] abundance; opulence; plenty. 풍만하다 abundant; opulent. **2** [몸이 비대함]. 풍만하다 plump; corpulent; voluptuous (▷ [육감적인] 이라는 느낌을 가짐); buxom; well-deve-

ㅍ

loped <breasts>; stout <lady>.

풍물 [फुंग्मुल] [**風物**] **1** 그는 전원의 풍물을 사랑한다 He loves rural scenery. 반딧불은 여름의 풍물이다 Fireflies bring us the real feeling of summer. **2** [그 고장의 생활과 관계가 깊은 것]. e.g. 독일의 풍물 the scenery and customs [scenes and manners] of Germany / things German. **3** [농악에 쓰이는 악기] farmers' musical instruments. **풍물시** a poem concerning a landscape; natural poetry.

풍미 [फुंग्मी] [**風靡**]풍미하다 overwhelm; dominate; predominate; sway; sweep; carry all <before one>.

풍부 [फुंग्बु] [**豊富**] (an) abundance; (an) opulence; (an) affluence; (a) plenty; (a) wealth; richness. 풍부하다 abundant; plentiful; plenteous; rich; ample; abound in [with]; <서술적> be fertile in <schemes>.

풍비 박산 [फुंग्बि बाक्सान] [**風飛雹散**] 풍비 박산하다 scatter [disperse / be scattered] (in all directions); [부서지다] break [be broken] to [into] fragments [splinters].

풍선 [फुंग्सौन] [**風船**] **1** [공기보다 가벼운 기체를 넣어 밀폐한 주머니] a balloon. **2** **풍선껌** <a piece of> bubble gum. e.g. 풍선껌을 부풀리다 blow a bubble.

풍성 [फुंग्सौंग] [**豊盛**] 풍성하다 [넉넉하다] abundant; plentiful; ample; affluent; opulent; exuberant

풍속 [फुंग्सोक] [**風俗**] [풍습] manners and customs; [풍기] (public) morals

풍속 [फुंग्सोक] [**風速**] wind velocity; the velocity of the wind.

풍수 [फुंग्सु] [**風水**] [民俗] [음양 오행설에 기초한 지술 (地術)] feng-shui; wind-and-water magic.

풍수지리설 [फुंग्सुजीरिसौल] [**風水地理說**] the theory of divination based on topography; Chinese geomantic principles.

풍습 [फुंग्सब] [**風習**] [풍속] manners and customs; [습관] a custom.

풍요 [फुंग्यो] [**豊饒**] richness; abundance; [비옥] fertility; productiveness; fruitfulness. 풍요하다 rich; affluent; fertile; productive; fruitful; abundant.

풍자 [फुंग्जा] [**諷刺**] a (stroke of) satire; a sarcasm; an innuendo <*pl.* ~(e)s>; an irony; a squib; a skit. 풍자하다 satirize; innuendo; lampoon(신랄히); squib.

풍족 [फुंग्जोक] [**豊足**] (an) abundance; (an) opulence;

(an) affluence; (a) plenty; (a) wealthy; richness. 풍족하다 abundant; opulent; affluent; plentiful; rich; wealthy

풍차 [फुंग्छा] [風車] a windmill.

풍채 [फुंग्छै] [風采] (one's personal) appearance; air; mien; getup; dash (씩씩한); presence.

풍치 [फुंग्छी] [風致] taste; [우아] elegance; (풍경의) scenic beauty.

풍토 [फुंग्थो] [風土] natural features <of a region>; climate

풍토병 [फुंग्थोब्यौंग] an endemic (disease); a local disease.

풍파 [फुंग्फा] [風波] **1** [바람과 물결] the wind and waves [sea]; (폭풍우) a storm; a tempest; (거친 파도) rough seas. **2** [인생의 고초] a storm. **3** [불화] (a) discord; a quarrel; a trouble; disturbances; dissensions.

풍향 [फुंगह्यांग] [風向] the direction of the wind.

풍화 [風化] [फुंगह्वा] [地質] weathering; aeration. 풍화하다 weather

프라이 [फ्राई] [튀김] fry. e.g. 달걀 프라이 fried eggs / <美>a sunny-side up. 새우 프라이 fried prawns / fried lobster.

프라이버시 [फ्राइबौशि] privacy.

프로 [फुरो] **1** 프로급의 <a player> on a professional level. **2** [퍼센트] percent

프로그래머 [फुरोगुरैमौ] [컴퓨터] a (computer) programmer.

프로그램 [फुरोगरैम] a program (me); a card.

프로덕션 [फुरोदौकस्यौन] a production; a (movie) studio <*pl.* ~s>; a film studio.

프로듀서 [फुरोदयूसौ] [映, 劇] a producer.

프로젝트 [फुरोजेकथ] a project.

프로포즈 [फुरोफोस] a proposal of marriage.

프로필 **1** [फुरोफिल] [옆모습] a profile; [인물 단평] a profile; a brief character sketch.

플라스틱 [फुल्लासथिक] (a) plastic; plastics.

피 [फि] **1** [혈액] blood. **2** [혈연, 겨레] blood; lineage; consanguinity. **3** <비유>. e.g. 새 발에 피 a drop in the bucket.

피격 [फिग्यौक] [被擊] e.g. 피격되다 be attacked [assailed / assaulted] <by>.

피고 (인) [फिगो इन] [被告(人)] (민사상의) a defendant; (형사상의) the accused; a prisoner at the bar.

피곤 [फिगोन] [疲困] fatigue; weariness; exhaustion; tiredness. 피곤하다 tired; weary; fatigued; exhausted.

피난 [फिनान] [避難] refuge; shelter; harborage; evacuation. 피난하다 seek safety in flight; take [seek] refuge <in a place / with a

person>; take [find] shelter <in>; flee <to a place> for safety; evacuate (다른 지방으로)

피동 [फिदोंग] [被動] passivity; passiveness.

피력 [फिर्यौक] [披瀝] 피력하다 express <one's opinion>; give expression [vent] to <one's thoughts>; make known; reveal

피로 [फिरो] [疲勞] fatigue; weariness; exhaustion. 피로하다 tired; weary; fatigued; exhausted.

피부 [फिबू] [皮膚] the skin.

피살 [फिसाल] [被殺] e.g. 피살되다 be killed [murdered].

피상 [फिसांग] [皮相] **1** [외관] an outward look. **2** [천박] superficiality.

피서 [फिसौ] [避暑] summering. 피서하다 summer <at / in>; pass [spend] the summer <at / in>. **피서지** [फिसौजी] a summer resort.

피습 [फिसुप] [被襲] 피습하다 be attacked; be assaulted; be set upon.

피신 [फिशिन] [避身] escape; flight; refuge. 피신하다 escape; get off [away]; flee; take refuge <in>; [숨다] conceal [hide] oneself.

ㅍ

피아노 [फिआनो] [건반 악기의 하나] a piano <*pl.* ~s>

피어나다 [फिऔनादा] **1** [불이 다시 일다] light [blaze] up (again); burn up; get lively. **2** [형편이 좋아지다] begin to prosper [flourish / thrive]. **3** [의식이 차츰 깨어나다] come to (oneself); come to life again; revive <from a swoon>. **4** [꽃 등이 피게 되다] begin to bloom [come out]; come [burst] into flower; effloresce (문화 등이) **피우다** [फिउदा] **1** [꽃을 피게 하다] make <flowers> open [bloom]. **2** [불을 피게 하다] kindle; burn; make(up). **3** (담배를) smoke; puff. **4** [냄새를 퍼뜨리다] emit; give out [off]; send forth [out].

피의자 [फिइजा] [被疑者] a suspected person; a suspect; a person under suspicion.

피임 [फिइम] [避姙] contraception; prevention of conception [maternity]; [산아 제한] birth control. 피임하다 prevent conception; practice birth control.

피자 [फिजा] pizza; (a) pizza pie.

피탈 [फिथाल] [被奪] 피탈하다 be robbed of <a thing>; have <something> taken away.

피투성이 [फिथूसौंगी] e.g. 피투성이의 bloodstained / blood-soaked / gory / bloody.

피폐 [फिफ्ये] [疲弊] impoverishment; exhaustion. 피폐하다 become [be] impoverished [exhausted].

피하다 [फिहादा] [避-] [회피하다] avoid <the heat>; escape; evade <punishment>; elude <payment>; dodge [duck] <a blow>; [막다] avert <danger>; (사람, 요구 등을) put off; (비바람을) take [seek / find] shelter <from>..

피해 [फिहे] [害] (무생물의) damage; (주로 사람의) an) injury; harm; casualties (사상).

피해자 [फिहैजा] a victim; a sufferer; the injured person.

피험자 [फिहोमजा] [被驗者] (시험의) an examinee; a testee; (실험의) a subject.

피혁 [फिह्यौक] [皮革] [짐승 가죽] hides (and skins); leather (무두질한)

핀잔 [फिन्जान] (a) scolding; a wipe; a snub; a rebuff.

필기 [फिल्गी] [筆記] [글씨를 씀] taking notes; [받아씀] notes. 필기하다 take a note [notes] of; write [note / put] down

필답 [फिल्दाप] [筆答] a written answer [response]. 필답하다 answer in writing.

필독 [फिलतोक] [必讀] required reading.

필력 [फिलल्यौक] [筆力] the power [force] of a brush stroke [the pen]; [문장의 힘] the force of one's written style.

필수 [फिल्सू] [必須] 필수의 indispensable / essential / requisite / mandatory.

필승 [फिलसंग] [必勝] (a) certain [sure / unfailing] victory.

필연 [फिर्यौन] [必然] **1** inevitability; necessity. e.g. 논리적 [물리적] 필연 logical [physical] necessity. 필연적인 inevitable / necessary. **2** <부사> certainly; surely; definitely; without doubt; necessarily; inevitably.

필요 [फिरयो] [必要] (a) necessity <for / of / to do>; (a) need <of / for / to do>; requirement. 필요하다 necessary; needful; needed; required; requisite; indispensable; essential.

필자 [फिल्चा] [筆者] the writer; the author.

필적 [फिल्चौक] [匹敵] a rival; a match; an equal. 필적하다 equal; rival; be a match <for>; be equal <to>; compare <with>; stand comparison <with>

필통 [फिल्थोंग] [筆筒] (꽂아 두는) a pencil vase; a pen [brush] stand; (넣고 다니는) a pencil case.

필히 [फिल्ही] [必-] certainly; surely; necessarily; by all means; at any cost.

핍박 [फिप्पाक] [逼迫] pressure <for money>; stringency <of the money market>; tightness <of money>. 핍박하다 be tight; get stringent

ㅍ

핏줄 [फिच्चुल] **1** a blood vessel; a vein e.g. 핏줄이 불거진 손 a veinous [veiny] hand. **2** lineage; stock; blood (relationship) e.g. 핏줄이 같다 be blood-related <to> / be of the same blood / be related by blood <to>.

핑계 [फिंग्ये] an excuse; a pretext; a pretense; a plea. 핑계하다 make a pretext [a pretense / an excuse] of; pretend <to be ill>; use <something> as pretext.

하[1] [हा] a **1** [하등]the low class [grade]; inferiority. e.g. 그는 중류의 하의 집안 출신이다 He comes from [belongs to] the lower middle class. **2** [상하 2 권의 하] the second volume; [상중하 3 권의 하] the third [last] volume.**3** [아래] e.g. 의 지휘[지도 / 감 독]하에 under the command [direction / supervision] of ... / under ....

하[2] [हा] [놀람] ha!; huh!; O!; oh!; Oh my goodness!; Dear me!; [의문] eh?; what? e.g. 하 돈을 잃어버렸다고 Say you lost your money, eh?

하강 [हागांग] [下降] a descent; a fall; (경기 등의) a decline; a downturn. e.g. 하강 도중에 on the way down. 하강하다 descend; go [come] down. e.g. 기구는 서서히 하강하고 있다 The balloon is gradually descending [coming down

하객 [हागैक] [賀客] a congratulator; a well-wisher.

하고 [हागो] [및] and; [함께] with; along [together] with. e.g. 아버지하고 아들 father and son. 그 사람 하고 함께 살다 live in the same house with him.

하교 [हाक्यो] [下校] e.g. 하교 도중에 톰을 만났다 On my way home from school I met Tom. 하교시에 비가 오기 시작했다 Just when school was over, it started to rain. 하교하다 come [return] home from school.

하급 [हागुप] [下級] a lower class [grade].

하나 [हाना] **1** (숫자의) one; a unit. e.g. 하나를 듣고 열을 알다be quick to understand / be quick on the uptake **2** [한 개] one; a piece. e.g. 흔히 쓰이는 동사가 하나 빠져 버렸다 One very common verb was left out. **3** [유일] a single one; only one. e.g.

단 하나의 the only / the sole <survivor> / the one (and only) / solitary / single / unique / exclusive. **4** [동일] the same. e.g. 하나의 (one and) the same / identical **5** [일체] one(body); one flesh. e.g. 하나로 만들다 make into one / unite (into one) / unify / merge.

하나하나 [हानाहाना] one ather another; one by one; one at a time; piece by piece; [개별적으로] individually; separately; minutely; in all particulars; fully; in detail.

하녀[हान्यौ] [下女] a maid; a maidservant; a servant girl.

하느님 [हानुनिम] 가톨릭, 기독교] God; the Almighty; the Lord; the Supreme Being; the Most High; a deity.

하는 수 없이 [हानन सु औप्शि] unavoidably; inevitably; for want of any other alternative; for lack of anything better; [마지 못해서] reluctantly; unwillingly.

하늘 [हानल] [천공] the sky; the blue; the heavens; the firmament; [상공] the skies; [공중] the air.

하늘거리다 [हानलकौरीदा] ⇨ 흐늘거리

하다못해 [हादामोथै] [심지어] so far as; to the extent of; even; [적어도] at (the) least; at the lowest; to say the least (of it); [별도리 없이] under the pressure of necessity; driven by necessity; [종국에는] in the end; finally. e.g. 그는 온갖 못된 짓을 하다못해 나중에는 살인까지 했다]He went to the extent of committing murder to top off the varieties of crimes he had perpetrated. / He went so far as to commit murder in the end.

하대 [हादै] [下待] [낮게 대접함] inhospitable treatment; a disrespectable reception; inhospitality. 하대하다 treat [receive] <a person> inhospitably; be inhospitable <towards>.

하도 [हादो] Too; too much; excessively; to excess; overly; very much; ever so much [hard / fast ...]. e.g. 하도 기뻐서 in the excess [fullness] of one's joy / through excess of joy / elated by joy / in one's joy / for joy

하드웨어 [हादुवेऔ] [컴퓨터] hardware.

하등 [हादुंग] [下等] [하급] [हागुप] a low(er) class [grade]; [열등] inferiority; [조잡] coarseness; [छैन्सोक] bad form; bad taste. e.g. 하등 low / lower <plant> / inferior / mean / coarse / vulgar / infamous / rotten.

ㅎ

하락 [हराक] [下落]가격의) [a fall [drop / decline] <in price>; depreciation; a slump (폭락); (품질의) deterioration; [증권] a sag; a downturn 하락하다fall (off); decline; come [go] down; depreciate; sink; [(가치가) 떨어지다] deteriorate; degrade; [증권] sag; show a downward [declining] tendency. e.g. 물가가 하락했다 Prices have come down [fallen]. **-하러** to; for; in order to [that ... may]; so as to <do>; for the purpose [sake] of. e.g. 사냥[등산]하러 가다 go (out) hunting [climbing

하루 [हारू] **1** [일수] a day. e.g. 하루의 일 a day's work. **2** [어느 날] one day. e.g. 하루 저녁 one evening. 하루는 근교의 몇몇 절에 가보았다 One day I visited some temples in the suburbs.

하루살이 [हारूसारी] a mayfly; a dayfly; an ephemera <*pl.* ~s, -rae

하루하루 [हारूहारू] every day; daily; from day to day; day ather [by] day. e.g. 하루 하루 나아지다 get better day by day.

하룻밤 [हारूप्पाम] [한 밤] a night; one evening [night]; [온 밤] all night (long); all the night through; [어느 날 밤] one night.

하류 [हार्यु] [下流] **1** (하천의) the lower reaches of a river [stream]. e.g. 배는 하류를 향해 나아가고 있었다 The boat was going downstream [down the river]. **2** [사회의 하층 계급] the lower classes.

하릴없다 [हारिल ओप्ता] [어쩔 수 없다] inevitable; unavoidable; inescapable; <서술적> cannot help <it>; <it> cannot be helped; cannot choose but <do>. e.g. 네게 비난을 받아도 하릴없다 know I deserve your reproaches.

하마터면 [हामाथौम्यौन] almost; nearly; as near as a toucher. e.g. 나는 하마터면 목숨을 잃을 뻔했다I came within an inch of being killed. / I very nearly lost my life.

하물 [हामुल] [荷物] = 짐

하물며 [हामुलम्यौ] (긍정) (how) much more; still more; (부정) much [still] less; to say nothing of. e.g. 나는 동요도 잘못 부르는데 하물며 오페라는 더 말할 것도 없다I cannot even sing children's songs well, to say nothing of [much less / let alone] opera

하반 [हाबान] [下半] the lower half; the latter [second] half. e.g. 하반기 the second [latter] half of the year; the half-year ending

December 31.

허상 [हसांग] [虛像] **1** a virtual image.**2** [참모습과는 다르게 만들어진 모습] a false image;(a) prêtense. e.g. 그들의 번영은 허상에 불과했다 Theirs was only a false prosperity.

허세 [हसे] [虛勢] (a) bluff; a false show of power [courage]. e.g. 허세를 부리다 bluff / put on a bold front

허송 [हसोंग] [虛送] passing time idly.허송하다 idle one's time [hours / life] away; pass one's time idly [in idleness

허송 세월 [हसोंगसेवॉल] [虛送歲月] ⇨ 허송 e.g. 그는 허송 세월을 보내고 있다He is idling his time away. / He is leading an idle life.

허수아비 [हसूआबी] **1** a scarecrow. **2** <비유>a(mere) figurehead; a dummy; a puppet. e.g. …을 허수아비로 만들다 make a puppet of <a person>.

허술하다 [हसुलहादा] **1** [초라하다]]\shabby; poor-looking; plain; humble; miserable. e.g. 허술하게 만들어진 가구 \shabby furniture / poorly made furniture.**2** [부주의하다] careless; negligent; inattentive; rude; rough; loose. e.g.허술한 방비]a loose defense.

허식 [हशिक] [虛飾] [과시] ostentation; display; [허세부림]]affectation.

허심 탄회 [हशिम थान्ह्वे] [虛心坦懷] frankness; candidness; open-mindedness [-heartedness]. 허심 탄회하다 open-minded[-hearted]; candid; frank; free and easy. e.g. 허심 탄회하게 [솔직히]frankly / [거리낌없이] candidly / [마음을 터놓고] with an open heart.

허약 [हयाक] [虛弱] weakness; infirmity; feebleness 허약하다 weak; weakly; infirm; delicate; feeble; frail; sickly (병약하다)]. e.g. 허약한 남자 a man in poor health.

허영 [हयोंग] [虛榮] vanity; vainglory.

허영심 [हयोंग्शिम] [虛榮心] vanity.

허용 [हयोंग] [許容] [용인] permission; allowance; approval; sanction; admission; tolerance. 허용하다 permit; approve; allow; admit; tolerate

허우적거리다 [हउचौक्कोरिदा] struggle; flounder; paw the air. e.g. 물에서 헤어나려고 허우적거리다 paw the air to get out of the water.

허울 [हउल] outward appear-

ㅎ

ance [features / show]; exterior. e.g. 허울만 번드르르한 물건 a gimcrack / a trumpery / a gewgaw.

허위 [हौवी] [虛僞] (a) falsehood; falsity; an untruth; a lie; fallacy.

허전하다 [हौजौनहादा] <서술적> feel empty; feel something lacking; miss something. e.g. 호주머니가 허전하다 have a light [lean / slender] purse / have empty pockets.

허점 [हौजौम] [虛點] a blind spot[point]; an unguarded point.

허탈 [हौथाल] [虛脫] (physical) collapse; prostration. 허탈하다 collapsed; prostrated.

허탕 [हौथांग] vain [fruitless] effort; vain attempt; lost labor. e.g. 모든 노력이 허탕이 되었다 All our efforts were in vain. **허투루** [경솔하게] carelessly; heedlessly; lightly; [아무렇게나] negligently; in a slovenly way; roughly. e.g. 허투루 볼 수 없는 사나이]a crathy[tricky] fellow / a sly dog. 허투루 보다 make [think] light of / make little account of / slight [neglect] <a person

허튼 소리 [हौथुन सोरी] a random remark; absurd remarks; a silly talk; nonsense; [잡소리] idle gossip; an empty prattle. e.g. 허튼 소리를 하다say silly things / talk nonsense.

허튼 수작 [हौथुन सुजाक] [-酬酌] (말) silly talk; idle talk; nonsense; (짓) a foolish act. e.g. 허튼 수작 하지 마라 Don't make yourself ridiculous. / Shame on you!

허풍 [हौफुंग] [虛風] a boast; a brag; tall [big] talk; a gasconade; a fanfaronade; <美> hot air. e.g. 그가 하는 말은 모두 허풍이다 Everything he says is exaggerated. 그건 허풍이다 That's just hot air.

허하다 [हौहादा] [虛-] [속이 비다] hollow; empty; void; vacant. e.g. 허한 느낌 a hollow feeling (inside of one). **2** [허약하다] weak(ly); infirm; delicate; feeble; frail. e.g. 몸이 허하다have a weak [delicate] constitution / bein delicate health. 기가 허하다 lack vitality [spirit].

허허[1] [हौहौ] [웃는 소리] ha! ha! e.g. 허허 웃으면서 <answer> with a(high) laugh. 허허 웃다 laugh aloud.

허허[2] [हौहौ] [놀람 등의 탄식 소리] Oh; Well; Why; Good gracious!; Heavens!; Dear me!; [슬픔을 나타내는 소리] Alas!; [일이 틀어졌을 때 내는 소리] Oops!; Damn it! e.g. 허허

이거 망쳐놨는 걸 Oh, I have made a mess of it!

허황 [हौह्वांग] [虛荒] unreliability; untrustworthiness; groundlessness; absurdity; nonsense. 허황하다 unreliable; untrustworthy; absurd; nonsensical; fantastic (al); wild <rumor>; groundless

헌금 [हौन्गुम] [獻金] a gith of money; a contribution; a donation; a subscription; (교회 등에서의) a collection; an offering.

헌납 [हौन्नाप] [獻納] [금품을 바침] presentation; offering; contribution; donation. 헌납하다 present <an airplane to the army>; offer; contribute; donate.

헌법 [हौन्पौप] [憲法] the constitution; the constitutional law.

헌신 [हौन्शिन] [獻身] self-sacrifice; devotion; dedication. e.g. 헌신적인 self-sacrificing / devoted.

헌혈 [हौन्ह्यौल] [獻血] blood donation; donating blood.

헐값 [हौल्गाप] [歇-] a give-away [wretched] price. 헐값의 dirt-[dog-] cheap / cheap as dirt. 헐값으로 사다buy <a thing> cheap as dirt / get <an article> for a mere song. 헐값으로 팔다 sell <something> for its scrap value / sell <an article> dirt-cheap.

헐겁다 [हौल्गौप्ता] loose (-fitting); baggy; too large.

헐다[1] [हौल्दा] (부스럼 등이) form [develop] a boil; break out in sores; be inflamed. e.g. 무릎이 헐었다I have got a boil on my knee. 다친 데가 헐었다 The wound was inflamed.

헐다[2] [हौल्दा] [낡아지다] become [get] old; wear [be worn] out; (옷 등이) become shabby. e.g. 헐어서 누더기가 되다 be worn to rags.

헐다[3] [हौल्दा] [허물다] break [pull / take / tear] down <a house>; demolish; destroy. e.g. 돌담을 헐다 demolish a stone wall.

헐떡거리다 [हौल्तौकौरीदा] pant; gasp(for breath); puff (and blow); breathe hard [heavily / with difficulty]; be out [short] of breath; be panting [gasping] for breath. e.g. 헐떡거리며 gasping (ly) / panting (ly) / between gasps / out of breath.

헐렁거리다 [हौल्लौंगकौरीदा] [헐거워서 흔들리다] be loose; fit [work] loose. e.g. 신이 헐렁거리다 one's shoes fit loose.

헐렁하다 [हौल्लौंगहादा] loose (-fitting); baggy.

헐레벌떡 [हौल्लेबौल्तौक] [헐떡거리며] puffing and blowing; gasping and panting;

out of breath; [황급히] hurry-scurry; helter-skelter. e.g. 헐레 벌떡 달려가다 run along panting and puffing.

헐리다 [**होल्लिदा**] be pulled [torn] down; be demolished [destroyed]. e.g. 헐리고 있는 건물 a building under demolition.

헐벗다 [**होल्बौत्ता**] **1** [사람이 누더기를 입다] <서술적> be in need [want] of clothes. e.g. 헐벗은 아이들 poorly [shabbily] clothed children.**2** [나무가 없다] <서술적> be bared [stripped] of leaves. e.g. 헐벗은 산 a bare [bald] mountain

험난 [**होम्नान**] [**險難**] [어려움] hardship; difficulty; adversity; [험준함] steepness; precipitousness. 험난하다 difficult; hard; arduous; tough; steep; precipitous

험담 [**होम्दाम**] [**險談**] abuse; (a) slander; calumny; [뒷전에서 하는 말] backbiting; malicious gossip; scandal 험담 잘하는 사람 a scandalmonger / a backbiter. 험담하다 speak ill of <a person>; talk scandal about; slander; abuse; calumniate; (뒷전에서) backbite.

험악 [**होमाक**] [**險惡**] 험악하다 dangerous; perilous; (날씨 등이) threatening <sky>; stormy; (사태가) serious; critical; grave. e.g.험악한 날씨 stormy [threatening / rough] weather.

험준 [**होमजुन**] [**險峻**] 험준하다 steep; precipitous; rugged; sheer. e.g. 험준한 산길 a steep [rugged] trail.

헛간 [**होक्कान**] [**-間**] a shed; a (storage) barn.

헛걸음 [**होक्कौरुम**] 헛걸음하다 go on a bootless [fool's] errand; make a visit <on a person> in vain; make a fruitless call <on a person>. e.g. 그가 집에 없을지 모르지만, 헛걸음할 셈치고 가 보는 것도 좋겠지 He may not be at home, but you might go just on chance.

헛구역 [**होक्कुयौक**] [**-嘔逆**] vomiturition. 헛구역질하다 try to vomit in vain.

헛기침 [**होक्कीछिम**] a dry cough. 헛기침하다 have a dry cough; (일부러) clear one's throat; give a cough; hawk; hem.

헛돈 [**होत्तोन**] money thrown away; wasted money. 헛돈 쓰다 waste [throw away] one's money <on>.

헛되다 [**होत्द्वेदा**] **1** [보람이나 뜻이 없다] vain; fruitless; ineffective; futile; unavailing; useless; <서술적> be in vain; be no good; come to nothing; prove fruitless. e.g.헛된 노력 a vain [fruitless / useless] effort / lost labor. **2** [허황하다] wild; groundless; false; untrue. 헛된 소문 a groundless [wild] rumor / a canard.

헛되이 [हौत्देई] [무익하게] in vain; vainly; uselessly; to no purpose; [보람없이] fruitlessly; futilely; to no avail; [목적도 없이] aimlessly; [한가하게] idly. e.g. 헛되이 세월을 보내다 pass one's time idly / live in idleness / idle one's time away.

헛디디다 [हौत्तीदीदा] miss one's foot [step]; lose one's footing; make a false step; slide down <a cliff>. e.g. 벼랑을 헛디뎌서 바다 속으로 떨어지다 step over the cliff into the sea.

헛소리 [हौस्सोरी] **1** [혼미중에 하는 소리] talking in delirium; delirious utterances. **2** [미덥지 않은 말] a falsehood; a lie; idle words; an empty talk; nonsense.

헛소문 [हौस्सुमुन] [-所聞] a groundless [false] rumor; a canard. 헛소문을 퍼뜨리다 set a false rumor afloat.

헛수고 [हौत्सुगो] fruitless [useless / vain] efforts; waste of labor; lost labor. e.g. 헛수고로 돌아가다 prove fruitless / end in a (mere) waste of labor.

헛웃음 [हौत्तुसुम] a feigned [an affected] laugh [smile]; a smirk; a (conscious) simper. e.g. 헛웃음 치다 affect [feign] a laugh / put on a feigned smile / simper.

헛일 [हौशिल] useless work; a wasted effort; waste of labor; lost labor.

헝겊 [हौंगौप] a piece of cloth; a patch; rags.

헝클다 [हौंगख्युल्दा] tangle; entangle; ravel; dishevel. 머리를 헝클다 dishevel one's hair. 실을 헝클다 tangle thread.

헝클어지다 [हौंगख्युरौजीदा] tangle; getz [become] tangled; be entangled; be in a tangle. e.g. 헝클어진 머리 tangled [matted] hair / disheveled [unkempt] hair.

헤드폰 [हेदुफोन] a headphone.

헤매다 [हेमैदा] **1** [돌아다니다] wander [roam / knock] about; hover <about / in>; stray about (길을 잃고) e.g. 여기저기를 헤매다 wander from place to place. **2**[어찌할 바를 모르다]. be puzzled [perplexed] <what to do>; be at a loss <what to do>; be quite embarrassed.

헤어나다 [हेऔनादा] escape from <danger>; get out of <a predicament>; extricate oneself from <difficulties>; free oneself from <a bondage>; find one's way out of <a fix>. e.g. 위기에서

헤어나다. get through [tide over] a crisis.

헤어스타일 **[हेऔसुथाइल]** a hair-style.

헤어지다 **[हेऔजीदा]** **1** [이별하다] part <from / with>; separate; be separated <from>; be parted <from>; [이혼하다] divorce oneself <from>. e.g. 아내와 헤어지다 divorce one's wife **2** [흩어지다] break up; disperse; be scattered. e.g. 졸업생들은 각처로 흩어졌다 The graduates were scattered in all directions.

헤엄 **[हेऔम]** swimming; a swim; a swimming stroke

헤치다 **[हेछिदा]** **1** [파헤치다] dig up; turn up. e.g. 나는 쓰레기를 헤치고 잃어버린 물건을 찾아냈다I searched through the debris and found what I had lost. **2** [흩어버리다] scatter; disperse; break up. e.g. 모인 사람을 헤치다 disperse a crowd. **3** [좌우로 물리치다] push aside; make one's way <through>; plow [edge / push / work / elbow] one's way <through>. e.g. 인파를 헤치고 나아가다 push [elbow / thrust] one's way through the crowd.

헤프다 **[हेफुदा]** **1** (물건이) not durable; soon used up; <서술적> do not stand long use [give a long service]; do not last long; go fast. e.g. 요새 돈이 헤프다 Money doesn't go far these days. **2** (씀씀이가) neconomical; wasteful; prodigal; unthrithy. e.g. 돈을 헤프게 쓰다 be too free with one's money / be wasteful of money. be careless with money.**3** (몸가짐이) loose; dissolute; dissipated. e.g. 몸가짐이 헤픈 여자 a loose [fast] woman.

헬리콥터 **[हेल्लिखोपथौ]** a helicopter

헷갈리다 **[हेक्कालिलदा]** **1** [뒤섞이다] be mixed (confusedly). e.g. 서류가 헷갈리지 않도록 하다 see that the papers do not get mixed. **2** [갈피를 못 잡다] be hardly distinguishable <from>; hardly tell [discriminate] <A from B>; [머리가 혼란하다] be thrown into confusion; be confused [perplexed]. e.g. 머리가 헷갈린다 I'm getting confused. / <美> My head is buzzy.

헹가래 **[हेंगारै]** tossing <a person>; hoisting <a person> shoulder-high 헹가래 치다 hoist <a person> shoulder-high / toss.

헹구다 **[हेंगुदा]** wash out; rinse; give <a thing> a rinse [swill].

혀 [ह्यौ] (사람의) a tongue; (동물의) a lingua. 혀를 내두르다 e.g. 그의 노래에는 동급생들도 혀를 내둘렀다 His classmates were filled with admiration for his singing. 그의 먹성이 좋은 것에 그녀는 혀를 내둘렀다 She was astoundded at his appetite. 혀를 내밀다 e.g. 그녀는 그의 등 뒤에서 혀를 내밀었다 She laughed at him [made a fool of him] behind his back.혀를 차다 click [clack] one's tongue; tut; be wonder-struck. e.g. 혀를 차는 소리 a tongue-clicking sound / a click [clack] of the tongue / (못마땅하여) Tut, tut.

혁명 [ह्यौगम्यौग] [革命] a revolution

혁신 [ह्यौग्शिन] [革新] [사회적,정치적 개혁 (a) reform; [쇄신] an) innovation

현 [ह्यौन] [現] [현재의] current; present; [현직의] incumbent. e.g. 현시점에서는 at present / at this point in time.

현격하다 [ह्यौन्ग्यौख्यादा] [懸隔-] far [wide] apart <from>; (widely) different <from>. e.g. 현격한 차이 a great disparity / a wide difference [gap].

현관 [ह्यौन्ग्वान] [玄關] [입구] the entrance; the porch (way); the (front) door

현금 [ह्यौन्गुम] [現金] cash; [현재 있는 금전] actual [ready] money; specie; [맞돈] prompt [spot] cash; ready funds.

현대 [ह्यौन्दै] [現代] the present age [day / generation]; modern times; today. 현대의 present-day / contemporary / present / current / of our time / modern / of the day

현대적 [ह्यौनदैजौग] [現代的] modern (-type); modernistic; up-to-date; up-to-the-minute.
modernization; updating.

현란 [ह्यौल्लान] [絢爛] 현란하다 gorgeous; brilliant; dazzling; (문체 등이) flowery; ornate; florid; gaudy. e.g. 현란한 문체a flowery [richly ornate] style.

현명하다 [ह्यौनमयौगहादा] [賢明-] wise; clever; intelligent; [분별 있다] judicious; sensible; prudent; discreet; well-advised. e.g. 현명한 방책 a wise policy.

현미경 [ह्यौन्मीग्यौग] a microscope.

현상 [ह्यौन्सांग] [懸賞] [상품, 상금 등을 걸기]a prize contest [competition]; offer of a prize [reward]. e.g. 소설의 현상 모집 a prize novel competition.

현상금 [ह्यौन्सांगुम] prize money; a reward; a prize <on his head>. e.g. 현상금을

걸다 offer a prize [reward] <for> / (범인 등에) set [put] a price on <an offender"s head>.

현상 [**हयौन्सांग**] [**現象**] a phenolmenon <*pl.* –na>; an appearance <in the sky>; [사건] a happening; [국면] a phase. 자연 [사회] 현상 a natural [social] phenomenon.

현세 [**हयौन्से**] [**現世**] [지금 세상] this (present) world; the transient life; [불교] the land of the living; this life.

현수막 [**हयौन्सुमाक**] [**懸垂幕**] (극장의) a drop curtain; (거리, 건물의) a banner; (방 등의) a hanging screen; a curtain; [플래카드] a placard.

현신 [**हयौन्शिन**] [**現身**] 현신하다 present oneself before a superior; put in one's appearance; appear.

현실 [**हयौन्शिल**] [**現實**] actuality; the actual; the realities of life; a hard fact (공론에 대하여) 현실의 [으로] actual (ly) / real (ly).

현실화 [**हयौन्शिर्हवा**] [**現實化**] actualization; realization; materialization. 현실화하다 actualize; realize; materialize; (물가 등을) readjust <prices> to a realistic level

현악 [**हयौन्आक**] [**弦樂, 絃樂**] string music.

현역 [**हयौन्यौक**] [**現役**] (군무의) active service [duty]; (휴직에 대하여) ser-vice on full pay; commission (군함의) e.g. 현역의 군인a serviceman on active duty.

현장 [**हयौन्जांग**] [**現場**] (사건의) the (actual) spot; the scene <of action>; (작업의) the scene of labor; a job site; (건축의) a building site; a construction field. e.g. 사고 [범죄]의 현장 the scene of the accident [crime].

현재 [**हयौन्जे**] [**現在**] [지금] now; presently; <at> the present time. 현재의 present / existing / current <prices>. 현재까지 up to now / up [down] to date. 현재는 [바로 지금] at present / now / at the present time / [지금 당장] for the time being.

현존 [**हयौनजोन**] [**現存**] 현존의 [지금도 살아 있는] living / [지금도 있는] (now) existent.

현존 하다 exist; be in existence; be extant; subsist

현지 [**हयौन्जी**] [**現地**] the spot; the field; the actual place; the (actual) locale. e.g. 현지의 on-the-spot.

현직 [**हयौन्जिक**] [**現職**] the present post [office]; the office now held. e.g. 현직의 incumbent / on the active list / in active service

현찰 [ह्यौन्छाल] [**現札**] [현재 가지고 있는 돈] (hard) cash; actual [ready] money; [현금이 되는 지폐] a (bank) note; bread; dough.

현충일 [ह्यौन्छुंगिल] [**顯忠日**] the Memorial Day.

현판 [ह्यौन्फान] [**懸板**] a tablet; a hanging board (with a picture or some calligraphy on it); a framed picture (그림으로 된)

현행 [ह्यौन्हैंग] [**現行**] 현행의 present / existing / current (▷ present 는 현재 행하여지고 있다는 뜻에서 그 시간이 강조되며, existing, current는 현재 통용되고 있다는 데서 그 존재가 문제가 된다는 뜻이 담김) / (법률, 규정 등이) in force / in operation. 현행대로 same as at present. e.g. 현행의 교통 법규로는[] under the present [current / existing] traffic regulations.

현혹 [ह्यौनहोक] [**眩惑**] dazzlement; bewilderment; a daze. 현혹하다 [당혹하게 하다] perpleK [혼란시키다] con-fuse; [판단을 그르치게 하다] delude; [유혹하다] seduce; tempt; make dizzy [giddy]; mystify [bewil-der] <a person>. **현황** [ह्यौन्हवांग] [**現況**] the present condition [state] <of>.

혈관 [ह्यौलग्वान] [**血管**] a blood vessel.

혈당 [ह्यौल्दांग] [**血糖**] blood sugar

혈색 [ह्यौल्सैग] [**血色**] one's complexion; color.

혈안 [ह्यौरान] [**血眼**] a blood-shot eye. e.g. 그들은 딸의 입학 시험 때문에 혈안이 되어 있다 They can't think of anything but their daughter's entrance examination.

혈압 [ह्यौराप] [**血壓**] blood pressure.

혈액형 [ह्यौरैख्यौंग] [**血液型**] a blood type; the type of one's blood.

혈연 [ह्यौर्योन] [**血緣**] a blood relative. e.g. 그는 나의 혈연이다 He is my own flesh and blood.

혈육 [ह्यौर्युक] [**血肉**] [자식] one's sons and daughters; [육친] one's own flesh and blood. 혈육의 형제 a brother of the same flesh and blood.

혈통 [ह्यौल्थोंग] [**血統**] blood; lineage; pedigree; family line; descent. e.g. 혈통이 좋은 집안 a family of good lineage.

혈혈단신 [ह्यौर्यौदान्शिन] [**孑孑單身**] being without a single human tie; being all alone; having no kith or kin. e.g. 나는 혈혈 단신이다 I stand all alone in the world.

혈흔 [ह्यौहुन] [**血痕**] a blood-stain. e.g. 혈흔이 묻은

ㅎ

손수건 a bloodstained handkerchief

혐오 [ह्यौमो] [嫌惡] hatred; dislike; disgust; aversion; abhorrence. 혐오하다 hate; loathe; detest. e.g. 그는 뱀을 본능적으로 혐오하였다 He instinctively hated [loathed] snakes. / He had an instinctive hated of snakes

혐오스럽다 [ह्यौमोसुरौप्ता] [嫌惡–] hateful; disgusting; detestable. e.g. 정치가의 독직만큼 혐오스러운 것도 없다 Nothing makes one's gorge rises like corruption in politicians.

혐의 [ह्यौमुइ] [嫌疑] [의심] suspicion; charge; accusation. e.g. 그는 살인의 혐의를 받고 있다 He is suspected of murder.

협공 [ह्यौप्कोंग] [挾攻] an attack on both flanks; a pincer attack [movement]; double envelopment. e.g. 도둑은 두 경비원에게 협공을 당하였다 The thief found himself [caught] between two guards.

협동 [ह्यौप्तोंग] [協同] cooperation; collaboration; union; combination. e.g. 협동의 communal / joint / concerted / united. 협동으로 in partnership <with> / jointly / communally. 협동하다 cooperate <with>; collaborate <in>; work together; act in concert [union] <with>; join forces [hands] <with>; team up <with>.

협력 [ह्यौमन्यौक] [協力] cooperation; collaboration; working together. 협력하다 cooperate <with>; work [pull] together; collaborate <with>; unite one's efforts <with>; make united [concerted] efforts; join forces [hands] <with>; team up <with>; play ball <with>.

협박 [ह्यौपाक] [脅迫] a threat; a menace; intimidation. 협박하다 threaten; intimidate; menace; blackmail; blackjack; bulldoze.

협상 [ह्यौप्सांग] [協商] [교섭] negotiation (s); bargainning; (a) conversation; [外交

협소 [ह्यौप्सो] [挟小] 협소하다 [폭이 좁다] narrow; [한정되다] limited; [면적이 작다] small

협약 [ह्यौब्याक] [協約] an agreement; a convention; a pact; [협상] an entente; an understanding

협의 [ह्यौबुइ] [協議] a conference; (a) consultation; (a) deliberation. (▷ conference 는 문제에 관하여 의견을 교환하는 일, consultation 은 전문가 등의 의견을 청하는 일 deliberation 은 정식의 심의, 토의) e.g. 문제에 대하여

협의를 계속하다 hold deliberations on a question.

협정 [ह्यौबजौंग] [**協定**] an agreement; a convention; a pact; a concordat

협조 [ह्यौबजो] [**協助**] help; aid; assistance; support (후원); cooperation (협력) e.g. 상호 협조 mutual help [aid] / cooperation / helping one another

협주곡 [ह्यौबजुगोग] [**協奏曲**] a concerto <*pl.* ~s -ti>. practice; small-bore cartridge practice; subcaliber firing.

협찬 [ह्यौबछान] [**協贊**] support; cooperation. e.g. 그 회사의 협찬으로 under the sponsorship of the company.

협회 [ह्यौबफ्वे] [**協會**] a society; an association.

혓바늘 [ह्यौत्बानल] a rash [an eruption] on the tongue. e.g. 혓바늘이 돋다 have eruption on one's tongue.

형[1] [ह्यौंग] [**型**] [양식](a) style; (a) type; a pattern; a make; [형식] form; mode; [종류] kind; stamp. e.g. 84년형 캐딜락[84] a 1984 model Cadillac.

형[2] [ह्यौंग] [**形**] **1** [형상](a) shape; [형식](a) form. V자 형의 V-shaped. 형이 망가지다 get out of shape / lose shape. **2** [만듦새] (a) cut; (a) make; [크기] (a) size. e.g. 포켓형의 사전 a dictionary of pocket size / a

형[3] [ह्यौंग] [**刑**] a penalty; [선고된 형] a sentence; [죄] (a) punishment. e.g. 종신형 a life sentence / imprisonment for life.

형[4] [ह्यौंग] [**兄**] **1** [나이가 많은 사람] one's older [elder] brother; **2** [친구간의 높임말] Mr. ...; [당신] you. 김 형Mr. Kim. 형씨 [हHey, pal! / Young man!

형광 [ह्यौंगग्वांग] [**螢光**] [理] fluorescence. 형광을 발하다 fluoresce.

형광등 [ह्यौंगवांगदुंग] a fluorescent light [lamp].

형국 [ह्यौंगगुग] [**形局**] **1** [형세] the situation; the state of things [affairs]. **2** [관상,풍수 지리의 겉모양] an aspect; a phase; a facet; a facies <단수P복수 동형>

형기 [ह्यौंगगी] [**刑期**] a prison term; a term of imprisonment [penal servitude]. e.g. 형기를 치르다 serve one's term of imprisonment / serve a prison term / do a jail term / do [serve] time <at>.

형법 [ह्यौंगबौब] [**刑法**] [法] <집합적> criminal [penal] law; (협의의) the Criminal Law Act; [형법전] the

Criminal [Penal] code.

형사 [ह्यौंगसा] [刑事] **1** [형법의 사건] a criminal [penal] case. e.g. 그 사건에서 형사상의 문제가 제기되었다 Some were prosecuted under the criminal law with the affair.**2** [경찰] a(police) detective; an operative; <美> a gumshoe; (수사계의) an investigator

형상 [ह्यौंगसांग] [形象] (a) shape; (a) form (▷ 추상적인 경우는 관사 없음)

형색 [ह्यौंगसैग] [形色] **1** [형상과 빛깔] form [shape] and color. **2** [용색] features; looks; appearance.

형성 [ह्यौंगसौंग] [形成] formation; (천체의) evolution. 형성하다 form; build (up); mold.

형세 [ह्यौंगसे] [形勢] [정세] the situation; the state of affairs [things]; the condition of affairs; the tide <of war>; how the land lies; the trend [run] of events; [전망] the prospects; the chances

형수 [ह्यौंगसु] [兄嫂] an elder brother's wife; a sister-in-law.

형식 [ह्यौंगशिग] [形式] (a) form; (a) formality; [哲] a mode; form.

형식적 [ह्यौंगशिकचौग] [形式的] formal; perfun-ctory <in-specttion

형용 [ह्यौंग्योंग] [形容] [생긴 모양] figure; shape; [서술] qualification; modification; description; [비유] a simile; a metaphor; figure of speech. 형용하다 [수식하다] qualify; modify; [비유적으로 말하다] express figuratively[metaphorically]. e.g. 그녀의 아름다움은 말로 형용할 수 없다 Words cannot describe her beauty.

형용사 [形容詞] [문법] an adjective

형제 [ह्यौंगजे] [兄弟] a sibling; brothers; [동포] brethren.

형제자매 [ह्यौंगजेजामै] [兄弟姉妹] brothers and sisters; brethren (동포). pattern <for a suit>.

형질 [ह्यौंगजील] [形質] **1** [형태와 성질] form and nature [quality]. **2** a character 유전[획득] 형질 an inherited [acquired] character.

형태 [ह्यौंगथै] [形態] **1** [사물의 생김새] (a) form; (a) shape. **2**configuration; <독> a Gestalt <*pl.* ~en>. **3** [生,言] morphology.

형통 [ह्यौंगथोंग] [亨通] 형통하다 go well[fine / smoothly / all right]; progress favorably. e.g. 만사 형통하였다 Everything [All] went well [favorably] with them. /

ㅎ

Everything turned out as they (had) wished.

형편 [ह्यौंगफ्यौन] [**形便**] **1** [상태] a state; (a) condition; a situation; the state of things [affairs]; an aspect; [사정] circumstances; reasons. e.g. 가정 형편 one's family circumstances [reasons]. **2** [살림 형세] living conditions; one's circumstances; (a) living. e.g. 형편이 넉넉하다[좋다] be well [comfortably] off / be in easy circumstances / be well-to-do.

형편없다 [ह्यौंगफ्यौनओप्ता] [**形便**-] [지독하다] terri-ble; dreadful; frightful; awful; wretched; [터무니 없다] exorbitant; unrea-sonn-able; absurd; nonsensical. e.g. 그의 문법은 형편없다 His grammar is simple terrible.

형형-색색 [ह्यौंगह्यौंग-सैगसैग] [**形形色色**] 형상과 종류의 가지가지. 의 장난감 [참고] 가지각색.

혜다 [ह्येदा] 1헤아리다 생각하다 2 세다

혜성 [ह्येसौंग] [**彗星**] a comet.

혜안 [ह्येआन] [**慧眼**] [총명한 눈] a quick [sharp / keen] eye; a piercing [penetrating] eye; a keen insight. 혜안의 quick-sighted / sharp-[keen- / clear-] sighted / keen [sharp-] eyed.

혜택 [ह्यैथैग] [**惠澤**] (a) benefit; (a) boon; (a) benefaction; (a) favor; grace. e.g. 혜택을 입다 [받다] owe <something to a person> / be indebted <to a person for something> / benefit [profit] <by something>.

호 [हो] with a whiff [puff]. 호하다 whiff; puff. e.g. 촛불을 호하고 끄다 whiff out a candlelight [candle].

호 [हो] [**號**] **1** [번호] a number; an issue (잡지, 신문의) e.g. 제1호 number one (略 No. 1, 1) / the first number. **2** [장신구의 크기] size; [실의 굵기] count. e.g. 2호 더 큰 모자a hat two sizes larger. 12호의 방적사 12-count cotton. **3** [항목] an item; a head. e.g. 제5조 제3항 제2호에 해당하다 come under Paragraph 2, Subsection 3, Section 5. **4** (비행기,배 등의) "the ...". 기선 부산호 the S.S. Pusan (Ho). (넬슨의 기함) 빅토리호 the Victory. **5** [본명,자 이외에 쓰는 이름] a pen name; a pseudonym. 호가 춘원인 작가 a writer with the pen name of Chunwon

호감 [होगाम] [**好感**] (a) good

feeling; (a) good will; (a) goodwill; [좋은 인상] a favorable [good] impression. e.g. 호감이 가는 amiable / affable / attractive / pleasing.

호객 **[होगैक]** [**呼客**] touting. 호객하다 tout; solicit patronage.

호구 **[होगू]** [입에 풀칠하기] bare [scanty] livelihood; [살아 나가기 living; livelihood; subsistence. 호구하다 gain a bare livelihood; keep the pot boiling; eke out a living; make one's living.

호구조사 **[होगुजोसा]** [**戶口調査**] census taking; a census. 호구 조사를 하다 take a census. **호기** **[होगी]** [**好機**] a good [golden / favorable] opportunity; a favorable [good] chance; a good time [occasion]; a most appropriate moment. e.g. 호기를 잡다[포착하다] seize [take] an opportunity / take time by the forelock / take the tide as it offers.

호기심 **[होगीशिम]** [**好奇心**] curiosity; inquisitiveness.

호되게 **[होद्वेगे]** severely; harshly; soundly; violently; mercilessly. e.g. 호되게 야단치다 scold <a person> scathingly [unsparingly] / give <a person> a good [sharp] scolding.

호되다 **[होद्वेदा]** severe; harsh; terrible; pitiless; merciless; cruel. e.g. 호된 더위 [추위] intense heat [cold].

호두 **[होदू]** a walnut.

호들갑떨다 **[होदुल्गापत्तोल्दा]** [과장해서 말하다] exaggerate; say extravagantly; make too much of <a matter>; [야단스럽게 말하다] say [speak] in a histrionic manner.

호락호락 **[होराकहोराक]** easily; readily; without ado. e.g. 호락호락 속아넘어가다 be deceived easily / be easily taken in [duped].

호랑이 **[होरांगी]** [**虎狼-**] **1** 벵골 호랑이a Bengal tiger. **2** [사납고 무서운 사람] a cruel [merciless] person; inhumanly sharp person. e.g. 호랑이 영감 a snarling old man.

호령 **[होर्यौंग]** [**號令**] a (word of) command; an order.

호르몬 **[होरुमोन]** [生] hormone

호리다 **[होरीदा]** **1** [넋을 잃게 하다] bewitch; enchant; fascinate; captivate.**2** [유혹하다] seduce; allure; entice. e.g. 여자를 잘 호리는 남자 a woman-killer / a Don Juan.

호리호리하다 **[होरीहोरीहादा]** slim; slender; thin; lean; lanky; weedy. e.g. 호리호리한 소녀 a slim girl.

호박 **[होबाग]** a pumpkin; a squash (호리병박 모양의)

e.g. 호박 같은 얼굴 a pumpkinlike [an ugly] face.

호봉 [होबोंग] [號俸] a pay step; a salary class

호사 [होसा] [豪奢] extravagance; luxury; sumptuousness; magnificence. 호사하다 repose in the lap of luxury; roll in luxury.

호사스럽다 [होसासुरोपता] [豪奢-] luxurious; extravagant; sumptuous; magnificent; grand.

호소 [होसो] [呼訴] (불평 등의) a complaint; (법 등에의) an appeal; a petition. 호소하다 (불평을) complain of; (정의,힘,무기 등에) appeal to <a sense of justice>; appeal [resort] to <arms>; have recourse to <violence>; appeal <to the eye, to the pictorial instinct, etc.>

호수 [होसू] [湖水] a lake

호수 [होसू] [號數] number; a register[serial] number. e.g. 집 호수 the number of a house

호스 [होसु] a hose; a hosepipe

호스텔 [होसथेल] a hostel

호스티스 [होसुथीसु] a hostess; a barmaid (여급)

호시탐탐 [होशिथामथाम] [虎視眈眈] with vigilant hostility; gloatingly. e.g. 그는 호시탐탐 공격의 기회를 노렸다He watched thirstily for a chance to attack.

호신 [होशिन] [護身] self-protection; self-defense. e.g. 호신용의[으로] for self-protection / for use in self-defense.

호신술 [होशिनसुल] the art of self-defense.

호연지기 [होयौनजीगी] [浩然之氣] 호연지기를 기르다 revive one's exhausted [spent] energy / refresh [recreate] oneself <with> / enliven one's spirits.

호우 [होउ] [豪雨] a heavy rain [rainfall]; a torrential [hard] rain; a downpour; cataracts [a deluge] of rain.

호위 [होवी] [護衛] a guard; an escort; a bodyguard; <집합적> guard; bodyguard; escort; convoy. 호위하다 guard; escort; (군함,군대가) convoy <a ship / supplies>.

호응 [होउंग] [呼應] **1** [부르고 대답함] hailing (to) each other. 호응하다 hail (to) each other. **2** [기맥 상통] acting in concert. 호응하다 act in concert [unison] <with>; be in sympathy <with>; respond to <a request>. 호응하여 in concert [cooperation] <with> / in response <to> / in collusion <with> 공모) e.g. 바다와 육지에서 서로

호응하여 적을 공격하였다 Land and sea forces attacked the enemy in concert. **3** [문법] concord; agreement. 시제의 호응 sequence of tenses.

호의 **[होउइ]** [**好意**] (a) good will; (a) goodwill; good wishes; friendliness; kindness; favor; courtesy. e.g. M씨의 호의 kindness of Mr. M. 호의로 [에서] out of courtesy / through kindness / out of good will

호의적 **[होउइजौग]** [**好意的**] friendly; amicable; kind; kindly.

호의호식 **[होउइहोशिग]** [**好衣好食**] dressing well and faring richly; high living; comfort; luxury. 호의호식하다 dress well and fare richly; live high [well / in clover].

호적 **[होजौग]** [**戶籍**] (등록) census registration; [호적부] a census [family] register.

호전 **[होजौन]** [**好轉**] a favorable turn [move]; a turn [change] for the better; improvement; a rally; pickup. 호전하다 take a favorable turn; change [take a turn] for the better; improve.

호젓하다 **[होजौत्हादा]** still; quiet; hushed; deserted; lonely; solitary; desolate.

호주 **[होजू]** [**戶主**] the head of a family [household]; the master of a house; a householder.

호주머니 **[होजुमौनी]** **1** [주머니] a pocket; a kick **2** [돈지갑] one's pocket; one's purse. e.g. 호주머니에 한푼도 없다 be penniless / have no money with one.

호출 **[होछुल]** [**呼出**] [불러냄] a call; calling out; [소환] a summons; citing; a subpoena (법원의) 자동 호출 an automatic calling.

호치키스 **[होछीखीस]** a stapler; a stapling machine; (상표명) a Hotchkiss (paper fastener).

호칭 **[होछीग]** [**呼稱**] a name; a title; a designation; an appellation. 호칭하다call; name; designate.

호탕 **[होथांग]** [**豪宕**] grandeur; magnanimity. 호탕하다 magnanimous; large-minded.

호텔 **[होथेल]** a hotel

호통 **[होथोंग]** hurling words of thunder; a yell. 호통을 치다 hurl words of thunder <at>; storm [nag / thunder / roar / snarl / snap] <at a person>; give <a person> a good scolding [blowing-up]

호평 **[होफ्योंग]** [**好評**] (a) favorable criticism; a favorable comment [reception / notice / opinion]; public favor. 호평의 of good repute / well-reputed. 호평이다 be popular / be highly [favorably] spoken of / enjoy [win / gain] popularity

호호 [होहो] [입김 뿜는 소리] blowing and blowing; in puffs [whiffs]. e.g. 추워서 손을 호호 불다 warm one's hands with one's breath / breathe upon one's hands to keep them warm.

호화 [होह्वा] [豪華] gorgeoussness; brilliancy; gaudiness; dazzling glamor; pomposity; sumptuousness. 호화 찬란하다 gorgeous; brilliant; gaudy; dazzling; pompous; sumptuous. e.g. 호화 찬란하게 치장하다be gorgeously dressed.

호화롭다 [होह्वारोपता] [豪華-] splendid; gorgeous; most luxurious; deluxe <car>; <a hotel> de luxe. e.g. 호화로운 식사 a sumptuous meal / a luxurious table.

호황 [होह्वांग] [好況] a prosperous condition; prosperity; a boom; a brisk market (시황의). e.g. 호황의 prosperous / favorable / brisk <market> / thriving [flourishing] <business>. 호황이다 be prosperous / be in a prosperous condition / boom / (물건이) be in good demand.

호흡 [होहुप] [呼吸] **1** a breath; breathing; respiration 호흡하다 breathe; respire. **2** [일을 함께 할 때의 장단] tone; time. e.g. 호흡이 맞다 be in rhythm / tune <with> / be in harmony <with> / hit it off together.

혹 [होक] (피부의) a wen; a lump; a bump; a swelling; a protuberance; (낙타의) a hump. e.g. 혹 떼러 갔다가 혹 붙이고 오다 <속담> go for wool and come home shorn.

혹독 [होक्तोक] [酷毒] severity; harshness; cruelty; rigor <of winter>. 혹독하다 [모질다] severe; hard; harsh; cruel; unfeeling; [엄하다] strict; stringent; rigorous; exacting

혹사 [होकसा] [酷使] driving hard; abuse; ill-usage; exploitation. 혹사하다 work [drive] <a person> hard; keep [hold / put] <a person's> nose [face] to the grindstone; sweat <one's employees

혹시 [होकशि] [或是] **1** [어쩌면] possibly; by some possibility; maybe; by (some) chance. e.g. 혹시 집에 계신가 하고 on the chance that I may find you at home. **2** [행여나] if; [걱정하여] lest ... should ...; for fear of ...[that ... may ...]. e.g.혹시 ... 하지나 않을까 하여 for fear of ...[that ... may

ㅎ

혹자 [**होक्चा**] [**或者**] [어떤 사람] some; someone; somebody; a certain [some] person; a Mr. So-and-so. e.g. 혹자는 이렇게 혹자는 저렇게 말한다 Some say one thing and others another.

혹평 [**होगप्यौंग**] [**酷評**] (a) severe [harsh / bitter / sharp / scathing / slashing] criticism; a cruel remark; strictures; hypercriticism

혹평하다 criticize sharply [bitterly / severely]; pass [offer] harsh [incisive] criticism <on>; speak bitterly [badly] of <a person>; say harsh things about <an opposition party>; hypercriticize; pound [score / beat] <a person> like anything.

혹하다 [**होक्हादा**] [**惑-**] **1** [유혹되다] be tempted; be seduced; [홀딱 빠지다] be infatuated with <a woman>; be captivated [fascinated] by <a woman's beauty>; fall a victim to <a woman's charms>; lose one's head over <a woman>; give oneself up <to>. e.g. 물욕에 혹하다 be blinded by love of gain.**2** [미혹되다] be deluded; be misled; be led into error; be trapped. e.g. 무당의 말에 혹하다 be deluded by a shaman's predictions.

혹한 [**होखान**] [**酷寒**] severe [bitter / intense] cold; a hard [severe] winter

혼 [**होन**] [**魂**] e.g. 혼을 부르다 call back the spirit of the dead.

혼기 [**होनगी**] [**婚期**] the marriageable age; nubility.

혼나다 [**होन्नादा**] [**魂-**] [놀라다] get frightened out of one's wits; be startled; [무서워하다] be scared [horrified]; [호된 경험을 겪다] have bitter experiences; have[get] the worst of it; have a hard [bad / rough / tough] time (of it) <with a person>; pay dearly <for>; have hard luck; suffer severely <from>; [꾸지람 듣다] catch it hot; burn one's fingers.

혼내다 [**होन्नेदा**] [**魂-**] [맛을 보이다] treat <a person> cruelly [badly]; give <a person> a hard [rough] time; do [serve] <a person> a bad [an ill] turn; give <a person> a raw deal; give it to <a person>(pretty) stiff; teach <a person> a lesson; put it across <a person>; tell off <a person>; [놀래 주다] frightened <a person> out of his wits; startle; horrify; scare

ㅎ

혼담 [होनदाम] [**婚談**] an offer of marriage.

혼돈 [होनदोन] [**混沌, 渾沌**] chaos; nebulosity; confusion. e.g. 혼돈 상태에 있다 be in a chaotic state / be in(a state of) chaos [confusion].

혼동 [होनदोंग] [**混同**] confusion; mixing. 혼동 하다 confuse [confound / mix up] <one thing with another>; mistake <one> for <the other>. e.g. 공과 사를 혼동하다 mix up public and private matters.

혼란 [होल्लान] [**混亂**] confusion; disorder; disorganization; disarrangement; chaos; pell-mell; mixup; a jumble; a pretty [nice / fine] kettle of fish. e.g. 정치적 혼란 political chaos.

혼령 [होल्यौंग] [**魂靈**] the spirit (of the dead); <a person's> departed soul; the soul.

혼례 [होल्लये] [**婚禮**] a marriage [wedding / nuptial] ceremony; a wedding; nuptials.

혼미 [होनमी] [**昏迷**] stupefaction; (bewildering) confusion; stupor.

혼비백산 [होनबीबैकसान] [**魂飛魄散**] 혼비 백산하 be frightened out of one's wits; be terrified out of one's senses. e.g. 혼비 백산하여 with one's heart in one's mouth.

혼사 [होनसा] [**婚事**] a matrimonial [marital / nuptial] matter; (a) marriage.

혼선 [होनसौन] [**混線**] **1** (전신, 전화국의) cross; contact; entanglement of wires. e.g. 혼선이 되고 있다 (전화가) The wires [lines] are mixed. / The lines are crossed. / (라디오가) The radio signals are jammed up. **2** [혼란] confusion.혼선하다 confuse. e.g. 회의에서는 이야기가 혼선된 것 같다 They seemed to be talking at cross-purposes at the conference.

혼성 [होनसौंग] [**混成**] mixture; composition; mixing; blending; contamination; hybridization; hybridism.

혼수[1] [होन्सू] [**婚需**] (물건) necessary articles for marriage; (비용) marriage expenses.

혼수[2] [होन्सू] [**昏睡**] **1** [정신 없이 깊이 잠듦] a deep sleep. **2** [의식을 잃음] a coma; a trance; stupor; sinking; lethargic sleep. e.g. 혼수 상태에 빠지다 fall [slip] into a comatose state [condition] / lapse into a coma

혼신 [होनशिन] [**渾身**] the whole body. e.g. 혼신의

힘을 다하여 with all one's might [strength] / with might and main.

혼용 [होनयोंग] [混用] 혼용하다 miK mingle; use <one thing> together with <another>. e.g. 한글과 한자를 혼용하다 mingle Hangul with Chinese characters.

혼인 [होनीन] [婚姻] marriage. ⇨ 결혼

혼자 [होनजा] [한 사람] one person; [홀몸] a single person; alone (단독으로); by oneself; for oneself (독력으로

혼잡 [होनजाब] [混雜] [혼란] confusion; disorder; [붐빔] crowdedness; con-gestion; a jam; a bustle. 혼잡하다 confused; disordered; crowded; congested; bustling; <美> jammed.

혼잣말 [होनजात्माल] talking to oneself; a soliloquy; a monologue.

혼탁 [होनथाग] [混濁] 1 [흐림]. 혼탁하다 (강 등이) turbid; muddy; (액체가) cloudy; (공기가) foul; (말소리가) thick. e.g. 흙먼지로 혼탁 해진 공기 air thick with dust. 2 [의식이 흐림]. 혼탁하다 e.g.그의 의식은 혼탁해 있다 His senses are muddled. / He is not fully conscious. / He is in a state of partial consciousness. 3 [세상의 문란]. 혼탁하다 e.g. 혼탁한 세상 the corrupt world.

혼합 [होनहाब] [混合] mixing; mixture; admixture. 혼합하다 mix [blend / mingle] <A with B>; compound; intermix.

혼혈 [होनहयौल] [混血] mixed blood [breed]; racial mixture.

홀- [होल-] [짝없음] single. e.g. 홀눈꺼풀 an eyelid with no fold. 홀몸 a single man [woman].

홀가분하다 [होलगाबुनहादा] light; free and easy; lighthearted (마음이). e.g. 홀가분한 복장 casual clothes.

홀대 [होलदै] [忽待] inhospitable [unkind] treatment; neglecting; slighting. 홀대하다 treat <a person> unkindly [inhospitably]; neglect [slight] <a person>. e.g. 손님을 홀대하다 treat a guest unkindly / neglect a guest.

홀딱 [होलताग] 1 [반한 모양] deeply; dead; madly. e.g. 홀딱 반하다 be deeply [dead / madly] in love <with> / lose one's heart <to>. 그는 2 [여지없이] fairly; nicely; completely; thoroughly. e.g. 홀딱 속아넘 어가다 be nicely [fairly] taken in. 돈을 홀딱 날리다 become (quite)

penniless. **3** [벗는 모양] <removing it> completely; entirely; quickly. e.g. 옷을 홀딱 벗다 strip oneself of all one's clothes / strip oneself bare [stark-naked]. (머리가) 홀딱 벗겨져 있다 be bald as an egg. **4** [뒤집히는 모양] <turning a thing> inside out. e.g. 바람에 홀딱 뒤집힌 우산 an umbrella blown inside [wrong side] out by the wind.

홀로 [होल्लो] alone; by oneself; single; single-handed (ly). ⇨ 혼자 e.g. 홀로되다 become a widow [a widower].

홀리다 [होल्लीदा] **1** (귀신 등에) be possessed <by / with>; be obsessed <by>; be bewitched <by>. e.g. 홀린 사람처럼 like one possessed. 무엇에 홀린 듯이 as if possessed by some devil or other. 여우 [귀신]에게 홀리다 be possessed by a fox [devil].**2** (이성에게) get infatuated [captivated / bewitched]. e.g. 여자에게 홀리다 get infatuated with a woman / be gone on a woman.**3** [현혹되다] get tempted; be deluded [tricked / deceived / seduced]. e.g. 돈에 홀려 나쁜 짓을 하다 be tempted by money to do wrong.

홀몸 [होलमोम] [단신] a single person; [독신] an unmarried person; (남자) a bachelor; (여자) a spinster

홀수 [होलसू] [-數] an odd [uneven] number.

홀아비 [होराबी] a widower.

홀연 [होरयौन] [忽然] suddenly; all of a sudden; all at once; unexpectedly; in an instant. e.g. 홀연 사라지다 vanish as if by magic.

홀쭉하다 [होलचोख्खादा] [가늘고 길다] lank; lanky; spindly; slender; spindling; [야위다] lean.

홈런 [होमरौन] [야구] a home run; a homer; a round-tripper; a circuit clout; a four bagger.

홍보 [होंगबो] [弘報] public information; public relations (▷ 단수 취급) (略 P.R.); publicity. 홍보하다 publicize.

홍수 [होंगसु] [洪水] **1** = 큰물. e.g. 홍수와 가뭄이 없는 비옥한 땅 fertile land free of flood and drought. **2** [많이 있음을 비유]. e.g. 편지의 홍수 a deluge [flood] of letters.

홍역 [होंग्यौग] [紅疫] the measles; rubeola. e.g. 홍역을 하다 catch[get / have] the measles. 홍역을 치르다 <비유> have bitter experiences / have a hard time (of it).

홍익인간 [होंगीगइनगान] [弘益

人間] devotion to the welfare of mankind. e.g. 홍익 인간의 이념 the humanitarian ideal.

홍일점 [होंगइलजौम] [**紅一點**] the only member of the fair sex <among>; the only woman in the company.

홍조 [होंगजो] [**紅潮**] [붉어진 얼굴] flushing; a glow. e.g. 홍조를 띠다 flush / (부끄러움 등으로) blush.

홍차 [होंगछा] [**紅茶**] black tea; <a cup of> tea.

홑몸 [होथमोम] **1** [홀몸] a single person; a person without encumbrances; a bachelor; a spinster (여자); bachelorhood; spinsterhood. **2** [임신하지 않은 몸] a woman who is not pregnant.

-화 [-हवा] [**靴**] shoes; boots. e.g. 스키화 ski boots. 신사[숙녀]화 men's [ladies's] shoes.

-화 [हवा] [**畵**] a picture; a drawing; a painting. e.g. 서양화 a Western painting

-화 [हवा] [**化**] -ization. 화하다 -ize e.g. 자동 화하다 automatize. 영화 화하다 cinematize <a novel> for the movies / make <a novel> into a movie [film].

화 [हवा] [**禍**] (serious) trouble; (an) evil; a curse; [불행] (a) misfortune; [재앙] (a) disaster; a calamity; woe. e.g. 화를 당하다 meet with a calamity / [살해되다] be killed.

화 [हवा] [**火**] **1** [성] pent-up resentment; anger; ire; wrath. e.g. 화가 나는 annoying / provoking / offensive / invidious / infernal.

화가 [हवागा] [**畵家**] a painter; an artist.

화근 [हवागुन] [**禍根**] the root of evil; a source of calamity. e.g. 화근을 없애다 cut off the evil at its root / eliminate [lay the axe to] the root of evil. 화근이 되다 form a source of calamity / be the ruin <of

화기애애 [हवागीऐऐ] [**和氣靄靄**] 화기 애애하다 harmonious; peaceful; happy <home>. e.g. 화기 애애한 가정 a happy [harmonious] family. 화기 애애한 모임 a congenial gathering

화끈 [हवाकुन] with a sudden flush [glow]; with a sudden flash of heat; with a burning sensation. e.g. (얼굴이) 화끈 달다 flush up (hotly) / blush / feel <with shame>. 화끈하다 hot; burning; flushing; glowing.

화끈거리다 [हवाकुनकौरीदा] feel hot [warm]; burn; flush; glow. e.g. 부끄러워서 얼굴이 화끈거리다 burn with shame. 귀가 화끈거린다 Running makes me hot. 추워서 볼이 화끈거린다 The cold air makes the cheeks glow.

화나다 [हवानादा] [火-] be angered [vexed / irritated / enraged / offended / provoked]; be riled <at>; feel irritated [injured]; be [feel] sore <at / about>.

화내다 [हवानेदा] [火-] get angry <about a thing / with [at] a person>; get mad <at a person / about a thing>; give vent to one's anger; blow one's top. e.g. 그것은 화낼 만한 일이 못된다 It's not worth getting angry about.

화단 [हवादान] [花壇] a flower bed; a flower garden; a parterre. e.g. 화단에 튤립을 심었다 I planted tulips in the flower bed.

화답 [हवादाब] [和答] a response. 화답하다 respond <in singing [reciting]>.

화두 [हवादू] [話頭] topic [subject] (of conversation). e.g. 화두를 돌리다 change to subject [topic of conversation] / shith the conversation.

화려 [हवारयौ] [華麗] splendor; magnificence; gorgeousness; brilliance; glory; glitter; (지나치도록) gaiety; gayety; showiness; gaudiness; flashiness. 화려하다 splendid; magnificent; gorgeous; ornate; gallant; gaudy; flowery; brilliant; gay; showy

화력 [हवारयौक] [火力] [불의 힘] heat; heating power. e.g. 화력이 세다[약하다] have a high [low] caloric value.

화로 [हवारो] [火爐] a (charcoal) brazier; a fire pot [box]. e.g. 화로에 손을 쬐다 warm one's hands over a brazier.

화면 [हवाम्यौन] [畵面] (그림의) a picture.

화목 [हवामोग] [和睦] harmony; concord; peace. 화목하 harmonious; peaceful; <서술적> be in harmony [concord]; be at peace with each other e.g. 화목하게 harmoniously / in harmony [peace] / happily / affectionately.

화물 [हवामुल] [貨物] freight; goods; cargo; [상품] commodities

화병 [हवाप्यौंग] [火病] a nervous disorder caused by one's pentup resent-ment.

화병 [हवाबयौंग] [花甁] a (flower) vase.

화보 [हवाबो] [畵譜] a picture book [album].

화분 [हवाबुन] [花盆] a flowerpot. e.g. 화분에 심은 장미 a potted rose / a rose planted in a pot.

화사 [हवासा] [華奢] [화려] gorgeousness; splendor;

brilliance; pomposity; gaudiness; [사치] luxury. 화사하다 gorgeous; splendid; brilliant; pompous; gaudy; luxurious; sumptuous.

화산 [**हवासान**] [**火山**] a volcano <*pl.* ~(e)s>.

화살 [**हवासाल**] an arrow; a shath; a clothyard shath (긴); a bolt (굵은); a dart (던지는).

화상 [**हवासांग**] [**火傷**] a burn (불에 덴); a scald (뜨거운 물에 덴). e.g. 화상을 입다 get [be] burnt / have [suffer] a burn / burn oneself / be [get] scorched (부젓가락 등으로) / get [be] scalded (뜨거운 물로) / scald oneself.

화상 [**हवासांग**] [**畵像**] **1** [초상] a portrait; one's likeness. e.g. v화상을 그리다 paint a person's portrait. **2** [TV] picture; screen. e.g. 화상이 비틀어졌다 The picture is distorted.

화석 [**हवासौग**] [**化石**] (작용) petrifaction; fossilization; (돌) a fossil.

화술 [**हवासुल**] [**話術**] the art of narration; the storyteller's art; narrative skill. e.g. 화술에 능한 사람 a master storyteller / a master of narrative / a man of great narrative power / a brilliant conversationalist

화신 [**हवाशिन**] [**化身**] (an) incarnation; (an) embodiment <of courage>; (a) manifestation. e.g. 악마의 화신 a devil incarnate.

화씨 [**हवाशी**] [**華氏**] Fahrenheit (略 Fahr., F.).

화약 [**हवायाग**] [**火藥**] gunpowder; powder.

화염 [**हवायोम**] [**火焰**] a flame; a blaze.

화요일 [**हवायोइल**] [**火曜日**] Tuesday (Tues., Tue.).

화원[**हवावॉन**][**花園**] **1** [꽃동산] a flower garden. **2** = 꽃가게.

화이트칼라 [**हवाइथखाल्ला**] an office worker; a white-collar worker. e.g. 화이트칼라의 white-collar.

화장 [**हवाजांग**] [**化粧**] (a) makeup; (a) toilet; dressing. e.g. 밑화장 a powder base / a foundation 화장하다 make up <one's face>; put on makeup; make one's toilet; paint [powder / embellish] one's face. e.g. 그녀는 화장실에서 화장하고 있다 She's in the ladies' room doing her face.

화장 [**हवाजांग**] [**火葬**] cremation. e.g. 전기 화장 electric cremation. 화장하다 cremate <the remains>; burn <the body> to ashes

화장실 [**हवाजांगशील**] [**化粧室**] [변소] (가정 등의) a bathroom; (극장P백화점 등의) a restroom; a toilet.

e.g. 화장실은 어디입니까 (개인의 집에서) Where can I wash my hands? / Where is the bathroom? (▷ 이 경우 toilet이라든가 water closet 이라고는 보통 말하지 않음) / (호텔, 백화점, 극장 등에서) Where is the restroom[the ladies' room / the gentlemen's room]?

화장지 [ह्वाजांगजी] [化粧紙] <a roll of> toilet paper [tissue]; bathroom tissue.

화장품 [ह्वाजांगफुम] [化粧品] cosmetics; toilet articles; makeup; a beauty product.

화재[1] [ह्वाजै] [火災] a fire; a conflagration (큰); a blaze (작은)

화재[2] [ह्वाजै] [畵才] artistic talent [skill]. e.g. 그는 화재가 있다 He is githed with artistic talent. / He has the makings of an artist.

화제 [ह्वाजे] [話題] a topic [subject](of conversation). e.g. 화제가 풍부하다 have a large [an ample] stock of topics.

화창 [ह्वाछांग] [和暢] balminess; brightness. 화창하다 balmy; bright; sunny.

화초[ह्वाछो][花草] a flowering plant; a flower.

화투 [ह्वाथू] [花鬪] Korean playing cards; 'flower cards'. 화투하다 play 'flower cards'; play Korean "*hwat'u*" cards

화폐 [ह्वाफ्ये] [貨幣] (통화) money; currency; (경화) a coin; <집합적> coinage.

화풀이 [ह्वाफुरी] [火-] venting of one's anger. e.g. 그것으로 화풀이가 된다면 얼마든지 나를 때려라 Beat me as much as you like, if it makes you feel better [give you any satisfaction].

화학 [ह्वाहाक] [化學] chemistry.

화합 [ह्वाहाब] [和合] harmony; concord; union; unity. e.g. 부부의 화합 conjugal harmony. 화합하다 harmonize <with>; be harmonious [harmonized]; agree <with each other>; be in accord <with> e.g. 화합하여 살다 live in perfect harmony.

화해 [ह्वाहै] [和解] amicable [friendly / peaceful] settlement; reconcilement; reconciliation; accommodation; [타협, 사화] composition; compromise. 화해하다 make up <with>; make peace <with>; come to terms <with>; reconcile oneself <with>; be [become] reconciled <with>; accommodate [compromise] <with>; (사건이) be settled amicably; come to an amicable settlement.

e.g. 화해할 수 있는[없는] reconcilable [irreconcilable

화형 [हवाहयौग] [火刑] (burning at) the stake; (fire and) faggot; burning to death.

화환 [हवाहवान] [花環] a wreath; a garland; a lei (목에 거는). e.g. 화환을 바치다 place [lay] a wreath <at the tomb / before a monument> / place a floral tribute <on the grave of>.

화훼 [हवाहवै] [花卉] a flowering plant.

확 [हवाग] [갑자기] suddenly; [잽싸게] in a flash; alertly; (힘차게) with a jerk. e.g. 확 당기다 [밀다] pull [push] with a (sudden) jerk.

확고 [हवाक्कों] [確固] firmness; determination. 확고하다 firm; definite; resolute; fixed; determined. e.g. 확고한 신념 a firm faith.

확답 [हवाकताब] [確答] a definite answer [reply]; a determinate reply; a categorical answer.

확대 [हवाकतै] [擴大] extension; augmentation; magnification; magnifying. 확대하다 magnify; scale up; [퍼지다] spread; expand; (사건 등이) assume serious proportions. e.g. 사진을 확대하다 enlarge a photograph.

확률 [हवागरयूल] [確率] probability.

확립 [हवांग्निप] [確立] establishment; settlement. 확립하다 establish <a theory>; build up; fiK settle e.g. 확립된 established <fame> / settled <habit>. 명성[신용]을 확립하다 establish one's reputation [credit].

확보 [हवाकपो] [確保] security; insurance; guarantee. 확보하다 secure <a seat / success>; make sure of <a copy of a book>; make good <one's position>; ensure [insure] <one's life>; assure <one's comfort>; guarantee; maintain <place and order>. e.g. 식량을 확보하다 secure foodstuffs. 교두보를 확보하다

확산 [हवागसान] [擴散] spread (ing); dissemination; proliferation; diffusion <of light, gas, etc.>.

확성기 [हवागसौगी] [擴聲器] a (loud) speaker; a megaphone; a speech amplifier; a speaking trumpet

확신 [हवागशिन] [確信] a conviction; a firm [confident] belief; assurance; confidence (자신).

확실 [हवाकशील] [確實] certainty; trustworthiness; reliability; authenticity. 확실하다 [틀림없다] certain; sure <method>; secure; positive; [믿을 만하다] reliable <news>; trust-worthy

<person>; [확정 되다] definite. from his ability, he is sure to succeed.

확실히 [हवाकशीरही] [確實-] certainly; surely; for certain; to be sure; positively; definitely; no doubt; doubtless; beyond doubt; decidedly

확약 [हवाग्याक [確約] a strict [definite] promise. e.g. 확약은 할 수 없다 I cannot make a definite promise. 확약하다 promise positively; make a definite promise; give one's word <to>; commit oneself <to>.

확언 [हवागऔन] [確言] a positive [definite] statement; assertion; affirmation. 확언하다 state [say] positively [definitely]; assert; affirm; commit oneself; lay down e.g. 그 점은 확언하기 어렵다 I am not positive about the point.

확연 [हवाग्यौन] [確然] 확연하다 definite; positive; sure; certain. 확연히 definitely; positively; surely; certainly.

확인 [हवागीन] [確認] confirmation; affirmation; certification; validation. 확인하다 confirm; affirm; certify; validate; identify; ascertain; make sure <of / that>. e.g. 시체를 확인하다 identify a corpse.

확장 [हवाकचांग] [擴張] extension <of one's premises>; expansion <of trade>; enlargement; aggrandizement; increment; dilation 확장하다 extend <one's domains>: expand <business>; enlarge; aggrandize; increase; dilate. e.g. 가로[거리]를 확장하다 widen a street.

확정 [हवाकचौग] [確定] decision; settlement. e.g. 확정적인 definite. 확정적으로 definitely / conclusively. 하다 decide upon <a matter>; settle; fiK confirm

확증 [हवाकचुंग] [確證] corroboration; confirmation; [증거] (a) corroborative [decisive / clear / convincing / positive] proof; conclusive evidence. e.g. 확증적(인) confirmatory / corroborative. 확증을 수반하지 않는 uncorroborated <confession>. …의 확증을 쥐다[잡다] secure [obtain] positive evidence of

확충 [हवागछुंग] [擴充] (an) expansion; (an) amplification; generalization; distribution; amplification. 확충하다 expand <productivity>; amplify. e.g. 교육 시설을 확충하다 expand [enlarge] educational facilities.

확확 [हवाख्हवाख] **1** (바람, 연기 등이) with great puffs; with [in] gusts. e.g.

바람이 확확 불다 have gust ather gust of wind. **2** (불길이) briskly; in flare-ups [blazes]; with flame ather flame; broilingly; scorchingly. e.g. (불이) 확확 타오르다 burn hot [briskly / furiously]. (뺨이나 얼굴이) 확확 달아오르다 flush up (hotly) / blush / feel <one's face> burning <with shame>.

환각 [हवानगाग] [幻覺] a hallucination; an illusion. e.g. 환각에 의해 보이는 상 a hallucinatory image

환갑 [हवानगाब] [還甲] the 60th anniversary of one's birth; one's 60th birthday.

환경 [हवान्ग्यौग] [環境] environment; surroundings; circumstances.

환골탈태 [हवानगोल्थालथै] [換骨奪胎] adaptation; modifycation; recasting.

환급 [हवानगुब] [還給] (a) refundment; (a) refund; (a) repayment; (a) reimbursement (상환, 보상). 환급하다 refund; repay; reimburse.

환기 [हवानगी] [換氣] ventilation; a change of air. e.g. 환기가 잘되다 [안되다] be well [badly / ill] ventilated.

환기 [हवानगी] [喚起] [불러 일으킴] awakening; evocation. 환기하다 awaken <one's sympathy>; call forth <great emotions>; rouse <romantic images>; aro-use <public attention>; excite <attention / curiosity>; evoke e.g. 주의를 환기하다 [시키다] call <a person's> attention <to a fact>.

환대 [हवानदै] [歡待] a hospitable [warm / cordial / hearty] reception; hospitality; hospitable treatment; welcome.

환락 [हवानल्लान] [歡樂] pleasure (s); merriment; mirth; merrymaking; gaieties. e.g. 인생의 환락 the pleasures of life.

환멸 [हवानम्यौल] [幻滅] disillusion; disillusionment. e.g. 환멸의 비애 a sad disillusionment / anguish [sorrow] of disillusionment.

환불 [हवानबुल] [還拂] (a) refundment; (a) refund; (a) drawback; (a) repayment. 환불하다 pay back; repay; refund; reimburse; rebate.

환산 [हवानसान] [換算] conversion; change. 환산하다 convert <won into dollars>; change <into>.

환상 [हवानसांग] [幻想] a fantasy; an illusion; a vision; a (day) dream; a reverie; a phantasm. e.g. 즐거운 환상 a sweet illusion.

환생 [हवानसैग] [還生] [다시 태어 남] rebirth; regeneration. 환생하다 be born again; be [get] reborn

환송 **[हवानसोंग]** **[歡送]** sending off; a send-off. 환송하다 give <a person> a hearty [good] send-off; farewell. e.g. 그들 모두가 그를 환송했다 They all gave him a hearty [cordial] send-off.

환심 **[हवानशिम]** **[歡心]** good graces; favor. 환심을 사다 curry favor with <a person>; win <a person's> favor; ingratiate oneself with <a person>; insinuate [ingratiate] oneself into <a person's> favor e.g. 여자의 환심을 사다 win a girl's heart.

환영 **[हवानयौंग]** **[歡迎]** (a) welcome; an ovation; (a) reception.

환원 **[हवानवौन]** **[還元]** **1** [복귀] restoration. 환원하다 restore <to its original state> e.g. 환원되다 be restored to <the former condition>. **2** [化] reduction; [분해] resolution; (산화물의) deoxidization. 환원하다 reduce <to>; deoxidize; (금속 등을) revive e.g. 환원되다 be reduced <to>. (원래의 상태로) 환원시키다 [化] revivify.

환율 **[हवानयूल]** **[換率]** = 환시세 e.g. 환율이 높다 [낮다] The exchange rate rules high [low].

환자 **[हवानजा]** **[患者]** a patient; a sufferer <from a cold>; a case <of cholera> (▷ 보통 치료를 받는 사람은 patient, 병에 걸린 사람은 case, sufferer를 씀); a victim <of a disease>; a subject <of operation>.

환장 **[हवानजांग]** **[換腸]** 환장하다 become [go] mad [crazy / insane]; go off [out of] one's mind [head]; lose one's mind [wits / reason]. e.g. 그 녀석은 완전히 환장했다 He's gone stone crazy.

환전 **[हवानजौन]** **[換錢]** exchange (of money); money changing. 환전하다 exchange <dollar into won / American money into Korean>; change <a 1,000-won note>

환절 **[हवानजौल]** **[換節]** [철이 바뀜] a change of seasons. **환절기** a change [turning-point] of season

환청 **[हवानछौंग]** **[幻聽]** an auditory hallucination. e.g. 환청이 들리다 hear things / suffer from auditory hallucinations.

환풍기 **[हवानफुंगी]** **[換風機]** a ventilation [ventilating] fan; an extractor fan.

환하다 **[हवानहादा]** **1** [밝다] bright; light e.g. 달빛이 환한 밤 a bright moonlight night. **2** [탁 트다] open; clear; unobstructed. e.g.

환히 보이다 get an unobstructed view / be fully exposed to view / be in plain sight. **3** [정통하다] <서술적> be familiar <with>; be versed <in>; be learned [well up] <in>; be conversant <with>; be posted up <in>. e.g. 사무에 환하다 be well versed in business methods.

환호 [**हवानहो**] [**歡呼**] a cheer; an ovation; an acclamation; a hurrah. e.g. 환호 속에서 amid (hearty) cheers. …에게 환호를 보내다 give <a person>

활 [**हवाल**] [무기] a bow; [궁술] archery

활기 [**हवालगी**] [**活氣**] vigor; spirit; energy; liveliness; animation; briskness; activity. e.g. 활기 있는 대화 a spirited [an animated] conversation / a lively talk.

활달 [**हवालताल**] [**豁達**] generosity; magnanimity; liberality; big-heartedness; large-[broad-] mindedness. 활달하다 generous; magnanimous; liberal; broad-minded; openhearted.

활동 [**हवालतोंग**] [**活動**] [활약] activity; action; operations; [노력] stre-nuous exertion; energy; service; [기능] function; working <of the bodily organs

활력 [**हवाल्लयौग**] [**活力**] vitality; energy; vital power [force / energies].

활발 [**हवालबाल**] [**活潑**] liveliness; briskness; sprightliness; activity; vivacity; animation; energy. 활발하다 lively; sprightly; active; brisk; full of life; corky; jazzy e.g. 활발한 동작 brisk [lively] move-ments.

활보 [**हवालबो**] 활보하다 stride; strut; swagger (about); walk with a swaggering gait e.g. 정계를 활보하다 move with bold strides in the political world / throw one's weight about in political circles.

활약 [**हवाल्याग**] [**活躍**] activity; action. e.g. 그녀의 활약상 her activity.

활용 [**हवाल्योंग**] [**活用**] **1** [응용] practical use; application. 활용하다 make use (of); put [turn] <knowledge> to practical use; apply; utilize. e.g. 새로운 방법을 산업에 활용하다 apply a new process in industry **2** = 어미 변화 (⇨ 어미(語尾)). e.g. 동사 'go'의 활용을 들어 보시오 Conjugate [Give the conjugation of] the verb 'go'. 활용하다 conjugate; inflect; decline.

활자 [**हवालजा**] [**活字**] (a) printing type; <집합적> type.

활주 [**हवालजू**] [**滑走**] gliding;

a glide; (빙상의) sliding; (비행기의) a ground run.

활주로 [हवालजुरो] a runway; a landing strip; (임시의) an airstrip. e.g. 비행기는 활주로를 달렸다 The plane taxied down the runway.

활짝 [हवालचाग] **1** [탁 트인 모양] widely; exceedingly (wide); broad; open; extensively. e.g. 활짝 열어 둔 창문 a wide-open window. **2** (웃음,꽃 등이) brightly; radiantly; happily. e.g. 활짝 웃다 beam <upon [at] a person> / smile radiantly / beam [be radiant] with joy **3** [날씨가 개거나 환히 밝은 모양] clearly; brightly. e.g. 활짝 갠 하늘 a bright, blue sky.

활활 [हवारहवाल] **1** [불타는 모양] in (fierce / great / tall) flames; in a blaze; (all) ablaze. e.g. 난로의 불이 활활 타오르고 있었다 A fire was blazing [burning brightly] in the fireplace **2** [부채질하는 모양] <fan oneself / use a fan> slowly and vigorously.**3** [새가 나는 모양] with great flaps of the wings. e.g. 활활 날아가다 fly with a steady flap of the wings.

홧김 [हवातकीम] [火 -] the influence of anger. e.g. 홧김에 under the influence of anger / in a fit of anger [rage / temper / the spleen]

황금 [हवांगुम] [黃金] = 금(金).
황금 만능주의 the almighty dollar principle; mammonism.

황급 [हवांगुब] [遑急] extreme urgency [haste]. 황급하다 urgent; pressing; hurried. 황급히 in great haste; hastily; in a great [violent / deuced / mortal] hurry. e.g. 황급히 달아나다 run away in a flurry / beat a hasty retreat.

황당 [हवांगदांग] [荒唐] absurdity; nonsense. ⇨ 황당무계 황당하다 absurd; preposterous; wild.

황량 [हवांगन्यांग] [荒凉] desolateness; dreariness; bleakness. 황량하다 desolate; bleak; deserted <village>. e.g. 우리들 앞에는 황량한 벌판이 펼쳐져 있다 There spread a desolate plain before us.

황망 [हवांगमांग] [慌忙] rush; hurry; flurry; restlessness. 황망하다 hurried; bustling; restless; flurried; confused. 황망히 hurriedly; flurriedly; in a hurry [flurry]; confusedly. e.g. 나는 황망히 떠나는 바람에 열쇠를 잊었다 I left in such a haste [flurry] that I forgot my keys.

황무지 [हवांगमुजी] [荒蕪地] waste [wild / barren / bad] land; a barren tract; a wilderness; a waste.

황사 [ह्वांगसा] [黃砂] yellow sand

황소 [ह्वांगसो] a bull. e.g. 황소같이 일하다 work like blazes [a horse / a tiger].

황실 [ह्वांगशिल] [皇室] the Imperial Household [Family].

황제 [ह्वांगजे] [皇帝] an emperor

황태자 [ह्वांगथैजा] [皇太子] the Crown Prince; the Prince Imperial; the Heir Apparent (to the Throne).

황폐 [ह्वांगफ्ये] [荒廢] desolation; (재해, 전쟁 등에 의한) devastation; (토지, 건물 등의) dilapidation; waste; ruin; abandonment. 황폐하다 be devastated; go to ruin; be laid waste; (건물이) go[fall] into decay; run waste.

황해 [ह्वांगहै] (黃海) (중국, 한반도 사이) [바다] the Yellow Sea

황혼 [ह्वांगहोन] [黃昏] dusk; (evening) twilight; crepuscule. e.g. 이제 인생의 황혼이다 I have reached the twilight years of my life [my twilight years].

황홀 [ह्वांगहोल] [무아경] rapture; ecstasy; trance. 황홀하다 charmed; enchanted. e.g. 너무나 아름다운 풍경에 나는 황홀했다 I was enchanted [enraptured] by the extremely beautiful scenery

홱 [ह्वैग] [갑자기] suddenly; [잽싸게] quickly; with dispatch; nimbly. e.g. 홱 돌아보다 turn right round.

횃불 [ह्वैतबुल] a (pine) torch; a flambeau <*pl.* ~x, ~s>; a torchlight; a link

회[1] [ह्वे] [回] [돌림 횟수] a time; (경기의) a round; a game; [야구] an inning; (연재물의) an instalment. e.g. 1 회 once / one time.

회[2] [ह्वे] [會] [조직] a society; an association (협회); a club (클럽). e.g. 문학회 a literary society [club].

회[3] [ह्वे] [膾] (생선회) slices of raw fish; sliced raw fish; (육회) minced raw beef.

회갑 [ह्वेगाब] [回甲] = 환갑. **회갑연** = 환갑 잔치 (⇨ 환갑).

회개 [ह्वेगै] [悔改] repentance; penitence. 회개하다 repent <of one's sins>; renounce one's former sins; be [become] penitent; reform oneself; turn over a new leaf. e.g. 잘못[비행]을 회개하다 acknowledge one's mistakes [misdeeds] and reform.

회견 [ह्वेग्यौन] [會見] an interview; an audience.

회계 [ह्वेग्ये] [會計] [금전의 출납에 관한 일] accounts. e.g. 그는 저 상점에서 회계를 담당하고 있다 He is in charge of the accounts at the store.

회고 [**हवेगो**] [**回顧**] recollection; retrospect; retrospection; review. 회고하다 recollect; retrospect; look back <upon / over / at>; recall; review <one's past life>; pass <one's life> in review e.g. 과거를 회고하다 look back upon one's old days

회관 [**हवेग्वान**] [**會館**] a hall; an assembly hall; a clubhouse

회귀 [**हवेग्वी**] [**回歸**] [한 바퀴 돌고 제자리로 돌아옴](a) revolution; (a) recurrence.

회담 [**हवेदाम**] [**會談**] a conversation; a talk; a parley; a conference (정식의).

회답 [**हवेदाब**] [**回答**] a reply; an answer; a response.

회동 [**हवेदोंग**] [**會同**] an assembly; a meeting; a gathering. 회동하다 meet (together); assemble; gather (together); have an assembly.

회로 [**हवेरो**] [**回路**] ⇨ 전기회로 e.g. 병렬 [직렬] 회로 a parallel [series] circuit.

회보 [**हवेबो**] [**會報**] a bulletin; a report; the transactions (학회의). e.g. 동창회 회보 an alumni [alumnae] bulletin (▷ alumnae는 여자 학교의).

회복 [**हवेबोग**] [**回復, 恢復**] **1** [본디 상태로 돌이킴] recovery; restoration; retrieval; rehabilitation; (시세의) recovery; reaction; [法] recovery 회복하다 get back; recover <strength>; regain <one's reputation>; restore <peace>; rehabilitate <one's character>; retrieve <one's honor / position>; get over <a loss>; repair <one's ex-hausted energies>; make good; (실지 등을) win back; 소송에 의해) replevy; be restored to <one's honor> e.g. 명예를 회복하다 restore one's good name. **2** [건강의 나아짐] recovery; recuperation. e.g. 건강의 회복 the return [restoration] of health.

회비 [**हवेबी**] [**會費**] a fee (일시적인); a membership fee (회원의); a subscription (▷ 회보 등을 예약하고 불입하는).

회사 [**हवेसा**] [**會社**] a company (Co.); a corporation; a firm; a concern (상사).

회상 [**हवेसांग**] [**回想**] recollection; [과거의 추억] reminiscence; retrospecttion; reflection. 회상하다 recollect; recall; call to mind; retrospect; remember; reflect on. e.g.. 과거를 회상하다 look back on the past / recall old times.

회수 [**हवेसु**] [**回收**] (a) withdrawal; (a) collection; recovery; call-back (판 물건의); drawing in (은행권 등의). 회수하다 withdraw <coins / books> from circulation; collect; draw back; call in; retire; reclaim <disused things>. e.g. 대출금을 회수하다 withdraw [draw in] loans / collect [call in] debts.

회식 [हवेशिग] [**會食**] dining together; mess (군인의). 회식하다 dine together; dine <with>; take a meal together; (군인 등이) have a mess <with>; mess <with>.

회심 [हवेशिम] [**會心**] congeniality; complacency. e.g. 회심의 미소를 짓다 [띠우다] have [smile] a smile of satisfaction / smile complacently / have a self-satisfied smile.

회오리바람 [हवेओरीबाराम] a whirlwind; an eddywind; a vertiginous wind; a cyclone; a (whirling) tornado <*pl.* ~(e)s>; a twister.

회원 [हवेवॉन] [**會員**] a member <of a society / an association>; <집합적> a membership.

회유 [हवेयू] [**懷柔**] conciliation; pacification; appeasement; [매수] winning over. 회유하다 conciliate; pacify; appease; placate; bring <a person> round; [매수하다] buy [win] <a person> over; draw [bring] over <a person> to one's side. e.g. 그를 어떻게든 회유해서 우리 편으로 할 수 있었다 We managed to win him over to our side.

회의 [हवेउइ] [**懷疑**] doubt; skepticism; incredulity; unbelief. e.g. 그들은 상관의 생각에 회의적이었다 They were skeptical about their boss's principles.

회의 [हवेउइ] [**會議**] a conference; a meeting; a council; a talk; a convention (대회); a congress (대표자 회의); a sitting (회기 중인); a session

회장 [हवेजांग] [**會長**] the president <of a society>; the chairman <of a committee>; a grand <of a club>. e.g. 그 협회는 김 박사를 회장으로 모시고 있다 The society is under the presidency of Dr. Kim.

회전 [हवेजॉन] [**回轉, 廻轉**] (a) revolution; (a) rotation; (a) gyration (선회). 회전하다 revolve; rotate; gyrate; turn [spin] round; go [move] round; run(기계가). e.g. 180도 회전하다 rotate in a 180-degree arc.

회지 [हवेजी] [**會誌**] a bulletin; the transactions (학회의). e.g. 동창회 회지 an alumni bulletin / an alumnae bulletin (여학 교의).

회진 [हवेजीन] [回診] a (doctor's) round of visits. 회진하다 make a round of visits <to one's patients>; go the round of <one's patients>; visit one's patients; make sick calls; go round the beds.

회초리 [हवेछोरी] a switch; a whip; a cane; a pointer (교사용). e.g. 회초리로 때리다 switch <a boy> (with a cane) / cane / lash [flog / whip / swish] <a boy> (with a switch). 회초리를 맞다 be whipped / be caned [lashed] / get the cane.

회춘 [हवेछुन] [回春] [도로 젊어짐] rejuvenation; restoration of youth. 회춘하다 grow [get] younger; be [become] rejuvenated; undergo rejuvenation; be restored to youth; become [grow] young again e.g. 회춘 시키다 rejuvenate / rejuvenize.

회충 [हवेछुंग] [蛔蟲] a mawworm; an intestinal worm; a roundworm; an ascarid [ascaris] <*pl.* ascarid (e)s>.

회칙 [हवेछीग] [會則] the regulations [rules / bylaws] of a society; the articles of an association; the constitution of a club.

회포 [हवेफो] [懷抱] one's inmost [intimate] thoughts; one's heart [mind]. e.g. 회포를 풀다 unburden [unbosom] oneself <to a person>.

회피 [हवेफी] [回避] evasion; avoidance; shirking; elusion; [法] refrainment. 회피하다 evade; avoid; shirk; dodge; shun; sidestep; elude <payment>; get around <the difficulty>. e.g. 책임을 회피하다 evade [shirk] one's responsibility / flee from responsibility

회한 [हवेहान] [悔恨] remorse; (a) regret; (a) repentance; contrition; compunction. e.g. 회한의 눈물 tears of remorse.

회합 [हवेहाब] [會合] a meeting; an assembly; a gathering; a party; a get-together. 회합하다 meet; gather; assemble; get together

회화[1] [हवेहवा] [會話] (a) conversation; a talk.

회화[2] [हवेहवा] [繪畫] pictures; paintings; drawings. e.g. 시의 회화적인 아름다움 the pictorial beauty of a poem.

획 [हवेग] [劃] (글자의) a stroke. e.g. 획을 긋다 make a stroke.

획기적 [हवेक्कीजौग] [劃期的] epoch-making; epochal. e.g. 획기적 사건[발견] an epoch-making event [discovery].

획득 [ह्वेकतुक] [獲得] acquisition; acquirement; possession; gain; taking. 획득하다 gain; acquire; obtain; secure; get; win; take <the first prize>.

획일적 [ह्वेगीलजौग] [劃一的] [한결같은] uniform; standardized; [한결같음] uniformity. e.g. 획일적인 교육 uniform education.

획일화 [ह्वेगीरह्वा] [劃一化] standardization.

횟수 [ह्वेत्सु] [回數] the number of times; frequency. e.g. 횟수를 거듭 하다 repeat <so many times>.

횡단 [ह्वेंगदान] [横斷] crossing; crosscutting; intersection; traversing. 횡단하다 cross; traverse; sail [go / travel / swim / make a journey] across; run [lie] across [through]; intersect; cut transversely

횡령 [ह्वेंगन्यौग] [横領] (a) usurpation; (a) seizure; dispossession; assumeption; (an) embezzlement; misappropriation; conversion (동산의 횡령하다 usurp; seize upon; jump <a claim>; embezzle; dispossess <a person of his property>; assume; appropriate unlawfully; misappropriate; help oneself to (the money); grab; convert (동산을). e.g. 재산을 횡령하다 seize upon <a person's> property / dispossess <a person> of his property.

횡설수설 [ह्वेंगसौलसुसौल] incoherent talks; disjointed remarks; jargon; gibberish; jabberwock(y); nonsense. 횡설수설하다 talk incoherently; make disjointed remarks; talk jargon [nonsense]; jargon; gibber; jabber. e.g. 그의 진술은 점점 횡설수설 해졌다 His statement be-came more and more incoherent [confused].

횡재 [ह्वेंगजै] [横財] a windfall; a godsend; an acquisition; a find; [크게 한몫보기] a killing; a cleanup; a bonanza (투기 등에서). 횡재하다 fall in with a piece of (good) luck; make a rare find; realize a windfall profit <of>; receive one's share of the windfall; make a killing [cleanup]; strike a bonanza.

횡포 [ह्वेंगफो] [横暴] oppresssion (압제); violence (폭력); tyranny (포학); high-handedness (위압).

효 [ह्यो] [孝] filial piety [devotion]; filial duty; obedience to parents. e.g. 부모에게 효를 다하다 tend one's parents with filial piety / be dutiful to one's parents.

효과 [ह्योग्वा] [效果] (an)

effect; effectiveness; avail; (the) good <of something>; efficacy (약 등의); efficiency (능률); [결과] a result; fruit.

효과적 **[ह्योग्वाजौग]** [**效果的**] [효과 있는] effective; effecttual; successful; efficacious (약 등이); [효과가 있음] effectiveness; effectuality; effectualness; efficacyousness.

효녀 **[ह्योन्यौ]** [**孝女**] a filial [dutiful] daughter.

효능 **[ह्योनुंग]** [**效能**] effect; efficacy; virtue; properties <of a medicine>; benefit; good; use.

효도 **[ह्योदो]** [**孝道**] filial piety [devotion]; filial duty; obedience to parents. 효도하다 be dutiful [obedient / devoted] to one's parents; be a good son [daughter]; practice filial piety toward one's parents; discharge one's filial duties.

효력 **[ह्योरयौग]** [**效力**] **1** (약 등의) (an) effect. e.g. 그 약은 그의 두통에 아무런 효력이 없었다 This medicine did not relieve [help] his headache. **2** [법률의 작용] effect; [유효성] validity. e.g. 그 계약의 효력이 발생하는 것은 1년 뒤부터이다 The contract will come into force ather one year.

효성 **[ह्योसौग]** [**孝誠**] filial piety [devotion / affection] e.g. 그녀는 어머니에게 효성스럽다 She shows great devotion [behaves filially] to her mother. / She is faithful to her mother.

효시 **[ह्योशि]** [**嚆矢**] [맨 처음] the beginning; the first; the first person <to do>; the pioneer <in>. e.g. 이것이 …의 효시였다 This was the first instance of

효심 **[ह्योशिम]** [**孝心**] filial affection; filial piety. e.g. 효심이 지극한 사람 a very dutiful person.

효용 **[ह्योयोंग]** [**效用**] [용도] use; [유용성] usefulness; utility.

효율 **[ह्योयूल]** [**效率**] the utility factor; efficiency; (엔진의) duty.

효자 **[ह्योजा]** [**孝子**] a dutiful [filial] child [son]; a good [devoted] son.

효행 **[ह्योहैग]** [**孝行**] filial conduct; a filial deed.

효험 **[ह्योहौम]** [**效驗**] (an) effect; efficacy; virtue; benefit. e.g. 효험이 없다 be inefficacious / be ineffective / do <a person> no good / have no effect

후 **[हू]** [**後**] **1** [사후]. e.g. 나는 그 후로 여기에 살아왔다 I have lived here since then. **2** [앞날] future. e.g. 2주일 후에 two weeks hence [from now].

후의 future / coming. 그 일은 후로 미룹시다 We will put it off till some other time. 천년 후의 세계는 어찌 될 것인가 What will become of the world a thousand years hence [from now]?

후각 [हूगाग] [**嗅覺**] the sense of smell; the smell; the olfactory sense.

후견 [हूग्यौन] [**後見**] [보좌] guardianship; wardship; tutelage; tutorage; [원조] assistance. e.g.. 후견을 받고 있다 be in [under] ward / be (placed) under the guardianship <for> / look ather <children> / have the wardship of <a person>.

후계 [हूग्ये] [**後繼**] succession. 후계하다 succeed <a person / to another's office>.

후계자 [हूग्यैजा] [**後繼者**] [대를 이을 사람] an heir (남자); an heiress (여자); an inheritor; (학문, 예능 등의) a successor.

후광 [हूग्वांग] [**後光**] a glory; an aureole [aureola]; a gloria; [광륜] a halo <*pl.* ~(e)s>; a nimbus <*pl.* – bi, ~es>; (태양의) a corona. e.g. 성자의 머리에 후광이 비치고 있다 The saint has a halo around his head. / A halo is visible around the saint's head.

후기[1] [हूगी] [**後記**] a postscript (略 P.S., p.s.). e.g. 편집 후기 the editor's postscript.

후기[2] [हूगी] [**後期**] [뒤의 기간] the latter period; the latter [second] half year; the second semester. e.g. 18세기 후기에 in the later [latter part of the] eighteenth century

후닥닥 [हूदाकताग] **1** [갑자기] suddenly; abruptly; all at once; [열쌔게] quickly; nimbly; alertly;(as) quick as thought. e.g. 후닥닥 뛰어가다 break into a run. **2** [서둘러] hastily; hurriedly; in a hurry; in haste; in a flurry. e.g. 계단을 후닥닥 오르다 [내리다] hurry upstairs [downstairs].

후대[1] [हूदै] [**後代**] the next [coming / oncoming] generation; [후세] ather [coming] age. e.g. 창립 자의 정신을 후대에 전하다 hand down the founder's spirit to future generations [posterity].

후대[2] [हूदै] [**厚待**] a warm [cordial / hearty] reception; kind [hospitable] treatment; hospitality. e.g. 후대를 받다 be kindly treated / be received warmly [cordially] / be accorded a cordial reception.

후덕 [हूदौग] [**厚德**] eminent

[high] virtue. 후덕하다 virtuous; of high virtue.

후들거리다 [हुदुलगौरीदा] tremble; quiver; quake; shake; shiver. e.g. 무릎이 후들거렸다 My knees shook [were about to give away]. / I felt wobbly about the knees.

후딱 [हुताग] quickly; rapidly; nimbly; agilely; alertly;(as) quick as thought. e.g. 후딱 해치우다 finish <one's work> quickly / dispatch <one's work> / make short work of <a thing / a person>.

후려치다 [हुर्योछीदा] give <a person> a sound thrashing [good licking]; hit <a person> hard; tan <a person's> hide (good). e.g. 상대의 칼끝을 후려 치다 knock away one's opponent's sword

후련하다 [हुर्यौनहादा] <feel> relieved; <feel one's mind> unburdened. e.g. 그가 단념했다는 말을 듣고 나는 속이 후련해졌다 I was delighted to learn that he'd given up.

후렴 [हुर्यौम] [後斂] (노래의) a burden; a refrain.

후루룩 [हुरुरुग] **1** [나는 소리] flap-flap; with a flutter. **2** [들이마시는 소리] slurping; sipping. e.g. 뜨거운 죽을 후루룩 마시다 sip (rice) gruel boiled hot. 후루룩하다=후루룩거리다.

후문[1] [हुमुन] [後聞] lingering rumors; anecdotes [stories / rumors] that are spread ather the event.

후문[2] [हुमुन] [後門] a back [rear] gate; a postern (gate); a back door.

후미지다 [हुमीजीदा] **1** (물굽이가) deeply indented; penetrated <far into the land>; deep <into the land>. e.g. 해안의 후미진 곳 a recess in the shoreline. **2** [깊숙하다] sequestered; secluded; retired; unfrequented; lonely. e.g. 후미진 곳 a recess / a nook / a quiet, secluded place / an out-of-the-way place.

후반[हुबान][後半] the latter half; the second half.

후배[हुबै][後輩] [경험, 나이가 뒤진 사람] younger men; the younger generation; [후진] one's junior.

후보 [हुबो] [候補] [입후보함] candidacy; candidature; a candidate (사람); (운동 팀의) substitution.

후보자 [हुबोजा] [候補者] a candidate <for the election>; an applicant <for a position>.

후불 [हुबुल] [後拂] [뒤에 치름] deferred payment; future [ather] payment.

후비다 [**हुबीदा**] dig up; grub; (귀, 코 등을) pick. e.g. 귀를 후비다 clean [pick] one's ears.

후사 [**हुसा**] [**厚謝**] [감사] hearty [sincere / warm] thanks; deep [heartfelt] gratitude; [사례] a handsome [liberal] recompense [reward]. 후사하다 recompense handsomely; thank heartily; reward warmly.

후세 [**हुसे**] [**後世**] [후대] ather [coming / future] ages; posterity; future generations.

후속 [**हुसोग**] [**後續**] succession. e.g. 후속의 following / succeeding.

후손 [**हुसोन**] [**後孫**] a descendant; a scion (명문의); <집합적> posterity; progeny.

후송 [**हुसोंग**] [**後送**] [후방으로 보냄]. 후송하다 send back (to the rear). e.g. 중상병은 후송되었다 Seriously wounded soldiers were sent back to the rear.

후예 [**हुए**] [**後裔**] a descendant; a scion; offspring <*pl.* ~(s)>.

후원 [**हुवोन**] [**後援**] support; backing; patronage; assistance; boosting; help; aid; favor. 후원하다 support; give [lend] support <to>; be [stand] behind <a movement>; give backing <to>; back up; patronize; help <a person>; aid; stand by <a person>; sponsor. e.g. 많은 친구가 그를 후원했다 Many(of his) friends backed him (up) [gave him support].

후일 [**हुइल**] [**後日**] 후일에 in (the) future / later on / some (other) day / some day or other. e.g. 사건의 후일담 a sequence [sequel] to the event.

후임 [**हुइम**] [**後任**] [뒤에 맡은 임무] the duty left over by one's predecessor; [후임자] a successor <to a post>; an incomer; a replacement. e.g. …의 후임으로 in succession to / to succeed <a person> / as (a) successor to / in place of.

후자 [**हुजा**] [**後者**] the latter. e.g. 전자와 후자 the former and the latter.

후줄근하다 [**हुजुलगनहादा**] (wet and) limp; flaccid; a little soggy. e.g. 후줄근해지다 become limp / droop / flap. 후줄근한 옷차림을 하고 있다 be sloppily dressed.

후진 [**हुजीन**] [**後進**] **1** [후배] a junior; a younger man [fellow]; <집합적> the rising [younger] generation. e.g. 후진을 기르다 train the younger [next] generation.**2** [미발달] underdevelopment; backwardness; lagging (behind). e.g. 문화적 후진 cultural backwardness / a cultural lag (지체). **3** [후퇴] backing; backward motion; retreat; [海] sternway. e.g. 전속 후진 <구령> Back full! 후진하다 back (away from); retrocede; (배가) go [move] astern; make sternway.

후천적 [हुछौनजौग] [後天的] a posteriori; acquired <immunity>; learned <behavior pattern>. e.g. 후천적으로 a posteriori. 성격은 후천적으로 형성된다 You can form your own personal character in the course of your lifetime.

후추 [हुछु] pepper; black pepper.

후텁지근하다 [हुथौपचीगुनहादा] sultry; sticky; stuffy. 오늘 밤은 몹시 후텁지근하다 It is very sultry [hot and humid] tonight.

후퇴 [हुथ्वे] [後退] [뒤로 물러남] backdown; (a) retreat; retrocession; regress; regression; retrogression; withdrawal; retirement; falling back; backdown 후퇴하다 retreat; go [fall] back; back (away); retrocede; recede; retrograde; backtrack; (배가) drop [move / go] astern.

후하다 [हुहादा] [厚-] (인심, 인정이) kind (hearted); tender (hearted); warm (hearted); hearty; cordial; hospitable; friendly; (보수, 대우 등이) generous; lenient; liberal; magnanimous; handsome; openhanded. e.g. 점수가 후하다 be liberal [generous] in marking <examination> papers / be an easy grader.

후환 [हुह्वान] [後患] future troubles. e.g. 후환이 두려워서 아무도 피해를 신고하지 않는다 No one reports the damage for fear of the consequences [of reprisals].

후회 [हुह्वे] [後悔] (a) repentance; (a) regret; penitence; remorse; contrition; compunction. 후회하다 [हुह्वेहादा] repent (of); regret; be sorry <for>; be penitent [repentant] <for>; feel regret <for>; feel remorse <for>. e.g. 죄를 후회하다 be penitent for one's sin.

훅 [हुक] **1** [들이마시는 소리] with a sip [slurp]; at a gulp [drath / draught]. e.g. 국을 훅 들이마시다 slurp up [gulp down] soup. **2** [부는 소리] with a whiff [puff] e.g. 촛불을 훅 불어 끄다 whiff [puff] out a candlelight [candle].

훈계 [हुनग्ये] [訓戒] (an) admonition; exhortation; a lecture; [타일러 주의시킴] caution; warning 훈계하다 admonish [exhort] <a person to do something>; caution [warn] <a person

ㅎ

against errors

훈련 [हुन्नयौन] [**訓練**] training; (a) drill; practice; exercise; (a) discipline; schooling. 훈련하다 train; drill; exercise; discipline; school.

훈련소 [हुन्नयौनसो] [**訓練所**] a training school [station / institute / center]. e.g. 육군 신병 훈련소 an army recruit [recruits'] training center / an army training camp for recruits.

훈민정음 [हुनमीनजौगम] [**訓民正音**] [한글] the Korean script.

훈장 [हुनजांग] [**勳章**] a décoration; an order (▷décoration 은 훈장 그 자체를 가리키며, order 는 훈장의 명칭 앞에 붙여 써서 수장자 (受章者) 의 한 사람이 되었다는 뜻을 내포함); a medal. e.g. 훈장을 달다[차다] wear a décoration

훈제 [हुनजे] [**燻製, 薰製**] smoking. e.g. 훈제의 smoked / smoke-dried / bloated. 훈제하다 smoke; bloat; kipper; dry <fish> in the smoke.

훈훈하다 [हुनहुनहादा] [**薰薰**-] comfortably warm; nice and warm. e.g. 훈훈한 방 a nice and warm room.

훌륭하다 [हुल्लयुंगहादा] **1** [멋지다] fine; handsome; nice; excellent; superb; spleendid; brilliant; magnificent; grand. e.g. 맛이 훌륭합니다 It's delicious [very good]. **2** [(태도 등이) 당당하다] stately; imposing; commanding. e.g. 훌륭한 풍채 commanding presence / imposing appearance. **3** [존경할 만하다] honorable; respectable; [가치 있다] worthy; [떳떳하다] decent; presentable. e.g. 훌륭한 일생을 보내다 lead a worthy [reputable] life.

훌쩍 [हुलचौक] **1** [가볍게 날거나 뛰는 모양] lightly; [단번에 뛰는 모양] with [at] a jump [bound]; [재빨리 움직이는 모양] nimbly; quickly. e.g. 담을 훌쩍 뛰어넘다 jump clean over the fence / fly over the fence at a bound. **2** (코를) sniffling; snivel(l)ing. e.g. 코를 훌쩍 들이마시다 sniffle / snivel. **3**[떠나가는 모양] aimlessly; without any definite purpose. e.g. 훌쩍 나가다 go out with no definite purpose [destination] in mind

훑다 [हुल्था] **1** (벼 등을) hackle; thrash; strip. e.g. 그가 밀이삭을 훑으면 밀알이 아래로 떨어졌다 As he stripped off the ears of wheat [stripped the wheat with his hands], the grains fell to the ground. **2** [제거하다] remove; scrub <off / away / out>. e.g.

생선속을 훑다 remove the guts from a fish / gut a fish.

훑어보다 [हुल्थौबोदा] **1** (위아래를) look <a person> up and down; stare [look hard] at <a person>; survey [search / study] <a person's face>; scrutinize [peruse] <a person's face>. e.g. 남의 위아래를 훑어보다 stare a person up and down / survey a person from head to foot. **2** [죽 살피다] look [go] over [through] <the page>; pass an eye over <the manuscript>; scan <a newspaper>. e.g. 서류를 대충 [쓱] 훑어보다 run one's eyes through[over] the papers.

훔쳐보다 [हुमच्यौबोदा] steal a glance [look] <at>; look [glance] furtively <at>. e.g. 슬쩍 훔쳐보다 steal a glance at.

훔치다 [हुमछीदा] [도둑질하다] steal <a thing from a person>; pilfer [filch / purloin] <articles from a shop>; make free with <another's possessions>; lith; sneak; hook; <美> swipe.

훗날 [हुन्नाल] [後-] 훗날에 in (the) future / later (on) / some (other) day.

훤칠하다 [ह्वॉनछीरहादा] strapping; tall; <서술적> be high in stature; have a full well-developed figure. e.g. 훤칠한 여자 a strapping girl.

훤하다 [ह्वॉनहादा] [흐릿하게 밝다] dimly white; light; gray; dimly-lit. e.g. 훤해지다 lighten / grow [get] light / turn gray / light up.

훨씬 [ह्वॉलशिन] fair; by far; a great deal; a lot; out [far] and away; by long [all] odds; by a long way; much <bigger, broader, etc.>. e.g. 훨씬 좋은 물건

훨훨 [ह्वॉरह्वॉल] **훼방** [ह्वैबांग] [毁謗] [방해] interruption; interference; intrusion; prevention; disturbance; trouble.

훼방하다 [ह्वेबांगहादा] interrupt; interfere with <a person>; thwart; hinder; disturb; stand in <another's> way; put a spoke in <another's> wheel.

훼손 [ह्वैसोन] [毁損] damage; (명예의) defamation of character. 훼손하다 damage; injure; impair; spoil; compromise. e.g. 명예를 훼손하다 defame / injure to a person's reputation.

휘 [ह्वी] **1** [바람 소리] whistling; with a puff [whiff]. e.g. 바람이 휘 불었다 The wind was whistling [hissing / piping]. / There was a gust of wind. **2** [숨소리] with a puff [sigh]. e.g. 숨을 휘 내쉬다 let out a long breath / puff out. 휘 한숨을 쉬다 give a heavy sigh.

휘갈기다 [हवीगाल्गीदा] (매 등을) give [whip / lash] <a person> a sound thrashing [good licking]; trail one's whip; hit hard; (글씨를) write hurriedly [hastily]; scribble; scrawl. e.g. 회초리로 등을 휘갈기다 lash <a person> on the back. 그는 종이에 주소를 휘갈겼다 He dashed off [hurriedly wrote] his add-ress on a sheet of paper.

휘감기다 [हवीगामगीदा] [감기어 붙다] twine [coil / wind] itself round; coil around; twist about; get wound [twisted] round. e.g. 담쟁이에 휘감긴 나무 a tree entwined with ivy.

휘감다 [हवीगामता] twine round; coil round; wind round [around]; entwine; tie [fasten] round. e.g. 부러진 다리에 붕대를 휘감다 swathe broken limb in bandages

휘날리다 [हवीनाल्लीदा] [나부끼다] wave; flutter; flap; fly; float; stream; (이름이) <one's name> resound; become famous [renowned / well-known]. e.g. 바람에 휘날리는 기 a streaming flag.

휘다 [हवीदा] [구부러지다] bend; curve; become bent [curved]; warp; [뒤틀 리다] crook; buckle (up); [낭창낭창하다] be pliant [pliable]; be flexible [supple]; yield (압력에); (손가락, 몸이) bend back (ward); lean backward (몸이). e.g. 가지가 휘도록 열매가 달린 나무 a tree overburdened [overbowed] with fruit

휘두르다 [हवीदुरुदा] 1 [돌리다] brandish; flourish; wield; wave (about); throw about; swing (around); sway. e.g. 팔을 휘두르다 throw one's arms about. **2** [제 뜻대로 하다] turn [twist] <a person> round one's (little) finger; have <a person> at one's beck and call. e.g. 남에게 휘둘리다 be turned [twisted] around a person's (little) finger / be at the mercy of a person

휘둥그레지다 [हवीदुंगगुरेजीदा] open <one's eyes> wide; <美> be pop-eyed. e.g. 놀라서 눈이 휘둥그레지다 stare [open one's eyes wide] with [in] wonder / be pop-eyed with alarm

휘말리다 [हवीमाल्लीदा] [휩쓸리다] be involved <in>; be embroiled <on>; (파도 등에) be engulfed; be swallowed up; be dragged in. e.g. 음모에 휘말리다 be entangled in a plot.

휘몰아치다 [हवीमोराछीदा] (바람이) blow violently [boisterously]; blow hard (and strong); bluster; rage; rave; roar; (눈이) fall in whirls; fall thick and fast. e.g. 휘몰아치는 눈 a swirling snow / whirls of snow / a blizzard.

휘발유 [हवीबारयू] Volatile oils; benzene; naphtha; gasoline.

휘어잡다 [हवीऔजापता] 1 [구부리어 거머잡다] hold <a thing> bent [doubled up] in one's hand; grasp; take[catch / grab / clutch] hold of. e.g. 버들가지를 휘어잡다 hold willow branches in one's hand. 2 [손아귀에 넣고 부리다] gain [win] <a person> over <to one's side>; have <a person> under one's control; bend <a person> to one's will. e.g. 여자를 휘어잡다 control a woman at will.

휘어지다 [हवीऔजीदा] bend; be bent; be crooked; be pliant; be supple. e.g. 철사가 휘어졌다 A wire got bent [bents].

휘젓다 [हवीजौत्ता] 1 [뒤섞다] stir (up) <coffee>; give <the porridge> a stir; beat up <cream>; churn <milk>. e.g. 스푼 [숟가락] 으로 휘젓다 stir <one's tea / coffee> with a spoon. 2 [흔들다] swing <one's arms>. e.g. 팔을 휘저으며 걷다 swing one's arms as one goes [walks].3 [어지럽게 하다] disturb; disarrange; upset; confuse; ruffle; (뒤져서) ransack <a drawer>; rummage [rout / root] <in a drawer>. e.g. 마음의 평화를 휘젓다 disturb the peace of mind.

휘청거리다 [हवीछौग गौरीदा] 1 [휘어지다] yield; give; bend; [낭창거리다] be pliant[pliable / flexible / supple]. e.g. 휘청거리는 지팡이 an elastic cane. 버들가지는 잘 휘청거린다 Willow twigs are pliable. 2 [힘이 없어 흔들리다] be unsteady; reel; be shaky <on one's legs>; be groggy (권투에서). e.g. 세게 얻어 맞고 휘청거리다 reel under a heavy blow.

휘파람 [हवीफाराम] a whistle.

휘황 [हवीहवांग] [**輝煌燦爛**] **찬란하다** [छाल्लानहादा] brilliant; bright; radiant; dazzling; glittering; res-plendent. e.g. 휘황 찬란한 보석 a brilliant [radiant] jewel.

휙 [हवैक] 1 [빨리 돌아가는 모양] with a swerve; with a jerk; with a whirl; [갑자기] suddenly; abruptly; with a jerk; [재빨리] quickly. e.g. 휙 뒤돌아 보다 turn right round / look round. 2 [바람 등이 세게] whizzing; whistling; with a whistle [whiz(z)]. e.g. 총알이 머리 위를 휙 지나갔다 A bullet whistled [whizzed] past me. 3 [힘껏] with full force; with all one's strength. e.g. 창을 휙 던지다 hurl [dart] a spear. 그는 트럭에서 짐을 휙 던졌다 He chucked the load off the truck.

휠체어 [हवैल्छेऔ] a wheel-chair.

휩싸다 [हवैपसादा] **1** [감아싸다] wrap <in>; lap <in>; tuck up <in>. e.g. 홑이불로 어깨를 휩싸다 tuck the bedcovers about one's shoulders / tuck the bed-covers in round one's shoulders **2** [비호하다] protect; shield; take <a person> under one's wings. e.g. 아버지가 노하면 어머니가 딸을 휩싸고 돌았다 The mother screened her daughter from her father's anger. **3** [온통 뒤덮다] cover <with>; veil <in>; shroud <in>; mantle <in>. e.g. 안개에 휩싸다 be veiled [folded / (en) shrouded] in mist.

휩싸이다 [हवैपसाइदा] **1** [감겨싸이다] be wrapped up <in>; be bundled [swaddled] <in>. e.g. 담요에 휩싸이다 be wrapped [tucked] up in a blanket. **2** [덮어 가려지다] be covered <with>; be veiled [enveloped / shrouded] <in>. e.g. 불길에 휩싸 이다 be enveloped in flames.

휩쓸다 [हवैपसुलता] **1** [일소하다] sweep away [off]; clear (away / off); clean out [away]; make a clean sweep <of>; (병, 재해 등이) sweep <over / through>; [풍미하다] overwhelm; sway. e.g. 경기를 휩쓸다 sweep [win] all the games [matches / bouts] / win a sweeping victory.**2** [설치다] overrun; rampage; rave [rage / ramp] about. e.g. 부랑배가 시내를 휩쓸다 Hoodlums tore the town up.

휩쓸리다 [हवैपसुल्लीदा] **1** (모조리) be swept away [off]; [말려들다] be involved [entangled] in; be drawn into. e.g. 인파에 휩쓸리다 be swept along in the crowd / be caught up into the crowd. **2** (설치는 힘에) be overrun; suffer a rampage.

휴가 [ह्यूगा] [**休暇**] a vacation; time off; [말미] a leave of absence; (a) furlough.

휴간 [ह्यूगान] [**休刊**] suspension [discontinuation] of publication

휴강 [ह्यूगांग] [**休講**] 휴강하다 give no lecture (for the day); absent oneself from school

휴게 [ह्यूगे] [**休憩**] (a) rest; a recess; a break; time-off; a time-out; [막간] an intermission; an interval. 휴게하다 rest; take a rest [recess]; take one's time off; take[have] a break.

휴게소 [**ह्यूगेसो**] a resting place; a rest area.

휴관 [**ह्यूग्वान**] [**休館**] closure <of a museum>. 휴관하다 close <a museum>. e.g. 미술관은 월요일에 휴관한다 The art museum is closed on Mondays.

휴교 [**ह्यूग्यो**] [**休校**] closure of a school. 휴교하다 close <a school> temporarily; be closed

휴대 [**ह्यूदै**] [**携帶**] carrying. e.g. 휴대용의 portable <radio> / hand <camera> / pocket <dictionary> / handy (to carry). 휴대하다 carry; bring [take] <a lunch> with one; have <a thing> with one; equip oneself with <a camera>; pack <a gun>. e.g. 무기를 휴대하다 carry [be armed with] a weapon

휴식 [**ह्यूशिक**] [**休息**] (a) rest; repose; relaxation; a respite; a breather. 휴식하다 rest (oneself); take a rest [respite / breather]; repose; relax.

휴양 [**ह्यूयांग**] [**休養**] (a) rest; a layoff; repose; relaxation; recreation; recuperation (병후의). 휴양하다 rest; take a rest; repose; relaK (병후에) recuperate; recruit (oneself). e.g. (병으로) 1년간 휴양하다 have a year's holiday to recruit [recuperate] <at

휴업 [**ह्यूऔब**] [**休業**] (점포 등의) suspension of business [operations]; closure; (회사, 공장의) a shutdown 휴업하다 (사람이) take a holiday; take a day off; (점포 등이) be closed (to business); suspend business (operations).

휴전 [**ह्यूजौन**] [**休戰**] suspension [cessation] of hostilities; an armistice; a truce; a cease-fire.

휴지[1] [**ह्यूजी**] [**休紙**] **1** [못 쓰는 종이] wastepaper; a scrap of paper; paper scraps. e.g. 휴지를 줍다 pick up wastepaper. **2** [뒤지] toilet [lavatory] paper [tissue]; a toilet roll (두루말이); [코푸는 종이] paper for wiping the nose; a paper handkerchief. e.g. 휴지로 코를 풀다 blow one's nose on tissue paper.

휴지[2] [**ह्यूजी**] [**休止**] a pause; a standstill; cessation; sus-pension; stoppage; discon-tinuance; a letup. e.g. 그 두 단어 사이에 보통 조금 휴지를 둔다 We usually make a slight pause between those two words

휴직 [**ह्यूजीक**] [**休職**] temporary retirement from office; a layoff (단기의). 휴직하다

retire temporarily from office; (명을 받고) be put [placed] on the half-pay list (군인이); be laid off; be suspended from duty [office].

휴학 [ह्यूहाक] [**休學**] temporary absence from school. 휴학하 withdraw [absent oneself] from school temporarily [for a time].

흉 [ह्यूंग] **1** [흉터] a scar. e.g. 흉이 있는 얼굴 a scarred face / a face with a scar / a face marked with wounds. **2** [흠] [हुम] a fault; a defect; a flaw; a blemish; a drawback. e.g. 흉 없는 사람은 없다 No one is free from faults. / There is no man but has some faults. / Nobody is perfect.

흉가 [ह्यूंगा] **凶家**] a house of ill [evil] omen; an ominous house; a haunted house.

흉계 [ह्यूग्ये] [**凶計**] a wicked [sinister] design; an evil scheme; a plot; a trick. e.g. 흉계를 꾸미다 devise wicked designs / hatch a plot / concoct tricks.

흉기 [ह्यूंगी] [**凶器**] a murder [death / lethal / mortal / deadly / dangerous] weapon.

흉내 [ह्यूंगनै] (an) imitation; mimicry; apery; impersonation; a takeoff. 흉내(를) 내다 imitate; copy; ape; follow <another's example>; mimic; take off; do a take-off <of>; follow suit; take a leaf out of <a person's> book.

흉년 [ह्यूंगन्यौन] [**凶年**] a bad year; a lean year; a year of bad harvest; a year of famine. e.g. 흉년이 들다 have a bad <rice> crop [harvest] / have a short crop [yield] <of rice> / be a bad year <for the rice crop>.

흉물 [ह्यूंगमुल] [**凶物**] an evil [a treacherous] person; a deep one; a snake. e.g. 흉물스럽다 be tricky / be sly / be wily / be crathy.

흉보다 [ह्यूंगबोदा] find fault with; pick out <another's> defects; speak ill of; run [cry / play] down; abuse; disparage; censure; criticize. e.g. 안 듣는 데서 흉보는 사람 a backbiter. 안 듣는 데서 흉보다 backbite <a person> / speak ill of <a person> behind his back [in his absence].

흉부 [ह्यूंगबु] [**胸部**] the breast; the chest; the thorax <*pl.* ~es, thoraces>; [動] the corselet

흉작 [ह्यूंगजाक] [**凶作**] a bad [poor] harvest [crop]; a scanty harvest; a failure of crops

흉잡다 [ह्यूंगजापता] find fault with; pick [point] out <another's> defects; pick a hole in <another's> coat [character]; disparage.

흉조 [ह्युंगजो] [凶兆] an ill omen; an evil sign. 흉조다 bode ill [evil] <to / for>.

흉측 [ह्युंगछुक] [凶測] 흉측하다 (성질이) atrocious; heinous; brutal; (용모가) very ugly[crude]; bad-[ugly-] looking; <비유> terrible; dreadful; awful; bitter. e.g. 뱀은 움직이는 꼴이 흉측해서 싫습니다 I don't like snakes because the way they move is revolting.

흉터 [ह्युंगथी] a scar; a seam <of an old wound>; a mark. e.g. 팔의 덴 자리에 흉터가 생겼다 The burn on my arm has left a scar.

흉하다 [ह्युंगहादा] [凶-] **1** [못생기다] ugly; bad-[ugly-] looking; plain; [보기 언짢다] unseemly; unsightly; ungainly; ugly. e.g. 다리에 보기 흉한 자국이 생겼다 An ugly scar remained [was left] on my leg. **2** [불길하다] ill; ill-omened; unlucky; inauspicious; sinister. e.g. 흉한 꿈 an unlucky dream. 흉한 예감 an ominous presentiment.

흉흉하다 [ह्युंगह्युंगहादा] [洶洶-] (인심이) panic-stricken; filled with alarm; <서술적> be in great alarm [fear] e.g. 그 소문으로 인심이 흉흉해졌다 The rumor aroused much fear in people's minds.

흐느끼다 [हुनुकीदा] sob; blubber; (아이 등이) whimper; whine. e.g. 흐느껴 우는 것 같은 바이올린 소리 the plaintive sound [the lament] of a violin.

흐느적거리다 [हुनुजौक्कौरीदा] swing; sway; shake; waver; flutter; (불꽃 등이) flicker; flare. e.g. (나뭇잎 등이) 바람에 흐느적거리다 be swayed by the wind / sway (about) to the wind / tremble [flutter] in the breeze.

흐려지다 [हुर्यौजीदा] **1** (하늘이) become cloudy [overcast]; be clouded [dull]; cloud up. e.g. 하루 종일 날씨가 흐려져 있었다 It was cloudy all day. **2** [선명하지 않게 되다] become dim; dim; be clouded; fog up; be obscured; be blurred; become foggy (사진이); become turbid [muddy / impure / thick]. e.g. 김으로 거울이 흐려졌다 The mirror was clouded (up / over) with steam. **3** [걱정스러운 빛이 있다] be gloomy. e.g. 심노 때문에 그의 마음은 흐려졌다 All his troubles have cast a cloud (of gloom) over his heart.

흐르다 [हुरुदा] **1** [유동하다]

stream; flow; run; course; trickle (졸졸); ooze (스며 나오다); drain (배수되다); (양초의 촛물이) run; gutter e.g. 그 강은 시내를 흐르고 있다 The river flows through the city. **2** [떠다니다] float; drith; [유랑하다] drith; wander; knock about. e.g. 흘러흘러 한국에 오다 drith to Korea. **3**[쏟아지다] fall; spill; get [be] spilt; [넘치다] overflow; run [flow] over <the brim>. e.g. 애교가 넘쳐 흐르다 be overflowing [beaming] with smiles.**4** [윤기, 광택이 나다]. e.g. 그의 얼굴에 기름이 흐른다 Grease exudes on[oozes out of] his face. / His face is sleek [slick].**5** [쏠리다] lapse [fall] <into>; run [incline / be inclined] <to>; lean [tend / trend] <toward>. e.g. 극단으로 흐르다 go to extremes [excess] / rush into extremes / go too far. **6** (세월이) pass <by / away>; elapse; go [roll / flow] by [on]. e.g. 그때부터 10 년이 흘렀다 Ten years have passed [elapsed] since then.

흐름 **[हुरूम]** [흐르는 것] flowing; (물줄기 등의) a flow; a stream; a current; (페인트 등의) run; running; (시대 조류의) the current [tendency / trend] of the times.

흐리다[1] **[हुरीदा]** **1** [혼탁하게 하다] make <water> muddy [turbid / roily]; roil; rile; make foul [impure]; contaminate.**2** [명예를 더럽히다] tarnish; sully; defile; blemish; stain; spot. e.g. 이름 [명예] 을 흐리다 tarnish [stain] one's name [honor].**3** (흔적을) blot out; blur (out); obscure; bedim. **4**[애매하게 하다] make vague [obscure / indistinct / ambiguous / hazy]. e.g. 대답을 흐리다 equivocate in replying / give a vague [a noncommittal / an evasive] answer. 그는 말꼬리를 흐리는 버릇이 있다 He has a way of slurring his word endings.

흐리다[2] **[हुरीदा]** [불분명하다] not clear; unclear; vague; dim; obscure; hazy; misty; foggy; [애매하다] ambiguous; equivocal; evasive. e.g. 의식이 흐리다 have a dim consciousness. **2** [희미하다] dim; clouded; foggy; obscure; blurred; smoked. e.g. 굴뚝 연기로 건물의 윤곽이 흐려지고 있다 The outline of the building is blurred by the smoke [emitted] from the chimney.**3** [탁하다] muddy; turbid; thick <puddles>; cloudy <wine>; (목소리가) thick; hoarse; [혼탁하다] foul; impure. e.g. 흐린 물 muddy water. **4** (날씨가) cloudy; clouded; overcast; murky. e.g. 흐린 하늘 a cloudy sky. **5** (시력이) dull; dim; blurred; bleary; bleared; dimmed; purblind. e.g. 눈이 흐리다 have bleared [dim] eyes.

흐리멍덩하다 [हुरीमौंगदौंगहादा] [분명치 않다] vague; dim; faint; obscure; indistinct; indeterminate; indecisive; indefinite; muddled; [애매하다] ambiguous; equivocal; evasive; dubious; noncommittal. e.g. 흐리멍덩한 눈 clouded [lack-luster / fishy] eyes / glazed [glassy / remote] eyes. **2**(귀가) dull; dim. e.g. 귀가 흐리멍덩하다 be hard [dull] of hearing / have a bad [poor] ear / have difficulty [be weak] in hearing.

흐릿하다 [हुरीथादा] **1** (날이) rather cloudy [overcast]. e.g. 흐릿한 날씨 rather cloudy [gray] weather.**2** [불분명하다] rather vague [dim / obscure / indistinct / hazy / ambiguous]; [뿌옇다] rather dim [clouded / blurred / smoked]; [둔탁하다] rather muddy [turbid / thick]. e.g. 달이 흐릿하게 보인다 The moon looks blurred. **3** (눈이) rather dim [dull / blurred / bleary]; (청력이) rather hard [dull] of hearing. e.g. 나이를 먹으면 눈이 흐릿해진다 Our sight grows dim with age.

흐물흐물 [हुमुरहुमुल] 물흐물하다 overripe; (too) soth; pulpy; pulpous; limp; flaccid; mushy. e.g. 흐물흐물해지다 be reduced to pulp / become pulpy [mushy / flabby / limp].

흐뭇하다 [हुमुथादा] 만족하다] gratifying; satisfying; satisfactory; gratified; [유쾌하다] pleasing; pleasant; [기쁘다] joyful; joyous; delightful; happy. e.g. 마음이 흐뭇해지는 편지 a heart-warming letter.

흐지부지 [हुजीबुजी] 흐지부지한 태도 a lackadaisical [lukewarm] attitude.

흐트러뜨리다 [हुथुरौतुरीदा] **1** (여기저기) scatter (about); strew; (군중 등을) disperse; scatter; break up. e.g. 물건들을 흐트러뜨려 놓다 leave things scattered [lying] about. **2** (머리칼 등을) dishevel <one's hair>; rumple up <one's hair>; muss (up) <one's hair>. e.g. 머리를 흐트러 뜨리고

with disheveled [unkempt] hair / with one's hair in disorder.

흐트러지다 [हुथुरौजीदा] **1** [흩어지다] disperse; scatter; be scattered (about). e.g. 비행기는 산산이 흐트러져 바다에 처박혔다 The air-plane plunged into the sea in pieces. **2** 머리칼 등이) be disheveled; be mussed (up); be in dis-array. e.g. 흐트러진 머리 [옷차림] disheveled [rum-pled] hair [clothing].

흑백 [हुकपैक] [黑白] **1** [흑과 백] black and white. **2** [선악] good and bad [evil]; [옳고 그름] right and wrong; [유죄와 무죄] guilt and innocence. e.g. 법정에서 흑백을 가리기로 하자 Let's argue the rights and wrongs of the case in court.

흑심 [हुकशीम] [黑心] black heart; an evil [a wicked] heart; an evil [a dark] design. e.g. 흑심을 품다 harbor an evil heart / cherish a dark design.

흑인 [हुगीन] [黑人] black; a Negro <*pl.* ~es>; (인종) the blacks

흑자 [हुकचा] [黑字] 경제의) the black; a black-ink balance [figure]; (무역상의) a surplus. e.g. 우리 회사는 흑자다[이 되었다] Our company is in [got into] the black.

흑흑 [हुखुक] [흐느껴 우는 소리]. 흑흑하다] sob; give a ob; whimper (어린아 이가).

흔들다 [हुनदुलदा] **1** [잇달아 움직이게 하다] wave <a flag, one's hand, etc.>; shake <a stick, a bell, a coat, etc.>; swing <a pen-dulum, a door, a ham-mock, etc.>; give a <hard / good> shake <to>; rock; wag. e.g. 병 [몸] 을 흔들다 shake a bottle [oneself]. **2** 감동, 동요시키다] stir up; agitate; instigate; disturb; upset; move. e.g. 민심을 흔들다 inflame [stir up] the popular passion.

흔들리다 [हुनदुल्लीदा] **1** (물체가) shake; quake; sway; wave; tremble (떨리다); vibrate (진동하다); (배 등이) pitch (세로); roll (가로); rock (전후로); (상하로) toss; heave; bob; (매단 것이) swing; (차 등이) joggle; (불꽃이) flicker; quiver. e.g. 바람에 흔들리는 갈대 reeds swaying in the wind.**2** [동요하다] shake; be shaken; be unsteady [shaky]; reel; vacillate; waver. e.g. 흔들리는 세계 경제 the unstable world economy.

흔적 [हुनजौक] [痕迹] 형적) traces; marks; vestiges; (발자취) tracks; evidences; signs.

흔전만전 [हुनजौनमानजौन] in

(great) plenty [abundance]; abundantly; plentifully; amply. e.g. 돈을 흔전만전 쓰다 lavish [waste / squander] money / make the money fly.

흔하다 [हुनहादा] **1** [많다] abundant; plentiful; rich; ample. e.g. 생선이 흔한 고장 a district rich [abund-ant] in marine products. **2** [아무 데나 있다] common; commonplace; ordinary; familiar; common (or) garden; stock. e.g. 흔해 빠진 이야기 an old story / a twice-told tale.

흔히 [हुनही] commonly; ordinarily; usually; generally; in general; othen; [통속적으로] popularly; vulgarly. e.g. 흔히 있는 실수 a common error.

흘기다 [हुलकीदा] look disapprovingly out of the corner of one's eyes <at>; cast a reproachful [disapproving] glance <at>; scowl <at>. e.g. 그는 번쩍이는 두 눈을 흘겨 만장의 청중을 노려 보았다 He glared at the whole audience with his eyes glittering.

흘러가다 [हुल्लौगादा] flow; run; float [drith] along; fly (시간이). e.g. 덧없이 흘러가는 청춘 시대 the flying years of youth

흘러나오다 [हुल्लौनाओदा] [유출하다] flow out; run out; effuse; stream [pour] out; gush forth (분출하다); ooze out (고름 등이). e.g. 호수에서 흘러나오는 강 a river which proceeds from the lake.

흘러내리다 [हुल्लौनेरीदा] **1** [떨어지다] fall; drop; run [stream / pour] down. e.g. 눈물이 그녀의 볼을 줄줄 흘러내렸다 Tears ran [streamed / coursed / rolled / trickled] down her cheeks. **2** [미끄러지다] slip [slide / glide] down; work down. e.g. 흘러내리는 바지를 치켜올리다 pull [hitch] up one's trousers. 내 양말이 흘러내린다 My socks are sliding down.

흘리다 [हुल्लीदा] **1** (액체를) let <water> flow [run out]; [쏟다] shed; spill; slop; pour over; [뚝뚝 떨어지게 하다] drop; let drop; drip; dribble. e.g. 눈물[피]을 흘리다 shed [drop] tears [blood]. **2** [잃어버리다] drop; lose. e.g. 지갑을 흘리다 lose one's purse. 돈을 흘리다 drop money. **3**[귀담아 듣지 않다] take no notice <of>; pay no attention <to>; give no heed <to>; be deaf to <a person's remonstrances>; let <an insult> go by. e.g. 농담으로 흘리다 take <it> as a joke. 그는 그녀의 말을 한쪽 귀로 듣고 한쪽

귀로 흘려 버렸다 He let her words go in one ear and out the other. / He took no heed of what she said.

흙 [हुक] [토양] earth; soil; [진흙] mud; [찰흙] clay; [지면] the ground.

흙먼지 [हुल्गमौनजी] dust; a cloud of dust; a dust storm. e.g. 앞사람들이 일으킨 흙먼지 dust stirred up by those in front

흙탕물 [हुल्गथांगमुल] muddy water. e.g. 흙탕물에 빠지다 slip into a muddy pool <on the road>.

흠 [हुम] [欠] **1** (물건의) a crack; a flaw; a disfigurement; a scratch; a speck; (과일의) a bruise. e.g. 찻잔의 가장자리에 난 흠 a nick in the lip [rim] of a teacup. **2** [결점] a fault; a defect; a flaw; a blemish; a mar; a stain; a blur. e.g. 그의 경력에 있어서의 흠 a blemish on his record.

흠모 [हुम्मो] [欽慕] admiration; adoration; reverence; high regard. 흠모하다. admire; adore; esteem; idolize; entertain a high regard <for>; make an idol of <a person>. e.g. 그는 여전히 동향인의 흠모를 받고 있다 He is still the idol of his countrymen.

흠뻑 [हुमपौक] fully; thoroughly; to the full; sufficiently; [마음껏] to one's heart's content; to one's satisfaction. e.g. 흠뻑 젖은 옷 dripping-wet clothes.

흠잡다 [हुमजापता] find fault with; cavil [carp] at; pick holes in; pick on <a person [thing]>. e.g. 흠잡을 데가 없다 be above reproach / be faultless [unimpeachable] / leave nothing to be desired / be perfect [ideal

흠집 [हुमजीब] [欠-] (신체의) a scar; (물건의) a crack; a flaw; a scratch; a fault. e.g. 흠집 있는 손 a scarred hand.

흠칫 [हुमछीत] cringing. e.g. 흠칫 놀라다 =흠칫하다 . 흠칫하다 shrink (back) <at / from>; hold [fall] back <from>; flinch <from>; cringe in surprise [fright].

흡기 [हुपकी] [吸氣] [들이마시기] inhalation of air [breath]; inspiration; (공기) air breathed in. 흡기하다 inhale; breathe in.

흡사 [हुपसा] [恰似] **1** a close [a near / an exact] resemblance; a striking likeness [resemblance]; close affinity.

흡사하다 be strikingly similar <to>; resemble closely; bear a close resemblance [a strong likeness] <to>; be the very picture of <one's father>; be as like as two peas [eggs]; be exactly alike; be an exact counterpart <of>; be a copy [replica] <of>. e.g. 이 꽃병은 내 것과 흡사하다 This vase is very similar to mine. / This vase looks almost exactly like mine. **2** <부사> just as; as if; as though; as it were. e.g. 흡사 죽은 것 같다 look as if dead / be more dead than alive.

흡수 [हुप्सु] [**吸收**] absorption; [흡인] imbibition; suction; (열의) decalescence; (빛의) extinction; [동화] assimilation. e.g. 영양의 흡수 absorption of nourishment.

흡연 [हुब्यौन] [**吸煙**] smoking (tobacco). e.g. 흡연으로 건강을 해치다 smoke oneself ill [sick].

흡입 [हुबीब] [**吸入**] inhalation; indrath; imbibition; suction. 흡입하다 inhale; breathe [draw] in; suck (in); imbibe.

흡족 [हुबचोक] [**洽足**] **1** [아주 넉넉함] sufficiency; ampleness. 흡족하다 sufficient; ample; enough; full. 흡족히 enough; sufficiently; fully; to the full; amply; in plenty. e.g. 흡족히 보답하다 reward amply [abundantly] paid. **2.** [만족함] satisfaction; gratification. 흡족하다 satisfactory; gratifying. 흡족히 satisfactorily; to one's satisfaction; to one's heart's content. e.g. 흡족히 여기다 be contented <with> / find <something> more than satisfactory.

흡착 [हुबछाग] [**吸着**] adsorption. 흡착하다 adsorb.

흡혈 [हुफ्यौल] [**吸血**] blood-sucking. 흡혈하다 suck blood

흥 [हुंग] [**興**] interest; fun; amusement; merriment; mirth; pleasure e.g. 흥이 나면 when fancy leads one. 흥이 깨지다 find one's fun spoiled <by> / one's enthusiasm is dampened <by>.

흥 [हुंग] <부사>. e.g. 코를 흥하고 풀다 blow one's nose with a hissing sound. (아이에게) 흥해 Blow, honey!

흥 [हुंग] <감탄사> hm(m); hum (ph); hem; h'm. e.g. 흥하고 코웃음 치다 turn up one's nose at <a person>.

흥건하다 [हुंगौनहादा] **1** (물 등이) brimful; full to the brim. e.g. 웅덩이에 물이 흥건하게 괴었다 A puddle is full of rainwater.흥건히 brimfully. **2** (국물 등이) juicy; watery; <서술적> <have> much juice in it. e.g. 김치 국물이 흥건하다 The kimchi is much juicy. 흥건히 juicily; waterily

흥겹다 [हुंग्योप्ता] [**興**-] delightful; merry; pleasant;

joyous; cheerful; exciting; gay; full of fun. e.g. 흥겨운 하루 a day full of fun / an exciting day.

흥나다 [हुंगनादा] [興-] get merry [excited]. e.g. 흥나서 춤추다 dance in one's mirth.

흥망 [हुंगमांग] [興亡] rise and fall; ups and downs; vicissitudes; existence; destinies (운명). e.g. 인생의 흥망성쇠 the vicissitudes [ups and downs] of life.

흥미 [हुंगमी] [興味] (an) interest; zest. e.g. 비상한 흥미 great [keen] interest.

흥미 진진 [हुंगमी जीनजीन] [興味津津] 흥미 진진하다 very [intensely] interesting; of great [absorbing] interest; full of interest; absorbing <book>.e.g. 흥미 진진한 화제 topic of great interest <to one>.

흥분 [हुंगबुन] [興奮] excitement; excitation; agitation; stimulation. e.g. 신경성 흥분 erethism 흥분하다 be excited; be aroused <to activity>; be [get] stimulated <into action>; be highly strung; be wrought [worked] up <over>; work oneself up <into a passion>; get warm [hot]; get a kick [thrill] <from

흥얼거리다 [हुंगऔल्गौरीदा] hum <a tune>; sing to oneself; croon <a song>. e.g. 그녀는 작은 목소리로 민요의 마디마디를 흥얼거리고 있었다 She was singing snatches of a folk song sothly to herself.

흥얼흥얼 [हुंगौरहुंगौल] humming; crooning e.g. 흥얼흥얼 혼자 노래하다 hum [croon] to oneself.

흥정 [हुंगजौग] [매매] buying and selling; purchase and sale; [거래] dealings; transactions; business; a bargain; [매매를 위한 값 등의 의논] bargaining; chaffering; haggling; [교섭] negotiation. e.g. 정치적 흥정 <oppose to any sort of> political compromise.

흥청거리다 [हुंगछौगौरीदा] [마껏 놀다] indulge in merry-making; make merry; be on the spree; [거드럭거리다] be highly elated; exult; crow; be puffed up; swagger. e.g. 부어라 마셔라 하며 흥청거리다 go [be] on the spree / revel it / have a high time.

흥청망청 [हुंगछौगमांगछौग] **1** [즐기는 모양] merrily; gaily. e.g. 흥청망청 놀기 a (hilarious) merrymaking / a spree / a racket / high jinks. 흥청망청 떠들며 놀다 indulge in a rowdy spree [boisterous merry-making] / have high jinks / go on the spree. **2** [낭비하는 모양] in pro-fusion. e.g.

ㅎ

돈을 흥청 망청 쓰다 spend money most lavishly [in profusion].

흥취 [हुंगच्वी] [興趣] interest; gusto; taste. e.g. 매우 흥취가 있다 be of absorbing interest. 아무런 흥취도 없다 have no attract-tive features.

흥하다 [हुंगहादा] [興-](나라 등이) rise; [번영,번창하다] thrive; flourish; prosper; boom; roar. e.g. 장사가
흥한다 Business booms [flourishes / prospers].

흥행 [हुंगहैग] [興行] (사업) public entertainment; the amusement [entertainment] industry; show business; (연예)(a) performance; (an) exhibition; a run; a show 흥행하다 give a performance; produce <a play>; show; exhibit; run <a show>. e.g. 연극을 흥행 하다 give [present] a play.

흥흥거리다 [हुंगहुंगौरीदा] 1 [흥겨워서 콧소리를 치다] hum; croon; sing through the nose; sing to oneself. e.g. 흥흥거리며 일하다 do work humming a tune. 2 [아이가 투정부리다] grumble; complain; whine; whimper.

흩날리다 [हुथनाल्लीदा] blow off [away]; be blown off; go to the winds; fly about [off]; scatter; flutter. e.g. 바람에 흩날리다 be blown off by the wind

흩뿌리다 [हुथ्पुरीदा] scatter; strew; sprinkle. e.g. 씨를 흩뿌리다 scatter seeds.

흩어지다 [हुथौजीदा] [분산하다] disperse; scatter; be scattered (about); [어질지다] be littered (up) <with>; be in disorder. e.g. 군중 경관이 오자 사방으로 흩어다 The crowd dispersed [scattered] when the police arrived.

희곡 [हवीगोन] [戯曲] a drama; a play. 희곡적[의] dramatic / dramatical. 희곡을 쓰다 write a drama.

희귀 [हवीग्वी] [稀貴]. 희귀 다 rare; infrequent. e.g. 희귀 물건 a rarity / a curiosity / a black swan / a white crow.

희극 [हवीगुन] [喜劇] a comedy; a farce (소극(笑劇)); a funny show.

희끗희끗 [हवीकुतहवीुत] (흰 빛깔이) spotted [speckled] with white; grizzled; grizzly. 희끗희끗하다 grizzled; (옷감 등이) pepper-and-salt e.g. 희끗희끗한 수염 a grizzled beard.

희다 [हवेदा] (빛깔이) white; (피부가) fair; (머리칼이) gray; hoary. e.g. 흰 얼굴 a fair [white] face.

희로애락 [हवीरोऐराक] [喜怒哀樂] joy, anger, sorrow, and pleasure [happiness];

joy and anger; (감정) emotion; feelings. e.g. 희로 애락을 얼굴에 나타지 않다 do not betray one's feelings [emotions].

희롱 [**ह्वेरोंग**] [**戯弄**] banter; raillery; rally; jeer; badinage; chaff; jest; a rag. e.g. 그녀는 그를 희롱 상대로 골랐다 She chose him as a partner to flirt with. 희롱하다 banter; chaff; tease <a person with his cowardice, a person with jest, etc.>; poke fun <at>; make a mock of; ridicule. e.g. 남을 희롱하다 tease a person in jest / josh a person. 그는 젊은 여자들을 희롱하기 좋아한다 He enjoys bantering with young women.

희망 [**ह्वीमांग**] [**希望**] [바람] (a) hope; [소망] a wish; (강한 소망) a desire; an aspiration; [기대] prospect; expectation; [요구] a request; a demand.

희미 [**ह्वीमी**] [**稀微**] dimness; faintness; [불분명함] vagueness; indistinctness; mistiness. 희미하다 [미약하다] dim; faint; vague; indistinct; misty; hazy. e.g. 희미한 소리 a faint sound.

희박 [**ह्वीबाक**] [**稀薄**] thinness; rarity; rarefaction. 희박하다 [엷다] thin; weak; [묽다] dilute (d) <solution>; (공기, 가스 등이) rare; rarefied; [성기다] sparse.

희비 [**ह्वीबी**] [**喜悲**] joy and sorrow. e.g. 나는 희비가 엇갈렸다 I have mixed feelings [emotions] about it. / Joy and grief [Sorrow and pleasure] alternated in my heart.

희생 [**ह्वेसैंग**] [**犧牲**] a sacrifice; (자기 희생) self-sacrifice; self-immolation; (남을 대신하는) a scape-goat. 희생하다 sacrifice; victimize; make a sacrifice [scapegoat / victim] of <a person> e.g. …을 희생하여 at the sacrifice of ... / at the cost[price / expense] of .... 자기 자신을 희생하다 sacrifice oneself / make a martyr of oneself.

희석 [**ह्वीसौक**] [**稀釋**] dilution; attenuation. 희석하다 dilute; attenuate. e.g. 희석한 커피 [차] weakened coffee [tea]. 우유를 물로 희석하다 water milk down / thin milk with water.

희소 [**ह्वीसो**] [**稀少**] scarcity; rarity. 희소의 rare. 희소하다 [**ह्वीसोहादा**] scarce; rare.

희소식 [**ह्वीसोशिक**] [**喜消息**] good [favorable / happy / glad] news; joyful [glad] tidings

희열 [**ह्वीयोल**] [**喜悅**] joy; happiness; delight; gladness

희한 [**ह्वीहान**] [**稀罕**] 희한하다 rare; uncommon; unusual; phenomenal; singular; extraordinary; curious (진

기하다); novel (신기하 다). e.g. 희한한 물건 a rare article / a rarity / a curiosity.

히죽히죽 [हीजुख़ीजुक] grinningly; with a broad grin. e.g. 히죽히죽 웃다 grin (broadly) <at>.

히터 [हीथौ] a heater. e.g. 전기 히터 an electric heater. 히터를 켜다[끄다] turn on [off] a heater.

히트 [हीथु] [대성공] a hit; a great (box-office) success. e.g. 기록을 깨는 대히트였다 It was a record-breaking hit.

힌두 [हीन्दु] 힌두의 Hindu / Hindoo.

힌두교 [हीन्दग्यो] [-教] Hinduism; Hindooism.

힌트 [हीथु] a hint; a tip-off. e.g. 힌트를 주다 give [drop / let fall] a hint.

힐 [हील] a heel. e.g. 하이[로]힐 high-[low-] heeled shoes.

힘 [हीम] **1** 체력] (physical) strength; energy; force; might; power. e.g. 힘만으로 by sheer strength. **2** [물리적인 힘] force; power; energy. e.g. 열의 힘 energy of heat / caloric force. **3** [작용] agency; action. e.g. 눈에 보이지 않는 힘 an invisible agency **4** [권세, 위력] power; force; authority; sway; influence; weight. e.g. 전통의 힘 the weight of tradition. **5** [능력] ability; power; faculty; capability; capacity; [재산] means. e.g. 힘 자라는 데까지 as far [much] as one can / to best of one's ability [power].

힘겨룸 [हीमग्यौरुम] a contest of strength. 힘겨룸하다 have a strength contest; have a trial of strength. e.g. 힘겨룸해 보자 Let's see who is the stronger, you or

힘겹다 [हीमग्यौप्ता] <서술적> be not strong enough <to do>; be beyond one's ability [power / reach]; be too much for one <to manage>. e.g. 힘겨운 여행 a hard journey

힘껏 [हीमक्कौत] with all one's strength [might]; with might and main; to the best of one's ability [power]. e.g. 힘껏 하다 do one's best [utmost] / do everything in one's power [as one can].

힘들다 [हीमदुल्दा] **1** [벅차다] laborious [arduous / strenuous / toilsome / troublesome / tough / painful]. e.g. 힘드는 일 a heavy [hard / laborious / toilsome / painful] task / a tough job **2** [어렵다] hard [difficult / hard going / tough sledding]. e.g. 힘든 문제 a difficult problem.

힘들이다 [हीमदुरीदा] **1** (체력, 노력을) put in one's strength [labo (u)r / efforts];

ㅎ

make efforts; exert oneself; ende-avor (u)r. e.g. 일에 힘들이다 throw oneself into one's work. **2** [애쓰다] take pains; take trouble; make (stren-uous) efforts; labor. e.g. 조금도 힘들이지 않고 without taking the least pains / without any effort / easily.

힘세다 [हीमसेदा] strong; power-ful; mighty. e.g. 그는 굉장히 힘세다 He is of Herculean strength. / He is as strong as a horse.

힘쓰다 [हीमसुदा] **1** [노력하다] exert oneself; make efforts; endeavor; strive; try hard; labor <to do / for / ather>. e.g. 어학 연구에 특히 힘쓰다 lay special emphasis (up) on the study of languages. **2** [돕다] do <a person> a service; help; aid; extend help <to>; lend a helping hand <to>; (영향을) use one's influence <for a person>. e.g. 남의 취직을 위해 힘쓰다 help <a person> find employment / assist <a person> to a posi-tion. **3** [체력을 발휘하다] put forth [out] one's strength <to do>. e.g. 힘써 밀 다 push with might and main.

힘없이 [हीमऑफ्शि] feebly; droo-pingly; dejectedly. e.g. 힘없이 대답하다 give a feeble answer / answer feebly [de-jectedly].

힘입다 [हीमीपता] owe; be indebted to <a person> fo <something>; be in <anot her's> debt. e.g. 아버지의 교육에 힘입어 성공하다 owe one's success to one's father's education.

힘있다 [हीमीत्ता] **1** [힘이 세다] strong; have strength. **2** (문장, 어조가) forceful powerful; heavy. e.g. 힘있는 문장 powerful sentences 힘있는 어조 a heavy accent **3** (지위, 권력으로 보아) influ ential; carry weight; have power. e.g. 힘있는 사람 an influential person / a person who carries some weight.

힘주다 [हीमजुदा] **1** (육체적으로 strain (at stool) (변소에서) bear down (분만 때에). **2** [강조하다] emphasize; put stress <on>. e.g. 힘주어 말하다 emphasize [lay stress on] one's words / speak with emphasis.

힘차다 [हीमछादा] **1** [활력이 넘치다] powerful; forceful forcible; vigorous; energetic full of strength. e.g. 그는 힘차게 노를 젓기 시작했다 He started to row with vigor [with all his might / energetically]. **2** [힘에 벅차다] laborious; tough; hard; difficult. e.g. 힘차게 떠밀다 shove hard.

ㅎ